THE
EXPOSITOR'S
BIBLE
COMMENTARY

THE EXPOSITOR'S BIBLE COMMENTARY

in Thirteen Volumes

When complete, the Expositor's Bible Commentary will include the following volumes:

To see which titles are available, visit www.zondervan.com.

THE
EXPOSITOR'S
BIBLE
COMMENTARY

REVISED EDITION

1 Chronicles ~ Job

Tremper Longman III & David E. Garland

General Editors

ZONDERVAN®

ZONDERVAN.com/
AUTHORTRACKER
follow your favorite authors

ZONDERVAN

The Expositors Bible Comentary: 1 Chronicles – Job Vol. 4

1 and 2 Chronicles — copyright © 2010 by Frederick J. Mabie
Ezra and Nehemiah — copyright © 2010 by Edwin M. Yamauchi
Esther — copyright © 2010 by Elaine Phillips
Job — copyright © 2010 by Jane H. Smick

Requests for information should be addressed to:

Zondervan, *Grand Rapids, Michigan 49530*

Library of Congress Cataloging-in-Publication Data
The expositor's Bible commentary: 1 Chronicles – Job / [general editors], Tremper Longman III and David E. Garland. — Rev.
    p. cm.
   Includes bibliographical references and index.
   ISBN 978-0-310-23496-8 (hardcover : alk. paper)
   1. Bible. N.T. — Commentaries. I. Longman, Tremper. II. Garland, David E.
BS2341.53.E96 2005
220.7 — dc22   2005006281

Interior design: Tracey Walker

Printed in the United States of America

19 20 / DCI / 32 31 30 29 28 27 26 25 24 23 22 21 20 19 18 17 16 15 14 13 12 11 10 9 8 7 6

CONTENTS

CONTRIBUTORS TO VOLUME FOUR

1 and 2 Chronicles: **Frederick J. Mabie** (PhD, University of California at Los Angeles), an independent scholar, currently resides in West Linn, Oregon.

Ezra and Nehemiah: **Edwin M. Yamauchi** (PhD, Brandeis University) has been teaching undergraduate and graduate courses in ancient history at Miami University in Oxford, Ohio, since 1969. He is the author of numerous books and articles on the ancient Near East, the Old Testament, the New Testament, and the early church.

Esther: **Elaine Phillips** (PhD, The Dropsie College for Hebrew and Cognate Learning) is professor of biblical studies at Gordon College in Wenham, Massachusetts.

Job: **Elmer B. Smick** (PhD, The Dropsie College for Hebrew and Cognate Learning) was professor of Old Testament Languages and Literature at Gordon-Conwell Theological Seminary in South Hamilton, Massachusetts.

General editor: **Tremper Longman III** (PhD, Yale University) is Robert H. Gundry professor of biblical studies at Westmont College in Santa Barbara, California.

General editor: **David E. Garland** (PhD, Southern Baptist Theological Seminary) is associate dean of academic affairs and William M. Hinson professor of Christian Scriptures at George W. Truett Seminary, Baylor University, in Waco, Texas.

PREFACE

Frank Gaebelein wrote the following in the preface to the original Expositor's Bible Commentary (which first appeared in 1979): "The title of this work defines its purpose. Written primarily by expositors for expositors, it aims to provide preachers, teachers, and students of the Bible with a new and comprehensive commentary on the books of the Old and New Testaments." Those volumes achieved that purpose admirably. The original EBC was exceptionally well received and had an enormous impact on the life of the church. It has served as the mainstay of countless pastors and students who could not afford an extensive library on each book of the Bible but who wanted solid guidance from scholars committed to the authority of the Holy Scriptures.

Gaebelein also wrote, "A commentary that will continue to be useful through the years should handle contemporary trends in biblical studies in such a way as to avoid becoming outdated when critical fashions change." This revision continues the EBC's exalted purpose and stands on the shoulders of the expositors of the first edition, but it seeks to maintain the usefulness of the commentary by interacting with new discoveries and academic discussions. While the primary goal of this commentary is to elucidate the text and not to provide a guide to the scholarly literature about the text, the commentators critically engage recent academic discussion and provide updated bibliographies so that pastors, teachers, and students can keep abreast of modern scholarship.

Some of the commentaries in the EBC have been revised by the original author or in conjunction with a younger colleague. In other cases, scholars have been commissioned to offer fresh commentaries because the original author had passed on or wanted to pass on the baton to the next generation of evangelical scholars. Today, with commentaries on a single book of the Old and New Testaments often extending into multiple volumes, the need for a comprehensive yet succinct commentary that guides one to the gist of the text's meaning is even more pressing. The new EBC seeks to fill this need.

The theological stance of this commentary series remains unchanged: the authors are committed to the divine inspiration, complete trustworthiness, and full authority of the Bible. The commentators have demonstrated proficiency in the biblical book that is their specialty, as well as commitment to the church and the pastoral dimension of biblical interpretation. They also represent the geographical and confessional diversity that characterized the first contributors.

The commentaries adhere to the same chief principle of grammatico-historical interpretation that drove the first edition. In the foreword to the inaugural issue of the journal *New Testament Studies* in 1954, Matthew Black warned that "the danger in the present is that theology, with its head too high in the clouds, may end by falling into the pit of an unhistorical and uncritical dogmatism. Into any new theological undertaking must be brought all that was best in the old ideal of sound learning, scrupulous attention to philology, text and history." The dangers that Black warned against over fifty years ago have not vanished. Indeed, new dangers arise in a secular, consumerist culture that finds it more acceptable to use God's name in exclamations than in prayer and that encourages insipid theologies that hang in the wind and shift to tickle the ears and to meet the latest fancy. Only a solid biblical foundation can fend off these fads.

The Bible was not written for our information but for our transformation. It is not a quarry to find stones with which to batter others but to find the rock on which to build the church. It does not invite us simply to speak of God but to hear God and to confess that his Son, Jesus Christ, is Lord to the glory of God the Father (Php 2:10-11). It also calls us to obey his commandments (Mt 28:20). It is not a self-interpreting text, however. Interpretation of the Holy Scriptures requires sound learning and regard for history, language, and text. Exegetes must interpret not only the primary documents but all that has a bearing, direct or indirect, on the grammar and syntax, historical context, transmission, and translation of these writings.

The translation used in this commentary remains the New International Version (North American edition), but all of the commentators work from the original languages (Hebrew and Greek) and draw on other translations when deemed useful. The format is also very similar to the original EBC, while the design is extensively updated with a view to enhanced ease of use for the reader. Each commentary section begins with an introduction (printed in a single-column format) that provides the reader with the background necessary to understand the Bible book. Almost all introductions include a short bibliography and an outline. The Bible text is divided into primary units that are often explained in an "Overview" section that precedes commentary on specific verses. The complete text of the New International Version is provided for quick reference, and an extensive "Commentary" section (printed in a double-column format) follows the reproducing of the text. When the Hebrew or Greek text is cited in the commentary section, a phonetic system of transliteration and translation is used. The "Notes" section (printed in a single-column format) provides a specialized discussion of key words or concepts, as well as helpful resource information. The original languages and their transliterations will appear in this section. Finally, on occasion, expanded thoughts can be found in a "Reflections" section (printed in a double-column format) that follows the Notes section.

One additional feature is worth mentioning. Throughout this volume, wherever specific biblical words are discussed, the Goodrick-Kohlenberger (GK) numbers have been added. These numbers, which appear in the *Strongest NIV Exhaustive Concordance* and other reference tools, are based on the numbering system developed by Edward Goodrick and John Kohlenberger III and provide a system similar but superior to the Strong's numbering system.

The editors wish to thank all of the contributors for their hard work and commitment to this project. We also deeply appreciate the labor and skill of the staff at Zondervan. It is a joy to work with them — in particular Jack Kuhatschek, Stan Gundry, Katya Covrett, Dirk Buursma, and Verlyn Verbrugge. In addition, we acknowledge with thanks the work of Connie Gundry Tappy as copy editor.

We all fervently desire that these commentaries will result not only in a deeper intellectual grasp of the Word of God but also in hearts that more profoundly love and obey the God who reveals himself to us in its pages.

David E. Garland, associate dean for academic affairs and
William M. Hinson professor of Christian Scriptures, George W.
Truett Theological Seminary at Baylor University

Tremper Longman III, Robert H. Gundry professor of biblical
studies, Westmont College

Bible Texts, Versions, Etc.

ASV	American Standard Version	NET	New English Translation (www.netbible.com)
AT	*The Complete Bible: An American Translation* (NT: E. J. Goodspeed)	NIV	New International Version
Barclay	*The New Testament, A New Translation*	NJB	New Jerusalem Bible
		NJPS	New Jewish Publication Society
Beck	*New Testament in Language of Today*	NKJV	New King James Version
		NLT	New Living Translation
BHK	*Biblia Hebraica Kittel*	Norlie	*New Testament in Modern English*
BHS	*Biblia Hebraica Stuttgartensia*	NRSV	New Revised Standard Version
CEV	Contemporary English Version	Phillips	*New Testament in Modern English,* J. B. Phillips
CSB	Christian Standard Bible		
ESV	English Standard Version	REB	Revised English Bible
GNB	Good News Bible (see also TEV)	Rieu	*Penguin Bible*
GWT	God's Word Translation	RSV	Revised Standard Version
JB	Jerusalem Bible	RV	Revised Version
KJV	King James Version	Tanakh	Tanakh, a Jewish translation of the Hebrew Bible
Knox	*Holy Bible: A Translation from the Latin Vulgate*		
		TCNT	Twentieth Century New Testament
MLB	Modern Language Bible		
Moffatt	*A New Translation of the Bible,* James Moffatt	TEV	Today's English Version
		TNIV	Today's New International Version
Montgomery	*Centenary Translation of the New Testament in Modern English*		
		UBS[4]	*The Greek New Testament,* United Bible Societies, 4th ed.
NA[27]	*Novum Testamentum Graece,* Nestle-Aland, 27th ed.		
		Weymouth	*New Testament in Modern Speech,* R. F. Weymouth
NAB	New American Bible		
NASB	New American Standard Bible	Williams	*The New Testament in the Language of the People,* C. B. Williams
NCV	New Century Version		
NEB	New English Bible		

Old Testament, New Testament, Apocrypha

Ge	Genesis	Mt	Matthew
Ex	Exodus	Mk	Mark
Lev	Leviticus	Lk	Luke
Nu	Numbers	Jn	John
Dt	Deuteronomy	Ac	Acts
Jos	Joshua	Ro	Romans
Jdg	Judges	1–2Co	1–2 Corinthians
Ru	Ruth	Gal	Galatians
1–2Sa	1–2 Samuel	Eph	Ephesians
1–2 Kgdms	1–2 Kingdoms (LXX)	Php	Philippians
1–2Ki	1–2 Kings	Col	Colossians
3–4 Kgdms	3–4 Kingdoms (LXX)	1–2Th	1–2 Thessalonians
1–2Ch	1–2 Chronicles	1–2Ti	1–2 Timothy
Ezr	Ezra	Tit	Titus
Ne	Nehemiah	Phm	Philemon
Est	Esther	Heb	Hebrews
Job	Job	Jas	James
Ps/Pss	Psalm/Psalms	1–2Pe	1–2 Peter
Pr	Proverbs	1–2–3Jn	1–2–3 John
Ecc	Ecclesiastes	Jude	Jude
SS	Song of Songs	Rev	Revelation
Isa	Isaiah	Add Esth	Additions to Esther
Jer	Jeremiah	Add Dan	Additions to Daniel
La	Lamentations	Bar	Baruch
Eze	Ezekiel	Bel	Bel and the Dragon
Da	Daniel	Ep Jer	Epistle of Jeremiah
Hos	Hosea	1–2 Esd	1–2 Esdras
Joel	Joel	1–2 Macc	1–2 Maccabees
Am	Amos	3–4 Macc	3–4 Maccabees
Ob	Obadiah	Jdt	Judith
Jnh	Jonah	Pr Azar	Prayer of Azariah
Mic	Micah	Pr Man	Prayer of Manasseh
Na	Nahum	Ps 151	Psalm 151
Hab	Habakkuk	Sir	Sirach/Ecclesiasticus
Zep	Zephaniah	Sus	Susanna
Hag	Haggai	Tob	Tobit
Zec	Zechariah	Wis	Wisdom of Solomon
Mal	Malachi		

Dead Sea Scrolls and Related Texts

CD	Cairo Genizah copy of the *Damascus Document*	4QpPs	*Pesher Psalms* (texts from Qumran)
DSS	Dead Sea Scrolls	4Q44 (4QDt^q)	Deuteronomy (texts from Qumran)
1QapGen	*Genesis Apocryphon* (texts from Qumran)	4Q174	*Florilegium* (texts from Qumran)
1QH	*Hôdāyōt* or *Thanksgiving Hymns* (texts from Qumran)	4Q252	*Commentary on Genesis A*, formerly *Patriarchal Blessings* (texts from Qumran)
1QIsa	Isaiah (texts from Qumran)		
1QM	*Milḥāmâ* or *War Scroll* (texts from Qumran)	4Q394	*Miqṣat Maʿaśê ha-Torah*^a (texts from Qumran)
1QpHab	*Pesher Habakkuk* (texts from Qumran)	4Q400	*Songs of the Sabbath Sacrifice* (texts from Qumran)
1QpMic	*Pesher Micah* (texts from Qumran)	4Q502	*Ritual of Marriage* (texts from Qumran)
1QS	*Serek Hayaḥad* or *Rule of the Community* (texts from Qumran)	4Q521	*Messianic Apocalypse* (texts from Qumran)
1QSa	*Rule of the Congregation* (texts from Qumran)	4Q525	*Beatitudes* (texts from Qumran)
		11QPs^a	*Psalms Scroll*^a
4QEzr	Ezra (texts from Qumran)	11Qtg Job	*Targum of Job*
4QpNa	*Pesher Nahum* (texts from Qumran)	11Q13	*Melchizedek* (texts from Qumran)

Other Ancient Texts

ʾAbot R. Nat.	ʾAbot of Rabbi Nathan	Ant.	*Jewish Antiquities* (Josephus)
Abraham	*On the Life of Abraham* (Philo)	Ant. rom.	*Antiquitates romanae* (Dionysius of Halicarnassus)
Ad.	*Adelphi* (Terence)		
Aeth.	*Aethiopica* (Heliodorus)	1 Apol.	*First Apology* (Justin Martyr)
Ag.	*Agamemnon* (Aeschylus)	Apol.	*Apologia* (Plato)
Ag. Ap.	*Against Apion* (Josephus)	Apol.	*Apologeticus* (Tertullian)
Agr.	*De Lege agraria* (Cicero)	Apos. Con.	*Apostolic Constitutions*
Alc.	*Alcibiades* (Plutarch)	Ascen. Isa.	*Ascension of Isaiah*
Alex.	*Alexander the False Prophet* (Lucian)	As. Mos.	*Assumption of Moses*
		Att.	*Epistulae ad Atticum* (Cicero)
Amic.	*De amicitia* (Cicero)	b. ʿAbod. Zar.	ʿAbodah Zarah (Babylonian Talmud)
An.	*De anima* (Tertullian)		
Anab.	*Anabasis* (Xenophon)	2–4 Bar.	*2–4 Baruch*
Ann.	*Annales* (Tacitus)	b. ʿArak.	ʿArakin (Babylonian Talmud)
Ant.	*Antigone* (Sophocles)	b. B. Bat.	Baba Batra (Babylonian Talmud)

b. B. Qam.	*Baba Qamma* (Babylonian Talmud)	*Comm. Matt.*	*Commentarium in evangelium Matthaei* (Origen)
b. Ber.	*Berakot* (Babylonian Talmud)	*Corrept.*	*De correptione et gratia* (Augustine)
b. Ḥag.	*Ḥagigah* (Babylonian Talmud)	*Cyr.*	*Cyropaedia* (Xenophon)
b. Hor.	*Horayot* (Babylonian Talmud)	*Decal.*	*De decalogo* (Philo)
b. Ḥul.	*Ḥullin* (Babylonian Talmud)	*Decl.*	*Declamationes* (Quintilian)
b. Ker.	*Kerithot* (Babylonian Talmud)	*Def. orac.*	*De defectu oraculorum* (Plutarch)
b. Ketub.	*Ketubbot* (Babylonian Talmud)	*Deipn.*	*Deipnosophistae* (Athenaeus)
b. Meg.	*Megillah* (Babylonian Talmud)	*Deut. Rab.*	*Deuteronomy Rabbah*
b. Menaḥ.	*Menaḥot* (Babylonian Talmud)	*Dial.*	*Dialogus cum Tryphone* (Justin Martyr)
b. Moʿed Qaṭ.	*Moʿed Qaṭan* (Babylonian Talmud)	*Diatr.*	*Diatribai* (Epictetus)
b. Ned.	*Nedarim* (Babylonian Talmud)	*Did.*	*Didache*
b. Nid.	*Niddah* (Babylonian Talmud)	*Disc.*	*Discourses* (Epictetus)
b. Pesaḥ.	*Pesaḥim* (Babylonian Talmud)	*Doctr. chr.*	*De doctrina christiana* (Augustine)
b. Roš Haš.	*b. Roš Haššanah* (Babylonian Talmud)	*Dom.*	*Domitianus* (Suetonius)
		Ebr.	*De ebrietate* (Philo)
b. Šabb.	*Šabbat* (Babylonian Talmud)	*E Delph.*	*De E apud Delphos* (Plutarch)
b. Sanh.	*Sanhedrin* (Babylonian Talmud)	*1–2 En.*	*1–2 Enoch*
b. Šebu.	*Shebuʿot* (Babylonian Talmud)	*Ench.*	*Enchiridion* (Epictetus)
b. Soṭah	*Soṭah* (Babylonian Talmud)	*Ep.*	*Epistulae morales* (Seneca)
b. Taʿan.	*Taʿanit* (Babylonian Talmud)	*Eph.*	*To the Ephesians* (Ignatius)
b. Yebam.	*Yebamot* (Babylonian Talmud)	*Epist.*	*Epistulae* (Jerome, Pliny, Hippocrates)
b. Yoma	*Yoma* (Babylonian Talmud)		
Bapt.	*De baptismo* (Tertullian)	*Ep. Tra.*	*Epistulae ad Trajanum* (Pliny)
Barn.	*Barnabas*	*Est. Rab.*	*Esther Rabbah*
Ben.	*De beneficiis* (Seneca)	*Eth. nic.*	*Ethica nichomachea* (Aristotle)
Bibl.	*Bibliotheca* (Photius)	*Exod. Rab.*	*Exodus Rabbah*
Bibl. hist.	*Bibliotheca historica* (Diodorus Siculus)	*Fam.*	*Epistulae ad familiares* (Cicero)
		Fid. Grat.	*De fide ad Gratianum* (Ambrose)
Bride	*Advice to the Bride and Groom* (Plutarch)	*Flacc.*	*In Flaccum* (Philo)
		Flight	*On Flight and Finding* (Philo)
Cels.	*Contra Celsum* (Origen)	*Fr. Prov.*	*Fragmenta in Proverbia* (Hippolytus)
Cic.	*Cicero* (Plutarch)		
Claud.	*Divus Claudius* (Suetonius)	*Gen. Rab.*	*Genesis Rabbah*
1–2 Clem.	*1–2 Clement*	*Geogr.*	*Geographica* (Strabo)
Comm. Dan.	*Commentarium in Danielem* (Hippolytus)	*Gorg.*	*Gorgias* (Plato)
		Haer.	*Adversus haereses* (Irenaeus)
Comm. Jo.	*Commentarii in evangelium Joannis* (Origen)	*Heir*	*Who Is the Heir?* (Philo)
		Hell.	*Hellenica* (Xenophon)

Hist.	*Historicus* (Polybius, Cassius Dio, Thucydides)	*m. Meg.*	*Megillah* (Mishnah)
		m. Mid.	*Middot* (Mishnah)
Hist.	*Historiae* (Herodotus, Tacitus)	*m. Naz.*	*Nazir* (Mishnah)
Hist. eccl.	*History of the Church* (Eusebius)	*m. Ned.*	*Nedarim* (Mishnah)
Hist. Rome	*The History of Rome* (Livy)	*m. Nid.*	*Niddah* (Mishnah)
Hom. Acts	*Homilies on Acts* (John Chrysostom)	*m. Pesaḥ.*	*Pesaḥim* (Mishnah)
Hom. Col.	*Homilies on Colossians* (John Chrysostom)	*m. Qidd.*	*Qiddušin* (Mishnah)
		m. Šabb.	*Šabbat* (Mishnah)
Hom. Jo.	*Homilies on John* (John Chrysostom)	*m. Sanh.*	*Sanhedrin* (Mishnah)
		m. Šeb.	*Šebiʿit* (Mishnah)
Hom. Josh.	*Homilies on Joshua* (Origen)	*m. Šeqal.*	*Šeqalim* (Mishnah)
Hom. Phil.	*Homilies on Philippians* (John Chrysostom)	*m. Sukkah*	*Sukkah* (Mishnah)
		m. Taʿan.	*Taʿanit* (Mishnah)
Hom. Rom.	*Homilies on Romans* (John Chrysostom)	*m. Tamid*	*Tamid* (Mishnah)
		m. Ṭehar.	*Ṭeharot* (Mishnah)
Hom. 1 Tim.	*Homilies on 1 Timothy* (John Chrysostom)	*m. Yoma*	*Yoma* (Mishnah)
		Magn.	*To the Magnesians* (Ignatius)
Hom. 2 Tim.	*Homilies on 2 Timothy* (John Chrysostom)	*Mand.*	*Mandate* (Shepherd of Hermas)
		Marc.	*Adversus Marcionem* (Tertullian)
Hom. Tit.	*Homilies on Titus* (John Chrysostom)	*Mem.*	*Memorabilia* (Xenophon)
		Midr. Ps.	*Midrash on Psalms*
Hypoth.	*Hypothetica* (Philo)	*Migr.*	*De migratione Abrahami* (Philo)
Inst.	*Institutio oratoria* (Quintilian)	*Mor.*	*Moralia* (Plutarch)
Jos. Asen.	*Joseph and Aseneth*	*Moses*	*On the Life of Moses* (Philo)
Joseph	*On the Life of Joseph* (Philo)	*Nat.*	*Naturalis historia* (Pliny the Elder)
Jub.	*Jubilees*	*Num. Rab.*	*Numbers Rabbah*
J.W.	*Jewish War* (Josephus)	*Oec.*	*Oeconomicus* (Xenophon)
Lam. Rab.	*Lamentations Rabbah*	*Onir.*	*Onirocritica* (Artemidorus Daldianus)
L.A.E.	*Life of Adam and Eve*		
Leg.	*Legum allegoriae* (Philo)	*Or.*	*Orationes* (Demosthenes)
Legat.	*Legatio ad Gaium* (Philo)	*Or.*	*Orationes* (Dio Chrysostom)
Let. Aris.	*Letter of Aristeas*	*Paed.*	*Paedagogus* (Clement of Alexandria)
Lev. Rab.	*Leviticus Rabbah*		
Liv. Pro.	*Lives of the Prophets*	*Peregr.*	*The Passing of Peregrinus* (Lucian)
m. ʾAbot	*ʾAbot* (Mishnah)	*Pesiq. Rab.*	*Pesiqta Rabbati*
m. Bek.	*Bekorot* (Mishnah)	*Pesiq. Rab Kah.*	*Pesiqta of Rab Kahana*
m. Bik.	*Bikkurim* (Mishnah)	*Phaed.*	*Phaedo* (Plato)
m. Giṭ.	*Giṭṭin* (Mishnah)	*Phil.*	*To the Philippians* (Polycarp)
m. Mak.	*Makkot* (Mishnah)	*Phld.*	*To the Philadelphians* (Ignatius)
		Phorm.	*Phormio* (Terence)

Planc.	*Pro Plancio* (Cicero)	*S. ʿOlam Rab.*	*Seder ʿOlam Rabbah*
Plant.	*De plantatione* (Philo)	*Somn.*	*De somniis* (Philo)
P. Oxy.	*The Oxyrhynchus Papyri*	*Spec.*	*De specialibus legibus* (Philo)
Pol.	*Politica* (Aristotle)	*Stat.*	*Ad populum Antiochenum de statuis* (John Chrysostom)
Pol.	*To Polycarp* (Ignatius)		
Posterity	*On the Posterity of Cain* (Origen)	*Strom.*	*Stromata* (Clement of Alexandria)
Praescr.	*De praescriptione haereticorum* (Tertullian)	*T. Ash.*	*Testament of Asher*
		T. Dan	*Testament of Dan*
Princ.	*De principiis* (Origen)	*T. Gad*	*Testament of Gad*
Prom.	*Prometheus vinctus* (Aeschylus)	*Tg. Neof.*	*Targum Neofiti*
Pss. Sol.	*Psalms of Solomon*	*Tg. Onq.*	*Targum Onqelos*
Pud.	*De pudicitia* (Tertullian)	*Tg. Ps.-J.*	*Targum Pseudo-Jonathan*
Pyth.	*Pythionikai* (Pindar)	*Theaet.*	*Theaetetus* (Plato)
Pyth. orac.	*De Pythiae oraculis* (Plutarch)	*t. Ḥul.*	*Ḥullin* (Tosefta)
Quaest. conv.	*Quaestionum convivialum libri IX* (Plutarch)	*T. Jos.*	*Testament of Joseph*
		T. Jud.	*Testament of Judah*
Quint. fratr.	*Epistulae ad Quintum fratrem* (Cicero)	*T. Levi*	*Testament of Levi*
		T. Mos.	*Testament of Moses*
Rab. Perd.	*Pro Rabirio Perduellionis Reo* (Cicero)	*T. Naph.*	*Testament of Naphtali*
		Trall.	*To the Trallians* (Ignatius)
Resp.	*Respublica* (Plato)	*T. Reu.*	*Testament of Reuben*
Rewards	*On Rewards and Punishments* (Philo)	*t. Soṭah*	*Soṭah* (Tosefta)
		Tusc.	*Tusculanae disputationes* (Cicero)
Rhet.	*Rhetorica* (Aristotle)	*Verr.*	*In Verrem* (Cicero)
Rhet.	*Volumina rhetorica* (Philodemus of Gadara)	*Virt.*	*De virtutibus* (Philo)
		Vis.	*Visions* (Shepherd of Hermas)
Rom.	*To the Romans* (Ignatius)	*Vit. Apoll.*	*Vita Apollonii* (Philostratus)
Rosc. com.	*Pro Roscio comoedo* (Cicero)	*Vit. beat.*	*De vita beata* (Seneca)
Sacrifices	*On the Sacrifices of Cain and Abel* (Philo)	*Vit. soph.*	*Vitae sophistarum* (Philostratus)
		y. ʿAbod. Zar.	*ʿAbodah Zarah* (Jerusalem Talmud)
Sat.	*Satirae* (Horace, Juvenal)		
Sera	*De sera numinis vindicta* (Plutarch)	*y. Ḥag.*	*Ḥagigah* (Jerusalem Talmud)
Serm.	*Sermones* (Augustine)	*y. Meg.*	*Megillah* (Jerusalem Talmud)
Sib. Or.	*Sibylline Oracles*	*y. Ned.*	*Nedarim* (Jerusalem Talmud)
Sim.	*Similitudes* (Shepherd of Hermas)	*y. Šabb.*	*Šabbat* (Jerusalem Talmud)
Smyrn.	*To the Smyrnaeans* (Ignatius)	*y. Soṭah*	*Soṭah* (Jerusalem Talmud)

Journals, Periodicals, Reference Works, Series

AASOR	Annual of the American Schools of Oriental Research	Arch	Archaeology	
AB	Anchor Bible	ARM	Archives royales de Mari	
ABD	Anchor Bible Dictionary	ASORMS	American Schools of Oriental Research Monograph Series	
ABL	Assyrian and Babylonian Letters Belonging to the Kouyunjik Collections of the British Museum	ASTI	Annual of the Swedish Theological Institute	
ABR	Australian Biblical Review	AThR	Anglican Theological Review	
ABRL	Anchor Bible Reference Library	ATLA	American Theological Library Association	
AbrN	Abr-Nahrain	AuOr	Aula orientalis	
ABW	Archaeology in the Biblical World	AUSDDS	Andrews University Seminary Doctoral Dissertation Series	
ACCS	Ancient Christian Commentary on Scripture	AUSS	Andrews University Seminary Studies	
ACNT	Augsburg Commentaries on the New Testament	BA	Biblical Archaeologist	
AcT	Acta theologica	BAGD	Bauer, Arndt, Gingrich, and Danker (2d ed.). Greek-English Lexicon of the New Testament and Other Early Christian Literature	
AfOB	Archiv für Orientforschung: Beiheft			
AIs	Ancient Israel, by Roland de Vaux			
AJBI	Annual of the Japanese Biblical Institute	BAR	Biblical Archaeology Review	
AJP	American Journal of Philology	BASOR	Bulletin of the American Schools of Oriental Research	
AJSL	American Journal of Semitic Languages and Literature	BBB	Bonner biblische Beiträge	
AnBib	Analecta biblica	BBR	Bulletin for Biblical Research	
ANEP	The Ancient Near East in Pictures Relating to the Old Testament	BDAG	Bauer, Danker, Arndt, and Gingrich (3d ed.). Greek-English Lexicon of the New Testament and Other Early Christian Literature	
ANET	Ancient Near Eastern Texts Relating to the Old Testament			
ANF	Ante-Nicene Fathers	BDB	Brown, Driver, and Briggs. A Hebrew and English Lexicon of the Old Testament	
AnOr	Analecta orientalia			
ANRW	Aufstieg und Niedergang der römischen Welt	BDF	Blass, Debrunner, and Funk. A Greek Grammar of the New Testament and Other Early Christian Literature	
AOAT	Alter Orient und Altes Testament			
AR	Archiv für Religionswissenschaft			

BEB	Baker Encyclopedia of the Bible	BZNW	Beihefte zur Zeitschrift für die neutestamentliche Wissenschaft
BECNT	Baker Exegetical Commentary on the New Testament	*CAD*	Assyrian Dictionary of the Oriental Institute of the University of Chicago
Ber	Berytus		
BETL	Bibliotheca ephemeridum theologicarum lovaniensium	CAH	Cambridge Ancient History
BETS	Bulletin of the Evangelical Theological Society	CahRB	Cahiers de la Revue biblique
		CANE	Civilizations of the Ancient Near East. Edited by J. Sasson. 4 vols. New York, 1995.
BGU	Aegyptische Urkunden aus den Königlichen Staatlichen Museen zu Berlin, Griechische Urkunden		
		CBC	Cambridge Bible Commentary
BI	Biblical Illustrator	*CBQ*	Catholic Biblical Quarterly
Bib	Biblica	CBQMS	Catholic Biblical Quarterly Monograph Series
BibInt	Biblical Interpretation		
BibOr	Biblica et orientalia	CGTC	Cambridge Greek Testament Commentary
BibS(N)	Biblische Studien (Neukirchen)		
Bijdr	Bijdragen: Tijdschrit voor filosofie en theologie	*CH*	Church History
		ChrT	Christianity Today
BIS	Biblical Interpretation Studies	*CIG*	Corpus inscriptionum graecarum
BJRL	Bulletin of the John Rylands University Library of Manchester	*CIL*	Corpus inscriptionum latinarum
		CJT	Canadian Journal of Theology
BJS	Brown Judaic Studies	ConBNT	Coniectanea biblica: New Testament Series
BKAT	Biblischer Kommentar, Altes Testament		
		ConBOT	Coniectanea biblica: Old Testament Series
BN	Biblische Notizen		
BR	Biblical Research	*COS*	The Context of Scripture
BRev	Bible Review	*CTJ*	Calvin Theological Journal
BSac	Bibliotheca sacra	*CTM*	Concordia Theological Monthly
BSC	Bible Student's Commentary	*CTQ*	Concordia Theological Quarterly
BSOAS	Bulletin of the School of Oriental and African Studies	*CTR*	Criswell Theological Review
		DBI	Dictionary of Biblical Imagery
BST	The Bible Speaks Today	*DDD*	Dictionary of Deities and Demons in the Bible
BT	The Bible Translator		
BTB	Biblical Theology Bulletin	DJD	Discoveries in the Judean Desert
BurH	Buried History	*DOTHB*	Dictionary of the Old Testament: Historical Books
BWANT	Beiträge zur Wissenschaft vom Alter und Neuen Testament		
		DOTP	Dictionary of the Old Testament: Pentateuch
BZ	Biblische Zeitschrift		
BZAW	Beihefte zur Zeitschrift für die alttestamentliche Wissenschaft	*DOTT*	Documents from Old Testament Times

DOTWPW	Dictionary of the Old Testament: Wisdom, Poetry & Writings	GNS	Good News Studies
DRev	Downside Review	GR	Greece and Rome
DSD	Dead Sea Discoveries	Grammar	A Grammar of the Greek New Testament in the Light of Historical
DukeDivR	Duke Divinity Review		Research (A. T. Robertson)
EA	El-Amarna tablets	GRBS	Greek, Roman, and Byzantine
EAEHL	Encyclopedia of Archaeological Excavations in the Holy Land		Studies
EBC	Expositor's Bible Commentary	GTJ	Grace Theological Journal
EBib	Études bibliques	HALOT	Koehler, Baumgartner, and Stamm. The Hebrew and Aramaic
ECC	Eerdmans Critical Commentary		Lexicon of the Old Testament
EcR	Ecumenical Review	HAR	Hebrew Annual Review
EDNT	Exegetical Dictionary of the New Testament	HAT	Handbuch zum Alten Testament
		HBD	HarperCollins Bible Dictionary
EgT	Eglise et théologie	HBT	Horizons in Biblical Theology
EGT	Expositor's Greek Testament	Hen	Henoch
EncJud	Encyclopedia Judaica	Herm	Hermeneia commentary series
ErIsr	Eretz-Israel	HeyJ	Heythrop Journal
ESCJ	Etudes sur le christianisme et le judaisme (Studies in Christianity and Judaism)	HNT	Handbuch zum Neuen Testament
		HNTC	Harper's New Testament Commentaries
EstBib	Estudios bíblicos	Holladay	A Concise Hebrew and Aramaic
ETL	Ephemerides theologicae lovanienses		Lexicon of the Old Testament
ETS	Evangelical Theological Society	Hor	Horizons
EuroJTh	European Journal of Theology	HS	Hebrew Studies
EvJ	Evangelical Journal	HSM	Harvard Semitic Monographs
EvQ	Evangelical Quarterly	HSS	Harvard Semitic Studies
EvT	Evangelische Theologie	HTKNT	Herders theologischer Kommentar zum Neuen
ExAud	Ex auditu		Testament
Exeg	Exegetica		
ExpTim	Expository Times	HTR	Harvard Theological Review
FAT	Forschungun zum Alten Testament	HTS	Harvard Theological Studies
		HUBP	Hebrew Union Bible Project
FCB	Feminist Companion to the Bible	HUCA	Hebrew Union College Annual
FF	Foundations and Facets	IB	Interpreter's Bible
FRLANT	Forschungen zur Religion und Literatur des Alten und Neuen Testaments	IBC	Interpretation: A Bible Commentary for Teaching and Preaching
GBS	Guides to Biblical Scholarship	IBHS	An Introduction to Biblical Hebrew
GKC	Genesius' Hebrew Grammar		Syntax

IBS	*Irish Biblical Studies*	*JETS*	*Journal of the Evangelical Theological Society*
ICC	International Critical Commentary		
		JJS	*Journal of Jewish Studies*
IDB	*Interpreter's Dictionary of the Bible*	*JNES*	*Journal of Near Eastern Studies*
IDBSup	*Interpreter's Dictionary of the Bible: Supplementary Volume*	*JNSL*	*Journal of Northwest Semitic Languages*
IEJ	*Israel Exploration Journal*	Joüon	P. Joüon, *Grammar of Biblical Hebrew,* trans. and revised by T. Muroaka
IJT	*Indian Journal of Theology*		
Imm	*Immanuel*		
Int	*Interpretation*	*JPOS*	*Journal of the Palestine Oriental Society*
ISBE	*International Standard Bible Encyclopedia,* 2d ed.		
		JPSBC	Jewish Publication Society Bible Commentary
IVPBBC	IVP Bible Background Commentary		
		JQR	*Jewish Quarterly Review*
IVPNTC	IVP New Testament Commentary	*JR*	*Journal of Religion*
		JRAS	*Journal of the Royal Asiatic Society*
JAAR	*Journal of the American Academy of Religion*	*JRelS*	*Journal of Religious Studies*
		JRS	*Journal of Roman Studies*
JAARSup	JAAR Supplement Series	*JSJ*	*Journal for the Study of Judaism in the Persian, Hellenistic, and Roman Periods*
JANESCU	*Journal of the Ancient Near Eastern Society of Columbia University*		
JAOS	*Journal of the American Oriental Society*	*JSNT*	*Journal for the Study of the New Testament*
JAOSSup	Journal of the American Oriental Society Supplement Series	JSNTSup	JSNT: Supplement Series
		JSOT	*Journal for the Study of the Old Testament*
Jastrow	Jastrow, *A Dictionary of the Targumim, the Talmud Babli and Yerushalmi, and the Midrashic Literature*		
		JSOTSup	JSOT: Supplement Series
		JSP	*Journal for the Study of the Pseudepigrapha*
JBL	*Journal of Biblical Literature*	*JSS*	*Journal of Semitic Studies*
JBMW	*Journal for Biblical Manhood and Womanhood*	*JSSEA*	*Journal of the Society for the Study of Egyptian Antiquities*
JBQ	*Jewish Biblical Quarterly*	*JTC*	*Journal for Theology and the Church*
JBR	*Journal of Bible and Religion*	*JTS*	*Journal of Theological Studies*
JCS	*Journal of Cuneiform Studies*	K&D	Keil and Delitzsch, *Biblical Commentary on the Old Testament*
JE	*Jewish Encyclopedia*		
Jeev	*Jeevadhara*	KAT	Kommentar zum Alten Testament
JES	*Journal of Ecumenical Studies*	KB	Koehler and Baumgartner, *Hebräisches und Aramäisches Lexicon zum Alten Testament* (first
JESHO	*Journal of the Economic and Social History of the Orient*		

	or second edition; third edition is *HALOT*)	NICOT	New International Commentary on the Old Testament
KEK	Kritisch-exegetischer Kommentar über das Neue Testament	*NIDBA*	*New International Dictionary of Biblical Archaeology*
KHAT	Kurgefasstes exegetisches Handbuch zum Alten Testament	*NIDNTT*	*New International Dictionary of New Testament Theology*
KTU	*Die keilalphabetischen Texte aus Ugarit*	*NIDOTTE*	*New International Dictionary of Old Testament Theology and Exegesis*
L&N	Louw and Nida. *Greek-English Lexicon of the New Testament: Based on Semantic Domains*	NIGTC	New International Greek Testament Commentary
LCC	Library of Christian Classics	NIVAC	NIV Application Commentary
LCL	Loeb Classical Library	NIVSB	Zondervan NIV Study Bible
LEC	Library of Early Christianity	*Notes*	*Notes on Translation*
LS	*Louvain Studies*	*NovT*	*Novum Testamentum*
LSJ	Liddell, Scott, and Jones. *A Greek-English Lexicon*	NovTSup	Novum Testamentum Supplements
LTP	*Laval théologique et philosophique*	*NPNF*	*Nicene and Post-Nicene Fathers*
MM	Moulton and Milligan. *The Vocabulary of the Greek Testament*	NTC	New Testament Commentary (Baker)
MSJ	*The Master's Seminary Journal*	NTD	Das Neue Testament Deutsch
NAC	New American Commentary	NTG	New Testament Guides
NBC	*New Bible Commentary*, rev. ed.	*NTS*	*New Testament Studies*
NBD	*New Bible Dictionary*, 2d ed.	NTT	New Testament Theology
NCB	New Century Bible	NTTS	New Testament Tools and Studies
NCBC	New Century Bible Commentary	OBO	Orbis biblicus et orientalis
		OBT	Overtures to Biblical Theology
NEA	*Near Eastern Archaeology*	*OJRS*	*Ohio Journal of Religious Studies*
NEAEHL	*The New Encyclopedia of Archaeological Excavations in the Holy Land*	OLA	Orientalia lovaniensia analecta
		Or	*Orientalia* (NS)
		OTE	*Old Testament Essays*
NEASB	*Near East Archaeological Society Bulletin*	OTG	Old Testament Guides
		OTL	Old Testament Library
Neot	*Neotestamentica*	OTS	Old Testament Studies
NewDocs	*New Documents Illustrating Early Christianity*	OtSt	Oudtestamentische Studiën
		PAAJR	*Proceedings of the American Academy of Jewish Research*
NIBC	New International Biblical Commentary	*PEGLMBS*	*Proceedings, Eastern Great Lakes and Midwest Bible Societies*
NICNT	New International Commentary on the New Testament	*PEQ*	*Palestine Exploration Quarterly*

PG	Patrologia graeca	ScrHier	Scripta hierosolymitana
PL	Patrologia latina	*SE*	*Studia evangelica*
PNTC	Pillar New Testament Commentary	SEG	Supplementum epigraphicum graecum
Presb	*Presbyterion*	*Sem*	*Semitica*
PresR	*Presbyterian Review*	SHANE	Studies in the History of the Ancient Near East
Proof	*Prooftexts: A Journal of Jewish Literary History*	SJLA	Studies in Judaism in Late Antiquity
PRSt	*Perspectives in Religious Studies*	*SJOT*	*Scandinavian Journal of the Old Testament*
PTMS	Pittsburgh Theological Monograph Series	*SJT*	*Scottish Journal of Theology*
PTR	*Princeton Theological Review*	SNT	Studien zum Neuen Testament
RB	*Revue biblique*	SNTSMS	Society for New Testament Studies Monograph Series
RBibLit	*Review of Biblical Literature*	SNTSU	Studien zum Neuen Testament und seiner Umwelt
RefJ	*Reformed Journal*		
RelSRev	*Religious Studies Review*	SP	Sacra pagina
ResQ	*Restoration Quarterly*	*SR*	*Studies in Religion*
RevExp	*Review and Expositor*	*ST*	*Studia theologica*
RevistB	*Revista bíblica*	Str-B	Strack, H. L., and P. Billerbeck, *Kommentar zum Neuen Testament aus Talmud und Midrasch*
RevQ	*Revue de Qumran*		
RevScRel	*Revue des sciences religieuses*		
RHPR	*Revue d'histoire et de philosophie religieuses*		
		StudBT	*Studia biblica et theologica*
RTR	*Reformed Theological Review*	SUNT	Studien zur Umwelt des Neuen Testaments
SAOC	Studies in Ancient Oriental Civilizations		
SBB	Stuttgarter biblische Beiträge	*SVF*	*Stoicorum veterum fragmenta*
SBJT	*Southern Baptist Journal of Theology*	SVT	Studia in Veteris Testamenti
		SwJT	*Southwestern Journal of Theology*
SBLDS	Society of Biblical Literature Dissertation Series	*TA*	*Tel Aviv*
SBLMS	Society of Biblical Literature Monograph Series	*TAPA*	*Transactions of the American Philological Association*
		TBT	*The Bible Today*
SBLSP	Society of Biblical Literature Seminar Papers	*TDNT*	Kittel and Friedrich. *Theological Dictionary of the New Testament*
SBLWAW	Society of Biblical Literature Writings from the Ancient World	*TDOT*	Botterweck and Ringgren. *Theological Dictionary of the Old Testament*
SBT	Studies in Biblical Theology		
ScEccl	*Sciences ecclésiastiques*	*TF*	*Theologische Forschung*
ScEs	*Science et esprit*		

THAT	Theologisches Handwörterbuch zum Alten Testament	VT	Vetus Testamentum
Them	Themelios	VTSup	Supplements to Vetus Testamentum
ThEv	Theologia Evangelica	WBC	Word Biblical Commentary
THKNT	Theologischer Handkommentar zum Neuen Testament	WBE	Wycliffe Bible Encyclopedia
		WEC	Wycliffe Exegetical Commentary
ThTo	Theology Today	WMANT	Wissenschaftliche Monographien zum Alten und Neuen Testament
TJ	Trinity Journal		
TLNT	Theological Lexicon of the New Testament	WTJ	Westminster Theological Journal
		WUNT	Wissenschaftliche Untersuchungen zum Neuen Testament
TLOT	Theological Lexicon of the Old Testament		
		YCS	Yale Classical Studies
TNTC	Tyndale New Testament Commentaries	ZABR	Zeitschrift für altorientalische und biblische Rechtgeschichte
TOTC	Tyndale Old Testament Commentaries	ZAH	Zeitschrift für Althebräistik
		ZAW	Zeitschrift für die alttestamentliche Wissenschaft
TQ	Theologische Quartalschrift		
Transeu	Transeuphratène	ZDPV	Zeitschrift des deutschen Palästina-Vereins
TS	Theological Studies		
TWOT	Theological Wordbook of the Old Testament	ZNW	Zeitschrift für die neutestamentliche Wissenschaft und die Kunde der älterern Kirche
TynBul	Tyndale Bulletin		
TZ	Theologische Zeitschrift	ZPEB	Zondervan Pictorial Encyclopedia of the Bible
UBD	Unger's Bible Dictionary		
UF	Ugarit-Forschungen	ZWT	Zeitschrift für wissenschaftliche Theologie
UT	Ugaritic Textbook		
VE	Vox evangelica		

General

AD	anno Domini (in the year of [our] Lord)	d.	died
		diss.	dissertation
Akkad.	Akkadian	ed(s).	editor(s), edited by, edition
Arab.	Arabic	e.g.	exempli gratia, for example
Aram.	Aramaic	esp.	especially
BC	before Christ	et al.	et alii, and others
ca.	circa (around, about, approximately)	EV	English versions of the Bible
		f(f).	and the following one(s)
cf.	confer, compare	fig.	figuratively
ch(s).	chapter(s)	frg.	fragment

Gk.	Greek	p(p).	page(s)
GK	Goodrick & Kohlenberger numbering system	par.	parallel (indicates textual parallels)
Heb.	Hebrew	para.	Paragraph
ibid.	*ibidem*, in the same place	q.v.	*quod vide*, referring to the text within a work
i.e.	*id est*, that is		
JPS	Jewish Publication Society	repr.	reprinted
Lat.	Latin	rev.	revised
lit.	literally	Samar.	Samaritan Pentateuch
LXX	Septuagint (the Greek OT)	s.v.	*sub verbo*, under the word
mg.	marginal note	Syr.	Syriac
MS(S)	manuscript(s)	Tg.	Targum
MT	Masoretic Text of the OT	TR	Textus Receptus (Greek text of the KJV translation)
n(n).	note(s)		
n.d.	no date	trans.	translator, translated by
NS	New Series	v(v).	verse(s)
NT	New Testament	vs.	versus
OT	Old Testament	Vul.	Vulgate

1 AND 2 CHRONICLES

FREDERICK J. MABIE

Introduction

1. DATE

The setting of the book(s) of Chronicles[1] is the postexilic community of Judea.[2] Nevertheless, the specific time of the writing of Chronicles remains open to debate. Proposals range from the Persian time frame (400s BC) to the Greek/Hellenistic time frame (300s–200s BC) to the Maccabean/Hasmonean time frame (100s BC). The attention given to temple worship and priestly duties would seem to imply a date following the dedication of the Second Temple (that is, after 516/15 BC).[3] In addition, the extent of the family line of Zerubbabel traced by the Chronicler (cf. 1Ch 3:19–24) would imply a date following the reforms of Ezra and Nehemiah (i.e., after the mid to low 400s BC).[4]

---

1. In this commentary the term "Chronicles" is frequently used in place of "1 and 2 Chronicles" since these books were originally one literary work (cf. the verse enumeration and midpoint identification employed by the Masoretic scribes). Consequently, the outline schema used in the commentary does not start over in 2 Chronicles, but rather continues the outline from 1 Chronicles to underscore this literary unity (see Outline, below).

2. The term "Judea" (also known by the Aramaic "Yehud"; cf. Ezr 5:8) is used to distinguish the small geographical area of the postexilic community from the larger tribal area of Judah.

3. Similarly, mention of the Persian daric coin at 1 Chronicles 29:7 would necessitate a date after the minting of this coin (ca. 515 BC).

4. The family tree of Zerubbabel (one of the early postexilic Judean leaders, ca. 537–20 BC) is noted in 1 Chronicles 3:19–21 and traces Zerubbabel's family line for two generations (Hananiah and Pelatiah), which would bring the time frame to the mid or low 400s BC. Conversely, some claim that Zerubbabel's family tree is traced for six or seven generations, which would amount to a later time frame. See the discussion in V. P. Hamilton, *Handbook on the Historical Books* (Grand Rapids: Baker, 2004), 477. For the approach of seven generations from the exile of King Jehoiachin (ca. 597 BC), see A. E. Hill, *1 & 2 Chronicles* (NIVAC; Grand Rapids: Zondervan, 2003), 41 (cf. 1Ch 3:17–24).

Moreover, the language and content of Chronicles does not seem to reflect a Greek setting, implying that the text was composed prior to 333 BC.[5] In addition, the use of Chronicles by other literary works from Maccabean/Hasmonean times (such as Sirach) implies that the text was in existence and seen as having some degree of authority prior to 180 BC.[6] In sum, these observations indicate a likely range of 430–340 BC for the writing of Chronicles, with some preference for the earlier side of this range (ca. 430–400 BC).[7]

The content of Chronicles extends from Adam (1Ch 1:1) through the Persian king Cyrus (cf. 2Ch 36:22–23). This noted, the genealogical section at the beginning of Chronicles (1Ch 1–9) actually extends *beyond* the time of the closing section of Chronicles (2Ch 36) and into the postexilic setting (as reflected in the family line of Zerubbabel; 1Ch 3:19–24).[8] In addition, this structure of Chronicles shows that while the *historical* time frame of Chronicles is clearly postexilic, the *theological* time frame of Chronicles is exilic.[9] That is to say, while the text was composed (or at least completed) after the exile, the book of Chronicles nevertheless *ends on the eve of the postexilic time frame.*[10] This contrast can be appreciated from the following overview of the postexilic time:

The Persian Empire and Postexilic Judea

Ruler	Reign (BC)	Significant Events of This Time
Cyrus	560–530	Founded Persian Empire; issued the Decree of Cyrus (539/538 BC), allowing conquered peoples (including Judeans) to return to their native countries *(Time of Daniel and Sheshbazzar; Second Temple foundation laid ca. 536 BC)*

---

5. S. Japhet, *I & II Chronicles: A Commentary* (OTL; Louisville, Ky.: Westminster John Knox, 1993), 42.

6. Along similar lines, a portion of a scroll of Chronicles was discovered at Qumran (4Q118), reflecting composition prior to the second century BC.

7. The earlier side of this range would place the writing of Chronicles prior to the havoc in the environs of Judea (and much of Canaan and Syria) in the early fourth century BC caused by Egyptian revolts against Persian hegemony.

8. In a sense, the literary-theological message of Chronicles is first told genealogically and then narratively (cf. Hamilton, *Handbook on the Historical Books*, 477). This fact has given rise to the view of a two-stage composition of Chronicles, that is, 1 Chronicles 10–2 Chronicles 36 (or 1Ch 10–2Ch 34) shortly after the Decree of Cyrus (ca. 530–500 BC) and 1 Chronicles 1–9 (and possibly 2Ch 35–36) following the reforms of Ezra and Nehemiah (ca. 450–400 BC; cf. F. M. Cross, "A Reconstruction of the Judean Restoration," *JBL* 94 [1975]: 4–18). While this is not necessarily a problematic view, the interrelationship across chs. 8, 9, and 10 of 1 Chronicles is not consistent with such a sharp literary break at 1 Chronicles 10.

9. W. Johnstone, *1 and 2 Chronicles; Volume 1: 1 Chronicles 1–2 Chronicles 9: Israel's Place among the Nations* (JSOTSup 253; Sheffield: Sheffield Academic, 1997), 10–11.

10. Thus Chronicles retells earlier (biblical) history to a different audience in a different *Sitz im Leben* (life setting).

Theological Setting of Chronicles: The Decree of Cyrus (539/538 BC)		
Cambyses	530–522	Conquered Egypt in 525 BC
Darius I	522–486	Increased strength of Persian Empire; unsuccessful attempt at conquering Greece *(Time of Haggai and Zechariah [perhaps also Malachi]; Second Temple completed and dedicated during the time of Zerubbabel, ca. 516/515 BC)*
Xerxes I (Ahasuerus)	486–465	Destroyed Babylon in 482 BC; another unsuccessful Greek invasion; Xerxes I was murdered in 465 BC *(Time of Esther)*
Artaxerxes I	465–424	Faced six-year Egyptian rebellion; signed a peace treaty with Greece *(Time of Ezra and Nehemiah)*
Historical Setting (Date of Writing/Completion) of Chronicles: Mid-Late 400s BC		
Darius II	423–404	Gained control of Asia Minor after Peloponnesian War
Artaxerxes II	404–358	Egypt regained independence; significant revolts in the west of the empire
Artaxerxes III	358–338	Reconquered Egypt
Darius III	336–333	Decline of the Persian Empire; falls to Alexander the Great in 333 BC

2. AUTHORSHIP

The most relevant factor that should be stressed on the topic of the authorship of Chronicles is that the book of Chronicles (along with much of the OT) lacks any notation of authorship. Thus it is anonymously authored and, from the vantage point of inspiration, such anonymity was clearly the intent of God.

The most common theme considered in the authorship of Chronicles is the issue of the relationship between the author(s) of Chronicles and Ezra-Nehemiah.[11] Among those who propose a common author for these works (namely, Ezra), the supporting evidence includes a degree of similarity in vocabulary and Hebrew syntax, a penchant for source citations and lists, a degree of overlapping ideological and theological concerns (such as the temple and priests), and Ezra-Nehemiah's picking up where 2 Chronicles ends (cf. 2Ch 36:23 and Ezr 1:1–4). Such factors also led to the early Jewish perspective (cf. the Babylonian Talmud) that Ezra was the author of Chronicles.[12]

---

11. For bibliography on the relationship of Chronicles and Ezra-Nehemiah, see Japhet (*I & II Chronicles*, 3–4), and R. L. Braun, *1 Chronicles* (WBC; Waco, Tex.: Word, 1986), xxv–xxvi, and xxviii. Also see the discussion in M. J. Selman, *1 Chronicles* (TOTC; Downers Grove, Ill.: InterVarsity Press, 1994), 65–69.

12. This view was likewise championed by Albright (cf. W. F. Albright, "The Date and Personality of the Chronicler," *JBL* 40 [1921]: 104–24) and permeated the earlier edition of this commentary (J. B. Payne, "1, 2 Chronicles," *EBC* first ed. [Grand Rapids: Zondervan, 1988], esp. 304–7).

In spite of such points of similarity, there are also a number of thematic distinctions between Chronicles and Ezra-Nehemiah, such as the level of attention directed to the Davidic monarchy (high in Chronicles, low in Ezra-Nehemiah), stress on the Sabbath (low in Chronicles, high in Ezra-Nehemiah), and interest in the prophetic office (high in Chronicles, low in Ezra-Nehemiah).[13] Such points of difference have caused a number of scholars to reject the view of a common author for Chronicles and Ezra-Nehemiah.[14]

All told, the issue of the authorship of Chronicles is likely to remain an unsettled area of biblical scholarship. Given that God saw fit to have Chronicles become a part of canonical biblical literature as an anonymous work, it seems fitting to refer to the (human) author as "the Chronicler" and focus interpretive energies on the theological message of the Chronicler.

3. HISTORICAL AND SOCIAL BACKGROUND

Following the destruction of Jerusalem in 586 BC and large-scale deportations of the citizens of Judah to Babylonia, the Babylonian king Nebuchadnezzar appointed Gedaliah as governor of Judah in Mizpah, to the north of Jerusalem (cf. 2Ki 25:22–24).[15] The establishment of this new administration prompted those who had scattered in battle or had fled to neighboring regions to return to Judah (cf. Jer 40:5–12). Yet before long Gedaliah was assassinated, which resulted in more deportations, more flights abroad (especially to Egypt), and a sparsely inhabited Judah. During this time Edom took advantage of Judah's dire situation by occupying the southern parts of what had been Judah, particularly in the region between Beersheba and Beth Zur.[16]

Meanwhile, the Nabateans settled in Transjordanian areas previously belonging to Edom as well as Cisjordan wilderness regions. All things considered, those who remained in the land ("the poorest people of the land"; cf. 2Ki 25:12; Jer 52:16) were concentrated in the central hill country to the north of Jerusalem over the course of the exilic period.[17] The end of the bleak exilic period begins with the absorption of the Babylonian Empire into the Persian Empire in 539 BC.[18]

---

13. Alternatively, the annalistic (or chronographic) nature of the text (see "Genre," below), particularly the integration or earlier documents written by a variety of authors, might explain the observable thematic differences. Thus, if Ezra played a role in the composition of Chronicles, it may have been primarily in the selectivity, shaping, and cohesion of preexisting texts with preexisting thematic and theological points of emphasis. On the issues of language and authorship, see M. Throntveit, "Linguistic Analysis and the Question of Authorship in Chronicles, Ezra and Nehemiah," *VT* 32 (1978): 9–36; W. G. E. Watson, "Archaic Elements in the Language of Chronicles," *Bib* 53 (1972): 191–207.

14. See S. Japhet, "The Supposed Common Authorship of Chronicles and Ezra-Nehemiah Investigated Anew," *VT* 18 (1968): 330–71.

15. For details concerning the fall of the southern kingdom, see comments at 2 Chronicles 36:11–19.

16. Cf. Ps 137; Ob 1–4; Arad Letter #24 (*COS*, 3.43K). In Hellenistic times this area came to be known as *Idumea*.

17. On options concerning the "seventy-year" period of the exile, see comments on 2 Chronicles 36:20–21.

18. On the time frame of the exilic period, see comments at 2 Chronicles 36:20–21. For the experiences of the exilic community in Babylonia, see R. Zadok, *The Jews in Babylonia during the Chaldean and Achaemenain Periods* (Haifa: Univ. of Haifa Press, 1979), and D. Smith, *The Religion of the Landless: The Social Context of the Babylonian Exile* (Bloomington, Ind.: Meyer-Stone, 1989).

Following the Persian takeover of the Babylonian Empire in 539 BC, all of what had been Judah (as well as the northern kingdom, "Israel") fell under one of the large administrative units of the Persian Empire (satrapies) known by the geographical description "Beyond the [Euphrates] River." Within this region was the small province of Judea (frequently referred to by the Aramaic *Yehud*; cf. Ezr 5:8).[19] Yehud was further divided into five or six districts (depending on whether Jericho is counted as a district) with the following administrative centers: Jerusalem, Beth Hakkerem, Mizpah, Beth Zur, and Keilah (cf. Neh 3). The Decree of Cyrus in 539/538 BC enabled those exiled to Babylonia to return to their homeland and rebuild what was left of Judea (see commentary at 2Ch 36:22–23; cf. Ezr 2:1–67; Ne 7:5–73).[20] While still clearly under the hegemony of the Persian Empire, Judea was nevertheless granted some degree of political autonomy under the governorship of Sheshbazzar and subsequent leaders. A partial list of the leaders of Yehud is summarized below:[21]

Governors of Postexilic Judea (Yehud)

Name	Dates
Sheshbazzar	538–20 BC
Zerubbabel	520–? BC
Elnathan	Late 6th century BC
Nehemiah	445–33 BC
Bagohi (or Bagavahya/Bagoas)	Ca. 408 BC
Yehezeqiah	4th century BC

19. Other Persian administrative districts in the vicinity of Judea/Yehud include Samaria to the north (stretching from the Jezreel Valley in the north to the border of Judea in the south from the Sharon Plain in the west to the Jordan River in the east), Gilead in the Transjordanian area to the east of Judea, the region of Kedar/Geshem/Edom to the south of Judea, Ashdod to the west of Judea on the coastal plain including some of the Shephelah (cf. Ne 2:10, 19; 4:1–12; Y. Aharoni, *The Land of the Bible* [rev. and enl.; trans. and ed. A. F. Rainey; Philadelphia: Westminster, 1988], 413–23; M. Avi-Yonah, *The Holy Land from the Persian to Arab Conquests [536 B.C. to A.D. 640]: A Historical Geography* [rev. ed.; Grand Rapids: Baker, 1977], 13–31. Finally, note that the proposal of Sanballat, Tobiah, and Geshem to "meet" in the "Plain of Ono" following the completion of the wall (cf. Ne 6) implies that this area was in the vicinity of the intersection of the borders of Samaria, Judea, and Ashdod.

20. On the political involvement of Persia within the affairs of the Judean community, see J. Cataldo, "Persian Policy and the Yehud Community during Nehemiah," *JSOT* 28 (2003): 240–52; J. L. Berquist, *Judaism in Persia's Shadow: A Social and Historical Approach* (Minneapolis: Fortress, 1995), esp. 131–240; and S. E. McEvenue, "The Political Structure in Judah from Cyrus to Nehemiah," *CBQ* 43 (1981): 353–64.

21. The dates of several of these leaders of Yehud are not certain. Note that the governors Yehezer and Ahzai may fill in some of the period between Elnathan and Nehemiah. See the analysis of data pertaining to postexilic leaders in C. Meyers and E. Meyers, *Haggai, Zechariah 1–9* (AB; Garden City, N.Y.: Doubleday, 1987), 9–15.

Before long, the euphoria following the Decree of Cyrus gave way to the reality of the bleak situation in Judea. Discouragement replaced hope as the returnees faced the daunting challenge of rebuilding homes and cities, reestablishing societal infrastructure (such as agricultural production), and rebuilding the Jerusalem temple. These challenges were exacerbated by episodes of internal and external opposition.[22]

Nonetheless, spurred on by the ministries of Haggai and Zechariah, work on the temple was restarted and completed in 516/515 BC (cf. Ezr 6:14–15), resulting in another high point of optimism within the postexilic community. In time, however, the situation in Judea again reached a state of despair, as reflected in the report that reached Nehemiah in the Persian citadel of Susa (cf. Ne 1:2–3).[23] These challenges lead to the appointment of Nehemiah as governor of Yehud (cf. Ne 5:14) and the commissioning of Ezra in the realm of religious affairs (cf. Ezr 7:25–26).[24]

The leadership and rebuilding organized by Nehemiah and the spiritual revival facilitated by Ezra fostered a new era of hope and optimism within Yehud. This mood of optimism is enhanced by territorial gains in the west and south, enhanced security, and the fortification and repopulation of Jerusalem.[25] However, the end of the Ezra-Nehemiah time frame is punctuated with instances of recurring spiritual

---

22. Most of this opposition stems from those whose heritage traced back to the mixed people groups, which resulted from the repopulation policies of the Assyrians. For detailed treatment of the postexilic setting, see L. L. Grabbe, "A History of the Jews and Judaism," in *The Second Temple Period: Yehud: A History of the Persian Province of Judah* (Library of Second Temple Studies; London: T&T Clark, 2004); C. E. Carter, *The Emergence of Yehud in the Persian Period: A Social and Demographic Study* (JSOTSup 294; Sheffield: Sheffield Academic, 1999); P. R. Ackroyd, *The Chronicler in His Age* (JSOTSup 101; Sheffield: Sheffield Academic, 1991). Also see the articles in O. Lipschits and M. Oeming, eds., *Judah and the Judeans in the Persian Period* (Winona Lake, Ind.: Eisenbrauns, 2006).

23. Note also that by this time it had become clear that Zerubbabel was unable to restore/inaugurate the Davidic covenant (as per Jer 31–33 and Eze 37). There is little to no stress on the Davidic lineage of Zerubbabel within Chronicles, perhaps reflecting a milieu wherein focus had shifted from an individual laden with messianic imagery (cf. the presentation of Zerubbabel in Hag 2:20–23) to the collective hope of the community of believers, as perhaps implicit in the repeated expression of "all Israel" (43 times) within Chronicles. Moreover, the repeated use of "all Israel" in Chronicles might also reflect an effort to transcend the political and sectarian points of division that had developed within the postexilic community and to instill a vision for those still abroad. The difficulty of this period may have been exacerbated by the taxation and tribute requirements imposed on Yehud by Persia (cf. Carter, *Emergence of Yehud*, 259). In any event, sundry economic difficulties were a given in the struggling Yehud.

24. These appointments take place in the mid-fifth century BC. For the historical context of these appointments see the earlier table, "The Persian Empire and Postexilic Judea," above. Note that the time frame of Ezra and Nehemiah (ca. 460–30 BC) is approximately 75–110 years after the Decree of Cyrus.

25. At the beginning of the time frame of Ezra and Nehemiah, the geographical extent of Yehud was largely centered in the central hill country, the Jordan valley (Jericho), and some cities in the Shephelah (cf. Ne 3:1–25; 11:29–36). By the end of the Ezra-Nehemiah period, the territory of Judea had expanded to the west and south and now extended from (approximately) Jericho-Bethel-Ono in the north to En Gedi-Beth Zur-Azekah in the south and from Emmaus and Azekah-Gezer-Ono in the west and to the Dead Sea-Jordan River in the east (see the city list in Ne 11:25–36). The summary notice of Nehemiah 11:30 describes Judean occupation as being "from Beersheba to the Valley of Hinnom." Note that the lack of security in and around Jerusalem is implied by the necessity of casting lots to determine who would occupy Jerusalem following the completion of the wall (cf. Ne 11).

and societal problems. The closing verses of Nehemiah lament the neglect of God's house (Ne 13:4–11), violation of the Sabbath (Ne 13:15–16), and intermarriage with foreigners (Ne 13:23–28[26]).[27] The issue of intermarriage implies spiritual compromise and fostered cultural fragmentation, as some within the Judean community became unable to speak the "language of Judah" (cf. Ne 13:24).[28] Thus, once again, a time of hope and promise in Judea gave way to more challenge and discouragement. In other words, waves of hope within the postexilic community repeatedly give way to periods of despair and discouragement—a cycle that can be visually seen in the following graph:

Cycles of Hope and Discouragement in Postexilic Judea

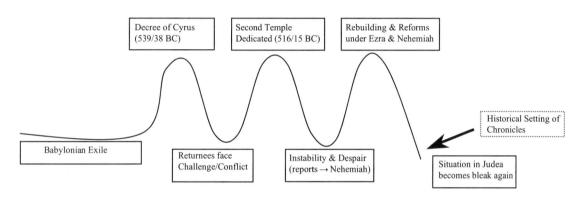

The manifold challenges facing those in Judean Yehud and the possibility that dispersed Judeans might opt to stay abroad might factor into the phrase that the Chronicler chose to end his work as follows: "Anyone of his [Yahweh's] people among you—may the LORD his God be with him, and let him go up." This final exhortation is an invitation to those still outside the Promised Land to come and rejoin "all Israel." As such, the *theological* setting of Chronicles is the eve of the postexilic setting—a hopeful contrast to the difficult *historical* situation in Judea. Thus, while the Chronicler's time frame may be one of

---

26. This intermarriage even included the son of the high priest.

27. Note that a number of the challenging aspects in Nehemiah 13 reflect an ongoing multinational/multiethnic presence in and around Jerusalem, a scenario that contributed to cultural-social fragmentation as well as spiritual compromises of various sorts. The continued fragmented nature of the broader Jewish community in the period following that of Ezra and Nehemiah is reflected in fifth-century BC Aramaic letters from the Elephantine corpus (cf. *COS*, 3.46–53).

28. The language of the postexilic context is referred to as Late Biblical Hebrew. On some of the distinctions and peculiar aspects of this stage of biblical Hebrew, cf. W. G. E. Watson, "Archaic Elements in the Language of Chronicles," *Bib* 53 (1972): 191–207; C. H. Gordon, "North Israelite Influence on Postexilic Hebrew," *IEJ* 5 (1955): 85–88; and S. Gevirtz, "Of Syntax and Style in the 'Late Biblical Hebrew'—'Old Canaanite Connection,'" *JANESCU* 18 (1986): 25–29.

disappointment, the Chronicler nonetheless proclaims a message of hope and possibility (also see "Literary Purpose and Theology," below).

4. GENRE

The OT books we know as 1 and 2 Chronicles have carried a variety of names over time.[29] For example, the name of Chronicles in the Greek translation of the OT (the Septuagint [LXX]) is *Paraleipomenōn tōn basileōn Iouda*, which means "[the] things omitted concerning the kings of Judah." The implication of this title may have influenced the relocation of Chronicles within the Christian Bible from the end of the OT to just after 1 and 2 Kings.[30] The resulting canonical placement unfortunately suggests that the purpose of Chronicles is simply to provide supplemental information for the texts in the Deuteronomic History (particularly Samuel and Kings), rather than having its own literary-theological message.[31]

By contrast, the name for Chronicles in the Hebrew Bible (*dibrê hayyāmîm*, meaning "the matters/ events of the days")[32] suggests a historical and annalistic purpose to the message of Chronicles. Similarly, the name for Chronicles in the Latin Vulgate is *Chronicon* (or *Chronikon*) *Totius Divinae Historiae*, meaning "Chronicle of the Total Divine History," suggesting a wide-ranging engagement of God's involvement in human history.[33]

One consideration in analyzing the genre of Chronicles is the fact that Chronicles has more in common with the genre of "annal" than it does with the genre of "chronicle." While both of these literary genres include individuals, records, and deeds, a chronicle is typically an abbreviated listing of historical events, while an annal features more sustained summaries of historical events with narrative shaping (including

---

29. On the different names attached to the book of Chronicles over time, see G. N. Knoppers and P. B. Harvey Jr., "Omitted and Remaining Matters: On the Names Given to the Book of Chronicles in Antiquity," *JBL* 121 (2002): 227–43.

30. Most ancient Hebrew manuscripts situate 1 and 2 Chronicles at the end of the final section of the Hebrew Bible (the Writings). The threefold division of the Hebrew Bible is as follows: (1) *Torah*/Law (Pentateuch [Genesis to Deuteronomy]; (2) *Nebiim*/Prophets (Former Prophets: Joshua, Judges, 1 and 2 Samuel, 1 and 2 Kings; Latter Prophets: Isaiah, Jeremiah, Ezekiel; and the twelve Minor Prophets [Hosea–Malachi]); and (3) *Ketubim*/Writings (balance of the OT). The term "Tanak" comes from the initial consonants of the Hebrew terms for these three sections. Jesus' words in Matthew 23:35 concerning the death of the priest Zechariah (probably referring to 2Ch 24:20–22) seems to imply that 2 Chronicles was understood as the end of the Hebrew canon during the time of Christ.

31. On the importance of approaching 1 and 2 Chronicles as an independent literary work, see T. Sugimoto, "Chronicles as Independent Literature," *JSOT* 55 (1992): 61–74.

32. This phrase is found at 1 Chronicles 27:24.

33. As Japhet notes, "God's rule of his people is expressed by his constant, direct, and immediate intervention in their history" (Japhet, *I & II Chronicles*, 44). Jerome's name for Chronicles in the Latin Vulgate gave rise to the name "Chronicles" used today. On the importance of genre in understanding points of contrast between Samuel/Kings and Chronicles, see R. Bruner, "Harmony and Historiography: Genre as a Tool for Understanding the Differences between Samuel-Kings and Chronicles," *ResQ* 46 (2004): 79–93.

a variety of genres and subgenres)[34] and an overall ideological purpose.[35] The narrative shaping of annals typically summarizes the deeds of rulers and people against the backdrop of divine blessing (or judgment).[36] In short, the genre of annal, like the text and content of Chronicles, features documentary details (what took place), ideological aspects (the significance of what took place), and literary elements (the shaping and stylistics of the account of what took place).

5. SOURCES

Chronicles, like the genre of annalistic literature discussed above, reflects the usage (selectivity) and shaping (literary-theological) of a wide range of sources from the administrative realm (e.g., kings and officials, military, taxation, royal assets) and the religious realm (e.g., temple officials, temple assets, temple procedures and responsibilities, prophetic oracles).[37] Kings of the biblical world often left detailed accounts of invasions, military maneuvers, political relationships, and the like in extensive royal annals.[38] The various references to source books in the OT indicate that this was also practiced in ancient Israel.[39]

Sources could later be consulted and referenced in the composition of additional literary works as reflected in Chronicles. Lastly, some ancient Near Eastern annals (such as those of Thutmose III)

---

34. Annals feature the use of other genres, such as lists, genealogies, cultic/temple records, and other archival documents (Kenton L. Sparks, *Ancient Texts for the Study of the Hebrew Bible* [Peabody, Mass.: Hendrickson, 2005], 408). Similarly, note that the book of Chronicles has a number of subgenres, including lists (e.g., kings, officials, cities, gatekeepers, temple items), genealogies (see the discussion of genealogies in the overview to 1 Chronicles 1–9), prophetic oracles, poetry, legal instruction, narrative, and speeches. On speeches and hortatory elements in Chronicles, see L. C. Allen, "Kerygmatic Units in 1 and 2 Chronicles," *JSOT* 41 (1988): 21–36. The variety of subgenres in Chronicles together with content the text shares with other biblical texts (esp. Samuel and Kings) has made identifying the macrogenre of Chronicles somewhat of a cottage industry.

35. Moreover, annals are "episodic" texts in that they summarize historical events at regular intervals without necessarily being chronologically exhaustive. Similarly, in the case of Chronicles, the text is historical, given that the overview of events and people are presented in a more or less chronological order against the implied backdrop of divine agency. In the words of Japhet (*I & II Chronicles*, 32), Chronicles is a presentation of consequent events, focused on the fortunes of a collective body, Israel, along a period of time within a defined chronological and territorial setting. The events do not constitute an incidental collection of episodes but are both selected and structured. They are represented in a rational sequence, governed by acknowledged and explicitly formulated principles of cause and effect, and are judged by stringent criteria of historical probability. The Chronicler wrote this history with full awareness of his task, its form and meaning.

36. That is, the ruler's deeds (or misdeeds) are commonly interwoven with references to divine favor and disfavor (cf. Sparks, *Ancient Texts*, 363).

37. Similarly, within the ancient Near Eastern literary setting, annals would commonly utilize chronicle accounts as sources. For example, in the Egyptian Middle Kingdom, miscellaneous records of temple and palace administration were recorded in documents known as "daybooks," which were utilized as sources for recording the accomplishments of individual rulers in annalistic accounts (see *CANE*, 2435). Such daybooks might be referenced as sources that could be consulted within an annalistic account, as evidenced in the fifteenth-century BC Annals of Thutmose III (cf. *CANE*, 2436).

38. Cf. the numerous inscriptions of the fifteenth-century BC Egyptian pharaoh Thutmose III and the seventh-century BC Assyrian monarch Sennacherib.

39. For example, note the reference to "the Book of the Wars of the LORD" in the book of Numbers (Nu 21:14) and the references to "the Book of Jashar/Yashar" in Joshua and Samuel (Jos 10:13; 2Sa 1:18).

use phraseology reminiscent of Chronicles and Kings, including the expression "as it is written in," to bring the reader's attention to earlier, authoritative texts. A selection of sources cited in Chronicles is as follows:[40]

- The Genealogical Records during the Reigns of Jotham King of Judah and Jeroboam King of Israel (1Ch 5:17)
- The Genealogies Recorded in the Book of the Kings of Israel (1Ch 9:1)
- The Book of the Annals of King David (1Ch 27:24)
- The Book of the Kings of Israel and Judah (2Ch 27:7; 35:27; 36:8)
- The Book of the Kings of Judah and Israel (2Ch 16:11; 25:26; 28:26; 32:32)
- The Book of the Kings of Israel (2Ch 20:34)
- Annotations [NASB: "Treatise"] on the Book of the Kings (2Ch 24:27)
- The Annals [NASB: "Records"] of the Kings of Israel (2Ch 33:18)
- The Written Instruction of David the King of Israel (2Ch 35:4)
- The Written Instruction of Solomon (2Ch 35:4)
- The Records of Samuel the Seer (1Ch 29:29)
- The Records of Nathan the Prophet (1Ch 29:29; 2Ch 9:29)
- The Records of Gad the Seer (1Ch 29:29)
- The Prophecy of Ahijah the Shilonite (2Ch 9:29)
- The Visions of Iddo the Seer (2Ch 9:29)
- The Records of Shemiah the Prophet and Iddo the Seer That Deal with Genealogies (2Ch 12:15)
- The Annotations [NASB: "Treatise"] of the Prophet Iddo (2Ch 13:22)
- The Annals of Jehu the son of Hanani (2Ch 20:34)
- The Words of David and of Asaph the Seer (2Ch 29:30)
- The Records of the Seers [= ḥôzāy; another term for *prophets*] (2Ch 33:19)

Beyond these directly noted sources, the intimate details reflected in temple organization, military structure, and the like imply that the Chronicler used other sources as well. Moreover, the genealogies of 1 Chronicles 1–9 clearly draw on genealogical sources that are not directly cited (esp. those of Genesis).[41] As the list of sources given above illustrates, a number of the sources referenced by the Chronicler have a prophetic connection, reflecting the role of the prophet in declaring the Word of God and mediating the covenant between Yahweh and Israel (also cf. 2Ch 26:22; 32:32). Similarly, note also the nearly identical

40. Note that some of these sources may be alternative names for the same document (such as variations of references to the "Book of the Kings"). For further examples of sources in Chronicles, see Hamilton, *Handbook on the Historical Books*, 2; Hill, *1 and 2 Chronicles*, 44; and Japhet, *I & II Chronicles*, 20. Note that Chronicles refers to sources at similar junctions as reflected in the book of Kings (e.g., 2Ch 12:15 and 1Ki 14:29; 2Ch 16:11 and 1Ki 15:23; 2Ch 20:34 and 1Ki 22:45; 2Ch 25:26 and 2Ki 14:18. See also J. A. Thompson, *1, 2 Chronicles* [NAC; Nashville: Broadman & Holman, 1994], 23).

41. Moreover, note that genealogical records often overlap with military counts (cf. 1Ch 7:9; 7:40). Also see the Overview on 1 Chronicles 1–9.

content shared between passages in Kings and sections of Isaiah and Jeremiah (e.g., Isa 36–39 and 2Ki 18–20; Jer 52 and 2Ki 25).

6. LITERARY PURPOSE AND THEOLOGY

Understanding Chronicles through the lens of an annal aids in the understanding of such variations of subgenre, content, and stylistics seen throughout Chronicles and allows interpretive attention to shift to the *purpose* of such literature. In short, annalistic literature such as Chronicles is not history for history's sake.[42] Instead, such texts arrange historical information (often gleaned from earlier texts; see "Sources") with an overarching political and/or religious agenda, such as teaching and inspiring the adoption of a certain perspective (e.g., spiritual, theological, political, ethnic) significant to the historical context (social, political, etc.) of the original audience (see "Historical and Social Background," above).[43] In the case of Chronicles, a theology of covenantal hope (much more than the oft-cited notion of "immediate retribution")[44] guides the selection, shaping, and structure of the text, with the goal of imparting this perspective to the Chronicler's readers and hearers.[45] This perspective makes the tone of the Chronicler's presentation of historical events didactic, almost sermonic, in its literary style and presentation.[46]

---

42. J. H. Walton, *Ancient Israelite Literature in Its Cultural Context: A Survey of Parallels between Biblical and Ancient Near Eastern Texts* (Grand Rapids: Zondervan, 1989), 114.

43. Ibid., 115–19. Walton prefers to call Chronicles a *chronographic text*.

44. Studies on the Chronicler all too frequently reflect an automaton parroting of a "retribution" hermeneutic for interpreting the Chronicler's presentation of the history of Judah. For example, Braun (*1 Chronicles*, xxxvii) makes the following declaration: "It needs to be stated that retribution is the major, if not the sole, yardstick used in writing the history of the post-Solomonic kings." Conversely, Selman (*1 Chronicles*, 62) is correct to conclude that "it seems therefore that immediate retribution is too narrow a term to express adequately the Chronicler's theology of judgment and blessing and it would be wise to revise substantially the use of the term." Selman, 63, is also correct to observe that the Chronicler emphasizes much more the "hope of restoration rather than the sad reality of retribution." Also see M. A. Thronveit, "Chronicles, Books of," in *Dictionary for Theological Interpretation of the Bible* (Grand Rapids: Baker Academic, 2005), 109–12. Again, while the Chronicler may "flatten" his summaries of certain historical events (e.g., not engaging the extended drama of David's becoming king over all Israel), the retribution approach has too many "exceptions" across the span of the Chronicler's work to justify its usage as a central interpretive principle. For a presentation of the retribution view, see R. B. Dillard, "Reward and Punishment in Chronicles: The Theology of Immediate Retribution," *WTJ* 46 (1984): 164–72.

45. Note that even the genealogical survey of the Chronicler (1Ch 1–9) exhibits selectivity (cf. the absence of various individuals such as Abel) and shaping (cf. the Chronicler's presenting of family lines such as that of Noah in such a way as to end with the person through whom God's redemptive plans will unfold; cf. 1Ch 1:5–27).

46. Cf. W. M. Schniedewind, *The Word of God in Transition: From Prophet to Exegete in the Second Temple Period* (JSOTSup 197; Sheffield: Sheffield Academic, 1995), 249–52.

The Chronicler's survey of events in the history of Judah (often, but not always, from a positive perspective)[47] is articulated through a theological framework centered on covenant.[48] In short, the book of Chronicles recounts the faithful acts of God as a means of provoking the seeking of God, hope in God, and covenantal faithfulness (obedience) within the Judean community.[49] Establishing continuity between the past and present is one of the ways in which the Chronicler weaves together this theological message of (covenantal) hope — as well as call to covenantal obedience — for his postexilic audience.[50] Note that the apostle Paul had a similar understanding of earlier biblical literature that showcased the faithfulness of God and simultaneously called God's people to obedience and perseverance: "For everything that was written in the past was written to teach us, so that through endurance and the encouragement of the Scriptures we might have hope" (Ro 15:4; cf. 1Co 10:11).

---

47. With respect to selectivity and shaping within the book of Chronicles, commentators frequently stress the Chronicler's tendency to cover the history of Judah from a positive light (e.g., David's affair with Bathsheba and treachery with Uriah are not mentioned in Chronicles). Dillard's remark is typical: "Any fault or transgression which might tarnish the image of David and Solomon has been removed" (R. B. Dillard, "The Chronicler's Solomon," *WTJ* 43 [1980]: 290). While the Chronicler's positive orientation is true to an extent given the text's orientation toward covenantal hope, this perspective is commonly overstated in studies on Chronicles. For example, the Chronicler includes a significant number of instances of covenantal unfaithfulness, including David's attempt to move the ark of the covenant that was not done "in the prescribed way" and was done without inquiring of God (see David's words at 1Ch 15:13; cf. 1Ch 13) and David's census that was "evil in the sight of God" (1Ch 21:7; cf. 1Ch 21). The latter is arguably more emphasized in Chronicles than Samuel (cf. Braun, *1 Chronicles*, 217). In addition, the opening phraseology of 1 Chronicles 20 reminds the reader via intertextuality (albeit subtly) of the unfortunate backdrop to this Ammonite battle (namely, the Bathsheba/Uriah incident; 2Sa 11). In addition to David, the reference to the prophecy of Ahijah (2Ch 10:15) invites the reader to review the glaring critique of Solomon vis-à-vis the Deuteronomic covenant in 1 Kings 10–11 that leads to the division of the Israelite kingdom. Similarly, the phraseology at 2 Chronicles 10:4 describes the labor required of Solomon with the same terminology used of the Egyptians in their bondage of the Israelites (e.g., Ex 6:6–9). Similar examples can be given for other Judean kings, such as Asa (cf. 2Ch 16) and Jehoshaphat (cf. 2Ch 19:1–3; 20:37). In addition, a number of important "positives" for Judah are *not* included in the Chronicler's account (see examples in Japhet, *I & II Chronicles*, 536).

48. The theological element of history gave rise to the phraseology *Heilsgeschichte* ("salvation history") in biblical studies, reflecting the purposeful activity of God within history (cf. Walton, *Ancient Israelite Literature in Its Cultural Context*, 120–22).

49. As Selman notes (*1 Chronicles*, 51), the Chronicler was a "theological optimist who wanted to bring fresh hope to his people." The Chronicler likewise shows that covenantal faithfulness extends to obedience to the covenantal structures established by God, particularly the Davidic monarchy/dynasty. For example, the stress of the poetic words of Amasai in 1 Chronicles 12:17–18 is that complete dedication, loyalty and service ("help") to David begets not only success (lit., "peace [upon] peace" or "supreme peace") for David but also success (again lit., "peace") upon those who are faithful to David. On the centrality of David within the Chronicler's message, see R. North, "Theology of the Chronicler," *JBL* 82 (1963): 369–81.

50. See P. R. Ackroyd, *The Chronicler in His Age*, 273–89. Also see idem, "The Chronicler as Exegete," *JSOT* 2 (1977): 2–32; W. M. Schniedewind, "The Chronicler as Interpreter of Scripture," in *The Chronicler as Author: Studies in Text and Texture* (ed. M. P. Graham and S. L. McKenzie; JSOTSup 263; Sheffield: Sheffield Academic, 1999), 158–80; J. Goldingay, "The Chronicler as Theologian," *BTB* 5 (1975): 99–121; S. Japhet, *The Ideology of the Book of Chronicles and Its Place in Biblical Thought* (Frankfurt: Peter Lang, 1989).

As Paul's writings suggest, the message of Chronicles of covenantal hope, seeking God, obedience, and faithful endurance transcends the Chronicler's time and percolates with meaning for God's people at all times. Similarly, the Chronicler is careful to emphasize that deeper *internal* issues, such as faithfulness, obedience, and personal purity, must coincide with *external* acts of worship.[51] Moreover, the Chronicler repeatedly draws focus to God so that the hope of his audience ("all Israel," not simply Judah)[52] is focused on God and his covenantal faithfulness and reconciling nature. As such, the temple is fundamental to the Chronicler's message of hope as the temple was both a tangible and symbolic image of divine presence, divine-human reconciliation, and divine-human fellowship (cf. 2Ch 7:12–22).[53]

Lastly, the final phrase of the Chronicler's work ("Let him go up") leaves the audience with a sense of anticipation of what might happen next and the realization that they (the Chronicler's original audience) are the ones who will finish this story! This final exhortation is an invitation to those still outside the Promised Land to come and rejoin "all Israel."[54] Thus, while the Chronicler's historical time frame may be one of disappointment (see "Date" and "Historical and Social Background," above), the Chronicler nonetheless proclaims a message of covenantal hope and possibility.[55] The Chronicler's review of historical events functions to shape the theological awareness of the postexilic Judean community—much as the book of Deuteronomy recaps history to the new generation waiting to enter the Promised Land who were born during the "exile" of the wilderness wanderings.[56] In both, there is the possibility and hope of entering the

---

51. As reflected in David's successful move of the ark (cf. 1Ch 15:12–15), Hezekiah's reforms (cf. 2Ch 29:11), and Josiah's reforms (cf. 2Ch 35:5).

52. Israelite unity is at the heart of the Chronicler's message of covenantal hope. While the Chronicler is largely silent on matters of the northern kingdom, the Chronicler incorporates praiseworthy aspects of those in the north in his genealogical survey (cf. 1Ch 5:20; 7:40) and in his narrative account, including the northern kingdom's mercy toward southern kingdom captives (cf. 2Ch 28:9–15), the positive response of some to Hezekiah's Passover invitation (cf. 2Ch 30:11), and even their efforts to destroy symbols of idolatry and syncretism (cf. 2Ch 31:1). The Chronicler's emphasis on the "good days" of Judah is consistent with his intent of spurring on hope and covenantal faithfulness for his audience, while his presentation of the shortcomings of even David and Solomon ensure that the focus of his audience is on God, not humanity.

53. Hence much of the Chronicler's presentation of the reigns of David and Solomon touches on the construction of the Jerusalem temple. Similarly, the Chronicler's detailed presentation of the roles of priests and Levites connects with their covenantal responsibilities to facilitate divine-human reconciliation and divine-human worship/fellowship as well as to instruct God's people concerning holiness and righteousness. The specific role of priests as teachers reflects the covenantal framework in which priests are charged by God to "teach the Israelites all the decrees the LORD has given them" (Lev 10:11; cf. Dt 33:8–11). The teaching of God's will infuses God's people with the spiritual direction needed to walk in a manner pleasing to him.

54. On the ending of Chronicles on a note of hope, see W. Johnstone, "Hope of Jubilee: The Last Word in the Hebrew Bible," *EvQ* 72 (2000): 307–14.

55. As noted (see "Date" and "Historical and Social Background"), the *theological* setting of Chronicles is the eve of the postexilic setting—a hopeful contrast to the difficult *historical* situation in Judea seen during the Chronicler's time period.

56. Recall that in the early decades of the return to Judea following the Decree of Cyrus in 539/538 BC, few returned. (Note that the families of Ezra, Nehemiah, and Esther obviously did not chose to return.) Also, recall Jeremiah's advice to those heading into exile to "settle down" and even to pray for the welfare of their new place of residence (Jer 29:5–7). Thus, many of the postexilic Judeans hearing the message of Chronicles would have been born in exile and have had little or no emotional-spiritual connection to the Promised Land.

land given by Yahweh and living as a covenantal community wholeheartedly in their commitment to him.[57] Thus the Chronicler ends his work with a message of the hope and possibility that comes with covenantal faithfulness, a note of covenantal hope also expressed by God through Jeremiah:

> "For I know the plans I have for you," declares the LORD, "plans to prosper you and not to harm you, plans to give you hope and a future. Then you will call upon me and come and pray to me, and I will listen to you. You will seek me and find me when you seek me with all your heart." (Jer 29:11–13)

7. SYNOPTIC ISSUES

Synoptic issues with Chronicles typically parallel passages from 2 Samuel, 1 Kings, or 2 Kings and less often involve sections from 1 Samuel, Ezra, Nehemiah, and the Psalter.[58] For better or worse, commentaries on Chronicles are often little more than a running comparison of synoptic issues featuring either a sustained apologia with frequent harmonization or a sustained string of unabashed speculation regarding the ideology behind the Chronicler's assumed "changes" to earlier texts.[59] Unfortunately such approaches come at the detriment of engaging the meaning and theological message of the Chronicler's text on its own terms.[60] Instead, the biblical texts with which Chronicles has parallel passages or differing thematic emphases (such as Samuel and Kings) reflect selectivity, shaping, and emphasis in line with their respective authorial intent in a given pericope. Thus, distinctions and differences in parallel texts (such as Kings and Chronicles) may simply reflect different approaches to telling the same story or reflect a different voice (such as thematic emphasis or theological point) drawn from one event.[61]

---

57. Note that both Deuteronomy and Chronicles exhort people to *remember* and *obey* their covenantal relationship with Yahweh while recounting the faithful acts of God. The recounting of the past sets the trajectory for considering the present and future. Moreover, in both there is the aftermath of divine judgment that involved prolonged time outside the land of promise as well as the presentation of hope and possibility for the future.

58. Helpful references for seeing parallel passages include J. D. Newsome, *A Synoptic Harmony of Samuel, Kings, and Chronicles* (Grand Rapids: Zondervan, 1986), and J. C. Endres et al., eds., *Chronicles and Its Synoptic Parallels in Samuel, Kings, and Related Biblical Texts* (Collegeville, Minn.: Liturgical, 1998).

59. Speculation may also be coupled with a preexisting hermeneutical-interpretive bent such as the "good" presentation of Judah or the (supposed) theme of immediate retribution (see note 44, above). For example, in referring to the Chronicler's coverage of the reign of Amaziah, Dillard notes the following: "Comments in his Kings *Vorlage* have been expanded to provide the theological rationale for weal or woe and to demonstrate once again the validity of the author's theology of immediate retribution" (Dillard, *2 Chronicles*, 202).

60. As noted by Braun (*1 Chronicles*, xxii), the synoptic approach is frequently laden with "artificiality and forced exegesis" and inadequately covers portions unique to Chronicles. This commentary strives to focus on the meaning of the Chronicler's text as received and with respect to its own biblical and theological agenda. As such, pertinent synoptic issues will not be ignored but will typically be addressed in the Notes section of the commentary. On approaching Chronicles on its own terms, see Sugimoto, "Chronicles as Independent Literature," 61–74.

61. Moreover, points of genre may affect the (re)telling of an account in synoptic passages (compare the poetic account of the crossing of the Sea in Ex 15 with the narrative account in Ex 14). On the importance of genre in understanding points of contrast between Samuel/Kings and Chronicles, see R. Bruner, "Harmony and Historiography: Genre as a Tool for Understanding the Differences between Samuel-Kings and Chronicles," *ResQ* 46 (2004): 79–93. Incidentally, different elements of detail, point of view, and literary style are not atypical for ancient Near Eastern texts reporting on the same event as reflected in the multiple works depicting Ramesses II's battle against the Hittites at Qadesh (cf. CANE, 2436).

While plausible suggestions can be given for instances of differences between parallel texts, the matter of the synoptic issue between Chronicles and other OT books is largely a philosophical-presuppositional area that goes hand in hand with one's view of the Bible vis-à-vis inspiration and inerrancy.[62] For evangelical readers of Chronicles the issue of potential differences between two biblical texts speaking on the same topic can be disconcerting and oftentimes motivates the drive for harmonization—even when such harmonization stretches the limits of plausibility. Yet the impulse to force solutions should be resisted; God does not need us to protect him or his Word. Moreover, forced and implausible solutions to synoptic difficulties will hardly change the mind of the skeptic. Thus it is often preferable to leave a point of interpretive tension as it is rather than to provide a forced solution.[63]

While interpretation is largely a presuppositional issue, there is a handful of categories wherein synoptic issues are typically addressed and that will be covered below.

Synoptic Issues Involving Numbers

Differences in numbers are one of the major categories treated in synoptic studies, though it should be noted that there is complete agreement in numbers between Chronicles and parallel texts in 195 out of 213 instances.[64] In several of the instances where numbers differ, the number reflected in Chronicles is actually the correct number. For example, the Hebrew text has "40,000" stalls for chariot horses at 1 Kings 4:26[5:6], while the text at 2 Chronicles 9:25 has the correct reading of "4,000" stalls (also cf. the LXX at 1Ki 10:26).[65]

In other cases, the difference simply reflects a distinction in the basis of counting or reckoning.[66] For example, the Chronicler has a different tabulation at 1 Chronicles 9:6 from that found at Nehemiah 11:6 (690 versus 468) that may relate to a different approach to counting ("men" is noted at Ne 11:6, whereas 1Ch 9:6 has "people"). Alternatively, the difference may simply be a factor of the time gap between the point in time utilized by the Chronicler and that utilized by Nehemiah.[67] Similar explanations can be posited for the difference in the enumeration of priests reflected in Chronicles and Nehemiah (1,760 in 1Ch 9:13 versus 1,192 in Ne 11:12–14).

---

62. As such, synoptic challenges are typically addressed via one's existing interpretive grid. With respect to the historical veracity of the Chronicler's account, see S. Japhet, "The Historical Reliability of Chronicles," *JSOT* 33 (1985): 83–107, and W. M. Schniedewind, "The Source Citations of Manasseh: King Manasseh in History and Homily," *VT* 41 (1991): 450–61. On the genealogical section of 1 Chronicles 1–9, see G. A. Rendsburg, "The Internal Consistency and Historical Reliability of the Biblical Genealogies," *VT* 40 (1990): 185–206. For an exegetical approach to synoptic issues, see W. E. Lemke, "The Synoptic Problem in the Chronicler's History," *HTR* 4 (1965): 349–63.
63. For a conservative evangelical methodology for engaging biblical challenges, see W. D. Barrick, "'Ur of the Chaldeans' (Gen 11:28–31): A Model for Dealing with Difficult Texts," *MSJ* 20 (2009): 7–18, esp. 17–18.
64. In the texts where there is a numerical difference, Chronicles has a higher number in eleven instances and a lower number in seven instances. See the helpful chart in Hill, *1 & 2 Chronicles*, 31.
65. In fact the NIV (rightly) corrects the MT 40,000 to 4,000 per 2 Chronicles 9:25.
66. See the extensive discussion in J. B. Payne, "Validity of Numbers in Chronicles," *NEASB* 11 (1978): 5–58.
67. Cf. Hill, *1 & 2 Chronicles*, 180.

Other synoptic issues involving numbers may be simply stylistic differences, such as rounding versus not rounding numbers as reflected in the following summaries of David's reign:

> He ruled over Israel forty years—seven in Hebron and thirty-three in Jerusalem. (1Ch 29:27)
> In Hebron he reigned over Judah seven years and six months, and in Jerusalem he reigned over all Israel and Judah thirty-three years. (2Sa 5:5)

In this example, the Chronicler opted to report David's reign in whole years ("seven years"), while the author of 2 Samuel also included the months ("seven years and six months"). Note that the Chronicler also includes the months of David's reign in his earlier genealogical survey (cf. 1Ch 3:4). Instances in rounding may also explain some differing numbers of military figures in synoptic accounts.[68]

Synoptic Issues Involving Perspective

In addition to the handling of numbers, synoptic differences may reflect a different point of reference or perspective that is not necessarily mutually exclusive (i.e., it can be both-and and is not necessarily either-or). For example, note the following statements regarding the ascension of Solomon:

> Solomon sat on the throne of his father David. (1Ki 2:12)
> Solomon sat on the throne of the LORD. (1Ch 29:23)

Note that these statements, while different, are both true.[69] The statement in Kings stresses God's faithfulness to fulfill his promise with respect to the Davidic covenant (see 2Sa 7:12), while the statement in Chronicles stresses the ultimate reality of God's universal kingship and (by extension) the role of the Israelite king as undershepherd to God. The Chronicler's manner of expressing Solomon's reign is consistent with his authorial intent (*Tendenz*) to emphasize that the people led by the king are *God's people* (cf. 2Ch 1:10), the kingdom is *God's kingdom* (cf. 1Ch 17:14; 2Ch 13:8), and that the king sits on *God's throne* (cf. 1Ch 29:23; 2Ch 9:8).[70]

Similarly, the Chronicler tends to emphasize the involvement of "all Israel" in important spiritual events in line with his focus on the whole covenantal community of Yahweh. For example, while the account of the taking of Jerusalem in Samuel (cf. 2Sa 5:6–10) focuses on the efforts of a small band of warriors, the Chronicler notes the involvement of "all the Israelites" in this important event (cf. comments on 1Ch 11:4–8).[71]

---

68. Such as the notation of 470,000 versus 500,000 men of Judah noted in Joab's census (cf. 1Ch 21:5 versus 2Sa 24:9). On the large numbers reflected here and other interpretive possibilities, see the extended discussion at 2 Chronicles 11:1.

69. Note that a difference in perspective may account for the oft-noted synoptic difference regarding "the LORD" (2Sa 24:1) versus "S/satan" (1Ch 21:1) in inciting David to conduct his ill-fated census. See a full discussion at 1 Chronicles 21:1–7.

70. Cf. Hill, *1 & 2 Chronicles*, 12.

71. Similarly, the Chronicler notes the involvement of the broader community in the relocation of the ark of the covenant to Jerusalem (cf. 1Ch 13 vs. 2Sa 6).

Lastly, the presentation of Manasseh in Chronicles emphatically shows the forgiving and reconciling nature of Yahweh experienced by Manasseh at the end of his days (cf. 2Ch 33)[72] in line with his message of covenantal hope for God's people, while the account in Kings summarizes the spiritual infidelity that characterized the vast majority of Manasseh's reign (cf. 2Ki 21) in line with his distinct authorial intent.[73]

Synoptic Issues Resulting from Scribal Error

Another area of synoptic differences may relate to errors in textual transmission. Although many evangelical believers hold to the view of the inerrancy of Scripture, the doctrine of inerrancy refers to the originally crafted manuscripts of biblical books (called "autographs") and does *not* extend into scribal/textual transmission of the biblical texts.[74] By the sovereign will of God, the transmission process was not inerrant; consequently, there may be variations in the manuscripts of biblical books in which only one reading is correct.

While these variations are statistically small, they do factor into a number of noted synoptic divergences.[75] For example, 2 Samuel 24:13 has "seven" years in the Hebrew text (MT) rather than "three" years as recorded at 1 Chronicles 21:12. Nonetheless, the NIV translates "three" at 2 Samuel 24:13, given the LXX at this verse as well as the parallel text here (see the NIV note), reflecting the likelihood of a scribal transmission error.[76] In addition, the similarity of certain Hebrew letters[77] likely brought about unintended spelling variations over time.[78] Moreover, the overlapping usage of some of these similar-looking letters as composite vowels, prefixes (verbal, definite article), consonants, suffixes (possessive/pronominal, direct object), and verbal inflection markers no doubt facilitated some of the transmission errors observed.

---

72. See commentary at 2 Chronicles 33:12–13.

73. Similarly, the account of Saul's death by his own hand at 1 Chronicles 10:4–5 is described in 2 Samuel 1:5–10 as coming by the hand of an Amalekite whom Saul asked to put him out of his misery as he lay upon his spear (2Sa 1:6–9; cf. 1Ch 10:5; 1Sa 31:4). While some try to present this as a contradiction, the account of 2 Samuel can easily be understood as providing additional details of Saul's final moments. In both scenarios, Saul has brought about his death. Note that the account in 2 Samuel has the same point of tension with the summary of Saul's death at 1 Samuel 31:4–5.

74. As the Chicago Statement on Biblical Inerrancy states, "Since God has nowhere promised an inerrant transmission of Scripture, it is necessary to affirm that only the autographic text of the original documents was inspired and to maintain the need of textual criticism as a means of detecting any slips that may have crept into the text in the course of its transmission. The verdict of this science, however, is that the Hebrew and Greek text appears to be amazingly well preserved, so that we are amply justified in affirming, with the Westminster Confession, a singular providence of God in this matter and in declaring that the authority of Scripture is in no way jeopardized by the fact that the copies we possess are not entirely error-free." See http://theapologeticsgroup.com/export/Articles/01_Inerrancy_Christian_Wordldview.pdf

75. Careful textual criticism often brings the correct reading to light.

76. Similarly, recall the issue of the number of stalls for chariot horses noted earlier.

77. For example, note the similarity of the following Hebrew letters: פ/ב/כ; ד/ר/ך; ה/ח/ת; י/ו/ז/ן; ג/נ.

78. Cf. the spelling variations noted in the Chronicler's genealogical summary in 1 Chronicles 1–9. See examples in Selman, *1 Chronicles*, 92 (n. 1). This noted, name and spelling variations may also reflect synchronic or diachronic changes in the Hebrew language (cf. examples in Hill, *1 & 2 Chronicles*, 183; Japhet, *I & II Chronicles*, 218–19).

8. BIBLIOGRAPHY

Braun, R. L. *1 Chronicles*. Word Biblical Commentary. Waco, Tex.: Word, 1986.

Day, J. "Asherah in the Hebrew Bible and Northwest Semitic Literature." *Journal of Biblical Literature* 105 (1986): 385–408.

Dillard, R. B. *2 Chronicles*. Word Biblical Commentary. Waco, Tex.: Word, 1987.

Hill, A. E. *1 & 2 Chronicles*. NIV Application Commentary. Grand Rapids: Zondervan, 2003.

Ishida, T., ed. *Studies in the Period of David and Solomon and Other Essays*. Winona Lake, Ind.: Eisenbrauns, 1982.

Japhet, S. *I & II Chronicles: A Commentary*. Old Testament Library. Louisville, Ky.: Westminster John Knox, 1993.

Johnstone, W. *1 and 2 Chronicles. Volume 1: 1 Chronicles 1–2 Chronicles 9: Israel's Place among the Nations*. Journal for the Study of the Old Testament Supplement Series 253. Sheffield: Sheffield Academic, 1997.

————. *1 and 2 Chronicles: Volume 2: 2 Chronicles 10–2 Chronicles 36: Guilt and Atonement*. Journal for the Study of the Old Testament Supplement Series 254. Sheffield: Sheffield Academic, 1997.

Keel. O. *The Symbolism of the Biblical World*. Translated by T. J. Hallet. Winona Lake, Ind.: Eisenbrauns, 1997.

Kitchen, K. *On the Reliability of the Old Testament*. Grand Rapids: Eerdmans, 2003.

Mabie, F. J. "2 Chronicles." Pages 286–393 in *Zondervan Illustrated Bible Backgrounds Commentary on the Old Testament*, volume 3. Grand Rapids: Zondervan, 2009.

McConville, J. G. *I and II Chronicles*. Daily Study Bible. Philadelphia: Westminster, 1984.

Provan, I., V. P. Long, and T. Longman III. *A Biblical History of Israel*. Louisville, Ky./London: Westminster John Knox, 2003.

Rainey, A. F., and R. S. Notley. *The Sacred Bridge: Carta's Atlas of the Biblical World*. Jerusalem: Carta, 2005.

Selman, M. J. *1 Chronicles*. Tyndale Old Testament Commentaries. Downers Grove, Ill.: InterVarsity Press, 1994.

————. *2 Chronicles*. Tyndale Old Testament Commentaries. Downers Grove, Ill.: InterVarsity Press, 1994.

Thiele, E. R. *The Mysterious Numbers of the Hebrew Kings*. 3rd ed. Grand Rapids: Zondervan, 1983.

Thompson, J. A. *1, 2 Chronicles*. New American Commentary. Nashville: Broadman & Holman, 1994.

9. OUTLINE

Text and Exposition

I. THE CHRONICLER'S GENEALOGICAL SURVEY OF ALL ISRAEL (1CH 1:1–9:44)

OVERVIEW

The genealogies of the Chronicler's account highlight both Israel's unique position of covenant with the Creator-God vis-à-vis the nations as well as God's ultimate plan of blessing for "all peoples on earth" (cf. Ge 12:1–3). There are two primary types of genealogies used by the Chronicler: vertical genealogies and horizontal genealogies. Vertical genealogies are careful to trace comprehensively the lineage of a particular part of a family line. In biblical genealogies vertical genealogies are used to focus on those in the chosen line of individuals through whom God is advancing his purposes (e.g., Ge 5:1–32; 11:10–26) and to show the legitimacy of covenantal roles and offices. For example, the Chronicler uses vertical genealogies to trace the lineage of Levitical priests (e.g., Levi-Kohath-Amram-Aaron-Eleazar; cf. 1Ch 6:1–15) and Davidic kings beginning with Solomon (1Ch 3:10–16). By contrast, horizontal genealogies provide supplementary information that provides breadth through a limited survey of descendants stemming from a single ancestor (cf. the line of Ishmael in Ge 25:12–18). For example, horizontal genealogies are used to provide information on the Edomites (cf. 1Ch 1:38–42) and the sons of David (1Ch 3:1–9).

Perhaps the most significant theological element conveyed through the Chronicler's genealogical survey is the notion of the continuity of Yahweh's covenantal promises. The Chronicler's genealogical survey reminds his audience of their connection with Abraham, Moses, and David, and the extension of his genealogy beyond the time of the exile (cf. Zerubbabel's family line; 1Ch 3:19–24) shows that God's promises are still in effect. In addition, the Chronicler's mention of the key tribal units from both sides of the long-divided Israelite kingdom acts as a powerful display of the Chronicler's message of tribal unity and covenantal hope. The Chronicler's strong message of unity is more striking when it is recalled that it had been about five hundred years since "all Israel" had existed as an independent unified nation.

Thus, while the Chronicler's genealogical survey reviews the past, it also works to produce hope in God at the present because of the covenantal possibilities for the future. Similarly, the image of continuity between the past and present facilitates hope that God is still at work through his people. This message of continuity is part of the Chronicler's message of hope and call to covenantal obedience for his postexilic audience. While the history of Judah is clearly punctuated with sin and unfaithfulness, it is nonetheless permeated by divine grace and faithfulness. Indeed, the Chronicler's genealogical survey echoes the words of Jeremiah that God's mercies are new each morning and that his faithfulness is great (cf. La 3:22–23, 31; see M. D. Johnson, *The Purpose of the Biblical Genealogies* [Cambridge: Cambridge Univ. Press, 1969]; also R. Wilson, *Genealogy and History in the Biblical World* [New Haven, Conn.: Yale Univ. Press, 1977]).

A. From Adam to the Sons of Israel (1Ch 1:1–2:2)

OVERVIEW

The first chapter of Chronicles is largely a succinct summary of the genealogical sections of the book of Genesis that brings the reader quickly from Adam to the descendants of Jacob's brother Esau. In between, the Chronicler provides snippets of ethnic and historical information that works ultimately to place Jacob/Israel in the midst of "the nations." This presentation both highlights Israel's unique position of covenant with the Creator-God vis-à-vis the nations as well as God's ultimate plan of blessing for "all peoples on earth" (cf. Ge 12:1–3).

[1]Adam, Seth, Enosh, [2]Kenan, Mahalalel, Jared, [3]Enoch, Methuselah, Lamech, Noah.
[4]The sons of Noah:

Shem, Ham and Japheth.

[5]The sons of Japheth:

Gomer, Magog, Madai, Javan, Tubal, Meshech and Tiras.

[6]The sons of Gomer:

Ashkenaz, Riphath and Togarmah.

[7]The sons of Javan:

Elishah, Tarshish, the Kittim and the Rodanim.

[8]The sons of Ham:

Cush, Mizraim, Put and Canaan.

[9]The sons of Cush:

Seba, Havilah, Sabta, Raamah and Sabteca.

The sons of Raamah:

Sheba and Dedan.

[10]Cush was the father of

Nimrod, who grew to be a mighty warrior on earth.

[11]Mizraim was the father of

the Ludites, Anamites, Lehabites, Naphtuhites, [12]Pathrusites, Casluhites (from whom the Philistines came) and Caphtorites.

[13]Canaan was the father of

Sidon his firstborn, and of the Hittites, [14]Jebusites, Amorites, Girgashites, [15]Hivites, Arkites, Sinites, [16]Arvadites, Zemarites and Hamathites.

[17]The sons of Shem:

Elam, Asshur, Arphaxad, Lud and Aram.

The sons of Aram:

Uz, Hul, Gether and Meshech.

[18]Arphaxad was the father of Shelah,

and Shelah the father of Eber.

[19]Two sons were born to Eber:

One was named Peleg, because in his time the earth was divided; his brother was named Joktan.

[20]Joktan was the father of

Almodad, Sheleph, Hazarmaveth, Jerah, [21]Hadoram, Uzal, Diklah, [22]Obal, Abimael, Sheba, [23]Ophir, Havilah and Jobab. All these were sons of Joktan.

[24]Shem, Arphaxad, Shelah,

[25]Eber, Peleg, Reu,

[26]Serug, Nahor, Terah

[27]and Abram (that is, Abraham).

[28]The sons of Abraham:

Isaac and Ishmael.

[29]These were their descendants:

Nebaioth the firstborn of Ishmael, Kedar, Adbeel, Mibsam, [30]Mishma, Dumah, Massa, Hadad, Tema, [31]Jetur, Naphish and Kedemah. These were the sons of Ishmael.

[32]The sons born to Keturah, Abraham's concubine:

Zimran, Jokshan, Medan, Midian, Ishbak and Shuah.

The sons of Jokshan:

Sheba and Dedan.

[33]The sons of Midian:

Ephah, Epher, Hanoch, Abida and Eldaah.

All these were descendants of Keturah.

[34]Abraham was the father of Isaac.

The sons of Isaac: Esau and Israel.

[35]The sons of Esau:

Eliphaz, Reuel, Jeush, Jalam and Korah.

[36]The sons of Eliphaz:

Teman, Omar, Zepho, Gatam and Kenaz; by Timna: Amalek.

[37]The sons of Reuel:

Nahath, Zerah, Shammah and Mizzah.

[38]The sons of Seir:

Lotan, Shobal, Zibeon, Anah, Dishon, Ezer and Dishan.

[39]The sons of Lotan:

Hori and Homam. Timna was Lotan's sister.

[40]The sons of Shobal:

Alvan, Manahath, Ebal, Shepho and Onam.

The sons of Zibeon:

Aiah and Anah.

[41]The son of Anah:

Dishon.

The sons of Dishon:

Hemdan, Eshban, Ithran and Keran.

[42]The sons of Ezer:

Bilhan, Zaavan and Akan.

The sons of Dishan:

Uz and Aran.

[43]These were the kings who reigned in Edom before any Israelite king reigned:
Bela son of Beor, whose city was named Dinhabah.

[44]When Bela died, Jobab son of Zerah from Bozrah succeeded him as king.

[45]When Jobab died, Husham from the land of the Temanites succeeded him as king.

[46]When Husham died, Hadad son of Bedad, who defeated Midian in the country of
Moab, succeeded him as king. His city was named Avith.

[47]When Hadad died, Samlah from Masrekah succeeded him as king.

[48]When Samlah died, Shaul from Rehoboth on the river succeeded him as king.

[49]When Shaul died, Baal-Hanan son of Acbor succeeded him as king.

[50]When Baal-Hanan died, Hadad succeeded him as king. His city was named Pau, and
his wife's name was Mehetabel daughter of Matred, the daughter of Me-Zahab.
[51]Hadad also died.

The chiefs of Edom were:

Timna, Alvah, Jetheth, [52]Oholibamah, Elah, Pinon, [53]Kenaz, Teman, Mibzar, [54]Magdiel
and Iram. These were the chiefs of Edom.

[2:1]These were the sons of Israel:

Reuben, Simeon, Levi, Judah, Issachar, Zebulun, [2]Dan, Joseph, Benjamin, Naphtali, Gad
and Asher.

COMMENTARY

1–4 The Chronicler begins his account of
Israel's history with the first man, Adam, perhaps
as a means of connecting his account with the
beginning of history vis-à-vis humankind as well as

the beginning point of the biblical canon (namely, Genesis). As such, the Chronicler's approach is similar to that used in Luke's gospel in presenting the Christ (cf. Lk 3:23–38) rather than Matthew's gospel, which begins with Abraham (cf. Mt 1:1–2). Note that this list of names moving from Adam to Noah and his sons is derived from the genealogy of Genesis 5.

5–27 This next major genealogical section draws from the "Table of Nations" of the book of Genesis (Ge 10:1–29) and as such summarizes the geopolitical expanse of the descendants of Noah following the flood (cf. Ge 10:1, 32). The Chronicler presents the genealogical summaries in reverse chronological (birth) order to focus on the divinely-chosen line of Shem-Abram/Abraham. The descendants of Japheth (vv.5–7; cf. Ge 10:2–5) are described as those who would occupy the Mycenaean coastal regions hugging the northern and northwestern shores of the Mediterranean Sea (e.g., Javan [= Greece]) as well as areas more inland (e.g., Tubal).

The descendants of Ham (vv.8–16; cf. Ge 10:6–20) occupy the northern areas of the African continent (e.g., Mizraim [= Egypt] and Cush) as well as the region of Syro-Canaan (e.g., Jebusites and Sidon) and farther north (e.g., Hamathites).

Lastly, the descendants of Shem (vv.17–27; cf. Ge 10:21–31 and 11:10–32) occupy the region of northeastern Canaan (e.g., Aram), Mesopotamia (e.g., Asshur [Assyria]), the area east of Mesopotamia (e.g., Elam), as well as desert regions (e.g., Sheba). Following this geopolitical summary, the summary of the "Semites" (descendants of Shem) is both retraced and expanded (cf. vv.24–27) in order to focus on the person and genealogical line of Abraham.

28–34 The Chronicler continues his genealogical presentation in such a way as to end with an individual central to God's redemptive plan

(here "Israel," i.e., Jacob). Thus, as the Chronicler did earlier with the summary of the sons of Noah and will do later with the sons of Isaac, he will first summarize the horizontal genealogy of Ishmael before turning to that of Isaac, and that of Esau before turning to that of Jacob/Israel. As noted above (see the Overview to chs. 1–9), horizontal genealogies provide a limited summary of descendants, whereas vertical genealogies trace the lineage of a particular part of a family line. The Chronicler's summary of the family line of Hagar/Ishmael is drawn from Genesis 25:12–18. The family of Ishmael settled in the wilderness regions to the south of what would become Israel (cf. Ge 25:18), while the other sons of Abraham were sent off to "the land of the east" (Ge 25:6).

1:35–2:2 As he did with the summary of the sons of Noah and Abraham, so the Chronicler will pursue the family line of Abraham-Isaac in such a way as to end with the person through whom God's redemptive plans will unfold. Thus the Chronicler first summarizes the genealogy of Esau before turning to the lineage of Israel/Jacob. The expanded coverage of the genealogy of Esau underscores the close connection historically and theologically between Jacob and Esau (cf. Mal 1:2–5; Ob 1; Ro 9:13), highlighting the notion of divine grace and God's engagement of the nations (cf. Ob 21). The summaries of Esau's lineage and the related histories of Edom and Seir (vv.35–54) closely reflect the content of Genesis 36.

The account of the two sons of Isaac spills into ch. 2 and ends with the listing of the actual twelve sons of Jacob/Israel (1Ch 2:1–2). These sons will constitute both the geographical organization of the future nation that will likewise be named "Israel" (the tribal territories). As such, 1 Chronicles 2:1–2 serves as both a conclusion to ch. 1 and an introduction to chs. 2 and following (cf. Japhet, 65; Selman, 95).

B. The Tribes of Israel (1Ch 2:3–9:1)

1. The Tribe of Judah (1Ch 2:3–4:23)

a. The Family Line of Judah Part One (1Ch 2:3–55)

OVERVIEW

After listing the twelve sons of Judah in 1 Chronicles 2:1–2, the Chronicler pursues the subsequent lineage of these tribes in the balance of chs. 2–8, with particular focus directed at the heritage of the tribes of Judah (1Ch 2:3–4:23) and Levi (1Ch 6:1–81). In addition, the Chronicler provides a detailed account of the tribe of Benjamin (though in separated blocks; cf. 1Ch 7:6–12; 8:1–40; 9:35–44), partly to provide the backdrop for the Saulide monarchy (ch. 10). Thus, even though Judah was the fourth-born son of Leah, the Chronicler treats the tribe of Judah first and most extensively. This preeminence of Judah relates to the Chronicler's attention to the Davidic monarchy (which shapes his presentation of Israel's history; cf. 1Ch 28:4), while the focus on the tribe of Levi relates to the Chronicler's interest in the covenantal role of priests and Levites within Judean society. See H. G. M. Williamson, "Sources and Redaction in the Chronicler's Genealogy of Judah," *JBL* 98 (1979): 351–59.

[3]The sons of Judah:

Er, Onan and Shelah. These three were born to him by a Canaanite woman, the daughter of Shua. Er, Judah's firstborn, was wicked in the LORD's sight; so the LORD put him to death. [4]Tamar, Judah's daughter-in-law, bore him Perez and Zerah. Judah had five sons in all.

[5]The sons of Perez:

Hezron and Hamul.

[6]The sons of Zerah:

Zimri, Ethan, Heman, Calcol and Darda—five in all.

[7]The son of Carmi:

Achar, who brought trouble on Israel by violating the ban on taking devoted things.

[8]The son of Ethan:

Azariah.

[9]The sons born to Hezron were:

Jerahmeel, Ram and Caleb.

[10]Ram was the father of

Amminadab, and Amminadab the father of Nahshon, the leader of the people of Judah. [11]Nahshon was the father of Salmon, Salmon the father of Boaz, [12]Boaz the father of Obed and Obed the father of Jesse.

¹³Jesse was the father of

Eliab his firstborn; the second son was Abinadab, the third Shimea, ¹⁴the fourth Nethanel, the fifth Raddai, ¹⁵the sixth Ozem and the seventh David. ¹⁶Their sisters were Zeruiah and Abigail. Zeruiah's three sons were Abishai, Joab and Asahel. ¹⁷Abigail was the mother of Amasa, whose father was Jether the Ishmaelite.

¹⁸Caleb son of Hezron had children by his wife Azubah (and by Jerioth). These were her sons: Jesher, Shobab and Ardon. ¹⁹When Azubah died, Caleb married Ephrath, who bore him Hur. ²⁰Hur was the father of Uri, and Uri the father of Bezalel.

²¹Later, Hezron lay with the daughter of Makir the father of Gilead (he had married her when he was sixty years old), and she bore him Segub. ²²Segub was the father of Jair, who controlled twenty-three towns in Gilead. ²³(But Geshur and Aram captured Havvoth Jair, as well as Kenath with its surrounding settlements — sixty towns.) All these were descendants of Makir the father of Gilead.

²⁴After Hezron died in Caleb Ephrathah, Abijah the wife of Hezron bore him Ashhur the father of Tekoa.

²⁵The sons of Jerahmeel the firstborn of Hezron:

Ram his firstborn, Bunah, Oren, Ozem and Ahijah. ²⁶Jerahmeel had another wife, whose name was Atarah; she was the mother of Onam.

²⁷The sons of Ram the firstborn of Jerahmeel:

Maaz, Jamin and Eker.

²⁸The sons of Onam:

Shammai and Jada.

The sons of Shammai:

Nadab and Abishur.

²⁹Abishur's wife was named Abihail, who bore him Ahban and Molid.

³⁰The sons of Nadab:

Seled and Appaim. Seled died without children.

³¹The son of Appaim:

Ishi, who was the father of Sheshan.

Sheshan was the father of Ahlai.

³²The sons of Jada, Shammai's brother:

Jether and Jonathan. Jether died without children.

³³The sons of Jonathan:

Peleth and Zaza.

These were the descendants of Jerahmeel.

³⁴Sheshan had no sons — only daughters.

He had an Egyptian servant named Jarha. ³⁵Sheshan gave his daughter in marriage to his servant Jarha, and she bore him Attai.

³⁶Attai was the father of Nathan,
   Nathan the father of Zabad,
³⁷Zabad the father of Ephlal,
   Ephlal the father of Obed,
³⁸Obed the father of Jehu,
   Jehu the father of Azariah,
³⁹Azariah the father of Helez,
   Helez the father of Eleasah,
⁴⁰Eleasah the father of Sismai,
   Sismai the father of Shallum,
⁴¹Shallum the father of Jekamiah,
   and Jekamiah the father of Elishama.

⁴²The sons of Caleb the brother of Jerahmeel:
   Mesha his firstborn, who was the father of Ziph, and his son Mareshah, who was the father of Hebron.
⁴³The sons of Hebron:
   Korah, Tappuah, Rekem and Shema. ⁴⁴Shema was the father of Raham, and Raham the father of Jorkeam. Rekem was the father of Shammai. ⁴⁵The son of Shammai was Maon, and Maon was the father of Beth Zur.
⁴⁶Caleb's concubine Ephah was the mother of Haran, Moza and Gazez. Haran was the father of Gazez.
⁴⁷The sons of Jahdai:
   Regem, Jotham, Geshan, Pelet, Ephah and Shaaph.
⁴⁸Caleb's concubine Maacah was the mother of Sheber and Tirhanah. ⁴⁹She also gave birth to Shaaph the father of Madmannah and to Sheva the father of Macbenah and Gibea. Caleb's daughter was Acsah. ⁵⁰These were the descendants of Caleb.

The sons of Hur the firstborn of Ephrathah:
   Shobal the father of Kiriath Jearim, ⁵¹Salma the father of Bethlehem, and Hareph the father of Beth Gader.
⁵²The descendants of Shobal the father of Kiriath Jearim were:
   Haroeh, half the Manahathites, ⁵³and the clans of Kiriath Jearim: the Ithrites, Puthites, Shumathites and Mishraites. From these descended the Zorathites and Eshtaolites.
⁵⁴The descendants of Salma:
   Bethlehem, the Netophathites, Atroth Beth Joab, half the Manahathites, the Zorites, ⁵⁵and the clans of scribes who lived at Jabez: the Tirathites, Shimeathites and Sucathites. These are the Kenites who came from Hammath, the father of the house of Recab.

COMMENTARY

3–8 The Chronicler gives the lineage of the tribe of Judah a position of literary and theological preeminence by his "fronting" of the genealogical summary of the fourth-born Judah together with his extended treatment of the descendants of Judah. This initial section gives the genealogical information for the five sons of Judah (v.4), building on earlier lists given in Genesis and Numbers (cf. Ge 46:12; Nu 26:19–22).

In addition, the broader summary of the tribal lineage of Judah reminds the reader of the sordid events of Genesis 38, which led to Judah's fathering of Perez and Zerah by his daughter-in-law Tamar. This in turn provides a vivid example of God's sovereign outworking of his will and elective purposes. For example, recall that Judah was the fourth-born of Jacob's less-favored wife, Leah, but nonetheless becomes the conduit for the Davidic dynasty (and the Messiah), despite Tamar's foray into pseudo-harlotry to ensure the continuity of her husband's line (cf. Ge 38:26–30). Moreover, Tamar's father's house in the land of Canaan (Ge 38:11) suggests she was not an Israelite.

Similarly, one of the genealogical lists likely referenced by the Chronicler (Ru 4:18–22; cf. 1Ch 2:10–12) illustrates that the Davidic line (and hence the messianic line) also included a Moabitess (Ruth), an astounding reflection of God's redemptive grace (recall Dt 23:3). Note that these details are reflected in Matthew's genealogical presentation of the Christ along with Rahab (likely the Canaanite harlot of Jos 2) and the unwed mother Mary (cf. Mt 1:1–16). All this reflects God's faithfulness and creative sovereignty to bring his plans to pass through—and despite—imperfect human beings (Ro 8:28).

This reality of God's providential workings would provide hope for the Chronicler's audience and subsequent readers of Chronicles. Together with the presentation of God's restorative grace is the reality of God's distaste for unfaithfulness and sin (vv.3, 7; cf. Ge 38:7; Jos 7:24–26; Selman, 95–96). Unfaithfulness by the descendants of Judah (particularly the monarchy) will ultimately play a large role in the eventual destruction of Jerusalem and exile to Babylonia.

9–17 Although Ram was not the oldest son of Hezron, he is treated with priority by the Chronicler, given his connection with David (v.15). Note that vv.10–12 in this section reflect the genealogy leading to David given in Ruth 4:18–22. For more on the theology of divine grace and sovereignty reflected in these genealogical summaries, see comments on vv.3–8. Lastly, note that this genealogical summary shows that the military leaders Joab, Abishai, and Amasa (vv.16–17) were related to each other as well as to King David.

18–24 Much of the balance of the genealogy of the sons of Hezron has little to no parallel data in the balance of the OT. The references to a certain descendant of Judah's being a "father" of a certain city (vv.21, 23, 24) probably reflect a position of leadership (such as a town elder) within that city. Note that this section provides the family lineage of Bezalel, who was given a "skill, ability and knowledge in all kinds of crafts" by Yahweh in the context of building the tabernacle in the wilderness during the time of Moses (cf. Ex 31:1–5). Solomon's later construction of the temple will draw a number of similarities between the tabernacle and the temple as well as between Solomon and Bezalel (see comments on 2Ch 1:10 and 2Ch 2:1).

25–41 The section outlining the descendants of Jerahmeel provides genealogical information on this little known family that is mostly situated in the southern regions of Judah (cf. "the Negev of

Jerahmeel," 1Sa 27:10). Particular attention seems given to women, even non-Israelite women, in this section (cf. Hill, 81). Note the inclusion of an Egyptian (Jarha) in this broader family line of Judah (recall Tamar [probably a Canaanite] and Ruth [Moabitess]). As Isaiah proclaims, God's ultimate redemptive plan includes Israelites, Egyptians, and Assyrians serving him shoulder to shoulder, with God saying of the Egyptians, "Blessed be Egypt my people" (cf. Isa 19:18–25).

42–55 The Chronicler continues his summary of the family line of Caleb begun earlier (cf. vv.18–24). A number of these descendants are connected with cities in the southern areas of Judah that play a significant role in the broader history of Israel (e.g., Hebron, v.42; Kiriath Jearim, v.53; Bethlehem, v.54). The Netophathites (v.54) are later associated with two of David's mighty men (cf. 2Sa 23:28–29; 1Ch 11:30), and the town of Netophah (about three miles south of Jerusalem) later served as a home to Levitical singers during the postexilic period (cf. Ne 12:27–28). Note that the Kenites (v.55) were not ethnically Israelites (cf. Ge 15:18–21) but were eventually "grafted in" to the tribe of Judah and the family of Israel, demonstrating God's transethnic redemptive plan (cf. Ge 12:1–3; Eph 2:19–22).

NOTES

6 Note that the names of Heman and Ethan are mentioned in the headings of Psalms 88 and 89, respectively. In these psalms they are noted as Ezrahites, which might reflect their backdrop as Zerahites (v.6) or disciples of the postexilic Ezra.

15 The Chronicler here refers to David as the seventh son of Jesse, whereas 1 Samuel 17:12–14 refers to David as the eighth son. While the reason for this difference is not certain, the account in Samuel may be counting a half-brother or even a child that died young. Another son may be mentioned at 1 Chronicles 27:18.

17 Jether, designated here as an "Ishmaelite" (הַיִּשְׁמְעֵאלִי, *hayyišmᵉʿēʾlî*), is described as an "Israelite" (הַיִּשְׂרָאֵלִי, *hayyiśrᵉʾēlî*) in 2 Samuel 17:25. The similarity of these terms suggests a textual transmission issue.

18 The references to Caleb (v.18; vv.42–55) are likely not the same Caleb associated with Joshua, since that Caleb is noted as being a "Kenizzite" and a son of Jephunneh (cf. Jos 14:6, 13–15).

55 While the reference to the "clans of the scribes" might refer to the location of a scribal guild in ancient Israel as reflected in the NIV, another possibility is that the term used here (וּמִשְׁפְּחוֹת סֹפְרִים, *ûmišpᵉḥôt sōprîm*) is actually a family gentilic designation, e.g., "clans of the Sophrites/Siphrites" (cf. Selman, 99).

b. The Line of David (1Ch 3:1–9)

OVERVIEW

The Chronicler provides a succinct portrait of the descendants of David and as such provides a summary of those charged with upholding the Davidic covenant (see comments on 1Ch 17:7–15). In this survey of the Judean royal line, the Chronicler develops his earlier genealogical summary leading to David (cf. 1Ch 2:10–17).

¹These were the sons of David born to him in Hebron:

The firstborn was Amnon the son of Ahinoam of Jezreel;

the second, Daniel the son of Abigail of Carmel;

²the third, Absalom the son of Maacah daughter of Talmai king of Geshur;

the fourth, Adonijah the son of Haggith;

³the fifth, Shephatiah the son of Abital;

and the sixth, Ithream, by his wife Eglah.

⁴These six were born to David in Hebron, where he reigned seven years and six months. David reigned in Jerusalem thirty-three years, ⁵and these were the children born to him there:

Shammua, Shobab, Nathan and Solomon. These four were by Bathsheba daughter of Ammiel. ⁶There were also Ibhar, Elishua, Eliphelet, ⁷Nogah, Nepheg, Japhia, ⁸Elishama, Eliada and Eliphelet — nine in all. ⁹All these were the sons of David, besides his sons by his concubines. And Tamar was their sister.

COMMENTARY

1–9 The first section of the Chronicler's summary of the Davidic line is a listing of the actual sons of David born in both Hebron (vv.1–4) and later in Jerusalem (vv.5–9). The genealogical information noted here was likely gleaned from similar listings in 2 Samuel (e.g., 3:2–5 and 5:13–16). The list of the six sons of David born in Hebron indicates six different wives/mothers (Ahinoam, Abigail, Maacah, Haggith, Abital, and Eglah). The fact that each wife is only associated with one son suggests that the Chronicler's information was drawn from a list of firstborn sons (Japhet, 94–95).

The thirteen sons born to David in Jerusalem (vv.5–9) include four sons born to Bathsheba (Heb. *Bat-šûaʿ*) and another nine sons born to unspecified wives. The Chronicler's later listing of the sons of David born in Jerusalem (cf. 1Ch 14:3–7) differs from this listing, suggesting the use of different genealogical sources by the Chronicler in weaving together his history of Judah. The Chronicler notes that these sons do not include those born by David's concubines (v.9). The mention of only one daughter of David (Tamar) does not necessarily mean that David had only one daughter, but rather that this is the one named daughter who figures (however ignominiously) into the canonical story line of the royal family (cf. 2Sa 13).

NOTES

1 The second son of Abigail is called "Kileab" in 2 Samuel 3:3, likely reflecting either a textual transmission issue or an alternative name used of this son.

5 The Chronicler's placement of Solomon in fourth (last) position in his listing of the sons of Bathsheba is similar to the Chronicler's earlier reversed sequences of genealogies. This arrangement places a successor in the final (emphatic) position (cf. the lineage of the sons of Noah, 1:5–27).

6–8 The sons Eliphelet and Nogah are not listed at 2 Samuel 5:14. The mention of a son named "Eliphelet" at v.8 has caused some to propose that dittography occurred during the scribal transmission process; however, the summary amount of "nine [sons] in all" (v.8) makes this view difficult and might suggest haplography on the part of the scribes copying Samuel.

c. Listing of Davidic Kings (1Ch 3:10–24)

¹⁰Solomon's son was Rehoboam,
    Abijah his son,
    Asa his son,
    Jehoshaphat his son,
    ¹¹Jehoram his son,
    Ahaziah his son,
    Joash his son,
    ¹²Amaziah his son,
    Azariah his son,
    Jotham his son,
    ¹³Ahaz his son,
    Hezekiah his son,
    Manasseh his son,
    ¹⁴Amon his son,
    Josiah his son.
¹⁵The sons of Josiah:
    Johanan the firstborn,
    Jehoiakim the second son,
    Zedekiah the third,
    Shallum the fourth.
¹⁶The successors of Jehoiakim:
    Jehoiachin his son,
    and Zedekiah.
¹⁷The descendants of Jehoiachin the captive:
    Shealtiel his son, ¹⁸Malkiram, Pedaiah, Shenazzar, Jekamiah, Hoshama and
    Nedabiah.
¹⁹The sons of Pedaiah:
    Zerubbabel and Shimei.

The sons of Zerubbabel:
  Meshullam and Hananiah.
  Shelomith was their sister.
²⁰There were also five others:
  Hashubah, Ohel, Berekiah, Hasadiah and Jushab-Hesed.
²¹The descendants of Hananiah:
  Pelatiah and Jeshaiah, and the sons of Rephaiah, of Arnan, of Obadiah and of Shecaniah.
²²The descendants of Shecaniah:
  Shemaiah and his sons:
  Hattush, Igal, Bariah, Neariah and Shaphat — six in all.
²³The sons of Neariah:
  Elioenai, Hizkiah and Azrikam — three in all.
²⁴The sons of Elioenai:
  Hodaviah, Eliashib, Pelaiah, Akkub, Johanan, Delaiah and Anani — seven in all.

COMMENTARY

10–16 The second section of the Chronicler's summary of the Davidic line is a listing of the kings of Judah; that is, of the southern kingdom during the divided kingdom period (ca. 930s BC–722/721 BC) as well as the time frame following the fall of the northern kingdom up to and including the fall of Judah (ca. 722/721 BC–586 BC). Thus this list is limited to kings who ruled over Judah rather than being an exhaustive list of all Davidic descendants.

17–24 The final section of the Chronicler's summary of the Davidic line is a summary of the royal line during and after the exile (ca. sixth to fifth/fourth century BC). For the Chronicler, the ability to trace these "sons" of David was important for facilitating hope in God's present and future plans for the house of David. This list clearly extends into the postexilic period, perhaps even to the time of the Chronicler. The leadership of Zerubbabel (v.19) corresponded with renewed prophetic hope that God was restoring the Davidic line in Judah (cf. Zec 4:1–14; Hag 2:20–23), a hope ultimately fulfilled in Christ (cf. Mt 22:42; Lk 1:32; Ac 15:16).

NOTES

15 On the spelling variations related to the sons of Josiah, see the discussions in Braun, 51–52, and Japhet, 97–98.

19–24 Zerubbabel's father is noted as "Pedaiah" in v.19 but noted as Shealtiel (cf. v.18) in Ezra 3:2 (cf. Mt 1:12). This issue cannot be resolved definitively but may relate to a dual understanding of father (birth father vs. one who raised/discipled him) or the outworking of a Levirate-marriage arrangement following an early death of Shealtiel (cf. Dt 25:5–10). But note that the LXX here has the reading "Shealtiel" here instead of "Pedaiah." See the fuller analysis of this issue in Selman, 100–101, and Japhet, 100. Although Zerubbabel did not fill the office of king (e.g., he is noted as "governor" in Hag 1:1; recall Jer 22:30), there was still hope of restoration of the Davidic dynasty. The hope of Yahweh's restoration of the Davidic dynasty may be reflected in the meaning of the names of Zerubbabel's sons. For example, Meshullam (v.19) means "restored," while Jushab-Hesed (v.20) means "[Covenant] lovingkindness/faithfulness returns." See other examples in Braun, 54, and Selman, 101.

d. The Family Line of Judah Part Two (1Ch 4:1–23)

OVERVIEW

The first part of ch. 4 (vv.1–23) provides additional genealogical details on the family line of Judah begun earlier (cf. 2:3–3:24) not found elsewhere in Scripture. The Chronicler's remark at v.22 implies that this family line information was drawn from old (preexilic) genealogical lists.

¹The descendants of Judah:
    Perez, Hezron, Carmi, Hur and Shobal.
²Reaiah son of Shobal was the father of Jahath, and Jahath the father of Ahumai and Lahad. These were the clans of the Zorathites.
³These were the sons of Etam:
    Jezreel, Ishma and Idbash. Their sister was named Hazzelelponi. ⁴Penuel was the father of Gedor, and Ezer the father of Hushah.
These were the descendants of Hur, the firstborn of Ephrathah and father of Bethlehem.
⁵Ashhur the father of Tekoa had two wives, Helah and Naarah.
⁶Naarah bore him Ahuzzam, Hepher, Temeni and Haahashtari. These were the descendants of Naarah.
⁷The sons of Helah:
    Zereth, Zohar, Ethnan, ⁸and Koz, who was the father of Anub and Hazzobebah and of the clans of Aharhel son of Harum.

⁹Jabez was more honorable than his brothers. His mother had named him Jabez, saying, "I gave birth to him in pain." ¹⁰Jabez cried out to the God of Israel, "Oh, that you would bless me and enlarge my territory! Let your hand be with me, and keep me from harm so that I will be free from pain." And God granted his request.
    ¹¹Kelub, Shuhah's brother, was the father of Mehir, who was the father of Eshton.
        ¹²Eshton was the father of Beth Rapha, Paseah and Tehinnah the father of Ir Nahash. These were the men of Recah.

¹³The sons of Kenaz:
    Othniel and Seraiah.

The sons of Othniel:

Hathath and Meonothai. ¹⁴Meonothai was the father of Ophrah.

Seraiah was the father of Joab,

the father of Ge Harashim. It was called this because its people were craftsmen.

¹⁵The sons of Caleb son of Jephunneh:

Iru, Elah and Naam.

The son of Elah:

Kenaz.

¹⁶The sons of Jehallelel:

Ziph, Ziphah, Tiria and Asarel.

¹⁷The sons of Ezrah:

Jether, Mered, Epher and Jalon. One of Mered's wives gave birth to Miriam, Shammai and Ishbah the father of Eshtemoa. ¹⁸(His Judean wife gave birth to Jered the father of Gedor, Heber the father of Soco, and Jekuthiel the father of Zanoah.) These were the children of Pharaoh's daughter Bithiah, whom Mered had married.

¹⁹The sons of Hodiah's wife, the sister of Naham:

the father of Keilah the Garmite, and Eshtemoa the Maacathite.

²⁰The sons of Shimon:

Amnon, Rinnah, Ben-Hanan and Tilon.

The descendants of Ishi:

Zoheth and Ben-Zoheth.

²¹The sons of Shelah son of Judah:

Er the father of Lecah, Laadah the father of Mareshah and the clans of the linen workers at Beth Ashbea, ²²Jokim, the men of Cozeba, and Joash and Saraph, who ruled in Moab and Jashubi Lehem. (These records are from ancient times.) ²³They were the potters who lived at Netaim and Gederah; they stayed there and worked for the king.

COMMENTARY

1–8 The additional genealogical details on the family tree of Judah listed here by the Chronicler build on the earlier treatment of the house of Caleb (cf. 1Ch 2:50–55). The particular focus on the line of Hur and Shobal likely reflects the Chronicler's postexilic setting, wherein the village of Zorah (cf. the Zorathites in v.2) was a place of resettlement for Judeans following the Babylonian exile. Establishing continuity between the past and present is one of the ways that the Chronicler weaves together his message of hope for his postexilic audience. References to a certain descendant of Judah's being a "father" of a certain city (e.g., v.4) probably indicate a position of leadership (such as a town elder) within that city.

9–10 This short commentary on Jabez does not fit into or connect with the surrounding genealogical material. In fact, these two verses contain the only mention of the person Jabez in the Bible. ("Jabez" at 1Ch 2:55 is a place name associated with scribes.) Given that Jabez does not have a clear connection to either the immediate or broader genealogical review of the Chronicler, this short passage was no doubt intended to provide a theological message vis-à-vis its literary placement within the genealogy of the Israelite tribes. (For possible connections with the subsequent material, see comments on vv. 13–16 and 34–43.)

The "honor" of Jabez seems to be his seeking of God through prayer, with God blessing him in a way that transcends the meaning of his name (a variation of the "pain" in which his mother bore him [v.9]). Thus the Chronicler's message may be that in light of the pain and reduced territory reflected in the postexilic setting, God's people should seek him in prayer and faithfulness (cf. Solomon's temple-dedication prayer [2Ch 6, esp. vv.22–39]).

11–12 The genealogy of Kelub (Chelub) is only found here in the Bible. The mention of "Ir Nahash" may suggest an early center of metalworking (copper) in the Arabah area. The metalworking for the bronze objects of the Jerusalem temple took place on the eastern side of the Jordan Valley midway between the Dead Sea and the Sea of Chinnereth (Galilee; see further comments on 2Ch 4:12–18).

13–16 This list highlights the descendants of Kenaz, the Kenizzites. Like the Kenites (cf. 1Ch 2:55) the Kenizzites were not ethnically Israel-

ites (cf. Ge 15:19; 36:40–43) but were eventually "grafted in" to the tribe of Judah and the family of Israel, thus demonstrating God's transethnic redemptive plan (cf. Ge 12:1–3; Eph 2:19–22). Note that Othniel (v.13) was the first of Israel's judges (cf. Jdg 3:9–11). Along with Caleb, Othniel helped expand the territorial extent of Israel (recall the prayer of Jabez [vv.9–10]).

17–20 The family line of Ezrah includes a particular focus on women within the lineage of Judah, including an Egyptian woman who may have hailed from Egyptian royalty (v.18; see Note). As Isaiah notes, God's ultimate redemptive plan includes Israelites, Egyptians, and Assyrians serving him shoulder to shoulder (cf. Isa 19:18–25). As noted above (see comments on 1Ch 2:25–41), the chosen line of Judah includes Egyptians (e.g., Bithiah here and Jarha at 1Ch 2:34–35), Canaanites (e.g., Tamar and perhaps Rahab), and Moabites (e.g., Ruth). This presentation highlights God's ultimate plan of blessing for "all peoples on earth" (cf. Ge 12:1–3).

21–23 Like the mention of the "city of copper" (Ir Nahash [v.12]) and the mention of a scribal depot located at Jabez (1Ch 2:55), the Chronicler provides details of the towns of the descendants of Shelah that were associated with particular guilds, including linen workers (v.21) and royal potters (v.23). The editorial remark in v.22 that "these records are from ancient times" suggests the Chronicler had access to rather early genealogical lists dating to preexilic times.

NOTES

1 "Carmi" may be another name for Caleb.

4–8 The family line of Ashhur should be compared with the family line of Caleb in 1 Chronicles 2:18–24. If the LXX is preferred at v.24 ("and Caleb married Ephrathah" vs. "Hezron died in Caleb Ephrathah"), it would mean that Ashhur was the younger brother (not son) of Hur (see Hill, 95).

10 The final line of Jabez's prayer may be better construed along the lines of "so that I will not cause pain" (cf. NKJV) rather than "so that I will be free from pain." Pechawer suggests that the prayer request of Jabez be translated, "If you would only bless me, then enlarge my territory that your hand may be with me, and provide me with pastureland so that I will not be in distress." This translation suggests that Jabez's prayer request had a single focus related to ample pastureland (see L. Pechawer, *The Lost Prayer of Jabez* [Joplin, Mo.: Mireh, 2001]).

18 The remark that Bithiah is a "daughter of Pharaoh" (בַת־פַּרְעֹה, *bat-parʿōh*) may be a reference to her Egyptian ancestry rather than a statement of her royal lineage (cf. "Bithiah," *ISBE*, 1:520). This noted, the boast of the Egyptian pharaoh Amenhotep III that no daughter of an Egyptian pharaoh was ever given in marriage is often inappropriately seen as a once-for-all "proof" that such a marriage (like the later marriage of Solomon to a daughter of Pharaoh; cf. 2Ch 8:11) could not have taken place. However, note that Amenhotep's claim was made more than four hundred years *before* Solomon's reign.

22 The specific association with Saraph and Moab is not completely clear in Hebrew. In addition to some kind of leadership role, it is possible that the text (via transposition of consonants) is actually referring to migratory *work* in Moab (as reflected in the story of Ruth) or is referring to *marriage* with Moabites (the root of "to rule" [בעל, *bʿl*; GK 1249] also refers to marriage; see Hill, 99).

REFLECTION

Despite the implicit message of popular books, the prayer of Jabez in 4:9–10 is not a formulaic blueprint for achieving spiritual blessings from on high. While Godwardness reflected in prayer transcends the Chronicler's time frame, the motivation to pray in order to *get* reflects a focus on self that is inconsistent with the example of Christ and the teachings of the NT (e.g., Lk 9:23; 1Co 13:5; Php 2:1–11).

2. The Tribe of Simeon (1Ch 4:24–43)

OVERVIEW

The second half of ch. 4 (vv.24–43) provides the genealogical summary of the tribe of Simeon, whose history was intertwined with that of Judah, given that Simeon's tribal territory was located within the tribal territory of Judah (cf. Jos 19:1–9).

²⁴The descendants of Simeon:
  Nemuel, Jamin, Jarib, Zerah and Shaul;
²⁵Shallum was Shaul's son, Mibsam his son and Mishma his son.
²⁶The descendants of Mishma:

Hammuel his son, Zaccur his son and Shimei his son.

[27]Shimei had sixteen sons and six daughters, but his brothers did not have many children; so their entire clan did not become as numerous as the people of Judah. [28]They lived in Beersheba, Moladah, Hazar Shual, [29]Bilhah, Ezem, Tolad, [30]Bethuel, Hormah, Ziklag, [31]Beth Marcaboth, Hazar Susim, Beth Biri and Shaaraim. These were their towns until the reign of David. [32]Their surrounding villages were Etam, Ain, Rimmon, Token and Ashan — five towns — [33]and all the villages around these towns as far as Baalath. These were their settlements. And they kept a genealogical record.

[34]Meshobab, Jamlech, Joshah son of Amaziah, [35]Joel, Jehu son of Joshibiah, the son of Seraiah, the son of Asiel, [36]also Elioenai, Jaakobah, Jeshohaiah, Asaiah, Adiel, Jesimiel, Benaiah, [37]and Ziza son of Shiphi, the son of Allon, the son of Jedaiah, the son of Shimri, the son of Shemaiah.

[38]The men listed above by name were leaders of their clans. Their families increased greatly, [39]and they went to the outskirts of Gedor to the east of the valley in search of pasture for their flocks. [40]They found rich, good pasture, and the land was spacious, peaceful and quiet. Some Hamites had lived there formerly.

[41]The men whose names were listed came in the days of Hezekiah king of Judah. They attacked the Hamites in their dwellings and also the Meunites who were there and completely destroyed them, as is evident to this day. Then they settled in their place, because there was pasture for their flocks. [42]And five hundred of these Simeonites, led by Pelatiah, Neariah, Rephaiah and Uzziel, the sons of Ishi, invaded the hill country of Seir. [43]They killed the remaining Amalekites who had escaped, and they have lived there to this day.

COMMENTARY

24–33 Following a brief genealogical sketch of the Simeonites (vv.24–27) that includes a brief notation on the small size of Simeon vis-à-vis Judah (v.27), the Chronicler enumerates the towns that were settled by the descendants of Simeon (cf. Jos 19:1–9). The tribal territory of Simeon occupied a small area completely surrounded by the tribal territory of Judah. Over the course of time Simeon was effectively subsumed into Judah and ceased to be a distinct tribal entity. This near landlessness of Simeon together with that of Levi reflects the prophetic "blessing" of Jacob on his sons, which includes the scattering of Levi and Simeon (Ge 49:5–7) in the light of their response to the situation with their sister Dinah (cf. Ge 34). The Chronicler's inclusion of the descendants of Simeon along with their long-lost tribal inheritance may be intended to instill hope that God's covenantal promises (land and otherwise) still have significance for his people.

34–43 Following a list of Simeonite clan leaders (vv.34–38), the Chronicler summarizes the successful tribal expansion of Simeon to the west (vv.39–41) and to the east/southeast (vv.42–43). The description of this expansion is reminiscent of the Danite tribal migration noted in Judges 17–18 (compare Jdg 18:7, 27–28 with vv.39–41 above). The exact location of the Hamites (vv.40–41; cf. 1Ch 1:8–16; Ge 10:6–20) is unknown, but their association with the Arabian Meunites (v.41) might imply the western or southwestern Negev region. The Meunites are also associated with the southern region of Transjordan and parts of the Sinai.

The reference to the time of Hezekiah (v.41) reflects Hezekiah's similar success in expanding Judah westward (cf. 2Ki 18:8). The expansion of the Simeonites to the east/southeast (vv.42–43) includes victory over areas to the south of the Dead Sea ("the hill country of Seir," v.42), as well as victory over the seminomadic Amalekites, who traversed the Negev and Sinai regions (v.43). Again (cf. comments on vv.13–16), this expansion of territory and pasturelands for the Simeonites is reminiscent of the prayer of Jabez (vv.9–10; also see Note on v.10).

3. The Transjordanian Tribes (1Ch 5:1–26)

OVERVIEW

As part of his survey of "all Israel," the Chronicler now turns his attention to the Transjordanian tribes of Reuben, Gad, and (part) Manasseh. Prior to Israel's entry into Canaan, Israel acquired land in Transjordan in conjunction with the defeat of Sihon and Og (cf. Nu 21:21–35; Dt 2:24–3:10). The area taken from Sihon extended from the border of Moab at the Arnon River/Wadi to the Jabbok River/Wadi and eastward to the border of the Ammonites. The allure of this region, given its agricultural richness and prime grazing areas (cf. Lot in Ge 13), prompted Reuben and Gad to seek the "land of Gilead" as their inheritance (Nu 32).

Although not well received initially (cf. Nu 32:6–15), this Transjordanian territory is ultimately allotted to Reuben, Gad, and part of Manasseh (cf. Nu 32:33). Although efforts were made to ensure that the Jordan River did *not* divide the tribes of Israel (cf. Jos 22:21–34), it nevertheless functioned as a barrier to tribal integration. As with the tribe of Simeon, these tribes had long ceased to exist within their original tribal territory by the time of the Chronicler. As such, the Chronicler's presentation of the genealogical material of these tribes continues his emphasis on showing continuity between the past and present that can foster hope within his postexilic audience. With this in mind, the Chronicler's remarks on God's blessing and enablement to those who cry out to him in prayer and trust (vv.20–22) stand in important contrast to the remarks on God's judgment of those who persist in covenantal unfaithfulness (vv.25–26).

a. The Tribe of Reuben (1Ch 5:1–10)

¹The sons of Reuben the firstborn of Israel (he was the firstborn, but when he defiled his father's marriage bed, his rights as firstborn were given to the sons of Joseph son of Israel;

so he could not be listed in the genealogical record in accordance with his birthright, ²and though Judah was the strongest of his brothers and a ruler came from him, the rights of the firstborn belonged to Joseph) — ³the sons of Reuben the firstborn of Israel:

Hanoch, Pallu, Hezron and Carmi.
⁴The descendants of Joel:
Shemaiah his son, Gog his son,
Shimei his son, ⁵Micah his son,
Reaiah his son, Baal his son,
⁶and Beerah his son, whom Tiglath-Pileser king of Assyria took into exile. Beerah was a leader of the Reubenites.
⁷Their relatives by clans, listed according to their genealogical records:
Jeiel the chief, Zechariah, ⁸and Bela son of Azaz, the son of Shema, the son of Joel. They settled in the area from Aroer to Nebo and Baal Meon. ⁹To the east they occupied the land up to the edge of the desert that extends to the Euphrates River, because their livestock had increased in Gilead.
¹⁰During Saul's reign they waged war against the Hagrites, who were defeated at their hands; they occupied the dwellings of the Hagrites throughout the entire region east of Gilead.

COMMENTARY

1–2 The Chronicler's genealogical summary of the tribal line of Reuben has an almost immediate digression that seeks to explain why the firstborn of Jacob's sons (namely, Reuben) was not afforded the typical benefits of the firstborn expected within the biblical world (note the repetition of "firstborn" in vv.1–3). As with the near landlessness of Simeon (see comments on 4:24–31), the basis for this demotion is based on an event within the story line of Genesis (the situation with Jacob's concubine Bilhah; cf. Ge 35:22) and anticipated in Jacob's prophetic "blessings" on his sons (cf. Ge 49:3–4). The demotion of Reuben is coupled with the promotion of Joseph, which also draws on the content of Genesis (cf. Ge 48:5; Dt 21:15–17).

While the Chronicler places the tribe of Judah in a sustained position of preeminence throughout his work (the "ruler" of v.2 would almost certainly be a reference to the Davidic monarchy), he is likewise careful to show the added level of respect and position afforded to the tribe of Joseph. Recall that "Judah" and "Joseph" (esp. "Ephraim") would ultimately serve as monikers for the southern kingdom and northern kingdom, respectively.

3–10 The Chronicler picks up his review of the tribe of Reuben by partially repeating the beginning of v.1 prior to the tangent regarding Reuben's loss of his firstborn privileges (see previous comment). While the sons of Reuben are also noted elsewhere (e.g., Ge 46:9), the information on the descendants of Joel (vv.4–6) is unique to Chronicles. The juxtaposition between the sons of Joel and the remark of the Assyrian captivity might imply unfaithfulness on the part of these Reubenites.

The geographical extent of the Reubenites of v.8 reflects Reuben's early territorial hub to the north of Moab (i.e., north of the Arnon River/Wadi) and west of Ammon, while the geographical markers in v.9 reflect eastward expansion by the tribe. Thus, as he did with the tribe of Simeon (see comments on 4:13–16, 34–43), the Chronicler highlights military successes and territorial expansions of the tribe of Reuben (vv.8–10), which resulted in additional pastureland for the tribe (recall the prayer of Jabez [4:9–10]; also see Note on 4:10).

The Hagrites as a people group (v.10; cf. vv.19–21) are only mentioned once outside Chronicles (Ps 83:6[7], in a list of nations committed to destroying God's people). Some have assumed the Hagrites to be in the lineage of Hagar, Ishmael's mother, but this is only conjecture. Note that two Hagrites are listed in the administration of David (cf. 1Ch 11:38; 27:31).

NOTE

8 The locations given in this verse are found in the mid-ninth-century-BC Moabite Stone (also known as the Mesha Stele; *COS*, 2.23; *ANET*, 320–21; cf. 2Ki 1:1; 3:4–27) as territory seized from Israel. This reality is reflected in later prophetic literature (cf. Isa 15–16; Jer 48).

b. The Tribe of Gad (1Ch 5:11–17)

> [11] The Gadites lived next to them in Bashan, as far as Salecah:
> [12] Joel was the chief, Shapham the second, then Janai and Shaphat, in Bashan.
> [13] Their relatives, by families, were:
> Michael, Meshullam, Sheba, Jorai, Jacan, Zia and Eber — seven in all.
> [14] These were the sons of Abihail son of Huri, the son of Jaroah, the son of Gilead, the son of Michael, the son of Jeshishai, the son of Jahdo, the son of Buz.
> [15] Ahi son of Abdiel, the son of Guni, was head of their family.
> [16] The Gadites lived in Gilead, in Bashan and its outlying villages, and on all the pasturelands of Sharon as far as they extended.
> [17] All these were entered in the genealogical records during the reigns of Jotham king of Judah and Jeroboam king of Israel.

COMMENTARY

11–17 The close connection between the Transjordanian tribes of Reuben (vv.1–10) and Gad is underscored by the Chronicler's introduction of Gad via their geographical proximity to "them" (i.e., the tribe of Reuben; v.11). Following the genealogical survey (vv.11–15), the tribe of Gad is described vis-à-vis their settlement within the fertile pasturelands of Gilead, Bashan, and Sharon. Gilead (vv.14, 16; cf. v.10) was another name for the Transjordanian region stretching between the Arnon River/Wadi in the south (the border of Moab) and the Yarmuk River/Wadi (cf. Nu 32:29). Bashan was previously the territory of Og (cf. Nu 21:21−35; Dt 2:24−3:10). The specific location of Sharon (v.16) is unknown, but its mention in the Moabite Stone implies southern Transjordan. The correlation of the genealogy of the Transjordanian tribes (who were part of the northern kingdom during the divided kingdom) with the reign of the southern king reflects the centrality of the line of Judah/David in the Chronicler's presentation of Israel's history.

c. Military Accomplishments of the Transjordanian Tribes (1Ch 5:18−22)

[18]The Reubenites, the Gadites and the half-tribe of Manasseh had 44,760 men ready for military service — able-bodied men who could handle shield and sword, who could use a bow, and who were trained for battle. [19]They waged war against the Hagrites, Jetur, Naphish and Nodab. [20]They were helped in fighting them, and God handed the Hagrites and all their allies over to them, because they cried out to him during the battle. He answered their prayers, because they trusted in him. [21]They seized the livestock of the Hagrites — fifty thousand camels, two hundred fifty thousand sheep and two thousand donkeys. They also took one hundred thousand people captive, [22]and many others fell slain, because the battle was God's. And they occupied the land until the exile.

COMMENTARY

18−22 Although the genealogy of the half-tribe of Manasseh has not yet been given (cf. vv.23−24), the Chronicler provides an account of the three Transjordanian tribes that intersects with the crux of his message, namely, God's faithfulness to effect covenantal blessings to those who seek him (vv.20−22). When God is sought and trusted by his people, the battle of his people becomes his own battle (v.22; cf. Dt 20:4; Lev 26:6−8).

The theme of God's faithfulness is stressed over and again by the Chronicler, no doubt for the encouragement of the postexilic community (cf. Jer 29:10−14; see comments on 2Ch 6:22−39). Conversely, as the summary of the genealogy of the Transjordanian tribes will show (5:25−26), God is also "faithful" to bring about covenantal consequences for disobedience and unfaithfulness. The specific background of the Hagrites (vv.19−21) is uncertain, and the proposed connection with the lineage of Hagar (Ishmael's mother) is only conjecture. On the large number of captives (v.21), see the extended discussion at 2 Chronicles 11:1.

d. Transjordanian Manasseh (1Ch 5:23–26)

²³The people of the half-tribe of Manasseh were numerous; they settled in the land from Bashan to Baal Hermon, that is, to Senir (Mount Hermon).
²⁴These were the heads of their families: Epher, Ishi, Eliel, Azriel, Jeremiah, Hodaviah and Jahdiel. They were brave warriors, famous men, and heads of their families. ²⁵But they were unfaithful to the God of their fathers and prostituted themselves to the gods of the peoples of the land, whom God had destroyed before them. ²⁶So the God of Israel stirred up the spirit of Pul king of Assyria (that is, Tiglath-Pileser king of Assyria), who took the Reubenites, the Gadites and the half-tribe of Manasseh into exile. He took them to Halah, Habor, Hara and the river of Gozan, where they are to this day.

COMMENTARY

23–24 Although the half-tribe of Manasseh was part of the previous section (cf. vv.18–22), the Chronicler now provides a formal genealogical sketch of the family line of Manasseh. The expansive settlement area of this part of the tribe of Manasseh occupied the northern and northeastern area of Transjordan, at one point extending as far north as Mount Hermon (v.23; cf. Dt 3:8). Note that the Chronicler includes positive remarks regarding individuals from northern tribes (e.g., v.24), which underscores his overall concern for "all Israel."

25–26 Although the Chronicler has pointed out the successes of the Transjordanian tribes as they sought him (cf. vv.20–22), this summary of their genealogy reflects the reality that ultimately these tribes were unfaithful to God (cf. 2Ki 17:7–17). In the light of the covenantal unfaithfulness of these tribes, God is "faithful" to bring about promised covenantal consequences for disobedience and unfaithfulness, including defeat by enemies (cf. Lev 26:14–17; Dt 28:48). The sovereign agency of God is seen in his use of the Neo-Assyrian king Tiglath-Pileser III (ca. 745–27 BC; spelled "Pil*n*eser" by the Chronicler and also noted by his throne name "Pul"), whom God "stirred up" both to defeat and disperse the Transjordanian tribes (v.26; cf. Isa 10:5).

4. The Tribe of Levi (1Ch 6:1–81)

OVERVIEW

The length of the Chronicler's treatment of the tribe of Levi is second only to his survey of the line of Judah (chs. 2–4). The extra attention afforded to these two tribes relates to their key role in ancient Israel: the Davidic dynasty through the tribe of Judah and priests and Levites through the tribe of Levi. The tribe of Levi was chosen by God to mediate matters of sacrifice, temple/tabernacle caretaking, music, and worship. In addition, priests and Levites served as teachers of God's law, will, and ways to God's covenantal people. It should be noted that the Chronicler is careful to maintain the distinction between Levites and priests throughout his genealogical survey with items pertaining to genealogy and settlement cities handled separately for each. While every priest was a Levite, not every Levite was a priest (see comments on vv.31–47 and vv.48–49 below).

¹The sons of Levi:

   Gershon, Kohath and Merari.
²The sons of Kohath:

   Amram, Izhar, Hebron and Uzziel.
³The children of Amram:

   Aaron, Moses and Miriam.

The sons of Aaron:

   Nadab, Abihu, Eleazar and Ithamar.
   ⁴Eleazar was the father of Phinehas,
   Phinehas the father of Abishua,
⁵Abishua the father of Bukki,
   Bukki the father of Uzzi,
⁶Uzzi the father of Zerahiah,
   Zerahiah the father of Meraioth,
⁷Meraioth the father of Amariah,
   Amariah the father of Ahitub,
⁸Ahitub the father of Zadok,
   Zadok the father of Ahimaaz,
⁹Ahimaaz the father of Azariah,
   Azariah the father of Johanan,
¹⁰Johanan the father of Azariah (it was he who served as priest in the temple Solomon built in Jerusalem),
¹¹Azariah the father of Amariah,
   Amariah the father of Ahitub,
¹²Ahitub the father of Zadok,
   Zadok the father of Shallum,
¹³Shallum the father of Hilkiah,
   Hilkiah the father of Azariah,
¹⁴Azariah the father of Seraiah,
   and Seraiah the father of Jehozadak.
¹⁵Jehozadak was deported when the LORD sent Judah and Jerusalem into exile by the hand of Nebuchadnezzar.
¹⁶The sons of Levi:

   Gershon, Kohath and Merari.

¹⁷These are the names of the sons of Gershon:
> Libni and Shimei.

¹⁸The sons of Kohath:
> Amram, Izhar, Hebron and Uzziel.

¹⁹The sons of Merari:
> Mahli and Mushi.

These are the clans of the Levites listed according to their fathers:

²⁰Of Gershon:
> Libni his son, Jehath his son,
> Zimmah his son, ²¹Joah his son, Iddo his son,
> Zerah his son
> and Jeatherai his son.

²²The descendants of Kohath:
> Amminadab his son, Korah his son,
> Assir his son, ²³Elkanah his son,
> Ebiasaph his son, Assir his son,
> ²⁴Tahath his son, Uriel his son, Uzziah his son and Shaul his son.

²⁵The descendants of Elkanah:
> Amasai, Ahimoth,
> ²⁶Elkanah his son, Zophai his son,
> Nahath his son, ²⁷Eliab his son,
> Jeroham his son, Elkanah his son
> and Samuel his son.

²⁸The sons of Samuel:
> Joel the firstborn
> and Abijah the second son.

²⁹The descendants of Merari:
> Mahli, Libni his son,
> Shimei his son, Uzzah his son,
> ³⁰Shimea his son, Haggiah his son
> and Asaiah his son.

³¹These are the men David put in charge of the music in the house of the LORD after the ark came to rest there. ³²They ministered with music before the tabernacle, the Tent of Meeting, until Solomon built the temple of the LORD in Jerusalem. They performed their duties according to the regulations laid down for them.

³³Here are the men who served, together with their sons:

From the Kohathites:
> Heman, the musician,
> the son of Joel, the son of Samuel,

³⁴the son of Elkanah, the son of Jeroham,
the son of Eliel, the son of Toah,
³⁵the son of Zuph, the son of Elkanah,
the son of Mahath, the son of Amasai,
³⁶the son of Elkanah, the son of Joel,
the son of Azariah, the son of Zephaniah,
³⁷the son of Tahath, the son of Assir,
the son of Ebiasaph, the son of Korah,
³⁸the son of Izhar, the son of Kohath,
the son of Levi, the son of Israel;
³⁹and Heman's associate Asaph, who served at his right hand:
Asaph son of Berekiah, the son of Shimea,
⁴⁰the son of Michael, the son of Baaseiah,
the son of Malkijah, ⁴¹the son of Ethni,
the son of Zerah, the son of Adaiah,
⁴²the son of Ethan, the son of Zimmah,
the son of Shimei, ⁴³the son of Jahath,
the son of Gershon, the son of Levi;
⁴⁴and from their associates, the Merarites, at his left hand:
Ethan son of Kishi, the son of Abdi, the son of Malluch, ⁴⁵the son of Hashabiah,
the son of Amaziah, the son of Hilkiah,
⁴⁶the son of Amzi, the son of Bani,
the son of Shemer, ⁴⁷the son of Mahli,
the son of Mushi, the son of Merari,
the son of Levi.

⁴⁸Their fellow Levites were assigned to all the other duties of the tabernacle, the house of God. ⁴⁹But Aaron and his descendants were the ones who presented offerings on the altar of burnt offering and on the altar of incense in connection with all that was done in the Most Holy Place, making atonement for Israel, in accordance with all that Moses the servant of God had commanded.

⁵⁰These were the descendants of Aaron:
Eleazar his son, Phinehas his son,
Abishua his son, ⁵¹Bukki his son,
Uzzi his son, Zerahiah his son,
⁵²Meraioth his son, Amariah his son,
Ahitub his son, ⁵³Zadok his son
and Ahimaaz his son.

⁵⁴These were the locations of their settlements allotted as their territory (they were assigned to the descendants of Aaron who were from the Kohathite clan, because the first lot was for them).

⁵⁵They were given Hebron in Judah with its surrounding pasturelands. ⁵⁶But the fields and villages around the city were given to Caleb son of Jephunneh.

⁵⁷So the descendants of Aaron were given Hebron (a city of refuge), and Libnah, Jattir, Eshtemoa, ⁵⁸Hilen, Debir, ⁵⁹Ashan, Juttah and Beth Shemesh, together with their pasturelands.

⁶⁰And from the tribe of Benjamin they were given Gibeon, Geba, Alemeth and Anathoth, together with their pasturelands.

These towns, which were distributed among the Kohathite clans, were thirteen in all.

⁶¹The rest of Kohath's descendants were allotted ten towns from the clans of half the tribe of Manasseh.

⁶²The descendants of Gershon, clan by clan, were allotted thirteen towns from the tribes of Issachar, Asher and Naphtali, and from the part of the tribe of Manasseh that is in Bashan.

⁶³The descendants of Merari, clan by clan, were allotted twelve towns from the tribes of Reuben, Gad and Zebulun.

⁶⁴So the Israelites gave the Levites these towns and their pasturelands. ⁶⁵From the tribes of Judah, Simeon and Benjamin they allotted the previously named towns.

⁶⁶Some of the Kohathite clans were given as their territory towns from the tribe of Ephraim.

⁶⁷In the hill country of Ephraim they were given Shechem (a city of refuge), and Gezer, ⁶⁸Jokmeam, Beth Horon, ⁶⁹Aijalon and Gath Rimmon, together with their pasturelands.

⁷⁰And from half the tribe of Manasseh the Israelites gave Aner and Bileam, together with their pasturelands, to the rest of the Kohathite clans.

⁷¹The Gershonites received the following:

From the clan of the half-tribe of Manasseh

they received Golan in Bashan and also Ashtaroth, together with their pasturelands;

⁷²from the tribe of Issachar

they received Kedesh, Daberath, ⁷³Ramoth and Anem, together with their pasturelands;

⁷⁴from the tribe of Asher

they received Mashal, Abdon, ⁷⁵Hukok and Rehob, together with their pasturelands;

⁷⁶and from the tribe of Naphtali

they received Kedesh in Galilee, Hammon and Kiriathaim, together with their pasturelands.

⁷⁷The Merarites (the rest of the Levites) received the following:

From the tribe of Zebulun

they received Jokneam, Kartah, Rimmono and Tabor, together with their
pasturelands;
[78]from the tribe of Reuben across the Jordan east of Jericho
they received Bezer in the desert, Jahzah, [79]Kedemoth and Mephaath, together
with their pasturelands;
[80]and from the tribe of Gad
they received Ramoth in Gilead, Mahanaim, [81]Heshbon and Jazer, together with
their pasturelands.

COMMENTARY

1–15 This initial section focuses on the lineage of Kohath, who represents the line of the Aaronic high priests. This genealogy reminds the audience that while Aaron, Moses, and Miriam were from the family of Levi, only the line of Aaron served as high priests. Within this family line, the two eldest sons of Aaron — Nadab and Abihu — violated God's holy space by not doing everything according to God's will ("unauthorized fire ... contrary to his [God's] command"; cf. Lev 10:1), and Eleazar became the son through whom the high priesthood transferred. This genealogical survey of the line of Kohath extends into exilic times via the mention of Jehozadak (v.15). Only the lines of Judah and Levi are traced by the Chronicler into the exilic time frame, further attesting to their critical role in the covenantal life of Israel.

16–30 Note that this section begins in the same way as the previous section (vv.1–15), that is, by reviewing the names of the sons of Levi (v.16; cf. v.1). In this section, the Chronicler's survey seems to reflect Levitical lists in earlier texts, such as Exodus 6:16–19 and Numbers 3:17–20. While the genealogy of each of the sons of Levi is developed by at least two generations, the line of Gershon and Merari is pursued for seven generations.

One of the peculiar aspects of this section is the fivefold mention of the name "Elkanah." (Only four are recorded in the NIV, as only one of the two mentions in v.26 is rendered.) The prophet Samuel's close connection with the ark of the covenant and priestly service at Shiloh during the days of Eli reflects his priestly descent through his father Elkanah (vv.27–28; cf. 1Sa 1–3). On the distinctions between priests and Levites, see comments on vv.31–47, 48–49.

31–47 This section of the Chronicler's survey of the family line of Levi focuses on David's organization of the musical branch of the Levites. In ancient Israel, numerous Levitical ministers are noted as being responsible for music and worship, including "joyful songs, accompanied by musical instruments: lyres, harps, and cymbals" (1Ch 15:16; cf. the 288 musicians counted during the time of David; 25:1–8). By contrast, with the exception of the blowing of trumpets (cf. 15:24; 2Ch 5:13), the priests did not play a role in the musical service of ancient Israel.

The presentation of this genealogy is in the reverse (ascending) order (compare vv.22–28). As such, the subsections of this genealogy end with Kohath (v.38), Gershon (v.43), and Merari (v.47) rather than beginning with each of these sons of Levi. The focal point of the Chronicler's overview of the Levitical musical corps is Heman the Kohathite (v.33; cf. 1Ch 15:16–17; 25:1, 4–5), with

Asaph the Gershonite being described as serving at his right hand (v.39), and Ethan the Merarite described as being at his left hand (v.44). All three of these worship leaders are associated with the sounding of bronze cymbals (cf. 15:19).

The musical leadership and worship example of these individuals made an impact on subsequent generations of Israelites (and Christians), as Heman is noted as the composer of Psalm 88, Asaph is credited with the authorship of twelve Psalms (Pss 50, 73–83), and Ethan is noted as the author of Psalm 89. Following the completion of the temple, music was one of the primary responsibilities of the Levites (cf. 1Ch 23:2–32; 25:1–7; 2Ch 5:7–13). For more remarks on the musical aspects of Israelite worship, see comments on 1 Chronicles 25:1–7 and 2 Chronicles 5:12–13. On the distinctions between priests and Levites, see next comment.

48–49 As these verses reflect and as previously noted, the Chronicler is careful to maintain the distinction between Levites and priests throughout his survey of the tribe of Levi, and while every priest was a Levite, not every Levite was a priest. In addition to the musical responsibilities of some Levites (see comments on vv.31–47), other Levites functioned as servants to the Levitical/Aaronic priests, especially in matters of the tabernacle/temple (v.48; cf. Nu 8:19). Similarly, the Chronicler elsewhere writes, "The duty of the Levites was to help Aaron's descendants in the service of the temple of the LORD: to be in charge of the courtyards, the side rooms, the purification of all sacred things and the performance of other duties at the house of God" (1Ch 23:28).

Levites were also called to be watchful stewards over God's Word (cf. Dt. 33:8–11) and were entrusted with the responsibility of carrying the ark of the covenant (cf. Nu 4:15; Dt 10:8–9; 1Ch 15:14–15). In the light of these various duties, Levites had titles such as doorkeepers/gatekeepers, scribes, secretaries, treasurers, and temple-work

supervisors (cf. 1Ch 23:2–32; 26:20–22; 2Ch 34:8–13).

By contrast, priests were descendants of the Aaronic Levitical family line (cf. Ex 28:1 and 1Ch 6:3–8) and were primarily responsible for the matters of temple service, particularly the sacrificial system and other aspects of worship that took place within the Most Holy Place (cf. v.49). As the Chronicler succinctly summarizes, "Aaron was set apart, he and his descendants forever, to consecrate the most holy things, to offer sacrifices before the LORD, to minister before him and to pronounce blessings in his name forever" (1Ch 23:13).

In addition, priests had the responsibilities of discerning between clean and unclean, and of teaching Israelites the ways of God (cf. Lev 10:10–11). The specific role of priests as teachers reflects God's covenantal framework, in which priests are charged by God to "teach the Israelites all the decrees the LORD has given them" (Lev 10:11; cf. the poetic [and prophetic] description of Levi's teaching and atonement commission in Dt 33:8–11 as well as the admonition directed at priests in Mal 2:1–9).

The teaching of God's will/law—both then and now—infuses God's people with the spiritual direction and energy needed to walk in a manner pleasing to him. Wise leaders of God's people (cf. Jehoshaphat in 2Ch 19:8–10) understood the key role of priests in the spiritual life of Israel. Given that there was not a functioning Davidic monarchy in the Chronicler's time, it was all the more imperative that the priests and Levites faithfully exercised their covenantal duties.

50–53 This list of Aaronic high priests is an abridged summary of the list of high priests given at 6:1–15 (e.g., 6:3–8) and functions as a point of reference to the distinctions between priests and Levites articulated in vv.48–49. Since Zadok and Ahimaaz (v.53) served during the reigns of David and Solomon, respectively, this review serves the Chronicler's ultimate focus on the Davidic dynasty and temple ministries served by the priests and Levites.

54–81 The Chronicler ends his summary of the tribe of Levi by giving a list of Levitical cities provided for both priestly and nonpriestly Levites. The tribe of Levi did not receive a landed inheritance like the balance of Israelite tribes. From a positive angle, this was because the Lord was their inheritance (cf. Nu 18:20–24). From a negative angle, this lack of a landed inheritance (like the near landlessness of Simeon; 1Ch 4:24–43) reflects the prophetic "blessing" of Jacob on his sons that includes the scattering of Levi and Simeon (Ge 49:5–7) in the light of their response to the situation with their sister Dinah (cf. Ge 34:1–31, esp. vv.25–31).

Continuing his trend of addressing matters of priest and Levite separately, the Chronicler initially lists the settlement towns and pasturelands granted to Levitical/Aaronic priests (vv.54–60), largely echoing the content of Joshua 21:1–42. The towns and pasturelands allotted to the priests were only located in Judah and Benjamin, presumably to provide proximity to places of communal worship. Unlike the Levitical/Aaronic priests, whose towns were only in the tribal areas of Judah and Benjamin, the nonpriestly Levites were granted towns and pasturelands dispersed across the tribal territories of Israel (vv.61–81). The mention of Hebron and Shechem as cities of refuge (vv.57, 67) reflected their function (along with six other towns spread throughout the territory of ancient Israel) as safe havens for those accused of killing another person unintentionally (cf. Jos 20:1–9).

NOTES

16 [6:1] In this verse and others (cf. vv.17, 20, 43, 62, and 71) the Hebrew text reads "Gershom" (גֵּרְשֹׁם, *gēršōm*) rather than Gershon (גֵּרְשׁוֹן, *gēršôn*), reflecting either a spelling variation on this name or a scribal transmission issue.

44 [29] In 16:42 and 25:1 the name "Jeduthun" replaces Ethan in lists of temple musical leaders. It is unclear whether this is an alternative name for Ethan or he was replaced by Jeduthun.

53 [38] The lineage of Zadok through Aaron (as noted here) is sometimes challenged on account of other OT genealogies. However, the lineage of Zadok can be plausibly traced through Aaron in conjunction with 1 Samuel 14:3 and 1 Chronicles 24:3 (as well as this verse[!]; see Hill, 139, esp. n. 16).

REFLECTION

The teaching of God's will—both then and now—infuses God's people with the spiritual direction and energy needed to walk in a manner pleasing to him. In the Israelite covenantal community, priests were especially entrusted with being stewards over God's Word, which included discerning that which was holy and teaching God's people "all the decrees the LORD has given them" (see Lev 10:10–11; Dt 33:8–11; Mal 2:1–9). Part of their commission included battling against those having zeal without knowledge as well as the ever-present human tendency to do what is right in our own eyes rather than doing God's revealed will.

The Scriptures show that teaching God's ways and God's Word facilitates wisdom and godly living (cf. Pr 2:1–9). To do what is pleasing to God is the fundamental tenet of the spiritual life, and that which is pleasing to God must be taught, learned, and applied. The description of believers in priest-like ways in the NT (e.g., Heb 4:16; 1Pe 2:5; Rev 1:6) underscores our corporate responsibility to teach, admonish, rebuke, encourage, and exhort one another in the ways of God (see Col 1:28; 3:16; Heb 3:13).

5. The Northern Tribes (1Ch 7:1–8:40)

OVERVIEW

In these chapters the Chronicler provides comparatively short genealogical snippets on several of the tribes to the north of Judah (note especially the brief treatment of Naphtali; v.13). With the exception of Benjamin these tribes would become part of the northern kingdom, following the division of the Israelite monarchy in the 930s BC, which probably explains the Chronicler's lack of detailed information. Similarly, note that the style of these genealogies differs from the preceding family line summaries provided by the Chronicler in that they read more like tribal military censuses.

Note too that this list (as well as the balance of 1Ch 1–9) does not include genealogical information for the tribes of Dan or Zebulun. Given the variety of listings of the twelve tribes across the Bible (including the absence of one or more tribes, and lists that include Joseph and one of his sons), these absences should not be overinterpreted. The Chronicler's genealogical coverage of the tribes of Israel totals twelve sons of Jacob, with the number twelve providing the important imagery of completion (i.e., "all Israel"), renewal, and unity sought by the Chronicler (recall Eze 37:1–28).

a. The Tribe of Issachar (1Ch 7:1–5)

¹The sons of Issachar:

Tola, Puah, Jashub and Shimron—four in all.
²The sons of Tola:

Uzzi, Rephaiah, Jeriel, Jahmai, Ibsam and Samuel—heads of their families. During the reign of David, the descendants of Tola listed as fighting men in their genealogy numbered 22,600.
³The son of Uzzi:

Izrahiah.

The sons of Izrahiah:

Michael, Obadiah, Joel and Isshiah. All five of them were chiefs. ⁴According to their family genealogy, they had 36,000 men ready for battle, for they had many wives and children.

> [5] The relatives who were fighting men belonging to all the clans of Issachar, as listed in their genealogy, were 87,000 in all.

COMMENTARY

1–5 The Chronicler's brief treatment of the genealogy of the tribe of Issachar reflects the style of a military census, and the mention of David may imply a census from that time (perhaps even David's ill-fated census of 1Ch 21; cf. 2Sa 24).

b. The Tribe of Benjamin Part One (1Ch 7:6–12)

> [6] Three sons of Benjamin:
>   Bela, Beker and Jediael.
> [7] The sons of Bela:
>   Ezbon, Uzzi, Uzziel, Jerimoth and Iri, heads of families — five in all. Their genealogical record listed 22,034 fighting men.
> [8] The sons of Beker:
>   Zemirah, Joash, Eliezer, Elioenai, Omri, Jeremoth, Abijah, Anathoth and Alemeth. All these were the sons of Beker. [9] Their genealogical record listed the heads of families and 20,200 fighting men.
> [10] The son of Jediael:
>   Bilhan.
> The sons of Bilhan:
>   Jeush, Benjamin, Ehud, Kenaanah, Zethan, Tarshish and Ahishahar. [11] All these sons of Jediael were heads of families. There were 17,200 fighting men ready to go out to war.
> [12] The Shuppites and Huppites were the descendants of Ir, and the Hushites the descendants of Aher.

COMMENTARY

6–12 The Chronicler's genealogical survey of the tribe of Benjamin is also the topic of ch. 8 and the end of ch. 9 (9:35–44). As such, the tribe of Benjamin receives the third largest coverage by the Chronicler (after Judah and Levi). While the genealogical information on the lineage of the tribe of Benjamin in chs. 8 and 9 largely focuses on the lineage before and after Saul, this genealogy is incomplete and does not directly include the Saulide family line.

NOTE

6–12 Note that the genealogical summaries of the tribe of Benjamin reflect notable variation in the four times in which they are found in the OT: Genesis 46:21; 1 Chronicles 7:6–12; 8; 9:35–44. Even the onset of the Benjamite genealogy here (cf. v.6) lacks the characteristic introduction of "[the] son[s] of" seen elsewhere. While the reason(s) for this variety is unknown, it may reflect Benjamin's geographical, familial, and theological position as a buffer between the later divided monarchy (and the subsequent efforts of the northern kingdom and southern kingdom to control the territory of Benjamin). This may imply the possibility of partial listings of those aligned to the northern kingdom or southern kingdom.

Alternatively (or perhaps additionally) these differences may reflect the sociological issues (divisions) related to the transfer from a Benjamin-based monarchy (that of Saul) to a Judah-based monarchy (Davidic dynasty), which was neither a fast nor a challenge-free transition (cf. 2Sa 3:1). (For a detailed discussion of textual issues pertaining to the Chronicler's summary of Benjamin, see Japhet, 172–73, 190–99.) Also note the differences in the descendents of Benjamin listed at 1 Chronicles 9:7–9 with the somewhat parallel listing at Nehemiah 11:7–9 (see remarks in Hill, 180). Some have considered the final part of v.12 to pertain to the tribe of Dan, but this possibility is not convincing.

c. The Tribe of Naphtali (1Ch 7:13)

> **13**The sons of Naphtali:
> Jahziel, Guni, Jezer and Shillem — the descendants of Bilhah.

COMMENTARY

13The Chronicler's summary of Naphtali is the most abridged of all the Israelite tribes, being limited to a single verse that echoes the content of Genesis 46:24 (cf. Nu 26:48–49).

d. The House of Joseph (1Ch 7:14–29)

i. The tribe of Cisjordan Manasseh (1Ch 7:14–19)

> **14**The descendants of Manasseh:
> Asriel was his descendant through his Aramean concubine. She gave birth to Makir the father of Gilead. **15**Makir took a wife from among the Huppites and Shuppites. His sister's name was Maacah.

Another descendant was named Zelophehad, who had only daughters. [16]Makir's wife Maacah gave birth to a son and named him Peresh. His brother was named Sheresh, and his sons were Ulam and Rakem. [17]The son of Ulam:

Bedan.

These were the sons of Gilead son of Makir, the son of Manasseh. [18]His sister Hammoleketh gave birth to Ishhod, Abiezer and Mahlah. [19]The sons of Shemida were:

Ahian, Shechem, Likhi and Aniam.

COMMENTARY

14−19 The Chronicler's treatment of the lineage of Joseph's son Manasseh continues his earlier description of the part of tribe of Manasseh that opted to settle in Transjordan (cf. 1Ch 5:23−24). This Cisjordanian or western component of the tribe of Manasseh implies at least one point of intermarriage between the line of Manasseh and surrounding people groups (i.e., through Manasseh's Aramean concubine [v.14] and perhaps Makir's wife Maacah [v.16; cf. Jos 12:5]). As noted above (see comments on 2:3−8), the mention of such intermarriage by the Chronicler seems to reflect his understanding of God's creative and faithful sovereignty rather than being a marker of spiritual compromise (as reflected at Ne 13:23−27).

As also seen in the genealogy of Benjamin (see Note on 7:6−12), this genealogical summary is an incomplete summary of earlier biblical data, such as that in Numbers 26:29−34 and Joshua 17:1−3 (see D. Edelman, "The Manassite Genealogy in 1 Chronicles 7:14−19," *CBQ* 53 [1991]: 179−201). Unlike most of the genealogical lists of this section (excepting the single sentence concerning Naphtali and the genealogy of Ephraim), the Chronicler's summary of Manasseh here does not include the military-type census numbers. Lastly, brief geographical data pertaining to both Manasseh and Ephraim are summarized by the Chronicler following his survey of the tribe of Ephraim (vv.28−29).

ii. The tribe of Ephraim (1Ch 7:20−27)

[20]The descendants of Ephraim:

Shuthelah, Bered his son,

Tahath his son, Eleadah his son,

Tahath his son, [21]Zabad his son and Shuthelah his son.

Ezer and Elead were killed by the native-born men of Gath, when they went down to seize their livestock. [22]Their father Ephraim mourned for them many days, and his relatives came to comfort him. ²³Then he lay with his wife again, and she became pregnant and gave birth to a son. He named him Beriah, because there had been misfortune in his family. ²⁴His daughter was Sheerah, who built Lower and Upper Beth Horon as well as Uzzen Sheerah.

²⁵Rephah was his son, Resheph his son,
   Telah his son, Tahan his son,
²⁶Ladan his son, Ammihud his son,
   Elishama his son, ²⁷Nun his son
   and Joshua his son.

COMMENTARY

20–27 The Chronicler's summary of the lineage of Joseph's son Ephraim is presented in tandem with that of Joseph's son Manasseh (cf. the summary of vv.28–29 below; also see Jos 17:14–18). Unlike the balance of genealogies in this chapter, the Chronicler provides settlement information for Ephraim (along with Manasseh) and does not include the military-like census numbers reflected in most of the other genealogies of this section. This divergence suggests that the Chronicler had a different set of sources (or additional sources) available for the prominent "House of Joseph."

Note that the Chronicler's summary of the tribe of Ephraim ultimately culminates with Joshua, the son of Nun, whom Yahweh used to deed the Promised Land and begin the process of occupying it—another way in which the Chronicler uses his genealogical summaries to draw attention to the covenantal hope(s) available for "all Israel."

iii. Settlement of Ephraim and Cisjordanian Manasseh (1Ch 7:28–29)

²⁸Their lands and settlements included Bethel and its surrounding villages, Naaran to the east, Gezer and its villages to the west, and Shechem and its villages all the way to Ayyah and its villages. ²⁹Along the borders of Manasseh were Beth Shan, Taanach, Megiddo and Dor, together with their villages. The descendants of Joseph son of Israel lived in these towns.

COMMENTARY

28–29 The geographical information summarized here reflects towns and settlements of both Ephraim and Manasseh, both of the "house of Joseph." These settlement towns partly reflect

Joshua 16–17, with updating to show that previously unconquered areas (cf. the listing of unconquered areas [Jdg 1:27–29]) were now under the control of these tribes. In fact, the majority of the towns listed here (e.g., Gezer, Beth Shan, Taanach, Megiddo, and Dor) were previously listed as towns out of which the Israelites were unable to drive out the Canaanites. Thus the Chronicler is possibly including these cities to foster hope in his audience in God's faithfulness to bring about the fullness of covenantal blessings as his people demonstrate obedience (see Jdg 3:1–4; see N. Na'aman, "Sources and Redaction in the Chronicler's Genealogies of Asher and Ephraim," *JSOT* 49 [1991]: 99–111).

e. The Tribe of Asher (1Ch 7:30–40)

30The sons of Asher:

Imnah, Ishvah, Ishvi and Beriah. Their sister was Serah.

31The sons of Beriah:

Heber and Malkiel, who was the father of Birzaith.

32Heber was the father of Japhlet, Shomer and Hotham and of their sister Shua.

33The sons of Japhlet:

Pasach, Bimhal and Ashvath. These were Japhlet's sons.

34The sons of Shomer:

Ahi, Rohgah, Hubbah and Aram.

35The sons of his brother Helem:

Zophah, Imna, Shelesh and Amal.

36The sons of Zophah:

Suah, Harnepher, Shual, Beri, Imrah, 37Bezer, Hod, Shamma, Shilshah, Ithran and Beera.

38The sons of Jether:

Jephunneh, Pispah and Ara.

39The sons of Ulla:

Arah, Hanniel and Rizia.

40All these were descendants of Asher — heads of families, choice men, brave warriors and outstanding leaders. The number of men ready for battle, as listed in their genealogy, was 26,000.

COMMENTARY

30–40 The Chronicler's summary of the genealogical line of Asher reflects the prototype of a military census also seen in this chapter in the summaries of Issachar and Benjamin. As he has done in his summaries of other tribes who ultimately become part of the northern kingdom (e.g., Reuben and Gad), the Chronicler includes information praising this tribe (e.g., v.40). As seen in the other genealogies of northern Cisjordanian tribes covered in this chapter (e.g., Issachar, Benjamin, and Manasseh), the Chronicler clearly has access to other genealogical information regarding the tribe of Asher. This supplemental information, along with biblical data such as Genesis 46:17–18, is woven together by the Chronicler to create this summary of the tribe of Asher (see D. Edelman, "The Asherite Genealogy in 1 Chronicles 7:30–40," *BR* 33 [1988]: 13–23).

f. The Tribe of Benjamin Part Two (1Ch 8:1–40)

OVERVIEW

The Chronicler's genealogical coverage of the tribe of Benjamin began with his earlier treatment of the northern Cisjordanian (western) tribes (cf. 7:6–12) and will be continued (actually repeated) at the close of the next chapter (cf. 9:35–44) as a lead-up to the Saulide monarchy (ch. 10). Despite the Chronicler's extended coverage of the tribe of Benjamin, the genealogical information is incomplete; consequently, certain points of familial relationship are unclear (see Note on 7:6–12 above).

[1]Benjamin was the father of Bela his firstborn,
  Ashbel the second son, Aharah the third,
    [2]Nohah the fourth and Rapha the fifth.
[3]The sons of Bela were:
  Addar, Gera, Abihud, [4]Abishua, Naaman, Ahoah, [5]Gera, Shephuphan and Huram.
[6]These were the descendants of Ehud, who were heads of families of those living in Geba and were deported to Manahath:
  [7]Naaman, Ahijah, and Gera, who deported them and who was the father of Uzza and Ahihud.
[8]Sons were born to Shaharaim in Moab after he had divorced his wives Hushim and Baara. [9]By his wife Hodesh he had Jobab, Zibia, Mesha, Malcam, [10]Jeuz, Sakia and Mirmah. These were his sons, heads of families. [11]By Hushim he had Abitub and Elpaal.
[12]The sons of Elpaal:
  Eber, Misham, Shemed (who built Ono and Lod with its surrounding villages), [13]and Beriah and Shema, who were heads of families of those living in Aijalon and who drove out the inhabitants of Gath.
[14]Ahio, Shashak, Jeremoth, [15]Zebadiah, Arad, Eder, [16]Michael, Ishpah and Joha were the sons of Beriah.
[17]Zebadiah, Meshullam, Hizki, Heber, [18]Ishmerai, Izliah and Jobab were the sons of Elpaal.

¹⁹Jakim, Zicri, Zabdi, ²⁰Elienai, Zillethai, Eliel, ²¹Adaiah, Beraiah and Shimrath were the sons of Shimei.

²²Ishpan, Eber, Eliel, ²³Abdon, Zicri, Hanan, ²⁴Hananiah, Elam, Anthothijah, ²⁵Iphdeiah and Penuel were the sons of Shashak.

²⁶Shamsherai, Shehariah, Athaliah, ²⁷Jaareshiah, Elijah and Zicri were the sons of Jeroham.

²⁸All these were heads of families, chiefs as listed in their genealogy, and they lived in Jerusalem.

²⁹Jeiel the father of Gibeon lived in Gibeon.

His wife's name was Maacah, ³⁰and his firstborn son was Abdon, followed by Zur, Kish, Baal, Ner, Nadab, ³¹Gedor, Ahio, Zeker ³²and Mikloth, who was the father of Shimeah. They too lived near their relatives in Jerusalem.

³³Ner was the father of Kish, Kish the father of Saul, and Saul the father of Jonathan, Malki-Shua, Abinadab and Esh-Baal.

³⁴The son of Jonathan:

Merib-Baal, who was the father of Micah.

³⁵The sons of Micah:

Pithon, Melech, Tarea and Ahaz.

³⁶Ahaz was the father of Jehoaddah, Jehoaddah was the father of Alemeth, Azmaveth and Zimri, and Zimri was the father of Moza. ³⁷Moza was the father of Binea; Raphah was his son, Eleasah his son and Azel his son.

³⁸Azel had six sons, and these were their names:

Azrikam, Bokeru, Ishmael, Sheariah, Obadiah and Hanan. All these were the sons of Azel.

³⁹The sons of his brother Eshek:

Ulam his firstborn, Jeush the second son and Eliphelet the third. ⁴⁰The sons of Ulam were brave warriors who could handle the bow. They had many sons and grandsons — 150 in all.

All these were the descendants of Benjamin.

COMMENTARY

1–28 The Chronicler's genealogical coverage of the tribe of Benjamin continues his brief (and partial) coverage of Benjamin treated earlier (cf. 7:6–12). Moreover, the Chronicler treats the lineage of the tribe of Benjamin again at the close of the final chapter of his genealogical survey of Israel (cf. 9:35–44).

The present survey of Benjamin includes a number of geographical markers. Note that several of these towns are listed in the postexilic lists of returnees and settlement patterns specified in Ezra and Nehemiah (cf. Ezr 2:1–39; Ne 7:6–38; 11:31–35). In addition, some of these cities associated with the tribe of Benjamin were originally part of the tribal inheritance of Dan (e.g., Aijalon [also a Levitical city; cf. Jos 19:42; 21:24], as well as Ono and Lod [implied in Jos 19:46]). Moreover, recall that Jerusalem (v.28) may have been originally part of the tribal inheritance of Benjamin (cf. Jos 18:28; Jdg 1:21; but also see Jos 15:8, 63). All this suggests a certain degree of fluidity regarding the geographical extent of the tribal boundaries (cf. the Danite tribal migration of Jdg 17–18 and the boundary changes anticipated in Eze 47:13–48:29).

29–40 The Chronicler's treatment of the line of Benjamin ends with a focus on the family line that will both culminate in and proceed from Saul. As noted above, the majority of this genealogical survey is reiterated at the end of the next chapter (compare vv.29–38 and 9:35–44) in order to set up the Chronicler's summary of the kingship of Saul (ch. 10).

This genealogy of the family line of Saul focuses on two cities: Gibeon (v.29) and Jerusalem (v.32). The city of Gibeon (also a Levitical city; cf. Jos 21:17) was located in the central hill country on the western side of the Benjamite plateau about five and a half miles northwest of Jerusalem. As with the cities noted in the first part of the chapter (vv.1–28), Gibeon was located at the intersection of important roads (passes) connecting the hill country with the Shephelah. The double mention of the city of Jerusalem within the genealogy of Benjamin (vv.28, 32; also cf. 9:3, 38) may be a subtle connection with the notion of Saulide/Benjamite (versus Davidic/Judahite) kingship as Jerusalem is listed among the tribal inheritance of both Benjamin and Judah (cf. Jos 18:28; Jdg 1:21; but also see Jos 15:8, 63).

NOTE

6–8 The significance of the Chronicler's mention of the "deportation" (vv.6–7) of some Benjamites to the city of Manahath (situated in the tribal territory of Judah to the south of Jerusalem) is uncertain but may be simply a reflection of the migration of part of the tribe, or a more serious issue of banishment as a result of tribal fidelity.

6. Genealogical Summary (1Ch 9:1)

¹All Israel was listed in the genealogies recorded in the book of the kings of Israel. The people of Judah were taken captive to Babylon because of their unfaithfulness.

COMMENTARY

1 This two-part verse summarizes the Chronicler's genealogical portrait of Israel in chs. 1–8 (note that the NIV section headings places the first part of v.1 with the previous section) and also succinctly summarizes the time frame just prior to his

own, namely, the captivity and exile. As will be portrayed throughout the balance of his theological summary of the southern kingdom (Judah), the root cause of the nation's captivity and exile was *unfaithfulness*.

C. Postexilic Resettlement (1Ch 9:2–34)

OVERVIEW

The Chronicler's listing of those in the postexilic setting who had resettled Jerusalem reflects important familial connections between the Chronicler's postexilic audience and the covenantal community of ancient Israel (cf. Hill, 178). Such continuity between the past (particularly the patriarchs and the tribes of Israel) and the Chronicler's present audience provides a tangible means for covenantal hope in the light of God's faithfulness.

²Now the first to resettle on their own property in their own towns were some Israelites, priests, Levites and temple servants.

³Those from Judah, from Benjamin, and from Ephraim and Manasseh who lived in Jerusalem were:

⁴Uthai son of Ammihud, the son of Omri, the son of Imri, the son of Bani, a descendant of Perez son of Judah.

⁵Of the Shilonites:

Asaiah the firstborn and his sons.

⁶Of the Zerahites:

Jeuel.

The people from Judah numbered 690.

⁷Of the Benjamites:

Sallu son of Meshullam, the son of Hodaviah, the son of Hassenuah;

⁸Ibneiah son of Jeroham; Elah son of Uzzi, the son of Micri; and Meshullam son of Shephatiah, the son of Reuel, the son of Ibnijah.

⁹The people from Benjamin, as listed in their genealogy, numbered 956. All these men were heads of their families.

¹⁰Of the priests:

Jedaiah; Jehoiarib; Jakin;

¹¹Azariah son of Hilkiah, the son of Meshullam, the son of Zadok, the son of Meraioth, the son of Ahitub, the official in charge of the house of God;

¹²Adaiah son of Jeroham, the son of Pashhur, the son of Malkijah; and Maasai son of Adiel, the son of Jahzerah, the son of Meshullam, the son of Meshillemith, the son of Immer.

¹³The priests, who were heads of families, numbered 1,760. They were able men, responsible for ministering in the house of God.

¹⁴Of the Levites:

Shemaiah son of Hasshub, the son of Azrikam, the son of Hashabiah, a Merarite; ¹⁵Bakbakkar, Heresh, Galal and Mattaniah son of Mica, the son of Zicri, the son of Asaph; ¹⁶Obadiah son of Shemaiah, the son of Galal, the son of Jeduthun; and Berekiah son of Asa, the son of Elkanah, who lived in the villages of the Netophathites.

¹⁷The gatekeepers:

Shallum, Akkub, Talmon, Ahiman and their brothers, Shallum their chief ¹⁸being stationed at the King's Gate on the east, up to the present time. These were the gatekeepers belonging to the camp of the Levites. ¹⁹Shallum son of Kore, the son of Ebiasaph, the son of Korah, and his fellow gatekeepers from his family (the Korahites) were responsible for guarding the thresholds of the Tent just as their fathers had been responsible for guarding the entrance to the dwelling of the LORD. ²⁰In earlier times Phinehas son of Eleazar was in charge of the gatekeepers, and the LORD was with him. ²¹Zechariah son of Meshelemiah was the gatekeeper at the entrance to the Tent of Meeting.

²²Altogether, those chosen to be gatekeepers at the thresholds numbered 212. They were registered by genealogy in their villages. The gatekeepers had been assigned to their positions of trust by David and Samuel the seer. ²³They and their descendants were in charge of guarding the gates of the house of the LORD — the house called the Tent. ²⁴The gatekeepers were on the four sides: east, west, north and south. ²⁵Their brothers in their villages had to come from time to time and share their duties for seven-day periods. ²⁶But the four principal gatekeepers, who were Levites, were entrusted with the responsibility for the rooms and treasuries in the house of God. ²⁷They would spend the night stationed around the house of God, because they had to guard it; and they had charge of the key for opening it each morning.

²⁸Some of them were in charge of the articles used in the temple service; they counted them when they were brought in and when they were taken out. ²⁹Others were assigned to take care of the furnishings and all the other articles of the sanctuary, as well as the flour and wine, and the oil, incense and spices. ³⁰But some of the priests took care of mixing the spices. ³¹A Levite named Mattithiah, the firstborn son of Shallum the Korahite, was entrusted with the responsibility for baking the offering bread. ³²Some of their Kohathite brothers were in charge of preparing for every Sabbath the bread set out on the table.

³³Those who were musicians, heads of Levite families, stayed in the rooms of the temple and were exempt from other duties because they were responsible for the work day and night.

³⁴All these were heads of Levite families, chiefs as listed in their genealogy, and they lived in Jerusalem.

COMMENTARY

2–34 The Chronicler's introductory statement on those who returned to their "own" property (v.2, *ªḥuzzâ* [GK 299]; cf. Jos 22:9) in the postexilic period includes individuals ("Israelites") associated with tribes from the house of Judah (i.e., Benjamin and Judah — the southern kingdom) as well as the house of Joseph (i.e., Ephraim and Manasseh — the northern kingdom). The Chronicler's mention of the key tribal units from both sides of the long-divided Israelite kingdom acts as a powerful display of the Chronicler's message of tribal unity and covenantal hope.

The Chronicler's strong message of unity is more striking when we recall that it had been 450 to 500 years since "all Israel" had existed as an independent, unified nation. While the Chronicler makes mention of these four tribes' returning to the land (vv.2–3), the list of specific individuals only includes names of those from Judah (vv.4–6) and Benjamin (vv.7–9). Part of the Chronicler's list of those returning to Jerusalem (vv.2–17) is similar to the listing in Nehemiah 11:3–20.

In addition to these Israelites from northern and southern tribes, the Chronicler mentions individuals central to the Israelite covenantal community (namely, priests, Levites, and temple servants). While some of these covenantal fiduciaries relocated to their "own" towns (Levitical and priestly cities [v.2]; cf. Ne 11:3),

a significant number resettled in Jerusalem, hub of the Israelite covenantal community (vv.10–34; recall Ne 11:1–2). The importance of priests as teachers of God's ways and will (cf. Lev 10:11; Dt 33:8–11), together with the musical worship and temple service provided by the Levites, underscores the Chronicler's emphasis on hope and covenantal renewal.

The Chronicler's list of priests and Levites includes extended details regarding the Levitical gatekeepers (vv.17–28). In these verses, the repeated stress of protecting and guarding Yahweh's holy space seems to reflect the importance of guarding and watching over all that pertains to God, as seen in earlier days (note the references to tribal forefathers, Phinehas, Samuel, and David within this section; e.g., vv.19–22). Such faithfulness ("positions of trust," v.22) on the part of these Levitical gatekeepers will foster God's presence with them as with Phinehas (v.20).

Beyond gatekeeping, the Chronicler mentions other temple and worship duties of Levites, including the caretaking of temple items (vv.29, 31–32) and music (v.33; see Johnstone, 1:119–29; for more on the specific duties and distinctions of priests and Levites, see comments on 6:31–47, 48–49). In closing this section, the Chronicler again makes mention of Jerusalem, the physical and metaphysical center of the Israelite covenantal community (v.34).

NOTES

6 The Chronicler gives a different tabulation (690) from that in Nehemiah 11:6 (468) that may relate to a different approach to counting ("men" is noted at Ne 11:6, whereas 1Ch 9:6 has "people"). Alternatively, the difference may be a factor of the temporal gap between the point in time utilized by the Chronicler and that utilized by Nehemiah (see Hill, 180). Similar explanations can be posited for the difference in the enumeration of priests reflected in Chronicles and Nehemiah (1,760 in 1Ch 9:13 vs. 1,192 in Ne 11:12–14).

24 The gates to the temple complex were located at the four compass points, with the eastern entrance (known as the King's Gate) being the main entrance since it faced the entrance to the temple proper.

D. The Line of Saul (1Ch 9:35–44)

³⁵Jeiel the father of Gibeon lived in Gibeon.

His wife's name was Maacah, ³⁶and his firstborn son was Abdon, followed by Zur, Kish, Baal, Ner, Nadab, ³⁷Gedor, Ahio, Zechariah and Mikloth. ³⁸Mikloth was the father of Shimeam. They too lived near their relatives in Jerusalem.

³⁹Ner was the father of Kish, Kish the father of Saul, and Saul the father of Jonathan, Malki-Shua, Abinadab and Esh-Baal.

⁴⁰The son of Jonathan:

Merib-Baal, who was the father of Micah.

⁴¹The sons of Micah:

Pithon, Melech, Tahrea and Ahaz.

⁴²Ahaz was the father of Jadah, Jadah was the father of Alemeth, Azmaveth and Zimri, and Zimri was the father of Moza. ⁴³Moza was the father of Binea; Rephaiah was his son, Eleasah his son and Azel his son.

⁴⁴Azel had six sons, and these were their names:

Azrikam, Bokeru, Ishmael, Sheariah, Obadiah and Hanan. These were the sons of Azel.

COMMENTARY

35–44 The purpose of the Chronicler's reiteration of the genealogical information presented at 8:29–38 is to set up the subsequent summary of the reign of Saul (or at least the closing moments of Saul's reign) in the following chapter. The Chronicler's pursuit of the line of Saul for several (twelve) generations after Saul provides hope for the line of Saul and the tribe of Benjamin that extends well beyond Saul's reign (cf. Selman, 131).

II. THE UNITED MONARCHY (1CH 10:1–2CH 9:31)

A. The Closing Moments of Saul's Reign (1Ch 10:1–14)

OVERVIEW

The Chronicler's interest in moving to the accounts of David and Solomon is reflected in the fact that his account of Saul begins in the closing moments of Saul's reign (ca. 1Sa 31). In addition, the Chronicler's account of David begins with the inauguration of all tribes, bypassing the seven-year drama of a divided kingdom, with the northern tribes aligning with the house of Saul and with Judah supporting David (cf. 2Sa 2–4).

The Chronicler's account of Saul shows the high cost of covenantal unfaithfulness, described as rejecting the word of the Lord (v.13; cf. 1Sa 13:14; 15:26). In fact, Samuel told Saul that God "would have established your kingdom over Israel for all time" (1Sa 13:13). Instead, Saul's unfaithfulness causes the Lord to seek a leader "after his own heart" (13:14).

[1]Now the Philistines fought against Israel; the Israelites fled before them, and many fell slain on Mount Gilboa. [2]The Philistines pressed hard after Saul and his sons, and they killed his sons Jonathan, Abinadab and Malki-Shua. [3]The fighting grew fierce around Saul, and when the archers overtook him, they wounded him.

[4]Saul said to his armor-bearer, "Draw your sword and run me through, or these uncircumcised fellows will come and abuse me."

But his armor-bearer was terrified and would not do it; so Saul took his own sword and fell on it. [5]When the armor-bearer saw that Saul was dead, he too fell on his sword and died. [6]So Saul and his three sons died, and all his house died together.

[7]When all the Israelites in the valley saw that the army had fled and that Saul and his sons had died, they abandoned their towns and fled. And the Philistines came and occupied them.

[8]The next day, when the Philistines came to strip the dead, they found Saul and his sons fallen on Mount Gilboa. [9]They stripped him and took his head and his armor, and sent messengers throughout the land of the Philistines to proclaim the news among their idols and their people. [10]They put his armor in the temple of their gods and hung up his head in the temple of Dagon.

[11]When all the inhabitants of Jabesh Gilead heard of everything the Philistines had done to Saul, [12]all their valiant men went and took the bodies of Saul and his sons and brought them to Jabesh. Then they buried their bones under the great tree in Jabesh, and they fasted seven days.

[13]Saul died because he was unfaithful to the LORD; he did not keep the word of the LORD and even consulted a medium for guidance, [14]and did not inquire of the LORD. So the LORD put him to death and turned the kingdom over to David son of Jesse.

COMMENTARY

1–7 Although Yahweh used Saul to temper the Philistine threat against his people (cf. 1Sa 9:16), it was not completely eradicated. In fact, Philistine dominance over Israel is reflected in the garrisons they were able to establish in Judah and Benjamin (cf. 1Sa 10:3–5; 13:3) as well as their ability to prohibit metalworkers in Israel (13:19–22). Despite this dominance, Saul had some success in pushing the

Philistines back to the coastal plain and reasserting Israelite control over the Negev (cf. 13:3–14:46). Nonetheless, there was "bitter war" between Israel and the Philistines "all the days of Saul" (14:52).

The Chronicler focuses on the final moments of the last extended battle narrative between Saul and the Philistines, which ends in his demise (for the full account see 1Sa 28–31). This conflict between the Israelites and the Philistines is unique in that it is centered in the environs of the Jezreel Valley rather than the typical location in the Shephelah or hill country, and it may relate to control of key trade routes that pass through the Jezreel and Beth Shan valleys. As the Chronicler succinctly summarizes, the Israelites were routed in this battle, Saul died, his sons were killed, and the Israelite army fled (vv.6–7). This victory gave the Philistines control over the important Jezreel-Harod-Beth Shan valleys (v.7), effectively driving a wedge between the Cisjordanian tribes (see J. M. Monson, *The Land Between* [Mountain Home, Id.: Biblical Backgrounds, 1996], 57).

8–12 The Chronicler shows the honor of the inhabitants of Jabesh Gilead in contrast to the dishonor of the Philistines. The displaying of the spoils of war or the body of an important enemy in a temple (v.10) was, in the biblical world, a means of thanking a deity for victory in battle (cf. v.9). The motivation behind the Jabesh Gileadites' rescuing the bodies of Saul and his sons for proper burial may well stem from Saul's efforts to save that city from a brutal assault by the Ammonites (1Sa 11:1–11).

13–14 The crux of the Chronicler's account of the history of Israel relates to the faithfulness or unfaithfulness of the people and leaders of the covenantal community. The Chronicler's account of Saul shows the high cost of covenantal unfaithfulness, evidenced by not heeding Yahweh's word and not seeking (or inquiring of) God's will and wisdom (vv.13–14). Worse, Saul instead sought the counsel of a "medium" (the "witch of Endor"; cf. 1Sa 28:5–25), a practice vehemently prohibited in the covenant (e.g., Lev 20:6).

All told, Saul's unfaithfulness causes the Lord to put Saul to death and seek a leader "after his own heart" (1Sa 13:14), to whom he would give the kingdom of his people (v.14). The agency of God in Saul's death at the hand of the Philistines is stressed by the Chronicler in a way similar to his description of the later division of the kingdom: "this turn of events was from God, to fulfill the word of the LORD" (2Ch 10:15).

NOTES

4–5 The account of Saul's death by his own hand noted here and at 1 Samuel 31:4–5 is described in 2 Samuel 1:5–10 as coming by the hand of an Amalekite, whom Saul asks to put him out of his misery as he lay upon his spear (2Sa 1:6–9; cf. 1Ch 10:5; 1Sa 31:4). While some try to present this as a contradiction, the account of 2 Samuel has simply provided additional details of Saul's final moments.

6 While all the "house" of Saul who stood with him on the battlefield at Gilboa died, Saul's son Ish-Bosheth/Ishbaal would later be anointed king by Saul's military commander (cf. 2Sa 2:8–10), beginning a seven-plus year struggle between the House of Saul and the House of David (2:8–4:12), a prototype for a divided kingdom in Israel. In addition, Jonathan's crippled son Mephibosheth would be later be brought to the royal palace and cared for by King David. As noted in the overview to 1Ch 10:1–14, the Chronicler's review of Saul's reign is brief and works to succinctly summarize the final event through which God "turned the kingdom over to David son of Jesse" (10:14).

8–12 Saul's motivation to aid the city of Jabesh Gilead likely stemmed from the close connection between the Benjamites and the city of Jabesh Gilead. Recall that two-thirds of the decimated tribe of Benjamin (four hundred men out of six hundred survivors) received their wives from the city of Jabesh Gilead in the aftermath of the Benjamite war (Jdg 19–21; cf. esp. 21:5–12). Thus two-thirds of Saul's kin (including perhaps his own mother or grandmother) could trace their lineage through the city of Jabesh Gilead, facilitating a unique and strong bond between this city and the tribe of Benjamin.

B. The Reign of David (1Ch 11:1–29:30)

1. David's Enthronement and Consolidation of Power (1Ch 11:1–12:40)

OVERVIEW

Having quickly dispatched with the reign of Saul, the Chronicler now begins his extended coverage of the reign of David. The Chronicler's account of David begins with David's inauguration by "all Israel" (1Ch 11:1–3), bypassing the seven years of drama between the house of Saul and the house of David (cf. 2Sa 2–4). The opening chapters of David's account (1Ch 11–12) present a clear image of unity in affirming the Lord's will in David's rise to power (cf. 11:2–3) and stress the depth and breadth of support enjoyed by David. This introductory unit begins and ends with David's enthronement at Hebron (1Ch 11:1–3; 12:38–40; see Selman, 137–38).

a. David's Coronation over All Israel (1Ch 11:1–3)

¹All Israel came together to David at Hebron and said, "We are your own flesh and blood. ²In the past, even while Saul was king, you were the one who led Israel on their military campaigns. And the LORD your God said to you, 'You will shepherd my people Israel, and you will become their ruler.'"
³When all the elders of Israel had come to King David at Hebron, he made a compact with them at Hebron before the LORD, and they anointed David king over Israel, as the LORD had promised through Samuel.

COMMENTARY

1 The Chronicler's account of David's reign begins with the clear portrayal of Israelite unity in the gathering of "all Israel" to David. This unity is reinforced with the declaration of the familial-ethnic oneness of the tribes of Israel ("we are your own flesh and blood"). The Chronicler's introduction to the Davidic monarchy does not address the seven years of intrigue (including a divided kingdom) that took place between the house of Saul and the house of David (cf. 2Sa 2−4), preferring to focus on the imagery of tribal unity that reflects his literary-theological intent.

2 The people of Israel had ample opportunity to observe God's hand of blessing on the life of David, particularly in military victories that began in earnest during the reign of Saul (e.g., 1Sa 18:6−9). The people here express recognition that David's elevation to "shepherd" and "ruler" is an element of divine election and sovereignty. The imagery of David as shepherd reflects the king's fiduciary role of protecting the flock (i.e., people) and leading them in righteousness (cf. Dt 17:14−20). The theological significance of the shepherd image is

also reflected in exilic and postexilic prophetic literature (e.g., Eze 34:1−31) and in Christ's self-revelation (cf. Jn 10:1−18). The reminder that these are *God's* people whom David will lead underscores the reality that David's authority has been delegated by God.

3 Although David was anointed king over Judah seven and a half years earlier (cf. 2Sa 2:11), this moment marked the beginning of David's reign over the whole nation. The total span of David's reign is usually marked from 1010−970 BC. The city of Hebron is located in the heart of the tribal territory of Judah; it is closely connected with the patriarchal era and was David's capital when he reigned over Judah. The Chronicler again (cf. v.2) makes God's will central to David's accession to the throne and includes another reference to the prophetic anticipation of David's rise to power (cf. 1Sa 16:1−13).

b. David's Taking of Jerusalem (1Ch 11:4−8)

⁴David and all the Israelites marched to Jerusalem (that is, Jebus). The Jebusites who lived there ⁵said to David, "You will not get in here." Nevertheless, David captured the fortress of Zion, the City of David.

⁶David had said, "Whoever leads the attack on the Jebusites will become commander-in-chief." Joab son of Zeruiah went up first, and so he received the command.

⁷David then took up residence in the fortress, and so it was called the City of David. ⁸He built up the city around it, from the supporting terraces to the surrounding wall, while Joab restored the rest of the city.

COMMENTARY

4−8 While the taking of Jerusalem recorded in Samuel (cf. 2Sa 5:6−10) focuses on the efforts of a small band of warriors, the Chronicler emphasizes the participation of the broader community in this

important accomplishment ("all the Israelites," v.4). The taking of Jerusalem and David's subsequent transfer of his capital from Hebron to Jerusalem ("the City of David," v.7) was a significant step in deepening solidarity across the tribes and constituencies of Israel for a number of reasons. It was:

- geographically central to the twelve tribes (in contrast to deep in the territory of Judah, as Hebron was)
- politically neutral, as it was taken from the Jebusites and was not occupied by any particular tribe (cf. Washington, D.C.)
- connected with the patriarch Abraham via the earlier names "Salem" (cf. Ge 14:18–20; Ps 76:2) and "Mount Moriah" (cf. Ge 22; 2Ch 3:1)
- earned by David (reflecting divine blessing; recall vv.2, 9) and advanced the fulfillment of

Yahweh's promise to Israel of land (previous efforts at taking Jerusalem [Jebus] were only temporarily successful [see, e.g., Jos 10; 15:63; Jdg 1:8, 21])

- a central location for religious and political power bases (cf. chs. 15–17; 2Sa 6–7)

All these factors worked together to minimize potential tribal jealousies, promote national and religious unity, and demonstrate the tangible blessing of God on the leadership of David. This account also shows the backdrop to the ascendancy of David's military leader Joab (v.6) and introduces two common synonyms used for Jerusalem, namely "Zion" (v.5) and the "City of David" (v.7).

c. David's Power and Support (1Ch 11:9–12:40)

[9]And David became more and more powerful, because the LORD Almighty was with him. [10]These were the chiefs of David's mighty men — they, together with all Israel, gave his kingship strong support to extend it over the whole land, as the LORD had promised — [11]this is the list of David's mighty men:

Jashobeam, a Hacmonite, was chief of the officers; he raised his spear against three hundred men, whom he killed in one encounter.

[12]Next to him was Eleazar son of Dodai the Ahohite, one of the three mighty men. [13]He was with David at Pas Dammim when the Philistines gathered there for battle. At a place where there was a field full of barley, the troops fled from the Philistines. [14]But they took their stand in the middle of the field. They defended it and struck the Philistines down, and the LORD brought about a great victory.

[15]Three of the thirty chiefs came down to David to the rock at the cave of Adullam, while a band of Philistines was encamped in the Valley of Rephaim. [16]At that time David was in the stronghold, and the Philistine garrison was at Bethlehem. [17]David longed for water and said, "Oh, that someone would get me a drink of water from the well near the gate of Bethlehem!" [18]So the Three broke through the Philistine lines, drew water from the well near the gate of Bethlehem and carried it back to David. But he refused to drink it; instead, he poured it out before the LORD. [19]"God forbid that I should do this!" he said. "Should I drink the blood of these men who went at the risk of their lives?" Because they risked their lives to bring it back, David would not drink it.

Such were the exploits of the three mighty men.

[20]Abishai the brother of Joab was chief of the Three. He raised his spear against three hundred men, whom he killed, and so he became as famous as the Three. [21]He was doubly honored above the Three and became their commander, even though he was not included among them.

[22]Benaiah son of Jehoiada was a valiant fighter from Kabzeel, who performed great exploits. He struck down two of Moab's best men. He also went down into a pit on a snowy day and killed a lion. [23]And he struck down an Egyptian who was seven and a half feet tall. Although the Egyptian had a spear like a weaver's rod in his hand, Benaiah went against him with a club. He snatched the spear from the Egyptian's hand and killed him with his own spear. [24]Such were the exploits of Benaiah son of Jehoiada; he too was as famous as the three mighty men. [25]He was held in greater honor than any of the Thirty, but he was not included among the Three. And David put him in charge of his bodyguard.

[26]The mighty men were:

Asahel the brother of Joab,
Elhanan son of Dodo from Bethlehem,
[27]Shammoth the Harorite,
Helez the Pelonite,
[28]Ira son of Ikkesh from Tekoa,
Abiezer from Anathoth,
[29]Sibbecai the Hushathite,
Ilai the Ahohite,
[30]Maharai the Netophathite,
Heled son of Baanah the Netophathite,
[31]Ithai son of Ribai from Gibeah in Benjamin,
Benaiah the Pirathonite,
[32]Hurai from the ravines of Gaash,
Abiel the Arbathite,
[33]Azmaveth the Baharumite,
Eliahba the Shaalbonite,
[34]the sons of Hashem the Gizonite,
Jonathan son of Shagee the Hararite,
[35]Ahiam son of Sacar the Hararite,
Eliphal son of Ur,
[36]Hepher the Mekerathite,
Ahijah the Pelonite,
[37]Hezro the Carmelite,
Naarai son of Ezbai,

³⁸Joel the brother of Nathan,
  Mibhar son of Hagri,
³⁹Zelek the Ammonite,
  Naharai the Berothite, the armor-bearer of Joab son of Zeruiah,
⁴⁰Ira the Ithrite,
  Gareb the Ithrite,
⁴¹Uriah the Hittite,
  Zabad son of Ahlai,
⁴²Adina son of Shiza the Reubenite, who was chief of the Reubenites, and the thirty
  with him,
⁴³Hanan son of Maacah,
  Joshaphat the Mithnite,
⁴⁴Uzzia the Ashterathite,
  Shama and Jeiel the sons of Hotham the Aroerite,
⁴⁵Jediael son of Shimri,
  his brother Joha the Tizite,
⁴⁶Eliel the Mahavite,
  Jeribai and Joshaviah the sons of Elnaam,
  Ithmah the Moabite,
⁴⁷Eliel, Obed and Jaasiel the Mezobaite.

^{12:1}These were the men who came to David at Ziklag, while he was banished from the presence of Saul son of Kish (they were among the warriors who helped him in battle; ²they were armed with bows and were able to shoot arrows or to sling stones right-handed or left-handed; they were kinsmen of Saul from the tribe of Benjamin):

³Ahiezer their chief and Joash the sons of Shemaah the Gibeathite; Jeziel and Pelet the sons of Azmaveth; Beracah, Jehu the Anathothite, ⁴and Ishmaiah the Gibeonite, a mighty man among the Thirty, who was a leader of the Thirty; Jeremiah, Jahaziel, Johanan, Jozabad the Gederathite, ⁵Eluzai, Jerimoth, Bealiah, Shemariah and Shephatiah the Haruphite; ⁶Elkanah, Isshiah, Azarel, Joezer and Jashobeam the Korahites; ⁷and Joelah and Zebadiah the sons of Jeroham from Gedor.

⁸Some Gadites defected to David at his stronghold in the desert. They were brave warriors, ready for battle and able to handle the shield and spear. Their faces were the faces of lions, and they were as swift as gazelles in the mountains.
⁹Ezer was the chief,
  Obadiah the second in command, Eliab the third,
¹⁰Mishmannah the fourth, Jeremiah the fifth,
¹¹Attai the sixth, Eliel the seventh,

¹²Johanan the eighth, Elzabad the ninth,

¹³Jeremiah the tenth and Macbannai the eleventh.

¹⁴These Gadites were army commanders; the least was a match for a hundred, and the greatest for a thousand. ¹⁵It was they who crossed the Jordan in the first month when it was overflowing all its banks, and they put to flight everyone living in the valleys, to the east and to the west.

¹⁶Other Benjamites and some men from Judah also came to David in his stronghold. ¹⁷David went out to meet them and said to them, "If you have come to me in peace, to help me, I am ready to have you unite with me. But if you have come to betray me to my enemies when my hands are free from violence, may the God of our fathers see it and judge you."

¹⁸Then the Spirit came upon Amasai, chief of the Thirty, and he said:

> "We are yours, O David!
>   We are with you, O son of Jesse!
> Success, success to you,
>   and success to those who help you,
>   for your God will help you."

So David received them and made them leaders of his raiding bands.

¹⁹Some of the men of Manasseh defected to David when he went with the Philistines to fight against Saul. (He and his men did not help the Philistines because, after consultation, their rulers sent him away. They said, "It will cost us our heads if he deserts to his master Saul.") ²⁰When David went to Ziklag, these were the men of Manasseh who defected to him: Adnah, Jozabad, Jediael, Michael, Jozabad, Elihu and Zillethai, leaders of units of a thousand in Manasseh. ²¹They helped David against raiding bands, for all of them were brave warriors, and they were commanders in his army. ²²Day after day men came to help David, until he had a great army, like the army of God.

²³These are the numbers of the men armed for battle who came to David at Hebron to turn Saul's kingdom over to him, as the Lᴏʀᴅ had said:

²⁴men of Judah, carrying shield and spear — 6,800 armed for battle;

²⁵men of Simeon, warriors ready for battle — 7,100;

²⁶men of Levi — 4,600, ²⁷including Jehoiada, leader of the family of Aaron, with 3,700 men, ²⁸and Zadok, a brave young warrior, with 22 officers from his family;

²⁹men of Benjamin, Saul's kinsmen — 3,000, most of whom had remained loyal to Saul's house until then;

³⁰men of Ephraim, brave warriors, famous in their own clans — 20,800;

³¹men of half the tribe of Manasseh, designated by name to come and make David king — 18,000;

³²men of Issachar, who understood the times and knew what Israel should do — 200 chiefs, with all their relatives under their command;

³³men of Zebulun, experienced soldiers prepared for battle with every type of weapon, to help David with undivided loyalty — 50,000;

³⁴men of Naphtali — 1,000 officers, together with 37,000 men carrying shields and spears;

³⁵men of Dan, ready for battle — 28,600;

³⁶men of Asher, experienced soldiers prepared for battle — 40,000;

³⁷and from east of the Jordan, men of Reuben, Gad and the half-tribe of Manasseh, armed with every type of weapon — 120,000.

³⁸All these were fighting men who volunteered to serve in the ranks. They came to Hebron fully determined to make David king over all Israel. All the rest of the Israelites were also of one mind to make David king. ³⁹The men spent three days there with David, eating and drinking, for their families had supplied provisions for them. ⁴⁰Also, their neighbors from as far away as Issachar, Zebulun and Naphtali came bringing food on donkeys, camels, mules and oxen. There were plentiful supplies of flour, fig cakes, raisin cakes, wine, oil, cattle and sheep, for there was joy in Israel.

COMMENTARY

11:9 The Chronicler emphasizes the theological reality that David's military and political successes are an outworking of God's blessing on his chosen king. The Chronicler uses the imagery of divine presence ("the LORD Almighty was with him") to express God's effectual blessing of David's efforts (also seen with the patriarchs, Moses, and Joshua; see the Reflection on divine presence in 2Ch 1).

10–47 The Chronicler's emphasis in this listing of warriors is the fierce loyalty and extensive accomplishments of the men who led David's military. As such, this list should be read together with the list of warriors and troops who join David enumerated in the next chapter. Even though the list focuses on a group of elite military leaders, the Chronicler begins by stressing that these military "chiefs" were aligned with "all Israel" vis-à-vis

David's rule "over the whole land," and that they were used of God to bring about what "the LORD had promised" (v.10).

The Lord's protective blessing on David and this group is reflected in the Chronicler's remark at the end of one of the vignettes (vv.12–14) that "the LORD brought about a great victory" (v.14), reflecting the fact that the faith of God's people should rest in their powerful God, not in powerful men. In addition, perhaps as a subtle precursor to Israel's role with respect to the nations, a number of non-Israelites are counted among David's elite military corps, including those of Moabite (v.46), Ammonite (v.39), and Hittite (v.41) descent.

The short account of David pouring out the water bravely obtained by his warriors (vv.15–19) can be incorrectly seen as an act of waste and ungratefulness on the part of David in the light of his men's risk. Instead, David's act of selfless *worship* to his superior (as it should be seen) aptly balances out the selfless act of courage displayed by the men to their superior. Thus a translation along the lines of "he poured it out *to* the LORD" or "he poured it out *in the presence of* the LORD" might better capture the sense of worship implied in David's act (cf. RSV; Selman, 143).

12:1 – 7 The initial group of men noted by the Chronicler as expressing allegiance to David hail from Saul's tribe, Benjamin (v.2). The Chronicler seems to be emphasizing the theme of tribal unity in this unexpected show of loyalty by the kinsman of Saul toward David, given the double mention of Saul in vv.1 – 2 and the listing of this group first. This ambidextrous group of Benjamites had particular military acumen in the areas of archery and sling shooting (v.2) and came to David while he was living in Philistine territory (cf. 1Sa 27:1 – 7).

8 – 15 In addition to David's support from some men from Saul's tribe of Benjamin (vv.1 – 7), the Chronicler notes that skilled warriors from the Transjordanian tribe of Gad aligned themselves with David. While the Benjamite warriors were skilled with arrows and slingshots (implying warfare from a distance), these Gadites had specialized skill in shields and spears (implying close combat). In addition, these Gadite soldiers were known for their ferocity ("faces of lions"), speed ("swift as gazelles"), and ability to navigate treacherous waters (v.15). The location of David's "stronghold in the desert" (v.8) is unknown, though it may have been Adullam (cf. 1Sa 22:1), En Gedi (cf. 1Sa 24:1), or a location in the wilderness of Ziph (cf. 1Sa 23:14).

16 – 17 In addition to kinsmen of Saul (vv.1 – 7) and soldiers from the tribe of Gad (vv.8 – 15), the Chronicler notes that others from the tribes of Benjamin and Judah aligned themselves with David during his time of political banishment. For reasons

that are not specified, David is concerned about the sincerity of these men and calls on God to act if they are planning treachery. In any case, David is interested in unity with these men ("unite with me") if indeed they have come in peace and with hearts to serve ("to help me," v.17; note the frequency of the term "help" in the broader context of this chapter).

As an aside, it is somewhat ironic that the Chronicler notes David's concern for genuine loyalty only with a group that includes men from his own tribe of Judah. On the possibilities of David's "stronghold" (v.16), see the comments on vv.8 – 15.

18 Following David's divine appeal in the light of his uncertainty of these men's motives (vv.16 – 17), the Chronicler notes that the "Spirit" came upon "Amasai, chief of the Thirty," the group of especially talented military leaders listed earlier (ch. 11). However, Amasai is not specifically listed in ch. 11, nor is David's eventual military commander Joab, so that list is not intended to include all of David's key military leaders. The stress of the poetic words of Amasai is that complete dedication, loyalty, and service ("help") to David begets not only success for David (lit., "peace upon peace/supreme peace" šālôm šālôm], translated "perfect peace" in Isa 26:3), but also success (again, lit., "peace") on those who are faithful to David. This call to unmitigated faithfulness to God through obedience and submission to the covenantal structures he has provided (including leadership) is central to the Chronicler's message.

19 – 21 In addition to those from Benjamin, Gad, and Judah noted above (vv.1 – 18), men from the northern tribe of Manasseh aligned themselves with David while he was at Ziklag. As an aside, the Chronicler reminds his audience that David was nearly part of the Philistine coalition that battled Israel in the environs of the Jezreel and Beth Shan valleys (cf. 1Sa 29). Since this was the battle that led to the death of Saul and his sons, this move by the Philistine leaders providentially prevented David from being implicated (directly or indirectly) in the death of the reigning king and his sons.

22 Following select highlights of capable soldiers pledging allegiance to David from the tribes of Benjamin, Gad, Judah, and Manasseh, the Chronicler summarizes that these were not isolated incidents, but part of a broader, national move of fidelity toward the leadership of David. The end result is a "great army, like the army of God," consisting of those who had risked everything to commit themselves to a fugitive currently banished from his homeland. This reality reflects the Chronicler's earlier statement that "David became more and more powerful, *because the LORD Almighty was with him*" (1Ch 11:9, emphasis added; cf. 11:2).

23–40 This section concludes the Chronicler's extended summary of the transition to Davidic rule

in Israel that began in ch. 11. As noted earlier (cf. 1Ch 11:10), this "turning over" of the kingdom from Saulide to Davidic rule was in accordance with the will of God ("as the LORD had said," v.23). As seen throughout the broader context of chs. 11 and 12, the Chronicler presents a vivid picture of tribal unity and dedication toward God's chosen king. The Chronicler notes that these battle-ready individuals from all the tribes of Israel "volunteered to serve" David and were "fully determined" (lit., "with a whole heart" [*belēbāb šālēm*]) to make David king over all Israel (v.38).

Moreover, the balance of the community ("all the rest of the Israelites") was likewise "of one mind" (lit., "one/unified heart" [*lēb 'eḥād*]) in affirming God's choice of David as king. This unity of purpose culminates in a celebratory meal reflecting the "joy in Israel" brought about by God (vv.39–40).

NOTES

12:18 [19] The expression "Then the Spirit came upon Amasai" [וְרוּחַ לָבְשָׁה אֶת־עֲמָשַׂי, *werûaḥ lōbeśâ 'et-ʿamāśay*] is possibly more accurately rendered "a spirit came upon [lit., 'clothed'] Amasai," as there is no definite article on S/spirit and it is not in construct with a proper noun (e.g., Spirit *of God*). Such a rendering would be akin to an individual's getting a surge of passion that prompts him to speak or act with conviction. This rare expression is also used of Gideon in his purging of Canaanite idolatry (Jdg 6:34) and by the Chronicler in introducing the words of Zechariah, also in the context of pagan idolatry (2Ch 24:20).

23–40 [24–41] On the possible nuance of "thousand" (אֶלֶף, *'elep*; GK 547) as a marker of a fighting unit rather than the number 1,000, see extended comments on 2 Chronicles 11:1.

2. Return of the Ark of the Covenant Initiated (1Ch 13:1–14)

OVERVIEW

Although this initial attempt to move the ark of the covenant ends negatively (cf. vv.9–12), the Chronicler nonetheless maintains his emphasis on

the unity of all Israel under David's leadership and closes this episode on a note of hope (v.14). Moreover, David's immediate attention to bringing the ark of the covenant to a position of physical and spiritual centrality for the community implies that David's reign will be marked by seeking God and by concern for the covenant (recall that the text of the covenant [the law of Moses] was housed within the ark; cf. Dt 10:1–5). These characteristics of spiritual faithfulness place David in sharp contrast to Saul (cf. 1Ch 10:13–14).

¹David conferred with each of his officers, the commanders of thousands and commanders of hundreds. ²He then said to the whole assembly of Israel, "If it seems good to you and if it is the will of the LORD our God, let us send word far and wide to the rest of our brothers throughout the territories of Israel, and also to the priests and Levites who are with them in their towns and pasturelands, to come and join us. ³Let us bring the ark of our God back to us, for we did not inquire of it during the reign of Saul." ⁴The whole assembly agreed to do this, because it seemed right to all the people.

⁵So David assembled all the Israelites, from the Shihor River in Egypt to Lebo Hamath, to bring the ark of God from Kiriath Jearim. ⁶David and all the Israelites with him went to Baalah of Judah (Kiriath Jearim) to bring up from there the ark of God the LORD, who is enthroned between the cherubim — the ark that is called by the Name.

⁷They moved the ark of God from Abinadab's house on a new cart, with Uzzah and Ahio guiding it. ⁸David and all the Israelites were celebrating with all their might before God, with songs and with harps, lyres, tambourines, cymbals and trumpets.

⁹When they came to the threshing floor of Kidon, Uzzah reached out his hand to steady the ark, because the oxen stumbled. ¹⁰The LORD's anger burned against Uzzah, and he struck him down because he had put his hand on the ark. So he died there before God.

¹¹Then David was angry because the LORD's wrath had broken out against Uzzah, and to this day that place is called Perez Uzzah.

¹²David was afraid of God that day and asked, "How can I ever bring the ark of God to me?" ¹³He did not take the ark to be with him in the City of David. Instead, he took it aside to the house of Obed-Edom the Gittite. ¹⁴The ark of God remained with the family of Obed-Edom in his house for three months, and the LORD blessed his household and everything he had.

COMMENTARY

1–4 Although this episode quickly moves from human celebration to divine judgment (cf. vv.8–12), the Chronicler nonetheless maintains his emphasis on the unity of all Israel. Thus David confers with his military leaders (v.1) and engages "the whole assembly of Israel" at Hebron and the rest of the Israelites "throughout the territories of Israel" (v.2). Moreover, David receives support from "the whole assembly" and approval from "all the people" (v.4) regarding the relocation of the ark of the covenant (also cf. vv.5–6).

While the loss of the ark is theologically connected with Yahweh's rejection of the Elide priesthood (cf. 1Sa 2:27–34; 3:11–14; 4:12–22), the Chronicler implies that it was subsequently neglected during the time of Saul (v.3). Given the connection between the ark and the presence of God in the midst of his people (cf. Ex 25:17–22; 1Sa 4:21–22), such neglect is a subtle but significant negative commentary on the spiritual priorities reflected in Saul's reign. Conversely, the implication of v.3 is that David's reign will be marked by seeking God and, by extension, attentiveness to the covenantal stipulations safeguarded within the ark. Ironically, the final remark of this section ("it seemed right to all the people," v.4) seems to anticipate that what was right *to God* was not being sufficiently considered by David and the people (cf. 15:13).

5–6 The Chronicler stresses the unity and involvement of the whole Israelite community in the moving of the ark of the covenant ("David assembled all the Israelites … David and all the Israelites"; also see previous comment). The priority given to this (attempted) move of the ark symbolizes the commitment of David and the Israelites to seek God and to obey his covenantal stipulations (contained in the ark; cf. Dt 10:1–5).

The description of Israelites "from the Shihor River in Egypt to Lebo Hamath" reflects the ultimate anticipated geographical extent of Israel and may imply that some of the descendants of Jacob were already in these outlying areas. The ark had been in Kiriath Jearim (also known as Baalath, Kiriath Baal, and Mahaneh Dan in the OT) for twenty years following its seven-month exile in Philistine territory during the time of Samuel and Eli (cf. 1Sa 4–6). Kiriath Jearim was located near the tribal boundaries of Benjamin, Judah, and Dan, approximately nine miles from Jerusalem.

Like the temple (cf. Dt 12:5; 2Ch 2:1), the ark is associated with the "Name" of Yahweh (v.6). Such "name theology" includes aspects of God's character and his covenantal relationship with Israel and humanity. On the cherubim guarding the ark, see comments on 2 Chronicles 3:10–13.

7–8 Following the example of the Philistines in getting the ark out of their territory (cf. 1Sa 5:1–6:12), the assembly places the ark on a "new cart" to move it from Kiriath Jearim. Despite the worship of David and the people, the celebration quickly moves to divine judgment after God's holiness is violated by Uzzah (vv.9–12). On the musical instruments noted here, see comments on 2 Chronicles 5:12–13.

9–13 While Uzzah's action seems well-intentioned, it is nonetheless an act of spiritual profanity that violates God's holy space (cf. Nu 4:15). This incident is reminiscent of the situation involving the two eldest sons of Aaron, who likewise violated God's holiness by offering "unauthorized fire before the LORD, contrary to his [the LORD's] command" (Lev 10:1). In both situations, the individuals did what was right in their own eyes rather than what was right in God's eyes and required in the light of his holiness. See the Reflection below.

Although David's reaction to Uzzah's death includes anger (v.11), David also gains a greater degree of the fear of the Lord and a greater recognition of the separation between a holy God and unholy humanity (v.12). Moreover, David's commitment to please God is reflected in his immediate stoppage of the ark's transfer and the subsequent careful steps of obedience taken in the later (successful) move of the ark to Jerusalem (cf. 1Ch 15:1–28).

14 Despite the rapid shift from celebration to judgment (vv.8–12), the Chronicler ends his summary of this incident on a note of blessing and promise. Ultimately, the Lord will also bless David, his household, and everything he has.

NOTE

9–10 The wrath of God also broke out against seventy men of Beth Shemesh who dared to look into the ark (1Sa 6:19–20).

REFLECTION

The sad story of Uzzah's fatal attempt to steady the ark of God is a painful lesson underscoring the necessity of doing what is right in God's eyes, not our own eyes. The tendency to do what seems good in our eyes is at the heart of human rebellion against the authority of God (cf. Ge 3:6). In anticipation of a settled covenantal community, the Israelites were instructed not to worship God "in their way" or "everyone as he sees fit" (cf. Dt 12:4, 8). Unfortunately, the early history of Israel demonstrated the power of this human tendency (cf. Jdg 17:6; 21:25).

Similarly, today too often the standard of determining what is "good" is approached from the vantage point of our own personal opinion (what is right in our eyes) rather than through the lens of biblical principles. Our cultural and social tendencies prompt us to affirm, approve, and praise the actions of others based on whether they mean well regardless of biblical accuracy, as though zeal without knowledge were a commendable trait. Yet, as this incident with Uzzah shows, what is right in our eyes is irrelevant and frequently disastrous (Dt 4:24; Heb 12:29). Indeed, we should not lose sight of the reality that the human heart is self-deceiving and mired in the noetic (cognitive) effects of the fall (Jer 17:9). Such theological awareness prompts believers to seek God's Word and grace in order to be transformed and alert to what is pleasing and acceptable in God's eyes (cf. Ro 12:1–2).

3. David's Family (1Ch 14:1–17)

OVERVIEW

This section of the Chronicler's work begins and ends with statements reflecting God's blessings on David both in Israel and in the surrounding nations (vv.2, 17). In between, the Chronicler details how God enabled David to defeat the Philistines, who had been in a position of power over Israel during the judges' time (cf. Jdg 13–16), the time of Eli and Samuel (cf. 1Sa 4–7), and the reign of Saul (cf. 1Sa 8–31). This chapter is out of chronological order, perhaps as a means of contrasting the house of David and the house of Saul. A number of parallels from this chapter will be seen later, during the early stage of Solomon's reign (e.g., cf. v.1 with 2Ch 2:11–14 and v.2 with 2Ch 1:1).

¹Now Hiram king of Tyre sent messengers to David, along with cedar logs, stonemasons and carpenters to build a palace for him. ²And David knew that the LORD had established him as king over Israel and that his kingdom had been highly exalted for the sake of his people Israel.

³In Jerusalem David took more wives and became the father of more sons and daughters. ⁴These are the names of the children born to him there: Shammua, Shobab, Nathan, Solomon, ⁵Ibhar, Elishua, Elpelet, ⁶Nogah, Nepheg, Japhia, ⁷Elishama, Beeliada and Eliphelet.

⁸When the Philistines heard that David had been anointed king over all Israel, they went up in full force to search for him, but David heard about it and went out to meet them. ⁹Now the Philistines had come and raided the Valley of Rephaim; ¹⁰ so David inquired of God: "Shall I go and attack the Philistines? Will you hand them over to me?"

The LORD answered him, "Go, I will hand them over to you."

¹¹So David and his men went up to Baal Perazim, and there he defeated them. He said, "As waters break out, God has broken out against my enemies by my hand." So that place was called Baal Perazim. ¹²The Philistines had abandoned their gods there, and David gave orders to burn them in the fire.

¹³Once more the Philistines raided the valley; ¹⁴so David inquired of God again, and God answered him, "Do not go straight up, but circle around them and attack them in front of the balsam trees. ¹⁵As soon as you hear the sound of marching in the tops of the balsam trees, move out to battle, because that will mean God has gone out in front of you to strike the Philistine army." ¹⁶So David did as God commanded him, and they struck down the Philistine army, all the way from Gibeon to Gezer.

¹⁷So David's fame spread throughout every land, and the LORD made all the nations fear him.

COMMENTARY

1–2 It is noteworthy that David accepts Phoenician assistance in the building of his palace (cf. Solomon in the building of Yahweh's temple [2Ch 2:3–16]). The Phoenicians were noted for supplying raw building materials and having the technical expertise to construct buildings and fabricate artistic objects with wood, metal, fabric, and stone.

The area of Tyre (Phoenicia or Lebanon more broadly) was a well-known source for quality lumber such as cedar. In the biblical world the wood of the slow-growing cedar tree was especially desired for important building projects, such as palaces and temples, given its fragrance and durability. Phoenician stonemasons were skilled in both construction techniques and specialty craftsmanship, such as dressed masonry (ashlar) and carved basalt orthostats (e.g., lion figures shaped from stone).

3–7 This list of David's sons is also found in the Chronicler's genealogical survey (cf. 3:1–9) and is noted here as another means of showing that God had established David in Jerusalem (v.2). Although God's design for marriage is one man to one woman, no negative comment is made by the Chronicler on the issue of David's polygamy, nor does Deuteronomy 17:17 necessarily prohibit polygamy as it speaks against a king's taking "many" wives (cf. Solomon, 1Ki 11:3).

8–16 In these two instances of David's success against the Philistines at the beginning of his reign, the Chronicler's emphasis is that David "inquired of [sought] God" (vv.10, 14) and that God "answered him" (vv.10, 14). David's seeking of God stands in sharp contrast to Saul, who either did not inquire of God (cf. 1Ch 10:13–14) or sought insight from pagan sources (cf. 1Sa 28:7–25). Moreover, the Chronicler illustrates that God brings success to David as "David did as God commanded him" (v.16), an important spiritual lesson for the Chronicler's audience and God's people at all times (cf. Johnstone, 1:180).

Israel's territorial conflicts with the Philistines and Ammonites stressed in Judges 10–16 are likely not far removed from the time of Samuel and dovetail with the establishment of the monarchy (cf. 1Sa 8:19–20). The Samson account (Jdg 13–16) stresses Philistine domination over Israel (cf. Jdg 14:4; 15:11, 20) and makes it clear that the Philistines have expanded from the coastal plain into the Shephelah and central hill country. Although the Philistine threat was tempered during the days of Samuel (cf. 1Sa 7:13; 9:16), it was not eradicated, and the Philistines maintained a position of hegemony over Israel (cf. 1Sa 10:3–5; 13:3, 19–22).

After realizing that David has reconsolidated the tribes of Israel, the Philistines attack twice (vv.8, 13) but are defeated and driven back. David's victory succeeds in removing the Philistine foothold in the hill country and part of the Shephelah (v.16). Following his first victory, David burns the abandoned Philistine idols (v.12), according to Deuteronomic instruction (cf. Dt 7:5–6; 12:1–3). Thus David's twofold victory over the Philistines at the beginning of his reign emphatically shows God's hand of protection and blessing over the king and the nation as David seeks him and obeys his Word (cf. vv.10–11, 14–16, 17).

17 This summary statement reflects the Chronicler's sustained focus on God's goodness in establishing and blessing the reign of David. This blessing is expressed via the position of respect and power attained by Israel during the reign of David and is likewise seen during the reigns of Solomon (2Ch 9:9, 24) and Jehoshaphat (cf. 2Ch 17:10–11).

NOTES

1 "Hiram" (חִירָם, *Ḥîrām*) is actually spelled "Huram" (חוּרָם, *Ḥûrām*) in Chronicles and "Hiram" (or "Hirom" [חִירוֹם, *Ḥîrôm*]) in Samuel and Kings (cf. 2Sa 5:11; 1Ki 5:1 [15], 10 [24], 18 [32]; 7:40).

11 As God did with Uzzah (13:11), so God "breaks out" against the Philistines. In the same way that the place where God broke out against Uzzah is renamed "Perez Uzzah" (13:11), so the name of the city where God breaks out against the Philistines is renamed "Baal Perazim" (v.11). Note that the word "Baal" here [בַּעַל, *baʿal*; GK 1251] is a title meaning "L/lord; M/master," as implied in the name here ("Lord who breaks through"), though its typical use in the OT (and the biblical world) is a shortened way of referring to the Syro-Canaanite storm god, Baal-Hadad.

15 While the specific meaning of the sound of marching in the treetops is unknown, it provokes the image of God (along with his angelic army) as supernaturally fighting for his covenantal people (cf. Dt 20:1–4).

4. Return of the Ark of the Covenant Completed (1Ch 15:1–16:43)

OVERVIEW

These chapters recount the successful move of the ark of the covenant to Jerusalem. In contrast to the well-intended but irreverent earlier attempt at moving the ark (ch. 13), David is now careful to take all requisite steps to ensure that the movement of the ark is done God's way (cf. vv.2, 15).

¹After David had constructed buildings for himself in the City of David, he prepared a place for the ark of God and pitched a tent for it. ²Then David said, "No one but the Levites may carry the ark of God, because the LORD chose them to carry the ark of the LORD and to minister before him forever."

³David assembled all Israel in Jerusalem to bring up the ark of the LORD to the place he had prepared for it. ⁴He called together the descendants of Aaron and the Levites:

⁵From the descendants of Kohath,
    Uriel the leader and 120 relatives;
⁶from the descendants of Merari,
    Asaiah the leader and 220 relatives;
⁷from the descendants of Gershon,
    Joel the leader and 130 relatives;
⁸from the descendants of Elizaphan,
    Shemaiah the leader and 200 relatives;
⁹from the descendants of Hebron,
    Eliel the leader and 80 relatives;
¹⁰from the descendants of Uzziel,
    Amminadab the leader and 112 relatives.

¹¹Then David summoned Zadok and Abiathar the priests, and Uriel, Asaiah, Joel, Shemaiah, Eliel and Amminadab the Levites. ¹²He said to them, "You are the heads of the Levitical families; you and your fellow Levites are to consecrate yourselves and bring up the ark of the LORD, the God of Israel, to the place I have prepared for it. ¹³It was because you, the Levites, did not bring it up the first time that the LORD our God broke out in anger against us. We did not inquire of him about how to do it in the prescribed way." ¹⁴So the priests and Levites consecrated themselves in order to bring up the ark of the LORD, the God of

Israel. ¹⁵And the Levites carried the ark of God with the poles on their shoulders, as Moses had commanded in accordance with the word of the Lord.

¹⁶David told the leaders of the Levites to appoint their brothers as singers to sing joyful songs, accompanied by musical instruments: lyres, harps and cymbals.

¹⁷So the Levites appointed Heman son of Joel; from his brothers, Asaph son of Berekiah; and from their brothers the Merarites, Ethan son of Kushaiah; ¹⁸and with them their brothers next in rank: Zechariah, Jaaziel, Shemiramoth, Jehiel, Unni, Eliab, Benaiah, Maaseiah, Mattithiah, Eliphelehu, Mikneiah, Obed-Edom and Jeiel, the gatekeepers.

¹⁹The musicians Heman, Asaph and Ethan were to sound the bronze cymbals; ²⁰Zechariah, Aziel, Shemiramoth, Jehiel, Unni, Eliab, Maaseiah and Benaiah were to play the lyres according to *alamoth*, ²¹and Mattithiah, Eliphelehu, Mikneiah, Obed-Edom, Jeiel and Azaziah were to play the harps, directing according to *sheminith*. ²²Kenaniah the head Levite was in charge of the singing; that was his responsibility because he was skillful at it.

²³Berekiah and Elkanah were to be doorkeepers for the ark. ²⁴Shebaniah, Joshaphat, Nethanel, Amasai, Zechariah, Benaiah and Eliezer the priests were to blow trumpets before the ark of God. Obed-Edom and Jehiah were also to be doorkeepers for the ark.

²⁵So David and the elders of Israel and the commanders of units of a thousand went to bring up the ark of the covenant of the Lord from the house of Obed-Edom, with rejoicing. ²⁶Because God had helped the Levites who were carrying the ark of the covenant of the Lord, seven bulls and seven rams were sacrificed. ²⁷Now David was clothed in a robe of fine linen, as were all the Levites who were carrying the ark, and as were the singers, and Kenaniah, who was in charge of the singing of the choirs. David also wore a linen ephod. ²⁸So all Israel brought up the ark of the covenant of the Lord with shouts, with the sounding of rams' horns and trumpets, and of cymbals, and the playing of lyres and harps.

²⁹As the ark of the covenant of the Lord was entering the City of David, Michal daughter of Saul watched from a window. And when she saw King David dancing and celebrating, she despised him in her heart.

^{16:1}They brought the ark of God and set it inside the tent that David had pitched for it, and they presented burnt offerings and fellowship offerings before God. ²After David had finished sacrificing the burnt offerings and fellowship offerings, he blessed the people in the name of the Lord. ³Then he gave a loaf of bread, a cake of dates and a cake of raisins to each Israelite man and woman.

⁴He appointed some of the Levites to minister before the ark of the Lord, to make petition, to give thanks, and to praise the Lord, the God of Israel: ⁵Asaph was the chief, Zechariah second, then Jeiel, Shemiramoth, Jehiel, Mattithiah, Eliab, Benaiah, Obed-Edom and Jeiel. They were to play the lyres and harps, Asaph was to sound the cymbals, ⁶and Benaiah and Jahaziel the priests were to blow the trumpets regularly before the ark of the covenant of God.

⁷That day David first committed to Asaph and his associates this psalm of thanks to the LORD:

⁸Give thanks to the LORD, call on his name;
  make known among the nations what he has done.
⁹Sing to him, sing praise to him;
  tell of all his wonderful acts.
¹⁰Glory in his holy name;
  let the hearts of those who seek the LORD rejoice.
¹¹Look to the LORD and his strength;
  seek his face always.
¹²Remember the wonders he has done,
  his miracles, and the judgments he pronounced,
¹³O descendants of Israel his servant,
  O sons of Jacob, his chosen ones.

¹⁴He is the LORD our God;
  his judgments are in all the earth.
¹⁵He remembers his covenant forever,
  the word he commanded, for a thousand generations,
¹⁶the covenant he made with Abraham,
  the oath he swore to Isaac.
¹⁷He confirmed it to Jacob as a decree,
  to Israel as an everlasting covenant:
¹⁸"To you I will give the land of Canaan
  as the portion you will inherit."

¹⁹When they were but few in number,
  few indeed, and strangers in it,
²⁰they wandered from nation to nation,
  from one kingdom to another.
²¹He allowed no man to oppress them;
  for their sake he rebuked kings:
²²"Do not touch my anointed ones;
  do my prophets no harm."

²³Sing to the LORD, all the earth;
  proclaim his salvation day after day.
²⁴Declare his glory among the nations,
  his marvelous deeds among all peoples.
²⁵For great is the LORD and most worthy of praise;
  he is to be feared above all gods.

²⁶For all the gods of the nations are idols,
>   but the LORD made the heavens.
²⁷Splendor and majesty are before him;
>   strength and joy in his dwelling place.
²⁸Ascribe to the LORD, O families of nations,
>   ascribe to the LORD glory and strength,
²⁹ascribe to the LORD the glory due his name.
Bring an offering and come before him;
>   worship the LORD in the splendor of his holiness.
³⁰Tremble before him, all the earth!
>   The world is firmly established; it cannot be moved.
³¹Let the heavens rejoice, let the earth be glad;
>   let them say among the nations, "The LORD reigns!"
³²Let the sea resound, and all that is in it;
>   let the fields be jubilant, and everything in them!
³³Then the trees of the forest will sing,
>   they will sing for joy before the LORD,
>   for he comes to judge the earth.

³⁴Give thanks to the LORD, for he is good;
>   his love endures forever.
³⁵Cry out, "Save us, O God our Savior;
>   gather us and deliver us from the nations,
that we may give thanks to your holy name,
>   that we may glory in your praise."
³⁶Praise be to the LORD, the God of Israel,
>   from everlasting to everlasting.

Then all the people said "Amen" and "Praise the LORD."

³⁷David left Asaph and his associates before the ark of the covenant of the LORD to minister there regularly, according to each day's requirements. ³⁸He also left Obed-Edom and his sixty-eight associates to minister with them. Obed-Edom son of Jeduthun, and also Hosah, were gatekeepers.

³⁹David left Zadok the priest and his fellow priests before the tabernacle of the LORD at the high place in Gibeon ⁴⁰to present burnt offerings to the LORD on the altar of burnt offering regularly, morning and evening, in accordance with everything written in the Law of the LORD, which he had given Israel. ⁴¹With them were Heman and Jeduthun and the rest of those chosen and designated by name to give thanks to the LORD, "for his love endures forever." ⁴²Heman and Jeduthun were responsible for the sounding of the trum-

pets and cymbals and for the playing of the other instruments for sacred song. The sons of Jeduthun were stationed at the gate.

⁴³Then all the people left, each for his own home, and David returned home to bless his family.

COMMENTARY

15:1–2 While David's previous attempt to move the ark was well-intentioned, it ultimately fell short of God's will and did not appropriately respect God's holiness (see comments on 1Ch 13:9–13). On this occasion, however, David is careful to make appropriate preparations (v.1; cf. v.12) and consult the covenantal teachings revealed through Moses (cf. v.15) that specified that Levites had the special responsibility of carrying the ark (cf. Nu 4:15–33; Dt 10:8–9).

3 While David appropriately involves the Levites in their covenantal role in moving the ark of the covenant (v.2), the Chronicler is also careful to stress that this spiritually significant step is an activity that involved the whole community ("all Israel").

4–15 In addition to the involvement of "all Israel" (v.3), David summons key individuals representing the priests and Levites. A similar group will be convened by Solomon to bring the ark to the newly constructed temple (2Ch 5:4–6). The Chronicler's emphasis is that the individuals who had particular responsibility in the holy things of God (priests and Levites) needed to be consecrated (vv.12–13), reflecting the Chronicler's broader work that deeper internal issues such as faithfulness, obedience, and personal purity must coincide with external acts of worship (cf. 2Ch 29:11; 35:5–6; Eph 4:1).

In addition, the Chronicler again notes David's newfound awareness of God's prescribed will regarding the moving of the ark (vv.13, 15) as well as his realization of the reason the previous attempt ended in divine judgment. While the priests are not carriers of the ark (aside from the ultimate movement of the ark into the Most Holy Place [cf. 2Ch 5:7–11]), they will be part of the broader procession that tangibly signifies the return of God's presence into the midst of the people.

16–24 In addition to their role as carriers of the ark of God (vv.2, 15), the Levites have responsibilities in areas of song and music to facilitate the worshipful atmosphere surrounding the movement of the ark of the covenant ("sing joyful songs accompanied by musical instruments"; for further details on Levites as musicians, see comments on 2Ch 5:4–6; on the musical instruments mentioned here [e.g., v.16], see comments on 2Ch 5:12–13; on the Levitical family lines involved in musical leadership, see comments at 1Ch 6:31–47). Levitical doorkeepers (vv.18, 23–24) work in conjunction with the priests to ensure the sanctity of sacred space and sacred objects. (On the distinctions between priests and Levites, see comments on 1Ch 6:48–49.)

25–28 The Chronicler continues his attention on the involvement of the whole Israelite community in relocating the ark of the covenant by noting that tribal leaders ("elders") and military leaders ("commanders") are part of the broader procession (v.25). Moreover, the Chronicler also stresses the atmosphere of celebration and worship accompanying the return of the ark of the covenant as it tangibly marks the return of God's presence (and God's favor) to Israel (vv.25–26; cf. Ex 25:17–22; 1Sa 4:12–22).

David's wearing of fine linen robes like the Levites' attire (v.27) may reflect his participation in the musical portion of the procession (cf. v.29), while the significance of his linen ephod is uncertain given that this article was associated with the Aaronic priesthood (cf. Ex 39:2–7, 22–27). Given that the Chronicler's summary of David's relocation of the ark has stressed that things were done according to God's will (e.g., vv.2, 15), it is unlikely that David's attire represents a violation of covenantal boundaries. Instead, the Chronicler's mention of this clothing more likely highlights the special regalia worn by the king to commemorate the joyous occasion. The Chronicler summarizes this joyful moment of David's reign by once again emphasizing the involvement of the whole covenantal community: "all Israel brought up the ark of the covenant of the LORD" (v.28).

Lastly, note the numerous points of connection between 1 Chronicles 15:12–16:42 and 2 Chronicles 5:12–13.

29 The final remark in the Chronicler's summary of David's relocation of the ark of the covenant to Jerusalem may be a subtly negative assessment of the spiritual apathy of the house of Saul. David's wife Michal, "daughter of Saul," unlike the wide array of Israelites mentioned in the chapter, expresses no joy at the return of the ark (and the related symbol of God's presence with his people), but rather expresses bitterness toward David.

16:1–3 Following the celebratory procession of priests, Levites, and "all Israel" (1Ch 15:3–28), the ark of the covenant is brought inside the temporary enclosure ("tent") built by David (v.1). In response to the ark's arrival in Jerusalem, worship ensues in the form of burnt offerings (signifying divine-human reconciliation; cf. Lev 1:1–17) and fellowship offerings (signifying divine-human communion; cf. Lev 3:1–16). A similarly joyful procession and sacrifices will accompany the ark's move from this location (in the City of David) to its permanent place within the Solomonic temple (2Ch 5:2–14; 7:1–22). David concludes the time with the people by giving a benediction as well as a gift of food, perhaps for the journey home. Similar nonpriestly blessings of God's people are given by Moses (Ex 39:43), Joshua (Jos 22:6), and Solomon (2Ch 6:3).

4–6 These verses (also see vv.37–38) briefly summarize the Levitical musicians who had particular responsibility in the realm of worship in music and song in the presence of the newly arrived ark (cf. 1Ch 15:17–21; on the musical responsibilities of the Levites, see comments on 2Ch 5:4–6, 12–13; for more details on the Levitical families of Heman, Ethan, and Asaph, see comments on 1Ch 6:31–47). Recall that the only musical responsibility of priests was the blowing of trumpets (cf. Nu 10:1–9).

7–36 Following the community-wide celebration and worship after the installation of the ark of God in Jerusalem, the Chronicler includes a psalm of thanksgiving and praise that has points of overlap with three psalms from the Hebrew Psalter: Psalms 105:1–15 (cf. vv.8–22), 96:1–13 (cf. vv.23–33), and 106:1, 47–48 (cf. vv.34–36). The three major sections of this psalm begin with an invitation to thanksgiving and praise: "Give thanks to the LORD" (v.8); "Sing to the LORD" (v.23); and "Give thanks to the LORD" (v.34).

In fact, the final section (vv.34–36), which may reflect the exilic/postexilic reality of dispersion ("Save us, O God our Savior; gather us and deliver us from the nations," v.35), is especially laden with praise and thanksgiving—a reality no doubt meant to resonate with the Chronicler's postexilic audience (cf. Php 4:4–7). Even the created realm is exhorted to join in the praise and exaltation of the Creator

God (vv.30–33). In addition, note that this worship poetry is preceded and followed by a brief list of Levites (most notably Asaph) appointed by David to serve before the ark in the realm of petition, thanksgiving, worship, and music (vv.4–6, 37–38).

The Chronicler's placement of this psalm of thanksgiving underscores the spiritually significant event of the return of the ark. The ark was a tangible reminder of God's ongoing presence in the midst of the Israelite community and also housed the covenantal texts outlining the relationship of blessing between God and Israel (cf. Ex 25:17–22; Dt 10:1–5). As such, the content of this psalm spans broadly across a number of themes significant to the life of the covenantal community.

The concept of covenant is central to this psalm as well as to the Chronicler's message as a whole. For example, note the repeated references to "covenant" and the covenantal name of God ("LORD" [Yahweh]), references to the patriarchs (vv.13, 16–17), mention of the land promised in the Abrahamic covenant (v.18), and reminder of God's protection of his people (vv.21–22). In short, the poet's declaration that Yahweh "remembers his covenant forever" (v.15) provides the theological foundation for the community's songs of joy, declarations of praise, and expressions of faith. Lastly, the psalmist makes clear that doxological truths are to be shared by God's people with all humankind:

- "make known among the nations what he has done" (v.8)
- "tell of all his wonderful acts" (v.9)
- "declare his glory among the nations; his marvelous deeds among all peoples" (v.24)

In response to this poetic expression of praise and thanksgiving, the Chronicler notes that "all the people" affirm the truths of the psalm ("Amen") and are invited to join in praising the God of the covenant ("Hallelujah" = "Praise the LORD").

37–38 These names complement the list of Levites given in verses 4–7 above and specify those who will serve on an ongoing basis in Jerusalem (City of David) in conjunction with the newly installed ark. The focus of these Levites appointed to serve in the presence of the ark is that of music, in contrast to the priests who serve in sacrificial ministry at Gibeon (vv.39–42; cf. Hill, 238).

39–42 In contrast to the emphasis on the musical ministry of those assigned to serve "before the ark" (vv.37–38), David appoints priests to serve at Gibeon in their covenantal responsibilities of sacrifices and offerings "in accordance with everything written in the Law of the LORD" (v.40). The city of Gibeon was located on the western side of the Benjamite plateau, about five and a half miles northwest of Jerusalem. Since the tabernacle (tent of meeting constructed during the time of Moses) and the bronze altar constructed by Bezalel (also from the time of Moses) were located at Gibeon, this location became a significant worship center prior to the construction of the Solomonic temple (cf. 1Ch 21:29; 2Ch 1:2–6; also see comments on 2Ch 1:3–5).

As well as noting the priests who will discharge their sacrificial duties, the Chronicler specifies that the Levitical families of Heman and Jeduthun were appointed to oversee music and worship at Gibeon. As noted in the earlier poetry (v.34), these Levites remind God's people of God's steadfast covenantal love ("his love endures forever," v.41). For more on the divisions and responsibilities of the Levitical families, see comments on 1 Chronicles 6:31–47.

43 The Chronicler concludes his extended summary of the transfer of the ark of the covenant to Jerusalem by noting David's blessing on his household. The Lord's blessing on David's household will occupy much of the following chapter (1Ch 17:3–14).

NOTES

15:20–21 The specific meanings of the musical terms *alamoth* (v.20 [עֲלָמוֹת, *ᶜālāmôt*; GK 6628]) and *sheminith* (v.21 [שְׁמִינִית, *šᵉmînît*; GK 9030]) are not certain but may have a particular significance with respect to stringed instruments. Note the use of these terms in the headings of several Psalms (e.g., Ps 46, *alamoth*; Pss 6; 12, *sheminith*).

16:1 The tent pitched by David for the ark of the covenant is not the same as the tent of meeting (the tabernacle in the wilderness) constructed during the time of Moses. The Mosaic tent and the bronze altar were located at Gibeon (note vv.39–42; cf. 1Ch 21:29; 2Ch 1:2–6).

7 The introduction to this psalm does not necessarily indicate that David was the author of this poetry, but rather emphasizes the responsibility of leading in thanksgiving and musical worship entrusted to these Levites by David (continuing the information on Levitical musical assignments preceding and following the psalm; e.g., vv.4–6 and 37–38; cf. Hill, 238). Also, note that the NIV's "this psalm" of v.7 is interpretive and not found in the Hebrew text (see the NASB's translation). Similarly, while this does not preclude Davidic authorship, note that none of the related Psalms (Pss 96; 105; 106) have a superscription indicating Davidic authorship. Recall that Asaph is credited with the authorship of twelve psalms (Pss 50; 73–83). On the Levitical families that were appointed leaders in the realm of music (including that of Asaph [v.7]), see comments on 1 Chronicles 6:31–47.

5. The Davidic Covenant (1Ch 17:1–27)

¹After David was settled in his palace, he said to Nathan the prophet, "Here I am, living in a palace of cedar, while the ark of the covenant of the LORD is under a tent."
²Nathan replied to David, "Whatever you have in mind, do it, for God is with you."
³That night the word of God came to Nathan, saying:

⁴"Go and tell my servant David,'This is what the LORD says: You are not the one to build me a house to dwell in. ⁵I have not dwelt in a house from the day I brought Israel up out of Egypt to this day. I have moved from one tent site to another, from one dwelling place to another. ⁶Wherever I have moved with all the Israelites, did I ever say to any of their leaders whom I commanded to shepherd my people, "Why have you not built me a house of cedar?"'

⁷"Now then, tell my servant David,'This is what the LORD Almighty says: I took you from the pasture and from following the flock, to be ruler over my people Israel. ⁸I have been with you wherever you have gone, and I have cut off all your enemies from before you. Now I will make your name like the names of the greatest men of the earth. ⁹And I will provide a place for my people Israel and will plant them so that they can have a home of their own and no longer be disturbed. Wicked people will not oppress them anymore, as they did at the beginning ¹⁰and have done ever since the time I appointed leaders over my people Israel. I will also subdue all your enemies.

"'I declare to you that the LORD will build a house for you: [11]When your days are over and you go to be with your fathers, I will raise up your offspring to succeed you, one of your own sons, and I will establish his kingdom. [12]He is the one who will build a house for me, and I will establish his throne forever. [13]I will be his father, and he will be my son. I will never take my love away from him, as I took it away from your predecessor. [14]I will set him over my house and my kingdom forever; his throne will be established forever.'" [15]Nathan reported to David all the words of this entire revelation.

[16]Then King David went in and sat before the LORD, and he said:

"Who am I, O LORD God, and what is my family, that you have brought me this far? [17]And as if this were not enough in your sight, O God, you have spoken about the future of the house of your servant. You have looked on me as though I were the most exalted of men, O LORD God.

[18]"What more can David say to you for honoring your servant? For you know your servant, [19]O LORD. For the sake of your servant and according to your will, you have done this great thing and made known all these great promises.

[20]"There is no one like you, O LORD, and there is no God but you, as we have heard with our own ears. [21]And who is like your people Israel—the one nation on earth whose God went out to redeem a people for himself, and to make a name for yourself, and to perform great and awesome wonders by driving out nations from before your people, whom you redeemed from Egypt? [22]You made your people Israel your very own forever, and you, O LORD, have become their God.

[23]"And now, LORD, let the promise you have made concerning your servant and his house be established forever. Do as you promised, [24]so that it will be established and that your name will be great forever. Then men will say, 'The LORD Almighty, the God over Israel, is Israel's God!' And the house of your servant David will be established before you.

[25]"You, my God, have revealed to your servant that you will build a house for him. So your servant has found courage to pray to you. [26]O LORD, you are God! You have promised these good things to your servant. [27]Now you have been pleased to bless the house of your servant, that it may continue forever in your sight; for you, O LORD, have blessed it, and it will be blessed forever."

COMMENTARY

1–2 The construction of a new temple or refurbishing of a religious shrine was an important task for a new king in the biblical world. David's words (v.1) indicate his commitment to honor God in this custom, while Nathan's words (v.2) reflect the reality that a prophet may speak nonprophetically.

3–6 Note that God's initial response to David's idea of building a temple ("a house" for God's dwelling) is not completely positive. This may relate to a culturally driven desire on the part of David to construct a shrine for God apart from God's directive (see comments on vv.1–2), since the centralization of worship is anticipated in Deuteronomy (cf. Dt 12:5). A similar issue may be behind the negative aspects surrounding the people's desire for a king (cf. 1Sa 8:6–8), which was likewise anticipated in covenantal texts (cf. Dt 17:14–20). The anticipation of a place where God would choose to cause his name to dwell (Dt 12:5) is coupled with the negative reality that human beings tend to approach God "in their way" (Dt 12:4) and "everyone as he sees fit" (Dt 12:8).

While the Lord implies that a temple will be built, the emphasis of the Lord's message to Nathan is that he is *not* like the gods of the nations and does not *need* an ornate dwelling place (vv.5–6). Nonetheless, God does reveal that David's son will be given the honor of overseeing the building of a *house* (i.e., temple) for God. Ultimately, however, God will build a *house* (i.e., dynasty) for David (see comments on vv.7–15).

7–15 Although David's idea to build a temple for God is not well received, God reveals through the prophet Nathan that David's son will be given the honor of building a *house* (i.e., temple) for God. Yet God further reveals through Nathan that he (Yahweh) will build a *house* (i.e., dynasty) for David (the Davidic covenant). This blessing is consistent with God's election of David (v.7), his ongoing presence with David (v.8), and his plans to strengthen David (v.8).

The primary emphasis of the Davidic covenant articulated via the prophet Nathan (cf. 2Sa 7:5–16) focuses on a specific son of David (namely, Solomon). For example, although David would not be the one to build the temple (2Ch 6:7–9; cf. 1Ch 17:1–4; 22:8–10; 28:2–4), his son/descendant (singular) will occupy the Davidic throne and build a temple for the Lord (vv.11–12; 22:6–11; 28:5–7). Note that Nathan uses the singular ("he," "his," etc.) to describe this anticipated son/descendant of David. That David and Solomon both understand this individual to be Solomon is reflected in David's later words to Solomon and the congregation (cf. 1Ch 22:6–11; 28:5–7) and Solomon's reply to God in 2 Chronicles 1:7–9.

Moreover, note how often Solomon refers to the Lord's "fulfilling" his word to David within the extended version of his temple-dedication prayer in 1 Kings 8:12–61 (see esp. 8:15, 20, 24). Similarly, Solomon's temple-dedication prayer begins with expressions of praise and with thanksgiving that focus on God's faithfulness to fulfill his Word, all of which echo aspects of the Davidic covenant (e.g., cf. 2Ch 6:4–10 with 1Ch 17:7–15). Beyond this one-generational promise to David, a layer of conditionality is connected with Solomon and subsequent Davidic leaders, as reflected in Yahweh's response to Solomon's temple-dedication prayer:

> The LORD said to him:
> "I have heard the prayer and plea you have made before me; I have consecrated this temple, which you have built, by putting my Name there forever. My eyes and my heart will always be there.
> "As for you, if you walk before me in integrity of heart and uprightness, as David your father did, and do all I command and observe my decrees and laws, I will establish your royal throne over Israel forever, as I promised David your father when I said, 'You shall never fail to have a man on the throne of Israel.'
> "But if you or your sons turn away from me and do not observe the commands and decrees I have given you and go off to serve other gods and worship them, then I will cut off Israel from the land I have given them and will reject this temple I have consecrated for my Name. Israel will then become a byword and an object of ridicule among all peoples. And though this temple is now imposing, all who pass by will be appalled and

will scoff and say, 'Why has the Lord done such a thing to this land and to this temple?' People will answer, 'Because they have forsaken the Lord their God, who brought their fathers out of Egypt, and have embraced other gods, worshiping and serving them—that is why the Lord brought all this disaster on them.'" (1Ki 9:3–9; cf. 2Ch 7:11–22)

This layer of conditionality is also reflected in David's summary of God's promise regarding Solomon spoken to the officials and leaders of the Israelite kingdom: "I will establish his kingdom forever if he is unswerving in carrying out my commands and laws" (1Ch 28:7). In addition, the dynamics of God's promises to David are cited by God in the midst of Solomon's later apostasy and cause the division of the kingdom to come *after* Solomon on account of Yahweh's promise to David (see 1Ki 11:9–40, esp. vv. 11–13, 31–34).

The messianic (and unconditional) application of the Davidic covenant is gleaned from the broader setting of Nathan's prophetic word to David and subsequent biblical revelation. For example, note the details of complete peace ("no longer be disturbed," v. 9; cf. 2Sa 7:10), never being oppressed and having all enemies subdued (vv. 9–10; cf. 2Sa 7:10–11), an everlasting kingdom (v. 14; cf. 2Sa 7:16), and perhaps even the motif of temple reflected in the person of Christ (cf. Jn 2:18–22).

In addition, the broader notion of the Davidic covenant is reinforced through the theological details provided via progressive revelation (cf. Isa 9:7; Lk 1:32; Heb 1:5). Thus God ultimately bases his commitment to preserve the house of David on account of his Word and his character rather than human effort. God's enduring promise to David is exalted in the poetry of Psalm 89 and the prophetic oracle of Jeremiah 33:

"Once for all, I have sworn by my holiness—
and I will not lie to David—

that his line will continue forever
and his throne endure before me like the sun;
it will be established forever like the moon,
the faithful witness in the sky." (Ps 89:35–37; cf. Ps 132:11–12)

The word of the Lord came to Jeremiah: "This is what the Lord says: 'If you can break my covenant with the day and my covenant with the night, so that day and night no longer come at their appointed time, then my covenant with David my servant—and my covenant with the Levites who are priests ministering before me—can be broken and David will no longer have a descendant to reign on his throne. I will make the descendants of David my servant and the Levites who minister before me as countless as the stars of the sky and as measureless as the sand on the seashore.'" (Jer 33:19–22)

This understanding of a fuller (and ultimately messianic) application of the Davidic covenant is also consistent with Solomon's response to God's question wherein he not only praises God for bringing his promises to David through him, but also asks that God will continue to bring forth the fullness of the Davidic covenant (see 2Ch 1:8–9). Similarly, the broad spectrum of Solomon's temple-dedication prayer reflects the balance between the fulfilling of God's Word (cf. esp. 2Ch 6:4–10, 15) and the prayer that God will continue to bring to pass the full measure of his promises (cf. 2Ch 6:16–17).

16–27 David's prayer in response to God's revelation of the "Davidic covenant" (cf. vv. 7–15) reflects his awe in the light of God's blessings already bestowed on him (vv. 16–17) as well as God's promise to establish his "house" (dynasty) into the future ("forever"). David's humility and awe are directly tied to God's singularity ("there is no one like you, O Lord," v. 20; cf. 2Ch 14:11; 20:6) and his choice of Israel to be his redeemed people (vv. 21–22). David understands God's blessing on his house as part of

God's broader relationship of blessing with his people, Israel, which in turn is a conduit to God's goodness and ways becoming known to all humankind ("Then men will say …" v.24).

NOTES

1–2 Examples of significant temple building or refurbishing projects in the biblical world include those of the Sumerian king Gudea (cf. *COS*, 2.155) and the Babylonian king Nabonidus (cf. *COS*, 2:123A).

7–15 While the phrase "Davidic covenant" is commonly used to describe Yahweh's word of promise to the house of David, the term "covenant" is actually not used in Nathan's oracle, nor is it used in the broader passage. David's response (vv.16–27) refers to "the promise" God has made (cf. vv.19, 23, 26).

6. David's Military Victories and Regional Hegemony (1Ch 18:1–20:8)

a. David's Victories to the North, East, South, and West (1Ch 18:1–14)

¹In the course of time, David defeated the Philistines and subdued them, and he took Gath and its surrounding villages from the control of the Philistines.

²David also defeated the Moabites, and they became subject to him and brought tribute.

³Moreover, David fought Hadadezer king of Zobah, as far as Hamath, when he went to establish his control along the Euphrates River. ⁴David captured a thousand of his chariots, seven thousand charioteers and twenty thousand foot soldiers. He hamstrung all but a hundred of the chariot horses.

⁵When the Arameans of Damascus came to help Hadadezer king of Zobah, David struck down twenty-two thousand of them. ⁶He put garrisons in the Aramean kingdom of Damascus, and the Arameans became subject to him and brought tribute. The LORD gave David victory everywhere he went.

⁷David took the gold shields carried by the officers of Hadadezer and brought them to Jerusalem. ⁸From Tebah and Cun, towns that belonged to Hadadezer, David took a great quantity of bronze, which Solomon used to make the bronze Sea, the pillars and various bronze articles.

⁹When Tou king of Hamath heard that David had defeated the entire army of Hadadezer king of Zobah, ¹⁰he sent his son Hadoram to King David to greet him and congratulate him on his victory in battle over Hadadezer, who had been at war with Tou. Hadoram brought all kinds of articles of gold and silver and bronze.

¹¹King David dedicated these articles to the LORD, as he had done with the silver and gold he had taken from all these nations: Edom and Moab, the Ammonites and the Philistines, and Amalek.

¹²Abishai son of Zeruiah struck down eighteen thousand Edomites in the Valley of Salt. ¹³He put garrisons in Edom, and all the Edomites became subject to David. The LORD gave David victory everywhere he went.

¹⁴David reigned over all Israel, doing what was just and right for all his people.

COMMENTARY

1–14 This summary of David's accomplishments (cf. 2Sa 8) provides a condensed overview of the political and military moves that expanded Israel's geographical boundaries and regional influence during the reign of David, as celebrated in the poetry of Psalms 60:6–12 and 108:7–13. These victories take place on all sides:

1. In the east against the Ammonites and Moabites (with the latter becoming tribute-paying vassals of David; cf. v.2)
2. In the west against the Philistines (v.1)
3. In the south against the Edomites (who become vassals and host Israelite garrisons; cf. vv.12–13)
4. In the north against the Arameans (Syrians) of Damascus (who pay tribute and allow Israelite garrisons in Damascus; cf. v.6) and in territory previously held by Hadadezer, king of Zobah, in the Beqa Valley (prompting the king of Hamath to seek peace; vv.9–10; cf. 2Sa 8:9–10)

This summary illustrates that David now controlled parts of the key trade routes passing on either side of Israel: the Coastal Highway to the west, and the Edom-to-Damascus portion of the Transjordanian King's Highway to the east. As the Chronicler emphasizes, it was the Lord who gave David (together with his designated military leaders such as Abishai, v.12; cf. 2Sa 8:13–14) victory "everywhere he went" (v.6; cf. v.13).

In turn, David dedicated the spoils of his victories to the Lord, some of which were later used by Solomon in constructing the temple (vv.8, 10–11; cf. 2Ch 2:1–5:1). It is interesting to consider Israel's control of Edom, Moab, and Ammon in the light of the injunctions against meddling with these "family members," as Yahweh had not given any of their land to the Israelites (cf. Dt 2:4–19). The Chronicler summarizes David's military and political accomplishments by showing the resulting blessing for "all Israel" as the king did what was "just and right for all his people" (v.14), which perhaps implies David's sensitivity to carefully follow God's law (cf. Dt 17:18–20).

NOTE

4 The remark about David's hamstringing the majority of the seized horses implies that cavalry and chariot warfare were not significantly developed in Israel at this time. By the time of Solomon, Israel had developed an impressive equine force (see comments on 2Ch 1:14).

b. David's Officials (1Ch 18:15–17)

¹⁵Joab son of Zeruiah was over the army; Jehoshaphat son of Ahilud was recorder; ¹⁶Zadok son of Ahitub and Ahimelech son of Abiathar were priests; Shavsha was secretary; ¹⁷Benaiah son of Jehoiada was over the Kerethites and Pelethites; and David's sons were chief officials at the king's side.

COMMENTARY

15–17 This list summarizes leaders entrusted to oversee particular sectors of government within David's royal administration, perhaps as an aspect of his "just and right" rule of "all Israel" (v.14; cf. Japhet, 351). In addition, such governmental needs would stem from the territorial expansions of David's kingdom (vv.1–13) and reflect the maturing of the Israelite nation. In addition to the royal princes (David's sons) who served in various leadership roles within the royal bureaucracy, the Chronicler notes two areas of administration (recorder and secretary [scribe]), two areas of military service (the regular army and the specialty wing of the Kerethites [Cretans] and Pelethites [Philistines]), and one area of religious oversight (priests).

NOTE

17 While the Chronicler refers to David's sons functioning as "chief officials" here, the book of Samuel notes that David appointed some of his sons "as priests" (2Sa 8:18 [כֹּהֲנִים, kōhᵃnîm; GK 3913]). The term "priests" is translated there (somewhat curiously) as "royal advisors" by the NIV, which removes the interpretive tension raised by the use of the term "priest" with respect to the non-Levitical sons of David. The lack of broader context on these appointments makes it impossible to determine whether this phraseology refers to a political or religious position. Indeed, the absence of further narrative attention on the role(s) of these sons within the biblical material would imply that these appointments did not violate divinely established roles (cf. G. J. Wenham, "Were David's Sons Priests?" *ZAW* 87 [1975]: 79–82).

c. David's Battles against the Ammonites (1Ch 19:1–20:3)

^{19:1}In the course of time, Nahash king of the Ammonites died, and his son succeeded him as king. ²David thought, "I will show kindness to Hanun son of Nahash, because his father showed kindness to me." So David sent a delegation to express his sympathy to Hanun concerning his father.

When David's men came to Hanun in the land of the Ammonites to express sympathy to him, ³the Ammonite nobles said to Hanun, "Do you think David is honoring your father by sending men to you to express sympathy? Haven't his men come to you to explore and spy out the country and overthrow it?" ⁴So Hanun seized David's men, shaved them, cut off their garments in the middle at the buttocks, and sent them away.

⁵When someone came and told David about the men, he sent messengers to meet them, for they were greatly humiliated. The king said, "Stay at Jericho till your beards have grown, and then come back."

⁶When the Ammonites realized that they had become a stench in David's nostrils, Hanun and the Ammonites sent a thousand talents of silver to hire chariots and charioteers from Aram Naharaim, Aram Maacah and Zobah. ⁷They hired thirty-two thousand chariots and charioteers, as well as the king of Maacah with his troops, who came and camped near Medeba, while the Ammonites were mustered from their towns and moved out for battle.

⁸On hearing this, David sent Joab out with the entire army of fighting men. ⁹The Ammonites came out and drew up in battle formation at the entrance to their city, while the kings who had come were by themselves in the open country.

¹⁰Joab saw that there were battle lines in front of him and behind him; so he selected some of the best troops in Israel and deployed them against the Arameans. ¹¹He put the rest of the men under the command of Abishai his brother, and they were deployed against the Ammonites. ¹²Joab said, "If the Arameans are too strong for me, then you are to rescue me; but if the Ammonites are too strong for you, then I will rescue you. ¹³Be strong and let us fight bravely for our people and the cities of our God. The LORD will do what is good in his sight."

¹⁴Then Joab and the troops with him advanced to fight the Arameans, and they fled before him. ¹⁵When the Ammonites saw that the Arameans were fleeing, they too fled before his brother Abishai and went inside the city. So Joab went back to Jerusalem.

¹⁶After the Arameans saw that they had been routed by Israel, they sent messengers and had Arameans brought from beyond the River, with Shophach the commander of Hadadezer's army leading them.

¹⁷When David was told of this, he gathered all Israel and crossed the Jordan; he advanced against them and formed his battle lines opposite them. David formed his lines to meet the Arameans in battle, and they fought against him. ¹⁸But they fled before Israel, and David killed seven thousand of their charioteers and forty thousand of their foot soldiers. He also killed Shophach the commander of their army.

¹⁹When the vassals of Hadadezer saw that they had been defeated by Israel, they made peace with David and became subject to him.

So the Arameans were not willing to help the Ammonites anymore.

> 20:1 In the spring, at the time when kings go off to war, Joab led out the armed forces. He laid waste the land of the Ammonites and went to Rabbah and besieged it, but David remained in Jerusalem. Joab attacked Rabbah and left it in ruins. 2David took the crown from the head of their king — its weight was found to be a talent of gold, and it was set with precious stones — and it was placed on David's head. He took a great quantity of plunder from the city 3and brought out the people who were there, consigning them to labor with saws and with iron picks and axes. David did this to all the Ammonite towns. Then David and his entire army returned to Jerusalem.

COMMENTARY

1–5 While David's military operations in the Transjordanian territories of Edom and Moab may have created concern for the leadership of Ammon with respect to David's motives, David's gesture toward the family of Nahash was a sincere gesture of sympathy and kindness. Nevertheless, his act was misinterpreted by the leadership of Ammon as a cover for espionage. The treatment of the Israelite delegation by the Ammonites was intended to cast a maximum shame on David's men (directed at their manhood) and, by extension, on David and Israel.

6–15 A good gesture gone awry (vv.1–5) prompts the forming of an anti-Israel coalition by the Ammonites, who hire Arameans from Beth Rehob and Zobah, mercenaries from Maacah and Tob, as well as chariots and horsemen from Aram Naharaim, Aram Maacah, and Zobah to battle against David (vv.1–15; cf. 2Sa 10:1–14). Joab's words to his military leaders are reminiscent of the words spoken to Joshua as the Israelites prepared to enter the Promised Land (cf. Dt 31:7–8; Jos 1:5–9). To be strong, biblically speaking, is to be immovably committed to obedience and trust in God.

Moreover, Joab reminds his warriors that their efforts ultimately protect their kin and people back home ("our people") as well as God's ultimate ownership of the land and cities (cf. Lev 25:23), espe-

cially Jerusalem (cf. Ps 48; cf. Selman, 195). Finally, note that Joab's exhortation is rooted in the notion of God's sovereign rule and ultimate goodness ("The LORD will do what is good in his sight"). While the Ammonites and Arameans retreat, two more series of battles (vv.16–19 and 1Ch 20:1–3) will be needed before the Ammonites are completely subdued.

16–19 After an initial setback at Medeba (vv.6–15), the Arameans regather their forces and send for help from other Arameans "beyond the River" in the territory of Hadadezer but lose again at Helam (in the Land of Tob) against the forces of "all Israel" rallied by David. Following this defeat the people of Hadadezer seek peace with David and refuse to help Ammon any longer, further solidifying David's position in northern Aram and Transjordan (v.19; cf. 2Sa 10:15–16). Such respect and submission from other nations is celebrated in Hebrew poetry such as Psalm 18 (= 2Sa 22, esp. vv.44–50// Ps 18:43–49 [18:44–50]). While the Arameans flee and become subject to David (v.19), one final battle is needed against the Ammonites (see 20:1–3).

20:1–3 While the Chronicler does not specifically mention the Bathsheba/Uriah affair that takes place as Joab completes the Israelite victory against the Ammonites (2Sa 11), the opening of this chapter ("In the spring, at the time when kings go off to war, Joab [*not* David] led out the armed forces ... but David remained in Jerusalem," v.1; cf. 2Sa 11:1) subtly reminds the reader of the unfortunate backdrop to this victory. Spring was the preferred time for warfare in the biblical world, given the rains of the fall and winter and the stifling heat of summer.

At some point during Joab's impending victory over the Ammonites, David arrives at the essentially vanquished city and assumes the scripted position of victor (note Joab's words in 2Sa 12:26–31). The Ammonites are subsequently put to forced labor, particularly in the area of timber.

NOTES

19:1–5 The account of this chapter may be providing details of the earlier victory over the Ammonites summarized above (cf. 1Ch 18:3–8).

18 The parallel text at 2 Samuel 10:18 notes that seven hundred charioteers were killed (vs. seven thousand here) and that forty thousand *horsemen* were also killed (vs. forty thousand *foot soldiers* here). On the latter, see the NASB's translation as the NIV has adopted the reading of "foot soldiers" at 2 Samuel 10:18 (following 1Ch 19:19; see Japhet, 361). On the broader issues of such disagreements in parallel texts, see "Synoptic Issues" in the Introduction.

20:2 Note that the LXX refers to this as the crown of the Ammonite god Milcolm, not the Ammonite king. This may explain the sizeable weight of the crown (approximately 65–75 pounds).

d. David's Additional Battles against the Philistines (1Ch 20:4–8)

⁴In the course of time, war broke out with the Philistines, at Gezer. At that time Sibbecai the Hushathite killed Sippai, one of the descendants of the Rephaites, and the Philistines were subjugated.
⁵In another battle with the Philistines, Elhanan son of Jair killed Lahmi the brother of Goliath the Gittite, who had a spear with a shaft like a weaver's rod.
⁶In still another battle, which took place at Gath, there was a huge man with six fingers on each hand and six toes on each foot — twenty-four in all. He also was descended from Rapha. ⁷When he taunted Israel, Jonathan son of Shimea, David's brother, killed him.
⁸These were descendants of Rapha in Gath, and they fell at the hands of David and his men.

COMMENTARY

4–8 These brief summaries of battles with the Philistines underscore David's continued dominance over even the formidable champions of the Philistine city-states. Each of these champions is directly or indirectly associated with the Rephaites (descendants of Rapha), an ethnic group noted for their massive physical size. Recall that Goliath was over nine feet tall, while the bed of King Og (who was "left of the remnant of the Rephaites" [Dt 3:11]) was thirteen feet long and six feet wide. While God is not specifically mentioned in these short vignettes, nor is David the one defeating these champions, the victory of David's men nonetheless reflects the Chronicler's earlier note that "the LORD gave David victory everywhere he went" (1Ch 18:6). Thus to oppose David or Israel was to oppose God (cf. Dt 20:4; see McConville, 65).

NOTE

5 The brother of Goliath is identified in the parallel passage in Samuel as Goliath himself, suggesting that the term "Goliath" may be a title for Philistine national champions.

7. David's Presumptuous Census and Selection of the Temple Site (1Ch 21:1–22:1)

OVERVIEW

Through the reality of David's sinfulness the Chronicler presents the backdrop to the place that God will choose to cause his name to dwell — a place of atonement, prayer, forgiveness, and reconciliation.

¹Satan rose up against Israel and incited David to take a census of Israel. ²So David said to Joab and the commanders of the troops, "Go and count the Israelites from Beersheba to Dan. Then report back to me so that I may know how many there are."

³But Joab replied, "May the LORD multiply his troops a hundred times over. My lord the king, are they not all my lord's subjects? Why does my lord want to do this? Why should he bring guilt on Israel?"

⁴The king's word, however, overruled Joab; so Joab left and went throughout Israel and then came back to Jerusalem. ⁵Joab reported the number of the fighting men to David: In all Israel there were one million one hundred thousand men who could handle a sword, including four hundred and seventy thousand in Judah.

⁶But Joab did not include Levi and Benjamin in the numbering, because the king's command was repulsive to him. ⁷This command was also evil in the sight of God; so he punished Israel.

⁸Then David said to God, "I have sinned greatly by doing this. Now, I beg you, take away the guilt of your servant. I have done a very foolish thing."

⁹The LORD said to Gad, David's seer, ¹⁰"Go and tell David, 'This is what the LORD says: I am giving you three options. Choose one of them for me to carry out against you.'"

¹¹So Gad went to David and said to him, "This is what the Lord says: 'Take your choice: ¹²three years of famine, three months of being swept away before your enemies, with their swords overtaking you, or three days of the sword of the Lord — days of plague in the land, with the angel of the Lord ravaging every part of Israel.' Now then, decide how I should answer the one who sent me."

¹³David said to Gad, "I am in deep distress. Let me fall into the hands of the Lord, for his mercy is very great; but do not let me fall into the hands of men."

¹⁴So the Lord sent a plague on Israel, and seventy thousand men of Israel fell dead. ¹⁵And God sent an angel to destroy Jerusalem. But as the angel was doing so, the Lord saw it and was grieved because of the calamity and said to the angel who was destroying the people, "Enough! Withdraw your hand." The angel of the Lord was then standing at the threshing floor of Araunah the Jebusite.

¹⁶David looked up and saw the angel of the Lord standing between heaven and earth, with a drawn sword in his hand extended over Jerusalem. Then David and the elders, clothed in sackcloth, fell facedown.

¹⁷David said to God, "Was it not I who ordered the fighting men to be counted? I am the one who has sinned and done wrong. These are but sheep. What have they done? O Lord my God, let your hand fall upon me and my family, but do not let this plague remain on your people."

¹⁸Then the angel of the Lord ordered Gad to tell David to go up and build an altar to the Lord on the threshing floor of Araunah the Jebusite. ¹⁹So David went up in obedience to the word that Gad had spoken in the name of the Lord.

²⁰While Araunah was threshing wheat, he turned and saw the angel; his four sons who were with him hid themselves. ²¹Then David approached, and when Araunah looked and saw him, he left the threshing floor and bowed down before David with his face to the ground.

²²David said to him, "Let me have the site of your threshing floor so I can build an altar to the Lord, that the plague on the people may be stopped. Sell it to me at the full price."

²³Araunah said to David, "Take it! Let my lord the king do whatever pleases him. Look, I will give the oxen for the burnt offerings, the threshing sledges for the wood, and the wheat for the grain offering. I will give all this."

²⁴But King David replied to Araunah, "No, I insist on paying the full price. I will not take for the Lord what is yours, or sacrifice a burnt offering that costs me nothing."

²⁵So David paid Araunah six hundred shekels of gold for the site. ²⁶David built an altar to the Lord there and sacrificed burnt offerings and fellowship offerings. He called on the Lord, and the Lord answered him with fire from heaven on the altar of burnt offering.

²⁷Then the Lord spoke to the angel, and he put his sword back into its sheath. ²⁸At that time, when David saw that the Lord had answered him on the threshing floor of Araunah

the Jebusite, he offered sacrifices there. ²⁹The tabernacle of the Lᴏʀᴅ, which Moses had made in the desert, and the altar of burnt offering were at that time on the high place at Gibeon. ³⁰But David could not go before it to inquire of God, because he was afraid of the sword of the angel of the Lᴏʀᴅ.

²²:¹Then David said, "The house of the Lᴏʀᴅ God is to be here, and also the altar of burnt offering for Israel."

COMMENTARY

21:1–7 While David's motivation for ordering this census is unspecified, the repeated connection to troops and elements of warfare implies a military-oriented census, which in turn implies a level of trust on the part of David in his troops rather than a complete trust in God. The Chronicler frequently highlights examples of complete trust in God (e.g., 2Ch 14:11; 20:12; 25:7–10) as well as breaches of complete trust in God (e.g., 2Ch 16:7–8; 28:16). The repulsion (v.3) and subsequent disobedience (v.6) of Joab toward David's command underscores the unfaithfulness reflected in David's request for the census. Note that Joab's admonition to David ("Why should he [you] bring guilt on Israel?" v.3) foreshadows the divine judgment that will strike the nation.

Despite the NIV's translation at v.1, the Chronicler does not necessarily have the personal being "Satan" in view. The term is rare in the OT and is only found here in Chronicles. The term S/ satan is a transliteration of the Hebrew term (שָׂטָן, śāṭān; GK 8477), meaning "adversary" or "accuser," with capitalization or its lack reflecting whether a general adversary (e.g., 2Sa 19:22) or *the* adversary/accuser (i.e., the devil) is in view. Use of this term wherein *the* (supernatural) adversary/devil is clearly in view is reflected in the first two chapters of Job (14x) and Zechariah 3:1–2 (4x). Note that in these occurrences in Job and Zechariah,

the term "Satan" has the Hebrew definite article (underscoring the notion of "*the* adversary"). However, the term in 1 Chronicles 21:1 does not have the Hebrew article. This has prompted some scholars to take the term as a proper name, but this is a significant distinction from the instances in Job and Zechariah that should not be minimized and may reflect the Chronicler's intent of signaling a human adversary.

In addition to the intended meaning of s/Satan, the parallel account in Samuel notes that "the Lᴏʀᴅ" incited David (cf. 2Sa 24:1), not Satan or an adversary as here. While this at first seems to be a perplexing difference, in biblical terms the will/ agency of God and a supernatural adversary can operate in parallel (cf. Job 1–2) as can the will/ agency of God and a human adversary (cf. 1Ki 11:14, 23). In fact, these last examples from Kings pertain to covenantal unfaithfulness on the part of a Davidic king (Solomon) and involve both God's agency and a human adversary: for example, "Then the Lᴏʀᴅ raised up against Solomon an adversary, Hadad the Edomite …" (1Ki 11:14). Moreover, the examples from Kings involve a clear scenario of guilt and deserved divine punishment as well as subsequent divine grace in limiting this judgment (cf. 1Ki 11:12–13, 34–36).

All told, while the translation "Satan" is certainly plausible, the translation "adversary" seems preferable (see J. Sailhamer, "1 Chronicles 21:1 — A Study of Inter-Biblical Interpretation," *TJ* 10 [1989]: 33–48; Braun, 216; McConville, 72–74). These uncertainties aside, this passage reminds the reader of the reality of the spiritual battle facing all God's people—whether against the "old self" (Eph 4:22–24) or "against the spiritual forces of evil in the heavenly realms" (Eph 6:12; cf. 2Co 10:3–5).

8–17 In the aftermath of his census, David realizes his actions and motives are "evil in the sight of God" (v.7) and he repents deeply. However, despite his earnest grief and repentance, divine judgment follows in the form of a divinely delivered plague ("the sword of the LORD," per the choice of David). The prophet ("seer") Gad mediates this choice of judgment (vv.9–13), and he will also mediate the path to God's grace and reconciliation (cf. vv.18–27). The outworking of God's judgment is especially difficult for David as he realizes that the consequences of his sin spill over onto his "sheep" (vv.14, 17). In the midst of David's vision of the destroying angel executing God's judgment (v.16), David gathers the elders to seek God and appeal for his grace and mercy (cf. "in wrath remember mercy," Hab 3:2). This said, God had already exercised mercy and grace even *before* David prayed (cf. v.15).

21:18–22:1 In the context of David's and the elders' seeking God's mercy (v.17), the Lord directs David (via the prophet Gad) to build an altar at the place where the Lord had *already* in grace held back the destroying angel, whose sword was extended over Jerusalem (vv.15–16). The location at the threshing floor of Ornan the Jebusite (spelled "Araunah" in 2Sa 24:18) is described as *chosen by God* to be the place of sacrifice and atonement for David's sin (note God's choice via Gad [v.18]; cf. 2Ch 7:12, a divine choice anticipated by Moses [Dt 12:5–7]). Thus David's decision (1Ch 22:1) regarding this location for the future Jerusalem temple is simply following God's previously announced choice.

Note that the chosen place for the temple connects with both divine grace and forgiveness (following David's sin) and a divine encounter (via the angel of Yahweh). Also, this place is associated with God's hearing the prayers of those who seek him in humility and obedience (cf. vv.17, 19, 26, 28). The chosen location for the temple is also connected with Mount Moriah (cf. 2Ch 3:1), which further associates this location with God's provision of a substitutionary sacrifice (Ge 22) and God's presence ("the mountain of the LORD"; Ge 22:14). Put together, the location chosen for the future temple is associated with a place of propitiation, divine grace and mercy, divine presence, prayer, sacrifice, and forgiveness.

Even though the owner is a Jebusite and David is king of the land, David insists on a fair price for the threshing floor and surrounding area that will eventually comprise the temple complex. The efficacy of David's sacrifice and God's sanctification of the altar is reflected in the divine fire that descends from heaven (v.26; cf. 2Ch 7:1), God answering David's prayer (v.26), and his command to the destroying angel to put his sword back into its sheath (v.27). God's grace and answer to David's plea prompt David to offer additional sacrifices (v.28).

While sacrifice are normally associated with the priests, the bronze altar, and the tabernacle (tent of meeting) situated at Gibeon (vv.29–30; cf. 1Ch 16:39–42), God specifically chooses the threshing floor of Ornan in Jerusalem for David's altar and sacrifice. The tabernacle will be relocated to Jerusalem once the temple is completed (cf. 2Ch 5:4–6).

NOTES

5 The census numbers here (1,100,000 men in "all Israel"; 470,000 men in Judah) differ from those recorded in 2 Samuel 24:9 (800,000 men in Israel; 500,000 men in Judah). While there are a number of plausible explanations for this divergence, the exact reason for the differences is not certain. For example, the difference in the numbers for Judah could be accounted for by a different convention of rounding (these numbers would appear to be rounded numbers), or the larger number in 2 Samuel may include the Levites initially omitted by Joab.

Note that the Chronicler refers to "all Israel" while the parallel text simply says "Israel," which perhaps implies that the Chronicler is incorporating an expanded group of individuals, possibly a combination of Benjamites and Levites or even foreigners living within the borders of Israel. Alternatively, the 1,100,000 may be a total number, with 470,000 from Judah and 630,000 from Israel. If this was the case, it may imply that the larger number in Samuel included the omitted Benjamites together with Levites living in the northern tribal territories. On these large numbers, see the extended discussion at 2 Chronicles 11:1 for other possible meanings for the term commonly translated "thousand," which would result in lower numbers of troops.

12 Note that 2 Samuel 24:13 has "seven" (שֶׁבַע, *šebaʿ*) years in the Hebrew text (MT) rather than "three" (שָׁלוֹשׁ, *šālôš*) years, as here. Nonetheless, the NIV renders "three" at 2 Samuel 24:13, given the LXX at this verse as well as the parallel text here (see NIV note), which together suggest a scribal transmission error in 2Sa 24:13.

25 The purchase price is noted as fifty shekels in 2 Samuel 24:24 and six hundred shekels here. The difference probably lies in the notation of the "threshing floor" in Samuel, whereas in Chronicles the "site" (i.e., the broader parcel of land used for the temple complex) is in view.

8. David's Preparations for the Temple and Leadership Transfer (1Ch 22:2−29:30)

OVERVIEW

The final chapters of 1 Chronicles (22−29) do not have a sustained parallel in the books of Samuel or Kings. The content of these chapters may provide expanded details corresponding to the time frame summarized in 1 Kings 2:1−12 (cf. E. Ball, "The Co-Regency of David and Solomon [1 Kings 1]," *VT* 27[1977]: 268−79). All in all, the Chronicler makes a clear shift in these chapters from a focus on David to a focus on David and his son (and designated heir) Solomon. This focus on David and Solomon is one of transition, largely within the context of David's expansive preparations for the Jerusalem temple and the requisite personnel (see J. W. Wright, "The Legacy of David in Chronicles: The Narrative Function of 1 Chronicles 23−27," *JBL* 110 [1991]: 229−42).

a. David's Preparation of Temple Materials and Craftsmen (1Ch 22:2–4)

²So David gave orders to assemble the aliens living in Israel, and from among them he appointed stonecutters to prepare dressed stone for building the house of God. ³He provided a large amount of iron to make nails for the doors of the gateways and for the fittings, and more bronze than could be weighed. ⁴He also provided more cedar logs than could be counted, for the Sidonians and Tyrians had brought large numbers of them to David.

COMMENTARY

2–4 In order to address the challenge of supplying skilled and unskilled workers common to large building projects in the biblical world, David taps into the resident aliens living within Israel. That some of the individuals are skilled in certain trades is reflected both here (v.2) and in the further details on the craftsmen noted later (cf. vv.15–16).

In addition to the provision of manpower, David also provides a significant amount of the raw materials necessary for the temple construction project (again, note the further details on precious metals, timber, and stone noted later; cf. v.14). The raw materials noted here reflect a combination of David's hegemony over the Philistines (iron), his economic-political alliance with Phoenicia (cedar), and his earlier military conquests (bronze; e.g., 18:8; see further remarks on these raw materials at 2Ch 2:7–9).

b. David's Initial Charge to Solomon and the Leaders of Israel (1Ch 22:5–19)

⁵David said, "My son Solomon is young and inexperienced, and the house to be built for the LORD should be of great magnificence and fame and splendor in the sight of all the nations. Therefore I will make preparations for it." So David made extensive preparations before his death.

⁶Then he called for his son Solomon and charged him to build a house for the LORD, the God of Israel. ⁷David said to Solomon: "My son, I had it in my heart to build a house for the Name of the LORD my God. ⁸But this word of the LORD came to me: 'You have shed much blood and have fought many wars. You are not to build a house for my Name, because you have shed much blood on the earth in my sight. ⁹But you will have a son who will be a man of peace and rest, and I will give him rest from all his enemies on every side. His name will be Solomon, and I will grant Israel peace and quiet during his reign. ¹⁰He is the one who will build a house for my Name. He will be my son, and I will be his father. And I will establish the throne of his kingdom over Israel forever.'

¹¹"Now, my son, the LORD be with you, and may you have success and build the house of the LORD your God, as he said you would. ¹²May the LORD give you discretion and understanding when he puts you in command over Israel, so that you may keep the law of the LORD your God. ¹³Then you will have success if you are careful to observe the decrees and laws that the LORD gave Moses for Israel. Be strong and courageous. Do not be afraid or discouraged.

¹⁴"I have taken great pains to provide for the temple of the LORD a hundred thousand talents of gold, a million talents of silver, quantities of bronze and iron too great to be weighed, and wood and stone. And you may add to them. ¹⁵You have many workmen: stonecutters, masons and carpenters, as well as men skilled in every kind of work ¹⁶in gold and silver, bronze and iron — craftsmen beyond number. Now begin the work, and the LORD be with you."

¹⁷Then David ordered all the leaders of Israel to help his son Solomon. ¹⁸He said to them, "Is not the LORD your God with you? And has he not granted you rest on every side? For he has handed the inhabitants of the land over to me, and the land is subject to the LORD and to his people. ¹⁹Now devote your heart and soul to seeking the LORD your God. Begin to build the sanctuary of the LORD God, so that you may bring the ark of the covenant of the LORD and the sacred articles belonging to God into the temple that will be built for the Name of the LORD."

COMMENTARY

5 This statement (largely repeated later at 29:1) reflects David's desire that the temple built for Yahweh bring together the apex of beauty and craftsmanship in such a way as to remind God's people of the beauty of God's holiness (cf. Ps 29:2). David's extensive preparations (also cf. v.14) and plans for the temple (plans received via divine revelation, cf. 1Ch 28:11–12, 19) underscore the Chronicler's perspective that the Jerusalem temple was in many ways a joint project of David and Solomon. David's concern for Solomon's youth and inexperience is likewise reflected in Solomon's own prayer for wisdom (1Ki 3:6–9).

6–10 The Chronicler's summary of David's charge to Solomon captures the essence of God's promissory word to David via the prophet Nathan (the Davidic covenant). David's exhortation provides additional insight into God's further revelation to him. Note that the expression "David will never fail to have a man to sit on the throne of the house of Israel," commonly associated with the Davidic covenant (cf. Jer 33:17), is *not* part of the recorded oracle of the prophet Nathan (1Ch 17; cf. 2Sa 7). Similarly, the prohibition indicated here that David cannot build the temple for Yahweh on account of the blood he has shed (v.8) and the divine promise regarding peace and rest during Solomon's reign are also not part of Nathan's recorded oracle. Presumably, such points of clarification are part of God's subsequent (i.e., progressive) revelation given to David. For a discussion of the Davidic covenant, see extended comments on 1 Chronicles 17:7–15.

11–13 David's charge to his son Solomon reflects the reality that the building of the temple for the Lord is a spiritual exercise as much as it is a building enterprise. The notion of "success" (vv.11, 13) is that which is pleasing in the eyes of the Lord, which in turn has a direct correlation to obedience and covenantal faithfulness (vv.12–13). Such obedience is enabled by God's presence (v.11) together with the gifts of wisdom and understanding that come from above (v.12). Moreover, success in temple building is consistent with God's promises to David regarding Solomon ("as he said you would," v.11; cf. 1Ch 17:11–12).

David's encouragement for Solomon to be strong and courageous and not afraid or discouraged will remind him of the same words spoken to Joshua as the Israelites prepared to enter the Promised Land (cf. Jos 1:5–9). As David's charge shows, to be strong and courageous biblically speaking is to be immovably committed to obedience and trust in God ("keep the law of the LORD your God … [be] careful to observe the decrees and laws that the LORD gave Moses"). In addition, the exhortation to "be strong and courageous" is inseparable from God's presence ("the LORD be with you," v.11)—a reality greater than any challenge Solomon might face as a leader.

Finally, note that David's charge to Solomon is reminiscent of the succession statements made in the leadership transition from Moses to Joshua (see Ex 24:12–14; 33:11; Nu 27:18–21; Dt 31:7–8, 14–15; 32:44; 34:9; see H. G. M. Williamson, "The Accession of Solomon in the Books of Chronicles," *VT* 26 [1976]: 351–61).

14–16 As reflected above (cf. vv.2–4), David takes extensive steps of preparation for the temple construction project, especially in the areas of raw materials (precious metals, stone, timber) and craftsmen able to work with each of these materials skillfully. Solomon's success (cf. v.13), however, will hinge on divine presence and enablement ("the LORD be with you," v.16; cf. vv.11–12, 17). On the massive quantities of gold, silver, bronze, and iron noted here, see comments on 2 Chronicles 3:8–9.

17–19 While the temple project is prepared by David and completed by Solomon, it is nonetheless an expression of the mutuality of the whole Israelite congregation and their "help" in the project. Note that David's charge to the leaders to devote their heart and soul to "seek" God is inseparably connected with their obedience to God's Word (see comments on 2Ch 14:4; cf. the words of Christ in Jn 15:10, 14). Moreover, as seen with Solomon (vv.11, 16), divine presence ("Is not the LORD your God with you?" v.18) is at the center of David's admonition to the leaders of Israel, as only God's enabling power can shape human hearts to his pleasure (cf. Php 2:13). Moreover, David's reminder of God's faithfulness to his covenantal promises ("has he not granted you rest … handed the inhabitants of the land over to me," v.18; cf. Dt 12:10) will encourage these leaders that God will complete the good work he has begun in the covenantal life of Israel (cf. Php 1:6). Also see the Reflection at 2 Chronicles 12.

NOTES

8 The Chronicler does not explain why David's many wars and shedding of much blood disqualifies him from the actual construction of the temple. Instead, the Chronicler's emphasis is on God's fulfilling his word to David through Solomon rather than the specifics of God's rejection of David as builder (vv.9–10).

11–13 Beyond the exhortation of being strong and courageous, both Solomon and Joshua are told that Yahweh will be with them and that God will not leave them or forsake them, and they are admonished to obey God's Word/law (see Jos 1:5–9; 1Ch 22:6–19; 28:20). In addition, the Chronicler notes that Yahweh made Solomon "exceedingly great," phraseology reminiscent of that applied to Joshua (1Ch 29:25; 2Ch 1:1; cf. Jos 3:7; 4:14).

c. David's Organization of Levitical Families (1Ch 23:1–32)

¹When David was old and full of years, he made his son Solomon king over Israel. ²He also gathered together all the leaders of Israel, as well as the priests and Levites. ³The Levites thirty years old or more were counted, and the total number of men was thirty-eight thousand. ⁴David said, "Of these, twenty-four thousand are to supervise the work of the temple of the LORD and six thousand are to be officials and judges. ⁵Four thousand are to be gatekeepers and four thousand are to praise the LORD with the musical instruments I have provided for that purpose."

⁶David divided the Levites into groups corresponding to the sons of Levi: Gershon, Kohath and Merari.

⁷Belonging to the Gershonites:
  Ladan and Shimei.
⁸The sons of Ladan:
  Jehiel the first, Zetham and Joel — three in all.
⁹The sons of Shimei:
  Shelomoth, Haziel and Haran — three in all.
  These were the heads of the families of Ladan.
¹⁰And the sons of Shimei:
  Jahath, Ziza, Jeush and Beriah.
  These were the sons of Shimei — four in all.
    ¹¹Jahath was the first and Ziza the second, but Jeush and Beriah did not have many
    sons; so they were counted as one family with one assignment.

¹²The sons of Kohath:
  Amram, Izhar, Hebron and Uzziel — four in all.
¹³The sons of Amram:
  Aaron and Moses.
  Aaron was set apart, he and his descendants forever, to consecrate the most holy
  things, to offer sacrifices before the LORD, to minister before him and to pronounce
  blessings in his name forever. ¹⁴The sons of Moses the man of God were counted as
  part of the tribe of Levi.
¹⁵The sons of Moses:
  Gershom and Eliezer.

¹⁶The descendants of Gershom:

Shubael was the first.

¹⁷The descendants of Eliezer:

Rehabiah was the first.

Eliezer had no other sons, but the sons of Rehabiah were very numerous.

¹⁸The sons of Izhar:

Shelomith was the first.

¹⁹The sons of Hebron:

Jeriah the first, Amariah the second, Jahaziel the third and Jekameam the fourth.

²⁰The sons of Uzziel:

Micah the first and Isshiah the second.

²¹The sons of Merari:

Mahli and Mushi.

The sons of Mahli:

Eleazar and Kish.

²²Eleazar died without having sons: he had only daughters. Their cousins, the sons of Kish, married them.

²³The sons of Mushi:

Mahli, Eder and Jerimoth — three in all.

²⁴These were the descendants of Levi by their families — the heads of families as they were registered under their names and counted individually, that is, the workers twenty years old or more who served in the temple of the Lord. ²⁵For David had said, "Since the Lord, the God of Israel, has granted rest to his people and has come to dwell in Jerusalem forever, ²⁶the Levites no longer need to carry the tabernacle or any of the articles used in its service." ²⁷According to the last instructions of David, the Levites were counted from those twenty years old or more.

²⁸The duty of the Levites was to help Aaron's descendants in the service of the temple of the Lord: to be in charge of the courtyards, the side rooms, the purification of all sacred things and the performance of other duties at the house of God. ²⁹They were in charge of the bread set out on the table, the flour for the grain offerings, the unleavened wafers, the baking and the mixing, and all measurements of quantity and size. ³⁰They were also to stand every morning to thank and praise the Lord. They were to do the same in the evening ³¹and whenever burnt offerings were presented to the Lord on Sabbaths and at New Moon festivals and at appointed feasts. They were to serve before the Lord regularly in the proper number and in the way prescribed for them.

³²And so the Levites carried out their responsibilities for the Tent of Meeting, for the Holy Place and, under their brothers the descendants of Aaron, for the service of the temple of the Lord.

COMMENTARY

1 This brief remark indicates a coregency between David and Solomon—a paradigm for regnal stability that was likely mimicked by a number of subsequent kings in Israel and Judah. While a few subsequent coregencies are indicated in the balance of Chronicles (as well as Kings), most regnal summaries do not specify a coregency between the previous and subsequent kings. The likelihood of coregencies is an important factor in engaging the challenges of specific dating during the divided kingdom period. Note that Solomon is later acknowledged as king and heir to the Davidic throne in a public ceremony in the midst of the Israelite congregation (cf. 29:21–25).

2–6 In the presence of the priests and key officials of the community (v.2), David articulates the responsibilities that will be undertaken by the main family lines of Levi (v.6) once a temple is established in Jerusalem (note vv.25–26). The various responsibilities of these Levites are divided between those who will supervise the temple service (v.4), those who will serve in the civil realm (officials and judges; v.4), the gatekeepers (v.5), and the musicians/worship leaders (v.5). The latter part of the chapter (cf. vv.24–27) reflects the significant diversity of service ultimately performed by the Levitical community.

As reflected here (v.5), Levitical ministers are noted as being responsible for music and worship accompanied by a variety of musical instruments, such as lyres, harps, and cymbals (cf. the 288 musicians noted at 25:1–8). Following the completion of the temple, music became one of the primary responsibilities of the Levites (cf. 25:1–7; 2Ch 5:7–13; for more remarks on the musical aspects of Israelite worship, see comments on 2Ch 5:12–13). In addition to the responsibilities of Levites noted here, other Levites functioned as servants to the Aaronic priests, especially in matters of the tabernacle/temple (see vv.28–32).

7–23 This short genealogical information lists the main family lines of Levi: the Gershonites (cf. vv.7–11), the Kohathites (vv.12–20), and the Merarites (vv.21–23). These Levitical families are organized by David in light of the transition from a worship setting that included a portable shrine and changing sites of worship, to a centralized worship setting at the Jerusalem temple (cf. vv.25–26; for specific remarks on these Levitical families, see comments on 6:1–15, 16–30, 31–47). The remark with respect to the line of Aaron (i.e., the priestly line [v.13]) underscores that the distinction between priests and Levites is not affected by David's organization of the clans of Levi (on the distinctions between priests and Levites, see comments on 6:48–49).

24–27 David's organization of the Levitical family lines listed by the Chronicler (vv.7–23) reflects expanded responsibilities for these descendants of Levi in light of the transition to centralized worship at the Jerusalem temple (vv.25–26). Despite these organizational changes, the distinction between priests (who are of Levi via the family line of Aaron) and Levites is not altered (on the distinctions between priests and Levites, see comments on 6:48–49). On the age of these Levites (twenty years and older; vv.24, 27) versus the earlier notation (thirty years and older), see Note on v.3.

28–32 This summary of the various duties of the nonpriestly Levites provides vivid insight into the daily responsibilities of the Levitical family lines. A key responsibility of Levites was to serve the priests ("Aaron's descendants," v.28; cf. v.32) in the various aspects of temple service, ranging from the preparation of the temple bread (bread of the Presence) to the purification of the vessels and implements associated with the sacrificial system (vv.28–29; cf. Nu 8:19). The Levites also had the distinct privilege of leading in acts of public praise and thanksgiving at the beginning and end of each day (v.30) as well as on the Sabbath and appointed days of community worship (v.31).

Most likely, such expressions of corporate thanksgiving were accompanied by the singing and music commonly associated with the Levites (see comments on 1Ch 6:31–47; 2Ch 5:4–6,

12–13). In the light of these manifold duties and functions, Levites bore a number of titles in ancient Israel, including singer/musician/choir director, door/gatekeeper, official/judge, scribe, secretary, and temple servant (cf. vv.2–6; 2Ch 34:8–13; on the distinctions between priests and Levites, see comments on 1Ch 6:48–49).

NOTE

3 David's organization of these Levites is noted here as involving men age thirty and older (v.3), though in the summary of these organizational details the Chronicler also notes the age of twenty and older (vv.24, 27; cf. 2Ch 31:17). While there is no certain explanation for this difference, one possibility is that the different ages of service reflect different time frames. The Chronicler's remark that Levites were enrolled beginning at the age of twenty "according to the last instructions of David" (v.27) may suggest that David later modified his earlier instructions. Another option is that Levites entered a type of "apprenticeship" program that began at age twenty, with full service beginning at age thirty (perhaps reflected in earlier instructions; cf. Nu 4:34–49 with Nu 8:24; also note the reference to teachers and students at 1Ch 25:8).

d. Priestly Divisions (1Ch 24:1–31)

¹These were the divisions of the sons of Aaron:

The sons of Aaron were Nadab, Abihu, Eleazar and Ithamar. ²But Nadab and Abihu died before their father did, and they had no sons; so Eleazar and Ithamar served as the priests. ³With the help of Zadok a descendant of Eleazar and Ahimelech a descendant of Ithamar, David separated them into divisions for their appointed order of ministering. ⁴A larger number of leaders were found among Eleazar's descendants than among Ithamar's, and they were divided accordingly: sixteen heads of families from Eleazar's descendants and eight heads of families from Ithamar's descendants. ⁵They divided them impartially by drawing lots, for there were officials of the sanctuary and officials of God among the descendants of both Eleazar and Ithamar.

⁶The scribe Shemaiah son of Nethanel, a Levite, recorded their names in the presence of the king and of the officials: Zadok the priest, Ahimelech son of Abiathar and the heads of families of the priests and of the Levites — one family being taken from Eleazar and then one from Ithamar.

⁷The first lot fell to Jehoiarib,
  the second to Jedaiah,
⁸the third to Harim,
  the fourth to Seorim,
⁹the fifth to Malkijah,
  the sixth to Mijamin,
¹⁰the seventh to Hakkoz,
  the eighth to Abijah,
¹¹the ninth to Jeshua,
  the tenth to Shecaniah,
¹²the eleventh to Eliashib,
  the twelfth to Jakim,
¹³the thirteenth to Huppah,
  the fourteenth to Jeshebeab,
¹⁴the fifteenth to Bilgah,
  the sixteenth to Immer,
¹⁵the seventeenth to Hezir,
  the eighteenth to Happizzez,
¹⁶the nineteenth to Pethahiah,
  the twentieth to Jehezkel,
¹⁷the twenty-first to Jakin,
  the twenty-second to Gamul,
¹⁸the twenty-third to Delaiah
  and the twenty-fourth to Maaziah.

¹⁹This was their appointed order of ministering when they entered the temple of the Lord, according to the regulations prescribed for them by their forefather Aaron, as the Lord, the God of Israel, had commanded him.

²⁰As for the rest of the descendants of Levi:
    from the sons of Amram: Shubael;
    from the sons of Shubael: Jehdeiah.
²¹As for Rehabiah, from his sons:
    Isshiah was the first.
²²From the Izharites: Shelomoth;
    from the sons of Shelomoth: Jahath.
²³The sons of Hebron: Jeriah the first, Amariah the second, Jahaziel the third and Jekameam the fourth.

²⁴The son of Uzziel: Micah;
> from the sons of Micah: Shamir.

²⁵The brother of Micah:
> Isshiah; from the sons of Isshiah: Zechariah.

²⁶The sons of Merari: Mahli and Mushi.
> The son of Jaaziah: Beno.

²⁷The sons of Merari:
> from Jaaziah: Beno, Shoham, Zaccur and Ibri.

²⁸From Mahli: Eleazar, who had no sons.

²⁹From Kish: the son of Kish:
> Jerahmeel.

³⁰And the sons of Mushi: Mahli, Eder and Jerimoth.

These were the Levites, according to their families. ³¹They also cast lots, just as their brothers the descendants of Aaron did, in the presence of King David and of Zadok, Ahimelech, and the heads of families of the priests and of the Levites. The families of the oldest brother were treated the same as those of the youngest.

COMMENTARY

1–19 Another aspect of the organization of personnel in anticipation of the temple (cf. 1Ch 23:2–32) is the matter of divisions and rotations of priestly service. While these priestly divisions are situated within the general context of David's preparations for Solomon's incoming administration (v.3; cf. chs. 22–29), they are also rooted in divine instruction previously given to Aaron (cf. v.19). In addition, the outworking of these priestly appointments advances via the casting of lots (cf. vv.5–18), reflecting both equity ("impartially," v.5) and divine involvement (cf. Pr 16:33). The casting of lots culminates in the appointment of twenty-four priestly divisions that constitute their "appointed order of ministering" in the context of temple service (vv.3, 19; on the backdrop to these divisions, see H. G. M. Williamson, "The Origins of the Twenty-Four Priestly Courses," SVT 30 [1979]: 251–68).

20–31 The Chronicler follows the appointments of the twenty-four Levitical priestly divisions (vv.1–19) with the backdrop for the division of the balance of (nonpriestly) Levitical families. Note that most of the names recorded here were also recorded in the preceding chapter (cf. 23:7–23). The addition of another generation to the names included here may imply subsequent refinement in the Levitical divisions.

Note that the Chronicler does not include the Levitical family line of Gershon in this listing. The reason for this omission is uncertain but may relate to this chapter's focus on those having particular duties at the Jerusalem temple. As with their priestly brethren (v.31; cf. vv.5–18), these Levites have their divisions determined by lot (cf. Pr 16:33) and without partiality (v.31).

NOTES

3 The unexpected appearance of Ahimelech with Zadok (instead of Abiathar, the father of Ahimelech) may be a result of Abiathar's support of Adonijah's uprising (cf. 1Ki 1:5–10; Selman, 231).

5 The expression "officials of the sanctuary and officials of God" (שָׂרֵי־קֹדֶשׁ וְשָׂרֵי הָאֱלֹהִים, *śārê-qōdeš wᵉśārê hāᵓlōhîm*) may be epexegetical (appositional), implying a translation along the lines of "officials of the sanctuary; that is, officials of/for God."

7–18 The twenty-four priestly divisions delineated in this chapter are only found here in the OT. Solomon is noted as carefully following these determined divisions (cf. 2Ch 8:14–15). Subsequent listings of specific priestly divisions (e.g., Ne 10:1–8) imply that there may have been a degree of fluidity in the actual number of divisions.

e. David's Organization of Levitical Musicians (1Ch 25:1–31)

¹David, together with the commanders of the army, set apart some of the sons of Asaph, Heman and Jeduthun for the ministry of prophesying, accompanied by harps, lyres and cymbals. Here is the list of the men who performed this service:

²From the sons of Asaph:

Zaccur, Joseph, Nethaniah and Asarelah. The sons of Asaph were under the supervision of Asaph, who prophesied under the king's supervision.

³As for Jeduthun, from his sons:

Gedaliah, Zeri, Jeshaiah, Shimei, Hashabiah and Mattithiah, six in all, under the supervision of their father Jeduthun, who prophesied, using the harp in thanking and praising the LORD.

⁴As for Heman, from his sons:

Bukkiah, Mattaniah, Uzziel, Shubael and Jerimoth; Hananiah, Hanani, Eliathah, Giddalti and Romamti-Ezer; Joshbekashah, Mallothi, Hothir and Mahazioth. ⁵All these were sons of Heman the king's seer. They were given him through the promises of God to exalt him. God gave Heman fourteen sons and three daughters.

⁶All these men were under the supervision of their fathers for the music of the temple of the LORD, with cymbals, lyres and harps, for the ministry at the house of God. Asaph, Jeduthun and Heman were under the supervision of the king. ⁷Along with their relatives — all of them trained and skilled in music for the LORD — they numbered 288. ⁸Young and old alike, teacher as well as student, cast lots for their duties.

⁹The first lot, which was for Asaph, fell to Joseph,

    his sons and relatives,   12

  the second to Gedaliah,

    he and his relatives and sons,   12

¹⁰the third to Zaccur,
    his sons and relatives,   12
¹¹the fourth to Izri,
    his sons and relatives,   12
¹²the fifth to Nethaniah,
    his sons and relatives,   12
¹³the sixth to Bukkiah,
    his sons and relatives,   12
¹⁴the seventh to Jesarelah,
    his sons and relatives,   12
¹⁵the eighth to Jeshaiah,
    his sons and relatives,   12
¹⁶the ninth to Mattaniah,
    his sons and relatives,   12
¹⁷the tenth to Shimei,
    his sons and relatives,   12
¹⁸the eleventh to Azarel,
    his sons and relatives,   12
¹⁹the twelfth to Hashabiah,
    his sons and relatives,   12
²⁰the thirteenth to Shubael,
    his sons and relatives,   12
²¹the fourteenth to Mattithiah,
    his sons and relatives,   12
²²the fifteenth to Jerimoth,
    his sons and relatives,   12
²³the sixteenth to Hananiah,
    his sons and relatives,   12
²⁴the seventeenth to Joshbekashah,
    his sons and relatives,   12
²⁵the eighteenth to Hanani,
    his sons and relatives,   12
²⁶the nineteenth to Mallothi,
    his sons and relatives,   12
²⁷the twentieth to Eliathah,
    his sons and relatives,   12
²⁸the twenty-first to Hothir,
    his sons and relatives,   12

²⁹the twenty-second to Giddalti, his sons and relatives,	12
³⁰the twenty-third to Mahazioth, his sons and relatives,	12
³¹the twenty-fourth to Romamti-Ezer, his sons and relatives,	12

1–7 Another aspect of the organization of personnel in anticipation of a centralized temple in Jerusalem (cf. 23:2–32; 24:1–31) relates to the branch of the Levites responsible "for the music of the temple of the LORD" (v.6). Following the completion of the temple, music was one of the primary responsibilities of the Levites (cf. 23:2–32; 2Ch 5:7–13). As reflected here, numerous (288; v.7) Levitical ministers had responsibility in the realm of music and worship, which featured "joyful songs, accompanied by musical instruments: lyres, harps and cymbals" (15:16).

As reflected in the earlier treatment of the musical branch of the Levites (cf. 6:31–47), prominence is attributed to Heman the Kohathite (vv.4–5; cf. 6:33; 15:16–17), who is noted as the "king's seer" (v.5). Heman was also blessed in conjunction with God's promises to exalt him (v.5). The musical leadership of these Levites affected subsequent generations of Israelites (and Christians), as reflected in the sixteen Psalms attributed to these three Levitical leaders (Heman: Ps 88; Asaph: Pss 50, 73–83; and Jeduthun [v.3]: Pss 39, 62, 77; for more remarks on the musical aspects of Israelite worship, see comments on 2Ch 5:12–13).

Of particular interest in this summary is the fourfold reference to aspects of prophetic ministry associated with these Levitical musical families (e.g., "the ministry of prophesying" [v.1]; "prophesied under the king's supervision" [v.2]; "prophesied, using the harp in thanking and praising the LORD"

[v.3]; and "Heman the king's seer" [v.5]). Similarly, note that the term "seer" applied to Heman here (v.5) is also used of Asaph (cf. 2Ch 29:30) and Jeduthun (cf. 2Ch 35:15; Heman and Asaph may be in view here as well).

While the oracle proclaimed through the Levite Jahaziel during the time of Jehoshaphat certainly shows that Levites may be used of God to receive and proclaim prophetic utterances (see 2Ch 20:14–17), the context here of Levites appointed to musical service at the Jerusalem temple suggests that the acts of "prophecy" discharged by these musical Levites relates to their role in the proclamation of God's truth through music rather than ecstatic utterances (cf. Japhet, 440–41). In line with this view, note that Moses' blessing of the Israelite tribes states that a responsibility of the tribe of Levi was teaching God's precepts and law (cf. Dt 33:10). As such, the singing of songs that proclaimed God's truth and exhorted God's people to obedience (cf. the theological content of the Psalms attributed to Heman, Asaph, and Jeduthun) functions in parallel to prophetic ministry.

8–31 As with their priestly brothers (cf. 24:5–18, 31) and their Levitical brothers (cf. 24:20–31), these Levitical musicians have their divisions determined by lot without partiality to age or stature (v.8; cf. Pr 16:33). The Levitical musicians appointed to musical ministry at the temple are organized into twenty-four divisions in analogy to the twenty-four divisions of Levitical-Aaronic priests appointed to minister at the Jerusalem temple (cf. 1Ch 24:1–19). This suggests that these Levitical musicians ministered in tandem with the twenty-four divisions of priests in the context of temple worship, feasts, and morning and evening sacrifice together with others who led in expressions of praise and thanksgiving (cf. 1Ch 23:30–31; note the superscriptions to Pss 92; 100; cf. Isa 30:29; Selman, 236; Hill, 310). When these roles are understood together, it is clear that David envisioned the temple as home to a vibrant tapestry of praise and worship, reflecting the splendor of God's goodness and holiness.

NOTE

1 The phrase translated "commanders of the army" (וְשָׂרֵי הַצָּבָא, *wᵉ śārê haṣṣābāʾ*) may actually be a reference to the "leaders of the host" of *Levites* (i.e., Levitical officers/leaders), rather than implying the involvement of David's military leaders in determining assignments for the Levitical corps of musicians. In support of this view, the term translated "army" (צָבָא, *ṣābāʾ*; GK 7372) is used elsewhere for the service of the Levites (cf. the translation "to serve" at Nu 4:1–3 and "service" at 8:24–25 [NIV]). As such the reference indicates the involvement of the Levitical family leaders in David's organization (cf. the expression "under the supervision of their fathers," v.6) by analogy to the involvement of the priestly leadership families in determining the priestly temple assignments (cf. 1Ch 24:5–6; cf. Japhet, 439–40).

f. Levitical Gatekeepers (1Ch 26:1–19)

¹The divisions of the gatekeepers:
From the Korahites: Meshelemiah son of Kore, one of the sons of Asaph.
²Meshelemiah had sons:
Zechariah the firstborn,
Jediael the second,
Zebadiah the third,
Jathniel the fourth,
³Elam the fifth,
Jehohanan the sixth
and Eliehoenai the seventh.
⁴Obed-Edom also had sons:
Shemaiah the firstborn,
Jehozabad the second,
Joah the third,
Sacar the fourth,
Nethanel the fifth,
⁵Ammiel the sixth,
Issachar the seventh

and Peullethai the eighth.
(For God had blessed Obed-Edom.)

⁶His son Shemaiah also had sons, who were leaders in their father's family because they were very capable men. ⁷The sons of Shemaiah: Othni, Rephael, Obed and Elzabad; his relatives Elihu and Semakiah were also able men. ⁸All these were descendants of Obed-Edom; they and their sons and their relatives were capable men with the strength to do the work — descendants of Obed-Edom, 62 in all.
⁹Meshelemiah had sons and relatives, who were able men — 18 in all.

¹⁰Hosah the Merarite had sons: Shimri the first (although he was not the firstborn, his father had appointed him the first), ¹¹Hilkiah the second, Tabaliah the third and Zechariah the fourth. The sons and relatives of Hosah were 13 in all.
¹²These divisions of the gatekeepers, through their chief men, had duties for ministering in the temple of the LORD, just as their relatives had. ¹³Lots were cast for each gate, according to their families, young and old alike.

¹⁴The lot for the East Gate fell to Shelemiah. Then lots were cast for his son Zechariah, a wise counselor, and the lot for the North Gate fell to him. ¹⁵The lot for the South Gate fell to Obed-Edom, and the lot for the storehouse fell to his sons. ¹⁶The lots for the West Gate and the Shalleketh Gate on the upper road fell to Shuppim and Hosah.

Guard was alongside of guard: ¹⁷There were six Levites a day on the east, four a day on the north, four a day on the south and two at a time at the storehouse. ¹⁸As for the court to the west, there were four at the road and two at the court itself.

¹⁹These were the divisions of the gatekeepers who were descendants of Korah and Merari.

COMMENTARY

1–11 Another aspect of the organization of personnel in anticipation of a centralized temple in Jerusalem (cf. 23:2–32; 24:1–31; 25:1–6) is the matter of ensuring the protection of the "sacred space" of the temple complex through the service of Levitical gatekeepers (doorkeepers). The repeated stress of protecting and guarding Yahweh's holy space in the Chronicler's earlier treatment of gatekeepers (cf. 9:17–28) reflects the importance of guarding and watching over all that pertains to God (see J. W. Wright, "Guarding the Gates: 1 Chron-

icles 26:1–19 and the Role of Gatekeepers in Chronicles," *JSOT* 48 [1990]: 69–81).

In addition to protecting each of the compass-point entrances to the temple complex (cf. vv.13–18; especially the eastern entrance, which faced the main temple entrance and received added protection; cf. v.17), gatekeepers worked with the priests to ensure the sanctity of sacred space and sacred objects (cf. 15:18, 23–24). In light of the critical importance of protecting holy space and holy things, the Chronicler earlier described the task of the gatekeepers as a "position of trust" (cf. 9:22). Similarly, here he describes the gatekeepers as being "very capable men" (v.6), "able men" (vv.7, 9), "capable men with the strength to do the work" (v.8), and in the case of one of the east gate guards a "wise counselor" (v.14). On the topic of sacred space, see comments on 2 Chronicles 2:1.

12–19 As with the priests (cf. 24:5–18, 31) and other Levites (cf. 24:20–31; 25:8–31), these Levitical gatekeepers had their particular service determined by lot (vv.12–18; cf. Pr 16:33). As noted above, the eastern gate received additional protection as it faced the main entrance to the temple (v.17).

g. Levitical Treasurers (1Ch 26:20–28)

²⁰Their fellow Levites were in charge of the treasuries of the house of God and the treasuries for the dedicated things.

²¹The descendants of Ladan, who were Gershonites through Ladan and who were heads of families belonging to Ladan the Gershonite, were Jehieli, ²²the sons of Jehieli, Zetham and his brother Joel. They were in charge of the treasuries of the temple of the LORD.

²³From the Amramites, the Izharites, the Hebronites and the Uzzielites:

²⁴Shubael, a descendant of Gershom son of Moses, was the officer in charge of the treasuries. ²⁵His relatives through Eliezer: Rehabiah his son, Jeshaiah his son, Joram his son, Zicri his son and Shelomith his son. ²⁶Shelomith and his relatives were in charge of all the treasuries for the things dedicated by King David, by the heads of families who were the commanders of thousands and commanders of hundreds, and by the other army commanders. ²⁷Some of the plunder taken in battle they dedicated for the repair of the temple of the LORD. ²⁸And everything dedicated by Samuel the seer and by Saul son of Kish, Abner son of Ner and Joab son of Zeruiah, and all the other dedicated things were in the care of Shelomith and his relatives.

COMMENTARY

20–28 This section of the Levitical personnel who will serve at the Jerusalem temple focuses on stewards of temple treasures and other items dedicated to Yahweh (v.20). While the specifics of the main temple treasures are not given, the Chronicler provides additional details concerning the "dedicated things." These separately kept treasures are connected with five individuals (Samuel, Saul, David, Abner, and Joab) and three groups of military leaders. Given the number of military leaders included in this list, most of these dedicated items originated from plunder following military victories (cf. v.27). A portion of these dedicated things will provide for the repair and maintenance of the temple complex (v.27), which suggests another aspect of David's preparation.

h. Levites Serving away from the Temple (1Ch 26:29–32)

²⁹From the Izharites: Kenaniah and his sons were assigned duties away from the temple, as officials and judges over Israel.
³⁰From the Hebronites: Hashabiah and his relatives—seventeen hundred able men—were responsible in Israel west of the Jordan for all the work of the LORD and for the king's service. ³¹As for the Hebronites, Jeriah was their chief according to the genealogical records of their families. In the fortieth year of David's reign a search was made in the records, and capable men among the Hebronites were found at Jazer in Gilead. ³²Jeriah had twenty-seven hundred relatives, who were able men and heads of families, and King David put them in charge of the Reubenites, the Gadites and the half-tribe of Manasseh for every matter pertaining to God and for the affairs of the king.

COMMENTARY

29–32 This final section of Levitical assignments focuses on those serving "away from the temple" (v.29) in the realm of civil service ("officials and judges"). The Chronicler notes that these individuals are engaged in civil service in various tribal territories ("west of the Jordan," v.30; "Reubenites, the Gadites, and the half-tribe of Manasseh" [in Transjordan], v.32). Twice the Chronicler notes that these "capable" (v.31) Levites are entrusted with a two-pronged service: *spiritual service* ("all the work of the LORD," v.30; cf. "every matter pertaining to God," v.32) and *royal service* ("the king's service," v.30; cf. "the affairs of the king," v.32). Given their mandate as officials and judges, presumably they have the responsibility to settle and enforce matters in the religious realm (e.g., Torah law) and the civil realm (perhaps in conjunction with civil obligations toward the royal infrastructure; recall 1Sa 8:11–17).

i. David's Military Leaders (1Ch 27:1–24)

¹This is the list of the Israelites—heads of families, commanders of thousands and commanders of hundreds, and their officers, who served the king in all that concerned the army divisions that were on duty month by month throughout the year. Each division consisted of 24,000 men.

²In charge of the first division, for the first month, was Jashobeam son of Zabdiel. There were 24,000 men in his division. ³He was a descendant of Perez and chief of all the army officers for the first month.

⁴In charge of the division for the second month was Dodai the Ahohite; Mikloth was the leader of his division. There were 24,000 men in his division.

⁵The third army commander, for the third month, was Benaiah son of Jehoiada the priest. He was chief and there were 24,000 men in his division. ⁶This was the Benaiah who was a mighty man among the Thirty and was over the Thirty. His son Ammizabad was in charge of his division.

⁷The fourth, for the fourth month, was Asahel the brother of Joab; his son Zebadiah was his successor. There were 24,000 men in his division.

⁸The fifth, for the fifth month, was the commander Shamhuth the Izrahite. There were 24,000 men in his division.

⁹The sixth, for the sixth month, was Ira the son of Ikkesh the Tekoite. There were 24,000 men in his division.

¹⁰The seventh, for the seventh month, was Helez the Pelonite, an Ephraimite. There were 24,000 men in his division.

¹¹The eighth, for the eighth month, was Sibbecai the Hushathite, a Zerahite. There were 24,000 men in his division.

¹²The ninth, for the ninth month, was Abiezer the Anathothite, a Benjamite. There were 24,000 men in his division.

¹³The tenth, for the tenth month, was Maharai the Netophathite, a Zerahite. There were 24,000 men in his division.

¹⁴The eleventh, for the eleventh month, was Benaiah the Pirathonite, an Ephraimite. There were 24,000 men in his division.

¹⁵The twelfth, for the twelfth month, was Heldai the Netophathite, from the family of Othniel. There were 24,000 men in his division.

¹⁶The officers over the tribes of Israel:
  over the Reubenites: Eliezer son of Zicri;
  over the Simeonites: Shephatiah son of Maacah;
¹⁷over Levi: Hashabiah son of Kemuel;
  over Aaron: Zadok;
¹⁸over Judah: Elihu, a brother of David;
  over Issachar: Omri son of Michael;
¹⁹over Zebulun: Ishmaiah son of Obadiah;
  over Naphtali: Jerimoth son of Azriel;
²⁰over the Ephraimites: Hoshea son of Azaziah;
  over half the tribe of Manasseh: Joel son of Pedaiah;
²¹over the half-tribe of Manasseh in Gilead: Iddo son of Zechariah;
  over Benjamin: Jaasiel son of Abner;

²²over Dan: Azarel son of Jeroham.

These were the officers over the tribes of Israel.

²³David did not take the number of the men twenty years old or less, because the LORD had promised to make Israel as numerous as the stars in the sky. ²⁴Joab son of Zeruiah began to count the men but did not finish. Wrath came on Israel on account of this numbering, and the number was not entered in the book of the annals of King David.

COMMENTARY

1–15 Another aspect of David's organization of personnel in anticipation of the handover of power to Solomon is the matter of the strength and security of the nation. The structure of this section implies that these military conscripts "served the king" (v.1) one month per year and thus are not fulltime soldiers (except in times of war). Of interest, at least six of the twelve listed division commanders are from Judah, while only two are from a northern tribal area (Ephraim); this fact suggests that David (of the tribe of Judah) wants to ensure an added level of loyalty within his military chain of command. The numbers listed for each division (24,000) may be rounded numbers or exact recruitment targets. On the possibility that the term translated "1,000" in this section may actually refer to a "military fighting unit" (such as a squad or platoon), see the extended comments on 2 Chronicles 11:1.

16–22 In addition to the rotating division commanders noted above (vv.1–15), the Chronicler also delineates military leaders at the tribal level. Although the Chronicler does not specifically state that David made these appointments, the broader context of chs. 24–27 suggests that David selected these tribal leaders as part of his organizational efforts.

Note that the Chronicler has omitted the tribes of Gad and Asher in this listing. There is no certain explanation for this omission, but given the variety of listing of the twelve tribes across the Bible (including the absence of tribes and lists that include both Joseph and one of his sons; see Braun, 260), these absences should not be over-interpreted. The fact that this list totals *twelve* tribal leaders (a total significant for the motif of *all Israel*) seems to be the most significant factor in tribal listings.

23–24 David's nonregistration of those twenty and younger (v.23) is connected with God's promise to Abraham concerning his descendants (cf. Ge 15:5) as well as David's ill-fated census (v.24). The Chronicler's mention of the census commissioned by David reminds the reader of the fundamental issue that covenantal faithfulness necessitates complete trust in God to fulfill his promises (e.g., v.23). Recall that David's census (cf. 21:1–22:1) implied a level of trust in his troops rather than complete trust in God (see comments on 21:1–7). On the topic of sources such as "the book of the annals of King David," see comments on 2 Chronicles 12:15 and the Introduction.

j. David's Officials (1Ch 27:25-34)

²⁵Azmaveth son of Adiel was in charge of the royal storehouses.

Jonathan son of Uzziah was in charge of the storehouses in the outlying districts, in the towns, the villages and the watchtowers.

²⁶Ezri son of Kelub was in charge of the field workers who farmed the land.

²⁷Shimei the Ramathite was in charge of the vineyards.

Zabdi the Shiphmite was in charge of the produce of the vineyards for the wine vats.

²⁸Baal-Hanan the Gederite was in charge of the olive and sycamore-fig trees in the western foothills.

Joash was in charge of the supplies of olive oil.

²⁹Shitrai the Sharonite was in charge of the herds grazing in Sharon.

Shaphat son of Adlai was in charge of the herds in the valleys.

³⁰Obil the Ishmaelite was in charge of the camels.

Jehdeiah the Meronothite was in charge of the donkeys.

³¹Jaziz the Hagrite was in charge of the flocks.

All these were the officials in charge of King David's property.

³²Jonathan, David's uncle, was a counselor, a man of insight and a scribe. Jehiel son of Hacmoni took care of the king's sons.

³³Ahithophel was the king's counselor.

Hushai the Arkite was the king's friend. ³⁴Ahithophel was succeeded by Jehoiada son of Benaiah and by Abiathar.

Joab was the commander of the royal army.

COMMENTARY

25-31 The Chronicler's listing of the royal officials charged with overseeing the various holdings of the house of David provides engaging insight into the economy, natural resources, and royal bureaucracy of ancient Israel. This list spans the gamut of viticulture, agriculture, horticulture, and animal husbandry, as well as the workers and storage needed to manage the logistics of these varied and dispersed royal assets. Thus this list suggests an impressive degree of state planning at the level of the production, storage, and distribution of royal holdings by the end of David's reign.

32-34 In addition to those who handled the royal holdings in different regions of the land (vv.25-31), the Chronicler also notes those with particular responsibility within the palace and to the royal family. This "inner circle" of David's cabinet provided a multitude of counsel and insight to the king (cf. Pr 15:22; note that the position of "king's friend" was possibly akin to "most trusted advisor").

David's relationship with several of these advisors changed for the worse in the context of the attempted coups of Absalom and Adonijah (Ahithophel: 2Sa 16:20–23; Joab: 2Sa 18:9–15; 1Ki 1:7; Abiathar: 1Ki 1:7). Ahithophel's replacement was necessitated both by his disloyalty to David and his subsequent suicide (cf. 2Sa 15:31; 16:20–23; 17:23).

Conversely, David's relationship with Hushai was no doubt deepened during the Absalom crisis (cf. 2Sa 15:32–37; 16:16–19), perhaps earning him the title "king's friend" (v.33).

NOTES

18 The reference to "Elihu, a brother of David" as the official over the tribe of Judah is intriguing, since he was not mentioned in the Chronicler's overview of Jesse's family (cf. 2:13–15). "Elihu" may be another name for "Eliab" (as reflected in the LXX) or perhaps the eighth son of Jesse not listed in the Chronicler's genealogy (cf. Hill, 320).

25–31 This list also reflects the societal costs of sustaining a royal bureaucracy, as anticipated by Samuel (cf. 1Sa 8:10–18)

k. David's Second Charge to Solomon and the Leaders of Israel (1Ch 28:1–10)

¹David summoned all the officials of Israel to assemble at Jerusalem: the officers over the tribes, the commanders of the divisions in the service of the king, the commanders of thousands and commanders of hundreds, and the officials in charge of all the property and livestock belonging to the king and his sons, together with the palace officials, the mighty men and all the brave warriors.

²King David rose to his feet and said: "Listen to me, my brothers and my people. I had it in my heart to build a house as a place of rest for the ark of the covenant of the LORD, for the footstool of our God, and I made plans to build it. ³But God said to me, 'You are not to build a house for my Name, because you are a warrior and have shed blood.'

⁴"Yet the LORD, the God of Israel, chose me from my whole family to be king over Israel forever. He chose Judah as leader, and from the house of Judah he chose my family, and from my father's sons he was pleased to make me king over all Israel. ⁵Of all my sons— and the LORD has given me many—he has chosen my son Solomon to sit on the throne of the kingdom of the LORD over Israel. ⁶He said to me: 'Solomon your son is the one who will build my house and my courts, for I have chosen him to be my son, and I will be his father. ⁷I will establish his kingdom forever if he is unswerving in carrying out my commands and laws, as is being done at this time.'

⁸"So now I charge you in the sight of all Israel and of the assembly of the LORD, and in the hearing of our God: Be careful to follow all the commands of the LORD your God, that you may possess this good land and pass it on as an inheritance to your descendants forever.

> [9]"And you, my son Solomon, acknowledge the God of your father, and serve him with wholehearted devotion and with a willing mind, for the LORD searches every heart and understands every motive behind the thoughts. If you seek him, he will be found by you; but if you forsake him, he will reject you forever. [10]Consider now, for the LORD has chosen you to build a temple as a sanctuary. Be strong and do the work."

COMMENTARY

1–8 Following his extensive preparations in workers, raw materials, and leadership (chs. 22–27), David now seeks to prepare the hearts of the leaders of the Israelite community to embrace Solomon's rule and strive for covenantal faithfulness and obedience. These leaders and officials include those designated by David as part of his leadership transitionary preparations (note esp. the listings of ch. 27).

In speaking to these community leaders David reiterates much of what he has said to Solomon earlier regarding his desire to build a temple for the Lord and God's choice of Solomon not only to build the temple but also to be David's heir and God's adopted regnal "son" (see comments on 22:6–10). The crux of David's heartfelt speech ("my brothers and my people," v.2) is wholehearted obedience to the covenantal framework established between Yahweh and his people ("be careful to follow *all* the commands of the LORD your God," v.8, emphasis added). David connects his exhortation to obedience with Israel's continued possession of the Promised Land (v.8) in a manner reminiscent of earlier biblical passages connected with Abraham, Moses, and Joshua (e.g., Ge 17:1–8; Dt 8:1; Jos 23:6–13).

One of the more striking aspects of David's speech is the emphatic stress on the agency of God in shaping the path of the nation:

- "But God said to me, 'You are not to build a house for my Name'" (v.3).
- "The God of Israel chose me" (v.4).
- "He chose Judah as leader" (v.4; cf. the "scepter" of Judah in Ge 49:8–12).
- "He chose my family" (v.4).
- "He was pleased to make me king" (v.4).
- "He has chosen my son Solomon" (v.5).
- "I have chosen him" (v.6).
- "I will be his father" (v.6).
- "I will establish his kingdom" (v.6).

This stress on God's expression of his will underscores that Solomon's imminent coronation as king and temple builder (note vv.12, 19) is part of God's sovereign design, which includes the reality that Solomon will be sitting "on the throne of the kingdom of the LORD over Israel" (v.5). While kings of the biblical world were seen as sovereign monarchs over nations and people, in the case of the Israelite covenantal community, the people led by the king are *God's people* (2Ch 1:10), the kingdom is *God's kingdom* (1Ch 17:14; 2Ch 13:8), the king is *God's son* (1Ch 22:10; 28:5–6), and the king sits on *God's throne* (1Ch 29:23; 2Ch 9:8; cf. Dillard, 12; Hill, 380). On the layer of conditionality suggested by David's summary of God's promise to him ("I will establish his kingdom forever if he is unswerving in carrying out my commands and laws ..."), see the extended discussion of the Davidic covenant at 17:7–15.

9–10 The essence of David's earlier private charge to Solomon (cf. 22:6–13) is now repeated in the presence of "all Israel" (v.8; see Selman, 250–52, for ways in which David's words here expand his original charge to Solomon). As with David's exhortation to the leaders of the people, the crux of David's charge is that of covenantal faithfulness ("wholehearted devotion" [$b^e l\bar{e}b \ \check{s}\bar{a}l\bar{e}m$]) and the grave consequence of covenantal unfaithfulness ("he will reject you forever," v.9).

Yet David makes it clear that biblical faithfulness cannot be fabricated; it must flow from pure motives, Godward thoughts, and a willing mind (vv.9–10). As David's charge implies, to "be strong" (v.10) biblically speaking is to be steadfastly committed to seeking God, obeying him, and faithfully carrying out his work (see related comments at 22:11–13).

Lastly, David's charge illustrates the role of the believer's mind in discerning and doing that which is pleasing to God (cf. Ro 12:2; 2Co 10:5): "acknowledge the God of your father" (v.9); "a willing mind" (v.9); "every motive behind the thoughts" (v.9); "consider now" (v.10).

l. David Gives the Temple Plans to Solomon (1Ch 28:11–19)

¹¹Then David gave his son Solomon the plans for the portico of the temple, its buildings, its storerooms, its upper parts, its inner rooms and the place of atonement. ¹²He gave him the plans of all that the Spirit had put in his mind for the courts of the temple of the LORD and all the surrounding rooms, for the treasuries of the temple of God and for the treasuries for the dedicated things. ¹³He gave him instructions for the divisions of the priests and Levites, and for all the work of serving in the temple of the LORD, as well as for all the articles to be used in its service. ¹⁴He designated the weight of gold for all the gold articles to be used in various kinds of service, and the weight of silver for all the silver articles to be used in various kinds of service: ¹⁵the weight of gold for the gold lampstands and their lamps, with the weight for each lampstand and its lamps; and the weight of silver for each silver lampstand and its lamps, according to the use of each lampstand; ¹⁶the weight of gold for each table for consecrated bread; the weight of silver for the silver tables; ¹⁷the weight of pure gold for the forks, sprinkling bowls and pitchers; the weight of gold for each gold dish; the weight of silver for each silver dish; ¹⁸and the weight of the refined gold for the altar of incense. He also gave him the plan for the chariot, that is, the cherubim of gold that spread their wings and shelter the ark of the covenant of the LORD.

¹⁹"All this," David said, "I have in writing from the hand of the LORD upon me, and he gave me understanding in all the details of the plan."

COMMENTARY

11–19 Following his charge to Solomon to serve God with "wholehearted devotion" (vv.9–10), David entrusts Solomon with the plans for the temple complex. David's plans and provisions for

Yahweh's temple are detailed (e.g., "the weight of gold for each gold dish ...," v.17) and wide-ranging (from architectural details [vv.11–12] to implements used in the Israelite sacrificial system [vv.17–18]). This degree of detail reflects the depth of David's dedication to the temple project (cf. 22:2–4, 14–16). Similarly, note that David's detailed organization of the priestly and Levitical divisions (v.13) occupies much of the content of chs. 23–26.

David's motivation for his vast preparatory efforts relate to both Solomon's inexperience as well as David's desire that the temple be "of great magnificence and fame and splendor in the sight of all the nations" (22:5; cf. 29:1). In short, David wants the beauty of the temple to reflect brightly the beauty of God's holiness (cf. Ps 29:2).

In addition, David's level of involvement in the temple project underscores the notion that the Jerusalem temple is in many ways a joint project of David and Solomon. As with the emphasis on the throne of Israel ultimately belonging to God (v.5), David emphasizes that the plans for the temple ("all this," v.19) have come through divine revelation. In fact, David's portrayal of this process (namely, "all that the Spirit had put in his mind [v.11] ... I have in writing from the hand of the LORD upon me, and he gave me understanding in all the details of the plan [v.19]") amounts to an insightful summary of the doctrine of verbal plenary inspiration.

NOTES

12 The relationship of this verse with v.19 (framing the details of the temple plans and provisions) supports the NIV's translation of "Spirit" (i.e., referring to *God's Spirit*) over translations that understand "spirit" (רוּחַ, *rûaḥ*; GK 8120) as referring to *David's mind* (e.g., RSV, NRSV, NASB, ESV).

18 The NIV's translation of the expression "chariot, that is, the cherubim" (הַמֶּרְכָּבָה הַכְּרֻבִים, *ham-merkābâ hakkᵉrubîm*) implies an appositional value to "chariot"—that is, another name for the cherubim rather than a separate object crafted for the temple (e.g., "chariot *of* the cherubim" [cf. ESV]). This term is only found here in conjunction with the ark of the covenant, so the intended meaning is uncertain. The image of the mobility of God's presence is underscored in the visions of Ezekiel (cf. Eze 1:4–28), including the image of "wheels" in association with cherubim (cf. Eze 10:1–20).

m. David Gives another Charge to Solomon (1Ch 28:20–21)

> ²⁰David also said to Solomon his son, "Be strong and courageous, and do the work. Do not be afraid or discouraged, for the LORD God, my God, is with you. He will not fail you or forsake you until all the work for the service of the temple of the LORD is finished. ²¹The divisions of the priests and Levites are ready for all the work on the temple of God, and every willing man skilled in any craft will help you in all the work. The officials and all the people will obey your every command."

COMMENTARY

20–21 David concludes his public exhortation by reiterating the charge to Solomon to be "strong and courageous" (v.20; cf. vv.9–10; 1Ch 22:11–13), an exhortation also reflected in the leadership transition from Moses to Joshua (e.g., Ex 24:12–14; 33:11; Nu 27:18–21; Dt 31:7–8, 14–15; 32:44; 34:9; Jos 1:5–9). Although David exhorts Solomon to be strong and courageous to complete the temple project, Solomon's ability to have such strength and courage completely hinges on divine presence and enablement ("the LORD my God is with you. He will not fail you or forsake you until all the work for the service of the temple of the LORD is finished," v.20; cf. 22:11–12, 16–17). As such, David's exhortation reflects the reality that the building of the temple for the Lord is a spiritual exercise as much as it is a building enterprise.

David's confidence in the help available to Solomon (v.21) reflects his careful organization of the priests and Levites (occupying the bulk of the content of chs. 23–26), as well as his earlier order to the leadership of Israel "to help his son Solomon" (cf. 22:17). Thus, while the temple project is prepared by David and completed by Solomon, the success of the project requires the dedication of the broader Israelite community.

n. Gifts for the Temple Project (1Ch 29:1–9)

[1]Then King David said to the whole assembly: "My son Solomon, the one whom God has chosen, is young and inexperienced. The task is great, because this palatial structure is not for man but for the LORD God. [2]With all my resources I have provided for the temple of my God—gold for the gold work, silver for the silver, bronze for the bronze, iron for the iron and wood for the wood, as well as onyx for the settings, turquoise, stones of various colors, and all kinds of fine stone and marble—all of these in large quantities. [3]Besides, in my devotion to the temple of my God I now give my personal treasures of gold and silver for the temple of my God, over and above everything I have provided for this holy temple: [4]three thousand talents of gold (gold of Ophir) and seven thousand talents of refined silver, for the overlaying of the walls of the buildings, [5]for the gold work and the silver work, and for all the work to be done by the craftsmen. Now, who is willing to consecrate himself today to the LORD?"

[6]Then the leaders of families, the officers of the tribes of Israel, the commanders of thousands and commanders of hundreds, and the officials in charge of the king's work gave willingly. [7]They gave toward the work on the temple of God five thousand talents and ten thousand darics of gold, ten thousand talents of silver, eighteen thousand talents of bronze and a hundred thousand talents of iron. [8]Any who had precious stones gave them to the treasury of the temple of the LORD in the custody of Jehiel the Gershonite. [9]The people rejoiced at the willing response of their leaders, for they had given freely and wholeheartedly to the LORD. David the king also rejoiced greatly.

COMMENTARY

1−5 David's final recorded speech in Chronicles is oriented to the "whole assembly" of Israel (v.1; cf. vv.10, 17−18, 20, 30) and the integral role the community will play in the construction of the Jerusalem temple. David's opening words declare that the temple is "for the LORD God" (v.1) and thus should have the finest of materials and craftsmanship so that the beauty of God's holiness is aptly reflected (vv.2−5; cf. 22:5, 14; Ps 29:2). Many of these materials were also used in the construction of the tabernacle during the time of Moses. David is also motivated to facilitate Solomon's success in the completion of such a monumental project. Note that David's observation of Solomon's youth and inexperience (v.1) is echoed by Solomon in his prayer for wisdom (1Ki 3:6−9).

David's speech also indicates that the vast supplies of precious materials and resources he devoted to the temple project (vv.2−4) are supplemented further by significant gifts from his personal treasure (v.5). David's gifts are a reflection of his devotion to God and the place that will be built in honor of *his God* (note the triple reference of "the temple of my God," vv.2, 3 [2x]). In the light of David's abundant personal gifts to the temple project, he challenges the congregation to follow his example—expressed as personal choice to show devotion to God ("who is willing to consecrate himself today to the LORD?" v.5; cf. Ro 12:1). On the staggering amount of gold and silver

dedicated by David, see comments on 2 Chronicles 3:8−9. The location of Ophir (v.4) is not certain; proposals range from India to coastal Africa (including Punt and Nubia; note that "Nub" means gold; see E. M. Yamauchi, *Africa and the Bible* [Grand Rapids: Baker Academic, 2004], 83−90). As with gold from Parvaim (cf. 2Ch 3:4−7), gold from Ophir designated high quality gold in the biblical world.

6−9 In the light of David's challenge to the people to follow his example of abundant generosity (v.5), the leaders of the Israelite community respond with their own display of generosity toward the Jerusalem temple project. The Chronicler emphasizes the "willing response" (v.9; cf. "willingly," v.6; "freely and wholeheartedly," v.9) of the community leaders and the resulting joy of both people and king (v.9). Note that the focus of the leaders' giving is Godward—"toward the work on the temple of God" (v.7); "to the LORD" (v.9).

These corporate acts of wholehearted freewill giving and joyful celebration work to transition David's description of the temple as the "temple of *my* God" (vv.2, 3 [2x]) to the Israelite community's embracing the temple as the "temple of *our* God." On the massive amount of gold and silver dedicated by the people, see comments on 2 Chronicles 3:8−9. The "daric" (v.7) was a Persian monetary unit used by the Chronicler to give a sense of comparison helpful to his postexilic audience.

o. David's Benedictory Prayer of Praise (1Ch 29:10−20)

---

¹⁰David praised the LORD in the presence of the whole assembly, saying,

"Praise be to you, O LORD,
    God of our father Israel,
    from everlasting to everlasting.

---

¹¹Yours, O Lᴏʀᴅ, is the greatness and the power
and the glory and the majesty and the splendor,
for everything in heaven and earth is yours.
Yours, O Lᴏʀᴅ, is the kingdom;
you are exalted as head over all.
¹²Wealth and honor come from you;
you are the ruler of all things.
In your hands are strength and power
to exalt and give strength to all.
¹³Now, our God, we give you thanks,
and praise your glorious name.

¹⁴"But who am I, and who are my people, that we should be able to give as generously as this? Everything comes from you, and we have given you only what comes from your hand. ¹⁵We are aliens and strangers in your sight, as were all our forefathers. Our days on earth are like a shadow, without hope. ¹⁶O Lᴏʀᴅ our God, as for all this abundance that we have provided for building you a temple for your Holy Name, it comes from your hand, and all of it belongs to you. ¹⁷I know, my God, that you test the heart and are pleased with integrity. All these things have I given willingly and with honest intent. And now I have seen with joy how willingly your people who are here have given to you. ¹⁸O Lᴏʀᴅ, God of our fathers Abraham, Isaac and Israel, keep this desire in the hearts of your people forever, and keep their hearts loyal to you. ¹⁹And give my son Solomon the wholehearted devotion to keep your commands, requirements and decrees and to do everything to build the palatial structure for which I have provided."

²⁰Then David said to the whole assembly, "Praise the Lᴏʀᴅ your God." So they all praised the Lᴏʀᴅ, the God of their fathers; they bowed low and fell prostrate before the Lᴏʀᴅ and the king.

COMMENTARY

10–20 This exquisite piece of poetic prayer spoken in the midst of the "whole assembly" (vv.10, 20) flows from the atmosphere of wholehearted giving and joyful celebration on the part of the king, leaders, and Israelite community (v.17; cf. vv.6–9). David's prayer radiates the recognition that all glory, honor, praise, and thanksgiving belong to God and God alone (vv.10–13, 20; note the number of times

"yours" and "you" appear in the prayer). Moreover, David's words over and again declare the reality that every good and perfect gift comes from God (vv.12, 14, 16; cf. Jas 1:17).

In addition, the Chronicler once again stresses that the kingdom of Israel is ultimately God's kingdom ("yours, O Lᴏʀᴅ, is the kingdom," v.11; "you are exalted as head over all," v.11; "you are the ruler of all things," v.12; also note v.23: "Solomon sat on the throne of the Lord" cf. 1Ch 17:14; 28:5; 2Ch 9:8; 13:8). David's simple response to these theological realities is one of awe and humility: "Who am I, and who are my people ... we are aliens and strangers in your sight ... our days on earth are like a shadow" (vv.14–15; recall David's similar response to God's promise of a Davidic dynasty [17:16]). For the Chronicler, the reminder of these divine qualities and covenantal truths provide the theological foundation for the rebuilding done by the postexilic community.

The crux of David's appeal to God is that God may continue the good work he has begun in the hearts of Solomon and the Israelite community: "Keep their hearts loyal to you ... give my son Solomon the wholehearted devotion to keep your commands, requirements and decrees" (vv.18–19; cf. Php 1:6). David's prayer is similar to Paul's understanding of God's effectual grace in the hearts of his children: "It is God who works in you to will and to act according to his good purpose" (Php 2:13). The "whole assembly" responds to God's goodness and sovereign rule in corporate praise and submission to God and God's chosen king (v.20).

NOTE

11 Note the similarity of David's declaration to the end of the Lord's Prayer reflected in some manuscripts: "Yours is the kingdom and the power and the glory forever" (Mt 6:13). Also note the points of similarity between David's broader prayer (vv.10–19) and David's other prayers of thanksgiving in 1 Chronicles (16:7–36; 17:16–27) as well as Psalm 145, which is attributed to David in the superscription of that psalm.

p. Solomon's Public Coronation (1Ch 29:21–25)

²¹The next day they made sacrifices to the Lord and presented burnt offerings to him: a thousand bulls, a thousand rams and a thousand male lambs, together with their drink offerings, and other sacrifices in abundance for all Israel. ²²They ate and drank with great joy in the presence of the Lord that day.

Then they acknowledged Solomon son of David as king a second time, anointing him before the Lord to be ruler and Zadok to be priest. ²³So Solomon sat on the throne of the Lord as king in place of his father David. He prospered and all Israel obeyed him. ²⁴All the officers and mighty men, as well as all of King David's sons, pledged their submission to King Solomon.

²⁵The Lord highly exalted Solomon in the sight of all Israel and bestowed on him royal splendor such as no king over Israel ever had before.

COMMENTARY

21–25 This celebration of the community's unity in giving wholeheartedly toward the temple project (vv.1–9; cf. David's expression of God's goodness [vv.10–20]) culminates in a time of sacrifice and fellowship "with great joy in the presence of the LORD." It is fitting that such sacrifice, fellowship, and joy in the context of engaging the presence of God takes place, as these characteristics anticipate the function of the Jerusalem temple. As with the precious materials gathered for the temple project (cf. vv.1–5), the amounts of the sacrifices noted here act as tangible symbols of the devotion and worship of David, Solomon, and the Israelite community (v.21; cf. 2Ch 7:4–5).

The assembled Israelite community also uses this occasion publicly to acknowledge Solomon as David's (and God's) chosen heir to the Davidic throne (v.22). This large-scale public enthronement in the presence of "all Israel" follows up on David's smaller ceremony anointing Solomon as king ("a second time," v.22; cf. 23:1). The Chronicler notes that "all Israel" obeyed Solomon (v.23) and that Yahweh "highly exalted Solomon in the presence of all Israel" (v.25), underscoring the fact that Solomon's strength and splendor were by-products of God's graciousness toward him and the house of David (cf. God's similar blessings on Joshua [Jos 3:7; 4:14]; on Solomon's enthronement on the throne *of the Lord* [v.23], see comments on vv.10–20).

NOTE

22 Since Zadok was already a priest (cf. 18:16), this anointing likely reflects a public investure of some sort, possibly his appointment as high priest (cf. Selman, 262).

q. David's Death and Regnal Summary (1Ch 29:26–30)

²⁶David son of Jesse was king over all Israel. ²⁷He ruled over Israel forty years — seven in Hebron and thirty-three in Jerusalem. ²⁸He died at a good old age, having enjoyed long life, wealth and honor. His son Solomon succeeded him as king.

²⁹As for the events of King David's reign, from beginning to end, they are written in the records of Samuel the seer, the records of Nathan the prophet and the records of Gad the seer, ³⁰together with the details of his reign and power, and the circumstances that surrounded him and Israel and the kingdoms of all the other lands.

COMMENTARY

26–30 The Chronicler's closing remarks on the reign of King David reflect God's blessings on him through a long life (cf. Ps 91:16; Pr 3:16), wealth (recall 1Ch 29:2–4), and honor. Recall that David's earlier prayer attributed such blessings of wealth, honor, and strength to God's goodness (cf. 29:12). The Chronicler's reference to the "kingdoms of all the other lands" (v.30) is likely a reference to David's victories over nations to the east, west, south, and north summarized in chs. 18–20.

Nonetheless, such God-given victories also work to "make known among the nations what [God] has done" (16:8; cf. 16:24). Such an element of outreach is reflected elsewhere in Chronicles (cf. 2Ch 17:10; 20:29–30). On the topic of sources such as the records of Samuel, Nathan, and Gad (v.29), see comments on 2 Chronicles 12:15 and the Introduction.

C. The Reign of Solomon and the Construction of the Temple (2Ch 1:1–9:31)

OVERVIEW

Following the Chronicler's extended treatment of the transition from Davidic to Solomonic rule (1Ch 22–29), the opening of this next section of his work (namely, 2 Chronicles) stresses God's favor on Solomon, including aspects of divine election, presence, and enablement. The Chronicler connects the favor shown by God to Solomon with the divine favor of the Davidic dynasty via similar statements (cf. 1Ch 11:9; 17:8). The literary shaping of the Chronicler's account of Solomon's reign is reflected by sustained points of repetition (mirroring):

A Solomon's God-given wisdom, wealth, and regional trading success (2Ch 1:7–17)
Note repetition of details between 2 Chronicles 1:12–17 and 9:23–28
> **B Solomon's wisdom facilitates good relations with the nations (2:1–18)**
> (Hiram King of Tyre: "The LORD loves his people," 2:11)
> (Hiram King of Tyre: "[God] has given David a wise son," 2:12)
> (Hiram King of Tyre: "Praise be to the LORD," 2:12)
> > **C Temple construction and dedication (3:1–7:22)**
> **B' Solomon's wisdom facilitates good relations with the nations (8:1–9:22)**
> (Queen of Sheba: "Your wisdom is true," 9:5)
> (Queen of Sheba: "Praise be to the LORD," 9:8a)
> (Queen of Sheba: "God has delighted in you," 9:8b)
A' Solomon's God-given wisdom, wealth, and regional trading success (9:23–28)
Note repetition of details between 2 Chronicles 9:23–28 and 1:12–17

The overlapping statements and themes work to "frame" the account of Solomon and draw attention to the role of divinely-gifted wisdom in the construction of the temple (as with Bezalel and the construction of the tabernacle) and in Israel's outreach to the nations (cf. Dt 4:6). The focal point of the Chronicler's summary of Solomon's reign is that of the "middle" chapters (2Ch 3–7), where he has situated the ultimate outworking of this divinely enabled wisdom and success, namely, in the construction and dedication of the Jerusalem temple — the place of divine presence, holiness, forgiveness, worship, and prayer "for all nations."

In addition to actual construction details, this "middle" section also includes the notation of starting and completing the temple (cf. 3:1 and 7:10), the deposit of the ark of the covenant into the temple (5:2–14), Solomon's declaration to the assembly (6:1–11) and dedicatory prayer (6:12–42), and the Lord's response to Solomon's prayer (7:1–3, 11–22). For a more elaborate proposal for the structuring of these chapters, see D. A. Dorsey, *The Literary Structure of the Old Testament* (Grand Rapids: Baker, 1999), 148.

1. Solomon Assumes the Davidic Throne (2Ch 1:1)

¹Solomon son of David established himself firmly over his kingdom, for the Lord his God was with him and made him exceedingly great.

COMMENTARY

1 The Chronicler begins his account of Solomon's reign by emphasizing God's favor on Solomon during the transition from Davidic to Solomonic rule in Israel. The theological notions of divine election, presence, and enablement are all succinctly noted within this opening statement of 2 Chronicles. In addition, this opening remark connects Solomon with the divine favor of the Davidic dynasty via similar statements of divine favor made concerning David (cf. 1Ch 11:9; 17:8).

The remark that Solomon "established himself firmly over his kingdom" is a succinct way of summarizing the details of Solomon's transition to power. (Note the similar summary statement at 1 Kings 2:46 following two chapters summarizing Solomon's actions at the beginning of his reign.) The Chronicler uses similar phraseology in several royal succession contexts, including Rehoboam (2Ch 12:1), Asa (15:8), Jehoshaphat (17:1), and Amaziah/Uzziah (25:3), and may imply challenges implicit in any regnal changeover. God's presence ("the Lord his God was with him") is the basis for Solomon's strength and success (also see Reflection below). As with Solomon's wisdom (see comments on 1:10), divine presence is directly connected to the building of the temple (cf. 1Ch 28:20).

2. Solomon and All Israel Worship at Gibeon (2Ch 1:2–6)

²Then Solomon spoke to all Israel — to the commanders of thousands and commanders of hundreds, to the judges and to all the leaders in Israel, the heads of families — ³and Solomon and the whole assembly went to the high place at Gibeon, for God's Tent of Meeting was there, which Moses the LORD's servant had made in the desert. ⁴Now David had brought up the ark of God from Kiriath Jearim to the place he had prepared for it, because he had pitched a tent for it in Jerusalem. ⁵But the bronze altar that Bezalel son of Uri, the son of Hur, had made was in Gibeon in front of the tabernacle of the LORD; so Solomon and the assembly inquired of him there. ⁶Solomon went up to the bronze altar before the LORD in the Tent of Meeting and offered a thousand burnt offerings on it.

COMMENTARY

2 Solomon's speech to all levels of the Israelite leadership emphasizes the breadth of unity and oneness that shapes this pilgrimage to Gibeon by the Israelite community. A gathering of a similar group of individuals was organized by David to announce that Solomon would build the temple for the Lord (1Ch 28:1–8) as well as the procession that accompanied David in moving the ark of the covenant from Kiriath Jearim to Jerusalem (1Ch 13 and 15).

3–5 The location of Gibeon at the intersection of important roads connecting the hill country with the Shephelah (low rolling hills in between the coastal region and the hill country) facilitated Gibeon's development and prominence from early times (recall Gibeon's description as "an important city, like one of the royal cities" in Jos 10:2). During the conquest period, the Hivite residents of Gibeon were indentured as temple servants as a result of their ruse on the Israelite leadership (see Jos 9).

The mention of a mass pilgrimage to a high place is at first startling in the light of the negative association of high places within biblical literature. However, prior to the construction of the temple, high places were often generic worship sites

not necessarily connected with pagan worship, and they reflect a noncentralized worship setting (cf. 1Ki 3:2). Because of the possibility that the Chronicler's audience would view Solomon's trip to a high place negatively, much is done to emphasize that the high place at Gibeon was a legitimate place of worship. Of particular importance, we learn here that the Tent of Meeting made by Moses "the LORD's servant" as well as the bronze altar for burnt offerings crafted by Bezalel (2Ch 1:5; cf. Ex 38:1–2) were at Gibeon (see also 1Ch 21:29).

The Tent of Meeting underscores continuity with Moses, while the bronze altar connects the site with the Israelite sacrificial system and the Aaronic priesthood (see 1Ch 16:39–40). These details combine to make it clear that the high place at Gibeon was not only a legitimate sacred place, but also an important site prior to the construction of the temple (note its description as the "great" or "most important" high place in the parallel text at 1Ki 3:4).

The strong negative connotation of high places begins after the completion of the Jerusalem temple, which inaugurated a time of centralized worship anticipated in Deuteronomy 12:13–14. From this point forward, high places become associated with the worship of foreign deities, idolatry, and syncretism. Subsequently, eradicating high places becomes a litmus test for the spiritual faithfulness of a given ruler.

6 Solomon's extensive sacrifice at Gibeon ("a thousand burnt offerings") is a tangible way of showing his reverence of God at the outset of his reign. Similarly abundant sacrifice is connected with the dedication of the temple (cf. 7:5). As reflected in the dedication of the temple, there is a close connection between sacrifice and prayer in this setting.

NOTES

3 The name "high place" (בָּמָה, *bāmâ*; GK 1195) reflects the fact that high places were commonly associated with hills or mountains in the broader OT world. (Note that the name "Gibeon" is a cognate of "hill," so it is likely that the high place at Gibeon was located on an elevated plateau [cf. D. L. Petter, "High Places," *DOTHB*, 417].)

4 This text clarifies that the ark of the covenant (which would normally be situated within the tent/tabernacle) was not located at Gibeon but had been relocated to Jerusalem by David from Kiriath Jearim (1Ch 13). Recall that the ark was in Kiriath Jearim for twenty years following its seven-month exile in Philistine territory during the time of Samuel and Eli (see 1Sa 4−6). The syntactical structure of v.4 implies this is a parenthetical remark intended for clarification.

REFLECTION

The idea of divine presence (as reflected in the Chronicler's note that the Lord God was "with" Solomon, 2Ch 1:1) is an important theological motif that threads it way through the pages of Scripture. In the beginning of the creation of humankind, the presence of God was up front and center, before being marred and lost through sin. From the opening chapters of Genesis to the closing chapters of Revelation, the redemptive plan of God is working to reestablish the fullness of divine presence to his people.

The promise (or reminder) of divine presence is reiterated to each of the patriarchs (Abraham, Isaac, and Jacob) at pivotal moments in their spiritual walk and is noted as that which sustained Joseph during his trials in Egypt (note the use of this concept in Ge 39). In addition, divine presence is arguably at the heart of the giving (and meaning) of the divine name in Exodus 3 (note the first instance of "I am/will be" within the passage is at 3:12: "I will be with you"). Divine presence is also proclaimed to Moses in the aftermath of the golden calf incident (Ex 33:14) and at the heart of what will facilitate Joshua's success as he readies the people to enter Canaan (see Jos 1:5−9).

Moreover, divine presence is at the crux of the presentation of the Messiah, Immanuel (which means "God with us"). The opening chapter of the gospel of John shows how the Word (God) became flesh and dwelt in the midst of humankind. Similarly, Jesus tells believers that he will always be with them (Mt 28:20). Indeed, the notion of abiding in Christ as he abides in us gets to the heart of the practice of the presence of God (cf. Jn 15).

The giving of the Spirit of God provides believers with the ongoing presence of God in everyday life. As John writes, "We know that we live in him and he in us, because he has given us of his Spirit" (1Jn 4:13). Finally, as human history is absorbed into the eschatological end-game of God, believers will enjoy the fullness of divine presence for eternity: "I heard a loud voice from the throne saying, 'Now the dwelling of God is with men, and he will live with them. They will be his people, and God himself will be with them and be their God'" (Rev 21:3).

3. Solomon's Dream Theophany and Request for Wisdom (2Ch 1:7–13)

⁷That night God appeared to Solomon and said to him, "Ask for whatever you want me to give you."

⁸Solomon answered God, "You have shown great kindness to David my father and have made me king in his place. ⁹Now, LORD God, let your promise to my father David be confirmed, for you have made me king over a people who are as numerous as the dust of the earth. ¹⁰Give me wisdom and knowledge, that I may lead this people, for who is able to govern this great people of yours?"

¹¹God said to Solomon, "Since this is your heart's desire and you have not asked for wealth, riches or honor, nor for the death of your enemies, and since you have not asked for a long life but for wisdom and knowledge to govern my people over whom I have made you king, ¹²therefore wisdom and knowledge will be given you. And I will also give you wealth, riches and honor, such as no king who was before you ever had and none after you will have."

¹³Then Solomon went to Jerusalem from the high place at Gibeon, from before the Tent of Meeting. And he reigned over Israel.

COMMENTARY

7 Solomon's dream (noted as such in the parallel passage at 1Ki 3) at Gibeon includes a theophany (appearance by God) and provides the setting for Solomon's reception of wisdom from above. Note that Solomon's temple building project is "framed" by revelatory dreams (here and at 7:12–22, following the completion of the temple).

8 Solomon's prayer (in answer to God's question) begins with an expression of gratefulness that focuses particularly on God's covenantal faithfulness and loyalty (ḥesed [GK 2876]; NIV: kindness) for his father David. Solomon phrases his thanksgiving in a way that draws on one element of the Davidic covenant ("[you] have made me king in his place"; cf. 2Sa 7:12), which will form the basis for the first part of Solomon's petition (see vv.9–10). Solomon's attitude of thanksgiving and declaration of God's covenantal faithfulness within a context of prayer and worship form a significant reminder and exhortation to the Chronicler's postexilic audience (cf. Solomon's prayer in conjunction with the dedication of the temple; 2Ch 6:14–42).

9 Following Solomon's expression of thanksgiving, Solomon asks for two things: (1) that God will continue to bring the fullness of the Davidic covenant to pass (v.9), and (2) that God will grant him wisdom and knowledge (v.10). As with the theme of divine favor (cf. 1:1), Solomon's words stress continuity with Yahweh's covenantal promises to David. In addition, the phraseology describing the people as being "as numerous as the dust of the earth" implies continuity with the Abrahamic covenant (cf. Ge 13:16; 28:14).

It is interesting to note that Solomon's words here together with the previous verse imply that while some aspects of the Davidic covenant have been fulfilled, other elements have not yet come to pass (compare David's prayer in 1Ch 17:16–27, esp. 17:23). In addition, both verses imply that Solomon understands himself as being part of God's promise to David. Indeed, the primary emphasis of the Davidic covenant articulated via the prophet Nathan in 1 Chronicles 17 (cf. 2Sa 7) focuses on a single son of David (namely, Solomon; see the full discussion at 1Ch 17:7–15 and related comments on 2Ch 6:4–11, 14–17; 21:7).

10 Solomon's request for wisdom and knowledge connects with his ability rightly to govern *God's people*. Although kings are typically thought of as sovereignly ruling over nations, people, and empires, in the case of the Israelite monarchy the Chronicler emphasizes that the people led by the king are *God's people*, the kingdom is *God's kingdom* (1Ch 17:14; 2Ch 13:8), the king is *God's son* (see 1Ch 22:10; 28:5–6), and the king sits on *God's throne* (1Ch 29:23; 2Ch 9:8; cf. Dillard, 12; Hill, 380).

In addition, in the broader context of 2 Chronicles Solomon's wisdom is interwoven with his construction of *God's temple*. As such, Solomon's wisdom connects him with Bezalel, who is also noted as being given wisdom and knowledge by God (lit., "wisdom of heart") for the task of constructing the tabernacle in the wilderness (cf. Ex 31:1–5; 35:30–35; 36:1). Perhaps with this motif of constructing a holy place for God's dwelling, Paul refers to himself as a "wise master builder" (1Co 3:10 [NASB]) within a context of discipleship and church building. Similarly, note Paul's role in ensuring that the right foundation has been established (namely, Christ; cf. Eph 2:19–22) and exhorting believers to construct their "temples" in holiness (cf. 1Co 6:12–20).

With respect to decision making, Solomon's request for wisdom is connected to his ability to govern (judge) God's people and facilitate an ordered, God-honoring society. It is significant to note that the term translated "govern" (GK 9149) is the verbal form of the noun "judge." The relationship between judgeship and kingship is stressed repeatedly at the outset of the Israelite monarchy (see 1Sa 8:1–22, esp. vv.5–6, 20). The overlap between the role of judge and king may imply that the office of king in Israel could be likened to a national (supratribal) judgeship. Along these lines, Solomon's first "wise" act is an act of judgeship (see 1Ki 3:16–28). In order to judge wisely, Solomon must be able to discern and apply God's will. This element of wisdom is paramount in leading a God-pleasing life for all believers (see Reflection, below).

11–13 Interestingly, God's response to Solomon's prayer focuses on the second part of that prayer—namely, the aspect of wisdom. God's response illustrates how he draws near to the humble and shows his propensity to do above and beyond what his people ask or think.

REFLECTION

The role of wisdom within one's spiritual life does not always receive the attention it ought — particularly with respect to the role of wisdom vis-à-vis the popular lingo of "spiritual formation." Biblical wisdom is not a matter of smarts, education, or the like, but rather the application of life-shaping divine truth that begins with the fear of the Lord (cf. Job 28:28; Ps 111:10; Pr 9:10). Biblical wisdom is much more functional than it is abstract and theoretical.

Put another way, wisdom involves cultivating a way of thinking — God's way — and helping others to do the same. Such thinking is part of the process of renewing our minds that facilitates Spirit-driven transformation, which (as Paul writes) enables us to discern God's good and perfect will (see Ro 12:2). Biblical wisdom involves skillfully applying God's Word to everyday life and thus connects intimately with one's spiritual walk, sanctification, spiritual fruit, and more. Note the close connection between wisdom and knowledge (the core of the second part of Solomon's prayer at 2Ch 1:10) and the spiritual life reflected in Paul's opening prayers for believers in Ephesus and Colossae:

> I keep asking that the God of our Lord Jesus Christ, the glorious Father, may give you the Spirit of wisdom and revelation, so that you may know him better. I pray also that the eyes of your heart may be enlightened in order that you may know the hope to which he has called you, the riches of his glorious inheritance in the saints. (Eph 1:17–18)

> For this reason, since the day we heard about you, we have not stopped praying for you and asking God to fill you with the knowledge of his will through all spiritual wisdom and understanding. And we pray this in order that you may live a life worthy of the Lord and may please him in every way: bearing fruit in every good work, growing in the knowledge of God, being strengthened with all power according to his glorious might so that you may have great endurance and patience, and joyfully giving thanks to the Father, who has qualified you to share in the inheritance of the saints in the kingdom of light. (Col 1:9–12)

As these verses show, biblical wisdom and knowledge directly connect to a growing intimacy with God, living a God-pleasing life, bearing spiritual fruit, and other key areas of the spiritual life. No wonder Moses prays that God will "teach us to number our days, that we may apply our hearts unto wisdom" (Ps 90:12 [KJV]), that Solomon himself writes, "wisdom is supreme; therefore get wisdom; though it cost all you have, get understanding" (Pr 4:7), and that Jesus defines the wise person as the one who heeds his words and practices them (Mt 7:24–27).

4. Solomon's Equine Force and Chariot Cities (2Ch 1:14)

¹⁴Solomon accumulated chariots and horses; he had fourteen hundred chariots and twelve thousand horses, which he kept in the chariot cities and also with him in Jerusalem.

COMMENTARY

14 Details of Solomon's horse and chariot trading are also found at 1 Kings 10:26, and the text at 2 Chronicles 9:25 (cf. 1Ki 4:26) adds the detail that Solomon had four thousand stalls for horses and chariots. In the light of the broader biblical background, Solomon's chariot-and-horse holdings are large, but within the range of those of other contemporary nations. In addition, the ratio of three horses to one chariot is what would be expected (two horses per chariot with one backup horse).

Prior to the time of Solomon, Israel exhibited no inclination to develop a chariot force or cavalry (cf. Jos 11:6–9; 1Ch 18:3–4). Solomon's development of a chariot force required a considerable amount of infrastructure, as reflected in the construction of chariot cities, the organization of workers (cf. 1Sa 8:11), and the organization of Solomon's taxation structure (which included provisions for chariot horses; cf. 1Ki 4:28). Solomon even arranged to have tribute paid in the form of horses (see 2Ch 9:24; 1Ki 10:25).

The text also notes that Solomon stationed chariots and horsemen in "chariot cities" as well as with him in Jerusalem. Solomon's chariot cities have long been identified as Hazor (in the far north), Megiddo (in the Jezreel Valley), and Gezer (in the Shephelah). Each of these cities has similar fortification plans that suggest a certain amount of state planning, including casemate walls (a double wall connected with crosswalls that can be used for storage or filled in during a siege) and gateways with three chambers on each side having nearly the same dimension.

The locations of these three sites are strategic and would facilitate protection of lucrative trade routes as well as defend against potential enemy incursions. Still, the biblical text never identifies these cities as chariot cities — they are simply mentioned as cities that Solomon fortified (cf. 1Ki 9:15–18; 2Ch 8:1–6). Other cities that have been mentioned as possible chariot cities include Lachish, Beersheba, Tell el-Hesi, Tell Abu Hawam, and Tell Qasile.

With respect to what has been called "Solomon's stables" at Megiddo, the original excavators at Megiddo identified an area with what seemed to be aisles and troughs as horse stables dating to the reign of Solomon. However, subsequent study has indicated that these structures likely date to the time of Omri and Ahab (a century or more later) and that they may even be the remains of storehouses rather than stables. Others argue that Solomon's stables lie beneath these later structures.

NOTE

14 The Hebrew text has "forty thousand" (אַרְבָּעִים אֶלֶף, *arbāʿîm ʾelep*) stalls at 1 Kings 4:26 [5:6], which the NIV rightly corrects to "four thousand," per 2 Chronicles 9:25 and the Septuagint (LXX) at 1 Kings 10:26.

A number of military texts from Egypt and Assyria from the fifteenth century to the ninth century BC make mention of chariot forces exceeding one thousand chariots. For example, the thirteenth-century battle between the Hittites and Egyptians involved about forty-five hundred chariots (*COS*, 2.5).

5. Solomon's Wealth (2Ch 1:15)

¹⁵The king made silver and gold as common in Jerusalem as stones, and cedar as plentiful as sycamore-fig trees in the foothills.

COMMENTARY

15 Israel's terrain is rocky throughout much of the country, especially in the Judean hill country where Jerusalem is located, and this provides a vivid image of the abundance of silver and gold enjoyed during Solomon's reign. Beyond gold and silver, Israel's prosperity during the reign of Solomon included the purchase of an abundance of the highly-valued cedar trees. The durability and pleasant scent of the cedar tree made it an especially popular wood for important building projects in the biblical world. However, cedar was rare in Israel and needed to be imported (usually from the Phoenician coast—cf. the OT expression "the cedars of Lebanon"), whereas the less-valued (see Isa 9:10) sycamore tree was widely distributed throughout Israel—enough to justify the appointment of an individual during David's reign who was in charge of olive and sycamore trees (1Ch 27:28). These raw materials (gold, silver, cedar) will occupy a central role in the construction of the temple.

6. Solomon's Regional Trade in Horses and Chariots (2Ch 1:16–17)

¹⁶Solomon's horses were imported from Egypt and from Kue—the royal merchants purchased them from Kue. ¹⁷They imported a chariot from Egypt for six hundred shekels of silver, and a horse for a hundred and fifty. They also exported them to all the kings of the Hittites and of the Arameans.

COMMENTARY

16 This verse reflects Solomon's skill in leveraging Israel's geographical location as a land bridge connecting the continents of Africa, Asia, and Europe. Although the idea of Solomon getting horses from Egypt is sometimes dismissed, there is clear evidence that regions of northeast Africa (Egypt, Kush, and Nubia) were known horse-breeding places both before and after the time of Solomon. A number of texts indicate that certain Egyptian horses (especially Nubian ones) were a large and prized breed, in contrast to the smaller horses common in the northern regions. Moreover, the prohibition against an Israelite king's getting horses from Egypt (Dt 17:14–20) would imply that a king would wish to do so! (see Y. Ikeda, "Solomon's Trade in Horses and Chariots in Its International Setting," in *Studies in the Period of David and Solomon and Other Essays* [ed. T. Ishida; Winona Lake, Ind.: Eisenbrauns, 1982], 215–38; L. A. Heidorn, "Horses of Kush," *JNES* 56 [1997]: 105–14).

With respect to Kue (Que), this term was not originally recognized as a place name (hence the translation "linen yarn" in the KJV and "in droves" in the ASV). It is now clear that Kue can be equated with Cilicia, in southeast Anatolia, known for ample pasturage for equine breeding.

17 As noted at v.16, Solomon's brokering of horses and chariots between Egypt to the south and Aramean states to the north reflects the growing international trade of ancient Israel, as well as Solomon's skill in leveraging Israel's geographical location as a land bridge connecting the kingdoms of the south (Egypt, Nubia, Kush) with those of the north (Aram/Syria, Mesopotamia, Hittite, etc.). While the data for prices of chariots are limited, it seems clear that the price point of 600 shekels of silver for a chariot is high. This fact suggests that these are no ordinary chariots, but rather richly appointed chariots utilized by royalty in processions and state ceremonies.

The price of 150 shekels paid by Solomon's royal merchants for a horse is on the high end of the broad range of horse prices, based on a variety of texts from the OT world. Ancient texts from this time record a wide range of prices corresponding to size, age, color, quality, pedigree, function, training, and the like (as is the case today). In short, the horses being brokered by Solomon's royal merchants were apparently of high quality.

Lastly, while Solomon's brokering of horses and chariots between Egypt and city-states to the north fits Israel's geographical location, Solomon's trading of horses between the northern region of Kue to Neo-Hittite and Aramean states seems unlikely at first since it would require that Solomon exerted control over these northern territories. Significantly, the Bible stresses that this is exactly what had begun during David's rule (cf. 2Sa 8:3–11; 1Ch 18:3–10). As a result, Solomon was able to build and fortify storage cities in Hamath (northern Aram/Syria), an ideal place for his "royal merchants" to rear and keep horses for trade because of its ample amount of pasturage, and at Tadmor, an oasis city on the main trade route between Mesopotamia and Canaan (2Ch 8:3–4; 1Ki 9:17).

NOTE

16–17 Instead of "Egypt" in these verses, some scholars have speculated that the text is referring to a different location in central Anatolia known as Musri. (The spelling in the Hebrew consonantal text would be similar: מצרי, *mṣry* [Musri]; מצרים, *mṣrym* [Egypt].) This view is partly due to the association of Musri and Que in at least one later Assyrian text. In this scenario, the horses are from the greater Anatolian area to the north, the chariots are from Egypt, and Solomon benefits from his location in the middle (see H. Tadmor, "Que and Musri," *IEJ* 11 [1961]: 143–50).

7. Solomon's Construction of the Jerusalem Temple (2Ch 2:1– 7:22)

a. Workers Conscripted and Phoenician Assistance Sought (2Ch 2:1–18)

¹Solomon gave orders to build a temple for the Name of the LORD and a royal palace for himself. ²He conscripted seventy thousand men as carriers and eighty thousand as stonecutters in the hills and thirty-six hundred as foremen over them.

³Solomon sent this message to Hiram king of Tyre:

"Send me cedar logs as you did for my father David when you sent him cedar to build a palace to live in. ⁴Now I am about to build a temple for the Name of the LORD my God and to dedicate it to him for burning fragrant incense before him, for setting out the consecrated bread regularly, and for making burnt offerings every morning and evening and on Sabbaths and New Moons and at the appointed feasts of the LORD our God. This is a lasting ordinance for Israel.

⁵"The temple I am going to build will be great, because our God is greater than all other gods. ⁶But who is able to build a temple for him, since the heavens, even the highest heavens, cannot contain him? Who then am I to build a temple for him, except as a place to burn sacrifices before him?

⁷"Send me, therefore, a man skilled to work in gold and silver, bronze and iron, and in purple, crimson and blue yarn, and experienced in the art of engraving, to work in Judah and Jerusalem with my skilled craftsmen, whom my father David provided.

⁸"Send me also cedar, pine and algum logs from Lebanon, for I know that your men are skilled in cutting timber there. My men will work with yours ⁹to provide me with plenty of lumber, because the temple I build must be large and magnificent. ¹⁰I will give your servants, the woodsmen who cut the timber, twenty thousand cors of ground wheat, twenty thousand cors of barley, twenty thousand baths of wine and twenty thousand baths of olive oil."

¹¹Hiram king of Tyre replied by letter to Solomon:

"Because the LORD loves his people, he has made you their king."

¹²And Hiram added:

"Praise be to the LORD, the God of Israel, who made heaven and earth! He has given King David a wise son, endowed with intelligence and discernment, who will build a temple for the LORD and a palace for himself.

¹³"I am sending you Huram-Abi, a man of great skill, ¹⁴whose mother was from Dan and whose father was from Tyre. He is trained to work in gold and silver, bronze and iron, stone and wood, and with purple and blue and crimson yarn and fine linen. He is

experienced in all kinds of engraving and can execute any design given to him. He will work with your craftsmen and with those of my lord, David your father.

¹⁵"Now let my lord send his servants the wheat and barley and the olive oil and wine he promised, ¹⁶and we will cut all the logs from Lebanon that you need and will float them in rafts by sea down to Joppa. You can then take them up to Jerusalem."

¹⁷Solomon took a census of all the aliens who were in Israel, after the census his father David had taken; and they were found to be 153,600. ¹⁸He assigned 70,000 of them to be carriers and 80,000 to be stonecutters in the hills, with 3,600 foremen over them to keep the people working.

COMMENTARY

1 The construction of Solomon's temple (building on David's preparations; cf. 1Ch 21–29) began in his fourth year as king (ca. 967 BC) during the spring month of Ziv (part of April and May) and was completed in the eleventh year of his reign (ca. 960 BC), a seven-year building process (cf. 1Ki 6:1; 2Ch 3:2). Unlike the account of Solomon's building activities in 1 Kings (e.g., 1Ki 7:1–12), the Chronicler only mentions Solomon's palace in passing. The central narrative focus of chs. 2–7 is the construction of the Jerusalem temple.

The temple is frequently described as a place for "the Name of the LORD" (cf. Dt 12:5). Such "name theology" includes aspects of God's character and his covenantal relationship with Israel and humankind. Thus the temple for Yahweh was to be a "house of prayer" not only for the Israelites, but also for all nations (cf. 2Ch 6:32–33; Isa 56:7). Although the temple facilitated closeness to and communion with the Creator God, the glory of God cannot be contained within its walls (2Ch 2:6).

In the broader context of 2 Chronicles, Solomon's wisdom is interwoven with his construction of *God's temple*. As such, Solomon's wisdom connects him with Bezalel, who is also noted as being given wisdom and knowledge by God (lit., "wisdom of heart"—obscured by the NIV's "skill") for the task of constructing the tabernacle in the wilderness (cf. Ex 31:1–5; 35:30–35; 36:1).

2 An ongoing challenge in the construction of large building projects in the biblical world was the supply of skilled and unskilled workers. Given this challenge, manpower requirements for such projects were commonly extracted from slaves, prisoners of war, and lower sectors of the society. In the case of larger empires the acquisition of human resources was a motivating factor for military excursions along with the perennial goal of obtaining financial assets such as gold and silver. In the aftermath of such military operations, both skilled and unskilled laborers would become part of an indentured workforce. In military annals from the biblical world, the number of individuals seized for work projects was listed together with other plunder obtained in battle.

One significant issue that arises from this passage is the question of whether the Israelites were subject to forced labor (corvée) in the context of Solomon's building projects. In the biblical text,

2 Chronicles 2:17–18 clarifies that the workers noted in 2:2 (153,600) were taken from the foreign population living within Israel. This number is connected with David's ill-fated census (cf. 1Ch 21:1–22:1). No doubt these workers were largely composed of the original people groups living in Canaan not conquered by the Israelites, including the Canaanites and Amorites, who eventually became forced labor (cf. Jos 16–17; Jdg 1; see the list at 2Ch 8:7–8).

Yet while the institution of corvée was certainly forced on foreign residents as part of Israel's royal projects, there is a lingering issue as to whether Solomon raised a corvée labor force from the Israelite population and, if so, whether it differed from that imposed on foreigners. On the one hand, texts such as the present verse and 2 Chronicles 8:9 (= 1Ki 9:22) indicate that Solomon did not impose slavery on Israelites. On the other hand, other texts (such as 1Ki 5:13) imply that Israelites were also conscripted for royal work projects (also cf. 1Ki 12:3–4), which would be consistent with the expectation of required national service in Samuel's description of kingship (see 1Sa 8:10–17).

Also, note the role of the difficult yoke of the northern kingdom in the breakup of the kingdom, including the stoning of the corvée officer Adoniram (cf. 1Ki 11:26–28; 12:1–18). The discovery of a seventh-century-BC seal that belonged to an Israelite corvée supervisor reflects the reality of this custom in ancient Israel. The title of the supervisor noted in this seal (something to the effect of "overseer of the corvée") is the same Hebrew expression as that found in the title noted of Adoniram (Adoram/Hadoram), the supervisor of corvée during the days of David, Solomon, and Rehoboam (cf. 2Sa 20:24; 1Ki 4:6; 5:14 [28]; 12:18; see N. Avigad, "The Chief of the Corvée," *IEJ* 30 [1980]: 170–73).

The difference may simply lie in the distinction between the slavery-style imposed labor placed on the foreign population and required national service expected of citizens. The drama of Rehoboam's confrontation with the northern kingdom elders may stem from the distinction between Jeroboam as an officer of the corvée (*sēbel*; GK 6023; cf. 1Ki 11:28) and Adoniram as the overseer of the forced labor gangs (*mas* or *mas-ʿōbēd*; see GK 4989 [cf. Jos 16:10; 1Ki 9:21; 2Ki 12:18; 2Ch 10:18]). This difference in terminology may well imply different categories of state workers. In short, Rehoboam may have been backing up his verbal rhetoric by sending the overseer of harsher work to the north (see A. F. Rainey, "Compulsory Labor Gangs in Ancient Israel," *IEJ* 20 [1970]: 191–202; *The Sacred Bridge*, 167–68; R. B. Dillard, "The Chronicler's Solomon," *WTJ* 43 [1980]: 289–300).

Certainly the conscription of citizens for national interests such as warfare and infrastructure projects was not uncommon in the biblical world. Similarly, special taxes might be imposed on the citizenry to help underwrite the cost of the raw materials and precious items associated with such projects. But the raising of a corvée from the citizenry carried a negative nuance that could be exploited by political rivals (as with Jeroboam), especially if northern tribes were treated differently from southern tribes.

3 The exchange of letters between Hiram and Solomon reflects standard ancient Near Eastern diplomatic correspondence. The shape and format of this letter may reflect an intent to highlight parallels between Solomon and Huram with Moses and Bezalel and Oholiab. As reflected here, such diplomatic correspondence typically contained expressions of respect, warmth, divine blessings, and even love. It is noteworthy that Solomon (like David; cf. 1Ch 22:1–5) readily seeks Phoenician assistance in the building of Yahweh's temple. The Phoenicians were noted for both supplying crucial building materials (cf. vv.7–8, below) as well as the technical expertise to construct buildings and to fashion raw materials into artistic objects. On cedar logs, see comment on vv.8–9.

4 This synopsis of aspects of temple worship reflects careful knowledge of worship instructions found in the Pentateuch, including the burning of incense (cf. Ex 30:1–8; see comments on 4:19–22), showbread (cf. Ex 25:30; Lev 24:5–9; see comments on 2Ch 4:8), sacrifice at morning and evening (cf. Ex 29:38–39; Nu 28–29), and calendar-oriented feasts and pilgrimages (cf. Ex 23:14–19; 31:3; Nu 10:10). Much of the calendar year of ancient Israel (as with other early societies) was largely organized around the agricultural cycle. Hence, various feasts were celebrated in conjunction with different points of the cycle of harvest(s), such as the seasonal feasts specified in Leviticus 23 and Numbers 28–29. But the notion of a weekly Sabbath was unique to Israel. Such calendar-based observances fostered a regular and systematic pattern of recognition of dependence on God and subsequent worship and celebration of his goodness.

5–6 Solomon's extensive efforts to build a temple for Yahweh (like those of David) are rooted in the greatness of God. Nonetheless, Solomon recognizes that no temple or even the sum of the created order ("the heavens, even the highest heavens") can house the glory of God. Instead, the temple will house what could be understood as a localization of divine glory. Solomon's response to the dilemma of building a dwelling for the infinite God "who is able … who then am I?" is similar to expressions of awe and humility expressed by Moses and David when they grasped the reality that they were unworthy and ill-equipped for the task God had set before them (cf. Ex 3:11; 2Sa 7:18).

7 The mention of precious metals and fabrics used in the construction of the Jerusalem temple underscores the notion that nothing but the best went into the construction of Yahweh's temple. Solomon readily seeks Phoenician assistance in sourcing and fashioning these precious metals and fabrics. Such localized specialties in crafts and technologies typically went hand in hand with the natural resources of a particular geographical area.

Thus, the resource of purple dye from the murex snail native to the shallow waters off the coast of Phoenicia and the plentiful supply of cedar trees in the interior of Phoenicia (Lebanon) facilitated guilds of craftsmen with finely developed skills for fashioning these items into high quality products. A veil woven of blue, purple, and scarlet yarn was also used in the Tent of Meeting (Ex 26:31–36).

8–9 Like the precious metals and materials sourced by Solomon (v.7), the Chronicler details the high quality wood used in the construction of Yahweh's temple. Cedar was an especially desired wood for important building projects such as temples and palaces, given its fragrance, durability, and ability to receive a fine finish. The area of Tyre (Phoenicia or Lebanon more broadly) was a well-known source for quality lumber such as cedar.

In addition to cedar, two other types of wood are mentioned. The first of these, "pine" (sometimes translated "cypress" or "fir"), was also a common type of tree in Phoenicia. The second type of wood, "algum" (a name transliterated from Hebrew and spelled "almug" in 1Ki 10:11–12; see NIV note on 2Ch 2:8) is uncertain but may be a type of sandalwood, ebony, or perhaps a pine or cypress variety, given the parallel of 1Ki 5:8. This lack of specificity aside, algum wood was likely a highly polishable quality wood, given its use in the temple project. This wood would be transported to Solomon via boats and rafts (see comments on 2Ch 2:16). Ultimately, the whole interior of the temple was covered in gold (cf. 3:4–7; 1Ki 6:15–22, 30).

10 Solomon's payment of agricultural products (and derivatives) is formidable and provides both rations for the Phoenician guest workers and payment for their services. The agricultural products supplied by Israel, such as wheat, barley, wine, and oil, were some of Israel's natural resources (especially of the northern tribal regions as well as portions of Transjordan), while the wood and fabrics supplied by Tyre were key natural resources of the region of Phoenicia. The cor (*kōr*) is a unit of dry measure equivalent to approximately 6.25 bushels, making the trade amounts in wheat and barley amount to 125,000 bushels each. The "bath" is a unit of liquid measure equivalent to approximately six gallons, making Solomon's shipments of wine and oil equal to about 120,000 gallons each.

11–12 Hiram's declaration of Yahweh's love for Solomon and his recognition of God's gracious elevation and enablement of Solomon as both ruler and temple builder are striking in the light of his position as king in a region dominated by the worship of Canaanite deities, such as Baal and Asherah. Comparable declarations are made by the Queen of Sheba (cf. 2Ch 9:7–9), the Persian king Cyrus (2Ch 36:22–23; cf. Ezr 1:2–3), the Babylonian king Nebuchadnezzar (cf. Da 4:34–35), and the (Medo-)Persian king Darius (cf. Da 6:25–27).

While these remarks could be understood as simply part of the protocol of ancient Near Eastern diplomacy, Yahweh's reception of praise and honor from Gentile nations and rulers both in a historical and an eschatological setting is reflected in a number of biblical passages. Hiram's words to Solomon closely connect with the content of David's prayer and interaction with God recorded at 1 Chronicles 22:6–13. On Solomon's wisdom noted by Hiram (v.12), see the comments on 2 Chronicles 1:10; 9:22–23.

13–14 The literal translation of Huram-Abi is "Huram my father," but the tag "father" is an honor-ific term rather than a familial designation. (Hiram's father's name was likely Abibaal.) While there are a variety of possibilities as to the specific nuance of this honorific designation, it seems that this title reflects Huram-Abi's position as a head craftsman or similar role that would be central to Solomon's building efforts. This seems to be the nuance of the term "father" used to describe Joseph's key role in Pharaoh's administration (cf. Ge 45:8) and used in the offer of religious leadership (albeit corrupt) extended to the Levite in Judges 17:10.

All this aside, note that Huram-Abi's main qualification is that he is a "[wise] man of great skill" (v.13), who will work with Solomon's "wise men" (v.14, lit. trans.). Unfortunately, the NIV obscures the passage's emphasis on wisdom by translating the Hebrew word for "wisdom" as "skill" in 2:13 and "wise men/wise ones" as "craftsmen" in 2:14, and it omits the second occurrence of "wise men/wise ones" in v.14.

15 On the agricultural items traded by Solomon, see comments on vv.7, 8–9, 10, above.

16 The transporting of wood by means of floating logs was a practical logistical option for city-states and nations that had access to seaports. The transportation of wood over sea is seen in Assyrian reliefs that show logs being towed by Phoenician ships. The ancient port city of Joppa is probably to be identified with Tell Qasile. Solomon's ability to transport this wood from the seaport inland to Jerusalem implies his full control over the coastal plain and Shephelah (low hills) from Joppa eastward to Jerusalem. The journey from Tyre to the port city of Joppa is approximately one hundred miles, and the trip inland to Jerusalem is another thirty or so miles. For more on Solomon's maritime trade, see comments on 8:17–18.

17–18 See the remarks on temple workers at 2:2, above.

NOTES

1 [1:18] In the Hebrew text (MT) 2 Chronicles 2:1–18=1 Chronicles 1:18–2 Chronicles 2:17.

3 [2] Note that Hiram (חִירָם, *Ḥîrām*) is technically spelled "Huram" (חוּרָם, *Ḥûrām*) in Chronicles. The spelling is typically "Hiram" elsewhere in the OT but is also attested as "Hirom" (חִירוֹם, *Ḥîrôm*) in 1 Kings 5:24, 32; 7:40.

10 [9] The selectivity of narrative accounts means that not all the details of such a transaction are given, such as the negotiation process and time line (as well as any adjustments in the arrangement made later), the payment particulars (i.e., one time vs. annual payment; government of Tyre vs. outsourced workers), and specific product details (such as the types, grades, and quantities of oils provided by Israel; the absence of barley and wine in Kings). On some of the differences in details recorded on this transaction versus that in Kings, see Dillard, 20, and Selman, 300–301.

13–14 [12–13] While the text here notes that the mother of Huram-Abi was from Dan and his father from the Phoenician city of Tyre, the parallel text in 1 Kings 7:14 connects the tribal affiliation of Huram-Abi with the tribe of Naphtali ("whose mother was a widow from the tribe of Naphtali") rather than Dan. This might relate to the Danite tribal migration (cf. Jdg 17–18), in which a portion of that tribe migrated to the Huleh Valley, north of the Sea of Galilee (Chinneroth) and adjacent to the tribal territory of Naphtali; that area was previously inhabited by those of Phoenician descent (cf. Jdg 18:7).

The texts of 1 Kings and 2 Chronicles may imply that Huram-Abi's mother had one parent from one tribe and one from the other, or one may indicate where the mother resided (i.e., Dan) and the other may indicate the tribal genealogy (i.e., Naphtali), as seen with the Ephraimite living in Benjamite territory in Judges 19–21. Either way, Huram-Abi functions as an ideal ethnic linchpin between Israel and Phoenicia.

17–18 [16–17] On the synoptic issues between these verses and 1 Kings 9:20–23 (cf. also 2Ch 8:7–10), the differences in numbers may reflect a different approach to describing the role(s) of the individuals in Solomon's workforce (e.g., worker/foreman/both). For different approaches on this issue, see Dillard, 22; Selman, 302–3; and Japhet, 546–47.

REFLECTION

The importance of a temple relates directly to the notion of *sacred space*—a place wherein the human realm could intersect with the divine realm and act as a conduit for divine presence and blessing. Since temples were understood to be sacred space (holy ground), the layout, features, and requisite rituals of these temples were connected to the attributes, provision, and strength of the deity. In Israel, the mediation of divine presence and holiness was the driving force behind the great importance attached to the proper procedures of approaching the holy space, usage of sanctified items, and human holiness.

The careful attention to the design of the temple structure and legal stipulations pertaining to entering the temple reflect the importance of properly navigating sacred space. Such procedure and protocols function to establish and maintain proper boundaries between the sacred and human realm. The importance of maintaining boundaries for sacred space is also reflected in the use of veils and doors to separate the innermost area of the temple. Such barriers reflect metaphysical and theological points of separation between a holy God and a fallen human race. Moreover, such barriers are reminders of the necessity of approaching—and worshiping— God on his terms within the temple context.

Likewise, for Christians our bodies are presented in the NT as temples in which the presence (Spirit) of God dwells (1Co 6:19). Thus Christians are admonished to keep their "temples" holy and pure in order to facilitate close communion and fellowship with God (cf. 1Co 6:15–20).

b. Temple Building Details (2Ch 3:1–17)

OVERVIEW

The design and features of Solomon's temple project have a number of points of connection (and shared vocabulary) with several Late Bronze and Iron Age temples throughout Syria and Canaan. The most distinguishing point of connection between these temples is that of the threefold (tripartite) structure within a rectangular footprint that included a courtyard (portico/porch; ʾûlām [GK 221]), a central temple chamber (main hall/ Holy Place; hêkāl [GK 2121]), and an inner sanctuary (Most Holy Place; dᵉbîr [GK 1808]).

This type of tripartite layout is reflected in more than two dozen Late Bronze and Iron Age temples in Syria and Canaan. For example, the ca. 1000 BC northwest-Syrian temple at the Aramaic capital of Ain Dara (ʾAin Derʿa) also featured a tripartite footprint, side storage rooms, and carved basalt orthostats with lions and cherubs/sphinxes (for more on cherubim, see comments on vv.10–13). In addition to similarity

in floor plan, there are several points of connection in the details of architecture and construction style, such as dressed masonry with interlaced wooden beams and ashlars (hewn blocks of building stone).

On the topic of Solomon's temple in its ancient Near Eastern context, see discussion and references in situ in F. J. Mabie, "2 Chronicles" (esp. chs. 3–7). See esp. W. G. Dever, *What Did the Biblical Writers Know and When Did They Know It? What Archaeology Can Tell Us about the Reality of Ancient Israel* (Grand Rapids: Eerdmans, 2001), esp. 145–55; V. Fritz, "What Archaeology Can Tell Us about Solomon's Temple," *BAR* 13 (1987): 38–49; E. Bloch-Smith, "'Who Is the King of Glory?' Solomon's Temple and Its Symbolism," in *Scripture and Other Artifacts* (ed. M. D. Coogan, J. C. Exum, and L. E. Stager; Louisville: Westminster John Knox, 1994), 18–31; Kitchen, 122–27. See sketches of Syro-Canaanite temples in Keel, 128–63.

¹Then Solomon began to build the temple of the LORD in Jerusalem on Mount Moriah, where the LORD had appeared to his father David. It was on the threshing floor of Araunah the Jebusite, the place provided by David. ²He began building on the second day of the second month in the fourth year of his reign.

³The foundation Solomon laid for building the temple of God was sixty cubits long and twenty cubits wide (using the cubit of the old standard). ⁴The portico at the front of

the temple was twenty cubits long across the width of the building and twenty cubits high.

He overlaid the inside with pure gold. [5]He paneled the main hall with pine and covered it with fine gold and decorated it with palm tree and chain designs. [6]He adorned the temple with precious stones. And the gold he used was gold of Parvaim. [7]He overlaid the ceiling beams, doorframes, walls and doors of the temple with gold, and he carved cherubim on the walls.

[8]He built the Most Holy Place, its length corresponding to the width of the temple—twenty cubits long and twenty cubits wide. He overlaid the inside with six hundred talents of fine gold. [9]The gold nails weighed fifty shekels. He also overlaid the upper parts with gold.

[10]In the Most Holy Place he made a pair of sculptured cherubim and overlaid them with gold. [11]The total wingspan of the cherubim was twenty cubits. One wing of the first cherub was five cubits long and touched the temple wall, while its other wing, also five cubits long, touched the wing of the other cherub. [12]Similarly one wing of the second cherub was five cubits long and touched the other temple wall, and its other wing, also five cubits long, touched the wing of the first cherub. [13]The wings of these cherubim extended twenty cubits. They stood on their feet, facing the main hall.

[14]He made the curtain of blue, purple and crimson yarn and fine linen, with cherubim worked into it.

[15]In the front of the temple he made two pillars, which together were thirty-five cubits long, each with a capital on top measuring five cubits. [16]He made interwoven chains and put them on top of the pillars. He also made a hundred pomegranates and attached them to the chains. [17]He erected the pillars in the front of the temple, one to the south and one to the north. The one to the south he named Jakin and the one to the north Boaz.

COMMENTARY

1 David's idea to build a temple for Yahweh was initially not well received by God, as God reminded David that he had not asked for a temple and reversed David's idea to build a "house" (temple) for God by promising to build a "house" (i.e., a *dynasty* [= the Davidic covenant]; see 1Ch 17:1–15) for David. Nevertheless, the notion of a temple was anticipated in Deuteronomy as an aspect of settling into the Promised Land (see Dt 12,

esp. 12:11). The location of the temple on Mount Moriah is connected with the place where Yahweh appeared to David (cf. 1Ch 21). In addition, this location is described as the place Yahweh has chosen for himself for the location of the temple (2Ch 7:12), a divine designation anticipated by Moses in Deuteronomy 12:5–7.

Moreover, the location of Mount Moriah connects with God's provision of a substitutionary sacrifice for Abraham (Ge 22), after which the area was called the "mountain of the LORD" (Ge 22:14). The location at the threshing floor of Ornan ("Araunah" in 2Sa 24:18) the Jebusite adds a further level of significance to the site of the Jerusalem temple. This location hearkens back to David and reminds the reader that the chosen place for the temple connects with both divine grace (following David's sin) and a divine encounter (via the angel of Yahweh). All told, careful narrative attention connects the temple location to Abraham, Moses, and David.

2 The construction of Solomon's temple began in his fourth year as king (ca. 967 BC), during the spring month of Ziv (part of April and May), and it was completed in the eleventh year of his reign (ca. 960 BC)—a seven-year building process (cf. 1Ki 6:1). The fact that Solomon did not begin the temple construction until his fourth year reflects the significant amount of preparation and planning that still needed to take place beyond that accomplished by David. It is tempting to see the length of time it took to build the temple against that of the royal palace (thirteen years) as a subtly negative commentary on Solomon's priorities, but this viewpoint is tenuous at best; the differing lengths of time may be due to a variety of factors (including the larger size of the royal palace complex).

3–4 The system of linear measurement used in ancient Israel was the result of standardizing commonly used measurements based on the length of fingers, hands (four fingers; length of the palm), and forearms. The Chronicler's statement here reveals that for his audience there would be more than one option for determining the length of the cubit. While it is difficult to unequivocally state which cubit standard the Chronicler had in view or to give the exact equivalent for the length of either cubit, the older standard cubit may have been somewhat longer (ca. 20–21 inches) than the more recent standard for the cubit (ca. 17–18 inches).

Note that references in Ezekiel may imply the opposite (see Eze 40:5; 43:13). If the older cubit is understood as the longer cubit and a mean of 20.6 inches is used per cubit, Solomon's temple would have been 103 feet long and 34 feet wide, not counting the portico/porch in the front of the temple (see 3:4), which measured 20 cubits by 20 cubits (ca. 34 feet by 34 feet). Alternatively, if the Chronicler intended the shorter cubit, the temple would have measured 87.5 feet long and 29 feet wide (using 17.5 inches to the cubit). By way of comparison, the playing area of a regulation tennis court (doubles playing area) is 78 feet long and 36 feet wide. On the length of the cubit, see A. Kaufman, "Determining the Length of the Medium Cubit," *PEQ* 116 (1984): 120–32.

The description of the temple is replete with notations of gold, both by type and amount of gold. Examples in the immediate context include "pure gold" (*zāhāb ṭāhôr*; v.4), "fine gold" (*zāhāb ṭôb*; v.5), gold from Parvaim (v.6), and, in the broader context of Chronicles, "pure gold" (*zāhāb sāgûr*; e.g., 2Ch 4:20, 22), "beaten gold" (*zāhāb šāḥûṭ*; e.g., 2Ch 9:15–16), and gold from Ophir (2Ch 8:18; cf. David's words in 1Ch 29:1–5). While the exact significance of each term (or geographic location) used in conjunction is not clear, the intended meaning and emphasis are clear—the temple built for Yahweh utilized top-quality gold sourced from locations known for special gold, reflecting the preciousness of God and the devotion of Solomon (also see comments on v.6).

5 The palm tree was a common symbol of fertility, life, and agricultural bounty in the ancient Near East and symbolized God's blessings on his people (see "Palm Tree," *DBI*, 622–23; for the related motifs of pillars, chains, and pomegranates found within the temple, see comments on vv.15–17).

6 The Chronicler emphasizes the precious metals, especially gold, that were used in the temple building project (cf. comments on 2:7–8; 4:20–22). The text mentions several grades of gold that increase in purity as one draws closer to the Most Holy Place (cf. Dillard, 28). The meaning of "Parvaim" is uncertain, but most likely it refers to a location, perhaps in Arabia. The reference to the gold of Parvaim, like the gold from Ophir (cf. below at 8:17–18), stresses the quality of the materials sourced for Yahweh's temple. The precious stones were likely used as settings (see 1Ch 29:2) or perhaps arranged together as a mosaic (also see comments on vv.3–4). Note that most Israelites would never see the inside of the temple, let alone the Most Holy Place. Thus these descriptions of the temple provided a window into this unseen world for the Israelites then, much as they do for us today.

7 See the remarks on cherubim at vv.10–13.

8–9 The dimensions of the Most Holy Place are approximately 30 feet by 30 feet (range = 28 by 28 to 35 by 35, depending on which cubit measurement is used; see comments on vv.3–4). This area is striking with respect to the amount of gold used throughout—600 talents in total. The weight of a talent is variously estimated in the range of 65 to 75 pounds. Using the midpoint of 70 pounds, the 600 talents used inside the Most Holy Place would be equivalent to 42,000 pounds (21 tons) of gold. The weight of the gold nails or pegs (50 shekels) amounts to more than one pound each. If these are the same nails as the type mentioned at 1 Chronicles 22:3, then the nails were made of iron and coated with gold.

While the amount of gold indicated here is obviously vast, it is not without points of comparison to other texts from the biblical world. For example, the tenth-century pharaoh Osorkon I enumerates gifts totaling 383 tons of gold and silver (over 10,000 talents of gold and silver) that he provided for the various gods and goddesses of Egypt, while Alexander the Great claims to have taken

7,000 tons (about 200,000 talents) from the Persian Empire. Thus, within this broader historical context, the amount of 600 talents of gold recorded in Solomon's temple project is not as staggering as it may at first seem (see A. R. Millard, "Does the Bible Exaggerate King Solomon's Golden Wealth?" *BAR* 15 [1989]: 20–34, and the sidebar in the article, "Where Did Solomon's Gold Go?" in Kitchen, 30).

The question of where Solomon got the gold used for the temple and where all the gold went in the subsequent history of Israel is a subject of much speculation. As noted later (see 9:13–14), Solomon received 666 talents of gold annually in tribute payments. Such tribute payments, along with profits earned via control of important trade routes, as well as taxation and gifts (such as the 120 talents of gold from both Hiram and the Queen of Sheba; cf. 1Ki 9:14; 2Ch 9:9), produced significant earnings for the Solomonic administration. Other royal ventures, such as the 450 talents of gold brought back from Ophir following the three-year maritime trading voyage (see 2Ch 8:18), also added to the royal treasury.

On the question of what happened to all this gold, as noted above, the Egyptian pharaoh Osorkon I contributed 383 talents of gold and silver as well as numerous other gifts to the gods and goddesses of Egypt in the tenth century BC (ca. 921 BC). This contribution took place early in Osorkon's reign (his fourth year), raising the question of the source of this immense amount of gold and silver, especially since there is no record of any significant campaigns by Osorkon during this time. When the broader historical context is considered, it becomes plausible that Osorkon I gifted gold and silver attained by his father pharaoh Shishak (Shoshenq I), who invaded the northern and southern kingdoms in ca. 926/925 BC a few years after the division of the kingdom and took "everything" from the house of Yahweh and the royal palace: "When Shishak king of Egypt attacked Jerusalem, he carried off the treasures of the temple of the LORD and the treasures of the royal palace. He took everything ...'" (2Ch 12:9).

In short, a vast portion of Solomon's gold recorded in the biblical material wound up in the hands of Pharaoh Shishak following this invasion. Not long after this invasion, Shishak died and his son Osorkon I assumed the throne in Egypt. Thus Osorkon I would have begun his reign with a large quantity of riches seized from Israel, which may well have formed the bulk of his contribution.

10–13 The two sculptured cherubim in the Most Holy Place receive little specific description beyond the coating of gold and the massive wingspan of the creatures. This wingspan extended the full width of the Most Holy Place (20 cubits; ca. 28 to 35 feet). The imagery of the expanse of the cherubim's wingspan may reflect God's comprehensive coverage (protection) over the ark, namely, his protective watching over his law delineating his covenantal relationship with Israel contained in the ark (cf. Ex 37:7–9; 1Ch 28:18; 2Ch 5:7–8). Moreover, the stationing of the cherubim facing the main temple hall suggests their fuller function as guardians of sacred space. Such a guardian role of cherubim is also reflected in Genesis 3:24, where these creatures guard the tree of life.

In the biblical material, cherubim are associated with the context and imagery of God's glory and majesty (cf. Ps 99:1; Eze 10:18–22). The imagery of fearsome supernatural creatures (referred to as sphinxes, griffins, and composite creatures) protecting the realm of deity and royalty is a common feature of temples and palaces from the biblical world. Within the broader motifs of the temple interior, the cherub, the sacred tree, and the lights conjure up images of the garden of Eden and the heavenly firmament (see E. Bloch-Smith, "Solomon's Temple: The Politics of Ritual Space," in *Sacred Time, Sacred Place: The Archaeology and the Religion of Israel*

[ed. B. M. Gittlen; Winona Lake, Ind.: Eisenbrauns, 2002]: 83–94).

14 The mention of a curtain or veil for the temple is unique to Chronicles, though there is precedent for a veil in the earlier tent of meeting (cf. Ex 26:31–37) and the later Herodian temple (cf. Mt 27:51). The use of curtains and veils reflects the importance of separating sacred space within a temple. The function of the curtain/veil was to provide a spatial barrier marking off the temple's Most Holy Place. Within the Israelite context, the curtain reflected the metaphysical and theological reality of separation between a holy God and a fallen human race. Moreover, such a barrier served to remind of the necessity of approaching—and worshiping—God on his terms. For the cherubim imagery within the curtain, see comments on vv.10–13.

15 The two free-standing pillars covered with polished bronze stationed in the front of Solomon's temple are noted as totaling 35 cubits in height (thus each column being about three stories tall). These impressive pillars included a five cubit (ca. 7 to 8 feet) capital, an ornate top that would have mostly overlapped the top portion of each pillar, thus creating a stylized arboreal image (see related remarks on palm trees at 3:5, chains and pomegranates at 3:16, and Asherah poles at 14:3).

16 The reference to interwoven chain ornamentation, also found on the pillar capitals (cf. 1Ki 7:17), may signify some aspect of God's character (such as his eternity) or may simply be a facet of Phoenician architectural style. These chains were at the top of the pillars and were adorned with pomegranates. Like palm trees (cf. 3:5), pomegranates were a symbol of fertility in the biblical world and one of the blessings of the Promised Land (cf. Dt 8:7–10). Images of pomegranates were frequently used as decorations of items as small as oil flasks and knives to as large as building columns. Note that the various motifs of the temple interior conjure up images of the primeval sacred space, the garden of Eden.

17 Since pillars were a common feature of a number of ancient Near East temples, it is possible that there is some type of symbolism expressed by these pillars, as perhaps implied by the names assigned to the pillars ("Jachin" and "Boaz," meaning approximately, "he establishes" and "strength is in him," respectively), representing Yahweh's undergirding of his nation and his people. In addition, the positioning of Josiah between the temple pillars may suggest that the pillars played a role in Israelite covenantal ceremonies (cf. 2Ki 23:1–3; see C. Meyers, "Jachin and Boaz in Religious and Political Perspectives," *CBQ* 45 [1983]: 167–78).

NOTES

14 The curtain/veil for the temple is only mentioned in this passage (the parallel passage in Kings notes only doors; cf. 1Ki 6:31–32; 2Ch 4:22). Presumably the temple had both doors and veil(s). The veil described here mimics the imagery and function of the veil of the tabernacle (Ex 26:31–33), specifically the separation of sacred space.

15 The notation in the account in 1 Kings 7:15 (cf. 2Ki 25:17) indicates a length of 18 cubits per pillar (36 total) versus the 35 cubits noted here (and in the LXX at Jer 52:21). The difference between the 18-cubit measurement and the 17.5-cubit measurement can be understood as related to the part of the capital extending beyond the top of the pillar (.5 cubit per pillar). For a helpful harmonization of 1 Kings 7:15–16 and 2 Chronicles 3:15, see Hill (388, fig. 9).

16–17 For a discussion of the many motifs featured in Solomon's temple, see E. Bloch-Smith, "Solomon's Temple: The Politics of Ritual Space," in *Sacred Time, Sacred Place: The Archaeology and the Religion of Israel* (ed. B. M. Gittlen; Winona Lake, Ind.: Eisenbrauns, 2002), 83–94. On broader ancient Near Eastern motifs reflected in Israel's worship, see Z. Zevit, *The Religions of Ancient Israel: A Synthesis of Parallelactic Approaches* (New York, N.Y.: Continuum, 2001). With respect to Christological connections implicit within the Israelite worship framework, see T. Longman III, *Immanuel in Our Place: Seeing Christ in Israel's Worship* (Phillipsburg, N.J.: P & R Publishing, 2001).

c. Temple Furnishings (2Ch 4:1–5:1)

¹He made a bronze altar twenty cubits long, twenty cubits wide and ten cubits high. ²He made the Sea of cast metal, circular in shape, measuring ten cubits from rim to rim and five cubits high. It took a line of thirty cubits to measure around it. ³Below the rim, figures of bulls encircled it—ten to a cubit. The bulls were cast in two rows in one piece with the Sea. ⁴The Sea stood on twelve bulls, three facing north, three facing west, three facing south and three facing east. The Sea rested on top of them, and their hindquarters were toward

the center. [5]It was a handbreadth in thickness, and its rim was like the rim of a cup, like a lily blossom. It held three thousand baths.

[6]He then made ten basins for washing and placed five on the south side and five on the north. In them the things to be used for the burnt offerings were rinsed, but the Sea was to be used by the priests for washing.

[7]He made ten gold lampstands according to the specifications for them and placed them in the temple, five on the south side and five on the north.

[8]He made ten tables and placed them in the temple, five on the south side and five on the north. He also made a hundred gold sprinkling bowls.

[9]He made the courtyard of the priests, and the large court and the doors for the court, and overlaid the doors with bronze. [10]He placed the Sea on the south side, at the southeast corner.

[11]He also made the pots and shovels and sprinkling bowls.

So Huram finished the work he had undertaken for King Solomon in the temple of God:

[12]the two pillars;

the two bowl-shaped capitals on top of the pillars;

the two sets of network decorating the two bowl-shaped capitals on top of the pillars;

[13]the four hundred pomegranates for the two sets of network (two rows of pomegranates for each network, decorating the bowl-shaped capitals on top of the pillars);

[14]the stands with their basins;

[15]the Sea and the twelve bulls under it;

[16]the pots, shovels, meat forks and all related articles.

All the objects that Huram-Abi made for King Solomon for the temple of the Lord were of polished bronze. [17]The king had them cast in clay molds in the plain of the Jordan between Succoth and Zarethan. [18]All these things that Solomon made amounted to so much that the weight of the bronze was not determined.

[19]Solomon also made all the furnishings that were in God's temple:

the golden altar;

the tables on which was the bread of the Presence;

[20]the lampstands of pure gold with their lamps, to burn in front of the inner sanctuary as prescribed;

[21]the gold floral work and lamps and tongs (they were solid gold);

[22]the pure gold wick trimmers, sprinkling bowls, dishes and censers; and the gold doors of the temple: the inner doors to the Most Holy Place and the doors of the main hall.

[5:1]When all the work Solomon had done for the temple of the Lord was finished, he brought in the things his father David had dedicated—the silver and gold and all the furnishings—and he placed them in the treasuries of God's temple.

COMMENTARY

1 The bronze altar, the centerpiece of the sacrificial system, was a raised platform on which offerings would be made to Yahweh. The dimensions of Solomon's altar (20 by 20 cubits; ca. 30–35 feet square) may include the size of the base, with the altar itself rising 10 cubits (ca. 15–17 feet) in a terraced fashion. The placement of the altar in the front of the temple suggests that God can only be approached once atonement has been made. A miniature example of a horned altar (used as an incense altar) was discovered at Megiddo (cf. *ANEP*, fig. 575).

2–4 The sea of cast metal (commonly referred to as the "Bronze Sea") was a massive caldron measuring in the vicinity of 15–17 feet across and 7–9 feet high (for details on volume, see comments on v.5; for issues regarding the size of a cubit, see comments on 3:3–4) and was used by the priests for washing (v.6). Beyond the huge size, the potential imagery of this "Sea" is compelling in the light of the biblical world, particularly with respect to the motifs of the sea and of bulls.

With respect to the motif of the sea, the connection between the divine realm, creation, and a watery abyss is present in a number of ancient Near Eastern texts. Such accounts feature a battle for preeminence between the storm god and the sea god (or goddess). The narration of these battles portrays the struggle against chaos (*Chaoskampf*) and the (ultimate) establishment of order (political, social, etc.). With respect to the motif of bulls, the bronze sea is replete with bull imagery, including the 300 bull images (ten per cubit) inscribed below the rim of the container and the twelve larger bulls on which the container rested.

The use of bulls catches the attention of OT scholars, given the connection between bovine animals and deities of the biblical world, such as the Canaanite Baal Hadad, Egyptian Hathor, and Babylonian Marduk. In addition, the biblical world has a number of deities associated with a cosmic ocean, such as the Canaanite deity Yamm (the Semitic term for "sea"; cf. the bronze "Sea"). In the OT, the understanding of the cosmic deep extends to the realm of God, as Yahweh is described as sitting enthroned over the flood as king forever (Ps 29:10) and praised as the one who "lays the beams of his upper chambers in [the] waters" (Ps 104:3). Such descriptions underscore Yahweh's mastery over the seemingly uncontrollable seas and thus foster trust and faith in Yahweh's power. The motif of the subjugation of chaotic forces in biblical passages connects with the notion that the created realm was founded on Yahweh's faithfulness, righteousness, and justice (cf. Pss 89; 93; see F. J. Mabie, "Chaos and Death," in *DOTWPW*).

5 The capacity of the bronze Sea is noted at 3,000 baths, which would amount to approximately 17,400 gallons (comparable to the capacity of a large above-ground swimming pool). The bronze Sea is described as being a handbreadth in thickness. A handbreadth was the measurement of the width of the palm (four fingers) and thus about three inches.

6 The ten basins used for washing each held forty baths of water (approximately 230 gallons; cf. 1Ki 7:38). These ten basins were used for the ceremonial washing of the utensils used within the sacrificial system. By contrast, the bronze Sea (see vv.2–4) was utilized for the ritual cleansing of priests involved in temple service. Both of these facets of washing reflect the importance of purity and cleanliness when approaching the presence of a holy God. For a description of the stands used in conjunction with these basins see 1 Kings 7:27–39.

7 While the tabernacle constructed during the time of Moses had one golden lampstand, the Solomonic temple had ten. The light from these golden lampstands against a room coated in fine gold would create a stunning reflection that would remind one of the brilliance and presence of the Creator God. As with the account of Moses' building of the tabernacle in the wilderness (Ex 25–40), the text frequently reminds the reader that these things were being done "according to the specifications for them," reflecting a careful concern that everything be done in accordance with God's will.

Like the tenfold increase in golden lampstands from tabernacle to temple (see v.7), there is also a tenfold increase in tables in the temple. Presumably, one of these tables was used to display the bread of the Presence (cf. 2Ch 4:19). The bread of the Presence is called "consecrated bread" at 2:4 and is sometimes translated as "showbread." Within the temple the showbread was arranged on the gold-covered acacia table by the Levites and replaced each Sabbath (cf. 1Ch 9:32; 23:29–32). The perpetual offering of a food item such as consecrated bread reflects a visible expression of the agricultural blessings given by God (cf. Ex 25:30; Lev 24:5–9) and was fundamentally an aspect of gratefulness and worship. The imagery of light via the lampstands (2Ch 4:7) and that of bread/food (cf. 4:19) reflect God's provision for his people as well as the blessing of obedience (cf. Dt 8:1–18).

9 Although not mentioned in the Chronicler's account, the courtyard for the priests may have been elevated to facilitate the public reading of God's Word (see Jer 36:10). The larger court was accessible to the general Israelite population of worshipers and pilgrims. The design of the tabernacle also included a single courtyard (cf. Ex 27:9–19). The later tradition of a court for women is not found within the biblical material.

10 For remarks on the Sea, see comments on vv.2–5.

11a The pots and shovels noted here were made of polished bronze (cf. v.16). Such utensils were used for the proper collection and cleanup of coals, ashes, blood, and similar items following a sacrifice, reflecting the importance of ceremonial purity and procedure. Such items are frequent discoveries in archaeological digs. For the various gold utensils within the temple, see comments on vv.19–22.

11b–17 This list summarizes the items fabricated by the Phoenician craftsman Huram-Abi for the Jerusalem temple (cf. vv.19–22). Thus, for comments on pillars and capitals (v.12), see 3:15–17; for comments on pomegranates (v.13), see 3:16; for comments on stands and basins (v.14), see 4:6; for comments on the Bronze sea and the twelve bulls (v.15), cf. 4:2–5; and for comments on pots, shovels, and meat forks (v.16a), see 4:11a.

The metalworking for the bronze objects of the Jerusalem temple (v.17) took place on the eastern side of the Jordan Valley midway between the Dead Sea and the Sea of Chinnereth (Galilee), perhaps under the supervision of Phoenician craftsman (2Ch 4:16). During this time, bronze objects were manufactured by extracting copper and mixing the copper with a small amount of tin for hardness (producing an alloy). Excavations at the Edomite Feinan mines (Khirbet en-Nahas) to the southeast of the Dead Sea have revealed numerous copper mines and copper-production slags dating from the eleventh to ninth centuries BC. Given Israel's hegemony over Edom, it is possible that these mines were used for Solomon's building projects.

Another significant copper mining site is Timna, located about seventy miles south of the Feinan mines on the western side of Arabah Valley, about fifteen miles north of Ezion Geber (cf. J. J. Bimson, "King Solomon's Mines? A Reassessment of Finds in the Aravah," *TynBul* 32 [1981]: 123–49; E. A. Knauf,

"King Solomon's Copper Supply," in *Phoenicia and the Bible* [Leuven: Orientalistiek, 1991]: 167–86).

18 While the Chronicler has been inclined to give the numbers associated with various items connected with the temple project, including the number of temple workers (2:17–18), the amount of gold used in the Most Holy Place (3:8), and the amount of water held by the Sea of cast metal (4:5), the amount of bronze used for the variety of items made for the temple was, effectively, beyond measure.

19–22 This is another summary statement of items fabricated for temple service (cf. vv.11–18), here focusing on items made of (or coated with) gold. The golden altar (v.19) is most likely that which was used to burn incense (for the bronze sacrificial altar, see comments on v.1). As with many items of the temple, the tabernacle in the wilderness constructed by Moses also had a golden altar of incense (see Ex 37:25–29). In addition to the gold altar, censers (v.22) were also used to hold and burn incense (cf. Ex 30:7; Lev 4:7; 16:12; for an example of an incense altar, see *ANEP*, fig. 575).

Incense bowls and incense altars were common in ancient Near Eastern temples, and incense censors were a part of the priestly array of various cultures of the biblical world. The burning of incense was a special spiritual function limited to priests

(cf. Ex 30:1–10; Nu 16:40; for discussion of the usage of incense, spices, and other fragrant items, see M. Haran, *Temples and Temple-Service in Ancient Israel* [Oxford: Clarendon, 1978], 230–45; for comments on the tables and bread of the Presence [v.19], see v.8; for comments on the lampstands [v.20], see v.7).

The gold noted in conjunction with the altar utensils (vv.21–22) reflects their supreme importance in the sacrificial system. No expense was spared in even the smallest details of the construction and furnishing of the temple complex (also see discussion at 2:7–8). The gold doors of the temple (v.22), like the veil (see comments on 3:7), were both works of art and functional means of protecting holy space (also see comments on 2:1).

5:1 Following the two summary sections of items crafted for the Jerusalem temple by Huram-Abi (see comments on 4:11–18, 19–22), the Chronicler notes that the items and treasures dedicated by his father David were likewise brought into the temple. The mention of David underscores the continuity between the two kings as well as the outworking of David's temple preparations (cf. 1Ch 18:10–11; 22:2–19; 29:2–5). Following this final step of furnishing, the next three chapters (2Ch 5:2–7:22) will highlight the dedication of the temple.

NOTES

1 See the Note on v.5.

2–4 Details of bulls aside, the reference to "bulls" below the rim differs from the description of "gourds" given at 1 Kings 7:24 and may suggest a textual issue. Note the similarity of these terms in Hebrew — בְּקָרִים, *beqārîm* ("bulls"), and פְּקָעִים, *peqāʿîm* ("gourds"). Alternatively, the description in Kings of these ornamental animal heads may simply be less specific.

5 The parallel text at 1 Kings 7:26 refers to two thousand baths, prompting a variety of explanations for the difference, including a different perspective in measuring (e.g., cylindrical in Chronicles versus hemispherical in Kings) and scribal/textual issues (which usually prefer the text in Kings). The dimensions noted for the basin are slightly different from what would be expected in light of *pi*, most likely a factor of the handbreath of thickness or some degree of rounding in the numbers reported here (see Dillard, 35).

d. Deposit of the Ark of the Covenant and Temple Dedication (2Ch 5:2 – 7:22)

OVERVIEW

The dedication of the temple is essentially one literary unit, beginning with the assembly of the leaders of Israel in 5:2 and closing with the dismissal of this assembly in 7:10, followed by a postscript indicating Yahweh's appearance and response to Solomon's temple-dedication prayer (7:11 – 22). The stress of Yahweh's response to Solomon's dedicatory prayer is that Deuteronomic covenantal blessings can be obtained and renewed through repentance, humility, and prayer. This emphatic message of hope and available reconciliation with God would have special significance for the Chronicler's postexilic audience, whose *Sitz im Leben* (life context) follows on the heels of the outworking of the divine threats noted in 7:19 – 22.

²Then Solomon summoned to Jerusalem the elders of Israel, all the heads of the tribes and the chiefs of the Israelite families, to bring up the ark of the Lord's covenant from Zion, the City of David. ³And all the men of Israel came together to the king at the time of the festival in the seventh month.

⁴When all the elders of Israel had arrived, the Levites took up the ark, ⁵and they brought up the ark and the Tent of Meeting and all the sacred furnishings in it. The priests, who were Levites, carried them up; ⁶and King Solomon and the entire assembly of Israel that had gathered about him were before the ark, sacrificing so many sheep and cattle that they could not be recorded or counted.

⁷The priests then brought the ark of the Lord's covenant to its place in the inner sanctuary of the temple, the Most Holy Place, and put it beneath the wings of the cherubim. ⁸The cherubim spread their wings over the place of the ark and covered the ark and its carrying poles. ⁹These poles were so long that their ends, extending from the ark, could be seen from in front of the inner sanctuary, but not from outside the Holy Place; and they are still there today. ¹⁰There was nothing in the ark except the two tablets that Moses had placed in it at Horeb, where the Lord made a covenant with the Israelites after they came out of Egypt.

¹¹The priests then withdrew from the Holy Place. All the priests who were there had consecrated themselves, regardless of their divisions. ¹²All the Levites who were musicians — Asaph, Heman, Jeduthun and their sons and relatives — stood on the east side of the altar, dressed in fine linen and playing cymbals, harps and lyres. They were accompa-

nied by 120 priests sounding trumpets. [13]The trumpeters and singers joined in unison, as with one voice, to give praise and thanks to the LORD. Accompanied by trumpets, cymbals and other instruments, they raised their voices in praise to the LORD and sang:

"He is good;
　his love endures forever."

Then the temple of the LORD was filled with a cloud, [14]and the priests could not perform their service because of the cloud, for the glory of the LORD filled the temple of God.

[6:1]Then Solomon said, "The LORD has said that he would dwell in a dark cloud; [2]I have built a magnificent temple for you, a place for you to dwell forever."

[3]While the whole assembly of Israel was standing there, the king turned around and blessed them. [4]Then he said:

"Praise be to the LORD, the God of Israel, who with his hands has fulfilled what he promised with his mouth to my father David. For he said, [5]'Since the day I brought my people out of Egypt, I have not chosen a city in any tribe of Israel to have a temple built for my Name to be there, nor have I chosen anyone to be the leader over my people Israel. [6]But now I have chosen Jerusalem for my Name to be there, and I have chosen David to rule my people Israel.'

[7]"My father David had it in his heart to build a temple for the Name of the LORD, the God of Israel. [8]But the LORD said to my father David, 'Because it was in your heart to build a temple for my Name, you did well to have this in your heart. [9]Nevertheless, you are not the one to build the temple, but your son, who is your own flesh and blood — he is the one who will build the temple for my Name.'

[10]"The LORD has kept the promise he made. I have succeeded David my father and now I sit on the throne of Israel, just as the LORD promised, and I have built the temple for the Name of the LORD, the God of Israel. [11]There I have placed the ark, in which is the covenant of the LORD that he made with the people of Israel."

[12]Then Solomon stood before the altar of the LORD in front of the whole assembly of Israel and spread out his hands. [13]Now he had made a bronze platform, five cubits long, five cubits wide and three cubits high, and had placed it in the center of the outer court. He stood on the platform and then knelt down before the whole assembly of Israel and spread out his hands toward heaven. [14]He said:

"O LORD, God of Israel, there is no God like you in heaven or on earth — you who keep your covenant of love with your servants who continue wholeheartedly in your way. [15]You have kept your promise to your servant David my father; with your mouth you have promised and with your hand you have fulfilled it — as it is today.

[16]"Now LORD, God of Israel, keep for your servant David my father the promises you made to him when you said, 'You shall never fail to have a man to sit before me on the

throne of Israel, if only your sons are careful in all they do to walk before me according to my law, as you have done.' [17]And now, O LORD, God of Israel, let your word that you promised your servant David come true.

[18]"But will God really dwell on earth with men? The heavens, even the highest heavens, cannot contain you. How much less this temple I have built! [19]Yet give attention to your servant's prayer and his plea for mercy, O LORD my God. Hear the cry and the prayer that your servant is praying in your presence. [20]May your eyes be open toward this temple day and night, this place of which you said you would put your Name there. May you hear the prayer your servant prays toward this place. [21]Hear the supplications of your servant and of your people Israel when they pray toward this place. Hear from heaven, your dwelling place; and when you hear, forgive.

[22]"When a man wrongs his neighbor and is required to take an oath and he comes and swears the oath before your altar in this temple, [23]then hear from heaven and act. Judge between your servants, repaying the guilty by bringing down on his own head what he has done. Declare the innocent not guilty and so establish his innocence.

[24]"When your people Israel have been defeated by an enemy because they have sinned against you and when they turn back and confess your name, praying and making supplication before you in this temple, [25]then hear from heaven and forgive the sin of your people Israel and bring them back to the land you gave to them and their fathers.

[26]"When the heavens are shut up and there is no rain because your people have sinned against you, and when they pray toward this place and confess your name and turn from their sin because you have afflicted them, [27]then hear from heaven and forgive the sin of your servants, your people Israel. Teach them the right way to live, and send rain on the land you gave your people for an inheritance.

[28]"When famine or plague comes to the land, or blight or mildew, locusts or grasshoppers, or when enemies besiege them in any of their cities, whatever disaster or disease may come, [29]and when a prayer or plea is made by any of your people Israel — each one aware of his afflictions and pains, and spreading out his hands toward this temple — [30]then hear from heaven, your dwelling place. Forgive, and deal with each man according to all he does, since you know his heart (for you alone know the hearts of men), [31]so that they will fear you and walk in your ways all the time they live in the land you gave our fathers.

[32]"As for the foreigner who does not belong to your people Israel but has come from a distant land because of your great name and your mighty hand and your outstretched arm — when he comes and prays toward this temple, [33]then hear from heaven, your dwelling place, and do whatever the foreigner asks of you, so that all the peoples of the earth may know your name and fear you, as do your own people Israel, and may know that this house I have built bears your Name.

[34]"When your people go to war against their enemies, wherever you send them, and when they pray to you toward this city you have chosen and the temple I have built for your Name, [35]then hear from heaven their prayer and their plea, and uphold their cause. [36]When they sin against you — for there is no one who does not sin — and you become angry with them and give them over to the enemy, who takes them captive to a land far away or near; [37]and if they have a change of heart in the land where they are held captive, and repent and plead with you in the land of their captivity and say, 'We have sinned, we have done wrong and acted wickedly'; [38]and if they turn back to you with all their heart and soul in the land of their captivity where they were taken, and pray toward the land you gave their fathers, toward the city you have chosen and toward the temple I have built for your Name; [39]then from heaven, your dwelling place, hear their prayer and their pleas, and uphold their cause. And forgive your people, who have sinned against you.

[40]"Now, my God, may your eyes be open and your ears attentive to the prayers offered in this place.

[41] "Now arise, O LORD God, and come to your resting place,
    you and the ark of your might.
  May your priests, O LORD God, be clothed with salvation,
    may your saints rejoice in your goodness.
[42] O LORD God, do not reject your anointed one.
    Remember the great love promised to David your servant."

[7:1]When Solomon finished praying, fire came down from heaven and consumed the burnt offering and the sacrifices, and the glory of the LORD filled the temple. [2]The priests could not enter the temple of the LORD because the glory of the LORD filled it. [3]When all the Israelites saw the fire coming down and the glory of the LORD above the temple, they knelt on the pavement with their faces to the ground, and they worshiped and gave thanks to the LORD, saying,

  "He is good;
    his love endures forever."

[4]Then the king and all the people offered sacrifices before the LORD. [5]And King Solomon offered a sacrifice of twenty-two thousand head of cattle and a hundred and twenty thousand sheep and goats. So the king and all the people dedicated the temple of God. [6]The priests took their positions, as did the Levites with the LORD's musical instruments, which King David had made for praising the LORD and which were used when he gave thanks, saying, "His love endures forever." Opposite the Levites, the priests blew their trumpets, and all the Israelites were standing.

[7]Solomon consecrated the middle part of the courtyard in front of the temple of the LORD, and there he offered burnt offerings and the fat of the fellowship offerings, because

the bronze altar he had made could not hold the burnt offerings, the grain offerings and the fat portions.

[8]So Solomon observed the festival at that time for seven days, and all Israel with him — a vast assembly, people from Lebo Hamath to the Wadi of Egypt. [9]On the eighth day they held an assembly, for they had celebrated the dedication of the altar for seven days and the festival for seven days more. [10]On the twenty-third day of the seventh month he sent the people to their homes, joyful and glad in heart for the good things the LORD had done for David and Solomon and for his people Israel.

[11]When Solomon had finished the temple of the LORD and the royal palace, and had succeeded in carrying out all he had in mind to do in the temple of the LORD and in his own palace, [12]the LORD appeared to him at night and said:

"I have heard your prayer and have chosen this place for myself as a temple for sacrifices.

[13]"When I shut up the heavens so that there is no rain, or command locusts to devour the land or send a plague among my people, [14]if my people, who are called by my name, will humble themselves and pray and seek my face and turn from their wicked ways, then will I hear from heaven and will forgive their sin and will heal their land. [15]Now my eyes will be open and my ears attentive to the prayers offered in this place. [16]I have chosen and consecrated this temple so that my Name may be there forever. My eyes and my heart will always be there.

[17]"As for you, if you walk before me as David your father did, and do all I command, and observe my decrees and laws, [18]I will establish your royal throne, as I covenanted with David your father when I said, 'You shall never fail to have a man to rule over Israel.'

[19]"But if you turn away and forsake the decrees and commands I have given you and go off to serve other gods and worship them, [20]then I will uproot Israel from my land, which I have given them, and will reject this temple I have consecrated for my Name. I will make it a byword and an object of ridicule among all peoples. [21]And though this temple is now so imposing, all who pass by will be appalled and say, 'Why has the LORD done such a thing to this land and to this temple?' [22]People will answer, 'Because they have forsaken the LORD, the God of their fathers, who brought them out of Egypt, and have embraced other gods, worshiping and serving them — that is why he brought all this disaster on them.'"

COMMENTARY

2 Solomon's gathering of leaders underscores the image of national unity and oneness at the dedication of the temple. A similar group of national lead- ers accompanied David in moving the ark of the covenant to Jerusalem (cf. 1Ch 13–16; cf. 28:1–8). The ark of the covenant is being relocated the short distance (about 500 meters) from the City of David (Zion) to the new palace-temple complex.

3 The festival of the seventh month is the autumn Feast of Tabernacles. Given the detail of 1 Kings 6:38 that the temple was completed in the eight month of Solomon's eleventh year, this would imply a gap of about eleven months from the time of completion to the dedicatory celebrations. This long stretch of time allowed for a vast amount of planning and preparation for the enormous dedicatory festivities as well as planning for the journey of the many attendees.

4–6 Solomon employs both Levites and priests for the handling and moving of the sacred objects, including the ark and the Tent of Meeting (the tabernacle in the wilderness). The mention of these groups implies differing responsibilities. In short, every priest must be a Levite; yet not every Levite would function as a priest. Levites (v.4) are most commonly described as musicians and as servants to (Levitical/Aaronic) priests (cf. Nu 8:19). As the Chronicler writes, "The duty of the Levites was to help Aaron's descendants in the service of the temple of the LORD: to be in charge of the courtyards, the side rooms, the purification of all sacred things and the performance of other duties at the house of God" (1Ch 23:28; cf. 6:48; 23:28–32). Thus Levites may have titles such as door/gatekeepers, scribes, secretaries, and temple work supervisors (cf. 2Ch 34:13).

In addition, Levites had the special responsibility of carrying the ark (Nu 4:15–33; Dt 10:8–9; cf. 1Ch 15:14–15), a reality no doubt reflected by the last passage. Beyond this, Levites performed musical service—which became one of their primary responsibilities once the ark of God was in its designated place as organized by David (cf. 1Ch 6:31–48; 23:2–32; 25:1–8).

By contrast, priests (vv.5, 7) were descendants of the Aaronic Levitical family line (Ex 28:1) and were primarily responsible for the matters of temple service, particularly the sacrificial system. They were also responsible for the ark at Jerusalem (cf. 1Ch 16:37–42). In addition, priests had the responsibilities of discerning between clean and unclean and teaching the Israelites the ways of God (cf. Lev 10:10–11 and the lament of Mal 2:1–9).

Last, while Levites are primarily associated with musical activity, there is one area of music set aside for priests—the blowing of trumpets (cf. v.13 below; 1Ch 15:24). The sacrifices in abundance (v.6) mirror and magnify those brought by David when he brought the ark of God to Jerusalem (cf. 1Ch 16:1–2). On the caretaking of priests and Levites by the community through offerings and tithes, see comments on 2 Chronicles 31:4–8.

7–11 The Aaronic/Levitical priests (v.7) take over from the Levites in bringing the ark into the Holy of Holies (= Most Holy Place; $d^eb\hat{i}r$ [GK 1808]; see the Overview to 3:1–17). The ark was placed between the wings of the cherubim within the Most Holy Place (vv.7–8). The wingspan of these cherubim extended the full width of the Most Holy Place (20 cubits; ca. 30–35 feet). The imagery of the expanse of the cherubs' wingspan over the ark likely reflects God's complete protection over the ark and the sacred inner sanctum (as holy space). This protection over the ark would visually portray God's protection over his Word, especially his covenantal relationship with Israel as inscribed on the two tablets placed within the ark (v.10).

No remark is made concerning the other two items previously kept in the ark, namely, the omer of manna (Ex 16:32–34) and Aaron's rod (Nu 17:10). It is possible that these items were removed or lost during the ark's transient period (including years in Philistine possession). The remark on priests' being consecrated regardless of their divisions (v.11) is a statement of unity that trumps established organizational structures established for the priesthood (cf.

1Ch 24: 3–19; for further discussion on the cherubim, see comments on 2Ch 3:10–13).

12–13 Music was an important dimension of worship in ancient Near Eastern cultures, and a wide variety of musical instruments were employed. Music was also used to motivate work, as attested in the use of music in the repairing and restoration of Yahweh's temple during Josiah's reforms (34:12–13). Stringed instruments ranged from those with three to ten strings mounted on wooden frames and having various shapes and sizes. Cymbals were typically forged from bronze, while trumpets were made of various metals, such as seen in the large silver trumpet found in King Tutankhamun's tomb.

As played out in the drama between Saul and David, musical instruments were understood as soothing to God and humans. In ancient Israel, numerous ministers are noted as being responsible for the music directed to Yahweh, as seen in this passage and the 288 musicians counted during the time of David (cf. 1Ch 25:1–8). As implied in the present passage, the role of the musician or singer was closely connected with priestly and military personnel. The priests were adorned in "fine linen," a symbol of purity and religious position. The blowing of trumpets (v.13) is the only musical activity performed by priests (see 1Ch 15:24). Typically, Levites performed musical service (see comments on 2Ch 5:4–6). The declaration that God's love endures forever is a key theological concept that incorporates the faithfulness of God and his commitment to his people and his covenant. On the cloud (v.13b), see comments on v.14.

14 After the declaration of God's attributes of goodness and love (*ḥesed*), the temple is filled with a cloud, reminiscent of the cloud that filled the tabernacle in the wilderness following its completion (cf. Ex 40:34–35). Similarly, at the beginning of ch. 6 Solomon notes that "the Lord has said that he would dwell in a dark cloud" (6:1). The cloud communicates the awesomeness of God's presence and his unapproachable glory.

In addition, the OT commonly portrays God's presence in conjunction with storm imagery (sometimes called a "storm theophany"), such as strong winds, lightning, dark clouds, and the like. For example, God is noted as one who surrounds himself with clouds (Ps 97:2; cf. Job 22:14), who walks on the wings of the wind (Pss 18:10[11]; 104:3), who uses clouds as his chariot (Ps 104:3), who causes clouds to burst with lightning (Job 37:11), who clears up the sky with his wind (Job 26:13), whose voice brings forth abundant rain (Job 38:34; Ps 78:23), and whose voice thunders, strikes, and shakes the earth (Ps 29:3–9). All of these facets of storm imagery showcase the power of God.

6:1–2 See previous comment on the cloud of God's presence. Solomon's intent is for the temple to be a permanent dwelling place for the Lord. However, Yahweh's response to Solomon's dedicatory prayer reflects the reality that the temple could (and would) be destroyed through disobedience and covenantal unfaithfulness (see 7:19–22).

3 After delivering his initial words to God while facing the completed temple, Solomon now turns to face the assembly and utters a blessing on the people before beginning his dedicatory prayer to Yahweh. This is reminiscent of the blessing given by David over the people in conjunction with the relocation of the ark of the covenant (cf. 1Ch 16:2).

4–11 Solomon's temple-dedication prayer begins with expressions of praise and thanksgiving that focus on God's faithfulness to fulfill his promise to David (compare vv.4–10 with 1Ch 17). Solomon's declaration of God's covenantal faithfulness within a context of prayer and thanksgiving would be a significant reminder to the Chronicler's postexilic audience.

Solomon extends his words of praise and gratefulness back to the exodus (v.5), which inaugurated God's covenantal relationship with the nascent nation of Israel (cf. Ex 19–24, esp. 19:3–6). In addition, the mention of God's choice of Jerusalem as the location of the temple (v.6) is likewise an element of God's fulfilling his Word (cf. 1Ch 28:4–6; see comments on 2Ch 3:1).

Following this expression of thanksgiving, Solomon praises God for bringing his Word to pass, especially in the matter of the completed temple (compare Solomon's prayer in 1:8–9). It is clear that Solomon understood himself as being part of God's fulfilling his promise to David. Indeed, the primary emphasis of the Davidic covenant articulated via the prophet Nathan in 1 Chronicles 17:4–14 (cf. 2Sa 7:5–16) focuses on a single son of David (namely, Solomon). For example, although David would not be the one to build the temple (vv.7–9; cf. 1Ch 17:1–4; 22:8–10; 28:2–4), his son/descendant would occupy the Davidic throne and build a temple for the Lord (vv.9–10; cf. 1Ch 17:11–12; 22:6–7; 28:5–7). The movement of the ark of the covenant to its rightful place within the temple (v.11) is the capstone to the momentous day (cf. 1Ch 22:19; for more discussion on the fulfillment of the Davidic covenant, see comments on 1Ch 17:7–15; 2Ch 1:9; 6:14–17).

12–13 The description of Solomon as standing, spreading out his hands, and kneeling reflect the variety of postures of worship attested in the OT (cf. 2Ch 29:29–30; Ne 9:1–3; Pss 5:7; 141:2). Such outward gestures and postures reflect submission to God, respect of his power, reverence, and the like. See examples in Keel, 308–23. Solomon's posture of kneeling declares his submission to the lordship and sovereignty of God in the presence of the Israelite assembly. The term for the platform used by Solomon (*kîyôr*; GK 3963) can refer to an elevated area used for official functions as reflected in the biblical world (cf. *ANEP*, fig. 576, p. 490).

14–17 Solomon again declares God as one who steadfastly keeps his Word (cf. 2Ch 6:4–11), most particularly with respect to God's covenantal relationship with Israel (a "covenant of love"—*habbᵉrît wᵉhaḥesed*) and God's delegation of leadership through the Davidic covenant. Note that the statement of v.16 is not found in the biblical texts typically associated with Yahweh's (initial) declaration of the Davidic covenant (e.g., 2Sa 7:5–16; 1Ch 17:4–14), but the notion of David's never failing to have a descendant sit on the throne of Israel is reflected in subsequent biblical passages (see esp. Jer 33:17) and must have been communicated to David in another setting not recorded in the biblical text.

The conditional undergirding of this statement, "if only your sons are careful in all they do to walk before me," is oftentimes glossed over in discussions of the Davidic covenant. The opening of v.16 and the closing statement of v.17 reflect the reality that this was not a certainty. The broader spectrum of 6:4–6:17 reflects the balance between God's Word being fulfilled (cf. esp. 6:4–10, 15) and the prayerful hope that God will bring to pass the full measure of his promises (cf. 6:16–17).

18–21 Solomon's statement that even the highest heavens cannot hold the Creator God (v.18) underscores that although God will localize his presence and glory in the Solomonic temple, no man-made, finite structure can house the infinite God. Yet God's ontological and epistemological accommodation to humankind in both the matter of the temple and even the matter of hearing Solomon's prayer (v.19) emphatically showcases God's grace and love toward his people.

The essence of Solomon's prayer is that God may hear both his prayer and the prayers of God's people (vv.19–21 and in the sections that follow). In his supplication, Solomon stresses the imagery of reconciliation and forgiveness within the physical setting of the temple (where the shedding of blood for sin will take place) and the metaphysical disposition of the Godward individual (who will seek God in prayerful contrition and repentance "toward" the place where God has caused his Name to dwell).

22–39 This long section details a number of scenarios wherein individuals, the nation as a whole, and foreigners might seek God in the context of prayer and the temple. The supplicatory refrain present in each of these scenarios is that God might "hear from heaven" (cf. 6:23, 25, 27, 30, 33, 35, 39). The consequences anticipated in several of these scenarios reflect covenantal judgments for unfaithfulness articulated in legal texts, particularly Deuteronomy 28 (e.g., defeat from enemies [v.25; cf. Dt 28:25, 48]; drought [v.24; cf. Dt 28:23–24]; famine, plague, blight, mildew, locusts [v.22; cf. Dt 28:21–22, 42], and captivity [v.36; cf. Dt 28:63–65]. Note that such divine chastening has a didactic function ("teach them the right way to live," v.27) as well as a sanctifying function ("so that they will fear you and walk in your ways," v.31).

In this section are two scenarios, unrelated to sin, in which Solomon asks God to hear from heaven: when a foreigner seeks God (vv.32–33) and when the nation goes out to war (vv.34–35). With respect to the foreigner seeking God (recall Isa 56:6–7), we are reminded that the temple is to be "a house of prayer for all nations" and that God's ultimate will is that all the peoples of the earth may know his name and fear him (v.33; cf. Ge 12:3). God's concern for all nations was a continuing message even within the disarray of the postexilic setting (cf. Zec 8:20–23). With respect to the nation going to war, covenantal faithfulness will ensure that Israel's enemies will be defeated (cf. Dt 28:7).

The final section (vv.36–39) deals with captivity and the reconciliation possible after such a drastic consequence. In this section, the theological reality of sin in humankind is declared ("for there is no one who does not sin," v.36), so that the confession of sin

is especially emphasized along with the way in which God must be sought ("if they turn back to you with all their heart and soul," v.38). When such an inner disposition of humility and contrition is shown, Solomon's prayer is that God would *hear*, *uphold*, and *forgive* his people (v.39)—a message of hope particularly apt for the Chronicler's postexilic audience.

40 Solomon summarizes the scenarios in which people might seek God (vv.22–39) in a manner similar to that which begins the section, namely, by asking that God's "eyes be open" toward his temple and that he hear the prayers offered at this holy place (cf. vv.20–21).

41–42 The final two verses in this section (not part of the parallel text in 1 Kings) function as a poetic summary similar to Psalm 132 (a royal psalm):

> Arise, O LORD, and come to your resting place,
>   you and the ark of your might.
> May your priests be clothed with righteousness;
>   may your saints sing for joy.
> For the sake of David your servant,
>   do not reject your anointed one. (Ps 132:8–10)

The contents of this psalm may reflect David's poetic celebration following his return of the ark of the covenant to Jerusalem (1Ch 16). Solomon's temple-dedication prayer ends with reference to David and the supplication that Yahweh's covenantal love extended to the Davidic line continue unabated in a setting of righteousness and joy.

7:1–3 The appearance of fire from heaven at the completion of Solomon's prayer visually showcases God's power and signifies his approval of Solomon's dedicatory prayer and offering. Similarly, fire came down from heaven following a number of important events, including David's sacrifice at the threshing floor of Ornan (the future location of the Jerusalem temple; cf. 1Ch 21:26), the inauguration of priestly service at the Tent of Meeting at Mount Sinai (cf. Lev 9:23–24), and Elijah's showdown with the prophets of Baal (cf. 1Ki 18:16–39, esp. 38).

As seen following the completion of the tabernacle during the time of Moses (cf. Ex 40:34–35) and the ark's earlier placement in the Most Holy Place (cf. 2Ch 5:11–14; see comments on 5:14), the glory of God is so intense that the priests are unable to enter the temple (v.2). Such a dramatic exposure to the power and glory of God causes the Israelite congregation to drop to their knees, put their faces to the ground, and worship the Creator God for his goodness (v.3; cf. 1Ki 18:39).

4–5 As with the bringing in of the ark of the covenant and Tent of Meeting into the temple (cf. 5:4–6) and the consecration of the courtyard (cf. 7:7), so the dedication of the Solomonic temple is accompanied with massive amounts of sacrifice, which here act as tangible symbols of the devotion and worship of Solomon and the Israelites. In like manner, Solomon's thousand burnt offerings at Gibeon offered at the outset of his reign (1:6) demonstrated his commitment to God in the presence of the Israelite assembly.

6 On the musical organization of ancient Israel and the distinct roles played by Levites and priests in the matter of music, see comments on 1 Chronicles 23:2–6; 2 Chronicles 5:4–6, 12–13. The antiphonal arrangement of the Levites and priests is reminiscent of Joshua's covenant-renewal ceremony at mounts Ebal and Gerizim, which also occurred in the context of an altar, burnt offerings, Levitical priests, and the ark of the covenant (cf. Jos 8:30–35).

7 Solomon also consecrated the broader area of the temple complex with a great number of different types of offerings (fellowship, grain, and burnt; cf. Lev 1–3). The burning of the fat portion of the fellowship offering implies that the broader animal

was used as part of the fifteen-day feast described in vv.8–10 (cf. the stipulations in Lev 3).

8–10 The notation that those assembled for the temple-dedication festival hailed "from Lebo Hamath to the Wadi of Egypt" (v.8) indirectly speaks to the geographical expanse and influence of Solomon's empire. The guest list for this festival included dignitaries from Lebo Hamath in the north to the Brook of Egypt (Wadi al-Arish) in the south. These place names are significant as they are used in early patriarchal promises concerning the geographical extent of the Promised Land. While the place Lebo Hamath is typically understood to be the southern border of Hamath, it is possible that the location of Lebo Hamath could be to the north of Hamath. Lebo Hamath means "Entrance to Hamath," and this expression could refer to the entrance from the perspective of Mesopotamia (wherein the entrance would be to the north of Hamath) rather than from a Canaanite/Israelite perspective (wherein the entrance would be on the southern side of Hamath). For further remarks on the extent of Solomonic geographical control, see comments on 9:26. On the specifics of the geographical extent of Israel at different time periods, see F. J. Mabie, "Geographical Extent of Israel," in *DOTHB,* 316–28.

The Chronicler expands on the account given in 1 Kings 8:65–66 related to the chronology and sequence of Solomon's festival celebration(s). Solomon's festival follows the pattern of the Feast of Tabernacles (Feast of Booths), which was celebrated from the fifteenth to the twenty-second of the seventh month (see Lev 23:33–43). The assembly on the eighth day of the Feast of Tabernacles (v.9) marked the end of the celebrations and was to be a solemn assembly (cf. Lev 23:36, 39). The Chronicler does not mention the Day of Atonement, which would have begun on the tenth day of the seventh month (cf. Lev 23:26–32). Following this protracted time of joyful celebration and solemnity, Solomon dismisses the people on the twenty-third day of the seventh month (v.10).

11–12 Solomon's second dream theophany takes place after the completion of the temple and the palace—about twenty years after his initial revelatory dream noted at 1:7 (see comments there). For God's choice of the temple location (v.12), see comments on 3:1.

13–16 God's response to Solomon's prayer in many ways mirrors the phraseology and content of Solomon's supplications, including the emphasis on hearing prayer and covenantal consequences, including drought, locusts, and plague (see comments on 6:12–42, esp. vv.22–39).

What is perhaps one of the most well-known verses of Chronicles and the OT as a whole (v.14, "If my people, who are called by my Name ...") is also simultaneously one of the more misappropriated verses in the Bible. In short, this verse is not a promissory statement being made to the United States or any country apart from the ancient covenant community of Israel. This statement is situated within covenantal particulars related to the Deuteronomic covenant (cf. v.13), matters of temple theology (and the interwoven Israelite sacrificial system; cf. vv.15–16), and the Davidic covenant (cf. vv.17–22). Note that all these features are directly applicable to the nation of Israel located within the specific geographical area of the Promised Land featuring a functioning temple in the city of Jerusalem and having a Davidic king on the throne. Moreover, the Chronicler is retelling something that had been told to Solomon about four centuries prior to the time of writing.

Given that the Chronicler is writing to those in Jerusalem with a functioning temple (the Second Temple, completed during the time of Zerubbabel, Haggai, and Zechariah, ca. 515 BC) and some degree (or hope) of Davidic leadership, there is certainly a secondary line of significance and application to the postexilic Judeans living in Israel. Beyond this expanded sense for Israel, this promise cannot be connected with any sense of direct divine promise that God will "heal" the United States or any other nation, although the notion of corporate (or national) humility and Godwardness is a wonderful image that God might sovereignly choose to bless. Notable examples of leaders described as humbling themselves or leading a time of national repentance include Rehoboam (12:6), Hezekiah (32:26), and especially the dramatic example of Manasseh (33:12). Such instances of repentance and humbling frequently accompany times of prayer and an earnest seeking of God.

God's name (v.16) designates the presence of God and incorporates aspects of God's character, such as his covenantal love, with Israel and his grace toward all humankind (cf. Dt 12:5).

17–22 A layer of conditionality is connected with Solomon and subsequent Davidic leaders, as reflected in Yahweh's response to Solomon's temple-dedication prayer. In addition, God cites the dynamics of his promises to David in the midst of Solomon's later apostasy and causes the judgment of the division of the kingdom to come after Solomon on account of Yahweh's promise to David (see the statements in 1Ki 11:9–40, esp. 11:11–13, 31–24).

God's closing words (vv.19–22) anticipate what will in time befall Israel in their earlier textual setting of 1 Kings 9:3–9 and in this textual setting (a century or so after this has happened); they remind the postexilic community that God does fulfill his Word and covenantal promises. On the matters of the conditional and unconditional (as well as the fulfilled and unfulfilled) layers of the Davidic covenant, see the detailed discussion at 1 Chronicles 17:7–15; 2 Chronicles 1:9; 6:4–11.

NOTES

5:12–13 Note the numerous points of connection between this section and David's bringing up of the ark to Jerusalem as recorded in 1 Chronicles 15:12–16:42.

6:42 In some manuscripts "God's anointed" (מְשִׁיחֶיךָ, *mᵉšîḥeykā*) is plural, perhaps implying God's blessing on the Davidic dynasty as a whole or the gamut of those anointed to various tasks within the broader covenantal community. However, note that the similar statement in Psalm 132:10 is singular (cf. Selman, 331, n. 1).

7:1–3 The burnt offerings and sacrifices noted here seem to relate back to those noted at 5:6.

8. Solomon's Building and Trading Activity (2Ch 8:1–18)

OVERVIEW

The presentation of the Solomonic accomplishments listed here is consistent with an ancient Near Eastern literary genre known as "summary inscription." In such texts, the information is not necessarily presented in a chronological/sequential format, and large gaps of time may be present between the events noted in one verse and those in the next. Such texts function to present a succinct list of the king's accomplishments during the course of his reign in a summary fashion. For a further discussion of the literary genre of Chronicles, see the Introduction.

[1]At the end of twenty years, during which Solomon built the temple of the LORD and his own palace, [2]Solomon rebuilt the villages that Hiram had given him, and settled Israelites in them. [3]Solomon then went to Hamath Zobah and captured it. [4]He also built up Tadmor in the desert and all the store cities he had built in Hamath. [5]He rebuilt Upper Beth Horon and Lower Beth Horon as fortified cities, with walls and with gates and bars, [6]as well as Baalath and all his store cities, and all the cities for his chariots and for his horses—whatever he desired to build in Jerusalem, in Lebanon and throughout all the territory he ruled.

[7]All the people left from the Hittites, Amorites, Perizzites, Hivites and Jebusites (these peoples were not Israelites), [8]that is, their descendants remaining in the land, whom the Israelites had not destroyed—these Solomon conscripted for his slave labor force, as it is to this day. [9]But Solomon did not make slaves of the Israelites for his work; they were his fighting men, commanders of his captains, and commanders of his chariots and charioteers. [10]They were also King Solomon's chief officials—two hundred and fifty officials supervising the men.

[11]Solomon brought Pharaoh's daughter up from the City of David to the palace he had built for her, for he said, "My wife must not live in the palace of David king of Israel, because the places the ark of the LORD has entered are holy."

¹²On the altar of the Lᴏʀᴅ that he had built in front of the portico, Solomon sacrificed burnt offerings to the Lᴏʀᴅ, ¹³according to the daily requirement for offerings commanded by Moses for Sabbaths, New Moons and the three annual feasts—the Feast of Unleavened Bread, the Feast of Weeks and the Feast of Tabernacles. ¹⁴In keeping with the ordinance of his father David, he appointed the divisions of the priests for their duties, and the Levites to lead the praise and to assist the priests according to each day's requirement. He also appointed the gatekeepers by divisions for the various gates, because this was what David the man of God had ordered. ¹⁵They did not deviate from the king's commands to the priests or to the Levites in any matter, including that of the treasuries.

¹⁶All Solomon's work was carried out, from the day the foundation of the temple of the Lᴏʀᴅ was laid until its completion. So the temple of the Lᴏʀᴅ was finished.

¹⁷Then Solomon went to Ezion Geber and Elath on the coast of Edom. ¹⁸And Hiram sent him ships commanded by his own officers, men who knew the sea. These, with Solomon's men, sailed to Ophir and brought back four hundred and fifty talents of gold, which they delivered to King Solomon.

COMMENTARY

1–2 The relationship between these verses and 1 Kings 9:10–14, where Solomon is described as giving Hiram twenty cities in the region of Galilee (the tribal territory assigned to Asher), is uncertain. One possibility is that the land was given to Hiram as collateral (temporary ceding of territory) during the massive flow of Phoenician supplies and workmanship into Israel (1Ki 9:10–14), with the return of this land following the settling of debts (via the significant quantities of Israelite agricultural products; cf. 2:3–16) recorded at 8:2.

3 Solomon's taking of Hamath Zobah and his subsequent building of storage cities (cf. vv.4–6) indicate a significant expansion of Israelite political control and economic hegemony achieved through the control of trade routes and the receipt of tribute payments and tax revenue. Solomon's geographical hegemony extended north, deep into northern Syria, and bordered the west bank of the Euphrates River to the northeast. The name of this area (Hamath Zobah) suggests that Hamath had gained prominence over the Aramean (or perhaps Neo-Hittite) kingdom of Zobah. David's earlier conflict with Zobah is noted in 1 Chronicles 18:3–6 (2Sa 8:3–8; also see comments on 2Ch 9:26).

4 Tadmor (also known as Palmyra) was an important caravan city in northern Syria nearly three hundred miles from Jerusalem. Tadmor was situated to the south of the region of Hamath on the diagonal trade route linking northeastern Aram and Mesopotamia on the end of the Aramean desert. As with Hamath Zobath (see comments on v.3), the fortification of Tadmor reflects Solomon's extensive control over important commercial trade routes.

5–6 The fortification of Upper and Lower Beth Horon as well as Baalath are related to national oversight of lucrative trade routes as well as protection of access routes to the heart of Israel. Lower Beth Horon (Beit Ur et-Tahta) and Upper Beth Horon (Beit Ur el-Foqa) were strategically located on the main east-west route linking the coastal highway and the central Judean hill country about twelve and fourteen miles from Jerusalem, respectively.

The designations "Upper" and "Lower" reflect the fact that Upper Beth Horon was approximately one thousand feet higher in elevation than Lower Beth Horon. Baalath (also known in the OT as Kiriath Jearim, Kiriath Baal, and Mahaneh Dan) was located on a secondary road leading from the coastal plain to the interior and was situated about six miles to the south of Upper and Lower Beth Horon, close to the boundary between the tribal territories of Judah and Dan. On Solomon's development of a chariot force see comments on 1:14. For the area of Lebanon and the extent of Solomonic hegemony, see the comments on 8:3 and 9:26.

7–10 On the organization of peoples conscripted for the nationalized labor force as well as the particular role played by Israelites in national service, see the extended discussion at 2:2.

11 The construction of a separate palace for the daughter of the Egyptian pharaoh provides a hint of Israelite-Egyptian relations during the Solomonic period. Solomon's alliance with Egypt is first noted in 1 Kings 3:1 and is connected with Solomon's marriage to the daughter of the Egyptian pharaoh, a scenario that implies a combination of Israelite strength and Egyptian weakness. The boast of the Egyptian pharaoh Amenhotep III that no daughter of an Egyptian pharaoh was ever given in marriage was made more than four hundred years before Solomon's reign and hence should not be used against the notion of Solomon's having an Egyptian princess as a wife.

The pharaoh in view is probably Siamun, one of the last pharaohs of the Twenty-First Dynasty. Around this time (although recorded in 1Ki 9:16), Egypt conquered the Canaanite-held Shephelah city of Gezer (an invasion supported by archaeological data) and gave the city to Solomon as a dowry for his daughter. Solomon's construction of a separate pal-

ace for the Egyptian princess reflects her high status within the royal harem (see A. Malamat, "A Political Look at the Kingdom of David and Solomon and Its Relations with Egypt," in *Studies in the Period of David and Solomon and Other Essays* [ed. T. Ishida; Winona Lake, Ind.: Eisenbrauns, 1982], 189–204).

12–16 Within the regnal summary of this chapter, these verses concisely summarize the crowning achievement of Solomon's reign—the construction of a functioning temple complex that operated in accordance with divine instructions revealed through Moses and David. Thus these verses condense much of the content of chs. 2–7. For more on calendar festivals and offerings, see comments on 2:4; 4:8; 7:8–10. On the distinctions between Levites and priests, see comments on 5:4–6, 12–13.

17–18 The port at Ezion Geber may have actually been located on a small island located at the head of the Gulf of Aqabah known as Jezirat Faraun, also referred to as Coral Island and Pharaoh's Island. This location, about eight miles south of modern-day Eilat, featured a natural harbor that was enhanced with a breakwater and boat mooring facilities. Another option for Ezion Geber is Tell el-Kheleifeh, a seaport on the northern shore of the Gulf of Aqabah; however, archaeological evidence from the time of Solomon is lacking. Some have identified Eilat/Elath/Elat with modern Aqabah, but this identification is not certain. In fact, it is possible that Ezion Geber and Eilat/Elath/Elat are names for the same place (see Note). With such an understanding the passage would read, "Then Solomon went to Ezion Geber (that is, Elath) on the coast of Edom" (cf. G. Pratico, "Where Is Ezion-Geber?" *BAR* 12 [1986]: 24–35). On the location of Ophir, see comments on 1Ch 29:1–5.

Solomon's arrangements for Phoenician expertise and craftsmanship extended to maritime trade, with the Phoenicians supplying both ships and experienced sailors. The Phoenicians were noted sailors in the ancient world. The Egyptian language even came to include the term "Byblos Ship" to denote high-quality vessels from Phoenicia (cf. L. Casson, *Ships and Seamanship in the Ancient World* [Baltimore: The Johns Hopkins Univ. Press, 1995]). Commercial shipping was attested in the ancient Near East from at least as early as the third millennium BC, including the shipping routes along the Mediterranean coast between Egypt and ports in Phoenicia (e.g., Byblos, Tyre, Sidon), Syria (e.g., Ugarit), and beyond (e.g., Anatolia and the Aegean world), as well as routes from Egypt to Arabia.

The description in 2Ch 9:21 of these ships as "ships of Tarshish" or "ships that go to Tarshish" (see NIV note in 9:21; cf. "trading ships" in NIV text) together with their three-year trading journey implies that these ships could manage the high seas and undertake long-distance sea travel. The specific location of Tarshish is uncertain but seems to be a distant western Mediterranean seaport (perhaps Tartessus, Spain). The trading connection between Phoenicia and Tarshish is reflected in the oracle against Tyre in Ezekiel 27 (e.g., Eze 27:12, 25; cf. Isa 23:1, 14). Trading vessels ranged from forty to eighty feet in length and could cover twenty-five to forty miles per day. In addition to the exchange of normal trade items such as agricultural products, metals, and timber, such maritime journeys also featured the acquisition of exotic cargo (note the apes and baboons mentioned at 9:21).

NOTES

1–2 For another proposal of how this passage might fill in further details from the account of Cabul in 1 Kings 9:10–14 and possibly parallel ancient Near Eastern accounts, see Kitchen, 113–15.

4 A textual issue raises the possibility that the city of Tamar to the south of the Dead Sea is intended here instead of Tadmor. In short, while the text here in v.4 and the indicated reading (*Qere*) of 1 Kings 9:18 is "Tadmor," the written text (*Kethiv*) of 1 Kings 9:18 is "Tamar." Tamar (En Haseva) is situated on a hill next to the southern bank of Nahal Hazeva at the intersection of major trade routes to the northwest (Beersheba, Arad, Hebron, Jerusalem), south (Ezion Geber), east (Edom), and west (Kadesh Barnea). This pivotal location kept Tamar near the center of regional social, political, military, and economic activities during the Iron Age. Tamar is mentioned in 1 Kings 9:17–18 as being fortified by Solomon, presumably to protect the valuable trade routes through the Negev and to protect the southern flank of Judah.

17 In the proposal that Ezion Geber is another name for Eilat (Elath), the conjunction "and" is understood as functioning as an epexegetical *waw* (ו, *w*), as is the case in 1 Chronicles 5:26: "Pul king of Assyria (that is, Tiglath-Pileser king of Assyria)," which is literally "Pul king of Assyria and Tiglath-Pileser king of Assyria." With such an understanding the passage would read, "Then Solomon went to Ezion Geber (that is, Elath) on the coast of Edom."

18 In the Chronicler's account Hiram sends ships to Solomon, while in 1 Kings 9:26–27 the text notes that Hiram sent sailors and Solomon built the ships. This difference of vantage point can probably be best understood in analogy to the temple, where the biblical text may in some instances (cf. 2Ch 8:16) note that "Solomon's work" was finished, but in actuality it was the work of Huram and others that was finished. Thus one can accurately state that "Solomon built the temple," "Huram-Abi built the temple," and "Phoenician craftsmen built the temple." Also, it is possible that ship-building materials were imported overland from Phoenicia (Tyre), with their final assembly accomplished under the oversight of Solomon's officials in/around Eilat/Elath/Elat.

9. Visit of the Queen of Sheba (2Ch 9:1–12)

[1]When the queen of Sheba heard of Solomon's fame, she came to Jerusalem to test him with hard questions. Arriving with a very great caravan—with camels carrying spices, large quantities of gold, and precious stones—she came to Solomon and talked with him about all she had on her mind. [2]Solomon answered all her questions; nothing was too hard for him to explain to her. [3]When the queen of Sheba saw the wisdom of Solomon, as well as the palace he had built, [4]the food on his table, the seating of his officials, the attending servants in their robes, the cupbearers in their robes and the burnt offerings he made at the temple of the LORD, she was overwhelmed.

[5]She said to the king, "The report I heard in my own country about your achievements and your wisdom is true. [6]But I did not believe what they said until I came and saw with my own eyes. Indeed, not even half the greatness of your wisdom was told me; you have far exceeded the report I heard. [7]How happy your men must be! How happy your officials, who continually stand before you and hear your wisdom! [8]Praise be to the LORD your God, who has delighted in you and placed you on his throne as king to rule for the LORD your God. Because of the love of your God for Israel and his desire to uphold them forever, he has made you king over them, to maintain justice and righteousness."

[9]Then she gave the king 120 talents of gold, large quantities of spices, and precious stones. There had never been such spices as those the queen of Sheba gave to King Solomon.

[10](The men of Hiram and the men of Solomon brought gold from Ophir; they also brought algumwood and precious stones. [11]The king used the algumwood to make steps for the temple of the LORD and for the royal palace, and to make harps and lyres for the musicians. Nothing like them had ever been seen in Judah.)

[12]King Solomon gave the queen of Sheba all she desired and asked for; he gave her more than she had brought to him. Then she left and returned with her retinue to her own country.

COMMENTARY

1 The visit and subsequent declarations of the Queen of Sheba showcase God's blessing on David's son, most notably in the areas of wisdom and wealth. The location of Sheba is identified with ancient Saba, a trading depot located in the vicinity of modern Yemen in the south of the Arabian peninsula, some 1,400 to 1,500 miles from Jerusalem. Sheba was famous for its wares, spice caravans, and trading skill. In addition, Sheba was noted in extrabiblical sources as having female rulers, as reflected here. The southern provinces of Arabia were noted for species of trees and shrubs whose aromatic resin was used to produce a number of spices, gums, and balms (cf. G. W. van Beek, "The Land of Sheba," in *Solomon and Sheba* [ed. J. B. Pritchard; London: Phaidon, 1974], 40–63).

2–3 On Solomon's wisdom (cf. vv.2–3, 5–7), see comments at 1:10; 9:22–23.

4 The Queen of Sheba was impressed by the food, setting, and attendants at Solomon's palace (v.4). Such royal banquets were an important aspect of life in the biblical world, as reflected in numerous texts and iconography. In these settings, the variety of dishes served, the number of guests that could be accommodated, the number of servants and attendants on hand, and the like all speak to wealth and prestige — and, by extension, evidence of divine favor and blessing.

5–9 On Solomon's wisdom (cf. vv.2–3, 5–7), see comments at 1:10; 9:22–23. The queen's declaration of Yahweh's delight and love for Solomon and Israel (vv.5–8) recalls the outreach element of divinely given wisdom reflected in Deuteronomy 4:6: "Observe them carefully, for this will show your wisdom and understanding to the nations, who will hear about all these decrees and say, 'Surely this great nation is a wise and understanding people.'"

The delighted and awed Queen of Sheba responds by giving Solomon 120 talents of gold (v.9). As noted above (see comments on 3:8–9), a talent of gold weighed in the range of 65 to 75 pounds, meaning that this gift exceeded four tons of gold. It is possible that this large "gift" was part of a broader commercial trading agreement/treaty negotiated between Solomon and the Queen of Sheba. It is interesting to note that Hiram is also recorded as having given Solomon 120 talents of gold (cf. 1Ki 9:14). For more on Solomon's massive acquisition of gold, see the extended comments on 3:8–9.

10–11 This parenthetical remark largely echoes earlier statements regarding Solomon's material acquisitions and building efforts. On gold from Ophir (v.10), see comments on 1Ch 29:1–5. On algumwood (vv.10–11) and other precious wood sourced for Solomon's building projects, see comments on 2:8–9. On music and musical instruments (v.11), see comments on 5:12–13. For the maritime efforts facilitating many of these acquisitions, see comments on 8:17–18.

12 Although the phraseology is uncertain, one possible understanding of this verse (as reflected in the NIV) is that Solomon gave the Queen of Sheba more than she had brought to him. Recall that the exchange of "gifts" may be part of a trade agreement.

10. Summary of Solomon's Wealth (2Ch 9:13–31)

[13]The weight of the gold that Solomon received yearly was 666 talents, [14]not including the revenues brought in by merchants and traders. Also all the kings of Arabia and the governors of the land brought gold and silver to Solomon.

[15]King Solomon made two hundred large shields of hammered gold; six hundred bekas of hammered gold went into each shield. [16]He also made three hundred small shields of hammered gold, with three hundred bekas of gold in each shield. The king put them in the Palace of the Forest of Lebanon.

¹⁷Then the king made a great throne inlaid with ivory and overlaid with pure gold. ¹⁸The throne had six steps, and a footstool of gold was attached to it. On both sides of the seat were armrests, with a lion standing beside each of them. ¹⁹Twelve lions stood on the six steps, one at either end of each step. Nothing like it had ever been made for any other kingdom. ²⁰All King Solomon's goblets were gold, and all the household articles in the Palace of the Forest of Lebanon were pure gold. Nothing was made of silver, because silver was considered of little value in Solomon's day. ²¹The king had a fleet of trading ships manned by Hiram's men. Once every three years it returned, carrying gold, silver and ivory, and apes and baboons.

²²King Solomon was greater in riches and wisdom than all the other kings of the earth. ²³All the kings of the earth sought audience with Solomon to hear the wisdom God had put in his heart. ²⁴Year after year, everyone who came brought a gift—articles of silver and gold, and robes, weapons and spices, and horses and mules.

²⁵Solomon had four thousand stalls for horses and chariots, and twelve thousand horses, which he kept in the chariot cities and also with him in Jerusalem. ²⁶He ruled over all the kings from the River to the land of the Philistines, as far as the border of Egypt. ²⁷The king made silver as common in Jerusalem as stones, and cedar as plentiful as sycamore-fig trees in the foothills. ²⁸Solomon's horses were imported from Egypt and from all other countries.

²⁹As for the other events of Solomon's reign, from beginning to end, are they not written in the records of Nathan the prophet, in the prophecy of Ahijah the Shilonite and in the visions of Iddo the seer concerning Jeroboam son of Nebat? ³⁰Solomon reigned in Jerusalem over all Israel forty years. ³¹Then he rested with his fathers and was buried in the city of David his father. And Rehoboam his son succeeded him as king.

COMMENTARY

13–14 This summary of Solomon's royal revenue (excluding profits made from trade and other income per v.14) is impressive and reflects the economic clout ancient Israel was able to develop by exerting hegemony over neighboring countries and regions. This regional hegemony enabled Israel to control numerous trade routes and leverage Israel's geographical position as a "land bridge" linking the continents of Africa, Asia, and Europe. These trade routes include those in the northern reaches of Syria (gateway to Mesopotamia), the Negev (gateway to trade with the Arabian states and access to maritime trade from Ezion Geber), the region of Transjordan (King's Highway; gateway to Damascus), and the Coastal Highway (also known as the Great Trunk Route and the Via Maris; gateway to Egypt in the south and Phoenicia to the north). The 666 talents of gold received by Solomon is equal to 46,620 pounds (23.3 tons), using 70 pounds to the talent (cf. A. R. Millard, "Solomon in All His Glory," *VE* 12 [1981]: 5–18; also see comments on 3:8–9).

15–16 These opulent ceremonial weapons were not intended for battle but instead provided tangible proof of a kingdom's wealth and prestige. Numerous gold ceremonial weapons have been uncovered in archaeological digs, particularly in the tomb of the Egyptian pharaoh King Tutankhamun. The palace known as the "Palace of the Forest of Lebanon" (v.16) is given further description in 1 Kings 7 and probably derives its name from dozens of cedar pillars inside the palace (which would create a tree-like appearance). This palace may have functioned as an alternative residence (such as a summer palace) for the king, as well as a more convenient place to meet trading partners and dignitaries from the north.

17–19 Solomon's regnal throne was a magnificent work of art that featured stylistics seen in other thrones from the biblical world. Given the Chronicler's remark at v.19, these common motifs and materials were brought together in such a way as to attain a level of elegance not seen before. Animal images such as the twelve lions on each side of the six steps to Solomon's throne and the lions stationed next to each armrest were also common ancient Near Eastern royal motifs, as these noble beasts project strength, power, and fortitude. Solomon's throne was also inlaid with ivory, a material prized in the ancient world for its smoothness and warmth. The use of ivory in art and architecture was an area of Phoenician expertise and was prominent in other royal buildings in the biblical world.

20 As with other statements in ch. 9, these remarks largely echo earlier statements regarding Solomon's material acquisitions and wealth. On the Palace of the Forest of Lebanon, see comments on vv.15–16. On the abundance of gold and silver during the time of Solomon, see comments on 1:15; 3:8–9. For specifics of gold articles, see comments on 4:19–22.

21 See comments on Solomon's maritime efforts at 8:17–18.

22–23 This statement functions as a conclusion that wraps up the visit of the Queen of Sheba and the wisdom aspect of that visit. It is significant to note that Solomon's wisdom is described at v.22 as being greater "than all other kings of the earth." Similarly, 1 Kings 4:30 notes that Solomon's wisdom was "greater than the wisdom of all the men of the East, and greater than all the wisdom of Egypt." This comparison implies an ample level of exposure to such wisdom traditions.

The description of Solomon's wisdom noted in 1 Kings 4:32–33 is similar to the areas of knowledge and expertise gained by those in the intelligentsia of ancient biblical cultures, such as scribes, merchants, and royalty. As with that of his Egyptian and Mesopotamian counterparts, Solomon's wisdom involved understanding the world in areas such as botany, zoology, music, law, diplomacy, flora, fauna, literature, and other elements of the cultured life. In addition to such areas of knowledge, wisdom for a king had particular functionality in the important areas of temple building and governing. With respect to governing, note that Solomon's request for wisdom is connected with his ability to judge (govern) God's people and facilitate an ordered society. See further comments on 1:10 above.

24 As noted earlier (cf. 9:9), God's blessing is reflected in the stream of foreign dignitaries bringing gifts and tribute payments to Israel (cf. Jehoshaphat [17:10–11]). On the related aspect of Solomon's control of key trade routes, see comments on 9:13–14.

25 On Solomon's horses and chariots, see comments on 1:14.

26 Solomon is noted as having authority over the regions across "the River" (southwest of the Euphrates) and over kings from Tiphsah on the Euphrates in the northeast to the border of Egypt in the southwest (cf. 1Ki 4:24 [5:4]). The geographical expansion that took place during the time of Solomon extended Israelite control over the Coastal

Highway in the west (along the Mediterranean Sea) and the Transjordanian King's Highway in the east — meaning that the King's Highway was controlled from the maritime port of Ezion Geber to Tiphsah on the Euphrates. This expansion allowed Israel to profit from the lucrative trade activity flowing between Egypt, Arabia, and Mesopotamia (1Ki 9:26–27; 10:14–29; for more on trade routes see comments on 2Ch 9:13–14).

This being noted, the northern boundary of Israel *on the coast* did not extend north of Sidon, though it clearly extended north of this point in the interior. Nevertheless, Judah and Israel are described as dwelling safely "from Dan to Beersheba" during the days of Solomon — the nomenclature for describing the north-south expanse of Israel even when Israel's geographical control extended much farther.

Solomon received resources from his twelve taxation districts, as well as tribute payment from vassals and trade route revenue from traveling merchants, traders, and "all the kings of Arabia," not to mention income from maritime trade and middleman operations such as horse brokering (see comments on 1:16–17). Solomon's districts indicate that Israel during Solomon's reign extended in the west to the Mediterranean Sea from just north of (and excluding) Joppa to the Mount Carmel region just south (and excluding) the Plain of Acco.

Finally, the structure of Solomon's taxation and administration districts is reminiscent of Egyptian governmental practice (see D. B. Redford, "Studies in Relations between Palestine and Egypt during the First Millennium BC, 1: The Taxation System of Solomon," in *Studies on the Ancient Palestinian World* [ed. J. W. Wevers and D. B. Redford; Toronto Semitic Texts and Studies 2; Toronto: Univ. of Toronto Press, 1972], 141–56).

27 For the abundance of silver and cedar in Jerusalem, see comments on 1:15.

28 On the acquiring of horses from Egypt, see the comments on 1:16–17.

29–31 This is the common literary formula for summarizing royal reigns in Kings and Chronicles (see that of David in 1Ch 29:26–30). These royal summaries provide basic regnal information, including the length of reign, name of successor, place of burial, and a reference to the source of the information and/or a reference to a source where more information about this king's reign can be gleaned. Oftentimes, the source is attributed to a specific prophet as here ("the records of Nathan the prophet"), thus implying a close link between the prophetic office and regnal annotations in ancient Israel. Moreover, these summaries set up the narrative(s) to follow by providing royal succession information.

NOTES

26 Solomon's districts imply three distinct districts in Transjordan (the Mishor/Tableland in the south; the central area from Jazer to Mahanaim including all of the eastern Jordan Valley; and the northern area from Ramoth Gilead to the Argob area of Bashan. On the topic of Solomon's districts, see A. Rainey, 174–79; P. S. Ash, "Solomon's District List," *JSOT* 67 [1995]: 67–86; R. S. Hess, "The Form and Structure of the Solomonic District List in 1 Kings 4:7–19," in *Crossing Boundaries and Linking Horizons: Studies in Honor of M. C. Astour* [ed. G. D. Young et al.; Bethesda, Md.: CDL, 1997], 279–92).

23–28 Note that most of the details of these verses repeat those found in 1:12–16. See the overview to 2 Chronicles 1–9, above.

III. THE REIGNS OF JUDEAN KINGS DURING THE DIVIDED MONARCHY (2CH 10:1–36:19)

OVERVIEW

Chapters 10–36 of 2 Chronicles constitute the final major section of the Chronicler's work: the account of the kingdom of Judah following the division of the kingdom in the 930s BC. This division created two political states, with Jeroboam as king of a new dynasty consisting of the northern tribes and Rehoboam as king of the tribes of Judah and Benjamin. In subsequent biblical literature, the northern kingdom is typically called "Israel" whereas the southern kingdom is typically called "Judah," after the most prominent tribe.

But note that biblical usage of "Israel" is varied and is used with some regularity in prophetic literature in anticipation of the eschatological restoration of the twelve tribes, and occasionally in narrative to refer to the southern kingdom (e.g., 21:2). Moreover, it is used of the southern kingdom following the fall of the northern kingdom. Biblical synonyms for the northern kingdom include variations of the most prominent tribe(s) of the north (e.g., house of Joseph, Ephraim, Manasseh) as well as the eventual capital city (Samaria).

In addition, some ancient Near Eastern texts refer to the northern kingdom as the land (or house) of Omri, the ninth-century military leader who inaugurated the Omride dynasty. Similarly, the "house of Ahab" is also used as a moniker for the northern kingdom (e.g., 21:6; 22:3). The primary synonym for the southern kingdom attested in the OT and ancient Near Eastern texts (such as the Tel Dan Stele) is the "house of David."

The division of the Israelite kingdom also entailed a variety of social, religious, and economic reper-

cussions. In the religious realm, Jeroboam established new religious shrines at Dan and Bethel (1Ki 12:26–33; 2Ch 11:15), while Jerusalem remained the religious capital of the southern kingdom. The golden calf shrines established by Jeroboam effectively nationalized covenantal unfaithfulness and pushed the northern tribes further from seeking God. Economically, both Israel and Judah were affected by a loss of tribute, trade revenue, and production in the aftermath of the division. These challenges were exacerbated by the frequent conflict between Israel and Judah, as noted at 12:15: "There was continual warfare between Rehoboam and Jeroboam" (cf. 1Ki 14:30; 15:6, 16).

While the capital of the Davidic dynasty remained at Jerusalem, the northern kingdom had several capital cities. The first administrative capital established by Jeroboam following the division of the kingdom was located at Shechem (Tell Balatah), located on the eastern side of the pass between Mount Ebal and Mount Gerizim (2Ch 10:1; 1Ki 12:25). The second northern kingdom capital was located at the Transjordanian town of Penuel, a move possibly connected with Shishak's invasion of parts of Jeroboam's territory a few years into his reign (cf. 2Ch 12:1–9; 1Ki 12:25). After Penuel, Jeroboam set up a capital at Tirzah (Tell el-Farah), located at the junction of important roads about six miles north of Shechem. Tirzah remained the capital city for subsequent northern kingdom rulers until the establishment of Samaria during the sixth year of Omri's reign (ca. 879 BC; cf. 1Ki 16:23–24). Note that Omri ruled for five years from Tirzah while battling against Tibni for control of the northern kingdom. Samaria remained the capital of the northern kingdom until its fall in 722/721 BC at the hands of the Assyrian army. For charts and a discussion of the chronology of this period, see Kitchen, 26–31.

A. The Reign of Rehoboam (2Ch 10:1–12:16)

1. Division of the Israelite Kingdom (2Ch 10:1–11:4)

[1]Rehoboam went to Shechem, for all the Israelites had gone there to make him king. [2]When Jeroboam son of Nebat heard this (he was in Egypt, where he had fled from King Solomon), he returned from Egypt. [3]So they sent for Jeroboam, and he and all Israel went to Rehoboam and said to him: [4]"Your father put a heavy yoke on us, but now lighten the harsh labor and the heavy yoke he put on us, and we will serve you."

[5]Rehoboam answered, "Come back to me in three days." So the people went away.

[6]Then King Rehoboam consulted the elders who had served his father Solomon during his lifetime. "How would you advise me to answer these people?" he asked.

[7]They replied, "If you will be kind to these people and please them and give them a favorable answer, they will always be your servants."

[8]But Rehoboam rejected the advice the elders gave him and consulted the young men who had grown up with him and were serving him. [9]He asked them, "What is your advice? How should we answer these people who say to me, 'Lighten the yoke your father put on us'?"

[10]The young men who had grown up with him replied, "Tell the people who have said to you, 'Your father put a heavy yoke on us, but make our yoke lighter'—tell them, 'My little finger is thicker than my father's waist. [11]My father laid on you a heavy yoke; I will make it even heavier. My father scourged you with whips; I will scourge you with scorpions.'"

[12]Three days later Jeroboam and all the people returned to Rehoboam, as the king had said, "Come back to me in three days." [13]The king answered them harshly. Rejecting the advice of the elders, [14]he followed the advice of the young men and said, "My father made your yoke heavy; I will make it even heavier. My father scourged you with whips; I will scourge you with scorpions." [15]So the king did not listen to the people, for this turn of events was from God, to fulfill the word the LORD had spoken to Jeroboam son of Nebat through Ahijah the Shilonite.

[16]When all Israel saw that the king refused to listen to them, they answered the king:

"What share do we have in David,
    what part in Jesse's son?
To your tents, O Israel!
    Look after your own house, O David!"

So all the Israelites went home. [17]But as for the Israelites who were living in the towns of Judah, Rehoboam still ruled over them.

[18]King Rehoboam sent out Adoniram, who was in charge of forced labor, but the Israelites stoned him to death. King Rehoboam, however, managed to get into his chariot and escape to Jerusalem. [19]So Israel has been in rebellion against the house of David to this day.

[11:1]When Rehoboam arrived in Jerusalem, he mustered the house of Judah and Benjamin—a hundred and eighty thousand fighting men—to make war against Israel and to regain the kingdom for Rehoboam.

[2]But this word of the LORD came to Shemaiah the man of God: [3]"Say to Rehoboam son of Solomon king of Judah and to all the Israelites in Judah and Benjamin, [4]'This is what the LORD says: Do not go up to fight against your brothers. Go home, every one of you, for this is my doing.'" So they obeyed the words of the LORD and turned back from marching against Jeroboam.

COMMENTARY

1 Rehoboam's journey to Shechem implies the importance of securing the support of the northern tribes—and that such support was not automatic (recall David's efforts in 1Ch 11:1–3; cf. 2Sa 5:1–3). The city of Shechem (Tell Bâlatah) was strategically located in the territory of Manasseh on the eastern side of the pass between Mounts Ebal and Gerizim. The significance of Shechem in the history of Israel is connected with important moments in the lives of Abraham (cf. Ge 12:6–7) and Jacob (cf. Ge 33:18–20; 34) and was the location of the renewing the covenant during the time of Joshua (Jos 24:25–26).

2–3 After falling out favor with Solomon (cf. 1Ki 11:26–40), Jeroboam had fled to Egypt and was a guest of the Egyptian pharaoh until the death of Solomon. The specifics of Jeroboam's time in Egypt are not detailed in the biblical text, but presumably the Egyptian pharaoh's hospitality toward Jeroboam would have come with some strings attached once he returned to Israel. While admit-

tedly speculative, Pharaoh Shishak's attack of both the southern kingdom and the northern kingdom (cf. 2Ch 12:1–12) may have partly related to an agreement not fulfilled by Jeroboam (see P. Galpaz, "The Reign of Jeroboam and the Extent of Egyptian Influence," *BN* 60 [1991]: 13–19). Lastly, the detail that the people sent for Jeroboam following the death of Solomon implies he was held in high regard despite his exile in Egypt. Similarly, recall the narrator's remark on Jeroboam's valor and his work ethic at 1Ki 11:28.

4 The request of those from the northern tribal areas for a reduction of their "heavy yoke" and "harsh labor" was a by-product of the significant national service and financial obligations (such as taxes) imposed by Solomon to aid his building and infrastructure projects. Of some irony, the phraseology of Jeroboam and "all Israel" used to describe their situation are the same expressions used to describe the conditions imposed on the Israelites during their time of bondage by the Egyptians (cf. Ex 6:6–9).

The request for this relief may have similarity to ancient Near Eastern decrees that were common at the outset of a king's reign. Such decrees (e.g., Misharum and Andurarum decrees) were designed to facilitate loyalty to the new king and often included popular proposals such as freedom from forced labor, forgiveness of debts, reduction of taxes, and the like. It should be noted that the northern tribes were not necessarily planning to revolt, as their request ends with the statement "… and we will serve you," which has the syntax of a result clause (e.g., "… so that we will serve you"). This syntax suggests that the initial intent of the northern tribes was to submit to the new Davidic king. On Solomon's use of foreign and Israelite workers in differing degrees of national service, see the detailed discussion at 2:2.

5 Rehoboam's initial response for the people to leave and report back in three days can be seen either positively (namely, that he was carefully considering the matter and planning to seek counsel on his decision) or negatively (namely, that he could have provided a gracious answer on the spot).

6–11 The two groups of counselors noted in this pivotal episode in ancient Israel's history may suggest some variation of a bicameral political structure within early Israel. In such a structure the advice posed by the two political groups would align with their particular role within the ancient society, such as military commanders, religious leaders, political advisors, and the royal family. In the setting of 2 Chronicles 10, the "young men" may have consisted of the royal princes aligned with Rehoboam, while the older group of counselors were associated with Solomon's administration.

The phraseology used with the first group ("young men") conjures an image of youthfulness; however, these men were not as youthful as we might presume. Rehoboam is forty-one years old, and these individuals are described as growing up with Rehoboam (1Ki 12:8; 14:21). Instead, the phraseology of "young" should be understood vis-à-vis their wisdom and experience as well as in comparison to the elders who served Rehoboam's father, Solomon. Unfortunately, Rehoboam rejected the advice of the elders before even hearing the advice of the younger men (v.8).

12–15 As the movement of vv.6–11 implies, Rehoboam opts for the harsher approach to the northern tribes and in so doing facilitates the division of the Israelite kingdom in approximately 930 BC. Yet the summary statement of this sobering moment in Israel's history ("this turn of events was from God," v.15) reminds us that even the actions of an unwise man fall under the sovereign will of God. Moreover, the Chronicler reminds the reader that God is careful to fulfill his Word, which was in turn delivered in the context of Solomon's persistent apostasy (cf. the full context of 1Ki 11).

16–19 While the impetus for the division of the Israelite kingdom was divinely scripted (cf. v.15), the division itself played out through the common human tendencies of pride, foolishness, and rebellion. The phraseology used in v.19 underscores that the crisis is much bigger than Rehoboam's folly (see comments at vv.12–15), as responsibility is also attached to "Israel" (the new nomenclature for the northern kingdom [see the Overview above]; v.19) as well as Solomon (implied in v.4 and the reference to the prophecy of Ahijah in v.15). The rallying call used by the northern tribal leaders (v.16) is reminiscent of the divisive words of Sheba in 2 Samuel 20:1–2 and (conversely) to the words of loyalty uttered to David in 1 Chronicles 12:18.

Rehoboam's ill-fated decision to send out Adoniram (v.18) may have been part of his mandate to make the yoke on the northern tribes even heavier than it was during the time of Solomon (vv.5–15), as Adoniram was the overseer of forced labor reserved for non-Israelites rather than the standard national service expected of Israelites. See further comments on 2:2.

11:1 The beginning of separate dynasties in the south and north is accompanied by a long on-and-off civil war between the two sides. Much of the battleground of this civil war amounts to conflict in and over the tribal territory of Benjamin. In addition to the reference to 180,000 fighting men noted here, the Chronicler records a number of large armies counted by different kings, including 1,100,000 during the time of David (not counting those of Benjamin or Levi; 1Ch 21:5–6); the army of 580,000 men of Judah and Benjamin raised by Asa (2Ch 14:8); the 1,160,000 soldiers counted by Jehoshaphat (17:14–18); the 300,000 recorded during the days of Amaziah (not counting another 100,000 hired from the northern kingdom; 25:5–6); and the 307,500 counted by Uzziah (26:13).

The number of troops noted in these battles is considerably higher than the listings of armies recorded in ancient Near Eastern annals. For example, the twelve-nation anti-Assyrian coalition (which included 10,000 troops from the northern kingdom) that successfully stalled the advance of the Assyrian army in ca. 853 BC was numbered at about 53,000 and did battle against the 120,000 troops that Shalmaneser III claimed to have brought to battle (cf. *COS*, 2:113B). Because archaeologists tend to believe that such large numbers are out of place in terms of assumed population levels, some biblical scholars have embraced options that reduce these figures for one reason or another. Yet it should be stressed that adjusting portions of the Bible that seem unlikely can be a slippery slope that can cause revisions of other "improbable" aspects of biblical content, such as the incarnation and resurrection from the dead.

This caveat noted, the issue of the authorial intent of the Spirit of God working through the human writer is the fundamental issue in any biblical passage. Such sensitivity to authorial intent involves exegetical thoroughness that includes engaging the characteristics of the type of literature of a given passage (genre). In Christian circles the word "genre" is sometimes cause for alarm, but it simply refers to the different types of literature found in the Bible, such as the different literary styles and expressions we encounter when reading a psalm, a proverb, a story in Samuel, priestly instruction in Leviticus, or a letter sent by the apostle Paul to an ancient congregation in the area of modern-day Turkey.

Similarly, biblical passages may use a wide variety of literary stylistics and idiom. By way of example, the various images used to describe the seed (descendants) God would give Abraham (e.g., numbered like the stars of the sky, the sand of the seashore, and the dust of the earth) are not intending to conjure up a specific number, but rather to facilitate the imagery of vastness. Any attempt to determine the promised number of Abrahamic descendants vis-à-vis the exact number of the images of stars, sand, and dust would be inconsistent with the authorial intent of these passages.

When considering the meaning (authorial intent) of the large numbers used in the descriptions of armies in the OT, the interpreter has two main options: taking the numbers as they stand, or understanding the numbers in the light of some combination of genre, idiom, and lexical factors that would change the nuance of these numbers. From the angle of genre, some propose that the large numbers reflect intentional hyperbole (overstatement). While the notion of intentional exaggeration sounds out of place in discussing biblical material, there are ample examples in the Bible of intentional overstatement. For example, in David's lament after the death of Saul and Jonathan he praises them as being "swifter than eagles" and "stronger than lions" (2Sa 1:23). In interpreting these statements it is clear that David's words underscore his desire to show honor and respect to Saul and Jonathan rather than to claim that Saul and Jonathan were able to run 75 to 100 mph (the speed of a dive of the golden eagle found in Israel) or embodied the literal strength of a lion. In such a view, large numbers were a normative means of expression in military battle summaries in the biblical world intended to convey a degree of shock and awe in the battle story. For more on this approach, see D. M. Fouts, "A Defense of the Hyperbolic Interpretation of Large Numbers in the Old Testament," *JETS* 40 (1997): 377–87.

In addition to the genre/literary convention approach, the use of "1,000" in these passages may be intended as an idiom of abundance rather than a specific numerical quantity. This idiomatic usage of the term translated "thousand" is seen in various instances. For example, in the oracle of hope directed to God's people in Isaiah 60:22, Yahweh's encouragement includes the statement that "the least of you will become a *thousand*, the smallest a mighty nation," which expresses the effect of divine enablement rather than numerical expansion. Similarly, since Hebrew has no word for "million," texts that refer to "a thousand thousands" could be intended to express an innumerable force. Nevertheless, while this idiomatic usage transcends a literal numerical quantity, it nevertheless creates the literal image of abundance.

Beyond the genre and idiom possibilities, another approach to this issue understands the lexical nuance intended by the term translated "thousand" (ʾelep; GK 547) as that of a military fighting unit or military chiefs/tribal leaders rather than

1,000 soldiers. That is to say, an expression currently translated as "580 *thousand*" (580,000) could actually be intended as "580 [military] *units/tribal leaders/officers*." Estimates for these military units range from ten to thirty soldiers each, perhaps in analogy to the units of the "three" and the "thirty" used to describe David's core military leadership (cf. 1Ch 11:10–47). Using this approach, a figure currently translated "580,000" (580 *thousand*) would instead be translated as 580 *units*, which would actually amount from 5,800 to 17,400 soldiers, depending on the estimate of the unit size. These lower numbers would fit better into assumed Iron Age population and military levels.

It is clear that the term translated "thousand" has a semantic domain beyond that of the numeral 1,000. This raises the distinct possibility that the intent of the Spirit of God was to communicate something other than a literal 1,000 soldiers. Of the alternative options noted above, the understanding of ʾelep as a military unit has the most merit.

2–4 Note that from the perspective of Yahweh, the divided tribes were still ultimately "brothers"— brothers of covenant. The final verse underscores what had been noted earlier (cf. 10:15)—that divine agency had been shaping the events at hand ("this is my doing"). Although Israel was in rebellion against the divinely established house of David (see 10:19), God's sovereignty was nonetheless in play in the division of the Israelite kingdom. The initial obedience of Rehoboam and the southern kingdom to God's will eventually gives way to disobedience and unfaithfulness (cf. 12:14).

NOTES

10:6–11 The advice of the elder advisors summarized in 1 Kings 12:7 expands the idea of Rehoboam's agreeing to the request for relief in national service by advising Rehoboam to "be a servant to these people and serve them"—a line of advice that resonates with the broader message of Scripture (cf. Mt 20:28; Mk 9:34–35; Jn 13:1–17).

11:1 Examples of the usage of אֶלֶף (ʾelep) as a tribal leader or chief include Numbers 10:4; Joshua 22:13−14, 21, 30 (cf. also Zec 9:7; 12:5−6). Similarly, several passages imply that ʾelep is a unit that is smaller than a tribe (cf. 1Sa 10:19; 23:23; Mic 5:2) and larger than a family (cf. Jdg 6:15). Such an understanding of ʾelep might shed some light on the "rout" that takes place at Ai (Jos 7:3−5). This defeat of the Israelites takes the lives of "about 36 men," a number that does not seem like much of a rout if they began with two or three *thousand* soldiers, but is much more understandable if they sent out two or three *units* totaling forty to sixty men. On this approach, see G. E. Mendenhall, "The Census Lists of Numbers 1 and 26," *JBL* 77(1958): 52−66. Similar approaches are proposed by J. W. Wenham, "Large Numbers in the Old Testament," *TynBul* 18 (1967): 19−53; J. B. Payne, "The Validity of Numbers in Chronicles," *BSac* 136 (1979): 109−28, 206−20. Also cf. *NIDOTTE* (1:416−18), and C. J. Humphreys, "The Number of People in the Exodus from Egypt: Decoding Mathematically the Very Large Numbers in Numbers I and XXVI," *VT* 48 (1998): 196−211.

2. Rehoboam's Fortifications and Administration (2Ch 11:5−23)

⁵Rehoboam lived in Jerusalem and built up towns for defense in Judah: ⁶Bethlehem, Etam, Tekoa, ⁷Beth Zur, Soco, Adullam, ⁸Gath, Mareshah, Ziph, ⁹Adoraim, Lachish, Azekah, ¹⁰Zorah, Aijalon and Hebron. These were fortified cities in Judah and Benjamin. ¹¹He strengthened their defenses and put commanders in them, with supplies of food, olive oil and wine. ¹²He put shields and spears in all the cities, and made them very strong. So Judah and Benjamin were his.

¹³The priests and Levites from all their districts throughout Israel sided with him. ¹⁴The Levites even abandoned their pasturelands and property, and came to Judah and Jerusalem because Jeroboam and his sons had rejected them as priests of the LORD. ¹⁵And he appointed his own priests for the high places and for the goat and calf idols he had made. ¹⁶Those from every tribe of Israel who set their hearts on seeking the LORD, the God of Israel, followed the Levites to Jerusalem to offer sacrifices to the LORD, the God of their fathers. ¹⁷They strengthened the kingdom of Judah and supported Rehoboam son of Solomon three years, walking in the ways of David and Solomon during this time.

¹⁸Rehoboam married Mahalath, who was the daughter of David's son Jerimoth and of Abihail, the daughter of Jesse's son Eliab. ¹⁹She bore him sons: Jeush, Shemariah and Zaham. ²⁰Then he married Maacah daughter of Absalom, who bore him Abijah, Attai, Ziza and Shelomith. ²¹Rehoboam loved Maacah daughter of Absalom more than any of his other wives and concubines. In all, he had eighteen wives and sixty concubines, twenty-eight sons and sixty daughters.

²²Rehoboam appointed Abijah son of Maacah to be the chief prince among his brothers, in order to make him king. ²³He acted wisely, dispersing some of his sons throughout the districts of Judah and Benjamin, and to all the fortified cities. He gave them abundant provisions and took many wives for them.

COMMENTARY

5–12 Rehoboam's fortified cities address the strategic threats to the southern kingdom from not only the northern kingdom but also foes to the east (e.g., Moab, Ammon), west (e.g., Philistines), and south (e.g., Egypt). The list of fifteen towns (vv.6–10) focuses on three main lines of fortification that are for the most part grouped accordingly: along the east/southeastern edge of the Judean hill country (e.g., Bethlehem); along the western edge of the Shephelah (e.g., Lachish); and along the southwestern edge of the Judean hill country (e.g., Hebron). In addition, Aijalon would protect from threats to the north via the Beth Horon Ridge (northern kingdom, Aram). All told, the focal point of Rehoboam's fortifications is the defense of access points to the capital city of Jerusalem. Excavations from several of these cities have uncovered fortifications that may date to Rehoboam's fortification efforts.

13–14 In the aftermath of the division, priests and Levites found themselves separated from the Jerusalem temple and rejected by the new northern dynasty (cf. comments on v.15). Some even opted to sacrifice personal security of land and possessions in order to gain proximity to the place where God caused his Name to dwell and show their allegiance to the Davidic dynasty that God had established.

15 In the northern kingdom, the division of the kingdom necessitated the development of political centers for the north (Shechem and Penuel) and alternative religious centers. Jeroboam's concern for the fidelity of his new subjects leads to his establishment of the infamous golden calf shrines in the northern region of the northern kingdom (the city of Dan) and at the southern region of the northern kingdom (the city of Bethel), as discussed in greater detail in the parallel passage of 1 Kings 12:26–33.

Jeroboam's choice of calf (bull) idols reflects the fact that bovines were commonly associated with divinity across the ancient Near East, given the bull's association with strength, power, and fertility. Thus Jeroboam's calves (like those of Aaron in Ex 32) may reflect syncretism with prevailing notions of expressing deity (namely, via bovines) in neighboring cultures. In any case, Jeroboam's idols may be primarily a violation of the second commandment (attempting to make an image of God).

Note that in the case of Aaron's golden calf in Exodus 32, the whole affair intersects the goal of readying a feast *to Yahweh* (cf. Ex 32:5) rather than to another god. It seems clear that the parallels drawn between these incidents are intended to catch the attention of the careful hearer/reader of God's Word. Thus, note the similarity between Jeroboam's words in 1 Kings 12:28 and the phraseology used by Aaron and the people in Exodus 32:4 in presenting the calf/calves to the people:

> "Here are your gods, O Israel, who brought
> you up out of Egypt." (1Ki 12:28)
> "These are your gods, O Israel, who brought
> you up out of Egypt." (Ex 32:4)

The intertextuality exhibited here implies that the writer of Kings wants his reader to understand the current crisis in the light of the earlier crisis during the time of Moses. In both cases, God's divinely chosen leadership was rejected and replaced, and the people at large opted to attempt to worship God on their terms rather than on his terms. The significance of goat idols noted in v.15 is uncertain, but they may represent satyr-like demons understood to traverse deserted wastelands.

16 Like the priests and Levites who left all they had to relocate to the southern kingdom (see vv.13–14), Godward individuals from the ten northern tribes opted to follow the example of the priests and Levites and migrate to the southern kingdom. Like the priests and Levites, these immigrants would have left farms, families, businesses, tribal allotments, and the like for the greater good of being in community with God's people pursuing his will. Also see the Reflection in ch. 12, below.

17 In comparison with the apostasy and syncretism of Jeroboam in the northern kingdom (see 11:13–15 above), the influx of the God-seeking people, priests, and Levites seems to stimulate a time of political strength and spiritual fervor in the southern kingdom. Unfortunately, this time of righteousness lasts only three years. The comments on 12:1 and 12:14 imply that the political strength attained in the southern kingdom facilitated the perilous step away from complete dependency on God and obedience to his ways (cf. 1Co 10:12).

18–23 In the context of the biblical world, Rehoboam's multiple wives and concubines tangibly displayed his power and wealth. Marriages were also a common component in political treaties, under the notion that the interweaving of family would increase loyalty and decrease the possibility of betrayal. Such "practical" reasons aside, the multiplying of wives was in direct contradiction to Deuteronomic warnings directed at kings (see Dt 17:17). Rehoboam's multiple wives are reminiscent of both his grandfather David's wives (cf. 2Sa 5:13; 1Ch 14:3) and those of his father, Solomon (1Ki 11:1–3). Likewise, Rehoboam took "many wives" for his sons (v.23), thus perpetuating the practice within the Davidic monarchy. Rehoboam's appointment of Abijah (son of his favorite wife, v.22) as chief priest further demonstrates Rehoboam's lack of commitment to the Mosaic law.

NOTES

5–12 The impressive brick fortification of Lachish Level IV may provide a glimpse into Rehoboam's fortification activities (see D. Ussishkin, "Lachish," *NEAEHL*, 3:897–911).

18 Abihail was likely Mahaloth's mother rather than another of Rehoboam's wives (cf. MT).

20 The reference to Absalom (vv.20–21) names David's son. Absalom had one daughter (Tamar; 2Sa 14:27), so it is usually assumed that Maacah was Absalom's granddaughter through Tamar. However, since the names of this family apparently have different spellings (e.g., Abishalom [1Ki 15:2, 10]; Micaiah [2Ch 13:2], which the NIV "corrects" to Maacah) and since Maacah was a known name for others, it is difficult to be certain on this issue.

3. Invasion of Pharaoh Shishak (2Ch 12:1–12)

¹After Rehoboam's position as king was established and he had become strong, he and all Israel with him abandoned the law of the LORD. ²Because they had been unfaithful to the LORD, Shishak king of Egypt attacked Jerusalem in the fifth year of King Rehoboam. ³With twelve hundred chariots and sixty thousand horsemen and the innumerable troops of Libyans, Sukkites and Cushites that came with him from Egypt, ⁴he captured the fortified cities of Judah and came as far as Jerusalem.

⁵Then the prophet Shemaiah came to Rehoboam and to the leaders of Judah who had assembled in Jerusalem for fear of Shishak, and he said to them, "This is what the LORD says, 'You have abandoned me; therefore, I now abandon you to Shishak.'"

⁶The leaders of Israel and the king humbled themselves and said, "The LORD is just."

⁷When the LORD saw that they humbled themselves, this word of the LORD came to Shemaiah: "Since they have humbled themselves, I will not destroy them but will soon give them deliverance. My wrath will not be poured out on Jerusalem through Shishak. ⁸They will, however, become subject to him, so that they may learn the difference between serving me and serving the kings of other lands."

⁹When Shishak king of Egypt attacked Jerusalem, he carried off the treasures of the temple of the LORD and the treasures of the royal palace. He took everything, including the gold shields Solomon had made. ¹⁰So King Rehoboam made bronze shields to replace them and assigned these to the commanders of the guard on duty at the entrance to the royal palace. ¹¹Whenever the king went to the LORD's temple, the guards went with him, bearing the shields, and afterward they returned them to the guardroom.

¹²Because Rehoboam humbled himself, the LORD's anger turned from him, and he was not totally destroyed. Indeed, there was some good in Judah.

COMMENTARY

1 Rehoboam and the southern kingdom as a whole begin transitioning to the time frame of the divided kingdom on the high note of the immigration of godly spiritual leaders and citizens to the south and an overall atmosphere of spiritual fervor for three years (see 11:16–17). However, once Rehoboam's strength and position are established, the southern kingdom abandons its initial orientation of "walking in the ways of David and Solomon" and no longer seeks to live life through the orientation of God's instruction (Torah/law).

Abandoning the Torah was the opposite of the covenanted fiduciary responsibility of the Israelite king, who was to read God's law "all the days of his life so that he may learn to revere the LORD his God and follow carefully" all the words of God's covenantal law (cf. Dt 17:14–20). This covenantal unfaithfulness (note this terminology in the next verse) is tantamount to "abandoning" Yahweh (see v.5) and underscores the clear link between obedience and genuine faith. The covenantal unfaithfulness of Rehoboam and Judah prompts God's response through the framework of the Deuteronomic covenant (cf. Dt 28:25 et al.; also cf. 1Ki 9:6–9).

2 As anticipated in the framework of the covenantal relationship between God and Israel and spelled out in numerous warning passages (e.g., Dt 28:25; 1Ki 9:6–9), God may choose to utilize the army of a foreign nation as a consequence for covenantal unfaithfulness. Shishak's invasion took place in the fifth year of Rehoboam (most likely 926 BC, as Rehoboam began his reign following the death of Solomon [ca. 931 BC], with the division of the kingdom happening shortly thereafter; 2Ch 12:2). The Chronicler notes in a handful of verses (cf. 11:17–12:1) that there was a three-year period in which Rehoboam was loyal to Yahweh (ca. 930–27), followed by apostasy, thus providing a context (theological and historical) for the time leading up to Shishak's invasion.

Since the last pharaoh of the Twenty-First Dynasty did not have a male son, he opted to promote a Libyan military commander named Sheshonq (biblical Shishak, variously spelled as Sheshonk, Shoshenq, and Shusheq) to a position of virtual heir to the throne. When Psusennes II died, Sheshonq become pharaoh, founding the Twenty-Second Dynasty in approximately 945 BC. Following his ascension to the Egyptian throne, Shishak/Sheshonq facilitated the reunification of Upper (Southern) and Lower (Northern) Egypt through deft political decisions, strategic priestly appointments, and political marriages.

3 The multiethnic African coalition raised by Shishak likely reflects a combination of Shishak's Libyan heritage (and the related Sukkites [Tjukten]) as well as Egyptian hegemony over Cush/Nubia to the south of Egypt (cf. F. Clancy, "Shishak/Shoshenq's Travels," *JSOT* 86 [1999]: 2–23). The area between the first and second cataracts of the Nile is referred to as Lower Nubia (since "Lower" relates to the flow of the Nile, Lower Nubia designates northern Nubia) and Upper (= southern) Nubia, the latter being known as "Cush" (Kush) to biblical writers, Assyrians, and Persians. Today, much of what was Lower Nubia is located in the southern area of Egypt (some of which is now under Lake Nasser following the construction of the dam outside Aswan). What was Upper Nubia now sits within the border of modern-day Sudan.

4 Because Rehoboam and Judah "abandoned" God and his Word (cf. vv. 1, 5), God "abandons" Judah to Shishak (cf. v. 5). The summary of Shishak's invasion in Chronicles provides additional details of Shishak's campaign over that disclosed in 1 Kings 14, including the extent of Shishak's invasion. Despite

different degrees of detail, both emphasize that Shishak took "everything" from the house of Yahweh and the royal palace (cf. 1Ki 14:26; 2Ch 12:9).

The details of Shishak's invasion are celebrated on the southwest wall of the Karnak temple in Thebes. Shishak's list includes a topographical inventory of more than 150 places in the form of place-name hieroglyphic ovals. Of this number, thirty or more name ovals are unreadable and a number of others are speculative reconstructions. The upper register of Shishak's list contains a number of towns in what was primarily northern kingdom territory (cf. *ANET*, 242–43), including places along the coastal highway (such as Socoh and Yaham), places in the Jezreel Valley (such as Taanach and Megiddo), towns in the Beth Shan Valley (including Beth Shan and Rehob), and places in Transjordan (such as Adam and Penuel). These victories restored Egyptian domination over important trade routes that traversed these areas.

In addition, Shishak records the defeat of several towns in southern kingdom territory, including Gibeon (central hill country) and Aijalon (one of Rehoboam's fortified cities in the Shephelah; cf. 11:5–12; 12:4). The lower register of Shishak's list focuses on towns in the southern region of Judah (the biblical Negev), perhaps aimed at reasserting Egyptian control over trade routes to Arabia. A stela (stone monument) discovered at Megiddo with the cartouche of Shoshenq almost certainly dates to this invasion. The absence of Jerusalem in Shishak's lists is noteworthy, though it is possible that references to Jerusalem were among the destroyed sections of the Karnak temple inscription.

Shishak's invasion of northern kingdom territory is intriguing, given Jeroboam's time in Egypt as a guest of the Egyptian pharaoh. This suggests that Shishak's invasion might be some type of reprisal against Jeroboam for failing to follow through with some kind of agreement. Recall that Jeroboam fled to Egypt to escape Solomon's wrath and was sheltered as a guest of Egypt by Pharaoh Sheshonq I (Shishak) until the death of Solomon (cf. 1Ki 11:26–40). For additional details of Shoshenq's [Shishak's] campaign into Israel and Judah, see K. Kitchen, *Third Intermediate Period* (2nd ed.; Warminster, UK: Aris and Phillips, 1986): 293–302, 432–47; J. Currid, *Ancient Egypt and the Old Testament* (Grand Rapids: Baker, 1997), 173–202.

5–8 In the aftermath of this covenantal unfaithfulness and God's judgment, the covenant functionary role of the prophet is reflected in Shemaiah's proclamation of the sin of the people and the resulting divine judgment (v.5; cf. Johnstone, 2:41–43). The king and the leaders of Israel respond to the prophet's indictment in a way anticipated in Solomon's temple-dedication prayer in 6:24–25 (12:6; also cf. v.12). While Jerusalem is not destroyed (v.7), the temple and palace treasuries are ravaged (see v.9) and the southern kingdom will now be under the hegemony of Egypt as a continuation of the consequence of abandoning God and his Word (v.8; also see comments on vv.2, 3, 4, 9).

9 The biblical accounts of Shishak's invasion of Judah emphasize that Shishak took "everything" from the house of Yahweh and the royal palace (cf. 1Ki

14:26). This ravaging of the treasures of the king and the temple dramatically reverses earlier statements heralding the wealth God had enabled Solomon to accumulate (cf. 2Ch 3:8–9; on the gold shields made during the time of Solomon, see comments on 9:15–16; also see comments above on ch. 12).

10–11 As a result of the loss of the hammered gold shields made by Solomon (see comments on 12:9 and 9:15–16), Rehoboam makes replacement shields out of a less precious metal (bronze) and institutes extra security measures to safeguard these less valuable shields.

12 As anticipated in Solomon's temple-dedication prayer, God abounds in mercy and forgiveness when his people seek him in humility and contrition (see comments on 6:22–39). This is a theme stressed over and again by the Chronicler, no doubt for the instruction and encouragement of the postexilic community still reeling from the sting of drastic divine judgment. Although there is some "good" to be found in Judah (cf. 11:2–4, 16–17; 12:5–7), Rehoboam is nonetheless described at the beginning of chapter 12 as abandoning God's covenantal law (cf. v.1), and he is summarized at the end of the chapter as doing evil because he did not set his heart on the Lord (v.14).

NOTE

4 Similarly, during the days of David and Solomon, Hadad the Edomite was sheltered in Egypt and even married the sister of the queen (cf. 1Ki 11:14–22).

4. Rehoboam's Regnal Summary (2Ch 12:13–16)

¹³King Rehoboam established himself firmly in Jerusalem and continued as king. He was forty-one years old when he became king, and he reigned seventeen years in Jerusalem, the city the LORD had chosen out of all the tribes of Israel in which to put his Name.

His mother's name was Naamah; she was an Ammonite. [14]He did evil because he had not set his heart on seeking the LORD.

[15]As for the events of Rehoboam's reign, from beginning to end, are they not written in the records of Shemaiah the prophet and of Iddo the seer that deal with genealogies? There was continual warfare between Rehoboam and Jeroboam. [16]Rehoboam rested with his fathers and was buried in the City of David. And Abijah his son succeeded him as king.

COMMENTARY

13 Like Solomon (1:1), Rehoboam is described as being firmly established on the Davidic throne. In addition to using this phraseology regarding Solomon and Jeroboam, the Chronicler also uses it in the royal succession contexts of Asa (15:8), Jehoshaphat (17:1), and Amaziah/Uzziah (25:3; on God's choice of Jerusalem, see comments on 3:1; on God's causing his Name to dwell in Jerusalem, see comments on 2:1; on the topic of the queen mother, see comments on 15:16; for the political marriage implied by Rehoboam's Ammonite mother [recall Solomon's international harem; 1Ki 11:1], see comments on 18:1). The country of Ammon traces its lineage back to Lot (Ge 19:38) and was located in the Transjordanian region to the east of the tribal areas of Reuben and Gad. All told, Rehoboam ruled over the southern tribes for 17 years (ca. 931/930–913 BC), while Jeroboam ruled over the northern tribes for about 21 years (ca. 931–910 BC; cf. Thiele, 80–81).

14 The fundamental issue behind Rehoboam's apostasy and covenantal unfaithfulness was his lack of setting his heart to seek God. This is opposite the demeanor of dependence, humility, and prayerfulness that God's king and God's people are to demonstrate. Conversely, despite his poignant instances of iniquity, David was a leader who set his heart to seek the Lord (1Sa 13:14). The distinc-

tion of whether a king sets his heart on seeking God will establish the trajectory of kings throughout the balance of the divided monarchy. Moreover, such a disposition ultimately determines the spiritual vibrancy and fruitfulness of our own lives (see Reflection).

15 A defining characteristic in Chronicles is its propensity to cite a wide range of sources. While some named sources may well be alternative names for the same document (e.g., variations of references to the "Book of the Kings"), the use of a variety of sources by the Chronicler is clear. These sources reflect the historiographical and theological purpose(s) of the Chronicler and also reflect a milieu in which earlier texts are referenced and seen as authoritative. As such, it is noteworthy to see the propensity for the source noted in Chronicles to have a prophetic connection.

Note also the overlapping content of certain prophetic texts with passages in Kings (e.g., Isa 36–39 and 2Ki 18–20; Jer 52 and 2Ki 25). In addition, Chronicles refers to sources at similar junctions as that reflected in the book of Kings (e.g., 2Ch 12:15 and 1Ki 14:29; 2Ch 16:11 and 1Ki 15:23; 2Ch 20:34 and 1Ki 22:45; 2Ch 25:26 and 2Ki 14:18). See additional remarks in the Introduction.

16 Despite the largely negative theological assessment of Rehoboam, he is afforded the honor being buried in the royal cemetery unlike other ungodly kings who were denied this privilege (e.g., Jehoram in 21:20). While little is known of ancient Israel's royal burial customs, the special treatment of kings in death and burial was common in the biblical world as reflected in the exquisite burial chambers in the Valley of the Kings in Thebes, Egypt. Following Rehoboam's death, his son Abijah assumes the throne in Judah, while Jeroboam is still ruling the northern kingdom.

REFLECTION

The Chronicler's comment that Rehoboam "did evil because he had not set his heart on seeking the LORD" (12:14) reflects the paramount value placed on the preparation of our hearts to pursue God in fellowship and obedience (cf. Dt 4:29; Mt 22:37). The distinction of whether a king set his heart on seeking God established the trajectory of his reign throughout the history of Israel. Similarly, such a disposition ultimately determines the spiritual vibrancy and fruitfulness of our own lives (Ps 19:14; Pr 4:23). Setting our heart to seek God goes hand in hand with serving God with all of our heart (cf. Dt 11:13–18), laying up God's Word in our heart (Ps 119:11), and applying our heart to understanding and walking in God's ways (cf. Dt 10:12). All told, believers today would do well to internalize David's charge to his son Solomon: "Devote your heart and soul to seeking the LORD your God" (1Ch 22:19).

B. The Reign of Abijah (2Ch 13:1–14:1)

OVERVIEW

The account of Abijah in Chronicles differs in tone and details from that recorded in the book of Kings, where the summary of Abijah's reign is succinct and summarized negatively (cf. 1Ki 15:3). In the longer account of Abijah's reign in Chronicles the focus is almost exclusively on an account of a battle between Abijah (of Judah) and Jeroboam (of Israel) in which Abijah gives a battlefield speech summarizing the northern kingdom's departure from God's will and covenantal framework (cf. 2Ch 13:4–9) and proclaiming Judah's obedience to Mosaic legislation and blessings of divine presence (cf. 13:10–12).

Abijah and Judah cry out to Yahweh at the start of the battle (cf. 13:14), and God brings victory to Abijah and Judah over Jeroboam and the north because of their reliance on him (cf. 13:15–18). In addition, the account in Chronicles stresses God's response to the prayers of his people and his protection of the Davidic kingdom (the "kingdom of the LORD," v.8). That Abijah's reign is ultimately characterized by his sin and lack of full commitment to Yahweh in Kings does not need to be seen as problematic in the light of this narrative account in Chronicles, as Rehoboam's reign is likewise highlighted by points of faith and obedience (e.g., 11:2–4, 16–17; 12:6–7) as well as his foolishness and ultimate departure from the ways of the Lord (e.g., 10:8–15; 12:1, 5, 14). The Chronicler's emphasis is consistent with his sustained message of hope and possibility directed to his postexilic audience. For more on the Chronicler's focus and intent, see the Introduction. On Abijah's specific portrayal, see D. G. Deboys, "History and Theol-ogy in the Chronicler's Portrayal of Abijah," *Bib* 71 (1990): 48–62.

---

[1]In the eighteenth year of the reign of Jeroboam, Abijah became king of Judah, [2]and he reigned in Jerusalem three years. His mother's name was Maacah, a daughter of Uriel of Gibeah.

There was war between Abijah and Jeroboam. [3]Abijah went into battle with a force of four hundred thousand able fighting men, and Jeroboam drew up a battle line against him with eight hundred thousand able troops.

[4]Abijah stood on Mount Zemaraim, in the hill country of Ephraim, and said, "Jeroboam and all Israel, listen to me! [5]Don't you know that the LORD, the God of Israel, has given the kingship of Israel to David and his descendants forever by a covenant of salt? [6]Yet Jeroboam son of Nebat, an official of Solomon son of David, rebelled against his master. [7]Some worthless scoundrels gathered around him and opposed Rehoboam son of Solomon when he was young and indecisive and not strong enough to resist them.

[8]"And now you plan to resist the kingdom of the LORD, which is in the hands of David's descendants. You are indeed a vast army and have with you the golden calves that Jeroboam made to be your gods. [9]But didn't you drive out the priests of the LORD, the sons of Aaron, and the Levites, and make priests of your own as the peoples of other lands do? Whoever comes to consecrate himself with a young bull and seven rams may become a priest of what are not gods.

[10]"As for us, the LORD is our God, and we have not forsaken him. The priests who serve the LORD are sons of Aaron, and the Levites assist them. [11]Every morning and evening they present burnt offerings and fragrant incense to the LORD. They set out the bread on the ceremonially clean table and light the lamps on the gold lampstand every evening. We are observing the requirements of the LORD our God. But you have forsaken him. [12]God is with us; he is our leader. His priests with their trumpets will sound the battle cry against you. Men of Israel, do not fight against the LORD, the God of your fathers, for you will not succeed."

[13]Now Jeroboam had sent troops around to the rear, so that while he was in front of Judah the ambush was behind them. [14]Judah turned and saw that they were being attacked at both front and rear. Then they cried out to the LORD. The priests blew their trumpets [15]and the men of Judah raised the battle cry. At the sound of their battle cry, God routed Jeroboam and all Israel before Abijah and Judah. [16]The Israelites fled before Judah, and God delivered them into their hands. [17]Abijah and his men inflicted heavy losses on them, so that there were five hundred thousand casualties among Israel's able men. [18]The men of Israel were subdued on that occasion, and the men of Judah were victorious because they relied on the LORD, the God of their fathers.

¹⁹Abijah pursued Jeroboam and took from him the towns of Bethel, Jeshanah and Ephron, with their surrounding villages. ²⁰Jeroboam did not regain power during the time of Abijah. And the LORD struck him down and he died.

²¹But Abijah grew in strength. He married fourteen wives and had twenty-two sons and sixteen daughters.

²²The other events of Abijah's reign, what he did and what he said, are written in the annotations of the prophet Iddo.

¹⁴:¹And Abijah rested with his fathers and was buried in the City of David. Asa his son succeeded him as king, and in his days the country was at peace for ten years.

COMMENTARY

1–2 Following Rehoboam's death, his son Abijah assumes the throne in Judah. Abijah reigns over the southern kingdom from ca. 913–11 BC and may have had a brief coregency with his father Rehoboam. Earlier, Rehoboam had appointed Abijah as chief prince, presumably to facilitate a stable regnal changeover (see 11:22). Meanwhile, Jeroboam is in his eighteenth year of rule in the northern kingdom.

3 The conflict that began between Jeroboam and Rehoboam (see 12:15) continues into the reign of Abijah, successor to Rehoboam in Judah. Even though Jeroboam's army is described as being double that of Abijah, the battle highlighted here implies that Abijah is on the offensive both militarily and theologically (on the latter, see comments at vv.4–12). God had previously disallowed battle between the north and south (cf. 11:2–4; on the large numbers of this battle, see the extended discussion at 11:1).

4–12 As with many narrative portions of the Bible, the speeches in Chronicles provide useful theological synthesis and underscore authorial intent in the selection and shaping of narrative details. Abijah's prophetlike speech from Mount Zemaraim teems with theological significance and reflects a keen understanding of the Davidic covenant (vv.5–8). Moreover, Abijah's speech reflects the necessity of complete obedience to God's covenantal stipulations concerning priestly service and sacrificial details (vv.9–11; recall Jeroboam's changes in matters of priests and spiritual service; cf. 10:15).

The location of Mount Zemaraim (v.4) is not certain but seems to be in the vicinity of Bethel near the border with Benjamin. Salt (v.5) was connected with the sealing of treaties and covenants in many cultures of the biblical world. Moreover, salt was an important element in the ancient world for preservation, and its use here would underscore God's commitment to preserve the house of David (note the similar expression in Nu 18:19).

13–17 The battle begins with an ambush by the troops of Jeroboam (v.13). In response, Judah cries out to the Lord while the priests blow their trumpets, reminiscent of the battle at Jericho (Jos 8). The trumpets were special trumpets constructed for priests as outlined in Numbers 10:1–9, and their use in military signaling is reflected in Israel's battle against the Midianites (cf. Nu 31:1–6). The victory illustrates the motif of God as a divine warrior who fights on behalf of his people (cf. Dt 20:4; see T. Longman III and D. Reid, *God Is a Warrior* [Grand

Rapids: Zondervan, 1995]; on the large number of casualties [v.17], see comments on 2Ch 11:1).

18 The victory of Judah over the significantly larger forces of the army of Jeroboam is attributed not to military stratagem or the like, but to their reliance on God. As Abijah noted at v.12, God is with his covenantal people, and to fight them is to "fight against the LORD." God's direct role in this battle is emphatically underscored within the language of the narrative—"God routed Jeroboam" (v.15), "God delivered them" (v.16), and "the LORD struck him [Jeroboam] down" (v.20).

19 Abijah's victory over Jeroboam gives Judah control of the two major north-south highways connecting Israel and Judah as well as control over the coveted Benjamin plateau together with a small portion of the Ephraimite hill country.

20 The remark that "Jeroboam did not regain power" may be related to Aramean pressure on the northern kingdom. Jeroboam died not long after this time and was succeeded by his son Nadab (ca. 910/909–909/908 BC), who was assassinated by his army commander Baasha while battling the Philistines. After his murder of Nadab, Baasha rules the northern kingdom for twenty-four years, largely overlapping with the reign of Asa in the southern kingdom.

21 While Jeroboam does not regain strength (v.20), Abijah grows in strength. Unfortunately, Abijah, like David, Solomon, and Rehoboam, expresses this strength in the ways of the biblical world by multiplying wives to himself, despite Deuteronomic warnings against this practice (see Dt 17:17). Note that Rehoboam had set this in motion by acquiring "many wives" for his sons (cf. 2Ch 11:23).

22 On the topic of prophetic regnal annotations, see comments on 12:15 and the Introduction.

14:1 This verse is the closing summary of the reign of Abijah covered in the previous chapter. Abijah is given the honor of being buried in the royal cemetery (also see comments on 12:16). The backdrop of the peace of this time frame began with the victory God gave Abijah over Jeroboam and the subsequent internal turmoil in the northern kingdom (cf. 13:15–20). Asa succeeds his father Abijah as ruler in the southern kingdom (ca. 911 BC) two years before the ascension of Nadab in the northern kingdom and enjoys a season of peace and stability lasting around one decade of his forty-one-year reign (ca. 910–870 BC), while the northern kingdom continues to face internal and external turmoil.

NOTES

13:1 In the book of Kings Abijah's name is spelled "Abijam," though the NIV still renders the name "Abijah." While this may simply be a spelling variation, it may also be a subtle commentary on the spiritual unfaithfulness of Abijah highlighted in Kings (cf. 1Ki 15:3), as the "-jam" (ם׳, *yām*) suffix would draw connection to the Canaanite sea god Yam ("my father is Yam[m]") while the "-jah" (ה׳, *yâ*) ending connects with the short form of the divine name Yah/Yahweh.

2 The king's mother's name is noted as "Micaiah" in Chronicles and "Maacah" in Kings (obscured by the NIV, which renders "Micaiah" as "Maacah" at 13:2). Also, his mother is described as the daughter of Uriel here (v.2), but she is noted as the daughter of Abishalom (Absalom) in 1 Kings. This difference probably functions in analogy to the flexible use of the Hebrew term for son (בֵּן, *bēn*; GK 1201), which can mean "son," "grandson," or simply "descendant." Thus Micaiah/Maacah might actually be both Abishalom/Absalom's granddaughter (or female descendant) as noted in Kings, and the daughter of Uriel as noted here. As with the Abijah/Abijam issue discussed in the previous note, Abijam's connection with Absalom noted in Kings may be intended by the writer of Kings as subtly negative commentary on the reign of Abijah/Abijam.

C. The Reign of Asa (2Ch 14:2–16:14)

1. Asa's Reforms and Military Strength (2Ch 14:2–8)

²Asa did what was good and right in the eyes of the Lord his God. ³He removed the foreign altars and the high places, smashed the sacred stones and cut down the Asherah poles. ⁴He commanded Judah to seek the Lord, the God of their fathers, and to obey his laws and commands. ⁵He removed the high places and incense altars in every town in Judah, and the kingdom was at peace under him. ⁶He built up the fortified cities of Judah, since the land was at peace. No one was at war with him during those years, for the Lord gave him rest.

⁷"Let us build up these towns," he said to Judah, "and put walls around them, with towers, gates and bars. The land is still ours, because we have sought the Lord our God; we sought him and he has given us rest on every side." So they built and prospered.

⁸Asa had an army of three hundred thousand men from Judah, equipped with large shields and with spears, and two hundred and eighty thousand from Benjamin, armed with small shields and with bows. All these were brave fighting men.

COMMENTARY

2 Asa is the first of the post-divided kingdom Judean kings to be described as doing what is right in God's eyes. Moreover, Asa is the first Judean king of this era to inaugurate significant reforms designed to eradicate syncretism and revitalize covenantal fidelity within the community (cf. 15:8–18). Thus the reign and reforms of Asa function as a sort of precursor to the later reformer kings in Judah, most notably Hezekiah and Josiah. Note that Asa, like Hezekiah (30:6–11), invites those situated within the northern kingdom to assemble in Jerusalem and publicly declare their loyalty to God's ways (cf. 15:9–15). By contrast, the final six or so years of Asa's reign (compare 15:19; 16:1, 13) are punctuated with compromise and ungodly behavior. For additional points of similarity between Asa and Hezekiah, see Selman, 384–87.

3 The destruction of idolatry and syncretistic worship commonly associated with Canaanite religious cults (high places, foreign altars, sacred stones, and Asherah poles) per Deuteronomic admonition (cf. Dt 16:21–22) was a cornerstone of Asa's religious reforms and was likewise seen in the reforms of Hezekiah (cf. 2Ch 31:1) and Josiah (cf. 34:3–7). A key attraction to the worship of Baal (Hadad) was his dominion over storms (i.e., rain), while a key attraction point for Asherah was her dominion over fertility.

Asherah was frequently tied to tree imagery (such as Asherah poles), perhaps in connection with the ancient Near Eastern motif of divine fruitfulness as well as that of the tree of life. Asherah poles were wooden cult symbols of Asherah in the form of both living trees and wooden poles/pillars. An Asherah pole would be erected, consecrated, and worshiped as a representative of the goddess. The Israelites were not immune to the allure of Asherah poles (cf. Dt 16:21 and Jer 17:2). The destruction of these poles by Asa suggests that the worship of Yahweh was being tainted with Asherah worship (see Day, 385–408).

Sacred stones could consist of rough stone or a finely shaped pillar, and such standing stones have widespread connection to religious settings in the world of the OT and even play a role in several passages involving covenant (cf. Ge 28:22; Ex 24:4; Jos 24:26). Presumably, the prohibition in Deuteronomy 16 relates to the risk of syncretistic worship as the Israelites enter the land of Canaan (see E. Stockton, "Sacred Pillars in the Bible," *ABR* 20 [1972]: 16 32; C. F. Graesser, "Standing Stones in Ancient Palestine," *BA* 35 [1972]: 34–63).

4 The portrayal of the Israelite king reading, writing, and living out the law of God is central to his role as a leader in God's covenantal framework:

> When he takes the throne of his kingdom, he is to write for himself on a scroll a copy of this law, taken from that of the priests, who are Levites. It is to be with him, and he is to read it all the days of his life so that he may learn to revere the LORD his God and follow carefully all the words of this law and these decrees and not consider himself better than his brothers and turn from the law to the right or to the left. Then he and his descendants will reign a long time over his kingdom in Israel. (Dt 17:18–20)

So part of the divinely intended role of the king is intimately related to the spiritual life of ancient Israel (note the statements of Jdg 17:6; 21:25). This spiritual leadership is described from a negative perspective in vv.3 and 5 (namely, removing, smashing, cutting down articles of idolatry) and from a positive one here (namely, seeking and obeying God). It should also be noted that Asa's charge for the people to "seek" God is inseparably connected with the admonishment to obey his Word ("his laws and commands"). The notion of seeking God apart from obedience is an unknown concept in the Bible (cf. the word of Christ in Jn 15:10, 14).

5 In addition to Asa's efforts to facilitate God-wardness and adherence to divine truth (orthodoxy) summarized in v.4, Asa takes specific steps to remove places associated with syncretism (heterodoxy; also see comments on v.3). The result of these efforts in covenantal obedience is God-given peace and stability within the southern kingdom. On high places, see comments on 1:3–5.

6–7 The cities fortified by Asa are likely the same strategically located cities fortified previously by Solomon and Rehoboam but destroyed by Shishak. Such fortifications protected access routes to key cities such as Jerusalem and also protected control over trade routes and highways. The granting of "rest" is a divine promise given to Israel and part of the broader notion of land theology (cf. Dt 12:10; for further details on previously fortified cities, see comments on 2Ch 8:5–6; 11:5–12).

8 One by-product of the rest and prosperity given by God (cf. v.7) is the development of a formidable army. It is possible that the distinctions of weaponry noted here (spears vs. bows; large shields vs. small shields) imply differing military specialties at the tribal level (cf. the differing capabilities of the tribes noted at 1Ch 12:1–38; on the large numbers noted here, see comments on 2Ch 11:1).

NOTE

3 [2] In this chapter the verse numbers in the Hebrew text (MT) are one lower than their English Bible counterpart. Asherah might be vocalized as "Athirat." However, this is uncertain given Athirat's connection with the sea (note her common title, "Lady Athirat of the Sea") and role as consort of El in the Ugaritic corpus (see summary in Day, 385–408 [esp. 387–88, 398–99]). Moreover, Asherah should be distinguished from the goddess Astarte, who is associated with the Mesopotamian goddess Ishtar. Asherah appears as a consort of El and is portrayed as the procreatress and mother of the gods of the pantheon (cf. Day, 389).

2. Invasion of Zerah the Cushite (2Ch 14:9–15)

⁹Zerah the Cushite marched out against them with a vast army and three hundred chariots, and came as far as Mareshah. ¹⁰Asa went out to meet him, and they took up battle positions in the Valley of Zephathah near Mareshah.

¹¹Then Asa called to the Lord his God and said, "Lord, there is no one like you to help the powerless against the mighty. Help us, O Lord our God, for we rely on you, and in your name we have come against this vast army. O Lord, you are our God; do not let man prevail against you."

¹²The Lord struck down the Cushites before Asa and Judah. The Cushites fled, ¹³and Asa and his army pursued them as far as Gerar. Such a great number of Cushites fell that they could not recover; they were crushed before the Lord and his forces. The men of Judah carried off a large amount of plunder. ¹⁴They destroyed all the villages around Gerar, for the terror of the Lord had fallen upon them. They plundered all these villages, since there was much booty there. ¹⁵They also attacked the camps of the herdsmen and carried off droves of sheep and goats and camels. Then they returned to Jerusalem.

COMMENTARY

9–10 Following Asa's early reforms and rebuilding, Zerah "the Cushite" brings a large army into the southwestern region of Judah. The location of Asa's battle with Zerah is Mareshah, one of Judah's fortified cities along the western edge of the Shephelah (see comments on 11:5–12), about thirty miles southwest of Jerusalem. The location of the Valley of Zephathah (v.10) is unknown, but the LXX's rendering ("the valley to the north of Mareshah," implying a Hebrew directive *heh* [ה] — i.e., to the north) might be a preferable reading to the MT's, reflected in the NIV ("in the valley of Zephathah near Mareshah"). This alternative reading would imply a ridge route that could be utilized by an advancing army (cf. Rainey, 196).

Although Egypt is not named within this account, the close connection between Cush/Nubia and Egypt as well as the inclusion of Libyans along with Cushites at 16:8 may imply that Zerah is the field general on behalf of an Egyptian pharaoh. Similarly, Cushites were used within Shishak's coalition that attacked Judah and Israel (cf. 12:3). Another possibility is that Zerah was a chief of an Arab coalition from the Sinai region. This alternative scenario reflects the absence of Egypt within the account, references to camels and herdsmen in the battle, and the pairing of Cushites with Midianites in biblical texts (cf. Hab 3:7).

11 Asa's prayer of complete reliance on God as the protector of Israel aptly reflects his broader demonstration of covenantal faithfulness (cf. vv. 1–8). As with Abijah's earlier prayer at the outset of battle against Jeroboam (cf. 13:14) and Jehoshaphat's later prayer (cf. 20:3–12), Asa's prayer shows Solomon's temple-dedication prayer in action (cf. 6:34–35). Asa notes in his prayer that he and the people of Judah are facing the army of Zerah "in [God's] name." The idea of the name of the Lord is inter-woven with aspects of God's character as well as his covenantal relationship with Israel. As Proverbs 18:10 notes, "The name of the LORD is a strong tower; the righteous run to it and are safe."

Similarly, Asa understands the crisis as *God's war* ("do not let man prevail against you"), and the Chronicler understands the outcome as *God's victory*: the Lord strikes them (v. 12); they are crushed before the Lord (v. 13); they suffer the terror of the Lord (v. 14). Like the victories brought to Abijah and Jehoshaphat, Asa's victory illustrates the motif of God as the divine warrior who fights on behalf of his covenantal people (cf. comments on 13:13–17).

12–15 Like God's direct intervention following the prayer of Abijah and the people (cf. 13:13–20), so God responds to Asa's prayer and enables him to defeat Zerah and his massive coalition. The exact location of Gerar is unknown, but its placement within the Table of Nations (Ge 10) implies the southern region of Canaan.

NOTE

9 [8] The translation "vast army" is literally an army of a "thousand thousands" (hence the translation "one million" in some versions), or thousands upon thousands. See comments and Note on 11:1.

3. Azariah's Prophecy and Asa's Further Reforms (2Ch 15:1–19)

¹The Spirit of God came upon Azariah son of Oded. ²He went out to meet Asa and said to him, "Listen to me, Asa and all Judah and Benjamin. The LORD is with you when you are with him. If you seek him, he will be found by you, but if you forsake him, he will forsake you. ³For a long time Israel was without the true God, without a priest to teach and without the law. ⁴But in their distress they turned to the LORD, the God of Israel, and sought him, and he was found by them. ⁵In those days it was not safe to travel about, for all the inhabitants of the lands were in great turmoil. ⁶One nation was being crushed by another and one city by another, because God was troubling them with every kind of distress. ⁷But as for you, be strong and do not give up, for your work will be rewarded."

⁸When Asa heard these words and the prophecy of Azariah son of Oded the prophet, he took courage. He removed the detestable idols from the whole land of Judah and Benjamin and from the towns he had captured in the hills of Ephraim. He repaired the altar of the LORD that was in front of the portico of the LORD's temple. ⁹Then he assembled all Judah and Benjamin and the people from Ephraim, Manasseh and Simeon who had settled among them, for large numbers had come over to him from Israel when they saw that the LORD his God was with him.

¹⁰They assembled at Jerusalem in the third month of the fifteenth year of Asa's reign. ¹¹At that time they sacrificed to the LORD seven hundred head of cattle and seven thousand sheep and goats from the plunder they had brought back. ¹²They entered into a covenant to seek the LORD, the God of their fathers, with all their heart and soul. ¹³All who would not seek the LORD, the God of Israel, were to be put to death, whether small or great, man or woman. ¹⁴They took an oath to the LORD with loud acclamation, with shouting and with trumpets and horns. ¹⁵All Judah rejoiced about the oath because they had sworn it wholeheartedly. They sought God eagerly, and he was found by them. So the LORD gave them rest on every side.

¹⁶King Asa also deposed his grandmother Maacah from her position as queen mother, because she had made a repulsive Asherah pole. Asa cut the pole down, broke it up and burned it in the Kidron Valley. ¹⁷Although he did not remove the high places from Israel, Asa's heart was fully committed to the LORD all his life. ¹⁸He brought into the temple of God the silver and gold and the articles that he and his father had dedicated.

¹⁹There was no more war until the thirty-fifth year of Asa's reign.

COMMENTARY

1–2 A second stage in Asa's spiritual reforms is initiated by the Spirit of God's coming upon the otherwise unknown prophet Azariah. The connection between the coming of the Spirit of God and a specific prophetic utterance is seen in the ongoing prophetic ministry of Ezekiel (cf. Eze 11:5–12) as well as in the episodic prophetic ministry of Zechariah (son of the priest Jehoiada during the time of Joash; cf. 2Ch 24:20). In such cases the prophet is fulfilling the covenantal fiduciary role of calling God's people to comprehensive obedience to God's Word and full dependence on him. Thus the content of Azariah's words to Asa reflects earlier

biblical motifs and covenantal texts, especially those of Deuteronomy, as seen here:

But if from there you seek the LORD your God, you will find him if you look for him with all your heart and with all your soul. When you are in distress and all these things have happened to you, then in later days you will return to the LORD your God and obey him. For the LORD your God is a merciful God; he will not abandon or destroy you or forget the covenant with your forefathers, which he confirmed to them by oath. (Dt 4:29–31)

Asa's response and obedience have a significant impact on others, including Judah as a whole (15:15;

cf. 14:2–7) and Israelites from northern kingdom territories (cf. 15:9–12). Also see comments on Asa's spiritual role at 14:4. On the significance of the expression "the LORD is with you" (v.2), see the Reflection on divine presence in ch. 1.

3–6 The temporal orientation of the prophet's remarks about a prolonged time when Israel was without the true God, without priests, without God's law, and in the midst of danger and international turmoil is not completely clear. Equally uncertain is Israel's return to God in the midst of these challenges (v.4). Part of the interpretive challenge in this section relates to the Hebrew syntax of these verses, especially the lack of any finite verbs in v.3 (there are only verbless clauses), which is the verse that sets the scene of this time frame. Typically, the broader context, use of adverbial particles (especially temporal particles), and choice of verbal conjugations work together to indicate the orientation (aspect) of the verbal action. However, in this setting the context is of little value, as the prophet's speech is a stand-alone section that can be understood as either a historical review or future reality, and the verbal data of Azariah's opening statement are unclear.

This noted, the verbs of v.4 (e.g., the suffix conjugation "he [translated "they" collectively] turned" followed by *waw* consecutives, "they sought"; "he was [they were] found") would favor a past aspect (time orientation), giving rise to the common view that the prophet was summarizing a spiritually dark time such as that reflected in the book of Judges. Alternatively, it is noteworthy that the translators of the Septuagint (LXX) translated v.4 with a future orientation, resulting in a close parallel between Azariah's prophecy of 15:3–7 to that of Hosea 3:4–5:

> For the Israelites will live many days without
> king or prince, without sacrifice or sacred stones,

without ephod or idol. Afterward the Israelites will return and seek the LORD their God and David their king. They will come trembling to the LORD and to his blessings in the last days.

Whether seen from a past or future orientation, the Chronicler's postexilic audience would no doubt appreciate the parallel to their own situation in the light of Judah's seventy years of captivity and the destruction of the Jerusalem temple and thus be likewise exhorted *to return and seek God.*

The role of priests as teachers reflects God's covenantal framework, in which priests are charged by God to "teach the Israelites all the decrees the LORD has given them" (Lev 10:11; cf. the poetic [and prophetic] description of Levi's teaching commission in Dt 33:8–11 and the admonition directed to priests in Mal 2:1–9). The teaching of God's will/law—both then and now—infuses God's people with the spiritual direction and energy needed to walk in a manner pleasing to him. Wise leaders such as Jehoshaphat understood the key role of priests in the spiritual life of Israel (cf. 2Ch 17:7–9).

7 The prophet's admonition to Asa to "be strong" is a function of one's spiritual—not physical—fortitude in times of challenge and uncertainty. This spiritual dimension of being strong is seen in Asa's response ("he took courage," v.8) as he embarks on leading the people in worship and spiritual renewal (vv.8b–15).

8 Asa's destruction of idols from the tribal territories of the southern kingdom and northern tribal areas ("the hills of Ephraim") is balanced with his repairs on the altar of the Jerusalem temple. These repairs on the altar function as a tangible act evidencing his inward disposition toward faithfulness and fidelity to God. The destruction of objects of idolatry and syncretistic worship per Deuteronomic admonition (cf. Dt 16:21–22) is a cornerstone of

Asa's religious reforms and is likewise seen in the reforms of Hezekiah (cf. 2Ch 31:1) and Josiah (cf. 34:3–7; for additional remarks on Asa's removal of idols and objects of syncretism, see comments on 14:3).

9–11 Asa responds to the exhortation of the prophet Azariah (vv.1–7) by taking steps to eradicate idolatry and ready the temple altar for offerings and worship (v.8). Once these steps of reform are accomplished, Asa organizes a significant gathering of the people from the southern kingdom (Judah and Benjamin) as well as Godward individuals who have migrated from the northern kingdom (Ephraim and Manasseh; recall a similar migration during the time of Rehoboam; cf. 11:16).

As mentioned above (see comments on 14:2), about two centuries later the Judean king Hezekiah will likewise invite those situated within the northern kingdom to assemble in Jerusalem and publicly declare their loyalty to his ways (cf. 30:6–11). Such assemblies during the united kingdom period (cf. 1Ch 15–16; 2Ch 5–7) marked significant moments in the spiritual life of the community of God's people. Lastly, on the newly refurbished altar the assembly offers to God sacrifices from plunder that was presumably seized following the battle with Zerah and his forces (cf. 2Ch 14:14–15).

12 The highlight of the gathering organized by Asa (vv.9–11) is the people's reaffirmation of the covenantal relationship with Yahweh based on fidelity and obedience. Their covenant is based on the oft-repeated notion of seeking God holistically ("with all their heart and soul," v.12), as seen in Solomon's temple-dedication prayer (see comments on 6:22–39), Yahweh's response to Solomon's prayer (cf. esp. 7:14), and Asa's earlier charge to the people of Judah (cf. 14:4). Moreover, the concept of seeking God is stressed in numerous passages in the book of Deuteronomy (cf. esp. Dt 4:29–31; 6:5;

10:12–21). All told, the seeking of God with all of one's being should be understood as a foundational element of rightly relating to God. This noted, v.15 (also cf. 15:2) shows that it is ultimately God who finds his children.

13 The idea of death for unfaithfulness and covenantal sin is not without precedent in the OT (see Lev 17:2–14 and Dt 13:6–11). But this death warning is even more restrictive in that it will be levied on those who do not seek Yahweh and is a by-product of the zeal of this covenant-renewing group led by Asa, not on the instruction of God.

14–15 The covenant of the people to seek God (see comments on v.12) and to eradicate those who do not do the same (v.13) is ratified by oath and celebrated by music and shouts of joy. The ratification of a covenant by oath is seen in Deuteronomy 29:9–15. Note that the postexilic spiritual renewal lead by Ezra was confirmed in writing (see Ne 9:1–10:39, esp. 9:38 and 10:28–29). The divine granting of "rest" was a key promise given to Israel and part of the broader notion of land theology (cf. Dt 12:10).

16 Another significant act of reform undertaken by Asa is the removal of his grandmother from the royal post of queen mother. The position of queen mother was a position of honor and influence. The queen mother held a significant official position in ancient societies such as Israel that could be exploited in various ways, as the examples of Bathsheba (cf. 1Ki 1–2), Maacah (cf. 1Ki 15), Jezebel (cf. 1Ki 16–2Ki 9), and Athaliah (cf. 2Ch 22–23) attest. See N. A. Andreasen, "The Role of the Queen Mother in Israelite Society," *CBQ* 45 (1983): 179–94. Some queen mothers were active in cultic affairs (as the ignominious examples of Maacah and Jezebel attest) and might hold various levels of administrative responsibility. That Athaliah was able to engineer an anti-Davidic coup and reign for six years in Judah implies a considerable amount of preexisting power, authority, and influence.

The Kidron Valley is located to the east of the old city of Jerusalem and is the location of the famed Gihon Spring. This valley as a focal point in the destruction of heterodoxy and idolatry continues into the later reforms of Hezekiah (cf. 29:15–17; 30:14) and Josiah (cf. 2Ki 23:1–15; for remarks on Asherah poles, see comments at 2Ch 14:3; also see comments on 15:8).

17 The reference to Asa's not removing the high places from Israel is not at variance with the comments on 14:3–5, as those pertain to high places in *Judah* (the southern kingdom), while this remark refers to high places in *Israel* (the northern kingdom). The statement extolling Asa's commitment to Yahweh mirrors the statement of Asa's doing what is right in God's eyes (cf. 14:2), providing literary framing around the accounts of Asa's spiritual leadership and reforms and separating these chapters (14 and 15) from the less flattering account of the final years of Asa's reign found in ch. 16.

18 Asa's dedication of items for the temple is similar to contributions made by David and Solomon given in the context of community worship and celebration. These items were obtained by his father Abijah and perhaps enhanced by the plunder seized from Asa's battle against the coalition led by Zerah (cf. 14:13–15). Likewise, Solomon brought into the temple gifts dedicated by David (cf. 5:1).

19 On the uncertainties regarding the specific time frame of peace enjoyed by Asa, see comments on 16:1.

NOTE

9 It is interesting that the tribe of Simeon here and during the time of Josiah (cf. 34:6) is regarded as a northern kingdom tribe, since the original tribal allotment of Simeon is found within the southwestern region of the tribal allotment of Judah (see Jos 19:1–9; cf. 15:26, 28–32). Like the tribe of Levi, Simeon's land status was different from the balance of the Israelite tribes (recall Ge 34:24–30; cf. 49:5–7) and this may in some way explain the shift reflected here. The genealogical section of the Chronicler implies some movement/migration by the tribe of Simeon (cf. 1Ch 4:34–43), which may have eventually expanded into the northern regions (recall the northern migration of the tribe of Dan; cf. Jdg 17–18; see L. J. Wood, "Simeon, the Tenth Tribe of Israel," *JETS* 14 [1971]: 221–25).

4. Asa's Battle with the Northern Kingdom and Treaty with Aram (2Ch 16:1–6)

¹In the thirty-sixth year of Asa's reign Baasha king of Israel went up against Judah and fortified Ramah to prevent anyone from leaving or entering the territory of Asa king of Judah.

²Asa then took the silver and gold out of the treasuries of the Lord's temple and of his own palace and sent it to Ben-Hadad king of Aram, who was ruling in Damascus. ³"Let there be a treaty between me and you," he said, "as there was between my father and

your father. See, I am sending you silver and gold. Now break your treaty with Baasha king of Israel so he will withdraw from me."

⁴Ben-Hadad agreed with King Asa and sent the commanders of his forces against the towns of Israel. They conquered Ijon, Dan, Abel Maim and all the store cities of Naphtali. ⁵When Baasha heard this, he stopped building Ramah and abandoned his work. ⁶Then King Asa brought all the men of Judah, and they carried away from Ramah the stones and timber Baasha had been using. With them he built up Geba and Mizpah.

COMMENTARY

1 Following decades of peace under Asa (cf. 15:19), as well as several years of peace during the latter years of Abijah's reign (cf. 13:20), conflict again breaks out between the northern kingdom and the southern kingdom. The dating reference of Baasha's attack (the thirty-sixth year of Asa; cf. reference to his thirty-fifth year at 15:19) is a challenging issue, as Baasha had been dead for about a decade by Asa's thirty-sixth year (cf. the date notations in 1Ki 15:33; 16:8). One possibility for reconciling this discrepancy is that the thirty-sixth year dating reference is based on the number of years since the division of the kingdom (cf. Thiele, 83–87). In this scenario, Baasha's attack actually takes place in the sixteenth year of Asa's reign (ca. 894 BC).

Ramah is located about seven miles north of Jerusalem on the important north-south watershed route connecting Jerusalem and Shechem (and beyond) in an area known as the central Benjamin plateau. Thus Baasha's advance would have a significant impact on the communication, trade, and security of Judah, as Baasha would now have control over key routes into the heartland of Judah.

2–3 Baasha's invasion of the region around Ramah (v.1) prompts Asa of the southern kingdom to hire the Arameans of Damascus (Ben-Hadad)

against the northern kingdom. This situation, when viewed in the light of 15:8–15 (and the rest that God had granted; cf. 15:15) implies that something has changed vis-à-vis Asa's and Judah's earlier faithfulness, spiritual fervor, and dependency on God.

Indeed, Asa's inclination to seek human help (namely, from Ben-Hadad) and not God's, together with his plundering of the temple treasury, is consistent with some weakening in his faith and character. Put another way, Asa is now more inclined to pillage the temple of Yahweh than to seek God in his temple when faced with a military threat (also seen in the later instance of Ahaz; cf. 28:16–21). This view is further supported by the words of the prophet Hanani noted in 16:7–9 (e.g., "you relied on the king of Aram and not on the Lord your God," 16:7).

4–5 After receiving payoff from Asa (cf. vv.2–3), the Aramean ruler Ben-Hadad invades the northern kingdom and takes a number of key cities in the Upper Galilee region, including cities surrounding the Huleh Valley (Dan, Ijon, Abel Beth Maachah), "all Kinnereth" (i.e., the environs of the Sea of Galilee; 1Ki 15:20), and "all the store cities of Naphtali." This attack from the north prompts Baasha to withdraw from Ramah. Asa subsequently fortifies Geba and Mizpah on his northern border (cf. v.6). For the next 175 years or so (through the fall of the northern kingdom in 722 BC), the border between the north and south remains fairly stable in the area between Bethel and Mizpah. See C. G. Rasmussen, *Zondervan NIV Atlas of the Bible* (Grand Rapids: Zondervan, 1989), 124–27.

6 Following the invasion by Ben-Hadad (see comments on vv.2–3 and 4–5), Baasha abandons his fortification of Ramah, which enables Asa to pillage Ramah for building materials that he then uses to fortify Geba and Mizpah. Geba, usually identified as Tell el-Ful, is located about six miles north of Jerusalem and guarded the important pass along which the eastern routes crossed. Mizpah (probably Tell en-Nasbeh) was situated about three miles west of Geba on the main east-west route in the hill country.

NOTES

2–3 This passage introduces the challenging issue of sorting through the various references to "Ben-Hadad" as the king of Aram/Damascus during the divided kingdom. It is likely that Ben-Hadad, meaning "son of [Baal] Hadad," was an Aramean regnal name that implied divine selection of the ruler ("son of god") and as such was utilized by multiple rulers. The reuse of a royal name was also attested in Assyria (e.g., Shalmaneser, Tiglath-Pileser) and Egypt (e.g., Thutmose, Amenhotep). This reuse of the name Ben-Hadad together with other uncertainties regarding Aramean chronology presents an ongoing challenge. One possible understanding of the sequence of Aramean kings is as follows:

Rezon	Time of Solomon, Rehoboam, Jeroboam (cf. 1Ki 11:23–25)
Tabrimmon	Time of Abijah, Jeroboam (noted in 1Ki 15:18)
Ben-Hadad I	Time of Asa, Baasha, Omri (2Ch 16:2–4; 1Ki 15:18–20)
Ben-Hadad II (Hadadezer; Assyrian: Adad-idri)	Time of Ahab, Joram, Jehoshaphat, Jehoram (1Ki 20:1–34; 22)
Hazael	Time of Jehu, Queen Athaliah, Joash (2Ki 8:7–15; 13:3–23)
Ben-Hadad III (Mari; Assyrian: Khadianu)	Time of Jehoash, Jeroboam II (2Ki 13:24–25)
Rezin (Assyrian: Rakhianu)	Time of Ahaz, Pekah, Isaiah (2Ki 15:37–16:9; Isa 7–9)

It is possible that another Ben-Hadad reigned briefly (ca. 845–41 BC) between the death of Hadadezer/Ben-Hadad II and the coup of Hazael. Rezin may have also used the title Ben-Hadad. For a discussion of Aramean chronology, see Wayne T. Pitard, *Ancient Damascus* (Winona Lake, Ind.: Eisenbrauns, 1987), 101–4. Also see the discussion in I. Provan, V. P. Long, and T. Longman III, *A Biblical History of Israel* (Louisville: Westminster John Knox, 2003), 367–68 n. 15.

5. Asa Rebuked by the Prophet Hanani (2Ch 16:7–10)

[7]At that time Hanani the seer came to Asa king of Judah and said to him:"Because you relied on the king of Aram and not on the LORD your God, the army of the king of Aram has escaped from your hand. [8]Were not the Cushites and Libyans a mighty army with great numbers of chariots and horsemen? Yet when you relied on the LORD, he delivered them into your hand. [9]For the eyes of the LORD range throughout the earth to strengthen those whose hearts are fully committed to him. You have done a foolish thing, and from now on you will be at war."

[10]Asa was angry with the seer because of this; he was so enraged that he put him in prison. At the same time Asa brutally oppressed some of the people.

COMMENTARY

7–8 The arrival of Hanani is the second recorded prophetic visit to Asa (the first from Azariah is recorded at 15:1–7). While the prophet Azariah's visit to Asa was full of the possibilities and blessings of seeking God and exercising covenantal obedience, this visit is full of rebuke and critique in the light of the lack of faith implied in Asa's request for help from the Arameans. Instead of relying on God, Asa has sought protection by pursuing a more tangible means to military aid—namely, by paying the Arameans a bounty pillaged from the temple treasury and royal treasury (cf. 16:2–3). Ultimately, as the prophet notes, to place trust in humankind or human institutions rather than completely in God is foolishness that reaps broad consequences (v.9). The phraseology of "seer" used with Hanani (cf. vv.7, 10) is an alternative (and earlier) term for "prophet" (see parenthetical remark at 1Sa 9:9).

9 The prophet poetically summarizes God's omniscience, omnipresence, and desire to bless and be gracious to those who seek him and fully rely on him. No one who relies on God will go unno-

ticed. Such an expression could easily function as a memorable point of exhortation to the Chronicler's postexilic audience faced with manifold challenges and pressures (cf. Zec 4:10). Conversely, as the prophet notes, placing trust in humankind or human institutions rather than in God is foolishness that reaps broad consequences. Asa's foolishness will reverse God's previous granting of peace (15:15), and the southern kingdom will now be at war without the complete protection of God.

10 Asa's reaction to the prophet and his message—namely, rage and imprisonment—and his subsequent oppression of God's people underscore that his heart has very much turned away from wholeheartedly seeking God and following his ways. Ironically, according to the reforms enacted by Asa himself earlier in his reign (cf. 15:12–15, esp. 15:13), he should have been put to death. Compounding the issue of Asa's relying on humans rather than God (cf. vv.7–9) is that the king once again has sought help from a human being rather than from God regarding his severe foot disease (see v.12, below).

NOTE

7 Note that the prophet Hanani is the father of the prophet Jehu, who ministered during the days of Asa's son Jehoshaphat and contributed to the royal annals (cf. 19:2; 20:34). With respect to the textual variant in this verse that has "Israel" in place of the second instance of "Aram" (G^L), see Dillard, 126.

6. Asa's Regnal Summary (2Ch 16:11–14)

> [11]The events of Asa's reign, from beginning to end, are written in the book of the kings of Judah and Israel. [12]In the thirty-ninth year of his reign Asa was afflicted with a disease in his feet. Though his disease was severe, even in his illness he did not seek help from the LORD, but only from the physicians. [13]Then in the forty-first year of his reign Asa died and rested with his fathers. [14]They buried him in the tomb that he had cut out for himself in the City of David. They laid him on a bier covered with spices and various blended perfumes, and they made a huge fire in his honor.

COMMENTARY

11–13 Compounding the issue of Asa's relying on humans rather than God (cf. vv. 7–9) is that the king once again seeks help from a human being rather than from God regarding his severe foot disease (v. 12). Although the biblical text does not directly connect Asa's compromise of not fully relying on God with his subsequent foot disease, it should be noted that Yahweh's covenantal judgments for unfaithfulness include numerous references to illness and disease (cf. Dt 28:21–22, 27–28, 35, 59–60). Conversely, Yahweh is described in the OT as the great Physician and Healer of his people (cf. Ex 15:26; Ps 103:3). Lastly, it is possible that the foot disease that hampered the final years of Asa's life (his thirty-ninth to forty-first year; vv. 12–13) fostered a coregency with his son Jehoshaphat.

The tone of Asa's lack of reliance on God in ch. 16 is at variance with the earlier summary of Asa's reforms and Godwardness (chs. 14–15), including statements that Asa's heart was fully committed to God "all his days" (15:17 NASB) and that he did "what was good and right in the eyes of the LORD" (14:2). While this is clearly not a point of contradiction to the Chronicler, it can be a point of tension for a later reader of the text.

Two approaches can be suggested to better understand this tension. One is that the time of Asa's reign until the events of ch. 16 (the final few years of his forty-one-year reign) was characterized by faithfulness to God and that ch. 16 is the unfortunate postscript to an otherwise faithful reign, which summarizes his compromise in faith in the light of military and personal challenge. The other possibility is that Asa's reign is a time overwhelmingly marked by faithfulness, but that this faithfulness is by no means perfect. The huge fire made in honor of Asa (cf. remarks on v. 14) shows that overall his reign is seen as deserving of honor.

14 A funerary pyre would be a statement of respect and honor for the deceased and was typically only available for those of high stature (cf. Jer 34:4–5). The withholding of honor is clearly connected to the absence of a funerary pyre for Jehoram (cf. 2Ch 21:19). Such fires were accompanied by spices and ointments as noted here and could also be seen as an aspect of purification of the dead, as reflected in the death customs of Egypt and Assyria. The notation that Asa had "cut out for himself" a tomb is unique in terms of regnal death notices in Chronicles.

D. The Reign of Jehoshaphat (2Ch 17:1–21:3)

OVERVIEW

The time frame of the reigns of Jehoshaphat and Jehoram in the southern kingdom coincides with what is known as the Omride dynasty in the northern kingdom. While the content of Kings engages the particulars of Omride rule in the north, the book of Chronicles is largely silent on matters pertaining to the northern kingdom. The Chronicler's account of Jehoshaphat is considerably longer than that found in Kings. A brief review of the Omride era will provide a helpful sense of the historical backdrop to the content of 2 Chronicles 17–20, particularly Jehoshaphat's alliances with rulers from the north.

Following several years of political division in the northern kingdom (including a divided northern kingdom as Omri ruled for five years from Tirzah while battling against Tibni), Omri emerged victorious, inaugurating the impressive (though contemptible) Omride dynasty (ca. 885–841 BC). While Omri's rule was relatively short (ca. 885–869 BC), his military and economic policies enhanced trade and diplomacy for Israel that lasted for several decades. In fact, a century after Omri's rise to power the area of northern Israel was still referred to as "the land of the house of Omri" in inscriptions of Assyrian kings such as Tiglath-Pileser III and Sargon II.

The era of the Omride dynasty in the northern kingdom was marked by political stability, including peace with the southern kingdom, as the episodes of 18:1–34 and 20:35–37 illustrate; expanded relations with Phoenicia, as reflected in the marriage alliance of Ahab and Jezebel (cf. 1Ki 16:31); and military strength, which allowed the northern kingdom to reassert control over lucrative trade routes on both sides of the Jordan River, including control over Moab as reflected in the Mesha Stele (cf. *COS*, 2:23; 2Ki 3). Israel's economic prosperity during this time is reflected in the ivory items discovered at Samaria dating to the tenth to eighth centuries BC (cf. 1Ki 22:39; Am 6:4). This peace and prosperity, however, facilitated social and religious degeneration. In light of this disintegration of covenantal fidelity, God raised the prophet Elijah to minister during the time of the Omride dynasty (covered extensively in Kings).

The backdrop to the Omride era in the northern kingdom and to the rule of Jehoshaphat in the southern kingdom is also marked by the rising threat from Assyria. This time of Assyrian dominance is distinguished from that beginning more than a century later under the Assyrian monarch Tiglath-Pileser III in 745 BC (a time period known as the Neo-Assyrian Empire; for this later period of Assyria's history, see Overview to 28:5–15). After a period of weakness, Assyria began expansionary measures in the late tenth century BC designed to facilitate tribute payments and exact control over trade routes throughout Mesopotamia, Anatolia, and the Levant.

The Assyrian king Adad-Nirari II ruled from ca. 911–891 BC and conducted numerous campaigns against the Aramean states. Tukulti-Ninurta II (ca. 890–884 BC), the son of Adad-Nirari II, continued military exploits around the northern border of Babylonia and along the Euphrates River heading north and even portions of southeastern Anatolia. Ashurnasirpal II (ca. 884–859 BC), the son of Tukulti-Ninurta II, used frequent military campaigns against city-states to the north, east, and south, as well as Neo-Hittite states (notably Carchemish) and Aramean states to fund an impressive array of public-works projects throughout Assyria. Ashurnasirpal II is contemporary with Omri and Ahab (partly) in the northern kingdom and Asa and Jehoshaphat in the southern kingdom. Shalmaneser III began the Assyrian custom of imposing on conquered areas regular (typically annual) tribute payments, no doubt a factor in the organizing of an anti-Assyrian coalition (cf. Rainey, 190–92; *ANET*, 275–78).

Shalmaneser III, the son of Ashurnarsipal II, ruled from ca. 859–824 BC and continued the aggression of previous Assyrian rulers with even greater tenacity, pushing farther into western territories. This prompted several states in the Levant to form a series of coalitions in the mid-ninth century BC to halt (or at least impede) these Assyrian incursions. The threat of Assyria under Shalmaneser III facilitated three years of peace between Aram and Israel insofar as the Assyrian threat took priority over local squabbles (cf. *ANET*, 278–79). Meanwhile, a coalition of twelve nations from the central and southern Levant included Hamath, Aram (Syria), Arvad, Ammon, Arabia, and Israel (under the leadership of Ahab, who is noted in the Kurkh Stele as providing 2,000 of the 3,930 chariots used by the coalition and 10,000 infantrymen).

Although Shalmaneser III claims victory over this coalition in the Kurkh Stele, the reality is that the coalition was effective in stemming Assyrian expansion to the west. After returning to Nineveh, Shalmaneser III did not cross the Euphrates for three years; when he did so, the Assyrian army met similar coalitions in several battles between ca. 850 and 841 BC. While these coalitions ultimately cracked and buckled under the Assyrian onslaught, they nevertheless evidenced impressive preparation and strategy in their attempts to stop Shalmaneser III.

However, by 841 BC (the eighteenth regnal year of Shalmaneser III), because of the political intrigue and upheaval in Syria and Canaan (including Jehu's revolt in the northern kingdom and Hazael's usurping of the throne in Damascus; see comments on 22:5–12), there was no coalition to oppose the Assyrian advance. Consequently, Assyria quickly gained dominance in the Levant from that point forward, conducting numerous campaigns in the west between 841 and 831 BC. Note that Jehu of the northern kingdom is portrayed on the Black Obelisk (in ca. 841 BC) as bowing down in the presence of Shalmaneser III (cf. *ANEP*, fig. 351). For further overview of Shalmaneser III's campaigns in the west between 841 and 831 BC, see Rainey, 208–9.

1. Jehoshaphat's Early Years (2Ch 17:1–19)

> ¹Jehoshaphat his son succeeded him as king and strengthened himself against Israel. ²He stationed troops in all the fortified cities of Judah and put garrisons in Judah and in the towns of Ephraim that his father Asa had captured.

³The L ORD was with Jehoshaphat because in his early years he walked in the ways his father David had followed. He did not consult the Baals ⁴but sought the God of his father and followed his commands rather than the practices of Israel. ⁵The L ORD established the kingdom under his control; and all Judah brought gifts to Jehoshaphat, so that he had great wealth and honor. ⁶His heart was devoted to the ways of the L ORD; furthermore, he removed the high places and the Asherah poles from Judah.

⁷In the third year of his reign he sent his officials Ben-Hail, Obadiah, Zechariah, Nethanel and Micaiah to teach in the towns of Judah. ⁸With them were certain Levites — Shemaiah, Nethaniah, Zebadiah, Asahel, Shemiramoth, Jehonathan, Adonijah, Tobijah and Tob-Adonijah — and the priests Elishama and Jehoram. ⁹They taught throughout Judah, taking with them the Book of the Law of the L ORD; they went around to all the towns of Judah and taught the people.

¹⁰The fear of the L ORD fell on all the kingdoms of the lands surrounding Judah, so that they did not make war with Jehoshaphat. ¹¹Some Philistines brought Jehoshaphat gifts and silver as tribute, and the Arabs brought him flocks: seven thousand seven hundred rams and seven thousand seven hundred goats.

¹²Jehoshaphat became more and more powerful; he built forts and store cities in Judah ¹³and had large supplies in the towns of Judah. He also kept experienced fighting men in Jerusalem. ¹⁴Their enrollment by families was as follows:

From Judah, commanders of units of 1,000:
Adnah the commander, with 300,000 fighting men;
¹⁵next, Jehohanan the commander, with 280,000;
¹⁶next, Amasiah son of Zicri, who volunteered himself for the service of the L ORD, with 200,000.
¹⁷From Benjamin:
Eliada, a valiant soldier, with 200,000 men armed with bows and shields;
¹⁸next, Jehozabad, with 180,000 men armed for battle.

¹⁹These were the men who served the king, besides those he stationed in the fortified cities throughout Judah.

COMMENTARY

1–2 The Hebrew expression for "Jehoshaphat ... strengthened himself" is used of Solomon at the outset of his reign (2Ch 1:1), but it is also used of Rehoboam in connection with his apostasy (see 12:1). The cities in Judah fortified by Jehoshaphat were likely those established by Solomon and Rehoboam (see comments on 8:5–6; 11:5–12), whereas those in Ephraim probably connected with earlier territorial gains achieved by Abijah (cf. 13:2–20) and Asa (cf. 15:8). While Jehoshaphat's military efforts in the tribal area of Ephraim might be seen as provocative, the relationship between the northern kingdom and southern kingdom is characterized as one of peace solidified via a political marriage alliance (see comments on 18:1).

3–4 The Lord's presence with Jehoshaphat (also noted at 20:17) is what will enable his success and obedience. The Chronicler stresses the clear biblical connection between seeking God and obeying his commands (see comments on 14:4 and note the words of Christ in Jn 15:10, 14). Jehoshaphat's vibrant relationship of obedience also relates to his avoidance of the practices of Israel (e.g., 18:4–6; on Israel's spiritual compromises, see comments on 11:15).

The plural of Baal ("Baals") is uncommon and may relate to the variety of deities pursued in Israel and the region of Syro-Canaan (recall that "Baal" is an honorific title meaning "lord" and typically was the shortened way of referring to the Syro-Canaanite storm god Baal-Hadad). The pressure to give honor to Baal was heightened by the northern kingdom's expanded relations with Phoenicia (as reflected in the marriage alliance of Ahab and Jezebel; cf. 1Ki 16:31) and the subsequent relationship of peace between the northern and southern kingdoms. The northern king Ahab even constructed a temple for Baal and put up Asherah poles in Samaria (cf. v.6; 1Ki 16:30–33; see comments on 2Ch 14:5).

5–6 As with Solomon, it is the Lord who established the kingdom for Jehoshaphat and blessed him with material wealth. Note that "the high places and the Asherah poles" were previously removed from Judah by Asa (cf. 14:3–5), but in the course of time the human tendency toward idolatry enabled their rebuilding (recall the unfaithfulness of Asa toward the end of his reign). Although Jehoshaphat removed these objects of idolatry, he is later critiqued for *not* removing high places (cf. 20:33; 1Ki 22:43), so presumably his eradication of high places is not complete, or his vigilance against

their removal and being rebuilt wanes over time. See additional remarks on high places at 1:3–5. For comments on Asherah and Asherah poles, see 14:3.

7–9 The notation of Jehoshaphat's third year (v.7) together with the date notation at 20:31 implies that Jehoshaphat had a coregency with Asa (likely connected with Asa's severe foot illness during the final three years of his reign; cf. 16:12–13). If so, Jehoshaphat's strong actions of reform take place following the death of Asa and during the initial year of his sole reign. Jehoshaphat dispatches a combination of royal officials, Levites, and priests to teach God's law throughout the region of Judah. A similar commissioning of Levites' teaching the law of God occurs during the postexilic ministry of Ezra and Nehemiah:

> The Levites—Jeshua, Bani, Sherebiah, Jamin, Akkub, Shabbethai, Hodiah, Maaseiah, Kelita, Azariah, Jozabad, Hanan and Pelaiah—instructed the people in the Law while the people were standing there. They read from the Book of the Law of God, making it clear and giving the meaning so that the people could understand what was being read. (Ne 8:7–8; cf. full context of 8:1–12)

It is noteworthy that these individuals go out to teach God's Word (in analogy to the *going forth* built into the Great Commission; cf. Mt 28:19–20), rather than expecting the people to come to them.

10–11 In addition to establishing Jehoshaphat's reign, the Lord facilitates peace for Jehoshaphat by causing the surrounding nations to fear God and realize his commitment to protect Judah. Note that the fear of the Lord facilitates peace (v.10), brings wealth from foreigners (v.11), and even spreads to the surrounding nations (20:29; recall that God did the same for David, Solomon, and Asa; cf. 1Ch 14:17; 2Ch 8–9; 14:14). The tribute brought from Philistines and Arabs, together with statements of military fortifications, implies that the southern kingdom now has hegemony over the caravan routes across the Arabah and Negev to the Coastal Highway.

This control provides a lucrative source of tax and tribute income for the southern kingdom during Jehoshaphat's administration. This economic and political stability in turn allows for further military strengthening, building projects, and governmental expansion (see 17:12–19). The Arabs noted here are likely seminomadic tribes in the desert regions to the south of the Judean Negev and portions of the Sinaitic and (perhaps) Arabian peninsulas.

12–19 These summary statements underscore the security and effectiveness of Jehoshaphat's reign. However, as chapter 18 shows, this divinely granted power and success do not preclude his entering into a political treaty with the apostate Israelite king Ahab via a marriage. The description of the Judean military commander Amasiah ("who volunteered himself for the service of the LORD") highlights a sense of dedication to serving God by serving God's king (note a similar atmosphere of service and commitment during David's reign; cf. 1Ch 29:5–9).

The forts and storage cities built (or rebuilt) by Jehoshaphat likely continue his fortification efforts noted in v.2 and probably overlap with many of those established earlier by Solomon and Rehoboam (see comments on 8:5–6; 11:5–12). On the large numbers of military recruits and the possibility that the Chronicler intends another nuance for the term "1,000," see comments on 11:1.

NOTES

1 It is possible that the expression "against Israel" (עַל־יִשְׂרָאֵל, ʿal-yiśrāʾēl) at the end of this verse is better translated as "over Israel," with "Israel" pertaining to God's people in the southern kingdom (cf. the use of "Israel" in the closing remarks of Jehoshaphat's reign [20:29]; also see discussion of northern kingdom versus southern kingdom terminology at 10:16–19). This would reflect a common meaning of the preposition used here (עַל, ʿal [GK 6584]; note its use in the similar expression in 2Ch 1:1: "Solomon ... established himself firmly *over* his kingdom") and better suits Jehoshaphat's peaceful relations with the northern kingdom.

3 The expression translated "early years" (הָרִאשֹׁנִים, hāriʾšōnîm) may actually refer to the early years of David (cf. the NASB's translation) rather than those of Jehoshaphat (as in the NIV; see Selman, 404 n. 1).

2. Jehoshaphat's Alliance with the Northern Kingdom (2Ch 18:1–19:3)

¹Now Jehoshaphat had great wealth and honor, and he allied himself with Ahab by marriage. ²Some years later he went down to visit Ahab in Samaria. Ahab slaughtered many sheep and cattle for him and the people with him and urged him to attack Ramoth Gilead. ³Ahab king of Israel asked Jehoshaphat king of Judah, "Will you go with me against Ramoth Gilead?"

Jehoshaphat replied, "I am as you are, and my people as your people; we will join you in the war." ⁴But Jehoshaphat also said to the king of Israel, "First seek the counsel of the LORD."

[5]So the king of Israel brought together the prophets—four hundred men—and asked them, "Shall we go to war against Ramoth Gilead, or shall I refrain?"

"Go," they answered, "for God will give it into the king's hand."

[6]But Jehoshaphat asked, "Is there not a prophet of the LORD here whom we can inquire of?"

[7]The king LORD Israel answered Jehoshaphat, "There is still one man through whom we can inquire of the LORD, but I hate him because he never prophesies anything good about me, but always bad. He is Micaiah son of Imlah."

"The king should not say that," Jehoshaphat replied.

[8]So the king of Israel called one of his officials and said, "Bring Micaiah son of Imlah at once."

[9]Dressed in their royal robes, the king of Israel and Jehoshaphat king of Judah were sitting on their thrones at the threshing floor by the entrance to the gate of Samaria, with all the prophets prophesying before them. [10]Now Zedekiah son of Kenaanah had made iron horns, and he declared, "This is what the LORD says: 'With these you will gore the Arameans until they are destroyed.'"

[11]All the other prophets were prophesying the same thing. "Attack Ramoth Gilead and be victorious," they said, "for the LORD will give it into the king's hand."

[12]The messenger who had gone to summon Micaiah said to him, "Look, as one man the other prophets are predicting success for the king. Let your word agree with theirs, and speak favorably."

[13]But Micaiah said, "As surely as the LORD lives, I can tell him only what my God says."

[14]When he arrived, the king asked him, "Micaiah, shall we go to war against Ramoth Gilead, or shall I refrain?"

"Attack and be victorious," he answered, "for they will be given into your hand."

[15]The king said to him, "How many times must I make you swear to tell me nothing but the truth in the name of the LORD?"

[16]Then Micaiah answered, "I saw all Israel scattered on the hills like sheep without a shepherd, and the LORD said, 'These people have no master. Let each one go home in peace.'"

[17]The king of Israel said to Jehoshaphat, "Didn't I tell you that he never prophesies anything good about me, but only bad?"

[18]Micaiah continued, "Therefore hear the word of the LORD: I saw the LORD sitting on his throne with all the host of heaven standing on his right and on his left. [19]And the LORD said, 'Who will entice Ahab king of Israel into attacking Ramoth Gilead and going to his death there?'

"One suggested this, and another that. [20]Finally, a spirit came forward, stood before the LORD and said, 'I will entice him.'

"'By what means?' the LORD asked.

[21]"'I will go and be a lying spirit in the mouths of all his prophets,' he said.

"'You will succeed in enticing him,' said the Lord. 'Go and do it.'

²²"So now the Lord has put a lying spirit in the mouths of these prophets of yours. The Lord has decreed disaster for you."

²³Then Zedekiah son of Kenaanah went up and slapped Micaiah in the face. "Which way did the spirit from the Lord go when he went from me to speak to you?" he asked.

²⁴Micaiah replied, "You will find out on the day you go to hide in an inner room."

²⁵The king of Israel then ordered, "Take Micaiah and send him back to Amon the ruler of the city and to Joash the king's son, ²⁶and say, 'This is what the king says: Put this fellow in prison and give him nothing but bread and water until I return safely.'"

²⁷Micaiah declared, "If you ever return safely, the Lord has not spoken through me." Then he added, "Mark my words, all you people!"

²⁸So the king of Israel and Jehoshaphat king of Judah went up to Ramoth Gilead. ²⁹The king of Israel said to Jehoshaphat, "I will enter the battle in disguise, but you wear your royal robes." So the king of Israel disguised himself and went into battle.

³⁰Now the king of Aram had ordered his chariot commanders, "Do not fight with anyone, small or great, except the king of Israel." ³¹When the chariot commanders saw Jehoshaphat, they thought, "This is the king of Israel." So they turned to attack him, but Jehoshaphat cried out, and the Lord helped him. God drew them away from him, ³²for when the chariot commanders saw that he was not the king of Israel, they stopped pursuing him.

³³But someone drew his bow at random and hit the king of Israel between the sections of his armor. The king told the chariot driver, "Wheel around and get me out of the fighting. I've been wounded." ³⁴All day long the battle raged, and the king of Israel propped himself up in his chariot facing the Arameans until evening. Then at sunset he died.

¹⁹:¹When Jehoshaphat king of Judah returned safely to his palace in Jerusalem, ²Jehu the seer, the son of Hanani, went out to meet him and said to the king, "Should you help the wicked and love those who hate the Lord? Because of this, the wrath of the Lord is upon you. ³There is, however, some good in you, for you have rid the land of the Asherah poles and have set your heart on seeking God."

COMMENTARY

1 Even though God established Jehoshaphat's kingdom (17:5) and gave him numerous blessings, including wealth (17:5; 18:1), safety and peace (17:10), and tribute from surrounding nations (17:11), Jehoshaphat nonetheless enters into the common means of gaining security in the biblical world—a treaty and political alliance by marriage. The increasing strength seen in the north during the Omride era may have motivated Jehoshaphat to seal peace with Ahab (see Overview to chs. 17–20). This act of diplomacy culminates in a political marriage treaty between Jehoshaphat's son Jehoram and

Ahab's daughter Athaliah (cf. 21:5–6). Such diplomatic marriage alliances were attested widely in the biblical world as a means to facilitate mutual trust and obligation. In addition, political marriages might result in potential heirs to the throne, as implied by Rehoboam's Ammonite mother.

2–3 Jehoshaphat's marriage alliance with Ahab facilitates Ahab's request for military aid from Judah against Aram. Although Aram and Israel (northern kingdom) had put aside their differences for several years to fight together against the Assyrians, once this threat was diminished (after the Battle of Qarqar, ca. 853 BC), Aram and Israel return to their prior hostilities. During this time, Ahab solicits Jehoshaphat's help to retake the strategically located Transjordanian town of Ramoth Gilead (likely Tell Ramith), which lies along the important trade route known as the King's Highway. Somewhat ironically, Jehoshaphat's response of faithfulness to Ahab (v.3) is reminiscent of Ruth's response of faithfulness to Naomi and Yahweh (cf. Ru 1:16–17).

4–27 Although Jehoshaphat has already committed himself to Ahab (v.3), he nonetheless requests that Yahweh be consulted prior to battle. Such prebattle divine inquiries (vv.5, 14), prophetic oracles (vv.5, 16, 19–22), prophetic drama (vv.23–24), and visions of the heavenly realm (vv.18–22) are seen elsewhere in the Bible (2Ki 3:11–19; 6:17; 2Ch 11:1–4; Jer 21:3–14; 28:1–17).

The kings gather at a threshing floor to hear the counsel of the prophets (v.9). The open flat area of threshing floors facilitated their use as a meeting place for ancient communities, in an analogous way to how a city gate functioned on a larger scale. As this account shows, in the context of doing God's work, strength is not found in numbers (cf. Ahab's showdown with Elijah; 1Ki 18:16–39); rather, strength comes from faithfully proclaiming a message from God. Note Micah's poetic presentation of the distinction between faithful and faithless prophets:

This is what the LORD says:
"As for the prophets
who lead my people astray,
if one feeds them,
they proclaim 'peace';
if he does not,
they prepare to wage war against him.
Therefore night will come over you, without visions,
and darkness, without divination.
The sun will set for the prophets,
and the day will go dark for them.
The seers will be ashamed
and the diviners disgraced.
They will all cover their faces
because there is no answer from God."
But as for me, I am filled with power,
with the Spirit of the LORD,
and with justice and might,
to declare to Jacob his transgression,
to Israel his sin. (Mic 3:5–8)

In addition, note Yahweh's harsh condemnation of lying prophets spoken through the prophet Jeremiah (cf. Jer 23:9–40). Simply claiming to have God's Spirit (cf. v.23) is irrelevant in terms of determining true and false prophets. The motif of lying spirits and supernatural enticement (2Ch 18:21) ultimately advances God's plans and purposes (cf. 1Sa 16:14–15; Eze 14:1–11; Job 1:6–2:7).

Ahab's treatment of the otherwise unknown prophet Micaiah (vv.23–27) is consistent with how other ungodly kings treated prophets delivering an unwanted message from God (cf. 16:7–10; Jer 37:16; 38:6). The Chronicler once again exhorts God's people to complete faithfulness to God's ways through the selection and shaping of his material. Lastly, recall that the veracity of the prophet's message (18:27) is one of the Deuteronomic criteria for determining a true prophet of Yahweh (cf. Dt 18:21–22).

28–34 Despite the ominous prophecy of Micaiah, Ahab and Jehoshaphat launch an attack on Ramoth Gilead that ends in defeat and the death of Ahab "at random" (vv.33–34), thus fulfilling God's word through Micaiah. Ahab's change of clothes (and instructions for Jehoshaphat not to remove his royal robes; v.29) may have been an attempt to thwart God's will as well as an attempt to put Jehoshaphat in harm's way.

Following the death of Ahab, Mesha of Moab rebels against the northern kingdom and seizes areas to the north of the Arnon, including the Medeba Plateau (cf. 2Ki 1:1; 3:4–27). Jehoshaphat's acceptance of Ahab's plan against the word of Yahweh's prophet both implies his imperfect faith and his likely position as the weaker partner in his alliance with the northern kingdom.

19:1–2 Thanks to God's intervention (cf. 18:31–32) Jehoshaphat's life is spared in the battle for Ramoth Gilead. Like his father Asa, Jehoshaphat receives a visit from a prophet in the aftermath of his compromise of full allegiance to God and his ways (cf. 16:7–10). This compromise is reflected in his marriage alliance with Ahab (18:1), his military assistance to a king who hated the Lord (19:2; cf. 18:3), and his implicit rejection of God's word by going forth to battle despite the prophecy of defeat (18:16, 28–34).

3 While Jehoshaphat's lack of complete fidelity to God is serious (v.2), he has not completely abandoned his commitment to the Lord. One of the ways in which Jehoshaphat is shown as seeking God is his tangible step to eradicate images of idolatry, such as Asherah poles within Judah (cf. 17:3–6; on Asherah poles, see comments on 14:3). The subsequent verses of this chapter (19:4–11) also reflect Jehoshaphat's desire to seek and honor God (cf. Elisha's later words at 2Ki 3:14).

NOTES

23 It is uncertain whether the expression רוּחַ־יְהוָה (*rûaḥ-yhwh*) should be translated "spirit from the Lord" (as in the NIV) or "Spirit of the Lord" (as reflected in the NASB). The NIV's rendering avoids connecting *the* Spirit of God with a false prophet.

28–34 Following the death of Ahab, Mesha of Moab rebels against the northern kingdom and seizes areas to the north of the Arnon, including the Medeba Plateau (cf. 2Ki 1:1; 3:4–27). The Mesha Stele (Moabite Stone; ca. 853 BC) notes that Mesha fortified several cities in this area, including Baal Meon, Kiriathaim, Medeba, and Bezer, presumably to prepare for attack from the northern kingdom (cf. *ANET*, 320–21). These fortifications made by Moab to the north of the Arnon may well be the reason that Joram (Jehoram) of the northern kingdom decides to attack Moab from the south "through the Desert of Edom" a few years later (2Ki 3:8).

As seen with the earlier battle at Ramoth Gilead, Jehoshaphat again assists an ungodly northern king (note the similarity of Jehoshaphat's request for a prophet of Yahweh in this later episode [2Ki 3:11] with 2Ch 18:6). Although the forces of Jehoshaphat and Joram gain some initial victories, Moab's quest for independence seems to have ultimately succeeded (cf. 2Ki 3:26–29), since Moab's control of this region is implied in the later prophetic oracles of Isaiah and Jeremiah (cf. Isa 15–16; Jer 48).

3. Jehoshaphat's Judiciary Reforms (2Ch 19:4–11)

⁴Jehoshaphat lived in Jerusalem, and he went out again among the people from Beersheba to the hill country of Ephraim and turned them back to the LORD, the God of their fathers. ⁵He appointed judges in the land, in each of the fortified cities of Judah. ⁶He told them, "Consider carefully what you do, because you are not judging for man but for the LORD, who is with you whenever you give a verdict. ⁷Now let the fear of the LORD be upon you. Judge carefully, for with the LORD our God there is no injustice or partiality or bribery."

⁸In Jerusalem also, Jehoshaphat appointed some of the Levites, priests and heads of Israelite families to administer the law of the LORD and to settle disputes. And they lived in Jerusalem. ⁹He gave them these orders: "You must serve faithfully and wholeheartedly in the fear of the LORD. ¹⁰In every case that comes before you from your fellow countrymen who live in the cities — whether bloodshed or other concerns of the law, commands, decrees or ordinances — you are to warn them not to sin against the LORD; otherwise his wrath will come on you and your brothers. Do this, and you will not sin.

¹¹"Amariah the chief priest will be over you in any matter concerning the LORD, and Zebadiah son of Ishmael, the leader of the tribe of Judah, will be over you in any matter concerning the king, and the Levites will serve as officials before you. Act with courage, and may the LORD be with those who do well."

COMMENTARY

4 Jehoshaphat's actions in going out to bring people to the Lord reflect the intended role of the king in the spiritual life of Israel (Dt 17:18–20). As mentioned above (see comments on 2Ch 17:7–9), it noteworthy that Jehoshaphat *goes out* to teach God's Word (in analogy to the *going forth* of the Great Commission; cf. Mt 28:19–20), rather than expecting the people to come to Jerusalem.

The city of Beersheba, located in the Negev, was the administrative seat of the southern region. Beersheba was also the common designation used to refer to the southern extent of Judah, as implied here. Notice that Jehoshaphat's itinerant ministry also includes those situated in part of the northern tribal area of Ephraim.

5–7 Jehoshaphat's judicial appointments following his outreach efforts (v.4) may reflect a correla-

tion between judicial overhaul and (lasting) spiritual renewal. Jehoshaphat's appointment of judges in the fortified cities of Judah and his exhortation to these judges suggest a reform of the judiciary in line with the covenantal fiduciary responsibilities of judges outlined in Deuteronomy 16:18–20:

Appoint judges and officials for each of your tribes in every town the LORD your God is giving you, and they shall judge the people fairly. Do not pervert justice or show partiality. Do not accept a bribe, for a bribe blinds the eyes of the wise and twists the words of the righteous. Follow justice and justice alone, so that you may live and possess the land the LORD your God is giving you.

These judiciary appointments along with the corollary appointments noted in vv.8–11 imply a centralization of the judicial system in the southern kingdom during the time of Jehoshaphat (see K. W. Whitelam, *The Just King: Monarchical Judicial Authority in Ancient Israel* [Sheffield: JSOT, 1979], 185–206; R. R. Wilson, "Israel's Judicial System in the Preexilic Period," *JQR* 74[1983]: 229–48). The fundamental exhortation given to these judicial appointees is that they carry out their responsibilities in the fear of the Lord—as this is what will prompt careful deliberations that are pleasing to God and absent of any perversion of justice.

8–10 Together with his appointment of judges charged with acting with integrity in the fear of the Lord (vv.5–7), Jehoshaphat also appoints selected Levites, priests, and family leaders within Jerusalem to handle appeals in Jerusalem from throughout Judah. Like the judicial appointments noted above, these appointments also seem to be in line with Deuteronomic law:

> If cases come before your courts that are too difficult for you to judge—whether bloodshed, lawsuits or assaults—take them to the place the LORD your God will choose. Go to the priests, who are Levites, and to the judge who is in office at that time. Inquire of them and they will give you the verdict. You must act according to the decisions they give you at the place the LORD will choose. Be careful to do everything they direct you to do. Act according to the law they teach you and the decisions they give you. Do not turn aside from what they tell you, to the right or to the left. (Dt 17:8–11)

These steps seem to reflect centralization of the judicial system in the southern kingdom. Again,

priests and Levites serve as teachers of God's ways and law. The role of priests as teachers reflects God's covenantal framework, in which priests are charged by God to "teach the Israelites all the decrees the LORD has given them" (Lev 10:11).

A similar commissioning of Levites is seen during the postexilic ministry of Ezra and Nehemiah (cf. Ezr 8:1–14). Like the commissioning of the judges (v.7), Jehoshaphat's crux exhortation given to these appointees is that they carry out their responsibilities faithfully in the fear of the Lord. Not to faithfully discharge this duty is sin (v.10) For remarks concerning the different responsibilities of Levites and priests, see comments on 5:4–6 and 5:12–13.

11 The particular appointment of Amariah and Zebadiah implies differing areas of responsibility pertaining to the executive branch (matters concerning the king) and the judicial-legal branch (matters concerning the Lord). The Levites function in a more generic role, perhaps akin to judicial clerks (cf. R. De Vaux, *Ancient Israel: Its Life and Institutions* [Grand Rapids: Eerdmans, 1997], 155). Jehoshaphat's exhortation to "courage" is similar to key exhortations given to those in watershed moments of spiritual leadership (as with Joshua; cf. Jos 1:5–9). A similar exhortation to take courage is given by Hezekiah to newly appointed military leaders in the midst of the Assyrian crisis (cf. 32:6–8; on the Lord's being "with" those who do well [v.11], see Reflection on divine presence in ch. 1).

4. Jehoshaphat's Battle against an Eastern Coalition (2Ch 20:1–30)

¹After this, the Moabites and Ammonites with some of the Meunites came to make war on Jehoshaphat.

²Some men came and told Jehoshaphat, "A vast army is coming against you from Edom, from the other side of the Sea. It is already in Hazazon Tamar" (that is, En Gedi). ³Alarmed, Jehoshaphat resolved to inquire of the LORD, and he proclaimed a fast for all Judah. ⁴The people of Judah came together to seek help from the LORD; indeed, they came from every town in Judah to seek him.

⁵Then Jehoshaphat stood up in the assembly of Judah and Jerusalem at the temple of the LORD in the front of the new courtyard ⁶and said:

"O LORD, God of our fathers, are you not the God who is in heaven? You rule over all the kingdoms of the nations. Power and might are in your hand, and no one can withstand you. ⁷O our God, did you not drive out the inhabitants of this land before your people Israel and give it forever to the descendants of Abraham your friend? ⁸They have lived in it and have built in it a sanctuary for your Name, saying, ⁹'If calamity comes upon us, whether the sword of judgment, or plague or famine, we will stand in your presence before this temple that bears your Name and will cry out to you in our distress, and you will hear us and save us.'

¹⁰"But now here are men from Ammon, Moab and Mount Seir, whose territory you would not allow Israel to invade when they came from Egypt; so they turned away from them and did not destroy them. ¹¹See how they are repaying us by coming to drive us out of the possession you gave us as an inheritance. ¹²O our God, will you not judge them? For we have no power to face this vast army that is attacking us. We do not know what to do, but our eyes are upon you."

¹³All the men of Judah, with their wives and children and little ones, stood there before the LORD.

¹⁴Then the Spirit of the LORD came upon Jahaziel son of Zechariah, the son of Benaiah, the son of Jeiel, the son of Mattaniah, a Levite and descendant of Asaph, as he stood in the assembly.

¹⁵He said: "Listen, King Jehoshaphat and all who live in Judah and Jerusalem! This is what the LORD says to you: 'Do not be afraid or discouraged because of this vast army. For the battle is not yours, but God's. ¹⁶Tomorrow march down against them. They will be climbing up by the Pass of Ziz, and you will find them at the end of the gorge in the Desert of Jeruel. ¹⁷You will not have to fight this battle. Take up your positions; stand firm and see the deliverance the LORD will give you, O Judah and Jerusalem. Do not be afraid; do not be discouraged. Go out to face them tomorrow, and the LORD will be with you.'"

¹⁸Jehoshaphat bowed with his face to the ground, and all the people of Judah and Jerusalem fell down in worship before the LORD. ¹⁹Then some Levites from the Kohathites and Korahites stood up and praised the LORD, the God of Israel, with very loud voice.

²⁰Early in the morning they left for the Desert of Tekoa. As they set out, Jehoshaphat stood and said, "Listen to me, Judah and people of Jerusalem! Have faith in the LORD your God and you will be upheld; have faith in his prophets and you will be successful." ²¹After consulting the people, Jehoshaphat appointed men to sing to the LORD and to praise him for the splendor of his holiness as they went out at the head of the army, saying:

"Give thanks to the LORD,
     for his love endures forever."

²²As they began to sing and praise, the LORD set ambushes against the men of Ammon and Moab and Mount Seir who were invading Judah, and they were defeated. ²³The men of Ammon and Moab rose up against the men from Mount Seir to destroy and annihilate them. After they finished slaughtering the men from Seir, they helped to destroy one another.

²⁴When the men of Judah came to the place that overlooks the desert and looked toward the vast army, they saw only dead bodies lying on the ground; no one had escaped. ²⁵So Jehoshaphat and his men went to carry off their plunder, and they found among them a great amount of equipment and clothing and also articles of value — more than they could take away. There was so much plunder that it took three days to collect it. ²⁶On the fourth day they assembled in the Valley of Beracah, where they praised the LORD. This is why it is called the Valley of Beracah to this day.

²⁷Then, led by Jehoshaphat, all the men of Judah and Jerusalem returned joyfully to Jerusalem, for the LORD had given them cause to rejoice over their enemies. ²⁸They entered Jerusalem and went to the temple of the LORD with harps and lutes and trumpets.

²⁹The fear of God came upon all the kingdoms of the countries when they heard how the LORD had fought against the enemies of Israel. ³⁰And the kingdom of Jehoshaphat was at peace, for his God had given him rest on every side.

COMMENTARY

1–2 Perhaps sensing weakness following the defeat of Jehoshaphat and Ahab at Ramoth Gilead (see comments on ch. 18), an eastern coalition joins forces against Jehoshaphat. This account (not found in 2Ki) has two areas of textual uncertainty regarding the details of this coalition. The first is that the Hebrew text has "Ammonites" in place of the NIV's "Meunites" (v.1). The NIV's "Meunites" reading is attested in the LXX and alleviates what would seem to be an unlikely expression (namely, "Moabites and Ammonites with some of the Ammonites"). Moreover, since this third part of the coalition is referred to as the "people of Seir" later in the passage (cf. v.22), this would also favor the reading of "Meunites."

The Meunites were an Arabian tribe living in the southern region of Transjordan and parts of the Sinai, a tribe of people who were able to control some of the trade routes stemming from the southern portion of the King's Highway. While the specific locations of some of the places noted in this passage are not known with certainty (e.g., the Pass of Ziz and the Desert of Jeruel; v.16), they are clearly locations within the hinterland area of the Dead Sea in the environs of the En Gedi oases. There is alarm in Judah when it is reported that the eastern coalition has reached En Gedi (only twenty-five miles southeast of Jerusalem). Nonetheless, this rebellion is thwarted by infighting prompted by Yahweh, who subsequently gives Jehoshaphat rest all around (vv.22-30).

The second textual uncertainty is that the Hebrew text has the coalition attacking "from Aram" (v.2), where the NIV has opted for "from Edom." While the manuscript support for "from Edom" is minimal, the rendering "from Edom" does make sense vis-à-vis the geographical setting of the battle. (Note that the coalition is described as coming "from the other side of the Sea," presumably the Dead Sea, perhaps via the Lisan). This noted, if Aram is indeed intended here, the passage would indicate that these eastern nations are being supported (if not incited) by Damascus, perhaps as a means of reprisal against Jehoshaphat in his help of Ahab's assault of Ramoth Gilead.

3-4 With the vast army from the eastern regions situated only about fifteen miles from Jerusalem (at En Gedi; v.2), Jehoshaphat wisely opts to seek the Lord through corporate prayer and fasting. The imagery of God's people gathered at the temple (in the new outer courtyard [v.5], to be distinguished from the courtyard for priests; 4:9) evokes the imagery of Solomon's temple prayer that anticipates God's people seeking him at the temple in times of war (cf. 6:34-35). This corporate gathering in fasting and prayer was also seen in earlier periods of national crisis (cf. Jdg 20:26) and is similar to the response of God's people in the light of Philistine oppression and the loss of the ark during the time of Samuel (cf. 1Sa 7:2-6). The Chronicler uses the

repetition of "all Judah" in this passage to emphasize the oneness of heart of the Judean community in seeking God during this time of uncertainty and danger (cf. v.13).

5-13 Jehoshaphat's prayer draws on God's cosmological (creation) power and his prior faithfulness in driving out the nations (as he gave his people the land), and calls on him to act in the current crisis. This prayer is similar to the corporate laments of the Psalter (e.g., Pss 44; 74). Once again, both the spirit and the specifics of Solomon's temple dedication permeate the prayer (compare vv.8-9 with 6:2-30; 7:13-15). In addition, Jehoshaphat's prayer reflects his knowledge of Israelite history, including Yahweh's specific prohibitions regarding the nations that make up the invading coalition (cf. Dt 2:1-23; recall the family connection Israel has to these nations through Lot and Esau).

Although Jehoshaphat has reformed the judiciary of Israel (cf. 2Ch 19:5-11), the king nonetheless recognizes that God is the ultimate judge of humankind (v.12). Jehoshaphat's statement of waiting faith ("our eyes are upon you," v.12) reflects his complete trust in God's strength and ability to deliver Judah (compare Asa's words in light of the invasion of the massive army of Zerah; 14:11).

14-17 In answer to the corporate prayer of Jehoshaphat and the assembled community, the Spirit of the Lord comes upon Jahaziel the son of Zechariah (cf. 1Ch 16:5). Note that the answer from God comes through a Levite (recall that the musical role of Levites might be accompanied by prophetic ministry; cf. 1Ch 25:1-7). Jahaziel's words portray the role of God as a divine warrior who fights on behalf of his covenantal people ("the battle is not yours, but God's," v.15; cf. vv.17, 22) as reflected in Deuteronomy:

> When you go to war against your enemies and
> see horses and chariots and an army greater than
> yours, do not be afraid of them, because the Lord

your God, who brought you up out of Egypt, will be with you. When you are about to go into battle, the priest shall come forward and address the army. He shall say: "Hear, O Israel, today you are going into battle against your enemies. Do not be faint-hearted or afraid; do not be terrified or give way to panic before them. For the LORD your God is the one who goes with you to fight for you against your enemies to give you victory." (Dt 20:1–4)

These truths undergird Jahaziel's statement of faith and impending divine deliverance (v.17) and bring to mind Moses' similar words of faith as the Israelites were backed up to the Sea of Reeds (cf. Ex 14:13–14), and Yahweh's words of encouragement to Joshua regarding Jericho ("I have delivered Jericho into your hands," Jos 6:2). The Lord's words to King Jehoshaphat and the people of Judah begin and end with the exhortation not to be afraid or discouraged (vv.15, 17), bringing to mind Yahweh's similar exhortation to Joshua (Jos 1:5–9) as well as the exhortation given by Hezekiah in the midst of the Assyrian crisis (2Ch 32:6–8). The promise of divine presence expressed by the prophet ("the LORD will be with you," v.17) will enable Jehoshaphat's obedience and success.

18–19 In response to Jahaziel's consoling prophecy (vv.14–17), the king and the people prostrate themselves in grateful worship accompanied by the loud sounds (singing?) of Levites. Levites played a key role in the worship celebration, especially Korahites, who were a subdivision of Kohathites (cf. 1Ch 6:31–48; 23:2–32). Singing and music will continue even as they march into battle (cf. vv.21–22) and following their return from victory (cf. vv.27–28).

20–23 Inspired by the word of God through Jahaziel, Jehoshaphat and the people set out in faith (recall the instructions of Jahaziel of 20:16) toward the Desert of Tekoa. Jehoshaphat's exhortation to the people to have faith is reminiscent of the prophet Isaiah's words to Ahaz during the Syro-Ephraimite

crisis (cf. Isa 7:9). Jehoshaphat reiterates Jahaziel's exhortation that connects aspects of applied faith (e.g., being strong and courageous; stepping out in obedience) and divinely granted success.

The men appointed by Jehoshaphat to lead singing to God and praise for the "splendor of his holiness" (v.21) are presumably Levites (on the musical service of Levites, cf. 1Ch 6:31–48; 23:2–32; 25:1–7). Going to battle in song is found in several key battles of faith in the OT and seems to underscore an especially intentional focus on God and his strength (cf. Jos 6:1–21; 2Ch 13:3–20). The refrain of thanks sung by the warriors ("Give thanks to the LORD, for his love endures forever"; cf. Ps 136:1) is used several times by the Chronicler and provides a summary of God's past goodness and also signifies the present and ongoing reality of God's *enduring* love for the Chronicler's postexilic audience and beyond.

As they begin to sing these words of praise and thanksgiving (v.22), God directly intervenes on the battlefield to bring to pass the prophetic word of Jahaziel that God would fight on behalf of his covenantal people ("the battle is not yours, but God's," v.15; cf. comments on vv.14–17). As a result of God's intervention ("the LORD set ambushes," v.22) and the resulting disarray between the eastern armies (v.23), the coalition armies destroy each other (a motif seen in other landmark OT battles; cf. Jdg 7:22; 1Sa 14:20; Eze 38:21). On the makeup of this coalition (men of Ammon, Moab, and Mount Seir; vv.22–23), see comments on vv.1–2.

24–26 Without any action on the part of Jehoshaphat's army, the eastern coalition is destroyed. The plundering of enemies is one of the ways in which God showed his sovereignty over the nations and his favor for his people (cf. Ex 12:35–36; Hag 2:22). It is likely that the location of the valley where the army assembled to praise God for his blessings was renamed Valley of

Beracah (= Valley of Blessing) in the light of the victory given by God.

27–28 The men return to Jerusalem in joy and return to the temple to continue corporate celebrations of worship, music, and song because Yahweh has fought for his people Israel (as anticipated at v.15 and reflected earlier at 17:10; see fur-

ther remarks on music and musical instruments at 5:12–13).

29–30 On God's establishing the king's dominion and bringing his fear to the surrounding nations, see comments on 17:10–11. The granting of "rest" was a key divine promise given to Israel and part of the broader notion of land theology (cf. Dt 12:10).

NOTE

2 Note the similarity of Edom and Aram in Hebrew consonantal writing: אֲרָם, *ʾrm* (Aram); אֱדֹם, *ʾdm* (Edom), which supports the possibility of a scribal transmission issue here. For a further geopolitical discussion of the question of "Edom" versus "Aram," see A. F. Rainey, "Mesha's Attempt to Invade Judah (2Chron 20)," in *Studies in Historical Geography and Biblical Historiography* (ed. G. Galil and M. Weinfeld; VTSup 81; Leiden: Brill, 2000), 174–76.

5. Jehoshaphat's Regnal Summary Part One (2Ch 20:31–34)

> [31]So Jehoshaphat reigned over Judah. He was thirty-five years old when he became king of Judah, and he reigned in Jerusalem twenty-five years. His mother's name was Azubah daughter of Shilhi. [32]He walked in the ways of his father Asa and did not stray from them; he did what was right in the eyes of the LORD. [33]The high places, however, were not removed, and the people still had not set their hearts on the God of their fathers.
>
> [34]The other events of Jehoshaphat's reign, from beginning to end, are written in the annals of Jehu son of Hanani, which are recorded in the book of the kings of Israel.

COMMENTARY

31–33 Jehoshaphat's regnal summary provides a strong but incomplete overview of his twenty-five-year reign in Judah (probably including a three-year coregency with Asa; cf. comments on 16:12–13). As such, the summary provides a fuller picture of the positive summary of his reign given at the beginning of the Chronicler's coverage of Jehoshaphat (cf. 17:3–6). While Jehoshaphat did

what was right in God's eyes (v.32) and walked in the ways of his father (who, likewise, had a positive but imperfect reign; cf. comments on 16:10–13), Jehoshaphat fell short in both his persistent alliances with ungodly Israelite kings (Ahab and Ahaziah) and in the touchstone area of high places.

The statement at v.33 should be understood together with the remark at 17:6, which states that

Jehoshaphat removed the high places from Judah. These statements imply that either Jehoshaphat's efforts were incomplete or that his vigilance in removing subsequent high places waned. For an example of the rebuilding of high places within Judah, recall that Jehoshaphat's father, Asa, had also removed high places from Judah but that more were built by the time Jehoshaphat was on the throne, vividly illustrating the Israelites' strong tendency toward idolatry and syncretism (cf. comments on 14:3–5). Thus the Chronicler attaches part of the responsibility for the nonremoval (and/or rebuilding) of high places on the sad reality that the people "had not set their hearts on the God of their fathers."

34 See the comment on sources and annals at 12:15 and the Introduction.

6. Jehoshaphat's Further Alliance with the Northern Kingdom (2Ch 20:35–37)

[35]Later, Jehoshaphat king of Judah made an alliance with Ahaziah king of Israel, who was guilty of wickedness. [36]He agreed with him to construct a fleet of trading ships. After these were built at Ezion Geber, [37]Eliezer son of Dodavahu of Mareshah prophesied against Jehoshaphat, saying, "Because you have made an alliance with Ahaziah, the Lord will destroy what you have made." The ships were wrecked and were not able to set sail to trade.

COMMENTARY

35–37 The pushing back of the Moabite/Ammonite/Meunite invasion (cf. 20:1–30) gave Jehoshaphat control of the region in the vicinity of the port city of Ezion Geber. Previous lucrative maritime trade from this port during the time of Solomon no doubt prompted Jehoshaphat's ill-fated attempt to restart maritime trade from this port through yet another ill-advised alliance with an ungodly northern kingdom king.

In short, this episode amounts to another example of faith compromise on the part of Jehoshaphat that reveals a heart not fully aligned with the ways of God. This prompts a prophetic rebuke from an otherwise unknown prophet (Eliezer), who announces God's coming judgment on this upstart maritime alliance. The connection with the time of Ahaziah of Israel places this maritime project in ca. 853 or 852 BC (cf. Thiele, 98–99). For additional details on Israelite maritime trade and the seaport at Ezion Geber, see commentary on 8:17–18.

NOTE

35–37 On the distinctions of the Chronicler's summary of this failed maritime alliance with the summary found in Kings, see Selman, 430.

7. Jehoshaphat's Regnal Summary Part Two (2Ch 21:1–3)

¹Then Jehoshaphat rested with his fathers and was buried with them in the City of David. And Jehoram his son succeeded him as king. ²Jehoram's brothers, the sons of Jehoshaphat, were Azariah, Jehiel, Zechariah, Azariahu, Michael and Shephatiah. All these were sons of Jehoshaphat king of Israel. ³Their father had given them many gifts of silver and gold and articles of value, as well as fortified cities in Judah, but he had given the kingdom to Jehoram because he was his firstborn son.

COMMENTARY

1–3 Following his death, Jehoshaphat is given the honor of being buried in the royal cemetery. While little is known of Israel's royal burial customs, the special treatment of kings in death and burial is commonplace in the ancient Near East, as reflected in the exquisite burial chambers in the Valley of the Kings in Thebes, Egypt. The Chronicler also provides an extended (and atypical) list of the sons of Jehoshaphat (brothers and/or half brothers of Jehoram) and the gifts and administrative oversight they were given by their father Jehoshaphat. In addition, note that Jehoshaphat is given the title "king of Israel" (v.2), which is usually used of rulers of the northern kingdom during the divided kingdom period.

E. The Reign of Jehoram (2Ch 21:4–20)

OVERVIEW

For some general comments on the reigns of Jehoshaphat and his son Jehoram, who succeeded him to the throne, see the Overview to 17:1–21:3.

⁴When Jehoram established himself firmly over his father's kingdom, he put all his brothers to the sword along with some of the princes of Israel. ⁵Jehoram was thirty-two years old when he became king, and he reigned in Jerusalem eight years. ⁶He walked in the ways of the kings of Israel, as the house of Ahab had done, for he married a daughter of Ahab. He did evil in the eyes of the LORD. ⁷Nevertheless, because of the covenant the LORD had made with David, the LORD was not willing to destroy the house of David. He had promised to maintain a lamp for him and his descendants forever.

⁸In the time of Jehoram, Edom rebelled against Judah and set up its own king. ⁹So Jehoram went there with his officers and all his chariots. The Edomites surrounded him and his chariot commanders, but he rose up and broke through by night. ¹⁰To this day Edom has been in rebellion against Judah.

Libnah revolted at the same time, because Jehoram had forsaken the Lord, the God of his fathers. ¹¹He had also built high places on the hills of Judah and had caused the people of Jerusalem to prostitute themselves and had led Judah astray. ¹²Jehoram received a letter from Elijah the prophet, which said:

> "This is what the Lord, the God of your father David, says: 'You have not walked in the ways of your father Jehoshaphat or of Asa king of Judah. ¹³But you have walked in the ways of the kings of Israel, and you have led Judah and the people of Jerusalem to prostitute themselves, just as the house of Ahab did. You have also murdered your own brothers, members of your father's house, men who were better than you. ¹⁴So now the Lord is about to strike your people, your sons, your wives and everything that is yours, with a heavy blow. ¹⁵You yourself will be very ill with a lingering disease of the bowels, until the disease causes your bowels to come out.'"

¹⁶The Lord aroused against Jehoram the hostility of the Philistines and of the Arabs who lived near the Cushites. ¹⁷They attacked Judah, invaded it and carried off all the goods found in the king's palace, together with his sons and wives. Not a son was left to him except Ahaziah, the youngest.

¹⁸After all this, the Lord afflicted Jehoram with an incurable disease of the bowels. ¹⁹In the course of time, at the end of the second year, his bowels came out because of the disease, and he died in great pain. His people made no fire in his honor, as they had for his fathers.

²⁰Jehoram was thirty-two years old when he became king, and he reigned in Jerusalem eight years. He passed away, to no one's regret, and was buried in the City of David, but not in the tombs of the kings.

COMMENTARY

4 As with Solomon (cf. 1:1), Jehoram "established himself firmly" over the kingdom. However, in the case of Solomon this description is tied to God's presence and blessing, while in Jehoram's case it is tied to his killing of all of his brothers (and/or half brothers). These individuals are named in v.2, which by twice noting that these were the sons of Jehoshaphat underscores the treachery of the act. The elimination of potential rivals or claimants to the throne (fratricide/regicide) was a somewhat common custom in the ancient Near East (the Hittites being especially famous for it). In addition to this incident, regicide is also seen in ancient Israel with Abimelech's murder of most of his brothers (cf. Jdg 9) and the murder of all Davidic descendants (except Joash) by Queen Athaliah (cf. 22:10).

5 Jehoram likely began a coregency with Jehoshaphat around 853 BC (the time frame of the Battle of Qarqar—perhaps a factor in the coregency) and began his sole reign in ca. 848 BC. The positing of a coregency addresses the various dating and regnal notations within Kings and Chronicles (see Thiele, 99–101; for more on this time frame, see Overview to 17:1–21:3).

6 Jehoram's wickedness was enhanced and inspired by his close association with the apostate northern kingdom (the "house of Ahab"). Jehoram's wife (Athaliah) was the daughter of the infamous Ahab and Jezebel of the northern kingdom (cf. 22:2; thus Athaliah was the granddaughter of Omri, founder of the Omride dynasty; see Overview to 17:1–21:3). The marriage of Jehoram and Athaliah was part of the political marriage treaty orchestrated by Jehoram's father, Jehoshaphat (see comments on 18:1). As noted above, such alliances show trust in human beings and political structures rather than complete trust in God and his ways. Moreover, such acts of spiritual compromise can have unexpected waves of consequences, as seen in the events of this chapter and the next. Athaliah, like her husband Jehoram (v.4), will kill Davidic heirs to the throne (cf. 22:10).

7 Despite the wickedness of the rule of Jehoram (and despite the disastrous events his wife will precipitate), God shows his commitment to preserve the house of David on account of *his* Word and *his* character. God's enduring promise to David is exalted in the poetry of Psalm 89 and the prophetic oracle of Jeremiah 33:

> "Once for all, I have sworn by my holiness—
>   and I will not lie to David—
> that his line will continue forever
>   and his throne endure before me like the sun;
> it will be established forever like the moon,

the faithful witness in the sky." (Ps 89:35–37; cf. Ps 132:11–12)

The word of the LORD came to Jeremiah: "This is what the LORD says: 'If you can break my covenant with the day and my covenant with the night, so that day and night no longer come at their appointed time, then my covenant with David my servant—and my covenant with the Levites who are priests ministering before me—can be broken and David will no longer have a descendant to reign on his throne. I will make the descendants of David my servant and the Levites who minister before me as countless as the stars of the sky and as measureless as the sand on the seashore.'" (Jer 33:19–22)

The Chronicler's narrative interlude provides a vivid reminder of hope that wickedness is temporary and that God will ultimately fulfill his Word. This reminder would have particular significance in light of the uncertainties and unknowns faced by the Chronicler's postexilic audience. For further remarks on the Davidic covenant, see comments on 1 Chronicles 17:7–15 and 2 Chronicles 1:9; 6:4–11.

8–10 The perceived weakness of Jehoshaphat's successor Jehoram (Joram) prompts Edom in the southeast and Libnah in the west to rebel against Judah (cf. 2Ki 8:20–22). Libnah (perhaps Tel Zayit, or Tel Bornat) was located in the Shephelah about midway between Azekah and Lachish, near the border with Philistia. The Chronicler notes similar hostility from the Philistines to the west and the Arabians to the south (see vv.16–17). Regardless of perceived weakness on the part of Judah, the ultimate theological reason for this upheaval is that "Jehoram had forsaken the LORD" (v.10).

11 Instead of being a spiritual leader regularly enriched in God's law (cf. the model for the king in Dt 17:18–20 and comments on 14:4), Jehoram led the people in wickedness and spiritual decay. Jehoram may have been the builder of the infamous Baal temple later destroyed during the early years of the reign of young Joash (cf. 23:16–17). The imagery of the people prostituting themselves produces a vivid picture of unfaithfulness and grave spiritual wickedness (cf. Lev 20:1–5; for more on high places and related objects of idolatry and syncretism, see comments on 2Ch 1:3–5; 14:3).

12–15 The letter from Elijah to Jehoram functions like a prophetic judgment oracle and contains a sweeping indictment of Jehoram, including his abandoning of the (largely) faithful ways of his forefathers (Asa [cf. 14:2; 15:1–19] and Jehoshaphat [cf. 17:3–6]), his adoption of the unfaithful and idolatrous ways characteristic of the northern kings (most detestably the "house of Ahab"; cf. 1Ki 16:30–33), and his murder (fratricide) of his "better" brothers. The prophet Elijah delivers a message of judgment that will touch every area of Jehoram's life and well-being (see comments on 2Ch 21:18–20).

Much of the attention given to this passage is directed to the unexpected detail of Elijah's delivering an indictment against a Judean king (in writing, no less)—unexpected since some understand, according to 2 Kings 2:1–12, that Elijah was already taken up to heaven by this time. It should be noted that this is the only appearance of Elijah in Chronicles, whose ministry efforts noted in Kings are directed against the wicked ways of the northern kingdom's Omride dynasty, particularly Ahab. However, Elijah's prophetic activity in the northern kingdom does not preclude his engagement with Judean kings, particularly if a king's actions (as here; cf. vv.6, 13) mimic that of the northern kings. Elijah likely spent some time in the southern kingdom during his flight to Mount Horeb (1Ki 19:3).

With respect to the chronological uncertainties, it is possible that Elijah's letter was written prior to his translation to heaven, prophetically mentioning the name and sins of the future king Jehoram (akin to Isaiah's mentioning the future Persian king Cyrus and his eventual role in the rebuilding of Jerusalem; cf. Isa 44:28; 45:13). While nothing in the text indicates this was the case, nothing in the text precludes the possibility either. Note that Elijah also prophesied the death of the northern king Ahaziah (cf. 2Ki 1:16–17).

In fact, the Israel-Judah regnal dating given in the context of this prophecy shows that Elijah was alive during at least some of Jehoram's reign in Judah. Given that Jehoram's fratricide and his dramatic steps toward pagan ways presumably happened early in his reign, the possibility of Elijah's writing this letter need not be a problematic issue. In addition, since 2 Kings 2–3 seems to portray Elisha's ministry as after the translation of Elijah, it is possible that Elijah and Elisha ministered together before Elijah was taken up. Alternatively, the account of 2 Kings 3 might be an instance of chronological disjunction vis-à-vis the events of 2 Kings 2 (cf. 2Ki 1:1 and the account of 2 Ki 3). Lastly, while 2 Kings 3:11 shows that Elisha was in the camp, it does not require that Elijah was already dead. All told, it cannot be said with certainty that Elijah was not alive at this time. For more discussion on this issue, see Dillard, 167.

16–17 Following Elijah's prophetic indictment (vv.12–15), God "aroused" the Philistines and Arabs to attack Jehoram. Thus, in addition to the rebellion of Edom and Libnah (see vv.8–10), Jehoram also faced attacks on Judah (including Jerusalem) from regional foes to the south and west, leading to the death of the older sons of Jehoram. The Arabs noted here were located in the desert regions to the south of the Judean Negev into portions of the Sinai Peninsula. The Cushites noted as "near" the Arabs might relate to the battle of Zerah, which would place them in the vicinity of Gerar, in the southern region of the Negev (cf. 14:9–13). These Arab raiders are credited with killing all of Jehoram's sons except Ahaziah (cf. 22:1). In addition to the difficulties of fighting battles on multiple fronts,

Judah's loss of these areas would entail the loss of tribute payments and caravan (trade) revenue.

18–20 The final words concerning the reign of Jehoram are strikingly negative:

- the Lord afflicts him with an incurable disease
- his condition worsens
- he dies in great pain
- no fire is made in his honor
- no one regrets his demise
- he is not given the honor of burial in the royal cemetery

Moreover, the typical information of resting with one's father, regnal succession information, and notations for where to find additional information are absent from these final remarks on Jehoram's reign. The portrayal of Jehoram is one of abject failure to be faithful to God. Conversely, this summary (and the next verse, 2Ch 22:1) shows the faithfulness of God to bring his word to pass (e.g., the prophetic indictment given through Elijah; cf. 21:14–15).

NOTE

17 The mention of Ahaziah in v.17 is actually "Jehoahaz" in the Hebrew text. Jehoahaz is another name for Ahaziah (cf. 22:1). Note that the components of these names (Ahaz and Jeho/[I]ah) are reversed (Jeho [Yeho] and -iah [Yah] are both shortened variations of the divine name, Yahweh): Yahweh-Ahaz// Ahaz-Yahweh, both referring to the strength of the Lord (Yahweh).

F. The Reign of Ahaziah (2Ch 22:1–9)

¹The people of Jerusalem made Ahaziah, Jehoram's youngest son, king in his place, since the raiders, who came with the Arabs into the camp, had killed all the older sons. So Ahaziah son of Jehoram king of Judah began to reign.

²Ahaziah was twenty-two years old when he became king, and he reigned in Jerusalem one year. His mother's name was Athaliah, a granddaughter of Omri.

³He too walked in the ways of the house of Ahab, for his mother encouraged him in doing wrong. ⁴He did evil in the eyes of the LORD, as the house of Ahab had done, for after his father's death they became his advisors, to his undoing. ⁵He also followed their counsel when he went with Joram son of Ahab king of Israel to war against Hazael king of Aram at Ramoth Gilead. The Arameans wounded Joram; ⁶so he returned to Jezreel to recover from the wounds they had inflicted on him at Ramoth in his battle with Hazael king of Aram.

Then Ahaziah son of Jehoram king of Judah went down to Jezreel to see Joram son of Ahab because he had been wounded.

⁷Through Ahaziah's visit to Joram, God brought about Ahaziah's downfall. When Ahaziah arrived, he went out with Joram to meet Jehu son of Nimshi, whom the LORD had anointed to destroy the house of Ahab. ⁸While Jehu was executing judgment on the

house of Ahab, he found the princes of Judah and the sons of Ahaziah's relatives, who had been attending Ahaziah, and he killed them. [9]He then went in search of Ahaziah, and his men captured him while he was hiding in Samaria. He was brought to Jehu and put to death. They buried him, for they said, "He was a son of Jehoshaphat, who sought the LORD with all his heart." So there was no one in the house of Ahaziah powerful enough to retain the kingdom.

COMMENTARY

1–2 Jehoahaz (also known as Ahaziah; see Note on 21:17) succeeded his father Jehoram in 841 BC and was killed within a year in the midst of Jehu's revolt (see comments on 22:7–9). The king's sons were killed in conjunction with God's inciting the Philistines and Arabs to attack Jehoram (see comments on 21:16–17), an outworking of the prophetic word delivered via letter from the prophet Elijah (cf. 21:12–15).

The significance of the group "the people of Jerusalem" is not certain but may be another term for the sociopolitical group known as "the people of the land," who figure into several succession narratives in ancient Judah. See the discussion on this group at 23:21. Ahaziah's mother (Jehoram's widow) is Athaliah, the northern kingdom daughter of Ahab and Jezebel and hence granddaughter of Omri, the military commander who inaugurated the Omride dynasty (which will end at the death of Ahaziah; for a review of this time frame, see the Overview to 2Ch 17:1–21:3). The marriage between Jehoram and Athaliah was part of the political marriage treaty orchestrated by Jehoshaphat (cf. 2Ch 18:1).

3–4 As with his father Jehoram, Ahaziah's wickedness and unfaithfulness were enhanced by his close association with the apostate northern kingdom (the "house of Ahab"; cf. 21:6) as well as the direct influence of his mother, Athaliah, daughter

of Ahab and Jezebel (see comments on vv.1–2). Instead of encouraging her son in the ways of wisdom and God (as with "Dame Wisdom" of the book of Proverbs), Ahaziah's mother "encouraged him in doing wrong." In addition to the evil influence of his mother, Ahaziah sought counsel from the northern kingdom "to his undoing." Also see comments on queen mothers at 15:16.

5–6 Ahaziah's reliance on the counsel of the ungodly (cf. vv.3–4) leads to his agreement to help the northern kingdom in battle alliance against Aram at the Transjordanian city of Ramoth Gilead, in similar manner to his grandfather Jehoshaphat (cf. 18:2–34). Ramoth Gilead (likely Tell Ramith) was situated along the King's Highway about thirty miles east of the Jordan River. Control over Ramoth Gilead meant control over the lucrative north-south trade caravans that passed through it.

The battle for Ramoth Gilead sets the scene for the outworking of divinely driven regnal changes in both Aram and the northern kingdom. Both of these changes were prophetically announced by Elijah (cf. 1Ki 19:15–18) and then reaffirmed via Elisha (cf. 2Ki 9:1–10).

7–9 The battle at Ramoth Gilead will lead to upheaval, military coups, and regnal changes in the Israel, Judah, and Aram. In the coup in the northern kingdom (known as "Jehu's revolt," ca. 841 BC), the military commander Jehu brings the Omride dynasty to an end by the assassination of Joram. In addition, Jehu kills Joram's Phoenician mother, Jezebel, and scores of priests and prophets of Baal and Asherah ("judgment on the house of Ahab," v.8), leading the narrator of Kings to depict Jehu as a liberator who freed Israel from the domination of a foreign queen mother (cf. 2Ki 9–10). Jehu also kills the Judah's king, Ahaziah, at Jezreel by the agency of God, as reflected in the statement "God brought about Ahaziah's downfall" (v.7).

The death of Ahaziah facilitates the rise to power of his mother, Queen Athaliah (daughter of Ahab and Jezebel), who in turn attempts to eliminate all male descendants of David (see comments on 22:10). Jezreel (Tel Yizra'l) is located on the eastern side of the Jezreel Valley (opposite Megiddo) near the base of Mount Gilboa. Note that Jehu's revolt at Jezreel plays into both the condemnation and message of hope in the prophetic message of Hosea (cf. Hos 1:4–5, 11; 2:22). As might be expected, Jehu's murder of Jezebel has a ruinous effect on the northern kingdom's relationship with Phoenicia, while his murder of Ahaziah ends the good relations between Israel and Judah. Jehu reigned in the northern kingdom for twenty-eight years (ca. 841–14 BC).

In addition to Jehu's killing Ahaziah and Joram, the Aramean official Hazael assassinated Ben-Hadad in Damascus and seized control of Aram. The Tel Dan Inscription indicates that King Hazael takes credit for the deaths of Joram and Ahaziah, implying that Jehu may have acted in collusion with Hazael/Aram (cf. COS, 2:39; see W. M. Schniedewind, "Tel Dan Stela: New Light on Aramaic and Jehu's Revolt," BASOR 302 [1996]: 75–90, esp. 82–85).

Regardless of any possible collusion between Jehu and Hazael, the net effect of the nearly simultaneous murders of the kings of Israel, Judah, and Aram fosters instability in the Levant that allows the Assyrian king Shalmaneser III to gain the upper hand in the region almost immediately. Note that Jehu is shown as prostrating before Shalmaneser III in a scene on the Black Obelisk, which indicates the northern kingdom's subservience to Assyria (see ANEP, fig. 351).

NOTES

2 The Hebrew text (MT) has Ahaziah becoming king at age forty-two (אַרְבָּעִים וּשְׁתַּיִם שָׁנָה, ʾarbāʿîm ûšᵉtayim šānâ), but the NIV is likely correct in rendering his age at twenty-two years old, based on 2 Kings 8:26 and the LXX^L's reading. (Other LXX manuscripts have twenty years old.) With respect to Athaliah as granddaughter of Omri, the Hebrew text refers to Athaliah as the "daughter" of Omri (בַּת, bat; GK 1426), but in analogy to the Hebrew term for "son," bat can mean "daughter," "granddaughter," or simply "female descendant."

6 Ramoth (NIV) is actually "Ramah" (רָמָה, rāmâ) in the Hebrew text (MT), but the NIV is likely correct. Similarly, "Ahaziah" in the NIV is "Azariah" in the MT (עֲזַרְיָהוּ ʿazaryāhû), and again the NIV's rendering is probably correct.

8 Note that Hebrew text (MT) is literally "sons of the brothers of Ahaziah" (בְּנֵי אֲחֵי אֲחַזְיָהוּ, bᵉnê ʾaḥê ʾaḥazyāhû)—but since his actual brothers are dead (recall 21:17; 22:1), the NIV's rendering of "relatives" is likely correct, since the Hebrew term for "brother" (GK 278) can also refer to family/kinsman.

9 Selman contends that the NIV unnecessarily adds "then" in this verse as an attempt to address sequential issues in the passage (Selman, 441).

G. The Coup and Rule of Queen Athaliah (2Ch 22:10–23:21)

1. Athaliah's Coup (2Ch 22:10–12)

¹⁰When Athaliah the mother of Ahaziah saw that her son was dead, she proceeded to destroy the whole royal family of the house of Judah. ¹¹But Jehosheba, the daughter of King Jehoram, took Joash son of Ahaziah and stole him away from among the royal princes who were about to be murdered and put him and his nurse in a bedroom. Because Jehosheba, the daughter of King Jehoram and wife of the priest Jehoiada, was Ahaziah's sister, she hid the child from Athaliah so she could not kill him. ¹²He remained hidden with them at the temple of God for six years while Athaliah ruled the land.

COMMENTARY

10 Athaliah takes the killing of her son Ahaziah by Jehu (cf. 22:7–9) as an opportunity to expand her power beyond her position as Queen Mother. In the aftermath of the chaos and instability within the southern kingdom, she proceeds to eliminate all Davidic claimants to the Judean throne (with the unintentional exception of Joash; cf. vv.11–12) and rules for about six years (ca. 841–36 BC). The six/seven–year reign of Athaliah is the only time ancient Judah or Israel is ruled by a queen.

Athaliah's ability to engineer this anti-Davidic coup and reign for about six years in Judah implies a considerable amount of preexisting power, authority, and influence. This dark episode in Judah's history provides the Judahites with a taste of exile without actually leaving the land. For more on the position of Queen Mother, see comments on 15:16. On the elimination of rival claimants to the throne, see comments on 21:4. For more details on

the series of events that facilitate Athaliah's coup, see comments on Jehu's revolt at 22:5–9.

11–12 In the midst of the disaster of the coup of Athaliah (cf. v.10), God ensures the survival of the Davidic line through Jehosheba (Jehoshebeath), the wife of the priest Jehoiada. The providential saving of this baby (cf. 2Ch 23:1; 24:1) recalls God's similar protection of the baby Moses (Ex 2:1–10) and baby Jesus (Mt 2:1–18). Providing some literary drama is the realization that Jehosheba is at some level related to Queen Athaliah (as daughter or step-daughter) but is nonetheless willing to risk everything to do what is right in the eyes of God. Similarly, the nurse of baby Joash also assumes enormous risk in going along with the plan (v.11). The hiding of Joash within the temple (v.12) provides both the spiritual-metaphysical sense of God's power and protection (cf. Pr 18:10) as well as the practical benefit of being the place where Jehoiada performs his daily duties as a priest.

2. Jehoiada's Counter-Coup and Installment of Joash (2Ch 23:1–21)

¹In the seventh year Jehoiada showed his strength. He made a covenant with the commanders of units of a hundred: Azariah son of Jeroham, Ishmael son of Jehohanan,

Azariah son of Obed, Maaseiah son of Adaiah, and Elishaphat son of Zicri. [2]They went throughout Judah and gathered the Levites and the heads of Israelite families from all the towns. When they came to Jerusalem, [3]the whole assembly made a covenant with the king at the temple of God.

Jehoiada said to them, "The king's son shall reign, as the LORD promised concerning the descendants of David. [4]Now this is what you are to do: A third of you priests and Levites who are going on duty on the Sabbath are to keep watch at the doors, [5]a third of you at the royal palace and a third at the Foundation Gate, and all the other men are to be in the courtyards of the temple of the LORD. [6]No one is to enter the temple of the LORD except the priests and Levites on duty; they may enter because they are consecrated, but all the other men are to guard what the LORD has assigned to them. [7]The Levites are to station themselves around the king, each man with his weapons in his hand. Anyone who enters the temple must be put to death. Stay close to the king wherever he goes."

[8]The Levites and all the men of Judah did just as Jehoiada the priest ordered. Each one took his men—those who were going on duty on the Sabbath and those who were going off duty—for Jehoiada the priest had not released any of the divisions. [9]Then he gave the commanders of units of a hundred the spears and the large and small shields that had belonged to King David and that were in the temple of God. [10]He stationed all the men, each with his weapon in his hand, around the king—near the altar and the temple, from the south side to the north side of the temple.

[11]Jehoiada and his sons brought out the king's son and put the crown on him; they presented him with a copy of the covenant and proclaimed him king. They anointed him and shouted, "Long live the king!"

[12]When Athaliah heard the noise of the people running and cheering the king, she went to them at the temple of the LORD. [13]She looked, and there was the king, standing by his pillar at the entrance. The officers and the trumpeters were beside the king, and all the people of the land were rejoicing and blowing trumpets, and singers with musical instruments were leading the praises. Then Athaliah tore her robes and shouted, "Treason! Treason!"

[14]Jehoiada the priest sent out the commanders of units of a hundred, who were in charge of the troops, and said to them: "Bring her out between the ranks and put to the sword anyone who follows her." For the priest had said, "Do not put her to death at the temple of the LORD." [15]So they seized her as she reached the entrance of the Horse Gate on the palace grounds, and there they put her to death.

[16]Jehoiada then made a covenant that he and the people and the king would be the LORD's people. [17]All the people went to the temple of Baal and tore it down. They smashed the altars and idols and killed Mattan the priest of Baal in front of the altars.

[18]Then Jehoiada placed the oversight of the temple of the LORD in the hands of the priests, who were Levites, to whom David had made assignments in the temple, to present

the burnt offerings of the LORD as written in the Law of Moses, with rejoicing and singing, as David had ordered. ¹⁹He also stationed doorkeepers at the gates of the LORD's temple so that no one who was in any way unclean might enter.

²⁰He took with him the commanders of hundreds, the nobles, the rulers of the people and all the people of the land and brought the king down from the temple of the LORD. They went into the palace through the Upper Gate and seated the king on the royal throne, ²¹and all the people of the land rejoiced. And the city was quiet, because Athaliah had been slain with the sword.

COMMENTARY

1–3 Following six years of successfully hiding the young Joash within the Jerusalem temple (22:11–12), Jehoiada "showed his strength," phraseology typically used only of kings at the beginning of their reigns (note that he is also buried with kings; cf. 24:16). Jehoiada begins to organize a pro-Davidic consortium consisting of military personnel, priests, family leaders, and Levites. Jehoiada initially makes a covenant with the military leaders (v.1) and then makes an additional covenant (v.3) with the full group once it has convened at the temple. Later, Jehoiada will present Joash with a copy of the covenant (v.11) and will oversee a covenant ceremony with the people of Judah (v.16). This emphasis on covenant reflects both the inherent risks of organizing a coup as well as the broader commitment to see the Davidic and Mosaic covenants upheld.

4–10 Jehoiada organizes the pro-Davidic group to take advantage of the double numbers and natural movement of personnel that happens at shift changes and thus to both maximize protection for the young Joash and minimize suspicion (v.8). The group is dispersed into key areas of the temple-palace complex, including the main courtyard (v.5), the palace (v.5), and entry/exit points (vv.4–5, 10). In the midst of these assignments, Jehoiada is careful to be faithful to covenantal restrictions concerning entry into the temple itself (v.6). The group is armed with weapons dating back to the time of David (vv.9–10) and given strict orders to protect the sole living Davidic descendant (v.7).

11 With layers of protection in place by Levites, military leaders, and others (cf. vv.4–10), Jehoiada begins the ceremony of publicly vesting and anointing Joash as king of Judah. A key element of this ceremony involves presenting Joash with a "copy of the covenant" (Heb. "copy of the *testimony*"; ʿēdût; GK 6343). While it is unclear whether this is a copy of the law (cf. Dt 17:18–20) or another significant document or symbol of the (Davidic or Mosaic) covenant, the emphasis is that the enthronement of Joash is meant to be in accord with God's Word and that his subsequent reign should likewise be faithful to covenantal stipulations.

12–13 The spectacle of sights and sounds and rejoicing at the scene of Joash's investiture finally catch the attention of Athaliah. Given Athaliah's rise to power through a murderous coup (cf. 22:10), her shouts of treason are somewhat ironic. See comments on "the people of the land" (v.13) at 23:21. On Levitical singers and musical instruments, see comments on 5:4–6, 12–13.

14–15 In light of the uprising associated with the enthronement of the Davidic king Joash,

Athaliah is quickly executed by order of the priest Jehoiada, who continues to function more as king (or judge) than priest (cf. vv. 1–3), but not before Athaliah is removed from the sacred temple complex. The Horse Gate was associated with death and judgment (cf. Jer 31:40).

16 The Chronicler continues the sustained emphasis on covenant during the transition from the rule of the usurper Athaliah to the Davidic king Joash. This pivotal time in Judah's history began with the priest Jehoiada's covenant with the military leaders (v. 1) and then his additional covenant with the fully convened group of military leaders, priests, Levites, and heads of families (v. 3). Afterward, Jehoiada presented Joash with a copy of the covenant (lit. "testimony") at his enthronement ceremony (v. 11). Here in v. 16 the covenant involves all the people and their relationship with Yahweh and as such functions as a covenantal renewal, reflecting the renewed commitment of the people to see the Davidic and Mosaic covenants upheld (cf. the covenant of the people during the time of Asa; 15:9–15).

17 The subsequent destruction of the temple of Baal, related objects of idolatry, and killing of the priest of Baal by the community ("all the people") following the covenantal renewal (v. 16) demonstrates the seriousness and zeal of the people to purge the land from idolatry and pagan worship. This is the only reference to "the temple of Baal" in Jerusalem (cf. 2Ki 11:18), and its exact location and history are unknown. The destruction of the temple of Baal is similar to the purging of Baalism in the northern kingdom orchestrated by Jehu some years earlier (cf. 2Ki 10:18–28), as well as the reforms under Asa (cf. 14:3), Hezekiah (cf. 31:1), and Josiah (cf. 34:3–7).

18–19 As final steps toward reorienting the life of the community in line with covenantal stipulations, Jehoiada (again, acting in a kinglike manner;

cf. 23:1, 14; 24:16) ensures that the oversight of temple worship functions in accordance with Mosaic and Davidic regulations (on the differing responsibilities of priests and Levites vis-à-vis temple service, see comments on 5:4–6, 12–13). Doorkeepers (or gatekeepers) work in conjunction with the priests to ensure the purity of the temple and the protection of sacred space (see Reflection on ch. 2).

20 As the final step of the king's investiture ceremony and celebration, the whole community participates in a procession to restore the new king on the throne of David in the royal palace. The full gamut of participants in this event (military, noblemen, governors, citizenry, priests) reflects the widespread support for the reforms enacted by the priest Jehoiada, culminating in the reign of Joash.

21 The group designated "the people of the land" factors into several significant regnal change narratives, including those about Joash (here), Josiah (33:25), and Jehoahaz (36:1). In addition, this group is noted several times in Jeremiah (cf. Jer 1:18; 34:19; 44:21) in a way that implies this was a group of regular citizens rather than officials empowered within the formal political structure. Nevertheless, the ability of this group to affect (and effect) regnal changes shows that "the people of the land" functioned as political power brokers regardless of their official status within the Judean kingdom.

While it is difficult to deduce their political and/or religious objectives completely, the pivotal nature of the biblical contexts into which they step implies that ideology was driving their participation in elevating kings. For example, "the people of the land" facilitate the coronation of Jehoahaz (36:1) following the death of Josiah at Megiddo (see comments on 35:20, 21–24). In putting Jehoahaz on the throne, "the people of the land" pass over the oldest son of Josiah (Eliakim), implying that they see Jehoahaz as a better fit for their agenda, which may have been pro-Babylonian and anti-Egyptian (as Josiah's actions at Megiddo reflect). This possibility is bolstered by the fact that Pharaoh Neco II deposes Jehoahaz after three months and replaces him with Eliakim (whose name he changes to Jehoiakim). Similarly, note the role of "the people of the land" in the political dynamics surrounding the assassination of Amon (33:24–25).

All told, the use of this expression in pivotal moments in Judah's history provides a degree of insight into the social dynamics in ancient Judah, including contrasting views of appropriate foreign policy and perhaps even tensions between urban and rural citizenry. For example, the reaction to the enthronement of Joash after deposing Queen Athaliah could be translated as "then all the people of the land rejoiced, but the city was quiet because Athaliah had been slain" (23:21; cf. 2Ki 11:20). Thus, rather than making two sets of positive remarks (namely, the people rejoiced and the city was quiet in the sense of *peaceful*), there could be one positive remark (the sociopolitical group "the people of the land" rejoice) versus a negative remark (the sociopolitical group represented by "the city" did not rejoice). If the latter option were the case, the different response might reflect this disenfranchisement of those in the city, who were implicit supporters of (and benefited from) Athaliah's reign.

In spite of this possibility, most likely v.21 offers two positive remarks, reflected in the use of "quiet" here, as in the sense of calm and peace following reforms and divine blessing during the reigns of Asa (cf. 14:4–6) and Jehoshaphat (cf. 20:30). Moreover, "the people of the land" may be the same group referred to as "the people of Jerusalem" in the succession narrative of Ahaziah (22:1–2) as well as the group "the people of Judah" noted in the succession narrative of Uzziah (26:1; see Dillard, 270; E. W. Nicholson, "The Meaning of the Expression עם הארץ in the Old Testament," *JSS* 10 [1965]: 59–66).

NOTES

5 The Foundation Gate is likely the same gate as the Sur Gate noted in the parallel account in Kings (2Ki 11:6).

11 It is of some irony that Jehoiada and his sons participate in this ceremony, given Joash's later brutal act against a son of Jehoiada (cf. 24:20–22).

H. The Reign of Joash (2Ch 24:1–27)

¹Joash was seven years old when he became king, and he reigned in Jerusalem forty years. His mother's name was Zibiah; she was from Beersheba. ²Joash did what was right in the eyes of the LORD all the years of Jehoiada the priest. ³Jehoiada chose two wives for him, and he had sons and daughters.

⁴Some time later Joash decided to restore the temple of the LORD. ⁵He called together the priests and Levites and said to them, "Go to the towns of Judah and collect the money

due annually from all Israel, to repair the temple of your God. Do it now." But the Levites did not act at once.

⁶Therefore the king summoned Jehoiada the chief priest and said to him, "Why haven't you required the Levites to bring in from Judah and Jerusalem the tax imposed by Moses the servant of the LORD and by the assembly of Israel for the Tent of the Testimony?"

⁷Now the sons of that wicked woman Athaliah had broken into the temple of God and had used even its sacred objects for the Baals.

⁸At the king's command, a chest was made and placed outside, at the gate of the temple of the LORD. ⁹A proclamation was then issued in Judah and Jerusalem that they should bring to the LORD the tax that Moses the servant of God had required of Israel in the desert. ¹⁰All the officials and all the people brought their contributions gladly, dropping them into the chest until it was full. ¹¹Whenever the chest was brought in by the Levites to the king's officials and they saw that there was a large amount of money, the royal secretary and the officer of the chief priest would come and empty the chest and carry it back to its place. They did this regularly and collected a great amount of money. ¹²The king and Jehoiada gave it to the men who carried out the work required for the temple of the LORD. They hired masons and carpenters to restore the LORD's temple, and also workers in iron and bronze to repair the temple.

¹³The men in charge of the work were diligent, and the repairs progressed under them. They rebuilt the temple of God according to its original design and reinforced it. ¹⁴When they had finished, they brought the rest of the money to the king and Jehoiada, and with it were made articles for the LORD's temple: articles for the service and for the burnt offerings, and also dishes and other objects of gold and silver. As long as Jehoiada lived, burnt offerings were presented continually in the temple of the LORD.

¹⁵Now Jehoiada was old and full of years, and he died at the age of a hundred and thirty. ¹⁶He was buried with the kings in the City of David, because of the good he had done in Israel for God and his temple.

¹⁷After the death of Jehoiada, the officials of Judah came and paid homage to the king, and he listened to them. ¹⁸They abandoned the temple of the LORD, the God of their fathers, and worshiped Asherah poles and idols. Because of their guilt, God's anger came upon Judah and Jerusalem. ¹⁹Although the LORD sent prophets to the people to bring them back to him, and though they testified against them, they would not listen.

²⁰Then the Spirit of God came upon Zechariah son of Jehoiada the priest. He stood before the people and said, "This is what God says:'Why do you disobey the LORD's commands? You will not prosper. Because you have forsaken the LORD, he has forsaken you.'"

²¹But they plotted against him, and by order of the king they stoned him to death in the courtyard of the LORD's temple. ²²King Joash did not remember the kindness

Zechariah's father Jehoiada had shown him but killed his son, who said as he lay dying, "May the LORD see this and call you to account."

²³At the turn of the year, the army of Aram marched against Joash; it invaded Judah and Jerusalem and killed all the leaders of the people. They sent all the plunder to their king in Damascus. ²⁴Although the Aramean army had come with only a few men, the LORD delivered into their hands a much larger army. Because Judah had forsaken the LORD, the God of their fathers, judgment was executed on Joash. ²⁵When the Arameans withdrew, they left Joash severely wounded. His officials conspired against him for murdering the son of Jehoiada the priest, and they killed him in his bed. So he died and was buried in the City of David, but not in the tombs of the kings.

²⁶Those who conspired against him were Zabad, son of Shimeath an Ammonite woman, and Jehozabad, son of Shimrith a Moabite woman. ²⁷The account of his sons, the many prophecies about him, and the record of the restoration of the temple of God are written in the annotations on the book of the kings. And Amaziah his son succeeded him as king.

COMMENTARY

1 Joash began his reign as a seven-year-old child, no doubt under the close guidance of Jehoiada the priest and the sociopolitical group known as "the people of the land" (see comments on this group at 23:21). Joash's long reign (ca. 835–796 BC) overlaps primarily with those of Jehu and Jehoahaz in the northern kingdom and reflects a time of Aramean resurgence under Hazael and Ben-Hadad and continued strength in Assyria, particularly under the rule of Shalmaneser III and Adad-Nirari III.

2 Like Rehoboam (chs. 11–12) and Asa (chs. 14–16), Joash begins his reign in an atmosphere of godliness but will turn to apostasy following the death of his mentor, the priest Jehoiada (vv.17–25).

3 The Chronicler makes no comment on the issue of Joash's polygamy, facilitated by his mentor Jehoiada. Certainly, polygamy was characteristic of many of Israel's kings. The instructions for Israelite kings in Deuteronomy 17:17 does not necessarily prohibit polygamy as it speaks against the king taking "many" wives (cf. the seven hundred wives and three hundred concubines of Solomon; 1Ki 11:3).

4 Joash's repair and restoration of the temple are similar to the later efforts of Hezekiah (29:3–36) and Josiah (34:8–13). Such refurbishing provided a tangible way for the ruler to show his devotion to God. As such, emphasis is placed on the involvement of many sectors of the community (cf. vv.9–12) as well as the skill and carefulness of those involved in the process of restoration (cf. v.13).

5–6 Despite Joash's noble idea to refurbish the temple (cf. v.4), he does not receive the expected cooperation of the priests in territory-wide fundraising. This lack of cooperation is somewhat ironic, given that Joash had grown up in the temple and was effectively raised by the priest Jehoiada (cf. 22:12). Joash's words to Jehoiada imply that he does not see the priest as adequately supporting his temple restoration efforts. The reference to the "tax imposed by Moses" (v.6) likely relates to the half-shekel "life-ransom" census tax noted in the tabernacle construction account (cf. Ex 30:11–16).

7 Joash's desire to refurbish the temple is made even more urgent by the Chronicler's reminder of the degree to which the temple's purity had been violated during the reign of Queen Athaliah. On the plural "Baals," see comments on 17:3–4.

8–9 Rather than the original plan that had priests and Levites going out to all Judah to collect funds for the temple refurbishing project (v.5), Joash has a collection chest constructed and placed just inside the entry area of the temple complex (see Note). This new approach fosters giving above and beyond the requisite census tax (see 2Ki 12:4 and v.10, below).

10–11 As a result of the proclamation made throughout Judah and the addition of a collection chest (vv.8–9), the whole community ("all the officials and all the people") begin to give generously and with joy. In addition to the expected census revenue (the half-shekel tax; cf. v.6), the parallel account also makes mention of extra contributions made in conjunction with personal vows, as well as other voluntary contributions (cf. 2Ki 12:4). The frequency with which the temple officials needed to empty the collection chest underscores the people's hearty generosity, as seen in earlier days (e.g., Ex 36:3–7).

12–14 The windfall of contributions (vv.10–11) enables the hiring of "diligent" (v.13) workers from the various trades, including masons, carpenters, and metal workers (vv.12–13) needed to refurbish the Jerusalem temple "according to its original design" (v.13), with money to spare. The extra funds are ultimately used for temple items (v.14), perhaps to replace items removed by Queen Athaliah (cf. v.7). The final remark that "burnt offerings were presented continually" within the newly refurbished temple "*as long as Jehoiada lived*" hints at the subsequent apostasy of Joash following the death of Jehoiada.

15 In the OT attaining old age was seen as a blessing from God (Ps 91:16) as well as a by-product of wisdom (Pr 3:16). Idealized ages for time of death include 110 in Egyptian thought and 120 in Mesopotamian thought. In the OT, a life lived to age 70 or 80 was considered normative (Ps 90:10; for the patriarchal-like age of Jehoiada at his death, cf. A. Malamat, "Longevity: Biblical Concepts and Some Ancient Near Eastern Parallels," AfOB 19 [1982]: 215–24).

16 Jehoiada's death notice (vv.15–16) reads more like a Judean regnal summary than a death notice for a priest. This final summary of his life reflects a number of subtle editorial strokes that work to portray Jehoiada's actions in a kinglike manner, including the phraseology that Jehoiada "showed his strength" (cf. 23:1), his leading in national covenant ratification (23:1, 3), his oversight of reforms to ensure adherence to Mosaic and Davidic instructions (cf. 23:18–19), his selection of wives for Joash (24:3), and his burial in the royal cemetery (v.16, an honor not given to Joash himself, cf. v.25). Thus, it can be argued that Jehoiada to an extent functioned as a surrogate king in a manner similar to Samuel during the reign of Saul (note that both were kingmakers with extensive national authority). Obviously, Joash's young age at his enthronement would have necessitated a significant degree of assistance with his royal responsibilities at the beginning of his reign.

17–18 After Jehoiada's death Joash turns full circle from doing "what was right in the eyes of the LORD" (v.2) and leading the temple repair efforts (vv.4–14) to "abandon the temple" and worship idols (v.18). Indeed, the death of Jehoiada creates a vacuum of godly counsel for the king, who long reigned under the watchful eye of the high priest. Now Joash opts to "listen" to the officials who come to visit and whose advice clearly includes compromise from the path established by Jehoiada.

The shared responsibility in the resulting apostasy and divine anger is reflected in a number of statements ("*they* abandoned" [v.18]; "*their* guilt" [v.18]; "bring *them* back" [v.19]; "*they* plotted against him [Zechariah]" [v.21]; "*Judah* had forsaken the LORD" [v.24]). Conversely, note that Joash and the people do not listen to the prophets whom God does send, and they even plot the murder of one of them (cf. vv.19–21; for remarks on Asherah poles [v.18] see comments on 14:3).

19 Despite his anger at the rapid abandonment of covenantal faithfulness by Joash and the Judeans, God emphatically demonstrates his love, patience, and grace for his covenantal people by repeatedly sending prophets to proclaim his word to urge the people to return to God in obedience. The summary of God's (unsuccessful) efforts to bring his people back to himself is reminiscent of the closing verses of Chronicles reflecting on the tragedy of the exile:

> The LORD, the God of their fathers, sent word to them through his messengers again and again, because he had pity on his people and on his dwelling place. [16]But they mocked God's messengers, despised his words and scoffed at his prophets until the wrath of the LORD was aroused against his people and there was no remedy. (2Ch 36:15–16)

20 After a number of prophetic visits, the Spirit of God comes on Zechariah, son of Jehoiada the priest, who delivers God's word of judgment. The connection between the coming of the Spirit of God and a specific prophetic utterance is seen in the ongoing prophetic ministry of Ezekiel (cf. Eze 11:5–12) as well as in the prophetic ministry of Azariah (cf. 2Ch 15:1–2).

21–22 Amazingly, the king and the people plot the murder of Zechariah, and the prophet is stoned to death (the punishment for a *false* prophet; cf. Dt 13:5; 18:20). What is especially striking about this low moment in the history of the Judean monarchy

is that Zechariah had been like a brother to Joash, as Jehoiada (Zechariah's father) had been a father figure to Joash from his days as an infant rescued from the murderous rampage of Athaliah (2Ch 22:10–12).

Moreover, Zechariah is killed in the same place that his father Jehoiada had arranged for the covert enthronement of Joash (23:4–13). Indeed, the Chronicler notes that Joash did not "remember" (a choice, not a mental lapse) "the kindness" (*ḥesed*; GK 2876) of Jehoiada. The outworking of both Zechariah's initial prophetic announcement of God's judgment (v.20) and his imprecatory prayer as he dies (v.22) will be seen in the balance of Joash's reign (vv.23–27).

23–24 In the aftermath of Zechariah's prophecy of divine judgment on Judah (v.20) and his prayer against Joash (v.22), the army of Aram attacks Judah. As noted above (see comments on 22:5–9), in the chaos following Jehu's revolt (ca. 841 BC) the Assyrian king Shalmaneser III was able to gain dominance in Syria and Canaan. However, a few years later (after 838 BC) Shalmaneser III turned his attention elsewhere, and Aram quickly became a regional power once again during the time of Jehu (cf. 2Ki 10:31–33).

In addition, Hazael invades the Shephelah and the Judean hill country and receives payment from the treasures of the palace and the temple (cf. 2Ki 12:17–18). As a result of this victory, Aram gains control of the Coastal Highway, the Transjordanian King's Highway, and western approaches to Judah. Note that the victory of the Arameans despite the smallness of their army is part of what God does for his people *when they are faithful* (cf. Lev 26:6–8), but unfaithfulness (as here) leads to defeat by one's enemies (cf. Lev 26:14–17).

25–26 In retaliation for Joash's murderous response to the prophetic word of Zechariah the son of Jehoiada (vv.20–22), the king's officials take advantage of Joash's weakened state and commit murder themselves. Later, they will be executed for this act of treachery (cf. 25:3). In contrast to the priest Jehoiada (24:16), Joash is not honored by interment in the royal cemetery. The notice that the palace officials who assassinate Joash are sons of foreign women might be intended to heap additional dishonor on the reign of Joash.

27 On the format and sources of regnal summaries, see comments on 12:15 and the Introduction.

NOTES

8 The NIV translates the location of the collection chest as "outside" the temple area. However, given that the parallel account in 2 Kings 12:9 [10] offers the more detailed description that the chest was placed אֵצֶל הַמִּזְבֵּחַ בַּיָּמִין בְּבוֹא־אִישׁ בֵּית יְהוָה (ʾēṣel hammizbēaḥ bayyāmîn bᵉbôʾ-ʾîš bêt yhwh), "beside the altar, on the right side as one enters the temple of the LORD" (i.e., *inside* the temple complex), the Hebrew syntax of this verse is worth reexamination. While one could simply posit the possibility that there were two collection bins — one just inside and one just outside the temple complex — the Hebrew text at 2 Chronicles 24:8 can be translated along the lines that the collection chest was placed "at the gate, facing the outside" (i.e., facing the entrance area so the people would see the collection chest as they arrived). As reflected here the Chronicler has condensed the details of this collection effort from the parallel account (see Selman, 452–54).

22 There is some uncertainty as to the intended meaning of the expression translated "May the LORD see this and call you to account" (יֵרֶא יְהוָה וְיִדְרֹשׁ, yēreʾ yhwh wᵉyidrōš), as the Hebrew phrase might suggest that Zechariah was praying that God would still *seek* Joash, not *judge* Joash (namely, "May the LORD see and seek"; cf. Selman, 456). However, the broader literary-historical context favors the NIV's translation as an imprecatory prayer.

I. The Reign of Amaziah (2Ch 25:1–28)

¹Amaziah was twenty-five years old when he became king, and he reigned in Jerusalem twenty-nine years. His mother's name was Jehoaddin; she was from Jerusalem. ²He did what was right in the eyes of the LORD, but not wholeheartedly. ³After the kingdom was firmly in his control, he executed the officials who had murdered his father the king. ⁴Yet he did not put their sons to death, but acted in accordance with what is written in the Law, in the Book of Moses, where the LORD commanded: "Fathers shall not be put to death for their children, nor children put to death for their fathers; each is to die for his own sins."

⁵Amaziah called the people of Judah together and assigned them according to their families to commanders of thousands and commanders of hundreds for all Judah and Benjamin. He then mustered those twenty years old or more and found that there were three hundred thousand men ready for military service, able to handle the spear and

shield. [6]He also hired a hundred thousand fighting men from Israel for a hundred talents of silver.

[7]But a man of God came to him and said, "O king, these troops from Israel must not march with you, for the LORD is not with Israel—not with any of the people of Ephraim. [8]Even if you go and fight courageously in battle, God will overthrow you before the enemy, for God has the power to help or to overthrow."

[9]Amaziah asked the man of God, "But what about the hundred talents I paid for these Israelite troops?"

The man of God replied, "The LORD can give you much more than that."

[10]So Amaziah dismissed the troops who had come to him from Ephraim and sent them home. They were furious with Judah and left for home in a great rage.

[11]Amaziah then marshaled his strength and led his army to the Valley of Salt, where he killed ten thousand men of Seir. [12]The army of Judah also captured ten thousand men alive, took them to the top of a cliff and threw them down so that all were dashed to pieces. [13]Meanwhile the troops that Amaziah had sent back and had not allowed to take part in the war raided Judean towns from Samaria to Beth Horon. They killed three thousand people and carried off great quantities of plunder.

[14]When Amaziah returned from slaughtering the Edomites, he brought back the gods of the people of Seir. He set them up as his own gods, bowed down to them and burned sacrifices to them. [15]The anger of the LORD burned against Amaziah, and he sent a prophet to him, who said, "Why do you consult this people's gods, which could not save their own people from your hand?"

[16]While he was still speaking, the king said to him, "Have we appointed you an advisor to the king? Stop! Why be struck down?"

So the prophet stopped but said, "I know that God has determined to destroy you, because you have done this and have not listened to my counsel."

[17]After Amaziah king of Judah consulted his advisors, he sent this challenge to Jehoash son of Jehoahaz, the son of Jehu, king of Israel: "Come, meet me face to face."

[18]But Jehoash king of Israel replied to Amaziah king of Judah: "A thistle in Lebanon sent a message to a cedar in Lebanon, 'Give your daughter to my son in marriage.' Then a wild beast in Lebanon came along and trampled the thistle underfoot. [19]You say to yourself that you have defeated Edom, and now you are arrogant and proud. But stay at home! Why ask for trouble and cause your own downfall and that of Judah also?"

[20]Amaziah, however, would not listen, for God so worked that he might hand them over to Jehoash, because they sought the gods of Edom. [21]So Jehoash king of Israel attacked. He and Amaziah king of Judah faced each other at Beth Shemesh in Judah. [22]Judah was routed by Israel, and every man fled to his home. [23]Jehoash king of Israel captured Amaziah king of Judah, the son of Joash, the son of Ahaziah, at Beth Shemesh.

Then Jehoash brought him to Jerusalem and broke down the wall of Jerusalem from the Ephraim Gate to the Corner Gate — a section about six hundred feet long. ²⁴He took all the gold and silver and all the articles found in the temple of God that had been in the care of Obed-Edom, together with the palace treasures and the hostages, and returned to Samaria.

²⁵Amaziah son of Joash king of Judah lived for fifteen years after the death of Jehoash son of Jehoahaz king of Israel. ²⁶As for the other events of Amaziah's reign, from beginning to end, are they not written in the book of the kings of Judah and Israel? ²⁷From the time that Amaziah turned away from following the LORD, they conspired against him in Jerusalem and he fled to Lachish, but they sent men after him to Lachish and killed him there. ²⁸He was brought back by horse and was buried with his fathers in the City of Judah.

COMMENTARY

1 Amaziah reigns for a twenty-nine year period (ca. 796–767 BC), most of which (about twenty-five years) is likely in coregency with Uzziah (Azaziah) following Amaziah's imprisonment in Samaria (cf. vv.17–24; for further details on the chronology of Uzziah's reign, see comments on 26:3). During Amaziah's reign, the Assyrian Empire begins to decline, which facilitates a time of peace and prosperity for Judah and Israel. For more details on this geopolitical change, see Overview to 26:1–23.

2 This verse gets to the heart of the inconsistencies seen in Amaziah's reign. On the one hand, he makes decisions based on the law of God (cf. v.2) and responds to the admonishment of a "man of God" by reversing course and stepping out in faith and reliance on God's strength (cf. vv.7–10). On the other hand, Amaziah adopts the gods of the Edomites as his own (cf. v.14), rejects the later admonishment of a prophet (cf. vv.15–16), and acts with pride and arrogance (cf. vv.17–19). God's ultimate decision to "destroy" and hand Judah over (vv.16, 20) shows the futility and destructive outcome of a spiritually compromised life.

3–4 One of Amaziah's first regnal acts is dealing with those who wronged his father (cf. 24:25–26; cf. Solomon's actions at the beginning of his reign [1Ki 2:44–46]). Despite the execution of the officials who assassinated his father, Amaziah stops short of exacting revenge on their broader families. The reason for this restraint is directly connected with obedience to the law, with Deuteronomy 24:16 quoted in support of Amaziah's decision.

5 As seen with other kings (most notably Solomon; cf. ch. 1), Amaziah ensures the proper administrative organization of his kingdom at the beginning of his reign. Amaziah's numbering of his fighting forces "twenty years old or more" is reminiscent of the war censuses in Numbers (cf. Nu 1:3; 26:2; on the large number of men noted here, see discussion at 2Ch 11:1).

6 In addition to the military conscription of those in Judah and Benjamin aged twenty and up (v.5), Amaziah also hires soldiers from the north (esp. Ephraim; cf. v.10). Amaziah's force of 300,000 is nearly half than that of Asa (580,000) and nearly one-fourth that of Jehoshaphat (1.16 million; on these large numbers of soldiers, see extended discussion at 2Ch 11:1). The hiring and use of mercenaries was a common practice in ancient Near Eastern military strategy, as reflected in the Amarna Letters' references to hiring Apiru (Habiru) and Nubian (Cushite) mercenaries. While pay for such hired mercenaries might include a negotiated payment (as with the hundred talents of silver noted here — about three shekels per soldier), the bulk of mercenary pay was obtained via plunder seized from battle (hence the anger and retaliation of the northern soldiers; cf. vv.10, 13).

7–10 As with his adherence to Mosaic law (cf. vv.3–4), Amaziah's response of faith to the man of God's admonishment is a positive highlight of his reign. Amaziah's hiring of the mercenary force from the northern kingdom (cf. v.6) implies a lack of wholehearted trust in God to fight for his people (cf. Dt 20:1–4 and comments on 2Ch 20:14–17). Conversely, the man of God announces that God will cause Amaziah's downfall if he continues down this path. Despite the significant monetary loss (v.9), Amaziah opts for the path of obedience and dismisses the hired troops from the north (v.10). While God gives Amaziah victory over the Edomites (vv.11–12), the dismissed mercenaries later cause havoc in retaliation for their loss of additional revenue via the plunder following victory (cf. v.13).

11–12 Amaziah's victory over the Edomites ("men of Seir"; cf. Ge 32:3; 36:8; Eze 35:15) takes place in the Valley of Salt (Wadi el-Milh), located within the Arabah to the south of the Dead (Salt) Sea. Later, Uzziah will build on Amaziah's victory over Edom by restoring Judean control over the port city of Elath, adjacent to Ezion Geber (cf. 26:2). Like the subsequent worship of the Edomite gods (v.14), the heinous act against the prisoners of war should be seen as repulsive.

13 Following a prophetic challenge, Amaziah had decided against using the mercenary troops

from Israel (vv.7–10). This decision prompts these troops to plunder Judean cities from "Samaria to Beth Horon." No doubt the soldiers were angered by the loss of a plundering opportunity even though they had already received about three shekels each (see comments on v.6). The expression "from Samaria to Beth Horon" may reflect the direction of the mercenaries' attack on Judean towns (coming from the north to the south/southwest).

These towns were plundered while the Judean army was away fighting the Edomites. This incident illustrates the spiritual reality that consequences may follow poor decisions, even if those decisions are later reversed. Lower Beth Horon (Beit Ur et-Tahta) and Upper Beth Horon (Beit Ur el-Foqa) were strategically located on the main east-west route linking the coastal highway and the central Judean hill country.

14 Following his victory at Edom, Amaziah takes the idols of the Edomite gods back to Jerusalem and worships them. While not specified, this might include worship of the Edomite god Qoš. The honoring or adoption of the gods of other peoples (even conquered peoples) was common in the biblical world. In the case of warfare, the victorious king might even mention in his battle report that he had received help from the deity of the conquered nation (cf. Cyrus's acknowledging the help of the Babylonian god Marduk in his taking of Babylon).

In addition, the plundering of enemy idols could also be used to underscore the victory of one national deity over another. This is reflected in the Moabite Stone (Mesha Stele), in which Mesha boasts that his god Chemosh (Kemosh) enabled him to seize religious objects connected with the worship of Israel's God (*COS*, 2:23). For a discussion of Edomite religious practices, see J. Barlett, *Edom and the Edomites* (JSOTSup 77; Sheffield: JSOT, 1989), 181–206.

15–16 Although God gave Amaziah victory over the Edomites, the king responds with idolatry. As God did earlier with Amaziah (vv.7–8) and with other Judean kings, such as Asa (cf. 16:7–13) and Joash (cf. 24:20–22), God sends a prophet to confront the king's covenantal unfaithfulness. While Amaziah responded in obedience to the earlier admonishment of the man of God (vv.9–10), here he follows the examples of Asa (cf. 2Ch 16:10) and Joash (cf. 2Ch 24:21–22) in rebuking the prophet and rejecting God's word. As announced by the prophet, God will bring about the destruction of Amaziah (v.16).

17 Amaziah's victory against the Edomites (vv.11–12) prompts him to challenge Jehoash (Joash) of the northern kingdom, a decision made in conjunction with poor advice received from his counselors (cf. Rehoboam [10:6–15]; Joash [24:17–19]). This ill-advised (but divinely prescribed; cf. 25:20) act of aggression results in the defeat of Judah, the capture of Amaziah, the breaking down of parts of the wall of Jerusalem, and the pillaging of the palace and temple (cf. vv.22–28).

18–19 Jehoash responds to Amaziah's challenge in poetic imagery that underscores the position of strength and numbers enjoyed by the northern kingdom over that of the southern kingdom at this time. A similar parable featuring olive and fig trees, vines, and thornbushes is used of Jotham to underscore the futility of the Shechemites' desire to anoint Abimelech as king (cf. Jdg 9:7–15).

20 As in the events with Rehoboam (cf. 10:15), the turn of events about to unfold is orchestrated by God in conjunction with the prophetic word delivered to Amaziah (vv.15–16). Like Joash (24:17–19), Amaziah will not listen to the prophetic word (25:16) but persists in unfaithfulness to Yahweh by seeking foreign gods.

21–23 The battle between Amaziah and Jehoash takes place at Beth Shemesh (Tell er-Rumeliah), a town in the Judean Shephelah about fifteen miles southwest of Jerusalem. This location is an unusual place for battle between Israel and Judah and may imply that the conflict has some connection with control of the Coastal Highway. Following this defeat and Amaziah's imprisonment in Samaria, the "people of Judah" make Uzziah (Azariah) king, beginning a lengthy coregency between Amaziah and Uzziah (ca. 792–767 BC; see comments on 22:1; cf. Thiele, 118–19). Under the circumstances of Amaziah's imprisonment, Judah is likely under the hegemony of the northern kingdom. In his assault of Jerusalem Jehoash destroys a sizable portion of the wall in the north/northwestern sector of the city.

24 As has been seen in other instances of covenantal unfaithfulness, God allows both military defeat and the looting of his own temple and the royal palace (cf. 12:9 [Rehoboam]; 16:2–3 [Asa]; 28:21 [Ahaz]; 2Ki 12:17–18 [Joash]; 2Ki 24:13 [Jehoiachin]). In addition to the plundering of the temple and palace, Jehoash takes hostages from Judah (including Amaziah; v.23), likely as a means to ensure continued influence and power over the southern kingdom.

25–26 This final paragraph covers Amaziah's final twenty-four years when his son Uzziah is (presumably) acting as his coregent. For nine of these years Amaziah is likely a prisoner of the northern king Jehoash. On these chronological issues, see further comments on v.1 and on 26:3. On the Chronicler's sources, see comments on 12:15 and the Introduction.

27 As with his father Joash (cf. 24:25), Amaziah's life ends by murder in the midst of conspiracy. In both cases, their rejection of God's prophetic word sets into action the events that lead to their demise (24:20, 22; 25:16, 20). The citadel of Lachish (Tell ed-Duweir) is located about thirty miles south/southwest of Jerusalem on the edge of the Shephelah, guarding passes from the Coastal Highway leading to the central hill country. The town of Lachish had a long history as a fortified city and would be an appropriate place for Amaziah to take refuge.

28 Given the association of his burial "with his fathers," the city of Judah would seem to be Jerusalem. On royal tombs, see comments on 21:20.

NOTES

13 Alternatively, Samaria might be the name of a Judean town. While there is no known town of Samaria in Judah, more than one town having the same name was common in Israel. Examples include Beth Shemesh, Jabneel, Rehob, Abel, Gedor, Gath, Ramah, Geba, Kanah, and Bethlehem.

17–18 The parable of Jehoash involving the "marriage" of the son of the thistle to the daughter of the cedar tree might imply that Amaziah's inquiry to Jehoash involved a political marriage alliance rather than a battle (as seen in the days of Jehoshaphat; cf. 18:1).

J. The Reign of Uzziah (2Ch 26:1–23)

OVERVIEW

The forty-year overlap between the reigns of Uzziah in Judah and Jeroboam II in Israel indicate a time of significant peace and prosperity for both kingdoms, aided by geopolitical realities such as weakness in Aram and regional distractions in Assyria. In addition to the prosperity of this period, the geographical extent of both Israel and Judah expanded considerably during the long reigns of these kings. In the northern kingdom, Jeroboam II extended the northern border of Israel to Lebo Hamath (including taking Damascus) and recaptured previously lost territory in Transjordan (cf. 2Ki 14:25, 28). In the southern kingdom, Uzziah was able to prevail over several Philistine cities in the west (including Gath and Ashdod), the Ammonites in the east, and Arabians and Meunites in the south. The Chronicler notes that these victories caused Uzziah's fame to spread "as far as the border of Egypt" (26:8).

Uzziah also rebuilt the Judean maritime port at Elath (26:2; cf. 2Ki 14:22) and fortified the southern Negev and wilderness regions (2Ch 26:10). As a result of these territorial gains by Israel and Judah, the combined geographical extent of the northern and southern kingdoms approximated the extent seen at the height of the united monarchy under David and Solomon. Moreover, the resulting control of trade routes enhanced the prosperity of both Israel and Judah.

The prosperity of this period is reflected in the numerous luxury items that have been discovered dating to this time, particularly in the environs of the northern kingdom capital of Samaria. For example, intricate carved ivory inlays of Phoenician design have been found in several northern kingdom sites, reflecting Israel's ongoing relationship with Phoenicia as well as the emergence of an affluent stratum of Israelite society. Similarly, vast amounts of ivory items (the Samaria Ivories) were found at the palace in Samaria, reflecting a propensity for luxury items within the Israelite leadership.

A sense of the administration of the northern kingdom can be gained to some extent by the (largely) administrative texts known as the Samaria Ostraca, which most likely date to the time of Jeroboam II. These short texts provide snippets of information on the storage and shipment of various products throughout Israel. The well-known seal of "Shema, servant of Jeroboam" with the relief of a roaring lion may have belonged to an official within Jeroboam's royal court. These aspects of peace and prosperity aside, a few years before the end of Uzziah's reign (745 BC), Tiglath-Pileser III began to reign in Assyria, ushering in what is known as the Neo-Assyrian Empire, a geopolitical development that brought radical change to Israel and Judah.

¹Then all the people of Judah took Uzziah, who was sixteen years old, and made him king in place of his father Amaziah. ²He was the one who rebuilt Elath and restored it to Judah after Amaziah rested with his fathers.

³Uzziah was sixteen years old when he became king, and he reigned in Jerusalem fifty-two years. His mother's name was Jecoliah; she was from Jerusalem. ⁴He did what was right in the eyes of the LORD, just as his father Amaziah had done. ⁵He sought God during the days of Zechariah, who instructed him in the fear of God. As long as he sought the LORD, God gave him success.

⁶He went to war against the Philistines and broke down the walls of Gath, Jabneh and Ashdod. He then rebuilt towns near Ashdod and elsewhere among the Philistines. ⁷God helped him against the Philistines and against the Arabs who lived in Gur Baal and against the Meunites. ⁸The Ammonites brought tribute to Uzziah, and his fame spread as far as the border of Egypt, because he had become very powerful.

⁹Uzziah built towers in Jerusalem at the Corner Gate, at the Valley Gate and at the angle of the wall, and he fortified them. ¹⁰He also built towers in the desert and dug many cisterns, because he had much livestock in the foothills and in the plain. He had people working his fields and vineyards in the hills and in the fertile lands, for he loved the soil.

¹¹Uzziah had a well-trained army, ready to go out by divisions according to their numbers as mustered by Jeiel the secretary and Maaseiah the officer under the direction of Hananiah, one of the royal officials. ¹²The total number of family leaders over the fighting men was 2,600. ¹³Under their command was an army of 307,500 men trained for war, a powerful force to support the king against his enemies. ¹⁴Uzziah provided shields, spears, helmets, coats of armor, bows and slingstones for the entire army. ¹⁵In Jerusalem he made machines designed by skillful men for use on the towers and on the corner defenses to shoot arrows and hurl large stones. His fame spread far and wide, for he was greatly helped until he became powerful.

¹⁶But after Uzziah became powerful, his pride led to his downfall. He was unfaithful to the LORD his God, and entered the temple of the LORD to burn incense on the altar of

incense. ¹⁷Azariah the priest with eighty other courageous priests of the LORD followed him in. ¹⁸They confronted him and said, "It is not right for you, Uzziah, to burn incense to the LORD. That is for the priests, the descendants of Aaron, who have been consecrated to burn incense. Leave the sanctuary, for you have been unfaithful; and you will not be honored by the LORD God."

¹⁹Uzziah, who had a censer in his hand ready to burn incense, became angry. While he was raging at the priests in their presence before the incense altar in the LORD's temple, leprosy broke out on his forehead. ²⁰When Azariah the chief priest and all the other priests looked at him, they saw that he had leprosy on his forehead, so they hurried him out. Indeed, he himself was eager to leave, because the LORD had afflicted him.

²¹King Uzziah had leprosy until the day he died. He lived in a separate house — leprous, and excluded from the temple of the LORD. Jotham his son had charge of the palace and governed the people of the land.

²²The other events of Uzziah's reign, from beginning to end, are recorded by the prophet Isaiah son of Amoz. ²³Uzziah rested with his fathers and was buried near them in a field for burial that belonged to the kings, for people said, "He had leprosy." And Jotham his son succeeded him as king.

COMMENTARY

1 The reference to the "people of Judah" as making Uzziah king is different from the typical regnal changeover format used in Chronicles. The (presumed) long coregency between Uzziah and Amaziah during Amaziah's imprisonment in Samaria (see comments on 25:1) and the murky circumstances of Amaziah's death (cf. 25:27) may have created some type of succession uncertainty, if not crisis, in Judah that necessitated the action of the community. The people of Judah may be the same group known as "the people of the land," who likewise step into Judean politics during times of regnal crisis. See the extended discussion on this sociopolitical group at 23:21.

2 Uzziah is able to take advantage of Amaziah's victory over Edom (25:11–12) and rebuild the port city of Elath. Solomon originally established this important maritime port city on the Gulf of Aqabah before the area was lost during the reign of Jehoram. The passage does not provide details of any seaborne trade that Judah was able to begin as a result of Uzziah's rebuilding of Elath. In any event, the port is lost again some decades later during the time of Ahaz (cf. 2Ki 16:6). A seal likely belonging to Uzziah's son Jotham indicates that Ezion Geber was an important center at the time of Uzziah and Jotham (see also comments on 8:17–18).

3 As noted at 25:21–23; 26:1, Uzziah (also spelled Ahaziah) was apparently made king in the aftermath of Amaziah's imprisonment in Samaria and had a lengthy coreign with Amaziah (the first twenty-four or twenty-five years of his fifty-five-year reign). In addition, Uzziah coreigned with his son Jotham during the final decade of his reign (ca. 750–740 BC), perhaps in conjunction with his skin ailment (see comments at v.19). All told, Uzziah's reign (including coregency) extended from ca. 792–740 BC. He reigned alongside Jeroboam II of the northern kingdom for forty out of his fifty-two years, a time of significant peace and prosperity for both Judah and Israel (see Overview to ch. 26).

4–5 Uzziah's reign is blessed in many respects as he learns the "fear of the LORD" from Zechariah and thus learns to do what was right in God's eyes. As reflected in the reign of Solomon (cf. chs. 8–9) and Jehoshaphat (cf. 17:10–11), the fear of the Lord facilitates success in battle (vv.6–7), wealth from foreigners (v.8), and "fame" among the surrounding nations (vv.8, 15). The comparison to Amaziah is double-edged, as Uzziah will likewise have a major incident of spiritual unfaithfulness leading to a permanent reduction in his regnal responsibilities (cf. Amaziah's lengthy imprisonment in Samaria with Uzziah's lengthy time in a secluded house in conjunction with his skin ailment; 2Ch 26:21). Indeed, although God blesses Uzziah in many areas ("God gave him success," v.5; "God helped him," v.7), ultimately Uzziah grows proud in the light of his power (v.16), and his downfall follows shortly thereafter.

6–8 Uzziah's dominance over areas to the east, west, and south of Judah enables the southern kingdom to leverage control over a number of primary and secondary trade routes and benefit from the related income. Uzziah's success in these battles is directly associated with God's enablement (recall v.5). The three mentioned Philistine cities are located on both spurs of the Coastal Highway and would facilitate trade revenue. Likewise, Uzziah's building efforts in Philistine areas would help ensure that trade revenue and tariffs remain stable.

Although the location of Gur Baal is unknown, Uzziah's conflict with these Arabs as well as the

Meunites (an Arabian tribe living in the southern region of Transjordan and parts of the Sinai) may connect with trade flowing through the wilderness region south of the Dead Sea as well as the southern portion of the King's Highway. Similarly, the tribute Uzziah receives from the Ammonites (located to the east of the Dead Sea and northeast to the territory of Moab) may be connected with the part of the King's Highway that passes through Ramoth-Ammon. Judah's domination over these regions along with Uzziah's fame spreading to Egypt is reminiscent of the geopolitical hegemony attained during David's and Solomon's reigns.

9–10 In addition to Uzziah's military successes (vv.6–8), he completes significant agricultural and building projects, including a number of towers in Jerusalem and beyond. Judah's trade and territorial expansion necessitate measures to ensure political and economic stability. These towers served as military outposts within the capital city in vulnerable areas of the Negev and wilderness region. Building remains including towers, cisterns, and probable storehouses have been found in sites such as Beersheba (administrative seat of the southern region located in the Negev) and likely date to Uzziah's time. Uzziah also undertakes efforts to enhance the administrative oversight of the royal lands and livestock.

11–13 Uzziah's continued dominance in the region (cf. vv.6–8) is (humanly speaking) aided by his well-organized and well-equipped military force. The significance of Judah's military during this time is reflected in the naming of Uzziah by the Assyrian king Tiglath-Pileser III as a key member of a mid-eighth-century BC coalition that attempted to stop the Assyrian advance into the Levant. Uzziah's accomplishment in organizing his army and equipping them with a variety of weapons reflects the prosperity and political stability of Judah at this time (see Overview to ch. 26). For remarks on understanding the large numbers of the military forces in Chronicles, see comments on 11:1.

15 In addition to his well-organized and well-equipped army, Uzziah pursues hardware advantages for his military force. Despite no shortage of effort and creativity, the specifics of these military machines are not clear. The notation that these machines were designed by skillful men together with the remark that Uzziah's fame spread far and wide following this description indicates that these were impressive devices. Although catapult-like devices are not known in the ancient world for another 200 to 300 years, the view that these machines were essentially shields ignores the clear sense that they were impressive devices requiring some degree of design and engineering. While the specifics are not known, the context of the passage indicates that these machines created, for a city under siege, a military advantage involving large stones and arrows.

16 The burning of incense was strictly limited to the Aaronic priesthood (cf. Ex 30:1–10; Nu 16:40); hence Uzziah's actions constitute covenantal unfaithfulness. Moreover, Uzziah's entry into the temple violates God's stipulations for his holy space that reserved entry to Levites (partial) and priests. Note that while other leaders such as Solomon offered sacrifices at the temple complex, their sacrificing took place on the altars *outside* the courtyard. Ultimately, Uzziah's self-absorption in the light of his God-gifted accomplishments (i.e., his pride) emboldens him to disregard the divinely established layers of boundaries for covenantal service (cf. Rehoboam's abandonment of God's law after "he had become strong"; 12:1). For additional remarks on incense, see commentary on 4:22.

17–18 Although potentially risking their lives, a group of eighty priests confront Uzziah with the covenantal requirements concerning incense and declare that his unfaithfulness will jeopardize

God's blessing on his rule. Uzziah's lack of a godly response to the rebuke from the priests will lead to his inability to discharge fully his regnal responsibilities (cf. vv.19–21).

19 Instead of acknowledging that the priests are correct and exiting the temple, Uzziah reacts consistently with the proud fool who does not receive a rebuke (cf. Pr 1:7; 12:15). While many translations render Yahweh's judgment on Uzziah as "leprosy" (ṣāraʿat; GK 7669), the term is used in biblical literature for a range of chronic and infectious skin diseases rather than as a technical term for the specific medical condition known today as leprosy (Hansen's disease; see E. V. Hulse, "The Nature of Biblical 'Leprosy' and the Use of Alternative Medical Terms in Modern Translations of the Bible," *PEQ* 107 [1975]: 87–105, esp. 90–93). The effect of Uzziah's condition renders him ritually unclean and necessitates his separation from the community as prescribed in legal texts such as Leviticus 13:46 and exemplified in the case of Miriam (cf. Nu 12:4–15).

20–21 Ironically, while Uzziah refuses to leave the temple when confronted by the priests, he becomes "eager to leave" in the light of God's judgment through a skin disease. That judgment lasts the balance of Uzziah's life (and even into his burial; cf. v.23)—a permanent visual reminder of the consequences of covenantal unfaithfulness. In addition, the ceremonial uncleanness brought about by the skin disease prohibits Uzziah from fully exercising his regnal responsibilities, prompting a coregency of approximately ten years (ca. 750–740 BC) between Uzziah and his son Jotham. After this, Uzziah has to live alone in a separate house (cf. Lev 13:46; Nu 5:1–3) and can never visit God's temple again.

22–23 On the use of sources in Chronicles, including prophetic sources as noted here, see comments on 12:15 and the Introduction. While Uzziah is largely remembered for the good aspects of his reign (cf. 26:4 – 15), the ceremonial uncleanness resulting from his skin disease prevents him from being buried in the royal cemetery. Instead he is buried "near" them on land owned by the royal crown.

K. The Reign of Jotham (2Ch 27:1 – 9)

[1]Jotham was twenty-five years old when he became king, and he reigned in Jerusalem sixteen years. His mother's name was Jerusha daughter of Zadok. [2]He did what was right in the eyes of the LORD, just as his father Uzziah had done, but unlike him he did not enter the temple of the LORD. The people, however, continued their corrupt practices. [3]Jotham rebuilt the Upper Gate of the temple of the LORD and did extensive work on the wall at the hill of Ophel. [4]He built towns in the Judean hills and forts and towers in the wooded areas.

[5]Jotham made war on the king of the Ammonites and conquered them. That year the Ammonites paid him a hundred talents of silver, ten thousand cors of wheat and ten thousand cors of barley. The Ammonites brought him the same amount also in the second and third years.

[6]Jotham grew powerful because he walked steadfastly before the LORD his God.

[7]The other events in Jotham's reign, including all his wars and the other things he did, are written in the book of the kings of Israel and Judah. [8]He was twenty-five years old when he became king, and he reigned in Jerusalem sixteen years. [9]Jotham rested with his fathers and was buried in the City of David. And Ahaz his son succeeded him as king.

COMMENTARY

1 Because of his skin disease (cf. 26:19), Uzziah had to live alone and separately, necessitating a coregency with his son Jotham from ca. 750 – 740 BC (cf. 26:21). Jotham's reign extended from approximately 750 – 732 BC, a time when the Neo-Assyrian Empire (745 – 650 BC) was reaching new heights of power and aggression (see Overview to ch. 26). In addition, Jotham likely served a coregency with his son Ahaz from ca. 735 – 732 BC (cf. Thiele, 133 – 34). The number of coreigns during the time from Amaziah to Hezekiah (some of which are specified, others deduced or assumed) creates a variety of chronological challenges for this period of the Judean monarchy (see, e.g., comments on 25:1, 25 – 26; 26:1, 3, 22 – 23; 28:1; 29:1).

During the time of Jotham's coregency with his father Uzziah, "Menahem the Samarian" (752 – 742 BC) is noted as paying Tiglath-Pileser III (also known as "Pul" in the OT) a thousand talents of silver (cf. 2Ki 15:19 – 20; *COS*, 2:117A). This payment coincides with the weakening of the northern kingdom following the death of Jeroboam II in 753 BC and the rise of the Neo-Assyrian Empire following the coronation of Tiglath-Pileser III in 745 BC, a regnal change that significantly reshapes the geopolitical landscape of the biblical world.

2 The summary evaluation of Jotham is similar to that of Uzziah (cf. 26:4). As with Uzziah (recall their long coregency; cf. v.1), Jotham "grew powerful" (v.6), enjoyed success in battle (v.5), and received tribute from foreign nations (v.5). Unlike Uzziah, however, Jotham did not grow proud and challenge Yahweh's covenantal bounds regarding temple service, but instead "walked steadfastly" (or better, "caused his ways to be ordered") before the Lord (v.6). Unfortunately, the people under Jotham's rule were not similarly inspired to pursue covenantal faithfulness.

3–4 Jotham continues the expansion and fortification efforts undertaken by his father Uzziah (see comments on 26:6–8, 9–10). In fact, the building projects of Uzziah and Jotham may be largely one and the same, given their extensive coregency. The building of forts and towers would help to protect Judah's interest in trade routes and provide overall national security. The hill of Ophel was located to the south of the city, abutting the earlier City of David. Although the exact locations of Jotham's fortifications outside Jerusalem are not specified, the reference to wooded areas implies fortifications in the central hill country to form a defensive perimeter around Jerusalem.

5 Jotham continues the domination of Ammon attained by his father, Uzziah (cf. 26:6–8). Since the northern kingdom retained the Transjordanian tribes (Gad, Reuben, and part of Manasseh) and exercised hegemony over Transjordanian nations such as Moab, Uzziah and Jotham's expansion of the southern kingdom's hegemony to Ammon is impressive and likely relates to the warmed relations between Israel and Judah during this time.

While the amount of tribute received by Uzziah from the Ammonites is not specified, the amount received by Jotham noted here is staggering. Estimates for the weight of a talent range between 65 and 75 pounds, meaning that Ammon's silver tribute is well over three tons. The *kor* (cor) is a unit of dry measure equal to approximately 6.25 bushels, making the amounts of wheat and barley total about 62,500 bushels each, about half the amount provided to Hiram by Solomon (2:10). Moreover, Judah's upper hand over Ammon provides Judah with continued direct access to the lucrative King's Highway. Control over this area would be lost again during the time of Ahaz (cf. 2Ki 16:6).

6 Jotham's success as king is based on his relationship with God and God's subsequent blessing. The NIV's rendering of the basis of Jotham's success (namely, "because he walked steadfastly before the LORD his God") might be better rendered along the lines of "because he caused his ways to be [rightly] ordered before the LORD his God" (cf. NASB, ESV, NKJV), suggesting his intentional effort to live in a manner pleasing to God (cf. Ro 12:2).

7–9 Jotham's reign extended from approximately 750–732 BC. His wars likely included several of the wars of Uzziah, given their coregency (cf. 26:6–8), as well as Judah's participation in the coalition against the Assyrian king Tiglath-Pileser III. On the historical particulars of this time frame, see Overview to ch. 26 and comments on 27:1. On the sources used by the Chronicler in regnal summaries, see comments on 12:15 and the Introduction.

NOTE

7–9 Jotham's wars may also include the Syro-Ephraimite crisis. See comments on 28:5–25.

L. The Reign of Ahaz (2Ch 28:1–27)

1. Introduction to the Reign of Ahaz (2Ch 28:1–4)

OVERVIEW

While the final decades of the ninth century BC had seen a decline in Assyrian dominance in the Levant, this situation changes dramatically with Tiglath-Pileser III's coming to the Assyrian throne in 745 BC. This time in Assyrian history is referred to as the Neo-Assyrian Empire (745–609 BC). Tiglath-Pileser III quickly strengthened the administrative infrastructure of Assyria's civil and military branches and set out on his first western campaign in 743 BC. In short measure, Assyria gained the upper hand over Urartu (in the northern region of modern-day Turkey and Armenia) and established a foothold in northern Syria following his defeat of Arpad. After the fall of Arpad in ca. 740 BC, Hamath and other Syrian (Aramean) city-states surrendered and were incorporated into the expanding Neo-Assyrian Empire.

Following these victories, Tiglath-Pileser III continued west and south. By the end of his first western campaign in ca. 738 BC, he had received tribute payments from numerous rulers in Syro-Canaan, including the Israelite king Menahem, the Arabian queen Zabibe, the Phoenician king Hiram, and the Aramean king Rezin (cf. 2Ki 15:19–20; *COS*, 2:117A). Tiglath-Pileser III was effective in using conquered areas as logistical bases and enlisting defeated leaders to provide military support. The expansion of the Neo-Assyrian Empire facilitated Assyrian control of trade routes, tribute payments, and access to agricultural and other natural resources of various regions.

[1]Ahaz was twenty years old when he became king, and he reigned in Jerusalem sixteen years. Unlike David his father, he did not do what was right in the eyes of the LORD. [2]He walked in the ways of the kings of Israel and also made cast idols for worshiping the Baals. [3]He burned sacrifices in the Valley of Ben Hinnom and sacrificed his sons in the fire, following the detestable ways of the nations the LORD had driven out before the Israelites. [4]He offered sacrifices and burned incense at the high places, on the hilltops and under every spreading tree.

COMMENTARY

1 Ahaz reigns from approximately 735–715 BC, including a presumed coregency with his father Jotham from ca. 735–732 BC and his son Hezekiah from 728/727 BC through ca. 715 BC (see further remarks on the chronological challenges of this period at 29:1). Ahaz's reign takes place during watershed moments in the history of both the southern kingdom (Judah) and the northern kingdom (Israel) vis-à-vis the Neo-Assyrian Empire that began under Tiglath-Pileser III in 745 BC (see Overview above). In a rapid departure from his father Jotham (cf. 2Ch 27:6), Ahaz becomes one of the most ungodly kings in the history of Judah's monarchy (note v.19), thus underscoring how quickly one generation can abandon the values of the previous generation.

2 Rather than follow in the ways of his father (v.1), Ahaz follows the ways of the apostate northern kingdom, which had long chosen to worship Syro-Canaanite deities such as Baal and Asherah. The plural of Baal may relate to the variety of deities pursued in Israel and the region of Canaan. ("Baal" is an honorific title meaning "lord" and was the shortened way of referring to the Syro-Canaanite storm god Baal-Hadad.)

A key attraction to Baal-Hadad was his presumed dominion over storms (i.e., rain), while a key attraction point for Asherah was her presumed dominion over fertility—both of which were key areas of concern for ancient societies such as Judah and Israel. But acts of spiritual compromise can have unexpected waves of consequences, as seen in the subsequent events of this chapter.

3 While strictly prohibited by God (cf. Lev 20:2–3; Dt 18:10), the practice of child sacrifice seems to have been considered the ultimate sacrifice to give to the gods in desperate situations (cf. 2Ki 3:26–27), as well as a means for divination practiced by Canaanites. The Valley of Ben Hinnom was located south of the Temple Mount and came to symbolize grave apostasy (Jer 32:35). During the reforms of Josiah this area was purged of its ignominious usage (cf. 2Ki 23:4–14). Ultimately the area became a city dump used for refuse and even the bodies of criminals; it was marked by constant fires and dreadful sights and smells. In the light of this imagery, the Hebrew expression for this valley (approximately "Gehenna") came to be used of hell itself (cf. Mt 10:28; Mk 9:43, 47; note that in these examples the NIV translates "Gehenna" as "hell").

4 This verse underscores the rampant extent of idolatry and syncretism "promoted" (cf. v.19) during the reign of Ahaz. See comments on high places at 1:3–5. On trees in conjunction with the worship of Asherah, see comments on 14:3.

NOTE

1 The age at which Ahaz died and Hezekiah became king (29:1) implies Ahaz became a father at a young age (approximately twelve or thirteen). While this is certainly biologically possible, some have posited that his coregency with father Jotham should be added to his reign of sixteen years (cf. Thiele, 133–34). Alternatively, some LXX manuscripts suggest he might have been twenty-five when he became king, which would also raise the age at which he became a father.

2. The Syro-Ephraimite Crisis (2Ch 28:5–25)

OVERVIEW

In the aftermath of Tiglath-Pileser III's campaign in ca. 738 BC wherein he received tribute payments from numerous rulers in Syro-Canaan, several western states (including Aram, Israel, Tyre, Ashkelon, and Gaza) began to form an anti-Assyrian coalition reminiscent of the twelve-nation coalition formed in the mid-ninth century to stem the advance of Shalmaneser III. Although some details are not completely clear, it appears that the formation of this coalition was impeded by the refusal of the southern king Ahaz to join the coalition, which leads to the invasion of Judah by Aram and Israel (28:5–6)—an episode known as the Syro-Ephraimite crisis (cf. 2Ki 15:29–30; 16:5–18; "Syro" refers to the nation of Syria/Aram, while "Ephraim" refers to the northern kingdom via its most prominent tribe).

This crisis is the historical context of Isaiah 7, which notes that Israel and Aram intended to install a new king, presumably one willing to join the anti-Assyrian coalition. Although the anti-Assyrian coalition fits the geopolitical context, it is possible that the invasion of Judah was simply a territorial conflict (note Isa 7:6, "Let us invade Judah; let us tear it apart and divide it among ourselves"), perhaps related to the Transjordanian gains attained by Uzziah and Jotham (cf. 2Ch 26:6–8 and 27:5).

In conjunction with Ahaz's request and pledge of vassalage to Assyria, Tiglath-Pileser III began his second western campaign in ca. 734 BC ("to Philistia" in Assyrian documents). Tiglath-Pileser III marched down the coastal plain and quickly defeated resistance in Phoenicia and Philistia. He then incorporated the Coastal Plain from the Plain of Sharon to Philistia into the newly-formed Assyrian province of Dor. Tiglath-Pileser III also received tribute from Edom, Moab, and Ammon.

Next (or perhaps on a separate campaign noted as "to Damascus"), the Assyrian army shifted their focus to Aram and Israel, beginning with a siege of Damascus. At the same time, Tiglath-Pileser III marched through much of the outlying areas of the northern kingdom and instituted the first set of deportations to be imposed on ancient Israel (2Ki 15:29). The devastation inflicted on this area may be reflected in the poetry of Isaiah 9:1 [8:23].

After the invasion of the northern areas of Israel, Damascus was completely isolated. It managed to hold out a bit longer but was completely destroyed in 732 BC and its king Rezin executed. Following the fall of Damascus, Hoshea assassinated Pekah and surrendered to Tiglath-Pileser III (2Ki 15:30). Tiglath-Pileser III took credit for the installation of Hoshea as king over what was left of Israel (cf. COS, 2:117C; 2:117F). Much of what had been the northern kingdom was incorporated into additional Assyrian provinces: Megiddo (Jezreel Valley north through the Galilee region), Gilead (Transjordan between the Dead Sea and the Sea of Galilee), Karnaim (north/northeast of the Sea of Galilee), and Hauran (east of the Sea of Galilee). In short, by 732 BC what was left of the northern kingdom was largely confined to the hill country of Manasseh and Ephraim.

After about five years of relative calm, the death of Tiglath-Pileser III in 727 BC inspired vassals in Canaan and Syria to seek to throw off the Assyrian yoke. Although Hoshea was initially loyal to Assyria and the new king Shalmaneser V (727–22 BC), he ultimately withheld tribute and explored rebellion against Assyrian hegemony, with some type of Egyptian support in view. The account in 2 Kings notes that Hoshea sent messengers to "So, king of Egypt" (2Ki 17:3–4), perhaps a short name for the pharaoh Osorkon IV or a reference to the capital city Sais established by the Pharaoh Tefnakht (see J. Day, "The Problem of 'So, King of Egypt' in 2 Kings 17:4," VT 42 [1992]: 289–301).

As a result, Shalmaneser V imprisoned Hoshea and attacked the "entire land" of Israel, culminating in a three-year siege of Samaria (2Ki 17:4–5; see B. Becking, The Fall of Samaria: An Historical and Archaeological Study [SHANE 2; Leiden: Brill, 1992], esp. 3–60). By 722 BC Shalmaneser V had taken Samaria, and his successor Sargon II (722–705 BC) oversaw the massive deportation (and repopulation) that followed (2Ki 17:6, 24–41; cf. *ANET*, 284–85). This deportation of the northern kingdom connects with the expression "the ten lost tribes," while the repopulation of the north with various people groups provides the backdrop for concern for genealogy in the postexilic community as well as the Samaritan issue(s) reflected in the NT.

Following the death of Shalmaneser V, Sargon II was faced with revolt in various parts of the Assyrian empire, including an anti-Assyrian coalition organized by Hamath, which likely delayed Sargon's completion of the defeat of Samaria. In addition to his claims of defeating Samaria, Sargon II claimed to be the subduer of Judah (cf. *ANET*, 285, 287). In ca. 710 BC Sargon II recorded a victory over Merodach-Baladan, king of Babylon, who then fled to Elam and plotted subsequent rebellion against Assyrian hegemony—a distraction to Sennacherib (the next Assyrian king) that would aid Hezekiah's preparation for rebellion. In addition, Assyria added the province of "Samaria" after the fall of the northern kingdom.

5Therefore the LORD his God handed him over to the king of Aram. The Arameans defeated him and took many of his people as prisoners and brought them to Damascus.

He was also given into the hands of the king of Israel, who inflicted heavy casualties on him. 6In one day Pekah son of Remaliah killed a hundred and twenty thousand soldiers in Judah — because Judah had forsaken the LORD, the God of their fathers. 7Zicri, an Ephraimite warrior, killed Maaseiah the king's son, Azrikam the officer in charge of the palace, and Elkanah, second to the king. 8The Israelites took captive from their kinsmen two hundred thousand wives, sons and daughters. They also took a great deal of plunder, which they carried back to Samaria.

9But a prophet of the LORD named Oded was there, and he went out to meet the army when it returned to Samaria. He said to them, "Because the LORD, the God of your fathers, was angry with Judah, he gave them into your hand. But you have slaughtered them in a rage that reaches to heaven. 10And now you intend to make the men and women of Judah and Jerusalem your slaves. But aren't you also guilty of sins against the LORD your God? 11Now listen to me! Send back your fellow countrymen you have taken as prisoners, for the LORD's fierce anger rests on you."

12Then some of the leaders in Ephraim — Azariah son of Jehohanan, Berekiah son of Meshillemoth, Jehizkiah son of Shallum, and Amasa son of Hadlai — confronted those who were arriving from the war. 13"You must not bring those prisoners here," they said, "or we will be guilty before the LORD. Do you intend to add to our sin and guilt? For our guilt is already great, and his fierce anger rests on Israel."

14So the soldiers gave up the prisoners and plunder in the presence of the officials and all the assembly. 15The men designated by name took the prisoners, and from the plunder they clothed all who were naked. They provided them with clothes and sandals, food and drink, and healing balm. All those who were weak they put on donkeys. So they took them back to their fellow countrymen at Jericho, the City of Palms, and returned to Samaria.

¹⁶At that time King Ahaz sent to the king of Assyria for help. ¹⁷The Edomites had again come and attacked Judah and carried away prisoners, ¹⁸while the Philistines had raided towns in the foothills and in the Negev of Judah. They captured and occupied Beth Shemesh, Aijalon and Gederoth, as well as Soco, Timnah and Gimzo, with their surrounding villages. ¹⁹The LORD had humbled Judah because of Ahaz king of Israel, for he had promoted wickedness in Judah and had been most unfaithful to the LORD. ²⁰Tiglath-Pileser king of Assyria came to him, but he gave him trouble instead of help. ²¹Ahaz took some of the things from the temple of the LORD and from the royal palace and from the princes and presented them to the king of Assyria, but that did not help him.

²²In his time of trouble King Ahaz became even more unfaithful to the LORD. ²³He offered sacrifices to the gods of Damascus, who had defeated him; for he thought, "Since the gods of the kings of Aram have helped them, I will sacrifice to them so they will help me." But they were his downfall and the downfall of all Israel.

²⁴Ahaz gathered together the furnishings from the temple of God and took them away. He shut the doors of the LORD's temple and set up altars at every street corner in Jerusalem. ²⁵In every town in Judah he built high places to burn sacrifices to other gods and provoked the LORD, the God of his fathers, to anger.

COMMENTARY

5–8 These verses constitute the beginning of the summary of what is known as the Syro-Ephraimite crisis (see Overview above). Note that the reason behind this crisis is that "Judah had forsaken the LORD" (v.6); thus God's anger is stirred (v.9) and he hands over his people to the kings of Aram and Israel (v.5). The large numbers of Judeans captured and (temporarily) deported from Judah include members of the royal family and the two most senior administrative officials, implying a dire situation in the southern kingdom. The imagery of captives, deportation, and exile reflects God's covenantal warnings (e.g., Dt 28:64–68) and anticipates the future Babylonian exile. For a detailed overview of interpretive options regarding large numbers such as these in the OT, see comments on 11:1.

9–11 In the midst of the sizable number of Judeans being brought captive to the northern

kingdom during the Syro-Ephraimite crisis (cf. vv.5–8), an otherwise unknown prophet rebukes the Israelite military leaders for planning to enslave their "fellow countrymen" (cf. Lev 25:39–46). The prophet reminds them that their victory over Judah was due to God's wrath and that they risk God's wrath by oppressing their brethren. This narrative interlude during the Syro-Ephraimite crisis shows the remnant of familial feelings between Judah and Israel (cf. 2Ch 11:1–4).

12–15 In light of the increasing unfaithfulness of Ahaz, it comes with some surprise that the northern kingdom (specifically, the military leaders of Ephraim; the northern king [Pekah] is absent from this account) emphatically responds to the prophet's rebuke and takes significant steps of kindness and mercy to remedy the situation and send their brethren back to Judah. The steps taken by the "assembly" of the northern kingdom, including returning plunder, clothing the unclothed, feeding the hungry, nursing wounds, and putting the weak on donkeys, together with the location of Jericho, are all reminiscent of the aspects of kindness shown in Jesus' parable of the good Samaritan (cf. Lk 10:25–37; see F. S. Spencer, "2 Chronicles 28:5–15 and the Parable of the Good Samaritan," *WTJ* 46 [1986]: 317–49).

16–18 Following the interlude featuring the prophet Obed and the acts of mercy and repentance of the northern kingdom (cf. vv.9–15), the text returns to the details of the Syro-Ephraimite crisis (also see comments on vv.5–8 and Overview above). In addition to the pressure on Judah from Aram and Israel to the north (vv.5–8), Ahaz also faces pressure in the south as the Edomites launch offensives into Judah (v.17). In addition, the Philistines seize several key Judean cities in the Shephelah, including Beth Shemesh, Aijalon, Soco, and Timnah (v.18). Note that most of these cities were located on the major passes (roads) leading into the central hill country.

Moreover, the Aramean king Rezin invades the port city of Elath, which is subsequently inhabited by Edomites (cf. 2Ki 16:6). The loss of Elath reversed the gains in this region achieved by Uzziah. All told, Judah's national and economic security is gravely threatened in the midst of this crisis. Faced with these threats and pressures, Ahaz makes the watershed decision to seek the help of the Assyrian king Tiglath-Pileser III:

> "I am your servant and vassal. Come up and save me out of the hand of the king of Aram and of the king of Israel, who are attacking me." And Ahaz took the silver and gold found in the temple of the LORD and in the treasuries of the royal palace and sent it as a gift to the king of Assyria. (2Ki 16:7–8; cf. 2Ch 28:16, 21; cf. *COS*, 2:117D; *ANET*, 282)

As noted above (v.9) and below (v.19), these pressures are a direct result of the unfaithfulness of Ahaz and Judah by failing to obey and fully trust the Lord (e.g., vv.1–5, 16, 21–25). While such covenantal consequences are intended to drive God's people to repentance, Ahaz instead pursues greater and greater levels of unfaithfulness (cf. vv.21–25).

19 This "humbling" of Ahaz and the southern kingdom is a direct result of the unfaithfulness of Ahaz and Judah to obey and fully trust the Lord (e.g., vv.1–5, 16, 21–25; cf. Isa 7:9–12). Moreover, Ahaz's sin in *promoting* wickedness (e.g., vv.2–4) is in direct opposition to his role as a covenant fiduciary charged with upholding and promoting righteousness in the land (cf. Dt 17:14–20). While "humbling" covenantal consequences are intended to drive God's people to repentance, Ahaz becomes more unfaithful (cf. vv.21–25, esp. v.22).

20–21 Once Tiglath-Pileser III had achieved his goal of dividing the nascent western coalition through the submission and allegiance of Ahaz, the Assyrian king only gave Ahaz "trouble" instead of the promised help (v.20). Rather than see the practical and theological folly of his reliance on humans (vs. God), Ahaz further attempted to curry favor with the Assyrian king by raiding the treasures of the temple and palace (as had been seen in prior instances of covenantal unfaithfulness; cf. 12:9 [Rehoboam]; 16:2–3 [Asa]; 2Ki 12:17–18 [Joash]; 2Ki 24:13 [Jehoiachin]), to no avail.

22 This is one of the saddest verses in all of Chronicles. As noted above (vv.9, 19), the judgment of God via the incursions of the surrounding nations is a direct result of the unfaithfulness of Ahaz (and Judah) to obey and trust the Lord fully. While such covenantal consequences are intended to drive God's people back to him in repentance, Ahaz instead becomes "even more *unfaithful*" (root *mˁl*; GK 5085) and pursues greater levels of wickedness by raiding the temple and palace treasuries, worshiping additional deities associated with the Arameans, and looting the temple for the furnishings of his many high places (cf. vv.21–25). By so doing Ahaz spurns the forgiving nature of the God, who abounds in mercy and forgiveness when his people seek him in humility and contrition (see comments on 6:22–39 and the examples of Rehoboam [12:12] and Manasseh [33:18–19]).

23 As part of his increased unfaithfulness, Ahaz turns to more idols rather than returning to the living God. The idea of a god as being primarily associated with a given nation or city (e.g., the gods of Damascus) was prevalent in the religious systems of the biblical world. Although Yahweh is frequently associated with Zion, Jerusalem, and Israel, the biblical material repeatedly describes Yahweh as directing the affairs of all nations and rulers. This said, the "gods of Damascus" might actually be *Assyrian*

gods adopted by the conquered Arameans (note the additional details provided in 2Ki 16:10–18). It is uncertain whether the notation to such pursuit of spiritual adultery as being the downfall of "all Israel" refers to Judah (as in v.19, where Ahaz is called the "king of Israel" instead of "king of Judah") or to the northern kingdom, whose population has likewise pursued idolatry (recall v.2). Note that Ahaz is the last king of Judah during the divided kingdom; after this only Judah remains.

24–25 As part of his increased unfaithfulness to Yahweh (see comments on vv.22 and 23), Ahaz loots the sacred objects of Yahweh's temple for his many pagan shrines (also see 2Ki 16:14–18), ultimately shutting the doors of God's temple. The reopening and purifying of that temple will be the first priority in the reforms of Ahaz's son Hezekiah (cf. 2Ch 29:3–36).

NOTE

19 The depth of Ahaz's unfaithfulness is underscored via a cognate infinitive absolute, which intensifies the meaning of the underlying root idea and thus produces the notion of a superlative of unfaithfulness ("most unfaithful"): וּמָעוֹל מַעַל, *ûmā'ôl ma'al* (cf. GK 5085, 5086).

3. Ahaz's Regnal Summary (2Ch 28:26–27)

> [26]The other events of his reign and all his ways, from beginning to end, are written in the book of the kings of Judah and Israel. [27]Ahaz rested with his fathers and was buried in the city of Jerusalem, but he was not placed in the tombs of the kings of Israel. And Hezekiah his son succeeded him as king.

COMMENTARY

26–27 On the sources referenced by the Chronicler in regnal summaries, see comments on 12:15 and the Introduction. In the light of his widespread

unfaithfulness, Ahaz is denied the honor of burial in the royal tombs. On the details of Hezekiah's reign, see comments on 29:1.

M. The Reign of Hezekiah (2Ch 29:1–32:33)

1. Hezekiah's Reforms and Temple Purification (2Ch 29:1–36)

¹Hezekiah was twenty-five years old when he became king, and he reigned in Jerusalem twenty-nine years. His mother's name was Abijah daughter of Zechariah. ²He did what was right in the eyes of the LORD, just as his father David had done.

³In the first month of the first year of his reign, he opened the doors of the temple of the LORD and repaired them. ⁴He brought in the priests and the Levites, assembled them in the square on the east side ⁵and said: "Listen to me, Levites! Consecrate yourselves now and consecrate the temple of the LORD, the God of your fathers. Remove all defilement from the sanctuary. ⁶Our fathers were unfaithful; they did evil in the eyes of the LORD our God and forsook him. They turned their faces away from the LORD's dwelling place and turned their backs on him. ⁷They also shut the doors of the portico and put out the lamps. They did not burn incense or present any burnt offerings at the sanctuary to the God of Israel. ⁸Therefore, the anger of the LORD has fallen on Judah and Jerusalem; he has made them an object of dread and horror and scorn, as you can see with your own eyes. ⁹This is why our fathers have fallen by the sword and why our sons and daughters and our wives are in captivity. ¹⁰Now I intend to make a covenant with the LORD, the God of Israel, so that his fierce anger will turn away from us. ¹¹My sons, do not be negligent now, for the LORD has chosen you to stand before him and serve him, to minister before him and to burn incense."

¹²Then these Levites set to work:

from the Kohathites,

Mahath son of Amasai and Joel son of Azariah;

from the Merarites,

Kish son of Abdi and Azariah son of Jehallelel;

from the Gershonites,

Joah son of Zimmah and Eden son of Joah

¹³from the descendants of Elizaphan,

Shimri and Jeiel;

from the descendants of Asaph,

Zechariah and Mattaniah;

¹⁴from the descendants of Heman,

Jehiel and Shimei;

from the descendants of Jeduthun,

Shemaiah and Uzziel.

¹⁵When they had assembled their brothers and consecrated themselves, they went in to purify the temple of the LORD, as the king had ordered, following the word of the LORD.

¹⁶The priests went into the sanctuary of the LORD to purify it. They brought out to the courtyard of the LORD's temple everything unclean that they found in the temple of the LORD. The Levites took it and carried it out to the Kidron Valley. ¹⁷They began the consecration on the first day of the first month, and by the eighth day of the month they reached the portico of the LORD. For eight more days they consecrated the temple of the LORD itself, finishing on the sixteenth day of the first month.

¹⁸Then they went in to King Hezekiah and reported: "We have purified the entire temple of the LORD, the altar of burnt offering with all its utensils, and the table for setting out the consecrated bread, with all its articles. ¹⁹We have prepared and consecrated all the articles that King Ahaz removed in his unfaithfulness while he was king. They are now in front of the LORD's altar."

²⁰Early the next morning King Hezekiah gathered the city officials together and went up to the temple of the LORD. ²¹They brought seven bulls, seven rams, seven male lambs and seven male goats as a sin offering for the kingdom, for the sanctuary and for Judah. The king commanded the priests, the descendants of Aaron, to offer these on the altar of the LORD. ²²So they slaughtered the bulls, and the priests took the blood and sprinkled it on the altar; next they slaughtered the rams and sprinkled their blood on the altar; then they slaughtered the lambs and sprinkled their blood on the altar. ²³The goats for the sin offering were brought before the king and the assembly, and they laid their hands on them. ²⁴The priests then slaughtered the goats and presented their blood on the altar for a sin offering to atone for all Israel, because the king had ordered the burnt offering and the sin offering for all Israel.

²⁵He stationed the Levites in the temple of the LORD with cymbals, harps and lyres in the way prescribed by David and Gad the king's seer and Nathan the prophet; this was commanded by the LORD through his prophets. ²⁶So the Levites stood ready with David's instruments, and the priests with their trumpets.

²⁷Hezekiah gave the order to sacrifice the burnt offering on the altar. As the offering began, singing to the LORD began also, accompanied by trumpets and the instruments of David king of Israel. ²⁸The whole assembly bowed in worship, while the singers sang and the trumpeters played. All this continued until the sacrifice of the burnt offering was completed.

²⁹When the offerings were finished, the king and everyone present with him knelt down and worshiped. ³⁰King Hezekiah and his officials ordered the Levites to praise the LORD with the words of David and of Asaph the seer. So they sang praises with gladness and bowed their heads and worshiped.

³¹Then Hezekiah said, "You have now dedicated yourselves to the LORD. Come and bring sacrifices and thank offerings to the temple of the LORD." So the assembly brought sacrifices and thank offerings, and all whose hearts were willing brought burnt offerings.

³²The number of burnt offerings the assembly brought was seventy bulls, a hundred rams and two hundred male lambs — all of them for burnt offerings to the Lord. ³³The animals consecrated as sacrifices amounted to six hundred bulls and three thousand sheep and goats. ³⁴The priests, however, were too few to skin all the burnt offerings; so their kinsmen the Levites helped them until the task was finished and until other priests had been consecrated, for the Levites had been more conscientious in consecrating themselves than the priests had been. ³⁵There were burnt offerings in abundance, together with the fat of the fellowship offerings and the drink offerings that accompanied the burnt offerings.

So the service of the temple of the Lord was reestablished. ³⁶Hezekiah and all the people rejoiced at what God had brought about for his people, because it was done so quickly.

COMMENTARY

1 The chronology of Hezekiah's reign in Judah is difficult because of unclear synchronism across various date markers in biblical passages and records from the ancient Near East. In addition, the number of coreigns that take place during the time from Amaziah to Hezekiah (some of which are specified; others deduced or assumed) adds to the chronological challenges of this period of the Judean monarchy (see comments on 25:1, 25–26; 26:1, 3, 22–23; 27:1; 28:1).

By way of example, 2 Kings 18:9–10 notes that the Assyrians under Shalmaneser V began their siege of Samaria (ca. 724 BC) in Hezekiah's fourth year and defeated Samaria (ca. 722 BC) in Hezekiah's sixth year. With these dates, this would imply that Hezekiah began to reign in about 728/727 BC. However, 2 Kings 18:13 records that the Assyrian king Sennacherib "attacked all the fortified cities of Judah and captured them" during Hezekiah's fourteenth year. Since this invasion is dated to 701 BC, this would imply that Hezekiah began to reign in about 715/714 BC. Hezekiah may have had a confrontation with Sennacherib while he was leading

military expeditions prior to his ascension to the Assyrian throne.

Other details, such as the length of Hezekiah's reign and the coordination of Hezekiah's reign with the third year of the reign of Hoshea of the northern kingdom (who assassinated Pekah in ca. 732 BC), add to the complexities of understanding how these time markers mesh. As seen in other instances, the first year of the regnal period of a king can be understood in at least three ways: the first year of a coreign, the first year of a solo reign, and the first full year following the king's official accession.

This is likely the situation here with Hezekiah's beginning a coregency with Ahaz in 728/727 BC and beginning his sole reign in 715/714 BC (see Provan, Long, and Longman, 272, 378 n. 858). Moreover, it is likely that Hezekiah served a coregency with his son Manasseh for the final decade of his reign (ca. 708–698 BC; see 33:1). All told, Hezekiah's twenty-nine-year reign (29:1) can be counted from the beginning of his coregency with his father Ahaz, resulting in a proposed reign for Hezekiah of 728/727–699/698

BC (coreign with Ahaz, 728/727−715/714 BC; sole reign, 715/714−709/708 BC; and a coregency with Manasseh, 708−698 BC).

2 Hezekiah's reign stands in juxtaposition to the reign of his father, Ahaz. Instead of being compared to the "kings of Israel" (28:3) and being "unlike David" (28:1), Hezekiah is described as doing what is right in God's eyes "just as his father David had done" (29:2). Instead of "promoting" wickedness in Judah (28:19), making objects of idolatry (28:24−25), and closing the doors of the temple (28:24), Hezekiah promotes a return to Yahweh (cf. 30:6−9), destroys objects of idolatry (31:1), and opens the doors of the temple (29:3). Instead of becoming "more unfaithful" during a time of duress (see 28:22), Hezekiah cries out to God in prayer (cf. 32:20 in the context of 32:1−23). In short, instead of being "most unfaithful" (cf. 28:19), Hezekiah is faithful and obedient to the Lord his God (31:20−21).

3 While what is in view regarding Hezekiah's "first" year is unclear (see comments on v.1), the emphasis is the speed with which Hezekiah acts (and hence his priorities) to open the doors of the temple closed by his father, Ahaz (cf. 28:24). The quickness of the reopening, purification, and dedication of the Jerusalem temple is celebrated with great joy by the community (cf. 29:36).

4−10 In conjunction with reopening the temple (v.3), Hezekiah convenes an assembly of those charged with covenantal functionary duties pertaining to the worship life of ancient Israel. The emphasis of this gathering is the consecration (*qdš*, GK 7727) of that which relates to the spiritual life of Israel: priests, Levites, and the temple (including the altar and other articles; cf. vv.18−19). Note that these reforms begin with the individuals consecrating themselves.

Hezekiah's speech also functions as a rallying call to faithfulness in the light of the disastrous (albeit covenantal) consequences of unfaithfulness. (Recall that speeches are a key facet of the Chronicler's means of expressing theological points of emphasis [cf. 13:4−12].) Hezekiah's focused commitment to restore Judah to faithfulness and nullify God's righteous anger against his people rises to the level of a covenant (v.10). Later, Hezekiah will convene an assembly of Judean officials (cf. vv.20−31) and finally the whole community (cf. 30:1−27) for worship and dedication at the Jerusalem temple.

11 Because the consecration of the temple can only happen with faithful (and consecrated; cf. vv.4−10) priests and Levites, Hezekiah exhorts these "sons" to act in a manner reflective of their covenantal calling (cf. Eph 4:1). This calling is a function of God's choice of Levi to serve him. On the differing responsibilities of priests and Levites vis-à-vis temple service, see comments on 5:4−6. On incense and temple service, see comments on 4:19−22.

12−14 This list of Levitical families includes the three subclans of Levi (Kohathites, Merarites, and Gershonites; cf. 1Ch 6:1−48; Nu 3:14−39) and the three families of Levitical musicians established by David (Asaph, Heman, and Jeduthun; cf. 1Ch 25:1−7). Between these sets of Levitical families is the mention of the descendants of Elizaphan, who was technically from the family of Kohath. His separate listing reflects his position of prominence as a "leader of the families of the Kohathites" (cf. Nu 3:30; on the responsibilities of priests and Levites regarding temple service, see comment on v.11).

15−16 While the command to purify the temple came by order of the king, the work of the priests and Levites ultimately sought to follow "the word of the LORD." This statement underscores the priority of adhering to Yahweh's covenantal stipulations reflected throughout the reign of Hezekiah (cf. Dt 12:4). Likewise, Hezekiah is described as organizing the Levites "in the way prescribed by David" and "by the LORD through the prophets" (cf. v.25).

Moreover, the account continues to emphasize the necessity of the purification and "cleanness" (i.e., holiness) of all things that pertain to the holy space of Yahweh's temple. For more on the topic of holy space, see the Reflection in ch. 2. The priests would necessarily play a key role in discerning between clean and unclean items (cf. Lev 10:10–11). In accordance with the careful emphasis on following God's revealed Word, only priests purified the inner part of the temple (v.16) because the Levites were excluded from the Most Holy Place.

17 The process of the cleansing of the temple and its altar and related items (cf. vv.18–19) takes two sets of eight days. Cleansing begins from the outside and progressively works toward areas of increasing holiness. The time required for the purification of the temple complex and the purification of sufficient priests necessitates a delay in the subsequent Passover celebration organized by Hezekiah (cf. 30:2–3, 15).

18–19 Following sixteen days of careful cleansing and purification of the temple, altar, and utensils (v.17), the priests and Levites finally removed the spiritual blight inflicted on the temple by Ahaz (cf. 28:21–25). This includes restoring of utensils previously removed from the temple for idolatrous worship (cf. 28:21, 24; cf. 36:18; Ezr 1:7–11). The consecration of the Jerusalem temple will prepare the way for an emphatic return to corporate worship in Israel (cf. vv.20–31 and 30:1–27).

20–24 Once the temple has been consecrated by the priests and Levites (vv.15–19), Hezekiah immediately ("early the next morning") convenes an assembly of Jerusalem city officials to participate in a temple (re-)dedication ceremony replete with the terminology and theology of the Israelite sacrificial system. Emphasis is placed on the making of a sin offering (vv.21, 23, 24[2x]) for the kingdom

(v.21), the sanctuary (i.e., the temple; v.21), Judah (v.21), and "all Israel" (v.24). For Mosaic instructions on burnt offerings (ʿōlâ; GK 6592) of animals from the herd or flock, see Leviticus 1:3–13. For sin offerings (ḥaṭṭāʾt; GK 2633) and the related laying of hands on the animal by people, priests, and community leaders (symbolizing the transfer of sin and substitutionary sacrifice; cf. v.23), see Leviticus 4:1–35.

The sacrifice of goats (v.23), the laying on of hands, and the sprinkling of blood are reminiscent of the Day of Atonement, which (as here) has particular application to the Most Holy Place and the altar (including the sprinkling of blood; cf. Lev 16:1–20). The sprinkling of the blood of lambs and goats on the altar (v.22) also functions as a component of fellowship offerings (cf. Lev 3:1–17; 17:5–6). The prominence of blood in the ceremony underscores that the shedding of blood is necessary to atone (kpr; GK 4105) for sin (Heb 9:21–22).

All together, these elements of the Israelite sacrificial system portray the forgiveness of sin, reconciliation, and atonement made available by God. Note that the sacrificial offerings are accompanied by (and followed by) singing and music (cf. vv.25–30). The final movement of Hezekiah's temple rededication ceremony (cf. vv.31–35) includes additional burnt offerings (vv.31–32, 35), thank offerings (v.31), peace/fellowship offerings (v.35), and drink offerings (v.35).

25–28 The stationing of Levitical musicians, singers, and trumpeting priests who accompany the sacrificial offerings works to present Hezekiah's temple (re-)dedication ceremony in parallel with Solomon's temple-dedication ceremony (e.g., 5:2–14; 7:4–7). Like Hezekiah's commitment to follow "the word of the LORD" noted earlier (cf. v.15), Hezekiah is careful to organize these groups "in the way prescribed by David" and "by the LORD through the prophets" (cf. v.25; also note vv.27 and 30) rather than by his own design (cf. Dt 12:4; on cymbals, harps, lyres, singers, and the trumpet responsibilities of priests, see comments on 5:4–6, 12–13; on worship postures such as bowing down [v.28], see comments on 6:12–13).

29–30 Following the completion of the sacrificial offerings (see comments on vv.20–24), Hezekiah leads the assembly in a solemn yet celebratory worship of God that is punctuated with another round of music and singing led by the Levites (cf. vv.25–28). Once again (cf. v.25) David is referenced in the light of Hezekiah's charge that the Levites praise God with the words of his worship songs (presumably Psalms; likewise those of Asaph). Recall earlier references to David's organization of the musical corps of the Levites with respect to their instrumental roles (v.25) and the instruments themselves (cf. v.27).

31–35 This final movement of Hezekiah's temple consecration and rededication ceremony includes additional burnt offerings (vv.31–32, 35), thank offerings (v.31; cf. Lev 7:11–16), peace/fellowship offerings (v.35; cf. Lev 3:1–16;

7:11–16) and drink offerings (v.35; cf. Lev 23:13; Nu 15:1–12). These additional offerings are provided by those "whose hearts were willing" (v.31) and highlight the image of corporate fellowship via the sharing of sacrificial meals and communion offerings (esp. the thank offerings [v.31] and peace/fellowship offerings [v.35]). In the midst of this otherwise perfect setting, there is a hint of critique directed at the priests (v.34; also cf. 30:3), which comes through the author's praise of the Levites as being "more conscientious" than the priests in consecrating themselves for temple service. This results is an insufficient number of priests to skin the burnt offerings — ironically, not a prescribed priestly or Levitical duty (see Lev 1:2–6).

36 In the afterglow of the ceremony culminating in a consecrated and functioning temple for God's people (v.35), there is a deep-seated atmosphere of gratefulness. As reflected at the beginning of the account (v.3), the quickness in which the temple is reopened, consecrated, and dedicated is an added measure of great joy celebrated by the king and the community as a whole.

NOTES

1 Thiele, 175–76, dates Hezekiah's rule from 715–686 BC, including a ten-year coreign with his son Manasseh (696–686 BC). A number of studies help shed light on the chronological questions of this time period (cf. H. Stigers, "The Interphased Chronology of Jotham, Ahaz, Hezekiah, and Hoshea," *BETS* 9 [1966]: 81–90; A. G. Vaughn, *Theology, History, and Archaeology in the Chronicler's Account of Hezekiah* [Atlanta: Scholars, 1999], 12–13; K. L. Younger Jr., "Assyrian Involvement in the Southern Levant at the End of the Eighth Century B.C.E.," in *Jerusalem in Bible and Archaeology: The First Temple Period* [ed. A. G. Vaughn and A. E. Killebrew; SBL Symposium 18; Atlanta: SBL, 2003], 235–63).

2 Note Hezekiah's similarity with Solomon (e.g., cf. Hezekiah's temple preparation and celebration of 29:4–36 with those of Solomon extending from 2Ch 5–7).

15 While Hezekiah's reforms reflect a priority of the revealed (and established) Word of God, God also uses Hezekiah to expand the OT canon. Note Proverbs 25:1: "These are more proverbs of Solomon, copied by the men of Hezekiah king of Judah." This statement implies that God uses Hezekiah's royal court (presumably scribes and priests) to canonize in written form what had been orally transmitted wisdom sayings of Solomon.

21 The multiples of seven in the sacrificial animals might be a picture of the completeness intended by the sacrifices.

34 It is possible that skinning may have been part of the broader responsibilities David assigned to the Levites as part of their temple service (cf. 1Ch 23:28–32).

2. Hezekiah's Passover Celebration (2Ch 30:1–31:1)

¹Hezekiah sent word to all Israel and Judah and also wrote letters to Ephraim and Manasseh, inviting them to come to the temple of the LORD in Jerusalem and celebrate the Passover to the LORD, the God of Israel. ²The king and his officials and the whole assembly in Jerusalem decided to celebrate the Passover in the second month. ³They had not been able to celebrate it at the regular time because not enough priests had consecrated themselves and the people had not assembled in Jerusalem. ⁴The plan seemed right both to the king and to the whole assembly. ⁵They decided to send a proclamation throughout Israel, from Beersheba to Dan, calling the people to come to Jerusalem and celebrate the Passover to the LORD, the God of Israel. It had not been celebrated in large numbers according to what was written.

⁶At the king's command, couriers went throughout Israel and Judah with letters from the king and from his officials, which read:

"People of Israel, return to the LORD, the God of Abraham, Isaac and Israel, that he may return to you who are left, who have escaped from the hand of the kings of Assyria. ⁷Do not be like your fathers and brothers, who were unfaithful to the LORD, the God of their fathers, so that he made them an object of horror, as you see. ⁸Do not be stiff-necked, as your fathers were; submit to the LORD. Come to the sanctuary, which he has consecrated forever. Serve the LORD your God, so that his fierce anger will turn away from you. ⁹If you return to the LORD, then your brothers and your children will be shown compassion by their captors and will come back to this land, for the LORD your God is gracious and compassionate. He will not turn his face from you if you return to him."

¹⁰The couriers went from town to town in Ephraim and Manasseh, as far as Zebulun, but the people scorned and ridiculed them. ¹¹Nevertheless, some men of Asher, Manasseh and Zebulun humbled themselves and went to Jerusalem. ¹²Also in Judah the hand of God was on the people to give them unity of mind to carry out what the king and his officials had ordered, following the word of the LORD.

¹³A very large crowd of people assembled in Jerusalem to celebrate the Feast of Unleavened Bread in the second month. ¹⁴They removed the altars in Jerusalem and cleared away the incense altars and threw them into the Kidron Valley.

¹⁵They slaughtered the Passover lamb on the fourteenth day of the second month. The priests and the Levites were ashamed and consecrated themselves and brought burnt offerings to the temple of the LORD. ¹⁶Then they took up their regular positions as prescribed in the Law of Moses the man of God. The priests sprinkled the blood handed to them by the Levites. ¹⁷Since many in the crowd had not consecrated themselves, the Levites had to kill the Passover lambs for all those who were not ceremonially clean and could not consecrate their lambs to the LORD. ¹⁸Although most of the many people who came from Ephraim, Manasseh, Issachar and Zebulun had not purified themselves, yet they ate the Passover, contrary to what was written. But Hezekiah prayed for them, saying, "May the LORD, who is good, pardon everyone ¹⁹who sets his heart on seeking God—the LORD, the God of his fathers—even if he is not clean according to the rules of the sanctuary." ²⁰And the LORD heard Hezekiah and healed the people.

²¹The Israelites who were present in Jerusalem celebrated the Feast of Unleavened Bread for seven days with great rejoicing, while the Levites and priests sang to the LORD every day, accompanied by the LORD's instruments of praise.

²²Hezekiah spoke encouragingly to all the Levites, who showed good understanding of the service of the LORD. For the seven days they ate their assigned portion and offered fellowship offerings and praised the LORD, the God of their fathers.

²³The whole assembly then agreed to celebrate the festival seven more days; so for another seven days they celebrated joyfully. ²⁴Hezekiah king of Judah provided a thousand bulls and seven thousand sheep and goats for the assembly, and the officials provided them with a thousand bulls and ten thousand sheep and goats. A great number of priests consecrated themselves. ²⁵The entire assembly of Judah rejoiced, along with the priests and Levites and all who had assembled from Israel, including the aliens who had come from Israel and those who lived in Judah. ²⁶There was great joy in Jerusalem, for since the days of Solomon son of David king of Israel there had been nothing like this in Jerusalem. ²⁷The priests and the Levites stood to bless the people, and God heard them, for their prayer reached heaven, his holy dwelling place.

³¹:¹When all this had ended, the Israelites who were there went out to the towns of Judah, smashed the sacred stones and cut down the Asherah poles. They destroyed the high places and the altars throughout Judah and Benjamin and in Ephraim and Manasseh. After they had destroyed all of them, the Israelites returned to their own towns and to their own property.

COMMENTARY

1 Once the temple has been restored to its consecrated and functioning status (ch. 29), Hezekiah invites those remaining in what had been the northern kingdom ("Ephraim and Manasseh") as well as Judah. This verse functions as a summary statement of the mission of the couriers detailed in vv. 5–12. Although they are received with scorn by some in the remnant of the northern kingdom (cf. vv. 10–11), Hezekiah's efforts not only tie into his religious reforms, but will also facilitate his later quest for political independence (recall that Ahaz had earlier made Judah an Assyrian vassal in conjunction with the Syro-Ephraimite crisis; cf. 28:16–23).

2–4 The time required for the purification of the temple complex (cf. 29:17–19) necessitated a delay in the subsequent Passover celebration organized by Hezekiah. In another subtly negative remark aimed at priests (cf. 2Ch 29:34), part of the extra time needed to consecrate the temple is attributed to an insufficient number of priests who took the steps to become ritually pure. Although ceremonial uncleanness was a valid reason for a delayed celebration (Nu 9:9–10), the critique implies apathy on the part of some of the priests.

In addition, the delay is connected to issues in convening an assembly (which will include those who journey from the north), an issue addressed to some extent in Mosaic law (cf. Nu 9:9–10). Passover was one of the three major pilgrimage festivals (along with the Feast of Tabernacles [also known as the Feast of Ingathering, the Feast of Booths, and Succoth] and Pentecost [also known as the Feast of Weeks, the Feast of Harvest, and First-fruits]; cf. Ex 23:14–17; Dt 16:1–17). As reflected here (cf. vv. 13, 21), Passover was closely connected with the seven-day Feast of Unleavened Bread (cf. Ex 23:15). Normally the Passover would be celebrated on the fourteenth day of the month of Abib (cf. Nu 9:1–3; 28:16–25). The officials who aided the king in making the decision to have a late Passover celebration are the same ones who helped dedicate the newly consecrated temple (cf. 2Ch 29:20–35).

The final statement (v. 4) underscores the theme of unity reflected in the early dedication ceremony (see comments at 29:31–35) and throughout the Passover celebration narrative. Also see comments on the Passover at v. 15.

5 Although the letter itself from King Hezekiah and the Judean officials does not actually mention Passover (cf. vv. 6–9), the invitation from these officials addresses the deeper issues of spirituality that get to the core of worshiping God on his terms (cf. Hezekiah's words to the priests and Levites; 29:4–11). Significantly, Hezekiah's invitation is not simply within his realm in Judah, but extends throughout what had been the territory of Israel before the division of the kingdom ("Beersheba to Dan"; cf. 1Ch 21:2; also see comments on 2Ch 9:26). As with other steps taken by Hezekiah and his officials (cf. 29:15–16, 25), this invitation revitalizes a neglected element of covenantal worship in accordance with God's Word ("according to what was written"). For details on the Feast of Passover, see comments on vv. 2–4 and 15.

6–9 As reflected in the phraseology "Beersheba to Dan" (v. 5), Hezekiah's couriers extend the invitation to celebrate Passover to those in Judah as well as those in the geographical region that was previously the northern kingdom ("Israel") before its fall to the Assyrian Empire (ca. 722/721 BC). The heart of Hezekiah's letter to the people of Judah and Israel is similar to his exhortation directed to the priests and Levites (cf. 29:4–11) in that it calls individuals to realign themselves with the stipulations of Yahweh's covenant. As such, the letter does not actually mention Passover but instead invites the community to engage the deeper issues of personal purity and spirituality that get to the core of worshiping God on his terms.

The exhortations in the letter are articulated both in the positive (e.g., "return to the LORD" [v. 6]; "submit to the LORD" [v. 8]; "come to the sanctuary" [v.8]; "serve the LORD your God" [v.8]) and in the negative (e.g., "do not be like your fathers and brothers, who were unfaithful" [v.7]; "do not be stiff-necked" [v.8]). The core of these exhortations is *returning to God*, which implies repentance and submission to his authority.

Hezekiah's letter begins and ends with this call to return to the Lord (cf. vv.6, 9). Returning to God is that which will cause God to return to his people (v.6) in graciousness and compassion (v.9; recall Solomon's temple-dedication prayer; e.g., 6:24–25, 36–39). The references to Assyria (v.6) and to those in captivity (v.9) imply that the letter was especially directed to those located in what had been the northern kingdom. The exhortation to return to God in the aftermath of exile would have added significance to the Chronicler's audience.

10–12 Although Hezekiah's invitation is received with scorn by some in the north, others begin the process of returning to God physically ("to Jerusalem") and metaphysically/spiritually ("humbled themselves"). In the south (v.12), the receptivity is more positive as there is "unity of mind" on the part of those in Judah in responding to the king's invitation to Passover and spiritual renewal in accordance with "the word of the LORD."

13 In response to Hezekiah's letter of invitation sent to those in Judah and the former territory of Israel (vv.6–9), a "very large crowd" of Godward individuals assembles in Jerusalem. As reflected in Mosaic law, Hezekiah's Passover is celebrated in conjunction with the seven-day Feast of Unleavened Bread (cf. Ex 23:14–17; Dt 16:1–17; for further details on Passover, see comments on vv.2–4, 15).

14 In parallel with the earlier actions taken by the assembly of priests and Levites (cf. 29:15–17), the assembly of Judeans and Israelites takes tangible steps in their return to God by removing and destroying items of idolatry and syncretism

throughout Jerusalem, most of which had been built by Ahaz (cf. 28:24–25). The destruction of such elements during Hezekiah's reign is similar to purges directed by Asa (cf. 14:3; 15:16), Joash (cf. 23:17), and Josiah (cf. 34:3–7) in Judah as well as Jehu in the northern kingdom (cf. 2Ki 10:18–28).

15 Following the destruction of items reflecting spiritual unfaithfulness (v.14), the Passover Feast begins with the sacrifice of the Passover lamb by the community (cf. Ex 12:6) in Jerusalem (cf. Dt 16:5–6). The Passover celebration hearkens back to Israel's deliverance in (and departure from) Egypt en route to inaugurating a covenantal relationship with Yahweh. Thus the Passover celebrates both God's gracious deliverance of his people *by means of blood* (Ex 12:13, 23; cf. 1Co 5:7; Jn 1:29) as well as the inauguration of a covenant confirmed *by means of blood* (Ex 24:3–8; cf. Mt 26:28; Heb 9:14).

These people are described as a chosen people belonging to God (Ex 19:5–6; cf. 1Pe 2:9; on the Feast of Passover beginning on the fourteenth day of the second month rather than the first month, see vv.2–4). Perhaps as a function of the zeal of the assembled group (vv.13–14) or the realization of their unholiness, the priests and Levites are "ashamed" and consecrate themselves (cf. 29:15–16).

16 The stationing of Levites and priests at the Passover Feast (v.16) is similar to Hezekiah's earlier temple (re-)dedication ceremony (cf. 29:25–28; cf. 5:2–14; 7:4–7) and organized "as prescribed in the Law of Moses" (cf. 29:15, 25–28), with the Levites functioning as ministerial servants to the priests in the realm of temple service. The sprinkling of the blood underscores the centrality of blood in God's deliverance of and covenant with Israel (see discussion at v.15).

17–20 Given the spiritually dark period in Judah during the rule of Ahaz and the persistent spiritual darkness in Israel, it is not surprising to learn that some in the assembly are not consecrated. This issue is addressed by the Levites' killing the Passover lambs of those who are ceremonially unclean, a practice also seen in Josiah's Passover (cf. 35:3–6). However, the matter is made more complicated when the whole community partakes of the Passover meal, "contrary to what was written" (v.18). Given the frequent refrain of Hezekiah's actions being shaped through written revelation (e.g., 29:15, 25; 30:12, 16; cf. 31:3, 21), this remark is nothing short of surprising. However, the outworking of this dilemma emphatically proclaims the principle that God's concern is fundamentally oriented toward the *inward* disposition of a person ("everyone who sets his heart on seeking God") as over against *outward* ritual ("not clean according to the rules of the sanctuary").

Note the similar stress on this principle by the prophet Isaiah, who ministered during the time of Hezekiah (cf. Isa 1:11–17). Hezekiah's prayer recalls the principle of God *hearing* ("the LORD heard Hezekiah") and *healing* ("and healed the people") underscored in Solomon's temple-dedication prayer (cf. 6:12–42). The pardon (v.18; lit., "atone"; *kpr*; GK 4105) and the healing (v.20; *rp'*; GK 8324) effected by God are spiritual in nature rather than physical (see Reflection below).

21 As reflected in the law, Hezekiah's Passover is celebrated in conjunction with the seven-day Feast of Unleavened Bread (cf. Ex 23:14–17; Dt 16:1–17). The "great rejoicing" of the community is fostered both by the covenantal reminders of the Passover celebration (see comments on v.15) and by the measure of divine grace experienced in the spiritual healing appropriated by those ceremonially unclean (vv.17–20). For remarks on Levitical musical instruments and the trumpet responsibilities of priests, see commentary on 5:4–6 and 5:12–13).

22 Hezekiah praises the Levites who have distinguished themselves throughout Hezekiah's temple

reforms (cf. 2Ch 29:12–19, 25–26, 29–30, 34; 30:16–17, 21) and thereby demonstrated both willing hearts and "good understanding" in their spiritual service to the Lord.

23 Hezekiah's Passover celebration is extended by an additional week by decision of the "whole assembly," suggesting a spirit of unity among the gathered individuals who, despite significant differences in their respective backgrounds (see v.25), are unified in their focus on worship and celebration. The two-week length of the festival echoes the duration of Solomon's temple dedication (cf. 7:8–10), which likewise featured community unity, unmitigated joy, and a sense of spiritual optimism.

This noted, Hezekiah's Passover is an anomaly in that it is celebrated in the second month rather than the first month (v.2), lasts for two weeks instead of the prescribed seven days (v.23), and includes unclean worshipers (e.g., vv.17–18). These details no doubt play into the summary statement that "there had been nothing like this in Jerusalem" (v.26).

24 The multitude of sacrificial animals acts as a tangible statement of the devotion and commitment of the community to God and to one other (cf. 1:6; 7:4–5).

25–26 The "entire assembly" of Hezekiah's Passover celebration consists of five rather divergent groups: (1) priests, (2) Levites, (3) pilgrims from what had been the northern kingdom, (4) "aliens" who also travelled down from the north, and (5) Judeans. The "aliens" from the north might refer to some combination of ethnic groups resettled in the north by the Assyrian Empire, individuals from the original inhabitants of the land of Canaan, or those whose genealogical background was impacted by mixed marriage. Such non-Israelites were included in the Mosaic regulations for Passover (cf. Nu 9:14).

Regardless of the specific identification of these "aliens," the emphasis here is the *oneness* and *unity* of the people in purpose, not their various differences (cf. Php 2:1–2), as reflected in the transethnic aspect of the Abrahamic promise (Ge 12:1–3). The deep unity of this diverse group along with the various anomalies of Hezekiah's Passover celebration (see comments on v.23) leads to the Chronicler's summary statement that "there had been nothing like this in Jerusalem" (v.26). Indeed!

27 At the conclusion of Hezekiah's protracted Passover celebration, the assembled worshipers are blessed by what are probably "Levitical priests" in the spirit of the priestly prayer (cf. Nu 6:22–27; Lev 9:22) rather than "priests and Levites" as in the NIV

(see Note). Note how Deuteronomy 10:8–9 says that one responsibility of Levites is to "pronounce blessings" in God's Name. Their prayer of blessing on the people is heard by God, which reflects the intention that the temple be a house of prayer for both Israelite and foreigner alike (6:20–21, 32–33, 40; 7:15).

31:1 At the end of the extended Passover celebration, the attendees from the northern kingdom travel around Judah and their own homeland destroying pagan worship shrines. This effort builds on earlier actions by priests and Levites (cf. 29:15–19) and the community within the environs of Jerusalem (cf. 30:14 and comments; on sacred stones and Asherah poles, see comments on 14:3; on high places see comments on 1:3–5).

NOTES

26 Second Kings does not mention Hezekiah's Passover and notes that Josiah's Passover is without parallel. But v.26 here only compares backward, not forward. Moreover, Hezekiah's Passover was an anomaly in that it was celebrated in the second month (v.2), not the first month as prescribed, and lasted for two weeks (v.23), not one week as prescribed (e.g., vv.17–18; also see comments on 35:17–19).

27 The translation here might be better rendered as a hendiadys: "Levitical priests" rather than the NIV's "the priests and the Levites"), as there is no conjunction ("and"; Heb.ו, *w*) between the two (cf. Dillard, 245).

REFLECTION

The reference to God's hearing and "healing" the land of Israel (cf. 7:14) and the Chronicler's remark that the Lord heard Hezekiah and healed the people (30:20) raises the issue of the biblical meaning of "healing" in these passages. Although the terminology of "heal" commonly brings to mind healing from physical ailments, in actuality these passages most likely refer to spiritual healing—namely, forgiveness and spiritual restoration. As such, the remark at 30:20 on Yahweh's healing the people is

connected with those who have set their hearts on seeking God (cf. 30:18–20). Similarly, an emphasis on spiritual healing is likely the intent of James 5:14–15:

> Is any one of you sick? He should call the elders of the church to pray over him and anoint him with oil in the name of the Lord. And the prayer offered in faith will make the sick person well; the Lord will raise him up. If he has sinned, he will be forgiven.

This passage is part of a series of closing exhortations beginning at James 5:7. In James 5:13–15, James gives a series of three questions followed by three commands. The first two, "Is anyone of you in trouble?" and "Is anyone happy?" each receive short commands reflecting a godly inward disposition: "He should pray" and "He should sing songs of praise," respectively. However, the third question, "Is any one of you sick?" receives a detailed response. The meaning of this third question-command sequence hinges on the nuance of two words typically rendered "sick" in Bible translations.

The first term translated "sick" (v.14; *astheneō*, GK 820) is the negated form of the verb "to strengthen" and thus is defined along the lines of "to be weak or powerless." Similarly, the nominal and adjectival forms of this term carry the meaning of "weak/weakness." This idea of "weakness" can have several nuances, including bodily weakness, spiritual weakness, and even economic weakness. The nuance of bodily weakness is understood, by extension, to be physical sickness, as seen in the Gospels in conjunction with the healing ministry of Christ. In fact, the healing ministry of Christ has likely influenced the nuance of physical sickness typically associated with James 5:14.

However, within the NT letters the *asthene*-word group overwhelmingly has the nuance of *spiritual weakness*. For example, in Romans 4:19 Paul notes that Abraham did not become *weak* in faith concerning the promise of God. Also, in 1 Corinthians 8:11–12 Paul notes that misuse of spiritual knowledge can ruin those who are *weak*. Moreover, the writer of Hebrews connects Christ's temptations with his ability to "sympathize with our *weaknesses*" (Heb 4:15; also see Ro 8:26; 14:1–2; 15:1; 1Co 9:22; 2Co 11:29–30; 1Th 5:14).

The second term typically translated "sick" in James 5:15 (*kamnō*) occurs in only one other place

in the NT, a place wherein the stress is that of spiritual weakness, not bodily sickness: "consider him who endured ... so that you will not grow weary and lose [*kamnō*] heart" (Heb 12:3).

With this notion of spiritual weakness in mind, note that James commands those who are weak to call for the elders of the church. Since a key requirement for an elder is spiritual strength, those who are *spiritually weak* are being told to seek out those who are *spiritually strong*. We see the other side of this relationship in Paul's farewell to the elders of Ephesus, wherein he exhorts these elders to "help the *weak*" (Ac 20:35; same term as Jas 5:13). The elders are instructed to pray for the individual and to anoint him/her with oil (an image portrayed in Ps 23 in conjunction with spiritual strengthening). The results of this prayer and anointing ("will make well ... will raise up ... will be forgiven") are those of spiritual restoration (cf. Ps 23).

In addition, these results are *guaranteed*. This makes perfect sense in the context of spiritual strengthening but does not make sense with regard to physical healing. In the following verses (Jas 5:16–20), James exhorts *all* believers to engage in the restoration process and stresses the great value of redirecting the spiritually weak. Ultimately, it is the Lord who forgives, restores, and strengthens the weak, and thus is the one who receives all the glory and honor (also see Ps 41:4; Isa 53:5).

The likelihood that these passages are speaking of spiritual healing rather than physical healing should in no way impede our desire or fervency to pray for the sick. Rather, this interpretation highlights an integral aspect of church life, namely, elders (and others who are spiritually strong) having an ongoing and active role in strengthening those wearied in their spiritual race. Lastly, James's exhortation reminds those who are spiritually weak of their responsibility to seek out those who are spiritually strong.

3. Hezekiah's Further Reforms (2Ch 31:2–21)

[2]Hezekiah assigned the priests and Levites to divisions — each of them according to their duties as priests or Levites — to offer burnt offerings and fellowship offerings, to minister, to give thanks and to sing praises at the gates of the LORD's dwelling. [3]The king contributed from his own possessions for the morning and evening burnt offerings and for the burnt offerings on the Sabbaths, New Moons and appointed feasts as written in the Law of the LORD. [4]He ordered the people living in Jerusalem to give the portion due the priests and Levites so they could devote themselves to the Law of the LORD. [5]As soon as the order went out, the Israelites generously gave the firstfruits of their grain, new wine, oil and honey and all that the fields produced. They brought a great amount, a tithe of everything. [6]The men of Israel and Judah who lived in the towns of Judah also brought a tithe of their herds and flocks and a tithe of the holy things dedicated to the LORD their God, and they piled them in heaps. [7]They began doing this in the third month and finished in the seventh month. [8]When Hezekiah and his officials came and saw the heaps, they praised the LORD and blessed his people Israel.

[9]Hezekiah asked the priests and Levites about the heaps; [10]and Azariah the chief priest, from the family of Zadok, answered, "Since the people began to bring their contributions to the temple of the LORD, we have had enough to eat and plenty to spare, because the LORD has blessed his people, and this great amount is left over."

[11]Hezekiah gave orders to prepare storerooms in the temple of the LORD, and this was done. [12]Then they faithfully brought in the contributions, tithes and dedicated gifts. Conaniah, a Levite, was in charge of these things, and his brother Shimei was next in rank. [13]Jehiel, Azaziah, Nahath, Asahel, Jerimoth, Jozabad, Eliel, Ismakiah, Mahath and Benaiah were supervisors under Conaniah and Shimei his brother, by appointment of King Hezekiah and Azariah the official in charge of the temple of God.

[14]Kore son of Imnah the Levite, keeper of the East Gate, was in charge of the freewill offerings given to God, distributing the contributions made to the LORD and also the consecrated gifts. [15]Eden, Miniamin, Jeshua, Shemaiah, Amariah and Shecaniah assisted him faithfully in the towns of the priests, distributing to their fellow priests according to their divisions, old and young alike.

[16]In addition, they distributed to the males three years old or more whose names were in the genealogical records — all who would enter the temple of the LORD to perform the daily duties of their various tasks, according to their responsibilities and their divisions. [17]And they distributed to the priests enrolled by their families in the genealogical records and likewise to the Levites twenty years old or more, according to their responsibilities and their divisions. [18]They included all the little ones, the wives, and the sons and daughters of the whole community listed in these genealogical records. For they were faithful in consecrating themselves.

¹⁹As for the priests, the descendants of Aaron, who lived on the farm lands around their towns or in any other towns, men were designated by name to distribute portions to every male among them and to all who were recorded in the genealogies of the Levites. ²⁰This is what Hezekiah did throughout Judah, doing what was good and right and faithful before the Lord his God. ²¹In everything that he undertook in the service of God's temple and in obedience to the law and the commands, he sought his God and worked wholeheartedly. And so he prospered.

COMMENTARY

2 Following the cleansing of the temple (ch. 29) and the celebration of Passover (ch. 30), Hezekiah organizes the corps of priests and Levites and reestablishes the pattern of financial support for temple personnel (vv.3–19). Hezekiah's assignments reflect the organization established in the Mosaic law and further developed under David and Solomon (cf. 1Ch 23:1–32; 25:1–6; 28:13; 2Ch 8:14–15; on the differing responsibilities of priests and Levites, see comments on 2Ch 5:4–6, 12–13).

3 This brief statement reflects Hezekiah's generosity toward the Lord's work (cf. David [1Ch 29:2–5] and Solomon [2Ch 3–4]) as well as Hezekiah's continued commitment to do that which was "written in the Law of the Lord" (cf. 29:15, 25; 30:12, 16; 31:21). Moreover, this brief synopsis of temple worship reflects Hezekiah's knowledge of instructions found in the Pentateuch, including morning and evening sacrifices (cf. Ex 29:38–39; Nu 28–29) and calendar-oriented feasts and pilgrimages (2Ch 31:3; cf. Ex 23:14–19; Nu 10:10; for additional details on calendar festivals, see comments on 2Ch 2:4).

4–8 In conjunction with his organization of priests and Levites into their designated areas of spiritual responsibility (cf. v.2), Hezekiah takes steps to reestablish the biblically mandated means of providing for these servants of the temple so that they may "devote themselves to the Law of the Lord"

(v.4). In light of the setting of Chronicles, this reminder not to neglect the caretaking of priests and Levites (cf. Dt 12:19; 14:27) would have added significance in the Second Temple period (cf. Ne 13:10; Mal 3:8). The generosity shown by the people (v.5; following the example of Hezekiah, v.3) is consistent with other outward aspects of spiritual fruit shown by the congregation (cf. 2Ch 30:12, 14; 31:1).

The reference to grain, new wine, and oil (v.5) is reflected in Mosaic literature as offerings appointed for priests (cf. Nu 18:12). In addition, priests received part of the offerings presented to God (Lev 6:16–18, 26; 7:6, 28–34; Nu 18:9), other gifts such as grain (Nu 18:9), the firstfruits from the land (Nu 18:13), and other animals and items devoted to the Lord (Nu 18:18–19). All this relates to the reality that priests did not have an inheritance in the land and thus were limited in their ability to grow crops or raise flocks and herds (cf. Nu 18:20). These were intended to provide for the sustenance of the priests and their families (cf. vv.9–10, 18; Nu 18:9–11, 13). While honey is not mentioned as a designated gift for priests, it could be an "above-and-beyond" gesture on the part of the givers.

With respect to Levites (recall that all priests were Levites, but not all Levites were priests; see comments on 5:4–6), they were granted "all the tithes in Israel as their inheritance" (vv.5–6; cf. Nu 18:21, 24). Like the priests, they did not receive a landed inheritance and thus would be unable to farm or pasture flocks (Nu 18:23–24; Dt 10:9; 18:1–2). Thus these tithes of the offerings of grain and animals presented by the Israelites were intended to provide sustenance for Levites and their families (cf. vv.9–10, 18; Nu 18:31; Dt 14:27–29). Note that Levites are instructed to set apart a tithe of the tithe they received ("the best part" [cf. Nu 18:25, 29–32], likely the "holy things dedicated to the LORD" in v.6), which would in turn go to the priests (Nu 18:28).

Hezekiah praises the people for obediently and abundantly responding to this call of God (vv.6–7; cf. Dt 14:22–29). In the light of their obedience and generosity, Hezekiah blesses the people (v.8), similar to David's (cf. 1Ch 16:2) and Solomon's (cf. 2Ch 6:3–11) blessings. Indeed, the storage and faithful disbursement of accumulated tithes (vv.11–18; cf. Dt 14:28–29) act as a means of appropriating God's blessing ("so that the LORD your God may bless you in all the work of your hands"; Dt 14:29). Note that tithes have also been appointed for "aliens, the fatherless, and the widows who live in your towns" (Dt 14:29).

9–10 In light of the "heaps" of provisions being set aside for the priests and Levites (vv.4–8), the chief priest tells Hezekiah that the priests and Levites have more than enough to eat "because the LORD has blessed his people" (cf. Dt 14:29). This great display of generosity is reminiscent of the generosity shown by the people during pivotal moments in Israel's history, including the construction of the Tent of Meeting (cf. Ex 36:2–7) and during David's preparation for the Jerusalem temple (cf. 1Ch 29:6–9).

11 In light of the "heaps" of provisions being set aside for the priests and Levites (vv.4–8), Hezekiah orders the construction of storage areas

in the temple complex. Hezekiah's efforts are either a revamping of existing side storage areas reflected in the tripartite design of Solomon's temple or the construction of additional storage capacity. In addition to foodstuffs as here, such storage rooms were used to store a wide variety of items needed by priests in their temple ministry. Such "side rooms" were under the charge of Levites (cf. 1Ch 23:28).

12–19 In conjunction with the construction of storage space (v.11) to handle the "heaps" of tithes and offerings, steps are taken to handle the logistics of distributing the tithes and offerings to the priests and Levites in Jerusalem and throughout Judah. Emphasis is placed on the carefulness and faithfulness of those overseeing the logistical effort as an aspect of spiritual service. Both the accounting of the tithes, contributions, and gifts and the distribution of these gifts are overseen by Levites (Conaniah and Kore the gatekeeper, respectively; vv.12, 14), appointed by King Hezekiah and the high priest Azariah (v.13).

Thus provisions are distributed to all who are eligible according to genealogical records, including priests in outlying towns (v.15; cf. Jos 21:1–42), males involved in temple service (v.16), priestly and Levitical families in Jerusalem (vv.17–18), and priestly and Levitical families in rural areas (v.19; cf. Jos 21:41–42; on the different provisions appointed to priests and Levites, see comments on vv.4–8; on other distinctions between priests and Levites, see comments on 5:4–6, 12–13).

20–21 This remarkable summary statement of praise (namely, "good and right and faithful … in everything … obedience … sought his God … worked wholeheartedly … prospered") closes out the Chronicler's account of Hezekiah's reforms and is similar to the opening statement about his reign (cf. 29:2). As such, these remarks "frame" the overwhelmingly positive events of Hezekiah's reign (chs. 29–31) and create a literary separation between these positive events and the following narrative (ch. 32), in which Hezekiah's imperfections surface. Hezekiah's reign is especially marked by an intense and sustained focus on "obedience to the laws and the commands" of God (e.g., 29:15, 25; 30:12, 16; 31:3).

NOTES

10 The relationship (if any) between the priest Azaziah and the priest of the same name who challenged King Uzziah some decades earlier (26:16–20) is uncertain.

16 The age of males three years old or more may be a textual issue. Note the age of thirty indicated at 1 Chronicles 23:3. Conversely, recall the young age of Samuel at the start of his time at Shiloh (1Sa 1:21–28).

17 On the age details of thirty and twenty for Levites, see Note at 1 Chronicles 23:3.

4. The Invasion of the Assyrian King Sennacherib (2Ch 32:1–23)

¹After all that Hezekiah had so faithfully done, Sennacherib king of Assyria came and invaded Judah. He laid siege to the fortified cities, thinking to conquer them for himself. ²When Hezekiah saw that Sennacherib had come and that he intended to make war on Jerusalem, ³he consulted with his officials and military staff about blocking off the water from the springs outside the city, and they helped him. ⁴A large force of men assembled, and they blocked all the springs and the stream that flowed through the land. "Why should the kings of Assyria come and find plenty of water?" they said. ⁵Then he worked hard repairing all the broken sections of the wall and building towers on it. He built another wall outside that one and reinforced the supporting terraces of the City of David. He also made large numbers of weapons and shields.

⁶He appointed military officers over the people and assembled them before him in the square at the city gate and encouraged them with these words: ⁷"Be strong and courageous. Do not be afraid or discouraged because of the king of Assyria and the vast army with him, for there is a greater power with us than with him. ⁸With him is only the arm of flesh, but with us is the LORD our God to help us and to fight our battles." And the people gained confidence from what Hezekiah the king of Judah said.

⁹Later, when Sennacherib king of Assyria and all his forces were laying siege to Lachish, he sent his officers to Jerusalem with this message for Hezekiah king of Judah and for all the people of Judah who were there:

¹⁰"This is what Sennacherib king of Assyria says: On what are you basing your confidence, that you remain in Jerusalem under siege? ¹¹When Hezekiah says, 'The LORD our God will save us from the hand of the king of Assyria,' he is misleading you, to let

you die of hunger and thirst. [12]Did not Hezekiah himself remove this god's high places and altars, saying to Judah and Jerusalem, 'You must worship before one altar and burn sacrifices on it'?

[13]"Do you not know what I and my fathers have done to all the peoples of the other lands? Were the gods of those nations ever able to deliver their land from my hand? [14]Who of all the gods of these nations that my fathers destroyed has been able to save his people from me? How then can your god deliver you from my hand? [15]Now do not let Hezekiah deceive you and mislead you like this. Do not believe him, for no god of any nation or kingdom has been able to deliver his people from my hand or the hand of my fathers. How much less will your god deliver you from my hand!"

[16]Sennacherib's officers spoke further against the LORD God and against his servant Hezekiah. [17]The king also wrote letters insulting the LORD, the God of Israel, and saying this against him: "Just as the gods of the peoples of the other lands did not rescue their people from my hand, so the god of Hezekiah will not rescue his people from my hand." [18]Then they called out in Hebrew to the people of Jerusalem who were on the wall, to terrify them and make them afraid in order to capture the city. [19]They spoke about the God of Jerusalem as they did about the gods of the other peoples of the world — the work of men's hands.

[20]King Hezekiah and the prophet Isaiah son of Amoz cried out in prayer to heaven about this. [21]And the LORD sent an angel, who annihilated all the fighting men and the leaders and officers in the camp of the Assyrian king. So he withdrew to his own land in disgrace. And when he went into the temple of his god, some of his sons cut him down with the sword.

[22]So the LORD saved Hezekiah and the people of Jerusalem from the hand of Sennacherib king of Assyria and from the hand of all others. He took care of them on every side. [23]Many brought offerings to Jerusalem for the LORD and valuable gifts for Hezekiah king of Judah. From then on he was highly regarded by all the nations.

COMMENTARY

1 In the time following Hezekiah reforms (chs. 29–31; Hezekiah's fourteenth year, see 2Ki 18:13; see comment on 2Ch 29:1), Judah faced a significant threat from the Assyrians. As noted above (cf. 30:1–11), in conjunction with his reforms Hezekiah began to restore relations with those remaining in the north (from "Beersheba to Dan") by inviting those who had not been deported to come to Jerusalem to celebrate Passover. In time, Hezekiah's religious reforms likely contributed to his desire to throw off the Assyrian yoke he inherited from his father, Ahaz.

Following the death of Sargon II and the ascension of Sargon's son Sennacherib (ca. 705 BC), Hezekiah took steps to assert Judean independence from Assyrian vassalage and prepared Judah for an

Assyrian invasion (vv.2–5; 2Ki 18:7). Hezekiah was not alone in his desire to gain independence from Assyrian hegemony as rebellion broke out in several parts of the Assyrian Empire. In addition, following the death of Sargon II, Merodach-Baladan II retook the throne of Babylon. At the same time (perhaps with some coordination), rebellion broke out in western states, including Judah.

This is the context in which Hezekiah imprisoned a pro-Assyrian Ekron king, Padi (recall the attempt by Pekah and Rezin to force Judah's participation in their anti-Assyrian coalition by installing a compliant king, the "Son of Tabeel"; cf. *COS*, 2:119B [quoted below in comments on vv. 21–22]; Isa 7:6). Note that 2 Chronicles 32:31; 2 Kings 18:20–21, 24 (= Isa 36:5–6, 9) and 2 Kings 20:12–19 (= Isa 39:1–8) imply some type of support for Hezekiah's rebellion against Assyria from Egypt and Babylon. Once he defeated the forces of Merodach-Baladan II, Sennacherib set off to deal with the western rebellion. Sidon and Ashkelon quickly surrendered, and Ammon, Moab, Edom, and Philistia are noted as paying tribute (cf. *ANET*, 287–88). During this campaign Sennacherib was met by a large Egyptian force (probably sent by Shebitku) en route to Ekron (*ANET*, 287), but the overall impact of the Egyptian force was limited as Sennacherib soon moved into the confines of Judah (see W. R. Gallagher, *Sennacherib's Campaign to Judah: New Studies* [Leiden: Brill, 1999], 160–216).

In the backdrop of Hezekiah's rebellion against Assyrian hegemony was Hezekiah's apparent alliance with Babylon (hinted at in v.31), which was likewise an Assyrian vassal by this time. As seen in earlier incidents involving Asa (cf. 16:1–9), Amaziah (cf. 25:7–10), and Ahaz (cf. 28:5–25), such attempts at military-political alliances were seen theologically as reflecting trust in human beings rather than God and his covenantal promises (contrast Jehoshaphat's faith in 20:12; cf. Dt 20:1–4).

Hezekiah's display of misdirected trust in Babylon drew the rebuke of the prophet Isaiah, ultimately foreshadowing the Babylonian captivity (cf. Isa 39:3–7; also see comments on v.31).

2–5 In light of the looming Assyrian invasion, Hezekiah took impressive steps to prepare Judah for the onslaught of the Assyrian army. Given that Hezekiah was coregent with his father Ahaz when the Assyrians destroyed and deported the northern kingdom (ca. 722/21 BC), Hezekiah's preparation reflects his firsthand knowledge of the significant threat posed by the Assyrian army. In addition, Hezekiah's careful planning and preparation efforts were aided by Sennacherib's distraction with Babylonian unrest, affording Hezekiah approximately four years of preparation time (ca. 705–701 BC).

In his preparations, Hezekiah pushed westward in order to control approaches to the hill country, including retaking territory in the Shephelah lost during the days of his father Ahaz (cf. 28:17–18), and defeating the Philistines "as far as Gaza" (2Ki 18:8). To the south and southeast Hezekiah deployed Simeonites to push back Edomites, Amalekites, and Meunites (cf. 1Ch 4:41–43). In addition, Hezekiah manufactured weaponry, made watchtowers, fortified key cities (v.5; cf. 2Ki 18:8), and strategically stored food provisions (see comments on vv.27–30).

In addition, Hezekiah fortified "the Millo" ("supporting terraces," 32:5; see NIV note) and also expanded the confines of the city of Jerusalem by what is known as the Broad Wall, described as "another wall outside" the original city wall (v.5). This twenty-foot-thick wall expanded the walled portion of Jerusalem toward the western hill and allowed the city to accommodate the rising population as the Assyrian invasion drew near (see M. Broshi, "The Expansion of Jerusalem in the Reigns of Hezekiah and Manasseh," *IEJ* 24 [1974]: 21–26).

Hezekiah's most impressive achievement, however, was the tapping into the upper outlet of the Gihon spring and channeling the water underground (via the Siloam Tunnel) to the western side of the City of David (vv.3–4, 30). As a result, Jerusalem had ongoing access to fresh water that was out of the view (and access) of the Assyrian army (vv.3–4; see additional details on this tunnel at vv.27–30).

6–8 In addition to his physical preparations and fortifications, Hezekiah sought to prepare the hearts of the military men who would defend Judah. As this section and the subsequent sections will show (cf. vv.9–19, 20–21), much of the Chronicler's summary of the Assyrian threat against Judah unfolded as a battle of words (speeches) and ideologies (cf. Selman, 508). Note that the people became "steadfast on account of the words of Hezekiah" (lit. trans. of v.8; NIV, "the people gained confidence"). Hezekiah encouraged the military leaders to be strong and courageous, words that would remind the people of the same words spoken to Joshua as the Israelites prepared to enter the Promised Land (cf. Dt 31:7–8; Jos 1:5–9).

In short, to be strong and courageous is to be immovably committed to obedience and trust in God. Note that Hezekiah's exhortation to "be strong and courageous" is rooted in the notion of God's presence with his covenantal people ("with us is the LORD our God," v.8), a reality greater than any weapon an army could muster. Also see the Reflection on divine presence in ch. 1.

9–19 The threat sent by Sennacherib was set within the Assyrian assault on the city of Lachish (Tell ed-Duweir; v.9), a well-fortified garrison city strategically located in the Judean Shephelah about thirty miles south/southwest of Jerusalem. This siege is depicted in over sixty linear feet of wall reliefs from Sennacherib's palace at Nineveh (see *ANEP* figs. 371–74). The reliefs provide a graphic

reenactment of the Assyrian assault on Lachish, including depictions of siege machinery, movable assault towers, battering rams, and soldiers wielding a variety of weapons (see D. Ussishkin, "The Assyrian Attack on Lachish: The Archaeological Evidence from the Southwest Corner of the Site," *TA* 17 [1990]: 53–86).

The message presented by the officers of Sennacherib was consistent with standard Assyrian practices of intimidation. As noted above (see comments on vv.6–8), the Chronicler's summary of the Assyrian threat against Judah unfolded as a battle of words (speeches) and ideologies. Ultimately the message of the Assyrians, delivered orally (vv.10–16), in writing (v.17), and even in the language of those in Jerusalem ("Judean," v.18), amounts to a religious taunt whose core message is the exact opposite of the exhortation delivered by Hezekiah (cf. vv.7–8). In fact, the words of the Assyrian officials (v.17) are reminiscent of the taunts of Goliath, who likewise mocked "the armies of the living God" (1Sa 17:26; cf. 1Sa 17:8–10, 45–47).

Note that the message from Sennacherib implies that the Assyrians were aware of Hezekiah's reforms (v.12) and even Hezekiah's faith in God's deliverance (vv.10–11). Fundamentally, the Assyrians construed the God of Israel as simply another projection of the human tendency to make a god in their own image ("the work of men's hands," v.19), rather than the living God. The sustained taunt of the Assyrian messengers sharply contrasts to the Chronicler's simple remark that Hezekiah and Isaiah "cried out in prayer to heaven about this" (v.20).

20 The remark that Hezekiah and Isaiah "cried out in prayer" to God contrasts with the sustained taunt of the Assyrian messengers sent by Sennacherib (vv.10–19; cf. Mt 6:7). This prayer of Hezekiah and Isaiah exemplifies much of the spirit of Chronicles, in which God is shown as faithful to those who seek him (cf. Solomon's temple-dedication prayer; 6:12–7:16).

21–22 The angelic messenger sent by God in response to the prayer of Hezekiah and Isaiah (v.20) decimated the Assyrian army (vv.21–22; cf. 2Ki 19:35) and immediately removed the threat looming over Jerusalem. Later, the son(s) of Sennacherib assassinated him (v.21), apparently in jealousy over the selection of Esarhaddon as heir to the Assyrian throne (cf. *ANET*, 288–89). However, although Jerusalem was spared as a result this divine deliverance (along with a payoff from the palace and temple treasuries; cf. 2Ki 18:14–16), Sennacherib's invasion brought devastation and massive deportations to the rest of Judah. This devastation was especially felt in the Shephelah, where much of Sennacherib's destruction took place (cf. 2Ki 18:13; Isa 36:1; a total of forty-six cities and countless villages, according to Sennacherib; cf. *ANET*, 288).

In addition, Sennacherib gave some of Judah's territory to the kings of Ashdod, Ekron, and Gaza and imposed massive tribute on Judah—the longest list of tribute from all of Sennacherib's inscriptions. The devastation brought upon Judah by the Assyrian army in 701 BC can be appreciated from this excerpt from Sennacherib's military annals:

> As for Hezekiah, the Judean, I besieged forty-six of his fortified walled cities and surrounding smaller towns, which were without number. Using packed-down ramps and applying battering rams, infantry attacks by mines, breeches, and siege machines, I conquered (them). I took out 200,150 people, young and old, male and female, horses, mules, donkeys, camels, cattle, and sheep, without number, and counted them as spoil. He himself, I locked up within Jerusalem, his royal city, like a bird in a cage. I surrounded him with earthworks, and made it unthinkable for him to exit by the city gate. His cities which I had despoiled I cut off from his land and gave them to Mitinti, king of Ashdod, Padi, king of Ekron and Silli-bel, king of Gaza, and thus diminished his land. [Another variation of this text includes Ashkelon as well.] I imposed dues and gifts for my lordship upon him, in addition to the former tribute, their yearly payment. He, Hezekiah, was overwhelmed by the awesome splendor of my lordship, and he sent me after my departure to Nineveh, my royal city, his elite troops (and) his best soldiers, which he had brought in as reinforcements to strengthen Jerusalem, with 30 talents of gold, 800 talents of silver, choice antimony, large blocks of carnelian, beds (inlaid) with ivory, armchairs (inlaid) with ivory, elephant hides, ivory, ebony-wood, box-wood, multicolored garments, garments of linen, wool (dyed) red-purple and blue-purple, vessels of copper, iron, bronze and tin, chariots, siege shields, lances, armor, daggers for the belt, bows and arrows, countless trappings and implements of war, together with his daughters, his palace women, his male and female singers. He (also) dispatched his messenger to deliver the tribute and to do obeisance. (*COS*, 2:119B)

Following Sennacherib's destruction, Judah's population in the Shephelah was dramatically reduced, while the population in and around Jerusalem grew from an influx of refugees, ultimately resulting in a more centralized and urban society, a demographic shift reflected in several prophetic oracles of the time (e.g., Micah). In short, although there was divine deliverance for Jerusalem, the devastation on the rest of Judah was drastic.

23 Although the invasion of Judah brought a significant amount of devastation, the ultimate, miraculous, divine deliverance of Jerusalem ("the LORD saved Hezekiah and the people of Jerusalem," v.22; cf. v.21) prompted an outflow of worship, offerings, and gifts. Moreover, Hezekiah's divinely enabled (partial) success against the Assyrian army earned him respect in the eyes of the nations.

NOTES

1 The reference in 2 Kings 19:9 to "Tirhakah, the Cushite king of Egypt" as coming to fight against Sennacherib, a degree of tension between Hezekiah's sizable monetary payoff to Sennacherib (cf. 2Ki 18:14–16) and the divine routing, and the subsequent retreat of the Assyrian army (2Ch 32:21–22; 2Ki 19:35–36) have given rise to the proposal that there were two distinct invasions by Sennacherib during the days of Hezekiah recounted in Kings and Chronicles. For a presentation of this view, see W. H. Shea, "Sennacherib's Second Palestinian Campaign," *JBL* 104 (1985): 401–18, esp. 416–18.

With respect to Tirhakah (Taharqa), he did not become pharaoh until about 690 BC, more than ten years after the time of the invasion of Sennacherib summarized above. Given these factors, the two-campaign theory proposes that there was an initial invasion of Judah by Sennacherib in 701 BC, wherein Hezekiah capitulated, paid off Sennacherib, and resumed his vassal status. This is the campaign reflected in Assyrian sources and comprising the biblical account in 2 Kings 18:13–16. The second campaign is postulated to have taken place in 688/687 BC, not long after Tirhakah assumed power in 690 BC, and spans 2 Kings 18:17–19:36. However, there are no known Assyrian sources indicating a battle with Judah during this time. For an overview of Tirhakah and other chronological issues, see A. G. Vaughn, *Theology, History, and Archaeology in the Chronicler's Account of Hezekiah* (Atlanta: Scholars, 1999), 7–14.

Although the two-campaign theory has some compelling factors and maintains sensitivity to the biblical material, the difficulties of having another Assyrian (and Egyptian) campaign to Judah little more than ten years after the massive destruction of 701 BC, the dating of Stratum III at Lachish, and the lack of mention of such a campaign in Assyrian sources favor maintaining the view of one campaign. With respect to Tirhakah, his presence in the campaign of 701 BC was likely as a field commander for the pharaoh Shebitku, and his title of "king" within the passage is best explained as a proleptic use of his later title of king/pharaoh (Vaughn, 8–14, 81–87). The shift of the text between the submission and payment of Hezekiah and the victory of Yahweh over the Assyrian forces should be seen as a combination of the ebb and flow of battle conditions as well as the increased reliance on Yahweh evidenced in the passage.

21 In order to close out the account, the death notice of Sennacherib is given, although his actual death does not come for another twenty years (681 BC; similarly, recall that the death notation for Terah is given well before his death [Ge 11:32]).

5. Hezekiah's Illness (2Ch 32:24–26)

²⁴In those days Hezekiah became ill and was at the point of death. He prayed to the LORD, who answered him and gave him a miraculous sign. ²⁵But Hezekiah's heart was proud and he did not respond to the kindness shown him; therefore the LORD's wrath was on him and on Judah and Jerusalem. ²⁶Then Hezekiah repented of the pride of his heart, as did the people of Jerusalem; therefore the LORD's wrath did not come upon them during the days of Hezekiah.

COMMENTARY

24–26 The nonspecific expression "in those days" (v.24) allows for the possibility that this illness happened earlier in Hezekiah's reign (cf. 2Ki 20:1–11; Isa 38:1–22). Ultimately, Hezekiah's more serious "illness" is that of pride (v.25; ditto the people of Jerusalem, v.26), since God resists the proud (v.25) but gives grace to the humble (v.26). The "sign" (v.24) given to Hezekiah is the backward movement of the sun's shadow (cf. 2Ki 20:8–11; Isa 38:7–8). Again prayer (v.24) and repentance (v.26) are central to God's expression of grace and healing and the Chronicler's message of true spirituality. As the instance of Manasseh shows, there is no limit to divine grace in the midst of human humility and contrition (cf. 2Ch 33:12–13).

6. Hezekiah's Wealth and Accomplishments (2Ch 32:27–31)

[27]Hezekiah had very great riches and honor, and he made treasuries for his silver and gold and for his precious stones, spices, shields and all kinds of valuables. [28]He also made buildings to store the harvest of grain, new wine and oil; and he made stalls for various kinds of cattle, and pens for the flocks. [29]He built villages and acquired great numbers of flocks and herds, for God had given him very great riches.

[30]It was Hezekiah who blocked the upper outlet of the Gihon spring and channeled the water down to the west side of the City of David. He succeeded in everything he undertook. [31]But when envoys were sent by the rulers of Babylon to ask him about the miraculous sign that had occurred in the land, God left him to test him and to know everything that was in his heart.

COMMENTARY

27–30 These verses function as (another) summary of Hezekiah's wealth, success, and accomplishments (cf. 31:20–21). Hezekiah's riches in treasures, buildings, animals, and agriculture are a function of divine blessing and favor. Moreover, such divine blessings have a close connection with wisdom (cf. Pr 3:13–18; 8:15–21) and thus place Hezekiah's blessings in parallel with those of David (1Ch 29:28) and Solomon (1Ch 29:25; 2Ch 1:11–12; 9:13–28).

Hezekiah's efforts at strategically storing needed food provisions (v.28) are reflected in the discovery of more than twelve hundred large storage containers (or pieces thereof) stamped with the notation "belonging to the king" (Heb. *lmlk*). These *lmlk* jars reflect a high level of state planning and an established logistical infrastructure for the production, delivery, and management of such royal foodstuffs. In addition to agricultural resources, Hezekiah organized efforts to care for the herds and flocks belonging to the Judean monarchy (v.29; see N. Na'aman, "Hezekiah's Fortified Cities and the LMLK stamps," *BASOR* 261 [1986]: 5–21).

As noted above (cf. comments on 32:2–5), Hezekiah's most impressive engineering achievement was the tapping into the upper outlet of the Gihon spring and channeling the water to the western side of the City of David (v.30; cf. vv.3–4). Since the only year-round source of water for Jerusalem (the Gihon Spring) is found outside the city walls (in the Kidron Valley), the lack of a safeguarded fresh water supply was an ongoing area of vulnerability for Jerusalem. To address this vulnerability Hezekiah set two teams of workmen about fifteen hundred feet apart to dig a tunnel far underground to channel the Gihon water supply to a collection pool within the city. The digging of this tunnel (known as Hezekiah's Tunnel as well as the Siloam Tunnel), was commemorated by the workers with an inscription (the Siloam Tunnel Inscription) placed deep within the tunnel in the area where the two teams met, connecting the full length of the tunnel (*COS*, 2:28). As a result, Jerusalem had ongoing access to fresh water that was out of the view (and access) of the Assyrian army (vv.3–4; see Y. Shiloh, "Jerusalem's Water Supply during Siege: The Rediscovery of Warren's Shaft," *BAR* 7 [1981]: 24–39).

31 Chronologically, this visit by the envoys of Babylon likely precedes the invasion of Sennach-erib. If this is the case, the emissaries of Mero-dach-Baladan II likely visit Hezekiah to explore cooperation in their common goal of throwing off the Assyrian yoke (recall that Babylon, like Judah, was an Assyrian vassal at this time). This visit may connect to the closely timed revolts of Babylon and alliance in the east and Judah and allies in the west following the death of Sargon II.

As reflected in earlier incidents involving Asa (cf. 16:1–9), Amaziah (cf. 25:7–10), and Ahaz (cf. 28:5–25), such attempts at military-political alliances are seen theologically as reflecting trust in man rather than God and his covenantal promises (contrast Jehoshaphat's faith in 20:12; cf. Dt 20:1–4). The notion of placing some confidence and trust outside of Yahweh is especially lamented in Chronicles and the prophetic literature (cf. Isa 31:1–3; 39:1–7). God's testing of Hezekiah's heart in the midst of the Assyrian crisis ultimately reveals imperfections in his trust and faith in Yahweh. Poignantly, the prophet Isaiah's rebuke of Hezekiah in the midst of this Babylonian visit ultimately foreshadows the Babylonian captivity (cf. Isa 39:3–7).

7. Hezekiah's Regnal Summary (2Ch 32:32–33)

³²The other events of Hezekiah's reign and his acts of devotion are written in the vision of the prophet Isaiah son of Amoz in the book of the kings of Judah and Israel. ³³Hezekiah rested with his fathers and was buried on the hill where the tombs of David's descendants are. All Judah and the people of Jerusalem honored him when he died. And Manasseh his son succeeded him as king.

COMMENTARY

32–33 On prophetic regnal annotations, see comments on 12:15 and the Introduction. Note the similarity of the expression "vision of the prophet Isaiah" here with the opening to the book of Isaiah (Isa 1:1). In the light of his overwhelmingly faithful reign, Hezekiah is buried with honor in the royal tombs.

N. The Reign of Manasseh (2Ch 33:1–20)

OVERVIEW

During the fifty-five-year reign of Manasseh, Judah was a vassal to three Assyrian monarchs: Sennacherib, Esarhaddon, and Assurbanipal. By way of a short historical sketch, during his final regnal years Sennacherib was engaged with the northern areas of his kingdom and Babylon until being assassinated by his sons in 681 BC following the appointment of his youngest son, Esarhaddon, as heir to the Assyrian throne (recall 32:21). Esarhaddon (681–667 BC) focused considerable effort attempting to conquer Egypt and eventually established Assyrian control over Lower (northern) Egypt, including Memphis and the Delta Region (ca. 671 BC). Esarhaddon's son Ashurbanipal (667–630 BC) took occupation of Egypt even farther by successfully penetrating as far south as Thebes (Luxor, or biblical No-Amon) in ca. 664 BC (cf. the oracle of Na 3). In these battles Ashurbanipal used troops supplied by vassals, including troops supplied by Manasseh of Judah (*ANET*, 294).

¹Manasseh was twelve years old when he became king, and he reigned in Jerusalem fifty-five years. ²He did evil in the eyes of the LORD, following the detestable practices of the nations the LORD had driven out before the Israelites. ³He rebuilt the high places his father Hezekiah had demolished; he also erected altars to the Baals and made Asherah poles. He bowed down to all the starry hosts and worshiped them. ⁴He built altars in the temple of the LORD, of which the LORD had said, "My Name will remain in Jerusalem forever." ⁵In both courts of the temple of the LORD, he built altars to all the starry hosts. ⁶He sacrificed his sons in the fire in the Valley of Ben Hinnom, practiced sorcery, divination and witchcraft, and consulted mediums and spiritists. He did much evil in the eyes of the LORD, provoking him to anger.

⁷He took the carved image he had made and put it in God's temple, of which God had said to David and to his son Solomon, "In this temple and in Jerusalem, which I have chosen out of all the tribes of Israel, I will put my Name forever. ⁸I will not again make the feet of the Israelites leave the land I assigned to your forefathers, if only they will be careful to do everything I commanded them concerning all the laws, decrees and ordinances given through Moses." ⁹But Manasseh led Judah and the people of Jerusalem astray, so that they did more evil than the nations the LORD had destroyed before the Israelites.

¹⁰The LORD spoke to Manasseh and his people, but they paid no attention. ¹¹So the LORD brought against them the army commanders of the king of Assyria, who took Manasseh prisoner, put a hook in his nose, bound him with bronze shackles and took him to Babylon. ¹²In his distress he sought the favor of the LORD his God and humbled himself greatly before the God of his fathers. ¹³And when he prayed to him, the LORD was moved by his

entreaty and listened to his plea; so he brought him back to Jerusalem and to his kingdom. Then Manasseh knew that the LORD is God.

¹⁴Afterward he rebuilt the outer wall of the City of David, west of the Gihon spring in the valley, as far as the entrance of the Fish Gate and encircling the hill of Ophel; he also made it much higher. He stationed military commanders in all the fortified cities in Judah.

¹⁵He got rid of the foreign gods and removed the image from the temple of the LORD, as well as all the altars he had built on the temple hill and in Jerusalem; and he threw them out of the city. ¹⁶Then he restored the altar of the LORD and sacrificed fellowship offerings and thank offerings on it, and told Judah to serve the LORD, the God of Israel. ¹⁷The people, however, continued to sacrifice at the high places, but only to the LORD their God.

¹⁸The other events of Manasseh's reign, including his prayer to his God and the words the seers spoke to him in the name of the LORD, the God of Israel, are written in the annals of the kings of Israel. ¹⁹His prayer and how God was moved by his entreaty, as well as all his sins and unfaithfulness, and the sites where he built high places and set up Asherah poles and idols before he humbled himself—all are written in the records of the seers. ²⁰Manasseh rested with his fathers and was buried in his palace. And Amon his son succeeded him as king.

1 Manasseh's long reign extended from ca. 708–643 BC and likely included a ten-year coregency with his father, Hezekiah, from 708–698 BC. As with Joash (24:1) and Josiah (34:1), Manasseh was enthroned at a very early age. During his fifty-five-year reign, Judah was a vassal to three Assyrian monarchs: Sennacherib, Esarhaddon, and Assurbanipal (see Overview).

2–8 The breadth and depth of Manasseh's wickedness closely resemble the pattern of his ungodly grandfather, Ahaz (e.g., 28:2–4, 22–25), rather than his godly father, Hezekiah. Manasseh's wickedness even exceeds that of the nations that previously lived in Canaan (v.9). The enumeration of Manasseh's wicked practices is the essence of Deuteronomic covenantal unfaithfulness:

> When you enter the land the LORD your God is giving you, do not learn to imitate the detestable ways of the nations there. Let no one be found among you who sacrifices his son or daughter in the fire, who practices divination or sorcery, interprets omens, engages in witchcraft, or casts spells, or who is a medium or spiritist or who consults the dead. Anyone who does these things is detestable to the LORD, and because of these detestable practices the LORD your God will drive out those nations before you. You must be blameless before the LORD your God. (Dt 18:9–13)

In addition to the common Israelite tendency to worship Baal and Asherah (given their connection to rain and fertility, v.3; see comments on Baal at 11:15; 28:2, and on Asherah and Asherah poles at 14:3), Manasseh also erected idolatrous altars to the "starry hosts" within the Jerusalem temple and in its courtyards (vv.4–5). Manasseh's actions reversed the consecration of the temple accomplished during Hezekiah's reforms (29:3–19).

The worship of aspects of the cosmos ("starry hosts," vv.3, 5), such as celestial bodies, was common in the biblical world, as reflected in the number of gods named after the moon, sun, and planets. Moreover, divination via celestial bodies was common, particularly in Mesopotamia. Manasseh's close ties to Assyria might imply that Manasseh had adopted the worship of Mesopotamian astral deities. Astral worship was also connected with Canaanite deities such as Asherah (note the connection between Baal/Asherah worship and the starry host in 2Ki 17:16). Ezekiel 8:16 and Jeremiah 19:1–14 imply that astral worship was taking place in the late Judean period.

On child sacrifice and the connection between the Valley of Ben Hinnom and Gehenna (v.6), see comments on 28:3. On high places (v.3), see comments on 1:3–5. All such actions of idolatry and disobedience put Judah in the position of forfeiting her residency in the Promised Land (vv.7–8; recall God's words in 7:19–22). In fact, Manasseh's apostasy is connected with God's intent to "wipe out Jerusalem" in a manner reminiscent of what happened to the northern kingdom (cf. 2Ki 21:10–15).

9 Manasseh's wicked ways even exceed the practices of the nations that previously lived in Canaan. Like Ahaz (cf. 28:19), Manasseh is guilty of leading God's people astray, the opposite of his regnal responsibilities within the covenantal framework (Dt 17:14–20).

10–11 As a consequence of his flagrant idolatry and refusal to repent, Manasseh is "exiled" in then Assyrian-controlled *Babylon*, which aptly foreshadows what will happen to the nation as a whole as a result of persistent covenantal unfaithfulness. As he did during the apostasy of Joash (cf. 24:19), the Lord speaks to Manasseh and the people of Judah (v.10), demonstrating his love, patience, and grace toward his covenantal people. The summary of God's efforts to bring his people back to himself is reminiscent of the closing verses of Chronicles reflecting on the Babylonian exile:

> The Lord, the God of their fathers, sent word to them through his messengers again and again,

because he had pity on his people and on his dwelling place. But they mocked God's messengers, despised his words and scoffed at his prophets until the wrath of the Lord was aroused against his people and there was no remedy. (2Ch 36:15–16)

There is nothing within the biblical material or inscriptions from Assyria that specifies the reason(s) behind Manasseh's imprisonment. Of course, theologically, the reason is covenantal unfaithfulness (vv.2–10). The remark that Manasseh is brought to Babylon with a hook in his nose and bound with bronze shackles implies some type of disloyalty on his part (see the image of Assyrian captives in *ANEP*, fig. 447). Similarly, this imagery is used by Yahweh to describe a consequence of covenantal disloyalty (cf. Isa 37:29; Eze 19:4; Am 4:2). Assyrian texts describe Manasseh as a loyal vassal who assisted with Assyrian building projects during the reign of Esarhaddon and contributed soldiers during the reign of Ashurbanipal.

12–13 Unlike Ahaz, who grew in unfaithfulness in the midst of divinely orchestrated distress (cf. 2Ch 28:19, 22), Manasseh responds to God in deep humility ("humbled himself greatly") and the fruit of repentance ("sought the favor of the Lord"; cf. vv.15–16). In addition, Manasseh seeks the Lord in earnest prayer that touches God's heart (v.13). This short summary of Manasseh's repentance and God's response (absent from the account in Kings) is perhaps one of the most hope-inducing passages in the OT. In short, these two verses emphatically show that God can restore *anyone* who seeks him in true repentance, regardless of the depth of darkness of that person's ungodliness.

As with the apostle Paul's statement of being the "worst" of sinners and yet experiencing God's grace (1Ti 1:16), Manasseh is arguably the worst of sinful Judean kings (cf. vv.2–9). But he too experiences God's forgiving grace. Note that a core principle in God's response to Solomon's temple-dedication prayer is reflected in the reconciliation granted to Manasseh (cf. 7:14, 11–22). Following his repentance and seeking of God, the Lord brings Manasseh back from exile in Babylon and restores his kingdom (cf. Nebuchadnezzar in Da 4), an act of graciousness that deepens Manasseh's understanding of God's strength and mercy.

14 Manasseh's rebuilding (or repairing) of the outer wall seems to be both a reflex of his heightened sense of his regnal responsibilities and perhaps is also a tangible outworking of God's "healing the land" in the light of Manasseh's humility and seeking of God (cf. 7:14). The description of this wall suggests it was connected with the Broad Wall constructed by Hezekiah (see comments on 32:5).

15–16 As a tangible reflection of his inner spiritual renewal, Manasseh begins to dismantle the numerous elements of idolatry and covenantal unfaithfulness that he had so intensely pursued earlier in his reign (cf. vv.2–9). In addition, Manasseh consecrates ("restores") the temple in order to reinstitute sacrificial worship, as his father Hezekiah had

done (29:3–35). Note that while Manasseh had previously "led Judah and the people of Jerusalem astray" (v.9), he now instructs Judah to serve Yahweh (v.16; cf. Asa in 14:4).

17 Although temple service and offerings have been established, the people do not abandon their propensity for sacrificing at the high places. While these high-place sacrifices are "only to the LORD," this practice is nonetheless against God's established parameters for centralized worship in Jerusalem (Dt 12:13–14; also see comments on high places at 2Ch 1:3–5).

18–20 While the specific *words* of Manasseh's prayer are not recorded, it is ultimately the disposition of his *heart* that draws God to him in forgiveness and restoration (see comments on vv.12–13; on Manasseh's horrendous sinful activity, see comments on vv.2–8, 9). The significance of Manasseh's unusual burial within "his palace" is unknown (see Dillard, 269; on the sources used in regnal annotations, including prophetic sources [here "seers"], see comments on 12:15 and the Introduction).

NOTE

3 The plural of Baal ("Baals") is uncommon and may relate to the variety of deities pursued in Israel and the region of Syro-Canaan. (Recall that "Baal" is an honorific title meaning "lord" and typically, but not exclusively, was the shortened way of referring to the Syro-Canaanite storm god Baal-Hadad.)

O. The Reign of Amon (2Ch 33:21–25)

²¹Amon was twenty-two years old when he became king, and he reigned in Jerusalem two years. ²²He did evil in the eyes of the LORD, as his father Manasseh had done. Amon worshiped and offered sacrifices to all the idols Manasseh had made. ²³But unlike his father Manasseh, he did not humble himself before the LORD; Amon increased his guilt.

²⁴Amon's officials conspired against him and assassinated him in his palace. ²⁵Then the people of the land killed all who had plotted against King Amon, and they made Josiah his son king in his place.

COMMENTARY

21 Amon's brief reign lasts from about 643–641 BC, a time of significant Assyrian power in the biblical world (see Overview to ch. 33).

22–23 Amon's reign is both parallel to and in stark contrast to that of his father, Manasseh. Like Manasseh, the sins of Amon are legion; but unlike Manasseh he does not humble himself and seek the Lord while he can be found. Sadly, one of the consequences of Manasseh's wicked years was his "discipling" of his son Amon in the realm of spiritual apostasy and idolatry. While Manasseh ultimately sought God in repentance (vv.12–13), Amon is assassinated just two years into his reign (v.24), ushering in the reign of Josiah (v.25).

24–25 The backdrop for Amon's assassination by his palace officials is not clear, but it may be part of a larger political objective (such as a coup or a result of different agendas regarding Judah's continued status as an Assyrian vassal). In addition, it may have related to disgust over Amon's idolatrous ways. Note that the "people of the land" retaliate against Amon's murderous officials and usher in the reign of Josiah. This is yet another regnal situation in which this sociopolitical group plays a pivotal role (see extended discussion on this group at 23:21).

P. The Reign of Josiah (2Ch 34:1–35:27)

OVERVIEW

Josiah's thirty-one-year reign extends from 641–609 BC, a time of decreasing Assyrian strength as a result of a series of revolts across the Assyrian Empire in the 670s through the 640s BC. By 665 BC Assyria had little choice but to recognize the independence of Egypt under the Assyrian-appointed pharaoh Psammetichus I (Psamtik I) and his successor, Neco II. Shortly after the death of Ashurbanipal (ca. 630 BC), Assyria fell into an advanced state of decline, instability, and geographical contraction, as evidenced by Babylon's declaration of independence in 626 BC by Nabopolassar (first ruler of the Neo-Babylonian period and father of Nebuchadnezzar) and an assault on Nineveh by the Medes the following year.

The looming demise of Assyria created a power vacuum in the ancient Near East that Egypt and Babylon were eager to fill, particularly with respect to control of the land bridge known as Israel. Moreover, as a result of the weakening of the Assyrian Empire during the reign of Josiah, Judah began to experience what might be described as "pseudo-independence." This newfound freedom likely played a significant role in the wide array of reforms enacted by Josiah in both Judah and the former territory of the northern kingdom (vv.6–7). Josiah's reforms took place in three periods: his eighth year (ca. 633 BC; v.3), his twelfth year (ca. 629 BC; v.3), and his eighteenth year (ca. 623 BC; v.8). Note that the prophetic ministries of Zephaniah and Jeremiah likely supported the reforms enacted by Josiah.

1. Josiah's Reforms (2Ch 34:1–33)

a. Introduction to Josiah's Reign (2Ch 34:1–2)

¹Josiah was eight years old when he became king, and he reigned in Jerusalem thirty-one years. ²He did what was right in the eyes of the LORD and walked in the ways of his father David, not turning aside to the right or to the left.

COMMENTARY

1 As with Joash (24:1) and Manasseh (33:1), Josiah's reign in Judah begins at an early age, following the assassination of Amon (33:24). As discussed above (see comments on 23:21; 33:24–25), Josiah's installation as king is facilitated by the "people of the land," a sociopolitical group who may have played a significant role in managing the affairs of Judah during Josiah's childhood and adolescent years. Josiah's thirty-one-year reign extended from 641–609 BC, a time of decreasing Assyrian strength (see Overview above).

2 Josiah is one of the few Judean kings noted as walking in the ways of David (cf. Jehoshaphat [17:3–4] and Hezekiah [29:2]), a direct function of his devotion to God's law (cf. 2Ki 23:25; Dt 17:18–20) and of his focused commitment to God (i.e., spiritual life direction; cf. Eph 4:1). Josiah's walk is described as singularly focused on the ways of God, that is, not turning aside to the right or left. Such is the phraseology used in Deuteronomy to describe a focused, disciplined, and God-pleasing spiritual life:

> So be careful to do what the LORD your God has commanded you; do not turn aside to the right or to the left. Walk in all the way that the LORD your God has commanded you, so that you may live and prosper and prolong your days in the land that you will possess. (Dt 5:32–33; cf. 17:20; 28:14)

b. Josiah's Destruction of Idolatry (2Ch 34:3–7)

³In the eighth year of his reign, while he was still young, he began to seek the God of his father David. In his twelfth year he began to purge Judah and Jerusalem of high places, Asherah poles, carved idols and cast images. ⁴Under his direction the altars of the Baals were torn down; he cut to pieces the incense altars that were above them, and smashed the Asherah poles, the idols and the images. These he broke to pieces and scattered over the graves of those who had sacrificed to them. ⁵He burned the bones of the priests on their altars, and so he purged Judah and Jerusalem. ⁶In the towns of Manasseh, Ephraim and Simeon, as far as Naphtali, and in the ruins around them, ⁷he tore down the altars and the Asherah poles and crushed the idols to powder and cut to pieces all the incense altars throughout Israel. Then he went back to Jerusalem.

COMMENTARY

3–5 Josiah's initial period of reform (eighth year; age sixteen) is focused on seeking God. The concept of seeking God with all of one's being should be understood as a foundational element of rightly relating to God (cf. Dt 4:29–31; 6:5; 10:12–21). The second phase of Josiah's reforms (twelfth year; age twenty) is focused on the destruction of articles of idolatry. Such destruction of idolatry and syncretistic worship (high places, foreign altars, sacred stones, and Asherah poles) per Deuteronomic admonition (cf. Dt 16:21–22) was a cornerstone of spiritual reforms and revival, as reflected in the efforts of Asa (2Ch 14:3–5) and Hezekiah (cf. 31:1).

6–7 In addition to Josiah's purging reforms in Judah and Jerusalem (cf. vv.3–5), Josiah pursues a similar line of destroying items of idolatry and syncretistic worship. The weakening of the Assyrian Empire greatly reduced (and eventually eliminated) Assyrian presence in what had been the northern kingdom and enables Josiah's reforms to stretch from his initial geographical confines in Judah ("from Geba to Beersheba," 2Ki 23:8) to cities in the former northern kingdom's tribal territories of Manasseh, Ephraim, Naphtali, and others "throughout Israel." The mention of "as far as Naphtali" implies Josiah's influence extended to the vicinity to the west and even north of the Sea of Chinnereth/Galilee.

In addition, Josiah seems to have expanded Judah west to the coast in the area north of Ashdod, as implied in the Yavneh [Yabneh] Yam Inscription (*ANET*, 568). This northern and western expansion of Judah's border (in what had been the Assyrian provinces of "Samaria" and "Megiddo") is further reflected in Josiah's ability to confront Pharaoh Neco II at Megiddo in the Jezreel Valley (35:20–27; see comments below).

NOTES

3–7 The timing of the three movements of Josiah's reforms may have some correlation with geopolitical events (see F. M. Cross Jr. and D. N. Freedman, "Josiah's Revolt against Assyria," *JNES* 12 [1953]: 56–58; for the association of Josiah's eighteenth year with 2Ki 23:4–20, see Selman, 529–30).

3–4, 7 See the discussion on Baal and Asherah at 14:3. The plural of Baal is uncommon and may relate to the variety of deities pursued in Israel and the region of Syro-Canaan. (Recall that "Baal" is an honorific title meaning "lord" and typically, but not exclusively, was the shortened way of referring to the Syro-Canaanite storm god Baal-Hadad.)

6 With respect to the tribe of Simeon's affiliation with the northern tribes, see Note at 15:9.

c. Josiah's Temple Repairs (2Ch 34:8–13)

⁸In the eighteenth year of Josiah's reign, to purify the land and the temple, he sent Shaphan son of Azaliah and Maaseiah the ruler of the city, with Joah son of Joahaz, the recorder, to repair the temple of the LORD his God.

⁹They went to Hilkiah the high priest and gave him the money that had been brought into the temple of God, which the Levites who were the doorkeepers had collected from the people of Manasseh, Ephraim and the entire remnant of Israel and from all the people of Judah and Benjamin and the inhabitants of Jerusalem. ¹⁰Then they entrusted it to the men appointed to supervise the work on the LORD's temple. These men paid the workers who repaired and restored the temple. ¹¹They also gave money to the carpenters and builders to purchase dressed stone, and timber for joists and beams for the buildings that the kings of Judah had allowed to fall into ruin.

¹²The men did the work faithfully. Over them to direct them were Jahath and Obadiah, Levites descended from Merari, and Zechariah and Meshullam, descended from Kohath. The Levites — all who were skilled in playing musical instruments — ¹³had charge of the laborers and supervised all the workers from job to job. Some of the Levites were secretaries, scribes and doorkeepers.

COMMENTARY

8–13 The final stage in Josiah's reforms covers the restoration of the temple (including the discovery of the "Book of the Law") as well as Josiah's grand celebration of Passover following the restoration of the temple (35:1–19). This third movement in Josiah's reforms receives considerable attention by the Chronicler (34:8–35:19), perhaps in view of similarities with the Chronicler's postexilic audience, including the reconnection of a long-separated community, the need for unity, the importance of a singular focus on God's Word and covenant, and a newly recommissioned temple.

Josiah's repair and restoration of the temple is similar to the earlier efforts of Joash (24:14) and Hezekiah (29:3–36). These temple repairs reverse the neglect of God's house (v.11), the most notable attested during the reigns of Manasseh and Amon. The Chronicler emphasizes the involvement of the whole community through the giving of funds by both Judeans and those from the prior northern kingdom tribal areas (v.9), the skill and commitment ("faithfulness") shown by those involved in the refurbishment process itself (cf. vv.10–13; vv.16–17; cf. 2Ki 22:7), and the oversight provided by the high priest and Levites (vv.9, 12–13). For additional remarks concerning Levitical duties, see comments on 5:4–6 and 5:12–13.

NOTES

8 On the timing of Josiah's reforms with geopolitical events, see Note on 34:3–7.

d. Discovery of the Book of the Law (2Ch 34:14–33)

¹⁴While they were bringing out the money that had been taken into the temple of the Lord, Hilkiah the priest found the Book of the Law of the Lord that had been given through Moses. ¹⁵Hilkiah said to Shaphan the secretary, "I have found the Book of the Law in the temple of the Lord." He gave it to Shaphan.

¹⁶Then Shaphan took the book to the king and reported to him:"Your officials are doing everything that has been committed to them. ¹⁷They have paid out the money that was in the temple of the Lord and have entrusted it to the supervisors and workers." ¹⁸Then Shaphan the secretary informed the king, "Hilkiah the priest has given me a book." And Shaphan read from it in the presence of the king.

¹⁹When the king heard the words of the Law, he tore his robes. ²⁰He gave these orders to Hilkiah, Ahikam son of Shaphan, Abdon son of Micah, Shaphan the secretary and Asaiah the king's attendant: ²¹"Go and inquire of the Lord for me and for the remnant in Israel and Judah about what is written in this book that has been found. Great is the Lord's anger that is poured out on us because our fathers have not kept the word of the Lord; they have not acted in accordance with all that is written in this book."

²²Hilkiah and those the king had sent with him went to speak to the prophetess Huldah, who was the wife of Shallum son of Tokhath, the son of Hasrah, keeper of the wardrobe. She lived in Jerusalem, in the Second District.

²³She said to them, "This is what the Lord, the God of Israel, says: Tell the man who sent you to me, ²⁴'This is what the Lord says: I am going to bring disaster on this place and its people—all the curses written in the book that has been read in the presence of the king of Judah. ²⁵Because they have forsaken me and burned incense to other gods and provoked me to anger by all that their hands have made, my anger will be poured out on this place and will not be quenched.' ²⁶Tell the king of Judah, who sent you to inquire of the Lord, 'This is what the Lord, the God of Israel, says concerning the words you heard: ²⁷Because your heart was responsive and you humbled yourself before God when you heard what he spoke against this place and its people, and because you humbled yourself before me and tore your robes and wept in my presence, I have heard you, declares the Lord. ²⁸Now I will gather you to your fathers, and you will be buried in peace. Your eyes will not see all the disaster I am going to bring on this place and on those who live here.'"

So they took her answer back to the king.

²⁹Then the king called together all the elders of Judah and Jerusalem. ³⁰He went up to the temple of the Lord with the men of Judah, the people of Jerusalem, the priests and the Levites—all the people from the least to the greatest. He read in their hearing all the words of the Book of the Covenant, which had been found in the temple of the Lord. ³¹The

king stood by his pillar and renewed the covenant in the presence of the LORD — to follow the LORD and keep his commands, regulations and decrees with all his heart and all his soul, and to obey the words of the covenant written in this book.

³²Then he had everyone in Jerusalem and Benjamin pledge themselves to it; the people of Jerusalem did this in accordance with the covenant of God, the God of their fathers.

³³Josiah removed all the detestable idols from all the territory belonging to the Israelites, and he had all who were present in Israel serve the LORD their God. As long as he lived, they did not fail to follow the LORD, the God of their fathers.

COMMENTARY

14–15 This episode often comes as a surprise to readers who cannot imagine a scroll of the OT being "lost" in the temple. However, the foundation and walls of temples in the biblical world were commonly used as repositories for dedicatory inscriptions, administrative documents, building plans, and religious texts. For example, in the palace of Sin-kasid at Uruk, clay tablets were inserted into the foundation of the temple every sixteen to seventeen inches. Texts discovered during a temple refurbishing project would later be reburied, as reflected in the actions of Assyrian king Tukulti-Ninurta I, who redeposited foundation tablets from the time of Adad-Nirari I into the wall of the temple at Assur (see R. S. Ellis, *Foundation Deposits in Ancient Mesopotamia* [New Haven/London: Yale Univ. Press, 1968], 94–97, 187–97). With this in mind, Hilkiah's "discovery" of the Book of the Law in conjunction with a wide array of temple repairs (vv.10–11) is not as peculiar as it may at first appear.

The "book" (vv.16, 18) that is discovered by the priest Hilkiah is referred to as "the Book of the Law of the LORD," (v.14), the "Book of the Law" (v.15), and the "Book of the Covenant" (v.30). Despite no shortage of speculation, the exact identification of this book is not possible to determine.

Points of comparison can be drawn with Exodus (e.g., Ex 20–24), Leviticus (e.g., Lev 26), Numbers (e.g., Nu 9–10), and Deuteronomy (e.g., Dt 28–31). Given the content of the subsequent narrative, it is probably preferable simply to conclude that some or all of the Pentateuch was discovered at this time.

16–18 Following a short summary of the faithfulness of those repairing the temple (cf. vv.10–11), the scribe Shaphan informs King Josiah of the discovery of "a book," which he then reads in the presence of the king. It is interesting that while the high priest Hilkiah discovers the book, he gives it to the secretary (lit., "scribe"; see Note).

19–21 Despite Josiah's earlier actions of reform (vv.3–7) and temple refurbishing (vv.8–13), the reading of God's Word revealed the degree to which he and his predecessors had fallen short of God's revealed will ("not acted in accordance with all that is written in this book," v.21). Josiah's response is to express grief via the cultural norms of the time (v.19). Notice that Josiah's desire to hear from God relates not only to his concern for Judah but also to his concern for the remnant of Israel (northern kingdom; cf. v.21). Moreover, Josiah's words and actions reflect an implicit recognition of the divine nature and divine authority vested in the Book of the Law of the Lord, and hence the guilt and culpability of the people with respect to the covenant. As Paul notes, the knowledge of God's law causes every mouth to be silenced and renders the whole world "guilty before God" (Ro 3:19 [KJV]).

22 While Josiah sends the scribe (Shaphan) and the high priest (Hilkiah) to "inquire" on behalf of God's people ("for me and for the remnant in Israel and Judah," v.21), they in turn go to the wife of "the keeper of the wardrobe"—the prophetess Huldah. Little is known about this prophetess who declares God's judgment on the nation. The officials of Josiah, however, clearly know of her and opt to seek her intercession in light of the crisis at hand (cf. Barak and Deborah, Jdg 4–5). Although not as commonly as with males, females are noted in various temple, palace, and prophetic roles in parts of the biblical world, including Mari, Mesopotamia, and Egypt.

23–28 The oracle of the prophetess Huldah begins in customary prophetic manner (e.g., something akin to "Thus saith the LORD") and quickly (and succinctly; vv.24–25) proclaims a disaster on the land and God's people that will be meted out according to the stipulations of the Book of the Covenant (e.g., Dt 28:15–68; cf. Lev 26:14–43). In addition to the prophecy of disaster declared against Judah, the prophetess has a separate message for the king that is actually longer than that addressed to Judah (vv.26–28). In short, the prophetess declares that Josiah will not experience the covenantal judgments decreed for Judah (v.28). As reflected in the account of Manasseh (see comments on 33:12–13), Josiah has sincerely humbled himself before God (v.27 [2x]) and displayed godly grief (a function of his responsive [lit., "soft"] heart; v.27).

Huldah's statement that Josiah will be "buried in peace" (v.28) has a degree of tension with the death of Josiah at the hand of the army of Pharaoh Neco (cf. 35:23–24), which hardly seems to be a peaceful demise. Nevertheless, the core emphasis of Huldah's prophecy pertaining to Josiah is that he will be spared the disaster to befall Judah ("your eyes will not see all the disaster …"). Moreover, the remark in question relates to his *burial* ("you will be buried in peace") rather than his means of death.

Alternatively, it is possible that Josiah's later trust and reliance on something apart from God (implicit in his actions to support the Babylonians; see comments on 35:20; 35:21–24) cause him to forfeit part of this promise in line with the dynamic aspect of God's sovereign will. Such a theological dynamic is reflected in Jeremiah's revelatory trip to the potter's house:

> Then the word of the LORD came to me: "O house of Israel, can I not do with you as this potter does?" declares the LORD. "Like clay in the hand of the potter, so are you in my hand, O house of Israel. If at any time I announce that a nation or kingdom is to be uprooted, torn down and destroyed, and if that nation I warned repents of its evil, then I will relent and not inflict on it the disaster I had planned. And if at another time I announce that a nation or kingdom is to be built up and planted, and if it does evil in my sight and does not obey me, then I will reconsider the good I had intended to do for it. (Jer. 18:5–10)

Similarly, note the implication of God's message through the prophet regarding the house of Eli:

> "Therefore the LORD, the God of Israel, declares: 'I promised that your house and your father's house would minister before me forever.' But now the LORD declares: 'Far be it from me! Those who honor me I will honor, but those who despise me will be disdained.'" (1Sa 2:30)

29–32 Despite the message of disaster proclaimed by the prophetess (vv.23–28), Josiah leads the full spectrum of constituents ("from the least to the greatest") of the Judean community—"elders," "men of Judah," "people of Jerusalem," "priests," and "Levites"—in a solemn ceremony of hearing God's law at the temple (recall Solomon's prayer [2Ch 6]) and renewing their commitment to the covenant (34:29–31). Josiah models this covenantal renewal in the presence of the people and Yahweh, stressing his commitment to follow God and keep his commands, regulations, and decrees as similarly commanded by Moses:

> These are the commands, decrees and laws the LORD your God directed me to teach you to observe in the land that you are crossing the Jordan to possess, so that you, your children and their children after them may fear the LORD your God as long as you live by keeping all his decrees and commands that I give you, and so that you may enjoy long life. (Dt 6:1–2)

The details of that which Josiah pledges to keep ("commands, regulations and decrees") found within "the Book of the Covenant" all reflect the increased dependence on a written text in Judean society and the heightened sense of the authority of the written Word of God. Similarly, note the repeated emphasis on doing what was "written"

during Josiah's Passover preparations (cf. 35:1–27). During the time of Ezra and Nehemiah, the people reaffirm their commitment to Yahweh's covenant in *writing* (cf. Neh 9:38).

Josiah commits to keep God's written instructions with "all his heart and all his soul," as likewise commanded by Moses (cf. Dt 6:5–9; 11:13). While not explicitly stated, Josiah's commitment reflects the biblical reality that loving God is inseparable from keeping God's Word: "Love the LORD your God and keep his requirements, his decrees, his laws and his commands always" (Dt 11:1; cf. Jn 15:10, 14; see Reflection below). Following his public declaration, Josiah leads the people also to pledge their commitment to covenantal obedience (v.32; cf. Johnstone, 2:244–45).

33 This summary note implies a continuation of Josiah's reform efforts to destroy objects of idolatry from within the territory of the former northern kingdom (cf. vv.3–7; see comments on 34:3–5; 34:6–7). The statement that the people "did not fail to follow the LORD" *while Josiah was alive* foreshadows the rapid downfall that will happen in Judah following his death (see ch. 36; cf. 12:14).

NOTES

14 For a summary of reasons that favor the book of Deuteronomy as the book that was discovered, see Dillard, 280, and Selman, 531–32. Commonly cited reasons include the emphasis on worship centralization chosen by God (cf. Dt 12:4–7), instructions concerning the destruction of items of idolatry and heterodoxy (e.g., 12:1–3), instructions concerning observing Passover (cf. 16:1–8), and public covenant-reading ceremonies (e.g., 31:7–13). However, none of these points of connection necessitate that Deuteronomy *alone* was discovered at this time.

15–18 Shaphan "the secretary" (הַסֹּפֵר, *hassōpēr*) is better rendered "the *scribe*," as reflected in most translations. As a scribe, Shaphan would be an heir of a rich intellectual heritage in the ancient Near East. As reflected in this episode, the influence of scribes penetrated the power structures of royalty, religion, and commerce in ancient cultures.

REFLECTION

The emphasis on obeying God with all one's heart and soul, central to Josiah's reforms (cf. Hiram's stress of love [2:11–12]), is an important theological principle of the spiritual life. Numerous texts in the Bible stress the necessity of obedience with respect to covenantal instructions and laws. Although often missed in Christian settings, love was a foundational element of OT law and was the basis for God's covenantal choice of Israel (see Dt 7:6–9; Jer 31:3). In fact, the key underlying ethic of Israel's law is arguably love—love of God and love of others. Thus Christ is able to summarize the Law and the Prophets as *loving God with all one's heart, soul, mind, and strength and loving one's neighbor as oneself*. Note this emphasis in Christ's words and Paul's teachings:

"Teacher, which is the greatest commandment in the Law?"

Jesus replied: "'Love the Lord your God with all your heart and with all your soul and with all your mind.' This is the first and greatest commandment. And the second is like it: 'Love your neighbor as yourself.' All the Law and the Prophets hang on these two commandments." (Mt 22:36–40)

Let no debt remain outstanding, except the continuing debt to love one another, for he who loves his fellowman has fulfilled the law. The commandments, "Do not commit adultery," "Do not murder," "Do not steal," "Do not covet," and whatever other commandment there may be, are summed up in this one rule: "Love your neighbor as yourself." Love does no harm to its neighbor. Therefore love is the fulfillment of the law. (Ro 13:8–10)

2. Josiah's Passover Celebration (2Ch 35:1–19)

¹Josiah celebrated the Passover to the LORD in Jerusalem, and the Passover lamb was slaughtered on the fourteenth day of the first month. ²He appointed the priests to their duties and encouraged them in the service of the LORD's temple. ³He said to the Levites, who instructed all Israel and who had been consecrated to the LORD: "Put the sacred ark in the temple that Solomon son of David king of Israel built. It is not to be carried about on your shoulders. Now serve the LORD your God and his people Israel. ⁴Prepare yourselves by families in your divisions, according to the directions written by David king of Israel and by his son Solomon.

⁵"Stand in the holy place with a group of Levites for each subdivision of the families of your fellow countrymen, the lay people. ⁶Slaughter the Passover lambs, consecrate yourselves and prepare the lambs for your fellow countrymen, doing what the LORD commanded through Moses."

⁷Josiah provided for all the lay people who were there a total of thirty thousand sheep and goats for the Passover offerings, and also three thousand cattle—all from the king's own possessions.

⁸His officials also contributed voluntarily to the people and the priests and Levites. Hilkiah, Zechariah and Jehiel, the administrators of God's temple, gave the priests twenty-six

hundred Passover offerings and three hundred cattle. [9]Also Conaniah along with Shemaiah and Nethanel, his brothers, and Hashabiah, Jeiel and Jozabad, the leaders of the Levites, provided five thousand Passover offerings and five hundred head of cattle for the Levites.

[10]The service was arranged and the priests stood in their places with the Levites in their divisions as the king had ordered. [11]The Passover lambs were slaughtered, and the priests sprinkled the blood handed to them, while the Levites skinned the animals. [12]They set aside the burnt offerings to give them to the subdivisions of the families of the people to offer to the LORD, as is written in the Book of Moses. They did the same with the cattle. [13]They roasted the Passover animals over the fire as prescribed, and boiled the holy offerings in pots, caldrons and pans and served them quickly to all the people. [14]After this, they made preparations for themselves and for the priests, because the priests, the descendants of Aaron, were sacrificing the burnt offerings and the fat portions until nightfall. So the Levites made preparations for themselves and for the Aaronic priests.

[15]The musicians, the descendants of Asaph, were in the places prescribed by David, Asaph, Heman and Jeduthun the king's seer. The gatekeepers at each gate did not need to leave their posts, because their fellow Levites made the preparations for them.

[16]So at that time the entire service of the LORD was carried out for the celebration of the Passover and the offering of burnt offerings on the altar of the LORD, as King Josiah had ordered. [17]The Israelites who were present celebrated the Passover at that time and observed the Feast of Unleavened Bread for seven days. [18]The Passover had not been observed like this in Israel since the days of the prophet Samuel; and none of the kings of Israel had ever celebrated such a Passover as did Josiah, with the priests, the Levites and all Judah and Israel who were there with the people of Jerusalem. [19]This Passover was celebrated in the eighteenth year of Josiah's reign.

COMMENTARY

1 Josiah's Passover celebration is a continuation of his spiritual reforms in Judah and portions of Israel, especially the covenantal renewal that takes place following the discovery and reading of the Book of the Covenant (cf. 34:3–32). Note that Josiah's Passover was celebrated in the same (eighteenth) year (cf. v.19) as his extensive temple repairs (which led to the discovery of the Book of the Covenant; cf. 2Ch 34:8). Various statements throughout the Passover account (e.g., "as prescribed," "as is written in the Book of Moses"; cf. vv.6, 12–13) and details

such as the normative fourteenth day of the first month (cf. Nu 9:1–3; 28:16–25; recall Hezekiah's delayed Passover [2Ch 30:2–4]) indicate that the rediscovered Book of the Covenant is central in the organizing of Josiah's Passover celebration.

Similarly, references to following Levitical procedures established by David or Solomon (e.g., vv.4, 15) reflect Josiah's desire to do everything in a God-pleasing manner. Passover was one of the three major pilgrimage festivals (along with the Feast of Tabernacles and Pentecost; see comments on 30:2–4). The

Passover Feast began with the sacrifice of the Passover lamb by the community (cf. Ex 12:6) in Jerusalem (cf. Dt 16:5–6), which hearkens back to Israel's deliverance in (and departure from) Egypt en route to inaugurating a covenantal relationship with Yahweh. Thus the Passover celebrates both God's gracious deliverance of his people *by means of blood* (Ex 12:13, 23; cf. 1Co 5:7; Jn 1:29) as well as the inauguration of a covenant confirmed *by means of blood* (Ex 24:3–8; cf. Mt 26:28; Heb 9:14). As reflected here (cf. v.17), Passover was closely connected with the seven-day Feast of Unleavened Bread (cf. Ex 23:15).

2–6 Josiah's priestly and Levitical appointments in conjunction with his Passover celebration (vv.2–5) are done in accordance with previously prescribed divisions and roles established by David and Solomon (cf. vv.4, 15) and thus continue the theme of obedience to God's law seen in Josiah's reign. On the differing responsibilities of priests and Levites regarding temple service, including the handling of the ark (which may have been removed during the apostasy of Manasseh or Amon), see comments on 5:4–6. On the Mosaic legal instruction and theological significance of the slaughter of the Passover lambs (v.6), see comments on v.1.

Josiah's exhortation that the Levites "consecrate" themselves (v.6) in conjunction with their role in the Passover celebration underscores the notion that deeper internal issues such as personal purity must coincide with external acts of worship. Moreover, as reflected in Hezekiah's Passover celebration (cf. 30:17–20), Levites (rather than the individual offerer) slaughter the Passover lambs.

7–9 The "voluntary" contributions of Passover offerings and more made by the king, royal officials, the high priest, temple administrators, and Levitical leaders reflect both the imagery of generosity as well as that of unity and fellowship enjoyed through the sharing of sacrificial meals and communion offerings. The massive amount of offerings and the

efforts to account for a large number of those in Judah as well as Israel no doubt play into the summary remark that the Passover had not been celebrated like this before (v.18). These numbers are about double the offerings noted in conjunction with Hezekiah's Passover celebration (cf. 30:24), but they pale in comparison to Solomon's temple-dedication offerings (cf. 7:5).

10–16 As also noted earlier (cf. vv.2, 5), Josiah is careful to carry out prescribed regulations regarding priests and Levites (v.10). Likewise, his efforts are again described as being in accordance with the divine instructions found in "the Book of Moses" (v.12; cf. comments on v.1; on the differing responsibilities of priests and Levites for temple service reflected here, see extended comments on 5:4–6). On the theological significance and Pentateuchal instructions concerning the slaughter of the Passover lambs (vv.6, 13), including the sprinkling of the blood (v.11), see comments on v.1.

Following the sacrifices, the people eat together in remembrance of God's great redemptive act (v.13). As also seen in Hezekiah's Passover celebration, but *not* a prescribed priestly or Levitical duty, the Levites skinned the Passover animals (v.11; see Lev 1:2–6). Another element of unity and community (cf. vv.7–9) is seen in the steps taken by the Levites to ensure that their gatekeeper brethren (v.15) and priestly brethren (v.14) have the necessary Passover preparations in order (v.14). For additional remarks concerning the musical duties of Levites, see comments on 5:4–6 and 5:12–13).

17–19 As reflected in Mosaic law, Josiah's Passover is celebrated in conjunction with the seven-day Feast of Unleavened Bread (v.17; cf. Ex 23:14–17; Dt 16:1–17). The Chronicler's remark that Josiah's Passover celebration is a singular event not before witnessed in the history of Israel is similar to the assessment given concerning Hezekiah's Passover celebration (cf. 30:26). In a sense, given the differences between these celebrations (including the anomalies reflected in Hezekiah's late but double-length Passover celebration; cf. ch. 30), both Josiah's "normative" celebration and Hezekiah's "nonnormative" celebration are unique categories unto themselves in the history of Judah and Israel. In addition, while Hezekiah's Passover celebration included some dedicated pilgrims from the former northern kingdom, Josiah's Passover clearly expands the imagery of reunification between northern kingdom and southern kingdom.

NOTES

1, 17 For additional references concerning Mosaic legal instruction on the celebration of Passover and the relationship between Passover and the Feast of Unleavened Bread, see Exodus 12:1-11, 14-16, 43-49; Leviticus 23:5-8; Numbers 28:16-25; Deuteronomy 16:1-8.

19 The timing of Josiah's Passover is sometimes questioned since the discovery of the scroll/Book of the Law (34:14-18) and the Passover celebration are both recorded as taking place in the same year (Josiah's eighteenth year; cf. 34:8; 35:19). Some scholars suggest there was insufficient time for Josiah to make the radical changes noted in 34:19-33 together with the Passover preparations indicated in 35:1-18. Yet, such a rapid response of reform and obedience is consistent with the urgency reflected in Josiah's response to the discovery of the scroll.

3. Josiah's Confrontation with Pharaoh Neco (2Ch 35:20-24)

OVERVIEW

Josiah's encounter with Pharaoh Neco II (also commonly spelled "Necho") took place in 609 BC, thirteen to fourteen years after the discovery of the "Book of the Law" and his subsequent Passover celebration. As noted above (see Overview to 34:1-35:27), the Assyrian Empire entered a rapid state of decline following the death of Ashurbanipal (ca. 630 BC), culminating in the declaration of independence of Babylon in 626 BC. Over the following decade the Babylonian ruler Nabopolassar (father of Nebuchadnezzar) began encroaching into the southern and western regions of Assyrian territory while the Medes were invading the northern parts of Assyrian territory. In ca. 613 BC the Medes and Babylonians joined forces to attack Nineveh, which fell in 612 BC after a three-month siege.

Despite the fall of Nineveh, a portion of the Assyrian army and leadership retreated from Nineveh to the city of Haran, about one hundred miles to the west, and began to reorganize what was left of their political-military structure. A couple of years later the Medes and Babylonians again joined forces to eradicate what was left of the Assyrian Empire in the vicinity of Haran. The Egyptians, under Pharaoh Psammetichus I (Psamtik I), attempted to assist the Assyrians at Haran, but ultimately the Assyrians retreated across the Euphrates River to Carchemish.

While the reasons for Egypt's support of its former enemy (Assyria) are unclear, it may involve a desire to attain a geopolitical status quo in the light of the quickly growing threat of the Neo-Babylonian Empire. In addition, the contraction of the Assyrian Empire had enabled Egypt to regain control over key trade routes passing through parts of Canaan (especially the Coastal Highway through Philistia and Phoenicia). Thus, supporting Assyria against the Babylonians and Medes would also enable Egypt to maintain its newfound hegemony over much of the Levant.

Following this battle, Psammetichus I died, and his son Neco II became ruler in Egypt and subse-

quently organized another large force to help the Assyrians at Carchemish in their attempt to retake the city of Haran. This was the conflict into which Josiah chose to insert himself and all Judah with him (see Donald B. Redford, *Egypt, Canaan, and Israel in Ancient Times* [Princeton, N.J.: Univ. of Princeton Press, 1992], 438–55; Rainey and Notley, 257–60).

> [20] After all this, when Josiah had set the temple in order, Neco king of Egypt went up to fight at Carchemish on the Euphrates, and Josiah marched out to meet him in battle. [21] But Neco sent messengers to him, saying, "What quarrel is there between you and me, O king of Judah? It is not you I am attacking at this time, but the house with which I am at war. God has told me to hurry; so stop opposing God, who is with me, or he will destroy you."
> [22] Josiah, however, would not turn away from him, but disguised himself to engage him in battle. He would not listen to what Neco had said at God's command but went to fight him on the plain of Megiddo.
> [23] Archers shot King Josiah, and he told his officers, "Take me away; I am badly wounded." [24] So they took him out of his chariot, put him in the other chariot he had and brought him to Jerusalem, where he died. He was buried in the tombs of his fathers, and all Judah and Jerusalem mourned for him.

COMMENTARY

20 Following his reforms and Passover celebration, Josiah inserts himself into a conflict involving Assyria, Egypt, and Babylon that will have dramatic implications for the future of Judah (see Overview, above). This sequence of events is reminiscent of Hezekiah's conflict with Assyria following his reforms and Passover celebration (ch. 32). Note the similar introductions to these episodes:

After all that Hezekiah had so faithfully done ... (32:1)
After all this, when Josiah had set the temple in order ... (35:20)

Josiah's encounter with Pharaoh Neco II takes place in 609 BC, thirteen to fourteen years after the discovery of the "Book of the Law" and his subsequent Passover celebration.

21–24 While plausible motives for Egypt's support of its former enemy Assyria likely involve the balance of power in the ancient Near East and control over trade routes in the Levant (see Overview), the motives for Judah's support of the Babylonian-Median coalition (implicit in Josiah's attempt to interfere with Egypt's aid of Assyria) are less clear. The message sent from Neco via envoy emphasizes that the Egyptians had no direct issue with Judah.

It is possible that Josiah was acting independently, with the goal of ensuring that the Assyrians would not return to their former strength and dominance over Judah. However, it seems most likely that Josiah's actions reflected some type of alliance between Judah and Babylon. Recall that such an alliance likely originated during the time of Hezekiah when both Judah and Babylon were vassals of Assyria and desired to throw off the Assyrian yoke (see comments on 32:1; 32:31). As seen with Hezekiah and in earlier incidents involving Asa (cf. 16:1–9), Amaziah (cf. 25:7–10), and Ahaz (cf. 28:5–25), such alliances imply inadequate allegiance to Yahweh and faith in human beings rather than God and his covenantal promises (cf. Isa 31:1–3; 39:1–7).

In the light of this issue of misdirected faith, it is noteworthy that the message sent from Neco is attributed as being from "God" (v.21) and that Josiah's persistence to engage Pharaoh Neco in battle is attributed to Josiah's not listening "to what Neco had said *at God's command*" (v.22, emphasis added). This verse suggests that God was providing Josiah the opportunity to repent of seeking security apart from the Lord.

Josiah's motive(s) aside, his attempt to stop the Egyptian army failed and cost him his life. Moreover, this episode cost Judah her closest taste of independence since Ahaz's submission to Assyrian vassalage over a century earlier (cf. 28:5–25). In addition, Neco's attempt to help Assyria retake Haran ultimately failed, and by late 609 BC the Assyrian Empire ceased to exist. The fall of Assyria came to the delight of many in the ancient Near East, as poetically captured by the prophet Nahum:

O king of Assyria, your shepherds slumber;
    your nobles lie down to rest.
Your people are scattered on the mountains
    with no one to gather them.
Nothing can heal your wound;
    your injury is fatal.
Everyone who hears the news about you
    claps his hands at your fall,
for who has not felt
    your endless cruelty? (Nah 3:18–19)

The ramifications of Josiah's decision to involve Judah in this conflict were enormous. After a long period of Assyrian vassalage, Judah had begun to experience independence (or at least pseudo-independence) during the reign of Josiah in light of the contraction of the Assyrian Empire. However, in the aftermath of Judah's battle with Neco at Megiddo, Josiah was killed in battle (vv.23–24) and Judah became an Egyptian vassal. Only a few years later (ca. 605 BC) Judah would become a Babylonian vassal. Thus in the span of about two decades Judah shifted from Assyrian vassalage to (pseudo-) independence to Egyptian vassalage to Babylonian vassalage.

Moreover, the final three kings of Judah after Jehoahaz (Eliakim/Jehoiakim, Jehoiachin, and Mattaniah/Zedekiah) were placed on the throne by Egypt or Babylonia. Judah's subsequent rebellions against vassalage would ultimately lead to the destruction and deportation of Judah.

NOTES

22 The city of Megiddo is situated above a key pass through the Mount Carmel foothills that connected international trade routes leading to Syria, Egypt, Mesopotamia, and Anatolia. Because of its strategic location (as well as the bottlenecking of the pass in the vicinity of Megiddo before opening to the Jezreel

Valley), the city was frequently a place of epic battle (hence the imagery of Armageddon [lit., "Mount of Megiddo"] in the book of Revelation as a place of epic spiritual battle).

23–24 Josiah's death shows a number of parallels with the death of Ahab of the northern kingdom, including each king disguising himself for battle (18:29; 35:22), death by archers (18:33; 35:23), and injury and removal from battle within a chariot (18:34; 35:24; see Selman, 542).

4. Josiah's Regnal Summary (2Ch 35:25–27)

25 Jeremiah composed laments for Josiah, and to this day all the men and women singers commemorate Josiah in the laments. These became a tradition in Israel and are written in the Laments.
26 The other events of Josiah's reign and his acts of devotion, according to what is written in the Law of the LORD — 27 all the events, from beginning to end, are written in the book of the kings of Israel and Judah.

COMMENTARY

25–27 In addition to the notation that Josiah is buried in the royal tombs and is greatly mourned (v.24), Josiah's death notice has several additional features that underscore his special reign in Judah. For example, Josiah's death prompts the writing of formalized liturgical laments (funerary dirges) commemorating Josiah by the prophet Jeremiah (cf. the book of Lamentations following the fall of Judah). The impact of the reign of Josiah on the soul of the Israelite community is reflected in the continued singing of these laments well after this time.

The most praiseworthy summary given of Josiah's reign over Judah is the mention of his "acts of devotion, according to what is written in the Law of the LORD." This statement captures what was directly and indirectly seen during the different phases of Josiah's reign—namely, a reverence for God's revealed will and a commitment to do what is pleasing in God's sight. On the notations of regnal sources (v.27), see comments at 12:15 and the Introduction.

NOTE

25 The book "Laments" is not extant and was likely a collection of songs of commemoration and mourning.

Q. The Reign of Jehoahaz (2Ch 36:1–3)

1 And the people of the land took Jehoahaz son of Josiah and made him king in Jerusalem in place of his father. 2 Jehoahaz was twenty-three years old when he became

king, and he reigned in Jerusalem three months. ³The king of Egypt dethroned him in Jerusalem and imposed on Judah a levy of a hundred talents of silver and a talent of gold.

COMMENTARY

1 Following the death of Josiah at Megiddo in 609 BC (cf. 35:23–24), his son Jehoahaz (also know as Shallum; cf. 1Ch 3:15; Jer 22:11) is elevated to the throne by the "people of the land." Given that Jehoahaz is the younger brother of Eliakim/Jehoiakim (later enthroned by Pharaoh Neco; see below), it is intriguing to see the sociopolitical group known as "the people of the land" once again imposing their will at a time of regnal crisis. See the extended discussion on this group at 23:21.

2–3 Jehoahaz is quickly "put in chains" (2Ki 23:33), "dethroned," and "carried off" by Pharaoh Neco. Thus, it is possible that Jehoahaz followed in the steps of his father Josiah's pro-Babylonian (and thus anti-Egyptian) policies (see comments on 35:21–24). Pharaoh Neco also extracts a tribute payment of gold and silver from Judah (v.3; cf. 2Ki 23:33–35). After Jehoahaz, the final leaders of Judah will be enthroned by decree of Egypt or Babylon. Jehoahaz's reign lasts only three months

before he is "dethroned" (vv.2–3) by Pharaoh Neco and "carried off" to Egypt (v.4). Pharaoh Neco replaces Jehoahaz with his older brother Eliakim, whose name is changed to "Jehoiakim." Judah would remain an Egyptian vassal until 605 BC.

In the ancient Near East the act of changing a name reflects a change of destiny—a destiny now being shaped by the one powerful enough to effect the name change—and carries with it the expectation of loyalty. This idea of a change of destiny enabled by the name changer and symbolized by the new name may shed light on passages such as Isaiah 62:2 and Revelation 2:17. The names given to Judean rulers by Pharaoh Neco and Nebuchadnezzar retain theophoric elements consistent with Israelite faith rather than incorporating foreign religious elements (cf. Da 1:6–7). For example, Eliakim and Jehoiakim are largely the same name, with a substitution of one theophoric element ("El[i]," God) with another ("Jeho," Yahweh).

NOTE

2–3 The observation that Jehoahaz is the younger brother of Eliakim/Jehoiakim is deduced from the age notations given in vv.2, 5 in light of Jehoahaz's three-month reign.

R. The Reign of Jehoiakim (2Ch 36:4–8)

OVERVIEW

Although Egypt initially assumed control of Syria and Canaan shortly after Josiah's death (609 BC),

Pharaoh Neco was later defeated at Carchemish by the Babylonian king Nabopolassar and his son Nebuchadnezzar (occasionally rendered as "Nebuchadrez-zar") in 605 BC (cf. *COS*, 1:137). The Egyptian army retreated south and was again routed by Nebu-chadnezzar at Hamath and subsequently withdrew to Egypt, leaving Syria and Canaan (including Judah)

under the control of the Neo-Babylonian Empire (cf. 2Ki 24:7). Around this time (ca. 605/604 BC), Nebuchadnezzar ascended the Babylonian throne (605/604–562 BC), assuming control of the rapidly expanding Neo-Babylonian Empire.

> ⁴The king of Egypt made Eliakim, a brother of Jehoahaz, king over Judah and Jerusalem and changed Eliakim's name to Jehoiakim. But Neco took Eliakim's brother Jehoahaz and carried him off to Egypt.
>
> ⁵Jehoiakim was twenty-five years old when he became king, and he reigned in Jeru-salem eleven years. He did evil in the eyes of the LORD his God. ⁶Nebuchadnezzar king of Babylon attacked him and bound him with bronze shackles to take him to Babylon. ⁷Nebuchadnezzar also took to Babylon articles from the temple of the LORD and put them in his temple there.
>
> ⁸The other events of Jehoiakim's reign, the detestable things he did and all that was found against him, are written in the book of the kings of Israel and Judah. And Jehoiachin his son succeeded him as king.

COMMENTARY

4–5 Following Josiah's death in the ill-fated battle at Megiddo (see comments on 35:21–24) Judah became a vassal of the Egyptian Empire. However, just three months after "the people of the land" enthroned Jehoahaz, Pharaoh Neco deposes Jehoahaz, brings him to Egypt, and replaces him with his older brother Eliakim, whose name is changed to "Jehoiakim" (see comments on the sig-nificance of name changing at vv.2–3). Given that Jehoahaz is quickly "dethroned" and "carried off" by Pharaoh Neco, Jehoahaz has probably followed in the steps of his father Josiah's pro-Babylonian (thus anti-Egyptian) policies (see comments on 35:21–24). Jehoiakim's eleven-year reign extended from 609–598 BC, during which time Egypt and Babylonia repeatedly battle for control of the Levant. As with Jehoahaz (although only noted at

2Ki 23:32), Jehoiakim does not walk in the God-honoring ways of his father Josiah but instead does evil in God's eyes.

6–8 On the details leading to Babylonian rule over Judah, see Overview above. Although Jehoia-kim is enthroned by Egypt as an Egyptian vassal, he has little choice but to submit to Babylonian rule. Thus Judah has now changed from being an involuntary vassal of Egypt to an involuntary vassal of Babylonia. A few years later (ca. 601/600 BC) Nebuchadnezzar attempts to invade Egypt, but the Babylonian army is unsuccessful. Given Egypt's suc-cessful defense of its border and the (temporarily) weakened Babylonian forces, Jehoiakim decides to rebel against Nebuchadnezzar (2Ki 24:1), per-haps with a view to restoring his prior allegiance to Egypt.

Because Nebuchadnezzar is preoccupied with rebellion elsewhere, his attack on Judah is delayed about two years (to late 598 BC). Despite the overt rebellion on the part of Jehoiakim, Nebuchadnezzar does not destroy Jerusalem but simply takes some of the holy objects from the temple *into exile* (v.7; cf. v.10; Da 1:1–2). This is the likely time when Jehoiakim is brought in shackles *into exile* in Babylon (v.6; recall Manasseh [cf. 33:10–11]). Note the significant prophetic ministry of Jeremiah during this time (cf. Jer 25:1–11; 36:1–31; 45:1–5). Ultimately, Jeremiah's message to submit to God's judgment in the form of the Babylonian yoke is rejected, leading to the eventual destruction of Jerusalem.

During the time frame of this attack by the Babylonian army (and perhaps after a short stint in Babylon), Jehoiakim dies (perhaps at the hands of those favoring submission to Babylon; recall Jeremiah's ministry) and is replaced by his son Jehoiachin, who quickly surrenders to Nebuchadnezzar. See J. Bright, *A History of Israel* (3rd ed.; Philadelphia: Westminster, 1981), 327; Long, Provan, and Longman, 277; on regnal summaries (v.8) and the sources that are referenced, see comments on 12:15 and the Introduction.

NOTE

6 Another possibility for the timing of Jehoiakim's exile to Babylon is in conjunction with Nebuchadnezzar's trip to Syria in 599 BC.

S. The Reign of Jehoiachin (2Ch 36:9–10)

⁹Jehoiachin was eighteen years old when he became king, and he reigned in Jerusalem three months and ten days. He did evil in the eyes of the LORD. ¹⁰In the spring, King Nebuchadnezzar sent for him and brought him to Babylon, together with articles of value from the temple of the LORD, and he made Jehoiachin's uncle, Zedekiah, king over Judah and Jerusalem.

COMMENTARY

9–10 Sometime within the broader setting of the Babylonian attack on Judah (ca. 598/597 BC) Jehoiakim dies and his son Jehoiachin (also known as "Jeconiah" and "Coniah"; cf. Jer 22:24–30) becomes king, only quickly to surrender to Nebuchadnezzar and subsequently be taken *into exile* to Babylon (recall Jehoiakim [v.6] and Manasseh [cf. 33:10–11])—all within three months of his enthronement. As with Jehoahaz (cf. 2Ki 23:32) and Eliakim/Jehoiakim (v.5), Jehoiachin's reign is characterized by covenantal unfaithfulness, as poetically reflected in this oracle of the prophet Jeremiah:

"As surely as I live," declares the LORD, "even if you, Jehoiachin son of Jehoiakim king of Judah, were a signet ring on my right hand, I would still pull you off. I will hand you over to those who seek your life, those you fear—to Nebuchadnezzar king of Babylon and to the Babylonians. I will hurl you and the mother who gave you birth into another country, where neither of you was born, and there you both will die. You will never come back to the land you long to return to."

> Is this man Jehoiachin a despised, broken pot,
>   an object no one wants?
> Why will he and his children be hurled out,
>   cast into a land they do not know?
> O land, land, land,
>   hear the word of the LORD!
> This is what the LORD says:
> "Record this man as if childless,
>   a man who will not prosper in his lifetime,
> for none of his offspring will prosper,
>   none will sit on the throne of David
>   or rule anymore in Judah." (Jer 22:24–30)

In the aftermath of Judah's surrender to Nebuchadnezzar, Jehoiachin, the queen mother, royal officials, military officers, artisans, and seven thousand soldiers are taken captive to Babylon (cf. 2Ki 24:12, 14–16). In addition, consecrated articles from the temple are taken *into exile* in Babylon (cf. v.7). In conjunction with taking Jehoiachin prisoner, Nebuchadnezzar appoints Mattaniah (whose name he changes to "Zedekiah"; see comments on name changing at 36:2–3) to the Judean throne (v.10; cf. 2Ki 24:14–17). Note that Zedekiah, like Jehoahaz and Eliakim/Jehoiakim, is a son of Josiah.

Despite this appointment of Zedekiah as king in Judah, archaeological findings (such as seal notations) together with biblical references (such as the manner in which Ezekiel dates his oracles and the tracing of the royal genealogy through Jehoiachin; cf. 1Ch 3:17–24) seem to reflect the understanding that Jehoiachin (in exile in Babylon) is seen as the true king over Judah. Jehoiachin is eventually released in about 562 BC during the reign of Amel-Marduk (Evil-Merodach) and treated with honor (2Ki 25:27–30). Although Jehoiachin and others are taken captive to Babylon (cf. v.10; cf. 2Ki 24:11–16) and Nebuchadnezzar plunders "all the treasures of the temple of the LORD and from the royal palace" (2Ki 24:13; cf. *COS*, 1:137), Jerusalem is spared.

NOTE

9 The Hebrew text here says that Jehoichin is eight years (not eighteen, as in the NIV), but note that he has five children five years later! This could easily happen at an early age with multiple wives and concubines. However, the NIV is justified in the rendering of eighteen years in the light of 2 Kings 24:8 and some LXX manuscripts.

T. The Reign of Zedekiah and the Fall of Jerusalem (2Ch 36:11–19)

¹¹Zedekiah was twenty-one years old when he became king, and he reigned in Jerusalem eleven years. ¹²He did evil in the eyes of the LORD his God and did not humble himself before Jeremiah the prophet, who spoke the word of the LORD. ¹³He also rebelled against King Nebuchadnezzar, who had made him take an oath in God's name. He became

stiff-necked and hardened his heart and would not turn to the LORD, the God of Israel. [14]Furthermore, all the leaders of the priests and the people became more and more unfaithful, following all the detestable practices of the nations and defiling the temple of the LORD, which he had consecrated in Jerusalem.

[15]The LORD, the God of their fathers, sent word to them through his messengers again and again, because he had pity on his people and on his dwelling place. [16]But they mocked God's messengers, despised his words and scoffed at his prophets until the wrath of the LORD was aroused against his people and there was no remedy. [17]He brought up against them the king of the Babylonians, who killed their young men with the sword in the sanctuary, and spared neither young man nor young woman, old man or aged. God handed all of them over to Nebuchadnezzar. [18]He carried to Babylon all the articles from the temple of God, both large and small, and the treasures of the LORD's temple and the treasures of the king and his officials. [19]They set fire to God's temple and broke down the wall of Jerusalem; they burned all the palaces and destroyed everything of value there.

COMMENTARY

11–13 Following Jehoiachin's surrender and removal to Babylon (cf. 2Ch 36:10), Nebuchadnezzar appoints Jehoiachin's uncle Mattaniah (son of Josiah and brother of Jehoahaz and Eliakim/ Jehoikim) as king in Judah and changes his name to "Zedekiah" (see comments on name changing at vv.2–3). His eleven-year reign in Judah begins in ca. 597 and ends in the downfall and destruction of Jerusalem (586 BC). As with Jehoahaz (cf. 2Ki 23:32), Eliakim/Jehoiakim (v.5), and Jehoiachin (v.9), Zedekiah's reign is characterized by covenantal unfaithfulness (v.12). The extended summary of Zedekiah's unfaithfulness draws on a broad theological backdrop of OT expressions used to describe the persistent rebelliousness of Israel (and humankind) against the authority of God (cf. Ne 9:16–17):

- "did evil in the eyes of the LORD" (v.12);
- "did not humble himself" (v.12);
- "rebelled" (v.13);

- "stiff-necked" (v.13);
- "hardened his heart" (v.13);
- "would not turn to the LORD" (v.13).

All these traits are in direct opposition to his role as king charged with upholding and promoting righteousness in the land (cf. Dt 17:14–20).

Zedekiah's rebellion against Nebuchadnezzar (v.13) will be a watershed moment in the history of Judah. Although Jehoiachin had surrendered to Nebuchadnezzar and was brought captive to Babylon along with numerous others (cf. vv.9–10 above), Judah continues to explore the possibility of throwing off Babylonian hegemony. This disposition on the part of Judah and Zedekiah may have been fostered by the strength and presence of Egypt under pharaohs Psammetichus II (Psamtik II, ca. 595–89 BC) and Apries (Hophra, ca. 589–70 BC), who sought to reestablish Egyptian influence in Syria and Canaan (see A. Malamat, "The Kingdom of Judah between Egypt and Babylon:

A Small State within a Great Power Confrontation," *ST* 44 [1960]: 65–77).

In addition, Zedekiah seems to have been the leader of a coalition of western states including Moab, Ammon, Edom, Tyre, and Sidon, which tested the waters of rebellion briefly in 594/593 BC (the context of Jer 27–28) before disintegrating at the arrival of Nebuchadnezzar. Nevertheless, Zedekiah and other western states rebel again a few years later (somewhere between 591 and 589 BC), perhaps emboldened by a show of strength in the region in 592 BC by Psammetichus II (note the inclusion of Egypt in the oracle of Eze 17). Nebuchadnezzar's response to this latest act of rebellion on the part of Judah, although delayed, is comprehensive and devastating.

14–16 Sadly, the depth of unfaithfulness is not limited to the ungodly reign of Zedekiah (cf. vv. 12–13) but is likewise seen in the hearts of both people and priests. The inclusion of priestly leaders is especially egregious, since a key covenantal responsibility of priests was to "teach the Israelites all the decrees the LORD has given them" (Lev 10:11; cf. Dt 33:8–11). This dereliction of duty on the part of priests is also an issue during the Chronicler's own time, as reflected in the divine message against priests delivered via the postexilic prophet Malachi:

> "And now this admonition is for you, O priests. If you do not listen, and if you do not set your heart to honor my name," says the LORD Almighty, "I will send a curse upon you, and I will curse your blessings. Yes, I have already cursed them, because you have not set your heart to honor me.
>
> "Because of you I will rebuke your descendants; I will spread on your faces the offal from your festival sacrifices, and you will be carried off with it. And you will know that I have sent you this admonition so that my covenant with Levi may continue," says the LORD Almighty. "My covenant

was with him, a covenant of life and peace, and I gave them to him; this called for reverence and he revered me and stood in awe of my name. True instruction was in his mouth and nothing false was found on his lips. He walked with me in peace and uprightness, and turned many from sin.

> "For the lips of a priest ought to preserve knowledge, and from his mouth men should seek instruction—because he is the messenger of the LORD Almighty. [8]But you have turned from the way and by your teaching have caused many to stumble; you have violated the covenant with Levi," says the LORD Almighty. [9]"So I have caused you to be despised and humiliated before all the people, because you have not followed my ways but have shown partiality in matters of the law." (Mal 2:1–9)

Unfortunately, as seen during the reign of Ahaz (cf. 28:22), the response of Zedekiah, priests, and the people to covenantal consequences for unfaithfulness (e.g., serving your enemies; cf. Dt 28:48; Lev 26:14–17) is to become "more and more unfaithful" (v. 14) rather than to repent and return to God. As reflected in Solomon's temple-dedication prayer, such acts of divine chastening have a didactic function ("teach them the right way to live," 2Ch 6:27) as well as a sanctifying function ("so that they will fear you and walk in your ways," 6:31) and thus are a facet of God's love and mercy for his children (cf. Heb 12:5–6). Moreover, the people also rebuff (v. 16: "mocked," "despised," "scoffed") another aspect of God's mercy, namely, the sending of prophetic messengers to admonish God's people to return to him in righteousness (vv. 15–16), as likewise reflected in God's message through Jeremiah:

> Again and again I sent my servants the prophets, who said, 'Do not do this detestable thing that I hate!' But they did not listen or pay attention; they did not turn from their wickedness or stop burning incense to other gods. Therefore, my fierce anger was poured out; it raged against the

towns of Judah and the streets of Jerusalem and made them the desolate ruins they are today. (Jer 44:4–6; cf. Ne 9:26–27)

All told, by increasing their unfaithfulness and rejecting God's messengers, the people of Judah spurn the gracious nature of their God, who abounds in mercy and forgiveness and desires for none to perish (cf. v.15; see comments on 6:22–39; recall the opposite response of Manasseh in 33:18–19). Thus there is "no remedy" (lit., no "healing"; recall the use of this imagery in Solomon's temple prayer, esp. 6:12–42, and Yahweh's response, esp. 7:14) for the looming wrath of God (v.16).

17–19 Following the relative leniency shown by Nebuchadnezzar during the previous acts of rebellion shown by Judah, it is now time for Yahweh to bring about what he specifically warned of during the temple-dedication ceremony:

> "But if you turn away and forsake the decrees and commands I have given you and go off to serve other gods and worship them, then I will uproot Israel from my land, which I have given them, and will reject this temple I have consecrated for my Name. I will make it a byword and an object of ridicule among all peoples. And though this temple is now so imposing, all who pass by will be appalled and say, 'Why has the LORD done such a thing to this land and to this temple?' People will answer, 'Because they have forsaken the LORD, the God of their fathers, who brought them out of Egypt, and have embraced other gods, worshiping and serving them—that is why he brought all this disaster on them.'" (2Ch 7:19–22; cf. 1Ki 9:6–9)

Moreover, the looming destruction of Jerusalem and Judah by a fierce nation from afar and the brutal affliction, captivity, and exile of the people are all specifically noted as covenantal judgments for unfaithfulness as seen in this excerpt from Deuteronomy 28:

> Because you did not serve the LORD your God joyfully and gladly in the time of prosperity,

therefore in hunger and thirst, in nakedness and dire poverty, you will serve the enemies the LORD sends against you. He will put an iron yoke on your neck until he has destroyed you.

> The LORD will bring a nation against you from far away, from the ends of the earth, like an eagle swooping down, a nation whose language you will not understand, a fierce-looking nation without respect for the old or pity for the young. They will devour the young of your livestock and the crops of your land until you are destroyed. They will leave you no grain, new wine or oil, nor any calves of your herds or lambs of your flocks until you are ruined. They will lay siege to all the cities throughout your land until the high fortified walls in which you trust fall down. They will besiege all the cities throughout the land the LORD your God is giving you.

> Because of the suffering that your enemy will inflict on you during the siege, you will eat the fruit of the womb, the flesh of the sons and daughters the LORD your God has given you. Even the most gentle and sensitive man among you will have no compassion on his own brother or the wife he loves or his surviving children, and he will not give to one of them any of the flesh of his children that he is eating. It will be all he has left because of the suffering your enemy will inflict on you during the siege of all your cities. The most gentle and sensitive woman among you—so sensitive and gentle that she would not venture to touch the ground with the sole of her foot—will begrudge the husband she loves and her own son or daughter the afterbirth from her womb and the children she bears. For she intends to eat them secretly during the siege and in the distress that your enemy will inflict on you in your cities.

> ... You who were as numerous as the stars in the sky will be left but few in number, because you did not obey the LORD your God. Just as it pleased the LORD to make you prosper and increase in number, so it will please him to ruin and destroy

you. You will be uprooted from the land you are entering to possess.

Then the LORD will scatter you among all nations, from one end of the earth to the other. There you will worship other gods—gods of wood and stone, which neither you nor your fathers have known. Among those nations you will find no repose, no resting place for the sole of your foot. There the LORD will give you an anxious mind, eyes weary with longing, and a despairing heart. You will live in constant suspense, filled with dread both night and day, never sure of your life. In the morning you will say, "If only it were evening!" and in the evening, "If only it were morning!"—because of the terror that will fill your hearts and the sights that your eyes will see. (Dt 28:47–57, 62–67)

The unfolding of this drama of judgment takes place as follows: In response to the most recent rebellion of Judah (see comments on vv.11–13), Nebuchadnezzar begins his assault on Judah in 588/587 BC. After wreaking havoc in the Judean Shephelah and the hill country, the Babylonian army begins an eighteen-month siege of Jerusalem, which is temporarily interrupted by the arrival of Egyptian troops under the command of Pharaoh Apries. The walls of Jerusalem are breached in July 586 BC. In the midst of the assault on Jerusalem, Zedekiah is captured while attempting to flee and is forced to watch the execution of his sons, and then is subsequently blinded and sent into exile (cf. 2Ki 25:4–7).

Once Jerusalem is taken, Nebuchadnezzar II gives the order to his commander (Nebuzaradan; cf. 2Ki 25:8) to destroy the royal palace, burn down the temple of Yahweh, and tear down the Jerusalem city wall. This massive demolishment of Jerusalem takes place in August 586 BC (v.19; cf. 2Ki 25:8–10). Moreover, the remaining valuables of the temple and palace are seized (v.18), and deportation to Babylon follows for those who survive the battle ("the remnant," v.20; note the massive merciless killing of v.17; cf. 2Ki 25:11–20; see O. Edwards, "The Year of Jerusalem's Destruction," *ZAW* 104 [1992]: 101–6).

NOTES

19 The "House of Bullae," discovered within the City of David in Jerusalem, yielded a number of seal impressions from the time of the destruction of Jerusalem. Personal names on these seals match the names of individuals mentioned in Chronicles, Kings, and Jeremiah (see examples of names in Kitchen, 19–21). Examples from Chronicles include "Zechariah," naming the Levite from the time of Josiah (34:12); "Pedaiah," naming a son of Jehoiachin (1Ch 3:17–18); and "Azariah," naming a son of Hilkiah (1Ch 6:13; 9:11).

17–19 The comprehensiveness of God's covenantal judgment on his land, his temple, and his people is emphasized by the fivefold use of the Hebrew particle *kōl/hakkōl* ("all/everything"; cf. GK 3972) in vv.17–21, as well as the use of the literary device of merismus (e.g., "neither young man nor young woman," v.17; "both large and small," v.18). Following the destruction of Jerusalem, Nebuchadnezzar II installs a non-Davidic official named Gedaliah as governor of what is left of Judah (cf. 2Ki 25:22). Gedaliah rules Judah from Mizpah, located about seven miles north of Jerusalem (cf. 2Ki 25:23). Gedaliah is later assassinated, prompting many of those still in Judah to flee to Egypt (cf. 2Ki 25:26).

IV. THE EXILIC PERIOD (2CH 36:20-21)

[20]He carried into exile to Babylon the remnant, who escaped from the sword, and they became servants to him and his sons until the kingdom of Persia came to power. [21]The land enjoyed its sabbath rests; all the time of its desolation it rested, until the seventy years were completed in fulfillment of the word of the LORD spoken by Jeremiah.

COMMENTARY

20–21 Following the destruction of the temple, the city of Jerusalem, and the city wall in August 586 BC (v.19; cf. 2Ki 25:8–10), deportation to Babylon ensued for the survivors ("the remnant," v.20). In the aftermath of the destruction of Jerusalem, the Chronicler offers a brief biblical-theological reflection of the exilic period. In a sense, while the exilic period is one of destruction and judgment, it is also a time of restoration and rest. Note that the Chronicler's words closely echo the aftermath of covenantal unfaithfulness spelled out by God in Leviticus 26:

> I will scatter you among the nations and will draw out my sword and pursue you. Your land will be laid waste, and your cities will lie in ruins. Then the land will enjoy its sabbath years all the time that it lies desolate and you are in the country of your enemies; then the land will rest and enjoy its sabbaths. All the time that it lies desolate, the land will have the rest it did not have during the sabbaths you lived in it. (Lev 26:33–35)

Yet within this same covenantal document the image of restoration, rest, and hope is also seen:

> "'For the land will be deserted by them and will enjoy its sabbaths while it lies desolate without them. They will pay for their sins because they rejected my laws and abhorred my decrees. Yet in spite of

this, when they are in the land of their enemies, I will not reject them or abhor them so as to destroy them completely, breaking my covenant with them. I am the LORD their God. But for their sake I will remember the covenant with their ancestors whom I brought out of Egypt in the sight of the nations to be their God. I am the LORD.'" (Lev 26:43–45)

Likewise, the ultimate hope following the restoration of the seventy-year exile (the time frame of the Chronicler's audience) is vividly summarized by the prophet Jeremiah:

> This is what the LORD says: "When seventy years are completed for Babylon, I will come to you and fulfill my gracious promise to bring you back to this place. For I know the plans I have for you," declares the LORD, "plans to prosper you and not to harm you, plans to give you hope and a future. Then you will call upon me and come and pray to me, and I will listen to you. You will seek me and find me when you seek me with all your heart. I will be found by you," declares the LORD, "and will bring you back from captivity. I will gather you from all the nations and places where I have banished you," declares the LORD, "and will bring you back to the place from which I carried you into exile." (Jer 29:10–14)

The beginning point and ending point of this seventy-year period (Jer 25:8–11; 29:10) is not exactly specified within the biblical material. The most likely possibility is that the destruction of the temple in 586 BC started the seventy-year period, which comes to a close with the dedication of the Second Temple (ca. 516 BC). Another possibility is that the end of the seventy-year period is connected with the Decree of Cyrus (539 BC; cf. 2Ch 36:22), which would imply a beginning point around the death of Josiah (609 BC), after which Judah became a pawn to the geopolitical interests of Egypt and Babylonia.

NOTE

21 Some prefer to see the "seventy" of Jeremiah's prophecy as signifying the *completeness* of God's judgment on his land, his temple, and his people. In this view it is unnecessary to seek an exact seventy-year stretch to see the fulfillment of this prophecy (see Japhet, 1074–76; Selman, 550–51). Also, the statement that the land could now enjoy its Sabbath *rests* might imply that the land had not been given the prescribed rests (one year for each seven years; cf. Lev 25:1–7) since Israel's inception as a nation. The seventy-year "Sabbath rest" period would equate to 490 years, a period corresponding to the start of the Israelite monarchy in about 1040 BC.

V. THE DECREE OF CYRUS (2CH 36:22–23)

> [22]In the first year of Cyrus king of Persia, in order to fulfill the word of the LORD spoken by Jeremiah, the LORD moved the heart of Cyrus king of Persia to make a proclamation throughout his realm and to put it in writing:
> [23]"This is what Cyrus king of Persia says:
> "'The LORD, the God of heaven, has given me all the kingdoms of the earth and he has appointed me to build a temple for him at Jerusalem in Judah. Anyone of his people among you — may the LORD his God be with him, and let him go up.'"

22–23 The death of Nebuchadnezzar in 562 BC set in motion the rapid downfall of the Babylonian Empire. Nebuchadnezzar's son Amel-Marduk (Evil-Merodach) was assassinated after two years, and the next two Babylonian kings only reigned for about five years before Nabonidus assumed the throne.

Nabonidus ruled Babylon from 556–539 BC, but his interest in the moon god Sin (rather than the expected Marduk, head of the Mesopotamian pantheon) caused political and religious friction. After a few years, Nabonidus departed for the Arabian oasis city of Tema (some five hundred miles from Babylon) and appointed his son Belshazzar to rule in his stead (cf. *ANET*, 562–63; 305–7). Meanwhile, the Persian Empire (539–533 BC) continued to gain strength, and by 546 BC Persia was controlling much of the southern region of Babylonia and closing in on Babylon. In 539 BC Cyrus the Persian (559–30 BC), contrary to Nabonidus, presented himself as a loyal worshiper of Marduk and liberator of the Babylonian people. As a result, Cyrus was able to conquer Babylon with hardly a fight.

By conquering the Babylonian Empire Cyrus inherited rule over the various people groups who had been exiled to Babylon (including Judeans). Within his first year he reversed the policy of the Babylonians and allowed deported peoples to return to their homeland. This proclamation (the Decree of Cyrus) is summarized in the closing verses of 2 Chronicles as well as the opening verses of Ezra. In addition, the Decree of Cyrus is preserved in at least two ancient monumental inscriptions (cf. *ANET*, 315–16; *COS*, 2:124). It is directly connected with the outworking of Jeremiah's prophetic oracle (v.22). See Jer 29:12–14 and comments on vv.20–21; see R. de Vaux, "The Decrees of Cyrus and Darius on the Rebuilding of the Temple," in *The Bible and the Ancient Near East* (trans. D. McHugh; London: Darton, Longman, and Todd, 1972), 63–96.

In addition to allowing exiled people groups to return to their homeland, Cyrus also sought to placate the gods of the conquered nations by allowing freedom of worship, as reflected in his respect of Marduk and his reverential words acknowledging Yahweh's sovereignty (v.23). Regardless of the sincerity of Cyrus, Yahweh is clearly using him to advance the divine plan (v.22; cf. Isa 44:28; 45:13), which included not only the return of the Judean people from exile, but also the return of the consecrated items from the temple from exile, and even the Persian funding of the rebuilding of Yahweh's temple (cf. Ezr 1:2–8; 6:1–12).

The final phrase of the Chronicler's work— "Let him go up"—leaves the reader with a sense of anticipation of what will happen next and the realization that they (the Chronicler's audience) are the ones who will finish this story! Thus the Chronicler ends his work with his sustained message of the hope and possibility that comes with faithfulness, as also expressed by God through Jeremiah:

> "'For I know the plans I have for you,' declares the Lord, 'plans to prosper you and not to harm you, plans to give you hope and a future. Then you will call upon me and come and pray to me, and I will listen to you. You will seek me and find me when you seek me with all your heart.'" (Jer 29:11–13)

EZRA AND NEHEMIAH

EDWIN M. YAMAUCHI

Introduction

1. BACKGROUND[1]

The Babylonian exile in the sixth century BC was preceded by earlier deportations from both Israel and Judah by the Assyrians beginning in the eighth century. Tiglath-Pileser III, who brought an end to the Aramean kingdom of Damascus in 732, also attacked Galilee and Gilead and began the first deportations of Israelites (2Ki 15:29) by carrying off at least 13,520 persons to Assyria (*ANET*, 283–84). Ten years later Sargon II claimed the capture of Samaria, the capital of the northern kingdom of Israel (2Ki 17:6; 18:10). Sargon boasted that he carried off 27,290 persons from Israel and replaced them with other populations

---

1. See E. M. Yamauchi, "The Eastern Jewish Diaspora under the Babylonians," in *Mesopotamia and the Bible* (ed. M. W. Chavalas and K. L. Younger Jr.; Grand Rapids: Baker, 2002), 356–77; idem, "The Reconstruction of Jewish Communities during the Persian Empire," *The Journal of the Historical Society* 4 (2004): 1–25.

from Mesopotamia and Syria (*ANET*, 284–87).[2] Cuneiform sources from Assyria, which have yielded about fifty Israelite names, indicate that some were recruited to serve in the armed forces. But since the Israelites had already departed from a strict devotion to Yahweh and had no compunction about intermarriage, they were soon assimilated and became the so-called "Lost Tribes of Israel."[3]

Ezra 4:2 reports that some of those whose offer to help was rejected were brought to the region by the Assyrian king Esarhaddon. Surveys by A. Zertal in the area of Samaria have identified the numerous new sites occupied by those brought into the area by the Assyrians, and have found at a number of sites a type of bowl with decorations similar to cuneiform writing—the first archaeological evidence of these newcomers.[4] Four Neo-Assyrian tablets, dated from 698–648 BC and found at Tell Hadid and Tel Gezer, bear witness to the persons from Babylon and Cutha[5] who were transported to Palestine by the Assyrians. According to Naʾaman and Zadok, "The tablets from Gezer indicate that the deportees continued to call their children by Babylonian names. These are indications that the deportees preserved certain characteristics of their former identity for (at least) half a century."[6]

Judah had escaped the attacks of Tiglath-Pileser III when Azariah (Uzziah) paid tribute to the king (*ANET*, 282), though Gezer was captured. But when Sennacherib attacked Judah in 701 BC, he deported numerous Jews, especially from Lachish.[7] His annals claim that he deported 200,150 from Judah (*ANET*, 22), but this number may be an error for 2,150.

After the fall of Nineveh in 612 BC, prophesied by Nahum, the Chaldeans established the Neo-Babylonian Empire. Their greatest king, Nebuchadnezzar (605–562 BC), attacked Jerusalem in his first year (Da 1:1) and carried off Daniel and his companions to Babylon. Though we have no extrabiblical evidence confirming this attack, the Chaldean Chronicles report the capture of Jerusalem in 597 (2Ki 24).

---

2. On the Israelites deported by the Assyrians and their fate, see K. L. Younger Jr., "The Deportations of the Israelites," *JBL* 117 (1998): 201–27. On the basis of the names found in the spectacular treasury of queens unearthed at Nimrud, S. Dalley has argued that two of the Assyrian queens or consorts may have been Israelite ("Recent Evidence from Assyrian Sources for Judaean History from Uzziah to Manasseh," *JSOT* 28 [2004]: 387–401). But see K. L. Younger Jr., "Yahweh at Ashkelon and Calah? Yahwistic Names in Neo-Assyrian," *VT* 52 (2002): 207–18.

3. The hope that the descendants of the ten northern tribes, who had been exiled by the Assyrians, would one day be regathered, as prophesied by Jeremiah and Ezekiel, generated the legend of "The Ten Lost Tribes," first among Jews and then among Christians. When Columbus first encountered American Indians, some people thought that they were members of these tribes. See A. H. Godbey, *The Lost Tribes—A Myth* (Durham, N.C.: Duke Univ. Press, 1930; repr., New York: KTAV, 1974); R. H. Popkin, "The Lost Tribes, the Caraites and the English Millenarians," *JJS* 37 (1986): 213–27; A. Gross, "The Expulsion and the Search for the Ten Tribes," *Judaism* 41 (1992): 130–47; S. Goldman, ed., *Hebrew and the Bible in America* (Hanover, N.H.: Univ. Press of New England, 1993); S. Gustafson, "Nations of Israelites," *Religion and Literature* 26 (1994): 31–53.

4. A. Zertal, "The Pahwah of Samaria (Northern Israel) during the Persian Period: Types of Settlement, Economy, History and New Discoveries," *Transeu* 3 (1990): 9–21.

5. The association with Cutha was the reason that later Jews called the Samaritans "Cuthites" or "Cuthaeans."

6. N. Naʾaman and R. Zadok, "Assyrian Deportations to the Province of Samerina in the Light of Two Cuneiform Tablets from Tel Hadid," *TA* 27 (2000): 182.

7. On Sennacherib's campaign in 701, see E. M. Yamauchi, "Tirhakah and Other Cushites," in *Africa and the Bible* (Grand Rapids: Baker, 2004), ch. 4.

After a revolt by the Jews, Nebuchadnezzar destroyed the city and its temple in either 587 or 586. Archaeological evidence of the destructiveness of these campaigns is abundant.[8]

In an influential monograph, H. M. Barstad has attempted to overturn the "Myth of the Empty Land," the impression given by the hyperbolic language of Chronicles that the deportations had left Palestine essentially desolate. He minimizes the effects of the Babylonian invasions, stresses the essential continuity of life in Judah, and characterizes Ezra and Nehemiah as giving a one-sided view that completely overlooks any possible contribution of those who remained in the land. Some have cited the discovery in Jerusalem at Ketef Hinnom[9] of the tomb of a wealthy family to support an element of continuity even after the destruction of the temple. But this case may be isolated rather than representative. Since it was the upper classes who were deported, thus leaving behind the poorest of the land (2Ki 25:12; Jer 39:10; 52:16) to work the vineyards and fields, it is not surprising that it was the returning exiles who provided the spiritual and political leadership that enabled Judaism to evolve. A. Faust and O. Lipschits refute Barstad's view that there was continuity in rural Judah.[10]

On the other hand, archaeological evidence confirms the biblical record that the Babylonians spared the cities of Benjamin, to the north of Jerusalem, and made Mizpah (Tell en-Nasbeh)[11] their provincial capital. Archaeological evidence and inscriptions reveal that the Phoenicians occupied the Philistine coast and that the Edomites occupied the area south of Hebron.[12]

One striking difference between the earlier Assyrian deportations and those of the Babylonians was that the former brought newcomers into the land of Israel, whereas the Babylonians did not do the same with the land of Judah. The biblical references to the numbers of people deported by the Babylonians are incomplete and have given rise to differing interpretations. In 597 BC Nebuchadnezzar carried of a total of 10,000 fighting men, craftsmen, and artisans (2Ki 24:14); he also deported 7,000 fighting men and 1,000 craftsmen (2Ki 24:16). On the other hand, Jeremiah enumerates for 597 BC only 3,023 captives (Jer 52:28),

---

8. L. Stager, "The Fury of Babylon," *BAR* 22 (1996): 56–69, 76–77; O. Lipschitz, "Nebuchadrezzar's Policy in 'attu-Land' and the Fate of the Kingdom of Judah," *UF* 30 (1998): 467–87; idem, "Judah, Jerusalem and the Temple 586–539 BC," *Transeu* 22 (2001): 129–42.

9. "Ketef Hinnom" means "Shoulder of Hinnom." In 1980 Gordon Franz, working under the direction of Gabriel Barkay, discovered two silver amulets dated to the seventy century BC and containing citations from the priestly blessing of Numbers 6:24–26. These citations are now the oldest biblical texts ever recovered. See G. Franz, "Archaeology is NOT a Treasure Hunt," *Bible and Spade* 18/2 (2005): 53–59; G. Barkay et al., "The Amulets from Ketef Hinnom: A New Edition and Evaluation," *BASOR* 334 (2004): 41–71; E. B. de Souza, "The Ketef Hinnom Silver Scrolls," *NEASB* 49 (2004): 27–38.

10. A. Faust, "Judah in the Sixth Century BCE: A Rural Perspective," *PEQ* 135 (2003): 37–53; O. Lipschits, "The Rural Settlement in Judah in the Sixth Century BCE: A Rejoinder," *PEQ* 136 (2004): 99–107. See also B. Oded, "Where is the 'Myth of the Empty Land' to be Found?" in *Judah and the Judeans in the Neo-Babylonian Period* (ed. O. Lipschits and J. Blenkinsopp; Winona Lake, Ind.: Eisenbrauns, 2003), 55–74.

11. J. Zorn, "Mizpah: Newly Discovered Stratum Reveals Judah's Other Capital," *BAR* 23/5 (1997): 28–38, 66; O. Lipschitz, "The History of the Benjamin Region under Babylonian Rule," *TA* 26 (1999): 155–90.

12. See J. Elayi and J. Sapin, eds., *Quinze ans de recherche (1985–2000) sur la Transeuphratène à l'époque perse* (Paris: Gabalda, 2000), chs. 2 and 3.

and for 586 BC 832 from Jerusalem (Jer 52:29). In 582, after the murder of the governor Gedaliah, 745 were deported for a grand total of 4,600 (Jer 52:30).

Population estimates for Judah have varied widely (from 250,000 to 80,000), as have estimates of the proportion of those deported (from 10 percent to 50 percent). Albertz[13] has recently calculated that 25 percent of a population of 80,000 was deported.

Onomastic evidence of Israelites deported by the Assyrians and of Judeans deported by the Babylonians has been compiled in a comprehensive reference work by R. Zadok.[14] These data indicate that in a few cases the Israelites retained their identity for a century. Initially, no doubt, the exiles were saddened and disoriented in their enforced exile, as poignantly expressed in Psalm 137:1–6.

Once the exiles were transported to their new homes, most were not reduced to a position of abject slavery but had considerable freedom.[15] Though the Babylonians did use slaves, they had more than enough of them from natural reproduction.[16] Some exiles became dependents of the palace or the temples; they worked the lands that belonged to these institutions.

The Judean exiles were settled in various communities in lower Mesopotamia.[17] Judging from the place names, they were settled on the ruins of earlier cities, such as at Tel Abib ("the mound destroyed by a flood"; Eze 3:15), Tel Mela' ("mound of salt"), and Tel Harša ("mound covered with potsherds"; Ezr 2:59). These lists also indicate that the exiles must have maintained some cohesion as members of local communities; those who returned went "each to his own town" (Ezr 2:1 = Ne 7:6). The descendants of the exiles evidently prospered, since those who returned brought with them numerous servants and animals and were able to make contributions for the sacred services (Ezr 2:65–69; 8:26–27; Ne 7:70–72).

Ezekiel provides an important source for what life was like in exile.[18] His book was subject to much skepticism by earlier scholars. Recent scholarship has restored respect for the integrity and authenticity of the book as an important source for the exile.[19] Ezekiel, who was probably exiled with Jehoiachin, settled on the Kebar River, an irrigation canal near Nippur. We note that he was married (Eze 24:18) and had his own house (8:1). He refers to both the elders of the house of Judah (8:1) and the elders of the house of Israel (14:1; 20:1), who met with him.

A fascinating light on the Jews in Mesopotamia during the later Persian period is shed by the Murashu Tablets, which were found in a room at Nippur in 1893. From 1898 to 1912 H. V. Hilprecht and A. T. Clay published 480 of these texts out of a reported total of 730 tablets. In 1974 Matthew Stolper wrote a dissertation using 179 hitherto unpublished Murashu texts from the University Museum in Pennsylvania

13. R. Albertz, *Israel in Exile: The History and Literature of the Sixth Century BCE* (Atlanta: Scholars, 2003), 88.

14. R. Zadok, *The Pre-Hellenistic Israelite Anthroponymy and Prosopography* (Leuven: Peeters, 1988).

15. B. Oded, *Mass Deportations and Deportees in the Neo-Assyrian Empire* (Wiesbaden: L. Reichert, 1979), 87.

16. M. A. Dandamaev, *Slavery in Babylonia* (Dekalb, Ill.: Northern Illinois Univ. Press, 1984), 457, 459, 652.

17. B. Oded, "The Settlements of the Israelite and the Judean Exiles in Mesopotamia in the 8th–6th Centuries BCE," in *Studies in Historical Geography and Biblical Historiography* (ed. G. Galil and M. Weinfeld; Leiden: Brill, 2000), 91–103.

18. See L. Allen, *Ezekiel 1–19* (WBC; Waco, Tex.: Word, 1990); idem, *Ezekiel 20–48* (WBC; Waco, Tex.: Word, 1994); D. I. Block, *The Book of Ezekiel: Chapters 1–24* (NICOT; Grand Rapids: Eerdmans, 1997); idem, *The Book of Ezekiel: Chapters 25–48* (NICOT; Grand Rapids: Eerdmans, 1998).

19. L. Boadt, "Ezekiel, Book of," *ABD*, 2:711–22.

and four from the British Museum. He reports that the total of texts and fragments is now known to be 879.[20] These texts date from the reigns of Artaxerxes I (464–424 BC) and Darius II (423–404), and mainly from the years 440–414. This archive is the largest single source for conditions in Achaemenid Babylonia.[21]

Murashu and his sons, who managed agricultural land held as estates and fiefs, loaned out money, equipment, and animals. They also collected taxes and rents. Studies of the names of their clients have demonstrated that some of their clients were Jews. No doubt many Jews adopted Babylonian names, particularly those in official positions. Such individuals include the leaders Sheshbazar/Shenazzar (Ezr 1:8; 5:14; 1Ch 3:18) and Zerubbabel (Ezr 3:2), Bilshan (Ezr 2:2), Hattush, Nekoda, Esther (Est 2:7), and Mordecai (Est 2:5). Extrabiblical evidence indicates that at times those with non-Jewish names gave their children Yahwistic names, and other parents with Yahwistic names gave their children non-Jewish (i.e., Babylonian, West Semitic, and even Iranian) names.[22]

Yahwistic names—that is, names ending in the theophoric element *Yh/Yw/Yhw* for Yahweh (spelled in Akkadian *ia-a-ma*)—are useful for identifying Jews and their families in the Murashu archive.[23] Examples include *Tobyaw* = Tobiah, *Banayaw* = Benaiah, and *Zabadyaw* = Zebadiah. Of those identified as Jews, thirty-eight bore Yahwistic names, twenty-three West Semitic names, six Akkadian names, and two Iranian names. The Jews, who were from twenty-eight settlements, constituted only about 3 percent of the twenty-five hundred individuals named in these records.[24] As these texts deal only with the countryside, they do not yield any information on the possible presence of Jews at Nippur itself.

The Jews appear as contracting parties, agents, witnesses, collectors of taxes, and royal officials. A "Gedaliah" served as a mounted archer, a "Hanani" managed the royal poultry farm, and a "Jedaiah" was an agent of a royal steward.[25] There seem to have been no social or commercial barriers between the Jews and the Babylonians. Their prosperous situation may explain why some chose to remain in Mesopotamia when the opportunity to return presented itself. At the same time their growing confidence may explain why, as Bickerman has shown in his analysis, the proportion of Yahwistic names grew larger in the second generation.[26]

A remarkable cuneiform tablet from the reign of Darius, dated to his twenty-fourth year (498 BC), lists in a sales contract a number of Jews[27] who lived in *uru ia-a-hu-du*, that is, "the city of Judah."[28] Many of

---

20. M. W. Stolper, *Entrepreneurs and Empire* (Leiden: Nederlands Historisch-Archaeologisch Instituut te Istanbul, 1985), 1.

21. R. Zadok, *The Jews in Babylonian during the Chaldean and Achaemenian Periods* (Haifa: Univ. of Haifa Press, 1979).

22. E. J. Bickerman, "The Generation of Ezra and Nehemiah," *Studies in Jewish and Christian History* 3 (1986): 316.

23. For studies of comparable Yahwistic names in the Elephantine papyri, see M. H. Silverman, "Hebrew Name-Types in the Elephantine Documents," *Or* 39 (1970): 465–91.

24. M. D. Coogan, *West Semitic Names in the Murašû Documents* (Missoula, Mont.: Scholars, 1976); G. Wallis, "Jüdische Bürger in Babylonien während der Achämeniden-Zeit," *Persica* 9 (1980): 129–85.

25. Cf. M. D. Coogan, "Life in the Diaspora," *BA* 37 (1974): 10.

26. Bickerman comments, "The break with syncretism occurred in the generation of Ezra, who, probably, was born about 500" ("The Generation of Ezra and Nehemiah," 322).

27. F. Joannès and A. Lemaire, "Trois tablettes cunéiformes à onomastique ouest-sémitiques (collection Sh. Moussaïeff)," *Transeu* 17 (1999): 17–34.

28. S. Talmon points out that this same expression was used of Jerusalem in a Babylonian chronicle ("'Exile' and 'Restoration' in the Conceptual World of Ancient Judaism," in *Restoration* [ed. J. M. Scott; Leiden: Brill, 2001], 130).

the names in Akkadian can be compared to Hebrew names found in the Scriptures: *Nêri-Yâma* = Neriah, "Yahweh is my light"; *Yâhû-azari* = Joezer, "Yahweh is my help"; *Abdu-Yâhû* = Obadaiah, "The slave of Yahweh"; *Nadabi-Yâma* = Nedabiah, "Yahweh is generous"; *Ṣaduqu* = Zadok, "Righteous"; *Naḥum* = Nahum, "Comforted"; and *Šamah-Yâma* = Shemaiah, "Yahweh has heard."

An important source of extrabiblical information on the Jewish diaspora in Egypt during the exilic period is the Aramaic documents from the Jewish community on the Elephantine Island near Aswan.[29] This was a military garrison serving under the Persian occupation of Egypt. We are not at all certain how these Jews came to serve in this capacity. B. Porten has pointed out the syncretistic aspects of their religion.[30] M. Silverman, however, argues that their religion was more assimilationist than syncretistic.[31]

Some of the Jewish deportees may have at first been awed by the great ziggurat, the magnificent temple of Marduk, and the fifty other temples in Babylon (Eze 20:32),[32] but most Jews seem to have dismissed the thousands of idols in Mesopotamia (Isa 46:1–2).

Deprived of the temple, the exiles laid emphasis on the observation of the Sabbath,[33] the laws of purity, prayer and confession (Da 9; Ezr 9; Ne 9), and fasting to commemorate the tragic events of the Babylonian attacks (Zec 7:3, 5; 8:19). Great stress was laid on studying and expounding the Torah, as we see in the calling of Ezra the scribe (Ezr 7:6), "a teacher well versed in the Law of Moses."

It has often been surmised that the development of synagogues probably began in Mesopotamia during the exile. The gatherings held under the auspices of Ezekiel (Eze 8:1; 14:1) have been seen as precursors to the synagogue assemblies. The reading, interpreting, and possibly translating of the Scriptures into Aramaic—which were to be important features of the later synagogue service—were part of the great meeting described in Nehemiah 8. But archaeological and inscriptional evidence for synagogues has not been found from the exilic period in Mesopotamia; the earliest evidence is from Ptolemaic Egypt.[34]

The Jews were hardly alone in experiencing the hardships of an enforced exile. Nor were they alone in attempting to maintain their identity, inasmuch as groups such as the Egyptians also tried to do so. But all of them, with the exception of the Jews, were eventually assimilated and disappeared as recognizable entities. Eph'al remarks, "The outstanding survival of the Jews in Babylonia as an entity-in-exile in the subsequent

---

29. B. Porten, *Archives from Elephantine* (Berkeley: Univ. of California Press, 1968); idem, *Jews of Elephantine and Arameans of Syene: Aramaic Texts with Translation* (Jerusalem: The Hebrew Univ. Press, 1976); idem, *The Elephantine Papyri in English* (Leiden: Brill, 1996).

30. Porten, *Archives from Elephantine*.

31. M. Silverman, "The Religion of the Elephantine Jews—A New Approach," in *The Proceedings of the Sixth World Congress of Jewish Studies, 1973* (ed. A. Shin'an; Jerusalem: World Congress of Jewish Studies, 1975), 377–88.

32. See D. J. Wiseman, *Nebuchadrezzar and Babylon* (Oxford: Oxford Univ. Press, 1985).

33. The Sabbath is mentioned fifteen times in Ezekiel. Individuals named "Shabbethai" appear in Ezra 10:15 and Nehemiah 8:7, in the Murashu texts (five individuals), and in the Elephantine papyri (three individuals). See H. A. McKay, *Sabbath and Synagogue* (Leiden: Brill, 1994); H. Weiss, *A Day of Gladness: The Sabbath among Jews and Christians in Antiquity* (Columbia, S.C.: Univ. of South Carolina Press, 2003).

34. M. Hengel, "Proseuche und Synagoge," in *Tradition und Glaube* (ed. G. Jeremias et al.; Göttingen: Vandenhoeck & Ruprecht, 1971), 157–84; cf. E. Yamauchi, "Synagogue," in *Dictionary of Jesus and the Gospels* (ed. J. B. Green et al.; Downers Grove, Ill.: InterVarsity Press, 1992), 781–84.

period—in contrast to the disappearance of all the other foreign ethnic groups there—remains, however, a problem demanding a fuller explanation."[35] No doubt the key to their survival was their faith in a God who, though having momentarily punished them, was nonetheless a faithful, covenant-keeping Lord, who would watch over them even in a foreign Diaspora and restore them to their Holy Land.

Unlike the fate of the members of the so-called "Ten Lost Tribes," who had already lapsed from the exclusive worship of Yahweh, the exiles from Judah who were transported to Mesopotamia were apparently repulsed by the rampant idolatry they beheld in Babylon. During the Assyrian period the recovery of over eight hundred idols, half of which came from Jerusalem, indicate that idolatry persisted in Judah despite the fulminations of the prophets. What the prophets by their preaching could not achieve, the trauma of the Babylonian exile accomplished. As Stern observes, "Another difference is, perhaps, even more meaningful: Since the beginning of the Persian period, in all the territories of Judah and Samaria, there is not a single piece of evidence for any pagan cults!"[36]

The exiles who chose to return to Judah found their territory much diminished. According to M. Avi-Yonah, "Its extent from north to south was about twenty-five miles, from east to west about thirty-two miles. The total area was about eight hundred square miles, of which about one third was an uncultivable desert."[37]

The tiny enclave of Judah was surrounded by antagonistic neighbors. North of Bethel was the province of Samaria. South of Beth-Zur, Judean territory had been overrun by Idumaeans (cf. comments on Ezr 2:22–35). The eastern boundary followed the Jordan River, and the western boundary the Shephelah (low hills). The Philistine coast had been apportioned to Phoenician settlers.[38]

The Persians did make Judah an autonomous province with the right to mint its own coins (see Note on Ne 5:15). The archaeological evidence of coins and jar handles with *YHD* (for Yehud—Judah) comes from Jerusalem, Jericho, Gezer, Tell en-Nasbeh, etc.—all sites within the area demarcated as Jewish territory by Ezra-Nehemiah.

The Jewish territory of Yehud belonged to the satrapy called Abar Nahara, "Beyond the River" (Ezr 4:10, 11, 16–17, 20). The governor of "Beyond the River," who came to investigate the conflict between the Jews and their neighbors, was Tattenai (Ezr 5:3, 6; 6:6, 13), a figure who appears in cuneiform sources as *Tattanu* and is known to have held this position in 486.[39]

35. I. Eph'al, "Western Minorities in Babylonia in the 6th–5th Centuries BC: Maintenance and Cohesion," *Or* 47 (1987): 88.
36. E. Stern, *Archaeology of the Land of the Bible II: The Assyrian, Babylonian and Persian Periods 732–332 BCE* (New York: Doubleday, 2001), 479. On the often-suggested Persian influence on Judaism, see my *Persia and the Bible* (Grand Rapids: Baker, 1990), ch. 12, where the problem of the late (ninth century AD) Zoroastrian eschatological texts is discussed. See also J. Barr, "The Question of Religious Influence: The Case of Zoroastrianism, Judaism and Christianity," *JAAR* 53 (1985): 201–33.
37. M. Avi-Yonah, *The Holy Land* (Grand Rapids: Baker, 1966), 19.
38. See A. Lemaire, "Populations et territoires de la Palestine à l'époque perse," *Transeu* 3 (1990): 31–74.
39. M.W. Stolper, "The Governor of Babylon and Across-the-River in 486 BC," *JNES* 48 (1989): 283–305.

2. REIGN OF ARTAXERXES I[40]

Nehemiah served as the royal cupbearer of Artaxerxes I (Ne 1:1; 2:1), the Achaemenid king who ruled from 464 to 424 BC, as an Elephantine papyrus[41] dated to 407 mentions the sons of Sanballat, the governor of Samaria and adversary of Nehemiah (see *ANET*, 492). Although whether Ezra came in the seventh year (Ezr 7:7) of Artaxerxes I or of Artaxerxes II (403–359) is controversial, the traditional view places Ezra before Nehemiah in the reign of Artaxerxes I (cf. below, "The Order").

Artaxerxes I was nicknamed "Longimanus." According to Plutarch (*Artaxerxes* 1.1), "The first Artaxerxes, among all the kings of Persia the most remarkable for a gentle and noble spirit, was surnamed the Long-handed, his right hand being longer than his left, and was the son of Xerxes." Longimanus was the third son of Xerxes and Amestris. His older brothers were named Darius and Hystaspes. Their father was assassinated in his bedchamber between August and December 465 BC by Artabanus, a powerful courtier. In the ensuing months Artaxerxes, who was but eighteen years old, managed to kill Artabanus and his brother Darius. Then Artaxerxes defeated his brother Hystaspes in Bactria. His first regnal year is reckoned from April 13, 464.

Beginning in 461 Artaxerxes lived at Susa.[42] He used the palace of Darius I until it burned down near the end of his reign. He then moved to Persepolis, where he lived in the former palace of Darius I.[43] He completed the Great Throne Hall begun by Xerxes, as a text in Old Persian and Akkadian indicates.[44] The only other extant Old Persian inscription of this king is an identical one-line text found on four silver dishes.

When Artaxerxes I came to the throne, he was faced with a major revolt in Egypt that was to last a decade. This rebellion was led by Inarus, a Libyan, and Amyrtaeus of Sais. They defeated the Persian satrap Achaemenes, the brother of Xerxes, and gained control of much of the Delta region by 462.

The Athenians, who had been at war with the Persians since the latter invaded Greece in 490 BC, sent two hundred triremes to aid the rebels (*Thucydides* 1.104). In 459 they helped capture Memphis, the capital of Lower Egypt. This situation may have led the Persians to support Ezra's return in 458 to secure a loyal buffer state in Palestine.

In 456 Megabyzus, the satrap of Syria, advanced against Egypt with a huge fleet and army (*Diodorus Siculus* 11.77.1–5). During eighteen months he was able to suppress the revolt and captured Inarus in 456. A fleet of forty Athenian ships with six thousand men sailed into a Persian trap. In spite of promises made by Megabyzus, Inarus was impaled in 454 at the instigation of Amestris, the mother of Artaxerxes I. Angered at this betrayal, Megabyzus revolted against the king from 449–446. If the events of Ezra 4:7–23 took place in this period, Artaxerxes I would have been suspicious of the building activities in Jerusalem.

---

40. See E. M. Yamauchi, *Persia and the Bible* (Grand Rapids: Baker, 1990), ch. 6.
41. A. E. Cowley, *Aramaic Papyri of the Fifth Century* (Oxford: Clarendon, 1923), 30.
42. Ibid., ch. 7.
43. Ibid., ch. 10.
44. R. G. Kent, *Old Persian* (rev. ed.; New Haven, Conn.: Yale Univ. Press, 1953), 113, 115.

How then could the same king have commissioned Nehemiah to rebuild the walls of the city in 445? By then both the Egyptian revolt and the rebellion of Megabyzus had been resolved.[45]

The long, forty-year reign of Artaxerxes I ended when he died from natural causes in the winter of 424 BC—a rarity in view of the frequent assassinations of Persian kings. He was buried in one of the four tombs, probably the second from the left, at Naqsh-i-Rustam, north of Persepolis.

3. CHRONOLOGY

Ezra 1:1 says that Cyrus issued a proclamation to the Jews in his first year. Since Cyrus entered Babylon on October 29, 539 BC, 539 was counted as his accession year. Babylonian and Persian scribes hold that his first *regnal* year over the Babylonians began on New Year's Day, Nisan 1 (March 24), 538.

The Jews used both a religious and a civil calendar. The former began the year in Nisan (March/April). Many scholars assume that the calendar of Judah was identical with the Babylonian calendar, which also began in the spring.

Nehemiah 1:1 declares that Nehemiah was in Susa in the month of Kislev in the twentieth year of Artaxerxes I. According to a Nisan calendar, this regnal year ran from April 13, 445, to April 2, 444; Kislev would be the ninth month from December 5, 445 to January 3, 444. But Nehemiah 2:1 mentions a mission to Jerusalem in the month of Nisan in the twentieth year. Scholars who assume a Nisan-to-Nisan calendar assume a scribal error here because in such a spring-to-spring year Nisan precedes rather than follows Kislev. As Nehemiah 5:14 sets Nehemiah's tenure as governor from the king's twentieth year to his thirty-second, many scholars propose that Nehemiah 1:1 must have originally read the "nineteenth" year—*teša˓ ˓eśrēh* ("nineteen") instead of *˓eśrîm* ("twenty"). Brockington,[46] however, believes that Nehemiah 2:1 should read the "twenty-first" year.

The Israelite civil year began in the fall with the seventh month, Tishri. Some scholars conclude from Nehemiah 1 and 2 that the Israelites in the postexilic period reverted to a fall-to-fall calendar, wherein the twentieth year of Artaxerxes I would have run from October 7, 445 to September 25, 444. No emendation would then be needed.

4. CANON

In the Hebrew Bible Ezra and Nehemiah were reckoned as one book. The division into two books dates to Origen; its division was followed by Jerome in the Vulgate and then adopted into the printed Hebrew Bibles. J. VanderKam expresses a minority view when he holds that both books took shape separately rather than as the result of a single author/editor.[47]

---

45. For a critical analysis of these traditions, see K. G. Hoglund, *Achaemenid Imperial Administration in Syria-Palestine and the Missions of Ezra and Nehemiah* (Atlanta: Scholars, 1992). See also R. J. Littman, "Athens, Persia and The Book of Ezra," *TAPA* 125 (1995): 251–59.

46. H. L. Brockington, *Ezra, Nehemiah and Esther* (London: Nelson, 1969), 127.

47. J. C. Vanderkam, "Ezra-Nehemiah or Ezra and Nehemiah?" in *Priests, Prophets and Scribes: Essays In Honour of Joseph Blenkinsopp* (ed. E. Ulrich et al.; Sheffield: Sheffield Academic, 1992), 55–75.

The books now called "Ezra" and "Nehemiah" were known under the single title of "Ezra" in the earliest Hebrew manuscripts from the tenth century till the fifteenth century. The Masoretic scribes treated the works as one. Their separation into two books appeared in a Hebrew manuscript dated 1448 and then in the printed Bomberg edition of 1525. Josephus (*Ag. Ap.*, 40 [8]) and the Talmud (*b. B. Bat.* 15a) also refer to the book of Ezra, but not to a separate book of Nehemiah.

The oldest manuscripts of the LXX (Vaticanus, Sinaiticus, Alexandrinus) treat Ezra-Nehemiah as one book, called Esdras B (see below, Esdras). Later manuscripts of the LXX, perhaps under Christian influence, treat Ezra and Nehemiah as two works. Melito of Sardis and Eusebius regarded Ezra-Nehemiah as one book. Origen (ca. AD 185–253) was the first Christian to distinguish between two books, which he called I Ezra and II Ezra, but he noted that they were one book in the Hebrew. Jerome in translating the Vulgate called the book of Nehemiah *liber secundus Esdrae*.

Wycliffe's Bible (1382) refers to "The First and Second Book of Esdras." Myles Coverdale's translation (1535) has "The First Boke of Esdras" and "The Second Boke of Esdras, otherwyse called the Boke of Nehemias." Luther adopted the title "Nehemiah." Although Ezra and Nehemiah were regarded as one book from at least the third century BC, the internal evidence indicates two separate compositions later combined (see Literary Form and Authorship).

Although some Palestinian manuscripts begin the historical section of the *Ketubim* (Writings) section with Chronicles and end it with Ezra-Nehemiah, the standard list as recognized by the Babylonian Talmud places Ezra-Nehemiah and Chronicles after Esther. Probably Ezra-Nehemiah was accepted into the Hebrew canon before Chronicles. Ezra-Nehemiah is omitted only from the canons of Theodore of Mopsuestia, of the Nestorians, and of certain Monophysite groups.

5. LITERARY FORM AND AUTHORSHIP

Lists and Documents

As in the closely related books of Chronicles, one notes the prominence of various lists in Ezra-Nehemiah. Evidently obtained from official sources, these lists comprise (1) the vessels of the temple (Ezr 1:9–11); (2) the returned exiles (Ezr 2:1–70; Ne 7:6–73); (3) the genealogy of Ezra (Ezr 7:1–5); (4) the heads of the clans (Ezr 8:1–14), (5) those involved in mixed marriages (Ezr 10:18–43), (6) those who helped rebuild the wall (Ne 3); (7) those who sealed the covenant (Ne 10:1–27); (8) residents of Jerusalem and other cities (Ne 11:3–36); and (9) priests and Levites (Ne 12:1–26). Genealogical lists of ancestors were especially important "during a period when people renewed their claims upon ancestral homes and needed evidence to substantiate their status in the community of the returnees."[48]

Also included in Ezra are seven official documents or letters (all except the first in Aramaic, the first being in Hebrew): (1) the decree of Cyrus (Ezr 1:2–4); (2) the accusation of Rehum and others against the Jews (4:11–16); (3) the reply of Artaxerxes I (4:17–22); (4) the report from Tattenai (5:7–17); (5)

---

48. H. Tadmor, "The Babylonian Exile and the Restoration," in *A History of the Jewish People* (ed. H. Ben-Sasson; Cambridge, Mass.: Harvard Univ. Press, 1976), 159.

the memorandum of Cyrus's decree (6:2b–5); (6) Darius's reply to Tattenai (6:6–22); and (7) the king's authorization to Ezra (7:12–26).

In a study directed by A. Millard, C. Hensley examined these "Ezra Documents" in the light of thirty-two contemporary Persian documents and letters. Hensley concluded:

> The result has been that all of the questions raised concerning the authenticity of the ED [Ezra Documents] are answered in the positive in the light of our present state of knowledge of Achaemenid Persia. The study of the historical context of the ED in matters both general and specific has demonstrated that the ED can be considered authentic Persian documents, as far as history is concerned.[49]

The final conclusion drawn by Hensley is that linguistically, stylistically, and historically the ED correspond perfectly to the nonbiblical documents of the Achaemenid period. An important cuneiform text examined by M. Heltzer corroborates the officials mentioned in Ezra 4 and indicates that one of the officials serving the Persians in this text was Jewish.[50]

The Book of Zerubbabel (Ezra 1–6)[51]

The introductory chapters of Ezra relate the story of the initial return of the Jews after Cyrus's conquest of Babylon, the laying of the altar under Sheshbazzar, and the completion of the temple under Zerubbabel; this section concludes with the celebration of the Passover. Williamson has suggested that Ezra 1–6 was composed after Chronicles about 300 BC as a polemic against the building of the Samaritan temple on Mount Gerizim.[52] Klein, however, believes that the collaborative attitude toward the Persians in this section is an argument against such a late date.[53] Clines would date the books of Chronicles and Ezra/Nehemiah within a few decades after the activities of Ezra and Nehemiah.[54]

The Ezra Memoirs (Ezra 7–10; Nehemiah 8–9)

The Ezra Memoirs (EM), which combines first- and third-person accounts, either stems directly from Ezra or from an editor who had access to a source by Ezra. Williamson argues that the EM is based on a report

---

49. C. Hensley, "The Official Persian Documents in the book of Ezra" (PhD diss.; University of Liverpool, 1977), 233. See also B. Conklin, "The Decrees of God and of Kings in the Aramaic Correspondence of Ezra," *Proceedings of the Eastern Great Lakes and Midwest Biblical Societies* 21 (2001): 81–89. Note, however, should be taken of a study that argues for a Hellenistic date for the Aramaic documents in Ezra 4–6: D. Schwiderski's *Handbuch des nordwestsemitischen Briefformulars: Ein Beitrag zur Echtheitsfrage der aramäistischen Briefe des Esrabuches* (Berlin: de Gruyter, 2000).

50. M. Heltzer, "A Recently Published Babylonian Tablet and the Province of Judah after 516 BCE," *Transeu* 5 (1992): 57–61.

51. See B. Halpern, "A Historiographic Commentary on Ezra 1–6," in *The Hebrew Bible and Its Interpreters* (ed. B. Halpern, W. H. Propp, and D. N. Freedman; Winona Lake, Ind.: Eisenbrauns, 1990), 81–142; B. Porten, "Theme and Structure of Ezra 1–6: From Literature to History," *Transeu* 23 (2002): 27–44.

52. H. G. M. Williamson, "The Composition of Ezra i–vi," *JTS* 34 (1983): 1–30.

53. R. W. Klein, "Ezra-Nehemiah, Books of," *ABD*, 2:733.

54. D. J. A. Clines, *Ezra, Nehemiah, Esther* (NCBC, Grand Rapids: Eerdmans, 1992), 14.

written by Ezra to Artaxerxes I.[55] Ezra, who was both a priest and a skilled scribe (Ezr 7:1–6), led a further group of nearly two thousand Jews in 458 BC from Babylon to their homeland. He was entrusted with considerable treasures and given extraordinary powers according to a letter of Artaxerxes I (7:12–26). In contrast to Nehemiah, Ezra's caravan proceeded without an armed escort. The journey took four months (7:9). When the problem of mixed marriages was brought to his attention, Ezra tore out his own hair (9:3) and then uttered a prayer confessing the sins of his people (9:6–15). An extraordinary convocation then gathered in the rain (Ezr 10:13) to hear Ezra's rebuke of their failings, which led to a dismissal of the foreign wives.

As Nehemiah 8 deals primarily with Ezra, a number of scholars believe that this chapter has been displaced. Williamson argues that the dating system used in this chapter is consistent with the Ezra materials where months are numbered, whereas in the Nehemiah Memoirs (NM) months are always referred to by name (Ne 1:1; 2:1; 6:15). The repositioning of Nehemiah 8 between Ezra 8 and 9 allows for Ezra's work to have been accomplished in a single year. He leaves Mesopotamia in the first month and arrives in Judah in the fifth month (Ezr 7:9). He then reads the Law in the seventh month (Ne 8:2), rather than thirteen years later after Nehemiah's arrival. He concludes by dealing with the problem of mixed marriages on the first day of the first month (Ezr 10:17). This rearrangement, however, assumes that the mention of Nehemiah (Ne 8:9) is a redactional addition, for the verb is singular, and that the list of the signatories to the covenant, including Nehemiah (Ne 10:1) was an invention. D. R. Daniels, who is not persuaded by Williamson's arguments, prefers to consider Nehemiah 8–10 as an integrated unit.[56]

Clines, who assigns Nehemiah 9 to the EM, places Nehemiah 8–9 after Ezra 8. Nehemiah 9, which is attributed to Ezra in the LXX, betrays a critical attitude toward kings (Ne 9:36–37), which contrasts with the generally favorable attitude toward the Persian monarchs found in the EM. Williamson suggests that Nehemiah 9:5b–37 (along with Isaiah 63:7–64:12 and Psalm 106, may have possibly arisen out of liturgies recited at the site of the ruined temple (Jer 41:4–5).[57]

The Nehemiah Memoirs (Nehemiah 1–7, 10–13)

The Nehemiah Memoirs (NM) are accepted by L. L. Grabbe, who is skeptical about the EM.[58] Williamson suggests that Nehemiah originally composed the memoirs in Aramaic as a report to Artaxerxes I after a year in office, and then revised it later to claim due credit for certain achievements, which had not been acknowledged. Although defensive and self-glorifying monuments from Egypt and elsewhere have been cited as parallels, the NM are not addressed to posterity as these were, but to God himself (Ne 5:19; 6:14; 13:14, 22, 29, 31). Williamson believes that the NM and EM were combined about 400 BC.

---

55. H. G. M. Williamson, "Exile and After: Historical Study," in *The Face of Old Testament Studies* (ed. D. W. Baker and B. T. Arnold; Grand Rapids: Baker, 1999), 259.

56. D. R. Daniels, "The Composition of the Ezra-Nehemiah Narrative," in *Ernten, was man sät (K. Koch Festschrift)* (ed. D. R. Daniels et al.; Neukirchen-Vluyn: Neukirchener, 1991), 311–28.

57. H. G. M. Williamson, "Laments at the Destroyed Temple," *BRev* 6/4 (1990): 12–17, 44.

58. L. L. Grabbe, *Judaism from Cyrus to Hadrian* (Minneapolis: Fortress, 1992), 1:98–99.

The Work of the Chronicler

Since the time of L. Zunz (1832) and F. C. Movers (1834), the view has grown, sponsored notably by C. C. Torrey, that the author of Chronicles was also the author/compiler of Ezra-Nehemiah. It had been a scholarly consensus for a century and a half that a so-called "Chronicler" was the author of both Chronicles and Ezra-Nehemiah. Writing early in the twentieth century Torrey regarded the Chronicler as manufacturing historical fiction. Only a few scholars today take the "minimalist" view that the exile is a fiction created by Jewish writers in the Hellenistic era.

While not as dismissive of the Chronicler's accuracy as was Torrey, a number of important scholars (J. Blenkinsopp, D. Talshir) still defend the thesis of a common authorship by the "Chronicler" of Chronicles and Ezra-Nehemiah. For example, in both Chronicles and Ezra-Nehemiah, the building of the first and second temples is described in parallel ways, and both works show great interest in sacred vessels and liturgical music.

Common verses. The verses at the end of Chronicles (2Ch 36:22–23) and at the beginning of Ezra (1:1–3a) are identical (cf. comment on Ezr 1:1); however, this feature may have been a device by the author of Chronicles (or less probably of Ezra) to dovetail the narratives chronologically.[59]

Common words and themes. Both Chronicles and Ezra-Nehemiah exhibit a fondness for lists; for the description of religious festivals; for such phrases as "fathers' houses [NIV, 'families']" (Ezr 2:59; 10:16; Ne 7:61; 10:34, and more than twenty times in Chronicles), "heads of fathers' houses" (frequently in Ezra-Nehemiah and more than twenty times in Chronicles), and "the house of God" (frequently in Ezra-Nehemiah and more than thirty times in Chronicles). Especially striking in these books is the prominence of the Levites and of temple personnel. The Levites, who are only twice mentioned in the books of Samuel (1Sa 6:15; 2Sa 15:24) and but once in the books of Kings (1Ki 8:4) are mentioned by name more than sixty times in Ezra and Nehemiah and about one hundred times in Chronicles.

The words for "singer," "gatekeeper," and "temple servants" (*nᵉtînîm*) are used almost exclusively in Ezra-Nehemiah and Chronicles (cf. comments on Ezr 2:41–43). Because of the Chronicler's interest in the temple and the cult, it is assumed that he was a Levite, or even a singer.

Common theology. Bowman expressed the critical consensus as follows:

> The conclusion that Ezra-Nehemiah was originally part of Chronicles is further supported by the fact that the same late-Hebrew language, the same distinctive literary peculiarities that mark the style of the Chronicler, are found throughout Ezra-Nehemiah. The same presuppositions, interests, points of view, and theological and ecclesiastical conceptions so dominate all these writings that it is apparent that Chronicles-Ezra-Nehemiah was originally a literary unit, the product of one school of thought, if not of a single mind, that can be called "the Chronicler."[60]

So widely established is the view that the Chronicler was responsible for Ezra-Nehemiah that so conservative a scholar as Wright simply states, "It does not seem necessary, then, to spend longer in justifying

---

59. H. G. M. Williamson, *Israel in the Books of Chronicles* (Cambridge: Cambridge Univ. Press, 1977), 9; see also idem, "Did the Author of Chronicles Also Write the Books of Ezra and Nehemiah?" *BRev* 3/1 (1987): 56–59.

60. R. A. Bowman, "The Book of Ezra and Nehemiah," *IB*, 3:552.

the commonly held view that the Chronicler wrote Ezra-Nehemiah in addition to the Books known as Chronicles."[61]

Estimates of the Chronicler's Accuracy

The widespread agreement that Ezra-Nehemiah and Chronicles came from the same pen contrasts with the great disagreement over the value of the Chronicler's own contributions. Conservatives regard the Chronicler's work in Ezra-Nehemiah as that of an editor who has compiled authentic sources. Radical critics, however, view the Chronicler as an imaginative author who wrote fiction.

The outstanding proponent of the latter view was C. C. Torrey, who expressed his views initially in *The Composition and Historical Value of Ezra-Nehemiah*, published in 1896, and continued to maintain them in *The Chronicler's History of Israel*, published in 1954, just two years before his death. According to Torrey the Chronicler was a highly imaginative writer but a poor historian who forged documents for apologetic purposes. Arguing from the failure of Ben Sirach (ca. 180 BC) to mention Ezra, Torrey held that Ezra was a fictitious character. The entire episode of the return was created as a religious polemic against Samaritans. Torrey maintained, "We have no trustworthy evidence that any numerous company returned from Babylonia, nor is it intrinsically likely that such a return took place."[62] Torrey considered the Aramaic of Ezra to be late; and because of the presence of Greek words for coins, he dated the work of the Chronicler to 250 BC. His radical conclusions influenced A. Loisy, G. Holscher, S. A. Cook, W. A. Irwin, and R. H. Pfeiffer.

H. Kellermann has offered a complex and radical analysis dividing the Ezra-Nehemiah materials into very precise categories: (1) an Ezra source, (2) a Nehemiah source, (3) the editorial work of the Chronicler, and (4) the work of a post-Chronicler redactor. In Kellermann's view the Chronicler had but a few scraps of information about Ezra. All other aspects of the Ezra story are fictional midrashim composed by the Chronicler with the aim of making Ezra overshadow Nehemiah. The Chronicler used the Nehemiah source because he approved of its anti-Samaritan bias but disapproved of Nehemiah's Zionist sympathies. The later redactor was a Zionist, a supporter of the Hasmoneans, who sought to counteract the Chronicler's attempt to minimize Nehemiah's role. Though ingenious and imaginative, Kellermann's reconstruction requires more faith than the narrative as it stands.[63]

Ezra as the Chronicler?

Because the last verses of Chronicles are identical with the first verses of Ezra, some scholars argue that Ezra was written by the Chronicler. Other scholars, using the same data, argue that the Chronicler was Ezra himself. The Talmud (*b. B. Bat.* 15a) states that Ezra wrote Chronicles—a view upheld by the church fathers and many of the older commentaries. This thesis, which was revived by A. von Hoonacker, received

61. J. S. Wright, *The Date of Ezra's Coming to Jerusalem* (rev. ed.; London: Tyndale, 1958), 11.
62. C. C. Torrey, *Ezra Studies* (Chicago: Univ. of Chicago Press, 1910; repr. New York: Ktav, 1970), 11.
63. See U. Kellermann, *Nehemia: Quellen, Überlieferung und Geschichte* (Berlin: A. Töpelmann, 1967).

the influential endorsement of W. F. Albright[64] and was upheld by Albright's disciples John Bright[65] and J. M. Myers.[66]

The view that Ezra was or may have been the Chronicler is widely held by evangelical scholars, such as E. J. Young, G. L. Archer Jr., R. L. Harris, and J. S. Wright. This view, however, poses problems. First, late Jewish tradition is not reliable. The genealogical data brings the work of the Chronicler down to about 400 BC (cf. Date). This chronology was not a problem for Albright, who dated Ezra's coming to 428 BC (cf. The Order). If Ezra was at least forty years old when he led the return, he would have been near seventy in about 400 BC. But on the traditional dating of his return in 458, Ezra would have been about one hundred—not impossible, but improbable.

Differences between Chronicles and Ezra–Nehemiah

Though earlier scholars—such as W. de Wette, E. König, W. Rudolph, and M. H. Segal—had pointed out differences between Chronicles and Ezra-Nehemiah, it was especially the important analysis of Sara Japhet that pointed out many of the differences not noted before. Japhet listed words used in Ezra-Nehemiah that are not found in Chronicles and that pointed to different uses of common terms. In the matter of theophoric names, the short form is used in Ezra-Nehemiah, but both short and long forms are used in Chronicles. Japhet concluded, "Our investigation of the differences between the two books, which was restricted to one field, has proven that the books could not have been written or compiled by the same author."[67] In a later review she affirmed that "there is every indication, in the array of literary differences of every possible kind, that these two books are distinct compositions; the author of one work could not have been the author of the other."[68]

In his monograph Williamson noted other differences. The Chronicles emphasize the role of Jacob, an emphasis lacking in Ezra-Nehemiah.[69] Conversely, the Sabbath is important in Nehemiah. "In contrast, the Sabbath plays no significant role in Chronicles, and is most noticeably absent at 2 Chronicles 36:11–16, where we should have expected a reference to it on the basis of Nehemiah's words."[70] Williamson observes:

> When we turn with this in mind to the Chronicler's account of Solomon's reign, however, far from using such a golden opportunity of driving home this important lesson to his readers, we find that he actually omits from 1 Kings 11:1ff. the very account to which Nehemiah refers. It is usually argued that this passage was omitted by the Chronicler because he wanted to make of Solomon an ideal figure. However, if Ezra-Nehemiah is an integral part of his work, that argument completely breaks down in view of Nehemiah 13:26. It seems far

64. W. F. Albright, "The Date and Personality of the Chronicler," *JBL* 40 (1921): 119–20.
65. J. Bright, "The Date of Ezra's Mission to Jerusalem," in *Yehezkel Kaufmann Jubilee Volume* (ed. M. Haran; Jerusalem: Magness, 1960), 81.
66. J. M. Myers, *Ezra-Nehemiah* (AB; Garden City, N.Y.: Doubleday, 1965), XLVIII.
67. S. Japhet, "The Supposed Common Authorship of Chronicles and Ezra-Nehemiah," *VT* 18 (1968): 330–71.
68. S. Japhet, "The Relationship between Chronicles and Ezra-Nehemiah," in *Congress Volume: Leuven 1989* (ed. J. A. Emerton; Leiden: Brill, 1991), 310.
69. Williamson, *Israel in the Book of Chronicles*, 64.
70. Ibid., 69.

more sensible to see here the divergent emphases of separate authors. Ezra-Nehemiah emphasizes Moses and the exodus, whereas Chronicles does not.[71]

Today most, but not all, scholars no longer maintain that a single Chronicler was the author of both Chronicles and Ezra-Nehemiah.[72]

The Freedman and Cross Reconstructions

In 1961 D. N. Freedman proposed that most of Chronicles was written about 515 BC by a monarchist wishing to establish the claims of the house of David at the time of the completion of the second temple. First Chronicles 1–9 and Ezra-Nehemiah were then later attached by a clericalist.[73]

F. M. Cross has proposed a similar but three-staged reconstruction in the composition and editing of Chronicles and Ezra-Nehemiah:[74]

(1) In stage one (which he calls Chr1) most of Chronicles (1Ch 10–2Ch 34) and the first part of Ezra (Ezr 1:1–3:13) were composed about 520 BC at the time of the foundation of the second temple in support of the messianic movement centered around Zerubbabel and Jeshua.

(2) In stage two (Chr2), written about 450 BC, shortly after Ezra's mission, an editor added the Aramaic source (Ezr 5:1–6:19) as a preface to the Ezra narratives (Ezr 7–10).

(3) In stage three (Chr3) a third editor added the Nehemiah memoirs and the genealogies of 1 Chronicles 1–9.

Cross's reconstruction is based on the assumption that papponymy (see below) was current among the high priests. He has to assume two haplographies in his reconstruction and the equation of Joiada and Jaddua. G. Widengren notes that Cross mistakenly assumes that Eliashib was the brother of Joiakim, whereas Nehemiah 12:10 indicates that Eliashib was the son of Joiakim.[75]

Conclusions

Though there are many complex relationships between Ezra-Nehemiah and Chronicles, we regard Nehemiah as the author of the Nehemiah memoirs, Ezra as the author of the Ezra memoirs, and a follower of Ezra as composing the narrative of the book of Zerubbabel, with a separate author as the Chronicler, the composer of Chronicles.

---

71. Ibid., 61.

72. See, e.g., R. Braun, *1 Chronicles* (WBC; Waco, Tex.: Word, 1986), xx; R. B. Dillard, *2 Chronicles* (WBC; Waco, Tex.: Word, 1987), xix.

73. D. N. Freedman, "The Chronicler's Purpose," *CBQ* 23 (1961): 59–62.

74. F. M. Cross, "A Reconstruction of the Judean Restoration," *JBL* 94 (1975): 4–18.

75. G. Widengren, "The Persian Period," in *Israelite and Judean History* (ed. J. H. Hayes and J. M. Miller; Philadelphia: Westminster, 1977), 507–9.

6. DATE

Advocates of Late Dates

Though not from the same pen, Ezra-Nehemiah and Chronicles form a series and are assigned closely related dates. The *terminus ante quem* for dating the work of the Chronicler is about 200 BC, as Ben Sirach (ca. 180 BC) in Sirach 47:8–10 draws on 1 Chronicles 23–29. Only Mowinckel has advocated a date as late as 200 BC. Torrey, who believed that the words for coins in Ezra 2:69; 8:27 and Nehemiah 7:70–72 (cf. commentary) were references to the Greek drachma, dated the work of the Chronicler to 250 BC.

Most critical scholars of the nineteenth and early twentieth centuries preferred a date about 300 BC because they believed that the Jaddua, in Nehemiah 12:10–11, 22, was the same Jaddua whom Josephus associated with Alexander the Great (cf. below on "The High Priests"). These scholars believed that the genealogy of 1 Chronicles 3:15–24 lists six generations beyond Zerubbabel (ca. 520 BC); at thirty years per generation, this approach would date the passage at about 340 BC.

Among those holding such a late date for the composition of Chronicles and Ezra-Nehemiah are L. W. Batten, R. A. Bowman, L. H. Brockington, J. de Fraine, K. Galling, F. Michaeli, M. Noth, W. O. E. Oesterley, H. W. Robinson, H. H. Rowley, H. E. Ryle, H. Schneider, and A. Weiser. Most of these critics have also advocated reversing the traditional order by placing Ezra after Nehemiah (cf. below on "The Order"). An exception is the conservative J. S. Wright, who, while advocating the traditional order of Ezra and Nehemiah, maintains this late date: "Unless strong evidence were forthcoming on other grounds, it would be reasonable to adopt 300 BC as the approximate date with a margin of up to about 30 years on either side of that date."[76]

Advocates of an Early Date

Other scholars have argued that the genealogies of 1 Chronicles 3:15–24 originally listed four generations instead of six after Zerubbabel, that is, about 400 BC. Alternatively other scholars have calculated six generations of the passage at twenty years per generation, which would yield the same date. Those who advocate such an early date for the Chronicler argue that the Jaddua of Nehemiah 12:10–11, 22 was either a young man who lived to a ripe old age till Alexander's era, or that he is not to be identified with the Jaddua of Josephus.

A date of about 400 BC for the Chronicler and Ezra-Nehemiah has been advocated most notably by W. F. Albright.[77] Cross adds the following consideration: "Other arguments can be put for dating Chr3 to circa 400. No hint of the conquest of Alexander is to be found, and perhaps more important, no reference to the suffering and chaos of the mid-fourth century BC when Judah joined in the Phoenician rebellion, harshly put down by Artaxerxes III and his general, Bagoas."[78] Williamson writes, "We may thus conclude

---

76. Wright, *Date*, 12.
77. See W. F. Albright, *The Biblical Period from Abraham to Ezra* (New York: Harper & Row, 1963). This position has also been defended by both Myers and Bright ("The Date of Ezra's Mission to Jerusalem," in *Yehezkel Kaufmann Jubilee Volume* [ed. M. Haran; Jerusalem: Magness, 1960], 80).
78. Cross, "A Reconstruction," 12.

that there is no compelling evidence for dating Chronicles later than the Persian period, or at least for a date later than the time at which the impact of Hellenism was first felt in Judah. Chronicles should thus be dated at some point within the fourth century BC."[79]

In conclusion, we would date the composition of the Ezra materials about 440, the Nehemiah memoirs about 430, and the Chronicles in the early fourth century BC.

7. THE HIGH PRIESTS[80]

The date and order of Ezra-Nehemiah are connected with the list and the identification of the high priests mentioned in Ezra-Nehemiah (Ezr 10:6; Ne 12:10–26). Advocates of a late date and of a reverse order assume that the list of high priests is relatively complete and that one can identify certain of these with those mentioned by Josephus.

Jeshua

Jeshua (Joshua) was the high priest who was the contemporary of Zerubbabel during the reign of Cyrus (Ezr 2:2; Hag 1:1, 12, 14; 2:2, 4; Zec 3:1, 3, 6, 9; 6:11).

Joiakim

He may have been one of Jeshua's sons, who helped with the construction of the temple (Ezr 3:9). Joiakim was evidently the high priest during the reign of Darius I (late sixth century BC). Those who assume that the list of priests is complete assume that the same Joiakim had an unusually long period in office, down to the mid-fifth century (Ne 12:10, 12, 26).[81]

Eliashib

Eliashib was the high priest at the time of Nehemiah; he assisted in the rebuilding of the wall of Jerusalem (Ne 3:1, 20–21; 13:28).

A priest named "Eliashib" was guilty of defiling the temple by assigning rooms to Tobiah the Ammonite (Ne 13:4, 7). Scholars disagree as to whether this Eliashib was the same as the high priest.

An "Eliashib" is the father of Jehohanan, who controlled a chamber to which Ezra withdrew after rebuking the people for intermarrying (Ezr 10:6).[82]

---

79. Williamson, *Israel in the Book of Chronicles*, 86.

80. For a comprehensive study of all these high priests and their successors, see J. C. Vanderkam, *From Joshua to Caiaphas: High Priests after the Exile* (Minneapolis: Fortress, 2004).

81. Josephus (*Ant.* 11.5.1–5) regarded Joiakim (Joakeimos) as the high priest but also has his contemporary, Ezra, designated as "chief priest"—a position also maintained in 1 Esdras 9:39–40. That Ezra was the high priest has been argued by K. Koch in "Ezra and the Origins of Judaism," *JSS* 19 (1974): 190–93.

82. While Myers identifies the Eliashib in Ezra 10:6 with the high priest, he is not regarded as the high priest by Blenkinsopp and Williamson.

Joiada

Joiada was the son of Eliashib (Ne 12:10–11, 22). It is uncertain from Nehemiah 13:28 whether Joiada or his father was high priest at the time of Nehemiah's second return. His son, who was married to Sanballat's daughter, was driven away by Nehemiah.

Johanan

Johanan was the son of Joiada and grandson of Eliashib.

1. Ezra 10:6 mentions that Ezra went to the chamber of "Jehohanan son of Eliashib."
2. Nehemiah 12:11 mentions the son of Joiada, named Jonathan, who was the father of Jaddua.
3. Nehemiah 12:22 mentions a Johanan after Joiada and before Jaddua, and v.23 identifies Johanan as the son of Eliashib.
4. Elephantine papyri refer to Johanan as high priest (*ANET*, 492).[83]
5. Josephus (*Ant.* 11.297–301 [7.1]) refers to a "Johanan" who killed his brother Jesus.[84]

Are all five the same individual? Scholars who say so reason that in Nehemiah 12:11 Jonathan is an error for Johanan and that Nehemiah 12:23 indicates that Johanan was the descendant (i.e., grandson) of Eliashib. They would argue that since the Elephantine papyri indicate that Johanan was high priest in 410 BC, it is more likely that Ezra came seven years later in the seventh year of Artaxerxes II (398 BC) rather than forty-eight years earlier under Artaxerxes I (458 BC).[85]

If these identifications are correct, this reasoning provides one of the strongest arguments for reversing the order of Ezra and Nehemiah. There are, however, a number of serious objections to such a reconstruction. For example, would Ezra have consorted with a known murderer, as he would have done if he had arrived in 398 BC? This would have been the case if we were to identify Ezra's Jehohanan with the Johanan of Josephus. Such an identification would be undermined if Jehohanan was the son of Eliashib and the brother of Joiada rather than the grandson of Eliashib. Jehohanan (Johanan), after all, was a most common name; it was used by fourteen different individuals in the OT, five in Maccabees, and seventeen in Josephus. In Ezra 10:6, moreover, Jehohanan is not identified as a high priest.

---

83. See Cowley, *Aramaic Papyri*, 30:18; 31:17 (dated 411–410 BC).
84. A silver coin with an inscription in paleo-Hebrew, *Yoḥanan Hakkōhēn*, "Johanan the Priest," has been dated by most scholars to the late fourth century BC, thus making this priest the grandson of the Johanan mentioned in the Elephantine papyri. See J. Betlyon, "The Provincial Government of Persian Period Judea and the Yehud Coins," *JBL* 105 (1986): 633–42; D. Barag, "Some Notes on a Silver Coin of Johanan the High Priest," *BA* 48 (1985): 166–68; idem, "A Silver Coin of Yohanan the High Priest and the Coinage of Judea in the Fourth Century BC," *Israel Numismatic Journal* 9 (1987): 4–21. L. S. Fried ("A Silver Coin of *Yoḥanan Hakkōhēn*," *Transeu* 26 (2003): 65–85) dates this coin to 378–68 and associates this Johanan with the one mentioned in the Elephantine papyri.
85. See Peter R. Ackroyd, *Israel under Babylon and Persia* (Oxford: Oxford Univ. Press, 1970), 193, 285–86.

C. G. Tuland concludes that three basic differences exclude the identification of the high priestly Jehohanan-Eliashib "set" found in the Aramaic papyri with the ordinary priest of Ezra: (1) the difference in rank and title; (2) the difference in office; (3) the difference in family relationship.[86]

Jaddua[87]

A "Jaddua," the son of Johanan, is mentioned in Nehemiah 10:21 [22]; 12:11, 22. Josephus (*Ant.* 11.302–7 [7.2–8.2]) identifies this Jaddua with the high priest at the time of Alexander's invasion of Palestine. Some conservative scholars try to maintain the traditional order of Ezra-Nehemiah by arguing that the biblical Jaddua may have been a young man about 400 BC who lived to an unusually advanced age in 333–332 BC. As this idea seems most unlikely, Josephus was probably mistaken and wrongly identified the Hellenistic Jaddua with his grandfather. Williamson notes that there are "strong grounds for believing that Josephus 'reduced' the Persian period by at least as much as two generations." He may have been misled because there was an Artaxerxes and a Darius both in the fifth century and in the fourth century.[88]

Inspired by the evidence of papponymy in the Samaria papyri, Cross has proposed a new reconstruction that offers a possible harmonization of the biblical and extrabiblical data.[89] Papponymy (the repetition of the same name in alternating generations so that grandsons are named after their grandfathers) was a common practice among leading Jewish families. B. Mazar argued that the name "Tobiah" alternates over nine generations.[90] In a recently published Ammonite inscription, the royal name Amminadab recurs over six generations. The Samaria papyri indicate that the name Sanballat alternated over six generations.

Cross's reconstruction assumes that a pair of similar names has fallen out of our extant sources. His reconstruction list would be as follows:

Name	Birth	Contemporary of
Jeshua	570	Zerubbabel
Joiakim	545	
Eliashib I	540	
Johanan I	520	Ezra
Eliashib II	495	Nehemiah
Joiada	470	
Johanan II	445	

(Continue on the next page)

---

86. C. G. Tuland, "Ezra-Nehemiah or Nehemiah-Ezra," *AUSS* 12 (1974): 58–59.
87. A late Persian coin with the name "Jaddua" has been found. See A. Spaer, "Jaddua the High Priest," *Israel Numismatic Journal* 9 (1986–87): 1–3.
88. See H. G. M. Williamson, "The Historical Value of Josephus' *Jewish Antiquities* XI.297–301," *JTS* 28 (1977): 48–67.
89. Cross, "A Reconstruction," 4–18.
90. B. Mazar, "The Tobiads," *IEJ* 7 (1957): 137–45, 229–38.

(Continued)

Jaddua I[91]	420	
Johanan III	395	
Jaddua II	370	Alexander

By this reconstruction Cross resolves two key issues. Ezra's contemporary is Johanan I, son of Eliashib I, and not Johanan II, who is mentioned in the Elephantine papyri, as advocates of a reverse order have maintained. The Jaddua mentioned by Nehemiah would have been the grandfather of Jaddua II, high priest at the time of Alexander.[92]

8. THE ORDER OF EZRA AND NEHEMIAH[93]

A most important controversy concerns the order of Ezra and Nehemiah. Traditionally Ezra arrived in the seventh year of Artaxerxes I (Ezr 7:7) in 458 BC, and Nehemiah arrived in the king's twentieth year (Ne 2:1) in 445 BC.

Critics have proposed a reverse order in which, after Nehemiah's arrival in 445, Ezra arrived in the seventh year of Artaxerxes II in 398. Artaxerxes II, or Memnon (404–359 BC), is well known from Xenophon's *Anabasis* as the king whose younger brother Cyrus led an unsuccessful revolt supported by Greek mercenaries.

Other scholars have favored an intermediate position that maintains the contemporaneity of the men but places Ezra later than the traditional order in the twenty-seventh or thirty-seventh year of Artaxerxes I, that is, in 438 or 428 BC. This conclusion is achieved by textual emendation of the number "seven."

There are numerous lines of argument that have been adduced in favor of the reverse order. We shall consider these arguments and, at the same time, the counterarguments of those who favor either the traditional or intermediate position.

---

91. Jaddua is a caritative or endearing form of the name "Joiada."

92. Though Cross's reconstruction has been widely adopted, it has been criticized by B. E. Scolnic, *Chronology and Papponymy: A List of the Judean High Priests of the Persian Period* (Atlanta: Scholars, 1999). Scolnic (273), who assumes there were vacancies in the office, concludes: "Cross' ingenious attempt to create additional high priests in the first part of the list is unnecessary. On the other hand, the addition of a Jaddua-Johanna pair in the latter part of the period seems to have more of a basis." The reconstruction has also been criticized by J. C. VanderKam, who believes that the list of high priests is complete. See his "Jewish High Priests of the Persian Period: Is the List Complete?" in *Priesthood and Cult in Ancient Israel* (ed. G. A. Anderson and S. M. Olyan; Sheffield: Sheffield Academic, 1991), 67–91.

93. For a more thorough discussion of this important issue, see the commentaries of Blenkinsopp and Williamson, and E. M. Yamauchi, "The Reverse Order of Ezra/Nehemiah Reconsidered," *Them* 5 (1980): 13–21; R. W. Green, "The Date of Nehemiah: A Reexamination," *AUSS* 28 (1990): 195–209; L. McFall, "Was Nehemiah Contemporary with Ezra in 458 BC?" *WTJ* 53 (1991): 263–93; A. Brown II, "Nehemiah and Narrative Order in the Book of Ezra," *BSac* 162 (2005): 175–94.

The List of High Priests

As this argument is one of the weightiest, it has been considered separately in the preceding section.

The Contemporaneity of Ezra and Nehemiah

(1) As the text stands, Nehemiah and Ezra are noted together in Nehemiah 8:9, at the reading of the law, and in Nehemiah 12:26, 36, at the dedication of the wall. Since Nehemiah's name is lacking in the 1 Esdras 9:49–50 parallel to Nehemiah 8:9, it has been argued that Nehemiah's name was inserted as a gloss. It has also been claimed that Nehemiah 12:26, 36 were added to the original text. J. A. Emerton has asserted, "No meeting between them is recorded and they never both play active parts in the same action; one is active, and at most, the other's name is mentioned in passing."[94]

(2) But it is not true that one can delete Ezra or Nehemiah's name from Nehemiah 12:36, as some have argued, for to do so would leave one of the processions without a leader.

That references to the contemporaneity of Ezra and Nehemiah are few is readily explicable. Bright points out that "the Chronicler's interests were predominantly ecclesiastical, and to these Nehemiah was peripheral. Nehemiah, on the other hand, intended his memoirs as a personal apologia, not as a history of the contemporary Jewish community; he was concerned exclusively with what he himself had done."[95] We also have other examples of contemporary OT figures who do not refer to each other, e.g., Jeremiah and Ezekiel, Haggai and Zechariah.

Meremoth the Son of Uriah of the Clan of Hakkoz

(1) Ezra 2:61–62/Nehemiah 7:63–64 lists the family of Hakkoz as one of those unable to prove its priestly status. In Ezra 8:33 a "Meremoth son of Uriah" from this family is designated as one of the priests in charge of the temple treasury. In Nehemiah 3:4, 21 a "Meremoth son of Uriah" builds a double portion of the wall. Without a priestly title he is evidently considered a layman. Supporters of the reverse order argue that Meremoth in his youth aided in the building of the wall and in his old age (forty-seven years later, in 398) served as a treasurer. They suggest that Meremoth's family must have regained its priestly status after Nehemiah's time at Ezra's coming.

(2) On the other hand, it can also be argued that the situation can be explained on the basis of the traditional order. Koch suggests, "It seems as if Ezra acknowledged Meremoth at the time of his arrival in Jerusalem, but deposed him shortly afterward while carrying out his investigation."[96]

Simpler is Kellermann's suggestion that despite similar names and patronymics, we here have to do with two individuals, one from a priestly family and one from a lay family. Though Meremoth is not a common name (three or four occurrences), Uriah is more common (six or seven occurrences).[97]

---

94. J. A. Emerton, "Did Ezra Go to Jerusalem in 428 BC?" *JTS* 17 (1966): 16.

95. Bright, "The Date of Ezra's Mission," 86.

96. Koch, "Ezra and the Origins of Judaism," 190.

97. U. Kellermann, "Erwägungen zum Problem der Esradatierung," *ZAW* 80 (1968): 55–87.

The Thirteen-year Gap

(1) As the present text is arranged, after Ezra's arrival in 458 and his activities in that first year, we hear nothing further about his ministry until the public reading of the law some thirteen years later (Ne 8:1−8).

(2) Archer responds: "Yet Nehemiah 8 only records a solemn reading of the law in a public meeting on the occasion of the Feast of Tabernacles. It by no means implies that Ezra had not been diligently teaching the law to smaller groups of disciples and Levites during the preceding twelve years."[98] Less satisfactory are suggestions that Ezra may have returned to Mesopotamia, or that he may have fallen out of favor with the Persians by being associated with the attempt to rebuild the wall (Ezr 4:7−23).

(3) As noted earlier (see above, The Ezra Memoirs [Ezra 7−10; Nehemiah 8−9]), Williamson addresses this problem by repositioning Nehemiah 8 earlier in the narrative, so that Ezra's reading of the law comes in his first year.

The Problem of Mixed Marriages

(1) Both Ezra (chs. 9−10) and Nehemiah (13:23−28) deal with the problem of mixed marriages. Ezra adopted a more rigorous approach by demanding the dissolution of all such marriages. Apart from the expulsion of Joiada, Nehemiah simply forbade future mixed marriages. Brockington holds that Ezra's handling most naturally follows Nehemiah's attempt and regards this factor as "the strongest argument" for the reverse order. Furthermore, others argue that the situation faced by Nehemiah must have been one of long standing, since he found the children speaking in foreign dialects (Ne 13:23−24).[99]

(2) As to the latter argument, if Ezra's reforms took place some twenty-five years before Nehemiah's actions on his second return after 432 BC, enough time would certainly have elapsed for children to have been born to renewed mixed marriages and reached some considerable age. The idea that a more rigorous handling of the problem should come later is purely subjective.

The Alleged Failure of Ezra

(1) Closely allied to the preceding argument is the often-expressed idea that if Ezra preceded Nehemiah, Ezra must have "failed," as Nehemiah had to correct the same abuse. Rowley, for example, avers, "It is curious that some of those who are zealous to defend the chronological order of Ezra and Nehemiah as it appears in the Bible are willing to do so at the cost of jettisoning the Biblical representation of the character of Ezra, and the reduction of him to the stature of an incompetent who had to be rescued by Nehemiah after his failure."[100] The converse argument could, of course, be made, that if Nehemiah preceded Ezra, the former must have failed.

---

98. G. L. Archer, *A Survey of Old Testament Introduction* (rev. ed.; Chicago: Moody Press, 1974), 412.
99. Brockington, *Ezra, Nehemiah and Esther*, 19−20.
100. H. H. Rowley, *Men of God* (London: Nelson, 1963), 242.

(2) It should be noted that God's spokesmen do not "fail" when they faithfully deliver God's messages. The people who disobey are the ones who "fail." In the short period of time during Nehemiah's absence after his first term, numerous abuses appeared that he had to correct during his second term (Ne 13:4–31).

Supporters of the Reverse Order

In 1889 M. Vernes first suggested the reverse order; A. van Hoonacker gave the view currency in publications from 1890–1924. The ablest exposition of this position was by H. H. Rowley in 1948, at a time when only a minority of scholars favored it.[101] Thereafter, however, this view came to predominate; and in 1970 W. F. Stinespring could affirm:

> Indeed, the placing of Ezra after Nehemiah may now be spoken of as part of "critical orthodoxy," having been incorporated into such works as *The International Critical Commentary*, *The Interpreter's Bible*, *The Interpreter's Dictionary of the Bible*, *The Oxford Annotated Bible*, and into much of the church-school literature of the leading Protestant churches in North America. The great German introductions of Eissfeldt and Sellin-Fohrer, now translated into English (1965 and 1968 respectively), have also joined the chorus of assent.[102]

Supporters of the Intermediate Date

Some scholars attempted to retain the contemporaneity of Ezra and Nehemiah and yet date Ezra later by emending the number "7" of Ezra 7:7 to read either "27" or "37." The former would date Ezra's arrival in 438, the latter in 428. The former emendation was proposed by J. Wellhausen in 1895, the latter by J. Markwart in 1896. The first alternative has had relatively few supporters.

More attractive is the reading "37." Since both the Hebrew words "thirty" and "seven" begin with the letter š, it has been argued that the former word may have dropped out. The most influential advocate here was Albright.[103] Bright offered a persuasive exposition of this view.[104] Though it avoids the objections raised against the reverse position, there is no textual support for the proposed emendation.

Supporters of the Traditional Order

The traditional order has never lacked defenders. In 1948 Rowley wrote: "Despite this impressive support [for the reverse order], this view has never been unchallenged, and there have always been scholars of eminence—even more numerous than its supporters—who have refused to adopt it, but have adhered to

101. H. H. Rowley, "The Chronological Order of Ezra and Nehemiah," in *Ignace Goldziher Memorial Volume* (ed. S. Löwinger and J. Smogyi; Budapest: Globus, 1948), 117–49; reprinted in his *The Servant of the Lord* (rev. ed.; Naperville, Ill.: Allenson, 1965), 135–68.

102. W. F. Stinespring, "Prolegomenon" to C. C. Torrey, *Ezra Studies* (repr. ed.; New York: Ktav, 1970), XIV.

103. Albright, *The Biblical Period*, 45–55, 62–65, 113.

104. Bright, "The Date of Ezra's Mission," 70–87.

the traditional view."[105] U. Kellermann's article, published in 1968, refuted point by point the arguments for the reverse order.[106]

Only a few recent scholars, such as R. Albertz, now support the reverse order of Ezra and Nehemiah. J. Bright in his influential history of Israel has favored an intermediate position that maintains the contemporaneity of the men but places Ezra later than the traditional order by a textual emendation of the seventh to the thirty-seventh year of Artaxerxes I, that is, in 428 BC. The overwhelming majority of current scholars now support the traditional order of Ezra's priority over Nehemiah. These include: J. Blenkinsopp, D. J. Clines, F. M. Cross, R. W. Klein, and H. G. M. Williamson. I believe that the traditional order of Ezra's arrival prior to Nehemiah in the seventh year of Artaxerxes I is the correct order.

9. TEXT

The Masoretic Text of Ezra/Nehemiah has been relatively well transmitted, with few corruptions. The differences between the identical lists of Ezra 2 and Nehemiah 7 can be explained by the difficulty of transmitting numbers and the confusion of certain letters.[107] Only three small fragments (4QEzr) of the Hebrew and Aramaic text of Ezra 4:2–11; 5:17; 6:1–5 have been found among the Dead Sea Scrolls.[108] Assuming that Ezra/Nehemiah was one book, only Esther goes unrepresented in the extant biblical scrolls from Qumran.[109]

The Hebrew of Ezra 1:1–4:7; 6:19–22; 7:1–11, 27–28; 8–10—that is, the non-Aramaic sections—and the Hebrew of Nehemiah 7:6–12:26—that is, the nonmemoir sections—belong to the same late Hebrew as the Hebrew of the Chronicles. But the Hebrew of the Nehemiah memoirs—Nehemiah 1:1–7:5; 12:27–13:31 (see above, Literary Form and Authorship)—is written in a more archaic Hebrew, according to R. Polzin.

The Aramaic sections that are found in Ezra 4:8–6:18 and 7:12–26 consist largely of official documents. Out of these sixty-seven verses, fifty-two are records or letters and only fifteen are narrative.[110] The author evidently found these documents in Aramaic and copied them with the insertion of connecting verses

---

105. Rowley, "The Chronological Order of Ezra and Nehemiah," 122.

106. Kellermann, "Erwägungen zum Problem," 55–87.

107. H. L. Allrik, "The Lists of Zerubbabel (Nehemiah 7 and Ezra 2) and the Hebrew Numerical Notation," *BASOR* 136 (1954): 21–27.

108. E. Ulrich, "Ezra and Qoheleth Manuscripts from Qumran (4QEzra, 4QQoh,a,b)," in *Priests, Prophets and Scribes: Essays In Honour of Joseph Blenkinsopp* (ed. by E. Ulrich et al.; Sheffield: Sheffield Academic, 1992), 139–57. See M. Abegg Jr., P. Flint, and E. Ulrich, *The Dead Sea Scrolls Bible* (New York: HarperSan Francisco, 1999), 634–35.

109. See J. C. VanderKam, *The Dead Sea Scrolls Today* (Grand Rapids: Eerdmans, 1994), 30. From Qumran have come copies of a manuscript 4Q550, which some have called "Proto-Esther." According to F. G. Martínez (*The Dead Sea Scrolls Translated* [Leiden: Brill, 1994], 507), the manuscript represents "five copies of a narrative work which might have been the source of the book of Esther." This work has also been called "The Tale of Bagasraw" by M. Wise, M. Abegg Jr., and E. Cook (*Dead Sea Scrolls: A New Translation* [New York: HarperSan Francisco, 1996], 437–39).

110. On the importance of such texts for the literary structure of Ezra-Nehemiah, see T. C. Eskenazi, "Ezra-Nehemiah: From Text to Actuality," in *Signs and Wonders: Biblical Texts in Literary Focus* (ed. J. C. Exum; Decatur, Ga.: Scholars, 1989), 165–98.

in Aramaic. The community he was writing for understood both Hebrew and Aramaic (cf. comment on Ne 8:8).

Aramaic, a northwest Semitic language originally of the Arameans of Syria, became widespread as an international language first among the Assyrians and especially in the Persian Empire. The dialect of Aramaic used between 700 BC and 200 BC is known as Imperial Aramaic. The phase includes inscriptions from Anatolia to Afghanistan and the passages in Ezra and in Daniel 2:4–7:28. Isolated Aramaic phrases appear in Genesis 31:47 and Jeremiah 10:11.[111]

Torrey had branded the Aramaic of Ezra and Daniel as late Aramaic from the third to second century BC,[112] but extrabiblical sources clearly show that he was mistaken. Of greatest importance are the contemporary fifth-century BC Aramaic papryi recovered from the Jewish garrison at Elephantine in Upper Egypt.[113] Myers notes, "The Aramaic of Ezra ... is that prevailing in the official documents of the Persian empire as may be seen from the Elephantine correspondence and other documents."[114] The Aramaic of both Ezra and Daniel reveals the strong influence of Akkadian and Persian in numerous loanwords and syntactic features, thus indicating its origin in the Persian rather than the Hellenistic period.[115]

Apart from Daniel, which like Ezra contains significant Aramaic passages, Ezra-Nehemiah is the only book in the Hebrew canon lacking a Targum, that is, an Aramaic paraphrase. This factor, along with calques—that is, Hebrew forms occurring in a manner expected of Aramaic morphology and syntax—is one that inclines D. Marcus to suggest that Nehemiah may have originally been composed in Aramaic.[116]

10. ESDRAS[117]

The relation of the Hebrew MT text of Ezra to its Greek translations is complicated by the presence of two rival Greek versions of Ezra. One version, now commonly called either I Esdras or simply Esdras, differs considerably and is included among the OT apocryphal books considered deuterocanonical by the

---

111. For biblical Aramaic, see F. Rosenthal, *A Grammar of Biblical Aramaic* (Wiesbaden: Harrassowitz, 1961). For nonbiblical Aramaic texts and inscriptions, see J. Margain, "L'Araméen d'empire," in *La Palestine à l'époque perse* (ed. E.-M. Laperrousaz and A. Lemaire; Paris: Les éditions du Cerf, 1994), 225–41. See also D. C. Snell, "Why Is There Aramaic in the Bible?" *JSOT* 18 (1980): 32–51; A. Millard, "Aramaic Documents of the Assyrian and Achaemenid Periods," in *Ancient Archives and Archival Traditions* (ed. M. Brosius; Oxford: Oxford Univ. Press, 2003), 230–40.

112. Torrey, *Ezra Studies*, 140–61.

113. B. Porten, *The Elephantine Papyri in English* (Leiden: Brill, 1996).

114. Myers, *Ezra-Nehemiah*, LXIII.

115. See Rosenthal, *Grammar of Biblical Aramaic*; I. Jerusalmi, *The Aramaic Sections of Ezra and Daniel* (rev. ed.; Cincinnati: Hebrew Union College, 1970); S. Kaufman, *The Akkadian Influence on Aramaic* (Chicago: Univ. of Chicago Press, 1975). On the issue of the Greek words in the Aramaic of Daniel, see E. M. Yamauchi, *Greece and Babylon* (Grand Rapids: Baker, 1967); idem, "Persia and the Greeks," ch. 11 of *Persia and the Bible*.

116. D. Marcus, "Is the Book of Nehemiah a Translation from Aramaic?" in *Boundaries of the Ancient Near Eastern World* (ed. M. Lubetski et al.; Sheffield: Sheffield Academic, 1998), 103–10.

117. See J. M. Myers, *I & II Esdras* (Garden City, N.Y.: Doubleday, 1974); Z. Talshir, *1 Esdras: From Origin to Translation* (Atlanta: Society of Biblical Literature, 1999); idem, *1 Esdras: A Text Critical Commentary* (Atlanta: Society of Biblical Literature, 2001).

Roman Catholic Church after the Council of Trent, though modern Catholic Bibles such as the JB and the NAB omit it.

Nomenclature

The confusing nomenclature of several books called "Ezra" or "Esdras" may best be set out in the following chart:

English Versions	Ezra	Nehemiah	1 Esdras	2 Esdras
Septuagint	Esdras beta	Esdras gamma	Esdras alpha	
Vulgate	1 Esdras	2 Esdras	3 Esdras	4 Esdras
Content			Greek paraphrase	Latin apocalypse

The Contents of 1 Esdras

First Esdras (1 Esdras), the first book of the Apocrypha, differs from the other apocryphal books in that it is largely a divergent account of the canonical books of Ezra-Nehemiah. It parallels the last two chapters of 2 Chronicles, all of Ezra, and thirteen verses of Nehemiah from the section on Ezra (Ne 7:73–8:12).

In striking contrast to Ezra-Nehemiah, the writer of 1 Esdras concentrates exclusively on the ministry of Ezra. In the parallel to Nehemiah 8:9, the name of Nehemiah is omitted. The Ezra narrative now found in Nehemiah 7:73–8:12 is placed in 1 Esdras 8:88–9:36 immediately after the events of Ezra 10, thus avoiding the gap of thirteen years found in the MT between Ezra's arrival and the reading of the law (see above, The Order of Ezra and Nehemiah: The Thirteen-Year Gap).

The principal novelty of 1 Esdras is a long story (3:1–5:6) about three young bodyguards of Darius who seek to answer the riddle of what is the strongest thing in the world. Zerubbabel, by giving "truth" as the answer, is allowed to lead the exiles back to their homes. Josephus followed 1 Esdras in constructing his history of this period. Though a few scholars have followed Torrey in believing that 1 Esdras has preserved a superior account to Ezra, most scholars conclude that it is a secondary and late adaptation that provides no independent historical information.[118] Williamson points out that 1 Esdras is a late, composite, and unreliable work.[119]

---

118. See Z. Talshir, "Ezra-Nehemiah and First Esdras: Diagnosis of a Relationship between Two Recensions," *Bib* 81 (2000): 566–73.

119. H. G. M. Williamson, "The Problem with First Esdras," in *After the Exile: Essays in Honour of Rex Mason* (Macon, Ga.: Mercer Univ. Press, 1996), 201–16.

1 Esdras and the LXX

The Greek text of 1 Esdras is written in elegant Greek, in contrast to the painfully literal text of LXX Ezra-Nehemiah. The latter had been considered by Torrey as the work of Theodotion (second century AD),[120] but it is more probably a Palestinian translation by a forerunner of Theodotion.

In the LXX, 1 Esdras precedes the LXX's translation of Ezra-Nehemiah; the former is therefore designated Esdras Alpha, the latter Esdras Beta. First Esdras should be dated about 150 BC.

1 Esdras and Josephus

Josephus, in *Antiquities* 11, followed 1 Esdras rather than the MT-LXX perhaps because of its superior Greek. Josephus compounded the errors of 1 Esdras in his narrative. Both Ezra and Nehemiah are placed in the reign of Xerxes instead of in the reign of Artaxerxes.[121]

2 Esdras = 4 Ezra

This pseudepigraphical work is preserved in its entirety only in Latin recensions of the seventh to thirteenth centuries AD. Most scholars believe that the original, central section, which is an apocalypse (chs. 3–14), was composed in Hebrew or Aramaic by a Jewish author about AD 100. We have but three verses of ch. 15 in Greek (*P. Oxy.* 1010). Commenting on 4 Ezra, J. H. Charlesworth writes:

> Among these the most brilliant and earliest, and the stimulus for most of the others, is *4 Ezra*.... The Jewish author—perhaps the author of the best work on theodicy ever written—attributed his work to the famous scribe of the Tanak [i.e., OT], the optimistic Ezra, but he did not have an answer for a world that had gone up in smoke.[122]

The work was translated into several languages, including an important Armenian version that goes back to a Greek original. Chapters 3–14 relate seven visions by which the angel Uriel instructs Ezra about the problem of evil and the destiny of souls after death. Second Esdras 14:1–48 describes how God commanded Ezra to dictate the Scriptures in forty days to five rapidly writing scribes, who produced twenty-four canonical books and seventy secret books. Columbus quoted 2 Esdras 6:42 to show Ferdinand and Isabella that the proportion of land to water was six parts to one in order to obtain financing for his voyages![123]

The first two chapters now included in 4 Ezra are sometimes designated 5 Ezra. This was clearly a separate Christian composition from the middle of the second century AD. Fifth Ezra was the source of

---

120. Torrey, *Ezra Studies*, 11–36, 66–82.

121. On Josephus's rewriting of Scriptures, see E. M. Yamauchi, "Josephus and the Scriptures," in *Fides et Historia* 13 (1980): 42–63; L. H. Feldman, *Josephus' Interpretation of the Bible* (Berkeley: Univ. of California Press, 1998).

122. J. H. Charlesworth, "Interpretation of the Tanak in Apocrypha and Pseudepigrapha," in *A History of Biblical Interpretation I: The Ancient Period* (ed. A. J. Hauser and D. E. Watson; Grand Rapids: Eerdmans, 2003), 270–71.

123. B. M. Metzger, "The Fourth Book of Ezra," in *The Old Testament Pseudepigrapha* (ed. J. H. Charlesworth; Garden City, N.Y.: Doubleday, 1983), 1:517–60, esp. 523.

a number of phrases in the Catholic liturgy: *Requiem aeternam dona eis, Domine*—"Give them eternal rest, Lord" (2:34)—and *Lux perpetua luceat eis*—"May the eternal light shine upon them" (2:35).

11. POSTBIBLICAL TRADITIONS[124]

It is striking that neither Philo nor the NT refers to Ezra or to Nehemiah. Some have detected allusions to the "holy city" of Nehemiah 11:1, 18 in Matthew 4:5, and a possible allusion to Nehemiah 9:6 in Acts 4:24.

Traditions about Ezra

Ben Sirach (Sir 49:11–13) in his catalog of famous men lists Nehemiah but not Ezra. Ben Sirach, however, was primarily concerned about men who were builders. According to some scholars Ben Sirach betrays a Sadducean bias and according to others an anti-Levitical one, either of which would explain Ezra's omission.[125]

The Talmud (*b. Meg.* 16b) tells us that Ezra was a disciple of the aged Baruch, who had been Jeremiah's scribe. The rabbis held that "if Moses had not anticipated him, Ezra would have received the Torah" (*b. Sanh.* 21b). *B. Baba Batra* 14b–16a credits Ezra with the authorship of the books of Ezra and Chronicles.

B. Baba Qamma 82a ascribes to Ezra ten *takkanot* ("regulations") covering such miscellaneous practices as (1) holding the court on Mondays and Thursdays, (2) washing clothes on Thursdays and not Fridays, (3) eating garlic on Friday, (4) the combing of a woman's hair before taking a ritual bath.[126]

The OT tells us nothing of Ezra's end. Josephus (*Ant.* 11.158 [5.5]) relates concerning Ezra that "it was his fate, after being honored by the people, to die an old man and be buried with great magnificence in Jerusalem." Later traditions spoke of his burial at Abu Ghosh or south of Nablus.[127]

From the eleventh century AD, Jews in Mesopotamia held that Ezra was buried near the Persian Gulf at al-ʿUzair (Arabic for "Ezra"), on the right bank of the Tigris in southern Iraq.[128]

Samaritan tradition preserved in the medieval *Liber Josuae* blames "the cursed Ezra" for the excommunication of the Samaritans from the Jewish community.[129] This tradition may stem from the OT period but more probably reflects later hostility between the two communities.

The high regard with which the Jews of Arabia held Ezra may be reflected in the strange accusation found in the Qurʾan 9:30: "And the Jews say: Ezra is the son of Allah, and the Christians say: The Messiah is the son of Allah." A late tradition holds that Ezra tried to persuade the Jews of Yemen in southwestern

---

124. See E. M. Yamauchi, "Postbiblical Traditions about Ezra and Nehemiah," in *A Tribute to Gleason Archer* (ed. W. Kaiser and R. Youngblood; Chicago: Moody Press, 1986), 167–76.

125. P. Hoffken, "Warum schwieg Jesus Sirach über Esra?" *ZAW* 87 (1975): 184–201; C. Begg, "Ben Sirach's Non-Mention of Ezra," *BN* 42 (1988): 14–18.

126. S. Zeitlin, "Takkanot Ezra," *JQR* 8 (1917–18): 62–74.

127. See L. H. Feldman, "Josephus' Portrait of Ezra," *VT* 43 (1993): 190–214; M. Munk, "Esra Hasofer nach Talmud und Misrasch," *Jahrbuch der jüdisch-literarischen Gesellschaft* 22 (1931): 228–29.

128. D. S. Sasson, "The History of the Jews in Basra," *JQR* 17 (1927): 407–69.

129. J. D. Pravis, *The Samaritan Pentateuch and the Origin of the Samaritan Sect* (Cambridge, Mass.: Harvard Univ. Press, 1968), 98.

Arabia to return to Palestine but that they refused to go because they knew the Second Temple would be destroyed.[130]

Traditions about Nehemiah

Nehemiah is extolled in Sirach 49:13 (dated ca. 180 BC): "The memory of Nehemiah also is lasting; he raised our fallen walls, and set up the gates and bars, and rebuilt our ruined houses." Second Maccabees (first century BC) has some curious traditions about Nehemiah. For example, 2 Maccabees 1:18 refers to "the festival of the fire given when Nehemiah, who built the temple and the altar, offered sacrifices"; 2:13 reports: "The same things are reported in the records and in the memoirs of Nehemiah, and also that he founded a library and collected the books about the kings and prophets, and the writings of David, and letters of kings about votive offerings."

Josephus (*Ant.* 11.183 [5.8]) speaks of Nehemiah's life and death as follows: "Then, after performing many other splendid and praiseworthy public services, Nehemiah died at an advanced age. He was a man of kind and just nature and most anxious to serve his countrymen; and he left the walls of Jerusalem as his eternal monument."[131]

12. PURPOSE AND VALUES

Unlike those deported by the Assyrians from Israel, those deported by the Babylonians from Judah steadfastly retained their faith in Yahweh during the ordeal of their exile and maintained their identity as a distinct religious community. When the exiles returned, they revived an exclusive loyalty to Yahweh, which was no longer compromised by the worship of other gods. As Stern reports, since the beginning of the Persian era, not a single piece of evidence has been found for any pagan cults in Judah and Samaria.[132]

Ezra, a priest and scribe, and Nehemiah, a layman, with contrasting personalities, were each able to contribute to the revival and reformation of the Jewish community. The message of Ezra assured the Jews that God can work sovereignly through human rulers to fulfill his will, and the message of Nehemiah underscores what can be accomplished by faithful leaders with the courage and vision to inspire others.

The Book of Ezra

The book of Ezra reveals the providential intervention of the God of heaven in behalf of his people. In Ezra 1 the Lord is sovereign over all kingdoms (v.2) and moves even the heart of a pagan ruler to fulfill his will (v.1). He accomplishes the refining of his people through mighty and calamitous events such as the conquest and the exile. He stirs the heart of his people to respond and raises men of God to lead his people (v.11).

---

130. L. Ginzberg, *The Legends of the Jews* (Philadelphia: JPS, 1928), 6:432.

131. See L. H. Feldman, "Josephus' Portrait of Nehemiah," *JJS* 43 (1992): 187–202.

132. Stern, *Archaeology of the Land*, 479.

In Ezra 3 we see that the service of God requires a united effort (v.1), leadership (v.2a), obedience to God's Word (v.2b), courage in the face of opposition (v.3), offerings and funds (vv.4–7), and an organized division of labor (vv.8–9). Meeting these requirements would result in a sound foundation for later work (v.11), tears and joy (vv.11–12), and praise and thanksgiving to the Lord (v.11).

Ezra 4 teaches that doing the work of God brings opposition: in the guise of proffered cooperation from those who do not share our basic theological convictions (vv.1–2) to complete work we alone are responsible for (v.3); and opposition from those who would discourage and intimidate us (v.4), from professional counselors who offer misleading advice (v.5), from false accusers (vv.6, 13), and from secular authorities (vv.7, 21–24). Far from being discouraged, however, we need to be alert and vigorous in the knowledge that by God's grace we can triumph over all opposition and accomplish his will with rejoicing (6:14–16).

Ezra experienced the good hand of God. As a scribe he was more than a scholar—he was an expounder of the Scriptures (7:6, 12). He believed that God could guide and protect from misfortune (8:20–22). As an inspired leader he enlisted others and assigned trustworthy men to their tasks (7:27–28; 8:15, 24). He regarded what he did as a sacred trust (8:21–28).

Ezra was above all a man of fervent prayer (8:21; 10:1), deep piety, and humility (7:10, 27–28; 9:3; 10:6).

The Book of Nehemiah[133]

The book of Nehemiah perhaps more than any other book of the OT reflects the vibrant personality of its author. G. Campbell Morgan comments, "The book thrills and throbs and pulsates with the tremendous force of this man's will."[134] He is seen to have many admirable characteristics.

(1) Nehemiah was a man of responsibility. That he served as the king's cupbearer (Ne 1:11–2:1) can only mean that he had proven himself trustworthy over a long period.[135]

(2) Nehemiah was a man of vision. The walls of Jerusalem had been in ruins for 141 years when Nehemiah learned of an abortive attempt to rebuild them (Ezr 4:23). He had a great vision of who God was and what he could do through his servants.

(3) Nehemiah was a man of prayer. His first resort was to prayer (Ne 1:5–11). He prayed spontaneously even in the presence of the king (2:4–5).

(4) Nehemiah was a man of action and cooperation. He would explain what needed to be done (2:16–17) and inspire others to join him (2:18). He knew how to organize the rebuilding work (ch. 3). In spite of opposition the people responded so enthusiastically that they mended the wall in less than two months (6:15). He inspired the people with his own example (5:14–18). Nehemiah, a layman, was able to cooperate with his contemporary Ezra, the scribe and priest, in spite of the fact that these two leaders were of entirely different temperaments. In reaction to the problem of mixed marriages, Ezra plucked out his own hair (Ezr 9:3), whereas Nehemiah plucked out the hair of the offenders (Ne 13:25)!

---

133. See R. Brown, *The Message of Nehemiah* (Downers Grove, Ill.: InterVarsity Press, 1998).

134. G. Campbell Morgan, *Living Messages of the Books of the Bible: Old Testament* (New York: Revell, 1912), 262.

135. See E. Yamauchi, "Was Nehemiah the Cupbearer a Eunuch?" *ZAW* 92 (1980): 132–42.

(5) Nehemiah was a man of compassion. He renounced his own privileges (Ne 5:18) and denounced the wealthy who had exploited their poorer brothers (5:8). He did this because of his reverence for God (5:9, 15).[136]

(6) Nehemiah was a man who triumphed over opposition. His opponents used every ruse to intimidate him. They started with ridicule (2:19; 4:2–3). They attempted slander (6:5–7). Hired prophets gave him misleading advice (6:10–14). Nehemiah responded with prayer (4:4), redoubled efforts (v.6), vigilance (v.9), and trust in God (v.14).

(7) Nehemiah was a man with right motivation. Although he justified his ministry, his primary motive was not to be judged aright by others or to be remembered by posterity. The last words of Nehemiah — "Remember me with favor, O my God" (13:31) — recapitulate a frequently repeated theme (5:19; 13:14, 22, 29). His motive throughout his ministry was to please and serve his divine Sovereign. His only reward would be God's approbation.[137]

13. BIBLIOGRAPHY

Commentaries

Ackroyd, Peter R. *Chronicles, Ezra, Nehemiah*. London: SCM, 1973.
Allen, Leslie C., and Timothy Laniak. *Ezra, Nehemiah, Esther*. New International Biblical Commentary. Peabody, Mass.: Hendrickson, 2003.
Blenkinsopp, J. *Ezra-Nehemiah*. Old Testament Library. Philadelphia: Westminster, 1988.
Bowman, R. A. "The Book of Ezra and Nehemiah." Pages 549–819 in *The Interpreter's Bible*. Vol. 3. Edited by G. A. Buttrick. Nashville: Abingdon, 1954.
Brockington, L. H. *Ezra, Nehemiah and Esther*. London: Nelson, 1969.
Clines, D. J. A. *Ezra, Nehemiah, Esther*. New Century Bible Commentary. Grand Rapids: Eerdmans, 1992.
Fensham, F. C. *The Books of Ezra and Nehemiah*. New International Commentary on the Old Testament. Grand Rapids: Eerdmans, 1982.
Kidner, D. *Ezra-Nehemiah*. Tyndale Old Testament Commentary. Leicester/Downers Grove, Ill.: InterVarsity, 1979.
Myers, J. M. *Ezra-Nehemiah*. Anchor Bible. Garden City, N.Y.: Doubleday, 1965.
Rabinowitz, Y. *Ezra*. Brooklyn: Mesorah, 1984.
———. *Nechemiah*. Brooklyn: Mesorah, 1990.
Slotki, J. *Daniel, Ezra and Nehemiah*. London: Soncino, 1951.
Williamson, H. G. M. *Ezra, Nehemiah*. Word Biblical Commentary. Waco, Tex.: Word, 1985.

Other Works

Avigad, N. *Bullae and Seals from a Post-Exilic Judean Archive*. Jerusalem: Hebrew University Press, 1976.
Briant, P. *From Cyrus to Alexander: A History of the Persian Empire*. Winona Lake, Ind.: Eisenbrauns, 2002.
Carradice, I., ed. *Coinage and Administration in the Athenian and Persian Empires*. Oxford: British Archaeological Reports, 1987.

---

136. See E. Yamauchi, "Two Reformers Compared: Solon of Athens and Nehemiah of Jerusalem," in *The Bible World: Essays in Honor of Cyrus H. Gordon* (ed. G. Rendsburg et al.; New York: Ktav, 1980), 269–92.

137. E. M. Yamauchi, "Nehemiah, A Model Leader," in *A Spectrum of Thought: Essays in Honor of Dennis F. Kinlaw* (ed. Michael Peterson; Wilmore, Ky.: Francis Asbury, 1982), 171–80; J. Maciariello, "Lessons in Leadership and Management from Nehemiah," *ThTo* 60 (2003): 397–407.

Coogan, M. D. *West Semitic Personal Names in the Murašû Documents.* Missoula, Mont.: Scholars, 1975.

Cowley, A. E. *Aramaic Papyri of the Fifth Century.* Oxford: Clarendon, 1923.

Deutsch, R., and A. Lemaire. *Biblical Period Personal Seals in the Shlomo Moussaieff Collection.* Tel Aviv: Archaeological Center, 2000.

De Vaux R. "The Decrees of Cyrus and Darius on the Rebuilding of the Temple." Pages 63–96 in *The Bible and the Ancient Near East.* Garden City, N.Y.: Doubleday, 1971.

———. *Ancient Israel.* New York: McGraw-Hill, 1961.

Driver, G. R. *Aramaic Documents of the Fifth Century B.C.* Oxford: Clarendon, 1954.

Hensley, L. V. "The Official Persian Documents in the Book of Ezra." Ph.D. dissertation. University of Liverpool, 1977.

Hestrin, R., et al. *Inscriptions Reveal: Documents from the Time of the Bible, the Mishna, and the Talmud.* Jerusalem: Israel Museum, 1973.

Hoerth, A., G. Mattingly, and E. Yamauchi, eds. *Peoples of the Old Testament World.* Grand Rapids, Mich.: Baker, 1994.

Japhet, S. "Sheshbazzar and Zerubbabel—Against the Background of the Historical and Religious Tendencies of Ezra-Nehemiah." *Zeitschrift für die alttestamentumliche Wissenschaft* 94 (1982): 66–98.

Kent, R. G. *Old Persian.* Rev. ed. New Haven: American Oriental Society, 1953.

Kenyon, K. M. *Digging Up Jerusalem.* London: Benn, 1974.

———. *Jerusalem.* London: Thames & Hudson, 1967.

Kraeling, E. *The Brooklyn Aramaic Papyri.* New Haven: Yale University Press, 1953.

Laperrousaz, E.-M., and A. Lemaire. *La Palestine à l'époque perse.* Paris: Les Éditions du Cerf, 1994.

Lemaire, A. "Populations et territoires de la Palestine à l'époque perse." *Transeuphratène* 3 (1990): 31–74.

Mazar, B. *The Mountain of the Lord.* Garden City, N.Y.: Doubleday, 1975.

Millard, A. R. "Assyrian Royal Names in Biblical Hebrew." *JSS* 21 (1976): 1–14.

Naveh, J. *The Development of the Aramaic Script.* Jerusalem: Israel Academy of Sciences and Humanities, 1970.

Porten, B. *Archives from Elephantine.* Berkeley: University of California Press, 1968.

Rainey, A. F. *The Scribe at Ugarit.* Jerusalem: Israel Academy of Sciences and Humanities, 1968.

Rosenthal, F. *A Grammar of Biblical Aramaic.* Wiesbaden: Harrassowitz, 1961.

Stern, E. *Archaeology of the Land of the Bible II: The Assyrian, Babylonian and Persian Periods (732–332 BCE).* New York: Doubleday, 2001.

Williamson, H. G. M. *Israel in the Book of Chronicles.* Cambridge: Cambridge University Press, 1977.

———. "Ezra and Nehemiah in the Light of the Texts from Persepolis." *Bulletin for Biblical Research* 1 (1991): 50–54.

Wightman, G. J. *The Walls of Jerusalem from the Canaanites to the Mamluks.* Mediterranean Archaeological Supplement 4. Sydney: Meditarch, 1993.

Yamauchi, E. *Africa and the Bible.* Grand Rapids, Mich.: Baker, 2004.

———. *Persia and the Bible.* Grand Rapids, Mich.: Baker: 1990.

———. "Ezra and Nehemiah, Books of." Pages 284–95 in *Dictionary of the Old Testament: Historical Books.* Edited by Bill T. Arnold and H. G. M. Williamson. Downers Grove, Ill.: InterVarsity Press, 2003.

14. OUTLINES

Ezra

I. The First Return from Exile and the Rebuilding of the Temple (1:1–6:22)
- A. The First Return of the Exiles (1:1–11)
  1. The Edict of Cyrus (1:1–4)
  2. The Return under Sheshbazzar (1:5–11)
- B. The List of Returning Exiles (2:1–70)
  1. Leaders of the Return (2:1–2a)
  2. Families (2:2b–20)
  3. Villagers (2:21–35)
  4. Priests (2:36–39)
  5. Levites and Temple Personnel (2:40–42)
  6. Temple Servants (2:43–58)
  7. Individuals Lacking Evidence of Their Genealogies (2:59–63)
  8. Totals (2:64–67)
  9. Offerings (2:68–69)
  10. Settlement of the Exiles (2:70)
- C. The Revival of Temple Worship (3:1–13)
  1. The Rebuilding of the Altar (3:1–3)
  2. The Festival of Booths (3:4–6)
  3. The Beginning of Temple Reconstruction (3:7–13)
- D. The Opposition to the Rebuilding (4:1–24)
  1. Opposition during the Reign of Cyrus (4:1–5)
  2. Opposition during the Reign of Xerxes (4:6)
  3. Opposition during the Reign of Artaxerxes I (4:7–23)
     a. The Letter to the King (4:7–16)
     b. The Letter from the King (4:17–23)
  4. Resumption of Work under Darius (4:24)
- E. The Completion of the Temple (5:1–6:22)
  1. A New Beginning Inspired by Haggai and Zechariah (5:1–2)
  2. The Intervention of the Governor Tattenai (5:3–5)
  3. The Report to Darius (5:6–17)
  4. The Search for the Decree of Cyrus (6:1–5)
  5. Darius's Order for the Rebuilding of the Temple (6:6–12)
  6. The Completion of the Temple (6:13–15)
  7. The Dedication of the Temple (6:16–18)
  8. The Celebration of the Passover (6:19–22)

15. MAPS AND CHARTS

Dates are given according to a Nisan-to-Nisan Jewish calendar. The Jewish dates are indicated with Roman numerals representing months, Arabic numerals representing days.

NISAN	YEAR			MODERN		EVENT	REFER-ENCE
Year	Month	Day		Month	Day		
539	VII	16		Oct.	12	Babylon falls	
	VIII	3		Oct.	29	Cyrus enters Babylon	Dan 5:30-31
538 to	III	24		Mar.	24 to	Cyrus's first regnal year	Ezra 1-4
537	III	11		Mar.	11		
537				spring		Return under Sheshbazzar	Ezra 1:11
	VII			Oct.	5 to	Building the altar	Ezra 3:1-3
				Nov.	2		
536 to	II			Apr.	29 to	Work on the temple resumed	Ezra 3:8
530				May	28	Opposition during Cyrus's reign	Ezra 4:1-5
520	VI	1		Aug.	29	Haggai speaks to Zerubbabel	Hag 1:1
	VI	1		Aug.–Dec.	(?)	Work resumed on temple under Darius	Ezra 5:1-2; Hag 1:14-15
515	XII			Mar.	12	Temple completed	Ezra 6:15
458	I	1		Apr.	8	Ezra departs	Ezra 7:7
	V	1		Aug.	4	Ezra arrives	Ezra 7:8-9
	IX	20		Dec.	19	People assemble	Ezra 10:9
	X	1		Dec.	29	Committee begins investigation	Ezra 10:16
446 to				Mar.	26 to	Nineteenth year of Artaxerxes	
445				Apr.	12		

(Continue on the next page)

(Continued)

445 to				Apr.	13 to	Twentieth year of Artaxerxes	Neh 1:1
444				Apr.	2		
445	I			Apr.–May		Nehemiah approaches the king	Neh 2:1
				Aug.	?	Nehemiah arrives	Neh 2:11
	VI	25		Oct.	2	Completion of the wall	Neh 6:15
	VII			Oct.	8 to	Public assembly	Neh 7:73
				Nov.	5		
	VII	15 to		Oct.	22 to	Feast of Booths	Neh 8:14
		22			28		
	VII	24		Oct.	30	Fast	Neh 9:1
433 to				Apr.	1 to	Thirty-second year of Artaxerxes	Neh 5:14
432				Apr.	19	Nehemiah's recall and return	Neh 13:6

Number of Month	**Jewish Name**	**Modern Name**
I	Nisan	Mar./Apr.
II	Iyyar	Apr./May
III	Sivan	May/June
IV	Tammuz	June/July
V	Ab	July/Aug
VI	Elul	Aug./Sept.
VII	Tishri	Sept./Oct.
VIII	Marcheshvan	Oct./Nov.
IX	Kislev	Nov./Dec.
X	Tebeth	Dec./Jan.
XI	Shebat	Jan./Feb.
XII	Adar	Feb./Mar.

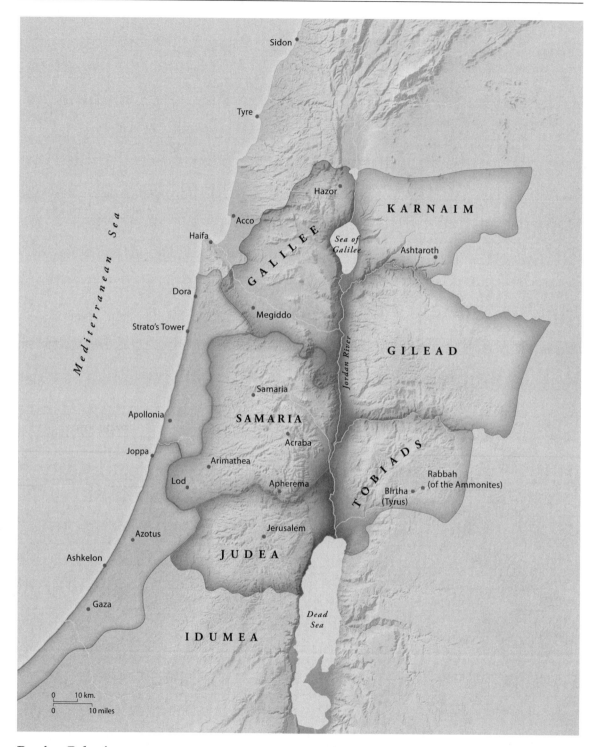

Persian Palestine

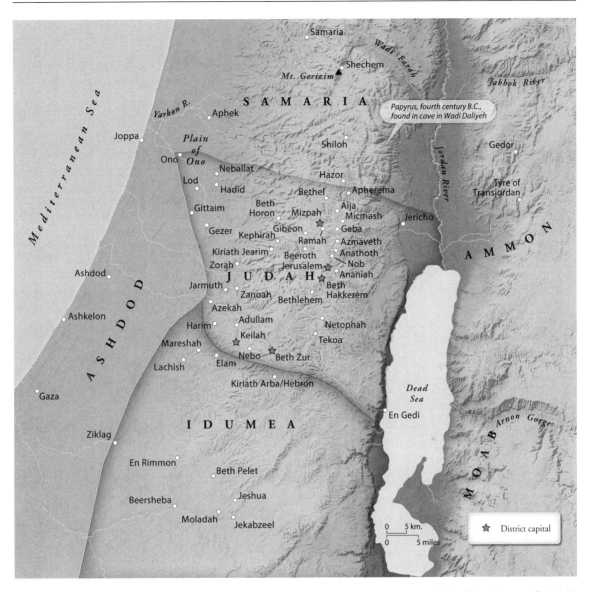

Samaria

Wadi Fārah

Shechem

Mt. Gerizim▲

Jabbok River

S A M A R I A

Papyrus, fourth century B.C., found in cave in Wadi Daliyeh

Yarkon R.

Aphek

Mediterranean Sea

Joppa

Plain of Ono

Shiloh

Gedor

Ono

Neballat

Hazor

Jordan River

Lod

Hadid

Bethel

Apherema

Tyre of Transjordan

Gittaim

Beth Horon

Mizpah

Aija

Micmash

Jericho

Gezer

Kephirah

Gibeon

Geba

A M M O N

Kiriath Jearim

Ramah

Azmaveth

Zorah

Beeroth

Jerusalem

Anathoth

Nob

J U D A H

Ananiah

Jarmuth

Zanoah

Beth Hakkerem

Azekah

Bethlehem

Harim

Adullam

Netophah

Keilah

Tekoa

Mareshah

Nebo

Beth Zur

Lachish

Elam

Ashdod

A S H D O D

Ashkelon

Kiriath Arba/Hebron

Gaza

I D U M E A

Dead Sea

En Gedi

Arnon Gorge

Ziklag

M O A B

En Rimmon

Beth Pelet

Beersheba

Jeshua

Moladah

Jekabzeel

0   5 km.
0   5 miles

☆   District capital

The Province of Judah

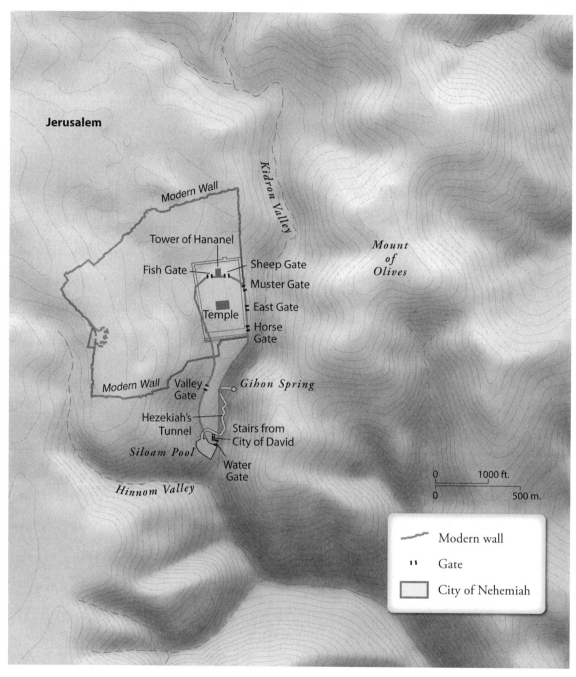

Jerusalem in the Time of Nehemiah

Text and Exposition

Ezra

I. THE FIRST RETURN FROM EXILE AND THE REBUILDING OF THE TEMPLE (1:1–6:22)

A. The First Return of the Exiles (1:1–11)

1. The Edict of Cyrus (1:1–4)

OVERVIEW

It had been nearly seventy years since the first deportation of the Jews by the Babylonians to Mesopotamia. Though the initial years must have been difficult, the second and third generation of Jews born in the exile had adjusted to their surroundings. Though some had become so comfortable that they refused to return to Judah when given the opportunity, still others, sustained by the examples and teachings of leaders such as Daniel and Ezekiel, retained their faith in the Lord's promises and their allegiance to their homeland.

> ¹In the first year of Cyrus king of Persia, in order to fulfill the word of the Lord spoken by Jeremiah, the Lord moved the heart of Cyrus king of Persia to make a proclamation throughout his realm and to put it in writing:
>
> ²"This is what Cyrus king of Persia says:
>
> "'The Lord, the God of heaven, has given me all the kingdoms of the earth and he has appointed me to build a temple for him at Jerusalem in Judah. ³Anyone of his people among you — may his God be with him, and let him go up to Jerusalem in Judah and build the temple of the Lord, the God of Israel, the God who is in Jerusalem. ⁴And the people of any place where survivors may now be living are to provide him with silver and gold, with goods and livestock, and with freewill offerings for the temple of God in Jerusalem.'"

COMMENTARY

1 Ezra 1:1–3a is virtually identical with the last verses of Chronicles (2Ch 36:22–23). (For the implications of this correspondence, see Introduction: Literary Form and Authorship.)

"In the first year" means the first regnal year of Cyrus, beginning in Nisan 538, after his capture of Babylon in October 539 (cf. Introduction: Chronology). Cuneiform texts record the Persian king's benefactions to Mesopotamian sanctuaries in the months following the capture of Babylon.

Cyrus, the founder of the Persian Empire and the greatest Achaemenid king, reigned over the Persians from 559 till 530 BC. He established Persian dominance over the Medes in 550, conquered Lydia and Anatolia in 547–46, and captured Babylon in 539.

Isaiah 44:28 and 45:1 speak of Cyrus as the Lord's "shepherd" and his "anointed"; other passages refer to him implicitly (Isa 41:2, 25; 45:18; cf. Jer 51:11). Daniel (Da 1:21; 6:28; 10:1) was in Babylon when Cyrus captured it.

"The word of the LORD spoken by Jeremiah" was the prophet's prediction (Jer 25:1–12; 29:10) of a seventy-year Babylonian captivity. The first deportations began in 605 BC, in the third year of Jehoiakim, according to Daniel 1:1. The seventieth year would be 536. We know that the Persian kings paid close heed to prophecies: Cambyses to Egyptian oracles, Darius and Xerxes to Greek oracles (*Herodotus* 8.133; 9.42, 151).

"Proclamation" (*qôl*) was an oral proclamation in the native language in contrast to the copy of the decree in 6:3–5, which was an Aramaic memorandum for the archives. In the case of the famous Behistun Inscription, Darius had copies sent throughout the empire in other languages, as we have copies in Akkadian from Babylon and on a papyrus in Aramaic from Elephantine, Egypt.

2 "The God of heaven" (*ʾelōhê haššāmāyim*; cf. Aram. *ʾelāh šemayyāʾ*) is a phrase that occurs primarily in the postexilic books. Seventeen of the twenty-two occurrences are in Ezra, Nehemiah, and Daniel. It appears also in apocryphal works (Tob 10:11–12; Jdt 5:8; 6:19; 11:17; cf. D. K. Andrews, "Yahweh the God of Heavens," in *The*

Seed of Wisdom [ed. W. S. McCullough; Toronto: Univ. of Toronto Press, 1964], 45ff.).

The holy city and the house of God are both prominent subjects in Ezra-Nehemiah. "Jerusalem" occurs eighty-six times, and the phrases "temple," "house of the LORD," and "house of God" appear fifty-three times. The phrase "a temple for him at Jerusalem in Judah" is literally, "a house for him in Jerusalem that is in Judah." The formulation "Jerusalem that is in Judah" is characteristic of Persian bureaucratic style. The Elephantine papyri (Cowley, 30:6) have "the temple of Yaw [i.e., Yahweh], the god, which is in the fortress of Yeb."

Cyrus instituted the enlightened policy of placating the gods of his subject peoples rather than carrying off their cult statues as the Assyrians, Elamites, Hittites, and Babylonians had done before. His generosity to the Jews was also paralleled by his benevolence to the Babylonians. Ultimately, however, it was the Lord who had "moved" his heart (v.1).

3 The religious orientation of the Achaemenid kings — Cyrus and his successors — is a controversial issue. Though we can be certain from his Behistun Inscription that Darius I was a follower of Zoroaster's god, Ahura Mazda, we cannot be certain of the religion of his predecessors, Cyrus and Cambyses. Mary Boyce and other scholars have claimed that Zoroastrianism influenced Cyrus (see Yamauchi, *Persia and the Bible*, ch. 12).

4 "Survivors" (*kol-hannišʾār*, "everyone who remains over") refers to those left over of the capture and deportation (cf. Ne 1:2). Regarding "may now be living," the Hebrew word for "living" (*gār*) is cognate to the word for "resident alien" (*gēr*). The deportees continued to be regarded as aliens, as were the Susians and Elamites who were "settled" in Samaria years after their deportation (4:10, 17).

"The people of any place" could mean non-Israelite neighbors as in the case of the exodus (Ex 3:21–22; 12:35–36). More probably it designates the many Jews, especially of the second and the third generation, who did not wish to leave the land of their birth.

"Freewill offerings" (nᵉdābâ, lit., "freewill offering") were voluntary giving (vv. 4, 6; 2:68–69; 3:5; 7:13–16; 8:28) and voluntary service (v. 5; 7:13), the keys to the restoration of God's temple and its service. A cognate form of nᵉdābâ was used of those who volunteered to join the community at Qumran (1QS 1, 6, et al.).

NOTES

1 The name of Cyrus in Hebrew is כּוֹרֶשׁ (kôreš; cf. Old Pers. kūruš, Akkad. kurašu, Gk. kyros). The title "king of Persia" in extant Old Persian texts appears first in the Behistun Inscription but is also found in the Nabonidus Chronicle. Because the Hebrew name for Cyrus is Koresh, Vernon Howell, the leader of the Branch Davidians at Waco, Texas, changed his name to "David Koresh." See J. D. Tabor and E. V. Gallagher, *Why Waco?* (Berkeley, Calif.: Univ. of California Press, 1995), 40.

The Assyrian king Esarhaddon declared in an inscription that the god Marduk reduced an original seventy-year period of depopulation for the city of Babylon and ordered its rebuilding in the eleventh year (cf. R. Borger, *Die Inschriften Asarhaddons Königs von Assyrien* [Graz: Archiv für Orientforschung, 1956], 15). For a discussion of the seventy-year period, see J. Applegate, "Jeremiah and the Seventy Years in the Hebrew Bible," in *The Book of Jeremiah and Its Reception* (ed. A. H. W. Curtis and T. Römer; Leuven: Leuven Univ. Press, 1997), 91–110.

There was also a return of Aramean exiles from the Syrian town of Neirab about 520 BC. See S. Timm, "Die Bedeutung der spätbabylonischen Texte aus *Nērab* für die Rückkehr der Judäer aus dem Exil," in *Meilenstein: Festgabe für Herbert Donner* (ed. M. Weippert and S. Timm; Wiesbaden: Harrassowitz, 1995), 276–88.

Earlier scepticism about the Cyrus decree was effectively countered by the citation of parallels from the decrees of Persian kings, most notably the Cyrus Cylinder (see E. J. Bickerman, "The Edict of Cyrus 1," *JBL* 65 [1946]: 249–75) and by R. de Vaux ("The Decrees of Cyrus," 63–96). It may also be argued from the analogy of the trilingual Xanthos Inscription that Jews could have aided the chancellery in adapting the king's proclamation for the intended audience as the Lycians did. See Briant, 704–9, 995–96.

4 M. D. Knowles, "Pilgrimage Imagery in the Returns in Ezra," *JBL* 123 (2004): 57–74, sees in Ezra 1 not an "exodus" but a "pilgrimage" motif.

2. The Return under Sheshbazzar (1:5–11)

⁵Then the family heads of Judah and Benjamin, and the priests and Levites — everyone whose heart God had moved — prepared to go up and build the house of the LORD in Jerusalem. ⁶All their neighbors assisted them with articles of silver and gold, with goods and livestock, and with valuable gifts, in addition to all the freewill offerings. ⁷Moreover, King Cyrus brought out the articles belonging to the temple of the LORD, which

Nebuchadnezzar had carried away from Jerusalem and had placed in the temple of his god. [8]Cyrus king of Persia had them brought by Mithredath the treasurer, who counted them out to Sheshbazzar the prince of Judah.

[9]This was the inventory:

gold dishes	30
silver dishes	1,000
silver pans	29
[10]gold bowls	30
matching silver bowls	410
other articles	1,000

[11]In all, there were 5,400 articles of gold and of silver. Sheshbazzar brought all these along when the exiles came up from Babylon to Jerusalem.

COMMENTARY

5–6 The Lord stirred not only the heart of the Persian king but also the hearts of many of the exiles who had maintained their faith in the Lord in spite of the devastation of their homeland. A vivid attestation to this faith is an inscription carved at Khirbet Beit Lei, five miles east of Lachish, first published in 1963 by J. Naveh. F. M. Cross ("The Cave Inscriptions from Khirbet Beit Lei," in *Near Eastern Archaeology in the Twentieth Century* [ed. J. A. Sanders; Garden City, N.Y.: Doubleday, 1970], 299–306) has translated the text as follows: "I am Yahweh thy God: I will accept the cities of Judah and will redeem Jerusalem." He has suggested that this may have been incised by a refugee to express his trust in God's faithfulness despite the desolation of the holy city (cf. La 3:22–24).

7 Conquerers customarily carried off the statues of the gods of conquered cities. The Hittites took the statue of Marduk when they conquered the city of Babylon. The Philistines took the ark of the Jews and placed it in the temple of Dagon (1Sa 5:2). But the ark was evidently destroyed by Nebuchadnezzar, as we no longer hear of it. Based on the legendary *Kebra Negast* tradition that the Queen of Sheba's son, Menelik, stole the ark from Solomon, Ethiopian Christians claim that they possess the ark in their cathedral in Aksum (see Yamauchi, *Africa and the Bible*, 100–105, 175–78).

As the Jews did not have a statue of the Lord, Nebuchadnezzar carried off the temple goods instead. The Hebrew of 2 Kings 24:13 indicates that he cut up the vessels of gold, no doubt the larger ones, to facilitate their transporting (cf. 2Ki 25:13; Jer 52:17). Jeremiah spoke of false prophets who prematurely predicted the return of these vessels (Jer 27:16–22a; 28:6), but he prophesied their ultimate return (27:22b). Belshazzar had the audacity to drink from some of the temple vessels (Da 5:23).

8 The Persian name "Mithredath" means "given by Mithra." Mithra(s) was the Persian god whose mystery religion became popular among Roman soldiers in the second century AD. Another official with the same name appears in 4:7. Mithradates was the name of the king of Pontus in northern Turkey who warred against the Romans (cf. R. A. Bowman, *Aramaic Ritual Texts from Persepolis* [Chicago: Univ. of Chicago Press, 1968], 32, 73, 78, for the name "Dat-Mithra"; see also Yamauchi, *Persia and the Bible*, ch. 14).

The word for "treasurer" is *gizbār*, from the Old Persian *ganzabara*. The word may be reflected in Gaspar (Caspar), the name of one of the Magi according to the apocryphal Gospel of the Hebrews.

Sheshbazzar, who had a Babylonian name (cf. Notes), was probably a Jewish official who served as a deputy governor of Judah under the satrap in Samaria (cf. Ezr 5:14; 1 Esd 2:12).

9–11 When the Assyrian and Babylonian conquerors carried off booty, their scribes made a careful inventory of it. The actual figures in the Hebrew text add up to 2,499 rather than 5,400, perhaps because only the larger and more valuable vessels were specified. The RSV follows 1 Esdras and gives figures of 1,000; 1,000; 29; 30; 2,410; and 1,000—a total of 5,469. The exact meanings of the Hebrew words for the objects are uncertain (cf. Notes).

We know nothing about the details of Sheshbazzar's journey, which probably took place in the spring of 537. Judging from Ezra's later journey (7:8–9), the trip probably took about four months. The caravan would have proceeded from Babylonia up the Euphrates River and then south through the Orontes Valley of Syria into Palestine.

NOTES

8 שֵׁשְׁבַּצַּר (*šēšbaṣṣar*, "Sheshbazzar") is a Babylonian name perhaps derived from one of the following Akkadian names:

(1) *Sin-ab-uṣur* ("Sin protect the father"; cf. LXX Sabanassaro, Sanabassaros; 1 Esd 2:5, 8). Sin was the moon god. This etymology is favored by Albright, Meyer, and Rosenthal.

(2) *Šamaš-ab-uṣur* ("Shamash protect the father") or *Šamaš-apla-uṣur* ("Shamash protect the son," favored by Brockington and Noth). Shamash was the sun god.

(3) *Šaššu-ab-uṣur* ("Shashu protect the father"). *Šaššu* is a variant for *Šamaš*. See R. Berger, "Zu den Namen שׁשׁבצר und שׁנאצר," *ZAW* 83 (1971): 98–100.

The proposal that Sheshbazzar is to be identified with Shenazzar (1Ch 3:18), the fourth son of Jehoiachin and therefore a royal descendant of David, should be abandoned. Josephus mistakenly identified him with Zerubbabel inasmuch as they both had a hand in laying the foundations of the temple (cf. Ezr 3:8–10 with 5:16).

9–10 אֲגַרְטְלִים (*ʾagarṭelîm*, "dishes") refers to a "basket with [a] pointed bottom" (cf. 2Ki 10:7) or "a basket-shaped libation cup."

מַחֲלָפִים (*maḥălāpîm*, "pans") occurs only here in the OT. In late Hebrew a related word is a technical term for the knives used in ritual slaughter of animals (so KJV, but cf. the RSV's "censers").

כְּפוֹרִים (*kepôrîm*, "bowls") occurs only here, in 8:27, and in 1 Chronicles 28:17. It is perhaps a late Hebrew word for מִזְרָק (*mizrāq*, "basin"; cf. Nu 4:14; 1Ki 7:40) or for קְעָרָה (*qeʿārâ*, "dish"; cf. Nu 4:7).

M. Segal ("Numerical Discrepancies in the List of Vessels in Ezra 1:9–11," *VT* 52 [2002]: 122–29) offers an explanation of how scribal errors in copying could have resulted in the discrepant figures.

P. R. Ackroyd ("The Temple Vessels—A Continuity Theme," *VTSup* 23 [1972]: 166–81) highlights the importance of this theme for the Jewish community.

During Pontius Pilate's rule as governor (AD 26–36), the leader of a rebellion of Samaritans led his followers to Mount Gerizim, where he promised to show them "the sacred vessels which were buried there, where Moses had deposited them" (Josephus, *Ant.* 18.85 [4.1]). See M. F. Collins, "The Hidden Vessels in Samaritan Traditions," *JSJ* 3 (1972): 97–116.

B. The List of Returning Exiles (2:1–70)

1. Leaders of the Return (2:1–2a)

> ¹Now these are the people of the province who came up from the captivity of the exiles, whom Nebuchadnezzar king of Babylon had taken captive to Babylon (they returned to Jerusalem and Judah, each to his own town, ²in company with Zerubbabel, Jeshua, Nehemiah, Seraiah, Reelaiah, Mordecai, Bilshan, Mispar, Bigvai, Rehum and Baanah).

COMMENTARY

1 The list of returning exiles in vv.1–70 almost exactly parallels the list in Nehemiah 7:6–73 (cf. 1 Esd 5:4–46). The list of localities indicates that people retained their memories of their homes and that exiles from a wide background of tribes, villages, and towns returned.

The KJV's colon after Zerubbabel (v.2) implies that all those who followed were among those returning with Zerubbabel in 537 BC. The NIV, NRSV, and other versions place a comma after Zerubbabel, thus leaving open the possibility, according to some scholars, that the list may include those who returned to Judah at a later date.

A comparison of Ezra 2 with Nehemiah 7 reveals a number of differences in both the names and the numbers that are listed. Though the lists of temple personnel show few variations, there are differences

in about half the cases of the lists of the laity. Of the 153 numbers, 29 are not the same in Ezra and Nehemiah. Many differences may be explained by assuming that a cipher notation was used with vertical strokes for units, horizontal strokes for tens, and stylized mems (the initial letter of the Hebrew word $m\bar{e}^{\,\circ}\hat{a}$) for hundreds. Single strokes could be overlooked or miscopied. H. L. Allrik ("The Lists of Zerubbabel [Nehemiah 7 and Ezra 2] and the Hebrew Numerical Notation," *BASOR* 136 [1954]: 27) states: "As for the lists in Nehemiah 7 and Ezra 2, while at first glance these textual-numerical differences may seem detrimental, actually they greatly enhance the value of the lists, as they bring out much of their real nature and age."

2a The list of eleven leaders in Ezra 2 is increased by the addition of "Nahamani" inserted before the name of Mordecai in Nehemiah 7:7 (cf. 1 Esd 5:8). On "Zerubbabel" see comments on 5:2.

"Jeshua" is a name similar to "Joshua" (Ne 8:17) and to the Greek "Jesus." It means "Yahweh is salvation." If he is the same as the Joshua of Haggai 1:1, he was the son of Jehozadak, the high priest carried into exile (1Ch 6:15), and the grandson of Seraiah, the high priest put to death by Nebuchadnezzar (2Ki 25:18–21; cf. Ezr 5:2; Ne 12:1, 10, 26; Zec 3:1).

"Nehemiah" was not the same person as the king's cupbearer (on the name see comment on Ne 1:1). "Seraiah" means "Yahweh is Prince." Nehemiah 7:7 has "Azariah." "Reelaiah" is paralleled in Nehemiah 7:7 by "Raamiah."

"Mordecai" is based on the name of the god of Babylon, Marduk (Jer 50:2). It is the name borne by Esther's uncle. "Bilshan" is probably the Akkadian *Bel-šunu* ("their Lord"). "Mispar" is paralleled in Nehemiah 7:7 by "Mispereth."

"Bigvai," a Persian name meaning "happy," was borne by the Persian governor of Judea addressed by the Jews of Elephantine: *B-g-w-h-y* (*Bagohi*). Josephus (*Ant.* 11.297 [7.1]) transliterated the name in Greek as *Bagoses*.

"Rehum" is a hypocoristicon (shortened form) for "(God) has been compassionate." Nehemiah 7:7 has "Nehum," which is probably a scribal error. The Murashu texts have a comparable name: *Raḥîm*.

The practice of giving Babylonian or Persian names to Jews in captivity (Est 2:7; Da 1:7) is richly illustrated by the archives of Murashu. According to M. D. Coogan ("Life in the Diaspora: Jews at Nippur in the Fifth Century BC," *BA* 37 [1974]: 11), "It was not considered a serious compromise of one's Jewish identity to give a child a name which was not Yahwistic, nor even of Hebrew or Aramaic linguistic stock."

NOTES

1 The simple, straightforward view of the lists in Ezra 2 and Nehemiah 7 as a list of the returnees under Zerubbabel is accepted by A. Alt, E. Meyer, F. Micheli, M. Noth, W. Rudolph, H. Schaeder, and G. Widengren. Other scholars (e.g., L. H. Brockington, R. J. Coggins, J. M. Myers, and R. North) doubt that so many people would have responded at first. Various alternative dates and explanations for the lists have therefore been proposed.

K. Galling ("The 'Gola List' according to Ezra 2//Nehemiah 7," *JBL* 70 [1951]: 149–58) has argued that the lists represent an official census drawn up in 519 BC for the governor Tattenai (Ezr 5) to show that the Jews could achieve the reconstruction of the temple.

J. E. Dyck ("Ezra 2 in Ideological Critical Perspective," in *Rethinking Contexts, Rereading Texts* [Sheffield: Sheffield Academic, 2000], 134), who offers a social science analysis of Ezra 2, dates the list to the time of Zerubbabel: "On this reading the list could be construed as a record of all the returnees from the time of Cyrus to Darius and not just a single return."

Some scholars date the lists to Nehemiah's time, arguing that the ending in Nehemiah 7:72b (7:73 in English versions)–8:1 provides a more satisfactory setting than Ezra 2:70–3:1. See especially the commentary by Williamson.

In the case of discrepant numbers, R. Klein ("Old Readings in I Esdras," *HTR* 62 [1969]: 99–107) notes that 1 Esdras supports Ezra thirteen times and Nehemiah but twice. He concludes that 1 Esdras preserves an older text than MT Ezra or the LXX. In some cases the 1 Esdras text can be used to correct some of the names and figures in the list.

In Ezra and Nehemiah there are about eighty different theophorous names bearing the divine element "iah" (for "Yahweh"), which are mentioned almost 270 times. We can compare these names with similar names of Jews from the contemporary communities in Egypt and Mesopotamia. At Elephantine in Egypt, of more than 160 Jewish names, only a few were nontheophorous.

A striking example of such faith implicit in a name is found in a seal dated paleographically to the sixth century BC. A father with the Babylonian name *Šawaš-šar-uṣur* ("Shamash protect the king") gave his daughter the Hebrew name *Yeho-yishma* ("Yahweh will hear"; N. Avigad, "Seals of the Exile," *IEJ* 15 [1965]: 223–30).

מְדִינָה (*medînâ*, "province") is used of an administrative area, either a satrapy or its subdivision. The "province" here is Babylonia (cf. 7:16). The word also appears in the Aramaic papyri (e.g., Cowley, 24:18, 35; 37:6; et al.; F. Charles Fensham, "Medina in Ezra and Nehemiah," *VT* 25 [1975]: 795–97).

2. Families (2:2b–20)

The list of the men of the people of Israel:	
³the descendants of Parosh	2,172
⁴of Shephatiah	372
⁵of Arah	775
⁶of Pahath-Moab (through the line of Jeshua and Joab)	2,812
⁷of Elam	1,254
⁸of Zattu	945
⁹of Zaccai	760
¹⁰of Bani	642
¹¹of Bebai	623
¹²of Azgad	1,222
¹³of Adonikam	666
¹⁴of Bigvai	2,056
¹⁵of Adin	454
¹⁶of Ater (through Hezekiah)	98
¹⁷of Bezai	323
¹⁸of Jorah	112
¹⁹of Hashum	223
²⁰of Gibbar	95

COMMENTARY

2b "The list of the men of the people of Israel" may have been of males only over the age of twelve, as 1 Esdras 5:41 makes explicit: "twelve or more years of age."

3 "The descendants of Parosh" represented the largest family of priests returning from Babylon. Members of this family returned with Ezra (8:3); some of them assisted in rebuilding the wall (Ne 3:25). "Parosh" means "flea" and may connote insignificance (cf. 1Sa 24:14). S. D. Goitein ("Nicknames as Family Names," *JAOS* 90 [1970]: 517) suggests, however: "Fleas are tormenting bloodsuckers, and the idea expressed in this name, or by-name, is that its bearer should be a constant plague to his enemies. A distinguished Arab family in Jerusalem is called *Barghūtī*, which means the same thing; Arabic *barghūth* and Hebrew *parʿōš* are identical phonetically and semantically."

Insect and animal names were common among the Hebrews (cf. comments on vv.5, 46; Ne 11:16; cf. Caleb ["dog"], Deborah ["bee"], Jonah ["dove"], Leah ["wild cow"], Rachel ["ewe"], et al.). An ostracon from the seventh century BC has the following names: Qore ("partridge"), Sorek ("bay horse"), and Qeres ("biting insect[?]"; Hestrin, *Inscriptions Reveal*, #138).

4 "Shephatiah" means "Yahweh has judged." The name occurs on seal #89 of the Moussaief collection, dated ca. 700 BC (Deutsch and Lemaire, 95), in the phrase *lšpṭyhw bn kšy*, "Belonging to Shepaṭyahu son of Kushi."

5 "Arah" means "wild ox." As the name appears elsewhere in 1 Chronicles 7:39 and Nehemiah 6:18 and has been found in documents from Mesopotamia, it may have been adopted during the exile.

6 "Pahath-Moab" means "governor of Moab" (cf. 8:4; 10:30; Ne 7:11; 10:14). This reference may signify the descendants of the tribe of Reuben who were deported from the province of Moab by Tiglath-Pileser III (cf. 1Ch 5:3–8).

7 "Elam" was the name of the country in southwestern Iran in the area of Susa (cf. v.31; 8:7; 10:2, 26; Ne 7:12; 10:14).

9 "Zaccai" may mean "pure" or may be a shortened form of "Zechariah" ("Yahweh has remembered").

10 "Bani" is a shortened form of "Benaiah" ("Yahweh has built"). Nehemiah 7:15 has "Binnui."

11 "Bebai" is "pupil of the eye"; cf. *Bi-bi-ya* in the Murashu texts (Coogan, 120).

12 "Azgad" ("Gad is strong") is either a reference to Gad, the god of fortune, or to the Transjordanian tribe of Gad. This name occurs only here and in Nehemiah 7:17. The greatest numerical discrepancy occurs here: Ezra lists 1,222 whereas Nehemiah lists 2,322.

13 "Adonikam" means "my Lord has arisen."

14 On "Bigvai" see comment on v.2.

15 "Adin" means "voluptuous."

16 "Ater" means "lefty" (cf. Jdg 3:15; 20:16). "Hezekiah" means "Yahweh is my strength."

17 "Bezai," a shorted form of "Bezalel," means "in the shadow of God."

18 "Jorah" is "autumn rain." Nehemiah 7:24 has "Hariph."

19 "Hashum" means "broad nose."

20 "Gibbar" is "strong man." Nehemiah 7:25 has "Gibeon."

3. Villagers (2:21-35)

OVERVIEW

Verses 21-35 list a series of villages and towns, most of them in Benjaminite territory north of Jerusalem. Why were some listed by their villages and not by families? Williamson (*Ezra, Nehemiah*, 34) believes that these may have represented "the poor of the land" (2Ki 25:12), who had no land or property in their own name.

Significantly, no references are to towns in the Negev south of Judah. When Nebuchadnezzar overran Judah (Jer 13:19), the Edomites (cf. Obadiah) opportunistically occupied the area. By the fifth century BC, Nabataean Arabs (Mal 1:2-5) were pressing on the Edomites, who moved west and occupied the area south of Hebron, later known as Idumaea (see K. G. Hoglund, "Edomites," in Hoerth, Mattingly, and Yamauchi, 335-47; Lemaire, 51-53).

[21]the men of Bethlehem	123
[22]of Netophah	56
[23]of Anathoth	128
[24]of Azmaveth	42
[25]of Kiriath Jearim, Kephirah and Beeroth	743
[26]of Ramah and Geba	621
[27]of Micmash	122
[28]of Bethel and Ai	223
[29]of Nebo	52
[30]of Magbish	156
[31]of the other Elam	1,254
[32]of Harim	320
[33]of Lod, Hadid and Ono	725
[34]of Jericho	345
[35]of Senaah	3,630

COMMENTARY

21 "Bethlehem," among the returnees may have been the ancestors of Jesus (Mic 5:2).

22 "Netophah," a city south of Jerusalem, was settled by Levites (1Ch 9:16).

23 "Anathoth," a village named after the Canaanite goddess Anath, was located three miles north of Jerusalem and was the home of the prophet Jeremiah (Jer 1:1). *Yalkut Shimoni*, a late collection of Jewish midrash, notes that because the people of Anathoth had conspired to murder the prophet (Jer 11:19), it was cursed (Jer 11:21-22). A midrash explains that as later descendants repented, they were numbered among the returning exiles.

24 "Azmaveth" was two miles farther north. Nehemiah 7:28 has "Beth-Azmaveth" ("the house of Azmaveth").

25 Here the Hebrew "Kiriath Arim" (cf. NIV margin) is probably an error for "Kiriath Jearim" ("village of the woods"), which is found in Nehemiah 7:29. The latter was the site eight miles northwest of Jerusalem where the ark rested (1Sa 6:21 – 7:1). "Beeroth" means "wells" and has been succeeded by modern Bireh, a site located twelve miles north of Jerusalem.

26 "Ramah" ("the height") was five miles north of Jerusalem. "Geba" was located east of Ramah.

27 "Michmash," eight miles northeast of Jerusalem, was the scene of Jonathan's exploit (1Sa 13:23).

28 "Bethel" ("house of God") was located at modern Beitin, twelve miles north of Jerusalem (cf. A. F. Rainey ["Bethel Is Still *Beitin*," *WTJ* 33 (1971): 175 – 88], who effectively refutes David Livingstone ["Location of Biblical Bethel and Ai Reconsidered," *WTJ* 33 (1970): 283 – 300]). Bethel, a border town, probably became a part of Judah in Josiah's reign. Cities such as Bethel, Mizpah, Gibeon, and Gibeah seemed to have escaped the Babylonian assault. Bethel, however, was destroyed in the transition between the Babylonian and Persian periods. Excavations reveal a small town on the site in Ezra's day.

29 "Nebo" was perhaps the same as Nob, which has been located on Mount Scopus, just to the east of Jerusalem (cf. Mordechai Cogan, "The Men of Nebo—Repatriated Reubenites," *IEJ* 29 [1979]: 37 – 39).

30 "Magbish" was perhaps southwest of Adullam.

31 On "Elam," see comment on v.7.

32 "Harim" means "dedicated to God." Compare the Arabic designation of what the Jews call the Temple Mount, the *Haram esh-Sharif*, "The Noble Sanctuary," and the English word "harem."

33 "Lod," modern Lydda, ten miles southeast of Jaffa, is today the site of the Israeli international airport.

34 "Jericho" is the famous oasis city just north of the Dead Sea.

35 "Senaah" means "the hated one." The largest number of returnees—3,630 (3,930 in Ne 7:38)—is associated with Senaah. Some have therefore suggested that this group did not come from a specific locality or family but represented low-caste people, as inferred from the meaning of the name. But others have interpreted it as a place name. (See Clines, 53; R. Zadok, "A Note on *snʾh*," *VT* 38 [1988]: 483 – 86.)

4. Priests (2:36 – 39)

OVERVIEW

These verses name four clans of priests numbering 4,289, or about one-tenth the total number of priests. Those named here may have been inspired by the hope of serving in a rebuilt temple.

³⁶The priests:

　the descendants of Jedaiah (through the family of Jeshua)　　　　973

[37]of	Immer	1,052
[38]of	Pashhur	1,247
[39]of	Harim	1,017

COMMENTARY

36 "Jedaiah" ("Yahweh has known") was a family of priests noted during the time of David (1Ch 24:7). The name appears as *Yadaʿyaw* in the Murashu texts (Coogan, 26).

37 "Immer" means "lamb" (cf. 1Ch 24:14).

38 "Pashhur" is derived from the Egyptian *Psh Ḥr* ("the portion of Horus"; cf. T. Meek, "Moses and the Levites," *AJSL* 56 [1939]: 113–20). The name is found on a number of inscriptions and seals (cf. Hestrin, *Inscriptions Reveal*, #61).

39 On "Harim," see comment on v.32.

5. Levites and Temple Personnel (2:40–42)

[40]The Levites:	
the descendants of Jeshua and Kadmiel (through the line of Hodaviah)	74
[41]The singers:	
the descendants of Asaph	128
[42]The gatekeepers of the temple:	
the descendants of Shallum, Ater, Talmon, Akkub, Hatita and Shobai	139

COMMENTARY

40 The Levites, descendants of Levi (Ge 29:34), may have originally been regarded as priests (Dt 18:6–8; cf. Jdg 17:7–13); but they became subordinate to the priestly descendants of Aaron, brother of Moses (Nu 3:9–10; 1Ch 16:4–42; 23:26–32). The Levites were then prohibited from offering sacrifices on the altar (Nu 16:40; 18:7). As the Levites had no inheritance in land, they lived in forty-eight Levitical cities and were supported by tithes (Dt 12:12, 18; 14:29; Tob 1:7). They were butchers, doorkeepers, singers (1Ch 15:22; 16:4–7), scribes and teachers (Ne 8:7, 9), and even temple beggars (2Ch 24:5–11). (See J. Schaper, *Priester und Leviten im achämenidischen Juda* [Tübingen: Mohr/Siebeck, 2000].)

41 "The singers" ("cantors," JB) are called "holy singers" in 1 Esdras 5:27 (cf. Ne 11:22–23; 12:29;

13:10). "Asaph" (lit., "he removed") was one of the three Levites appointed by David over the temple singers.

42 "Gatekeepers" are mentioned thirteen times in Ezra-Nehemiah, nineteen times in Chronicles. They are usually regarded as Levites (1Ch 9:26; 2Ch 8:14; 23:4; Ne 12:25; 13:22) but are sometimes differentiated from them (2Ch 35:15; cf. Jacob Liver, *Chapters in the History of the Priests and Levites* [Jerusalem: Magnes, 1968]).

At times as many as four thousand gatekeepers were mentioned (1Ch 23:5). Their primary function was to tend the doors and gates of the temple (1Sa 3:15; 1Ch 9:17–32) and perform other menial tasks (2Ch 31:14). The psalmist said he would rather be a doorkeeper in the house of his God than dwell in the tents of the wicked (Ps 84:10; cf. the English word "janitor," which comes from the Latin *janua*, "door").

The 139 gatekeepers listed here belonged to six small clans. "Shallum" means "complete" and "Talmon" means "brightness." The name "Akkub" ("protected") appears eight times in the Murashu texts as ʿaqqûb (Coogan, 32–33).

NOTES

41 מְשֹׁרְרִים (mᵉšōrᵉrîm, "singers") is a Polel participle of the verb שִׁיר (šîr, "to sing"). At Ugarit there was a guild of musicians called šrm.

42 שֹׁעֲרִים (šōˤᵃrîm) are "gatekeepers." At Ugarit, watchmen of the temple gates were called tgrm.

6. Temple Servants (2:43–58)

⁴³The temple servants:
the descendants of
Ziha, Hasupha, Tabbaoth,
⁴⁴Keros, Siaha, Padon,
⁴⁵Lebanah, Hagabah, Akkub,
⁴⁶Hagab, Shalmai, Hanan,
⁴⁷Giddel, Gahar, Reaiah,
⁴⁸Rezin, Nekoda, Gazzam,
⁴⁹Uzza, Paseah, Besai,
⁵⁰Asnah, Meunim, Nephussim,
⁵¹Bakbuk, Hakupha, Harhur,
⁵²Bazluth, Mehida, Harsha,
⁵³Barkos, Sisera, Temah,
⁵⁴Neziah and Hatipha

> 55The descendants of the servants of Solomon:
>   the descendants of
>   Sotai, Hassophereth, Peruda,
>   56Jaala, Darkon, Giddel,
>   57Shephatiah, Hattil,
>   Pokereth-Hazzebaim and Ami
> 58The temple servants and the descendants of the servants of Solomon   392

COMMENTARY

43 A long list of names (thirty-five in Ezra, thirty-two in Nehemiah) follows the heading "temple servants"; but the clans must have been small, averaging about nine members. The temple servants and the sons of Solomon's servants together numbered 392 (v.58)—more than the total of the Levites, gatekeepers, and singers (vv.40–42). Though of a menial status, they must have served God with true devotion.

The Hebrew word for temple servants (*nᵉtînîm,* "Nethinim") occurs only in 1 Chronicles 9:2 and in Ezra-Nehemiah (cf. Notes). The Nethinim occupied a special quarter in Jerusalem (Ne 3:26, 31; 11:21) and enjoyed exemption from taxes (Ezr 7:24). They participated in the rebuilding of the wall (Ne 3:26) and signed Nehemiah's covenant (Ne 10:29).

"Hasupha" ("quick") appears only here and in Nehemiah 7:46; likewise "Tabbaoth" ("signet ring").

45 "Labanah" means "white" (cf. the name "Lebanon").

"Hagabah" ("locust") may be derived from a root that in Arabic means "to cover," that is, alluding to the covering of the ground by locust swarms (cf. Agabus in Ac 11:28). The discovery of an inscription on a jar fragment from Tell el-Ful with this name has led E. Puech ("The Tell el-Ful Jar Inscription and the *Nᵉtînîm,*" *BASOR* 261 [1986]: 69–72) to suggest that some families of the Nethinim may have persisted until the first century BC. (See B. A. Levine, "Later Sources on the *Nᵉtînîm,*" *Orient and Occident* [ed. H. A. Hoffner, Jr.; Kevelaer: Butzon & Bercker, 1973], 101–7.)

46 "Shamlai" (*Kethiv*) is probably an error for "Shalmai" (*Qere,* NIV), which means "well-being" (cf. Ne 7:48).

"Hanan" ("[God] is gracious") is derived from the verb *ḥānan* ("to be gracious"). The name is found on seal #48 of the Moussaieff Collection (Deutsch and Lemaire, 54), dated ca. 700 BC, as *lḥnn kslyh,* "Belonging to Ḥanan (son of) Kisl(i)yah." Derivatives of this root are the components of numerous names borne by fifty-one persons in the OT, including Baalhanan, Elhanan, Hananel, Hanani, Hananiah, Hannah, Hanun, Henadad, Jehohanan, Johanan, and Tehinnah (cf. the Punic names Hanno and Hannibal of Carthage). "Johanan" ("Yahweh is gracious") has given us the name John. The woman's name "Hannah" gives us "Anna," "Ann," "Nan," and "Nancy."

47 "Giddel," a shortened form of "Geddeliah," means "Yahweh has made great."

48 "Rezin" is an Aramaic name that means "prince" (cf. Pr 14:28). It was borne by the kings of Damascus (Isa 7:8).

49 "Besai" is from Besodiah ("in the counsel of Yahweh").

50 "Asnah," an Egyptian name, means "he who belongs to Nah." "Meunim" seems to be related to the Maonites (Jdg 10:12), an Arab tribe south of the Dead Sea subdued by Uzziah (2Ch 26:7). A city near Petra is named Maʿan. "Nephussim" refers to a Bedouin tribe descended from Ishmael (Ge 25:15; 1Ch 1:31; 5:18–22).

51 On "Bakbuk" ("bottle") Goitein ("Nicknames as Family Names," *JAOS* 90 [1970]: 518) comments:

> This, no doubt, was originally a nickname. Baqbuq is a bottle, an earthenware container of bulging, protuberant form … one might assume that the nickname characterized a fat man with a protuding belly, and this is indeed what Martin Noth … tentatively suggests. But instead of the shape of the vessel, the sound of the word might have been intended. In Arabic, *baqbaq* designates the gurgling, bubbling sound of water poured out from a bottle, and figuratively, the prattle of a chatterbox. Thus the original Mr. Baqbūq might have received his by-name because of his ceaseless *baq, baq, baq, baq, baq*.

"Hakupha" means "humpbacked."

52 "Bazluth" is "onion." "Mehida" is possibly an error for Mehira ("bought"). "Harsha" means "deaf" or "dumb."

53 For "Barkos," see Notes. "Sisera" is a name borne by the Canaanite general who fought Deborah (Jdg 4–5).

54 "Neziah" is "faithful," and "Hatipha" means "snatched"—as a captive in childhood?

55 The phrase "the descendants of the servants of Solomon" occurs only in this passage and in Nehemiah 7:57, 60; 11:3. Note that the phrase does not appear in Chronicles. These may be the descendants of the Canaanites whom Solomon enslaved (1Ki 9:20–21). But B. A. Levine ("The Nᵉtînîm," *JBL* 82 [1963]: 209) argues that they were instead the descendants of the royal officers who were merchants in the service of Solomon (1Ki 9:22, 27).

"Hassophereth" is a feminine form that means "the scribe." Women scribes were rare. N. Avigad ("Hebrew Seals and Sealings and Their Significance for Biblical Research," *VTSup* 40 [1988]: 14) remarks on a stamped jar handle found by B. Mazar at the Temple Mount with the inscription, "Belonging to Ḥannah, daughter of ʿAzaryah": "This is the first seal impression belonging to a woman; all the others belonged to men. The impression of a woman's seal proves that her seal was indeed used for sealing and not as a mere piece of jewelry."

Goitein ("Nicknames," 517–18) remarks:

> Serving as a copyist or as a clerk was not a common occupation for a woman, but it was not entirely unknown even to Jewish or Islamic society in the Middle Ages. Cf.… an Iraqi Jew of noble descent whose family name was *Ibn an Nāsikha*, son of the female copyist. The colophon of an exactly and beautifully written codex of the Pentateuch from Yemen, written by Miriam, the daughter of the renowned scribe Benayah, contained this remark: "Please be indulgent of the shortcomings of this volume; I copied it while nursing a baby."

57 For "Shephatiah" see v.4. "Hattil" means "babbler." "Pokereth-Hazzebaim" is "huntress of the gazelles." For "Ami," Nehemiah 7:59 has "Amon" ("faithful").

58 An analysis of the figures in these lists yields the following percentages of the total (v.64):

Category	Percentages
Families	53.2
Villagers	29.6
Priests	14.7
Levites	0.2
Singers	0.4
Gatekeepers	0.5
Temple servants & descendants of the servants of Solomon	1.4
Total	**100.0**

NOTES

43 נְתִינִים (*nᵉtînîm*, "temple servants"), only in the plural, is derived from the verb נָתַן (*nātan*, "to give, devote, dedicate"; cf. 8:20). Some scholars compare them with the *ytnm*, a special group with the priests at Ugarit.

E. A. Speiser ("Unrecognized Dedication," *IEJ* 13 [1963]: 69–73) has compared the Nethinim with the Babylonian *širkūtu* (derived from the verb *šarāku[m]*, "to present, grant"), who were dedicated by their masters or fathers to the gods and lived in special quarters. Though without biblical support, many scholars follow the rabbinic tradition (*b. Yebam.* 79a) in viewing the Nethinim as the descendants of the Gibeonites, whom Joshua made "woodcutters and water carriers for the entire community" (Jos 9:21–23, 27). According to Ezra 8:20 it was David who dedicated the Nethinim as temple servants to the Levites (cf. Nu 31:28–30).

An analysis of the thirty-five names of the Nethinim in Ezra 2:43–54 indicates that fifteen, or 45 percent, are not attested elsewhere in the OT or in epigraphic onomastica. Moreover, 68 percent of the names are of foreign origin, as are 33–40 percent of the names of the sons of Solomon's servants. Whereas in preexilic times 90 percent of the priests and 82 percent of the Levites bore theophorous names, only 20 percent of the Nethinim had such names (cf. J. P. Weinberg, "*Nᵉtînîm* und 'Söhne der Sklaven Salomos' im 6.–4. Jh. v.u.Z.," *ZAW* 87 [1975]: 361ff.).

The majority of commentators (J. Wellhausen, E. Meyer, R. Kittel, R. de Vaux, J. Montgomery, S. Mowinckel, et al.) view the Nethinim as the descendants of foreign slaves dedicated to the temple service. An example of such a practice from Mesopotamia was the dedication by Nabonidus of 2,850 captives from Que as servants of the temples of Nabu and Nergal (cf. L. Mendelsohn, "State Slavery in Ancient Palestine," *BASOR* 85 [1942]: 14–17; M. Haran, "The Gibeonites, the Nethinim, and the Sons of Solomon's

Servants," *VT* 11 [1961]: 159–69). B. A. Levine ("The Nethinim," *JBL* 82 [1963]: 207–12), however, has argued that the Nethinim were originally the "dedicated" members of a cultic guild rather than slaves.

46 Jeffrey H. Tigay, in a study of hundreds of theophoric names both in the Scriptures and in extrabiblical sources, demonstrates that the overwhelming (more than 90 percent) number of names attest monotheistic allegiance to Yahweh; only a small percentage contain the names of foreign gods (see J. H. Tigay, "What's in a Name? Early Evidence of Devotion Exclusively to Yahweh," *BRev* 20/1 [2004]: 35–48, 50–51; cf. idem, *You Shall Have No Other Gods: Israelite Religion in the Light of Hebrew Inscriptions* [HSS; Atlanta: Scholars, 1986]). This impression is also confirmed by the evidence of seals. N. Avigad ("Hebrew Seals," 8) comments, "The worship of foreign gods, of which the Israelite people is often accused by the prophets, was apparently not so deep-rooted and widespread as to affect their personal names, at least not in Judah. In the entire corpus of Hebrew seals we find only one or two seals bearing a Ba'al name."

Yahwistic names are useful for identifying Jews in the Murashu archive. The Jews appear as contracting parties, agents, witnesses, collectors of taxes, and royal officials. A "Gedaliah" served as a mounted archer, a "Hanani" managed the royal poultry farm, and a "Jedaiah" was an agent of a royal steward. Their prosperous situation may explain why some chose to remain in Mesopotamia. At the same time their growing confidence may explain why, as E. J. Bickerman has shown in his analysis, the proportion of Yahwistic names grew larger in the second generation: "The break with syncretism occurred in the generation of Ezra, who, probably, was born about 500" ("The Generation of Ezra and Nehemiah," *Studies in Jewish and Christian History* 3 [1986]: 322).

53 בַּרְקוֹס (*barqôs*, "Barkos") is compounded with the name of the Edomite deity Qos (Qaus, Koze; T. C. Vriezen, "The Edomite Deity Qaus," *OtSt* 14 [1965]: 330–53). In 1960 Crystal Bennett found a seal at Umm El-Biyara near Petra with the name of Qos Gabar, an Edomite king ("Fouilles d'Umm el-Biyara," *RB* 73 [1966]: 398ff.). M. Rose ("Yahweh in Israel-Qaus in Edom?" *JSOT* 1 [1977]: 28–34) has argued that Qaus was originally an Arab god adopted by the Edomites. (See A. Lemaire, "Épigraphie et religion in Palestine à l'époque achéménide," *Transeu* 22 [2001]: 97–113.)

7. Individuals Lacking Evidence of Their Genealogies (2:59–63)

[59]The following came up from the towns of Tel Melah, Tel Harsha, Kerub, Addon and Immer, but they could not show that their families were descended from Israel:
[60]The descendants of
  Delaiah, Tobiah and Nekoda   652
[61]And from among the priests:
The descendants of Hobaiah, Hakkoz and Barzillai (a man who had married a daughter of Barzillai the Gileadite and was called by that name).
[62]These searched for their family records, but they could not find them and so were excluded from the priesthood as unclean. [63]The governor ordered them not to eat any of the most sacred food until there was a priest ministering with the Urim and Thummim.

COMMENTARY

59 "Tel Melah" ("mound of salt") is possibly a mound strewn with salt (cf. Jdg 9:45). "Tel Harsha" is "mound of potsherds." "Kerub" is "meadow" (cf. Akkad. *ḳirbu*). The Hebrew of "Addon" is "Addan" ("strong [place]").

The Hebrew word *tel* corresponds with the Akkadian *tillu* and the Arabian *tell* and designates hill-like mounds made from the remains of ruined cities built one on top of the other in layer-cake-like fashion. Tel-Abib (Eze 3:15) means the "mound of a flood," that is, a place destroyed by a flood (Akkad. *abūbu*).

The Jewish exiles were settled along the Kebar River (Eze 1:1) near the city of Nippur, a city in southern Mesopotamia that was the stronghold of rebels. The Jews were probably settled on the mounds of ruined cities depopulated by the Babylonians.

Of the exiles who returned, members of three lay families and three priestly families were unable at this time to prove their descent. Some may have derived from proselytes; others may have temporarily lost access to their genealogical records.

60 "Delaiah" is "Yahweh has drawn." The name is found on Moussaief seal #45 (Deutsch and Lemaire, 51), dated to the seventh century BC as *lhlʾl bn dlyhw*, "Belonging to Hilʾel son of Delayahu."

"Tobiah" ("Yahweh is good") was the name also of one of Nehemiah's chief adversaries (Ne 2:10, 19). This name appears on Moussaief seal #50 (Deutsch and Lemaire, 56), dated to the seventh century BC as *ṭbyhw ḥby* "Ṭobiyahu (son of) Ḥubbi." The name also appears in the Murashu texts as *Ṭobyaw* (Coogan, 26).

The total of 652 people who could not prove their genealogies represents but 1.5 percent of the total number given in v.64.

61 "Hobaiah" means "Yahweh has hidden." Barzillai ("man of iron") of Gilead in Transjordan helped David during his flight from his son Absalom (2Sa 17:27–29; 19:31–39; 1Ki 2:7). That the bridegroom took the name of his wife's father recalls the Mesopotamian *errēbu* ("to enter") marriage arranged by a father who had only daughters. Their children belonged to the wife's family (cf. Ge 29–31; 1Ch 2:34–36).

62 Genealogies figure prominently in Chronicles, Ezra, and Nehemiah. The knowledge of relationships was highly regarded in ancient times, and it is important in many societies today. A. S. Kirkbride related "that on one occasion, while he was in an Arab encampment, an Arab got up and related the history of his forebears back to forty generations, and that there were others in the assembly who obviously could have done the same" (cited in *The Biblical Archaeologist Reader* [ed. G. E. Wright and D. N. Freedman; Garden City, N.Y.: Doubleday, 1961], 63, n. 18).

63 "The governor" here probably refers to either Sheshbazzar or Zerubbabel. The Hebrew word (cf. Notes) is used in Nehemiah 7:65 of Zerubbabel and in Nehemiah 8:9; 10:1[2] of Nehemiah. "The most sacred food" (*qōdeš haqqodāšîm*), as in Leviticus 2:3, refers to the most holy part of the offering—the portion of the priests.

"The Urim [ʾûrîm] and Thummim [tummîm]," objects kept in the breastplate of the high priest, were used for divining God's will. In the Pentateuch they are associated with Levi (Dt 33:8), Aaron (Ex 28:30; Lev 8:8; cf. Sir 45:10), and Eleazar (Nu 27:21). The Urim and Thummim were probably two small objects made of wood, bone, or stone, perhaps of different colors or with different inscriptions, that would give a "yes" or "no" answer. The high priest would reach into his breastplate and extract one of the objects. The LXX translated the terms with abstractions: "Lights" and "Perfections"; elsewhere it translates the terms as "Manifestation" and "Truth." (See C. Van Dam, *Urim and Thummim* [Winona Lake, Ind.: Eisenbrauns, 1997].)

According to rabbinic tradition, Urim and Thummim were used "only for the King, for the Court, or for one of whom the congregation had need" (*m. Yoma* 7.5). The rabbis held that "since the

destruction of the first temple the Urim and the Thummim ceased" (*t. Soṭah* 13.1). They held that Ezra 2:63 expressed not a historical possibility but an eschatological hope (*b. Soṭah* 48a–b). Elsewhere in the Talmud (*b. Šebu.* 16a) we read that Ezra had to reconsecrate the temple without benefit of the Urim and Thummim. Rashi (on Ex 28:30) held that when the high priest sought an answer, letters of the names of the tribes on the breastplate would light up to give counsel!

NOTES

62 An ostracon from Arad dated to the late seventh century BC has an eleven-line list of names, such as "Shemaiahu son of Micaiahu … Tanhum son of Jedaiahu, Gealiahu son of Jedaiahu" (cf. Hestrin, *Inscriptions Reveal*, #137).

63 "Governor" is the Hebrew word תִּרְשָׁתָא (*tiršāta᾽*), which the KJV merely transliterates as "Tirshatha." W. T. In der Smitten ("Der Tirschata' in Esra-Nehemiah," *VT* 21 [1971]: 618–20) has proposed that the word means "the circumcised one," identifying Nehemiah and Zerubbabel as Jews. But the word does not imply a contemptuous nickname. Earlier E. Meyer had proposed the meaning "palace eunuch" from the New Persian word *tārash*. Perhaps the best explanation is "the one to be feared or respected," that is, "Excellency," assumed from the Old Persian *tarsa*, a view favored by I. Scheftelowitz, W. Rudolph, and K. Galling.

On the "Urim and Thummim," E. Lipinski ("Urīm and Tummīm," *VT* 20 [1970]: 495–96) cites an Assyrian text in which the god's answer was divined through two dice, called *aban erēši* ("the desirable die") and *aban la erēši* ("the undesirable die"). The text reads, "conjuration to foretell the future by means of a white stone (alabaster) and a black stone (Haematite)."

8. Totals (2:64–67)

[64]The whole company numbered 42,360, [65]besides their 7,337 menservants and maidservants; and they also had 200 men and women singers. [66]They had 736 horses, 245 mules, [67]435 camels and 6,720 donkeys.

COMMENTARY

64 The given total of 42,360 is considerably more than the sum of the actual figures given, as may be seen from a chart of the figures in Ezra 2, Nehemiah 7, and 1 Esdras 5.

Categories	Ezra	Nehemiah	1 Esdras
Men of Israel	24,144	25,406	26,390
Priests	4,289	4,289	2,388
Levites, singers, etc.	341	360	341
Temple servants	392	392	372
Men of unproven origin	652	642	652
Totals	29,818	31,089	30,143

The difference of about twelve thousand between the given total and the actual total presents a problem. Were these unspecified twelve thousand people women and/or children? (1 Esdras 5:41 explicitly states that its given total included "all those of Israel, twelve or more years of age.") If there were relatively few women among the returnees, the pressures for intermarriage would have been considerable.

Other scholars suggest that the numbers explicitly enumerated represent returnees from Judah and Benjamin, while the remainder were from other tribes. Laperrousaz and Lemaire, 19, judge that the total number of fifty thousand inhabitants would be realistic for the limited extent of the province of Judah. The number of those who remained in the land is unknown. (Cf. also Lemaire, 38.)

Many have questioned whether such a large group of about fifty thousand (42,360 + 7,337 slaves = 49,697) would have joined the initial return under Sheshbazzar. Some scholars have therefore suggested that the totals include other people who came later. But surely the initial response would have been indeed the greatest for the many who had harbored memories of their homeland and who had nurtured hope in the fulfillment of prophecy.

Modern experiences in repatriating Jews to Israel have consistently shown enthusiastic responses in large numbers when such opportunities were presented. The first of these efforts was "Operation Magic Carpet," which in 1950 airlifted fifty thousand Yemenite Jews to Israel. At one time, Baghdad was one-fifth Jewish. "Operation Ezra and Nehemiah" in 1951 and 1952 transported one hundred thirty thousand Iraqi Jews to Israel, which severely depleted the number of Jews in the country. There are fewer than twenty Jews living in Baghdad and fewer than one hundred in Iraq. Operation Moses airlifted fourteen thousand Falashas, the Black Jews of Ethiopia, to Israel in 1985. A second airlift, called "Operation Solomon," brought fourteen thousand more Falashas to Israel. Operation Exodus in 1989 brought more than seven hundred thousand Jews out of the Soviet Union to Israel.

65 The ratio of slaves one-to-six is relatively high; that so many slaves would return with their masters speaks highly of the relatively benevolent treatment of slaves by the Jews. Unlike the Code of Hammurabi, which permitted a master to kill his own slave with impunity, the Mosaic code denounced such a killing as murder. See H. L. Ellison, "The Hebrew Slave," *EvQ* 45 (1973): 30–35; J. M. van der Ploeg, "Slavery in the Old Testament," *VTSup* 26 (1974): 72–87; N. Lemche, "The Hebrew Slave," *VT* 25 (1975): 129–44.

The male and female singers listed here may have been secular singers who sang at weddings, funerals, etc. (2Ch 35:25), as distinct from the male temple singers of v.41.

66 "Horses" in the OT are usually associated with the military and royalty, who had a monopoly on these animals. The horses listed here may have been a donation from Cyrus for the nobility.

"Mules" are hybrid offspring of donkey stallions and equine mares. They combine the strength and size of the horse with the patience and surefootedness of the ass. They were not originally bred in Palestine; Solomon had to import them (1Ki 10:25; 2Ch 9:24). As precious animals, they were used by the royalty and wealthy (1Ki 1:33; Isa 66:20).

67 The "camels" mentioned in the OT were the one-humped Arabian camels as distinct from the two-humped Bactrian camels. The camel can carry its rider and about four hundred pounds and can travel three or four days without drinking.

"Donkeys" were surefooted and able to live on poor forage. They were used to carry loads, women, or children. Sheep, goats, and cattle are not mentioned. They would have slowed the caravan. (See G. S. Cansdale, *All the Animals of the Bible Lands* [Grand Rapids: Zondervan, 1970]; O. Borowski, *Every Living Thing: Daily Use of Animals in Ancient Israel* [Walnut Creek, Calif.: Alta Mira, 1998].)

9. Offerings (2:68–69)

⁶⁸When they arrived at the house of the Lord in Jerusalem, some of the heads of the families gave freewill offerings toward the rebuilding of the house of God on its site. ⁶⁹According to their ability they gave to the treasury for this work 61,000 drachmas of gold, 5,000 minas of silver and 100 priestly garments.

COMMENTARY

68 The caravan probably followed the Euphrates River up to a point east of Aleppo, crossed west to the Orontes River Valley, then traveled south to Hamath, Homs, and Riblah. They would then have either passed through the Beqaʾa Valley in Lebanon or have proceeded east of the Anti-Lebanon Mountains to Damascus and then to Palestine. The former route was followed by the Assyrian and Babylonian armies (Jer 39:5–7; 52:9–10, 26–27).

As the people were expending most of their savings, their giving demonstrated a true spirit of dedication to God's service (cf. Ex 36:5–7; 2Co 9:6–7).

69 The parallel passage in Nehemiah 7:70–72 gives a fuller and more systematic description than the account in Ezra. In Ezra the gifts come from the heads of the clans but in Nehemiah from three sources: the governor, the chiefs of the clans, and the rest of the people. The differences in the parallel accounts are as follows:

Ezra	Nehemiah
61,000 drachmas (or darics) of gold	Governor: 1,000 drachmas (or darics) of gold
5,000 minas of silver	Chiefs: 20,000 drachmas (or darics) of gold 2,200 minas of silver
	People: 20,000 drachmas (or darics) of gold 2,000 minas of silver

"Drachmas" translates the Hebrew *darkᵉmônîm* (cf. Ne 7:70–72). Another Hebrew word—ᵃʳ*darkōnîm*—is used for coins in Ezra 8:27 and 1 Chronicles 29:7. The "drachma" was the Greek silver coin worth a day's wage in the late fifth century BC. More probably the coin intended here was the Persian daric, a gold coin probably named either after Darius I, who began minting the coin, or after the Old Persian word for gold, *dari*. It was famed for its purity, which was guaranteed by the king. It was 98 percent gold with a 2 percent alloy for hardness. It was three-quarters of an inch in diameter and weighed 8.42 grams, or a little less than one-third of an ounce. Its value equaled the price of an ox or a month's wages for a soldier.

Since the coin was not in use until the time of Darius I (522–486 BC), its occurrence here in 537 BC has been labeled anachronistic. Its use is better viewed as a modernization of earlier values (perhaps the Median shekel) in terms current at the time of the book's composition. The total of 61,000 darics equals some 1,133 pounds of gold (about the same if the term represented the Greek drachma).

A "mina" equaled 1.26 pounds of silver; 5,000 minas would be 6,300 pounds of silver. In the sexa-gesimal system that originated in Mesopotamia, sixty shekels made a mina, and sixty minas a talent. A shekel, about one-third of an ounce of silver, was the average monthly wage. Hence a mina would equal five years' wages and a talent three-hundred-years' wages (cf. R. Loewe, "The Earliest Biblical Allusion to Coined Money?" *PEQ* 87 [1955]: 141–50; J. Weingreen, "Coins," *DOTT*, 232; Naster, "Were the Labourers of Persepolis Paid by Means of Coined Money?" *Ancient Society* 1 [1970]: 129–34). An important survey of the different types of Persian coins by I. Carradice ("The 'Regal' Coinage of the Persian Empire," in Carradice, 73–93) includes numerous plates.

NOTES

68 Temples in the ancient Near East had to be rebuilt on the same site. The Aramaic papyrus in Cowley, 32:8 (ca. 408 BC), refers to the rebuilding of the Jewish temple at Elephantine "in its place as it was before."

69 A belief that the Chronicler intended the Greek drachma led C. C. Torrey to date the Chronicler's work to 250 BC. The discovery of Greek coins in Palestine already in the Persian period undermines Torrey's argument. W. F. Albright (*Recent Discoveries in Bible Lands* [New York: Funk & Wagnalls, 1955], 105) noted:

> Most interestingly of all has been the finding (mostly outside of excavations) of many Atticizing coins following the drachma standard, belonging to the fifth and fourth centuries BC. This is one of the many recent discoveries which prove that Torrey and his followers are wrong in holding that the references to "drachmas" in the work of the Chronicler (including Ezra) belong to the Greek period.

E. Stern ("Israel at the Close of the Period of the Monarchy," *BA* 38 [1975]: 53) comments, "Indeed, the earliest coins discovered in Israel were minted in the mid-6th century, only some thirty years after the destruction of the Temple in 586." (For further discoveries of Greek coins, see Stern, *Archaeology*, 340, 555–59, 564.) Later in the Persian period, Judean authorities were permitted to mint their own small, silver coins with the name of the province Yehud in archaic Hebrew script (cf. Y. Meshorer, *Jewish Coins of the Second Temple* [Tel-Aviv: Am-Hassefer, 1967], 36–43).

10. Settlement of the Exiles (2:70)

70 The priests, the Levites, the singers, the gatekeepers and the temple servants settled in their own towns, along with some of the other people, and the rest of the Israelites settled in their towns.

COMMENTARY

70 Later Nehemiah would be compelled to move people by lot to reinforce the population of Jerusalem, as the capital city had suffered the severest loss of life at the time of the Babylonian attacks. The survivors, who came for the most part from towns in the countryside, naturally preferred to resettle in their hometowns.

C. The Revival of Temple Worship (3:1–13)

1. The Rebuilding of the Altar (3:1–3)

¹When the seventh month came and the Israelites had settled in their towns, the people assembled as one man in Jerusalem. ²Then Jeshua son of Jozadak and his fellow priests and Zerubbabel son of Shealtiel and his associates began to build the altar of the God of Israel to sacrifice burnt offerings on it, in accordance with what is written in the Law of Moses the man of God. ³Despite their fear of the peoples around them, they built the altar on its foundation and sacrificed burnt offerings on it to the LORD, both the morning and evening sacrifices.

COMMENTARY

1 "The seventh month" would be Tishri (September–October), about three months after the arrival of the exiles in Palestine. Tishri is one of the most sacred months of the Jewish year. According to the Mishnah and Talmud the first day of Tishri is the New Year's Day (Rosh Hashanah) of the civil calendar, proclaimed with the blowing of trumpets and a holy convocation (Lev 23:24). Ten days later the Day of Atonement (Yom Kippur) is observed (Lev 23:27). From the fifteenth to the twenty-second day, the Feast of Tabernacles (Succoth) is celebrated (Lev 23:34–36). "Assembled as one man" and similar expressions of the unity of Israel are found in Numbers 14:15; Judges 6:16; 20:1, 8, 11; 1 Samuel 11:7; and 2 Samuel 19:14.

2 Jeshua, the priest, took precedence over Zerubbabel, the civil leader, in view of the nature of the occasions (cf. v.8; 5:2; Hag 1:1; on the high priests in Ezra/Nehemiah see Introduction: The High Priests). Scholars have seen a tension between this statement and that of 5:16, which says it was Sheshbazzar who laid the foundations for the temple. Moreover, Haggai, who mentions Zerubbabel (Hag 1:1), does not mention Sheshbazzar. B. Halpern ("A Historiographic Commentary on Ezra 1–6," in *The Hebrew Bible and Its Interpreters* [ed. B. Halpern, W. H. Propp, and D. N. Freedman; Winona Lake, Ind.: Eisenbrauns, 1990], 103), citing Mesopotamian parallels, suggests, "In any case, if Sheshbazzar did lay a foundation around 538, years of exposure to the elements and vegetation would have necessitated clearing, reorientation by the builders with regard to directional bearings, extensive repair, and a ceremony invoking the god's aid in the completion of the project, cursed by a previous failure."

Zerubbabel's name indicates that he was born in Babylon. He began his leadership of the exiles under Cyrus and continued until the reign of Darius I. He was of royal Davidic descent, the grandson of Jehoiachin (1Ch 3:17–24). Though he is not given a title in Ezra, Haggai explicitly names him the "governor of Judah" (Hag 1:1; 2:2).

During their long stay in Babylon, the Jews were not able to offer any sacrifices, as this could only be done in Jerusalem. Instead they were surrounded by a myriad of pagan temples. About fifty temples are mentioned in Babylonian texts, together with one hundred eighty open-air shrines for Ishtar, three hundred daises for the Igigi gods, and twelve hundred daises for the Anunnaki gods. (See E. Yamauchi, "Babylon," in *Major Cities of Bible Times* [ed. R. K. Harrison; Nashville: Nelson, 1985], 32–48; cf. also D. J. Wiseman, *Nebuchadnezzar and Babylon* [Oxford: Oxford Univ. Press, 1985].) Thus, the first task of the returned exiles in the midst of hostile neighbors was to erect once more an altar to sacrifice to the Lord.

The "enemies" did not have anything to fear from the rebuilding of the temple, as they did from the rebuilding of the wall (as we will see in Nehemiah). Sincerely or not, they had at first offered their help to rebuild the temple (4:2). The rejection of this aid naturally aroused their hostility.

The phrase "the man of God" occurs seventy-five times in the OT. It is used of Moses in Deuteronomy 33:1; Joshua 14:6; 1 Chronicles 23:14; 2 Chronicles 30:16; Psalm 90:title; and elsewhere. David is so described in Nehemiah 12:36.

3 "Despite their fear" is literally "for with fear" or "for in fear." The Hebrew word *ʾêmâ* means a terror inspired by humans (Pr 20:2) or animals (Job 39:20). The LXX reads *en kataplēxei* ("in consternation").

"The peoples around them" (*ʿammê hāʾᵃrāṣôt*) is literally "peoples of the lands" (cf. comment on 4:4).

NOTES

1 Because of the similarity of the phrases in this verse and in Nehemiah 8:1, some scholars have concluded that both passages describe the same assembly. But the assemblies described in Ezra 3 and Nehemiah 8 pursue entirely different matters.

2 In Ezra, Zerubbabel is listed as the son of Shealtiel, but in 1 Chronicles 3:19 he is listed as the son of Pedaiah, the brother of Shealtiel. See S. Japhet, 72, for a discussion of this difficulty. She considers Sheshbazzar, who is called "the prince of Judah" (Ezr 1:8), the first governor of Judah. Jewish interperters such as Abrahm ibn Ezra considered "Sheshbazzar" and "Zerubbabel" two names of one individual. The Talmud (cf. Rabinowitz, *Ezra*, 100) even identified Zerubbabel with Nehemiah.

Since Zerubbabel was of Davidic origin, some scholars have considered him a royal vassal and a possible messiah, but this assertion goes beyond the evidence. (See N. Na'aman, "Royal Vassals or Governors?" *Hen* 22 [2000]: 35–44; W. H. Rose, *Zemah and Zerubbabel: Messianic Expectations in the Early Postexilic Period* [Sheffield: JSOT, 2000].)

2. The Festival of Booths (3:4–6)

⁴Then in accordance with what is written, they celebrated the Feast of Tabernacles with the required number of burnt offerings prescribed for each day. ⁵After that, they presented the regular burnt offerings, the New Moon sacrifices and the sacrifices for all the appointed sacred feasts of the LORD, as well as those brought as freewill offerings to

the LORD. ⁶On the first day of the seventh month they began to offer burnt offerings to the LORD, though the foundation of the LORD's temple had not yet been laid.

COMMENTARY

4 J. L. Rubenstein observes, "The passage emphasizes that the Sukkot sacrifices inaugurated the regular functioning of the cult; thereafter Sabbaths, new moons and other festivals would be observed in the proper way (3:4–5)" (*The History of Sukkot in the Second Temple and Rabbinic Periods* [Atlanta: Scholars, 1995], 33). The English word "tabernacle" is derived from the Latin Vulgate's *tabernaculum* ("tent"). The original Hebrew word *sukkôt* refers to the "huts" constructed for the feast, which is sometimes simply called "the feast" or "the feast of the LORD." Originally a joyous harvest celebration (Ex 23:14–16; 34:22–23; Lev 23:33–43; Nu 29:12–40; Dt 16:13–16), this feast is the only one possibly referred to in the historical books (1Sa 1:1–3; 1Ki 12:32).

Jews today celebrate this feast by building a hut covered with an open roof of branches, decorated with fruits and vegetables. Following Leviticus 23:40, Jews also use the palm, willow, and myrtle as the "lulav" ("shoot" or "young branch"), a Mishnaic term applied to all trees, but especially the palm branch used at *sukkôt*, and the "ethrog" (a name of uncertain origin), a yellow citron known in Israel only from Hellenistic times. During each of the nine days of the feast, the lulav and the ethrog are held in the hands and waved in all directions. The "burnt offerings" were the holocausts prescribed for morning (Lev 1:13) and evening (Nu 28:3–4).

5–6 The New Moon marked the first day of the month and was a holy day (Nu 28:11–15; cf. Col 2:16; cf. B. Z. Wacholder and D. B. Weisberg, "Visibility of the New Moon in Cuneiform and Rabbinic Sources," *HUCA* 42 [1971]: 227–41). "The appointed sacred feasts" include such festivals as Passover, Weeks (Pentecost), and the Day of Atonement (Lev 23).

The renewal of the "freewill offerings" (cf. 1:4) fulfilled the promise of Jeremiah 33:10–11. Note that the revival of the services preceded the erection of the temple itself. As Leviticus 17:3–4 seems to prohibit sacrificing outside the tabernacle (later reinterpreted to mean the temple), the Talmud stated that special permission was needed for these sacrifices. According to Rabinowitz (*Ezra*, 104, n. 1), "This has aroused periodic speculation among the late Rabbinic authorities concerning the feasibility of bringing sacrifices in postexilic and even contemporary times."

3. The Beginning of Temple Reconstruction (3:7–13)

⁷Then they gave money to the masons and carpenters, and gave food and drink and oil to the people of Sidon and Tyre, so that they would bring cedar logs by sea from Lebanon to Joppa, as authorized by Cyrus king of Persia.

⁸In the second month of the second year after their arrival at the house of God in Jerusalem, Zerubbabel son of Shealtiel, Jeshua son of Jozadak and the rest of their brothers (the priests and the Levites and all who had returned from the captivity to Jerusalem)

began the work, appointing Levites twenty years of age and older to supervise the building of the house of the LORD. ⁹Jeshua and his sons and brothers and Kadmiel and his sons (descendants of Hodaviah) and the sons of Henadad and their sons and brothers—all Levites—joined together in supervising those working on the house of God.

¹⁰When the builders laid the foundation of the temple of the LORD, the priests in their vestments and with trumpets, and the Levites (the sons of Asaph) with cymbals, took their places to praise the LORD, as prescribed by David king of Israel. ¹¹With praise and thanksgiving they sang to the LORD:

> "He is good;
>> his love to Israel endures forever."

And all the people gave a great shout of praise to the LORD, because the foundation of the house of the LORD was laid. ¹²But many of the older priests and Levites and family heads, who had seen the former temple, wept aloud when they saw the foundation of this temple being laid, while many others shouted for joy. ¹³No one could distinguish the sound of the shouts of joy from the sound of weeping, because the people made so much noise. And the sound was heard far away.

COMMENTARY

7 As with the first temple, the Phoenicians cooperated by sending timbers and workers (1Ki 5:7–12). Ancient Phoenicia, modern Lebanon, was renowned for its cedars and other coniferous trees. Both the Mesopotamians and the Egyptians sought its timbers either by trade or conquest. Cedars, mentioned seventy-one times in the OT, can grow to a height of one hundred twenty feet with a girth of thirty to forty feet. Their fragrant wood resists rot and insects. The forests of Lebanon were coveted both by the ancient Egyptians (*ANET*, 227) and the Assyrians (*ANET*, 275). (See J. Brown, *The Lebanon and Phoenicia* [Beirut: American Univ. of Beirut, 1969].)

Sidon, modern Saida, twenty-eight miles south of Beirut, was one of the greatest of all the Phoenician cities (Ge 10:19; 1Ki 5:6; 16:31; 1Ch 22:4). After the conquest of Tyre by Nebuchadnezzar following a thirteen-year siege, Sidon became promi-

nent (*Herodotus* 6.96–98; 8.67; see N. Jidejian, *Sidon, through the Ages* [Beirut: Dar el-Machreq, 1971].)

Tyre, modern *Ṣûr*, is located only a dozen miles north of the Israeli border. Renowned for its maritime trade (Eze 26:4–14), the island of Tyre was later transformed into a peninsula in Alexander the Great's conquest of it. (See H. J. Katzenstein, *The History of Tyre* [2nd ed.; Jerusalem: Ben-Gurion Univ. of the Negev, 1997].)

Because of their excellent harbors and supplies of timbers, the Phoenicians became the most daring seamen in the ancient world. (See W. A. Ward, "Phoenicians," in Hoerth, Mattingly, and Yamauchi, 83–206; J. Elayi, "The Phoenician Cities in the Persian Period," *JANESCU* 12 [1980]: 13–28; G. E. Markoe, *The Phoenicians* [Berkeley: Univ. of California Press, 2000]; R. Gore and R. Clark, "Who Were the Phoenicians?" *National Geographic* 206/4 [October 2004]: 26–49.)

8-9 The second month, Iyyar (April/May), was the same month in which Solomon began building his temple (1Ki 6:1). As the Jews probably returned to Palestine in the spring of 537 BC, the second year would be the spring of 536.

Previously the age limit for the Levites was thirty (Nu 4:3) or twenty-five years (Nu 8:24). Here it was reduced to twenty (1Ch 23:24, 27; 2Ch 31:17), no doubt because of the scarcity of Levites. Verses 8-10 indicate that Zerubbabel and Jeshua were involved in laying the foundation of the second temple, but 5:16 describes Sheshbazzar as also laying the foundation. On the apparent conflict, see the comment on 5:16.

10 "Trumpets" ($h^a \bar{s}\bar{o}\bar{s}r\hat{o}t$) appears twenty-nine times, always in the plural, except in Hosea 5:8. Of these occurrences sixteen are in 1 and 2 Chronicles. The trumpets were made of beaten silver (Nu 10:2). According to Josephus (*Ant.* 3.291 [12.6]), the trumpet was "in length a little short of a cubit; it is a narrow tube, slightly thicker than a flute." Except perhaps for their use at the coronation of Joash (2Ki 11:14; 2Ch 23:13), the trumpets were always blown by priests (Nu 10:8; 1Ch 15:24; 16:6; Sir 50:16). Trumpets were most often used on joyous occasions such as here and at the dedication of the rebuilt walls of Jerusalem (Ne 12:35; cf. 2Ch 5:13; Ps 98:6).

The designation "cymbals" ($m^e\bar{s}iltayim$) appears thirteen times; all its occurrences are in 1 and 2 Chronicles except the ones here and in Nehemiah 12:27. The cymbals were also played by priests and Levites. (See T. C. Mitchell, "The Music of the Old Testament Reconsidered," *PEQ* 124 [1992]: 124-43; idem, "And the Band Played On ... But What Did They Play On?" *BRev* 15/6 [1999]: 32-39; J. Braun, *Music in Ancient Israel/Palestine: Archaeological, Written and Comparative Sources* [Grand Rapids: Eerdmans, 2002].)

11 "They sang" (from Heb. *'nh*, "to answer") is taken by the NRSV in the sense of antiphonal singing by a choir divided into two groups singing responsively.

"He is good," a constant refrain in the Scriptures (1Ch 16:34; 2Ch 7:3; Pss 106:1; 136:1; Jer 33:10-11), implies the goodness of a covenant-keeping God (cf. A. R. Millard, "'For He Is Good,'" *TynBul* 17 [1966]: 115-17).

"Love" translates *hesed*, which more precisely means "steadfast love." (N. Glueck's monograph *Hesed in the Bible* [Cincinnati: Hebrew Union College Press, 1967] has been superseded by K. D. Sakenfeld's *The Meaning of Hesed in the Hebrew Bible* [Missoula, Mont.: Scholars, 1978].)

12-13 Loud shouting—"a great shout" expresses great jubilation or intense purpose (cf. 10:12; cf. Jos 6:5, 20; 1Sa 4:5; Ps 95:1-2). The NEB has "shouted at the top of their voices"; the TEV adds, "so loud that it could be heard for miles."

The tears and outcries expressed the deep emotion of the occasion. The Israelis reacted similarly when they reached the Wailing Wall in their war against the Arabs in 1967. Traditionally Hebrews showed their emotions by weeping out loud (cf. 10:1; Ne 1:4; 8:9). V. Hamp ("*bākhāh*," *TDOT*, 2:117) observes, "Like the Gk. *klaiō* and *dakryō*, and the Lat. *fleo* and *lacrimo*, Heb. *bkh*, 'weeping,' comes from the mouth and voice.... Orientals do not weep quietly, but are quite inclined to loud weeping and lamenting, thus explaining the frequent connection of *bkh*, 'weeping,' with *qôl*, 'the voice,' in the OT" (cf. T. Collins, "The Physiology of Tears in the Old Testament," *CBQ* 33 [1971]: 18-38, 185-97).

Whereas the elders were overcome with sadness, remembering the splendors of Solomon's temple, the younger returnees shouted with great excitement at the prospect of a new temple. The God who had permitted judgment was also the God who had brought them back and would enable them to complete this project. A Babylonian cornerstone reads, "I started the work weeping, I finished it rejoicing" (cf. Ps 126:5: "Those who sow in tears will reap with songs of joy").

D. The Opposition to the Rebuilding (4:1–24)

OVERVIEW

This chapter summarizes various attempts to thwart the efforts of the Jews. In vv.1–5 the author describes events under Cyrus (539–530 BC), in v.6 under Xerxes (485–465), in vv.7–23 under Artaxerxes I (464–424). He then reverts in v.24 to the time of Darius I (522–486), when the temple was completed (cf. Hag 1–2). The author drew on Aramaic documents from v.8 to 6:18, with a further Aramaic section in 7:12–26.

1. Opposition during the Reign of Cyrus (4:1–5)

[1]When the enemies of Judah and Benjamin heard that the exiles were building a temple for the LORD, the God of Israel, [2]they came to Zerubbabel and to the heads of the families and said, "Let us help you build because, like you, we seek your God and have been sacrificing to him since the time of Esarhaddon king of Assyria, who brought us here."

[3]But Zerubbabel, Jeshua and the rest of the heads of the families of Israel answered, "You have no part with us in building a temple to our God. We alone will build it for the LORD, the God of Israel, as King Cyrus, the king of Persia, commanded us."

[4]Then the peoples around them set out to discourage the people of Judah and make them afraid to go on building. [5]They hired counselors to work against them and frustrate their plans during the entire reign of Cyrus king of Persia and down to the reign of Darius king of Persia.

COMMENTARY

1–2 As most of the exiles were from Judah, their descendants became known as Jews (from Lat. *Iudaeus* = Old French *Ieu* = Middle English *Iewe*). "Judith," the name of an apocryphal book, means "Jewess."

Benjamin, the small tribe occupying the area immediately north of Judah, was the only tribe besides Judah that remained loyal to Rehoboam when the ten northern tribes rebelled. Saul, the first king of Israel, came from this tribe, as did Saul of Tarsus (Php 3:5).

The people who proffered their help were evidently from the area of Samaria, though they are not explicitly described as such. After the fall of Samaria in 722 BC, the Assyrian kings kept importing from Mesopotamia and Syria inhabitants who "worshiped the LORD, but ... also served their own gods" (2Ki 17:24–33). The newcomers' influence doubtless diluted further the faith of the northerners, who had already apostasized from the sole worship of the Lord in the tenth century. (In contrast, when the Babylonians deported the Jews in the sixth century, they did not take pagan settlers from elsewhere into Judah.)

Even after the destruction of the temple, worshipers from Shiloh and Shechem in the north came to offer cereals and incense at the site of the ruined temple (Jer 41:5). Moreover, the northerners did not abandon faith in Yahweh, as we see from the Yahwistic names given to Sanballat's sons, Delaiah and Shelemaiah (Cowley, 30:29). But they retained Yahweh not as the sole God, but as one god among many gods; Sanballat's name honors the moon god Sin. Though Ezra-Nehemiah does not explicitly mention the syncretistic character of the northerners, evidence suggests that the inhabitants of Samaria were syncretists. (We should, however, distinguish the syncretistic inhabitants of Samaria from the strictly monotheistic Samaritans by calling the former "Samarians.")

K. L. Younger Jr. has discussed the gods worshiped by these newcomers in the light of cuneiform evidence (see his "Recent Study on Sargon II, King of Assyria: Implications for Biblical Studies," in *Mesopotamia and the Bible* [ed. M. W. Chavalas and K. L. Younger Jr.; Grand Rapids: Baker, 2002], 288–329; idem, "The Repopulation of Samaria [2Ki 17:24, 27–31] in Light of Recent Study," in *The Future of Biblical Archaeology: Reassessing Methodologies and Assumptions* [ed. J. K. Hoffmeier and A. Millard; Grand Rapids: Eerdmans, 2004], 254–80).

In 1962 the Taʾamireh Bedouins who had found the Dead Sea Scrolls discovered a cave in Wadi Daliyeh with fourth-century BC papyri. In 1963 Paul Lapp found there a great mass of skeletons, numbering between two hundred to three hundred men, women, and children—the remains of the leading families of Samaria who had fled in 331 BC from Alexander the Great. Though most of the names were Yahwistic, others included the names of such deities as Qos (Edomite), SHR (Aramaic), Chemosh (Moabite), Baʾal (Canaanite), and Nebo (Babylonian). (See F. M. Cross, "A Report on the Samaria Papyri," *VTSup* 40 [1988]: 17–26.)

3 "You have no part with us" is literally "it is not for you and for us," a Hebrew idiom (cf. Jdg 11:12; 2Ki 3:13; Mk 1:24; Jn 2:4). The Jews tried tactfully to reject the aid proffered by the northerners by referring to the provisions of the king's decree. Nonetheless, their response understandably aroused hostility and determined opposition. M. Cogan, in "'For We, Like You, Worship your God': Three Biblical Portrayals of Samaritan Origins" (*VT* 38 [1988]: 289), contrasts the rebuff in Ezra 4:1–5 with the welcoming attitude of Hezekiah to the northern Israelites to celebrate the Passover in Jerusalem recorded in 2 Chronicles 30.

4 "The peoples around them" is ʿam hāʾāreṣ (lit., "the people of the land"; cf. Notes). Josephus (*Ant.* 11.19 [2.1], 84–87 [4.3]) describes these opponents explicitly as Cuthaeans or Samaritans. They were called Cuthaeans after Cutha, a sacred city in Babylonia, at least some of whose deportees the Assyrians resettled in Samaria. In the later passage from Josephus, the Jews declined their cooperation "since none but themselves had been commanded to build the temple.... They would, however, allow them to worship there."

"To discourage" is literally "to weaken the hands," a Hebrew idiom (cf. Jer 38:4). As a participle the verb rāpâ indicates a continuing process. The opposite idiom is "to strengthen the hands" (Ezr 6:22; Ne 6:9; Isa 35:3; Jer 23:14).

Regarding "make them afraid," the verb bālāh means "to terrify" and often describes the fear aroused in a battle situation (Jdg 20:41; 2Sa 4:1; 2Ch 32:18; Da 11:44).

5 On the hiring of counselors, compare the hiring of Balaam (Dt 23:4–5; Ne 13:2) and the hiring of the prophets to intimidate Nehemiah (Neh 6:14). "Down to the reign of Darius king of Persia" passes over the intervening reign of Cambyses (529–522 BC), who conquered Egypt in 525, and that of the usurper, the Pseudo-Smerdis, who seized power in 522 for seven months (see Yamauchi, *Persia and the Bible*, ch. 3, "Cambyses," and ch. 4, "Darius").

NOTES

1 See E. Yamauchi, "*yᵉhûdî*," *NIDOTTE*, 2:415–17; idem, "Jews in the New Testament," in *Layman's Bible Dictionary* (ed. T. Butler; Nashville: Holman, 1991), 794–95.

2 אֵסַר חַדֹּן (*ʾēsar ḥaddōn*, "Esarhaddon," for the Akkad. *Aššur-aḫ-iddin*, "Assur has given a brother") was the Assyrian king (680–669 BC) who succeeded Sennacherib (2Ki 19:37; Isa 37:38). (A. R. Millard, 1–14, demonstrates that Assyrian royal names have been preserved with remarkable accuracy in the Hebrew.) In "The Political Background of Zerubbabel's Mission and the Samaritan Schism" (*VT* 41 [1991]: 313), O. Margalith notes that Esarhaddon does not mention the area of Samaria in surviving reports. The deportations under Esarhaddon were probably connected with his conquest of Egypt in 671 (cf. *ANET*, 290; see Yamauchi, *Africa and the Bible*, 133–38).

4 The phrase עַם־הָאָרֶץ (*ʿam-hāʾāreṣ*, "people of the land"; "peoples around," NIV) and its plural variants עַמֵּי הָאָרֶץ (*ʿammê-hāʾāreṣ*, "peoples of the land"; 10:2, 11; Ne 9:24; 10:31–32) and עַמֵּי הָאֲרָצוֹת (*ʿammê-hāʾᵃrāṣôt*, "peoples of the lands"; 3:3; 9:1, 2, 11; Ne 9:30; 10:30) occur between sixty and seventy times in the OT. Scholars have speculated that the phrase designates "foreign-born landowners" (Alt), "the landed nobility" (Daiches), "the rural population" (Gordis), "people of Judah who were collaborators of Samaria" (Rothstein), etc. E. W. Nicholson ("The Meaning of the Expression עַם הָאָרֶץ in the Old Testament," *JSS* 10 [1965]: 59–66) points out that the phrase seems to mean different groups at different times and situations.

In 2 Kings 23:30 it designates landowning citizens; but during the exilic period, it often connoted the דַּלַּת הָאָרֶץ (*dallat hāʾāreṣ*, "the poor of the land"; 2Ki 25:12; Jer 40:7; 52:16), whom Gedaliah allowed to take possession of abandoned lands. These people felt that God had given them such lands (cf. Eze 11:15; 33:24). The exiles' return would understandably bring tensions between those who had stayed and occupied the lands and the former landowners (cf. E. Janssen, *Juda in der Exilzeit* [Göttingen: Vandenhoeck & Ruprecht, 1956], 49, 121). In Ezra-Nehemiah, except possibly for Nehemiah 9:30, the phrase seems to refer to non-Jewish inhabitants of the land, principally the people of Samaria (cf. H. C. Vogt, *Studien zur nachexilischen Gemeinde in Esra-Nehemiah* [Werl: Dietrich-Coelde, 1966], 152; Williamson, *Israel in the Book of Chronicles*, 55).

In the NT period the rabbis used the phrase *ʿam-hāʾāreṣ* of the common people who were ignorant of the ritual rules and who neglected tithing (cf. Jn 7:49; Lk 18:9–14). S. Zeitlin ("The *ʿam haarez*," *JQR* 23 [1932–33]: 45–61) ascribes the hostility between the *ʿam-hāʾāreṣ* and the rabbis to the fact that the farmers had to support the priests and Levites with their tithes, whereas the developing urban population in the Maccabean period was free from such obligations.

2. Opposition during the Reign of Xerxes (4:6)

⁶At the beginning of the reign of Xerxes, they lodged an accusation against the people of Judah and Jerusalem.

COMMENTARY

6 "Xerxes" (*ʾaḥašwērôš*; the "Ahasuerus" of Esther in KJV, NRSV) is the Hebrew transliteration of the Old Persian *Xšayāršā*, the son of Darius. He is best known for his unsuccessful invasion of Greece (see Yamauchi, *Persia and the Bible*, ch. 5, "Xerxes"). When Darius died at the end of 486 BC, Egypt rebelled, and Xerxes had to march west to suppress the revolt. The Persians finally regained control by the end of 483. A. F. Rainey ("The Satrapy 'Beyond the River,'" *Australian Journal of Biblical Archaeology* 1 [1969]: 57) comments about this verse, "Nothing is known about this incident beyond the brief biblical reference, but its timing to coincide with the Egyptian rebellion cannot be accidental."

"Accusation" (*śiṭnâ*, lit., "hostility") occurs only here and in Genesis 26:21, where it is the name of a well the herdsmen of Isaac and Gerar quarreled over.

NOTE

6 Josephus (*Ant.* 11.121 [5.1]) incorrectly made Ezra a friend of Xerxes and (ibid., 159 [5.6]) called Nehemiah a cupbearer of Xerxes.

J. Morgenstern ("Jerusalem 485 BC," *HUCA* 27 [1956]: 101–79; 28 [1957]: 15–47; 31 [1960]: 15–47) postulated a destruction of Jerusalem in 485 BC, in the reign of Xerxes, as the immediate background of Ezra-Nehemiah. Most scholars have dismissed this scenario as based on too many speculations, but S. G. Sowers, "Did Xerxes Wage War on Jerusalem?" *HUCA* 67 (1996): 43–53, suggests that Darius or Xerxes may have attacked Jerusalem.

3. Opposition during the Reign of Artaxerxes I (4:7–23)

a. The Letter to the King (4:7–16)

⁷And in the days of Artaxerxes king of Persia, Bishlam, Mithredath, Tabeel and the rest of his associates wrote a letter to Artaxerxes. The letter was written in Aramaic script and in the Aramaic language.

⁸Rehum the commanding officer and Shimshai the secretary wrote a letter against Jerusalem to Artaxerxes the king as follows:

⁹Rehum the commanding officer and Shimshai the secretary, together with the rest of their associates — the judges and officials over the men from Tripolis, Persia, Erech and Babylon, the Elamites of Susa, ¹⁰and the other people whom the great and honorable Ashurbanipal deported and settled in the city of Samaria and elsewhere in Trans-Euphrates.

¹¹(This is a copy of the letter they sent him.)

To King Artaxerxes,

From your servants, the men of Trans-Euphrates:

[12]The king should know that the Jews who came up to us from you have gone to Jerusalem and are rebuilding that rebellious and wicked city. They are restoring the walls and repairing the foundations.
[13]Furthermore, the king should know that if this city is built and its walls are restored, no more taxes, tribute or duty will be paid, and the royal revenues will suffer. [14]Now since we are under obligation to the palace and it is not proper for us to see the king dishonored, we are sending this message to inform the king, [15]so that a search may be made in the archives of your predecessors. In these records you will find that this city is a rebellious city, troublesome to kings and provinces, a place of rebellion from ancient times. That is why this city was destroyed. [16]We inform the king that if this city is built and its walls are restored, you will be left with nothing in Trans-Euphrates.

COMMENTARY

7 There were three Persian kings named "Artaxerxes": Artaxerxes I (464–424 BC), Artaxerxes II (403–359 BC), and Artaxerxes III (358–337 BC). The king in this passage is Artaxerxes I (see Yamauchi, *Persia and the Bible*, ch. 6, "Artaxerxes I").

Some scholars claim that the parallel account in Josephus (*Ant.* 11.21–25 [2.1]), which substitutes "Cambyses" for "Artaxerxes I," gives the correct order. Williamson (*Israel in the Book of Chronicles*, 50) points out that "at Ezra iv, however, it seems likely that the author has grouped by theme rather than by chronology. Josephus' corrections, therefore, which rest from one point of view on accurate historical knowledge, result in the end in unhistorical confusion" (cf. also C. G. Tuland, "Josephus, *Antiquities*, Book XI: Correction or Confirmation of the Biblical Post-Exilic Records?" *AUSS* 4 (1966): 176–92).

"Bishlam" (*bišlām*) is rendered by the LXX as *en eirēnē* (i.e., revocalizing the Hebrew as *bišᵉlôm*,

"with the approval of"). The author of the letter would then be Tabeel writing with the approval of Mithredath. On "Mithredath" see the comment on 1:8. "Tabeel" means "God is good" (cf. Isa 7:6).

Near Eastern kings used an elaborate system of informers and spies. Egyptian sources speak of the "ears and eyes" of the Pharaoh. Sargon II of Assyria had agents in Urartu whom he ordered, "Write me whatever you see and hear." The efficient Persian intelligence system is described by Xenophon (*Cyropaedia* 8.2.10–12). The King's Eye and the King's Ear were two distinct officials who reported to the monarch (cf. J. Balcer, "The Athenian Episkopos and the Achaemenid 'King's Eye,'" *AJP* 98 [1977]: 252–63; A. L. Oppenheim, "The Eyes of the Lord," *JAOS* 88 [1968]: 173–79). But God's people could take assurance in their conviction that God's intelligence system is not only more efficient than any king's espionage network but is in fact omniscient (cf. 2Ch 16:9; Zec 4:10).

The letter was probably dictated in Persian to a scribe, who translated it into Aramaic and wrote it down in Aramaic script (see Introduction: Text). Aramaic was written in an alphabet borrowed from the Phoenicians. In the eighth century BC, this became a distinct script that remained quite uniform till after Alexander's conquests, when a variety of scripts were developed for such Aramaic dialects as Nabataean, Palmyrenean, Syriac, and Mandaic (cf. Naveh, *The Development*; on the style and form of letters in Aramaic, see J. M. Lindenberger, *Ancient Aramaic and Hebrew Letters* (2nd ed.; Atlanta: Society of Biblical Literature, 2003).

8 Rehum ("merciful"), "the commanding officer" (Aram. *bᵉᶜēl ṭᵉᶜēm*, lit., "master of a decree"; cf. Akkad. *ṭêmu*, "order"), was an official with the role of a "chancellor" or a "commissioner" (cf. Driver, #3:7–8). "Shimshai" means "my sun" (cf. Samson [Heb. *šimšôn*]). The Akkadian name *Šam-ša-a* occurs in the Murashu texts (Coogan, 125).

Rehum dictated and Shimshai wrote the letter in Aramaic. It would then have been read in a Persian translation before the king (v.18). According to Herodotus (3.128), royal scribes were attached to each governor to report directly to the Persian king. A. L. Oppenheim ("A Note on the Scribes in Mesopotamia," *Studies in Honor of Benno Landsberger* [ed. H. C. Guterbock and T. Jacobsen; Chicago: Univ. of Chicago Press, 1965], 253) comments, "Equally crucial is the scribe's position as the king's secretary, because in this capacity he exercised control over the communication of written information to the ruler" (cf. Rainey).

A letter from the reign of Ashurbanipal (*ABL*, no. 1250) warns, "Whoever you are, scribe, who is going to read [the preceding letter], do not conceal anything from the king, my lord. Speak kindly (of me) before the king, my lord, so that Bēl and Nabu should speak kindly of you to the king."

9 "Associates" is the plural of the Aramaic *kᵉnāt* and is found in 4:17, 23; 5:3, 6; 6:6–13 (cf. Driver, #3:7). The Neo-Babylonian *kinatātu* or *kinattātu* were persons supported by the same fief, often children of the same parents. Persian bureaucracy reflected prominently the principle of collegiality; each responsibility was shared among colleagues.

"Judges" (Aram. *dînāyēʾ*) is transliterated by the KJV as "Dinaites." There was a tribe in western Armenia known as the *Dai-ia-e-ni*. But the word should be revocalized as *dayyānayyāʾ* ("judges") as in the Elephantine papyri.

"Persia" (Aram. *ᵃdpārsāyēʾ*) was transliterated by the KJV as "Apharsites." The Assyrians first encountered the Medes and the Persians in the reign of Shalmaneser III (858–824 BC).

"Erech" (Aram. *ʾarkᵉwāyēʾ*; "Archevites," KJV) was a great city (Ge 10:10) of the Sumerians called Uruk, famed as the home of the legendary Gilgamesh. Excavations at the site, now called Warka, have produced the earliest examples of writing.

In the reign of the Assyrian king Ashurbanipal, a major revolt took place from 652–648 BC involving Shamash-shum-ukin, brother of the king and the ruler over Babylonia. After a long siege, Shamash-shum-ukin hurled himself into the flames. Doubtless these men of Babylonia and the other cities were descendants of the rebels the Assyrians deported to the west (cf. H. W. F. Saggs, *The Greatness That Was Babylon* [New York: Hawthorn, 1962], 132).

"Elamites of Susa" (Aram. *šûšankāyēʾ dehāwēʾ ᶜēlmāyēʾ*) was mistakenly transliterated in the KJV as three nationalities: "Susanchites, the Dehavites, and the Elamites." The second, however, is not the name of a people but is to be revocalized *dᶜhûʾ*, "that is" (cf. Rosenthal, 21, par. 35). "The people of Susa" is in apposition to "the Elamites"; Susa was the major city of Elam in southwestern Iran. Because of Susa's part in the revolt, Ashurbanipal brutally destroyed Susa in 640 BC. So thorough was the Assyrian destruction of Susa's ziggurat that only recently have excavators recognized its location. (See Yamauchi, *Persia and the Bible*, ch. 7, "Susa"; P. Amiet, *Suse: 6,000 ans d'histoire* [Paris: Musée du Louvre, 1988]; O. Harper, J. Aruz, and F. Tallon, eds., *The Royal City of Susa* [New York: Metropolitan Museum of Art, 1992]; M. A. Dandamayev, "Susa, the Capital of Elam, and Babylonian Susa," in *Festschrift für Burkhart Kienast* [ed. G. J. Selz; Münster: Ugarit, 2003], 7–14.)

10 Ashurbanipal, the last great Assyrian king (669–633 BC), was famed for his large library at Nineveh. He is not named elsewhere in the Bible but was probably the king who freed Manasseh from exile (2Ch 33:11–13). He may be the unnamed Assyrian king who, according to 2 Kings 17:24, deported people to Samaria.

The descendants of such deportees, removed from their homelands nearly two centuries earlier, still commonly stressed their origins. Probably the murder of the Israelite king Amon (640–642 BC) was the result of an anti-Assyrian movement inspired by the revolt in Elam and Babylonia (cf. W. W. Hallo, "From Qarqar to Carchemish," *BA* 23 [1960]: 60–61). The Assyrians may then have deported the rebellious Samarians and replaced them with the rebellious Elamites and Babylonians. After Esarhaddon had defeated the Nubian Tirhakah (Taharqa) of the Twenty-Fifth Dynasty and had conquered Lower (i.e., northern) Egypt, Ashurbanipal pursued him all the way to Thebes in Upper Egypt (i.e., southern Egypt), an event noted by Nahum (Na 3:8–9) as a warning to Nineveh, the Assyrian capital (see Yamauchi, *Africa and the Bible*, 138–40).

11 "Trans-Euphrates" (Aram. *ʿabar-nahᵃrâ*, lit., "across the river" [i.e., the Euphrates River], corresponding to Akkad. *eber nāri*) is a phrase that first appeared in the reign of Esarhaddon. Palestinians defined the "land across the River" as Mesopotamia

(Jos 24:2–3, 14–15; 2Sa 10:16). Mesopotamians saw it as including Syria, Phoenicia, and Palestine (1Ki 4:24). The Persians also called this area *Athura* ("Assyria"), hence the name "Syria."

When Cyrus conquered Babylon in 539 BC, he appointed Gubaru as governor of Babylon and the "land beyond the River." This designation became the official title of the fifth satrapy (Ezr 5:3; 6:6; Ne 2:7; et al.).

12 The Aramaic word for "repairing" (*yaḥîṭû*) is from either the root *ḥwṭ* ("to repair") or the root *yḥṭ* ("to lay"). S. Smith ("Foundations: Ezra iv.12; v.16; vi.3," in *Essays in Honour of J. H. Hertz* [ed. I. Epstein, E. Levine, and C. Roth; London: Edward Goldstone, 1942], 394–95) suggests a relation with the Akkadian *ḥāṭu*, which describes the process of searching for old foundations. He compares the Aramaic *uššayyāʾ* ("foundations") with the Akkadian *uššu*, derived from the Sumerian *Uš*, a word used to designate the lower foundations as usually understood. Smith believes this approach resolves the alleged contradiction between the laying of the foundation by Sheshbazzar (Ezr 5:16) and by Zerubbabel (Hag 2:15–18), which he holds was a ceremonial foundation (cf. ibid., 387–96, and comments on Ezr 5:3).

13 "Taxes" (Aram. *mindâ*; cf. 7:24; elsewhere *middâ* [4:20; 6:8]) is derived from the Akkadian *mandattu, maddattu*, a fixed annual tax paid by the provinces into the imperial treasuries. The word appears in the Elephantine texts as the rent due from the royal domains in Egypt to the Persians (cf. Cowley, 10:3–4; Driver, 33–34, 76; J. N. Postgate, *Taxation and Conscription in the Assyrian Empire* [Rome: Pontifical Biblical Institute, 1974], 119; C. Tuplin, "The Administration of the Achaemenid Empire," in Carradice, 109–66; M. Heltzer, "Again on Some Problems of the Achaemenid Taxation in the Province of Judah," *Archäologische Mitteilungen aus Iran* 25 [1992]: 173–75).

"Tribute" (Aram. *bᵉlô*; cf. Akkad. *biltu*) was the rent tax in Babylonia (Driver, 8:5, 70). Some scholars interpret this word as an impost or duty charged on merchandise ("custom," NRSV) or as a poll tax (cf. Brockington).

"Duty" (Aram. *hᵃlāk*; cf. Akkad. *ilku*, "feudal service") derives from the Akkadian verb *alāku* (lit., "to go"), as used in the Akkadian phrase *ana ḫarrān šarrim alākum* ("to go in the king's way"; cf. Code of Hammurabi 26, 68–69; Postgate, *Taxation*, 86).

Estimates suggest that annually the Persian king collected twenty to thirty-five million dollars in taxes. The archive of the Egibi family sheds light on the collection of taxes in Mesopotamia under the Persians from 521–487 BC. (See K. Abraham, *Business and Politics under the Persian Empire* [Bethesda, Md.: CDL, 2004].)

14 "We are under obligation to the palace" is literally "we eat the salt of the palace." Salt was made a royal monopoly by the Ptolemies in Egypt, and perhaps also by the Persians (Porten, 86, n. 121). It was used in the ratification of covenants (Lev 2:13; Nu 18:19; 2Ch 13:5; cf. S. H. C. Trumbull, *The Covenant of Salt* [New York: Scribner's Sons, 1899],

17ff.). The English word "salary" is derived from the Latin *salarium*, the ration of salt given to soldiers (cf. the expression "a man who is not worth his salt"). For the significance of salt in world civilizations, see M. Kulansky, *Salt: A World History* (New York: Penguin, 2003).

15–16 "The archives" (Aram. *sᵉpar dokrānayyāʾ*; v.15) is literally "book of the records" (cf. Ezr 6:1–2; Est 2:23; 6:1). There were evidently several repositories of such documents at the major capitals. The Greek physician Ctesias, who served at the court of Artaxerxes II, used the royal archives, which preserved documents for centuries. Berossus in the third century BC used the Babylonian Chronicles, which covered events from the Assyrian to the Hellenistic eras (cf. R. Drews, "The Babylonian Chronicles and Berossus," *Iraq* 37 [1975]: 39–55). (See J. A. Black and W. J. Tait, "Archives and Libraries in the Ancient Near East," in *Civilizations of the Ancient Near East* [ed. J. Sasson et al.; New York: Scribner's Sons, 1995], 4:2197–2209; E. Posner, *Archives in the Ancient World* [Cambridge, Mass.: Harvard Univ. Press, 1972].)

NOTES

7 The Aramaic spelling of אַרְתַּחְשַׁשְׂתְּאֹ (ʾartaḥšaštaʾ, "Artaxerxes") in the Elephantine texts is ארתחששש (ʾrthššš). The original Old Persian name was *Artaxšathra*, which means "great [*arta*] kingdom [*xšathra*]."

D. B. Weisberg (*Guild Structure and Political Allegiance in Early Achaemenid Mesopotamia* [New Haven, Conn.: Yale Univ. Press, 1967], 15) has published a text (YBC 3499) from Uruk, from the fourth year of the reign of Cyrus, which confirms that local craftsmen in Mesopotamia were addressed in Aramaic: *ina lišānišunu iqbū* ("spoke in their language as follows").

8 The word for "secretary" is סָפְרָא (Aram. *sāprāʾ*, "scribe"; cf. vv.9, 17, 23; 7:12, 21). The Elephantine papyri have the phrases *spry ʾwṣrʾ* ("scribes of the treasury") and *spry mdyntʾ* ("scribes of the province"; Cowley, 2:12; 17:1, 6; Porten, 51, 55). סֹפֵר (*sōpēr*) is the corresponding Hebrew word (cf. 7:6, 11; Ne 8:1, 4, 9, 13; 12:26, 36; 13:13). The Neo-Babylonian official (Akkad. *sipiru*) was a royal scribe capable of reading and interpreting a language other than Akkadian. An important text from the Persian period contains names of similar officials and indicates that one of them was a Jew. (See M. Heltzer, "A Recently Published Babylonian Tablet and the Province of Judah after 516 BCE," *Transeu* 5 [1992]: 57–61.)

9 R. Achenbach ("Die Titel der pesischen Verwaltungsbeamten in Esra 4,9b [MT★]," *ZAH* 13 [2000]: 134–44) contends that the terms in this verse rendered as ethnic names were originally the titles of Persian officials but were later misunderstood in the transmission of the MT.

10 אָסְנַפַּר (ʾosnappar, "Ashurbanipal") is the Aramaized form of the Akkadian *Aššur-bān-apal* ("Ashur has made a son"). The shift of the final *l* to an *r* may be a sign of Persian influence, as in the Old Persian *Babiruš* for Babylon; the loss of medial *rh* may be the result of scribal or oral ellipsis (cf. Millard, 11).

b. The Letter from the King (4:17–23)

> [17] The king sent this reply:
>
> To Rehum the commanding officer, Shimshai the secretary and the rest of their associates living in Samaria and elsewhere in Trans-Euphrates:
>
> Greetings.
>
> [18] The letter you sent us has been read and translated in my presence. [19] I issued an order and a search was made, and it was found that this city has a long history of revolt against kings and has been a place of rebellion and sedition. [20] Jerusalem has had powerful kings ruling over the whole of Trans-Euphrates, and taxes, tribute and duty were paid to them. [21] Now issue an order to these men to stop work, so that this city will not be rebuilt until I so order. [22] Be careful not to neglect this matter. Why let this threat grow, to the detriment of the royal interests?
>
> [23] As soon as the copy of the letter of King Artaxerxes was read to Rehum and Shimshai the secretary and their associates, they went immediately to the Jews in Jerusalem and compelled them by force to stop.

COMMENTARY

17 "Greetings" is the Aramaic *šᵉlām* (cf. Heb. *šālôm*, Arab. *salām*).

18 As the king was probably illiterate, documents would be read to him. Darius I related, "And it was inscribed and was read off before me" (cf. Est 6:1).

"Translated" is literally "read separately," that is, distinctively, but probably meaning here that the letter was translated from Aramaic into Persian (cf. comments on 4:8 and Ne 8:8).

19 There was some truth in the accusation. Jerusalem had rebelled against the Assyrians and then the Babylonians in 701, 597, and 587 BC (2Ki 18:7, 13; 24:1; et al.).

20 According to the *Qere* reading of the Hebrew text of 1 Kings 9:18, Solomon rebuilt Tadmor, the important oasis in the Syrian desert that controlled much of the Trans-Euphrates area. His international prestige is reflected in his marriage to a pharaoh's daughter (1Ki 3:1; 7:8).

21–23 After provincial authorities had intervened, the Persian king ordered a halt to the Jewish attempt to rebuild the walls of Jerusalem (see comment on Ne 1:3). Most scholars would date the episode of vv.7–23 before 445 BC. The forcible destruction of these recently rebuilt walls rather than the destruction by Nebuchadnezzar would then be the basis of the report made to Nehemiah. Bowman, Olmstead, and Rudolph place this incident in the context of the revolt of the satrap Megabyzos against Artaxerxes I. Megabyzos was the king's brother-in-law and his greatest general.

To "compelled them by force to stop," the LXX adds "with horses and an (armed) force."

4. Resumption of Work under Darius (4:24)

²⁴Thus the work on the house of God in Jerusalem came to a standstill until the second year of the reign of Darius king of Persia.

COMMENTARY

24 The writer, after a long digression detailing opposition to Jewish efforts, returns to his original subject—rebuilding the temple (vv.1–3).

According to Persian reckoning, the second regnal year of Darius I began on Nisan 1 (April 3) 520 BC and lasted till February 21, 519. In that year the prophet Haggai (Hag 1:1–5) exhorted Zerubbabel to begin rebuilding the temple on the first day of the sixth month (August 29). Work began on the temple on the twenty-fourth day of the month—September 21 (Hag 1:15). (See J. Finegan, *Handbook of Biblical Chronology* [rev. ed.; Peabody, Mass.: Hendrickson, 1998], 267.)

The date is significant. During his first two years, Darius fought numerous battles against nine rebels, as recounted in his famous Behistun Inscription (cf. Kent, 107–8, 116–34; G. Cameron, "The Monument of King Darius at Bisitun," *Arch* 13 [1960]: 162–71; Yamauchi, *Persia and the Bible*, 131–34). Only after the stabilization of the Persian Empire could efforts to rebuild the temple be permitted.

The rebuilding of a temple with its completion after a delay follows a pattern attested in Mesopotamia, for example, in the reign of Nabonidus, the last Neo-Babylonian king. (See V. A. Hurowitz, *I Have Built You an Exalted House: Temple Building in the Bible in the Light of Mesopotamian and North-West Semitic Writings* [Sheffield: JSOT, 1992].)

NOTE

24 Though most scholars have now accepted the priority of Ezra as coming before Nehemiah in the seventh year of Artaxerxes I (see Introduction: The Order of Ezra and Nehemiah—The List of High Priests), one scholar who has argued for the reverse order, with Ezra's coming in the seventh year of Artaxerxes II (= 398 BC), is L. Dequeker ("Darius the Persian and the Reconstruction of the Jewish Temple in Jerusalem [Ezr 4,24],"in *Ritual and Sacrifice in the Ancient Near East* [ed. J. Quaegebeur; Louvain: Peeters, 1993], 67–92).

The Persian kings are not listed in chronological order in this chapter. But the author discussed these kings for his purposes and was not ignorant about their histories. Williamson (*Ezra, Nehemiah*, 59), writes: "We may thus conclude that our author has consciously given this section a literary setting at variance with its strict historical setting, but that this was much to his purpose and that he has left clear literary markers to indicate what he was doing." A. Brown II ("Chronological Anomalies in the Book of Ezra," *BSac* 162 [2005]: 42) comments, "Ezra's use of anachrony signals that thematic development is again overriding chronological presentation."

E. The Completion of the Temple (5:1–6:22)

1. A New Beginning Inspired by Haggai and Zechariah (5:1–2)

¹Now Haggai the prophet and Zechariah the prophet, a descendant of Iddo, prophesied to the Jews in Judah and Jerusalem in the name of the God of Israel, who was over them. ²Then Zerubbabel son of Shealtiel and Jeshua son of Jozadak set to work to rebuild the house of God in Jerusalem. And the prophets of God were with them, helping them.

COMMENTARY

1 Beginning on August 29, 520 BC (Hag 1:1) and continuing till December 18 (Hag 2:1–9, 20–23), the prophet Haggai delivered a series of messages to stir the people to commence work on the temple. Two months after Haggai's first speech, Zechariah joined him (Zec 1:1).

Haggai 1:6 describes the deplorable situation: housing shortages, disappointing harvests, lack of clothing and jobs, and inadequate funds—perhaps as a result of inflation (see comments on Ne 5). Money went into bags full of holes.

Haggai rebuked the people with a paronomasia (play on words). He proclaimed that because the Lord's house had remained "a ruin" (*ḥārēb*; Hag 1:4, 9), the Lord would bring "a drought" (*ḥōreb*; 1:11) on the land. Though perhaps hyperbolically, Haggai's prophecy implies that little progress had

been made in the sixteen years since the first foundation was laid.

Some scholars have held that there is an "irreconcilable difference" between Ezra 3:10 and the references in Haggai 2:18 and Zechariah 4:9; 8:9, as the former speaks of the foundation of the temple in 536 BC, the latter in 520. It is possible, however, to have more than one foundation ceremony for a particular building. J. S. Wright (*The Building of the Second Temple* [rev. ed.; London: Tyndale, 1958], 17) notes a Hittite ritual that speaks of the refoundation of a building (*ANET*, 356) and Akkadian rituals that tell of founding anew the temple in question (cf. also F. I. Andersen, "Who Built the Second Temple?" *ABR* 6 [1958]: 1–35; A. Gelston, "The Foundation of the Second Temple," *VT* 16 [1966]: 232–35.

2 "Zerubbabel" is a Babylonian name after the Akkadian *zēr-bābili* ("seed of Babylon," referring to his birth in exile, probably before 570 BC). Here and in Ezra 3:2; Nehemiah 12:1; and Haggai 1:1, he is described as the son of Shealtiel—son of Jehoiachin, the second-to-last king of Judah (1Ch 3:17). Though replaced by Zedekiah, Jehoiachin was regarded as the last legitimate king of Judah. Zerubbabel was the last of the Davidic line to be entrusted with political authority by the occupying powers.

In 1 Chronicles 3:19, however, Zerubbabel is listed as a son of Pedaiah, another son of Jehoiachin and brother of Shealtiel. Pedaiah may have married the widow of his dead brother, Shealtiel, in a levirate marriage (Dt 25:5–6). Note that the genealogy of Zerubbabel (as the son of Shealtiel) parallels the genealogy of Jesus (Mt 1:12; Lk 3:27).

Jeshua's father, Jozadak, had been carried off to Babylon by Nebuchadnezzar (1Ch 6:15; cf. Ezr 3:2, 8–9; 4:3; Hag 1:1, 12, 14).

NOTE

1 חַגַּי (*ḥaggay*, "Haggai," meaning "Festal," i.e., born on a feast) was a popular name. It was borne by eleven individuals at Elephantine and by four in the Murashu texts (Coogan, 23).

זְכַרְיָה (*zᵉkaryâ*, "Zechariah," i.e., "Yahweh has remembered") is described here as the "son" of Iddo, whereas according to Zechariah 1:1 he was the grandson of Iddo. The word "son" can designate a descendant. Iddo may have been the priest mentioned in Nehemiah 12:4 as one of those who returned with Zerubbabel. The Zechariah of Nehemiah 12:16 may have been a descendant of the prophet. Or it is possible that this Zechariah was the same as the prophet. In this case the prophet Zechariah was also the head of a priestly family.

2. The Intervention of the Governor Tattenai (5:3–5)

³At that time Tattenai, governor of Trans-Euphrates, and Shethar-Bozenai and their associates went to them and asked, "Who authorized you to rebuild this temple and restore this structure?" ⁴They also asked, "What are the names of the men constructing this building?" ⁵But the eye of their God was watching over the elders of the Jews, and they were not stopped until a report could go to Darius and his written reply be received.

COMMENTARY

3–5 A. T. Olmstead ("Tattenai, Governor of 'Across the River,'" *JNES* 3 [1944]: 46) pointed to a document that can be dated to June 5, 502 BC, which cites *Ta-at-tanni* as the *paḥat* ("governor") who was subordinate to the satrap over *Ebir-nari*. From the Persian perspective, "Across the River" was the area west of the Euphrates, including Syria and Palestine. The earliest known use of the title comes from the fourth year of Cyrus the Great, or 535 BC. We learn that Tattenai was a subordinate of *Uštānu*, governor of the combined satrapy of Across-the-River and Babylonia. Earlier scholars, relying on Herodotus (3.89), placed the separation of the two areas in the reign of Darius. But the cuneiform tablet from the British Museum (BM 74554) published by M. W. Stolper ("The Governor of Babylon and Across-the-River in 486 BC," *JNES* 48 [1989]: 289) indicates that the partition took place later in the reign of Xerxes.

Shethar-Bozenai may have functioned as a Persian official known as the *patifrasa* ("inquisitor") or *frasaka* ("investigator"). According to Cowley (37:5; cf. Porten, 54), a complaint was lodged before the "investigators" of the Egyptian satrap Arsames.

"Structure" (Aram. *ʾuššarnāʾ*) is rendered "wall" by the KJV and ASV and "structure" in the NRSV and NIV. The former rendering suggests an advanced stage in the rebuilding of the temple, the latter that Zerubbabel was fortifying the city. C. G. Tuland ("*ʾUššayyāʾ* and *ʾUššarnā*," *JNES* 17 [1958]: 269–75),

however, notes that the word — derived from the Old Persian *⋆ācdṛna* (with the asterisk indicating a reconstructed form; see Rosenthal, 58–59) — appears in the Aramaic papyri (Cowley, 26:5, 9, 21; 27:1, 18; 30:1, 11), where it means "material" or "equipment." He therefore suggests that the clause here means, "Who gave you a decree to build this house and to complete this (building) material?" Tuland concludes that Tattenai's investigations were thus made at an early stage, when the Jews were still gathering building materials (but see v.8).

The Persian governor gave the Jews the benefit of the doubt by not stopping the work while the inquiry (vv.3–5) was proceeding. Some scholars have suggested that Zechariah was promoting Zerubbabel as a messianic figure to lead a revolt against the Persians; evidently, however, from Tattenai's tolerant stance no such revolt took place.

On the "elders" see Ezra 5:9; 6:7–8, 14; Jeremiah 29:1; Ezekiel 8:1; 14:1. There was also an assembly of elders among the Egyptian exiles in Babylonia.

3. The Report to Darius (5:6–17)

⁶This is a copy of the letter that Tattenai, governor of Trans-Euphrates, and Shethar-Bozenai and their associates, the officials of Trans-Euphrates, sent to King Darius. ⁷The report they sent him read as follows:

To King Darius:
Cordial greetings.

⁸The king should know that we went to the district of Judah, to the temple of the great God. The people are building it with large stones and placing the timbers in the walls. The work is being carried on with diligence and is making rapid progress under their direction.

⁹We questioned the elders and asked them, "Who authorized you to rebuild this temple and restore this structure?" ¹⁰We also asked them their names, so that we could write down the names of their leaders for your information.

¹¹This is the answer they gave us:

"We are the servants of the God of heaven and earth, and we are rebuilding the temple that was built many years ago, one that a great king of Israel built and finished. [12]But because our fathers angered the God of heaven, he handed them over to Nebuchadnezzar the Chaldean, king of Babylon, who destroyed this temple and deported the people to Babylon.

[13]"However, in the first year of Cyrus king of Babylon, King Cyrus issued a decree to rebuild this house of God. [14]He even removed from the temple of Babylon the gold and silver articles of the house of God, which Nebuchadnezzar had taken from the temple in Jerusalem and brought to the temple in Babylon.

"Then King Cyrus gave them to a man named Sheshbazzar, whom he had appointed governor, [15]and he told him, 'Take these articles and go and deposit them in the temple in Jerusalem. And rebuild the house of God on its site.' [16]So this Sheshbazzar came and laid the foundations of the house of God in Jerusalem. From that day to the present it has been under construction but is not yet finished."

[17]Now if it pleases the king, let a search be made in the royal archives of Babylon to see if King Cyrus did in fact issue a decree to rebuild this house of God in Jerusalem. Then let the king send us his decision in this matter.

COMMENTARY

6–7 That such inquiries were sent directly to the king has been vividly confirmed by the Elamite texts from Persepolis, where in 1933–34 several thousand tablets and fragments were found in the fortification wall. Some two thousand fortification tablets were published in 1969 by Hallock. Dating from the thirteenth to the twenty eighth year of Darius (509–494 BC), they deal with the transfer and payment of food products.

In 1936–38 additional Elamite texts were discovered in the treasury area of Persepolis. Over one hundred of these texts were published by Cameron in 1948, 1958, and 1965. They date from the thirtieth year of Darius to the seventh year of Artaxerxes I (492–458 BC). In addition to payment in kind, they include supplementary payment in silver coins, an innovation introduced around 493 BC (see Yam-auchi, *Persia and the Bible*, 189–90; Williamson, "Ezra and Nehemiah," 50–54).

8 The interpretation of the phrase "large stones" (Aram. *ʾeben gᵉlāl*; cf. Akkad. *aban galâla*) is controverted. The LXX has "choice" or "splendid" stones (cf. 1Ki 7:9–11); 1 Esdras 6:9 (KJV) has "polished and costly" stones. The translation "large" has been suggested because *gᵉlāl* means "rolling," that is, they were such large stones that they were placed on rollers. Others believe *gᵉlāl* refers to the circular motion involved in polishing the stone. Williamson (*Ezra, Nehemiah*, 70) translates this as "dressed stone" and observes, "But the contexts often suggest that, whatever its etymology, the meaning 'smoothed (stone) polished (by a specific technique)' (*CAD* sub *galālu*) is appropriate."

"Placing the timbers in the walls" may refer to interior wainscoting (1Ki 6:15–18) or to logs alternating with the brick or stone layers in the walls (1Ki 6:36). The latter was a device widely used in earthquake zones.

9–12 According to 1 Kings 6:1, Solomon began building the temple in the fourth year of his reign. The project lasted seven years (6:38). Since Solomon employed Phoenician craftsmen (7:13–45), the temple evidently incorporated elements of foreign inspiration.

In 1936 a ninth-century temple was discovered at Tell Tainat (Tayinat) east of Antioch, which, though two-thirds the size of Solomon's temple, had a similar tripartite plan. Other parallels include a Late Bronze Canaanite temple at Hazor and a ninth- or tenth-century royal chapel at Hamath. An even closer parallel is the temple at ʿAin Dara (northwest of Aleppo) discovered by a shepherd and excavated by a Syrian archaeologist between 1980 and 1985. (See A. A. Assaf, *Der Tempel von ʿAin Dara* [Mainz: Philipp von Zabern, 1990].) The temple was constructed between 1300 and 1000 BC. On the basis of numerous parallels, J. Monson ("The New ʿAin Dara Temple: Closest Solomonic Parallel," *BAR* 6/3 [2000]: 35) concludes: "Simply put, the date, size and numerous features of the ʿAin Dara temple provide new evidence that chronologically anchors the Temple of Solomon in the cultural traditions of the tenth century BCE."

In response to the challenge of the Persian authorities, the Jewish elders declared that they were the servants of the God of heaven and earth and recounted the building of the first temple by Solomon, which must have been an object of national pride. They then confessed that because of their fathers' sins, God had been provoked into using the pagan Babylonians in chastising them, just as Jeremiah had warned.

The Chaldeans inhabited the southern regions of Mesopotamia and established the Neo-Babylonian Empire (626–539 BC). Their origins are obscure. There may have been some original kinship with the Arameans, who came to occupy adjacent territories to the north of the Chaldeans. The Chaldeans were consistently distinguished from the Arameans in the Assyrian documents (cf. 2Ki 24:2; Jer 35:11).

In the late seventh century BC, the Chaldeans with the Medes, led by Nabopolassar, the father of Nebuchadnezzar, overthrew the Assyrians. In 1956 Wiseman published the Chronicles of Chaldean Kings, which gives us vital information for the first ten years of Nebuchadnezzar's reign. Of the fall of Jerusalem on March 16, 597, the Chronicles laconically report:"He then captured its king (Jehoiachin) and appointed a king of his own choice (Zedekiah)" (cf. 2Ki 24:17). Unfortunately, the extant Chaldean Chronicles do not cover Nebuchadnezzar's final attack on Jerusalem.

Scholars are divided as to the year of Jerusalem's final capture. Second Chronicles 36:11 informs us that Zedekiah reigned eleven years (from 597 BC). Scholars (e.g., Albright, Freedman, Tadmor, Wiseman) who believe the Jews used a calendar beginning in Nisan (April) date the fall of Jerusalem to the summer of 587 BC. Others (e.g., Horn, Malamat, Redford, Saggs, Thiele), believing that the Jews used a calendar beginning in Tishri (September), place the fall in the summer of 586 BC. The latter date might accord better with Ezekiel 33:21, which says that the Judean exiles in Babylonia heard of the disaster from a fugitive in December 586. (See K. Freedy and D. Redford, "The Dates in Ezekiel in Relation to Biblical, Babylonian and Egyptian Sources," *JAOS* 90 [1970]: 462–85.)

13 For the title "king of Babylon," see the comments on Nehemiah 13:6. In cuneiform contracts in Mesopotamia and in Syria, Darius is also designated "king of Babylon."

14 Cyrus appointed Sheshbazzar "governor" (*peḥâ*, derived from Akkad. *pīḫatu*). The LXX has "the treasurer who was over the treasury." Both Sheshbazzar and Zerubbabel were "governors" (v.14; Hag 1:1; 2:2). Both are said to have laid the foundation of the temple (v.16; 1:3; 3:2–8; Hag 1:1, 14–15; 2:2–4, 18).

Some scholars conclude that an editor has telescoped the work of the two men and placed in retrospect the work done later by Zerubbabel in the time of Darius and credited it to Sheshbazzar in the age of Cyrus. That such an erroneous ascription was made lacks support. Sheshbazzar was probably an elderly man of about fifty-five to sixty years at the time of the return, whereas Zerubbabel was probably a younger contemporary of about forty (cf. Myers, 28).

Second, Sheshbazzar may have been viewed as the official Persian "governor," whereas Zerubbabel served as the popular leader (3:8–11; see Japhet, 66–98, perhaps explaining why the Jews mentioned Sheshbazzar here when speaking to the Persian authorities). Whereas the high priest Joshua is associated with Zerubbabel, no priest is likewise associated with Sheshbazzar.

15–17 It was important that the temple be built on its original "site" (v.15). Although Sheshbazzar presided over the laying of its foundation (v.16) in 536 BC, so little actually was accomplished that Zerubbabel evidently had to preside over a second foundation some sixteen years later.

The fate of Sheshbazzar is uncertain. Though some have suggested that he returned to Mesopotamia, more probably, in view of his advanced age, he died soon after his return to Jerusalem.

Though there are references to Zerubbabel in Nehemiah 7:7; 12:1, 47, they are retrospective and yield no further information about his activities after the dedication of the temple. Some have therefore speculated that Zerubbabel might have been suspected of planning a revolt against the Persians. There is no evidence whatever for the assertion that he was executed. Yet since we hear no more of him and since none of his family succeeded him, it is likely that the Persians did strip the Davidic house of its political prerogatives. Zerubbabel may have been summoned back to Persia, since one of his descendants, Hattush, returned with Ezra (8:2; 1Ch 3:19–22).

NOTES

6 אֲפַרְסְכָיֵא (Aram. ᵃparseḵāyēᵓ, "officials"; cf. 6:6) is transliterated "Apharsachites" in the KJV as the name of people. This is probably a variant of אֲפַרְסַתְכָיֵא (ᵓᵃparsatḵāyēᵓ) in 4:9 and describes a kind of official. Rosenthal, 58, suggests a derivation from the Persian frasaka ("investigator").

7 שְׁלָמָא כֹלָּא (šᵉlāmāᵓ kōllāᵓ, "cordial greetings") is literally "well-being completely."

8 אָסְפַּרְנָא (ᵓ āsparnāᵓ, "with diligence") is a loanword from the Persian asprna, which means "exactly, perfectly, eagerly." The adverb is also found in 6:8, 12; 7:17, 21, 26.

12 נְבוּכַדְנֶצַּר (Nᵉbûkadneṣṣar, "Nebuchadnezzar"; Akkad. Nabū-kudurri-uṣur) means "Nabu protect my boundary stone" or "Nabu has protected the succession rights." The Hebrew form נְבוּכַדְרֶאצַּר (Nᵉbûkadreᵓṣṣar, "Nebuchadrezzar"), used in Jeremiah and Ezekiel, is closer to the Akkadian. The variant used here in Ezra may be derived from an Aramaic form. Nebuchadnezzar, who reigned from 605–562 BC, is mentioned almost a hundred times in the OT. (See E. Yamauchi, "Nebuchadnezzar," *NIDBA*, 332–34; D. J. Wiseman, *Nebuchadrezzar and Babylon* [Oxford: Oxford Univ. Press, 1991].)

16 Hensley, 219, resolves the problem concerning the laying of the foundation thus: "It is sufficient to point out here that יהב (*Y-H-B*) is better understood in the sense of 'administer.' Thus Sheshbazzar is involved in the work as the official representative of the king, while Zerubbabel is the local authority in charge of the actual work."

17 בֵּית גִּנְזַיָּא (Aram. *bêt ginzayyā*ʾ, "the royal archives, house of treasures") comes from the Persian *ganza* ("treasure"; cf. the plural of גִּזְבָּר [*gizbār*, "treasurer"] in 7:21 from the Pers. *bara*, "bearer"). The *Genizah* was the storeroom where the Jews deposited worn-out Scriptures. The most important document of the Mandeans is called the *Ginza*.

4. The Search for the Decree of Cyrus (6:1–5)

> [1]King Darius then issued an order, and they searched in the archives stored in the treasury at Babylon. [2]A scroll was found in the citadel of Ecbatana in the province of Media, and this was written on it:
>
> Memorandum:
>
> [3]In the first year of King Cyrus, the king issued a decree concerning the temple of God in Jerusalem:
>
> Let the temple be rebuilt as a place to present sacrifices, and let its foundations be laid. It is to be ninety feet high and ninety feet wide, [4]with three courses of large stones and one of timbers. The costs are to be paid by the royal treasury. [5]Also, the gold and silver articles of the house of God, which Nebuchadnezzar took from the temple in Jerusalem and brought to Babylon, are to be returned to their places in the temple in Jerusalem; they are to be deposited in the house of God.

COMMENTARY

1 "The archives" (Aram. *bêt siprayyā*ʾ) is literally "house of books." The phrase then reads "in the house of the books where the treasures were laid up." Many Elamite documents were found in the so-called treasury area of Persepolis, along with precious stone objects and other such things.

2 Diodorus (2.32.4) declared that the Persians had "royal parchments" recording their history. Persian officials wrote on scrolls of papyrus and leather, as discoveries made in Egypt show.

"Citadel" (Aram. *bîrtā*ʾ) is probably from the Akkadian *bīrtu* ("fortress"). Widengren ("Persian

Period," in *Israelite and Judean History* [ed. J. H. Hayes and J. M. Miller; Philadelphia: Westminster, 1977], 499) comments on this verse: "Important documents were thus preserved in a fortress. This was a tradition which continued for many centuries, for in the Sassanian period, documents were still kept in the so-called *diz i nipišt*, 'the fortress of the archives.' Such a detail adds to the reliability of the story as to how the document was found."

Media was the homeland of the Medes in northwestern Iran. An Indo-European tribe related to the Persians, the Medes, after the rise of Cyrus in

550 BC, became subordinate to the Persians. The name was retained down to the NT era (Ac 2:9; see Yamauchi, *Persia and the Bible*, ch. 1, "The Medes".)

"Ecbatana" (Aram. *ʾaḥmᵉtāʾ*; "Achmetha," KJV; Old Pers. *Hagmatana*, "gathering place"; Akkad. *Agmatanu*, Gk. *Agbátana*) was the capital of Media. Its ancient name is still preserved in the name of the modern Hamadan. This is the sole OT reference to the site. There are numerous references in the apocryphal books (Tob 3:7; 7:1; 14:12–13; Jdth 1:1–4; 2 Macc 9:1–3; see Yamauchi, *Persia and the Bible*, ch. 8, "Ecbatana").

In "The Decrees of Cyrus," 89, de Vaux observed, "Now we know that it was the custom of the Persian sovereigns to winter in Babylon and depart in the summer to Susa or Ecbatana … and we also know that Cyrus left Babylon in the spring of 538 B.C…. A forger operating in Palestine without the information which we possess could hardly have been so accurate."

The Aramaic memorandum of the decree of Cyrus in vv. 3–5 is comparable with the Hebrew version of the king's proclamation (*qôl*) in 1:2–4. In contrast with the latter, the Aramaic is written in a more sober, administrative style without reference to Yahweh (see Hensley, 86–88). A similar "memorandum" (Aram. *dikrônâ*; cf. Egyp. Aram. *zkrn*) in the Aramaic papyri deals with Persian permission to rebuild the Jewish temple at Elephantine, which Egyptians had destroyed. This response was from the Persian governor, Bagohi, and the son of Sanballat, Delaiah, to a petition from the Jewish garrison serving the Persians on the island of Elephantine near Aswan in Upper Egypt. (See Cowley, 32 = B. Porten, *Jews of Elephantine and Arameans of Syene, Fifth Century B.C.E.* [Jerusalem: Hebrew Univ. Press, 1976], 98–99.) It reads as follows:

Memorandum of Bagohi and Delaiah. They said to me: "Let [this] indeed be a memorandum for you to say in Egypt before Arsames about the altar-house of the God of Heaven which [was] built in Elephantine the fortress, formerly, before Cambyses, which that wicked Vidranga demolished in year 14 [i.e., 408 BC]: to rebuild it on its site as it was formerly and they shall offer the meal-offering and the incense upon that altar as was [formerly] done."

3 "Ninety feet high and ninety feet wide" is literally "sixty cubits its height and sixty cubits its width." The cubit was the distance from the elbow to the fingertip, or slightly less than eighteen inches. No length is given here. These dimensions contrast with those of Solomon's temple, which was but twenty cubits wide by thirty cubits high by sixty cubits long (1Ki 6:2). Bowman, 552, suggests that the dimensions should be corrected to make the building thirty cubits high and twenty cubits wide, as with Solomon's temple.

The dimensions are probably not descriptions of the temple as built, however, but specifications of the outer limits of a building the Persians would support. The Second Temple was manifestly not as grandiose as the first (3:12; Hag 2:3).

Kenyon has identified as the only visible remains of Zerubbabel's building a straight joint of stones with heavy bosses about 108 feet north of the southeastern corner of the temple platform, which Dunand confirmed as similar to Persian masonry found in Phoenicia (cf. M. Dunand, "Byblos, Sidon, Jerusalem," *VTSup* 17 [1969]: 64–70; Kenyon, *Digging Up Jerusalem*, 111–12, 177–78).

4 Though the preserved text has the Aramaic word *ḥadat* ("new," KJV), most translations accept the emendation *ḥad*, "one," which makes far better sense. The same kind of construction is mentioned in 1 Kings 6:36 and 7:12. Such use of timber beams with masonry is attested at Ras Shamra, Tell Tainat, Troy, Mycenae, Tiryns, Knossos, et al. H. C. Thomas ("A Row of Cedar Beams," *PEQ* 92 [1960]: 61) remarks, "The most probable explanation is that protection against shock, and particularly earthquake shock, lies at the heart of this problem."

In 1973 French archaeologists discovered at Xanthos in Lycia in southwestern Turkey a cult foundation charter written in Greek, Lycian, and Aramaic and dated to the fourth century BC, a period when the area was controlled by a Persian satrap. The charter provided some striking parallels with the decree of Cyrus (see Briant, 704–9).

1. The Xanthos charter, though issued in response to a local request, would nonetheless have received ratification from the Persian court.
2. As in Ezra, amounts of sacrifices, names of priests, and responsibility for the upkeep of the cult are specified.

3. As in Ezra, gods were invoked to curse those who disregarded the decree of local gods.

A. R. Millard ("A Decree of a Persian Governor," *BurH* [June 1974]: 88) observes:

Most obvious is the similarity of wording between Greek and Lycian requests and the satrap's Aramaic answer. Such resemblances in the Ezra passages, thought to show a forger's hand, are signs of normal practice. This practice explains how the Persian king or officer appears to know in detail about the cult in question; his information stems from its adherents.... The further objection that the Persians would have paid no attention to such details falls away.

5. Darius's Order for the Rebuilding of the Temple (6:6–12)

⁶Now then, Tattenai, governor of Trans-Euphrates, and Shethar-Bozenai and you, their fellow officials of that province, stay away from there. ⁷Do not interfere with the work on this temple of God. Let the governor of the Jews and the Jewish elders rebuild this house of God on its site.

⁸Moreover, I hereby decree what you are to do for these elders of the Jews in the construction of this house of God:

The expenses of these men are to be fully paid out of the royal treasury, from the revenues of Trans-Euphrates, so that the work will not stop. ⁹Whatever is needed — young bulls, rams, male lambs for burnt offerings to the God of heaven, and wheat, salt, wine and oil, as requested by the priests in Jerusalem — must be given them daily without fail, ¹⁰so that they may offer sacrifices pleasing to the God of heaven and pray for the well-being of the king and his sons.

¹¹Furthermore, I decree that if anyone changes this edict, a beam is to be pulled from his house and he is to be lifted up and impaled on it. And for this crime his house is to be made a pile of rubble. ¹²May God, who has caused his Name to dwell there, overthrow any king or people who lifts a hand to change this decree or to destroy this temple in Jerusalem.

I Darius have decreed it. Let it be carried out with diligence.

COMMENTARY

6 "Stay away from there" (Aram. *raḥîq min tammâ*) is literally "to be distant from there," an idiom found also in the Egyptian Aramaic papyri (Cowley, 13:16; 25:4; 67:5; Kraeling, 1:7).

7 On "on its site" see comment on 5:15. When Babylonian kings such as Nebuchadnezzar and Nabonidus rebuilt temples, they searched carefully to discover the exact outlines of the former buildings. An inscription of Nabonidus (cited by R. Ellis, *Foundation Deposits in Ancient Mesopotamia* [New Haven, Conn.: Yale Univ. Press 1968], 181) reads: "I discovered its [i.e., the Ebabbara in Sippar] ancient foundation, which Sargon, a former king, had made. I laid its brick foundations solidly on the foundation that Sargon had made, neither protruding nor receding an inch."

8 "Treasury" (Aram. *niksîn*, Akkad. *nik[k]assū*; 7:26), literally "possessions, properties," occurs frequently in extrabiblical Aramaic with a wide variety of meanings. Here it seems to mean royal "funds."

As the accounts in Haggai and Zechariah do not speak of support from the Persian treasury, some have questioned the promises made here. Extrabiblical evidence, however, makes it clear that Persian kings consistently helped restore sanctuaries in their empire. As noted above, the memorandum concerning the rebuilding of the Jewish temple at Elephantine written by Bagoas, governor of Judah, and Delaiah, governor of Samaria, relates that they were "to rebuild it on its site as it was formerly and they shall offer the meal-offering and the incense upon that altar as was [formerly] done" (Cowley, 32; *ANET*, 492). Kraeling, 107, sees this memorandum as "a directive presumably suggesting that the rebuilding be done at government expense," with a hint of government subsidies for the offerings.

Cyrus repaired the Eanna temple at Uruk and the Enunmah at Ur. Cambyses gave funds for the temple at Sais in Egypt according to the important inscription of Udjahorresnet. (See J. Blenkinsopp, "The Mission of Udjahorresnet and Those of Ezra and Nehemiah," *JBL* 106 [1987]: 409–21.) The temple of Amon at Hibis in the Khargah Oasis, excavated in 1941 by H. Winlock, was rebuilt from top to bottom by order of Darius. See Tuplin, "The Administration of the Achaemenid Empire," in Carradice, 150–52.

9 A lamb was offered every morning and evening; also two were offered on the Sabbath, seven each at great feasts and at the beginning of each month, and fourteen every day during the Feast of Tabernacles (Lev 1:3, 10; Nu 28–29).

The "burnt offering" (lit., "holocaust") differed from the "welfare" or "fellowship" sacrifice (v.3) in that the sacrifice was wholly consumed on the altar. In the welfare sacrifice only the suet or fat was burned (Lev 3), with the meat divided between priest and sacrificer (Lev 7:11–36; see R. de Vaux, *Ancient Israel*, 417ff., 426ff.).

"Wheat" was offered as fine flour, either alone (Lev 5:11–13) or mixed as dough (Lev 2:1–3) or as cakes (Lev 2:4). "Salt" was offered with all oblations (Lev 2:13; Mk 9:49). "Wine" was poured out as a libation (Ex 29:40–41; Lev 23:13, 18, 37). "Oil" was used in the meal offerings.

Antiochus the Great gave the Jews money to complete the temple and large gifts of wine, oil, incense, wheat, and salt for sacrifices (Josephus, *Ant.* 12.140 [3.31]). Concerning "without fail," A. T. Olmstead ("A Persian Letter in Thucydides," *AJSL* 49 [1933]: 161) cites the parallel of a letter from Xerxes to the Spartan Pausanias (*Thucydides* 1.129.3): "And let neither night nor day hinder you from taking care to accomplish anything of what you have promised me, neither for expense of gold and silver let them be hindered."

That the Persian monarchs were interested in foreign cults is shown clearly by the ordinances of Cambyses and Darius I regulating the temples and priests in Egypt. On the authority of Darius II (423–404 BC), a letter was written in 419 to the Jews at Elephantine (Cowley, 21) concerning the keeping of the Feast of Unleavened Bread (*ANET*, 491).

10 "Sacrifices pleasing" (Aram. *nîḥôḥîn*) is literally sacrifices of "sweet smell" (cf. Ge 8:21; Da 2:46). In pagan religions the sacrifices were viewed literally as nourishment for the gods, but not in the worship of Yahweh (Eze 44:7; see E. Yamauchi, "Anthropomorphism in Ancient Religions," *BSac* 125 [1968]: 29–44).

Darius commanded that the Jews be allowed to "pray for the well-being of the king and his sons." In the Cyrus Cylinder the king asks, "May all the gods whom I have resettled in their sacred cities ask daily Bel and Nebo for a long life for me" (*ANET*, 316). The Jews of Elephantine wrote to the Persian governor of Judah, Bagoas, that if he helped them get their temple rebuilt, "the meal-offering, incense and burnt offering will be offered in your name, and we shall pray for you at all times, we, and our wives, and our children" (Cowley, 30:26; *ANET*, 492). Herodotus (1.132) reported that among the Persians anyone who offered a sacrifice had to pray for the king.

11 Decrees and treaties customarily had appended a long list of curses against anyone who might disregard them, as in the curses of the Vassal Treaties of Esarhaddon. (See D. J. Wiseman, *The Vassal Treaties of Esarhaddon* [London: British School of Archaeology in Iraq, 1958].)

Anyone who would change Darius's decree would be "impaled" on a beam from his own house. The OT cites the hanging or fastening of criminals (Ge 40:22; 41:13; Nu 25:4; et al.). According to Deuteronomy 21:22–23, a criminal was stoned and his corpse hung on a "tree" (cf. 2Sa 21:6, 9). Esther 2:23; 5:14, and 9:14 speak of the seventy-five-foot-high gallows that Haman planned for Mordecai but on which Haman's ten sons were hung after they were slain. According to *Herodotus* (3.159), Darius I impaled three thousand Babylonians when he took Babylon—an act that Darius himself recorded in the Behistun Inscription (Kent, 127–28; see also Yamauchi, *Persia and the Bible*, 131–35, 145–48).

"A pile of rubble" (Aram. *newālû*; "dunghill," KJV, NRSV) is a word of uncertain etymology. Hensley, 56–57, following Nöldeke, suggests it may mean that the house was to be "confiscated" (cf. 1Ki 14:10; 2Ki 10:27; Job 20:7; Da 2:5; 3:29; Zep 1:17).

12 At the end of his famous Behistun Inscription, Darius warned: "If thou shalt behold this inscription or these sculptures, (and) shalt destroy them and shalt not protect them as long as unto thee there is strength, may Ahuramazda be a smiter unto thee, and may family not be unto thee, and what thou shalt do, that for thee may Ahuramazda utterly destroy!"

NOTE

10 J. Kegler ("Die Fürbitte für den persischen Oberherrn im Tempel von Jerusalem [Ezra 6,10]," in *Gott an den Rändern: Sozialgeschichtliche Perspektiven auf die Bibel* [ed. U. Bail and R. Jost; Gütersloh: Kaiser, Gütersloher, 1996], 73–82) has an interesting discussion of intercessions and sacrifices for foreigners, especially foreign rulers, including such texts as Jeremiah 29:7; 1 Maccabees 7:33; 12:11; and Baruch 1:10–13.

Such acts were expressions of loyalty to the imperial rulers that, when stopped, signaled revolt, as in AD 66 against the Romans.

6. The Completion of the Temple (6:13–15)

¹³Then, because of the decree King Darius had sent, Tattenai, governor of Trans-Euphrates, and Shethar-Bozenai and their associates carried it out with diligence. ¹⁴So the elders of the Jews continued to build and prosper under the preaching of Haggai the prophet and Zechariah, a descendant of Iddo. They finished building the temple according to the command of the God of Israel and the decrees of Cyrus, Darius and Artaxerxes, kings of Persia. ¹⁵The temple was completed on the third day of the month Adar, in the sixth year of the reign of King Darius.

COMMENTARY

13–14 Work on the temple made little progress because of opposition and the preoccupation of the returnees with their own homes (Hag 1:2–3). Because they had placed their own interests first, God sent them famine as a judgment (1:5–6, 10–11). Spurred by the preaching of Haggai and Zechariah, and under the leadership of Zerubbabel and Joshua, a new effort was begun (1:12–15).

The reference to "Artaxerxes" seems out of place, for this king did not contribute to the rebuilding of the temple. His name may have been inserted here because he contributed to the work of the temple at a later date under Ezra (7:21 26).

15 "Adar," the last Babylonian month, was February-March. The temple was finished on March 12, 515 BC, a little over seventy years after its destruction. As the renewed work on the temple had begun on September 21, 520 BC (Hag 1:4–15), sustained effort had continued for over four years.

According to Haggai 2:3 the older members, who could remember the splendor of Solomon's temple, were disappointed when they saw the smaller size of Zerubbabel's temple (cf. 3:12).

Nonetheless this rebuilt temple, though not as grand as the first, lasted much longer. H. T. Frank (*Bible, Archaeology, and Faith* [Nashville: Abingdon, 1971], 220) observes, "it was large and so well built as to serve as a fairly successful fortress on several occasions over the next five hundred years. The longevity of this Temple and the fact that the Maccabees undertook only strengthening of its defenses and no thoroughgoing rebuilding bespeak of adequacy and also of accumulated splendor."

The general plan of the Second Temple resembled the first. The *hêkāl* ("Holy Place") was furnished with a table for the showbread, the incense altar, and one menorah instead of Solomon's ten (see Mazar, 104ff.). But the *d^ebîr* ("the Most Holy Place") was left empty, since the ark of the covenant had been lost through the Babylonian conquest. According to the Mishnah (*Yoma* 5.2), "after the Ark was taken away a stone remained there from the time of the early Prophets, and it was called 'Shetiyah.'"

According to the legendary *Kebra Negast* of the Ethiopian Orthodox Church, the son of Solomon by the Queen of Sheba, Menelik, stole the ark of the covenant. The Ethiopians claim that it is now preserved in a cathedral in Aksum (see Yamauchi, *Africa and the Bible*, 100–105, 178).

7. The Dedication of the Temple (6:16–18)

¹⁶Then the people of Israel — the priests, the Levites and the rest of the exiles — celebrated the dedication of the house of God with joy. ¹⁷For the dedication of this house of God they offered a hundred bulls, two hundred rams, four hundred male lambs and, as a sin offering for all Israel, twelve male goats, one for each of the tribes of Israel. ¹⁸And they installed the priests in their divisions and the Levites in their groups for the service of God at Jerusalem, according to what is written in the Book of Moses.

COMMENTARY

16 For the dedication of Solomon's temple, see 1 Kings 8. This verse and v.19 emphasize that the leadership of the returned exiles was responsible for the completion of the temple.

"With joy" (Aram. *ḥedwâ*) occurs here; it is identical with the Hebrew form, found only in 1 Chronicles 16:27 and Nehemiah 8:10. In the former passage we read that "joy," together with "strength," is found in God's "place," that is, his sanctuary.

"Dedication" (Aram. *ḥanukkâ*) occurs here, in v.17, and in Daniel 3:2–3; for the corresponding Hebrew word, see Numbers 7:10–11, 84, 88; 2 Chronicles 7:9; Nehemiah 12:27. The Jewish holiday in December that celebrates the discovery of pure oil, its prolongation, and the rededication of the temple captured by the Jews from the Seleucids is known today as Hanukkah.

17 The number of victims sacrificed was small compared to the thousands in similar services under Solomon (1Ki 8:5, 63), Hezekiah (2Ch 30:24), and Josiah (2Ch 35:7). Nonetheless they represented a real sacrifice under the prevailing conditions.

18 This verse ends the Aramaic section that began in 4:8; another Aramaic section begins at 7:12.

As there were more priests than necessary for services in the Jerusalem temple, they were divided into courses (*mišmarot*). Twenty-one courses are mentioned in Nehemiah 10:3–9 (twenty-four in 1Ch 24:1–19). As the priests served for a week at a time, they would normally serve at Jerusalem twice a year. John the Baptist's father was a priest serving at the temple when he was struck dumb (Lk 1:5, 8).

In 1962 fragments of a synagogue inscription listing the twenty-four courses were found at Caesarea (cf. M. Avi-Yonah, "The Caesarea Inscription of the Twenty-Four Priestly Courses," *The Teacher's Yoke* [ed. E. J. Vardaman; Waco, Tex.: Baylor Univ. Press, 1964], 46–57). Numerous *mišmarot* (a word not found in the Bible but in the Dead Sea Scrolls and in rabbinic writings) have been found among the Dead Sea Scrolls, where a solar rather than a lunar calendar was observed. These include such texts as 4Q325 ("Priestly Service: Sabbath, Month, and Festival—Year One"), 4Q326 ("Priestly Service: Sabbath, Month, and Festival—Year Four"),

4Q328 ("Priestly Service As the Seasons Change"), 4Q329 ("Priestly Rotation on the Sabbath"), 4Q329a ("Priestly Service on the Passover"), etc.

(See M. Wise, M. Abegg Jr., and E. Cook, tr., *The Dead Sea Scrolls: A New Translation* [New York: HarperSanFrancisco, 1996], 317–22.)

8. The Celebration of the Passover (6:19–22)

19On the fourteenth day of the first month, the exiles celebrated the Passover. **20**The priests and Levites had purified themselves and were all ceremonially clean. The Levites slaughtered the Passover lamb for all the exiles, for their brothers the priests and for themselves. **21**So the Israelites who had returned from the exile ate it, together with all who had separated themselves from the unclean practices of their Gentile neighbors in order to seek the LORD, the God of Israel. **22**For seven days they celebrated with joy the Feast of Unleavened Bread, because the LORD had filled them with joy by changing the attitude of the king of Assyria, so that he assisted them in the work on the house of God, the God of Israel.

COMMENTARY

19 This date would have been about April 21, 515 BC. Since the destruction of the temple by Titus in AD 70, Jews have not been able to sacrifice Passover lambs but have substituted eggs and roasted meat. (See J. B. Segal, *The Hebrew Passover from Earliest Times to AD 70* [New York: Oxford Univ. Press, 1963].) Only the Samaritans continue to slaughter lambs, for their place of worship is on Mount Gerizim (cf. Jn 4:20), though their temple has also been destroyed.

20 "Ceremonially clean" (Hithpael of *ṭāhēr*; GK 3197) is used almost exclusively of ritual or moral purity; the word occurs with its derivatives 204 times in the OT. Mostly these words appear in the priestly literature: about 44 percent in Leviticus and Numbers, about 16 percent in Exodus, and about 14 percent in Chronicles and Ezekiel.

21 The returning exiles were not uncompromising separatists; they were willing to accept those who would separate themselves from the syncretism of the foreigners introduced into the area by the Assyrians. Gentiles (such as Rahab and Ruth) who themselves were willing to join (cf. Ex 12:44–48) were accepted as members of the elect community. The same openness is expressed by Nehemiah (Ne 10:28). The repeated reference to "Israel" (twelve times in Ezr 1–6) was designed to include more than just those who had been deported from Judah.

"The unclean practices" (*ṭumʾâ*; GK 3240) are literally "uncleanness, filthiness." The antonym of *ṭāhēr* is *ṭāmēʾ*("to be unclean"). It and its derivatives occur 279 times in the OT, about 64 percent in Leviticus and Numbers and 15 percent in Ezekiel. Idolatry defiled the land (Eze 36:18; cf. Ge 35:2). The Lord asked Judah, "How can you say, 'I am not defiled; I have not run after the Baals'?" (Jer 2:23). Israel had been rendered unclean by the idols she had made (Eze 22:4; 36:25).

22 The title "king of Assyria" for a Persian king is most unusual and is considered by some scholars an error. Blenkinsopp, 133, suggests that there may be a deliberate allusion to the joyous account of the Passover celebrated by Hezekiah and the remnant who had escaped from the hand of the king of Assyria (2Ch 30:6). J. Fleishman concludes:

> Therefore, one can say that the metonymic phrase "King of Assyria" in Ezra 6:22 is a coded term. It is a literary didactic ploy by which the

narrator wished to make the reader think and contemplate the history of Israel from the days of the kings of Assyria until the days of their heir, Darius I, as well as to examine the contrary policy of the rulers of the Persian Empire and even more, the Lord God of Israel who motivated these kings.

See his "On the Meaning of the Term מלך אשור 'The King of Assyria' in Ezra 6:22," *JANESCU* 26 (1998): 45; cf. idem, "An Echo of Optimism in Ezra 6:19–22," *HUCA* 69 (1998): 29.

II. EZRA'S RETURN AND REFORMS (7:1–10:44)

A. Ezra's Return to Palestine (7:1–8:36)

1. Preparations (7:1–10)

¹After these things, during the reign of Artaxerxes king of Persia, Ezra son of Seraiah, the son of Azariah, the son of Hilkiah, ²the son of Shallum, the son of Zadok, the son of Ahitub, ³the son of Amariah, the son of Azariah, the son of Meraioth, ⁴the son of Zerahiah, the son of Uzzi, the son of Bukki, ⁵the son of Abishua, the son of Phinehas, the son of Eleazar, the son of Aaron the chief priest — ⁶this Ezra came up from Babylon. He was a teacher well versed in the Law of Moses, which the LORD, the God of Israel, had given. The king had granted him everything he asked, for the hand of the LORD his God was on him. ⁷Some of the Israelites, including priests, Levites, singers, gatekeepers and temple servants, also came up to Jerusalem in the seventh year of King Artaxerxes.

⁸Ezra arrived in Jerusalem in the fifth month of the seventh year of the king. ⁹He had begun his journey from Babylon on the first day of the first month, and he arrived in Jerusalem on the first day of the fifth month, for the gracious hand of his God was on him. ¹⁰For Ezra had devoted himself to the study and observance of the Law of the LORD, and to teaching its decrees and laws in Israel.

COMMENTARY

1 "After these things" refers to the completion and dedication of the temple in 515 BC (cf. ch.

6). The identity of the Artaxerxes mentioned here has been disputed. If he was Artaxerxes I, as the traditional view maintains—a view I believe is correct—Ezra arrived in Palestine in 458 BC. If he was Artaxerxes II, Ezra arrived in 398 (see Introduction: Chronology *and* The Order). The traditional view assumes a gap of almost sixty years between the events of ch. 6 and ch. 7. The only recorded event during this interval concerns opposition in Xerxes' reign (485–465 BC; cf. 4:6).

The genealogy of Ezra given in vv. 1–5 is an extraordinary one that lists his ancestors back sixteen generations to Aaron, brother of Moses. One can compare the list of 1 Chronicles 6:3–15, where twenty-three high priests are listed from Aaron to the exile.

"Ezra" (*ᶜezrāʾ*) is a shortened form of "Azariah," a name that occurs twice in the list of his ancestors. The Greek form is "Esdras."

"Seraiah" (*śᵉrāyâ*, "Yahweh is Prince") was the high priest under Zedekiah who was killed in 587 BC by Nebuchadnezzar (2Ki 25:18–21; Jer 52:24) some 129 years before Ezra's arrival.

"Azariah" (*ᶜazaryâ*, "Yahweh has helped") is the name of about twenty-five OT individuals, including one of Daniel's companions (Da 1:6–7).

"Hilkiah" (*ḥilqîyâ*, "my portion is Yahweh") was the high priest under Josiah (2Ki 22:4).

2 On "Shallum" see the comment on 2:42.

"Zadok" (*ṣādôq*, "righteous") was a priest under David whom Solomon appointed chief priest in place of Abiathar, who supported the royal rebel Adonijah (1Ki 1:7–8; 2:35). Ezekiel regarded the Zadokites as free from idolatry (Eze 44:15–16). The Zadokites held the office of high priest till 171 BC. The Sadducees were named after Zadok, and the Qumran community looked for the restoration of the Zadokite priesthood. (See J. R. Bartlett, "Zadok and His Successors at Jerusalem," *JTS* 19 [1968]: 1–18.)

"Ahitub" (*ᵃḥîṭûb*, "my brother is good") was the grandfather of Zadok (Ne 11:11).

3 "Amariah" (*ᵃmaryâ*) means "Yahweh has spoken."

4 "Zerahiah" (*zᵉraḥyâ*) means "Yahweh has shone forth"; "Uzzi" (*ᶜuzzî*), "[Yahweh is] strength"; and "Bukki" (*buqqî*), "vessel [of Yahweh]."

5 "Abishua" (*ᵃbîšûaᶜ*, "my father is salvation") was the great grandson of Aaron (1Ch 6:4–5 [5:30–31]).

"Phinehas" (*pînᵉḥās*), from the Egyptian *pʾ-nḥsy* ("the Nubian"), was the grandson of Aaron. Moses married a Negro woman from the Sudan; she is called "Ethiopian" in the KJV and "Cushite" in the NIV and NRSV (Nu 12:1; see Yamauchi, *Africa and the Bible*, ch. 2, "Moses' Cushite Wife").

"Eleazar" (*ʾelʿāzār*) is "God has helped." The Greek transliteration is "Lazarus" (Jn 11). The latter's town of Bethany is known today by the Arabic name Al-Azariyeh.

6 "A teacher" (*sōpēr*) is literally "a scribe" (cf. Aram. *sāpar* [4:8, 17, 23; 7:12, 21]; Akkad. *šāpirum*; see comment on 4:8; see also Rainey). Scribes served kings as secretaries, such as Shaphan under Josiah (2Ki 22:3). Others took dictation, as Baruch who wrote down what Jeremiah spoke (Jer 36:32; cf. N. Avigad, "Baruch the Scribe and Jerahmeel the King's Son," *BA* 42 [1979]: 114–18). We have the seal impression of this Baruch son of Neraiah. From the exilic period the scribes were scholars who studied and taught the Scriptures. In the NT period they were addressed as "rabbis."

"Well versed" (*māhîr*) is a word that literally means "quick" or "swift." It occurs in only three other passages: Psalm 45:1, "a skillful writer"; Proverbs 22:29, "skilled in his work"; and Isaiah 16:5, "speeds the cause of righteousness." The phrase also occurs in the Aramaic Story of Ahiqar found at Elephantine (Ahiqar 1:1): *spr ḥkym w-mhry* ("a scribe wise and skilled"). A reflection of the root meaning of *māhîr* may be the apocryphal tradition in 2 Esdras 14:24: "In the meantime equip yourself with a good supply of writing tablets and engage ... these five because they can write rapidly."

"The hand of the LORD his God was on him" is a striking expression of God's favor (cf. also vv.9, 28; 8:18, 22, 31; Ne 2:8, 18).

7–9 Most scholars assume that the seventh year of Artaxerxes I should be reckoned according to the Persian custom of dating regnal years from spring to spring (Nisan to Nisan, which was also the Jewish religious calendar). Thus Ezra would have begun his journey on the first day of Nisan (April 8, 458) and arrived on the first day of Ab (August 4, 458; see Introduction: Chronology *and* The Order; cf. also J. Finegan, *Handbook of Biblical Chronology* [rev. ed.; Peabody, Mass.: Hendrickson, 1998], #336).

The journey took 119 days (including an eleven-day delay indicated by 8:31), or four months. Spring was the most auspicious time for such journeys; most ancient armies went on campaigns during this season. Though the direct distance between Baby-lon and Jerusalem is about five hundred miles, the travelers would have had to traverse nine hundred miles going northwest along the Euphrates River and then south. The relatively slow rate of fewer than ten miles per day is explicable by the presence of children and the elderly.

The full phrase "the gracious hand of his God was on him" occurs here, in 8:18, 22, and in Nehemiah 2:8, 18. Ezra 7:28 and 8:31 omit "gracious." The phrase denotes God's permanent help and grace that rest on a person or a congregation

10 "Ezra had devoted himself" (lit., "Ezra set his heart"). He is described as a scribe who was learned in the law of Moses (v.6), as a "teacher of the Law of the God of heaven" (v.12). He not only studied the Scriptures but also taught and interpreted them (Ne 8). Bible study was not merely an intellectual discipline but also a personal study for his own life and for the instruction of his congregation.

NOTES

6 See C. Schams, *Jewish Scribes in the Second-Temple Period* (Sheffield: JSOT, 1998), 46–60.

9 The average rate of travel in antiquity was about fifteen to twenty miles per day. See E. Yamauchi, "On the Road with Paul: The Ease and Dangers of Travel in the Ancient World," *Christian History* 14/3 (1995): 16–19.

2. The Authorization by Artaxerxes (7:11–26)

[11]This is a copy of the letter King Artaxerxes had given to Ezra the priest and teacher, a man learned in matters concerning the commands and decrees of the LORD for Israel:
[12]Artaxerxes, king of kings,

To Ezra the priest, a teacher of the Law of the God of heaven:

Greetings.

[13]Now I decree that any of the Israelites in my kingdom, including priests and Levites, who wish to go to Jerusalem with you, may go. [14]You are sent by the king and his

seven advisers to inquire about Judah and Jerusalem with regard to the Law of your God, which is in your hand. [15]Moreover, you are to take with you the silver and gold that the king and his advisers have freely given to the God of Israel, whose dwelling is in Jerusalem, [16]together with all the silver and gold you may obtain from the province of Babylon, as well as the freewill offerings of the people and priests for the temple of their God in Jerusalem. [17]With this money be sure to buy bulls, rams and male lambs, together with their grain offerings and drink offerings, and sacrifice them on the altar of the temple of your God in Jerusalem.

[18]You and your brother Jews may then do whatever seems best with the rest of the silver and gold, in accordance with the will of your God. [19]Deliver to the God of Jerusalem all the articles entrusted to you for worship in the temple of your God. [20]And anything else needed for the temple of your God that you may have occasion to supply, you may provide from the royal treasury.

[21]Now I, King Artaxerxes, order all the treasurers of Trans-Euphrates to provide with diligence whatever Ezra the priest, a teacher of the Law of the God of heaven, may ask of you — [22]up to a hundred talents of silver, a hundred cors of wheat, a hundred baths of wine, a hundred baths of olive oil, and salt without limit. [23]Whatever the God of heaven has prescribed, let it be done with diligence for the temple of the God of heaven. Why should there be wrath against the realm of the king and of his sons? [24]You are also to know that you have no authority to impose taxes, tribute or duty on any of the priests, Levites, singers, gatekeepers, temple servants or other workers at this house of God.

[25]And you, Ezra, in accordance with the wisdom of your God, which you possess, appoint magistrates and judges to administer justice to all the people of Trans-Euphrates — all who know the laws of your God. And you are to teach any who do not know them. [26]Whoever does not obey the law of your God and the law of the king must surely be punished by death, banishment, confiscation of property, or imprisonment.

COMMENTARY

11 Many conservative Christians regard the Letter of Artaxerxes I permitting Ezra's return in 458 (or 457) BC as the *terminus a quo*, the beginning point, of Daniel's first 69 weeks (Da 9:24−27). If each week represented a solar year, then 69 times 7 years equals 483 years, added to 457 BC equals AD 26 — that is, the traditional date for the beginning of Christ's ministry. Others, however, regard the commission of the same king to Nehemiah in 445 BC as the starting point (Ne 1:1, 11; 2:1−8). From this date by computing according to a lunar year of 360 days, the same date of AD 26 is reached. H. W. Hoehner ("Chronological Aspects in the Life of Christ VI: Daniel's Seventy Weeks and New Testament Chronology," *BSac* 132 [1975]; 47−65), however, believes that the prophecy can be calculated to arrive at AD 29, when he believes Jesus' ministry began. (See also P. Maier, "The Date of the Nativity and the Chronology of Jesus' Life," in *Chronos, Kairos, Christos* [ed. J. Vardaman and E. M. Yamauchi; Winona Lake, Ind.: Eisenbrauns, 1989], 120–21.)

12 The text of the decree in vv.12–26 is in Aramaic (see Introduction: Text). This Aramaic document recording the commission given to Ezra by Artaxerxes I bears every indication that it reflects an official document. (See K. Koch, "Der Artaxerxes-Erlass im Esrabuch," in *Meilenstein: Festgabe für Herbert Donner* [ed. M. Weippert and S. Timm; Wiesbaden: Harrassowitz, 1995], 87–98.) Against the criticisms of D. Janzen ("The Mission of Ezra and the Persian Temple Community," *JBL* 119 [2000]: 619–43) that the letter authorizing Ezra's mission (7:12–26) is not authentic, R. C. Steiner ("The *mbqr* at Qumran, the *episkopos* in the Athenian Empire, and the Meaning of *lbqr⁾* in Ezra 7:14: On the Relation of Ezra's Mission to the Persian Legal Project," *JBL* 120 [2001]: 630) concludes, "In short, the legal component of Ezra's mission and even the term for it fit squarely into the fifth century BCE."

The phrase "king of kings" (Aram. *melek malkayyā⁾*) originally occurred in Akkadian as *šar šarrāni* (cf. *bēl šarrāni*), used by Assyrian kings from the time of Tukulti-Ninurta I as their empires incorporated many kingdoms. It was then adopted by Neo-Babylonian kings such as Nebuchadnezzar (Eze 26:7; Da 2:37, 47). The Achaemenid kings from Darius I on used the Old Persian phrase *xšāyathiya xšāyathiyānām*; the deposed king of Iran was known in modern Persian as *Shahinshah* ("king of kings"). The rabbis applied to God the title "King of the king of kings."

"The Law" (Aram. *dātā⁾*) is derived from the Persian *dāta*. R. N. Frye ("The Institutions," *Beiträge zur Achämenidengeschichte* [ed. G. Walser; Wiesbaden: Franz Steiner, 1972], 92) places the decree in its broader historical context as follows:

Darius was actively concerned not only with his own "imperial" laws, to be promulgated throughout the empire, but also with the local laws and traditional practices in various provinces.... Darius wrote to his satrap in Egypt Aryandes to collect the wise men of the realm to make a new code of laws. Although the work was not finished before his death, the successors of Darius continued to be interested in the codification of the laws of their subject peoples. It is in this light that one must understand the efforts of Ezra (7, 11) and Nehemiah (8, 1) to codify the Mosaic law, which was not accomplished till the reign of Artaxerxes I.

"Greetings" (Aram. *gᵉmîr*) means "perfect" as an adjective and "completely" as an adverb. According to Slotki's comment on this, this expression would correspond to the rabbinic term *wegomer* ("etc."), referring to the other titles of respect attached to Ezra's name. Others see it as an adjective ("perfect") with an omitted word ("scribe") understood, or with the word *šᵉlām* ("greetings," i.e., "hearty [greetings]"; cf. NIV).

13 Note the use of the term "Israelites" rather than "Judeans." Ezra's aim was to make a united Israel of those who returned. W. J. Dumbrell ("Malachi and the Ezra-Nehemiah Reforms," *RTR* 35 [1976]: 45) observes:

The Ezra narratives in both books [i.e., Ezra and Nehemiah] use the term Israel some twenty-four times. It is the key term of the edict of Artaxerxes with which Ezra is armed (cf. Ezr 7:13). Likewise emphasized is the term "God of Israel" throughout the Ezra material. On the other hand Judah as a term occurs only four times in the Ezra material, and then only as a geographical term (Ezr 7:14, 9:9, 10:7, 9). Though necessarily in the more administratively geared book of Nehemiah the term Judah appears frequently, where a theological point has to be made it is the term Israel which is used (cf. in Nehemiah's prayer in 1:6 and again in 13:3).

14 "Seven advisers" corresponds with the Persian tradition (*Herodotus* 1.31; 3.84; 7.8; 8.67; Xenophon, *Anabasis* 1.6.4–5; cf. Est 1:14 on the seven princes "who had special access to the king").

15–16 Critics ask whether the Persian king would be so generous. The Persian treasury had ample funds, and such benevolence was a well-attested policy. First Esdras 8:13 adds, "all the gold and silver belonging to the Lord of Israel which can be found in the province of Babylon." Though this phrase would hardly be in the king's letter, it expresses the truth found in Haggai 2:8: "'The silver is mine and the gold is mine,' declares the LORD Almighty."

There are close parallels to the directive of vv.15–16 in the Elephantine letters, that is, in the so-called Passover Papyrus, in which Darius II ordered the Jews to keep the Feast of Unleavened Bread (Cowley, 21; *ANET*, 491), and also in the temple reconstruction authorization: "Let meal-offering, incense and burnt-offering be offered upon the altar of the God Yahu in your name" (Cowley, 31; *ANET*, 492).

The custom of sending gifts to Jerusalem from the Jews in the Diaspora was to continue down through the Roman Empire (Josephus, *Ant.* 18.312–13 [9.1]) until the Jewish-Roman War, when the Romans diverted these contributions to the temple of Jupiter.

18–19 See the comments on 5:17 and 6:1.

20–21 There are over three hundred travel texts from Persepolis. According to R. T. Hallock (*Persepolis Fortification Tablets* [Chicago: University of Chicago, 1969], 6): "The travel-ration texts report the daily operations of a highly developed system of travel, transport, and communication.... The travel-ration texts also, by their very existence, imply an elaborate system for the transference of credits." A later set of treasury texts, dating from the thirtieth year of Darius I to the seventh year of Artaxerxes I

(492–458 BC), records the disbursement of silver in lieu of part of the rations. (See G. G. Cameron, *The Persepolis Treasury Tablets* [Chicago: Univ. of Chicago Press, 1948].)

Williamson ("Ezra and Nehemiah," 52) draws out the significance of the latter set for our passage in Ezra: "And this, then, leads straight back ... to the text of Ezra 7:15–20, where Ezra is given cash to enable him to buy both animals and other materials for the sacrificial cult. The different manner in which these grants were paid to the Jews by Darius and Artaxerxes is thus neatly explained by factors which we could only have learned about from the two collections of Elamite texts from Persepolis which come in between." He further comments (59):

> Ezra's letters are addressed "to all the treasurers of Beyond the River" (Ezr 7:21). In the light of the administrative structures probably to be deduced from the Aramaic texts considered above, we may say that these are likely, strictly speaking, to have been "sub-treasurers" (*ʾpgnzbrʾ*), who were actually responsible for making the payments, and who operated under the authority of the treasurer of the satrapy.

Some critics question how literally the Persian king's promise should be taken, as Haggai 1:8–11 indicates that work on the temple was delayed because of a lack of contributions from the Jewish community. Perhaps the provincial officials did not cooperate in carrying out the royal commands. Commenting on Cyrus's earlier decree, R. North ("Civil Authority in Ezra," in *Studi in onore di Edoardo Volterra* [Milan: A Giuffre, 1971], 388) suggests: "Cyrus merely said the Jews could draw on tax-funds paid in by the Syrian population ... ultimately their disbursement would depend much on the good will of local Samaritan treasurers."

22 A "talent" (*kikkār*, "circle") in the Babylonian sexagesimal system was sixty minas, with a mina being sixty shekels. A talent weighed about seventy-five pounds. One hundred talents was an enormous sum—about three-quarters of a ton of silver. This amount, together with a talent of gold, was the tribute that Pharaoh Neco imposed on Judah (2Ki 23:33).

A "cor" was a donkeyload, about six and one-half bushels. The total amount of wheat, six hundred fifty bushels, was relatively small. The grain would be used in meal offerings. A "bath" was a liquid measure of about six gallons; therefore the amount of oil was six hundred gallons. "Salt without limit" is literally "salt without prescribing (how much)" (see comments on 4:14; 6:9). A close parallel is the benefaction of Antiochus III as recorded by Josephus (*Ant.* 12.140 [3.3]):

> In the first place we have decided, on account of their piety, to furnish them for their sacrifices an allowance of sacrificial animals, wine, oil and frankincense to the value of twenty-thousand pieces of silver, and sacred *artabae* of fine flour in accordance with their native law, and one thousand-four hundred and sixty *medimni* of wheat and three hundred and seventy-five *medimni* of salt.

23 The urgency of the Persian king's command—"with diligence"—is reflected in a letter from Xerxes to Pausanias, the Spartan commander (*Thucydides* 1.129.3): "And let neither night nor day hinder you from taking care to accomplish anything of what you have promised me, neither for expense of gold and silver let them be hindered ... *boldly* execute both my affairs and yours, whatever is finest and best for both" (emphasis mine).

"Wrath against the realm of the king" speaks of Egypt's revolt against the Persians in 460 BC and Egypt's temporary expulsion of the Persians in 459 with the aid of the Athenians. In 458, when Ezra returned to Palestine, the Persians were involved in suppressing the revolt (see Introduction: Reign of Artaxerxes I). We do not know how many "sons"

the king had at this time, but he ultimately had eighteen, according to Ctesias (*Persika* 44).

24 Priests and other temple personnel were often given exemptions from enforced labor or taxes. An important letter of Darius to Gadates, the Persian governor in Ionia (western Turkey), rebuked him for disregarding his orders concerning the "gardeners of the sacred sanctuary of Apollo at Aulai" (see Briant, 492–93). After praising him for transplanting fruit trees, the king warned his governor: "But because my religious dispositions are being nullified by you, I shall give you, unless you make a change, a proof of a wronged (King's) anger. For the gardeners sacred to Apollo have been made to pay tribute to you; and land which is profane they have dug up at your command" (C. W. Fornara, ed., *Archaic Times to the End of the Peloponnesian War* [Baltimore: Johns Hopkins Univ. Press, 1977], 37).

Antiochus III granted exemptions to the Jews: "the priests, the scribes of the temple and the temple-singers shall be relieved from the poll-tax and the crown-tax and the salt-tax which they pay" (Josephus, *Ant.* 12. 142–43 [3.3]). Some seven centuries after Ezra (i.e., in the third century AD), Jewish rabbis cited this verse to claim exemption from Parthian taxes: "You have transgressed against the writings, as it is written, *It shall not be lawful to impose upon them* [priests and Levites] *minda, belo, and halakh*, and Rav Judah explained *Minda* means the portion of the king, *belo* is the poll-tax, and *halakh* is the *annona* [corvee, or forced labor]" (J. Neusner, *There We Sat Down* [Nashville: Abingdon, 1972], 64).

25 "Magistrates" (Aram. *šāpṭîn*, a loanword from the Heb. *šōpᵉṭîm*) is the literal name of the book of Judges. Royal judges under the Persians had tenure for life but were subject to capital punishment for misconduct in office (*Herodotus* 3.31; 5.25; 7.194). On the administering of justice, 1QapGen 20:13 reads, "For you are Lord and Master over all, and have power to mete out justice to all the kings of the earth."

26 "The law of the king" may be compared with the Akkadian phrase *data ša šarri*. G. Cameron ("Ancient Persia," in Robert C. Dentan, ed., *The Idea of History in the Ancient Near East* [New Haven, Conn.: Yale Univ. Press, 1955], 77–97) observes: "As early as his second regnal year, Darius' collection of existing laws was in use among the Babylonians, where, for the unusual guarantee by the seller, there is substituted the phrase: 'According to the king's law they shall make good.'"

The extensive powers given to Ezra—"must surely be punished by death"—are striking and extend to secular realms. Hensley, 225, cites a parallel from early Buddhist history: "Asoka's Rock Edict V grants basically the same authority to officials throughout his kingdom, also to regulate religious affairs." Some suggest that the implementation of these provisions may have involved Ezra in much traveling, which would explain the

silence about Ezra's activities between 458 and 445. Though some have questioned the wide authority given to Ezra, extrabiblical parallels show that it was Persian policy to encourage both moral and religious authority that would enhance public order.

An outstanding parallel to the king's commissioning of Ezra is found in a similar commission of Darius I, who sent Udjahorresenet, a priest and scholar, back to Egypt. He ordered the codification of the Egyptian laws in Demotic and Aramaic by the chief men of Egypt—a task that took from 518–503. On the reverse side of the Demotic Chronicle we are told, "Darius decrees that the wise men among the soldiers, the priests, and scribes, assemble and write down all Egyptian laws having been in force until the year 44 of Amasis (526 BC)." (See N. J. Reich, "The Codification of the Egyptian Laws by Darius and the Origin of the 'Demotic Chronicle'," *Mizraim* 1 [1933]: 180.)

NOTES

14 שְׁלִיחַ (*šelîaḥ*, "sent") is a passive participle that designates an ambassador or emissary; cf. the Greek ἀπόστολος (*apostolos*, "apostle"), which is derived similarly from the word "to send."

23 אַדְרַזְדָּא (*ʾadrazdāʾ*, "with diligence"), a hapax legomonon (i.e., occurs only here), derives from the Persian *drazdā* ("diligently").

24 זַמָּרַיָּא (*zammārayyāʾ*, "singers") is a hapax legomenon, the corresponding Hebrew word being *mešōrerîm*.

25–26 M. Heltzer ("The Right of Ezra to Demand Obedience to 'The Laws of the King' from Gentiles of the V Satrapy [Ez 7:25–26]," *ZABR* 4 [1998]: 192–96) argues from a Greek text from Ephesus, which dates either to the late Persian or early Hellenistic era, that Ezra had the right to demand obedience to the "laws of the King" from Jews and Gentiles in the entire satrapy, and that he had the power to try Gentiles for any crimes against the Jewish cult.

26 On this verse, see Yamauchi, *Persia and the Bible*, 105–9, and J. Blenkinsopp, "The Mission of Udjahorresnet and Those of Ezra and Nehemiah," *JBL* 106 (1987): 409–21.

3. Ezra's Doxology (7:27–28)

²⁷Praise be to the LORD, the God of our fathers, who has put it into the king's heart to bring honor to the house of the LORD in Jerusalem in this way ²⁸and who has extended his good favor to me before the king and his advisers and all the king's powerful officials. Because the hand of the LORD my God was on me, I took courage and gathered leading men from Israel to go up with me.

COMMENTARY

27–28 Here is the first occurrence of the first person for Ezra, a trait characterizing the "Ezra Memoirs" that continue to the end of ch. 9 (see Introduction: Literary Form; Authorship).

The Hebrew resumes in v.27. "Praise" (*bārûk*, lit., "blessed"; cf. the name "Baruch") opens the prayers the Jews recite today: "Blessed are Thou, O LORD, our God." Paul expressed his belief in Christ's deity by applying the corresponding Greek word (*eulogētos*) to him in 2 Corinthians 11:31 (cf. H. J. Schoeps, *Paul* [Philadelphia: Westminster, 1961], 152). Ezra recognized fully that the ultimate source of the favor granted by the king was the sovereign grace of God (cf. 6:22).

"To bring honor" (*pā'ēr*, the Piel infinitive of a relatively rare root, used fourteen times in the OT) can mean "to glorify." Man can beautify, but only God can endow with true glory (cf. Isa 60:7b, "I will glorify my glorious house" [NRSV]).

Later passages show that Ezra was primarily a priest and scholar rather than an administrator. Yet the assurance that God had called him and had opened the doors gave Ezra the courage and strength to undertake this great task.

4. Heads of Families Who Returned with Ezra (8:1–14)

¹These are the family heads and those registered with them who came up with me from Babylon during the reign of King Artaxerxes:
²of the descendants of Phinehas, Gershom;
of the descendants of Ithamar, Daniel;
of the descendants of David, Hattush ³of the descendants of Shecaniah;
of the descendants of Parosh, Zechariah, and with him were registered 150 men;
⁴of the descendants of Pahath-Moab, Eliehoenai son of Zerahiah, and with him 200 men;
⁵of the descendants of Zattu, Shecaniah son of Jahaziel, and with him 300 men;
⁶of the descendants of Adin, Ebed son of Jonathan, and with him 50 men;
⁷of the descendants of Elam, Jeshaiah son of Athaliah, and with him 70 men;
⁸of the descendants of Shephatiah, Zebadiah son of Michael, and with him 80 men;

⁹of the descendants of Joab, Obadiah son of Jehiel, and with him 218 men;
¹⁰ of the descendants of Bani, Shelomith son of Josiphiah, and with him 160 men;
¹¹of the descendants of Bebai, Zechariah son of Bebai, and with him 28 men;
¹²of the descendants of Azgad, Johanan son of Hakkatan, and with him 110 men;
¹³of the descendants of Adonikam, the last ones, whose names were Eliphelet, Jeuel and Shemaiah, and with them 60 men;
¹⁴of the descendants of Bigvai, Uthai and Zaccur, and with them 70 men.

COMMENTARY

1 Verses 1–14 list those people who accompanied Ezra from Mesopotamia, including the descendants of fifteen individuals. The figures of the men listed total 1,496 in addition to the individuals named. There were also a considerable number of women and children (v.21). An additional group of about forty Levites (vv.18–19) and of 220 "temple servants" (v.20) is also listed.

2 On "Phinehas" see the comment on 7:5. "Gershom" ("sojourner") was also the name of the elder son of Moses and Zipporah (Ex 2:22). "Ithamar" ("isle of palms") was also the name of the fourth son of Aaron (Ex 6:23). For "Hattush," compare the Akkadian *ḥa-an-ṭu-šu* in the Murashu texts (Coogan, 125).

3 "Shecaniah" means "Yahweh has taken up his abode." On "Parosh," see comment on 2:3.

"Zechariah" ("Yahweh has remembered") was the name of about thirty individuals in the Bible, including the prophet and the father of John the Baptist (Lk 1:5–67).

4 On "Pahath-Moab," see comment on 2:6. "Eliehoenai" ("to Yahweh are my eyes") is found only here and in 1 Chronicles 26:3 (cf. Ps 25:15).

5 The Hebrew lacks "Zattu" (cf. 2:8), but the name is preserved by the LXX and 1 Esdras. "Jahaziel" means "May God see!"

6 On "Adin," see comment on 2:15. "Ebed" (lit., "slave") is probably a shortened form of "Obadiah"

("slave of Yahweh"). It is found only here and in Judges 9:26 (see E. Yamauchi, "The Slaves of God," *BETS* 9 [1966]: 31–49). "Jonathan" ("Yahweh has given") is the name of sixteen individuals in the OT.

7 On "Elam," see 2:7. "Jeshaiah" means "Yahweh has saved." "Athaliah" ("Yahweh is exalted") was also the name of a famous queen, daughter of Ahab and Jezebel (2Ki 11).

8 On "Shephatiah," see 2:4. "Zebadiah" means "Yahweh has given." "Michael" ("Who is like God?") is the name of ten OT individuals, including the archangel.

9 "Joab" means "Yahweh is father." "Jehiel" means "May God live!"

10 The Hebrew omits Bani (see 2:10), but the name is retained by the LXX and 1 Esdras. "Josiphiah" ("May Yahweh add!") appears only here, but it is a name closely related to Joseph. "Shelomith" means "complete" or "reward." Though feminine in form, it is usually a man's name, as here. The Greek form is "Salome."

11 On "Bebai," see 2:11; on "Zechariah," see comment on v.3 above.

12 On "Azgad," see 2:12. "Johanan" ("Yahweh has been gracious") is the name of thirteen OT individuals. "Hakkatan" ("the little one") appears only here.

13 "The last ones" can mean that these three leaders were the last in the list, that is, the latest to arrive (cf. NEB). Blenkinsopp, 162–63, however, believes it most probable that "we are being told that with these three the entire family group had made *aliyah* ['the return'], leaving none behind in Babylon."

"Eliphelet" means "my God is escape." "Jeuel" is "Yahweh has stored up." "Shemaiah" ("Yahweh has heard") is the name of twenty-eight individuals in the Bible.

14 On "Bigvai," see 2:2. "Uthai" is perhaps hypocoristic for "(Yahu) has shown himself supreme." "Zaccur" ("remembered") is based on an emendation of the Hebrew Zabbud.

5. The Search for Levites (8:15–20)

¹⁵I assembled them at the canal that flows toward Ahava, and we camped there three days. When I checked among the people and the priests, I found no Levites there. ¹⁶So I summoned Eliezer, Ariel, Shemaiah, Elnathan, Jarib, Elnathan, Nathan, Zechariah and Meshullam, who were leaders, and Joiarib and Elnathan, who were men of learning, ¹⁷and I sent them to Iddo, the leader in Casiphia. I told them what to say to Iddo and his kinsmen, the temple servants in Casiphia, so that they might bring attendants to us for the house of our God. ¹⁸Because the gracious hand of our God was on us, they brought us Sherebiah, a capable man, from the descendants of Mahli son of Levi, the son of Israel, and Sherebiah's sons and brothers, 18 men; ¹⁹and Hashabiah, together with Jeshaiah from the descendants of Merari, and his brothers and nephews, 20 men. ²⁰They also brought 220 of the temple servants—a body that David and the officials had established to assist the Levites. All were registered by name.

COMMENTARY

15 "The canal that flows toward Ahava" probably flowed into either the Euphrates or the Tigris (cf. in Eze 1:1 the "River" Kebar, which was also a canal). Bowman, 552, suggests the modern *Meᶜn*, classical Maschana or Scenae, on the eastern bank of the Tigris River, which was near the beginning of two caravan routes. "Three days" would be from the ninth to the twelfth of Nisan, as the actual journey began on the twelfth (cf. v.31).

Brockington, 99, suggests "that Levites were perhaps not very numerous in Babylon because at the time of the deportations they were not in Jerusalem but remained scattered about the land near the shrines which had been closed during Josiah's reform." As for any Levites who were in Babylon, having been entrusted with many menial tasks, they may have found a more comfortable way of life in exile. Only about thirty-eight Levites from two families were willing to join Ezra's caravan. The service of God requires dedication and sometimes moving from a comfortable situation (Ezr 8:18–19).

A rabbinic midrash on Psalm 137 relates the legend that there were Levites in the caravan but that they were not qualified to officiate because when Nebuchadnezzar had ordered them to sing for him the songs of Zion, "they refused and bit off the ends of their fingers, so that they could not play on the harps."

16 "Eliezer" means "my God is help." "Ariel" ("Lion of God") appears only here as a personal name (cf. 2Sa 23:20; 1Ch 11:22). Elsewhere it is a cryptic name for Jerusalem (Isa 29:1–2, 7).

The Hebrew lists two chiefs and a third man of learning with the name "Elnathan." First Esdras 8:43 lists only two men by this name. It appears on the Lachish Ostracon III, in the Murashu texts as *ʾēlnatan* (Coogan, 13), and on a postexilic bulla as *ʾlntn* (Avigad, 6, fig. 5).

"Jarib" is a shortened form of "Joiarib" ("May Yahweh contend!"). "Nathan" is shortened from "Elnathan." "Meshullam" ("rewarded") is the name of nineteen OT individuals. Here he may be the same person who opposed the marriage reforms (10:15).

"Men of learning" is literally "those who cause to understand" (cf. 1Ch 25:8; 2Ch 35:3; Ne 8:7–9).

17 "Iddo" ("strength") is a shortened form of *ʾAdôn.*

The name "Casiphia" may be related to the word for "silver" (Aram. *kaspāʾ*); the person designated here may have been named after a guild of silversmiths. The NIV has not translated the phrase *hammāqôm* ("the place"), which occurs twice after Casiphia. As this phrase has been used for the temple (Dt 12:5; 1Ki 8:29), some have wondered whether the Babylonian exiles had a sanctuary, similar to that attested for the Jewish community in Elephantine, Egypt. Ackroyd (in loc.) speculates, "Since the word for 'place' is often used in the sense of 'holy place' it is natural to see here a reference to a sanctuary at this particular town."

18 "Sherebiah" possibly means "Yahweh has sent scorching heat" (cf. *Yišribyaw* [Coogan, 28, 85]). "A capable man" is literally "a man of insight." "Mahli" means "shrewd."

19 "Hashabiah" ("Yahweh has taken account") is the name of eleven OT individuals, primarily Levites. On "Jeshaiah," see v.7. "Merari" means "bitterness."

20 On "temple servants," see comment on 2:43. Humanly speaking, the dedication of this group is remarkable. Socially they were a caste of mixed origins and were inferior to the Levites in status. But God's Spirit had motivated them to respond in larger numbers than the Levites.

NOTE

15 See J. Schaper, *Priester und Leviten im achämenidischen Juda* (FAT 31; Tübingen: Mohr Siebeck, 2000).

6. Prayer and Fasting (8:21–23)

²¹There, by the Ahava Canal, I proclaimed a fast, so that we might humble ourselves before our God and ask him for a safe journey for us and our children, with all our possessions. ²²I was ashamed to ask the king for soldiers and horsemen to protect us from enemies on the road, because we had told the king, "The gracious hand of our God is on everyone who looks to him, but his great anger is against all who forsake him." ²³So we fasted and petitioned our God about this, and he answered our prayer.

COMMENTARY

21 For the association of fasting and humbling oneself, see Psalm 35:13.

"A safe journey" (*derek yᵉšārâ*) is literally "a straight way" unimpeded by obstacles and dangers (cf. v.31). First Esdras 8:50 has *euodian* ("favorable journey"). The Jews before travel offer a prayer called *tephillath hadderech* ("prayer of the road"). Bowman, 638, reports that this verse was the text of John Robinson's last sermon at Leiden before the Pilgrims sailed in 1620.

"Children" (*ṭap*, as in Dt 1:39) designates those younger than twenty, with a stress on the younger ages. Such "little ones" are most vulnerable in times of war (cf. Dt 20:14; Jdg 21:10; Eze 9:6). The vast treasures the returnees were carrying—"our possessions"—offered tempting bait for robbers.

22 Scripture speaks often of unholy shame (Jer 48:13; Mic 3:7) and sometimes of a sense of holy shame. Ezra was quick to blush with such a sense of holy shame (cf. 9:6). Ezra had gone out on a limb by proclaiming his faith in God's ability to protect the caravan. Having done so, he was embarrassed to ask for human protection.

Grave dangers faced travelers between Mesopotamia and Palestine. Clines, 111, comments: "To lead a company of 5,000, including women and children, in a four-month trek through uninhabited regions was a hazardous business ... especially when the company was carrying vast quantities of money and precious objects."

Some thirteen years later Nehemiah was accompanied by an armed escort. The difference, however, does not mean that Nehemiah was a man of lesser faith (cf. Ne 2:9).

23 Fasting implies an earnestness that makes one oblivious to food (for the association of fasting and prayer, see Ne 1:4; Da 9:3; Mt 17:21 [NIV note]; Ac 14:23).

7. The Assignment of the Precious Objects (8:24–30)

²⁴Then I set apart twelve of the leading priests, together with Sherebiah, Hashabiah and ten of their brothers, ²⁵and I weighed out to them the offering of silver and gold and the articles that the king, his advisers, his officials and all Israel present there had donated for the house of our God. ²⁶I weighed out to them 650 talents of silver, silver articles weighing 100 talents, 100 talents of gold, ²⁷20 bowls of gold valued at 1,000 darics, and two fine articles of polished bronze, as precious as gold.

²⁸I said to them, "You as well as these articles are consecrated to the LORD. The silver and gold are a freewill offering to the LORD, the God of your fathers. ²⁹Guard them carefully until you weigh them out in the chambers of the house of the LORD in Jerusalem before the leading priests and the Levites and the family heads of Israel." ³⁰Then the priests and Levites received the silver and gold and sacred articles that had been weighed out to be taken to the house of our God in Jerusalem.

COMMENTARY

24 This rendering implies that Sherebiah, Hashabiah, and ten others were the twelve leading priests. But according to vv.18–19, they were the leaders of the Levites at Casiphia. The verse can be rendered, "I set apart twelve of the leading priests *besides* Sherebiah, Hashabiah, and ten of their brothers" (emphasis mine). According to v.30, both priests and Levites were entrusted with the sacred objects.

25 "Offering" (*t°rûmâ*) means literally "what is lifted" (i.e., "dedicated," or "given" for the cult; cf. Ex 25:2; 35:5; Lev 7:14; Dt 12:6). Note that the offerings came not only from the Jews but also from the king and his court.

26 For comparison, 650 talents equals close to twenty tons of silver. These are enormous sums worth millions of dollars. Many scholars think that these are exaggerated figures or that there have been scribal errors in the copying of the numbers. According to Williamson (*Ezra, Nehemiah*, 119), "It is thus probable that an originally 'reasonable' list has been transmitted inaccurately, either out of a desire to magnify the glory of the temple by exaggerating the value of

the offerings or, more probably in view of the second item and the evidence of chap. 1, by an error through misunderstanding of figures or weights."

27 "Darics" (*°darkōnîm*) appears only here and in 1 Chronicles 29:7. On its significance see comment on 2:69 (cf. Ne 7:70–72), where the word *dark°mônîm* is used. According to Myers, 67, if this is the Persian gold daric, then one thousand darics would weigh about eighteen and a half pounds; if the silver daric, about twelve and a fifth pounds. "Polished bronze" (*muṣhāb*) is found only here in the OT, possibly from a by-form of the root of gold. This kind of bronze may have been orichalc, a bright yellow alloy of copper highly prized in ancient times.

28 Both people and objects were sacred and "consecrated" (*qōdeš*) to God.

29–30 Ezra carefully weighed out the treasures and entrusted them to others. He instilled a sense of the holiness of the mission and the gravity of each individual's responsibility. Each was responsible to guard his deposit, his "talent." The data were carefully recorded and rechecked at the journey's end (v.34).

NOTES

26 In the case, however, of huge sums, ascribed also to Solomon, texts from Egypt and Mesopotamia indicate that there is evidence for such huge sums. See D. J. Wiseman, "A Late Babylonian Tribute List?" *BSOAS* 30 (1967): 499; A. R. Millard, "Does the Bible Exaggerate King Solomon's Golden Wealth?" *BAR* 15/3 (1989): 20–29, 31, 34.

8. The Journey and Arrival in Jerusalem (8:31–36)

³¹On the twelfth day of the first month we set out from the Ahava Canal to go to Jerusalem. The hand of our God was on us, and he protected us from enemies and bandits along the way. ³²So we arrived in Jerusalem, where we rested three days.

³³On the fourth day, in the house of our God, we weighed out the silver and gold and the sacred articles into the hands of Meremoth son of Uriah, the priest. Eleazar son of Phinehas was with him, and so were the Levites Jozabad son of Jeshua and Noadiah son of Binnui. ³⁴Everything was accounted for by number and weight, and the entire weight was recorded at that time.

³⁵Then the exiles who had returned from captivity sacrificed burnt offerings to the God of Israel: twelve bulls for all Israel, ninety-six rams, seventy-seven male lambs and, as a sin offering, twelve male goats. All this was a burnt offering to the LORD. ³⁶They also delivered the king's orders to the royal satraps and to the governors of Trans-Euphrates, who then gave assistance to the people and to the house of God.

COMMENTARY

31 "We set out" (*nāsaʿ*) means literally to "pull up stakes" (i.e., of tents). After an initial three-day encampment (v.15), another eight days elapsed while Levites for the caravan were gathered. The actual departure was on the twelfth day. The journey was to take four months (see comment on 7:9).

According to A. T. Olmstead (*History of Palestine and Syria* [New York: Scribner's, 1931], 585), "The Mesopotamian plains were in their full spring beauty, and Ezra must often have recalled Second Isaiah's prophecy that the desert would blossom like the crocus." The route between Babylonia and Syria is described by Strabo (16.1.26–27).

32 Nehemiah also "rested three days" after his arrival in Palestine (Ne 2:11).

33 Ezra 2:61–62//Nehemiah 7:63–64 lists Meremoth the son of Uriah of the clan of Hakkoz as one of those who was not able to prove his priestly status. In Ezra 8:33 Meremoth the son of Uriah is listed as the priest in charge of the temple treasury. In Nehemiah 3:4, 21, we also have a Meremoth the son of Uriah, who builds a double portion of the wall. The latter is not given a priestly title. Despite the similar names and patronymics

(father's name), it is possible that we have to do with two individuals, one from a priestly and one from a lay family. Though Meremoth is not a common name (three or four occurrences), Uriah is more common (six or seven occurrences).

Supporters of the reverse order, who place Ezra's coming in the reign of Artaxerxes II (in 398 BC, rather than in the reign of Artaxerxes I in 458 BC) suggest that Meremoth in his youth helped build the wall in 445 BC, and then in his old age, forty-seven years later, served as a treasurer. They also suggest that Meremoth's family must have regained its priestly status after Nehemiah's time at Ezra's coming.

In supporting the traditional order of Ezra's coming before Nehemiah, Klaus Koch, who considers the passages (Ezr 2//Ne 7; Ezr 8, but not Ne 3) to refer to the same individual, suggests the following scenario: (1) Meremoth was *the* (chief) *priest* when Ezra arrived in 458 BC and was acknowledged as such; (2) "But in the course of Ezra's inquiries Meremoth was removed and his whole division disqualified. Ezra himself acted as high priest." Ezra was therefore titled "the priest" (Ezr 10:10, 16–18;

Ne 8:9; 12:26). (See K. Koch, "Ezra and Meremoth: Remarks on the History of the High Priesthood," in *Shaʾarei Talmon* [ed. M. Fishbane and E. Tov; Winona Lake, Ind.: Eisenbrauns, 1992], 110.)

"Eleazar" ("God has helped") is *ʾeP̄adar* in the Murashu texts (Coogan, 14). On "Phinehas," see the comment on 7:5. "Jozabad" means "Yahweh has given." "Noadiah" means "Yahweh has kept his appointment." In Nehemiah 6:14 it is the name of a prophetess.

34 According to Babylonian tradition (e.g., in the Hammurabi Law Code), almost every transaction, including sales and marriages, had to be recorded in writing. Ezra may have had to send back a signed certification of the delivery of the treasures.

35 The animal sacrifices were made as a thanksgiving to God for his mercies and as a sin offering to acknowledge their unworthiness for such mercies. Compared with the offerings of the returnees under Zerubbabel (6:17), when many more exiles were involved, the offerings on this occasion, except for the identical number of male goats, were far less.

36 "Satraps" (*ʾaḥašdarpᵉnîm*) comes from the Persian *xšathrapāna* (cf. Gk. *satrapēs*; see Est 3:12; 8:9; 9:3; Da 3:2−3, 27; 6:1−4, 6−7).

B. Ezra's Reforms (9:1−10:44)

1. The Offense of Mixed Marriages (9:1−6a)

¹After these things had been done, the leaders came to me and said, "The people of Israel, including the priests and the Levites, have not kept themselves separate from the neighboring peoples with their detestable practices, like those of the Canaanites, Hittites, Perizzites, Jebusites, Ammonites, Moabites, Egyptians and Amorites. ²They have taken some of their daughters as wives for themselves and their sons, and have mingled the holy race with the peoples around them. And the leaders and officials have led the way in this unfaithfulness."

³When I heard this, I tore my tunic and cloak, pulled hair from my head and beard and sat down appalled. ⁴Then everyone who trembled at the words of the God of Israel gathered around me because of this unfaithfulness of the exiles. And I sat there appalled until the evening sacrifice.

⁵Then, at the evening sacrifice, I rose from my self-abasement, with my tunic and cloak torn, and fell on my knees with my hands spread out to the LORD my God ⁶and prayed.

COMMENTARY

1 Ezra had reached Jerusalem on the first day of the fifth month (7:9). The measures dealing with intermarriage were announced on the seventeenth day of the ninth month (cf. 10:8 with 10:9), or four and a half months after his arrival.

Those who brought Ezra's attention to this problem were probably the ordinary members of the community rather than the leaders, who themselves were guilty (v.2). When those in positions of responsibility fall, they lead many others astray. Those guilty of intermarriage were among the returnees (v.4). Humanly speaking, there may have been reasons for such intermarriages, such as a disparity between the number of returning men and available Jewish women. (See the Reflection on Intermarriage at the end of ch. 10.)

"The neighboring peoples" (ʿammê hāʾarāṣôt, lit., "peoples of the lands") included the pagan newcomers who were brought into Samaria by the Assyrians and who had infiltrated south, and Edomites and others who had encroached on former Judean territories.

The eight groups listed designate the original inhabitants of Canaan before the Hebrew conquest (Ex 3:8, 17; 13:5; 23:23, 28; Dt 7:1; 20:17; Jos 3:10; 9:1; 12:8; Jdg 3:5; 1Ki 9:20). Only the Ammonites, Moabites, and Egyptians were still extant in the postexilic period (cf. 2Ch 8:7; Ne 9:8; cf. J. C. L. Gibson, "Some Important Ethnic Terms in the Pentateuch," *JNES* 20 [1961]: 217–38; on the Canaanites, see K. N. Schoville, "Canaanites and Amorites," in Hoerth, Mattingly, and Yamauchi, 157–82).

Though many have identified the "Hittites" (ḥittî, which occurs forty-eight times in the OT) and the sons of ḥēṭ (Ge 10:15; 1Ch 1:13) with the Anatolian Hittites (see A. Kempinski, "Hittites in the Bible," *BAR* 5 [1979]: 20–45), there are serious problems with such an identification. According to H. A. Hoffner, the editor of the *Chicago Hittite Dictionary*, there is no strong textual or archaeological evidence to support it (see H. A. Hoffner, "Hittites," in Hoerth, Mattingly, and Yamauchi, 127–56). He believes that the names are homonymous but refer to different peoples.

"Perizzites" is perhaps a designation for villagers from pᵉrāzâ ("hamlet"). The "Jebusites" occupied the city of Jerusalem (Jos 15:8; 18:16, 28), which was known as the city of Jebus (Jdg 19:10; 1Ch 11:4–5) before its capture by David. As the name Araunah (2Sa 24:16) can be interpreted as Hurrian, and as the Amarna Letters (fourteenth century BC) indicate that the chief of Jerusalem was *Abdi-ḫepa*, a man with a Hurrian name, E. A. Speiser ("Hurrians and Hittites," in *The World History of the Jewish People* [ed. B. Netanyahu; New Brunswick: Rutgers Univ. Press, 1964] 1:158–61) has argued that the peoples in the conquest lists known as Jebusites, Hivites, and Hittites should be considered as branches of the Horites or Hurrians. (For a critique see R. de Vaux, "Les Ḫurrians de l'histoire et les Horites de la Bible," *RB* 74 [1967]: 481–503.)

"Ammonites," the descendants of Lot by an incestuous union with his younger daughter (Ge 19:38), occupied the area around Rabbath Ammon, modern Amman in Transjordan (see R. W. Younger, "Ammonites," in Hoerth, Mattingly, and Yamauchi, 293–316).

"Moabites," the descendants of Lot by his elder daughter (Ge 19:37), occupied the area of Moab east of the Dead Sea. Ruth was a Moabitess (Ru 1:4; see G. L. Mattingly, "Moabites," in Hoerth, Mattingly, and Yamauchi, 317–34).

According to the Pentateuch, intermarriage with Egyptians was legitimate (see J. K. Hoffmeier, "Egyptians," in Hoerth, Mattingly, and Yamauchi, 251–90).

"Amorites" derives from the Akkadian *Amurru* ("Westland," or Syria; see K. N. Schoville, "Canaanites and Amorites," in Hoerth, Mattingly, and Yamauchi, 157–82).

First Esdras 8:66 reads "Edomites" instead of "Amorites," a reading that requires only minor changes: hāʾadōmî instead of hāʾemōrî. Because of the stereotyped nature of the list, the emendation is probably incorrect.

Though the Edomites are not mentioned by name in Ezra-Nehemiah, the harsh condemnation of them in Scripture (2Ch 25:11 ["men of Seir," NIV]; Ps 137:7; Eze 25:12–14; Obadiah; Mal 1:4) suggests that the Edomites took advantage of the Babylonian conquest of Judah (see K. G. Hoglund, "Edomites," in Hoerth, Mattingly, and Yamauchi, 335–47).

2 "The holy race" is literally "the holy seed." B. A. Levine ("Some Indices of Israelite Ethnicity," *Ethnicity in Ancient Mesopotamia* [ed. W. H. Van Soldt, R. Kalvelagen, and D. Katz; Leiden: Nederlands Instituut voor het Nabije Oosten, 2005], 193) observes:

> Taking biblical traditions at face value, a prevalent epitome of the ethnic character of ancient Israel is that of Israel as the "seed" of common ancestors. Among the appellations of the Israelites are: "seed of Israel/Jacob," "seed of Abraham," and variations of the same, "seed of Ephraim" (Isa 7:15), and "seed of the household of Israel" (Jer 23:8).... We also find usage that is clearly affected by religious themes, such as "the holy seed" (Isa 6:13), and "seed whom YHWH has blessed" (Isaiah 61, cf. Isa 65:23). We even find the image of "Godly seed" (Mal 2:15).

"Leaders" derives from *śar* ("official, chief, leader"; "princes," KJV). The "officials" (*seǧanîm*, plural of *segen* from Akkad. *šaknu*; cf. Jer 51:23, 28, 57) probably served the Persian government as tax collectors.

"Have led the way" is literally "their hand had been first." The leaders led or were "first," but in the wrong direction (cf. 10:18; Ne 6:18).

"In this unfaithfulness" derives from *maʿal* ("an act of unfaithfulness" or "breach of faith"; cf. 10:6; Lev 5:15; Jos 22:16; Da 9:7). In Chronicles "it nearly always refers to an offense against the Jerusalem temple and the purity of its service (e.g., 2Ch 26:16)" (Williamson, *Israel in the Book of Chronicles*,

53). Marrying those who did not belong to Yahweh was infidelity for the people of Israel, who were considered to be the bride of Yahweh.

3 Note the use of the first person: "When I heard this, I tore my tunic and cloak." Rending one's garments commonly expressed distress or grief (cf. Ge 37:29, 34; Est 4:1; Job 1:20; Isa 36:22; Jer 41:5; Mt 26:65). It is still practiced by some Jews after bereavement.

Ezra's act of pulling out his own hair is unique in the Bible. In the apocryphal Additions to Esther 14:2, we read, "all the places of her joy she filled with her torn hair." Elsewhere the head was shaved (Job 1:20; Eze 7:18; Am 8:10). Nehemiah demonstrates how different his personality was from Ezra's: when confronted with the same problem of intermarriage, instead of pulling out his own hair, Nehemiah pulled out the hair of the offenders (Ne 13:25)!

The word "appalled" is *mešômēm* (a Polel participle from *šmm*), which means "to be appalled or stupefied, to be reduced to shuddering" (cf. Da 4:19; 8:27). Rare is the soul who is so shocked at disobedience that he is appalled. (The English word originally meant "to make pale.")

Ezra's influence was not due to his official position but to the moral outrage he demonstrated. According to N. H. Snaith ("The Date of Ezra's Arrival in Jerusalem," *ZAW* 63 [1952]: 58), "his part was not an executive part, but comparable to that of Mahatma Gandhi in modern times. He is scandalized; he prays and he fasts (Ezr 9:3–5; 10:6)."

4 Those with a proper perception of God's holiness will tremble at his word (see Heb 12:18–29, esp. v.21). Blenkinsopp, 178, calls attention to the use of the verbal noun *ḥārēd* ("who trembled") in Isaiah 66:2, 5, where it denotes a group of devout "quakers" with eschatological beliefs.

The "evening sacrifice" took place at about 3:00 p.m. (cf. Ex 12:6; Ac 3:1). The informants had probably visited Ezra in the morning, so that he must have sat in this position for many hours. The time of the evening sacrifice was also the appointed time for prayer and confession.

5–6a "Self-abasement" (*ta‘anît*) means "mortification, humiliation." It is used only here in the OT.

In later Hebrew it meant fasting, as in the *Megillat Ta‘anit* ("The Scroll of Fasting"), a rare Aramaic document from the NT period. Thus the NRSV translates, "I got up from my fasting."

NOTES

1 On the Hittites in ancient Anatolia (Turkey), see J. G. Macqueen, *The Hittites and Their Contemporaries in Asia Minor* (rev. ed.; New York: Thames & Hudson, 1986); T. Bryce, *The Kingdom of the Hittites* (Oxford: Clarendon, 1998).

2 D. Böhler ("Das Gottesvolk als Altargemeinschaft," in *Gottesstadt und Gottesgarten: Zu Geschichte und Theologie des jerusalemer Tempels* [ed. O. Keel and E. Zenger; Freiburg: Herder, 2000], 211–13) denies that the prohibition against mixed marriage was based on ethnic purity but argues that it was based on concern for cultic purity by comparing the occurrence of "seed" in Ezra 9:2 with the phrase in Nehemiah 9:2, "seed of Israel" ("Israelite descent," NIV).

2. Ezra's Confession and Prayer (9:6b–15)

OVERVIEW

Ezra's prayer may be compared with that of Nehemiah (Ne 9:5b–37) and Daniel (Da 9:4–19). The following elements are included: a general confession (v.6), sins of former times (v.7), a recital of God's mercy and goodness (vv.8–9), a further confession of Israel's sins (vv.10–12), and a final confession of guilt and the appeal (vv.13–15).

"O my God, I am too ashamed and disgraced to lift up my face to you, my God, because our sins are higher than our heads and our guilt has reached to the heavens. ⁷From the days of our forefathers until now, our guilt has been great. Because of our sins, we and our kings and our priests have been subjected to the sword and captivity, to pillage and humiliation at the hand of foreign kings, as it is today.

⁸"But now, for a brief moment, the LORD our God has been gracious in leaving us a remnant and giving us a firm place in his sanctuary, and so our God gives light to our eyes and a little relief in our bondage. ⁹Though we are slaves, our God has not deserted us in our bondage. He has shown us kindness in the sight of the kings of Persia: He has granted us new life to rebuild the house of our God and repair its ruins, and he has given us a wall of protection in Judah and Jerusalem.

¹⁰"But now, O our God, what can we say after this? For we have disregarded the commands ¹¹you gave through your servants the prophets when you said: 'The land you are entering to possess is a land polluted by the corruption of its peoples. By their detestable practices they have filled it with their impurity from one end to the other. ¹²Therefore, do not give your daughters in marriage to their sons or take their daughters for your sons. Do not seek a treaty of friendship with them at any time, that you may be strong and eat the good things of the land and leave it to your children as an everlasting inheritance.'

¹³"What has happened to us is a result of our evil deeds and our great guilt, and yet, our God, you have punished us less than our sins have deserved and have given us a remnant like this. ¹⁴Shall we again break your commands and intermarry with the peoples who commit such detestable practices? Would you not be angry enough with us to destroy us, leaving us no remnant or survivor? ¹⁵O LORD, God of Israel, you are righteous! We are left this day as a remnant. Here we are before you in our guilt, though because of it not one of us can stand in your presence."

COMMENTARY

6b For "I am too ashamed and disgraced," the Hebrew uses two closely related words. The first one (*bôš*) means "I am ashamed," as in 8:22. The second one (a passive of *kālam*) means "to be humiliated or confounded," connoting the pain that accompanies shame. (H. W. M. Van Grol's "Schuld und Scham: Die Verwurzelung von Esra 9,6–7 in der Tradition" [*EstBib* 55 (1997): 29–52] is a thorough study of these two words.) The latter has a more active "ring" in that it means "to be dishonored, be put to shame"; the former has a more passive connotation. Ezra felt both an inner shame before God and an outward humiliation before others for the sins of his people.

These two verbs often occur together, as in Jeremiah 3:25, "Let us lie down in our shame, and let our disgrace cover us," and Jeremiah 31:19, "After I strayed, I repented; after I came to understand, I beat my breast. I was ashamed and humiliated because I bore the disgrace of my youth." Van Grol believes

that Ezra's words reflect Ezekiel 36:32: "I want you to know that I am not doing this for your sake, declares the Sovereign LORD. Be ashamed and disgraced for your conduct, O house of Israel!" Fensham, 128, comments, "It is as if Ezra has realized that immediately in front of him are all the cumulative iniquities which have heaped up through history. What an extraordinary view of sin!"

7 D. W. Thomas ("The Sixth Century BC: A Creative Epoch in the History of Israel," *JSS* 6 [1961]: 36) comments: "The language of bombast and self-glorification which is characteristic, for example, of the Assyrian records, contrasts remarkably with the acknowledgement of national failure which runs through the writing of the Hebrew historians."

"From the days of our forefathers" shows that the Jews were conscious of their corporate solidarity, unlike the individual emphasis of modern Christianity.

Ezekiel 21:16 vividly describes "the sword" (*ḥereb*; cf. Ne 4:13b) of Yahweh at work as an instrument of his judgment; though the king of Babylon wielded the sword, it was actually Yahweh himself who exercised divine judgment. Contrary to the view of scholars that Ezra/Nehemiah is devoid of eschatology, J. G. McConville ("Ezra-Nehemiah and the Fulfilment of Prophecy," *VT* 36 [1986]: 223) writes:

> My main conclusion is that, on the contrary, the books express deep dissatisfaction with the exiles' situation under Persian rule, that the situation is perceived as leaving room for a future fulfillment of the most glorious prophecies of Israel's salvation and that the cause of the delayed fulfillment is the exiles' sin.

After the conquest of Judah by the Babylonians in 605 BC, the Jews fell successively under the Persians, Alexander the Great, the Ptolemies, the Seleucids, the Romans, the Byzantines, the Arabs, the Turks, and the British. Only for about a century from the Maccabean Revolt in 165 BC till Pompey's intervention in 63 BC did the Jews enjoy autonomy—that is, until the establishment of the independent state of Israel in 1948.

8 In the archaic English of the KJV, "space" usually refers to a period of time. (The NIV has "for a brief moment." See Ge 29:14; Lev 25:8; Dt 2:14; Ac 5:7; 19:8; Rev 8:1.)

"Has been gracious" (*teḥinnâ*) means a prayer for grace in all but two passages of its twenty-four occurrences in the OT (e.g., in Solomon's prayer [1Ki 8:30, 38, 49]). Here in v.8 it signifies the Lord's grace or mercy for the remnant of his people.

"A remnant" (*pelêṭâ*) is literally "those who have escaped" (cf. Ge 45:7)."A firm place" (*yātēd*) is literally a "nail" or a "peg," as a nail driven into a wall (cf. Isa 22:23) or a tent peg into the ground (Isa 33:20; 54:2). The LXX renders the word *stērigma*

("establishment"). The RSV translates "a secure hold," the NRSV "a stake," the NEB "foothold."

An increase in light—"gives light to our eyes"—means vitality and joy (1Sa 14:27, 29; Pss 13:3 [4]; 19:8 [9]; Pr 15:30; 29:13; Ecc 8:1).

"Relief" (*miḥyâ*) is a relatively rare word that occurs but eight times, including once here and in v.9 ("new life"), where it means "relief, reviving." Elsewhere it means "to save lives" (Ge 45:5), "emergence of raw flesh" (Lev 13:10, 24), "subsistence" (Jdg 6:4 ["living thing," NIV]; 17:10 ["food," NIV]); "living" (2Ch 14:13 [12];"recover," NIV]).

The Jewish commentator Slotki, 166, observes poignantly:"A little grace had been granted by God to his people; a small remnant had found its weary way back to its home and driven a single peg into its soil; a solitary ray of light was shining; a faint breath of freedom lightened their slavery. How graphically Ezra epitomizes Jewish experience in these few words!"

9 The Achaemenid Persian kings were favorably disposed to the Jews: Cyrus (539–530 BC) gave them permission to return (Ezr 1). His son Cambyses (529–522), not named in the Bible, also favored them, as we learn from the Elephantine papyri. Darius I (522–486) renewed the decree of Ezra (Ezr 6). Darius's son Xerxes (485–465) granted Jews privileges and protection (Est 8–10). Artaxerxes I (464–424) gave authorizations to Ezra (Ezr 7) and Nehemiah (Ne 1–2).

"New life" is the same word translated "relief" (v.8)."To repair" is literally "to cause to stand."

"Ruins" (*ḥorbâ*, "waste, desolate places") occurs forty-two times in the OT. The verbal form means "to dry up, be in ruins, lay waste," or "to make desolate." Isaiah had prophesied that the Lord would raise up the ruins of Jerusalem (Isa 44:26). The city's ruins would break forth into singing (Isa 52:9; cf. 58:12; 61:4).

"A wall of protection" (*gādēr*; LXX *phragmos*, "fence") is used of a low fence around a sheep-fold (Nu 32:16) or of a wall bordering a path (Nu 22:24). The qualifying phrase "in Judah and Jerusalem" indicates a metaphorical reference in the sense of "protection" (RSV; cf. Zec 2:1–5). Some critics take this reference to a wall as an argument for the priority of Nehemiah over Ezra, assuming an allusion to the wall that Nehemiah had repaired in his day. But most scholars (e.g., Ackroyd, Brockington, Bright, Kellermann) agree that the reference here is not to be taken literally.

10–11 On these two verses compare Leviticus 18:24–26; Deuteronomy 7:1–6; 2 Kings 17; 23:8–16; Ezekiel 5:11; Romans 3:19.

"Polluted by the corruption" (*niddâ hîʾ bᵉniddat*) is literally "polluted (land), it is by the pollution." *Niddâ* (GK 5614) can mean menstrual flow (so Lev 12:2) or perversion (so Lev 20:21). (There is a tractate in the Mishnah called *Niddah*, which deals with menstrual blood and its polluting effects.) Here it refers to both the corruption of Canaanite idolatry and the immoral practices associated with it (cf. 2Ch 29:5; La 1:17; Eze 7:20; 36:17). The noun *ṭumʾâ* ("impurity") occurs thirty-six times in the OT, including twice in Ezra (see comment on 6:21).

The texts of Ugarit (Ras Shamra), on the Syrian coast across from Cyprus, have revealed the beliefs and practices of the Canaanites. See G. R. Driver, *Canaanite Myths and Legends* (Edinburgh: T&T Clark, 1956); C. H. Gordon, "Poetic Legends and Myths from Ugarit," *Berytus* 25 (1977): 5–133; M. D. Coogan, *Stories from Ancient Canaan* (Philadelphia: Westminster, 1978); C. Craigie, *Ugarit and the Old Testament* (Grand Rapids: Eerdmans, 1983); L. Day, "Ugaritic," in *Beyond Babel: A Handbook for Biblical Hebrew and Related Languages* (Atlanta: Society of Biblical Literature, 2002), 223–41.

12 Verses 10–12 are not drawn from a single quotation but from many passages (Dt 11:8–9; Pr 10:27; Isa 1:19; Eze 37:25).

13 "You have punished us less than our sins" is literally "you have withheld beneath our iniquities" (cf. Job 11:6).

14 "Angry" is related to the word *ʾap*, which means both "nose" and "anger." For the association see Ezekiel 38:18, "My anger will rise up in my nose" ("my hot anger will be aroused," NIV), and Psalm 18:7–8, "because he was angry, smoke rose from his nostrils." When God's anger came on the Israelites, it was because they had failed to perform their covenantal responsibilities (cf. Dt 7:4; 11:17; 29:25–28; Jos 23:16; Jdg 2:20).

15 A proper sense of God's holiness sheds light on our unworthiness (cf. Isa 6:1–5; Lk 5:8). For comparable passages of national lament, see Psalms 44, 60, 74, 79–80, 83, 85, 90, 108, 126, 129, and 137.

NOTES

7 *Ḥereb*, "sword," which occurs 407 times, is the most frequently named weapon in the OT. See E. Yamauchi, "732 חרב," *TWOT*, 1:320–21.

10 A. Schenker (*Studien zu Propheten und Religionsgeschichte* [Stuttgart: Katholisches Bibelwerk, 2003], 132–39) believes that Ezra's objection to mixed marriages was based not on Exodus 34:16 or on Deuteronomy 7:3, but on Leviticus 18 and 20—that is, not on prohibition against exogamous marriages but on avoiding pollution. By contrast, C. Hayes, "Intermarriage and Impurity in Ancient Jewish Sources," *HTR* 92 (1999): 6–7, believes that Ezra's prohibition rested on Deuteronomy 7:6.

3. The People's Response (10:1–4)

OVERVIEW

We have the following chronological indicators in this chapter. Verse 9 indicates that the people assembled on the twentieth day of the ninth month (Kislev) of the first year, which would have been December 19, 458, amid the cold, rainy season.

According to v.16, the examining committee began its work ten days later, on the first day of the tenth month (Tebet). The committee completed its work in three months (v.17), on the first day of the first month (Nisan), that is, March 27, 457.

¹While Ezra was praying and confessing, weeping and throwing himself down before the house of God, a large crowd of Israelites — men, women and children — gathered around him. They too wept bitterly. ²Then Shecaniah son of Jehiel, one of the descendants of Elam, said to Ezra, "We have been unfaithful to our God by marrying foreign women from the peoples around us. But in spite of this, there is still hope for Israel. ³Now let us make a covenant before our God to send away all these women and their children, in accordance with the counsel of my lord and of those who fear the commands of our God. Let it be done according to the Law. ⁴Rise up; this matter is in your hands. We will support you, so take courage and do it."

COMMENTARY

1 Hereafter Ezra is spoken of in the third person. (On the interchange between the first-person memoirs and the third-person narrative, see Introduction: Literary Form; Authorship.)

"Weeping," not silently but aloud (cf. comment on 3:12; Ne 1:4; Joel 1:12–17), like laughing, is contagious. The people also "wept bitterly," literally, "wept with a great weeping" (a Heb. idiom; cf. Jer 8:18–22).

"Throwing himself down" (*mitnappēl*, a Hithpael participle) implies that Ezra kept on "throwing himself down" on the ground. The prophets and other leaders used object lessons, even bizarre actions, to attract people's attention (Isa 7:3; 8:14, 18; Jer 19; 27). Note that women and children are mentioned. Entire families were involved.

2 Ezra, the wise teacher, waited for his audience to draw their own conclusions about what should be done. Kidner, 69–70, comments, "Instead of whipping a reluctant people into action, Ezra has pricked their conscience to the point at which they now urge him to act."

The Shecaniah here is distinct from that of 8:3 (see comment there). Possibly his father is the same Jehiel mentioned in vv.21 and 26, as he also was of the family of Elam (see comment on 2:7). Perhaps Shecaniah was grieved that his father had married a non-Jewish mother. Six members of the clan of Elam were involved in intermarriages (v.26).

3 "Make a covenant" (*kārat bᵉrît*, lit., "to cut a covenant") derives from the practice of cutting a sacrificial animal. Originally it may have involved passing between the pieces, with the implied curse that whoever did not keep the covenant should be cut up like the animals (Ge 15:9–18; cf. W. F. Albright, "The Hebrew Expression for 'Making a Covenant' in Pre-Israelite Documents," *BASOR* 121 [1951]: 21–22). The name of the modern Jewish organization Bnei Berit means "sons of the covenant."

"All these women and their children" reflects the fact that in ancient societies, as in ours, mothers were given custody of their children when marriages were dissolved. When Hagar was dismissed, Ishmael was sent with her (Ge 21:14). In Babylonia divorced women were granted custody of their children and had to wait for them to grow up before remarrying (Codex Hammurabi 137; *ANET*, 172).

In Greek divorces, however, the children remained with their fathers.

In "the counsel of my lord," the NIV has chosen to read the word for "lord" as vocalized *ᵃdōnî* ("my lord," i.e., Ezra) rather than as *ᵃdōnāy* ("Lord"). This reading is also adopted by the KJV, RV, and NEB. The general context, however, favors the rendering that the "counsel" is not simply that of Ezra but of the Lord (cf. Ps 33:11; Pr 19:21; Isa 19:17; Jer 49:20; 50:45).

4 "Rise up." Shecaniah gave a clarion call to action. Weeping was not enough. Courageous and painful decisions had to be made. The people themselves had to respond. Compare David's exhortation, "Arise and be doing! The LORD be with you!" (1Ch 22:16, lit. trans.).

4. The Calling of a Public Assembly (10:5–15)

⁵So Ezra rose up and put the leading priests and Levites and all Israel under oath to do what had been suggested. And they took the oath. ⁶Then Ezra withdrew from before the house of God and went to the room of Jehohanan son of Eliashib. While he was there, he ate no food and drank no water, because he continued to mourn over the unfaithfulness of the exiles.

⁷A proclamation was then issued throughout Judah and Jerusalem for all the exiles to assemble in Jerusalem. ⁸Anyone who failed to appear within three days would forfeit all his property, in accordance with the decision of the officials and elders, and would himself be expelled from the assembly of the exiles.

⁹Within the three days, all the men of Judah and Benjamin had gathered in Jerusalem. And on the twentieth day of the ninth month, all the people were sitting in the square before the house of God, greatly distressed by the occasion and because of the rain. ¹⁰Then Ezra the priest stood up and said to them, "You have been unfaithful; you have married foreign women, adding to Israel's guilt. ¹¹Now make confession to the LORD, the God of your fathers, and do his will. Separate yourselves from the peoples around you and from your foreign wives."

¹²The whole assembly responded with a loud voice: "You are right! We must do as you say. ¹³But there are many people here and it is the rainy season; so we cannot

stand outside. Besides, this matter cannot be taken care of in a day or two, because we have sinned greatly in this thing. [14]Let our officials act for the whole assembly. Then let everyone in our towns who has married a foreign woman come at a set time, along with the elders and judges of each town, until the fierce anger of our God in this matter is turned away from us." [15]Only Jonathan son of Asahel and Jahzeiah son of Tikvah, supported by Meshullam and Shabbethai the Levite, opposed this.

COMMENTARY

5 The Hebrew word for "oath" ($\check{s}^e b\hat{u}^c\hat{a}$) and "swear" ($\check{s}b^c$) is related to the word for "seven" (cf. Ne 5:12–13; 10:29). Another Hebrew word sometimes translated "oath" in the KJV is $\hat{a}l\hat{a}$ (e.g., Ge 24:41; 26:28; Dt 29:12), which more properly connotes the implicit "curse" (Zec 5:3).

Ezra first enlisted the aid of the leaders of the priests, Levites, and laity and had them swear an oath. The oath, a solemn declaration made under divine sanction, could be assertive, exculpatory, or promissory. An assertive oath called God to witness to the truth of a statement (1Ki 18:10; Ro 1:9; Php 1:8). An exculpatory oath sought to clear a person from an accusation (e.g., Codex Hammurabi 20, 23, 103; *ANET*, 167, 170). An oath could be promissory about future undertakings, as was the case here.

In biblical oaths the implied curse for nonfulfillment is often expressed in the vague statement, "May the LORD deal with me, be it ever so severely, if …" (Ru 1:17; 2Sa 3:35; 1Ki 2:23). On rare occasions the full implications of the curse are spelled out (Nu 5:19–31; Job 31; Pss 7:4–5; 137:5–6). Peter progressively denied Christ (Mt 26:70), denied with an oath (v.72), and finally cursed—that is, called down curses on—himself (v.74).

6 Such complete fasting—"he ate no food and drank no water" (cf. Ne 1:4)—was twice observed by Moses (cf. Ex 34:28; Dt 9:18). The people of Nineveh also had a total fast after Jonah's preaching (Jnh 3:7). But such fasts were rare. Ordinary fasts involved abstaining from eating only (1Sa 1:7; 2Sa 3:35). The Mishnah (*Ta͑an.* 1.4ff.) prescribes fasting from eating and drinking during daylight to pray for rain. Muslims observe a complete fast from food and drink during the daylight hours for the month of Ramadhan.

"He continued to mourn" (Hithpael of $\hat{a}bal$), though often referring to the mourning rites for the dead (Ge 37:34; 2Sa 13:31–37), also describes the reaction of those who are aware of the threat of deserved judgment (Ex 33:4; Nu 14:39; 1Sa 15:35; 16:1).

"The room" typifies chambers in the temple area that were used as storerooms (8:29; Ne 13:4–13). Jeremiah's prophecy was read in such a room before an assembly (Jer 36:10).

The identification of the names "Jehohanan son of Eliashib" and their relationship to the same names found in other sources is a complex issue that has an important bearing on the question of the order of Ezra and Nehemiah (see Introduction: The High Priests).

7 While Ezra continued to fast and pray, the chiefs and elders ordered all the exiles to assemble in Jerusalem. Though Ezra had been vested with great authority (7:25–26), he used it sparingly and influenced the people by his example.

8 As the territory of Judah had been much reduced, the most distant inhabitants would not be more than fifty miles from Jerusalem. The borders were Bethel in the north, Beersheba in the south, Jericho in the east, and Ono in the west. All could travel to Jerusalem "within three days."

"Would forfeit" (from *ḥērem*; GK 3049) means to ban from profane use and to devote, either to destruction (e.g., Ex 22:20; Dt 13:13–17) or for use in the temple as here (cf. Lev 27:28–29; Jos 6:18–19; 7:1–26). This verse, which is the earliest attestation of excommunication, is probably a modification of the more ancient capital punishment, "to be cut off from Israel" (Ge 17:14; Ex 12:15). W. Horbury ("Extirpation and Excommunication," *VT* 35 [1985]: 28) points out that in the Qumran Damascus Document a period of exclusion expressly replaces the death penalty (cf. Nu 15:34–35 with CD 12.4–6).

9 Usually Judah alone is mentioned, but a few passages also refer to the exiles who came from or settled in the area of Benjamin north of Jerusalem (1:5; 4:1).

"In the square" (*birᵉḥôb*) means "in a wide space." The KJV's "street" is misleading, though the word has this meaning in modern Hebrew. The plaza or square was either in the outer court of the temple or more probably in the open space before the Water Gate (Ne 3:26; 8:1).

"Greatly distressed" is the Hiphil participle of a relatively rare verb (*rāᶜad*) that occurs only here, in Daniel 10:11, and in Psalm 104:32. Related nouns appear in Exodus 15:15; Job 4:14; Psalms 2:11; 48:6; 55:5; and Isaiah 33:14. The trepidation of the people was caused by two distinct reasons: their transgressions and the weather.

"The rain" (*gᵉšāmîm*, plural of intensity) indicates heavy torrential rains. The ninth month, Kislev (November-December), is in the middle of the rainy season, which begins with light showers in October and lasts to mid-April (see E. Yamauchi,

"Ancient Ecologies and the Biblical Perspective," *Journal of the American Scientific Affiliation* 32 [1980]: 193–203).

December and January are also cold months in Jerusalem, with temperatures in the fifties and even forties. Sometimes it gets so cold that it snows (2Sa 23:20; Ps 147:16–17; Pr 31:21; 1Mc 13:22).

The assembly was shivering, not only because they were drenched but also because they sensed a sign of divine displeasure in the abnormally heavy rains (cf. 1Sa 12:17–18; Eze 13:11, 13). Blenkinsopp, 193, comments, "This is one of the more realistic scenes in the book which could hardly have been invented."

10 Ezra was not only a scribe (7:11–12, 21) but also a priest (*kōhēn*, a word reflected in many Jewish names today: Cohen, Cohn, Kahane, Kahn, et al.).

The sins and failures of the exiles were great enough; they added insult to injury by marrying pagan women, thus "adding to Israel's guilt" (cf. 2Ch 28:13). In Exodus 9:34; Judges 3:12; 4:1, the Hebrew idiom is "added" to sin or do evil.

11 "Confession" (*tôdâ*) almost always means "thanksgiving"; its present occurrence and that in Joshua 7:19 are exceptions. A better translation than "foreign wives" might be "pagan wives," implying not only a different nationality but also adherence to a different religion.

12 The Lord so convicted the hearers that what Ezra had said was right that they spontaneously and unitedly responded in an extraordinary manner, "with a loud voice" (cf. 3:12; 2Ch 15:14; Ne 9:4), thereby acknowledging their need to do something about the situation.

The NIV's "You are right! We must do as you say" is literally, "As you have said, so it is for us to do." The Hebrew word *kēn* is an adverb that means "so." In modern Hebrew it means "yes.

13 A spokesman for the people nonetheless pointed out the practical difficulties in view of the inclement weather. "Sinned" (*pāšaʿ*) connotes an act of revolt or rebellion (cf. 1Ki 12:19).

14 The "elders" (*zᵉqēnîm*) were the older men of the community who had beards (*zāqān*). They formed a governing council in every village (1Sa 30:26–31). At Succoth there were seventy-seven elders (Jdg 8:14). The elders at the gate of the town served as magistrates (Dt 19:12; 21:3, 19; Ru 4:1–12).

In addition there were also "judges" (*šōpᵉṭîm*) appointed in every town (Dt 16:18–20; cf. de Vaux, *Ancient Israel*, 137–38, 152–53, 156, 161–62).

"The fierce anger" (*ḥᵃrôn ʾap*, lit., "glow of the nose") is a phrase used only of God's wrath (cf. Ex 32:12; Nu 25:4; Dt 13:17; Jos 7:26; Ne 9:17, et al.).

15 The truth of the narrative is indicated by the candor with which the opposition to the reform measures is recorded. Why these four men opposed the measure is unclear. Perhaps they were protecting themselves or their relatives. Perhaps they viewed the measures of separation as too harsh. Less probably they were fanatics who wished no delay in implementing the measure.

"Asahel" means "God has made" or "God has acted." "Jahzeiah" ("May Yahweh see!") is found only here. "Tikvah" ("hope") is found otherwise only in 2 Kings 22:14 (cf. "Yah is my hope" in Cowley, 68:1).

On Meshullam's name, see the comment on 8:16. If this is Meshullam the son of Bani in v.29, he himself had married a pagan wife.

"Shabbethai" occurs only here and in Nehemiah 8:7 and 11:16. It may mean one born on the Sabbath. The name occurs nine times in the Murashu texts (Coogan, 34–35) as *šabbatay*, three times in the Elephantine texts (Cowley, 2:21; 58:3; Kraeling, 8:10) and once in a Hermopolis text. (See B. Porten, "The Religion of the Jews of Elephantine in Light of the Hermopolis Papyri," *JNES* 28 [1969]: 116–17, 121.) The Akkadian *Ša-ba-ta-ai* meant "one born on the day of the full moon."

NOTES

5 On oaths see: K. van der Toorn, "Herem-Bethel and Elephantine Oath Procedure," *ZAW* 98 (1986): 282–85; L. H. Schiffman, "The Law of Vows and Oaths (Nu 30,3–16) in the Zadokite Fragments and the Temple Scroll," *RevQ* 15 (1991–92): 199–214; T. C. Cartledge, *Vows in the Hebrew Bible and the Ancient Near East* (Sheffield: JSOT, 1992); D. R. Worley, "Fleeing to Two Immutable Things: God's Oath-Taking and Oath-Witnessing," *ResQ* 36 (1994): 223–36; S. Lafont, ed., *Jurer et maudire: Pratiques politiques et usages juridiques du serment dans le Proche-Orient ancien* (Paris: L'Harmaatan, 1996).

14 See J. McKenzie, "The Elders in the Old Testament," *Bib* 40 (1959): 522–40; H. Reviv, *The Elders in Ancient Israel* (Jerusalem: Magness, 1989). On the concept of the "aged" in different societies, see E. Yamauchi, "Attitudes toward the Aged in Antiquity," *NEASB* 45 (2000): 1–9.

The New Testament word for "elder" is *presbyteros*, which probably originally designated the older leaders of the house churches. See A. E. Harvey, "Elders," *JTS* 25 (1974): 318–32.

15 Later in church history after the Decian persecutions (ca. AD 250), Christians such as the bishop of Rome were divided among those who were willing to welcome the *lapsi* back, the rigorists under Novatian, who refused to accept them back, and Cyprian the bishop of Carthage, who was willing to accept them back, provided they showed due contrition by acts of penance.

5. Investigation of the Offenders (10:16–17)

¹⁶So the exiles did as was proposed. Ezra the priest selected men who were family heads, one from each family division, and all of them designated by name. On the first day of the tenth month they sat down to investigate the cases, ¹⁷and by the first day of the first month they finished dealing with all the men who had married foreign women.

COMMENTARY

16 For "Ezra the priest selected," the Hebrew reads "Ezra the priest, with certain heads of fathers' houses … were separated" (cf. KJV). The NIV and NRSV follow 1 Esdras 9:16 and the Syriac.

17 The committee began its work ten days after the assembly had met in the rain. They completed their work three months later on March 27, 457.

The investigating elders and judges did their work carefully and thoroughly. They discovered that about a hundred couples were involved. Williamson (*Ezra, Nehemiah*, 157) observes, "Ezra takes no more personal involvement than is absolutely necessary. He prefers to delegate the actual decision-making to the community's own leaders."

6. The List of Offenders (10:18–43)

¹⁸Among the descendants of the priests, the following had married foreign women:

From the descendants of Jeshua son of Jozadak, and his brothers: Maaseiah, Eliezer, Jarib and Gedaliah. ¹⁹(They all gave their hands in pledge to put away their wives, and for their guilt they each presented a ram from the flock as a guilt offering.)
²⁰From the descendants of Immer:
Hanani and Zebadiah.
²¹From the descendants of Harim:
Maaseiah, Elijah, Shemaiah, Jehiel and Uzziah.
²²From the descendants of Pashhur:
Elioenai, Maaseiah, Ishmael, Nethanel, Jozabad and Elasah.

²³Among the Levites:

Jozabad, Shimei, Kelaiah (that is, Kelita), Pethahiah, Judah and Eliezer.
²⁴From the singers:
Eliashib.
From the gatekeepers:
Shallum, Telem and Uri.

²⁵And among the other Israelites:

From the descendants of Parosh:
Ramiah, Izziah, Malkijah, Mijamin, Eleazar, Malkijah and Benaiah.
²⁶From the descendants of Elam:
Mattaniah, Zechariah, Jehiel, Abdi, Jeremoth and Elijah.
²⁷From the descendants of Zattu:
Elioenai, Eliashib, Mattaniah, Jeremoth, Zabad and Aziza.
²⁸From the descendants of Bebai:
Jehohanan, Hananiah, Zabbai and Athlai.
²⁹From the descendants of Bani:
Meshullam, Malluch, Adaiah, Jashub, Sheal and Jeremoth.
³⁰From the descendants of Pahath-Moab:
Adna, Kelal, Benaiah, Maaseiah, Mattaniah, Bezalel, Binnui and Manasseh.
³¹From the descendants of Harim:
Eliezer, Ishijah, Malkijah, Shemaiah, Shimeon, ³²Benjamin, Malluch and Shemariah.
³³From the descendants of Hashum:
Mattenai, Mattattah, Zabad, Eliphelet, Jeremai, Manasseh and Shimei.
³⁴From the descendants of Bani:
Maadai, Amram, Uel, ³⁵Benaiah, Bedeiah, Keluhi, ³⁶Vaniah, Meremoth, Eliashib,
³⁷Mattaniah, Mattenai and Jaasu.
³⁸From the descendants of Binnui:
Shimei, ³⁹Shelemiah, Nathan, Adaiah, ⁴⁰Macnadebai, Shashai, Sharai, ⁴¹Azarel, Shelemiah, Shemariah, ⁴²Shallum, Amariah and Joseph.
⁴³From the descendants of Nebo:
Jeiel, Mattithiah, Zabad, Zebina, Jaddai, Joel and Benaiah.

COMMENTARY

18 Among those involved were the descendants of Jeshua, the high priest (see 2:2). On "Jozadak," see comment on 3:2. "Maaseiah" ("the work of Yahweh") is the name of twenty-one OT persons. The name "Gedaliah" ("Yahweh has shown himself to be great") occurs twice in the Murashu texts as *Gadalyaw* (Coogan, 19).

19 For the symbolic handshake ("they all gave their hands"), see 2 Kings 10:15; Lamentations 5:6 ("We submitted to," NIV); and Ezekiel 17:18.

According to Leviticus 5:14–19, a "ram" was the guilt offering for a sin committed unwittingly. Though the offenders may not have fully realized the gravity of their offense, they had no excuse;

the Scriptures plainly set forth God's standards on marriage.

20 "Hanani" is a shortened form of "Hananiah" ("Yahweh has been gracious"). Nehemiah's brother bore this name (Ne 1:2). It occurs twelve times in the Murashu texts as Ḥananī (Coogan, 25). On "Immer," see comment on 2:37; on "Zebadiah," see comment on 8:8.

21 On "Harim" see comment on 2:32; on "Maaseiah," see comment on v.18 above. "Elijah" means "Yahweh is my God." On "Shemaiah" see comment on 8:13; on "Jehiel," see comment on 8:9. "Uzziah" means "Yahweh is (my) might."

22 On "Pashhur" see comment on 2:38. "Elioenai" is "my eyes are toward my God." Coogan, 124, believes this name is patterned after the Akkadian itti-dX-īnāya. On "Maaseiah" see comment on v.18. Ishmael means "May God hear!"; "Nethanel," "God has given." "Elasah" ("God has made") occurs only here and in Jeremiah 29:3.

23 "Shimei" is the shortened form of "Shemaiah" ("Yahweh has heard"). It appears on a bulla as š-m-ʿ-y (Avigad, 7). "Kelita" means "crippled, dwarfed one"; "Pethahiah" means "Yahweh has opened (the womb)."

24 "Telem" ("brightness") occurs only here. "Uri" is the shortened form of "Uriah" (8:33).

Only one singer and three gatekeepers were involved. There is no representative of the Nethinim (2:43–54) or of the descendants of Solomon's servants (2:55–57). The lowest classes were the least involved in intermarriage; the pagan women were probably not attracted to them.

25 "Ramiah" ("Yahweh is exalted") occurs only here, as does "Izziah" ("Yahweh sprinkled"). "Malkijah" means "Yahweh is my king." "Mijamin" ("luck") is literally "from the right hand," a contraction of Miniamin (Ne 12:17).

In place of the second "Malkijah," the NRSV inserts "Hashabiah" following 1 Esdras 9:26. "Bena-

iah" is "Yahweh has built" (cf. Banāyaw in the Murashu texts; Coogan, 15).

26 The name "Mattaniah" ("the gift of Yahweh") occurs seven times in the Murashu texts as Mattan-yas (Coogan, 29) and on a seventh-sixth century BC bulla M-t-n-y-h-w (K. O. Connell, "An Israelite Bulla from Tell el-Ḥesi," IEJ 27 [1977]: 197–99).

27 "Abdi," a shortened form of "Obadiah" ("servant of Yahweh"), occurs in the Murashu texts as ʿabdiya (Coogan, 31). "Jeremoth" means "swollen"; "Zabad" means "he has given" (cf. Coogan, 20). "Aziza" ("strong one") occurs only here.

28 "Hananiah" ("Yahweh has been gracious") is the name of fourteen OT individuals. It occurs three times in the Murashu texts as Ḥananyaw; (Coogan, 25). "Zabbai" is perhaps a shortened form of "Zebadiah" ("Yahweh has given"). "Athlai," a shortened form of "Athaliah" ("Yahweh is exalted"), occurs only here.

29 "Malluch" means "counselor"; "Adaiah" means "Yahweh has adorned himself." "Jashub" ("he will return") occurs only here and in Numbers 26:24 and 1 Chronicles 7:1. It occurs in the Murashu texts as yašúb (Coogan, 84). "Sheal" ("ask" or "may [God] grant") occurs only here. The name Š-ʾ-l occurs on a seal (Avigad, 9).

30 "Adna" means "pleasure"; "Kelal" means "perfection." "Bezalel" ("in the shadow of God") occurs only here and in Exodus 31:2 of the skilled craftsman who helped build the tabernacle. On "Binnui," see comment on 2:10. "Manasseh" ("Yahweh causes to forget") occurs also in v.33.

31 "Ishijah" ("May Yahweh forget") occurs only here. On "Malkijah," see comment on v.25; on "Shemaiah," see comment on 8:13. "Shimeon," derived from "Shemaiah" ("Yahweh has heard"), in Greek became the name "Simon." In the Murashu texts it appears as šamaʿōn (Coogan, 35, 85).

32 "Benjamin" means "son of the right hand;" "Shemariah" means "Yahweh has preserved."

33 Both "Mattenai" and "Mattattah" (only here) mean "gift of God." "Jeremai" is a hypocoriston (pet name) of Jeremiah. One of the seals published by Avigad, 7, has *l-y-r-m-y h-s-p-r* ("[seal] of Jeremai the scribe").

34 "Maadai" occurs only here (cf. Moadiah ["Yahweh assembles or promises"] in Ne 12:5). "Amram" is "people are exalted." "Uel" ("will of God") occurs only here.

35 Both "Bedeiah" ("branch of Yahweh") and "Keluhi" ("Yahweh is perfect") occur only here.

36 "Vaniah" (possibly Pers. *Vānyah* ["worthy of love"]) occurs only here.

37 "Jaasu" ("May Yahweh make!") occurs only here.

38 The NIV and NRSV follow the LXX and 1 Esdras 9:34 in emending the Hebrew from *ûbānî ûbinnûy* ("and Bani and Binnui"; cf. KJV) to *ûmibᵉnê binnûy* ("and from the descendants of Binnui").

39 "Shelemiah" means "Yahweh has restored."

40 "Machnadebai" is possibly a corruption of "possession of Nebo" (cf. Brockington, 119–20). "Shashai" occurs only here (cf. Cowley, 49:1). "Sharai," possibly a shortened form of "Sherebiah" (8:18), occurs only here.

41 "Azarel" means "God has helped."

42 "Joseph" is "May (God) add (prosperity)!"

43 "Nebo" possibly derives from the name of the Babylonian god Nabu. It occurs only here as a personal name. "Jeiel" ("God has healed") is the name of ten OT individuals, almost all of which appear in Chronicles. "Mattithiah" means "gift of Yahweh." "Zebina" ("purchased [as a child]") occurs in the Murashu texts six times as *Zabīn* and five times as *Zabīnā* (Coogan, 22–23, 72). "Jaddai," a shortened form of "Jedaiah" ("Yahweh has cared for"), occurs only here.

"Joel" means "Yahweh is God." On "Benaiah" see comment on v.25.

7. The Dissolution of the Mixed Marriages (10:44)

44All these had married foreign women, and some of them had children by these wives.

COMMENTARY

44 The book of Ezra ends abruptly and on a rather negative note. The Hebrew text reads literally: "And there were of them [masculine plural] wives, and they [*wayyāsîmû*] put down children." The Hebrew verb cannot mean "bear" children and is thus unintelligible. The ancient versions (LXX, Vulgate, Syriac) all interpret this to mean that some of these wives had borne children. First Esdras 9:36 reads, "they sent them away with their children," a rendering adopted by the NEB and placed in the margin of the NIV.

Some of the marriages produced children, but they were not accepted as a reason for halting the proceedings. As it was just under eight months from the time of Ezra's arrival (August 4) to the committee's findings (March 27), the offspring mentioned here must be either: (1) a few prematurely born babies, which suggestion is not too likely; (2) the offspring of mixed marriages contracted in Mesopotamia; or (3) the offspring of mixed marriages contracted by those who had returned earlier to Palestine.

Comparing the number of offenders to the numbers listed in the categories of people who returned with Zerubbabel (cf. Ne 7) results in the following percentages:

Classes	Those Who Returned	Those Who Intermarried	Percentages
Priests	4,289	17	0.4
Levites	74	6	8.1
Singers	128	1	0.8
Gate-keepers	139	3	2.2
Laity	24,144	84	0.3
Totals	28,774	111	0.4

J. Myers ("Ezra and Nehemiah," in *Encyclopaedia Judaica* [New York: Macmillan, 1972], 6.1120) makes some cogent comments on the list of offenders:

111 names appear in the unemended text of the list of those guilty of marriage infraction, an exceptionally small number in a community of some 30,000 persons. It is probably a truncated list, including representative names and pointing to the involvement of all classes, as the schematic arrangement may indicate. For the most part members of the upper classes are named, which also seems to reflect the genuineness of the list since they alone were in a position to contract such marriages and stood to benefit most from them.

REFLECTION

Mixed Marriages

Both Ezra (Ezr 9–10) and Nehemiah (Ne 13:23–28) dealt with the problem of mixed marriages. Ezra adopted a more rigorous approach by demanding the dissolution of all such marriages. Apart from the expulsion of Joiada, Nehemiah simply forbade future mixed marriages.

Marriage with foreigners as such was not prohibited in the Torah. Joseph was given an Egyptian wife, Asenath (Ge 41:45). Moses married both Zipporah, a Midianite, and a Cushite woman (Nu 12:1). Ruth, a Moabitess, had an honored place in Jesus' genealogy (Mt 1:5). There was, however, always the danger that marriage with non-Israelite women could lead to apostasy, as in the case of the numerous foreign wives of Solomon (1Ki 11:1–3).

Malachi, who prophesied in the early fifth century prior to Ezra's mission, indicates that some Jews had broken off marriages to their wives to marry women who were "daughters of a foreign god" (Mal 2:10–16). J. M. Sprinkle ("Old Testament Perspectives on Divorce and Remarriage," *JETS* 40 [1997]: 537–38) suggests that the mixed marriages in Ezra-Nehemiah had followed first marriages with Jewish wives who were then divorced—a possible but hypothetical interpretation.

The situation for the returning exiles was probably aggravated by demographic and economic factors. A. C. Welch (*Post-Exilic Judaism* [Edinburgh: William Blackwood & Sons, 1935], 251) suggests: "As has already been noted, the lists of the men of the Return and the natural probabilities of the case prove that the large proportion of the newcomers were males, who must have had difficulty in finding wives among their fellow-Jews." J. Myers (*The World of Restoration* [Englewood Cliffs, N.J.:

Prentice-Hall, 1968], 88–89) proposes that economic factors motivated the members of the upper classes, who were most prominent in contracting intermarriages.

Though the actions of Ezra and later of Nehemiah may strike some readers as harsh, they were more than racial or cultural measures and were necessary to preserve the spiritual heritage of Israel. Both from the principle and from exceptions to the rule, warnings against intermarriage were clearly concerned not so much about racial miscegenation as about spiritual adultery. H. Maccoby ("Holiness and Purity: The Holy People in Leviticus and Ezra-Nehemiah," in *Reading Leviticus: A Conversation with Mary Douglas* [ed. J. F. A. Sawyer; Sheffield: Sheffield Academic, 1996], 163) concludes, "Ezra's decision was at a watershed in the history of Judaism, when the future of monotheism was at stake. It was a matter of deep principle, not of ethnic exclusivism, to reject marital links with the 'people of the land.'"

D. Bossman ("Ezra's Marriage Reform: Israel Redefined," *BTB* 9 [1979]: 32–38) argues that Ezra's purification of the people followed a "priestly ideal of separation from all that is unclean." According to the later Mishnah (*m. Qidd.* 4:4): "If a man would marry a woman of priestly stock, he must trace her family back through four mothers, which are, indeed, eight: her mother, mother's mother, and mother's father's mother, and this one's mother; also her father's mother and this one's mother, her father's father's mother, and this one's mother."

What happened to a Jewish community that was lax concerning intermarriage can be seen from the example of the Elephantine settlement contemporary with Ezra and Nehemiah. Intermarriages took place among both lay leaders and priests. According to Porten, 174, "Some of the pagans who married Jews may have, like the early Samaritans, continued to worship their ancestral god(s) at the same time that they adopted the worship of YHW. Conversely, some of these Jews occasionally expressed devotion to the god(s) of their spouses at the same time that they continued to revere YHW." The Jews at Elephantine worshiped not only Yahweh but also the goddess Anath-Yahweh (cf. Jer 7:16–18; B. Porten, "The Religion of the Jews of Elephantine in Light of the Hermopolis Papyri," *JNES* 28 [1969]: 116–21).

J. Myers (*The World of the Restoration*, 122) concludes: "It is not accidental that Jewish communities in exile gradually disintegrated—for example, the one at Elephantine.... A pure cult with a pure people conducted in their religious and domestic affairs in a pure language was essential."

Perhaps no topic in Ezra-Nehemiah has been the subject of more scholarly discussion than the question of the "mixed marriage" issue in Ezra and in Nehemiah. Two works that survey the vast literature on the issue are D. Janzen, *Witchhunts, Purity and Social Boundaries: The Expulsion of the Foreign Women in Ezra 9–10* (Sheffield: JSOT, 2002), 10–19, and A. Philip Brown II, "The Problem of Mixed Marriage in Ezra 9–10" (*BSac* 162 [2005]: 437–58), based on ch. 6 of his dissertation, "A Literary and Theological Analysis of the Book of Ezra," which is available online at: http://bible.org/series/literary-and-theological-analysis-book-ezra. See also C. Hayes, "Intermarriage and Impurity in Ancient Jewish Sources," *HTR* 92 (1999): 3–36.

Nehemiah

I. NEHEMIAH'S FIRST ADMINISTRATION (1:1–12:47)

A. Nehemiah's Response to the Situation in Jerusalem (1:1–11)

1. News of the Plight of Jerusalem (1:1–4)

OVERVIEW

The walls of Jerusalem that had been destroyed by Nebuchadnezzar remained in ruins for almost a century and a half, despite abortive attempts to rebuild them (Ezr 4:6–23). Such a lamentable situation obviously made Jerusalem vulnerable to her numerous enemies. Yet from a mixture of apathy and fear the Jews failed to rectify this glaring deficiency. They needed the dynamic catalyst of an inspired leader; such a man was Nehemiah.

¹The words of Nehemiah son of Hacaliah:

In the month of Kislev in the twentieth year, while I was in the citadel of Susa, ²Hanani, one of my brothers, came from Judah with some other men, and I questioned them about the Jewish remnant that survived the exile, and also about Jerusalem.

³They said to me, "Those who survived the exile and are back in the province are in great trouble and disgrace. The wall of Jerusalem is broken down, and its gates have been burned with fire."

⁴When I heard these things, I sat down and wept. For some days I mourned and fasted and prayed before the God of heaven.

COMMENTARY

1 Though the books of Ezra and Nehemiah were bound together from the earliest times, "the words of" indicates the title of a separate composition (cf. Jer 1:1; Am 1:1; see Introduction: Canon). The Nehemiah Memoir (NM) is based on a first-person account, perhaps originally a report to his king, Artaxerxes I, after a year in office. Williamson (*Ezra, Nehemiah*, xxiv) comments, "It has long been recognized—and is today universally agreed—that substantial parts of the book of Nehemiah go back to a first-person account by Nehemiah himself (or someone writing under his immediate direction)."

The name "Nehemiah" means "the comfort of Yahweh" or "Yahweh has comforted"; it contains the same verbal root found in the names "Nahum" and "Menahem." The name appears as *Neḥemyahu* on an ostracon from Arad dated to the seventh century BC (cf. Y. Aharoni, "The 'Nehemiah' Ostracon from Arad," *ErIsr* 12 [1975]: 72–76). The name of the city, Capernaum, where Jesus ministered, was originally *Kᵉfar Nahum*, "The village of Nahum."

"Hacaliah" is contracted from "wait for Yahweh" (cf. Zep 3:8). Such an imperative form is highly unusual. The name occurs only here and in 10:1–2. The reference to his paternal sepulchers in Jerusalem (2:3, 5) may mean that Nehemiah came from a prominent family.

For "the month of Kislev," see Introduction: Chronology.

"Susa" was the major city of Elam, the area of southwestern Iran. Susa was located in a fertile alluvial plain one hundred fifty miles north of the Persian Gulf. In the Achaemenid period it served as a winter palace for the kings (Kislev = November-December), but the area became intolerably hot during the summer months.

Daniel (Da 8:2) saw himself in a vision at Susa. It was the site of the story of Esther. Ezra 4:9–10 refers to the men of Susa who were deported to Samaria. At Susa, Artaxerxes I received the embassy of Callias (449 BC) that ended Greek-Persian hostilities. In his reign the palace that Darius I had built at Susa burned to the ground. Though no inscription attests to the building activity of Artaxerxes I, he may have begun the small palace in the Donjon area of the Ville Royale completed by his successor, Darius II. From this small hypostyle hall have come all the fragments of stone bas reliefs now on display at the Louvre (see Yamauchi, *Persia and the Bible*, ch. 7, "Susa"; P. Amiet, *Suse: 6000 ans d'histoire* [Paris: Musée du Louvre, 1988]; O. Harper, J. Anz, and F. Tallon, eds., *The Royal City of Susa* [New York: Metropolitan Museum of Art, 1992]).

2 "Hanani" is the shortened form of "Hananiah" ("Yahweh is gracious"). Here and in 7:2 it designates the brother of Nehemiah. The Elephantine papyri mention a Hananiah who was the head of Jewish affairs in Jerusalem. Some scholars believe that this Hananiah can be identified with Nehemiah's brother and assume that he succeeded Nehemiah (ca. 427 BC; see C. G. Tuland, "Hanani-Hananiah," *JBL* 77 [1958]: 157–61; Porten, 130). But this is such a common name, with seven or eight different individuals bearing this name in Ezra-Nehemiah and two more at Elephantine, that such an identification is uncertain.

"The Jewish remnant" is literally "Jews who had escaped" (cf. Ezr 4:12). "Jews" (*yᵉhûdîm*, Gk. *andres Iouda*) became the name of the people of Israel after the exile.

3 The lack of a city wall meant that the people were defenseless against their enemies. K. Kenyon (*Digging Up Jerusalem*, 170) has noted:

> The effect on Jerusalem was much more disastrous and far-reaching than merely to render the city defenseless.... The whole system of terraces down the [eastern] slope, dependent on retaining walls buttressed in turn by the fill of the next lower terrace, was ultimately dependent on the town wall at the base, forming the lowest and most substantial of the retaining walls.

Most scholars, however, do not believe that Nehemiah's distress was caused by the condition of walls torn down one hundred forty years before his time but rather by the episode of Ezra 4:7–23. According to this passage Jews had attempted to rebuild the walls earlier, in the reign of Artaxerxes I. But after the protest of Rehum and Shimshai, the king ordered the Jews to desist. There was considerable suspicion of such attempts because of the revolt of Megabyzus. Josephus in his embellishment of the narrative adds the following details:

They said that these were in a bad way, for the walls had been torn down to the ground and the surrounding nations were inflicting many injuries on the Jews, overrunning the country and plundering it by day and doing mischief by night, so that many had been carried off as captives from the country and from Jerusalem itself, and every day the roads were found full of corpses. (*Ant.* 11.161)

4 Nehemiah "sat down" (cf. Ezr 9:3). Slotki, 183, comments: "The custom of mourners being seated (cf. Ps 137:1; Job 2:13) has survived among Jews,

the bereaved sitting on low stools during the seven days of mourning."

Nehemiah "mourned" (cf. comment on Ezr 10:6). Daniel mourned three weeks for the sins of his people (Da 10:2).

Nehemiah also "fasted." During the exile fasting became a common practice and included solemn fasts to commemorate the taking of Jerusalem and the murder of Gedaliah (Est 4:16; Da 9:3; 10:3; Zec 7:3–7; 8:19).

On "God of heaven" see comment on Ezra 1:2.

NOTE

1 The twentieth year of Artaxerxes I would have been 445 BC. As the Babylonian/Persian year began in the spring, there is a problem with the mention of Kislev (November-December) as coming in the twentieth year before Nisan (March-April; 2:1) of the same year. A number of explanations have been proposed, from the existence of an error in 1:1 for the nineteenth year to the use of a different calendar, which began in Tishri (September-October) in the fall, like the current Jewish calendar, which celebrates Rosh Ha-Shanah ("The Head of the Year") in Tishri (see Blenkinsopp, 205).

"Citadel" is *bîrâ*, a word derived from Akkadian *bîrtu*. It appears fifteen times in postexilic books in the Hebrew Bible. It occurs ten times in Esther in association with Susa. It appears once in Aramaic at Ezra 6:2. In a speculative article, D. Bodi ("La clémence des Perses envers Néhémie et ses compatriotes: faveur ou opportunisme politique?" *Transeu* 21 [2001]: 69–86) argues that the Persian king sent Nehemiah to fortify Jerusalem so that he could have a refuge for his army in case it was defeated.

2. Nehemiah's Prayer (1:5–11)

⁵Then I said:

"O Lord, God of heaven, the great and awesome God, who keeps his covenant of love with those who love him and obey his commands, ⁶let your ear be attentive and your eyes open to hear the prayer your servant is praying before you day and night for your servants, the people of Israel. I confess the sins we Israelites, including myself and my father's house, have committed against you. ⁷We have acted very wickedly toward you. We have not obeyed the commands, decrees and laws you gave your servant Moses.

⁸"Remember the instruction you gave your servant Moses, saying, 'If you are unfaithful, I will scatter you among the nations, ⁹but if you return to me and obey my commands, then

even if your exiled people are at the farthest horizon, I will gather them from there and bring them to the place I have chosen as a dwelling for my Name.'

[10]"They are your servants and your people, whom you redeemed by your great strength and your mighty hand. [11]O Lord, let your ear be attentive to the prayer of this your servant and to the prayer of your servants who delight in revering your name. Give your servant success today by granting him favor in the presence of this man."

I was cupbearer to the king.

COMMENTARY

5 "Awesome" (*nôrāʾ*) is a Niphal participle from the verb *yārēʾ* ("to fear, revere"). Yahweh is the one to be feared (cf. Dt 7:21; Da 9:4).

"Who keeps his covenant of love" is literally "who keeps covenant and steadfast love." The latter word, *ḥesed* (GK 2876) denotes the quality that honors a covenant through thick and thin (cf. comment on Ezr 3:11).

6 The Scriptures often use anthropomorphic figures of speech — e.g., "let your ear be attentive" — without sharing in the anthropomorphic concepts of pagan mythology (cf. comment on Ezra 6:9; cf. E. Cherbonnier, "The Logic of Biblical Anthropomorphism," *HTR* 55 [1962]: 187–210; E. Yamauchi, "Anthropomorphism in Ancient Religions," *BSac* 125 [1968]: 29–44).

Nehemiah did not exclude himself or members of his own family in his confession of sins. A true sense of the awesomeness of God reveals the depths of our own sinfulness (Isa 6:1–5; Lk 5:8).

7 "Commands" (*miṣwōt*, used 180 times in the OT, including 43 in Deuteronomy) is the usual word for commandment, as in the Ten Commandments (Ex 24:12).

"Decrees" (*ḥuqqîm*) indicates something prescribed as the statute of Joshua (Jos 24:25) and the commandment to keep the Passover (Ex 12:24).

"Laws" (*mišpāṭîm*) indicates legal decisions or judgments (Zec 7:9; cf. D. J. Wiseman, "Law and Order in Old Testament Times," *VE* 8 [1973]: 5–21). On the prominence of Moses in Ezra-Nehemiah, see Ezra 3:2; 7:6; Nehemiah 1:8; 8:1, 14; 9:14; 10:29; 13:1.

8 "Remember," a key word, recurs frequently in the book (4:14; 5:19; 6:14; 13:14, 22, 29, 31).

On "if you are unfaithful," Slotki, 185, comments: "The original does not include 'if' and is more forceful: 'you will deal treacherously, I will scatter you,' expressing an inescapable sequel." In the centuries following the Babylonian conquest, Jews were scattered farther and farther. In the NT period there were more Jews in the Diaspora than in Palestine (Jn 7:35; Ac 2:9–11; Jas 1:1; 1Pe 1:1).

9 "I will gather them" is a frequently made promise (Dt 30:1–5; Isa 11:12; Jer 23:3; 29:14; 31:8–10; Eze 11:17; 20:34, 41; 36:24; Mic 2:12).

The phrase "a dwelling for my Name" recalls Deuteronomy 12:5: "the place the LORD your God will choose ... to put his Name there for his dwelling." Parallels are found in extrabiblical sources, e.g., in the Amarna Letters: "Behold the king has set his name [Akkad. *šakan šumšu*] in the land of Jerusalem." Shamshi-Adad I of Assyria boasted, "Thus I placed my great name ... in the land of Lebanon."

10 Though they had sinned and failed, they were still God's people and his possession, a people for his treasure by virtue of his redemption (cf. Dt 4:34; 9:29).

11 Fensham, 157, remarks, "With the expression *this man* at the end of the prayer Nehemiah shows the big difference between his reverence for his God and his conception of his master, the Persian king. In the eyes of the world Artaxerxes was an important person, a man with influence, who could decide on life or death. In the eyes of Nehemiah, with his religious approach, Artaxerxes was just a man like any other man."

On the concern of Nehemiah, Williamson (*Ezra, Nehemiah*, 173) comments quite appositely: "Nehemiah was no doubt aware that if he was to have any success, Artaxerxes would need to overturn his previous decree (Ezr 4:21); to make such a request could be highly dangerous even for a royal favorite (cf. Est 4:11–16)." The interval between the first news and his approach to the king (comparing in 1:1 the month of Kislev with in 2:1 the month of Nisan) meant that Nehemiah had been praying about the matter for four months.

"Cupbearer" (*mašqeh*, a Hiphil participle of the verb *šāqâ*) literally means "one who gives [to someone] something to drink." It occurs twelve times in the OT in the sense of "cupbearer," e.g., in 1 Kings 10:5 and 2 Chronicles 9:4 of Solomon's attendants. In the Joseph story it occurs nine times (Ge 40:1–41:9), but its significance is obscured by

the KJV, which translates the word "butler," derived from the French *boteler*. That the cupbearer could have other responsibilities as well is indicated by Tobit 1:22: "Now Ahikar was cupbearer, keeper of the signet, and in charge of administration of the accounts, for Esarhaddon had appointed him second to himself."

Varied sources suggest something about Nehemiah as a royal cupbearer.

1. He would have been well trained in court etiquette (cf. Da 1:4–5).
2. He was probably a handsome individual (cf. Da 1:4, 13, 15; Josephus, *Ant.* 16, 230 [8.1]).
3. He would certainly know how to select the wines to set before the king. A proverb in the Babylonian Talmud (*b. B. Qam.* 92b) states, "The wine belongs to the master but credit for it is due to his cupbearer."
4. He would have to be a convivial companion, willing to lend an ear at all times.
5. He would have great influence as one with the closest access to the king, able to determine who was allowed to see his master.
6. Above all, Nehemiah had to be one who enjoyed the unreserved confidence of the king. The great need for trustworthy court attendants is underscored by the intrigues endemic to the Achaemenid court. Xerxes, father of Artaxerxes I, was killed in his own bedchamber by Artabanus, a courtier.

NOTE

11 For archaeological evidence of Persian wine services, see P. R. S. Moorey, "Metal Wine-Sets in the Ancient Near East," *Iranica Antiqua* 15 (1980): 181–97.

Some scholars have accepted the Septuagint's reading that Nehemiah was a eunuch and the evidence of Ctesias that many Persian cupbearers were eunuchs. But the Septuagint's reading is an obvious error, and Ctesias is an unreliable source. See E. Yamauchi, "Was Nehemiah the Cupbearer a Eunuch?" *ZAW* 92 (1980): 132–42.

B. Nehemiah's Journey to Palestine (2:1–20)

1. The King's Response (2:1–8)

[1]In the month of Nisan in the twentieth year of King Artaxerxes, when wine was brought for him, I took the wine and gave it to the king. I had not been sad in his presence before; [2]so the king asked me, "Why does your face look so sad when you are not ill? This can be nothing but sadness of heart."

I was very much afraid, [3]but I said to the king, "May the king live forever! Why should my face not look sad when the city where my fathers are buried lies in ruins, and its gates have been destroyed by fire?"

[4]The king said to me, "What is it you want?"

Then I prayed to the God of heaven, [5]and I answered the king, "If it pleases the king and if your servant has found favor in his sight, let him send me to the city in Judah where my fathers are buried so that I can rebuild it."

[6]Then the king, with the queen sitting beside him, asked me, "How long will your journey take, and when will you get back?" It pleased the king to send me; so I set a time.

[7]I also said to him, "If it pleases the king, may I have letters to the governors of Trans-Euphrates, so that they will provide me safe-conduct until I arrive in Judah? [8]And may I have a letter to Asaph, keeper of the king's forest, so he will give me timber to make beams for the gates of the citadel by the temple and for the city wall and for the residence I will occupy?" And because the gracious hand of my God was upon me, the king granted my requests.

COMMENTARY

1 "The twentieth year" would have been April 13, 445 to April 1, 444. There was a delay of about four months from Kislev (November-December), when Nehemiah first heard the news (1:1), to Nisan (March-April), when he felt prepared to broach the subject to the king. There are various explanations for this. The king may have been absent in his other winter palace at Babylon. Perhaps the king was not in the right mood. Even though Nehemiah was a favorite of the king, he would not have rashly blurted out his request. We know it was politic to make one's requests during auspicious occasions, such as birthday parties, or when rulers were in a generous mood (Ge 40:20; Est 5:6; Mk 6:21–25; Josephus, *Ant.* 18.289–93 [8.7]). It is certain that Nehemiah did not ask in haste but carefully bided his time, constantly praying to God to grant the proper opening.

"When wine was brought for him, I took the wine" indicates it was Nehemiah's turn to pour the wine. He was not "the" only cupbearer. (In 1:11 the definite article is lacking; see J. J. Modi, "Wine among the Ancient Persians," *Asiatic Papers* [Bombay: Royal Asiatic Society, 1905–1929]: 3:231–46.)

2 Persian works of art, such as the great treasury reliefs from Persepolis, indicate that those who came into the king's presence did so with great deference, placing the right hand with palm facing the mouth so as not to defile the king with one's breath (cf. R. Ghirshman, *The Art of Ancient Iran* [New York: Golden, 1964], 205–6; R. N. Frye, "Gestures of Deference to Royalty in Ancient Iran," *Iranica Antiqua* 9 [1972]: 102–7).

Regardless of one's personal problems, the king's servants were expected to keep their feelings hidden and to display a cheerful countenance before him. So far Nehemiah had managed to do this; now his burden for Jerusalem betrayed itself, no doubt in his eyes. Artaxerxes seemed to trust Nehemiah to such a degree, however, that no suspicious thought seemed to have crossed his mind; rather, he perceived that it was not a matter of illness and was thus concerned to discover what was distressing his cupbearer.

The NAB's "I was seized with great fear" expresses well the anxiety that must have gripped Nehemiah—not so much for the king's question, but in anticipation of the request that he was to make, well knowing that the king himself had stopped the Jewish efforts at rebuilding the wall (Ezr 4:17–23).

3 "May the king live forever!" was a common form of address to kings (1Ki 1:31; Da 2:4; 3:9). Note that Nehemiah did not mention Jerusalem by name—"the city"—as he wished to arouse the king's sympathy by stressing first the desecration of ancestral tombs.

4 "Then I prayed to the God of heaven" is the most beautiful example of spontaneous prayer in the Scriptures. Before turning to answer the king, Nehemiah uttered a brief prayer to God. Despite his trepidation Nehemiah knew that he stood not only in the presence of an earthly monarch but also before the King of the heavens. One of the most striking characteristics of Nehemiah is his recourse to prayer (cf. 4:4, 9; 5:19; 6:9, 14; 13:14). Those who are the boldest for God have the greatest need to be in prayer.

5 Fortified by his appeal to God and confident in the quality of his past service, Nehemiah was encouraged to make his bold request to the king. Nehemiah still did not mention Jerusalem by name but referred to it as "the city in Judah."

6–7 The word for "queen" (*šēgal*) comes from the root *šgl* ("to lie with" or "to ravish" a woman). It is used only here in v.6 and in Psalm 45:9. Though the word may simply mean a concubine (cf. the LXX's *pallakē*, "concubine"), the definite article indicates that she was the queen or the chief woman of the harem. Ctesias (#44) reports that the queen's name was Damaspia and that the king had at least three concubines (F. W. König, *Die Persika des Ktesias ton Knidos* [Graz: Archiv fur Orientforschung, 1972], 80–81, 124). Some have taken the queen's presence to conclude that this was a private audience and have even argued that this is one reason for considering Nehemiah a eunuch (cf. Notes). According to Daniel 5:2, however, royal women could be present on a public occasion.

The LXX and the Vulgate can be interpreted to mean that both the queen and the king spoke sympathetically to Nehemiah. Perhaps like Esther (Est 4–5), she may have influenced the king. Rainey, 18, cites a letter from Ashur to Ugarit: "Now then, read the tablets that I have sent to you before the queen, and make entreaty before the queen with my favourable words." Extrabiblical sources reveal that the Achaemenid court was notorious for the great influence exercised by the royal women. Especially domineering was Amestris, the cruel wife of Xerxes and mother of Artaxerxes I. Darius II was dominated by his sister and wife, Parysatis.

In addition to safe-conduct letters (v.7), Nehemiah probably asked for a brief leave of absence, which was later extended. Nehemiah 5:14 implies that he spent twelve years on his first term as governor of Judah. In the thirty-second year he returned to report to the king and then returned to Judah for a second term (13:6).

8 The chief forester's name, "Asaph," means "[Yahweh] has gathered." *Pardēs* ("forest") is a loanword from Persian (Old Pers. *paradayadām*; Avestan *pairidaēza*) that originally meant "beyond the wall," hence an enclosure, a pleasant retreat, or a park. Such a park surrounded the tomb of Cyrus at Pasargadae with canals watering the grass and trees of every species (see Yamauchi, *Persia and the Bible*, 332–34). The Hebrew word occurs in the OT only here, in Song of Songs 4:13 ("orchard"), and in Ecclesiastes 2:5 ("parks"). The Greek transliteration *paradeisos* is used here in the LXX and also of the garden of Eden (Ge 3:8–10, 23–24; cf. also Xenophon, *Oec.* 4.13–14).

The location of the king's forest, where Nehemiah was to obtain timber for the gates, is unclear. Some place it in Lebanon, famed for its forests of cedars and other coniferous trees. Solomon obtained such cedars for his temple (1Ki 5:6, 9; 2Ch 2:8–9, 16), as did Zerubbabel for the rebuilding of the temple (Ezr 3:7) and Darius for his palace at Susa (Kent, 77–97).

J. Brown (*Ancient Israel and Ancient Greece: Religion, Politics, and Culture* [Minneapolis: Fortress, 2003], 150; see idem, *The Lebanon and Phoenicia* [Beirut: American Univ. of Beirut, 1969], 175–212), is certain that this forest can only be that of Lebanon: "Here alone do we have testimony to the Persian bureaucracy, in which an official (with a West Semitic name) must grant permission for all logging in the *pardes*."

M. Heltzer ("Some Questions about Royal Property in the Vth Satrapy and Profits of the Royal Treasury," *Transeu* 19 [2000]: 128–29), suggests a closer location: "We can only propose the Carmel range or its eastern part, or possibly the Gilboa mountains, but by all means not very far from the coast, since the trees (trunks) were transported to the mouth of the river Yarkon, because they had to be transported from there to Jerusalem."

Others believe the king's forest should be identified with Solomon's Garden at Etham, located about six miles south of Jerusalem and well-known for its fine gardens (Josephus, *Ant.* 8.186 [7.3]; cf. 2Ki 25:4; Ecc 2:5–9; Jer 39:4; 52:7). In the construction of city gates, indigenous oak, poplar, or terebinth (Ge 12:6; Jos 19:33; Jdg 4:11; Hos 4:13) would most likely be used, not costly imported cedars from Lebanon.

Ordinarily in the Neo-Babylonian and Persian eras the word "citadel" signified a provincial capital. A. Lemaire believes that after the destruction of the walls of Jerusalem by Nebuchadnezzar (2Ki 25:10) the provincial governor's capital remained at Mizpah, the undamaged site to the north of Jerusalem, where Gedaliah was established as the Babylonian governor (Jer 40:4–6). (See A. Lemaire, "Nabonidus in Arabia and Judah in the Neo-Babylonian Period," in *Judah and the Judeans in the Neo-Babylonian Period* [ed. O. Lipschits and J. Blenkinsopp; Winona Lake, Ind.: Eisenbrauns, 2003], 292; J. R. Zorn, "Mizpah: Newly Discovered Stratum Reveals Judah's Other Capital," *BAR* 23/5 [1997]: 28–38, 66.)

NOTES

6 The presence of the queen has been used as an argument that Nehemiah was a eunuch. In 1:11 in place of the οἰνοχόος (*oinochoos*, "cupbearer") of the LXX Codex A, both א B have εὐνοῦχος (*eunouchos*, "eunuch"). Though it is true that there were many eunuchs at the Achaemenid court and that some cup-bearers were eunuchs—for example at Herod's court (Josephus, *Ant.* 16.229–31 [8.l]), the arguments used to support the thesis that Nehemiah was a eunuch are not convincing (see E. Yamauchi, "Was Nehemiah the Cupbearer a Eunuch?" 132–42).

8 For the use of the "Cedars of Lebanon" prior to the Persian era, see J. Elayi, "L'exploitation des cèdres du Mont Liban par les rois assyriens et néo-babyloniens," *JESHO* 31 (1988): 14–41.

The Greek word παράδεισος (*paradeisos*) during the intertestamental period acquired the sense of the abode of the blessed dead in such OT pseudepigrapha as *Testament of Levi* 18:10. It appears three times in the NT: Luke 23:43; 2 Corinthians 12:4; and Revelation 2:7.

2. The Journey to Palestine (2:9–10)

> [9]So I went to the governors of Trans-Euphrates and gave them the king's letters. The king had also sent army officers and cavalry with me.
> [10]When Sanballat the Horonite and Tobiah the Ammonite official heard about this, they were very much disturbed that someone had come to promote the welfare of the Israelites.

COMMENTARY

9 The text implies that Nehemiah set out immediately. Unlike Ezra (Ezr 8:22), Nehemiah was accompanied by an armed escort—not, however, because his faith was weaker than Ezra's, but because he was a royal Persian governor.

10 The name "Sanballat" derives from the Akkadian *Sin-uballiṭ*, which means "Sin [the moon god] has given life." His epithet "the Horonite" has been the subject of much speculation. It either means: (1) Horonaim in Moab (Jer 48:34); (2) either upper or lower Beth Horon, two key cities twelve miles northwest of Jerusalem that guarded the main road to Jerusalem (Jos 10:10; 16:3, 5; 1 Macc 3:15–16; 7:39); (3) Hauran, east of the Sea of Galilee; or (4) Harran, the city in northwestern Mesopotamia, where Abraham and Terah tarried (Ge 11:31–32). Harran's deity was the moon god, Sin.

Sanballat was the chief political opponent of Nehemiah (v.19; 4:1, 7; 6:1–2, 5, 12, 14; 13:28). Although not called governor, he had that position over Samaria (cf. 4:2). An important Elephantine papyrus dated to 407 BC (Cowley, 30; *ANET*, 492)—a letter to Bagoas, the governor of Judah—refers to "Delaiah and Shelemiah, the sons of Sanballat the governor [*peḥah*] of Samaria." It is interesting that Sanballat's sons both bear Yahwistic names. In Cowley, 32 (cf. *ANET*, 492), Bagoas and Delaiah authorized the Jews to petition the satrap Arsames about rebuilding their temple at Elephantine.

In 1962 the same Beduoins who discovered the Dead Sea Scrolls found a cave in Wadi ed-Daliyeh, northwest of Jericho, which contained fourth-century BC papyri. With them were the grim remains of about two hundred men, women, and children from Samaria who unsuccessfully tried to flee from the troops of Alexander the Great. The data from the Samaria papyri include a Sanballat who was probably the grandson of Nehemiah's foe (R. W. Klein, "Sanballat," *IDBSup*, 781–82; F. M. Cross, "A Report on the Samaria Papyri," *VTSup* 40 [1988]: 17–26).

Cross's student, D. M. Gropp, wrote a dissertation on nine of the Samaria papyri, which were slave conveyances. An analysis of these names by J. Zsengellér ("Personal Names in the *Wadi ed-Daliyeh* Papyri," *ZAH* 9 [1996]: 189) sheds interesting light on the religious background of three levels of the Samarian society in the fourth century BC as follows:

(a) The lowest end, at the same time, the largest part of the society is formed by the *remnant of Israel*, yahwistic in the preexilic and northern sense of the word....

(b) On the basis of Ezra 4,1–3, we can also identify a group which derives its origin from the deportation of Esarhaddon, consequently ethnically foreign in origin, but religiously belonging to the new yahwistic environment.... In view of the Samaria papyri, they can be considered as belonging mostly to the middle-class....

(c) The top of the hierarchy, the political elite, consists of the descendants of the Assyrian deportees. At the beginning of the Persian period they probably practised a totally pagan or syncretistic cult, but among them, too, Yahwism spread gradually.

"Tobiah" means "Yahweh is good"; the name appears in the Murashu documents as *Ṭûbiâma*. He may have been a Judaizing Ammonite, but more probably he was a Yahwist Jew, as indicated by his name and that of his son, Jehohanan (6:18). Some scholars speculate that Tobiah descended from an aristocratic family who owned estates in Gilead and was influential in Transjordan and Jerusalem even as early as the eighth century BC (B. Obed, "The Historical Background of the Syro-Ephraimite War

Reconsidered," *CBQ* 34 [1972]: 161). B. Mazar ("The Tobiads," *IEJ* 7 [1957]: 137–45, 229–38; cf. idem, *The Mountain of the Lord*, 66–68) has correlated varying lines of evidence to reconstruct the history of the Tobiad family to cover nine generations.

"Official" (ʿebed) is literally "slave" or "servant" (cf. v.19; 13:1–3). This word is often used of high officials both in biblical and extrabiblical texts (e.g., 2Ki 22:12; 24:10–11; 25:23; Jer 36:24; La 5:8). It is used of a Tobiah in Lachish Letter 3.19–21—"And a letter of Tobiah, the servant of the king"—who is also cited in Letter 5.7–10 as "Tobiah, the arm of the king." Mazar believes that this Tobiah was an ancestor of Nehemiah's contemporary.

Tobiah was married to the daughter of Shecaniah (cf. 3:29; 6:18); and his son Jehohanan married the daughter of Meshullam, son of Berekiah, leader of one of the groups repairing the wall (cf. 3:4, 30; 6:18). Tobiah also was closely related to the priest Eliashib (13:4–7). Josephus (*Ant.* 12.160 [4.2]) said that a later Tobiah was a leader of Jewish Hellenizers under Ptolemy II, as confirmed by the important Zenon papyri.

The region of Ammon is located in Transjordan around the modern capital of Jordan, Amman (Ezr 9:1). Tobiah was no doubt the governor of Ammon or Transjordan under the Persians. His grandson Tobiah is called "the governor of Ammon." The site of ʿArâq el-Emîr ("caverns of the prince"), about eleven miles west of Amman, was the center of the Tobiads. The visible remains of a large building on top of the hill (Qasr el-ʿAbd, "castle of the slave," 60 by 120 feet) have been interpreted as a Jewish temple built by a later Tobiad. On two halls are inscriptions with the name "Tobiah" in Aramaic characters. The date of the inscriptions is much disputed. Mazar favored the sixth-fifth century BC; Naveh, 62–64, the fourth century; Cross, the fourth-third century; and P. W. Lapp ("Soundings at ʿArâq el-Emo [Jordan]," *BASOR* 165 [1962]:

16–34; idem, "The Second and Third Campaigns at ʿArâq el-Emir," *BASOR* 171 [1963]: 8–39), who reexcavated the site in 1961–62, the third-second century (cf. also C. C. McCown, "The ʿArâq el-Emir and the Tobiads," *BA* 20 [1957]: 63–76; M. Hengel, *Judaism and Hellenism* [Philadelphia: Fortress, 1974], 1:49, 267–77).

The usual reason given for why Sanballat and Tobiah "were very much disturbed" was political rivalry. The authority of the Samaritan governor in particular was threatened by Nehemiah's arrival. But on the possibility of a religious schism in the fifth century BC, see Note.

NOTE

10 S. Mittmann ("Tobia, Sanballat und die persische Provinz Juda," *JNSL* 26 [2000]: 1–50) suggests that the enemies of Nehemiah, Tobiah and Sanballat, were members of families who had been repatriated with other exiles and then placed respectively by the Persian authories over Ammon and over Hauran.

Scholars have doubted Josephus's account of the origin of the Samaritan temple and have dated its origin to the Hellenistic era. But according to G. N. Knoppers ("'The City Which Yahweh Has Chosen'," in *Jerusalem in Bible and Archaeology: The First Temple Period* [ed. A. G. Vaughn and A. E. Killebrew; Atlanta: SBL, 2003], 318), "Beneath the second century BCE sacred precinct on Mount Gerizim, Naveh and Magen discovered an older layer, which they date to the second half of the fifth century and identify as the Samaritan temple mentioned (but misdated) by Josephus."

An important recent study of the archaeological, inscriptional, and numismatic evidence is I. Magen's "Mount Gerizim and the Samaritans," in *Early Christianity in Context—Monuments and Documents* (ed. F. Manns and E. Alliata; Jerusalem: Franciscan, 1993), 91–148. Magen, 135, reports: "The recent numismatic material originating from Samaria has established that the Samaritans had begun to create a distinctive religious, political, and national tradition in the fifth century BCE."

Though most of the names in the Wadi ed-Daliyeh papyri are Yahwistic, there are also names that are Edomite (Qos), Moabite (Kemosh), Babylonian (Nabu), Aramean (Sahar), etc. (see Laperrousaz and Lemaire, 41–45; Lemaire, 64–67). The fourth-century Samarian coins also contain Greek influence. (See Y. Meshorer and S. Qedar, *The Coinage of Samaria in the Fourth Century BCE* [Jerusalem: Numismatic Fine Arts, 1991].)

Archaeological evidence of foreign religious influence—especially Egyptian, and Phoenician in the north—particularly along the coast, is summarized by J. Kamlah in "Zwei nordpalästinische 'Heiligtümer' der persischen Zeit und ihre epigraphischen Funde," *ZDPV* 115 (1999): 163–90.

3. Nehemiah's Nocturnal Inspection of the Walls (2:11–16)

[11]I went to Jerusalem, and after staying there three days [12]I set out during the night with a few men. I had not told anyone what my God had put in my heart to do for Jerusalem. There were no mounts with me except the one I was riding on.

> ¹³By night I went out through the Valley Gate toward the Jackal Well and the Dung Gate, examining the walls of Jerusalem, which had been broken down, and its gates, which had been destroyed by fire. ¹⁴Then I moved on toward the Fountain Gate and the King's Pool, but there was not enough room for my mount to get through; ¹⁵so I went up the valley by night, examining the wall. Finally, I turned back and reentered through the Valley Gate. ¹⁶The officials did not know where I had gone or what I was doing, because as yet I had said nothing to the Jews or the priests or nobles or officials or any others who would be doing the work.

COMMENTARY

11–12 After the long journey, a few days of rest ("three"; v.11) were necessary (cf. Ezr 8:32). Such was Nehemiah's discretion that he took only a few men into his confidence at first (v.12). He acted with great care by going out at night, no doubt by moonlight, to inspect the situation firsthand.

13 Nehemiah did not make a complete circuit of the walls but only of the southern area to see how much was preserved. Jerusalem was always attacked where she was most vulnerable—from the north; thus, there was probably little preserved in that direction.

According to 2 Chronicles 26:9, Uzziah fortified towers in the west wall, on the Tyropoeon Valley. In the excavations of 1927–28, M. Crowfoot discovered remains of a gate with towers from the Persian and Hellenistic periods, which A. Alt (*Kleine Schriften* [Munich: Beck, 1959] 3:326–47) identified with the Valley Gate (see Mazar, 167, 182, 193; see also the map in the Introduction).

"Jackal Well" (*ʿên hattannîn*) is literally "spring of the dragons," the mythical water monsters (Ge 1:20–21; Ex 7:9; Ps 74:13; Jer 51:34; Eze 29:3). The NIV and RSV emend to read *tannîm* ("jackals"; cf. La 4:3; Mic 1:8); NRSV has "Dragon's Spring"). Many scholars suggest this was the *ʿên rogel* (Arab. Bir ʿAyub), at the junction of the Hinnom

and Kidron valleys 275 yards south of the tip of the southeastern ridge of Jerusalem (Kenyon, *Digging Up Jerusalem*, 152; W. H. Mare, *The Archaeology of the Jerusalem Area* [Grand Rapids: Baker, 1987], 108). J. Braslavi ("En-Tannin," *ErIs* 10 [1971]: 90–93) argues, however, that this must be the major spring of Jerusalem, the Gihon, and that the name "Tannin" is derived from the serpentine course of the waters of the spring to the Pool of Siloam. Braslavi believes that the En-Rogel had been buried beneath the debris of the earthquake of Uzziah's reign and would not have been visible to Nehemiah.

"The Dung Gate" (*šaʿar hāʾašpōt*; cf. 3:13–14; 12:31; 2Ki 23:10) led to the rubbish dump in the Hinnom Valley. It was situated about five hundred yards from the Valley Gate (3:13). Mazar interprets the Hebrew as *š-p-w-t*, a by-form of "Tophet," the "place of burning," where infant sacrifices were conducted in the days of Manasseh (2Ki 23:10): "We may therefore conclude that the gate in question led from the City of David to the 'burning place' of Tophet in the valley of Hinnom" (Mazar, 194–95).

Some propose a gate in the southwestern corner, but most scholars prefer the great gate in the southeastern corner (cf. J. Simons, *Jerusalem in the Old Testament* [Leiden: Brill, 1952], 123–24). According to Josephus (*J.W.* 5.145 [4.2]), the Herodian Jerusalem had a "Gate of the Essenes," which was used by the Essenes to reach the *Bethso*, or latrines. This gate cannot be identified with Nehemiah's "Dung Gate," however; it is to be located much farther north, on the grounds of the Jerusalem University College. (See Y. Yadin, "The Gate of the Essenes and the Temple Scroll," in *Jerusalem Revealed* [ed. Y. Yadin; Jerusalem: Israel Exploration Society, 1975], 90–96; B.-G. Pixner, "An Essene Quarter on Mount Zion?" *Studia Hierosolymitanna* 1 [1976]: 255–57; R. M. Mackowski, *Jerusalem City of Jesus* [Grand Rapids: Eerdmans, 1980], 62–66.)

14 "The Fountain Gate" was possibly in the southeastern wall facing toward En-Rogel. According to 2 Kings 20:20 (2Ch 32:30), Hezekiah diverted the overflow from his Siloam Tunnel to irrigate the royal gardens (2Ki 25:4) located at the junction of the Kidron and Tyropoeon valleys. Kenyon (*Jerusalem*, 69–71, 77), therefore, associates this gate with the Pool of Siloam or the adjacent Birket el-Hamra.

"There was not enough room." Kenyon's excavations between 1961 and 1967 on the eastern slopes of Ophel, the original hill of Jerusalem just south of the temple area, revealed the collapse of the terraces, which she identifies as the enigmatic "Millo" that David and Solomon had to keep repairing. She writes (*Jerusalem*, 107–8): "The tumble of stones uncovered by our Trench 1 is a vivid sample of the ruinous state of the eastern side of Jerusalem that balked Nehemiah's donkey. The event shows that the sight of this cascade of stones persuaded Nehemiah that he could not attempt to restore the quarter of Jerusalem on the eastern slope of the eastern ridge, or the wall that had enclosed it."

15 The NIV and NRSV indicate that Nehemiah retraced his steps and reentered the city at the Valley Gate on the western slope of Ophel.

16 "Nobles" (*ḥōrîm*) comes from the root "to be free" (cf. 4:14, 19; 5:7; 6:17; 7:5; 13:17) and denotes the clans' notable men who directed public affairs (cf. J. van der Ploeg, "Les nobles israelites," *OtSt* 9 [1951]: 54).

NOTE

13 The Hebrew translated "examining" is שֹׁבֵר (*šōbēr*, "breaking"). Rashi, the medieval Jewish commentator, suggested that Nehemiah was breaking the walls to bring conditions to the attention of the people! The Hebrew should be emended to read *śōbēr* ("examining"; cf. v.15).

4. Nehemiah's Exhortation to Rebuild the Walls (2:17–18)

17Then I said to them, "You see the trouble we are in: Jerusalem lies in ruins, and its gates have been burned with fire. Come, let us rebuild the wall of Jerusalem, and we will no longer be in disgrace." **18**I also told them about the gracious hand of my God upon me and what the king had said to me.

They replied, "Let us start rebuilding." So they began this good work.

COMMENTARY

17 The walls and gates of Jerusalem had lain in ruins since their destruction by Nebuchadnezzar some 140 years before, despite attempts to rebuild them. The leaders and people had evidently become reconciled to this sad state of affairs. It took an outsider to assess the situation and rally the people to renewed efforts. *Ḥerpâ* appears seventy times in the OT either as "abuse," "scorn," or, as in this case, "disgrace" (cf. 1:3; 4:4; 5:9).

18 Nehemiah could personally attest that God was alive and active in his behalf. He had come, moreover, with royal sanction and authority. What was required and what Nehemiah provided were vision and decisive leadership. Nehemiah was clearly a mover, a shaker, and a doer.

5. The Opposition of Sanballat, Tobiah, and Geshem (2:19–20)

¹⁹But when Sanballat the Horonite, Tobiah the Ammonite official and Geshem the Arab heard about it, they mocked and ridiculed us. "What is this you are doing?" they asked. "Are you rebelling against the king?"

²⁰I answered them by saying, "The God of heaven will give us success. We his servants will start rebuilding, but as for you, you have no share in Jerusalem or any claim or historic right to it."

COMMENTARY

19 On Sanballat and Tobiah, see comments on v.10. "Geshem" (*gešem*, so also in 6:1–2), meaning "bulky" or "stout," is a common North Arabian name, *Jasuma*, found in various Arabic inscriptions, including Safaitic, Lihyanite, Thamudic, and Nabataean.

Biblical and extrabiblical documents indicate that Arabs became dominant in the Transjordanian area from the Assyrian to the Persian periods (cf. Ge 25:13; Isa 60:7; Jer 49:28–33). Sargon II resettled some Arabs in Samaria in 715 BC (*ANET*, 286). Classical sources reveal that the Arabs enjoyed a

favored status under the Persians. (See Israel Eph'al, *The Ancient Arabs* [Jerusalem/Leiden: Magnes/Brill, 1982].)

A Lihyanite inscription from Dedan (modern *Al-ʿulā*) in northwestern Arabia reads: "*Jašm* son of *Šahr* and *ʿAbd*, governor of Dedan." This *Jašm* is identified by Winnett and Albright with the biblical Geshem (F. V. Winnett, *A Study of the Lihyanite and Thamudic Inscriptions* [Toronto: Univ. of Toronto Press, 1937], 50–51; W. F. Albright, "Dedan," in *Geschichte und Altes Testament* [Tübingen: J. C. B. Mohr, 1943], 1–12). In 1979 at Tayma in Arabia, a new Aramaic inscription was discovered bearing the name "Gashm ben Shahr," perhaps the grandfather of Geshem (see F. M. Cross, "A New Aramaic Stele from Tayma," *CBQ* 48 [1986]: 387–94).

In 1947 several silver vessels, some with Aramaic inscriptions dating to the late-fifth century BC, were discovered at Tell el-Maskhūta near Ismaila by the Suez Canal. One inscription bore the name "Qaynu the son of Gashmu, the king of Qedar." The son of Geshem records an offering to the goddess "Han-Ilat." Geshem was thus in charge of a powerful north-Arabian confederacy of tribes that controlled vast areas from northeastern Egypt (LXX Ge 45:10: "the land of Gesem of Arabia" instead of "the land of Goshen") to northern Arabia to southern Palestine. Geshem may have been opposed to Nehemiah's development of an independent kingdom because he feared it might interfere with his lucrative trade in myrrh and frankincense (see Yamauchi, *Africa and the Bible*, 91–97).

It is noteworthy that Edomites, who occupied the territory southeast of Judah, are not mentioned as a foe, though they are denounced particularly by the prophet Obadiah for taking advantage of the Babylonian occupation of Judah. Epigraphic evidence indicates the integration of Edom into the Persian-ruled territory of greater Arabia. A. Lemaire ("Nabonidus in Arabia and Judah," 290) concludes: "The disappearance of the kingdom of Edom means that, from 552 on, southward, the province of Judah had a border with Arabia. This political context explains the mention of Geshem/Gashmu, the Arab, in the book of Nehemiah (2:19; 6:1,2,6) and accords with Herodotus's tradition of Arab control of southern Palestine."

20 Nehemiah appealed to historical claims to reject the interference of the Samaritan, Ammonite, and Arabian leaders in the affairs of Jerusalem. By his great confidence and dependence on God for success, he inspired the leaders and the people to a task they had considered beyond their abilities.

NOTE

19 On the basis of the discovery of Edomite pottery north and south of Nahal Beʾer Sheba, some scholars have suggested that Edomites were establishing their control as early as the seventh-sixth century BC. But these artifacts may have been left by travelers and traders (see J. R. Bartlett, "Edomites and Idumaeans," *PEQ* 131 [1999]: 102–14). The region south of Hebron became known as Idumaea. John Hyrcanus forcibly converted the Idumaeans to Judaism. Herod the Great came from this background.

C. List of the Builders of the Wall (3:1–32)

OVERVIEW

This chapter, which was probably based on an independent source, describes the effective organization by Nehemiah of work crews to repair sections of the city wall, beginning at the Sheep Gate in the north and proceeding in a counterclockwise direction for the mile and a half circuit of the wall. Some cities, such as Bethlehem, are not represented; some segments of society, such as "the nobles" of Tekoa, refused to participate (v.5), but others repaired double sections (v.27). Archaeological evidence indicates that Nehemiah must have abandoned areas on the steep eastern slope of Ophel. Only one crew was needed to repair the southern half of the western wall (from the Valley Gate to the Dung Gate). On the other hand, the eastern section required twice as many work crews as the western section.

This text is one of the most important in the OT for determining the topography of Jerusalem. Though some locations are clear, others are not. Opinions differ about whether the wall enclosed the southwestern hill today called "Mount Zion" (the maximalist view; cf. R. Grafman, "Nehemiah's 'Broad Wall,'" *IEJ* 24 [1974]: 50–51; H. Geva, "The Western Boundary of Jerusalem at the End of the Monarchy," *IEJ* 29 [1979]: 84–91) or only the original settlement—including the temple area—of the southeastern hill of Ophel (the minimalist view).

The excavations of Kenyon from 1961–1967 have demonstrated that the southwestern hill was settled only in the Hellenistic period. H. G. M. Williamson ("Nehemiah's Walls Revisited," *PEQ* 116 [1984]: 81–88), comparing Nehemiah 3:8 with 12:38, concludes that though there was a preexilic wall that enclosed the Mishneh (the maximalist view), Nehemiah rebuilt a much more constricted wall (the minimalist view), following perhaps a wall but newly started (Ezr 4). (See also N. A. Bailey, "Nehemiah 3:1–32: An Intersection of the Texts and the Topography," *PEQ* 122 [1990]: 34–40.)

Scholars who still express their support for the maximalist position include E.-M. Laperrousaz ("Jérusalem à l'époque perse [étendue et statut]," *Transeu* 1 [1989]: 55–65) and A. Lemaire (31–74).

Some forty-one parties are named as participating in the reconstruction of forty-two sections. The towns listed as the homes of the builders seem to have represented the administrative centers of the Judean province.

All together, ten gates are listed as follows:

1. The Sheep Gate (v.1);
2. The Fish Gate (v.3);
3. The Old (Jeshanah) Gate (v.6);
4. The Valley Gate (v.13);
5. The Dung (Ashpot) Gate (v.14);
6. The Fountain Gate (v.15);
7. The Water Gate (v.26);
8. The Horse Gate (v.28);
9. The East Gate (v.29);
10. The Inspection Gate (v.31).

The account suggests that most of the rebuilding was concerned with the gates, as the enemy's assaults were concentrated on these structures.

According to the maximalist position, the circuit of walls would have been about two and a half miles, enclosing some 220 acres. According to the minimalist position, the circuit would have been just under two miles, enclosing about 90 acres. Each of the forty-two sections would then average about 250 feet, though an exceptionally long section of 1,500 feet is mentioned (v.3). Some sections were short (vv.21–23); double sections were worked by some groups (e.g., v.27).

Clearly, not all the sections of the walls or buildings in Jerusalem were in the same state of disrepair. Kenyon (*Digging Up Jerusalem*, 179) deduces a selective policy of destruction from 2 Kings 25:9 and concludes: "One can therefore accept as probable that quite a lot of the domestic buildings of Jerusalem survived (except those on the eastern slope): the hovels and the least important possibly completely, the medium scale houses probably capable of easy repairs, only the grand houses seriously destroyed."

1. The Northern Section (3:1–7)

¹Eliashib the high priest and his fellow priests went to work and rebuilt the Sheep Gate. They dedicated it and set its doors in place, building as far as the Tower of the Hundred, which they dedicated, and as far as the Tower of Hananel. ²The men of Jericho built the adjoining section, and Zaccur son of Imri built next to them.

³The Fish Gate was rebuilt by the sons of Hassenaah. They laid its beams and put its doors and bolts and bars in place. ⁴Meremoth son of Uriah, the son of Hakkoz, repaired the next section. Next to him Meshullam son of Berekiah, the son of Meshezabel, made repairs, and next to him Zadok son of Baana also made repairs. ⁵The next section was repaired by the men of Tekoa, but their nobles would not put their shoulders to the work under their supervisors.

⁶The Jeshanah Gate was repaired by Joiada son of Paseah and Meshullam son of Besodeiah. They laid its beams and put its doors and bolts and bars in place. ⁷Next to them, repairs were made by men from Gibeon and Mizpah — Melatiah of Gibeon and Jadon of Meronoth — places under the authority of the governor of Trans-Euphrates.

COMMENTARY

1 "Eliashib the high priest" was the son of Joaikim (see Introduction: The High Priests). His house is mentioned in vv.20–21. It was fitting that the high priest should set the example. Among the Sumerians the king himself would carry bricks for the building of the temple.

"The Sheep Gate" (cf. v.32; 12:39) was no doubt located in the northeastern section of the wall near the Birah fortress. John 5:2 locates it near the Bethesda Pool. The Sheep Gate was the only gate that was "sanctified" by the priests. It was used to bring in sheep for sacrifices at the temple.

"The Tower of the Hundred" (*migdal hammē'â*) occurs only here and in 12:39. What the "hundred" refers to is unclear—either its height, one hundred cubits, or one hundred steps, or a military unit (cf. Dt 1:15). Wightman, 71, offers this interpretation:

The name might be associated with the "commanders of the hundreds of the Carians," or simply

"commanders of the hundreds," mentioned several times in the Old Testament (2 Kgs. 11:4, 9, 19; 1 Chr. 28:1). Thus the Tower of the Hundred might have been the garrison post of one of the foreign mercenary divisions in Jerusalem during the 7th and early 6th centuries BC.

"The Tower of Hananel" is also mentioned in Jeremiah 31:38 and Zechariah 14:10 as the most northern part of the city. Some scholars (Brockington, 119–20) believe that "the Tower of the Hundred" may be a popular name for "the Tower of Hananel." But Wightman, 73, believes that these names designated two separate towers, with the Tower of Hananel to the west of the Tower of the Hundred (as rendered by the NIV). The towers were associated with "the citadel by the temple" (2:8) in protecting the vulnerable northern approaches to the city.

2 "Zaccur," short for "Zechariah," was a Levite who later signed the covenant (10:12).

3 "The Fish Gate" (cf. 12:39) was known in the days of the first temple (Zep 1:10) as one of Jerusalem's main entrances (2Ch 33:14). It may be the same as the Gate of Ephraim, which led out to the main road north from Jerusalem that then descended to the coastal plain through Beth Horon. Though some scholars would place the Fish Gate near the present-day Damascus Gate, Wightman, 73, suggests a location just south of the northwest corner.

Members of the "sons of Hassenaah" family appear in Ezra 2:35 (Ne 7:38) in the list of those returning from captivity. This group is the largest one enumerated (3,630 in Ezra; 3,930 in Nehemiah).

4 "Meremoth son of Uriah, son of Hakkoz," repaired a second section (v.21) and later signed the covenant (10:5). A priest named Meremoth the son of Hakkoz had difficulty establishing his lineage (Ezr 2:59, 61) but was entrusted with the treasures by Ezra (Ezr 8:33).

"Meshullam" also repaired a second section (v.30) and signed the covenant (10:20). Nehemiah complained that he had given his daughter to a son of Tobiah (6:18). He may have been one of the men who accompanied Ezra (Ezr 8:16).

5 "Tekoa" was a small town five miles south of Bethlehem, famed as the home of the prophet Amos (Am 1:1). Tekoa does not appear in the list of those who returned with Zerubbabel (Ezr 2:21–35).

"Nobles" ($^{}addîrîm$) is literally "exalted ones, majestic ones" (cf. 10:29; 2Ch 23:20; Jer 14:3; 25:34–36; Na 2:5). These aristocrats disdained manual labor; they "would not put their shoulders to the work." The Hebrew for "shoulders" ($sawwā^{}r$, "neck") specifically refers to the back of the neck. The expression is drawn from the imagery of oxen that refuse to yield to the yoke (Jer 27:12). The common phrase "to backslide" is derived from the KJV's rendering of Hosea 4:16: "For Israel slideth back as a backsliding heifer."

"Their supervisors" ($^{}adōnêhem$) comes from $^{}adôn$ (with pronominal suffix), a word used in the OT of an earthly lord about 300 times and of the divine Lord 30 times. The related $^{}adōnāy$ is used 449 times of the Lord (cf. *TDOT*, 1:59–72; *TWOT*, 1:12–13). The ASV, RSV, and NRSV render the word as "their [divine] Lord." But the RV translates "their lord"; NEB, "their governor"; and TEV (like the NIV), "the supervisors."

In a remarkable coincidence six centuries later, complaining about Tekoans who had disregarded his mobilization orders and were seeking refuge in En-gedi, Bar Kochba warned, "Concerning every man of Tekoa who will be found at your place — the houses in which they dwell will be burned and you (too) will be punished" (Y. Yadin, *Bar Kochba* [New York: Random House, 1971], 125).

6 "The Jeshanah [$y^{e}šānâ$] Gate" was situated in the northwestern corner and is identified with the Corner Gate of 2 Kings 14:13 and Jeremiah 31:38. Its name has been interpreted in three ways: (1) literally as "The Old Gate" (KJV); (2) as the gate to Jeshanah, lying on the border between Judea and Samaria (2Ch 13:19); (3) as calling for an emendation to "Mishneh" ("second quarter" or "new quarter"), since the names of the gates were derived from what was outside the walls (see Avi-Yonah, "Walls of Nehemiah — A Minimalist View," *IEJ* 4 [1954]: 242–43). The gate would then have led to the area of expansion (Zep 1:10; cf. "Gate of the New Quarter," JB).

7 "Mizpah" ($mispâ$, "Lookout Point") is identified with Tell en-Nasbeh, excavated by W. F. Badé (cf. vv.7, 15, 19). See J. Zorn, "Mizpah: Newly Discovered Stratum Reveals Judah's Other Capital," *BAR* 23/5 (1997): 28–38, 66.

"Under the authority" ($l^{e}kissē^{}$) is literally "to the chair" or "throne." Fragments of a lion's paw and a bronze cylinder that belonged to the foot of a Persian throne similar to those depicted at Persepolis were found in Samaria. M. Tadmor ("Fragments of an Achaemenid Throne from Samaria," *IEJ* 24 [1974]: 42) remarks, "A throne of the Achaemenid kings might have belonged to their representative, the governor of Samaria."

The phrase can be interpreted in different ways: (1) as the satrap's residence in Jerusalem; (2) as the satrap's residence at Damascus or Aleppo; or (3) interpreting "chair" as a symbol for the jurisdiction of the governor over the places from which the builders came, such as Gibeon and Mizpah (so NIV, RV, RSV, NRSV).

NOTES

1 An important study is G. J. Wightman, *The Walls of Jerusalem*; for a critical review see D. Bahat, *PEQ* 130 (1998): 51–62. Kenyon's excavations yielded only a minimal amount of Persian wares in a fill on the eastern slopes. A. D. Tushingham (*Excavations in Jerusalem 1961–1967: Volume I* [Toronto: Royal Ontario Museum, 1985], 33–38) suggests that these wares may have come from tombs. The Persian materials from the later excavations by Y. Shiloh were likewise meager (see A. De Groot and D. T. Ariel, eds., *Excavations at the City of David 1978–1985 Directed by Yigal Shiloh III: Stratigraphical, Environmental, and Other Reports* [Jerusalem: Hebrew Univ. Press, 1992], 50; *Excavations at the City of David 1978–1985 Directed by Yigal Shiloh V: Extramural Areas* [Jerusalem: Hebrew Univ. Press, 2000], 59–61). The only substantial wares from the Babylonian and early Persian eras from Jerusalem were found by G. Barkay in burial caves at Ketef Hinnom, southwest of Jerusalem, in excavations conducted between 1975 and 1989 (see G. Barkay, *Ketef Hinnom* [Jerusalem: Israel Museum, 1986]).

7 Z. Kallai (*Biblical Historiography and Historical Geography* [Frankfurt am Main: Peter Lang, 1998], 84) comments, "The interpretation of Nehemiah 3:7 which suggested that Mizpah was directly subject to the authority of the governor of Abar-Nahara does not stand up to examination."

2. The Western Section (3:8–13)

⁸Uzziel son of Harhaiah, one of the goldsmiths, repaired the next section; and Hananiah, one of the perfume-makers, made repairs next to that. They restored Jerusalem as far as the Broad Wall. ⁹Rephaiah son of Hur, ruler of a half-district of Jerusalem, repaired the next section. ¹⁰Adjoining this, Jedaiah son of Harumaph made repairs opposite his house, and Hattush son of Hashabneiah made repairs next to him. ¹¹Malkijah son of Harim and Hasshub son of Pahath-Moab repaired another section and the Tower of the Ovens. ¹²Shallum son of Hallohesh, ruler of a half-district of Jerusalem, repaired the next section with the help of his daughters.

¹³The Valley Gate was repaired by Hanun and the residents of Zanoah. They rebuilt it and put its doors and bolts and bars in place. They also repaired five hundred yards of the wall as far as the Dung Gate.

COMMENTARY

8 "One of the goldsmiths" reflects the Hebrew *ben* ("son of," i.e., a member of a guild; cf. I. Mendelsohn, "Guilds in Ancient Palestine," *BASOR* 80 [1940]: 17–21). The industrial district of the goldsmiths and perfumers may have been located outside the walls (cf. vv.31–32).

"Perfume-makers" translates *raqqāḥîm*, which occurs only here, with the feminine form in 1 Samuel 8:13. The KJV translates the word "apothecaries." Mazar, 194, discovered at Tell Garsen by Ein Gedi evidence of perfume manufacture from the balsam ointment from Stratum V (ca. 630–582 BC). On ancient perfumes, see A. Brenner, "Aromatics and Perfumes in the Song of Songs," *JSOT* 25 (1983): 75–81; P. Faure, *Parfums et aromates de l'antiquité* (Paris: Fayard, 1987); K. Nielsen, "Ancient Aromas Good and Bad," *BRev* 7/3 (1991): 26–33.

"They restored" comes from *ʿāzab*, which means "to abandon" (cf. LXX's *katelipon*, "they left"). Some scholars cite words in cognate languages to support their belief that the word here must be a homonym meaning "to restore" or "to fortify" (cf. Akkad. *ušezib*, Ugar. *ʿdb*, Sabean *ʿdb*, etc.; see R. Gordis, *The Word and the Book* [New York: Ktav, 1976], 205). But Williamson ("Nehemiah's Walls Revisited," 82–83; cf. idem, "A Reconsideration of עזב II in Biblical Hebrew," *ZAW* 97 [1985]: 74–85) takes the term literally to mean that Nehemiah abandoned areas as far as the Broad Wall.

"The Broad Wall" (*haḥômâ hārᵉḥābâ*) is usually understood as a thick wall, but R. Grafman ("Nehemiah's 'Broad Wall,'" *IEJ* 24 [1974]: 50–51) interprets the phrase to mean a long, extensive wall. In 1970–71 N. Avigad ("Excavations in the Jewish Quarter of the Old City of Jerusalem, 1971 [Third Preliminary Report]," *IEJ* 22 [1972]: 193–200), discovered in the Jewish Quarter of Jerusalem a wall seven and one-half yards thick, three hundred yards west of the temple area, and cleared it for some forty-four yards. The wall is dated to the early seventh century BC and was probably built by Hezekiah (2Ch 32:5).

M. Broshi ("The Expansion of Jerusalem in the Reigns of Hezekiah and Manasseh," *IEJ* 24 [1974]: 21–26) surmises that the great expansion to and beyond the Broad Wall that caused a three-to-fourfold expansion of the city was occasioned by the influx of refugees from the fall of Samaria in 722 BC. Avigad believes that the wall, which curves to the west, turned southward to enclose the Pool of Siloam. But Kenyon (*Digging Up Jerusalem*, 148) holds that the wall must have turned to the east, as she found no evidence of an early settlement on the southwest hill. (On the wall, see N. Avigad, "Excavations in the Jewish Quarter," 129–40.)

9–10 "Rephaiah" ("Yahweh has healed") had charge of half the central district, one of the five districts of Judea. "Harumaph" ("split nose" or "flat nose") is found only here. It made sense to have him and others repair the sections of the wall nearest their homes.

11 If "Malkijah son of Harim" is the individual mentioned in Ezra 10:31, the reference could support the contemporaneity of Ezra and Nehemiah. "Hasshub," short for "Hashabiah" ("Yahweh has considered"), was one who sealed the covenant (10:23).

"Another section" clearly indicates that our list is only partial, as no first section is mentioned.

The NIV's "Tower of the Ovens" (*migdal hattannûrîm*) is preferable to the alternative translation, "tower of the furnaces" (KJV). This tower is mentioned only here and was located on the western wall, perhaps in the same location as the one Uzziah built at the Corner Gate (2Ch 26:9). The ovens may have been those situated in the bakers' street (Jer 37:21) or were possibly the kilns in the potters' quarter.

12 "Hallohesh" (*hallôḥēš*) is not a proper name but a participle that means "whisperer," in the sense of a snake charmer or an enchanter (Ps 58:5; Ecc 10:11). F Michaeli (*Les livres des Chroniques, d'Esdras et de Néhémie* [Neuchâtel: Delachaux et Niestlé, 1967], 316) comments, "It indicates, perhaps, a kind of guild rather than a family. He is the only person whose daughters are said also to work on the wall. Were these his actual daughters, or were they women practicing divination?"

"With the help of his daughters" is a unique reference to women working at the wall. When the Athenians attempted to rebuild their walls after the Persians had destroyed them, it was decreed that "the whole population of the city, men, women, and children, should take part in the wall-building" (*Thucydides* 1.90.3). Less likely is the attempt to translate the word "daughters" as "dependent" villages (cf. 11:25–31).

13 Avi-Yonah (*The Holy Land* [Grand Rapids: Baker, 1966], 22) comments: "The fact that Hanun and the inhabitants of Zanoah repaired a gate — a task usually left to a community rather than an individual — suggests that part of a district is meant here, with Hanun as its 'ruler.'"

"Five hundred yards" (lit., "a thousand cubits" — about 1,720 feet) is an extraordinary length, but probably most of the section was less damaged.

On the "Dung Gate," see comment on 2:13. Almost all scholars identify this gate with the one found by Bliss in the central (Tyropoeon) valley west of the Siloam Pool at the southern extremity of Ophel.

3. The Southern Section (3:14)

14The Dung Gate was repaired by Malkijah son of Recab, ruler of the district of Beth Hakkerem. He rebuilt it and put its doors and bolts and bars in place.

COMMENTARY

14 "Recab" ("rider") was also the name of the father of an ascetic clan, the Recabites (Jer 35).

"Beth Hakkerem" ("house of the vineyard") is mentioned in Jeremiah 6:1 as a fire-signal point. Y. Aharoni ("Beth-haccherem," in *Archaeology and Old Testament Study* [ed. D. W. Thomas; London: Oxford Univ. Press, 1967], 171–84) has identified the site with Ramat Rahel, two miles south of Jerusalem, which he excavated from 1954 to 1962. The site seems to have been the residence of a district governor in the Persian period.

4. The Eastern Section (3:15–32)

15The Fountain Gate was repaired by Shallun son of Col-Hozeh, ruler of the district of Mizpah. He rebuilt it, roofing it over and putting its doors and bolts and bars in place. He also repaired the wall of the Pool of Siloam, by the King's Garden, as far as the steps going down from the City of David. [16]Beyond him, Nehemiah son of Azbuk, ruler of a half-district of Beth Zur, made repairs up to a point opposite the tombs of David, as far as the artificial pool and the House of the Heroes.

[17]Next to him, the repairs were made by the Levites under Rehum son of Bani. Beside him, Hashabiah, ruler of half the district of Keilah, carried out repairs for his district. [18]Next to him, the repairs were made by their countrymen under Binnui son of Henadad, ruler of the other half-district of Keilah. [19]Next to him, Ezer son of Jeshua, ruler of Mizpah, repaired another section, from a point facing the ascent to the armory as far as the angle. [20]Next to him, Baruch son of Zabbai zealously repaired another section, from the angle to the entrance of the house of Eliashib the high priest. [21]Next to him, Meremoth son of Uriah, the son of Hakkoz, repaired another section, from the entrance of Eliashib's house to the end of it.

[22]The repairs next to him were made by the priests from the surrounding region. [23]Beyond them, Benjamin and Hasshub made repairs in front of their house; and next to them, Azariah son of Maaseiah, the son of Ananiah, made repairs beside his house. [24]Next to him, Binnui son of Henadad repaired another section, from Azariah's house to the angle and the corner, [25]and Palal son of Uzai worked opposite the angle and the tower projecting from the upper palace near the court of the guard. Next to him, Pedaiah son of Parosh [26]and the temple servants living on the hill of Ophel made repairs up to a point opposite the Water Gate toward the east and the projecting tower. [27]Next to them, the men of Tekoa repaired another section, from the great projecting tower to the wall of Ophel.

[28]Above the Horse Gate, the priests made repairs, each in front of his own house. [29]Next to them, Zadok son of Immer made repairs opposite his house. Next to him, Shemaiah son of Shecaniah, the guard at the East Gate, made repairs. [30]Next to him, Hananiah son of Shelemiah, and Hanun, the sixth son of Zalaph, repaired another section. Next to them, Meshullam son of Berekiah made repairs opposite his living quarters. [31]Next to him, Malkijah, one of the goldsmiths, made repairs as far as the house of the temple servants and the merchants, opposite the Inspection Gate, and as far as the room above the corner; [32]and between the room above the corner and the Sheep Gate the goldsmiths and merchants made repairs.

COMMENTARY

15 "The Fountain Gate" (*šaʿar hāʿayin*) may also be translated "Spring Gate." This gate may have faced the En-Rogel spring (see comment on 2:13). R. Weill identified it with a gate he discovered in 1923–24 in the eastern wall between the southern end of the city and the double wall of the Siloam Pool.

Mazar, 174, however, derives the name from its location at the point at which the Siloam tunnel emerged from the ground with water from the Gihon Spring, the fountain par excellence of Jerusalem.

"Col-Hozeh" (lit., "everyone a seer") may indicate that the family practiced divination (cf. M. Jastrow, "Rōʾeh and Hōzeh in the Old Testament," *JBL* 28 [1909]: 42–56).

The "Pool of Siloam [šelaḥ, 'sent'; 'Siloah,' KJV]," a canal or water channel, is probably to be associated with the water of šilōaḥ (Gk. *Silōam*). Isaiah 8:6 has the prophet accusing the Judeans of rejecting "the gently flowing waters of Shiloah." In 2005 the earliest phase of this pool, built by Hezekiah, was uncovered by E. Shukron and R. Reich below the staircase of the Siloam Pool of the NT era (cf. Jn 9:7). They uncovered three sets of stairs each with five steps from this pool, which was located southeast of the Byzantine pool at the exit of the Siloam tunnel. (See H. Shanks, "The Siloam Pool Where Jesus Cured the Blind Man," *BAR* 31/5 [2005]: 15–23.)

The "King's Garden" would have been located outside the walls where the Kidron and Hinnom valleys converge (2Ki 25:4).

16 "Azbuk" ("Buq is mighty") occurs only here. Beth Zur was a district capital twenty miles south of Jerusalem. Excavations conducted in 1931 and 1957 reveal that occupation was resumed in the fifth century BC and was sparse during the Persian period.

First Kings 2:10 and 2 Chronicles 21:20; 32:33 confirm that David was buried in the city area (2:5; cf. also Ac 2:29). The so-called "Tomb of David" on Mount Zion, venerated today by Jewish pilgrims, is in the Coenaculum building, constructed in the fourteenth century AD. Such a site for David's tomb is mentioned no earlier than the ninth century AD (see J. Finegan, *The Archaeology of the New Testament: The Life of Jesus and the Beginning of the Early Church* [rev. ed.; Princeton: Princeton Univ. Press, 1992], 236–42).

"The House of the Heroes" (*bêt haggibbōrîm,* lit., "house of the mighty men, champions" [1Sa 17:51], "warriors" [Isa 21:17]) may have been the house of David's mighty men, which served later as the barracks or the armory.

17–18 "Keilah" (v.17) was a city southwest of Jerusalem and eight miles northwest of Hebron situated near the border with the Philistines. It played an important role in David's early history (1Sa 23:1). For "Binnui" (v.18; cf. v.24; Ezr 2:10; 8:33) most Hebrew manuscripts read "Bavvai."

19 The last part of the verse is difficult to translate. The NAB reads, "the Corner, opposite the ascent to the arsenal"; the JB has, "opposite the slope up to the Armoury towards the Angle"; the NEB renders, "opposite the point at which the ascent meets the escarpment."

20 "Baruch" is literally "blessed." A feminine form, barūkā, occurs in the Murashu texts (Coogan, 16; cf. barik, idem, 69–70).

"Zealously" (heḥᵉrâ) is from the root "to glow, burn," usually used of anger but also of zeal, as here.

21 The residences of the high priest and his colleagues were located along the eastern wall of the city, corresponding with the retaining wall of the temple area above the Kidron Valley.

22 The Hebrew word kikkār ("the surrounding region") signifies something round as (1) a loaf of bread (1Sa 10:3); (2) a weight, namely a talent (1Ki 10:10); or (3) the lower plain of the Jordan Valley (Ge 13:10). Here it means the environs or surrounding territory.

23–24 On Benjamin (v.23), see comment on Ezra 10:32. The name "Hasshub" also occurs in v.11, so we have either two men with the same name or two sections about the same man. An ostracon with the name "Hasshub" was found in the Yarkon basin near Tel Aviv (J. Kaplan, "The Archaeology and History of Tel Aviv-Jaffa," *BA* 35 [1972]: 87). "Ananiah" ("Yahweh has manifested himself") occurs only here as a personal name; it occurs in 11:32 as a site. On "Henadad" (v.24), see Ezra 3:9.

25 "Palal" (possibly "[God] has judged") is found only here. "Uzai," perhaps short for "Azaniah" ("Yahweh has heard"), is also found only here. "Pedaiah" ("Yahweh has ransomed") occurs in the Murashu texts as *padayaw* (Coogan, 33).

"The upper palace" was probably the old palace of David. Like Solomon's palace it would have a guardhouse (Jer 32:2). The "Gate of the Guard" (12:39) was probably located nearby.

26 "Ophel" ("swelling" or "bulge," hence a hill) was specifically the northern part of the southeast hill of Jerusalem that formed the original city of David, just south of the temple area (2Ch 27:3; 33:14). Parts of the "wall of Ophel" were discovered by Charles Warren in 1867–1870.

"The Water Gate" was a gate, not of the city, but of the palace-temple complex. It was so named because it led to the main source of water, the Gihon Spring. It must have encompassed a large area, for the reading of the law took place there (8:1, 3, 16; 12:37). Other gates of the palace-temple were (1) the East Gate (v.29), (2) the Inspection Gate (v.31), and (3) the Gate of the Guard (12:39; cf. 1 Macc 4:57; 2 Macc 1:8).

"The projecting tower" was on the crest of the Ophel Hill. In 1923–25 R. A. S. Macalister discovered a large stepped-stone structure, which supported a large building above it. Some would identify it with the "great projecting tower." Kenyon dated the substructure to the fourteenth–thirteenth century BC and different parts of the structure to the tenth, eighth, and second centuries BC. J. Cahill, however, on the basis of the pottery found in Y. Shiloh's excavations, dates all the parts of the stepped-stone structure to the thirteenth-twelfth century (see J. Cahill, "Jerusalem in David and Solomon's Time," *BAR* 30/6 [2004]: 22–24).

Excavations in 1978 at the base of the tower revealed "for the first time in Jerusalem a Persian-period ceramic layer within clear stratigraphical context — solid archaeological evidence for that resettlement of the Babylonian exiles in the City of David" (Y. Shiloh, "City of David: Excavation 1978," *BA* 42 [1979]: 168).

27 The common people of Tekoa did double duty whereas the nobles of Tekoa shirked their responsibility (see v.5).

28 Athaliah entered "the entrance of the Horse Gate of the king's house" (NRSV; 2Ch 23:15) and was slain there. Jeremiah 31:40 states that the "Horse Gate," in the easternmost part of the city, was a gate through which one could reach the Kidron Valley.

29 The "East Gate" may have been the predecessor of the present "Golden Gate" (see Bowman, 694; S. Steckoll, *The Gates of Jerusalem* [New York: Praeger, 1968], 29–33). A storm that opened up a crack permitted the clandestine viewing of the arch of an earlier gate below the Golden Gate (G. Giacumakis, "The Gate below the Golden Gate," *NEASB* 4 [1974]: 23–26; J. Fleming, "The Undiscovered Gate beneath Jerusalem's Golden Gate," *BAR* 9/1 [1983]: 24–37).

30 "The sixth son of Zalaph" is an unparalleled expression. Perhaps the text is a corruption for "inhabitants of Zanoah."

31 Some of the goldsmiths apparently inhabited an area to the east of the walls of the temple area; others, however, worked on sections in the west (see v.8 above). Myers, 111, suggests that the "house" was not a residence but a building where temple functions were performed.

"The Inspection Gate" was in the northern part of the eastern temple. The word for "inspection," *mipqād*, is found in only four other passages besides this verse: (1) in 2 Samuel 24:9 and Chronicles 21:5, where it means "numbering, mustering"; (2) in 2 Chronicles 31:13, where it refers to the "appointment" of supervisors; and (3) in Ezekiel 43:21, where it means the "appointed" place for the sin offering to be burned.

32 This verse brings us to the northeastern corner of Jerusalem or back to the point of departure near the Sheep Gate (v.1).

NOTE

15 Divination (i.e., the art of foretelling the future) was widely practiced in the ancient world in Mesopotamia, Egypt, Canaan, Greece, and Rome. There are also references to such practices in Israel. See O. Eissfeldt, "Wahrsagung im Alten Testament," in *La divination en Mésopotamie et dans les régions voisines* (Paris: Presses Universitaires de France, 1966), 141–46; A. Caquot, "La divination dans l'ancien Israël," in *La Divination* (ed. A. Caquot and M. Leibovici; Paris: Presses Universitaires de France, 1968), 1:83–114; J. R. Porter, "Ancient Israel," in *Divination and Oracles* (ed. M. Loewe and C. Blacker; London: George Allen & Unwin, 1981), 215–32.

D. Opposition to the Rebuilding of the Walls (4:1–23 [3:33–4:17])

1. The Derision of Sanballat and Tobiah (4:1–5 [3:33–37])

¹When Sanballat heard that we were rebuilding the wall, he became angry and was greatly incensed. He ridiculed the Jews, ²and in the presence of his associates and the army of Samaria, he said, "What are those feeble Jews doing? Will they restore their wall? Will they offer sacrifices? Will they finish in a day? Can they bring the stones back to life from those heaps of rubble — burned as they are?"

³Tobiah the Ammonite, who was at his side, said, "What they are building — if even a fox climbed up on it, he would break down their wall of stones!"

⁴Hear us, O our God, for we are despised. Turn their insults back on their own heads. Give them over as plunder in a land of captivity. ⁵Do not cover up their guilt or blot out their sins from your sight, for they have thrown insults in the face of the builders.

COMMENTARY

1 [3:33] The enumeration of the MT does not correspond to the English; 4:1 [3:33] (see Notes). On "Sanballat," see the comment on 2:10.

"Became angry" derives from *ḥārâ*, which means "to be hot," as in "his nose became hot," that is, his anger broke out (Ge 30:2; cf. 3:20; Ezr 10:14).

"Was greatly incensed" (from *kāʿas*) means "to be irritated" (cf. the reaction of Sanballat and his colleagues when they first heard of Nehemiah's arrival [2:19]).

Rabinowitz (*Nehemiah*) comments on this verse, "Not even the enemies of the settlers believed at first that this one man, Nehemiah, could make a difference. As they watched the efforts of his labor bear fruit, their concern turned to mockery and, finally, extreme anger. The realization that the Jews were actually completing the wall enraged them."

2 [3:34] "The army" translates ḥêl, which often means "strength, wealth," but at times "army" (Ex 14:4; 2Ki 6:14; Est 8:11; Eze 17:17). The LXX interprets it as part of a taunt: "So this is Samaria's strength, that the Judeans build a city!" Disputes between rival Persian governors were frequent, for example, the rivalry between the satraps Tissaphernes and Pharnabazus in western Asia Minor.

Sanballat rapidly fired five derisive questions to taunt the Jews and discourage them from their efforts.

(1) "What are those feeble Jews doing'?" The word "feeble" (ᵃmēlāl) is used only here in the sense of "frail, miserable, withered, powerless." The JB renders the phrase "pathetic Jews" (cf. the cognate words ᵃmulâ, "hot, feverish, weak" [Eze 16:30], and ᵓumlal, "to be frail, be in anguish, languish" [Ps 6:3]).

(2) "Will they restore their wall?" The word translated "restore" usually means "to abandon" (see comment on 3:8).

(3) "Will they offer sacrifices?" The Jews eventually succeeded in offering sacrifices (12:43).

(4) "Will they finish in a day?" Despite the furious activity of the Jews, the work seemed so great that it could hardly be finished in a short time.

(5) "Can they bring the stones back to life ... burned as they are?" Fire had damaged the stones, which were probably limestone, and had caused much of the stone to crack and disintegrate.

3 [3:35] On Tobiah, see the comment on 2:10. The word translated "fox" (šûʿāl) occurs elsewhere in the OT (in Jdg 15:4; Ps 63:10; SS 2:15; La 5:18; Eze 13:4). In some contexts it may designate "jackal." The jackal usually hunts in packs, whereas the fox is normally a nocturnal and solitary animal. The context, therefore, suggests that a fox is intended: the point of the sneer is that any wall the Jews built would be so flimsy that even the light footsteps of a solitary fox would collapse it (cf. G. Cansdale, *All the Animals of the Bible Lands* [Grand Rapids: Zondervan, 1970], 124–26; H. Hoehner, "The Meaning of 'Fox,'" in *Herod Antipas* [Grand Rapids: Zondervan, 1972], 343–47).

4–5 [3:36–37] Compare 6:9, 14; 13:29. As in the imprecatory psalms (Pss 69:22–28; 79:12; 94; 109:14; 137:8–9; cf. *ZPEB*, 4:938–39), Nehemiah did not personally take action against his opponents but called down the vengeance of God. Ackroyd, 277–78, remarked, "To understand such violent language, we need to appreciate fully the sense of the divine purpose at work, so that opposition is not seen in human terms but as opposition to God himself." Nehemiah's prayer borrows from the language of Jeremiah (Jer 12:3; 17:18; 18:21–23).

NOTES

1 [3:33] The verses of the EV do not follow the versification of the MT. The correspondences are as follows:

Masoretic Text	English Versions
3:33	4:1

(Continue on the next page)

(Continued)

3:38	4:6
4:1	4:7
4:17	4:23

2 **[3:34]** H. Tadmor ("Some Aspects of the History of Samaria during the Biblical Period," *Jerusalem Cathedra* 3 [1983]: 9) comments: "The reference to the 'army of Samaria' ... is of special interest. It indicates that in the Persian Empire, as in the Assyrian Empire that preceded it, Samaria was the site of a military garrison (cf. Josephus, *Ant.* 11.321; 342; 345). This is in contrast to Jerusalem, which preserved its status as a temple city and enlisted a 'home guard' from among its population only during periods of emergency."

2. The Threat of Attack (4:6–15 [3:38–4:9])

⁶So we rebuilt the wall till all of it reached half its height, for the people worked with all their heart.

⁷But when Sanballat, Tobiah, the Arabs, the Ammonites and the men of Ashdod heard that the repairs to Jerusalem's walls had gone ahead and that the gaps were being closed, they were very angry. ⁸They all plotted together to come and fight against Jerusalem and stir up trouble against it. ⁹But we prayed to our God and posted a guard day and night to meet this threat.

¹⁰Meanwhile, the people in Judah said, "The strength of the laborers is giving out, and there is so much rubble that we cannot rebuild the wall."

¹¹Also our enemies said, "Before they know it or see us, we will be right there among them and will kill them and put an end to the work."

¹²Then the Jews who lived near them came and told us ten times over, "Wherever you turn, they will attack us."

¹³Therefore I stationed some of the people behind the lowest points of the wall at the exposed places, posting them by families, with their swords, spears and bows. ¹⁴After I looked things over, I stood up and said to the nobles, the officials and the rest of the people, "Don't be afraid of them. Remember the Lord, who is great and awesome, and fight for your brothers, your sons and your daughters, your wives and your homes."

¹⁵When our enemies heard that we were aware of their plot and that God had frustrated it, we all returned to the wall, each to his own work.

COMMENTARY

6 **[3:38]** "The people worked with all their heart" is literally "the people had a heart to work."

7 **[4:1]** On Sanballat and Tobiah, see comment on 2:10. On the Arabs, see comment at 2:19; on the Ammonites, at Ezra 9:1. Josephus (*Ant.* 11.174 [5.8]) also mentions the Moabites.

Ashdod, along with Ashkelon, Gaza, Ekron, and Gath, was one of the five major Philistine cities in the Late Bronze Age (Jos 11:22; 13:3). Ashdod was overrun by the Assyrians in the eighth century BC (Isa 20:1). As the prophets foretold (Jer 25:20; Zep 2:4; Zec 9:6), Ashdod was then captured by the Neo-Babylonians (*ANET*, 308). With the Persian conquest alternate patches of the Palestinian coast were parceled out to the Phoenician cities of Tyre and Sidon, which provided ships for the Persian navy.

The site of Tel Ashdod was excavated from 1962–1972 by M. Dothan ("Ashdod," in *EAEHL*, 1:103–19). Ashdod was the most important city on the Philistine coast. As it was inland, it had a separate harbor at the coastal site of Ashdod-Yam. Stern, 407, reports:

> At Ashdod, a Persian-period occupation level (Stratum V) was uncovered in two separate areas. This stratum was almost totally destroyed by Hellenistic buildings, but in one area, remains of a large structure, possibly a public building, were discovered. It was built in brick on stone foundations. Despite the meager architectural remains, the excavator, M. Dothan, succeeded in distinguishing three superimposed Persian-period phases dating from the end of the 6th to the 4th centuries BCE. The two areas yielded many finds associated with this period, including an ostracon that mentions a shipment of wine.

8–9 [2–3] "Plotted together" (v.8) comes from *qāšar*, which means "to tie up," hence "to conspire" (cf. 1Ki 15:27; 16:20).

"Trouble" (*tôʿâ*, "confusion, chaos, perversion") occurs here and in Isaiah 32:6. Notice the balance between prayer and posting a guard (v.9).

10 [4] "Laborers," *sabbāl* ("burden bearer, porter"), occurs only here and in 1 Kings 5:15; 2 Chronicles 2:2, 18; 34:13.

"Is giving out" (from *kāšal*, "to stumble, to totter"; cf. Isa 3:8) depicts a worker tottering under the weight of his load and ready to fall at any step. The complaint, couched in poetic form in two lines of five words each, may reflect a song sung by the builders. Myers, 122, renders the refrain as follows:

> The strength of the burden bearer is drooping.
>> The rubbish heap so vast;
> And we are unable by ourselves
>> To rebuild the wall.

11 [5] "Enemies" (plural of *ṣar*, "adversary") would cause harm. A different word is used in v.15 (q.v.). Nehemiah must have had good sources of information to learn of these plots. The text indicates that the vigilance of Nehemiah and his fellow Jews forestalled any attempt at violent attack.

12 [6] "Ten times over" is an idiomatic expression for "again and again" (Ge 31:41). The NRSV emends *tāšûbû* ("you turn") to *yēšᵉbû* ("they live") and translates "from all the places where *they live* they will come up against us" (emphasis mine). This corresponds with the LXX's "They are coming against us from all sides."

13 [7] "The exposed places" (plural of *ṣᵉḥîaḥ*) derives from the verb *ṣāḥaḥ*, which means "to be white," thus a bare or exposed place. The word occurs only here and in Ezekiel 24:7; 26:4, 14. The related word *ṣᵉḥîḥâ* ("bare, scorched land") occurs only in Psalm 68:6. Nehemiah posted men conspicuously in those areas most vulnerable along the wall—"the lowest points."

14–15 [8–9] The best way to dispel fear—"Don't be afraid of them" (v.14; cf. Dt 3:22; 20:3; 31:6)—is to remember the Lord, who alone is to be feared. "Enemies" (v.15) is the plural of *ʾōyēb* (cf. Ezr 8:22, 31; Ne 5:9; 6:1, 16; 9:27–28).

3. The Rebuilding of the Walls (4:16–23 [10–17])

¹⁶From that day on, half of my men did the work, while the other half were equipped with spears, shields, bows and armor. The officers posted themselves behind all the people of Judah ¹⁷who were building the wall. Those who carried materials did their work with one hand and held a weapon in the other, ¹⁸and each of the builders wore his sword at his side as he worked. But the man who sounded the trumpet stayed with me.

¹⁹Then I said to the nobles, the officials and the rest of the people, "The work is extensive and spread out, and we are widely separated from each other along the wall. ²⁰Wherever you hear the sound of the trumpet, join us there. Our God will fight for us!"

²¹So we continued the work with half the men holding spears, from the first light of dawn till the stars came out. ²²At that time I also said to the people, "Have every man and his helper stay inside Jerusalem at night, so they can serve us as guards by night and workmen by day." ²³Neither I nor my brothers nor my men nor the guards with me took off our clothes; each had his weapon, even when he went for water.

COMMENTARY

16 [10] "My men" derives from *na⁽ar*, which can mean "boy, youth" (Ge 19:4); "young men" (1Sa 30:17); "servants" (Ge 22:3); "a young man bearing armor" (1Sa 14:1); and the member of a personal military retinue (1Sa 21:2, 4). The term is used of the bodyguard of Nehemiah in 5:10 and 13:19.

"Spears" (*r⁽māḥîm*) designates lances or spears with long shafts used as thrusting weapons (Nu 25:7–8; 1Ki 18:28). "Shields" (*māginnîm*) were small and round and were made of wood and wickerwork, for they were combustible (Eze 39:9). From 2 Chronicles 18:33 it seems that *širyôn* ("armor") primarily designated breastplates of metal, or more probably of mail, joined to a lower appendage. In some cases such cuirasses may have been made of leather (cf. 1Sa 17:38; 1Ki 22:34; 2Ch 26:14).

17 [11] "Weapon" translates *šelaḥ*, a "missile" or "javelin." The literal meaning would be that the burden-bearers were so loaded that they could

carry their loads with one hand and their weapons with the other. Others construe the meaning that the weapons were kept close at hand.

18–19 [12–13] "Swords" were worn in a sheath (1Sa 17:51) hung on a girdle (1Sa 17:39; 18:4; 25:13; Ps 45:3). The trumpet mentioned here is the *šôpār*, or ram's horn (Jos 6:4, 6, 8, 13), used for signaling as in times of attack (Nu 10:5–10).

The MT and Vulgate suggest that a single trumpeter accompanied Nehemiah; but the LXX and Peshitta, reading "next to him" (i.e., the builder), suggest a system of alarms. Josephus (*Ant.* 11.177 [5.8]) claims that Nehemiah stationed trumpeters at intervals of five hundred feet.

20 [14] For the concept of the "holy war" in which God fights for his people, see de Vaux, *Ancient Israel*, 258–67 (cf. Jos 10:14, 42; Jdg 4:14; 20:35; 2Sa 5:24).

21 [15] Work usually ceased at sunset (Dt 24:15; Mt 20:1–12). To work "till the stars came out" (cf.

Job 9:9) indicates the earnestness of the people's efforts.

22 [16] "His helper" is literally "his young man" or "servant" (cf. v.16 above). Though the ratio of returning slaves to free men was relatively high (see Ezr 2:65), it is improbable that each builder had a servant. More plausibly each builder had a young man as an assistant. Even those from outside Jerusalem stayed in the city at night so that some of them could serve as sentries.

23 [17] The last three words of this verse — ʾîš šilḥô hammāyim — are notoriously difficult to interpret; they are literally "each man his weapon the water." Several possible interpretations of this puzzling phrase follow:

(1) The NIV's rendering is similar to that of the RV: "every one (went with) his weapon (to) the water," and the JPS's "every one that went to the water had his weapon." This technique would parallel the way Gideon's selected men drank their water with weapons in hand as an indication of their vigilance.

(2) Many scholars would emend the word *hammāyim* ("water") to *bîmînô* ("in his right hand"); cf. the NEB's "each keeping his right hand on his weapon" and the NRSV's "each kept his weapon in his right hand").

(3) The Vulgate took the word *šilḥô* not in the sense of "his weapon" but as a verb meaning "stripped himself": *unusquisque tantum nudabatur ad baptismum* ("every one stripped himself when he was to be washed"). This sense was followed by the KJV: "every one put them off for washing."

(4) The LXX omitted the phrase altogether.

(5) The medieval commentator Rashi (1040–1105) interpreted the phrase to mean, "None of us disrobed [even to launder our garments] in water."

Though the precise meaning of the verse is not clear, the implication is that constant preparedness was the rule. According to Josephus (*Ant.* 11.178 [5.8]), Nehemiah "himself made the rounds of the city by night, never tiring either through work or lack of food and sleep, neither of which he took for pleasure but as a necessity." Williamson (*Ezra, Nehemiah*, 229) well summarizes the import of this verse: "Whether awake or asleep, however, Nehemiah and his immediate entourage ... set an example of constant vigilance. With a weapon to hand and dressed at all times for action, they could not be accused of laying harder burdens on others than they themselves were willing to shoulder."

E. Social and Economic Problems (5:1–19)

1. The Complaints of the Poor (5:1–5)

OVERVIEW

The economic crisis faced by Nehemiah is described in ch. 5, in the middle of his major effort to rebuild the walls of Jerusalem. Since the building of the wall lasted only fifty-two days (6:15), many scholars have considered it unlikely that Nehemiah would have called a great assembly (v.7) in the midst of such a project. Taking v.14 as retrospective, they suggest that the assembly was called only after the rebuilding of the wall.

Nevertheless, the economic pressure created by the rebuilding program may have brought to light problems long simmering that had to be solved before work could proceed. E. Neufeld ("The Rate of Interest and the Text of Nehemiah 5:11," *JQR* 44 [1953–54]: 203–4) holds this position.

Among the classes affected by the economic crisis were (1) the landless, who were short of food (v.2); (2) the landowners, who were compelled to mortgage their properties (v.3); (3) those forced to borrow money at exorbitant rates because of oppressive taxation (v.4); and (4) those forced to sell their children into slavery (v.5).

> ¹Now the men and their wives raised a great outcry against their Jewish brothers. ²Some were saying, "We and our sons and daughters are numerous; in order for us to eat and stay alive, we must get grain."
>
> ³Others were saying, "We are mortgaging our fields, our vineyards and our homes to get grain during the famine."
>
> ⁴Still others were saying, "We have had to borrow money to pay the king's tax on our fields and vineyards. ⁵Although we are of the same flesh and blood as our countrymen and though our sons are as good as theirs, yet we have to subject our sons and daughters to slavery. Some of our daughters have already been enslaved, but we are powerless, because our fields and our vineyards belong to others."

COMMENTARY

1 The gravity of the situation is underscored in that the wives joined in the protest as the people ran short of funds and supplies to feed their families. Williamson (*Ezra, Nehemiah*, 236) notes, "Nehemiah had forbidden the men to return home from Jerusalem while the wall was being built, the farms may have been severely understaffed during the crucial period of ingathering." It is significant that their complaints were not lodged against the foreign authorities but against their own fellow countrymen who were exploiting their poorer brethren at a time when both were needed to defend the country.

2 Some would prefer to read *rabbîm* ("numerous") as *ʿōrᵉbîm* ("taken for pledge"), as in v.3 (cf. Ex 21:2; Lev 25:39–41; Dt 15:12). Thus the NEB renders "daughters as pledges."

3 Economic conditions forced even owners of considerable property to mortgage to the aggran-

dizement of the wealthy few (cf. Isa 5:8). The rich got richer, the poor poorer.

The economic situation was aggravated by the natural conditions that had produced a famine. Some seventy-five years earlier the prophet Haggai had referred to a time of drought, when food was insufficient (Hag 1:5–11). Such hardships were considered expressions of God's judgment (Isa 51:19; Jer 14:13–18; Am 4:6). In times of dire need the wealthy usually had enough stored up to feed themselves. It was the poor who suffer because of the huge rise in prices caused by scarcities.

4 K. G. Hoglund (*Achaemenid Imperial Administration in Syria-Palestine and the Missions of Ezra and Nehemiah* [Atlanta: Scholars, 1992], 212–14) suggests that heavy military expenditures by the Persians at this time may have raised the need for even greater tax revenue. It is estimated that the Persian king collected the equivalent of twenty million darics a year in taxes. As A. T. Olmstead (*History of the Persian Empire* [Chicago: Univ. of Chicago Press, 1948], 298) points out: "Little of this vast sum was ever returned to the satrapies. It was the custom to melt down the gold and silver and to pour it into jars which were then broken and the bullion stored." At Susa alone, Alexander found nine thousand talents of coined gold (about two hundred seventy tons) and forty thousand talents of silver (about twelve hundred tons) stored up as bullion.

As coined money was increasingly taken out of circulation, inflation became rampant. As M. Dandamayev ("Achaemenid Babylonia," in *Ancient Mesopotamia* [ed. I. M. Diakonoff; Moscow: Nauka, 1969], 308) observes:

> Documents from Babylonia show that many inhabitants of this satrapy too had to mortgage their fields and orchards to get silver for the payment of taxes to the king. In many cases they were unable to redeem their property, and became landless hired labourers; sometimes they were compelled to give away their children into slavery.

The acquisition of land by the Persians and its alienation from production helped produce a 50 percent rise in prices (W. H. Dubberstein, "Comparative Prices in Later Babylonia," *AJSL* 56 [1939]: 20–43).

5 "Some of our daughters have already been enslaved [from *kābaš*, 'to subjugate']." As *kābaš* can mean "to rape a woman" (cf. Est 7:8), the JB renders "have even been raped." But the context favors the rendering "enslaved." In times of economic distress, families would borrow funds using members of the family as collateral. If a man could not repay the loan and its interest, his daughters, his sons, his wife, or even the man himself could be sold into bondage. A Hebrew who fell into debt would serve his creditor as "a hired worker" (Lev 25:39–40). He was to be released in the seventh year (Dt 15:12–18), unless he chose to stay voluntarily. The Code of Hammurabi (#117, *ANET*, 170–71) limited such bondservice to three years.

The ironic tragedy of the situation for the exiles was that at least in Mesopotamia, their families were together. Now, because of dire economic necessities, their children were being sold into slavery.

NOTES

4 An extensive discussion of taxes and tributes may be found in Briant, 399–410. The extensive archive of the Egibi family sheds detailed light on the collection of taxes in the late Persian Empire. See also K. Abraham, *Business and Politics under the Persian Empire* (Bethesda: CDL, 2004); Tuplin, "The Administration of the Achaemenid Empire," in Carradice, 137–43, 153–58.

5 On slavery among the Hebrews and the ancient Near East, see E. Lipinski, "L'esclave hébreu," *VT* 26 (1976): 120–24; M. A. Dandamaev, *Slavery in Babylonia* (DeKalb, Ill.: Northern Illinois Univ. Press, 1984); J. M. Lindenberger, "How Much for a Hebrew Slave? The Meaning of Mišneh in Deut. 15:18," *JBL* 110 (1991): 479–82; G. C. Chirichigno, *Debt Slavery in Israel and the Ancient Near East* (Sheffield: JSOT, 1993); J. Van Seters, "The Law of the Hebrew Slave (Ex 21:2–11; Lev 25:39–46; Deut 15:12–18," *ZAW* 4 (1996): 534–46; C. Pressler, "Wives and Daughters, Bond and Free: Views of Women in the Slave Laws of Exodus 21:2–11," and R. Westbrook, "The Female Slave," in *Gender and Law in the Hebrew Bible and the Ancient Near East* (ed. V. Matthews et al.; Sheffield: Sheffield Academic, 1998), 147–72, 214–38.

2. The Cancellation of Debts (5:6–13)

⁶When I heard their outcry and these charges, I was very angry. ⁷I pondered them in my mind and then accused the nobles and officials. I told them, "You are exacting usury from your own countrymen!" So I called together a large meeting to deal with them ⁸and said: "As far as possible, we have bought back our Jewish brothers who were sold to the Gentiles. Now you are selling your brothers, only for them to be sold back to us!" They kept quiet, because they could find nothing to say.

⁹So I continued, "What you are doing is not right. Shouldn't you walk in the fear of our God to avoid the reproach of our Gentile enemies? ¹⁰I and my brothers and my men are also lending the people money and grain. But let the exacting of usury stop! ¹¹Give back to them immediately their fields, vineyards, olive groves and houses, and also the usury you are charging them — the hundredth part of the money, grain, new wine and oil."

¹²"We will give it back," they said. "And we will not demand anything more from them. We will do as you say."

Then I summoned the priests and made the nobles and officials take an oath to do what they had promised. ¹³I also shook out the folds of my robe and said, "In this way may God shake out of his house and possessions every man who does not keep this promise. So may such a man be shaken out and emptied!"

At this the whole assembly said, "Amen," and praised the LORD. And the people did as they had promised.

COMMENTARY

6 Nehemiah "was very angry." There are times when we must speak out against social injustices (cf. Mt 21:18–19; Mk 11:12–18; Lk 19:45–48; Eph 4:26).

7 "Pondered" renders the Niphal of *mālak* ("to take counsel with oneself"); the NEB renders "I mastered my feelings."

"Accused" derives from *rîb*, which means "to dispute, quarrel, conduct a lawsuit with." The NEB renders "reasoned with"; the NRSV has "brought charges against."

The Hebrew word *maššāʾ*, which occurs only here and in 10:31[32], does not really mean "usury," which connotes the exaction of interest, often at exorbitant rates; rather, it means to impose a burden or claim for repayment of debt. Compare the related word *maššāʾâ* ("secured loan based on security"; Dt 24:10; Pr 22:26).

A seventh-century BC letter written in Hebrew on an ostracon from Meṣad Hashavyahu, on the coast of Israel, bears the poignant plea of a poor farmer whose garment had been taken by the governor's officer but had not been returned, in contravention of Exodus 22:26–27 (see J. Naveh, "A Hebrew Letter From the Time of Jeremiah," *Arch* 15/2 [1962]: 108–11).

The OT passages (Ex 22:25–27; Lev 25:35–37; Dt 23:19–20; 24:10–13) prohibiting the giving of loans at interest were not intended to prohibit commercial loans but rather the charging of interest to the impoverished so as to make a profit from the helplessness of one's neighbors (E. Neufeld, "The Prohibition against Loans at Interest in Ancient Hebrew Laws," *HUCA* 26 [1955]: 355–412; cf. Josephus, *Ant.* 4.266 [8.25]). Clines, 168, notes that despite the prohibition, there were attested instances of such practices according to Psalm 15:5 and Proverbs 28:8 (cf. Eze 18:8, 13, 17).

8 Though it was possible to use a poor brother as a bondservant, he was not to be sold as a slave (Lev 25:39–42). The sale of fellow Hebrews as slaves to Gentiles was a particularly callous offense and was always forbidden (Ex 21:8). Joseph's brothers nonetheless sold him to the Egyptians. We know from Joel 3:6 that Jews were being sold to Greeks (ca. 520 BC; cf. J. M. Myers, "Some Considerations Bearing on the Date of Joel," *ZAW* 74 [1962]: 177–95). The people's guilt was so obvious that "they kept quiet," having no rebuttal or excuse (cf. Jn 8:7–10). Blenkinsopp, 259, observes: "Phoenicians, Greeks, and Arabs, all of whom had commercial interests in the province, were involved in the lucrative slave trade (cf. Eze 27:13; Joel 3[4]:3, 4–8; Am 1:9), and it would be unremarkable if the assimilationist Judean aristocracy also had a hand in it."

9 Failure to treat others, especially fellow believers, with mercy is an insult to our Maker and a blot on our testimony (cf. Pr 14:31; 1Pe 2:12–15).

10 The granting of loans is not condemned, nor is the making of profit (cf. Sir 42:1–5a). But

the OT condemns the greed and avarice that seeks profit at the expense of people (Ps 119:36; Isa 56:9–12; 57:17; Jer 6:13; 8:10; 22:13–19; Eze 22:12–14; 33:31). In view of the urgency of the situation, Nehemiah urged the creditors to relinquish their rights to repayment with interest. Solon, the great Athenian reformer (594 BC), adopted a similar policy (cf. E. Yamauchi, "Two Reformers Compared: Solon of Athens and Nehemiah of Jerusalem," in *The Bible World* [ed. G. Rendsburg et al.; New York: Ktav, 1980], 269–92).

11 "The hundredth part" (*mēʾâ*) literally means the "hundred" pieces of silver. But in the context it must mean 1 percent, that is, per month, or as the Vulgate translates it, *centesiman pecuniae.*

12–13 On "oath" (v.12), see comment on Ezra 10:5. *Ḥōṣen* (v.13; cf. Akkad. *ḥuṣannu*) means "robe, sash, girdle." The KJV and RV translate the word "lap." Here it probably refers to the fold of the robe or the sash in which objects were kept.

On "Amen" compare Numbers 5:22 and Deuteronomy 27:15–26, where the people also assented to an oath and its curse formula by saying "Amen." "Amen" is derived from the verbal root *ʾmn*, which means in the Hiphil "to believe, trust" and in the Niphal "to be reliable."

"Amen" occurs in the OT only twenty-four times, with twelve of these occurrences in Deuteronomy 27:15–26. It is used in passages that praise God (e.g., 1Ch 16:36; Ne 8:6; cf. 1Co 14:16) and in doxologies (e.g., Pss 41; 72; 89; 106).

NOTES

7 The OT passages on loans and interest have had an enormous impact on Western civilization, as they were later interpreted for many centuries to prohibit the lending of money at interest.

The Jewish rabbis permitted loans at interest to Gentiles but condemned usury among fellow Jews as tantamount to denying God and to the shedding of blood. Moneylenders were classed together with gamblers, pigeon trainers, and Sabbath traders and were excluded from serving as witnesses (*m. Sanh.* 3:3). A legal fiction called *prosbul*, ascribed to Hillel the Elder, avoided the abrogation of debts on the sabbatical year by assigning the debts to courts (*m. Šeb.* 10:3).

Charging interest was a sufficiently accepted practice, for Jesus mentioned investments as sources of income without condemnation in his parable of the talents (Mt 25:14–30). The servant who buried his talent in the ground (v.25), rather than putting it on deposit with a banker (*trapezitēs*, v.27) to earn interest, was rebuked. In the parable of the pounds (Lk 19:11–27), the master entrusted each of ten servants with a *mina* (one hundred drachmas). One servant earned for his master an astounding 1000 percent increase, and another a 500 percent increase, but the third simply kept his money in a cloth and was rebuked by the master for not having "placed it on deposit" *epi trapezan* (v.23).

Early church councils, such as the councils of Elvira (AD 305), Arles (314), and Nicaea (325), condemned clerics who made money by offering loans at interest. Later councils, such as those of Carthage (345) and Aix (789), also condemned laymen who loaned money at interest. Medieval councils, such as the Third Lateran (1179), the Second of Lyons (1274), and of Vienne (1311), absolutely condemned moneylending, with the ironic result that the Jews became the moneylenders of Europe. Luther, Melanchthon, and Zwingli also condemned loans with interest.

Among early Muslims, prohibitions were enacted against *riba*, or usurious loans (Qurʾan 2:275–78; 3:130; 4:160–61; 30:39; 7:157). Before Muhammad died, he exhorted the Arabs to remain united, proclaimed the duties of married couples, and abolished the blood feud and usury. To get around this prohibition, modern Islamic banks do not charge or pay interest but instead offer *mudarabah* or "sleeping partnerships," which allow profits.

8 D. M. Gropp (*Wadi Daliyeh II: The Samaria Papyri from Wadi Daliyeh* [Oxford: Clarendon, 2001], 7) comments: "In the deeds of slave sale, slaves are sold outright 'in perpetuity' (ʿlmʾ) and are inherited by the buyer's children. Since sellers, slaves, and buyers tend to bear Yahwistic names, this outright sale directly violates Leviticus 25:39–47 (compare also Jer 34:8–17). The Samarians did not make the required distinction between their brothers and foreigners."

3. Nehemiah's Unselfish Example (5:14–19)

¹⁴Moreover, from the twentieth year of King Artaxerxes, when I was appointed to be their governor in the land of Judah, until his thirty-second year — twelve years — neither I nor my brothers ate the food allotted to the governor. ¹⁵But the earlier governors — those preceding me — placed a heavy burden on the people and took forty shekels of silver from them in addition to food and wine. Their assistants also lorded it over the people. But out of reverence for God I did not act like that. ¹⁶Instead, I devoted myself to the work on this wall. All my men were assembled there for the work; we did not acquire any land.

¹⁷Furthermore, a hundred and fifty Jews and officials ate at my table, as well as those who came to us from the surrounding nations. ¹⁸Each day one ox, six choice sheep and

some poultry were prepared for me, and every ten days an abundant supply of wine of all kinds. In spite of all this, I never demanded the food allotted to the governor, because the demands were heavy on these people.

¹⁹Remember me with favor, O my God, for all I have done for these people.

COMMENTARY

14 The thirty-second year of Artaxerxes I ran from April 1, 433 BC, to April 19, 432 BC. Nehemiah served his first term as governor for twelve years before being recalled to court (13:6), after which he returned for a second term of indeterminate length.

Provincial governors normally assessed the people in their provinces for their support, e.g., "food allotted to the governor." But Nehemiah, like Paul, bent over backwards and sacrificed even what was normally his due to serve as an example to the people (1Co 9; 2Th 3:8).

15 "Governors" is the plural of *peḥâ* (the same in Aram.), which is used of Sheshbazzar (Ezr 5:14), Zerubbabel (Hag 1:1, 14; 2:2), and various Persian officials (Ezr 5:3, 6; 6:6–7, 13; 8:36; Ne 2:7, 9; 3:7 et al.).

Nehemiah was certainly not referring here to Ezra and Zerubbabel. K. Galling ("Serubbabel und der Wiederaufbau des Tempels," in *Verbannung und Heimkehr* [ed. A. Kuschke; Tübingen: J. C. B. Mohr, 1961], 96) believes that Judah did not have governors before Nehemiah and suggests that this refers to governors of Samaria. New archaeological evidence, however, confirms that the reference is to previous governors of Judah.

"Placed a heavy burden" means literally "made heavy [the burden of taxation]." The KJV's "were chargeable" is an inadequate rendering. Persian practice usually exempted temple personnel, thus making the burden on the laity much heavier.

"Forty shekels of silver from them in addition to food and wine" is literally "of them for bread and wine after [ʾaḥar] forty shekels of silver." The NIV follows the lead of the KJV/RSV/NRSV ("besides") in rendering the preposition "in addition." Other scholars and versions follow the Vulgate, which reads "daily," that is, the cost of feeding the entourage amounted to about forty shekels per day (cf. comment on v.2).

If the governors themselves were extortionate, their "assistants" often proved even more oppressive (cf. Mt 18:21–35; 20:25–28).

16 Nehemiah's behavior as governor was guided by principles of service rather than by opportunism. In the Roman period honest governors like Cicero were exceptional. Roman governors who came to Palestine were rapacious (cf. Josephus, *J.W.* 2.272–73 [14.1]).

17 When Solomon became king, he sacrificed 22,000 oxen and 120,000 sheep and held a great seven-day feast for the assembly (1Ki 4:23; 8:62–65). A text found at Nimrud has Ashurnasirpal II feasting 69,574 people for ten days (D. J. Wiseman, "A New Stele of Aššurnasirpal II," *Iraq* 14 [1952]: 24–44).

As part of his social responsibility, a governor or ruler was expected to entertain lavishly. R. North ("Civil Authority in Ezra," in *Studi in onore di Edoardo Volterra* [Milan: A Giuffre, 1971], 436) comments, "The generosity of Nehemiah as of wealthy Bedouin sheiks is felt to consist in the fact that they let any number of poor relations come to dinner."

18 Compare Nehemiah's daily provisions with Solomon's (1Ki 4:22–23). The people of Judah were afraid to present a defective sheep to Nehemiah's predecessor, but they were not above offering such an animal to the Lord (Mal 1:8).

"Poultry" (*ṣippᵒrîm*, "birds") was domesticated in the Indus River valley by 2000 BC and was brought to Egypt by the reign of Thutmose III (fifteenth century BC). Poultry was known in Mesopotamia and Greece by the eighth century. The earliest evidence in Palestine is the celebrated seal of Jaazaniah (dated ca. 600 BC), which depicts a fighting cock.

The meat listed here would perhaps be sufficient to provide one meal for six hundred to eight hundred persons, including the one hundred fifty Jews and officials mentioned in v.17.

19 Some have suggested that Nehemiah's memoirs were inscribed as a memorial set up in the temple (cf. 13:14, 22, 31). According to Sirach 17:22, "one's almsgiving is like a signet ring with the Lord, and he will keep a person's kindness like the apple of his eye" (cf. Heb 6:10). A striking parallel to Nehemiah's prayer is found in Nebuchadnezzar II's prayer to his god: "O Marduk, my lord, do remember my deeds favorably as good [deeds], may (these) my good deeds be always before your mind" (*ANET*, 307). An even more apposite parallel are the words of Udjahorresnet, an Egyptian official who aided both Cambyses and Darius (M. Lichtheim, ed., *Ancient Egyptian Literature III: The Late Period* [Berkeley: Univ. of California Press, 1980], 39–40):

> I am a man who is good in his town. I rescued its inhabitants from the very great turmoil when it happened in this land. I defended the weak against the strong. I rescued the timid man when misfortune came to him. I did for them every beneficence when it was time to act for them.
>
> O great gods who are in Sais! Remember all the benefactions done by the chief physician, Udjahorresne. And may you do for him all benefactions! May you make his good name endure in this land forever!

NOTES

15 In 1974 a collection of about seventy bullae (clay seal-impressions) and two seals from an unknown provenance were shown to N. Avigad. On the basis of this evidence, Avigad, 35 (cf. Talmon, *IDBSup*, 325, 327) reconstructed a list of the governors of Judah (see also H. G. M. Williamson, "The Governors of Judah under the Persians," *TynBul* 39 [1988]: 59–82). Evidence is now also available from coins (see P. Machinist, "The First Coins of Judah and Samaria," in *Achaemenid History VIII: Continuity and Change* [ed. H. Sancisi-Weerdenburg, A. Kuhrt, and M. C. Root; Leiden: Nederlands Instituut voor het Nabije Oosten, 1994], 365–80).

Name	Source	Date
Sheshbazzar	Ezra 1:8; 5:14	538 BC
Zerubbabel	Haggai 1:1, 14	515 BC
Elnathan	bulla and seal	late sixth century BC

(Continue on the next page)

(Continued)

Yeho‘ezer	jar impression	early fifth century BC
Ahzai	jar impression	early fifth century BC
Nehemiah	Nehemiah 5:14; 12:26	445–433 BC
Bagohi	Cowley, 30:1	408 BC
(Bagoas)		
Yehezqiyah	coins	330 BC

19 On Udjahorresnet, see Yamauchi, *Persia and the Bible*, 104–8; J. Blenkinsopp, "The Mission of Udjahorresnet and Those of Ezra and Nehemiah," *JBL* 106 (1987): 409–21.

F. The Completion of the Walls despite Opposition (6:1–19)

OVERVIEW

A description of further attempts to frustrate the efforts of Nehemiah is recorded in ch. 6. C. J. Barber (*Nehemiah and the Dynamics of Effective Leadership* [Neptune, N.J.: Loizeaux, 1976], 97, notes that Nehemiah's enemies resorted "first to intrigue (Nehemiah 6:1–4), then to innuendo (6:5–9), and finally to intimidation (6:10–14) to achieve their end."

1. Attempts to Ensnare Nehemiah (6:1–9)

[1]When word came to Sanballat, Tobiah, Geshem the Arab and the rest of our enemies that I had rebuilt the wall and not a gap was left in it — though up to that time I had not set the doors in the gates — [2]Sanballat and Geshem sent me this message: "Come, let us meet together in one of the villages on the plain of Ono."

But they were scheming to harm me; [3]so I sent messengers to them with this reply: "I am carrying on a great project and cannot go down. Why should the work stop while I leave it and go down to you?" [4]Four times they sent me the same message, and each time I gave them the same answer.

[5]Then, the fifth time, Sanballat sent his aide to me with the same message, and in his hand was an unsealed letter [6]in which was written:

"It is reported among the nations — and Geshem says it is true — that you and the Jews are plotting to revolt, and therefore you are building the wall. Moreover, according to these reports you are about to become their king [7]and have even appointed prophets to make this proclamation about you in Jerusalem: 'There is a king in Judah!' Now this report will get back to the king; so come, let us confer together."

⁸I sent him this reply: "Nothing like what you are saying is happening; you are just making it up out of your head."

⁹They were all trying to frighten us, thinking, "Their hands will get too weak for the work, and it will not be completed."

⌊But I prayed,⌋ "Now strengthen my hands."

COMMENTARY

1–4 On Sanballat, Tobiah, and Geshem (v.1), see comments on 2:10, 19. "Ono" (v.2) was located seven miles southeast of Joppa near Lod (Lydda). It was in the westernmost area settled by the returning Jews (Ezr 2:33; Ne 7:37; 11:35). There is disagreement among scholars as to whether or not Ono was part of Judah. Some of them believe that the Valley of Ono was neutral territory between the provinces of Ashdod and Samaria. Fensham, 200, believes that it was probably hostile to the Jews. According to Allen and Laniak, 116, "The area was under Sidonian control and was not part of the province of Judah." Blenkinsopp, 268, avers, "We should assume that *at that time* it lay outside the territory of Judah, in spite of the presence of people from Ono in the list of repatriates." Stern, 203, on the basis of the discovery of seal impressions, believes that Ono belonged to Judah. Though unconvinced by the archaeological evidence, Williamson (*Ezra, Nehemiah*, 255) believes on the basis of Ezra 2:33 that Ono was part of the province of Judah. In any case, Nehemiah recognized the invitation as a trap (cf. Jer 41:1–3; 1 Macc 12:39–53; 16:11–24).

Nehemiah's sharp reply (v.3) may seem like a haughty rebuff to a reasonable invitation, but he correctly discerned the insincerity of his enemies and their evil designs. His own utter dedication to the great enterprise of the wall made that task his top pri-ority. He refused to be distracted with lesser matters that would divert and dissipate his energies. Nehemiah's foes were persistent (v.4), but he was equally persistent in steadfastly resisting their blandishments.

5–7 Letters during this period were ordinarily written on a papyrus or leather sheet, rolled up, tied with a string, and sealed with a clay bulla (seal impression). The latter was intended to seal the letter and to guarantee its authenticity. Sanballat obviously intended that the contents should be made known also to the public at large (v.5). The Persian kings did not tolerate the claims of pretenders to kingship (v.6; cf. the Behistun Inscription of Darius 16–18 [Kent, 120]).

On v.7, compare vv.12 and 14. Usurpers such as Jeroboam (1Ki 11:29–31) and Jehu (2Ki 9:1–3) hired false prophets. Such mercenary prophets were condemned by Amos (7:10–17). U. Kellermann (*Nehemia: Quellen, Überlieferung und Geschichte* [Berlin: A. Töpelmann, 1967], 156–59), who has argued that Nehemiah was of Davidic descent, believes there may have been some basis for the accusation "there is a king" (cf. Zec 6:9–14). Others are sharply critical of such an assumption.

8–9 Nehemiah does not mince words in his reply. He calls the report a lie (v.8). He may well have sent his own messenger to the king to assure him of his loyalty. "Making it up" is from *bādāʾ*, which occurs only here and in 1 Kings 12:33. The JB renders, "It is a figment of your own imagination."

"Their hands will get too weak" (v.9) uses the verb *rāpâ* ("to become slack"). The Hebrew idiom "to cause the hands to drop" means to demoralize, as in Ezra 4:4. Jeremiah was accused of "weakening [*mᵉrappēʾ*] the hands of the soldiers" (Jer 38:4; "discouraging the soldiers," NIV). Lachish Ostracon VI speaks of people in Jerusalem "who weaken the hands of the land and make the city slack so that it fails."

The Hebrew has an imperative: "strengthen." The NRSV inserts "O God" to indicate that this expression is a prayer—an interpretation to be preferred to the LXX, Vulgate, and Syriac, which have "I strengthened my hands" (cf. the NEB's "So I applied myself to it with greater energy"; cf. Pss 28:7–8; 29:11; 46:1; Isa 40:31). The NIV adds the words, "But I prayed."

NOTES

6 The variant *Gashmu* (cf. NIV margin) is closer to the original Arabian form of the name than "Geshem."

2. The Hiring of False Prophets (6:10–14)

¹⁰One day I went to the house of Shemaiah son of Delaiah, the son of Mehetabel, who was shut in at his home. He said, "Let us meet in the house of God, inside the temple, and let us close the temple doors, because men are coming to kill you—by night they are coming to kill you."

¹¹But I said, "Should a man like me run away? Or should one like me go into the temple to save his life? I will not go!" ¹²I realized that God had not sent him, but that he had prophesied against me because Tobiah and Sanballat had hired him. ¹³He had been hired to intimidate me so that I would commit a sin by doing this, and then they would give me a bad name to discredit me.

¹⁴Remember Tobiah and Sanballat, O my God, because of what they have done; remember also the prophetess Noadiah and the rest of the prophets who have been trying to intimidate me.

COMMENTARY

10 Since Shemaiah had access to the temple, Bowman, 694, suggests that he was probably a priest, "possibly one of those who were particularly friendly with Tobiah (cf. vss. 12, 18–19; 13:7–9)."

"Was shut in" (*ʿāṣûr*) means "shut up" or "imprisoned" (cf. Jer 36:5). The significance of the phrase here is obscure. Three proposals have been suggested: (1) that Shemaiah had an ecstatic seizure (cf. 1Ki 22:10; Isa 8:11; Eze 3:14), (2) that Shemaiah was shut up temporarily because of ritual impurity (cf. 1Ki 14:10; Jer 33:1), or (3) that Shemaiah had shut himself up as a symbolic action to indicate that his own life was in danger and to suggest that both must flee to the temple.

The last suggestion makes the most sense. Most people would interpret Shemaiah's words as a ruse in which he pretended to be in personal danger and tried as a friend of Nehemiah to get him to take refuge in the temple. Shemaiah could legitimately have proposed that Nehemiah should take refuge in the temple area at the altar of asylum (Ex 21:13; 1Ki 1:50–53; 2:28–34; 8:64; 2Ki 16:14), but not for him to take refuge in "the house of God," the temple building itself.

A. L. Ivry ("Nehemiah 6,10: Politics and the Temple," *JSJ* 3 [1972]: 38) suggests an even more complex plot: "It would appear that Shemaiah is indeed suggesting something much more plausible and more diabolical than refuge in the temple, viz., commandeering and possession of it. This is the 'sin' against which Nehemiah reacts so sharply."

11–12 Even if his life were genuinely threatened, Nehemiah was not a coward who would run into hiding (v.11). Nor would he transgress the law to save his life. As a layman he was, of course, not permitted to enter the sanctuary (Nu 18:7; cf. Ex 29:33; 33:20). When King Uzziah dared to offer incense in the sanctuary, he was stricken with leprosy (2Ch 26:16–20). That Shemaiah proposed a course of action contrary to God's Word revealed him as a false prophet (Mt 24:3–10).

13 Had Nehemiah wavered in the face of the threat, his leadership would have been discredited, and morale among the people would have plummeted.

14 In the OT only three other women are mentioned as being prophetesses: (1) Miriam (Ex 15:20), (2) Deborah (Jdg 4:4), and (3) Huldah (2Ki 22:14; 2Ch 34:22). The rabbinic traditions add another four: Sarah, Hannah, Abigail, and Esther. The prophets and prophetesses in Nehemiah's time may have favored a policy of accommodation and objected to his work as divisive (cf. Isa 9:15; 28:7; Jer 2:26; 27:9–10; 28:9, 15–17; 29:24–32; Eze 13:2, 17; Am 7:14; Mic 3:5–11)

NOTE

14 A scholar who is critical of Nehemiah and offers a postmodern deconstruction of the text imagines the following scenario: "I tend to see [Noadiah] (in my mind's eye, that is, my imagination) as a strong personality regularly opposing Nehemiah with powerful and denigratory words. As he built that wall and as he laboured to dominate the whole enterprise week after week, there was always *that woman* Noadiah within earshot denouncing his imperial ways." (See R. Carroll, "Coopting the Prophets: Nehemiah and Noadiah," in *Priests, Prophets and Scribes* [ed. E. Ulrich et al.; Sheffield: Sheffield Academic, 1992], 96–97.) For a feminist perspective on prophetesses in the Hebrew Scriptures, see S. Ackerman, "Why Is Miriam Also among the Prophets? And Is Zipporah among the Priests?" *JBL* 121 (2002): 47–80.

3. The Completion of the Walls (6:15–19)

[15]So the wall was completed on the twenty-fifth of Elul, in fifty-two days. [16]When all our enemies heard about this, all the surrounding nations were afraid and lost their self-confidence, because they realized that this work had been done with the help of our God.

> [17] Also, in those days the nobles of Judah were sending many letters to Tobiah, and replies from Tobiah kept coming to them. [18] For many in Judah were under oath to him, since he was son-in-law to Shecaniah son of Arah, and his son Jehohanan had married the daughter of Meshullam son of Berekiah. [19] Moreover, they kept reporting to me his good deeds and then telling him what I said. And Tobiah sent letters to intimidate me.

COMMENTARY

15 The date "twenty-fifth of Elul" (the sixth month) would have been October 27, 445 BC. Archaeological investigations indicate that the circuit of the wall in Nehemiah's day was much reduced. Kenyon found what she believes was part of Nehemiah's wall on the crest of the rock scarp on the summit of Ophel: "It was solidly built, ca. 2.75 metres thick, but its finish was rough, as might be expected in work executed so rapidly" (Kenyon, *Jerusalem*, 111; idem, *Digging Up Jerusalem*, 183–84).

Remarkably, the walls neglected for nearly a century and a half were rebuilt in less than two months' time when the people were galvanized into action by the catalyst of Nehemiah's leadership. One might have expected a description of the celebration and the dedication of the wall immediately on its completion, but we do not encounter this event until 12:27.

16 "Lost their self-confidence" is literally "were much cast down in their own eyes." Some scholars would emend *wayyippᵉlû* ("were much cast down") to *wayyipālᵉ* ("it was a wonderful thing"; cf. the JB's "they were deeply impressed"). The context, however, favors the unemended text. The rapid completion of the wall despite such odds could only have been accomplished with God's aid, and knowledge of this fact thoroughly discomfited Nehemiah's enemies (cf. 1Ch 14:17).

17–18 Tobiah was doubly related to influential families in Judah. He was married to the daughter of Shecaniah, and his son Jehohanan was married to the daughter of Meshullam, who had helped repair the wall of Jerusalem (3:4, 30).

19 Tobiah's friends and relatives acted as a "fifth column" within the city. They attempted both to propagandize on behalf of Tobiah and to act as an intelligence system for him. Tobiah himself kept on trying to frighten Nehemiah.

G. The List of Exiles (7:1–73a)

1. Provisions for the Protection of Jerusalem (7:1–3)

> [1] After the wall had been rebuilt and I had set the doors in place, the gatekeepers and the singers and the Levites were appointed. [2] I put in charge of Jerusalem my brother Hanani, along with Hananiah the commander of the citadel, because he was a man of integrity and feared God more than most men do. [3] I said to them, "The gates of Jerusalem are not to be opened until the sun is hot. While the gatekeepers are still on duty, have

> them shut the doors and bar them. Also appoint residents of Jerusalem as guards, some at their posts and some near their own houses."

COMMENTARY

1 On the gatekeepers, see Ezra 2:42; on the singers, see 2:41; and on the Levites, see 2:40. The gatekeepers normally guarded the temple gates (1Ch 9:17–19; 26:12–19); but because of the danger in the city, they were appointed to stand guard at the city gates along with the singers and the Levites. Allen and Laniak, 121, observe, "In another emergency situation Nehemiah ordered Levites to guard certain city gates (13:22), although in that case it was to resolve a religious problem." The Mishnah (*Mid.* 1:1) lists the locations in the temple at which the Levites were to stand guard.

2 "Hanani" (see comment on 1:2) is a shortened form of the name "Hananiah." Hanani was placed in charge of Jerusalem, that is, over Rephaiah and Shallum, who were over sections of the city (3:9, 12). Others view Hanani as the military governor under Nehemiah. The Hebrew phrase translated "along with Hananiah" may be interpreted in two ways: to denote two different individuals, or as explanatory, that is, "my brother Hanani, viz., Hananiah." Most English versions (KJV, RSV, NRSV, NEB, JB, NAB, NIV) translate the phrase to designate two individuals.

On "the citadel" (*bîrâ*), see comment on 1:1. The KJV consistently translates the word as "palace," but it was actually a fortress.

Theoretically, garrisons were directly controlled by the king, and their commanders were "enrolled upon the king's list" (Xenophon, *Cyropaedia* 8.6.9). In practice, however, governors such as Nehemiah could appoint their own men.

"A man of integrity" (*ʾîš ʾemet*, lit., "a man of truth") is used once elsewhere, in the plural in Exodus 18:21: "select ... trustworthy men" (cf. Paul's praise of Timothy [Php 2:19–21]).

3 Normally the gates were opened at dawn, but this was to be delayed until the sun was high in the heavens (Ge 18:1; Ex 16:21; 1Sa 11:9). Allen and Laniak, 124, surmise, "Evidently the gates were open for only half of the day, perhaps because there were not enough gatekeepers to keep them open for longer periods." According to Williamson (*Ezra, Nehemiah*, 266–67, 270), the gates were to be closed during the heat of the day, while people took a siesta. One famous historical episode of AD 410 that may illustrate the need for a special guard at this time was the attack by Alaric on a gate in Rome while the guards were dozing.

The OT distinguishes the sun from the stars not by its great light but by its heat (Ex 16:21; 1Sa 11:9; Ps 121:6; Isa 49:10). Inhabitants of the Near East are particularly conscious of the sun's heat during the summer (Ps 32:4).

NOTE

2 "Hananiah" occurs five times in the OT (cf. comment on Ezr 10:28). It also appears as *Hanana* on a bulla (Avigad, 5, #3). Both the long form *Ḥananyaw* and the short form *Hanani* appear in the Murashu texts (Coogan, 111).

2. Nehemiah's Discovery of the List (7:4–5)

⁴Now the city was large and spacious, but there were few people in it, and the houses had not yet been rebuilt. ⁵So my God put it into my heart to assemble the nobles, the officials and the common people for registration by families. I found the genealogical record of those who had been the first to return. This is what I found written there.

COMMENTARY

4 "Large and spacious" (*raḥᵃbat yādayim ûgᵉdolâ*) is literally "wide of two hands and large." This expression means extending to the right and left. *Rāḥāb* designates something "extensive" or "widespread," as the "wide sea" (Job 11:9; Ps 104:25), the "broad land" (Ex 3:8; Ne 9:35), and the "extensive" city of Babylon (Jer 51:58). As the actual circuit of the walls of the city had been contracted, the expressions must be relative to the number of people who could still be housed once the damaged houses were rebuilt. Allen and Laniak, 122, comments, "Even with the postexilic capital reduced to the eastern hill (having lost its western suburb), it must have had the air of a ghost town after most of the wall builders left Jerusalem and went home."

5 On "registration by families," compare v.64; see Ezra 2:62 and 8:1, 3.

3. The List of Exiles (7:6–69)

a. Families (7:6–25)

⁶These are the people of the province who came up from the captivity of the exiles whom Nebuchadnezzar king of Babylon had taken captive (they returned to Jerusalem and Judah, each to his own town, ⁷in company with Zerubbabel, Jeshua, Nehemiah, Azariah, Raamiah, Nahamani, Mordecai, Bilshan, Mispereth, Bigvai, Nehum and Baanah):

The list of the men of Israel:

⁸the descendants of Parosh	2,172
⁹of Shephatiah	372
¹⁰of Arah	652
¹¹of Pahath-Moab (through the line of Jeshua and Joab)	2,818
¹²of Elam	1,254
¹³of Zattu	845
¹⁴of Zaccai	760

[15]of Binnui	648
[16]of Bebai	628
[17]of Azgad	2,322
[18]of Adonikam	667
[19]of Bigvai	2,067
[20]of Adin	655
[21]of Ater (through Hezekiah)	98
[22]of Hashum	328
[23]of Bezai	324
[24]of Hariph	112
[25]of Gibeon	95

COMMENTARY

6–7 The following list of names is essentially the same as that found in Ezra 2:1–70. See the commentary on that section for the nature of the list and the reasons for the numerous variations in names and discrepancies in numbers.

"Raamiah" (v.7) means "Yahweh has thundered" (Ezr 2:2 has "Reelaiah"). "Nahamani" is a variant form for "Nehemiah." It does not occur in Ezra 2:2. The name is found in the Murashu texts as *na-aḥ-ma-nu* (Coogan, 78). "Nehum" is probably an error for "Rehum," which appears in the Ezra list.

10 Ezra 2:5 lists 775.

11 Ezra 2:6 lists 2,812.

13 Ezra 2:8 lists 945.

15 Ezra 2:10 has "Bani" and lists 642.

16 Ezra 2:11 lists 623.

17 Ezra 2:12 lists 1,222.

18 Ezra 2:13 lists 666.

19 Ezra 2:14 lists 2,056.

20 Ezra 2:15 lists 454.

22 Ezra 2:19 lists 223.

23 Ezra 2:17 lists 323.

24 "Hariph" means "sharp" or "autumn." Ezra 2:18 has "Jorah."

25 Ezra 2:20 has "Gibbar," which may be a corruption of "Gibeon."

b. Villagers (7:26–38)

[26]the men of Bethlehem and Netophah	188
[27]of Anathoth	128
[28]of Beth Azmaveth	42
[29]of Kiriath Jearim, Kephirah and Beeroth	743
[30]of Ramah and Geba	621
[31]of Micmash	122

³²of Bethel and Ai	123
³³of the other Nebo	52
³⁴of the other Elam	1,254
³⁵of Harim	320
³⁶of Jericho	345
³⁷of Lod, Hadid and Ono	721
³⁸of Senaah	3,930

COMMENTARY

26 Ezra 2:21–22 has "the men of Bethlehem 123, of Netophah 56," which numbers would total 179.

28 Ezra 2:24 has simply "Azmaveth."

32 Ezra 2:28 lists 223.

33 Ezra 2:29 has simply "Nebo."

37 Ezra 2:33 lists 725.

38 Ezra 2:35 lists 3,630.

c. Priests (7:39–42)

³⁹The priests:	
the descendants of Jedaiah (through the family of Jeshua)	973
⁴⁰of Immer	1,052
⁴¹of Pashhur	1,247
⁴²of Harim	1,017

COMMENTARY

39–42 The names and numbers are identical with the parallel passage in Ezra 2:36–69. Perhaps the lists of priests were kept more accurately than those of the laity.

d. Levites (7:43)

⁴³The Levites:	
the descendants of Jeshua (through Kadmiel through the line of Hodaviah)	74

COMMENTARY

43 The small number of Levites who returned is striking. When Ezra was about to leave Mesopotamia, he found not one Levite in the company; so he delayed his departure until he could enlist some Levites (Ezr 8:15–20).

e. Temple Staff (7:44–60)

⁴⁴The singers:

  the descendants of Asaph   148

⁴⁵The gatekeepers:

  the descendants of Shallum, Ater, Talmon, Akkub, Hatita and Shobai   138

⁴⁶The temple servants:
the descendants of
  Ziha, Hasupha, Tabbaoth,
  ⁴⁷Keros, Sia, Padon,
  ⁴⁸Lebana, Hagaba, Shalmai,
  ⁴⁹Hanan, Giddel, Gahar,
  ⁵⁰Reaiah, Rezin, Nekoda,
  ⁵¹Gazzam, Uzza, Paseah,
  ⁵²Besai, Meunim, Nephussim,
  ⁵³Bakbuk, Hakupha, Harhur,
  ⁵⁴Bazluth, Mehida, Harsha,
  ⁵⁵Barkos, Sisera, Temah,
  ⁵⁶Neziah and Hatipha

⁵⁷The descendants of the servants of Solomon:

the descendants of
  Sotai, Sophereth, Perida,
  ⁵⁸Jaala, Darkon, Giddel,
  ⁵⁹Shephatiah, Hattil,
  Pokereth-Hazzebaim and Amon

⁶⁰The temple servants and the descendants of the servants of Solomon   392

COMMENTARY

44 Ezra 2:41 lists 128.

45 Ezra 2:42 lists 139.

47 Ezra 2:44 has "Siaha" instead of "Sia."

48 The Hebrew manuscripts we have of Ezra 2:46 have "Shamlai," which is probably an error for "Shalmai."

52 Ezra 2:50 includes "Asnah," which is lacking in Nehemiah.

57 Ezra 2:55 has "Hassophereth" and "Peruda" instead of "Perida."

59 Ezra 2:57 has "Ami" instead of "Amon."

f. Individuals without Evidence of Their Genealogies (7:61–65)

[61]The following came up from the towns of Tel Melah, Tel Harsha, Kerub, Addon and Immer, but they could not show that their families were descended from Israel:

[62]the descendants of

Delaiah, Tobiah and Nekoda 642

[63]And from among the priests:

the descendants of

Hobaiah, Hakkoz and Barzillai (a man who had married a daughter of Barzillai the Gileadite and was called by that name).

[64]These searched for their family records, but they could not find them and so were excluded from the priesthood as unclean. [65]The governor, therefore, ordered them not to eat any of the most sacred food until there should be a priest ministering with the Urim and Thummim.

COMMENTARY

61 On these towns see the comment on Ezra 2:59.

62 Ezra 2:60 lists 652.

63–65 See the comments on Ezra 2:61–63.

g. Totals (7:66–69)

[66]The whole company numbered 42,360, [67]besides their 7,337 menservants and maidservants; and they also had 245 men and women singers. [68]There were 736 horses, 245 mules, [69]435 camels and 6,720 donkeys.

COMMENTARY

67 Ezra 2:65 lists two hundred men and women singers.

68 Most Hebrew manuscripts lack this verse. On vv.66–69, see comments on Ezra 2:64–67.

4. Offerings for the Work (7:70–72)

⁷⁰Some of the heads of the families contributed to the work. The governor gave to the treasury 1,000 drachmas of gold, 50 bowls and 530 garments for priests. ⁷¹Some of the heads of the families gave to the treasury for the work 20,000 drachmas of gold and 2,200 minas of silver. ⁷²The total given by the rest of the people was 20,000 drachmas of gold, 2,000 minas of silver and 67 garments for priests.

COMMENTARY

70 "Drachmas" (*darkᵉmônîm*) were Greek coins weighing about three-tenths of an ounce; "1,000 drachmas" would weigh about 19 pounds. As a drachma was ordinarily a silver coin, the Hebrew word may designate the Persian daric. The Persians also had silver coins known by the Greek word *siglos*, adapted from the Mesopotamian **šekel** (see comment on Ezra 2:69). On the earliest recovered coins, see Machinist, "The First Coins of Judah and Samaria," in *Achaemenid History VIII: Continuity and Change* (ed. H. Sancisi-Weerdenburg, A. Kuhrt, and M. C. Root; Leiden: Nederlands Instituut voor het Nabije Oosten, 1994), 365–80.

71–72 The weight of "20,000 drachmas" (v.71) would be about 375 pounds; "2,200 minas" about 2,550 pounds; and "2,000 minas" (v.72) about 2,500 pounds.

5. Settlement of the Exiles (7:73a)

⁷³The priests, the Levites, the gatekeepers, the singers and the temple servants, along with certain of the people and the rest of the Israelites, settled in their own towns.

COMMENTARY

73a Many returning exiles may not have been from Jerusalem, whose population no doubt suf-

fered the greatest casualties in the Babylonian attacks. These people naturally returned to their hometowns, thereby leaving Jerusalem underpopulated (cf. 11:1–24).

Blenkinsopp, 281, comments:

> The first part of Nehemiah (1:1–7:5a) records a time of trials and eventual triumph over opposition with the securing of the city and the reform of social ills. Only then is the entire community in its divinely ordained divisions, clerical and lay, presented as a community which obediently attends to the law and observes the festivals. This community on behalf of which God has made up his mind is constituted by repatriated Jews and those who choose to join them.

H. Ezra's Preaching and the Outbreak of Revival (7:73b–10:39)

1. The Public Proclamation of the Scriptures (7:73b–8:12)

OVERVIEW

The traditional view sees the reading of the law by Ezra as the first reference to him in about thirteen years since his arrival in 458 BC. Since Ezra was commissioned to teach the law (Ezr 7:14, 25–26), it seems strange that there was such a long delay in the proclamation of it. Other scholars have argued that Nehemiah 8 is out of place, inasmuch as 1 Esdras 9:37–55 (which parallels Ne 7:73–8:13a) and Josephus (who follows Esdras) place the reading of the law after Ezra 10. These scholars believe that the reading of the law took place soon after Ezra's arrival (see Introduction: The Ezra Memoirs).

When the seventh month came and the Israelites had settled in their towns, [8:1] all the people assembled as one man in the square before the Water Gate. They told Ezra the scribe to bring out the Book of the Law of Moses, which the LORD had commanded for Israel.

[2] So on the first day of the seventh month Ezra the priest brought the Law before the assembly, which was made up of men and women and all who were able to understand. [3] He read it aloud from daybreak till noon as he faced the square before the Water Gate in the presence of the men, women and others who could understand. And all the people listened attentively to the Book of the Law.

[4] Ezra the scribe stood on a high wooden platform built for the occasion. Beside him on his right stood Mattithiah, Shema, Anaiah, Uriah, Hilkiah and Maaseiah; and on his left were Pedaiah, Mishael, Malkijah, Hashum, Hashbaddanah, Zechariah and Meshullam.

[5] Ezra opened the book. All the people could see him because he was standing above them; and as he opened it, the people all stood up. [6] Ezra praised the LORD, the great God; and all the people lifted their hands and responded, "Amen! Amen!" Then they bowed down and worshiped the LORD with their faces to the ground.

[7] The Levites — Jeshua, Bani, Sherebiah, Jamin, Akkub, Shabbethai, Hodiah, Maaseiah, Kelita, Azariah, Jozabad, Hanan and Pelaiah — instructed the people in the Law while the

people were standing there. [8]They read from the Book of the Law of God, making it clear and giving the meaning so that the people could understand what was being read.

[9]Then Nehemiah the governor, Ezra the priest and scribe, and the Levites who were instructing the people said to them all, "This day is sacred to the LORD your God. Do not mourn or weep." For all the people had been weeping as they listened to the words of the Law.

[10]Nehemiah said, "Go and enjoy choice food and sweet drinks, and send some to those who have nothing prepared. This day is sacred to our Lord. Do not grieve, for the joy of the LORD is your strength."

[11]The Levites calmed all the people, saying, "Be still, for this is a sacred day. Do not grieve."

[12]Then all the people went away to eat and drink, to send portions of food and to celebrate with great joy, because they now understood the words that had been made known to them.

COMMENTARY

7:73b–8:1 The phrase "all the people assembled as one man" is identical with Ezra 3:1, which also refers to an assembly called in the seventh month of the year. The object of that meeting, however, was to restore the altar of burnt offerings and sacrificial worship. Possibly Ezra had instituted the practice of holding such assemblies on the seventh month, Tishri, the beginning of the civil year. But it is worth noting that in this instance, as in others, it was the people themselves who took the initiative. According to Williamson's (*Ezra, Nehemiah*, 298) perceptive analysis:

> There was to be no place here for a purely liturgical reading that could wash over the consciousness of the congregation.... Perhaps more than in anything else, Ezra's importance lies in the fact that he put the Bible of his day into the hands of the laity; it was no longer the exclusive preserve of the "professionals." Much of the shape of Judaism thereafter was determined by this fundamental achievement.

"In the square before the Water Gate," which gate led to the Gihon Spring, may denote the same location as the broad place before the house of the Lord (Ezr 10:9); but it is not to be confused with the Water Gate in Herod's temple (*m. Mid.* 1:4). First Esdras 9:38 places the plaza in front of the sacred gate or the first port that is toward the east.

Assemblies were held by the city gates (Jdg 19:15; 2Ch 32:6). A plaza measuring 64 feet by 31 feet has been uncovered by the gate at Dan. Mazar has found a broad plaza in front of the Huldah Gates of the temple.

There have been at least four views about what "the Book of the Law of Moses" represented: (1) a collection of legal materials (so R. Kittel, M. Noth, G. von Rad); (2) the priestly code (W. H. Kosters, H.-J. Kraus, A. Kuenen, A. Lods, E. Meyer, W. O. E. Oesterley, B. Stade); (3) Deuteronomic laws (R. Bowman, B. Browne, U. Kellermann, W. Scott); and (4) the Pentateuch (W. F. Albright, J. Bright, F. Cross, O. Eissfeldt, S. Mowinckel, W. Rudolph,

J. Sanders, H. Schaeder, E. Sellin, J. Wellhausen). Ezra could certainly have brought back with him the Torah, that is, the Pentateuch. This view is the one now favored by most scholars (see Clines, 183; R. Rendtoff, "Noch einmal: Esra und das 'Gesetz,'" *ZAW* 111 [1999]: 89–91).

B. Waltke ("The Samaritan Pentateuch and the Text of the Old Testament," in *New Perspectives on the Old Testament* [ed. J. B. Payne; Waco, Tex.: Word, 1970], 234) writes: "Finally, the Pentateuch itself must be older than the fifth century. If the scribal scholars of the second Jewish commonwealth found it necessary to modernize the Pentateuch to make it intelligible to the people (cf. Ne 8) in the fifth century, then obviously the original Pentateuch antedates this period by many years." Two silver amulets discovered in 1980 in a tomb at Ketef Hinnom in Jerusalem, citing the priestly benediction from Numbers (6:24–26), are dated to the seventh century BC (see E. B. de Souza, "The Ketef Hinnom Silver Scrolls," *NEASB* 49 [2004]: 27–38).

2 "The first day of the seventh month" was the New Year's Day of the civil calendar (Lev 23:23–25; Nu 29:1–6), celebrated also as the Feast of Trumpets (Rosh Hashanah) with a solemn assembly and cessation from labor. A striking omission is the lack of reference to Yom Kippur, which according to Leviticus 23 falls on the tenth day of this month. The omission of this rite, during which the high priest enters the Most Holy Place, according to Williamson (*Ezra, Nehemiah*, 293), was deliberate, as Ezra's exposition was aimed at the laity, not at the priests.

"Women" did not participate in ordinary meetings but were brought together with children on such solemn occasions (Dt 31:12; Jos 8:35; 2Ki 23:2).

"All who were able to understand" is rendered "children old enough to understand" by the JB (cf. v.3; 10:29).

3 "Daybreak" (*hāʾôr*) is literally "the light" (cf. Ge 44:3; Jdg 16:2; 19:26; Job 3:3–8; 24:14; Ps 139:11–12; Isa 58:8). The KJV translates the word "morning." At 4:21 the KJV also translates as "morning" *šaḥar*, which actually is the dawn—the light that appears a good hour before sunrise (Ps 139:9; Joel 2:2).

The people evidently stood for about five hours attentively listening to the exposition of the Scriptures. Christian missionaries have reported similarly rapt audiences attentive to the gospel's proclamation for extended periods of time.

4 "Platform" (*migdal*) usually means a "tower." Here it indicates a platform capable of holding Ezra and thirteen others. The JB renders it "dais."

"Shema" is a shortened form of "Shemaiah" (see comment on Ezr 8:13). "Anaiah" ("Yahweh has answered") was one of those who signed the covenant (10:22). "Mishael" ("Who is what God is?") was also the name of one of Daniel's friends (Da 1:6, et al.). "Hashbaddanah" is perhaps a corruption of "Yahweh has considered (men)," found only here.

5 The "book" was a scroll rather than a codex (a book), which did not become popular until the early Christian centuries. It is the hypothesis of Roberts and Skeat that it was the influence of Christians that popularized the codex or book form, both because it was cheaper (one could write on both sides), and handier (cf. C. H. Roberts and T. C. Skeat, *The Birth of the Codex* [London: Oxford Univ. Press, 1983]).

The rabbis deduced from "the people all stood up" that the congregation should stand at the reading of the Torah. In Eastern Orthodox churches the congregation stands throughout the service.

6 "Worshiped the Lord" is literally "blessed the Lord." In Jewish synagogues a benediction is pronounced before the reading of each scriptural section.

On "the great God," compare 9:32 (also Dt 10:17; Jer 32:18; Da 9:4). The Jews customarily "lifted their hands" in worship (cf. comment on Ezr 9:5; cf. Pss 28:2; 134:2; 1Ti 2:8).

The repetition "Amen! Amen!" connotes the intensity of feeling behind the affirmation (2Ki 11:14; Lk 23:21). The "Amen" as a congregational response is known from the time of David (see 1Ch 16:36). It was later used in the synagogue (b. Ber. 5.4; 8.8) and in the church (1Co 14:16). According to G. Dalman (*The Words of Jesus* [Edinburgh: T&T Clark, 1902], 226), "Amen is affirmation, Amen is curse, Amen is making something one's own. When he utters the word 'Amen,' the hearer affirms the wish that God may act, places himself under divine judgment, and joins in praise to God."

"Bowed down" (from *qādad*) occurs fifteen times in the OT (e.g., Ge 24:26, 48; 43:28; Ex 4:31; 12:27; et al.), always followed by the verb "to worship." The KJV renders it "bowed their heads"; it may mean "kneel down."

"Worshiped" is from the verb *hāwâ* (GK 2556), exclusively in the Hishtaphael stem as *hištaḥ°wâ*. The verb occurs 170 times in the OT, mostly of the worship of God, gods, or idols. Originally it meant to prostrate oneself on the ground, as the frequently accompanying phrase, *ārṣâ* ("to the ground"; e.g., in v.6), indicates. The verb is used relatively rarely of an individual's worship of God (Ge 22:5; 24:26, 48). Such private acts of worship often involved actual prostration "to the earth," as with Abraham's servant (Ge 24:52), Moses (Ex 34:8), Joshua (Jos 5:14), and Job (Job 1:20). There are also three cases of spontaneous communal worship in Exodus (4:31; 12:27; 33:10). In 2 Chronicles 20:18 Jehoshaphat and the people "fell down in worship before the LORD" when they heard his promise of victory (see H. H. Rowley, *Worship in Ancient Israel* [London: SPCK, 1967]).

7 On "the Levites" see 2 Chronicles 35:3 and comment on Ezra 2:40. "Jamin" means "right

hand" or "good luck." "Hodiah" means "Yahweh is splendor." "Pelaiah" is "Yahweh has acted wonderfully." "Instructed" literally means "causing to understand" (cf. v.8; Ezr 8:16; Ps 119:34, 73, 130; Isa 40:14).

8 "They read" is from *qārā*, which means "to call, proclaim," here "to read aloud" (Ex 24:7; Dt 17:19; 2Ki 5:7; cf. Arab. *Qur'an*, "recitation," the name of the Islamic scriptures). Reading in the ancient world was done aloud (Ac 8:28; cf. G. Hendricksson, "Ancient Reading," *Classical Journal* 25 [1929–30]: 182–96; W. P. Clark, "Ancient Reading," *Classical Journal* 26 [1930–31]: 698–700).

"Making it clear" (*mepōrāš*) translates the Pual participle of the verb *pāraš*, a form that occurs only here (cf. the Aram. Pael passive participle *mepāraš* in Ezr 4:18). Many would derive its meaning from the sense "to separate, to determine," hence "to make clear" (cf. the RSV's "clearly").

Rabbinic tradition from the epoch of Rab (AD 175–247) has understood this word as referring to translation from Hebrew into an Aramaic Targum. Thus the Babylonian Talmud (*Meg.* 3a) comments: "What is meant by the text: 'And they read in the book, in the law of God, *mephôraš*, and gave the sense and caused them to understand the meaning'? 'And they read in the book, in the Law of God': this indicates the Hebrew text; *mephôraš*: this indicates the targum" (see R. le Deaut, *Introduction à la litterature targuminque* [Rome: Pontifical Biblical Institute, 1966], 23; M. McNamara, *Targum and Testament* [Grand Rapids: Eerdmans, 1972], 79–80).

This latter view has been adopted by the JB's "translating" and the NAB's "interpreting"; it is also listed in the margins of the RSV and NIV. But the Talmudic comment is clearly anachronistic, as we have no evidence of targums from such an early date. The earliest extant targums are from Qumran and include a targum on Leviticus 16 and one on

Job 3–5, both from Cave 4. An extensive targum on Job comes from Cave 11. This targum, dated to 150–100 BC, may possibly be the Job Targum that Gamaliel ordered hidden (*b. Šabb.* 115a). A. van der Kooij in a thorough study of the word in Qumran texts and targums ("Nehemiah 8:8 and the Question of the 'Targum'-Tradition," in *Tradition of the Text* [ed. G. J. Norton and S. Pisano; Göttingen: Vandenhoeck & Ruprecht, 1991], 89), concludes: "From all this it follows that Nehemiah 8.8 does not testify to a 'targum'-tradition. Our text does not refer to the practice of an oral translation into Aramaic, when the Law was read publically."

9 Those scholars who place Ezra after Nehemiah deny the two men's contemporaneity and excise the reference to Nehemiah as an interpolation. But the fact that Nehemiah is omitted in the parallel in 1 Esdras 9:49 is hardly significant, as he is ignored throughout the work.

On mourning (cf. Ezr 10:6; Est 9:22; Isa 57:18–19; 60:20; 61:2–3; 66:10; Jer 31:13; 1 Macc 3:47–51; 4:38–40) and weeping (cf. Ezr 3:12; 10:1; Ne 1:4), see E. Feldman, *Biblical and Post-Biblical Defilement and Mourning* (New York: Yeshiva Univ. Press, 1977).

The powerful exposition of the Word of God can bring deep conviction of sin. Repentance, however, must not degenerate into a self-centered remorse but instead must elicit joy in God's forgiving goodness (cf. 2Co 2:5–11).

10 "Choice food" (*masmannîm*, from *šaman*, "to be fat") means delicious, festive food prepared with much fat (the LXX has *lipasmata*, "fat"). Another Hebrew word for "fat" (*ḥēleb*) is used metaphorically for the "best" in Numbers 18:12, 29–30, 32, and the "finest" in Psalm 81:16 [17] and 147:14. The fat of sacrificial animals was offered to God as the tastiest element of the burnt offering (Lev 1:8, 12), the peace offering (Lev 4:8–10), and the trespass offering (Lev 7:3–4). The fat was not to be

consumed in these cases (cf. J. Heller, "Die Symbolik des Fettes im AT," *VT* 20 [1970]: 106–8). "Sweet drinks" (*mamtaqqîm*) occurs only here and as "sweetness" in Song of Songs 5:16.

"Send some to those who have nothing prepared" reflects the Jews' tradition of remembering the less fortunate on joyous occasions (2Sa 6:19; Est 9:22; cf. 1Co 11:20–22). Here was one example of the social conscience and concern of the Jews (Ex 23:11; Lev 19:10; 23:22; Dt 14:28–29; 26:12–13; Job 29:12, 16; 31:16–19; Ps 112:9; Sir 4:1, 3–8; 7:32; 29:20; see C. van Leeuwen, *Le développement de sens social en Israel avant 1'ère chrétienne* [Assen: Van Gorcum, 1955].) On the Jewish influence on the development of charity and alms, see B. Becknell, "Almsgiving, The Jewish Legacy of Justice and Mercy" (Ph.D. diss., Miami University, 2000).

"The joy" (*ḥedwâ*, only here and in 1Ch 16:27; of the Aram. in Ezr 6:16), that is, our joy in the Lord as we eat and labor before him, will sustain us (Dt 12:7, 12, 18; 14:26; 16:11, 14). "Strength" (*māʿôz*; GK 5057) means "stronghold, fortress" (cf. Pss 27:1; 37:39; Jer 16:19). On this basis, G. C. I. Wong ("A Note on 'Joy' in Nehemiah VIII 10," *VT* 45 [1995]: 384) has argued for "the joy of the LORD" as a subjective genitive, that is, the Lord's joy in us, as that meaning makes more sense. He suggests, "In other words, it is Yahweh's joy over his people that is the basis for the hope that they will be saved or protected from his anger."

11 "Be still" (*ḥassû* from *has*) means "hush, be quiet," as in Judges 3:19.

12 On the day after Sukkoth (Tabernacles), the Jews celebrate a festival called *Simhat Torah* ("rejoicing over the Torah"), in which they parade in a circle inside the synagogue seven or more rounds with a different person holding the scrolls of the Torah each time. Children carry flags with inscriptions extolling the Word of God.

NOTES

6 The verb for worship הִשְׁתַּחֲוָה (*hištaḥᵃwâ*), formerly analyzed as a Hithpael of שָׁחָה (*šāḥâ*), is thought to be cognate with the Ugaritic *ḥwy* ("to bow down"; see G. R. Driver, "Studies in the Vocabulary of the Old Testament," *JTS* 31 [1929–30]: 279–80; D. Ap. Thomas, "Notes on Some Terms Relating to Prayer," *VT* 6 [1956]: 229–30; E. Yamauchi, "619 חוה [*ḥāwāh*]," *TWOT*, 1:267–69).

Prostration was a common act of self-abasement performed before relatives, strangers, superiors, and especially royalty (Ge 23:7, 12; 33:3, 6–7; Ex 18:7; Ru 2:10; 1Sa 20:41; 2Sa 9:6, 8). Vassals in the Amarna Letters wrote to the pharaoh: "Beneath the feet [of the king ...] seven times, and seven times [I fall]" (cf. *ANET*, 483).

The Greek word προσκυνέω (*proskyneō*, which is used to translate *hištaḥawâ* 148 times in the LXX) had a semantic development similar to the Hebrew word. Like it, *proskyneō* can mean either "I prostrate" or "I worship." In Mark 5:6 the KJV translates "worshipped" when "prostrated" would have been more appropriate (cf. Mk 5:22, 33). Muslims, who pray five times a day facing Mecca, must as part of the prescribed ritual prostate themselves with their heads touching the ground.

8 M. McNamara ("Interpretation of Scripture in the Targumim," in *A History of Biblical Interpretation I: The Ancient Period* [ed. A. J. Hauser and D. F. Watson; Grand Rapids: Eerdmans, 2003]) summarizes the targumic evidence from Qumran as follows:

> The first Aramaic translations may have been for private or scholastic, rather than liturgical, use. The Qumran scrolls include a "Reworked Pentateuch" (4Q364–67, 4Q158) in a late Hasmonean or early Herodian hand, which carries a running text of the Pentateuch interspersed with exegetical additions and omissions, a targum of Job (4Qtg. Job and 11Qtg. Job), possibly from the second century BCE, and fragments of a targum of Leviticus (4Qtg. Lev.), from the first century BCE.

2. The Festival of Booths (8:13–18)

¹³On the second day of the month, the heads of all the families, along with the priests and the Levites, gathered around Ezra the scribe to give attention to the words of the Law. ¹⁴They found written in the Law, which the Lord had commanded through Moses, that the Israelites were to live in booths during the feast of the seventh month ¹⁵and that they should proclaim this word and spread it throughout their towns and in Jerusalem: "Go out into the hill country and bring back branches from olive and wild olive trees, and from myrtles, palms and shade trees, to make booths"—as it is written.

¹⁶So the people went out and brought back branches and built themselves booths on their own roofs, in their courtyards, in the courts of the house of God and in the square by the Water Gate and the one by the Gate of Ephraim. ¹⁷The whole company that had returned from exile built booths and lived in them. From the days of Joshua son of Nun until that day, the Israelites had not celebrated it like this. And their joy was very great.

> [18]Day after day, from the first day to the last, Ezra read from the Book of the Law of God. They celebrated the feast for seven days, and on the eighth day, in accordance with the regulation, there was an assembly.

COMMENTARY

13 Notice that the people in this revival had an insatiable appetite to learn more about the Scriptures.

14 "Booths" (*sukkôt*) were not "tabernacles," that is, tents (as the KJV translates in Lev 23:34, following the Vulgate) but booths made out of branches. This feast, celebrated from the fifteenth of Tishri (September–October) for seven days (Lev 23:39–43), was one of the three great feasts (along with Passover and Pentecost) during which all Jewish men were to assemble in Jerusalem. It was a joyous agricultural festival that celebrated the completion of the harvest. The rabbis said, "He who has not seen Jerusalem during the Feast of Tabernacles does not know what rejoicing means" (see Ex 23:16; Dt 16:13; Ezr 3:4; the feast of Jn 7 was the Feast of Booths; cf. 7:2).

15 With the exception of palms and other leafy trees, the trees mentioned here are not the same as those prescribed in Leviticus 23:40. The latter included the willow, which is omitted here.

The olive tree (*Olea europaea, Eleagnus augustifolia*) is widespread in Mediterranean countries. According to Deuteronomy 8:8 it was growing in Canaan before the conquest. It takes an olive tree thirty years to mature, so its cultivation requires peaceful conditions.

"Tree of oil" (*ʿēṣ šemen*) is commonly regarded as the "wild olive tree" (*Olea europaea oleaster*). But this view is questionable, since according to 1 Kings 6:23, 31–32 its wood was used as timber, whereas

the wood of the wild olive tree would have been of little value for use in making the temple's furniture. Also, the oleaster contains little "oil." The phrase may have meant a resinous tree, such as the fir. The KJV renders the phrase as "pine."

"Myrtles" (*hᵃdas, Myrtus communis*) are evergreen bushes with a pleasing odor (Isa 41:19; 55:13; Zec 1:8, 10–11). "Palms" (from *tāmār, Phoenix dactylifera*) are date palms (cf. Ex 15:27; Lev 23:40; Nu 33:9; Ps 92:12; SS 7:8; Joel 1:12). Such trees were common around Jericho (Dt 34:3; 2Ch 28:15). "Shade trees" (*ʿēṣ ʿābōt*) means literally "leafy trees" (Eze 6:13; 20:28; see H. N. Moldenke and A. L. Moldenke, *Plants of the Bible* [Waltham, Mass.: Chronica Botanica, 1952]; *Fauna and Flora of the Bible* [London: United Bible Societies, 1972]).

Later Jewish celebrations of the Feast of Booths include the waving with the right hand of the *lulav*, made of branches of palms, myrtles, and willows, and the holding in the left hand of the ethrog, a citrus native to Palestine.

16 "Roofs" in Palestine were flat so that one could walk on them (Jos 2:6; 1Sa 9:25–26; 2Sa 11:2; Mk 2:4; Ac 10:9). "Courtyards, in the courts" renders the plural of *ḥāṣēr*, which occurs in the singular 120 times and in the plural twenty-five times in the OT. Near Eastern houses were built around a court (see H. K. Beebe, "Ancient Palestinian Dwellings," *BA* 31 [1968]: 38–58; H. Orlinsky, "*Ḥāṣēr* in the Old Testament," *JAOS* 59 [1939]: 22–37).

The important Temple Scroll from Qumran has God describing an ideal temple in great detail. Columns 40–46 describe the outer court as follows: "On the roof of the third story are columns for the constructing of booths for the Festival of Booths to be occupied by the elders, tribal chieftains, and the commanders of thousands and hundreds" (cf. Ne 8:16–17; J. Milgrom, "The Temple Scroll," *BA* 41 [1978]: 111).

On "the square by the Water Gate," see comments on 3:26; 8:1, 3; 12:37.

"The Gate of Ephraim" was a gate of the oldest rampart of Jerusalem, four hundred cubits east of the Corner Gate (2Ki 14:13; 2Ch 25:23). It was restored by Nehemiah (12:39).

17 The statement "from the days of Joshua son of Nun" hardly means that no celebration of the Feast of Booths had taken place since then, as such celebrations are mentioned after the dedication of Solomon's temple (1Ki 8:65; 2Ch 7:9) and after the return of the exiles (Ezr 3:4). It must mean that the feast had not been celebrated before with such exceptional joyousness (Slotki, 185) or strictness of observance.

The great joy compares to that experienced at the renewal of the Passover under Hezekiah (2Ch 30:26) and at the revival under Josiah (2Ki 23:22; 2Ch 35:18).

18 "Assembly" (*caṣeret*) is a solemn or festal assembly (cf. Lev 23:36; Nu 29:35; Dt 16:8; 2Ki 10:20; Joel 1:14).

REFLECTION

Problematic is the relationship between what is described in Nehemiah 8 and 9 (see comment on 9:37) and the origins of the synagogue. Many scholars have suggested that synagogues developed in the exile after the destruction of the temple. Ackroyd (*Israel under Babylon and Persia* [Oxford: Oxford Univ. Press, 1970], 28) cautions: "But this is purely a supposition"; he then adds, "Nehemiah 8 perhaps provides us with a picture of a stage in the evolution of the institution, with reading and exposition specially stressed."

Actual epigraphic evidence for a synagogue, however, is first attested not in Babylon or Palestine but in Egypt (under Ptolemy III, 247–221 BC), where two Greek inscriptions mention προσευχήν (*proseuchēn*, "[the house] of prayer"). Compare Acts 16:13, which M. Hengel ("Proseuche und Synagoge," in *Tradition und Glaube* [ed. G. Jeremias et al.; Göttingen Vandenhoeck & Ruprecht, 1971],

157–84) interprets *proseuchēn* as a reference to a synagogue. The word *synagōgē*, which originally meant the congregation itself rather than the building, first appears in first-century AD Palestine.

On this subject, see J. G. Griffiths, "Egypt and the Rise of the Synagogue," *JTS* 38 (1987): 1–15; L. L. Grabbe, "Synagogues in Pre-70 Palestine," *JTS* 39 (1988): 401–10; I. Levinskaya, "A Jewish or Gentile Prayer House? The Meaning of ΠΡΟΣΕΥΧΗ," *TynBul* 41 (1990): 154–59; F. G. Hüttenmeister, "'Synagoge' und 'Proseuche' bei Josephus und in anderen antiken Quellen," in *Begegnungen zwischen Christentum und Judentum in Antike und Mittelalter* (ed. D. Koch et al.; Göttingen: Vandenhoeck & Ruprecht, 1993), 163–81; L. I. Levine, "The Nature and Origin of the Palestinian Synagogue Reconsidered," *JBL* 115 (1996): 425–48; R. Hachlili, "The Origin of the Synagogue: A Reassessment," *JSJ* 28 (1997): 34–47.

3. A Day of Fasting, Confession, and Prayer (9:1–5a)

OVERVIEW

Interestingly, the ninth chapters of Ezra, Nehemiah, and Daniel are each devoted to confessions of national sin and prayers for God's grace. M. Gilbert, in a perceptive analysis ("La place de la Loi dans la prière de Néhémie 9," in *De la Tôrah au Messie* [ed. M. Carrez, J. Doré, and P. Grelot; Paris: Desclée, 1981], 310), highlights several keys to this confessional prayer. He notes that the giving generosity of Yahweh is stressed by the occurrence of the verb *nātan* ("to give") fourteen times: "He gives the land, the Law, the manna, water, his Spirit, the oppressors, but also the deliverers.... No biblical text, it seems, uses so frequently the verb 'to give.'" He also observes that another theme is the land (*hāʾāreṣ*), which occurs thirteen times. Moreover, Yahweh is addressed directly as "you" (*ʾattâ*) ten times.

H. Van Grol ("'Indeed, Servants We Are,'" in *The Crisis of Israelite Religion* [ed. B. Becking and M. C. A. Korpel; Leiden: Brill, 1999], 209–27) compares Nehemiah 9 with Ezra 9 and 2 Chronicles 12. This prayer of confession has been compared to Psalm 136 and to the apocryphal "Prayer of Manasseh," the wicked king who reigned fifty-five years (2Ki 21:1–18; 2Ch 33:1–20). This short text, which is not included in Catholic versions such as the NAB and JB, has been called by Bruce Metzger (*An Introduction to the Apocrypha* [New York: Oxford Univ. Press, 1957], 123) "One of the finest pieces in the Apocrypha." Blenkinsopp, 302, calls attention to a somewhat similar text from Qumran (4Q 504–506), "The Words of the Heavenly Lights," composed of prayers for the days of the week, which also recall God's mercy in creation and history, confess Israel's rebelliousness, and ask for forgiveness. They speak as well of Moses' having atoned for their sin. (See G. Vermes, *The Dead Sea Scrolls in English* [3rd ed.; London: Penguin, 1990], 217–20; F. G. Martínez, *The Dead Sea Scrolls Translated* [Leiden: Brill, 1994], 414–18.)

[1]On the twenty-fourth day of the same month, the Israelites gathered together, fasting and wearing sackcloth and having dust on their heads. [2]Those of Israelite descent had separated themselves from all foreigners. They stood in their places and confessed their sins and the wickedness of their fathers. [3]They stood where they were and read from the Book of the Law of the LORD their God for a quarter of the day, and spent another quarter in confession and in worshiping the LORD their God. [4]Standing on the stairs were the Levites — Jeshua, Bani, Kadmiel, Shebaniah, Bunni, Sherebiah, Bani and Kenani — who called with loud voices to the LORD their God. [5]And the Levites — Jeshua, Kadmiel, Bani, Hashabneiah, Sherebiah, Hodiah, Shebaniah and Pethahiah — said: "Stand up and praise the LORD your God, who is from everlasting to everlasting.'"

COMMENTARY

1 Many scholars find it strange to have a day of penance following a festival of joy and consider the events of this chapter to have originally followed Ezra 10. There would thus have been a three-week interval between Ezra 10:17 and Nehemiah 9:1. Williamson (*Ezra, Nehemiah*, 308–10) has argued that this chapter originally followed Ezra 8, with the result that "the entire recorded work of Ezra is fitted into exactly one year." (See also H. G. M. Williamson, "Structure and Historiography in Nehemiah 9," in *Proceedings of the Ninth World Congress of Jewish Studies* [Jerusalem: Magnes, 1988], 117–31; idem, "Laments at the Destroyed Temple," *BRev* 6 [1990]: 12–17, 44.)

"Sackcloth" (*śaq*) was a goathair garment that covered the bare loins during times of mourning and penance (Ge 37:34; 2Sa 3:31; 21:10; 1Ki 21:27; Est 4:14; Isa 58:5; Da 9:3). "Dust" (*ʾᵃdāmâ*) occurs 221 times in the OT. It originally indicated reddish-brown earth. Joshua 7:6, Lamentations 2:10, and Ezekiel 27:30 also mention the placing of *ʿāpār* ("ashes," often rendered "dust") on one's head (cf. also 2Sa 13:19 [*ʾēper*, "ashes"]; Job 2:12). At the excavations at Beersheba in 1970–71, A. Rainey ("Dust and Ashes," *TA* 1 [1974]: 77–83, summarized as "The Archaeology of Dust and Ashes," *BAR* 1 [1975]: 14, 16) noticed that the streets were composed of gray ash made from the broom tree. The mourner could simply sit on the ground and pick up ashes and dust to place on one's head as a sign of mourning (1Sa 4:12; 2Sa 1:2; 15:32).

2 "Those of Israelite descent" is literally "the seed of Israel" (cf. Ezr 9:2). On "had separated themselves" see Ezra 9:1; 10:8, 11, 16. On "confessed," see 1:6 (cf. Ezr 10:1; Da 9:20).

3 The congregation spent about three hours in the study of Scriptures and three hours in the worship of the Lord (see comment on 8:6). The Qumran Manual of Discipline (1QS 6) prescribes: "In any place where is gathered the ten-man quorum, someone must always be engaged in study of the Law day and night, continually, each one taking his turn. The general membership will be diligent together for the first third of every night of the year, reading aloud from the Book, interpreting Scripture, and praying together" (M. Wise, M. Abegg Jr., and E. Cook, trans., *The Dead Sea Scrolls: A New Translation* [New York: HarperSanFrancisco, 1996], 134).

4 "Shebaniah" possibly means "turn, pray, O Yahweh." "Bunni" is short for "Benaiah" ("Yahweh has built"). On "Sherebiah," see comment on Ezra 8:18. "Kenani," short for "Kenaniah" ("Yahweh strengthens"), occurs only here.

The "stairs" (*maʿᵃlēh*, "ascent") perhaps led to the platform mentioned in 8:4. On "loud voices," see the comment on Ezra 10:12.

5a According to the Hebrew text, this prayer is ascribed to the Levites. Five of the names here are the same as those in v.4. In accordance with "Stand up and praise the Lord," Jews begin their prayers with *Barukh* ("Blessed") and stand for the benediction (cf. v.3).

NOTES

1 On ritual actions to express mourning among Hebrews, see M. Jastrow, *Dust, Earth, and Ashes as Symbols of Mourning among the Ancient Hebrews* (Chicago: American Oriental Society, 1899); E. Feldman, *Biblical* *and Post-Biblical Defilement and Mourning* (New York: Yeshiva Univ. Press, 1977); G. A. Anderson, *A Time to Mourn, A Time to Dance: The Expression of Grief and Joy in Israelite Religion* (University Park: Pennsylvania State Univ. Press, 1991); B. A. Levine, "Silence, Sound, and the Phenomenology of Mourning in Biblical Israel," *JANESCU* 22 (1993): 89–106.

4. A Recital of God's Dealings with Israel (9:5b–31)

"Blessed be your glorious name, and may it be exalted above all blessing and praise. [6]You alone are the LORD. You made the heavens, even the highest heavens, and all their starry host, the earth and all that is on it, the seas and all that is in them. You give life to everything, and the multitudes of heaven worship you.

[7]"You are the LORD God, who chose Abram and brought him out of Ur of the Chaldeans and named him Abraham. [8]You found his heart faithful to you, and you made a covenant with him to give to his descendants the land of the Canaanites, Hittites, Amorites, Perizzites, Jebusites and Girgashites. You have kept your promise because you are righteous.

[9]"You saw the suffering of our forefathers in Egypt; you heard their cry at the Red Sea. [10]You sent miraculous signs and wonders against Pharaoh, against all his officials and all the people of his land, for you knew how arrogantly the Egyptians treated them. You made a name for yourself, which remains to this day. [11]You divided the sea before them, so that they passed through it on dry ground, but you hurled their pursuers into the depths, like a stone into mighty waters. [12]By day you led them with a pillar of cloud, and by night with a pillar of fire to give them light on the way they were to take.

[13]"You came down on Mount Sinai; you spoke to them from heaven. You gave them regulations and laws that are just and right, and decrees and commands that are good. [14]You made known to them your holy Sabbath and gave them commands, decrees and laws through your servant Moses. [15]In their hunger you gave them bread from heaven and in their thirst you brought them water from the rock; you told them to go in and take possession of the land you had sworn with uplifted hand to give them.

[16]"But they, our forefathers, became arrogant and stiff-necked, and did not obey your commands. [17]They refused to listen and failed to remember the miracles you performed among them. They became stiff-necked and in their rebellion appointed a leader in order to return to their slavery. But you are a forgiving God, gracious and compassionate, slow to anger and abounding in love. Therefore you did not desert them, [18]even when they cast for themselves an image of a calf and said, 'This is your god, who brought you up out of Egypt,' or when they committed awful blasphemies.

[19]"Because of your great compassion you did not abandon them in the desert. By day the pillar of cloud did not cease to guide them on their path, nor the pillar of fire by night to shine on the way they were to take. [20]You gave your good Spirit to instruct them. You

did not withhold your manna from their mouths, and you gave them water for their thirst. ²¹For forty years you sustained them in the desert; they lacked nothing, their clothes did not wear out nor did their feet become swollen.

²²"You gave them kingdoms and nations, allotting to them even the remotest frontiers. They took over the country of Sihon king of Heshbon and the country of Og king of Bashan. ²³You made their sons as numerous as the stars in the sky, and you brought them into the land that you told their fathers to enter and possess. ²⁴Their sons went in and took possession of the land. You subdued before them the Canaanites, who lived in the land; you handed the Canaanites over to them, along with their kings and the peoples of the land, to deal with them as they pleased. ²⁵They captured fortified cities and fertile land; they took possession of houses filled with all kinds of good things, wells already dug, vineyards, olive groves and fruit trees in abundance. They ate to the full and were well-nourished; they reveled in your great goodness.

²⁶"But they were disobedient and rebelled against you; they put your law behind their backs. They killed your prophets, who had admonished them in order to turn them back to you; they committed awful blasphemies. ²⁷So you handed them over to their enemies, who oppressed them. But when they were oppressed they cried out to you. From heaven you heard them, and in your great compassion you gave them deliverers, who rescued them from the hand of their enemies.

²⁸"But as soon as they were at rest, they again did what was evil in your sight. Then you abandoned them to the hand of their enemies so that they ruled over them. And when they cried out to you again, you heard from heaven, and in your compassion you delivered them time after time.

²⁹"You warned them to return to your law, but they became arrogant and disobeyed your commands. They sinned against your ordinances, by which a man will live if he obeys them. Stubbornly they turned their backs on you, became stiff-necked and refused to listen. ³⁰For many years you were patient with them. By your Spirit you admonished them through your prophets. Yet they paid no attention, so you handed them over to the neighboring peoples. ³¹But in your great mercy you did not put an end to them or abandon them, for you are a gracious and merciful God.

COMMENTARY

5b "Your glorious name" is literally "the name of your glory." The Hebrew word for glory (*kābôd*) comes from a root that means "weighty," and then by extension "honored."

The RSV and NRSV connect v.5b with what the Levites said in v.5a and insert at the beginning of v.6, "And Ezra said," following the LXX (cf. the other prayers of Ezra [Ezr 7:27–28a; 9:6–15]).

Myers, 167, comments, "This prayer psalm is a marvelous expression of God's continued faithfulness to his covenant despite the nation's equally continued apostasy."

The prayer reviews God's grace and power (1) in creation (v.6), (2) in Egypt and at the Red Sea (vv.9–11), (3) in the desert and at Sinai (vv.12–21), (4) at the conquest of Canaan (vv.22–25), (5) through the judges (vv.26–28), (6) through the prophets (vv.29–31), and (7) in the present situation (vv.32–37). Allen and Laniak, 133, comment, "Verses 6–25 presented kaleidoscopic pictures of divine grace: common grace, prevenient grace, and forgiving grace."

6b Ezra's prayer begins notably with the affirmation, "You are alone the LORD," which, though not in the same words as the famous Shema of Deuteronomy 6:4, expresses the central monotheistic conviction of Israel's faith (cf. 2Ki 19:15; Ps 86:10; Isa 37:16).

"The highest heavens" is literally "the heaven of heavens" (cf. Dt 10:14; 1Ki 8:27; 2Ch 2:6; 6:18; Ps 148:4). *Ṣābāʾ* (plural *ṣᵉbāʾōt*) literally means "army, host, warriors." The NIV interprets the host here as stars (cf. Ge 2:1), but the last clause may indicate that angels are meant (cf. 1Ki 22:19; Pss 103:20–21; 148:2). Elsewhere the KJV transliterates the word in the phrase "the Lord of Sabaoth" (Ro 9:29; Jas 5:4), which means "the Lord of hosts." The expression, which occurs three hundred times in the OT, is especially prominent in the prophetic books of this period, where it occurs fourteen times in Haggai, fifty-three in Zechariah, and twenty-four in Malachi.

Not only men but also "the multitudes of heaven" worship before the Lord. These "multitudes" include the *bᵉnê ʾelîm* (lit., "sons of gods"; Ps 29:1–2), rendered by the RV "sons of the mighty" and which probably means angels (cf. Ps 89:6 [7]). According to Psalm 97:7, even "all you gods" bow down before him.

7 On "chose" (from *bāḥar*; GK 1047), R. Rendtorff has an interesting observation. He writes, "There is still another remarkable peculiarity in Nehemiah 9: it is the only time in the Hebrew Bible that the verb בחר 'to elect' is used in reference to Abraham (v.7)" ("Nehemiah 9: An Important Witness of Theological Reflection," in *Tehillah le-Moshe: Biblical and Judaic Studies in Honor of Moshe Greenberg* [ed. M. Cogan, B. L. Eichler, and J. H. Tigay; Winona Lake, Ind.: Eisenbrauns, 1997], 112).

"Ur of the Chaldeans" (*ʾûr kaśdîm*) is found only here and in Genesis 11:28, 31; 15:7. As the Chaldeans do not appear in Mesopotamia until centuries after Abraham's time, the term "Chaldeans" was added as a later explanatory gloss (see E. Yamauchi, "Chaldea, Chaldeans," *NIDBA*, 123–25).

According to Genesis 17:4–5, "Abram" ("the father is exalted") was changed to "Abraham" ("the father of a multitude").

8 "Faithful" (*neʾᵉmān*) is used only a few times of individuals, for example, of Moses (Nu 12:7) and Samuel (1Sa 3:20, untranslated in the NIV). Whether the reference alludes to Abraham's faith in believing that God would grant him a son (Ge 15:6) or in being willing to sacrifice Isaac (Ge 22) is unclear. Sirach 44:20 and 1 Maccabees 2:52 favor the latter (cf. Jas 2:21–23 with Ro 4:16–22).

On the different people groups, see v.24 and the comments on Ezra 9:1. The latter verse lists surrounding populations and so includes also Ammonites, Moabites, and Egyptians.

"Girgashites" is a Canaanite tribe mentioned seven times in the OT. It is of uncertain identity (cf. the Qarqisha in Hittite records; the Ugaritic personal name *grgš*).

On "because you are righteous," see Ezra 9:15; Psalm 119:137; Lamentations 1:18.

9 The "Red Sea" (*yam-sûp*, "Sea of Reeds") was probably one of the Bitter Lakes that the Suez

Canal now passes through. See J. K. Hoffmeier, *Israel in Egypt* (New York: Oxford Univ. Press, 1996), 200–210.

10 "Signs" (plural of *ʾôt*, used eighty times) indicates "miracles, signs of confirmation or warning." It is often used with the plural of *môpet* ("wonder"), especially of events connected with the plagues of Exodus (Ex 7:3; Dt 4:34; 6:22; 7:19; Pss 78:43; 105:27; 135:9; Isa 8:18; Jer 32:20–21).

"How arrogantly" renders the Hiphil of *zyd* (cf. Ex 18:11; Dt 1:43; 17:13; 18:20; Jer 50:29). On "you made a name," compare v.5 (also 1:9, 11; Isa 63:12, 14).

11 On "you divided the sea ... and they passed through it," see Exodus 14:21–29; Psalm 78:13; 1 Corinthians 10:1–2; and Hebrews 11:29; and on "you hurled their pursuers," see Exodus 15:4; Isaiah 43:16–17.

12 On "you led them with a pillar of cloud," see v.19; Exodus 13:21–22; Numbers 14:14; Deuteronomy 1:33; Psalms 78:14; 105:39; Isaiah 42:16; 58:8.

13 On regulations, etc., see the comment on 1:7. Laws (*tôrôt*) is the plural of *tôrâ*, which means "instruction, law," and later, as the Torah, the Scriptures par excellence — the Pentateuch.

14 On "your holy Sabbath," compare Exodus 20:8–11; 31:13–17; Deuteronomy 5:15; Ezekiel 20:12. According to the Talmud, "The Sabbath outweighs all the commandments of the Torah" (*y. Ned.* 38b; cf. 10:31; 13:15–22).

15 "Bread from heaven" (Ex 16:4, 10–35; Pss 78:24; 105:40; Jn 6:32, 51, 58; see Borgen, *Bread from Heaven* [Leiden: Brill, 1965]), water from the rock (Ex 17:6; Nu 20:8; Ps 105:41), and "take possession" (see v.23; Dt 11:31; Jos 1:11) recall significant events from Israel's past.

"You had sworn with uplifted hand" is literally "lifted up your hand" (i.e., as in an oath; cf. 5:13; Ex 6:8; Eze 20:6; 47:14).

16 "Became arrogant" (from *zyd*, used in v.10) "and stiff-necked" (see vv.17, 29; cf. a similar phrase in 3:5) is a figure borrowed from the driving of stubborn oxen who resist guidance (Ex 32:9; Dt 10:16; 2Ki 17:14; 2Ch 36:13; Jer 7:26).

17 The forefathers "refused to listen" (cf. 1Sa 8:19; Jer 11:10) and "failed to remember the miracles" (cf. Mk 6:52).

Seven Hebrew manuscripts and the LXX read *beamiṣrāyim* ("in Egypt") instead of *bemiryām* ("in their rebellion"). Numbers 14:4 reports the proposal of "appointed a leader."

"A forgiving God" (lit., "a God of pardons") renders the plural of *selîḥâ*, a rare word that occurs only here, in Psalm 130:4, and in Daniel 9:9. In Modern Hebrew it is used in the expression "Excuse me." God is "gracious" (cf. v.31; Ex 34:6; 2Ch 30:9; Pss 86:15; 103:8; 145:8; Joel 2:13; Jnh 4:2).

18 The "image of a calf" recalls Exodus 32:4–8 and Deuteronomy 9:16. "Blasphemies" translates *neʾāṣôt* (only here, in v.26, and Eze 35:12), which means "abuses, aspersions" ("provocations," KJV).

19 "Compassion" renders *raḥamîm*, which is cognate with *reḥem* ("womb"). The two adjectives that describe Allah, "merciful and compassionate," in the opening lines of the Qur'an are cognate Arabic words (*raḥmān, raḥîm*).

20 The "good Spirit" and the "manna" recall Numbers 11. On "their thirst," see v.15; Isaiah 21:14; 44:3.

21 In the desert wanderings the people "lacked nothing" (cf. Dt 2:7, 8:4), and their "clothes" (plural of *śalmâ*, specifically a "mantle"; cf. 1Ki 10:25) "did not wear out" (cf. Dt 29:5[4]; contrast Jos 9:13). The absence of natural deterioration evidenced God's special guidance. "Become swollen" can mean "blistered"; *bāṣaq* occurs only here and in Deuteronomy 8:4.

The medieval commentator Rashi (AD 1040–1105) explained that the clouds of glory that protected the Israelites in the desert rubbed against their clothing and cleaned and ironed them (Rabinowitz, *Nehemiah*, 155).

22 Some would interpret *l[e]pē'â* (lit., "to a corner"; "even the remotest frontiers," NIV) in the sense of "quarter by quarter," others as "adjoining land" (i.e., Transjordan).

Sihon refused the Israelites passage through his land, which was in Transjordan between the Jabbok and the Arnon rivers (Nu 21:21–33; Dt 2–3; Jdg 11:19–21, Pss 135:11; 136:19–20). Excavations between 1968 and 1971 at Tel Hesban did not reveal any settlements earlier than the seventh century BC, so the location of Sihon's Heshbon remains uncertain.

"Og" was the Amorite king of Bashan with sixty cities (Dt 3:3–5; Jos 13:12). His defeat was one of the great victories of the Israelites (Jos 9:10; Pss 135:11; 136:20). The Babylonian Talmud (*b. Nid.* 61a) claims Og was the brother of Sihon. "Bashan," called Batanea in the NT period, was the fertile area north of Gilead in Transjordan.

23 On God's promise to Abraham, see Genesis 22:17; 26:4; Exodus 32:13; Deuteronomy 1:10; 10:22; 28:62; Judges 2:1; 1 Chronicles 27:23; Acts 7:5 (see A. A. MacRae, "Abraham and the Stars," *JETS* 8 [1965]: 97–100).

24 "Their sons went in and took possession" recalls Genesis 22:17; 26:4; Exodus 32:13; Deuteronomy 1:8; 10:22; 28:62; 1 Chronicles 27:23. On "you subdued before them the Canaanites," see v.8; Deuteronomy 9:3; Judges 1:4. On "along with their kings," see Deuteronomy 7:24; Joshua 11:12, 17.

25 The list of land, cities, etc., corresponds to the lists in the covenant at Sinai and its renewal (Dt 6:10–11; Jos 24:13). "Fortified cities" (plural of *bāṣûr*) designates such sites as Jericho (Jos 6), Lachish (Jos 10:32), and Hazor (Jos 11:11; cf. also Dt 3:5; 9:1; Jos 14:12). "Fertile land" is literally "fat [*š[e]mēnâ*] land" (cf. v.35). A related phrase, "the good

land," appears in Numbers 14:7; Deuteronomy 8:7; Joshua 23:13; 1 Kings 14:15.

The lack of rainfall during much of the year made it necessary for almost every house to have its own well or cistern to store water from the rainy seasons (2Ki 18:31; Pr 5:15). By 1200 BC the technique of waterproofing cisterns was developed, permitting the greater occupation of the central Judean hills. (See V. H. Matthews, *Manners and Customs in the Bible* [Peabody, Mass.: Hendrickson, 1988], 45–46; J. King and L. E. Stager, *Life in Biblical Israel* [Library of Ancient Israel; Louisville, Ky.: Westminster John Knox, 2001], 123–27.)

The chief cultivated trees of Palestine were the olive, fig, apple, almond, walnut, mulberry, sycamore, and pomegranate (cf. Dt 8:8; 2Ki 18:32). Date palms grew in the Jordan Valley, especially at Jericho (see comment on 8:15). When they entered the land of Canaan, the Israelites were warned not to cut down any fruit trees (Dt 20:20). The Egyptian story of Sinuhe (early second millennium BC) says of Canaan: "Figs were in it, and grapes. It had more wine than water. Plentiful was its honey, abundant its olives. Every kind of fruit was on its trees" (*ANET*, 19).

Šāman ("grew fat"; "well-nourished," NIV) is used but four other times in the OT (Dt 32:15 [2x]; Isa 6:10; Jer 5:28). It always implies physical satiety and spiritual insensitivity. There is a similar connotation with the use of *ḥeleb* ("fat"). In Job 15:27 the godless man has hidden his face in "fat"; the eyes of the wicked "gleam through folds of fat" (NEB; Ps 73:7). The heart of the godless is "gross like fat" (RSV; Ps 119:70; "gross and fat," NRSV).

"They reveled" (Hithpael of *ʿādan*, used only here) means "to luxuriate, to enjoy the good life."

26 Putting the law "behind their backs" (cf. 1Ki 14:9; Eze 23:35), the forefathers "killed [the] prophets" (see 1Ki 18:4; 19:10, 14; 2Ch 24:20–22; Jer 26:20–23; Mt 23:37; Lk 11:47), thus committing "awful blasphemies" (see comment on v.18, above).

27 When God "handed them over" (cf. Eze 39:23), "they cried out" to him (cf. Jdg 4:3; Ps 107:6, 28); and "from heaven [he] heard" (see 2Ch 6:21, 23, 25, 30, 33). He gave them "deliverers" (*môšîʿîm*, "saviors"), that is, "judges" such as Samson, Gideon, et al. (Jdg 2:16–18; 3:9, 15, et al.; 2Ki 13:5). The English "judges," the Latin *judices*, and the Greek *kritai* are all misleading translations of the Hebrew *šōpᵉṭîm*, who were military leaders rather than judicial magistrates.

28 The history of the "judges" is a cyclical story of deliverance, apostasy, and then deliverance (Jdg 3:7, 12; 4:1; 6:1; 8:33–34; et al.).

29 The ordinances of God are such that "a man will live if he obeys them" (cf. Lev 18:5; Ps 119:25;

Eze 20:11). The people "stubbornly ... turned their backs" (lit., "they presented a stubborn shoulder"; cf. the similar expressions in 3:5 and 9:16; also Hos 4:16; Zec 7:11).

30 By his "Spirit" (cf. Zec 7:12) and through his "prophets" (see 2Ki 17:13; 2Ch 24:19), God appealed to the people, but they "paid no attention" (cf. 1Sa 8:19). So he "handed them over" (see Jdg 6:1; 13:1; 2Ki 13:3; Ps 106:41; Jer 20:4–5; Eze 7:21).

31 God "did not put an end" to the erring people (see Jer 4:27; 30:11; 46:28). Significantly, Nehemiah's long recital of Israelite history excludes any reference to the reigns of Saul, David, and Solomon.

NOTES

6b The ancients worshiped the stars and planets, a practice forbidden in the Torah (Dt 17:3). The observation of celestial phenomena by the ancient Mesopotamians led to the development of astrology. See Yamauchi, *Persia and the Bible*, ch. 13, "The Magi"; idem, "The Episode of the Magi," in *Chronos, Kairos, Christos* (ed. J. Vardaman and E. M. Yamauchi; Winona Lake, Ind.: Eisenbrauns, 1989), 15–40; L. Ness, *Written in the Stars: Ancient Zodiac Mosaics* (Warren Center, Penn.: Shangri-La, 1999); F. Rochberg, *The Heavenly Writing: Divination, Horoscopy, and Astronomy in Mesopotamian Culture* (Cambridge: Cambridge Univ. Press, 2004).

22 On the excavations at Heshbon, see L. T. Geraty, "Heshbon, The First Casualty in the Israelite Quest for the Kingdom of God," in *The Quest for the Kingdom of God: Studies in Honor of George E. Mendenhall* (ed. H. B. Huffmon, F. A. Spina, and A. R. W. Green; Winona Lake, Ind.: Eisenbrauns, 1983), 243; L. T. Geraty and D. Merling, *Hesban after 25 Years* (Berrien Springs, Mich.: Andrews Univ. Press, 1994).

5. Confession of Sins (9:32–37)

³²"Now therefore, O our God, the great, mighty and awesome God, who keeps his covenant of love, do not let all this hardship seem trifling in your eyes—the hardship that has come upon us, upon our kings and leaders, upon our priests and prophets, upon our fathers and all your people, from the days of the kings of Assyria until today. ³³In all that has happened to us, you have been just; you have acted faithfully, while we did wrong. ³⁴Our kings, our leaders, our priests and our fathers did not follow your law; they did not

pay attention to your commands or the warnings you gave them. [35]Even while they were in their kingdom, enjoying your great goodness to them in the spacious and fertile land you gave them, they did not serve you or turn from their evil ways.

[36]"But see, we are slaves today, slaves in the land you gave our forefathers so they could eat its fruit and the other good things it produces. [37]Because of our sins, its abundant harvest goes to the kings you have placed over us. They rule over our bodies and our cattle as they please. We are in great distress.

COMMENTARY

32 "Now" marks the transition from a survey of the past to a supplication for the present situation. God is "mighty" (cf. 1:5; Dt 10:17; Da 9:4), and he "keeps his covenant of love" (see 1:5; Dt 7:9; 1Ki 8:23; 2Ch 6:14; Ps 89:28).

K. Baltzer (*The Covenant Formulary* [rev. ed.; Philadelphia: Fortress, 1971], 43–47) compares Nehemiah 9–10 with the covenantal formula found in the Pentateuch and in Hittite sovereignty treaties.

Treaty Form	Nehemiah 9–10
Title/Preamble	(missing)
Antecedent history	9:7–37
Stipulations: basic	10:29b
Stipulations: specific	10:30–39
Witnesses	9:38–10:29a
Curses and Blessings	10:29 (the curse is implied, and future blessings are not specified)

The nation suffered "hardship" (*telāʾâ*; cf. Ex 18:8; Nu 20:14; La 3:5).

One of the "kings of Assyria" was Shalmaneser III (858–824 BC), who is not mentioned in the OT. He reported that he defeated Ahab at the important battle of Qarqar in 853 (*DOTT*, 46–47). The first Assyrian king to expand his empire to the Mediterranean was the great Tiglath-Pileser III, also know as Pul. He attacked Phoenicia in 736, Philistia in 734, and Damascus in 732 (ibid., 53ff.). Early in his reign (752–742), Menahem of Israel paid tribute to him (2Ki 15:19–20; *ANET*, 283–84). During his campaigns against Damascus, Pul also ravaged Gilead and Galilee and destroyed Hazor and Megiddo (2Ki 15:29; *ANET*, 284).

Shalmaneser V (727–722) laid siege to Samaria—a task completed by Sargon II (721–705). Sargon's commander carried on operations against Ashdod (Isa 20:1). Sennacherib (704–681) failed to take Jerusalem in 701 (2Ki 18:13–17) but captured Lachish (*DOTT*, 64–73). Esarhaddon (681–669) conquered Egypt and extracted tribute from Manasseh of Judah (2Ki 19:37; Isa 37:38; Ezr 4:2; *DOTT*, 73–75). Ashurbanipal (669–633) was probably the king who freed Manasseh from exile and restored him as a puppet king (2Ch 33:13; Ezr 4:9). (See W. W. Hallo, "From Qarqar to Carchemish: Assyria and Israel in the Light of New Discoveries," *BA* 23 [1960]: 34–61.)

33–34 In all that happened God had "been just" (v.33; cf. 2Ch 12:6; Ezr 9:15; Ps 119:137; Jer 12:1; Da 9:14), but the people still "did not pay attention" (v.34).

35 A. R. Millard ("'For He Is Good,'" *TynBul* 17 [1966]: 115–17) notes that "goodness" is used in extrabiblical covenants with the connotation of friendship. It is an attribute of God's covenantal faithfulness, in a "spacious" (see comment on 7:4; cf. Ex 3:8; Jdg 18:10; 1Ch 4:40; Isa 22:18) and "fertile" (*š^emēnâ*, "fat"; see v.25) land. Yet the people did not turn from their "evil ways" (cf. Dt 28:20; Jdg 2:19; Ps 106:39; Isa 1:16; Jer 4:4; 21:12; 23:2, 22; Hos 9:15; Zec 1:4).

36 The people were "slaves" (see comments on Ezr 9:9; Ne 5:5) in the fruitful land God had given their forefathers (see 10:35, 37; Isa 1:19; Jer 2:7). L. L. Grabbe (*Judaism from Cyrus to Hadrian* [Minneapolis: Fortress, 1992], 1:56) comments, "Despite the often alleged beneficence of the Persian rule, this prayer asserts that they are still 'servants' (9:36: *ʿᵃbādîm*) in their land and in great distress because they are still under the rulership of a foreign power which reaches down to their cattle and even their own bodies (9:37)."

37 On taxes, see comment on 5:4.

The term *g^ewîyâ* ("bodies"; GK 1581), used thirteen times in the OT, characterizes human beings in weakness, oppression, or trouble (e.g., Ge 47:18 – 19). It is also used of a "corpse" (1Sa 31:10, 12; Ps 110:6; Na 3:3) or of a "carcass" (Jdg 14:8 – 9). The Persian rulers drafted their subjects into military service. Possibly some Jews accompanied Xerxes on his invasion of Greece.

The prayer of Ezra in Nehemiah 9:5 – 37 has had a profound impact on the Jewish synagogue service (so J. Liebreich, "The Impact of Nehemiah 9.5 – 37 on the Liturgy of the Synagogue," *HUCA* 32 [1961]: 227 – 37).

NOTE

32 On the Assyrians, see W. C. Gwaltney Jr., "Assyrians," in Hoerth, Mattingly, and Yamauchi, 77 – 106. On the campaigns of Sennacherib, Esarhaddon, and Ashurbanipal, see Yamauchi, *Africa and the Bible*, 122 – 25, 133 – 40.

6. A Binding Agreement (9:38 [10:1])

38 "In view of all this, we are making a binding agreement, putting it in writing, and our leaders, our Levites and our priests are affixing their seals to it."

COMMENTARY

38 [10:1] "Making" is literally "cutting"; see comment on Ezra 10:3. "A binding agreement" translates *ᵃmānâ* (GK 591), which occurs only here and in 11:23, where it means a "royal prescription." The word is related to "amen," and its root has the connotation of constancy. The KJV and RV translate it "sure covenant." The usual word for covenant (*b^erît*) appears in 1:5; 9:8, 32; 13:29; and in Ezra 10:3. The Qumran community evidently practiced an annual renewal of their covenant with God. See Helmer Ringgren, *The Faith of Qumran* (Philadelphia: Fortress, 1963), 225 – 27.

The Old Aramaic inscription of Panammu I, dated to the eighth century BC, has a similar expression: *ʾmn krt* (*ʾmōn krīt*, "a sure covenant struck"; cf. J. Fitzmyer, *The Aramaic Inscriptions of Sefire* [Rome: Pontifical Biblical Institute, 1967], 32–33).

M. J. Boda (*Praying the Tradition: The Origin and Use of Tradition in Nehemiah 9* [Berlin: de Gruyter, 1999]) believes that Nehemiah 9 was part of a Persian-period covenant ceremony, a suggestion criticized by B. Becking ("Nehemiah 9 and the Problematic Concept of Context [*Sitz im Leben*]," in *The Changing Face of Form Criticism for the Twenty-First Century* [ed. M. A. Sweeney and E. Ben Zvi; Grand Rapids: Eerdmans, 2003], 253–68).

a. A List of Those Who Sealed It (10:1–29 [2–30])

[1]Those who sealed it were:

Nehemiah the governor, the son of Hacaliah.

Zedekiah, [2]Seraiah, Azariah, Jeremiah,
[3]Pashhur, Amariah, Malkijah,
[4]Hattush, Shebaniah, Malluch,
[5]Harim, Meremoth, Obadiah,
[6]Daniel, Ginnethon, Baruch,
[7]Meshullam, Abijah, Mijamin,
[8]Maaziah, Bilgai and Shemaiah.
These were the priests.

[9]The Levites:

Jeshua son of Azaniah, Binnui of the sons of Henadad, Kadmiel,
[10]and their associates: Shebaniah,
Hodiah, Kelita, Pelaiah, Hanan,
[11]Mica, Rehob, Hashabiah,
[12]Zaccur, Sherebiah, Shebaniah,
[13]Hodiah, Bani and Beninu.

[14]The leaders of the people:

Parosh, Pahath-Moab, Elam, Zattu, Bani,
[15]Bunni, Azgad, Bebai,
[16]Adonijah, Bigvai, Adin,
[17]Ater, Hezekiah, Azzur,
[18]Hodiah, Hashum, Bezai,
[19]Hariph, Anathoth, Nebai,
[20]Magpiash, Meshullam, Hezir,
[21]Meshezabel, Zadok, Jaddua,
[22]Pelatiah, Hanan, Anaiah,

²³Hoshea, Hananiah, Hasshub,
²⁴Hallohesh, Pilha, Shobek,
²⁵Rehum, Hashabnah, Maaseiah,
²⁶Ahiah, Hanan, Anan,
²⁷Malluch, Harim and Baanah.

²⁸"The rest of the people — priests, Levites, gatekeepers, singers, temple servants and all who separated themselves from the neighboring peoples for the sake of the Law of God, together with their wives and all their sons and daughters who are able to understand — ²⁹all these now join their brothers the nobles, and bind themselves with a curse and an oath to follow the Law of God given through Moses the servant of God and to obey carefully all the commands, regulations and decrees of the LORD our Lord.

COMMENTARY

1 [2] This list is a legal one bearing the official seal and containing a roster of eighty-four names arranged according to the following categories: leaders, priests, Levites, and laymen. Nehemiah heads the list. Some scholars have explained the absence of Ezra's name by supposing that Ezra may have been the author of the agreement. Zedekiah may be identified with Zadok the scribe (13:13), as the latter is a shortened form of the longer name.

2 [3] Verses 2–8 contain twenty-one names, most of which recur in 12:1–7. "Jeremiah" ("May Yahweh raise up!") is the name of five persons in the OT, including the prophet.

6 [7] "Baruch" ("blessed") was also the name of Jeremiah's scribe. A seal with the latter's name and patronymic has been published by N. Avigad ("Baruch the Scribe and Jerahmeel the King's Son," *BA* 42 [1979]: 114–18). On the subject of seals, see L. Gorelick and E. Williams, *Ancient Seals and the Bible* (Malibu, Calif.: Undena, 1983); O. Keel, "Ancient Seals and the Bible," *JAOS* 106 (1986): 307–11; idem, *Corpus der Stempelsiegel-Amulette aus Palästina/Israel: von den Anfängen bis zur Perserzeit* (Freiburg/Göttingen: Universtätsverlag/Vandenhoeck & Ruprecht, 1995).

7 [8] "Abijah" ("Yahweh is my father") is the name of nine individuals in the OT. It occurs in the Murashu texts as *ʾabī-ya-a-ma*, that is, *ʾabîyaw* (Coogan, 12).

8 [9] "Maaziah" ("Yahweh is a refuge") occurs only here and in 1 Chronicles 24:18. "Bilgai" ("cheerfulness") occurs only here.

In Ezra 2:36–39 four priestly families are listed; in the later list of 1 Chronicles 24:7–18, we have the arrangement of twenty-four courses that served as the basis of the rotation for priestly service (Lk 1:8). J. Liver (*Chapters in the History of the Priests and Levites* [Jerusalem: Magness, 1968], ix) suggests that it may have been Nehemiah himself who established the twenty-four-course arrangement.

9 [10] Of the Levites seventeen are mentioned by name. "Azaniah" ("Yahweh has heard") occurs only here.

10 [11] "Associates" is literally "brothers."

11 [12] "Mica" is a shortened form of "Michael" ("Who is like God?"). "Rehob" ("spacious") occurs only here and in 2 Samuel 8:3, 12 as a personal name.

13 [14] "Beninu" ("our son") occurs only here.

14 [15] Of the leaders of the people listed here (vv.14–27), twenty are also found in the lists of Ezra 2 and Nehemiah 7. For the etymology of these names, see comments on Ezra 2.

19 [20] "Anathoth," a name derived from the Canaanite goddess Anath, is also the name of the home city of Jeremiah (Jer 1:1). As a personal name it occurs only here and in 1 Chronicles 7:8. "Nebai," a name of unknown meaning, occurs only here.

20 [21] "Magpiash," a name of unknown significance, occurs only here. "Hezir" means "swine" (cf. 1Ch 24:15). On animal names as nicknames, see comment on Ezra 2:3. The related noun $h^a z\hat{i}r$ occurs only seven times in the OT. Leviticus 11:7 and Deuteronomy 14:8 forbid the eating of swine's flesh. Isaiah 65:4; 66:3, 17 describe apostate Jews who ate swine's flesh in heathen sacrifices. In Psalm 80:13 [14] an enemy is described as being like a wild boar, and in Proverbs 11:22 a beautiful woman without discretion is likened to a golden ring in a pig's snout. Antiochus IV sought to compel Jews to eat pork (1 Macc 1:47; 2 Macc 6:18; cf. Mt 7:6; 2Pe 2:22). (See Alfred von Rohr, "The Cultic Role of the Pig in Ancient Times," in *In Memoriam Paul Kahle* [ed. M. Black and G. Fohrer; Berlin: A. Topelmann, 1968], 201–7.)

Archaeological evidence indicates that pigs were raised in Palestine in rural areas, especially in the coastal areas where the Philistines settled, such as Tel Miqne, Tel Batash, and Ashkelon. But they were absent from Iron Age I Judean sites, probably because of the Jewish prohibition against pork. See B. Hesse, "Pig Lovers and Pig Haters: Patterns of Palestinian Pork Production," *Journal of Ethnobiology* 10 (1990): 195–225.

22 [23] "Pelatiah" means "Yahweh delivers."

23 [24] "Hoshea" means "May Yahweh save!" (cf. the name of the prophet Hosea).

24 [25] On the name "Hallohesh" see comment on 3:12. "Pilha" ("millstone") occurs only here, as does "Shobek" ("victor").

26 [27] "Ahiah" ("my brother is Yahweh") occurs in the Murashu texts as $\hat{}ah\bar{i}yaw$ (Coogan, 12). "Anan" (short for Ananiah ["Yahweh has manifested himself"]) occurs only here.

28 [29] On Levites, see comment on Ezra 2:40; on gatekeepers and singers, see comment on 2:41; on temple servants, see comment on 2:43; and on wives and children, see comment on Nehemiah 8:2–3.

29 [30] This verse recalls Deuteronomy 27–29; see comments on Ezra 10:5 and Nehemiah 5:13. "A curse" (ʾālâ) means an adjuration with an imprecation of grievous punishments in case of failure to keep the oath. (See J. Pedersen, *Der Eid bei den Semiten* [Strasbourg: Trubner, 1914]; A. D. Crown, "Aposiopesis in the Old Testament and the Hebrew Conditional Oath," *AbrN* 4 [1963–64]: 96–111; M. G. Kline, "Oath and Ordeal Signs," *WTJ* 27 [1965]: 115–39.) Clines, 211, comments, "No one could any longer plead that his neglect of the law was of no consequence, nor could anyone doubt that his personal response to the will of God would in some way contribute to the welfare of his society as a whole."

NOTE

1 [2] A. Sivertsev ("Sects and Households: Social Structure of the Proto-Sectarian Movement of Nehemiah 10 and the Dead Sea Sect," *CBQ* 67 [2005]: 59–78), who holds that Nehemiah 10 was a covenant, seeks the origins of some of the later sects, such as the Qumran community, in Babylonian roots.

b. Provisions of the Agreement (10:30–39 [31–40])

i. Mixed marriages (10:30 [31])

> ³⁰"We promise not to give our daughters in marriage to the peoples around us or take their daughters for our sons.

COMMENTARY

30 [31] On mixed marriages, see the Reflection at the end of the commentary on Ezra 10.

ii. Commerce on the Sabbath (10:31a [32a])

> ³¹"When the neighboring peoples bring merchandise or grain to sell on the Sabbath, we will not buy from them on the Sabbath or on any holy day.

COMMENTARY

31a [32a] "Merchandise," from *maqqāḥôt*, is only found here. "Grain" translates *šeber* ("victuals," KJV). The provisions of vv. 31–34 may have been a code drawn up by Nehemiah to correct the abuses listed in ch. 13 (e.g., vv. 15–22).

Though the Sabbath passages in the Torah (Ex 20:8–11; Dt 5:12–15) do not explicitly prohibit trading on the Sabbath, this is clearly understood in Jeremiah 17:19–27 and Amos 8:5. Sivertsev ("Sects and Households," 76) notes some striking parallels from Qumran's Damascus Document:

> Similar to Nehemiah's laws, CD 12:8–11 prohibits a member of the sect from selling animals, clean birds, or "anything from his granary or his press" to Gentiles. Somewhat earlier, the same text states that "no one should stay in a place close to Gentiles on the Sabbath." It further requires that "no one shall violate the Sabbath for the sake of wealth or profit on the Sabbath" (11:14–15).

iii. The sabbatical year (10:31b [32b])

> Every seventh year we will forgo working the land and will cancel all debts.

COMMENTARY

31b [32b] According to the Mosaic legislation (Ex 23:10–11; Lev 25:2–7), in the seventh year the land was to lie fallow, and collection of debts was not to take place (Dt 15:1–3).

F. Mezzacasas ("Esdras; Nehemias y el año Sabatico," *RevistB* 23 [1961]: 1–9, 82–96) argues from parallels with Deuteronomy 31:10–11 that Nehemiah 8–10 is set in the context of a sabbatical year. He concludes that this year is 430/429 BC. Extrabiblical references include 1 Maccabees 6:49, 54; Philo (*Spec.* 2.104); and Josephus (*Ant.* 3.280–81 [12.3]; 12.378 [9.5]; 13.234 [8.2]; 14.202 [10.6], 206 [10.6], 475 [16.1]; 15.7 [1.1]; *J.W.* 1.60 [2.4]). The Romans misrepresented the Sabbath and the sabbatical year as indications of laziness. According to Tacitus (*Histories* 5.4): "They were led by the charms of indolence to give over the seventh year as well to inactivity."

Inasmuch as most of the topics addressed in ch. 10 correspond with those found in ch. 13, (1) mixed marriages (10:30 = 13:23–30), (2) Sabbath observance (10:31 = 13:15–22), (3) wood offering (10:34 = 13:31), (4) firstfruits (10:35–36 = 13:31), (5) Levitical tithes (10:37–38 = 13:10–14), and (6) neglect of the temple (10:39 = 13:11), Williamson (*Ezra, Nehemiah*, 331) concludes, "Nehemiah 10 followed Nehemiah 13 from a historical point of view."

iv. Offerings for the temple and its staff (10:32–39 [33–40])

[32]"We assume the responsibility for carrying out the commands to give a third of a shekel each year for the service of the house of our God: [33]for the bread set out on the table; for the regular grain offerings and burnt offerings; for the offerings on the Sabbaths, New Moon festivals and appointed feasts; for the holy offerings; for sin offerings to make atonement for Israel; and for all the duties of the house of our God.

[34]"We — the priests, the Levites and the people — have cast lots to determine when each of our families is to bring to the house of our God at set times each year a contribution of wood to burn on the altar of the LORD our God, as it is written in the Law.

[35]"We also assume responsibility for bringing to the house of the LORD each year the firstfruits of our crops and of every fruit tree.

[36]"As it is also written in the Law, we will bring the firstborn of our sons and of our cattle, of our herds and of our flocks to the house of our God, to the priests ministering there.

[37]"Moreover, we will bring to the storerooms of the house of our God, to the priests, the first of our ground meal, of our grain offerings, of the fruit of all our trees and of our new wine and oil. And we will bring a tithe of our crops to the Levites, for it is the Levites who collect the tithes in all the towns where we work. [38]A priest descended from Aaron is to accompany the Levites when they receive the tithes, and the Levites are to bring a tenth of the tithes up to the house of our God, to the storerooms of the treasury. [39]The people of Israel, including the Levites, are to bring their contributions of grain, new wine and oil

to the storerooms where the articles for the sanctuary are kept and where the ministering priests, the gatekeepers and the singers stay.
"We will not neglect the house of our God."

COMMENTARY

32 [33] Exodus 30:13–14 states that a "half shekel is an offering to the LORD" from each man twenty years old and older as a symbolical ransom. Later Joash used the annual contributions to repair the temple (2Ch 24:4–14). In the NT period Jewish men everywhere sent an offering of a half shekel (actually its equivalent) for the temple in Jerusalem (Mt 17:24).

Several explanations have been suggested why the offering should be a one-third shekel rather than a half shekel.

1. Some maintain that the half shekel of Exodus (30:16; 38:25–28) was meant as a onetime offering for the construction of the tabernacle and therefore has no bearing on the offering in Nehemiah 10:32.
2. Others argue that the offering was reduced from one-half to one-third because of economic impoverishment.
3. Some argue that the later shekel was based on a heavier standard, thus one-third of the later shekel was equal to one-half of the earlier shekel. That is, the later Babylonian-Persian shekel was twenty-one grams, whereas the former Phoenician shekel was fourteen grams, hence one-third the former was equal to one-half the latter.

The weights of the Babylonian shekel varied from 8.3 grams to 16.7 grams, with an average of 11.42 grams. According to Kenyon (*Digging Up Jerusalem*, 103): "The surprising point to emerge is that the weight of 4 shekels in absolutely mint condition gave a shekel value of 11.34 grammes, and this can be taken as the standard in use in Jerusalem in the reign of Zedekiah, immediately before the Babylonian destruction of the city." A third of a shekel would normally weigh about four grams or about one-eighth of an ounce.

33 [34] "The bread set out on the table" (*leḥem hammaᶜᵃreket*) is literally "bread of arrangement" ("shewbread," KJV) and consisted of twelve cakes of fine flour arranged in two rows of six set out each Sabbath (Lev 24:6–7). Elsewhere they are also called (*leḥem happāním*, "bread of the face"), that is, bread set before the presence of God (Ex 25:30; 1Sa 21:6 [7]; 1Ki 7:48; cf. A. H. de Boer, "An Aspect of Sacrifice I: Divine Bread," *VTSup* 23 [1972]: 27–36). Brockington, 184, comments that "*in meaning* it was both a reminder to men of the presence of God and a token gift by men to God of that which was a daily necessity." (See E. Yamauchi, "The Daily Bread Motif in Antiquity," *WTJ* 28 [1966]: 145–56.) In pagan cults such food was meant literally to provide nourishment for the gods. (See E. Yamauchi, "Anthropomorphism in Ancient Religions," *BSac* 125 [1968]: 29–44.)

On "regular grain offerings," see Exodus 29:38–41; Numbers 28:3–8. On "burnt offerings," compare Ezra 8:35.

"The Sabbaths, New Moon festivals and appointed feasts" recall Numbers 28:9–16. "To make atonement" translates *kipper* (Piel of *kāpar*), which means "to cover, wipe away" one's sin, hence to expiate. It describes the effect of the sin offerings and trespass offerings (Lev 4:20; Nu 5:8).

34 [35] "Lots" (plural of *gôrāl*) were used frequently to determine the will of the Lord to (1) apportion the land among the tribes (Nu 26:55; Jos 14:2; 18:10); (2) detect a guilty person (Jos 7:14; 1Sa 14:42; Jnh 1:7); (3) choose the first king, Saul (1Sa 10:19–21); (4) settle disputes (Pr 18:18); (5) determine the courses of the priests, singers, and gatekeepers (1Ch 24:5; 25:8; 26:13; Lk 1:9); (6) determine who should dwell in Jerusalem (Ne 11:1); and (7) choose the replacement of Judas Iscariot (Ac 1:26).

In a secular connection, Haman cast lots to determine the time to act against the Jews (Est 3:7; 9:24). Roman soldiers cast lots to gain the garment of Jesus (Mt 27:35; Mk 15:24; Lk 23:34; Jn 19:24).

Though there is no specific reference to a wood offering in the Pentateuch, the perpetual burning of fires would have required a continual "contribution of wood" (cf. 13:31; Lev 6:12–13). Josephus mentions "the festival of wood-offering" on the fourteenth day of the fifth month (Ab), when all the people were accustomed to bringing wood for the altar (*J.W.* 2.425 [17.6]). The Mishnah (*m. Taʿan.* 4.5) lists nine times when certain families brought wood. See further J. Epstein, "Die Zeiten des Holzopfers," *Monatschrift für Geschichte und Wissenschaft des Judentums* 78 (1934): 97–103; L. I. Rabinowitz, *Torah and Flora* (New York: Sanhedrin, 1977), 64–69.

Jubilees 21:13 specifies: "And of these kinds of wood lay upon the altar under the sacrifice, and do not lay [thereon] any split or dark wood, [but] hard and clean without fault, a sound and new growth, and do not lay [thereon] old wood, for there is no longer fragrance in it as before."

Columns 23–25 of the Temple Scroll from Qumran describe the celebration of the wood-offering festival. The provision of wood for the six days is assigned as follows: (1) first day, Levi and Judah; (2) second day, Benjamin and Joseph's sons, Ephraim and Manasseh; (3) third day, Reuben and Simeon; (4) fourth day, Issachar and Zebulun; (5) fifth day, Gad and Asher; and (6) sixth day, Dan and Naphtali (see J. Milgrom, "The Temple Scroll," *BA* 41 [1978]: 108; Y. Yadin, *The Temple Scroll* [London: Weidenfeld and Nicholson, 1985], 101–11).

35 [36] The offerings of the "firstfruits" were brought to the temple for the support of the priests and Levites (Ex 23:19; 34:26; Lev 19:23–24; Nu 18:13; Dt 26:1–11; Eze 44:30). Actually, the Torah stipulated only seven kinds of plants for the firstfruits. The promise to bring the firstfruits of "every tree" was an act of exceptional piety.

36 [37] The firstborn of men and beasts (Ex 13:1–16) and the firstfruits of field and garden (Lev 19:23–25) were to be given to God. They could be set free for secular use only by redemption (Ex 13:13, 15; 34:20; Lev 27:26–33; Nu 3:44–51; 18:15–17; Dt 14:23–26). M. Tsevat (*TDOT*, 2:126) says, "It is not only the best that belongs to God, but also the first. It would be presumptuous for man to enjoy something without first giving God his portion."

37 [38] On "storerooms," see Ezra 8:29; 10:6. "Ground meal" (*ʿărîsâ*) is mixed dough at the first stage (Nu 15:20–21). On "offferings" (*tᵉrûmâ*), see Ezra 8:25; Nehemiah 10:39; 12:44; 13:5. Literally it means "what is lifted." ("heave offering," KJV; cf. Ex 29:27–28). These contributions were for the maintenance of the priests.

"New wine" is *tîrôš*, which the LXX always translates *oinos* ("wine") and not *gleukos* ("new wine"), the term used in Acts 2:13. Though *tîrôš* can refer to freshly pressed grape juice (Isa 65:8; Mic 6:15), it can still be intoxicating (Hos 4:11).

The word is an archaic term often used in summaries of agricultural products (Ge 27:28; Dt 7:13; 11:14; 18:4; 2Ki 18:32; Jer 31:12) and is used exclusively in the Qumran texts. *Yiṣhār* is an archaic term for olive oil used in the same lists of agricultural products as *tîrôš*.

"A tithe of our crops" is literally "tithe of our land." The practice of giving a tenth was an ancient one (Ge 14:20; 28:22). The law of Moses decreed that one-tenth of the planted crops was holy to the Lord (Lev 27:30; Nu 18:23–32). There is no reference here to a tithe of cattle (as in Lev 27:32–33). Earlier in the fifth century BC, the prophet Malachi accused the Israelites of robbing God by withholding tithes and offerings (Mal 3:8). Tithes were meant for the support of the Levites (13:10–12; Nu 18:21–32). A tithe of this tithe was to go to the priests. But we know from Josephus that later on the priests collected the tithes for themselves. But not everyone paid his tithe. And because the tithe was originally expressed in terms of agricultural produce, the burden of the tithe fell disproportionately on farmers (see J. Jeremias, *Jerusalem in the Time of Jesus* [Philadelphia: Fortress, 1969], 106–7).

38 [39] The Levites were to give in their turn "a tenth of the tithes" they received (Nu 18:25–32). Chambers in the outer courts of the temple were used as "storerooms" for silver, gold, and other objects (cf. vv.39–40; 12:44; 13:4–5, 9; Ezr 8:29; 1 Macc 4:38).

39 [40] *Dāgān* means "grain" and cereal crops. Formerly people referred to a "corn" of salt. But "corn" in America means maize or Indian corn. In the KJV "corn" occurs 101 times; it is uniformly replaced by "grain" in the RSV and NRSV.

The people pledged that they would "not neglect" God's house. The prophet Haggai (Hag 1:4–9) had accused the people of neglecting the temple.

In an instructive analysis, David J. A. Clines ("Nehemiah 10 as an Example of Early Jewish Biblical Exegesis," *JSOT* 21 [1981]: 111) writes: "Nehemiah 10, despite its forbidding portal of 27 verses of proper names, is in reality a small treasure house of post-exilic interpretations of earlier Israelite law." Inasmuch as circumstances change over time, it has always been necessary to interpret biblical precepts in order to apply them to different situations. The later Pharisees debated these issues, which were eventually recorded in the Mishnah (ca. AD 200), which was in turn expounded in the later Babylonian and Palestinian Talmuds. Clines discerns five types of legal developments: (1) the creation of facilitating law (10:35); (2) revision of facilitating law (10:39); (3) creation of a new prescription from a precedent (10:33); (4) redefinition of categories, always in the direction of greater comprehensiveness (10:36); and (5) integration of potentially competing prescriptions (10:36–40).

NOTE

31 [32] An example of the later disputes involving Jews and their relationship to Gentiles is found in the Mishnah (*m. Šabb.* 1:7): "The School of Shammai say: They may not sell aught to a gentile or help him to load his beast or raise [a burden] on his shoulders unless there is time for him to reach a place near by [the same day]. And the School of Hillel permits it."

I. The New Residents of Judah and Jerusalem (11:1–36)

1. Selection of the New Residents (11:1–2)

¹Now the leaders of the people settled in Jerusalem, and the rest of the people cast lots to bring one out of every ten to live in Jerusalem, the holy city, while the remaining nine were to stay in their own towns. ²The people commended all the men who volunteered to live in Jerusalem.

COMMENTARY

1 On "lots," see comments on 10:34. Lots were made out of small stones or small pieces of wood. The pre-Islamic Arabs used wooden arrows without points (cf. Eze 21:21; Hos 4:12). They were shaken (Pr 16:33) and cast (Ob 11; Na 3:10) on the ground (1Ch 24:31; Eze 24:6; Jnh 1:7). Lots are also described as "coming out" (Nu 33:54; Jos 19:1, 17; 1Ch 24:7; 25:9; 26:14).

"The holy city" (cf. v.18) is a rare use in a historical narrative of the phrase that is usually found in prophetic texts (e.g., Isa 48:2; 52:1; Da 9:24; Joel 3:17). The designation is also used in the NT (Mt 4:5; 27:53; Rev 11:2). The Arabic name for Jerusalem is *al-Quds* ("The Holy [City]").

"The remaining nine" is literally "the nine of the hands [or 'parts']." According to Sirach 49:13, "The memory of Nehemiah also is lasting, he raised for us the walls that had fallen, and set up the gates and bars and rebuilt our ruined houses." Josephus (*Ant.* 11.181 [5.8]) asserts, "But Nehemiah, seeing that the city had a small population, urged the priests and Levites to leave the countryside and move to the city and remain there, for he had prepared houses for them at his own expense."

The practice of redistributing populations was also used to establish Greek and Hellenistic cities. The practice involved the forcible transfer from rural settlements to urban centers. The city of Tiberias, on the western shore of the Sea of Galilee, was populated through such a process by Herod Antipas in AD 18 (Josephus, *Ant.* 18.36–38 [2.3]).

Estimates of the population of Jerusalem in Nehemiah's day vary. The total number of new male settlers to supplement those already in the city (Ne 11:6–19) is about 3,000. This would imply a total population of 11,000–12,000 (according to E.-M. Laperrousaz, "Jérusalem à l'époque perse [étendue et statut]," *Transeu* 1 [1989]: 56–57; cf. Laperrousaz and Lemaire, 125). D. E. Gowan (*Bridge between the Testaments* [Pittsburgh, Pa.: Pickwick, 1976], 20) suggests 8,000. M. Broshi ("La population de l'ancienne Jérusalem," *RB* 92 [1975]: 9–10, 13), who multiplies an area of 120 dunams (a dunam equaling 1,000 square meters) by 40 persons, arrives at a figure of 4,800. This is quite a drop from an area of 500 dunams (125 acres) and 20,000 people during the time of Josiah (ca. 609 BC). C. E. Carter ("The Province of Yehud in the Post-Exilic Period," in *Second Temple Studies II: Temple and Community in the Persian Period* [ed. T. C. Eskenazi and K. H. Richards; Sheffield: JSOT, 1994], 129–36) has proposed a radically minimalist number for Judah in general, and for Jerusalem in particular. He estimates a population of Judah in Nehemiah's day as only 17,000 and Jerusalem as only 1,250–1,500.

Archaeological surveys indicate a drop of over 75 percent of the number of occupied sites as a result of the Babylonian conquest of Judah. I. Milevski ("Settlement Patterns in Northern Judah during the Achaemenid Period, according to the Hill Country of Benjamin and Jerusalem Surveys," *Bulletin of the Anglo-Israel Archaeological Socioety* 15 [1996–97]: 20) concludes:

> Nevertheless, in the proximity of Jerusalem, the decrease in the number of sites is less than that of the rest of the Land of Benjamin. The majority of sites are concentrated along the ancient roads which linked Jerusalem with its relatively close surround-

ings. This situation may be reflected in Nehemiah 11, which tells the story of the resettlement of Jerusalem by relocating a tenth part of the town and village population to the capital of the province.

2 In addition to those chosen by lot, some men volunteered, from a sense of duty, to live in Jerusalem (v.2). Evidently most would have preferred to stay in their native towns and villages (cf. Ezr 2:1). "Commended" (lit., "blessed") is a word usually used of God but at times, as here, of people (cf. 1Ch 16:2; 2Ch 6:3; 30:27).

NOTE

1 Broshi's estimate used a population coefficient of 40 persons per dunam (1,000 square meters), which would be then equal to 400 per hectare (10 dunams = 10,000 square meters = 2 1/2 acres). Such coefficients can vary from 25 to 500 per hectare. J. R. Zorn ("Estimating the Population Size of Ancient Settlements: Methods, Problems, Solutions, and a Case Study," *BASOR* 295 [1994]: 44), on the basis of a detailed study of the excavation results from Mizpah, cautions: "If, as we have suggested, the population of Tell en-Nasbeh was between 800 and 1000, the density coefficient will be between 470 and 590 in the Stratum 3C town. This is significantly higher than the most recent figures cited in table 1, and provides a caution against using such general estimates when the habitation pattern and settlement type of a site are not known."

2. The Provincial Leaders (11:3–24)

a. A Topical Statement (11:3–4a)

³These are the provincial leaders who settled in Jerusalem (now some Israelites, priests, Levites, temple servants and descendants of Solomon's servants lived in the towns of Judah, each on his own property in the various towns, **⁴**while other people from both Judah and Benjamin lived in Jerusalem):

COMMENTARY

3–4a These verses succinctly preview the specifics of vv.4b–36. Verses 3–19 are a census roster that can be compared with the list in 1 Chronicles 9:2–21 of the first residents in Jerusalem after the return from Babylonia. About half the names in the two lists are identical.

b. From Judah (11:4b–6)

From the descendants of Judah:

Athaiah son of Uzziah, the son of Zechariah, the son of Amariah, the son of Shephatiah, the son of Mahalalel, a descendant of Perez; [5]and Maaseiah son of Baruch, the son of Col-Hozeh, the son of Hazaiah, the son of Adaiah, the son of Joiarib, the son of Zechariah, a descendant of Shelah. [6]The descendants of Perez who lived in Jerusalem totaled 468 able men.

COMMENTARY

4b "Athaiah" ("Yahweh has shown himself preeminent") occurs only here. "Mahalalel" means "God is one who illuminates." "Perez" ("Breach") was also the name of one of the twin sons born to Judah (Ge 38:29).

5 "Hazaiah" ("Yahweh has seen") occurs only here. For "Shelah" the MT has "Shilonite," that is, an inhabitant of Shiloh, which belonged to the northern kingdom rather than to Judah. The word, therefore, should be revocalized to indicate a descendant of Shelah, Judah's third son (Nu 26:20).

6 "Able men" (ʾanšê-ḥāyil) literally means "men of valor." These were originally valiant, free men whose later descendants became wealthy and served in the armed forces (cf. v.14; 2:9; 4:2; 2Ki 15:20; Ezr 8:22).

c. From Benjamin (11:7–9)

[7]From the descendants of Benjamin:

Sallu son of Meshullam, the son of Joed, the son of Pedaiah, the son of Kolaiah, the son of Maaseiah, the son of Ithiel, the son of Jeshaiah, [8]and his followers, Gabbai and Sallai — 928 men. [9]Joel son of Zicri was their chief officer, and Judah son of Hassenuah was over the Second District of the city.

COMMENTARY

7 For "Benjamin," see comment on Ezra 4:1. "Joed" ("Yahweh is witness") occurs only here. "Kolaiah" ("voice of Yahweh") occurs only here and in Jeremiah 29:21. "Ithiel" ("God is with me") occurs only here and in Proverbs 30:1.

8 "Gabbai" derives from the verb "to be high" (cf. Ugar. gby; Gabābēl, "Bel is exalted" [Coogan, 70]).

9 "Zicri" is short for Zechariah. "The Second District" translates mišneh, which some English versions transliterate as "Mishneh." Like the "market district" (*maktēš*) in Zephaniah 1:11 (probably the Tyropoeon Valley area), the Mishneh was a new suburb to the west of the temple area. Excavations by B. Mazar and N. Avigad indicate that the city had spread outside the walls in this direction by the late eighth century BC before the "broad wall" was built about 700 BC by Hezekiah (see comment on 3:8; cf. Y. Yadin, *Jerusalem Revealed* [Jerusalem: Israel Exploration Society, 1975], 8, 41–44; also Zep 1:10–11).

NOTE

7 Benjamin provided twice as many men (928) as Judah (468) to protect the city of Jerusalem. There are many parallels between the names found in Nehemiah 11:3–19 and a similar but not identical list in 1 Chronicles 9:2–17, for example, "Sallu son of Meshullam" (Ne 11:7) = "Sallu son of Meshullam" (1Ch 9:7). For the complex relationship between the lists, see Williamson (*Ezra, Nehemiah*, 344–50); G. N. Knoppers, "Sources, Revisions, and Editions: The Lists of Jerusalem's Residents in MT and LXX Nehemiah 11 and 1 Chronicles 9," *Proof* 20 (2000): 141–68.

d. From the Priests (11:10–14)

¹⁰From the priests:

Jedaiah; the son of Joiarib; Jakin; ¹¹Seraiah son of Hilkiah, the son of Meshullam, the son of Zadok, the son of Meraioth, the son of Ahitub, supervisor in the house of God, ¹²and their associates, who carried on work for the temple — 822 men; Adaiah son of Jeroham, the son of Pelaliah, the son of Amzi, the son of Zechariah, the son of Pashhur, the son of Malkijah, ¹³and his associates, who were heads of families — 242 men; Amashsai son of Azarel, the son of Ahzai, the son of Meshillemoth, the son of Immer, ¹⁴and his associates, who were able men — 128. Their chief officer was Zabdiel son of Haggedolim.

COMMENTARY

10 To be qualified as a priest, one had to establish his descent through genealogical records, which would trace one's ancestry all the way back to Aaron, Moses' brother, the first priest. Hence, priestly genealogies play an important role in the books of Ezra (7:1–5), Nehemiah (11:10–14), and Chronicles (1Ch 6:1–15, 50–53; 9:10–13). The genealogy of 1 Chronicles 5:27–41 extends back twenty-five generations!

11 "Seraiah" was the descendant of the high priest taken prisoner by Nebuchadnezzar (2Ki 25:18–21). See also 10:2; 12:1, 12; Ezra 2:2.

"Supervisor" translates *nāgîd* ("chief, leader, prince"). Pashhur, who had Jeremiah put in stocks (Jer 20:1–2), was such a "chief officer."

12 "Pelaliah" ("Yahweh has interposed") occurs only here. "Amzi" ("my strong one") is an abbreviated form of "Amaziah." It occurs here and in 1 Chronicles 6:46.

13 "Ahzai" is a shortened form of "Ahaziah" ("Yahweh has grasped"), which occurs only here.

14 "Able men" (*gibbôrê ḥayil*) is literally "mighty men of valor" (cf. 2:9; 4:2; 11:6; 1Ch 9:13; Ezr 8:22). "Zabdiel" ("God has given") occurs only here and in 1 Chronicles 27:2. "Haggedolim" means "the great ones."

NOTE

10 One of the most important priests was Zadok, high priest during the reigns of David and Solomon. Both the Sadducees and the Qumran community claimed descent from Zadok. On high priests and their genealogies, see J. Blenkinsopp, "The Judaean Priesthood during the Neo-Babylonian and Achaemenid Periods: A Hypothetical Reconstruction," *CBQ* 60 (1998): 25–43; G. N. Knoppers, "The Priestly Genealogies and the High Priesthood," in *Judah and the Judeans in the Neo-Babylonian Period* (ed. O. Lipschits and J. Blenkinsopp; Winona Lake, Ind.: Eisenbrauns, 2003), 109–33; J. C. VanderKam, *From Joshua to Caiaphas: High Priests after the Exile* (Minneapolis: Fortress, 2004).

e. From the Levites (11:15–18)

¹⁵From the Levites:

Shemaiah son of Hasshub, the son of Azrikam, the son of Hashabiah, the son of Bunni; ¹⁶Shabbethai and Jozabad, two of the heads of the Levites, who had charge of the outside work of the house of God; ¹⁷Mattaniah son of Mica, the son of Zabdi, the son of Asaph, the director who led in thanksgiving and prayer; Bakbukiah, second among his associates; and Abda son of Shammua, the son of Galal, the son of Jeduthun. ¹⁸The Levites in the holy city totaled 284.

COMMENTARY

15 For "Hasshub," see the comment on 3:11. In 1957 J. Kaplan found an ostracon with this name at Tell Abu Zeitun along with fifth-century BC Attic sherds. "Azrikam" means "my help has arisen."

16 "The outside work" (*ḥiṣônâ*) is literally "lying outside, outer" (cf. 1Ch 26:29). Slotki, 251, explains

that it refers to "duties outside the Temple but connected with it; e.g. providing materials for repairing the fabric of the building."

17 "Mica" is short for Michael (cf. comment on 10:11) or possibly for Michaiah ("Who is like Yahweh?"). The latter name appears in the

Murashu texts as *Mīkayaw* (Coogan, 28). "Asaph" was one of the three leaders of the temple choirs (cf. 1Ch 25:1–2; Pss 50; 73–83). "Bakbukiah" possibly means "the bottle of Yahweh" (see the comment on Ezra 2:51). The name "Abda" ("slave" or "servant," i.e., of Yahweh, as in the name "Obadiah" [1Ch 9:16]) occurs here and in 1 Kings 4:6. It occurs nine times in the Murashu texts as ʿ*abdā*

(Coogan, 31). "Galal" means "tortoise." On animal names, see the comment on Ezra 2:3. "Jeduthun" was the chief of one of the three choirs (1Ch 16:42; 25:1; 2Ch 5:12; Pss 39; 62; 77).

18 The relatively small number of Levites (284) compared to the priests (1,192—the total of 822, 242, and 128 in vv.12–13) is striking, as in Ezra 2:40.

f. From the Temple Staff (11:19–24)

¹⁹The gatekeepers:

Akkub, Talmon and their associates, who kept watch at the gates—172 men.
²⁰The rest of the Israelites, with the priests and Levites, were in all the towns of Judah, each on his ancestral property.
²¹The temple servants lived on the hill of Ophel, and Ziha and Gishpa were in charge of them.
²²The chief officer of the Levites in Jerusalem was Uzzi son of Bani, the son of Hashabiah, the son of Mattaniah, the son of Mica. Uzzi was one of Asaph's descendants, who were the singers responsible for the service of the house of God. ²³The singers were under the king's orders, which regulated their daily activity.
²⁴Pethahiah son of Meshezabel, one of the descendants of Zerah son of Judah, was the king's agent in all affairs relating to the people.

COMMENTARY

19 On "the gatekeepers," see comment on Ezra 2:42. Blenkinsopp, 326, observes, "The 1 Chron. 9 list provides much more information: they were Levites, they guarded the King's Gate to the east, they were established by Samuel and David and functioned on a rota system, they had responsibility for the temple's security and for its furniture and utensils, and they lodged in the temple precincts."

20 "Ancestral property" (*naḥᵃlâ*) designates the inalienable hereditary possession including land, buildings, and movable goods acquired either by

conquest or inheritance (Ge 31:14; Nu 18:21; 27:7; 34:2; 1Ki 21:3–4). The word is used at Ugarit in connection with individuals concerned with the administration of landed property. But in the OT it describes the land of Canaan as the possession of both Yahweh and Israel, including the individual holdings of tribes and families. It also designated Israel as Yahweh's special possession (Dt 4:20; 9:26, 29; 1Ki 8:51–53). H. O. Forshey ("The Construct Chain *naḥᵃlat YHWH/ᵖᵉlōhîm*," *BASOR* 220 [1975]: 51) comments: "There is no parallel elsewhere in the ancient Near East to this use of *nahᵃlāh* as an appellative of the covenant community."

21 On "the temple servants," see comment on Ezra 2:43; on "Ophel," see comment on Nehemiah 3:26. "Gishpa," perhaps a corruption of Hasupha (Ezr 2:43), occurs only here.

22 On "the singers," see comment on Ezra 2:41.

23 David regulated the services of the Levites, including the singers (1Ch 25). The Persian king Artaxerxes I may have given a royal stipend so that the choir of Levites might sing and pray for "the well-being of the king" (Ezr 6:10).

24 "Zerah," short for "Zerahiah" (Ezr 7:4), means "Yahweh has shone forth" (cf. Akkad. *Zaraḫ-šameš*, "The sun [god] has shone forth" [Coogan, 23, 72–73]). "The king's agent" is literally "was at the king's hand." Clines, 219, believes

this may have been the name of a governor who succeeded Nehemiah. But Blenkinsopp, 327, suggests, "he may have been a local official reporting to the central government via the satrapal and provincial authorities and representing the interests of the local population." M. Heltzer ("*Nehemiah* 11,24 and the Provincial Representative at the Persian Royal Court," *Transeu* 8 [1994]: 119), on the basis of Egyptian and Greek officials at the Persian court, suggests that Pethahiah represented the Jews at the imperial court in Persia. He surmises that "there were representatives of the provinces (and possibly satrapies), who were appointed in various ways, being themselves aristocrats according to their origin ... [whose] function was to represent before the king the interests of the local population."

3. Places Settled by Those from Judah (11:25–30)

OVERVIEW

This important list corresponds to earlier lists of Judean cities. All these names also appear in Joshua 15 with the exception of Dibon, Jeshua, and Meconah. The list, however, is not comprehensive, as several cities listed in Ezra 2:20–34 and Nehemiah 3 are lacking. The limits of the Judean settlement after the return from Babylon have been confirmed by archaeological evidence.

The settlements to the south were in areas that were outside the boundary of the province of

Yehud, under the influence if not control of the Edomites or Arabs. Stern, 445, suggests that at the beginning of the Persian period, "Jewish villages may still have existed alongside Edomite ones, with Edomites gaining possession of them only later.... A possible explanation for this is that in this period Edomite settlement had not yet become consolidated into an independent administrative unit, and at the beginning of the period the inhabitants of the area were not among the enemies of Judah."

[25]As for the villages with their fields, some of the people of Judah lived in Kiriath Arba and its surrounding settlements, in Dibon and its settlements, in Jekabzeel and its villages, [26]in Jeshua, in Moladah, in Beth Pelet, [27]in Hazar Shual, in Beersheba and its settlements, [28]in Ziklag, in Meconah and its settlements, [29]in En Rimmon, in Zorah, in

Jarmuth, 30Zanoah, Adullam and their villages, in Lachish and its fields, and in Azekah and its settlements. So they were living all the way from Beersheba to the Valley of Hinnom.

COMMENTARY

25 "Kiriath Arba" ("city of four [giants]") was the archaic name of the city of Hebron (Ge 23:2; Jdg 1:20), the important city twenty miles south of Jerusalem. Brockington, 195, comments, "its mention is surprising because it must already have been firmly in Edomite possession, where it remained until Maccabean times (1 Mac. 5.65)." As Hebron is the traditional site of the burial of Abraham, Sarah, and other patriarchs, Jewish zealots of the Gush Emunim party have established a settlement on the outskirts of Arab Hebron known as Kiryat Arba. "Its settlements" is literally "its daughters" (cf. Nu 21:25, 32; 32:42; Jos 15:45, 47; 1Ch 2:23; 2Ch 13:19).

26 "Jeshua" is Tell es-Satweh (?), northeast of Beersheba. "Moladah" was not far from Beersheba (Jos 15:26); it was occupied by the Idumaeans and perhaps was the same as Malatha (Josephus, *Ant.* 18.147 [6.2]). "Beth Pelet," a site near Beersheba (Jos 15:27), means "house of refuge."

27 "Hazar Shual" means "enclosure of a fox [or jackal]" (see comment on 4:3; cf. Jos 15:28; 1Ch 4:28).

According to Genesis 21:25–31, "Beersheba" means "well of the seven" or "well of the oath." About thirty miles south of Hebron, Beersheba represented the southernmost limit of population, as in the expression "from Dan to Beersheba" (Jdg 20:1; cf. 1Ch 21:2). Tel Beersheba, east of the modern city, was excavated by Y. Aharoni from 1969 to 1976. He discovered a well sixty-five feet deep, but no material remains earlier than the early Iron Age. The settlement was destroyed by Sennacherib in 701 BC and only resettled in the Persian period.

Some forty Aramaic ostraca have been recovered from the mid-fourth century BC, though no buildings of this period have been discovered (cf. Y. Aharoni, "Beersheba, Tel," *EAEHL* 1:160–68).

28 "Ziklag" is celebrated as the town given to David by Achish, king of Gath (1Sa 27:6), and taken by the Amalekites (1Sa 30:1). "Meconah," a town near Ziklag, is of uncertain location, possibly Tell esh-Shārîʿah.

29 "En Rimmon" ("spring of the pomegranate") was probably Tell Halif, nine and a half miles north-northeast of Beersheba (cf. Jos 15:32; 19:7; 1Ch 4:32) (see J. D. Seger and O. Borowski, "The First Two Seasons at Tell Halif," *BA* 40 [1977]: 156–66). "Zorah" is Sartah on the northern side of the Wadi es-Sarar ("valley of Sorek"), the home of Manoah, Samson's father (Jdg 13:2). "Jarmuth," eight miles northeast of Eleutheropolis (Beit-Jibrin), was one of five Canaanite cities in the south that attempted to halt Joshua's invasion (Jos 10:3–5).

30 "Zanoah" was a village in the Shephelah district of low hills between Judah and the area of Philistia (Jos 15:34). The men of Zanoah repaired the Valley Gate (Ne 3:13). The site has been identified with Khirbet Zānûʿ, three miles southeast of Beth Shemesh. "Adullam" was the city between Jerusalem and Lachish where David hid in a cave from Saul (1Sa 22:1).

"Lachish" is Tell ed-Duweir, a great Judean city midway between Jerusalem and Gaza. The site was excavated between 1932 and 1938 by James Starkey. New excavations were conducted under D. Ussishkin from 1973–1977. See the following works by

Ussishkin: "Excavating at Tel Lachish 1973–77," *TA* 5 (1978): 1–97; "Answers at Lachish," *BAR* 5/6 (1979): 16–39; *The Conquest of Lachish by Sennacherib* (Tel Aviv: Tel Aviv Univ. Press, 1982); "The Assyrian Attack on Lachish," *TA* 17 (1990): 53–86.

The Assyrian king Sennacherib failed to take Jerusalem in 701 BC but did capture Lachish, a feat depicted on famous reliefs now in the British Museum. The city was later captured by Nebuchadnezzar (Jer 34:7) and was then resettled during Nehemiah's time for a Persian governor, identified as Geshem by G. E. Wright ("Judean Lachish," *BA* 18 [1955]: 9–17). An inscribed Arabic incense altar from Nehemiah's time has been found at Lachish (see F. M. Cross, "Two Notes on Palestinian Inscriptions of the Persian Age," *BASOR* 193 [1969]: 19–24).

"Azekah" is Tell Zakariyeh. Lachish and Azekah are mentioned together and in this order also in Jeremiah 34:7. One of the Lachish ostraca presents this dramatic message as Nebuchadnezzar's forces were approaching: "And let [my lord] know that we are watching for the signals of Lachish, according to all the indications which my lord hath given, for we cannot see Azekah" (*ANET*, 322). The discovery and excavation of Persian period settlements in Judah is limited. Persian period pottery was found at Khirbet Drusiye and Khirbet Hauran. Stern, 442, writes, "According to Rahmani, these settlements should be interpreted as *ḥaṣerîm* ('daughters' or 'fenced villages') of Azekah and Adullam (Ne 11:30)."

"Hinnom" is the valley southwest of Jerusalem (the NT's "Gehenna"; cf. L. R. Bailey, "Gehenna: The Topography of Hell," *BA* 49 [1986]: 187–91). The direct distance from Jerusalem to Beersheba is only forty miles.

4. Places Settled by Those from Benjamin (11:31–35)

³¹The descendants of the Benjamites from Geba lived in Micmash, Aija, Bethel and its settlements, ³²in Anathoth, Nob and Ananiah, ³³in Hazor, Ramah and Gittaim, ³⁴in Hadid, Zeboim and Neballat, ³⁵in Lod and Ono, and in the Valley of the Craftsmen.

COMMENTARY

31 "Geba" ("height") is Jeba, six miles northeast of Jerusalem (cf. Jos 18:24; Ezr 2:26; Ne 7:30). Geba, the traditional northern limit of Judah (2Ki 23:8; Zec 14:10), was fortified by Asa (1Ki 15:22).

"Micmash" is Mukhmas, seven miles northeast of Jerusalem (cf. Ezr 2:27; Ne 7:31). Micmash was the location of the strategic pass to the Jordan Valley, where Saul and Jonathan fought the Philistines (1Sa 13–14).

"Aija," an alternative name for "Ai" ("ruins"), has been identified with et-Tell, just three miles southeast of Bethel. But some scholars reject this identification, since according to Joshua 7–8 the city of Ai was taken by the Hebrews under Joshua, yet the excavations by J. Callaway at et-Tell between 1964 and 1970 did not uncover any Late Bronze remains. Nor has anything later than 1050 BC appeared at et-Tell.

"Bethel" ("house of God") is Beitin, a site partially excavated by W. F. Albright and J. L. Kelso between 1934 and 1960. Kelso (*The Excavation of Bethel* [Cambridge: American Schools of Oriental Research, 1968], 52) observed: "The data in Ezra and Nehemiah parallel the archaeological finds.... Bethel was the northernmost town listed with the Benjaminites in Nehemiah 11:31ff. but it was not listed at all among the people rebuilding the walls of Jerusalem. The tiny post-exilic village was doubtless close to the springs beneath the built-up area of modern Beitin."

32 "Anathoth" is Anata, three miles north of Jerusalem and the birthplace of Jeremiah (Jer 1:1; cf. Ezr 2:23; Ne 7:27). Nob, probably Mount Scopus, is just north of the Mount of Olives, where the sanctuary was established after the destruction of Shiloh (Jer 7:14; see 1Sa 21:1–9; Isa 10:27–32). "Ananiah" was probably Bethany (i.e., "house of Ananiah"), which lay two miles east of Jerusalem. Today the Arabs call the village *el-Azirîyeh*, after Lazarus.

33 "Hazor" is Khirbet Hazzur, west of Beit Hanina, which is north of Jerusalem. "Gittaim" ("two winepresses"; cf. 2Sa 4:3) is probably at Râs *AbūḤamīd* near Ramleh.

34 "Hadid" ("sharp") is el-Haditheh, three to four miles northeast of Lydda near the mouth of the Aijalon Valley (cf. Ezr 2:33, Ne 7:37). It was called Adida in the Hellenistic era (1 Macc 12:38). "Zeboim" ("hyenas") was possibly north of Lydda, perhaps Khirbet Sabieh. "Neballat" is Beit Nebala, four miles east of Lydda. The name may have preserved that of an Assyrian governor of Samaria (seventh century BC), Nabu-uballit.

35 "Lod" (Gk. "Lydda," Arab. "Ludd") is today the site of Israel's international airport, ten miles from the coast (cf. Ezr 2:33; Ne 7:37). Peter healed Aeneas at Lydda (Ac 9:32–38). It became a rabbinical center in the Talmudic period.

"Ono" is Kafr ʿAnā, five and one-half miles northwest of Lydda. The enemies of Nehemiah tried to lure him to a conference there (Ne 6:2; 7:37).

"The Valley of the Craftsmen" (*gê haḥᵃrāšîm*; cf. 1Ch 4:14) may be the Wadi esh-Shellal, the broad valley between Lod and Ono. The name may preserve the memory of the Philistine iron monopoly (1Sa 13:19–20). In any case the oak trees of the nearby Sharon plain would have been useful to artisans working in either wood or iron (see M. Har-El, "The Valley of the Craftsmen," *PEQ* 109 [1977]: 75–86).

NOTE

35 Z. Kallai (*Biblical Historiography and Historical Geography* [Frankfurt am Main: Peter Lang, 1998], 87) remarks, "In the district of Lod, in *Mōdîʾîn*, was the focus of the Hasmonaean revolt, a fact inconceivable unless there was a large concentration of Jewish population there, closely associated with the settlement centres in the mountain region and the lowlands."

5. Transfer of Levites from Judah to Benjamin (11:36)

[36]Some of the divisions of the Levites of Judah settled in Benjamin.

COMMENTARY

36 Certain divisions of Levites, who had been located in Judah, were now transferred to Benjamin to rectify the disproportion presumably discovered in Nehemiah's census.

J. Lists of Priests and the Dedication of the Wall (12:1–47)

1. Priests and Levites from the First Return (12:1–9)

¹These were the priests and Levites who returned with Zerubbabel son of Shealtiel and with Jeshua:

Seraiah, Jeremiah, Ezra,
²Amariah, Malluch, Hattush,
³Shecaniah, Rehum, Meremoth,
⁴Iddo, Ginnethon, Abijah,
⁵Mijamin, Moadiah, Bilgah,
⁶Shemaiah, Joiarib, Jedaiah,
⁷Sallu, Amok, Hilkiah and Jedaiah.

These were the leaders of the priests and their associates in the days of Jeshua. ⁸The Levites were Jeshua, Binnui, Kadmiel, Sherebiah, Judah, and also Mattaniah, who, together with his associates, was in charge of the songs of thanksgiving. ⁹Bakbukiah and Unni, their associates, stood opposite them in the services.

COMMENTARY

1 "Shealtiel" was the father of Zerubbabel according to this verse and Ezra 3:2, 8; Haggai 1:1; but 1 Chronicles 3:17–19 lists him as the uncle of Zerubbabel. On this issue, see comment on Ezra 5:2.

"Jeshua" was the high priest from in the late sixth century BC (cf. Ezr 2:2; Ne 7:7; 12:10, 26). "Seraiah" (cf. 11:11; 12:12) is called Azariah in 1 Chronicles 9:11 (cf. comment on Ezr 2:2). On "Jeremiah," see comment on 10:2.

This "Ezra" is, of course, not the same Ezra who returned eighty years later. On the name, see comment on Ezra 7:1.

2 On "Amariah," see Ezra 7:3; on Malluch, see Ezra 10:29; and on "Hattush," see Ezra 8:2.

3 On "Shecaniah," see comment on Ezra 8:3. On "Rehum," see comment on Ezra 2:2; in this verse it may be a corruption of "Harim" (cf. Ezr 2:39; Ne 7:42). On "Meremoth," see comment on Ezra 8:33.

4 "Iddo" (from ʿ*dāyāʾ*, "timely") is the same name as that of the prophet Zechariah's grandfather (Zec 1:1). On "Abijah," see comment on 10:7.

5 On "Mijamin," see comment on Ezra 10:25 (cf. "Miniamin," v.17; see Coogan, 77). "Moadiah" means "Yahweh assembles" (cf. v.17). "Bilgah" ("brightness") occurs only here, in v.18, and in 1 Chronicles 24:14.

6 On "Shemaiah," see comment on Ezra 8:13; on "Jedaiah," see comment on Ezra 2:36.

7 "Amok" means "deep, unsearchable." On "Hilkiah," see comment on Ezra 7:1.

According to Josephus (*Ant.* 7.365 [14.7]) the rotation of twenty-four priestly houses was established at the time of David, but modern scholars believe that this system was established at a much later time. There are twenty-two heads of priestly houses mentioned here in vv.1–7. Inscriptions listing the twenty-four courses of the priests probably hung in hundreds of synagogues in Palestine. Thus far only fragments of two such inscriptions have been recovered—one found at Ashkelon in the 1920s and fragments from Caesarea in the 1960s (dated to the third and fourth century AD; see M. A. Avi-Yonah, "The Caesarea Inscription of the Twenty-Four Priestly Courses," in *The Teacher's Yoke*

[ed. E. J. Vardaman et al.; Waco, Tex.: Baylor Univ. Press, 1964], 46ff.).

8 On "Jeshua," see comment on Ezra 2:2; on "Kadmiel," see comment Ezra 2:40; on "Sherebiah," see comment on Ezra 8:18; on "Judah," see comment on Ezra 3:9; and on "Mattaniah," see comment on Ezra 10:26.

9 On "Bakbukiah" ("bottle of Yahweh"?) see comment on Ezra 2:51. "Unni," short for "Anaiah" (cf. 8:4), occurs only here and in 1 Chronicles 15:18, 20. The singing was in antiphonal fashion, with two sections of the choir standing opposite each other (cf. v.24; 2Ch 7:6; Ezr 3:11).

"Services" (*mišmārôt*, "wards" or "divisions") is the title of a work from Qumran that discusses in detail the rotation of the priestly families' service in the temple according to the sect's solar calendar, which was synchronized with the lunar calendar. (See M. Wise, M. Abegg Jr., and E. Cook, trans., *The Dead Sea Scrolls, A New Translation* [New York: HarperSanFrancisco, 1996], 317–22.)

NOTES

7 H. G. M. Williamson ("The Origins of the Twenty-Four Priestly Courses: A Study of 1 Chronicles xxiii–xxvii," *VTSup* 30 [1979]: 251–68) dates the origin of the twenty-four priestly courses to the Persian period.

8 הַיְדוֹת (*huyyᵉdôt*, "thanksgiving") is an unusual form for הוֹדָיוֹת (*hôdāyôt*). The *Hodayoth* at Qumran were "Thanksgiving Hymns."

2. High Priests and Levites since Joiakim (12:10–26)

¹⁰Jeshua was the father of Joiakim, Joiakim the father of Eliashib, Eliashib the father of Joiada, ¹¹Joiada the father of Jonathan, and Jonathan the father of Jaddua.
¹²In the days of Joiakim, these were the heads of the priestly families:
of Seraiah's family, Meraiah;
of Jeremiah's, Hananiah;

¹³of Ezra's, Meshullam;
   of Amariah's, Jehohanan;
¹⁴of Malluch's, Jonathan;
   of Shecaniah's, Joseph;
¹⁵of Harim's, Adna;
   of Meremoth's, Helkai;
¹⁶of Iddo's, Zechariah;
   of Ginnethon's, Meshullam;
¹⁷of Abijah's, Zicri;
   of Miniamin's and of Moadiah's, Piltai;
¹⁸of Bilgah's, Shammua;
   of Shemaiah's, Jehonathan;
¹⁹of Joiarib's, Mattenai;
   of Jedaiah's, Uzzi;
²⁰of Sallu's, Kallai;
   of Amok's, Eber;
²¹of Hilkiah's, Hashabiah;
   of Jedaiah's, Nethanel.

²²The family heads of the Levites in the days of Eliashib, Joiada, Johanan and Jaddua, as well as those of the priests, were recorded in the reign of Darius the Persian. ²³The family heads among the descendants of Levi up to the time of Johanan son of Eliashib were recorded in the book of the annals. ²⁴And the leaders of the Levites were Hashabiah, Sherebiah, Jeshua son of Kadmiel, and their associates, who stood opposite them to give praise and thanksgiving, one section responding to the other, as prescribed by David the man of God.

²⁵Mattaniah, Bakbukiah, Obadiah, Meshullam, Talmon and Akkub were gatekeepers who guarded the storerooms at the gates. ²⁶They served in the days of Joiakim son of Jeshua, the son of Jozadak, and in the days of Nehemiah the governor and of Ezra the priest and scribe.

COMMENTARY

10–11 On the complex problem of the identification of these high priests, see Introduction: The High Priests. Most scholars believe that this list of high priests is incomplete, but J. C. VanderKam ("Jewish High Priests of the Persian Period: Is the List Complete?" in *Priesthood and Cult in Ancient Israel* [ed. G. A. Anderson and S. M. Olyan; Sheffield: Sheffield Academic, 1991], 67–91) believes that it was complete.

12 All but one of the twenty-two priestly families listed in vv.1–7 are repeated in this later list, which dates to the time of Joiakim, the high priest in the late sixth and early fifth century BC. "Meraiah," probably from Amariah, occurs only here.

13 On "Meshullam," see comment on Ezra 8:16; on "Amariah," see comment on Ezra 7:3; and on "Jehohanan," see comment on Ezra 10:6.

14 On "Jonathan," see comment on Ezra 8:6. For "Shecaniah" the Hebrew manuscripts read "Shebaniah," but probably in error (see v.3).

15 On "Harim," see comment on Ezra 2:32; on "Adna," see comment on Ezra 10:30. For "Meremoth" (LXX, Syr.) the Hebrew manuscripts read "Meraioth," but probably in error (cf: 10:5). "Helkai," contracted from "Hilkiah" ("my portion is Yahweh"), occurs only here.

17 "Zicri" is short for Zechariah. "Miniamin" ("luck") is literally "from the right hand" (cf. Coogan, 28). On "Moadiah," see comment on v.5. "Piltai" ("[God is] deliverance") occurs only here.

20 For "Sallu" the MT has "Sallai," but probably in error (cf. v.7). "Eber" was also the eponym of the Hebrews (Ge 10:21).

21 On "Hashabiah," see comment on Ezra 8:19.

22 On the identification of "Eliashib," "Joiada," "Johanan," and "Jaddua" with those mentioned in the extrabiblical sources, see Introduction: The High Priests.

"Darius the Persian" was either Nothus (Darius II, 423–404 BC), or Codomannus (Darius III, 335–331 BC), the king whose empire Alexander the Great conquered. The fact that a high priest called "Jaddua" is mentioned by Josephus (*Ant.* 11.302 [7.2]) has caused some scholars to favor the later king. A "Johanan" appears, however, as the high priest in an Elephantine papyrus dated to 407 BC (*ANET*, 492), thus favoring an identification with Darius II. But the Samaria papyri have persuaded scholars that the "Jaddua" in Nehemiah was not the Jaddua in Josephus but the grandfather of the latter. (See F. M. Cross, "The Discovery of the Samaria Papyri," *BA* 26 [1963]: 121; idem, "Aspects of Samaritan and Jewish History in Late Persian and Hellenistic Times," *HTR* 59 [1966]: 203ff.)

23 The "book of the annals" (*sēper dibrê hayyāmîm*, lit., "book of the words [or 'deeds'] of the days," or "chronicles"; cf. Ne 7:5) may have been the official temple chronicle containing various lists and records. Compare the annals of the Persian kings (Ezr 4:15; Est 2:23; 6:1; 10:2); "the book of the annals of the kings of Israel," mentioned eighteen times in 1 and 2 Kings; and "the book of the annals of the kings of Judah," mentioned fifteen times in 1 and 2 Kings.

24 On "who stood opposite," see comment on v.9. On "as prescribed by David," see 1 Chronicles 16:4; 23:27–31; 2 Chronicles 8:14.

25 From 11:17 we would have expected Mattaniah and Bakbukiah to be associated with the leaders of the choirs mentioned in v.24, rather than with the gatekeepers of v.25. On "gatekeepers," see comment on Ezra 2:42 (cf. Ne 3:1).

26 This is one of the few explicit references to the contemporaneity of Ezra and Nehemiah (see Introduction: The Order of Ezra and Nehemiah).

NOTE

22 Williamson (*Ezra, Nehemiah*, 365) argues here that Darius was designated as "the Persian" in opposition to the enigmatic "Darius the Mede" of the book of Daniel. On Darius I, see Yamauchi, *Persia and the Bible*, ch. 4. On Darius the Mede, see ibid., 58–59.

3. Dedication of the Walls of Jerusalem (12:27–43)

[27]At the dedication of the wall of Jerusalem, the Levites were sought out from where they lived and were brought to Jerusalem to celebrate joyfully the dedication with songs of thanksgiving and with the music of cymbals, harps and lyres. [28]The singers also were brought together from the region around Jerusalem — from the villages of the Netophathites, [29]from Beth Gilgal, and from the area of Geba and Azmaveth, for the singers had built villages for themselves around Jerusalem. [30]When the priests and Levites had purified themselves ceremonially, they purified the people, the gates and the wall.

[31]I had the leaders of Judah go up on top of the wall. I also assigned two large choirs to give thanks. One was to proceed on top of the wall to the right, toward the Dung Gate. [32]Hoshaiah and half the leaders of Judah followed them, [33]along with Azariah, Ezra, Meshullam, [34]Judah, Benjamin, Shemaiah, Jeremiah, [35]as well as some priests with trumpets, and also Zechariah son of Jonathan, the son of Shemaiah, the son of Mattaniah, the son of Micaiah, the son of Zaccur, the son of Asaph, [36]and his associates — Shemaiah, Azarel, Milalai, Gilalai, Maai, Nethanel, Judah and Hanani — with musical instruments prescribed by David the man of God. Ezra the scribe led the procession. [37]At the Fountain Gate they continued directly up the steps of the City of David on the ascent to the wall and passed above the house of David to the Water Gate on the east.

[38]The second choir proceeded in the opposite direction. I followed them on top of the wall, together with half the people — past the Tower of the Ovens to the Broad Wall, [39]over the Gate of Ephraim, the Jeshanah Gate, the Fish Gate, the Tower of Hananel and the Tower of the Hundred, as far as the Sheep Gate. At the Gate of the Guard they stopped.

[40]The two choirs that gave thanks then took their places in the house of God; so did I, together with half the officials, [41]as well as the priests — Eliakim, Maaseiah, Miniamin, Micaiah, Elioenai, Zechariah and Hananiah with their trumpets — [42]and also Maaseiah, Shemaiah, Eleazar, Uzzi, Jehohanan, Malkijah, Elam and Ezer. The choirs sang under the direction of Jezrahiah. [43]And on that day they offered great sacrifices, rejoicing because God had given them great joy. The women and children also rejoiced. The sound of rejoicing in Jerusalem could be heard far away.

COMMENTARY

27 On "dedication" ($h^a nukk\hat{a}$), compare the dedication of the temple by Solomon (1Ki 8) and the dedication of Zerubbabel's temple (Ezr 6:16). The dedication of the wall culminates the efforts of the people under Nehemiah's inspired leadership.

Great enthusiasm must have characterized their march to the joyful music.

After the recapture of the temple by Judas Maccabeus from the Seleucids on Kislev 25, 165 BC, the temple was again rededicated (2 Macc 1:18) —

an act that formed the basis of the Jewish holiday of Hanukkah.

"Cymbals" (*mᵉṣiltayim*) were used for religious ceremonies (2Sa 6:5; 1Ch 16:42; 25:1; 2Ch 5:12; 29:25; Ezr 3:10). Cymbals have been recovered from Beth Shemesh and from Tell Abu Hawam.

"Harps" (*nᵉbālîm*) occurs twenty-seven times. The KJV translated the word twenty-three times as "psaltry" (cf. Vul. *psalterium*) and four times as "viol." The instrument was used mainly in religious ceremonies (e.g., 1Sa 10:5; 2Sa 6:5; 1Ch 15:16, 20, 28; Ps 150:3), with a few exceptions (Isa 5:12; 14:11; Am 5:23). The harp was an instrument with strings of varying lengths. As harps are usually large instruments, Williamson (*Ezra, Nehemiah*, 367, 372) and Blenkinsopp, 341, prefer to translate the word as "lutes."

"Lyres" (*kinnōrôt*) occurs forty-two times. The LXX renders it twenty times as *kithara* and seventeen times as *kinura*. The KJV renders the term as "harp," the RSV and NRSV as "lyre." The lyre was an instrument with strings of the same length but of different diameters and tensions (see Ge 4:21; 1Sa 16:16, 23; 1Ch 15:16, 21, 28; Pss 137:2, 149:3; 150:3; Isa 23:16; cf. Da 3:5, 7, 10, 15). Blenkinsopp, 341, prefers "zithers." (See T. C. Mitchell and R. Joyce, "The Musical Instruments in Nebuchadnezzar's Orchestra," in *Notes on Some Problems in the Book of Daniel* [ed. D. J. Wiseman et al.; London: Tyndale, 1965], 19–22.)

Clines, 230, comments, "With vocal music from the front of the procession, and instrumental music from the rear (cf. 'Singers in front, minstrels last', Ps 68:25), the whole procession must have been enveloped in stereophonic sound."

28 "Netophathites" were from Netophah, a town near Bethlehem (1Ch 2:54; 9:16; Ezr 2:22; Ne 7:26). The site is perhaps Khirbet Bedd Faluh near the spring ʿAin en-Natuf.

29 "Beth Gilgal" was perhaps the Gilgal near Jericho (Jos 4:19–20) or the Gilgal of Elijah (2Ki 2:1), some seven miles north of Bethel.

30 On "purified," compare Ezra 6:20; see also comments on Nehemiah 13:9, 22, 30. The verb *ṭāhēr* occurs ninety-four times. It is used almost exclusively of ritual or moral purity, most frequently of the purification necessary to restore someone who had contracted impurity to a state of purity so that he might participate in ritual activities (Lev 22:4–7). The Levites are said to have cleansed all that was holy in the temple (1Ch 23:28) and the temple itself (2Ch 29:15) during the times of revival. Ritual purification was intended to teach God's holiness and moral purity (Lev 16:30).

31 There were two great processions, starting probably from the area of the Valley Gate (2:13, 15; 3:13) in the center of the western section of the wall. The first procession led by Ezra (v.36) and Hoshaiah (v.32) moved in a counterclockwise direction on the wall; the second with Nehemiah moved in a clockwise direction. They met between the Prison Gate and the Water Gate and then entered the temple area (cf. Ps 48:12–13).

"To the right" translates *yāmîn*. This procession went to the south. The Semites oriented themselves facing eastward; so the right hand represented the south (cf. the name of Yemen in southern Arabia; see Jos 17:7; 1Sa 23:24; Job 23:9).

32 "Hoshaiah" ("Yahweh has saved") occurs here and in Jeremiah 42:1; 43:2.

33–34 "Ezra" here is not Ezra the scribe (v.36).

35 On "trumpets," see comment on Ezra 3:10. Each choir was composed of seven priests blowing trumpets and the Levites playing on other musical instruments. "Asaph" was the founder of one of the three guilds of Levitical musicians (1Ch 25:1–2).

36 "Milalai," lacking in the LXX, is perhaps an error for "Gilalai," which occurs only here, as does "Maai." "Judah" is lacking in the LXX. On "Ezra the scribe," see comment on Ezra 7:1–6.

37 On the "Fountain Gate," see comment on 3:15; on the "Water Gate," see comment on 3:26.

The procession went around the southern end of the walls, then north up the eastern wall to the Water Gate near the Gihon Spring.

38 "The second choir" is literally "the second thanks," that is, the thanksgiving choir. "In the opposite direction" (*lᵉmôl*, to be emended to *lîśᵉmōl*) is literally "to the left" but means "northward" (so Jos 19:27; Isa 54:3; Eze 16:46; cf. Note on v.31).

The procession led by Nehemiah went northward in a clockwise direction around the northwestern sections of the wall. On the "Tower of the Ovens," see comment on 3:11; on "Broad Wall," see comment on 3:8.

39 On the "Ephraim Gate," see comment on 8:16. This gate is not mentioned as in need of repair in ch. 3. It stood between the Broad Wall and the Jeshanah Gate. On the "Jeshanah Gate," see comment on 3:6; on the "Fish Gate," see comment on 3:3; on the "Tower of Hananel," see comment on 3:1; and on the "Tower of the Hundred," see comment on 3:1.

Some scholars suggest that *maṭṭārâ* ("Gate of the Guard"; cf. "the courtyard of the guard" in Jer 32:2) be emended to *mipqād*, to make it the "Inspection Gate." On the latter, see comment on 3:31.

40 Other nations had such solemn processions, too. The famous fifth-century BC reliefs from the staircase of Darius's Apadana depict representatives from many nations bearing gifts for the royal treasury (cf. Yamauchi, *Persia and the Bible*, 347–56; R. Ghirshman, *The Art of Ancient Iran* [New York: Golden, 1964]; E. F. Schmidt, *Persepolis III* [Chicago: Univ. of Chicago Press, 1970]). In Athens, every fourth year the Panathenaic festival featured a procession from the Agora to the Acropolis for the presentation of a new garment for the statue of Athena (see N. Yalouris, *Classical Greece: The Elgin Marbles of the Parthenon* [Greenwich, Conn.: New York Graphic Society, 1960]). The famous Altar of Peace of Augustus depicts a solemn procession of the imperial family, senators, and priests (see D. Earl, *The Age of Augustus* [New York: Crown, 1968], 120ff., figs. 51, 53, 113–16).

42 "The choirs sang" is literally "the singers made [themselves] heard." "Jezrahiah" means "Yahweh shines forth" (cf. "Izrahiah" in 1Ch 7:3).

43 Note that the word "joy/rejoicing" appears five times in this verse. Fensham, 257, has called attention to the view that Psalm 147 was composed on this occasion. "The LORD builds up Jerusalem; he gathers the exiles of Israel" (Ps 147:2); "for he strengthens the bars of your gates and blesses your people within you" (147:13). At the dedication of the temple (Ezr 3:13), the sound of joy was also loud, but it was commingled with weeping as well.

NOTES

27 Some scholars (e.g., Michaeli, Gelin) believe that vv.27–34 on the dedication of the wall should be placed after 6:15–16, which describes the completion of the wall. Myers, 167, suggests that this passage "logically joins clearly with Nehemiah 11:36 of which it is a continuation." For the view that the נֵבֶל (*nēbel*) was not a harp but "a reed instrument with a windbag made of an animal hide," see Miriam Aharoni, "The Askos: Is It the Biblical Nebel?" *TA* 6 (1979): 95–97.

31 The MT reads וְתַהֲלֻכֹת (*wᵉtahᵃlukōt*, "festal procession"). The NIV's "one was to proceed" reflects an emendation to וְהָאַחַת הֹלֶכֶת (*wᵉhāᵓaḥat hōleket*, "and the one went in procession").

The word translated "choirs" is *tôdô̂t*, the plural form of *tôdâ*, "thanksgiving song" or "thanksgiving offering." The translation as "thanksgiving choir" is found in the Vulgate and in the Syriac Peshitta. M. J. Boda ("The Use of *tôdô̂t* in Nehemiah XII," *VT* 44 [1994]: 391) argues against the majority of translators and commentators in holding that even in this context the word should be understood as "offerings" rather than "choirs." He concludes, "The two processions that encircled the city of Jerusalem on their way to the temple were led by the sacrifices that were to be offered in the temple."

4. Regulations of the Temple Offerings and Services (12:44–47)

⁴⁴At that time men were appointed to be in charge of the storerooms for the contributions, firstfruits and tithes. From the fields around the towns they were to bring into the storerooms the portions required by the Law for the priests and the Levites, for Judah was pleased with the ministering priests and Levites. ⁴⁵They performed the service of their God and the service of purification, as did also the singers and gatekeepers, according to the commands of David and his son Solomon. ⁴⁶For long ago, in the days of David and Asaph, there had been directors for the singers and for the songs of praise and thanksgiving to God. ⁴⁷So in the days of Zerubbabel and of Nehemiah, all Israel contributed the daily portions for the singers and gatekeepers. They also set aside the portion for the other Levites, and the Levites set aside the portion for the descendants of Aaron.

COMMENTARY

44–45 "Storerooms" (v.44) translates *niškâ*, which occurs only here, in 3:30, and in 13:7. On "contributions," see comment on 10:37, 39.

The people of Judah were "pleased" (i.e., it gave them great joy) to contribute their offerings to support the priests and Levites (cf. 2Co 9:7). "Ministering" is literally "standing" (cf. Dt 10:8, "to stand before the LORD to minister" to him).

46 Asaph, a founder of one of the three musical guilds, was a Gershonite Levite to whom David entrusted the "service of song" in the tabernacle (cf. 1Ch 6:39; 2Ch 29:30; 35:15; Pss 50; 73–83).

47 On "Zerubbabel," see comment on Ezra 2:2; 3:2, 8; 4:2–3; Nehemiah 7:7; 12:1. "Contributed" translates a participle implying continued giving. "The daily portions" is literally "the matter of the day in its day" (cf. E. Yamauchi, "The Daily Bread Motif in Antiquity," *WTJ* 28 [1966]: 145–56). On "the Levites set aside," see comment on 10:37–38.

II. NEHEMIAH'S SECOND ADMINISTRATION (13:1–31)

A. Abuses during His Absence (13:1–5)

1. Mixed Marriages (13:1–3)

[1]On that day the Book of Moses was read aloud in the hearing of the people and there it was found written that no Ammonite or Moabite should ever be admitted into the assembly of God, [2]because they had not met the Israelites with food and water but had hired Balaam to call a curse down on them. (Our God, however, turned the curse into a blessing.) [3]When the people heard this law, they excluded from Israel all who were of foreign descent.

COMMENTARY

1 The reference "the Book of Moses" is to Deuteronomy 23:3–6 (cf. Nu 22–24). On marriages to Ammonites and Moabites, see comment on Ezra 9:1. On the general subject of intermarriage, see the Reflection after Ezra 10.

2 "Balaam" (*bilʿām*) was the seer summoned by Balak, the king of Moab, to curse Israel (Nu 22–24). He came from Pethor, probably Pitru in northwestern Mesopotamia (Nu 22:5). Though hired to curse the Israelites, through the inspiration of Yahweh he blessed them instead. Later, however, he led Israel into the worship of the Moabite god at Peor (Nu 25:1–3; 31:16; cf. Rev 2:14). In the NT his name is symbolic of avarice (2Pe 2:15; Jude 11).

A remarkable Aramaic inscription referring to Balaam, dated to the sixth century BC, was found inscribed on wall plaster at Deir Alla in Transjordan. See J. Hoftijzer, "The Prophet Balaam in a 6th-Century Aramaic Inscription," *BA* 39 (1976):

11–17; J. A. Hackett, *The Balaam Text from Deir ʿAlla* (Chico, Calif.: Scholars, 1984); H. J. Franken, "Balaam at Deir Alla and the Cult of Baal," in *Archaeology, History and Culture in Palestine and the Near East* (ed. T. Kapitan; Atlanta: Scholars, 1999), 183–202.

Curses had a dynamic power of their own once uttered and could not simply be recalled. They could, however, be canceled by blessings (cf. Jdg 17:1–2; see C. H. Gordon, *Adventures in the Nearest East* [London: Phoenix, 1957], 165–69; E. M. Yamauchi, *Mandaic Incantation Texts* [New Haven, Conn.: American Oriental Society, 1965; repr., Piscataway, N.J.: Gorgias, 2005], 1–67).

3 The same term for "foreign descent" (*ʿēreb*; "mixed multitude," KJV) is used in Exodus 12:38. There, however, the mixed multitude was welcomed, as they had agreed to the worship of Yahweh, whereas it is implied that this was not the case here.

NOTE

1 In 1980 Gabriel Barkay found two silver amulets in a seventh-century BC burial at Ketef Hinnom ("The Shoulder of Hinnom") just south of Jerusalem. These scrolls contain the oldest citation of the priestly blessing of Numbers 6:24–25, "The LORD bless you and keep you; the LORD make his face shine upon you and be gracious to you," and also a citation of Deuteronomy 7:9, "keeping his covenant of love to … those who love him and keep his commands." See G. Barkay, "The Priestly Benediction on Silver Plaques from Ketef Hinnom in Jerusalem," *TA* 19 (1992): 139–200; G. Barkay et al., "The Challenges of Ketef Hinnom: Using Advanced Technologies to Reclaim the Earliest Biblical Texts and Their Context," *Near Eastern Archaeology* 66 (2003): 162–71; idem, "The Amulets from Ketef Hinnom: A New Edition and Evalution," *BASOR* 334 (2004): 41–71; E. B. De Souza, "The Ketef Hinnom Silver Scrolls: A Suggestive Reading of Text and Artifact," *NEASB* 49 (2004): 27–38.

2. Tobiah's Occupation of the Temple Quarters (13:4–5)

> **4**Before this, Eliashib the priest had been put in charge of the storerooms of the house of our God. He was closely associated with Tobiah, **5**and he had provided him with a large room formerly used to store the grain offerings and incense and temple articles, and also the tithes of grain, new wine and oil prescribed for the Levites, singers and gatekeepers, as well as the contributions for the priests.

COMMENTARY

4 Some scholars identify "Eliashib" with the high priest of that name (cf. 3:1, 20; 13:28; see Introduction: The High Priests). Others argue that it is unlikely for a high priest to have been placed in charge of storerooms.

The word rendered "closely associated" (*qārôb*) is used in Ruth 2:20 to indicate that Boaz was related to Naomi and Ruth. We do not know exactly how Tobiah (cf. comment on 2:10) was related or associated with Eliashib.

5 During Nehemiah's absence from the city to return to the Persian king's court, Tobiah had used his influence with Eliashib to gain entrance into a chamber ordinarily set aside for the storage of tithes and other offerings (Nu 18:21–32; Dt 14:28–29; 26:12–15). The storerooms mentioned in vv.4–5, 13 were evidently in the inner court of the temple. Those mentioned in 10:38–39 and Zechariah 3:7 were parts of the outer court. Elsewhere we read of the chamber of Jehohanan (Ezr 10:6) and of Meshullam (Ne 3:30).

One of the Aramaic letters from the governors of Judah and Samaria to the Jews of Elephantine (Cowley, 32; *ANET*, 492) instructs that "the meal-offering and incense" were "to be made on that altar as it used to be" (cf. B. Porten, *Jews of Elephantine and Arameans of Syene, Fifth Century B.C.E.* (Jerusalem: Hebrew Univ. Press, 1976)]). Frankincense (*lᵉbônâ*, "incense" [NIV]), like myrrh, is a resin derived from trees that grow only in Somalia and in southern Arabia (cf. Gus W. van Beek, "Frankincense and Myrrh," *BA* 23 [1960]: 70–95; N. Green, *Frankincense and Myrrh* [London: Longman, 1981]; see also Yamauchi, *Africa and the Bible*, 90–97; idem, *Persia and the Bible*, 484–85).

B. Nehemiah's Return (13:6–7)

⁶But while all this was going on, I was not in Jerusalem, for in the thirty-second year of Artaxerxes king of Babylon I had returned to the king. Some time later I asked his permission ⁷and came back to Jerusalem. Here I learned about the evil thing Eliashib had done in providing Tobiah a room in the courts of the house of God.

COMMENTARY

6 The thirty-second year of Artaxerxes I ran from April 1, 433 to April 19, 432 BC. This verse and 5:14 indicate that Nehemiah's first term ran for about twelve years, till 433/432. We do not know the exact length of his second term, but it must have ended before 407 BC, when according to the Elephantine papyri Bagohi (Bigvai) was governor of Judah. Some scholars suggest that after Nehemiah's first term, he may have been succeeded by his brother Hanani (see comment on 1:2; 7:2), whom they would identify with the Hananiah mentioned in the Passover Papyrus of 419 BC (*ANET*, 491).

The Elephantine papyri provide us with an interesting parallel to Nehemiah's absence ("some time later"). Arsames, the satrap of Egypt, left his post in the fourteenth year of Darius I (414/413 BC) and was still absent at the Persian court in the seventeenth year (407/406). As in Nehemiah's circumstances, internal conflict and a breakdown of order took place during the governor's absence (see Cowley, 27, 30).

7 Zerubbabel's temple had two courtyards (Zec 3:7; cf. Isa 62:9; 1 Macc 4:38, 48). Hecataeus of Abdera, a Greek historian of the fourth century BC, described the inner court as being five hundred cubits long and one hundred cubits wide (see Josephus, *Ag. Ap.* 1.198 [22]); however, he may have known of these dimensions only by hearsay.

C. Nehemiah's Expulsion of Tobiah (13:8–9)

⁸I was greatly displeased and threw all Tobiah's household goods out of the room. ⁹I gave orders to purify the rooms, and then I put back into them the equipment of the house of God, with the grain offerings and the incense.

COMMENTARY

8 Nehemiah was a man of a volcanic temperament who quickly expressed his indignation by taking action (vv.25–28; cf. 5:6–13). Contrast the reaction of Ezra, who "sat appalled" (Ezr 9:3). Kidner, 129, comments: "If on his first visit he had been a whirlwind, on his second he was all fire and earthquake to a city that had settled down in his absence to a comfortable compromise with the gentile world." Nehemiah's action reminds us of Christ's furious expulsion of the moneychangers from the temple area (Mt 21:12–13; Mk 11:15–16; Lk 19:45–46; Jn 2:13–22).

"Household goods" (*kᵉlî*) include "vessels, equipment, implements," etc. (cf. Ge 45:20; the KJV's "stuff" means movable property).

9 On "to purify," see comment on 12:30 (cf. Lev 12; 14:4–32; 17:15–16). Though only a single chamber used by Tobiah has been mentioned before (vv.5, 7–8), the plural "rooms" here shows that other chambers were involved.

D. Reorganization and Reforms (13:10–31)

1. Offerings for the Temple Staff (13:10–14)

¹⁰I also learned that the portions assigned to the Levites had not been given to them, and that all the Levites and singers responsible for the service had gone back to their own fields. ¹¹So I rebuked the officials and asked them, "Why is the house of God neglected?" Then I called them together and stationed them at their posts.

¹²All Judah brought the tithes of grain, new wine and oil into the storerooms. ¹³I put Shelemiah the priest, Zadok the scribe, and a Levite named Pedaiah in charge of the storerooms and made Hanan son of Zaccur, the son of Mattaniah, their assistant, because these men were considered trustworthy. They were made responsible for distributing the supplies to their brothers.

¹⁴Remember me for this, O my God, and do not blot out what I have so faithfully done for the house of my God and its services.

COMMENTARY

10 It appears that Nehemiah was correcting an abuse of long standing. Strictly speaking the Levites had no holdings (Nu 18:20, 23–24; Dt 14:29; 18:1); but some may have had private income (Dt 18:8). The Levites' dependence on the faithful support of the people may explain the reluctance of many Levites to return from exile (see comment on Ezra 8:15). For the complaints of those who found little material advantage in serving the Lord, see Malachi 2:17; 3:13–15.

11 Nehemiah's rebuke of the officials here recalls his earlier rebuke of the selfish wealthy who exploited the less fortunate in granting them usurious loans. Less than a century before, the prophet

Haggai had rebuked the people for attending to their own houses and neglecting the rebuilding of the house of God (Hag 1:1–9).

12 On tithes, see comment on 12:44. Temples in Mesopotamia also levied tithes for the support of their personnel.

13 On the nature of the profession "scribe," see comment on Ezra 7:6.

"In charge of the storerooms" is literally "I made treasurers over the treasuries" (cf. Ezr 8:33–34). Of the four treasurers, one was a priest, one a Levite, one a scribe, and one a layman of rank. They all needed to be "trustworthy" (*ne'ĕmān*; cf. 9:8, "faithful"; see also 1Sa 22:14; Pr 25:13; Isa 8:2; Jer 42:5) "for distributing the supplies." This requirement would ensure that supplies were distributed equitably, just as the early church appointed deacons for this purpose (Ac 6:1–5).

The committee of Ezra 8:33 consisted of two priests and two Levites. J. Schaper ("The Temple Treasury Committee in the Times of Nehemiah and Ezra," *VT* 47 [1997]: 200–220), who believes that there is continuity between the two committees, has argued that they must have been entrusted not only with the collection of tithes but also with taxes for the Persian treasury.

14 Nehemiah was concerned that God would remember him (cf. v.31; 5:19) and "not blot out" (see Ex 17:14; 32:32) what he had done "faithfully" (the plural of *ḥesed*; GK 2876), that is, his good deeds inspired by steadfast love (see comment on 1:5).

2. The Abuse of the Sabbath (13:15–22)

[15]In those days I saw men in Judah treading winepresses on the Sabbath and bringing in grain and loading it on donkeys, together with wine, grapes, figs and all other kinds of loads. And they were bringing all this into Jerusalem on the Sabbath. Therefore I warned them against selling food on that day. [16]Men from Tyre who lived in Jerusalem were bringing in fish and all kinds of merchandise and selling them in Jerusalem on the Sabbath to the people of Judah. [17]I rebuked the nobles of Judah and said to them, "What is this wicked thing you are doing — desecrating the Sabbath day? [18]Didn't your forefathers do the same things, so that our God brought all this calamity upon us and upon this city? Now you are stirring up more wrath against Israel by desecrating the Sabbath."

[19]When evening shadows fell on the gates of Jerusalem before the Sabbath, I ordered the doors to be shut and not opened until the Sabbath was over. I stationed some of my own men at the gates so that no load could be brought in on the Sabbath day. [20]Once or twice the merchants and sellers of all kinds of goods spent the night outside Jerusalem. [21]But I warned them and said, "Why do you spend the night by the wall? If you do this again, I will lay hands on you." From that time on they no longer came on the Sabbath. [22]Then I commanded the Levites to purify themselves and go and guard the gates in order to keep the Sabbath day holy.

Remember me for this also, O my God, and show mercy to me according to your great love.

COMMENTARY

15 Grapes were, of course, trodden by foot (Isa 16:10; 63:2), but not normally on the Sabbath. There was always the temptation on the part of merchants to violate the Sabbath rest; this was especially true of non-Jewish merchants (see comment on 10:31; cf. Isa 56:1–8; 58:13; Jer 17:21; Am 8:5). The high regard for the ideal of the Sabbath was, however, expressed by many parents in naming their children "Shabbethai" (see comment on Ezr 10:15; cf. Ne 8:7; 11:16). On the later development of Sabbath observances, see H. A. McKay, *Sabbath and Synagogue* (Leiden: Brill, 1994).

The word translated "food" (*ṣāyid*, "provisions") occurs only here, in Joshua 9:5, 14; Job 38:41; Ps 132:15.

16 Tyre, modern Ṣûr, is located only a dozen miles north of the border between Israel and Lebanon. The Tyrians supplied some of their famous cedars for the rebuilding of the temple (Ezr 3:7). Tyre was renowned for its far-flung maritime trade (Eze 26:5, 14). Originally an island, Tyre was transformed into a peninsula by Alexander's siege causeway (cf. H. J. Katzenstein, *The History of Tyre* [Jerusalem: Schocken, 1973]; idem, "Tyre in the Early Persian Period [539–486 BCE]," *BA* 42 [1979]: 23–36).

The Tyrians also exported fish. Most of the fish, which included sardines, were either dried, smoked, or salted. Fish were an important part of a person's diet (Lev 11:9; Nu 11:5; Dt 14:9; Isa 19:8; Mt 15:34; Lk 24:42). They were sold at the market by the Fish Gate (2Ch 33:14; Ne 3:3; 12:39; Zep 1:10).

17 Nehemiah rebuked especially the nobles who were the leaders (cf. vv.11, 25; cf. 5:7). "Desecrating" (*ḥālal*) means to turn what is sacred into common use, to profane (cf. Mal 2:10–11).

18 On the "Sabbath," see comment on v.15 (cf. also Isa 58:13; Eze 20:13, 16; 22:8, 26; 23:38).

19 The gates began to cast long "evening shadows" even before sunset, when the Sabbath began. The Israelites, like the Babylonians, counted their days from sunset to sunset. (The Egyptians reckoned their days from dawn to dawn.) The precise moment at which the Sabbath began was heralded by the blowing of a trumpet by a priest. According to the Mishnah (*m. Sukkah* 5:5): "On the eve of Sabbath they used to blow six more blasts, three to cause the people to cease from work and three to mark the break between the sacred and the profane." Josephus (*J.W.* 4.582 [9.12]) describes the point on the parapet of the temple where the priests stood "in the afternoon of the approach, and on the following evening of the close, of every seventh day, announcing to the people the respective hours for ceasing work and for resuming their labors." Mazar's excavations by the temple mount recovered a stone from the parapet that had fallen to the ground in Titus's siege and bore the inscription *lᵉbeit hat-teqᶜiah*, "for the place of the blowing [of the trumpet]" (Mazar, 138–39).

20 When the gates were shut on the Sabbath eve, the persistent merchants carried on their activities outside the gates for two weeks until Nehemiah noticed them (v.21).

21 Nehemiah was not a man of idle words. He meant what he said and was not averse to backing up his words with force (v.25).

22 The Sabbath was sanctified not just negatively by a cessation of ordinary labor but also positively by a consecration of that day to joyous gatherings. Fasting and mourning were not to be observed on the Sabbath (*Jub.* 50:12; Jdt 8:6; CD 8.13; *m. Taᶜan.* 3:7). According to G. F. Moore (*Judaism in the First Christian Centuries of the Christian Era* [Cambridge, Mass.: Harvard Univ. Press, 1927], 1:37–38):

As the Scribes learned from Isaiah 58:13 that God meant the sabbath to be set apart from other days not only by the things that were not done on it, but by what was done, that it was a day for men to enjoy themselves on, and in accordance with the notions of feast days in the Scriptures, gave a front place in this enjoyment to more sumptuous eating and drinking than on other days.

NOTES

15 For the process of treading grapes, see J. King and L. E. Stager, *Life in Biblical Israel* (Louisville, Ky.: Westminster John Knox, 2001), 98–101.

16 Tyre, along with cities to the north such as Sidon and Byblos, were the harbors of the ancient Phoenicians, the ancient world's most active maritime traders. See M. Bikai, "The Phoenicians: Rich and Glorious Traders of the Levant," *Arch* 43/2 (1990): 22–26, 28–30; W. A. Ward, "The Phoenicians," in Hoerth, Mattingly, and Yamauchi, 183–206; G. E. Markoe, *Phoenicians* (Berkeley: Univ. of California Press, 2000).

19 "When evening shadows fell on the gates" is literally, "When the gates began to grow dark." צָלַל (*ṣālal*, "become dark, shady") appears in the Qal only here. In the Hiphil ("to give shade") it occurs in Ezekiel 31:3 and possibly in Jonah 4:6.

On the exact significance of "when the Sabbath was over," see J. H. Tigay, "*LIPNÊ HAŠŠABĀT* and *ʾAHAR HAŠŠABĀT* 'On the Day before the Sabbath' and 'On the Day after the Sabbath,'" *VT* 28 (1978): 362–65.

3. Mixed Marriages (13:23–29)

[23]Moreover, in those days I saw men of Judah who had married women from Ashdod, Ammon and Moab. [24]Half of their children spoke the language of Ashdod or the language of one of the other peoples, and did not know how to speak the language of Judah. [25]I rebuked them and called curses down on them. I beat some of the men and pulled out their hair. I made them take an oath in God's name and said: "You are not to give your daughters in marriage to their sons, nor are you to take their daughters in marriage for your sons or for yourselves. [26]Was it not because of marriages like these that Solomon king of Israel sinned? Among the many nations there was no king like him. He was loved by his God, and God made him king over all Israel, but even he was led into sin by foreign women. [27]Must we hear now that you too are doing all this terrible wickedness and are being unfaithful to our God by marrying foreign women?"

[28]One of the sons of Joiada son of Eliashib the high priest was son-in-law to Sanballat the Horonite. And I drove him away from me.

[29]Remember them, O my God, because they defiled the priestly office and the covenant of the priesthood and of the Levites.

COMMENTARY

23 Ezra had dealt with the same problem of intermarriage some thirty years before, according to the traditional dating (see Introduction: The Order, and the Reflection after Ezr 10). On "Ashdod," see comments on v.24 and on 4:7.

Ammon was the area in Transjordan around the city of Amman (cf. see comment on Ezr 9:1). Tobiah, Nehemiah's enemy, was influential in that area (cf. see comment on Ne 2:10). The Ammonites worshiped the god Molech (Milcom) by sacrificing children in fire (Lev 18:21; 2Ki 23:10, 13). Extensive archaeological evidence of the burning of thousands of young children has come to light in the Phoenician colony of Carthage.

Excavations have uncovered some Ammonite inscriptions from the ninth to the seventh century BC that feature the god Milcom (Jer 32:35; "Molech," NIV), to whom the children were offered (see S. H. Horn, "The Ammonite Citadel Inscription," *BASOR* 193 [1969]: 2–13). One seal was owned by an exile who returned from Assyria in the seventh century BC (cf. N. Avigad, "Seals of the Exile," *IEJ* 15 [1965]: 223–30). An ostracon from about 500 BC from Heshbon, southwest of Amman, indicates the mixed nature of the population, as a fragmentary name list has two West Semitic names, one Babylonian name, and one Egyptian name (cf. J. Naveh, "Hebrew Texts in Aramaic Script in the Persian Period?" *BASOR* 203 [1971]: 27–32).

The Moabites worshiped Chemosh, to whom they sacrificed their children (Nu 21:29; 2Ki 3:27). On the worship of Chemosh and of Milcom, see J. W. McKay, *Religion in Judah under the Assyrians* (Naperville, Ill.: Allenson, 1973), 39–41, 106–7.

24 Zechariah 9:6 declares, "Foreigners [*mamzēr*] will occupy Ashdod." The word *mamzēr* means "bastard" (cf. Dt 23:3); the RSV and NRSV render it "a mongrel people."

Myers, 216, comments: "Nehemiah observed it first in the speech of children—an interesting point, since the mothers naturally taught their children to speak the only language they knew." The Hebrews recognized other people as foreigners by their languages (cf. Dt 3:9; Jdg 12:6; Ps 114:1; Isa 33:4–19; Eze 3:5–6).

The excavations at Ashdod have uncovered an ostracon from Nehemiah's age in Aramaic script that reads *krm zbdyh* ("[from the] vineyard of Zebadiah"). The name Zebadiah means "Yahweh has given" (cf. Ezr 8:8; 10:20; see J. Naveh, "An Aramaic Ostracon from Ashdod," *ʿAtiqot* 9/10 [1967]: 200–201). Unfortunately the inscription is too brief to shed any light on the Ashdodite language. Possibly the dialect was Phoenician. In the Persian period the Philistine-Palestinian coastal area was divided into several jurisdictions. Ashkelon was under the Tyrians; Ashdod was the center of the Persian province. In 1964 F. M. Cross published an ostracon from Nebi Yunis in modern Ashdod with the Phoenician name *Bʿlṣd*, dating from about 350–300 BC. This name *Baʿlíṣíd* ("my lord is Sid") may, however, be a Persian loanword in Aramaic (cf. F. M. Cross, "An Ostracon from Nebi Yunis," *IEJ* 14 [1964]: 185).

"One of the other peoples" (*ʿam wāʿām*, "people and people") is a late Hebrew idiom (cf. Ezr 10:14; Est 1:22; 3:12; 8:9).

25 On Nehemiah's rebuke of the others, see vv.11, 17. Contrast the action of Ezra (Ezr 9:3), who pulled out his own hair, with Nehemiah's here. Plucking the hair from another's beard was an action designed to show anger, express an insult, and mark someone to scorn (2Sa 10:4; Isa 50:6; cf. Code of Hammurabi 127; *Herodotus* 2.121). The *semirasus* ("half-shaven") marked the lowest type of slave or prisoner at Rome.

Nehemiah's action was designed to prevent future intermarriages ("you are not to give"), whereas Ezra dissolved the existing unions. On the bearing of these different approaches on the chronological order of Ezra and Nehemiah, see Introduction: The Order.

26 Solomon was Israel's outstanding king in wealth and political achievements (1Ki 3:12–13; 2Ch 1:12). He reigned for forty years (1Ki 11:42), from 971–931 (see K. A. Kitchen, "How We Know When Solomon Ruled," *BAR* 27/5 [2001]: 32–37, 58). He built the magnificent temple (1Ki 6:1–38) and an even more splendid palace for himself (1Ki 7:1). His fame spread beyond his borders so that the queen of Sheba in southwestern Arabia traveled fourteen hundred miles to test his fabled wisdom (1Ki 10:1–3; cf. J. B. Pritchard, ed., *Solomon and Sheba* [London: Phaidon, 1974]). His international prestige is demonstrated in that he was given the daughter of a pharaoh (probably Siamun) in marriage (1Ki 3:1; 7:8; 9:16, 24; 11:1; 2Ch 8:11)—the only firmly attested instance in which a king of Egypt gave his daughter in marriage to an alien. (See K. A. Kitchen, *The Third Intermediate Period in Egypt* [rev. ed.; Warminster: Aris & Phillips, 1999], 281–83, 531–32, 574; A. R. Green, "Solomon and Siamun," *JBL* 97 [1978]: 353–67.)

According to 1 Kings 11:3, Solomon had seven hundred wives and three hundred concubines, among whom were Moabite, Ammonite, Edomite, Sidonian, and Hittite women (1Ki 11:1). The mother of Rehoboam, Solomon's successor, was an Ammonite princess. Hellenistic sources suggest that Solomon also married the daughter of Hiram of Tyre.

Solomon began his reign humbly by asking for wisdom from the Lord (1Ki 3:3–15). In later years, however, his foreign wives led him to worship other gods, so that he built a high place for Chemosh, the god of the Moabites on the Mount of Olives (1Ki

11:7). McKay (*Religion in Judah*, 95–96) notes later examples of foreign queens who led Israel astray:

Rehoboam's wife, Maacah, daughter of Abishalom, whose name is certainly not Yahwistic, erected an image to Asherah in the city (1Ki 15:10–13); Ahab's marriage to Jezebel brought the Sidonian Baal and Asherah to Samaria (1Ki 16:32–33); and in consequence of Jehoram's marriage to Ahab's daughter, Athaliah, a temple for the Sidonian Baal was erected in Jerusalem (2Ki 8:18; 11:1ff.).

27 On "terrible wickedness," cf. 2 Samuel 13:16; Jeremiah 26:19.

28 We do not know the name of "one of the sons of Joiada son of Eliashib the high priest." The Hebrew is ambiguous, as the phrase high priest could refer to either Joiada or Eliashib. In the latter case Eliashib was still alive (see Introduction: The High Priests). More probably the epithet "high priest" designates Joiada (cf. 12:10). The offending son would then have been a brother of the man who succeeded Joiada as high priest, Johanan II (12:22–23). He was married to a daughter of Sanballat.

According to Leviticus 21:14, the high priest was not to marry a foreigner. The expulsion of Joiada's son may have followed this special ban or the general interdict against intermarriage. Such a union was especially rankling to Nehemiah in the light of Sanballat's enmity (see comment on 2:10).

Josephus tells a similar story of Manasseh, brother of the high priest Jaddua, who married a "Nikaso," the daughter of a "Sanballat." After Manasseh was expelled from Jerusalem, he built a temple on Mount Gerizim (*Ant.* 11.302–12[7.2–8.2]). Josephus, however, dates this story to the period of Darius III and Alexander the Great. Most scholars regard Josephus's account as a garbled version of the situation cited in Nehemiah, though the discovery of the Samaritan papyri and the possibility of papponymy proposed by Cross has suggested the possibility that there were as many as three Sanballats, each separated by a generation. D. R. Schwartz ("On Some Papyri and Josephus' Sources and Chronology for the Persian Period," *JSJ* 21 [1990]: 186) concludes: "Josephus combined stories about two different Sanballats, whom we may today call, with Cross, Sanballat I (the father-in-law) and Sanballat III (of Alexander's day)."

NOTES

23 On Ammon and Ammonites, see R. W. Younker, "Ammonites," in Hoerth, Mattingly, and Yamauchi, 293−316; L. G. Herr, "What Ever Happened to the Ammonites?" *BAR* 19/6 (1993): 26−35, 68; O. Lipschits, "Ammon in Transition from Vassal Kingdom to Babylonian Province," *BASOR* 335 (2004): 37−52. On Moabites, see G. Mattingly, "Moabites," in Hoerth, Mattingly, and Yamauchi, 317−34.

26 On Solomon in the Scriptures and various (Jewish, Arabic, Ethiopian, European) traditions, see Yamauchi, *Africa and the Bible*, ch. 3.

28 On the relationships between the "Sanballats" found in Nehemiah, the Elephantine papyri, and in the Wadi ed-Daliyeh Samaria papyri, see D. M. Gropp, "Sanballat," *Encyclopedia of the Dead Sea Scrolls* (ed. L. H. Schiffman and J. C. VanderKam; Oxford: Oxford Univ. Press, 2000), 2:823−25.

Archaeologists have recently uncovered remains of a pre-Hellenistic shrine on Mount Gerizim that some scholars have dated to the seventh century BC and others to the fifth century BC. See I. Magen, "Mount Gerizim and the Samaritans," in *Early Christianity in Context—Monuments and Documents* (ed. F. Manns and E. Alliata; Jerusalem: Franciscan, 1993), 91−148.

The date of the Samaritan schism from the Jews is much debated. Some place it as early as the time of Nehemiah, and others as late as the second century AD. For a summary article, see R. T. Anderson, "Samaritans," *ABD*, 5:940−47. See further A. D. Crown, ed., *The Samaritans* (Tübingen: Mohr, 1989); A. D. Crown, R. Pummer, and A. Tal, eds., *A Companion to Samaritan Studies* (Tübingen: Mohr, 1993); A. D. Crown, *A Bibliography of the Samaritans* (Metuchen, N.J.: Scarecrow, 1993).

4. Provisions of Wood and Firstfruits (13:30−31)

[30]So I purified the priests and the Levites of everything foreign, and assigned them duties, each to his own task. [31] I also made provision for contributions of wood at designated times, and for the firstfruits.
Remember me with favor, O my God.

COMMENTARY

30 "Duties" (*mišmārôt*, "divisions") refers to the assignment of particular duties to groups of priests and Levites, possibly on a rotating basis.

31 On the wood offering, see comment on 10:34; on firstfruits, see comment on 10:35.

The last words of Nehemiah—"Remember me with favor"—recapitulate an often-repeated theme running through the final chapter (vv.14, 22). His motive throughout his ministry was to please and to serve his divine Sovereign.

REFLECTION

Nehemiah provides us with one of the most vivid patterns of leadership in Scriptures.

1. *He was a man of responsibility*, as shown by his position as the royal cupbearer.
2. *He was a man of vision*, confident of who God was and what he could do through his servants. He was not, however, a visionary but a man who planned and then acted.
3. *He was a man of prayer*, who prayed spontaneously and constantly even in the presence of the king (2:4–5).
4. *He was a man of action and cooperation*, who realized what had to be done, explained it to others, and enlisted their aid. Nehemiah, a layman, was able to cooperate with his contemporary, Ezra the scribe and priest, in spite of the fact that these two leaders were of entirely different temperaments.
5. *He was a man of compassion*, who was moved by the plight of the poorer members of society so that he renounced even the rights he was entitled to (5:18) and denounced the greed of the wealthy (5:8).
6. *He was a man who triumphed over opposition*. His opponents tried ridicule (4:3), attempted slander (6:4–7), and spread misleading messages (6:10–14). But through God's favor Nehemiah triumphed over all difficulties.

For more on Nehemiah, see E. Yamauchi, "Nehemiah: A Model Leader," in *A Spectrum of Thought* (ed. M. L. Peterson; Wilmore, Ky.: Francis Asbury, 1982), 171–80; J. Maciariello, "Lessons in Leadership and Mangement from Nehemiah," *ThTo* 60 (2003): 397–407.

ESTHER

ELAINE PHILLIPS

Introduction

1. GENERAL OVERVIEW

The Scroll (Megillah) of Esther is a splendid narrative full of delicious ironies and reversals. Because the plot is so beguilingly engaging, the reader easily overlooks the complexity and richness that are packed into this text. The narrative is at the same time bitingly sarcastic as it pokes fun at the entire Persian court and horrifyingly ominous as one man's wounded pride and hatred spell potential disaster for the entire Jewish people. The text raises timely and perplexing questions about ethnicity, gender, violence, and adherence to traditional orthodoxy.

It is also brimming with ambiguity at every turn. What are we to make of the choices and activities of Vashti, Ahasuerus (Xerxes), Mordecai, and Esther? Apart from the thoroughly evil Haman, every major figure in the narrative has garnered an astonishingly wide range of character assessments from centuries of commentators. Likewise, the communities represented, from the vast Persian Empire to the Jews of the diaspora, elicit both praise and scorn. Even God himself is subjected to scrutiny. How are we to understand his apparent absence from the stage of human events?

2. THEMATIC EMPHASES

The theological questions and moral challenges of this text emerge within an exquisitely structured narrative that is interwoven with a web of social, cultural, and political themes. A probe into these themes sheds light on the development of the characters and plot.

Honor and Shame

Honor and shame emerge as significant issues for members of the Persian court.[1] Individual honor is most ostentatiously lodged in the person of the king. The splendid royal trappings are overwhelmingly present in the first chapter in which the king's banquets are occasions for the pretentious display of wealth and status. The word for honor, $y^e q\bar{a}r$, surfaces repeatedly throughout the narrative (e.g., 1:4, 20; 6:3–11).[2] The reader cannot miss the messages about Xerxes. He is defined and he defines himself in the realm by his own splendor and his status. Nevertheless, the distinction between honor that is deserved and honor that is contrived and superficial is soon evident. The pomp and pageantry of the court scene are accompanied by actions and advice that expose the ridiculous excesses and intemperate decisions of members of that court and, in effect, undermine entirely the façade of honor. The king's lapses are both funny, as he depends on servants to figure out where his next queen will come from, and ominous, when he neglects to honor Mordecai and instead appoints an egotistical butcher as "second-in-command."[3]

The culture of the Persian court manifestly did not hold women in high esteem. They were excluded from public contexts unless bidden to come and were treated as objects;[4] and when they had served their purpose, their status changed from "young women" to "concubines" (Est 2:14). Vashti's shocking assertiveness eliminates her from the court, the scene of honor, while Esther seemingly plays a passive role in her initial appearances in the narrative and thereby wins a place of honor.

As the plot develops, the driving conflict between Haman and Mordecai has also to do with honor. Haman craves the public obeisance that accompanies his exalted position; shame and honor teeter on the balance for him as Mordecai refuses to do homage and Haman rages and seethes over the affront. Later, it is his blind obsession with his own presumed recognition as "one whom the king delights to honor" that determines the details of his public humiliation while honoring Mordecai.

Honor and shame were part of the fabric of national identity as well; the tenuous existence of the Jewish community separated from their homeland was a source of potential shame. Exile in the world of the ancient Near East meant loss of honor and was perceived as a matter of divine punishment.[5] In this narrative, the "legalized" annihilation of the Jewish people is likewise representative of honor destroyed. Thus the subsequent decree affording them the right of self-defense and the success of that operation restore their

---

1. See Lillian R. Klein, "Honor and Shame in Esther," in *A Feminist Companion to Esther, Judith and Susanna* (FCB 7; ed. Athalya Brenner; Sheffield: Sheffield Academic, 1995), 149–75; and Timothy S. Laniak, *Shame and Honor in the Book of Esther* (SBLDS 165; Atlanta: Scholars, 1998) for extensive treatments.
2. The term is used primarily in late biblical Hebrew (*TDOT*, 6:279–87). See commentary on ch. 1.
3. In regard to the portrayal of the court as unworthy of allegiance, see David G. Firth, "The Book of Esther: A Neglected Paradigm for Dealing with the State," *OTE* 10 (1997): 18–26.
4. See Timothy K. Beal, *The Book of Hiding: Gender, Ethnicity, Annihilation, and Esther* (London/New York: Routledge, 1997), 27–28; and Joshua Berman, "*Hadassah Bat Abihail*: The Evolution from Object to Subject in the Character of Esther," *JBL* 120 (2001): 647–69.
5. Laniak, *Shame and Honor*, 173.

honor.[6] In this framework, Levenson sees Mordecai and Esther as allegorizations of Israel's national destiny. Mordecai is transformed from refugee to prime minister, and Esther from orphan to royalty.[7]

Power and Presence

Interwoven with honor is authority. The Persian kingship with its pomp and power is at the center of the narrative. It is telling that words related to the Hebrew root meaning "to rule" (*mlk*) are used more than 250 times in 167 verses.[8] Nevertheless, the king is astonishingly impotent. While he is obsessed with honor and authority, he does not independently exercise the latter. Instead, the will of others repeatedly becomes the law. The king is characteristically driven by rage whenever his power and honor are threatened. In a similar manner, the consequences of Memucan's speech (1:16–20) and the scurrilous activities of Haman are indicative of the dangers when power is threatened.

In contrast, the initially powerless Esther comes to control the king. Her royal attire and demeanor overwhelm the king as she comes into his presence, and he will give up to half of his kingdom in order to satisfy her wishes (5:3, 6; 7:2). Subsequently, she wields royal power, especially in her denouncement of Haman, the elevation of Mordecai, and the measures taken to ensure the security of the Jewish population empirewide.

Those with authority are prominently in the presence of the monarch. The Hebrew idiom "before the face of …" appears repeatedly. Initially, those favored individuals include a group of seven named eunuchs who serve in the king's presence (1:10), additional notable individuals who "understand the times" (1:13), and seven named princes of Media and Persia who sit first in the kingdom and see "the face of the king" (1:14). In the course of five years, however, there is an insidious change, and only Haman is named as empowered (3:1); the rest have been silenced.[9]

It seems that those who have prominent positions "in the presence of the king" are exempt from the rule of the golden scepter (4:11). Haman freely approaches the king to get authorization to obliterate the people of Mordecai. By contrast, Esther must still operate under the scepter even after Haman's demise (8:4). That Esther and Mordecai both have access to the presence of the king by the end of the narrative is indicative of their firmly established authority.

Margins and Boundaries

Even though royal honor and power characterize those who are "inside," a fascinating aspect of this narrative is that major developments take place on boundaries between inside and outside. The restricted palace precincts are defined around the person of the king, but they are perilously close to the open public square and unseemly activities in that arena are unsettling. Mordecai lives his public life in the king's gate—clearly

6. Michael V. Fox, *Character and Ideology in the Book of Esther* (2nd ed.; Grand Rapids: Eerdmans, 2001), 295.
7. Jon D. Levenson, *Esther* (OTL; Louisville: Westminster John Knox, 1997), 16, 56.
8. Sandra Beth Berg, *The Book of Esther: Motifs, Themes and Structure* (SBLDS 44; Missoula, Mont.: Scholars, 1979), 69–71.
9. Yoram Hazony (*The Dawn: Political Teachings of the Book of Esther* [rev. ed.; Jerusalem: Shalem, 2000], 48–50) suggests that this totalitarian maneuver was really a crackdown in response to the foiled assassination plot.

a boundary area between the court and the outside, but one where power is exercised.[10] The eunuchs, whose very existence blurs the gender boundary, play significant mediating roles across boundaries and guard the way into the palace (1:10–12; 2:3, 8–9, 21; 4:4–16).[11] Even the city itself is demarcated between Susa and the citadel of Susa, and there are distinct differences between the populations of each.

Esther repeatedly operates across thresholds. She is the only character in the narrative with both Hebrew and Babylonian names, Hadassah and Esther, indicative of her identity with both contexts. In a moment of extreme tension, she transgresses a legal boundary as she enters the king's presence uninvited. In her marginal and precarious position she proves strategically clever by using her wits, persuasive rhetoric, and beauty.[12]

Beal has explored other, less obvious boundaries that add to the fascination of the entire text. Among them are Mordecai's precarious existence between a writing that preserves his deed of honor and one that will murder him, and the king's insomnia, on the boundary between desire for and inability to sleep.[13] Even the Megillah itself exists a bit on the margins, both in terms of canonical status and usage, particularly in the Christian communities (see below, secs. 3 and 10).

Law and Justice, Obedience and Disobedience[14]

The nature and function of "the word of the king" and the law ($d\bar{a}t$; GK 2017) are key factors at all levels of the narrative. Persian political theology meant that the word of the king, an imitation of the gods, unified the realm. Thus Haman's description of the Jews as those who do not keep the laws of the king makes them sound particularly threatening. In this context, it is essential that the "laws of Persia and Media" were irrevocable (1:19; also 8:8),[15] and it is equally essential that there were mechanisms in order to get around these unchangeable laws. The unjust law mandating the annihilation of the Jews (3:14; 4:3, 8) is overridden by a second one (8:14, 17), and the pattern of measure-for-measure justice, foundational to biblical legislative and prophetic texts, is highlighted as the language of that second edict mirrors the first.

Ironically, in a court that is manifestly short on true justice, there are edicts for the consumption of wine, marital relations, language, the deposition of the first queen, and the prolonged preparation of the royal

---

10. Trials were conducted (Dt 21:19; 22:15) and critical developments unfolded at gates (2Sa 15:1–2). Xenophon, *Cyropaedia* 8.1.6, and Herodotus, *History* 3.120, indicate that Persian officials had to stay at the gate of the palace.

11. On the crucial but often overlooked roles of the eunuchs in the wider Persian culture, see Pierre Briant, *From Cyrus to Alexander: A History of the Persian Empire* (trans. Peter T. Daniels; Winona Lake, Ind.: Eisenbrauns, 2002), 268–77; and Carol M. Bechtel, *Esther* (IBC; ed. James L. Mays; Louisville, Ky.: John Knox, 2002), 12–13.

12. See Laniak, *Shame and Honor*, 165.

13. Beal, *Book of Hiding*, 33, 79, 124.

14. See Berg (*The Book of Esther*, 72–82, 100) for further discussion of the unifying theme of obedience and disobedience in the context of unjust authority. See also A. Kay Fountain, *Literary and Empirical Readings of the Books of Esther* (Studies in Biblical Literature 43; New York: Peter Lang, 2002), 138–42, who summarized the key uses of the term *dāt* in the text.

15. André LaCocque, *The Feminine Unconventional: Four Subversive Figures in Israel's Tradition* (Minneapolis: Fortress, 1990), 51–52. See further below (Historicity of the Narrative) on the irrevocability of the laws of the Persians and Medes.

concubines.[16] Nevertheless, the web of Persian legal endeavor is repeatedly undermined; the king's laws are shown to be foolish and dangerous enterprises, and he is effectively controlled by those around him.

Disobedience on the part of key characters drives the action forward. Vashti's refusal to comply with the king's summons prepares the way for the rest of the story. As Mordecai identifies with the Jewish community, he disobeys the king's order to bow before Haman. This disobedience in turn serves as the basis for Haman's accusation that the Jews do not obey the king's laws. While Esther is obedient to Mordecai and to Hegai, she too chooses identity with her people and disobeys the king's edict (4:11), thereby risking her life. That choice turns the patterns upside down. Mordecai obeys her; she gains access into the sphere of power in the presence of the king; and she becomes a commanding queen, both in presence and in word.

Writing and the (False) Sense of Permanence

Closely related to the matter of law is the significance of writing. In fact, few OT texts are so focused on writing as this one, as indicated even in its title Megillah (Scroll).[17] Vashti's punishment is written as an irrevocable decree to stave off disorder in the kingdom. Nevertheless, while she is "written out" of the court and out of the story, she is remembered (2:1), and the memory has to be addressed. Mordecai's deed is recorded in the king's chronicles, but while that writing recognized him as a loyal subject, his deed is forgotten. Instead, Haman's decree in response to Mordecai's insolence is intended to obliterate him. The symmetrical laws of annihilation and self-defense are written for distribution in a system designed for efficiency.

The profusion of writing at the end of the narrative to establish the festival may demonstrate the potential for bureaucratic overwriting when new institutions arise. Finally, the recital of all the events is likewise written in the national chronicles. Writing purportedly demonstrates power and makes things public and permanent. Yet each written text, so fundamental to the development of this plot, is never entirely sufficient.[18]

Anti-Semitism

For reasons that are not articulated, Mordecai commands Esther not to reveal her ethnic identity—a possible indication that there is widespread and longstanding antipathy toward the Jews that will later serve as fertile ground in which to sow Haman's decree. It is evident that Haman expects extensive public

---

16. David J. A. Clines, *The Esther Scroll: The Story of the Story* (JSOTSup 30; Sheffield: Sheffield Academic, 1984), 11, 16. T. Cuyler Young Jr., "The Consolidation of the Empire and Its Limits of Growth under Darius and Xerxes," in *The Cambridge Ancient History* (2nd ed.; Cambridge: Cambridge Univ. Press, 1988), 4:81–83, describes the rigidity and legal protocol in the court of the Persian king, whose very word was the law.

17. Clines, *The Esther Scroll*, 24. See also Beal, *Book of Hiding*, 24–32; 79–84; Bechtel, *Esther*, 14–16, on the power of the written word; and the deconstructionist approach of Mieke Bal, "Lots of Writing," *Semeia* 54 (1991): 77–102.

18. Danna Nolan Fewell, "Introduction: Writing, Reading, and Relating," in *Reading between Texts: Intertextuality and the Hebrew Bible* (Louisville: Westminster John Knox, 1992), 11–12.

participation in his plan to annihilate the Jews.[19] While the populace of Susa is thrown into an uproar by the decree of the king and Haman (3:15), the reasons for that "confusion" are not presented, and there is an equally significant part of the empire that decides to attack the Jews even in the face of the second decree.

3. TEXTS, PLACE IN THE CANON, AND CANONICITY

The text of Esther poses particular challenges in that there are two extant Greek versions, which are, at points, significantly different from each other as well as being embellished beyond the Hebrew text (MT). Josephus produced an additional popular rendition of the narrative (*Ant.* 11.184–296 [6.1–13]). The more accessible and longer of the Greek versions, designated the *B*-Text, appears in the Septuagint (LXX). Broadly speaking, it consists of six major additions (107 verses), all of which enhance the theological or the dramatic content of the text by naming God and describing his intervention outright, reporting Mordecai's apocalyptic dream and eventually its interpretation, inserting prayers of Mordecai and Esther, describing Esther's audience with the king, and presenting the texts of the royal edicts.[20] As a result of the additions, God and Mordecai are central in the text instead of Esther, and the narrative structure emphasizes different key themes.[21] There are further significant modifications within the narrative of the LXX beyond these six distinct units. Many of these modifications clarify apparent ambiguities in the Hebrew text.

The second Greek text, designated the *A*-Text,[22] is noticeably shorter. It does have the six additions that characterize the LXX, but once those additions are removed it does not have any indication of the irrevocability of the laws of the Persians and Medes — a detail that changes rather markedly the development of the narrative. Once Haman is dead, Mordecai simply asks that the edict be revoked, the king gives Mordecai the affairs of the kingdom, and there is no subsequent conflict between those enemies of the Jews who are still intent on their destruction and the Jews who kill in self-defense. The two days of fighting in Susa, which serves in the MT as the basis for two festival days, is absent. Further, the text omits the profusion of doublets, which serve as a built-in device to emphasize the two days.

---

19. Joseph Fleishman, "Why Was Haman Successful at Winning King Ahasuerus' Approval to Exterminate the Jews in the Persian Empire?" *HUCA* 68 (1997): 35–49 (Heb.); and Hazony, *The Dawn*, ch. 9, titled "Anti-Semitism." For the alternative view that Persia was not a threatening environment, see Clines, *The Esther Scroll*, 39–46; and Kenneth Craig, *Reading Esther: A Case for the Literary Carnivalesque* (Louisville: Westminster John Knox, 1995), 124–25.

20. Carey A. Moore, *Daniel, Esther, and Jeremiah: The Additions* (AB 44; Garden City, N.Y.: Doubleday, 1977), 153–54; and Charles V. Dorothy, *The Books of Esther: Structure, Genre, and Textual Integrity* (Sheffield: Sheffield Academic, 1997), 91–92.

21. Elias Bickerman, "Notes on the Greek Book of Esther," *PAAJR* 20 (1950): 101–33; idem, *Four Strange Books of the Bible* (New York: Schocken, 1967), 218–34; Carey A. Moore, ed., *Studies in the Book of Esther* (New York: Ktav, 1982), lxvi.

22. For summaries of the nature of this text as well as various proposed explanations of its relationship to the MT and LXX, see Carey A. Moore, "A Greek Witness to a Different Text of Esther," *ZAW* 79 (1967): 351–58; Clines, *The Esther Scroll*, 71–72; Emanuel Tov, "The 'Lucianic' Text of the Canonical and the Apocryphal Sections of Esther: A Rewritten Biblical Book," *Text* 10 (1982): 1–25; Michael V. Fox, *The Redaction of the Books of Esther: On Reading Composite Texts* (SBLMS 40; Atlanta: Scholars, 1991); Karen H. Jobes, *The Alpha-Text of Esther: Its Character and Relationship to the Masoretic Text* (Atlanta: Scholars, 1996); Dorothy, *The Books of Esther*, 13–41; and Kristin De Troyer, *The End of the Alpha Text of Esther: Translation and Narrative Technique in MT 8:1–17, LXX 8:1–17; and AT 7:14–41* (Septuagint and Cognate Studies 48; Atlanta: SBL, 2000). The wide range of opinions drawn from the same data indicates that determining literary dependence is extremely risky business!

In sum, the *A*-Text presents neither Esther as the primary character, nor the Esther narrative as an etiology for the festival and a mandate for its perpetual establishment, both of which purposes seem clearly to be goals of the MT. The extent of the differences among the early versions of Esther may have been due to ancient translators' varying views as to its authoritative value and the freedom they felt to modify and amplify the story.[23] These issues are of considerable importance with regard to the matters of canon and the purposes of the Scroll to be discussed below. Their complexity, however, merits a separate treatment, which is beyond the scope of this commentary; therefore, the Greek additions will simply be noted at the points where they appear, and the possible implications of those additions as well as other significant changes in the LXX will be briefly addressed.

As early as the redaction of the Mishnah (AD 220), there is evidence of an Aramaic translation (*targum*) of Esther: *M. Megillah* 2:1 reads, "One who reads a *targum* [has not fulfilled the obligation to read the Megillah]." It is unclear when the Targums that are extant were written down; proposed dates range from the fifth to the eighth centuries.[24] Esther is the only text outside the Torah that has two Targums devoted to it. The first one carefully reproduces the Hebrew text but intersperses material that effectively serves as a grammatical and interpretive commentary. The end result is about twice as long as the Hebrew text. The second Targum is even more expanded, reflecting both the popularity of the Esther narrative and further development of creative embellishments that accompany the story. In both cases, there is evident concern to give religious practice and belief a higher profile. The second Targum shares a number of its expansions with the exegetical developments in both the Babylonian Talmud and the Talmud of the Land of Israel or Jerusalem Talmud, as well as *Midrash Esther Rabbah*.

The book of Esther is positioned in the Hebrew Bible with the five Megillot (Scrolls), those texts specifically read on the occasions of the Jewish festivals.[25] Esther is read on Purim, Song of Songs on Passover, Ruth at the Feast of Weeks or Pentecost, Lamentations on the Ninth of Av in mourning for the destruction of the temple, and Ecclesiastes at the Feast of Tabernacles. According to the pattern established in the Septuagint, English translations place the book following Ezra and Nehemiah because of its chronological and historical relationship with the events recorded in those books.

Any discussion of the canonical status of Esther must recognize both the complications noted above regarding the texts of Esther and the complexities regarding the matter of the canon itself.[26] Data adduced as evidence regarding the canonicity of the Hebrew text of Esther include a somewhat vague reference in Josephus (*Ag. Ap.* 1:8:32–42) and a rabbinic dispute in the fourth century AD as to whether Esther, along

---

23. See Moore, *Additions*, 167; and Bickerman, "Notes on the Greek Book of Esther," 101–33.

24. Bernard Grossfeld, ed. and trans., *The Two Targums of Esther, Translated, with Apparatus and Notes* (Collegeville, Minn.: Michael Glazier, 1991), 8–24.

25. The order among these books varies slightly depending on the codex. See Lewis B. Paton, *A Critical and Exegetical Commentary on the Book of Esther* (ICC; New York: Scribner, 1908), 1–2.

26. See Ste[phen G. Dempster, "Torah, Torah, Torah: The Emergence of the Tripartite Canon," in *Exploring the Origins of the Bible: Canon Formation in Historical, Literary, and Theological Perspective* (ed. Craig A. Evans and Emanuel Tov; Grand Rapids: Baker, 2008), 87–128; Lee Martin McDonald, *The Biblical Canon: Its Origin, Transmission, and Authority* (Peabody, Mass.: Hendrickson, 2007) for varying evangelical positions regarding the basic definition of canon, evaluation of the evidence for a recognized canon, and suggested dates for establishment of the Hebrew Bible canon.

with Qoheleth (Ecclesiastes) and Song of Songs, "defiles the hands." The relevant portion of *b. Megillah* 7a reads: "R. Judah said in the name of R. Samuel: Esther does not defile the hands. Are we to infer from this that Samuel was of the opinion that Esther was not composed under the inspiration of the holy spirit? It was composed to be recited but not to be written."

The standard explanation of this cryptic expression has been that "defiling the hands" implied that a given text was considered canonical. It may be, however, that in declaring that a scroll made the hands unclean and thus required the hands to be washed after every contact, the sages were protecting the given scroll from casual and irreverent treatment. Berlin suggests that the expression had to do with whether the text was read publicly on the Sabbath or festivals (by someone who might defile the scroll with unclean hands).[27] The discussion may also have addressed the relative ritual status of these works based on their lack of the Tetragrammaton.[28]

In sum, the questions that the rabbis raised in the fourth century concerning Esther are not conclusive evidence that its canonical status was still unsettled at that point. By the time the Mishnah was redacted, an entire tractate (Megillah) was given over to regulations for reading the text at Purim, and a baraita (*b. B. Bat.* 14b) listing ostensibly canonical texts cites Esther.

The very fact that the translators of the Septuagint felt constrained to augment the narrative they had suggests that it did hold canonical status fairly early and was troubling because of its supposed lack of religious content. The nature of the additions is curious but may be a subtle indication that the core narrative of the Hebrew text was not to be tampered with. For example, Mordecai's challenge to Esther (4:14) would seem to be an obvious place to modify with deliberate and direct allusions to the intervention of God, but the LXX did not do so. That statement was preserved and then Mordecai's prayer was attached afterward.

Further compounding the issues related to canonicity are the absence of any fragments of the text of Esther as we know it from the Dead Sea texts[29] and the apparent ambivalence of the early church regarding the status of Esther. Significant among the church fathers who accepted Esther were Clement of Rome and Origen. Athanasius and Theodore of Mopsuestia viewed it with suspicion, and Melito of Sardis left it out of his list.[30]

---

27. Adele Berlin, *Esther* (JPSBC; Philadelphia: Jewish Publication Society, 2001), 43–44.

28. Michael J. Broyde, "Defilement of the Hands, Canonization of the Bible, and the Special Status of Esther, Ecclesiastes, and Song of Songs," *Judaism* 44 (1995): 65–79. See *b. Sanh.* 100a.

29. There is considerable debate as to whether six Aramaic fragments from Qumran that appear to be narratives of Jews in the Persian court are related to an early form of the Esther story. See R. Eisenman and M. Wise, "Stories from the Persian Court," in *The Dead Sea Scrolls Uncovered* (Rockport, Maine: Element, 1992): 99–103; J. T. Milik, "Les modèles araméens du livre d'Esther dans la grotte 4 de Qumran," *RevQ* 15/16 (1992–1993): 321–406; Michael Wechsler, "Two Para-Biblical Novellae from Qumran Cave 4: A Reevaluation of 4Q550," *DSD* 7:2 (2000): 130–72; and Kristin De Troyer, "Once More, the So-Called Esther Fragments of Cave 4," *RevQ* 19:3 (2000): 401–22. It seems that even an indirect connection is tenuous at best.

30. Carey A. Moore (*Esther: A New Translation with Introduction and Commentary* [AB; New York, Doubleday, 1971], xxv–xxviii) presents the data regarding Esther's acceptance by the early church. See also Beckwith, *The Old Testament Canon*, 295–97; Bernhard W. Anderson, "The Place of the Book of Esther," *JRelS* 30 (1950): 33; Frederic W. Bush, *Ruth, Esther* (WBC 9; Dallas, Word: 1996), 275; and Sid Leiman, *The Canonization of Hebrew Scripture: The Talmudic and Midrashic Evidence* (Hamdon, Conn.: Archon, 1976), 48, 160 n. 239.

4. LITERARY CONSIDERATIONS: GENRE, UNITY OF THE TEXT, STRUCTURE, LANGUAGE

There is considerable lack of agreement when it comes to determining the genre of the text.[31] In fact, some scholars are hesitant to attach a singular genre label to the text because it manifests such a rich array of literary features.[32] A definitive characteristic of the story is the rollicking satire on the inept Persian court in stark combination with the ominous dread of genocide.[33] Claiming that the humor is laced with improbabilities and exaggerations, some have called the text a literary farce.[34] Variations on this theme include a burlesque on the Persian court scene[35] and a carnivalesque fusion of parody and ambivalence.[36] Talmon lodged Esther within the wisdom tradition, calling it a "historicized wisdom-tale" that focused on the wisdom of a courtier, Mordecai, to accomplish his purposes.[37] Gordis rejected Talmon's conclusions and suggested that a Jewish author, posing as a Gentile writer, composed a "simulated royal chronicle."[38]

Because the plot development appears in a purportedly historical context, a number of suggestions range in the vicinity of historical novel[39] or novella, the latter in recognition of its brevity. These genres include diaspora novella[40] and deliverance novella.[41] While "novel" has been one of the most frequent designations, Baldwin suggested that it was an anachronistic reflection of the popularity of that genre in the nineteenth century.[42] The tangle of legislative language at the end has given rise to the label "festal etiology."[43] Each of these categories implies that the work is primarily fiction, driving a wedge between

---

31. For summaries and critiques of the major proposals, see Joyce Baldwin, *Esther: An Introduction and Commentary* (TOTC; ed. D. J. Wiseman; Downers Grove, Ill.: InterVarsity Press, 1984), 32–36; Fox, *Character and Ideology*, 141–52; and Bush, *Ruth, Esther*, 298–300.

32. See J. A. Loader, "Esther as a Novel with Different Levels of Meaning" *ZAW* 90 (1978): 417–21; Dorothy, *The Books of Esther*, 327, 341–43; and Laniak, *Shame and Honor*, 169–72.

33. Clines, *The Esther Scroll*, 32; Bush, *Ruth, Esther*, 316; idem, "The Book of Esther: *Opus non gratum* in the Christian Canon," *BBR* 8 (1998): 49.

34. Beal, *Book of Hiding*, ix; Daniel F. Polish, "Aspects of Esther: A Phenomenological Exploration of the Megillah of Esther and Origins of Purim," *JSOT* 85 (1999): 99–103.

35. Berlin, *Esther*, xviii–xx.

36. Craig, *Reading Esther*, 30–44, 147–68.

37. Shemaryahu Talmon, "'Wisdom' in the Book of Esther," *VT* 13 (1963): 419–55.

38. Robert Gordis, "Religion, Wisdom and History in the Book of Esther: A New Solution to an Ancient Crux," *JBL* 100 (1981): 375–78.

39. Moore, *Esther*, lii–liii; Levenson, *Esther*, 25.

40. W. Lee Humphreys, "The Story of Esther and Mordecai: An Early Jewish Novella," in *Saga, Legend, Tale, Novella, Fable: Narrative Forms in Old Testament Literature* (ed. G. Coats; JSOTSup 35; Sheffield: JSOT, 1985: 97–113); André LaCocque, "Haman in the Book of Esther," *HAR* 11 (1987): 208–9; idem, *The Feminine Unconventional*, ch. 5.

41. Dorothy, *The Books of Esther*, 322–24.

42. Baldwin, *Esther*, 33–34.

43. See Fox, *Character and Ideology*, 151–52. Dorothy, *The Books of Esther*, 321, rejects this label and says the justification for Purim was tacked on. See also Humphreys, "The Story of Esther and Mordecai," 112–13.

literary art and historical veracity.[44] Nevertheless, a substantial case can be made for reliable narrative historiography.[45] Given the remarkable representation of this historical context, the best label might simply be "historical narrative."[46]

The unity of Esther has been repeatedly challenged. Earlier theories, prompted by the popularity of source criticism and the striking abundance of doublets in this text, posited two or three separate sources, shaped around the individual characters of Esther, Mordecai, and Vashti and woven together into one narrative.[47] While that approach has been discounted, the distinctively administrative and anticlimactic tone of the final chapters of the MT has persuaded a number of commentators that the original narrative ended somewhere in ch. 8.[48] The parts of ch. 9 that have been dismissed, however, are essential for the main theme of the narrative, which is the complete reversal of the threat against the Jews as a people. They demonstrate justice and action taken against "Jew-haters" and address the need to commemorate that event.[49] That so many critics have found narrative infelicities in ch. 9 may actually attest to its authenticity. It is what it purports to be: the description of the daunting process of instituting a new festival.

It is only when the Hebrew text is read in its entirety that an overarching chiastic structure is evident. A complex web of reversals emerges, and a major thread that weaves them together is a succession of ten banquets.[50] The outer frame of the chiastic structure consists of pairs of these feasts. The first chapter describes the king's lavish banquets, the first one for the military and nobility and the second one specifically for the residents of Susa. Correspondingly, the Scroll closes with the first and second celebrations of Purim (also a festival for drinking), on the fourteenth and (for Susa) fifteenth of Adar. The chiasm has as its central turning point the insomnia of the king (6:1), which occurs between the two private banquets of Esther. The king's insomnia and the subsequent exchange between Xerxes and Haman are so utterly beyond the scope of anyone's plans and schemes, whether for good or for ill, that they serve as stunning witnesses to the sovereign working of God. Placement at the center of the narrative is a subtle indicator of this witness.

---

44. Humphreys, "The Story of Esther and Mordecai," 86–88.

45. Iain Provan, V. Philips Long, and Tremper Longman III, *A Biblical History of Israel* (Louisville: Westminster John Knox, 2003), 75–93.

46. Forrest S. Weiland, "Historicity, Genre, and Narrative Design in the Book of Esther," *BSac* 159 (April–June 2002): 151–65; and Mervin Breneman, *Ezra, Nehemiah, Esther* (NAC 10; Nashville: Broadman & Holman, 1993), 287.

47. Bickerman, *Four Strange Books*, 172; Hans Bardtke, *Das Buch Esther* (KAT XVII/5; Gultersloh: Mohn, 1963), 248–52; and Henri Cazalles, "Note sûr la composition du rouleau d'Esther," in *Lex Tua Veritas* (ed. H. Gross and F. Mussner; Trier: Paulinus, 1961), 17–29.

48. See Bush, *The Book of Esther*, 41; [*Ruth, Esther*, 1996: 279–94]; Dorothy, *The Books of Esther*, 313–38; Clines, *Esther Scroll*, 39–63; and evaluation of Clines' position in Levenson, *Esther*, 125–32.

49. André LaCocque, "The Different Versions of Esther," *BibInt* 7 (1999): 301–22, esp. 304, 312; Berg, *The Book of Esther*, 31–47; and Lisbeth S. Fried, "Towards the *Ur*-Text of Esther," *JSOT* 88 (2000): 49–57.

50. Berg, *The Book of Esther*, 31–57; and Levenson, *Esther*, 8. The banquet (*mišteh*) was a special occasion for eating and drinking. The term is used forty-six times in the biblical text; twenty of them are in Esther, several of which further emphasize the drinking aspect by calling the event a *mišteh hayyayin*, a "drinking feast of wine."

A term that repeatedly surfaces in recent commentaries on Esther is "peripety," referring to the sudden and unexpected reversal of events.[51] These patterned repetitions and reversals both move the narrative forward and drive home the fact of God's sovereign presence in the lives of his people. The principle is articulated explicitly in 9:1 — (lit.) "and it was overturned." The narrator has made certain that the audience perceives the peripety by using similar phrases in both the event and its opposite. The anti-Jewish decree is overturned by its verbal parallel, giving the Jews the right to self-defense.

Further examples of linguistic correspondence include the promotion of Haman mirrored by that of Mordecai, and the giving of the signet rings to each of these individuals. The counterparts to the celebratory nature of the banquet are mourning and fasting. After the king agrees to sponsor the nefarious decree of Haman, they sit down to drink together, while Mordecai and the Jews throughout the realm go into mourning. Esther's extreme fast of three days, which also includes abstinence from drinking, is called in preparation for two of the most tense banquet scenes we might imagine. Additional evidence of perceived symmetry and balance is the distinct motif of measure-for-measure justice.[52]

The most significant reversals in the complex chiasm have to do with unexpected acquisitions and losses of honor, presented in terms of rising and falling. Haman's promotion is reversed in two ways; Haman is raised again, but this time on the pole he intended for Mordecai, and Mordecai is exalted to Haman's political position. The motif of falling becomes ominously more frequent as the narrative progresses and surfaces repeatedly in regard to Haman's demise and the fear of the Jews' "falling" on the people. The shame of the Jews is reversed; those who hate them are both defeated and shamed, and Haman's sons are hung as Haman had been. Significantly, the first and last instances of "fall" (3:7 and 9:24) have to do with the lot.

Repetition occurs on the large scale, as the stylistic backdrop for the reversals in the chiasm, but it is not limited to that medium. There is an overabundance of pairs of words, repeated indications of events, and sets of statements and requests.[53] The doublets are evident in the description of the Persian court, which is characterized by particularly rich and excessive vocabulary to convey the opulence of the court. The word pairs (dyads) are representative of Persian "officialese" and may be part of the humorous satire on the royal scene.[54] These pairs lead up to the critical "petition and request" pattern of the king's invitations to

---

51. See Berg, *The Book of Esther*, 104–5; Fox, *Character and Ideology*, 158–63; and Judith Rosenheim, "Fate and Freedom in the Scroll of Esther," *Proof* 12 (1992): 131. Medieval Jewish commentators were aware of the structural parallelism evident in the reversals and cited multiple examples of them (Barry Dov Walfish, *Esther in Medieval Garb: Jewish Interpretation of the Book of Esther in the Middle Ages* [Albany, N.Y.: State Univ. of New York Press, 1993], 63–65).

52. William T. McBride, "Esther Passes: Chiasm, Lex Talio, and Money in the Book of Esther," in *"Not in Heaven": Coherence and Complexity in Biblical Narrative* (ed. J. P. Rosenblatt and J. C. Sitterson, Jr.; Bloomington, Ind.: Indiana Univ. Press, 1991), 211–23; 254–60; Jack M. Sasson, "Esther," in *The Literary Guide to the Bible* (ed. Robert Alter and Frank Kermode; Cambridge: Cambridge Univ. Press, 1987), 341; and Polish, "Aspects of Esther," 88–91.

53. For classifications of the duplications, see Athalya Brenner, "Looking at Esther through the Looking Glass," in Brenner, *A Feminist Companion*, 72–73; and Polish, "Aspects of Esther," 86–90.

54. Levenson, *Esther*, 11–12. The word pairs are not limited to Esther; Nehemiah responded to Artaxerxes with the same pattern (Ne 2:5).

Esther to state her case (5:3, 6; 7:2). It is also possible that these verbal pairs and the pairs of feasts are all adumbrations of the two-day celebration of Purim.[55]

Furthermore, perhaps the two letters at the end, rather than being indicative of a separate and inferior document, continue the emphasis on double attestations. The ubiquitous duality also may reinforce the theme of dual loyalty with which Jews in the diaspora context have always wrestled.[56] At several key points, dyads are replaced by triplets, most notably in the context of sanctioning and effecting violence (3:13; 7:4; 8:11; 9:5).[57] They in turn give way to fourfold verbal "strings" of jubilation (8:16–17; 9:19, 22).[58]

In addition to the peculiar and repeated appearance of pairs, there is an overabundance of passive verb forms in critical contexts. Esther's early appearances are almost exclusively described in this manner; she is acted upon by larger, nameless forces. This same anonymity has a wider circle than just Esther and the young women. It pervades the court scenes of the narrative, thus divesting the bureaucracy of accountability.[59] The passive forms allow for ambiguity in regard to who is responsible for what transpires. Implicit in this stylistic device may be an acknowledgment of the unnamed Divine Orchestrator.

5. PURPOSES OF THE TEXT

This discussion presupposes that the MT is the foundational text and is to be read as a unit. With that in mind, it is clear that there are two interrelated primary intentions. One is the establishment of the annual celebration to commemorate the deliverance of Jews across the empire from annihilation. Reading the story would become an integral part of that commemoration. Chapter 9 firmly establishes the two-day festival. This emphasis is particularly important because Purim, unlike the major Jewish festivals, had not been instituted at Sinai.

Nevertheless, some see the connection between the deliverance narrative (chs. 1–8) and the festival observance as secondary and contrived.[60] Scholars of the nineteenth century proposed creative hypotheses that attempted to explain satisfactorily why the story of a *Jewish* deliverance would be connected to what they assumed was a preexisting pagan celebration, whether it was of Assyrian, Babylonian, or Persian origin. The nature of this hypothetical festival was as tentative as its proposed point of origin. Some suggested the New Year, others a spring festival, and still others connected it with Farvardigan, a feast in memory of the dead.

Among the favored hypotheses—dependent on the identification of Mordecai and Esther, Haman and Vashti, with Babylonian and Elamite deities—were varied proposals that the Esther narrative was reworked Babylonian mythology of some stripe, in which there was a feast celebrating victories of Marduk and

55. Berg, *The Book of Esther*, 40.

56. Edward L. Greenstein, "A Jewish Reading of Esther," in *Judaic Perspectives on Ancient Israel* (ed. J. Neusner, B. A. Levine, and E. S. Frerichs; Philadelphia: Fortress, 1987), 237.

57. Each of the verses cited includes "destroy, kill ... annihilate" except 9:5, which reads "struck ... killing ... destroyed."

58. Ibid., 239.

59. Bush, *Esther*, 307.

60. See Baldwin, *Esther*, 21–22, and Berg, *The Book of Esther*, 3–5.

Ishtar.[61] What does seem to be clear is that the Akkadian term *puru(m)*, which can be traced through both Assyrian and Babylonian texts, meant "lot" and secondarily "fate."[62] The practice of casting lots in order to determine the outcome of events has a long history and bears a central role in this narrative.

According to Abraham Cohen, Haman's use of *pûr* (GK 7052) demonstrates his conviction that *he* could control the fate of the Jews by casting the lot. This is an act of defiance against God, who in the end controls all the "coincidences" as they unfold. The very name of the holiday, "Purim," indicates the centrality of the inversion from chance, to which Haman appeals, and Providence, which prevails at every step. Thus *"the 'pur' is nothing less than the intentional symbol of chance-fate."*[63] Further, the Scroll may have served as a protest against Zoroastrian dualism and the accompanying fatalistic view of reality. This hypothesis does away with the idea that the text is a late rationalization for the adoption of an existing Persian holiday. It is notable that Haman appeals to a historical reality when he describes the people as separated and scattered (3:8). If Jewish exclusiveness was a real phenomenon, it is unlikely that the Jews would have easily adopted a Persian holiday.[64]

Following the work of Cohen, Judith Rosenheim claims that the issues of fate (determinism) and freedom are the fabric of this story, but she reverses the implications of casting the lot. In Persian culture, the results of casting *pûr* were perceived as evidence of the predetermined decisions of a pagan deity. Thus the lot did not indicate random chance. Instead, Haman was consulting his gods. Given this wider socioreligious context, it is important that this narrative unfolds as it does, with God apparently silent and thus *not* predictable, but sovereignly free to reverse the date that had been set by casting the lot and to do so particularly in conjunction with the Passover. *Pûr* is central to the narrative because it represents both fate and chance (thus the plural, *pûrim*) and the ambiguity in determining which one is "controlling" the future.[65]

Because there was a mandate to commemorate the event, it was necessary to establish recitation of the narrative so that it would be "remembered and observed" (9:28). It is *this* requirement that draws together the narrative of chs. 1–8 with the legislation regarding the feast. It must be told and heard to recapture the experience from generation to generation.[66] Esther is to be read annually so that Israelites will relive blotting out the memory of their archenemy until the kingdom of God comes.[67] Medieval Jewish commentators saw the narrative of Esther as a foretaste of the final redemption, when the forces of evil, epitomized in Amalek, will be finally destroyed. Thus the narrative took on cosmic proportions.[68] Through the

---

61. Paton (*Esther*, 77–94) presents a survey and assessment of theories regarding the origin of the festival and the composition of Esther up to the time of his study in 1908.

62. See Julius Lewy, "The Feast of the 14th Day of Adar," *HUCA* 14 (1939): 144; William W. Hallo, "The First Purim," *BA* 46/1 (1983): 19–26; and LaCocque, *The Feminine Unconventional*, 64.

63. Abraham D. Cohen, "'*Hu Ha-goral*': The Religious Significance of Esther," *Judaism* 23 (1974): 89.

64. Ibid., 90–94.

65. Rosenheim, "Fate and Freedom," 127–29.

66. Bush, *Ruth, Esther*, 329; and Michael Wechsler, "The Purim–Passover Connection: A Reflection of Jewish Exegetical Tradition in the Peshitta Book of Esther," *JBL* 117 (1998): 321–27.

67. LaCocque, "Haman in the Book of Esther," 213–15.

68. Walfish, *Esther in Medieval Garb*, 93–94.

succeeding centuries Purim plays, known as *purimspiels*, have become an integral part of this commemorative aspect.[69]

The narrative not only authenticates the festival, however; it is the one biblical text focused solely on life in the diaspora. Unlike the rest of the postexilic literature that emphasizes return to the land, this narrative presents the complexities involved with the choice to remain in the dispersion and the vulnerability of those diaspora communities.[70] On the one hand, the close of this story presents the reader with a fully "integrated" Mordecai, apparently devoid of tension between his association with the pagan court and life among the "people of God." Instead, both he and Esther creatively use the mechanisms of the existing system for the benefit of their people.[71] On the other hand, there is no mistaking the fundamentally untrustworthy nature of the pagan realm. The opening farcical tone of the narrative simply intensifies the forthcoming shock as pride and egotism quickly mutate into murderous hatred.

Throughout the history of the Jews in the diaspora, in both Eastern and Western contexts, the tide has turned against them with an appalling frequency, and attempts at self-defense have themselves been deemed illegal.[72] Ironically, extensive cultural assimilation, viewed as a protection, has often resulted in a backlash of catastrophic proportions, of which the last two centuries of western European history are the most recent sobering reminder. In sum, the text of Esther is vital; it demonstrates a "theology … for the dispersion" in which Jewish *action* is as necessary as trust in God's providence.[73] It has prepared Jews for their precarious existence in those scattered communities for centuries to come. In that regard, it is an absolutely essential part of the canon.

Esther is tremendously important for readers in every imaginable context. For those who feel themselves removed from narratives of God's miraculous interventions that are so different from their own experiences, Esther's story describes life "under the sun" (cf. Ecclesiastes), complete with ambiguities and the messiness created by sin. It also attests to the reversals that are part of life's experience, perhaps in its own way preparing for the great reversal from death to life eternal through the unlikely means of the crucified Messiah. Jesus' earthly ministry was replete with teaching that emphasized reversal of human expectations, the exaltation of the humble, and the first becoming last.[74] The beginning and end of the gospel message is the resurrection, the greatest of all reversals.

---

69. As a riveting example of a drama that weaves together the interminable horror of pogroms for Jews in the diaspora and a *purimspiel* on the occasion of Purim, see Elie Wiesel, *The Trial of God* (New York: Schocken, 1979).

70. Levenson, *Esther*, 15–16; idem, "The Scroll of Esther in Ecumenical Perspective," *JES* 13 (1976): 446–47; Berg, *The Book of Esther*, 68; Bush, *Ruth, Esther*, 312–14.

71. W. Lee Humphreys, "A Lifestyle for Diaspora: A Study of the Tales of Esther and Daniel," *JBL* 92 (1973): 211–23, esp. 215–16. See also Hazony, *The Dawn*; Firth, "The Book of Esther," 18–26.

72. See esp. Joan Peters, *From Time Immemorial: The Origins of the Arab-Jewish Conflict over Palestine* (New York: Harper & Row, 1984); and H. H. Ben-Sasson, ed., *A History of the Jewish People* (Cambridge, Mass.: Harvard Univ. Press, 1976), ch. 27, "Effects of Religious Animosity on the Jews."

73. LaCocque, "Haman in the Book of Esther," 209–10.

74. The Sermon on the Mount (Mt 5–7) encapsulates many of these reversals. See also Luke 6:20–36; 9:23–25; 13:22–30; 14:11.

Esther also challenges all readers to consider in what manner God has prepared them "for such a time as this" and just what those "times" might be in each of our lives. One message of the text has to do with living faithfully in systems that may be significantly at odds with *our* faith traditions. Finally, the text is a sober call to be mindful of the Hamans inside and out that would wreak havoc with truth, justice, and peace for God's people.

6. THEOLOGICAL AND MORAL/ETHICAL CHALLENGES

In rabbinic tradition, Esther was read as a book of divine concealment based on the lexical connection with Deuteronomy 31:18, "I will surely hide [*hastēr ʾastîr*] My face" (NASB; cf. *b. Ḥul.* 139b). God's apparent absence and the choices of Mordecai and Esther have engendered a range of assessments of the book's theological significance.[75] There are scholars who have labeled the work "secular" and claim it primarily reflects cultural compromise followed by excessive nationalism, neither of which is exemplary. In this context, the absence of God's name, the lack of evident prayer and piety, and the questionable behavior of Esther are all seen as evidence that she and Mordecai represent a diaspora community that was decidedly irreligious. It was not intent on keeping the covenant, had lost a sense of the presence of God, and was fundamentally disobedient in remaining in the diaspora.[76]

This view, however, misses several issues that significantly affect the interpretation of the text. First, while postenlightenment thought easily establishes a dichotomy between secular nationalism and religious intention, this dichotomy was unthinkable in antiquity.[77] "Loyalty to the community was inseparable from loyalty to the deity who called it into being; group identity and devotion to God went together ... atheism was almost unknown in the ancient world. Virtually all believed that there really was a divine sphere."[78] Second, God is characteristically present in more subtle ways in narratives that have to do with foreigners. This presence is evident in the Joseph and Ruth stories as well as Esther.

Fox articulates four indications of God's presence and activity in the narrative, the sum of which makes a good case that both the characters of the drama and the author(s) identify themselves as members of God's covenantal community.

1. There are allusions to God's activity (4:14; 6:13; 9:1) and appeals for his intervention (4:3, 16).
2. The whole array of what are often termed "coincidences" is cumulatively significant. The most notable of these coincidences is the king's insomnia, but they appear from beginning to end in the narrative.

---

75. See Berg, *The Book of Esther*, 88, n. 57; Beal, *Book of Hiding*, 116−17; Leila Leah Bronner, "Esther Revisited: An Aggadic Approach," in Brenner, *A Feminist Companion*, 180−81.

76. F. B. Huey Jr., "Esther" (EBC; ed. Frank E. Gaebelein; Grand Rapids: Zondervan, 1988), 4:786−87; Ronald W. Pierce, "The Politics of Esther and Mordecai: Courage or Compromise?" *BBR* 2 (1992): 75−89. Fox ("The Religion of the Book of Esther," *Judaism* 39/2 [1990]: 135−47, esp. 136−36) listed those who view it as secular.

77. Fox, "The Religion of the Book of Esther," 135; idem, *Character and Ideology*, 236.

78. E. P. Sanders, *Judaism: Practice and Belief 63 BCE−66 CE* (London: SCM, 1992), 144. See also Gordis, "Religion, Wisdom and History," 371.

3. The comprehensive structure built around the unexpected reversal of human expectations attests to divine control of circumstances and the hope for ultimate justice.

4. Finally, preservation of the Jewish people and the necessity of war to counter raw evil are vital themes in the context of the covenant.[79]

Presuming that the text does reflect God's providential orchestrating of the critical events and the main characters' awareness of his doing so, then why did the narrator not overtly state the name of God and attribute these activities to him? Medieval Jewish exegetes posed explanations ranging from the author's concern not to offend Persian authorities to the fear of profaning the name of God during the frivolity that came to characterize the Purim festival.[80] These possibilities have continued to surface in recent treatments,[81] but the latter suggestion is problematic in that it assumes the celebration of the festival prior to the composition of the text.[82] Further, excessive drinking in conjunction with the festival developed only in the fourth century AD in Babylon, so there would be no inherent connection between frivolity and Purim.[83]

More substantially, the ambiguity regarding God's presence in the narrative allows for wide-ranging application. The numerous providential coincidences are lodged in contexts that demanded responsible and faithful human choices and action.[84] In the face of recurring divine silence, God's people are compelled to choose between the imperfect alternatives that arise in the real ambiguities of life, just as Esther and Mordecai did. At the same time, people of faith are confident that God will address injustice and suffering and will preserve his people in his wisdom and in his time.[85] This divine involvement is extremely important, as the text would be—and has been—read and reread through centuries filled with pain and suffering for God's people.

Turning to the issue of responsible actions, there are those who have suggested that both Mordecai and Esther suffer severe moral lapses that result in the silent disapproval of God.[86] That Mordecai is living in Susa, to say nothing of serving in some capacity in the court, instead of having returned with the exiles, is posited as evidence of his disobedience. It is significant, however, that both Ezra and Nehemiah, at the outset of their individual stories, are also in high-profile positions in Susa. In fact, it is telling that those

---

79. Fox, "The Religion of the Book of Esther," 139–43. See also David Beller, "A Theology of the Book of Esther," *ResQ* 39 (1997): 1–15.

80. Walfish, *Esther in Medieval Garb*, 76–79.

81. Fox, "The Religion of the Book of Esther," 137–38.

82. Gordis, "Religion, Wisdom and History," 363.

83. Eliezer Segal, "Human Anger and Divine Intervention in Esther," *Proof* 9 (1989): 252, n. 1.

84. Beller, "Theology of the Book of Esther," 1–15.

85. Karen Jobes, *Esther* (NIVAC; Grand Rapids: Zondervan, 1999), 45. See also Harold Fisch, "Esther: Two Tales of One City," in *Poetry with a Purpose* (Bloomington, Ind.: Indiana Univ. Press, 1988), 13.

86. Huey, "Esther," 785–88; idem, "Irony as the Key to Understanding the Book of Esther," *SwJT* 32 (1990): 36–39; Forrest S. Weiland, "Literary Clues to God's Providence in the Book of Esther," *BSac* 160 (January–March 2003): 34–47. Paton (*Esther*, 96) had likely the most vitriolic commentary on Esther, to whose unlikely Persian queen he attributed evil character and motives.

events take place just about a generation after the crisis narrated in the book of Esther. Perhaps the wave of pro-Jewish sentiment and the pattern set by Mordecai's position helped pave the way for the prominent roles that both Ezra and Nehemiah held in the Persian court prior to their respective returns to Judea.

A further charge against Mordecai centers on his willingness—perhaps to further his own interests— to send Esther into the "den of iniquity" that was the Persian court. Moreover, he forbids Esther, once she finds herself in that context, to reveal her identity with God's covenantal people. These actions could smack of his complete disregard for the spiritual aspects of his heritage and his intended assimilation to the dominant culture. Contrary to this picture, however, there are indications early in the text that he is not so callous. In the absence of Esther's parents, he has cared for her and adopted her as his daughter. The description of Esther emphasizes her extraordinary beauty, which far exceeds the criteria for being rounded up; being taken is unavoidable. Once she is trapped in the harem, Mordecai's concern for her is evident in his daily walk outside the palace.

Critics of Esther have risen in several quarters. From a feminist perspective, she is a seriously deficient role model in contrast to Vashti, who courageously refuses to be an "object" in the king's possession and forfeits her crown as a result. Esther, by way of contrast, passively does what she is told, allows herself to be controlled by one man after another, and exercises manipulative feminine wiles as a powerful queen. These features of the narrative have prompted some readers to view the text as unpleasantly subversive![87]

Further, Esther seems to have had no qualms about entering the harem and participating in a contest the sole focus of which was to satisfy the pagan and lascivious king's sexual appetite. From the outset of Israel's history, intermarriage with the Canaanites was forbidden (Dt 7:1–4) because of the temptation to idolatry. The same motivation was behind the severe measures during the reforming activities of Ezra and Nehemiah (Ezr 9:1–2; Ne 13:23–27), when foreign wives were put away. These measures were enacted in the mid-fifth century BC, about a generation after the time of Xerxes and Esther. The determinative factor, however, was that Esther is "taken" as part of the roundup of young women to fill the king's harem.[88] Further, Rosenheim suggests that, while the most obvious interpretation has Esther indeed proving herself to be a more memorable sexual partner than all the other candidates, possibly the king is intrigued with her specifically because she does not capitulate to his whims.[89] After all, he has access to a full harem for those pleasures.

Somewhat more favorable presentations attribute to Esther a "character transformation" from initial passivity to forthright courage.[90] More accurately, however, she is an *actor* from the outset within the wider machinery of the royal household and the court. She "wins favor"—a more dynamic expression than the usual "find favor"—with key people. She successfully acts as an intermediary between Mordecai and the king (2:22–23). When it comes time to move into the public arena, she is ready to do so and proves

---

87. The character and choices of Esther are addressed extensively in feminist readings of the text. See particularly Brenner's *Feminist Companion.*
88. See Danna Nolan Fewell, "Introduction," 15–16.
89. Rosenheim, "Fate and Freedom," 131–32. For further discussion of Esther's active and exemplary participation in the unfolding events, see Leila L. Bronner, "Reclaiming Esther: From Sex Object to Sage," *JBQ* 26/1 (1998): 3–10.
90. As examples, see Fox, *Character and Ideology,* 196–99; Jobes, *Esther,* 138; and Humphreys, "The Story of Esther and Mordecai," 106.

extraordinarily strategic about the entire operation by enlisting the support of the Jewish people as well as her maidens, confronting the king and Haman, arranging for self-defensive measures for the Jewish populations, and instituting the festival.

Further questions arise to which there are no easy answers, primarily because the text, which serves up a clear picture of Haman's thoughts and intentions, has not exposed Mordecai in the same way. Is Mordecai's refusal to bow to Haman from true religious conviction or a proud response to a longstanding ethnic feud? Does he sanction wholesale brutality when the tables turn around? Individual Jews and Jewish communities have lived for millennia in an uncertain world of political intrigue and hostility. When faced with the prospect of genocide, covert, defensive, and punitive actions are necessary. To do nothing when it was within the power of Esther and Mordecai to address the situation would have been irresponsible. The contemporary applications are unmistakable.[91] In sum, the ethical and moral challenges facing these characters are reminders of the choices fallible human beings must make in situations that present multiple alternatives, all of which have evil bound up within them.[92]

7. HISTORICAL CONTEXTS

While the narrative is located in the postexilic diaspora context, it reverberates with echoes from the entirety of Israelite covenantal history. The immediate context is shaped by the Persian Empire, which had, under Cyrus the Great, conquered Babylon in 539 BC.[93] Cyrus was followed by Cambyses (530–522), who moved against and into Egypt to secure for the Persian Empire what Nebuchadnezzar had conquered for Babylon. On his way back from Egypt, however, he died under rather curious circumstances (Herodotus 3.62–66) and, after a time of turmoil, was succeeded by Darius I (522–486).

It was under the rule of Darius, along with the Seven Great Houses of nobles, that the empire underwent significant administrative changes, including the establishment of twenty satrapies and regional codification of laws. Darius also dealt with rebellious provinces, carried out a major campaign to win Egypt, and escalated the conflict with Greece. Finally, he began to build a new capital at Persepolis, although Susa remained the administrative center (Herodotus 3.80–89).[94]

Prior to the death of Darius, Xerxes[95] was crown prince and governor of Babylon. Upon becoming king (486–465), he attempted to hold Egypt in subservience and was compelled to put down a rebellion

---

91. Jonathan Magonet, "The Liberal and the Lady: Esther Revisited," *Judaism* 29 (1980): 174–75; Firth, "The Book of Esther," 18–26.

92. Jobes, *Esther*, 111–14.

93. For assessment of Herodotus's account (*History of the Persian Wars*, Book I) of the rise of Cyrus, see Briant, *From Cyrus to Alexander*, 15–16, 31–44. Political, economic, and religious aspects of the Persian period are ably summarized by Young, "The Consolidation of the Empire," 53–111. On Cyrus's policy of restoring national gods and temples, see Amelie Kuhrt, "The Cyrus Cylinder and Achaemenid Imperial Policy," *JSOT* 25 (1983): 83–97.

94. Briant, *From Cyrus to Alexander*, 111–71. Berlin (*Esther*, xxxiii) notes that Darius likely made Susa the winter capital because of the blistering summer heat.

95. On the equivalence of Xerxes and the biblical Ahasuerus, see commentary on 1:1. See Edwin Yamauchi (*Persia and the Bible* [Grand Rapids: Baker, 1990], 187–239) and Moore (*Esther*, xxxv–xli) for general historical summaries of the reign of Xerxes.

in Babylon (Herodotus 7.4–7).[96] He spent the next four years mustering a massive force for the attack on Greece—a venture that desolated Athens but ended in his defeat at Salamis (Herodotus 7.8, 20–21; 8.50–51, 86). Although the sources are sparse, there may be indications that Xerxes' reign took a turn toward intolerance of other religions and cultures.[97] According to Herodotus (7.37–39; 8.118; 9.108–13), Xerxes was a cruel and lascivious despot,[98] a characterization that fits well with the Esther narrative. When he was assassinated, Artaxerxes I (464–425 BC) took the throne. In a departure from the MT, the text of the Septuagint places the events of Esther during the reign of Artaxerxes.[99]

As God's covenantal people, the Israelites lived in full awareness that obedience to the covenant meant shalom in the Promised Land, while disobedience and idolatry would result in exile (Lev 26:33–35). After repeated prophetic pronouncements and warnings, they were indeed deported to Babylon, and Nebuchadnezzar destroyed the temple (2Ch 36:10–21). Also in accordance with the prophets (cf. Jer 25:11–12), after seventy years a number of Jews (42,360, according to Ezr 2:64) returned to the land in response to the decree of Cyrus (2Ch 36:22–23; Isa 44:28–45:3). In the presentation of this event are clear echoes of the exodus (Ezr 1:6; Isa 43:16–19; 48:20–21). The returnees eventually completed the work on the temple in 516 BC (Ezr 6:14–16), struggled to establish themselves around Jerusalem and in the small geographical area of Judah (Ne 6), and contended with the surrounding populations (Ezr 4; Ne 1:3). This group in Judah, however, was a small percentage of the Jewish population empirewide—a fact that is evident in the Esther narrative.

Moving beyond the immediate chronological context, this text is rich with historical and theological connections. The primary one is, without question, the longstanding enmity between Israel and Amalek. Mordecai was of the tribe of Benjamin, and one of his ancestors bore the name "Kish." The reader is supposed to connect that information to King Saul, whose father was Kish. Haman, however, is also explicitly linked to a venerable line—that of Agag! The astute audience would recognize some significant unfinished business from the early period of the Israelite monarchy when King Saul was commanded by the Lord to obliterate the Amalekites, whose king was Agag (1Sa 15). This command was not capricious; the judgment on the Amalekites was a fulfillment of God's declaration in Exodus 17:14 that he would erase the memory of the Amalekites for their attack on Israel as described earlier in the chapter.[100] The assault of the Amalekites was brutal and directed against those who were weak and straggling behind the Israelites (Dt 25:17–19).

---

96. There is some question regarding the date of the Babylonian rebellion, but William Shea ("Esther and History," *Concordia Journal* 13/3 [1987]: 237) has made a good case that it was during the fifth year of Xerxes. See also Briant, *From Cyrus to Alexander*, 525.

97. Robert J. Littman, "The Religious Policy of Xerxes and the Book of Esther," *JQR* 65 (1975): 145–55.

98. For the view that the biographies of Herodotus are significantly shaped according to conventional and stereotypical presentations of tyrants, see John G. Gammie, "Herodotus on Kings and Tyrants: Objective Historiography or Conventional Portraiture?" *JNES* 45 (1986): 171–95; and Briant, *From Cyrus to Alexander*, 515–18, 525–42.

99. This identification is also followed by Josephus (*Ant.* 11.6.1[6:184–186]). See Karen H. Jobes, "How an Assassination Changed the Greek Text of Esther," *ZAW* 110 (1998): 75–78, for a suggested explanation of the change.

100. Berlin (*Esther*, xxxviii) noted the oxymoron of a written text about erasing permanently the memory of Amalek.

Underlying that military encounter is an earlier hostility: Amalek was a descendant of Esau (Ge 36:12). The fleeting mention of a king Agag in the oracle of Balaam (Nu 24:7) is a further adumbration of the forthcoming conflict. Saul disobeyed the Lord and left Agag alive. This confrontation between Mordecai and Haman revisits that old ethnic tension, this time shot through with the apparent injustice of Haman's rise to power while Mordecai remains unrecognized. That Saul took plunder instead of completely destroying it as commanded is "set right" in the Esther narrative by the pointed statement that the Jews do *not* take plunder, even though they have been authorized to do so (Est 8:11; 9:10, 15–16).

Additional biblical connections sharpen the enmity expressed against the Jews by Haman. The decree to destroy, kill, and annihilate the Jews was written on the thirteenth day of the first month (3:12–13), the day before Passover. Instead of celebrating on that festive occasion, the Jewish population of the Persian realm was thrown into mourning. The corporate remembrance of both brutal oppression and subsequent deliverance would reverberate through the entire Jewish community, both on that occasion and as the narrative was read in the intervening centuries. The two days of commemorating the deliverance were established as the fourteenth and fifteenth of Adar, the last month of the year, and also are parallel to the celebration of Passover on the fourteenth and fifteenth of the Nisan, the first month. Both commemorations are to be kept forever.[101]

Further, connections with the context of Egypt and exodus may be found in the parallels between the Joseph narrative and Esther/Mordecai. These connections range from mirroring the actual language to the broad themes represented.[102] In each case, the presence of God is muted; after all, both accounts are set in a foreign country.

8. HISTORICITY OF THE NARRATIVE

The style of the narrative, with its concern for dates, numbers, names, and procedures, indicates that it was intended to be read as history.[103] Furthermore, in many details the correspondence between Esther and extrabiblical sources is remarkable—a point conceded by most scholars.[104] Nevertheless, even though it has been increasingly demonstrated that the author represents Persian customs, language, names, and court matters in a plausible manner, this plot and these characters are otherwise unattested, leaving many to suggest that the text was intended as some form of historical fiction.

It should, however, give the skeptic pause that Purim is indeed adopted and practiced with enthusiasm—something inexplicable if the basis is entirely fabricated. The essence of the narrative is God's deliverance of his people from a very real catastrophe in the making. The message of hope is severely diminished if that deliverance never happened.

---

101. LaCocque, "Haman in the Book of Esther," 215.

102. See Susan Niditch, *Underdogs and Tricksters* (San Francisco: Harper & Row, 1987), ch. 5; Berg, *The Book of Esther*, 123–26.

103. Regardless of genre label, if the book purports to be history, it is important to assess its historical accuracy (Baldwin, *Esther*, 16).

104. As representative examples, see Paton, *Esther*, 65; Moore, *Esther*, xli; Gordis, "Studies in the Esther Narrative," *JBL* 95 (1976): 44; Talmon, "'Wisdom' in the Book of Esther," 422; Berg, *The Book of Esther*, 2.

Virtually every introduction to the text addresses the alleged inaccuracies from one perspective or the other by providing a list of the problems—occasionally categorizing them according to their degree of improbability, and either indicating why they are insoluble or marshalling evidence to demonstrate that they ought to be viewed as red herrings.[105] The primary extrabiblical source is Herodotus, but unfortunately his narrative ends shortly after Xerxes' campaign to the West, which comes at just about the time the Esther story takes off.[106] Some additional details may be found in works by Xenophon (*Cyropaedia*) and Ctesias of Cnidus (*History of Persia*), although their reliability is somewhat questionable. The writings of the latter are partially preserved by Diodorus of Sicily and Photius, a ninth-century patriarch of Constantinople, in *The Bibliotheca*. There are also Persian inscriptions and archaeological evidence that illuminate our understanding of the period. The intent here is to survey again the major issues. Additional alleged inaccuracies will be treated in the appropriate commentary sections.

It has been noted that the likelihood of Esther's becoming queen was slim because the queen was supposed to be chosen from among the seven families whose nobles had participated in the overthrow of the Magi when Darius came to power (Herodotus 3.70–71, 84). The record in Herodotus, however, reflects an agreement reached among those conspirators just one generation before Xerxes, not a longstanding tradition. That agreement would omit the line of Cyrus itself, and yet the roster of Darius's four wives included two daughters of Cyrus, one of whom was Atossa (3.88), and Xerxes was the son of Atossa. This objection carries little weight.

More challenging is the fact that there is no external corroboration of Mordecai's position as second in the empire. There is an undated cuneiform document from the Persian period that refers to Marduka, who was thought to be in high office either late in the reign of Darius I or at the beginning of Xerxes' rule. First published by Ungnad[107] and referred to repeatedly by subsequent scholars, it was hailed as evidence of the well-positioned Mordecai represented in the biblical text. Nevertheless, more recent appraisals of the text question whether the Marduka of this text was really as prominent as initially thought and whether he was in office after 502 BC.[108] Given the religious significance of Marduk, it is not unusual to find the variants of that name woven into a number of personal names from the period.[109]

The most challenging problem is the identity of Vashti, ostensibly the reigning queen only until her deposition in 483 BC, in relationship to the notorious Amestris, Xerxes' wife, whom Herodotus (9.108–12) described as participating in a royal intrigue after the campaign to Greece in 480. One possibility is simply to state that neither Esther nor Vashti rose to the surface in Herodotus's records of royal women, of which

---

105. For contrasting presentations of the issues that have been deemed most significant, see Shea, "Esther and History," 234–48, and Fox, *Character and Ideology*, 147–50.

106. It is worth noting that Herodotus's account of Egyptian pharaohs and history is both sketchy and imaginative (see 2.100–111); therefore, while helpful, his reliability in providing accurate background for Esther should be viewed with the requisite caution.

107. Arthur Ungnad, "Keilinschriftliche Beitrage zum Buch Ezra und Ester," *ZAW* 58 (1940–1941): 240–44.

108. See Clines, "In Quest of the Historical Mordecai," *VT* 41/2 (1991): 129–36; Ran Zadok, *The Jews in Babylonia during the Chaldean and Achaemenian Periods according to the Babylonian Sources* (Haifa: Univ. of Haifa Press, 1979), 69–70.

109. Carey A. Moore, "Archaeology and the Book of Esther," *BA* 38 (1975): 74; Yamauchi, *Persia and the Bible*, 235–36; idem, "Mordecai, the Persepolis Tablets, and the Susa Excavations," *VT* 42 (1992): 272–75.

there may have been quite a number if the circumstances in 9.108 reflect a pattern for Xerxes. Amestris, after all, was a much more colorful character, and Herodotus tended to go for color! He noted in passing (7.114) that in her old age Amestris buried alive fourteen sons of notable Persians as a thank offering to the god of the netherworld. The narrative of her cruelty to the wife of Masistes (9.112) is equally horrifying. Amestris was still alive and influential when her son, Artaxerxes, came to power after the assassination of Xerxes. It appeared she had not lost her knack for brutality, as she crucified one Inaros, beheaded fifty Greeks, and buried alive Apollonides from Cos.[110]

It may be possible, however, that Amestris and Vashti were the same individual.[111] Names are notoriously fluid in transition from one language to another. While the name "Vashti" does not look much like "Amestris," it represents the English version of the Hebrew rendition of a Persian name. When Herodotus put the Persian name into Greek, substitutions of letters were necessary because neither the first nor the second consonant had an equivalent in Greek.[112] Amestris was not only Xerxes' wife but also the daughter of one of his commanders, Otanes, who *was* one of the aforementioned seven (7.61). She had already borne Xerxes two sons, and Artaxerxes, the third, was born in 483. These circumstances may have meant practically that while she could be banished from Xerxes' bedroom and deprived of the crown, there were limits on the banishment and good political reasons for keeping her in the extensive royal household.[113]

Shortly after these events, Xerxes headed off to wage war on the western front and was thus occupied for the next three years. It could be that 2:1 (lit., "after these things"; NIV, "later") refers to this passage of time and that the wholesale roundup of young women did not commence until his return. We do know that Esther's first entrance (after a year of preparation) occurred in the seventh year of the king, which would have been 479 BC (2:16). In the meantime, Herodotus dishes up a tidbit about Xerxes' dalliance with his niece, Amestris' jealousy, and her cunning and brutal revenge (9.108–12). It may be that after all *these* events, Xerxes was more than ready for a new queen! Perhaps his remembering Vashti and what she had done (2:1) was not entirely with fondness if that memory included her activities in the intervening three years. In any case, the narrative in Herodotus does not state that Amestris was queen from the seventh to the twelfth years of Xerxes' reign; doing so would be overstatement.

While the irrevocability of the law of the Persians and the Medes seems cumbersome and truly unrealistic in our conception of jurisprudence, it is important to place the unchangeable royal word in its theological and political culture—one in which gods gave unalterable mandates and kings imitated the gods.[114] It seems that the Jews were sufficiently impressed with this phenomenon to write it into both Daniel and

---

110. Ctesias, *Persica*, quoted by Photius, *The Bibliotheca* (trans. N. G. Wilson; London: Duckworth, 1994), 54–78.

111. This reconstruction is dependent on the work of Shea ("Esther and History," 234–48) and J. Stafford Wright ("The Historicity of the Book of Esther," in *New Perspectives on the Old Testament* [ed. J. Barton Payne; Waco, Tex.: Word, 1970], 37–47). While they reach somewhat different conclusions with regard to how the events may have unfolded, they both note that the deposition of Vashti may not have been complete banishment from the royal precincts. Instead, she could have still been operating viciously on the fringes.

112. Wright ("The Historicity of the Book of Esther," 41–42) articulates the details of how this substitution might work.

113. Wright (ibid., 43) suggests that Vashti's reason for not appearing at Xerxes' party may have been because she was in some stage of pregnancy at the time.

114. Bickerman, *Four Strange Books*, 192.

Esther.[115] In Esther, both $w^e l\bar{o}^{\circ} ya^c \breve{a} b\hat{o}r$ (1:19 with reference to the same principle in 8:3) and $^{\circ} \hat{e}n\ l^e h\bar{a}\breve{s}\hat{i}b$ (8:8; see 8:5) indicate this unchangeable nature of the law. See the commentary sections.

It has been further suggested that the narrative is unrealistic in presupposing that a decree such as Haman's could be effected in the Persian Empire. Appeal has been made to Cyrus's edict to respect the gods and temples of foreigners in order to demonstrate that the empire was relatively benevolent. The Cyrus inscription, however, might better be interpreted as a standard piece of propaganda that reflected a relatively localized practice on the part of Cyrus and affecting primarily those groups in the immediate area of Babylon.[116] In addition, Cyrus preceded Xerxes by about half a century.

9. DATE AND AUTHORSHIP

The data that are available to determine the general date of Esther's composition have led scholars to land in one of two camps. On the one hand, the text itself demonstrates some distance from the events that are the focus of the narrative. The apparent need to identify Xerxes in the introduction may signal something about imperial change in the interim. Likewise, that the days were remembered and observed in every generation (9:28) might be indicative that the festival had been established for a considerable time.[117] It is, however, equally possible that, as one of the four sets of pairs (generations, families, provinces, and cities), $b^e kol\ d\hat{o}r\ w\bar{a}d\hat{o}r$ (9:28) is a stylistic clue to the comprehensive observance. Until recently, most scholars have dated the book to the Hellenistic period, notably the third or second centuries BC.[118]

On the other hand, the anonymous author or authors evidence clear knowledge of the Persian court, customs, and language—factors that suggest composition in the later Persian period. The narrative contains words from Old Persian: $part^e m\hat{i}m$ ("nobles"), $^{\circ a} \d{h}a\breve{s}darp^e n\hat{i}m$ ("satraps"), $b\hat{i}tan$ ("palace"; cf. 1:3, 5; 3:12; 6:9; 7:7, 8; 8:9). These words were no longer used in the Hellenistic period, and they are not found in Hebrew texts of that period. In addition, Esther does not contain Greek terms.[119] The possible evidence of redactional stages in the development of the text also complicates the discussion of date and authorship. Levenson claimed it was written perhaps in the fourth century BC for eastern Jewish communities but did not become part of Palestinian Jewish texts until the second century.[120]

Of the identity of the author(s), there is nothing definitive to be said apart from locating him or them in the eastern diaspora. A baraita in *b. Baba Bathra* 15a indicates that the Men of the Great Assembly wrote Esther, along with Ezekiel, the Twelve Minor Prophets, and Daniel. Rashi added that Esther, Ezekiel, and Daniel may have been written by the Men of the Great Assembly to give these texts more credence since

---

115. LaCocque, *The Feminine Unconventional*, 52. See also Young, "Consolidation of the Empire," 104–5. Another angle on the perceived irrevocability of the Persian king's word is also evident in Ezra 6:11–12. Anyone who would dare to go against it faced certain death.

116. See Baldwin, *Esther*, 17–18; and Kuhrt, "The Cyrus Cylinder," 83–97.

117. Fox, *Character and Ideology*, 132.

118. Paton (*Esther*, 60–61) notes that this position was unanimous among "modern critics." See also A. E. Morris, "The Purpose of the Book of Esther," *ExpTim* 42 (1930/1931): 124–28.

119. Michael Helzer, "The Book of Esther: Where Does Fiction Start and History End," *BRev* 9 (1992): 27; Berlin, *Esther*, 42.

120. Levenson, *Esther*, 26–27.

each of the named individuals was functioning outside the land. Augustine attributed the text to Ezra. Significant numbers of early Jewish and Christian writers in antiquity suggested that Mordecai was the author.[121]

10. ESTHER IN JEWISH AND CHRISTIAN INTERPRETIVE TRADITION

That Josephus presented a significant rewriting of Esther (*Ant.* 11.6.1–13 [184–296]) and 1 Clement (55) referred to her as a woman of faith who humbled herself in order to save the twelve tribes indicate the narrative's recognition in the first century AD. The popularity of the story and the inevitable embellishments that resulted were evident already in the additions to the LXX and the Targums, in the large number of Esther scrolls, and in the extensive medieval literature on Esther.[122]

The sages discussed its importance. "Between the Temple service and reading the Megillah, the reading takes precedence; between reading Torah and reading the Megillah, the Megillah takes precedence; between reading the Megillah and the obligation to bury dead, the latter takes precedence" (*b. Meg.* 3b). "Women were under obligation to read the Megillah because they profited from the miracle" (*b. Meg.* 4a). The rabbis considered the rescue a miracle. "Our rabbis taught: forty-eight prophets and seven prophetesses prophesied to Israel and they did not take away or add to what was written in the Torah except for the reading of the Scroll" (*b. Meg.* 14a).

As part of a discussion with R. Johanan, who said that only Torah would remain, while the Prophets and Writings would cease, R. Shimon b Lakish (ca. AD 300) said Esther and Torah would remain and based the assertion on the occurrence in both Deuteronomy 5:22 and Esther 8:3 of the verbal root *yāsap*, meaning "to add" (*y. Meg.* 1:5; 70d). Maimonides echoed this position some nine hundred years later: "When Messiah comes and the Prophets and Writings pass away, only Esther and the Torah will remain."[123]

Paton presented a comprehensive survey of both Christian and Jewish scholarship on the book of Esther from late antiquity through the beginning of the twentieth century.[124] Several Christian commentators from the Middles Ages drew on the expositions of Esther by Rashi and ibn Ezra; and even though Luther's outright hostility to the book is notorious, he also saw in it good examples.[125] Between the Reformation and the Enlightenment, the text was addressed with careful exegetical methods and generally viewed with favor by certain segments of the church that saw themselves persecuted by others!

This assessment changed with the onset of the Enlightenment, however, when the actions of Jewish intolerance and nationalism in the book were deemed revolting.[126] Bernhard Anderson was one of the first post-Holocaust scholars to begin to "reinstate" Esther and acknowledge the importance of the text

---

121. Paton, *Esther*, 60.

122. Walfish's treatment in *Esther in Medieval Garb* of every identified medieval Hebrew commentary makes it clear that most of the interpretations suggested by modern exegetes have a very long history.

123. Gershom Scholem, *The Messianic Idea in Judaism* (New York: Schocken, 1971), 54–55.

124. Paton, *Esther*, 97–118. For a recent survey of the strongest negative opinions regarding Esther, see Mark A. Roberts, *The Book of Esther* (The Communicator's Commentary; ed. Lloyd Ogilvie; Dallas: Word, 1993), 311–12. Roberts himself was ambivalent about the book.

125. Bickerman, "Notes on the Greek Book of Esther," 102. The reference to Luther comes from his *Table Talk*, in *Luther's Works* (v. 22 in Weimar edition 1912), 208.

126. Bickerman, *Four Strange Books*, 212–18; Paton, *Esther*, 111–18.

as a realistic presentation of the problem ever confronting the Jews: the meaning of the election of Israel and the "scandal of particularity." Nevertheless, he stated that faithful Christian ministers would not take their texts from Esther. It "may be left aside as one of those unfortunate detours away from the road, first blazed by the prophets, which led toward enlightenment."[127] Bush observed that anti-Semitism was thinly veiled as commentaries criticized the narrative for its judaizing, nationalism that rejoiced in the massacre of Gentiles, vindictiveness and revenge against those who persecute Jews, and characters who demonstrate pride, fear, and hatred.[128]

Especially in the post-Holocaust world, this text should compel Christians, whose actions have all too often mirrored those of Haman's followers, to reassess the subtle and not-so-subtle ways in which anti-Semitism continues to be fostered in contemporary cultures. Furthermore, as those whose "citizenship is in heaven" (Php 3:20), we also live as a minority in a dangerous world where comfortable circumstances could radically and rapidly change. Thus this narrative of relief and deliverance, effected through the unfailing providence of God using fallible human beings, is a vital part of the "great and precious promises" (2Pe 1:4).

11. SELECTED BIBLIOGRAPHY

Commentaries

Baldwin, Joyce. *Esther: An Introduction and Commentary*. Tyndale Old Testament Commentaries. Edited by D. J. Wiseman. Downers Grove, Ill.: InterVarsity Press, 1984.

Bush, Frederic W. *Ruth, Esther*. Word Biblical Commentary. Vol. 9. Dallas: Word, 1996.

Gordis, Robert. *Megillat Esther: The Masoretic Text with Introduction, New Translation and Commentary*. New York: Ktav, 1974.

Jobes, Karen. *Esther*. NIV Application Commentary. Grand Rapids: Zondervan, 1999.

Levenson, Jon D. *Esther*. The Old Testament Library. Louisville: Westminster John Knox, 1997.

Moore, Carey. *Esther: A New Translation with Introduction and Commentary*. Anchor Bible. New York: Doubleday, 1971.

Paton, Lewis B. *A Critical and Exegetical Commentary on the Book of Esther*. International Critical Commentary. New York: Scribner, 1908.

Other Works

Beal, Timothy K. *The Book of Hiding: Gender, Ethnicity, Annihilation, and Esther*. London/New York: Routledge, 1997.

Berg, Sandra Beth. *The Book of Esther: Motifs, Themes and Structure*. Society of Biblical Literature Dissertation Series 44. Missoula, Mont.: Scholars, 1979.

Berman, Joshua. "Hadassah Bat Abihail: The Evolution from Object to Subject in the Character of Esther." *Journal of Biblical Literature* 120/4 (2001): 647–69.

Brenner, Athalya, ed. *A Feminist Companion to Esther, Judith and Susanna*. Feminist Companion to the Bible. Vol. 7. Sheffield: Sheffield Academic, 1995.

Briant, Pierre. *From Cyrus to Alexander: A History of the Persian Empire*. Translated by Peter T. Daniels. Winona Lake, Ind.: Eisenbrauns, 2002.

Clines, David J. A. *The Esther Scroll: The Story of the Story*. Journal for the Study of the Old Testament Supplement Series 30. Sheffield: Sheffield Academic, 1984.

Fox, Michael V. *Character and Ideology in the Book of Esther*. 2nd ed. Grand Rapids: Eerdmans, 2001.

---

127. Anderson, "The Place of the Book of Esther," 42.

128. Bush, *Ruth, Esther*, 332–33.

Gordis, Robert. "Studies in the Esther Narrative." *Journal of Biblical Literature* 95 (1976): 43–58.

Haupt, Paul. "Critical Notes on Esther." *American Journal of Semitic Languages and Literature* 24 (1907–1908): 97–186 (reprinted in C. Moore, *Esther*, 1–90).

Hazony, Yoram. *The Dawn: Political Teachings of the Book of Esther*. Rev. ed. Jerusalem: Shalem, 2000.

Klein, Lillian R. "Honor and Shame in Esther." Pages 149–75 in *A Feminist Companion to Esther, Judith and Susanna*. Edited by Athalya Brenner. Sheffield: Sheffield Academic, 1995.

Laniak, Timothy S. *Shame and Honor in the Book of Esther*. Society of Biblical Literature Dissertation Series 165. Atlanta: Scholars, 1998.

Moore, Carey A., ed. *Studies in the Book of Esther*. New York: Ktav, 1982.

Olmstead, A. T. *History of the Persian Empire*. Chicago: University of Chicago Press, 1948.

Rosenheim, Judith. "Fate and Freedom in the Scroll of Esther." *Prooftexts* 12 (1992): 125–49.

Shea, William H. "Esther and History." *Concordia Journal* 13/3 (1987): 234–48.

Torrey, C. C. "The Older Book of Esther." *Harvard Theological Review* 37 (1944): 1–40.

Walfish, Barry Dov. *Esther in Medieval Garb: Jewish Interpretation of the Book of Esther in the Middle Ages*. Albany, N.Y.: State University of New York Press, 1993.

Yamauchi, Edwin. *Persia and the Bible*. Grand Rapids: Baker, 1990.

12. OUTLINE

Text and Exposition

I. HONOR AND SHAME: INSIDE, OUTSIDE, AND ON THE BOUNDARIES (1:1–2:23)

OVERVIEW

The introduction to King Xerxes is intentionally grandiose. His name is presented twice at the outset—a stylistic touch that sets the stage for the continuous procession of dyads through the description of the Persian court (cf. Levenson, 10–11). The geopolitical ("127 provinces") and geographical ("from India to Cush") extent of his reign is articulated. He ostensibly controlled both military and diplomatic forces, and the display of his wealth took a long time! Honor and royalty are linked repeatedly throughout the chapter; names, titles, and positions seem to be of primary importance, but the reader will become aware that, in truth, the text is poking a good deal of fun at the upper crust of the Persian monarchy.

A. The Trappings of Honor (1:1–8)

1. The King in His Empire (1:1–4)

¹This is what happened during the time of Xerxes, the Xerxes who ruled over 127 provinces stretching from India to Cush: ²At that time King Xerxes reigned from his royal throne in the citadel of Susa, ³and in the third year of his reign he gave a banquet for all his nobles and officials. The military leaders of Persia and Media, the princes, and the nobles of the provinces were present. ⁴For a full 180 days he displayed the vast wealth of his kingdom and the splendor and glory of his majesty.

COMMENTARY

1 The story begins with *wayᵉhî bîmê* ("it happened in the days of ..."), a phrase that also commences the narrative of Ruth ("it happened in the days of the judges ..."). By itself *wayᵉhî* introduces several of the historical biblical texts, and on three separate occasions it explicitly connects with the preceding narratives (*wayᵉhî ʾaḥᵃrê môt*, "it happened after the death of ..."; Jos 1:1; Jdg 1:1; 2Sa 1:1). Here there is no preceding narrative, and some have proposed that it is a conventional, perhaps archaizing formula intended to suggest the distant past (Paton, 121; Moore, *Esther*, 3; Fox, 15; see also Baldwin, 55). In rabbinic tradition, the Men of the Great Assembly said that *wayᵉhî* in the text indicates the approach of trouble; this verse is the prime example among many others (*b. Meg.* 10b).

The king's name in the MT is *ʾăḥašwērôš*, rendered "Ahasuerus" in some English translations. It is the Hebrew equivalent of the Persian *Khshayarsha*, of which Xerxes is the Greek transliteration (Paton, 41–45). *ʾăḥaš* appears as part of the larger word translated as "satraps" (*ʾăḥašdarpᵉnîm*, "protectors of the realm" [BDB]) in 8:9 and 9:3; the construct form is found in 3:12 and Ezra 8:6. *ʾăḥaštᵉrānîm* occurs in Esther 8:10, 14 in parallel with *hārekeš* and possibly means "royal." Finally, the same form is part of a word in 1 Chronicles 4:6. It may simply be an official title or a generic name meaning "chief of rulers" (Moore, *Esther*, 3–4; cf. H. S. Gehman, "Notes on the Persian Words in the Book of Esther," *JBL* 43 [1924]: 321–28).

The description that unfolds fits well with what we know of Xerxes (Herodotus 3.97; 7.9, 65, 69–70). In 486 BC, Xerxes inherited a vast domain from Darius I, who had added India (*hōddû* in Hebrew) to the empire. An inscription on the foundation stone of Xerxes' palace at Persepolis attests to the extent of his realm (*ANET*, 316–17; see Carey A. Moore, "Archaeology and the Book of Esther," *BA* 38 [1975]: 70; idem, *Esther*, 4). India and Cush represented the southeastern and southwestern corners, respectively (Adele Berlin, *Esther* [JPS Bible Commentary; Philadelphia: Jewish Publication Society, 2001], 6). The parallel expression "from Dan to Beersheba" is a standard biblical designation of the full extent of geopolitical territory. In this case, the designations were representative of the whole known world (Bush, 353) and established the universal sovereignty and therefore supreme honor of Xerxes (Laniak, 38–39).

The number of provinces has been the focus of a good deal of skeptical commentary (Paton, 71–72; Clines, 275). Herodotus (3.89–96) indicated there were twenty satrapies in the Persian Empire under Darius. A *mᵉdînâ* ("province"), however, was a smaller entity than a satrapy, as is evident from 3:12, which mentions both terms. Given the importance for Xerxes of consolidating Persia's hold on the vast empire, citing the number of provinces instead of satrapies made it sound more impressive (Baldwin, 56). Daniel 6:1–2, referring to the Medo-Persian conquest of Babylon, indicates 120 *ʾăḥašdarpᵉnayyāʾ*. Apart from the possible propaganda engine evident here, it is, from a literary standpoint, another mechanism for poking fun at the king, who ruled 127 provinces but lapsed in his own palace garden.

2 After the pointed identification of the king, the second verse resumes the narrative and emphasizes the matter of his royal dominion in additional ways. *Kᵉšebet* (lit., "sitting") on his royal throne might refer to his sitting securely after putting down the rebellions noted by Herodotus (Moore, *Esther*, 5; although see Fox, 16, for the position that this mention simply means that he ruled in Susa).

Ancient Persia had four capitals: Ecbatana, Susa, Persepolis, and Babylon. Susa (Heb. *šûšan*) had been chosen by Darius I as the main administrative center, and the acropolis to the west of the lower city was fortified (Olmstead, 163–71; Yamauchi, 279–303). Susa served as the winter residence for the Persian kings (Gordis, *Megillat Esther*, 21). There is a consistent distinction made between the *bîrâ* ("citadel") and the "city" (3:15; 4:16; 8:14).

3 The third year of Xerxes' reign (483 BC) may have had particular significance, given the wider geopolitical context in which he found himself. The date of his encounter with Egypt was 485 (cf. Herodotus 7.7). A subsequent intensive diplomatic effort, lasting four years and including a gathering of nobles (Herodotus 7.8, 20–21), was likely designed to inspire confidence across the empire that he could next go to war successfully against Greece and to enlist support for that endeavor (Moore, *Esther*, 12; Baldwin, 57). The presence of armed forces (*ḥêl*) among the other notables may be an indicator of this intent. Xerxes left Susa in 481 and arrived in Sardis in the fall. After wintering there, the battles of Thermopylae and Salamis were engaged in 480.

The banquet (*mišteh*) prepared by Xerxes was an occasion characterized by excess and a vehicle for wielding power. It would likely have occurred during the winter because of the intense summer heat in Susa. If so, the banquet's end, culminating in the seven-day festival, may have coincided with the springtime New Year's festival, in which all Susa would have been involved.

Vast numbers of guests attended banquets in antiquity; Ashurbanipal, at his own recording, invited close to seventy thousand people to the celebration of the completion of one of his palaces (Elias Bickerman, *Four Strange Books of the Bible* [New York: Schocken, 1967], 185). Characteristically, at royal celebrations large quantities of food were distributed (cf. 2Ch 30:23–24; 31:3–19; Ne 5:14–18; see Berlin, 4). Here there is no mention of food; the entire focus was drinking, and the significant details of ch. 1 have also to do with drinking (Beal, 17). Because some of it was excessive, by the king's own authorization, it undermined the superficial displays of honor (Klein, 154–55).

The pairs of words that characterize the descriptions in this first chapter appear here in increasingly widening circles. "His nobles and officials" (lit., "servants") may have been local bureaucrats. They were joined by "military leaders from Persia and Media," and finally more distant "princes and nobles of the provinces." The NIV has translated *śārîm* as "nobles" (see BDB) and *partᵉmîm* as "princes." Just how to define and connect these groups is unclear because of the absence of the *waw* conjunction before *ḥêl* ("armed forces") and *partᵉmîm*.

4 In the Hebrew text, "showing" is the first word; Xerxes was establishing his splendor before whole entourages of notables he needed to impress. The verbal pairs, double constructs, and other forms of redundancy (Levenson, 13) highlight the inconceivable wealth of the kingdom. Literally, the double construct pairs read "riches of the glory of his kingdom" (*ᶜōšer kᵉbôd malkûtô*) and "honor of the crown of his greatness" (*yᵉqār tipᵊᵉret gᵉdûlātô*) and should be interpreted dynamically as tremendous wealth and extraordinary splendor, the *essence* of the Persian kingdom. Each individual term in the description is heavily freighted with connotations of honor and the resultant status and awe (Laniak, 46–47).

In saying (lit.) "for many days, in fact, 180 days!" the narrator registers astonishment at the amount of time the banquet lasted. This equivalent of six months is viewed as a literary exaggeration designed to demonstrate the excesses of the Persian monarchy. It is unlikely, however, that all the princes, servants, army personnel, and diplomats were carousing together for the full 180 days. Instead, this celebration was an ongoing diplomatic effort to woo broad support for the attack on Greece, and groups were arriving in succession.

Prior to this grandiose introduction to Ahasuerus (Xerxes) with which the Hebrew text (MT) commences, the LXX both revises the historical context and puts the narrative into a more distinctly theological framework. It first names Artaxerxes (464–425 BC) as the Persian monarch and then identifies Mordecai as a Benjamite in captivity exiled by Nebuchadnezzar from Jerusalem (587 BC). This latter identification appears in the MT in 2:5–6. The main focus of the introduction in the LXX is to report an apocalyptic dream in which Mordecai saw two dragons ready to fight amidst appalling tribulation. The righteous people cried out to God, and a small stream became a mighty river, light arose, and the lowly were exalted. The audience and Mordecai are left to ponder the implications of this dream until the end of the LXX, where it is interpreted.

In the meantime, at this juncture Mordecai overheard two eunuchs of the king plotting his assassination and reported it to Artaxerxes. The matter was examined, the eunuchs were hanged, and Mordecai was brought to serve in an official capacity in the court. In another key diversion from the MT, we learn here that Haman determined to harm Mordecai and his people because of what happened to the two eunuchs, thus tying together aspects of the plot that are left ambiguous in the MT.

NOTES

1 The syntactical form הוּא אֲחַשְׁוֵרוֹשׁ (hûᵓ ᵓᵃḥašwērôš) indicated to the early Jewish sages that the king could be identified with a series of named, evil biblical characters (b. Meg. 11a).

In Daniel 2:49 and Ezra 2:1, מְדִינָה (mᵉdînâ) refers to a small area around Jerusalem that was within the larger satrapy of Trans-Euphrates (see also Ne 1:3). Representatives from the surrounding region who lived in Jerusalem were designated "heads of the province" (Ne 11:3). Specific regions around Babylon (Ezr 7:16; Da 3:1–3, 12, 30) as well as Elam (Da 8:2), Judah (Ezr 5:8), and Media (Ezr 6:2) are each designated as the province (mᵉdînâ) belonging to that named city (see Hess, NIDOTTE, 2:853). For further discussion of satraps and satrapies in the Persian Empire, see Briant, 63–67.

2 מַלְכוּת (malkût) is used extensively in later Hebrew (Esther, Daniel, and Chronicles) to indicate Persian royal power, kingdom, or reign. It appears characteristically in the construct state and serves as an adjective—in this case, "his royal throne."

בִּירָה (bîrâ, "citadel"), used only in postexilic books, is a late loanword from Assyrian/Persian. Most references are to Susa or to the fortress in it (Ne 1:1; Da 8:2), though several texts use the word in regard to the Jerusalem temple and the fortress nearby (1 Chr 29:1, 19; Ne 2:8; 7:2; see Schoville, NIDOTTE, 1:654–55; BDB). The precise understanding of bîrâ is difficult, but it likely comes from Assyrian birtu ("fortress") and might best be translated as "capital city" or "acropolis" (Berg, 19, n. 5).

3 Putting off the Greek campaign until the fifth year may have been due to the rebellion in Babylon, though dating that event is difficult (see the summary of the issues in Shea, 236–37). Herodotus 7.61–88 gives an extensive and colorful description of Xerxes' armed forces, who hailed from all parts of the empire. Yamauchi, 196, cites possible figures of 150,000 to 210,000 for the number of military personnel Xerxes took to battle, so these guests would have been representative heads of the army or perhaps more broadly aristocracy (cf. Ne 4:2; 1Ki 10:2). Each class of guests was documented, just as later those who received the official communications were likewise listed (Laniak, 39).

4 The primary term for "honor" in the book of Esther is יְקָר (yᵉqār; GK 3702). Honor "appears as a major theme in later OT writings whose literary settings are the imperial courts of Gentile rulers" (Yarchin, NIDOTTE, 2:523). The adjectival form יָקָר (yāqār) means "precious, costly, rare," or "valuable." Honor, linked repeatedly in Esther with royalty, is demonstrated by an interweaving of substance, status, and splendor. In the public arena, respect for status, awe in the face of splendor, and dependence for largesse (substance) all enhanced the reputation of a given individual. The king's royal banquet was clearly an occasion to honor himself. None of these facets was static; status was always changing and being challenged (Laniak, 17–20, 36–40).

2. The King's Liberality in Susa (1:5–8)

⁵When these days were over, the king gave a banquet, lasting seven days, in the enclosed garden of the king's palace, for all the people from the least to the greatest, who were in the citadel of Susa. ⁶The garden had hangings of white and blue linen, fastened with cords of white linen and purple material to silver rings on marble pillars. There were couches of gold and silver on a mosaic pavement of porphyry, marble, mother-of-pearl and other costly stones. ⁷Wine was served in goblets of gold, each one different from the other, and the royal wine was abundant, in keeping with the king's liberality. ⁸By the king's command each guest was allowed to drink in his own way, for the king instructed all the wine stewards to serve each man what he wished.

COMMENTARY

5 The separate, seven-day feast for all the people remaining (*hannimṣᵉʾîm*) in Susa indicates that the previous enterprise had been staged primarily for foreigners whom the king was trying to impress. With this event, he may have been thanking the local population that had hosted "tourists" for half a year. In the Hebrew text, the successive nouns in construct at the end of the verse take the reader step by step into the interior—"in the courtyard of the garden of the pavilion [*bîtan*] of the king." The syntax intimates that this access was a special occasion.

6 The description of the inner quarters provides a rich feast for the imaginative eye. From ceiling to floor, the columns, draperies, and parquet flooring were the sumptuous backdrop for couches on which guests would lounge. The words in the long list are exotic and the identity of materials is difficult, creating the impression of something almost surreal. The rugged syntax conveys a sense of wonder at the opulence.

At the same time, the repetitious dyads poke fun at the officious Persian court, and, furthermore, those who knew the prophetic message as part of their heritage would be painfully aware

of the injustice inherent in this system (Baldwin, 55). *Tᵉkēlet*, deep blue or violet material, was used extensively in conjunction with the tabernacle and temple (Ex 25–28; 35–39; 2Ch 2–3). Perhaps the author intends a subtle contrast between the dwellings of the King of the universe and this "king."

7 In keeping with the extravagant surroundings, the drinking that characterized this event in the Persian court was from exquisite and singularly unique vessels. This detail finds echoes in Xenophon (*Cyropaedia* 8.8.18), who reported that the Persians had as many drinking cups as possible. Furthermore, the royal wine was flowing freely (lit., "according to the king's hand")—a fact that has ominous implications, as drinking consistently precedes or accompanies disaster in this text.

8 The drinking process as described here is a microcosm of the real nature of both the empire and its ruler. On the surface, all details were controlled by law (*dāt*), but the law, in fact, means that the king lets people do as they wish—a matter that will find sobering expression in Haman's being allowed to write whatever decree he wants (Levenson, 46).

NOTES

5 In neo-Assyrian inscriptional evidence from the time of Sennacherib and Esarhaddon, the *bitanu* (an Akkadian loanword from West Semitic) was an open structure, a "small building used for certain prestigious purposes, in fact reserved for royalty." The Assyrians adopted from the West the architectural innovation of gardens in conjunction with the palace for the pleasure of the king (Leo Oppenheim, "On Royal Gardens in Mesopotamia," *JNES* 24 [1965]: 330–31). These features likely carried over into the Babylonian and Persian periods. The Persians were famous for their gardens and parks (Yamauchi, 332–33).

6 חוּר (*ḥûr*), related to a verbal form meaning "to be white" (used in Isa 29:22), occurs only in Esther. These white hangings are of כַּרְפַּס (*karpas*) and תְּכֵלֶת (*tᵉkēlet*). The former is used only here in the biblical text; it may be cotton or fine linen (BDB). Driver suggested that the word order be emended because *ḥûr* is indicative of color and, together with *tᵉkēlet*, should modify *karpas*, the material ("Problems and Solutions," *VT* 4 [1954]: 235).

These luxuriant hangings were bound with cords and fastened to גְּלִילֵי כֶסֶף (*gᵉlîlê kesep*), a part of the furnishings that could be either silver rods or rings. In the light of Song of Songs 5:14, "rods" is most likely (Haupt, 105). While the material of which the alabaster columns are made is identifiable, three of the four components of the inlaid floor are *hapax legomena*. The only one that occurs elsewhere is שֵׁשׁ (*šēš*, "alabaster") in Song of Songs 5:15 and, in an alternative form (*šayiš*), in 1 Chronicles 29:2. They may all be some form of marble (Haupt, 105). בַּהַט (*bahaṭ*), perhaps from the Egyptian *behiti*, may be prophyry (BDB); דַּר (*dar*), perhaps from *drr*, "to flow abundantly" or "shine," could be pearl or mother of pearl (BDB); and סֹחָרֶת (*sōḥāret*) is simply said to be a stone used in paving (BDB).

8 אֵין אֹנֵס (*ʾên ʾōnēs*) most likely means "there was no restraint," although the expression is used only here in biblical Hebrew. In later usage, *ʾōnēs* means "compulsion, force," or "unavoidable interference" (Jastrow, 1:29). Both early and more recent commentators have wrestled with the two contradictory clauses. The Second Targum stated that there was a custom by which guests were compelled to drink a large containerful at one draught, but in this case that rule did not apply. John Gray suggested that כַּדָּת (*kaddāt*) could mean "flagons" (*The Legacy of Canaan* [Leiden: Brill, 1956], 226), but that meaning would remove one of the ironic twists of the story.

B. Royal Honor Threatened and the Assertive Queen Banished (1:9–22)

1. Vashti's Refusal to Cross a Boundary (1:9–12)

⁹Queen Vashti also gave a banquet for the women in the royal palace of King Xerxes. ¹⁰On the seventh day, when King Xerxes was in high spirits from wine, he commanded the seven eunuchs who served him — Mehuman, Biztha, Harbona, Bigtha, Abagtha, Zethar and Carcas — ¹¹to bring before him Queen Vashti, wearing her royal crown, in order to display her beauty to the people and nobles, for she was lovely to look at. ¹²But when the

attendants delivered the king's command, Queen Vashti refused to come. Then the king became furious and burned with anger.

COMMENTARY

9 On the possible identity of Vashti with Amestris, see the Introduction: Historicity of the Narrative. The narrator presents the banquet for women as a parallel to the ongoing feast of the king. The sentence commences with *gam* ("also"), and the words used for giving a banquet (*ʿāśᵉtâ mišteh*) are the same here as in the case of the king's banquet. At the same time, the contrast between the simplicity of this statement and the effusive description of the king's banquets is not to be missed. Vashti's separate banquet sets the stage for the ongoing separate worlds in which the king and his queen operated (Levenson, 46–47), makes her refusal to be the lone woman at the king's drinking party understandable, and also is an adumbration of Esther's private banquets (Fox, 17–18).

10 The number seven plays a significant role in these early stages of the narrative. To be brought by seven eunuchs on the seventh day may suggest that the king intends Vashti's appearance as the grand finale to days of basking in admiration and honor. Thus it is utterly humiliating when she refuses to come. The command via seven eunuchs emphasizes again that everything about this court is overdone, but according to official protocol (Fox, 20).

The seven names are mirrored in the names that appear in v.14 (see below). While *sārîs* can refer to someone who was not a eunuch (see Yamauchi, 262–63; cf. Ge 37:36; 39:1, where Potiphar, who had a wife, is called a *sārîs*), it is likely that the attendants of the king who have access to the harem are eunuchs (see Briant, 268–77). The eunuchs, the princes, and later Haman's sons are named. In an

intriguing internal modification of the narrative, the LXX includes the name of Haman with the eunuchs.

After seven days, the king's condition is distinctly affected by the wine. The expression *ṭôb lēb* can be translated anywhere on the spectrum from "cheerful" to "drunk." It appears in other biblical contexts where intoxication is connected to impending destruction (Jdg 16:25; 1Sa 25:36; 2Sa 13:28; see Levenson, 47).

11 As a consummate act of self-aggrandizement in an already overextended parade, the king determines to show off another possession, his queen. That the eunuchs are commanded "to bring" Vashti indicates it is simply expected she will display her beauty before the people and princes. It is telling that the term "to show" is used with regard to both Vashti and the king's possessions (Est 1:4). Vashti must wear a royal crown, the specific mention of which prompted rabbinic commentators to suggest that this was *all* she was to be wearing (*b. Meg.* 12b; *Est. Rab.* 3.13–14; First and Second Targums).

12 While the text does not explicitly state why Vashti refuses, it is not difficult to surmise that she is loathe to show herself, clothed or otherwise, before a large group of men well under the influence of their wine. Herodotus (5.18; see also 3.32; 9.110) attributes to Persians the claim that wives and concubines generally joined them in banqueting, so this audience may not have included only men. Nevertheless, Vashti does have her own festivities going on simultaneously.

The king's wrath is described in doublets, even the sound of which indicates his sputtering (*yiqṣōp*) with rage and the anger smoldering within him (*bāᵃrâ bô*). That his reaction has to do with honor is clear in the advice from Memucan that follows.

NOTES

9 The meaning of Vashti's name is either "best" or "beloved" (Moore, *Esther*, 8; Baldwin, 60). On another level, a listening audience might be aware of the homophony between וְהַשְׁתִיָּה (*wᵉhaššᵉtîyâ*, "and the drinking") in the previous verse and וַשְׁתִּי (*waštî*) here.

11 כֶּתֶר (*keter*), translated "crown," is used only in the book of Esther; in one occurrence, it refers to the headdress on the king's horse (6:8).

2. Consulting the Sages (1:13–15)

> ¹³Since it was customary for the king to consult experts in matters of law and justice, he spoke with the wise men who understood the times ¹⁴and were closest to the king — Carshena, Shethar, Admatha, Tarshish, Meres, Marsena and Memucan, the seven nobles of Persia and Media who had special access to the king and were highest in the kingdom. ¹⁵"According to law what must be done to Queen Vashti?" he asked. "She has not obeyed the command of King Xerxes that the eunuchs have taken to her."

COMMENTARY

13–14 The crucial question from the king to his counselors is interrupted by an elaborate parenthetical note on the decision-making body in the governmental structure—another jab at the excessively regulated and farcical nature of the entire court (Gordis, "Studies in the Esther Narrative," 53; Bush, 344). The text not only attests to the king's procedure (*dᵉbar*) of deferring to those whose knowledge of judicial procedure (*dāt wādîn*) was their livelihood; it also drops momentarily the crisis of honor to note the names of those who advise him in these delicate circumstances.

Maintaining seven official legal advisers seems to have been regular practice in the Persian court (Herodotus 3.31, 84, 118; Ezr 7:14). These wise men (*ḥᵃkāmîm*), also styled as "those who understood the times," came from within the ranks of those who were experts in *dāt wādîn* and had immense potential for influencing the king, as they were in his presence and were seated first in the kingdom. The precise nature of their expertise is debated. The same expression appears in 1 Chronicles 12:32 regarding members of the tribe of Issachar who, because they understood what Israel ought to do, were among those who came to Hebron to make David king. The position clearly required possessing a degree of political savvy in that case.

Wise men were a traditional institution in the courts, and several of these names were found in the Persepolis Tablets (A. R. Millard, "The Persian Names in Esther and the Reliability of the Hebrew Text," *JBL* 96 [1977]: 481–88). Ibn Ezra suggests that "those who understood the times" were astrologers and *dāt* in this case referred to the "laws of the heavens" (Walfish, 114–15, 273, n. 46) — an interpretation that has continued to hold some sway (Baldwin, 61; Levenson, 50–51). Nevertheless, nothing in the immediate context suggests that astrology contributed significantly (Paton, 151–53; Bush, 350). Rosenheim, 134–35, proposed that because fate appeared to be dependent on cause-and-effect connections, and increased knowledge about causes might allow someone partially to control outcomes, "those who understood the times" wielded significant power in the Persian hierarchy.

Here, however, it seems that their wits are likewise beclouded with wine. As will become evident, those who "understand the times" and fear a women's uprising miss the conspiracy that Mordecai the Jew uncovers.

The names of these ministers and the eunuchs listed in 1:10 are similar when read in reverse order (Clines, 116–17). Although there are several aberrations in the reversed patterns, the general order might constitute a literary device hinting from another perspective at the reversals that characterize the entire narrative. Seven eunuchs are to bring Vashti; seven advisers will determine her fate.

15 That the king has to ask how to handle his rebellious wife and expects some sort of response "according to the law" adds to the hilarious tone of the narrative. From their inability to respond with a legal protocol, it seems that nothing similar has ever happened before. This, therefore, sets up the appearance of the situation's being all that much more shocking!

NOTES

13 The terms דָּת (*dāt*) and דִּין (*dîn*) are not synonymous. *Dāt* was a loanword from Old Persian that primarily referred to a decree or royal command (T. Cuyler Young Jr., "The Consolidation of the Empire and Its Limits of Growth under Darius and Xerxes," in *The Cambridge Ancient History* [2nd ed.; Cambridge: Cambridge Univ. Press, 1988], 4:94–99), whereas *dîn* indicated legislative issues (Haupt, 109).

14 On the complications in the transmission of these names, see Haupt, 110–11; Moore, *Esther*, 8–10; and Millard, 481–88.

3. Memucan's Advice Heeded (1:16–22)

16Then Memucan replied in the presence of the king and the nobles, "Queen Vashti has done wrong, not only against the king but also against all the nobles and the peoples of all the provinces of King Xerxes. **17**For the queen's conduct will become known to all the women, and so they will despise their husbands and say, 'King Xerxes commanded Queen

Vashti to be brought before him, but she would not come.' ^{18}This very day the Persian and Median women of the nobility who have heard about the queen's conduct will respond to all the king's nobles in the same way. There will be no end of disrespect and discord.

^{19}"Therefore, if it pleases the king, let him issue a royal decree and let it be written in the laws of Persia and Media, which cannot be repealed, that Vashti is never again to enter the presence of King Xerxes. Also let the king give her royal position to someone else who is better than she. ^{20}Then when the king's edict is proclaimed throughout all his vast realm, all the women will respect their husbands, from the least to the greatest."

^{21}The king and his nobles were pleased with this advice, so the king did as Memucan proposed. ^{22}He sent dispatches to all parts of the kingdom, to each province in its own script and to each people in its own language, proclaiming in each people's tongue that every man should be ruler over his own household.

COMMENTARY

16–17 Vashti has publicly dishonored the king, and her action could be presented as having severe repercussions for male honor, official and otherwise. Memucan's speech moves the bright spotlight of humiliation from focusing solely on the king to include all the men — a brilliant maneuver for someone close to the king and responsible for his reputation (Carol M. Bechtel, *Esther* [IBC; ed. James L. Mays; Louisville, Ky.: John Knox, 2002], 24). Those at the highest ranks (*haśśārîm*) in this tenuous, honor-holding sphere have the most to lose (Laniak, 48–49).

Memucan's tone is that of near panic, probably because he knows that gossip spreads like wildfire: "all" the nobles, "all" the people, "all" the provinces. While the women who have gathered for Vashti's feast will likely be part of the feared newsflash, the verse indicates that everyone will be talking about the scandal; the suffix on the infinitive construct is masculine plural (*bᵒomrām*). Vashti's offense is presented as worse than impropriety. The

Hebrew verb is *ᶜwh*, related to a common nominal form, *ᶜāwōn*, most frequently rendered "sin."

18 According to Memucan's worst-case scenario, the women of nobility will hear of the queen's shocking behavior and brazenly use it to shame their own husbands, who, because honor was woven into the very fabric of the culture, could only respond with rage (*qeṣep*). This verse is not redundant of the previous statement but is a subtle indicator of class distinctions; even the noblewomen will shame *their* husbands (Gordis, *Megillat Esther*, 24).

While the general inebriation could have accounted for some of the apparently excessive anger, the prospect of public humiliation because of public disobedience lies at the bottom of the rage. An expression of anger in that cultural context would not only have be acceptable; it would have in fact been expected (Laniak, 56–57). This result is also expressed in a doublet, "shame and rage" (*bizzāyôn wāqāṣep*).

19 Subtly indicative of the impersonal political and legal machinery, the recurring pattern of passive verbal forms begins with the issuance of the royal decree. The edict is to be issued from the king, and it is to "be written in the laws of Persia and Media." The next clause, $w^el\bar{o}$ ' $ya^ca\underline{b}\hat{o}r$, is syntactically challenging. The subject of the previous clause, the "royal decree," requires another passive verb to carry over as the subject here—"it must not be transgressed," although this expression might be interpreted, "so that it [this particular edict] will not pass away." The immediately preceding referent, the laws of the Medes and the Persians, would seem to require a plural verbal form—"they do not pass away"—if the intent is to indicate their dependable irrevocability.

Here and in Daniel 6 are the only clear references to the irrevocability of these laws (see Introduction: Historicity of the Narrative), but the occurrence in this context is essential to the story as it exists in the MT.

Memucan's advice makes permanent and *public* Vashti's own refusal to be in the king's presence at the banquet. It also effectively removes her from any sphere where she might in the future exercise power. It is no accident that at this point in the text she is no longer called "Vashti, the Queen." Her position will be given to one who will, in the fondest hopes of Memucan, the king, and the rest of the nobles present, have a more pliable disposition.

20 In this finale of Memucan's speech, full of the requisite bowing and scraping, there is a modification in the nature and implications of the decree. The only way to achieve the restoration of male honor will be through the demonstration of obedience by *all* the women of the empire; therefore, not only does the decree banish Vashti, but it also vainly attempts to address Memucan's real concern to compel all women to give respect ($y^eq\bar{a}r$) to their husbands, from the greatest to the least. In his presentation, it will only have to be heard (another passive form of the verb) for proper hierarchy and honor to be restored!

21–22 In a land where law was supposedly so important, this one comes into effect because it "seemed good" to an inebriated king and his princes (Baldwin, 62). He determines to issue the decree regarding Vashti and, in a vain bid to bolster the expected empire-wide results, an odd and unenforceable mandate is added (Fox, 23). The literal rendition of the last two clauses is, "every man is to be ruling in his own house and speaking the language of his people." The NIV has changed the subject of $m^edabb\bar{e}r$ from "every man" to the previously referenced dispatch that will reach each location. Reading it that way, however, simply repeats what has just been said, namely, that the text is written in the language of each location to which it was sent.

This mandate might be better understood in the light of the subculture described in Nehemiah 13:23–24, where intermarriage had resulted in families' speaking the language of Gentile mothers instead of Hebrew, and it may testify to a significant degree of intermarriage and to the power that resides in language. (See Gordis, "Studies in the Esther Narrative," 53; Levenson, 52; and Bea Wyler, "Esther: The Incomplete Emancipation of a Queen," in Brenner, 117.) Writing for each political entity ($m^ed\hat{\imath}n\hat{a}$) *and* language ($l\bar{a}\check{s}\hat{o}n$) is an indication that the coverage is indeed to be comprehensive. Although Aramaic was the international language, no doubt there were many languages from all parts of the empire represented at the king's gathering. This measure assured the reception of the decree. A further contributor to that certainty was the efficiency of the postal system (Herodotus 5.52–53; 8.98).

NOTES

16 The *A*-Text of the LXX, while omitting the list of advisers' names from v.14, identifies Memucan as Bougaios, establishing that he is the same as Haman "son of Hammedatha the Bougaean." This identity is also suggested in the First Targum and *b. Meg.* 12b and was adopted by a number of medieval Jewish commentators. It solved the exegetical problem posed by Haman's inexplicable and sudden rise to power (Walfish, 33).

18 The difficult syntax of the first part of this verse has been addressed in a number of ways. The major problem is that תֹּאמַרְנָה (*tōʾmarnâ*, "they will say") has no explicit object. Although some emend the text, doing so is unnecessary. אֲשֶׁר (*ʾašer*), generally translated in this context as "who," can also be translated "that." In other words, it could read "... the noble women of Persia and Media will say *that* they have heard the scandal about the queen...." This use of אֲשֶׁר is frequent in late biblical Hebrew (Gordis, "Studies in the Esther Narrative," 45–47). It is also possible that the direct object is simply elided because it is already clear in the context (Bush, 351). On ellipsis in biblical Hebrew, see *IBHS*, 11.4.3.

22 סֵפֶר (*sēper*) is an Assyrian loanword and originally meant "message" (Haupt, 113; Paton, 162). לִהְיוֹת (*lihyôt*), infinitive construct plus *lamed*, introduces the contents of the dispatches, as it will in 3:13 and 8:13. The Second Targum on 1:16 humorously reflects the possible connection with Nehemiah 13:23–24 by stating that Memucan had his own domestic issues to resolve, for he had taken for a wife a Persian woman who was richer than he was and she refused to speak with him except in her own language!

C. Mobilizing for a New Queen (2:1–23)

OVERVIEW

This section is a critical transition between the court excesses described in the first chapter and the grim narrative details that will unfold in the rest of the story. The excesses are still here, but change is in the offing, and after this chapter nothing is languid any longer!

1. Vacancy: Search for Replacement (2:1–4)

¹Later when the anger of King Xerxes had subsided, he remembered Vashti and what she had done and what he had decreed about her. ²Then the king's personal attendants proposed, "Let a search be made for beautiful young virgins for the king. ³Let the king appoint commissioners in every province of his realm to bring all these beautiful girls into the harem at the citadel of Susa. Let them be placed under the care of Hegai, the king's eunuch, who is in charge of the women; and let beauty treatments be given to them. ⁴Then let the girl who pleases the king be queen instead of Vashti." This advice appealed to the king, and he followed it.

COMMENTARY

1 "After these things" (NIV "later") is often used to start a new section of narrative in Hebrew (Bush, 359), and the focus does shift at this point, with the anger of Xerxes serving as the "connector." Once his wrath subsides, he remembers three things, each mention of which is preceded by the Hebrew particle *ʾēt*, emphasizing their distinctiveness: Vashti, what she had done, and what had been decreed against her. The narrator skillfully keeps the king's responsibility out of these matters; they all have to do with what *Vashti* has done and what the nameless bureaucracy has decreed.

Almost four years have transpired, and the war with Greece has offered the king another humiliation. Given the ubiquitous availability of women from the harem and the evidence from Herodotus that Xerxes was self-indulgent in this regard, it is unlikely that Xerxes is pining for feminine companionship. Whether the number was symbolic or factual, sources indicate that Persian kings maintained 360 concubines, and they were "employed" (Briant, 280–85). In light of the abundance of women, there seems to have been something particularly significant about the role of this Persian queen. If Amestris and Vashti were the same person, she may have continued to make her presence known on the margins of the royal court.

2 The young servants of the king make the decision recorded in this verse as well but do it adroitly to make it appear that Xerxes himself will choose the new queen (v.4: "the girl who pleases the king

..."). The recommended procedure may have represented one these young men themselves had experienced. Herodotus describes occasions on which young boys were rounded up to become eunuchs and girls were sent as presents to the king (3.48; 6.32). The criteria, repeated in v.3, are articulated as *nᵉʿārôt bᵉtûlôt ṭôbôt marʾeh*, "young women, virgins, beautiful." Each term narrows the field and sets this scene up as one of antiquity's beauty pageants.

3 The roundup of beautiful young virgins will be conducted in the same officious manner as the rest of the Persian bureaucracy. A "commission," responsible for getting all the likely prospects to the harem at Susa, is appointed to gather them from each province. The description of the operation makes it clear that local populations, which include Mordecai, have no choice in the matter. One can imagine the confusion once all these young women begin converging on the area of the citadel. The text implies large numbers with "every" (*kol*) province and "every" (*kol*) young woman. Once there, the beauty treatments follow (see 2:12).

4 The attendants defer to the king's approval (lit., "pleasing in the king's eyes") regarding both the acceptability of their plan and the ultimate selection of the young woman. The plan has two stages. The first is gathering all the beautiful virgins; the second is the contest. The servants seem to be aware that the last thing the king wants is an ambitious woman. The roundup is necessary and will demonstrate that the king is firmly in control.

NOTES

1 The word indicating the subsiding of the king's anger, שֹׁך (*šōk*, the infinitive construct from *škk*; GK 8896), is rarely used, but it does appear in Esther 7:10 and Genesis 8:1, in the latter case describing the waters subsiding after the flood. In that context, it follows *God's* remembering.

2 The third masculine plural יְבַקְשׁוּ (yᵉbaqšû, "let them seek") without an antecedent is the equivalent of a passive (Bush, 357; see GKC, 144f.; Joüon, 155b). בְּתוּלָה (bᵉtûlâ; GK 1435) indicates a young woman of marriageable age who is under the guardianship of her father (Walton, *NIDOTTE*, 1:781–84). It does not have to mean "virgin." (Note the word's use in Esther 2:17–19 and Joel 1:8.)

3 The syntax of the second clause is awkward because אֶת (ʾet) is followed by כֹּל (kōl) and then "young women, virgins" without the definite article. The variations in the vocalization of Hegei here and Hegai in v.8 are inconsequential. The final clause of the verse begins with an infinitive absolute and is subordinate to preceding verb—an increasingly common pattern in later Hebrew (*IBHS*, 35.5.2.d; see GKC, 113z; Joüon, 123x).

2. Outside: The Jewish Diaspora (2:5–7)

> [5]Now there was in the citadel of Susa a Jew of the tribe of Benjamin, named Mordecai son of Jair, the son of Shimei, the son of Kish, [6]who had been carried into exile from Jerusalem by Nebuchadnezzar king of Babylon, among those taken captive with Jehoiachin king of Judah. [7]Mordecai had a cousin named Hadassah, whom he had brought up because she had neither father nor mother. This girl, who was also known as Esther, was lovely in form and features, and Mordecai had taken her as his own daughter when her father and mother died.

COMMENTARY

5 The word order of the Hebrew text is significant. The verse begins with ʾîš yᵉhûdî, a Jewish man, who is "in the citadel of Susa." These identifying marks appear even before his name, and they hint at the conflict that follows by setting up the Jewish counterpoint to the Persian king and key members of his court. The focus of this verse is Jewishness and genealogy. Mordecai is repeatedly called "Mordecai the Jew," pointedly distinguishing him in the Diaspora context. Mordecai was a common name, appearing on cuneiform tablets, Elamite texts, and a tablet noting the payment made to Persian officials, one of whom was *Marduka*, the name of a scribe. See the Introduction: Historicity of the Narrative.

The primary question regarding the genealogy is the impossible age of Mordecai if the relative clause of v.6 refers to *his* being taken into exile rather than the last-named individual in the genealogy, Kish. Because the former is unlikely for a narrator seemingly so careful about detail, it is more probable that Kish was the individual taken into exile and these forebears of Mordecai had names that reflected earlier generations of the family tree. It was not unusual for clan names to continue throughout generations. If such is the case here, then for Mordecai to be a responsible man caring for his cousin and functioning in the king's gate in the 480s, he may have been born in exile to Jair in about 520. Jair's birth might date to approximately 550, and his father, Shimei, may have been born shortly after Kish was taken into exile in 597.

Attention is directed toward the Kish who was the father of King Saul (1Sa 9:1; 1Ch 8:33) in order to prepare for Haman's ties with Agag. It is that longstanding enmity between the Amalekites (the people of Agag) and the Israelites that makes the crisis between Mordecai and Haman understandable. Both are descendants of royalty — King Agag and Saul, Israel's first king.

6 The literal rendition of this verse is, "who was exiled from Jerusalem with the group of exiles which was exiled with Jeconiah, king of Judah, whom Nebuchadnezzar, king of Babylon, took into exile." The first two verbs are passive, and the last one refers to Nebuchadnezzar, who caused the exile of the people. The exile shaped these characters whose lives mirrored the national experience of Israel. Just as the people had no choice but were taken into exile, so also Esther had no choice but was taken into the harem. Mordecai's ancestors had lived in Jerusalem, and their exile in 597 along with Jeconiah (also known as Jehoiachin) indicates that theirs was an upper class family (2Ki 24:8–16; Jer 29:1–2). The eunuchs, nobles, and officials of the king were taken in that wave.

7 Again, word order is significant. The verse begins with *wayehî 'ōmēn*, "he was caring for," a noun used in regard to guardianship of children (Nu 11:12; Isa 49:23). It is related to *amen*, which has in its semantic range "trustworthiness." This clause is important in establishing the exemplary character of Mordecai.

"Hadassah … [that is] Esther" is the only character to have two names, indicative of her two worlds, initially separated, and one of which is hidden. Nevertheless, she will publicly fuse them in the power center of the Persian Empire. The very complexity of these unfolding processes is even captured in the names themselves. At the simplest

level, "Hadassah" means "myrtle" (*hadas*). That name alone carried significant associations. In the prophetic symbolism of Isaiah 55:13, the myrtle would replace the desert thorn. In postexilic times, myrtle was carried on the Feast of Tabernacles (Ne 8:15) to symbolize peace and thanksgiving (Baldwin, 66).

A more challenging question has to do with the meaning of "Esther" and the possible relationship between the two names. Esther has popularly been identified with Ishtar, the goddess of both love and war (see Julius Lewy, "The Feast of the 14th Day of Adar," *HUCA* 14 [1939]: 128–30). If this is intended as a "literary nickname," it is a good choice, as Esther proves herself in both realms! A better etymology, however, derives the name from Old Iranian *stara*, meaning "star" (see Ran Zadok, "Notes on Esther," *ZAW* 98 [1986]: 107; Bush, 364). There may be an even simpler relationship. Based on his study of the preservation of Old Persian forms, Abraham S. Yahuda ("The Meaning of the Name Esther," *JRAS* [1946]: 174–78; repr. in Moore, *Studies in the Book of Esther*, 268–72) concluded that "Esther" is the Persian equivalent of "Hadassah" and itself means myrtle. While the Persian for myrtle is *as*, the name as it appears in the text preserves an older and longer form, the Medic *astra*, via Old Persian.

The verse emphasizes the absence of Esther's parents by twice indicating that both have died and intimating that, apart from Mordecai, she would have been deserted. Even though Esther is Mordecai's cousin, she is sufficiently younger so that he adopts her as his daughter. The doublet describing Esther emphasizes her beauty — "beautiful of form" (*yepat-tōʾar*) and "lovely in appearance" (*tôbat marʾeh*). In other words, her extraordinary beauty far exceeds the qualifications for being rounded up in the net; her inclusion would have been unavoidable.

NOTES

5 אִישׁ יְהוּדִי (ʾîš yᵉhûdî) should not be understood as Judean or Judahite, a resident of the independent state of Judah or someone from that tribal area. Mordecai was a resident of Susa and was of the tribe of Benjamin; the appellation indicates his Jewishness. That later in the narrative (8:17) people adopted Judaism (mityahᵃdîm) without changing locations corroborates this interpretation.

6 An אֲשֶׁר (ᵃšer) clause of which the antecedent is the last name in a list appears in 2 Chronicles 22:9 and Ezra 2:61 (see Shea, 243). The mention of Shimei, hardly a positive figure among the descendants of Saul (2Sa 16:5–8), is curious. Perhaps there were still those in the family of Saul who resisted the Davidic monarchy and out of clan pride maintained this name among their descendants.

The list in 1 Chronicles 9:3 of those who settled in Jerusalem indicates that the range of tribes were represented there. They included Judah, Benjamin, Ephraim, and Manasseh.

7 Because Mordecai and Esther were cousins, the rabbinic sources (*b. Meg.* 13a, Targums, and *Midrash Esther Rabbah*) read "took her for a daughter" as "took her for a wife" by exchanging בַּת (*bat*) for בַּיִת (*bayit*), which secondarily can mean "wife." Centuries of Jewish interpreters have wrestled with the moral implications of Esther's position as wife to both Mordecai and the king (Walfish, "Kosher Adultery? The Mordecai–Esther–Ahasuerus Triangle in Talmudic, Medieval and 16th Century Exegesis," in *The Book of Esther in Modern Research* [ed. Sidnie White Crawford and Leonard J. Greenspoon; London: T&T Clark, 2003], 111–36).

3. Esther in the Harem (2:8–11)

> [8]When the king's order and edict had been proclaimed, many girls were brought to the citadel of Susa and put under the care of Hegai. Esther also was taken to the king's palace and entrusted to Hegai, who had charge of the harem. The girl pleased him and won his favor. Immediately he provided her with her beauty treatments and special food. He assigned to her seven maids selected from the king's palace and moved her and her maids into the best place in the harem.
>
> [10]Esther had not revealed her nationality and family background, because Mordecai had forbidden her to do so. [11]Every day he walked back and forth near the courtyard of the harem to find out how Esther was and what was happening to her.

COMMENTARY

8 The tone of this verse is determined by three passive verbs. The word and decree are heard, many young women are gathered, and Esther is taken. Given even a modicum of Jewish values as part of her upbringing by her parents and the subsequent nurturing of Mordecai, this occasion would have been one for anguish and shame (Klein, 157–58). The importance of Hegai for Esther's advancement is indicated in the dual mention of his name at this point; she is given into the care (*yad*) of Hegai. The contrast between Mordecai's role as nurturing guardian (*ʾōmēn*) and Hegai's position as "keeper [*šōmēr*] of the women" is noteworthy.

9 Continuing the stylistic pattern of doublets, Esther is pleasing to Hegai and wins his favor. The expression *tíśśāʾ ḥesed*, occurring only in Esther, has a sense of active "gaining" rather than the more subdued "finding" grace, favor, or kindness—the customary idiom. Esther is astute enough to know when to acquiesce and when to engage actively in social interactions; she is a success even before Xerxes sees her (Clines, 288). *Ḥesed* (GK 2876) is used in conjunction with *ḥēn* ("favor" or "grace"; GK 2834) as Esther captures the heart of the king (2:17). The same pair of words occurs in Genesis with regard to Joseph. The audience of the Esther narrative would have undoubtedly made the connection.

Hegai's attention to Esther moves her quickly forward in the process; as overseer of the treatments and special food (*mānôt*), Hegai gives her the best attendants and situates them in the best location in the harem. *Mānôt* is also used in 1 Samuel 1:4–5 with reference to Elkanah's distribution of portions of the sacrifice to his wives and children. The seven selected maids are likely those whom Hegai is reserving for the young woman who might, in his estimation, become Vashti's successor. That Esther alone receives their attention is suggested by the use of "her" prior to treatments and portions but not with these attendants. The other candidates get all the other kinds of care, but not the specially chosen attendants. By virtue of knowing the king, Hegai recognizes Esther as a good candidate for Vashti's replacement (Bush, 364).

10 The contention that it is not realistic to think Esther could conceal her identity because there would have been checks on her background may read a contemporary mindset into the Persian context. See in this regard Josiah Derby, "The Paradox in the Book of Esther," *JBQ* 23 (1995): 116–19. After all, the officials in charge of large numbers of beautiful women would hardly be likely to pay attention to much more than the preparations necessary to make them pleasing to the king (Haupt, 117). Because the text does not give an explicit reason for hiding Esther's identity, it leaves a sense of danger and nameless dread that sets the stage for what Haman devises in the chapters that follow (Fox, 32; Bush, 368). His extreme reaction against all Jews in response to Mordecai's insult suggests that anti-Semitism is already lurking in dark corners. If so, hiding their identity would be a prudent thing to do. It also explains Mordecai's abiding concern to keep himself apprised of Esther's welfare in the court (v.11).

11 Mordecai's continued care for Esther is manifested in his daily presence outside (lit., "in front of") the courtyard of the harem, where he checks on her welfare (*šālôm*), perhaps through connections he maintains in the harem. Mordecai will soon become apprised of the long process, perhaps trying his patience as it goes on for a year! The word (*yādaʿ*, "know") also appears in v.22 in regard to his learning of the plot against the king. While it has been argued that his presence would unquestionably give away Esther's nationality, that assertion is not necessarily correct. He could very likely obtain information about a favored young woman without divulging his relationship to her. The bustle of activities in the rooms of the gate and the ebb and flow of people could allow him to maintain an appropriately subdued profile until it comes time to reveal his own identity. After all, Haman does not notice him until his disobedience is actually pointed out (3:4–5).

NOTE

11 J. Stafford Wright ("The Historicity of the Book of Esther," in *New Perspectives on the Old Testament* [ed. J. Barton Payne; Waco, Tex.: Word, 1970], 45) suggests that Mordecai was a eunuch, since he had access to the women's quarters, frequented the gate area where other eunuchs were (v.21), and seems not to have had a wife or family (v.7). His sitting in the gate could indicate that he had already engaged in political activity, perhaps with the intent of effecting significant change (Hazony, 29–30). That he is adept at getting information becomes evident both in terms of the plot against Xerxes and the details of the conversation between Haman and the king. The participle מִתְהַלֵּךְ (*mithallēk*) in this case is indicative of the frequent nature of his manifest care (Joüon, 121–22).

4. "All the King's Women" (2:12–14)

OVERVIEW

Following on the previous "what would happen," the process is detailed, and the excesses continue the satire on the extravagant Persian court (Bush, 368). The next four verses repeatedly use the terminology "to enter into" with regard to the candidate's visit to the king, intimating sexual activity. It is an OT euphemism for intercourse (Ge 16:2; 29:21; Ru 4:13). On the surface, it appears that the criteria for being chosen as Vashti's replacement are two: beauty and ability to satisfy the king's sexual appetite.

> [12] Before a girl's turn came to go in to King Xerxes, she had to complete twelve months of beauty treatments prescribed for the women, six months with oil of myrrh and six with perfumes and cosmetics. [13] And this is how she would go to the king: Anything she wanted was given her to take with her from the harem to the king's palace. [14] In the evening she would go there and in the morning return to another part of the harem to the care of Shaashgaz, the king's eunuch who was in charge of the concubines. She would not return to the king unless he was pleased with her and summoned her by name.

COMMENTARY

12 Each young woman has a turn after a year of preparation. The treatment period (*yᵉmê mᵉrûqêhen*) is "prescribed" (*dāt*) with oil massages for six months and spices for another six, no doubt to soften and perfume the skin. The association of myrrh with sexual attraction and love is particularly evident in the Song of Songs (SS 1:13; 4:6, 14; 5:1, 5, 13; see also Pr 7:17).

The importance of oiling skin in a hot and dry climate cannot be overestimated. Examples of cosmetic burners have been found at several sites in ancient Israel, the primary one being Lachish.

These were filled with a combination of spices and used by women to fumigate themselves and their clothes, ostensibly to make them more desirable (W. F. Albright, "The Lachish Cosmetic Burner and Esther 2:12," in *A Light unto My Path: Old Testament Studies in Honor of Jacob M. Myers* [ed. H. N. Bream, R. D. Helm, and C. A. Moore; Philadelphia: Temple Univ. Press, 1974], 25–32).

13–14 The "rules of the contest" are that each candidate can ask for anything she wishes to take with her to the king's palace, presumably in order to make herself memorable enough to be summoned again by name. That presumption, of course, assumes that the contestants *want* to be recalled. It may also be that whatever they ask for is their "payment"; the story does not indicate what the items might have been or whether they could keep them. After one night with the king, the woman is a concubine, and if she is not summoned (passive) by name, she spends the rest of her life in the harem, reduced to essential widowhood (Baldwin, 68).

That the women are brought to the king in the evening is a notable detail; Esther's later daytime arrival (5:1) is clearly an aberration in more ways than one. It is not entirely clear where a young woman goes when she leaves the king's bedroom in the morning. "Another part of the harem" is literally "the second house of women," but the grammar is somewhat awkward (see Notes). Perhaps this is yet another of the manifold ways in which the text emphasizes *two*. Wherever they are located, there is a special separate keeper for the used concubines.

Xerxes was out of Susa for the duration of the war. Now that he is back, his pleasure is the primary concern, and the harem has to operate accordingly.

NOTES

12 In the context of his narrative about Smerdis, Herodotus (3.69) notes that the wives of Persian nobles came to them by turns.

The function of the incense burners has been elucidated by names of spices inscribed on numerous examples from Southern Arabia and a nineteenth-century description of the process as it was still used at that time. This should be read, however, with Clines, 289, who cautions about applying material from nineteenth-century Ethiopia to the Persian period. The verbal root מרק (*mrq*) connotes rubbing, scouring, and cleansing (BDB; *HALOT*).

14 If the young women were taken to a "second harem," there should be a definite article on שֵׁנִי (*šēnî*) to modify "harem." But שֵׁנִית (*šēnît*) may mean "again" and modify the verb "returned" with the omission of the final letter—a construction that is not unusual (Gordis, "Studies in the Esther Narrative," 54; though Haupt, 118, discounts the idea).

5. The Turn of Esther (2:15–18)

> ¹⁵When the turn came for Esther (the girl Mordecai had adopted, the daughter of his uncle Abihail) to go to the king, she asked for nothing other than what Hegai, the king's eunuch who was in charge of the harem, suggested. And Esther won the favor of

everyone who saw her. ¹⁶She was taken to King Xerxes in the royal residence in the tenth month, the month of Tebeth, in the seventh year of his reign.

¹⁷Now the king was attracted to Esther more than to any of the other women, and she won his favor and approval more than any of the other virgins. So he set a royal crown on her head and made her queen instead of Vashti. ¹⁸And the king gave a great banquet, Esther's banquet, for all his nobles and officials. He proclaimed a holiday throughout the provinces and distributed gifts with royal liberality.

COMMENTARY

15 In one of the Scroll's characteristic parentheses, Esther's Jewish identity is given just as she is about to cross the threshold into the king's palace, not a likely place for a young Jewish woman. She is, the reader is reminded, the daughter of Abihail and adopted daughter of Mordecai, but she will emerge as the queen (Berman, 650). Her strategy is contrasted with that of the other candidates. She distances herself from the tawdry flamboyance of the court, and her success is due to her restraint in taking with her only what Hegai, who knows the king's tastes, advises. Chances are that Hegai also knows women quite well and knows precisely what will enhance Esther's already distinctive beauty. The narrative is reserved, but the reader is to surmise that she expects to engage in the same activity as all the others, albeit in a significantly different manner without the excess of adornment.

While Esther won favor in connection with Hegai, who oversaw her and was her superior for that period of time (see v.9), more publicly she wins grace (ḥēn)—a probable testimony both to her stunning beauty and to her demeanor. There is a hint here that the route to the king's bedroom may have customarily involved a bit of a parade.

16 Here is the final instance in which Esther is taken. Even though the narrative depicts her passiv-ity in the human sphere, providentially it is at this point that she reaches the place she is supposed to be (see 4:14) in order for the deliverance of the Jews to take place. She is taken "to King Xerxes in his royal residence [bêt malkûtô]" in the tenth month of the seventh year of his reign. Four years had elapsed since the removal of Vashti. This fact fits well with the intervening interval on the battlefront. If Xerxes had only just returned from war when the mobilization for young women began, then presumably Hegai has moved Esther to the front of the line.

17 The king's response to Esther is striking. Whereas the emotional focus of the preceding narrative was his pleasure (ḥāpēṣ) in regard to the women brought to him, the king "loves" (ʾhb) Esther. Not only that—she wins grace *and* favor (ḥēn wāḥesed) above all the virgins who have visited him. The narrative has prepared for this development by indicating that Esther won ḥesed in the eyes of Hegai and ḥēn from all who were around her. Now both expressions come together to describe her complete conquest of the king. He places on her head the crown, the same diadem that Vashti refused to wear (1:11).

18 Appropriate for a coronation, there is an immense court celebration and there are empire-wide ramifications. The great banquet for nobles and officials, specifically noted as being for Esther, closes the look at the seemingly innocuous side of the Persian court. In the context of this third banquet, there are subtle contrasts with Vashti. She refused the crown; Esther wears it. Vashti banqueted with the women; the king prepares this banquet for Esther.

There are also parallels with the end of the narrative. Just as the provinces enjoyed a holiday (*ḥᵃnāḥâ*, "rest") at this point, so after the deliverance from their enemies the Jews will have rest (*nôaḥ*), both on the fourteenth and fifteenth days of Adar (9:16–18). The king's generosity is likewise mirrored by giving gifts as part of the initial and subsequent Purim celebrations (9:19).

Máśʾēt (GK 5368) means something "lifted up" and could imply exemption from military and forced labor requirements or amnesty (Bush, 358). That the war with Greece, for which vast numbers of troops and provisions had been mobilized (Herodotus 7.60–100), was recently over could have something to do with sending military conscripts home. More likely, however, the mention of *máśʾēt* in the context of a great feast specifically refers to gifts of food (see Jer 40:5; Am 5:11). That the word indicates a remission of taxes is an interpretation based on the reinstatement of taxation in Esther 10:1. While this interpretation is possibly correct (see Herodotus 3.67), the two occasions may not be connected.

NOTES

16 Tebeth, corresponding to December/January, is a wet and cold month even in Susa.

17 It is unclear just what אהב (*ʾhb*; GK 170) means in this context. It is a generic word for "love." Judith Rosenheim (131, 142–43) presents the possibility that Esther does not conquer Xerxes by seductive wiles and sexual expertise but by something distinctive and therefore challenging about her character. She depicts Esther as operating very much in the sphere of Hellenistic virtues. Levenson, 62, notes that there is no mention in the text that Xerxes marries Esther, perhaps to downplay an apparent violation of biblical norms.

6. Doings at the Gate (2:19–23)

¹⁹When the virgins were assembled a second time, Mordecai was sitting at the king's gate. ²⁰But Esther had kept secret her family background and nationality just as Mordecai had told her to do, for she continued to follow Mordecai's instructions as she had done when he was bringing her up.

²¹During the time Mordecai was sitting at the king's gate, Bigthana and Teresh, two of the king's officers who guarded the doorway, became angry and conspired to assassinate King Xerxes. ²²But Mordecai found out about the plot and told Queen Esther, who in turn reported it to the king, giving credit to Mordecai. ²³And when the report was investigated and found to be true, the two officials were hanged on a gallows. All this was recorded in the book of the annals in the presence of the king.

COMMENTARY

19 The two parts of this verse represent an odd juxtaposition. Clearly, the second gathering of virgins sets the context for Mordecai's presence at the gate, but there is no indication as to what precisely it represents, when it occurs, or why. The *waw* conjunction before "when [they] were assembled" suggests a connection to what has just transpired. In that case, perhaps there is a large assemblage of virgins as part of the celebrations, but why they are gathered is not clear. If the king is indeed pleased with Esther, maintaining an overextended harem will not be necessary. But it is also possible that the king's attendants who know him well have a regular routine for keeping the harem full.

Because eunuchs were integral to the process of herding virgins, and because the two would-be assassins discovered by Mordecai at the gate are eunuchs (v.21), the narrator may have felt it important to note this particular event as background for that discovery. It might also be that "second" is yet another linguistic indicator of the "twos" in the text, always moving toward two days for Purim.

The significant element for the continuing story is Mordecai's position in the king's gate, a locus of authority where administrative and judicial activities occurred and where information abounded, leading to both intrigue and bids for power. The gate marked a boundary; guards were an integral part of gate areas, and those guards were often eunuchs. Mordecai's presence at the gate is noted multiple times (2:21; 3:2; 5:9, 13; 6:10, 12), but the narrative does not indicate when or how he achieved that prominence.

The early versions suggest that Mordecai had already been strategically positioned there. Equally possible, Esther may have gotten him the appointment to give him a means of access to her now

that she is royalty and his previous avenues into the harem are no longer sufficient to reach the queen. If the second gathering of virgins has to do with major changes in the harem's structure, this occasion would be a good one to get him repositioned. At the same time, the uproar is good cover for the workings of the plot.

20 That Esther's secrecy regarding her people and kin and Mordecai's command to keep silent in that regard are reiterated intimate the ominous and undefined nature of some threat. Mordecai seems to have been keenly aware of potential danger and, given the nature of his daily activities, he is likely privy to a good deal of subsurface menace. This text is striking in its demonstration of the depth of nurturing represented by 'ōmēn (Mordecai's guardianship of Esther). The term reappears here from the initial description of their relationship. Even though Esther's status has changed radically, she still does what Mordecai tells her to do. This obedience reaches its critical point when he changes course and exhorts her to reveal her identity.

21 After the parenthetical note of v.20, the narrative resumes. The repetition of the fact that Mordecai is in the gate stresses its importance. In those chaotic days when there are more young virgins milling about, officials who are eunuchs are guarding the gate. Among them are Bigthana and Teresh, the former of whom may be the same as Bigtha (1:10), one of the royal eunuchs commanded to fetch Vashti. The reason for their anger is not given, but it is sufficient to hatch the assassination plot. Because they are "keepers of the threshold," they have access into the king's private chambers. In fact, Xerxes was ultimately assassinated in 465 BC because one of his attendants allowed the captain of the bodyguard into his bedroom (Diodorus Siculus 11.69; Ctesias, *Persica* 29).

22 The covert nature of Mordecai's discovery is implied in the passive (lit.) "the matter was known to Mordecai"; his sources are not divulged. As a loyal subject of the king, he informs Esther, who in turn tells the king but gives Mordecai the credit. Although it might strain credulity to think he would have this kind of access and their relationship still would not be known, it is conceivable that anyone who became aware of an assassination plot and was indeed loyal to the king, who had developed communication avenues in and out of various levels of court activities, and who would like to contemplate advancement in the political sphere might use some of that intricate network to get the information where it ought to be. It is noteworthy that at this point Esther has no problem getting a message to the king.

23 In keeping with Persian impersonal bureaucracy, the matter is investigated, the two instigators are found and hung, and a notice is written—all recorded in the passive voice. This event may account for a further degree of latent hostility between Mordecai and the others at the gate, who have little inclination to protect him later (3:4).

Hanging "on wood" (ʿal-ʿēṣ) would have meant either impalement or crucifixion in the Persian period. It is unlikely it denotes death by hanging; more likely the hanging is public humiliation by exposure of the body after death (Laniak, 61; Bush, 373). The same would be true of Haman's intent to shame Mordecai by hoisting his body on such a high and exposed stake. This punishment by hanging is an adumbration of what will ultimately happen to the scoundrel Haman and his sons.

"Recorded ... in the presence of [lipnê] the king" does not necessarily mean that he watches it happen but that it is ready to be presented to him; in other words, it is at his disposal. The same is true of the lots being cast lipnê Haman (3:7); the act fulfills his orders (Haupt, 122). Nevertheless, that the king should have acknowledged the event but does not is a problem of honor that readers and hearers of the story will take note of (Laniak, 68). Because Persian kings were careful to give rewards, it was a noticeable affront when Mordecai is not rewarded—hence the king's immediate concern to honor Mordecai in ch. 6. It is a matter of the *king's* honor as well.

NOTES

19 Paton, 186–88, presents a comprehensive summary of the scholarly opinions as to what the second gathering of virgins might have meant. They range from its being a parade of "latecomers" to the king's insatiable appetite that necessitates a constant supply of new material even though Esther has become queen. "Second" is not in the Greek versions but that is possibly due to the inability of the ancient translators to make sense of the text. Gordis ("Studies in the Esther Narrative," 47–48; *Megillat Esther*, 30) suggests that it was a second procession that simply accentuated Esther's overwhelming beauty above all the others. Elizabeth Groves ("Double Take: Another Look at the Second Gathering of Virgins in Esther 2:19a," in *The Book of Esther in Modern Research* [ed. Sidnie White Crawford and Leonard J. Greenspoon; London: T&T Clark, 2003], 91–111) makes the case that it was a dramatic necessity, thus giving another indication of the king's reckless use of women and Esther's understandable apprehension at appearing before him after thirty days (4:11).

20 The final clause is awkward in Hebrew. A most literal rendition is: "as she was during her upbringing with him," reading בְּאָמְנָה (bᵉʾomnâ) as an infinitive construct with a third feminine singular suffix (without *mappiq*).

23 Chronicles were kept in the Persian Empire (Herodotus 7.100; 8.85, 90). Herodotus 8.85 is particularly helpful in that it recorded two men by name, Theomestor and Phylacus, the latter of whom was named a benefactor of the king and was given much land.

II. THE CONFLICTS—"FOR SUCH A TIME AS THIS" (3:1–4:17)

A. Mordecai Threatens the Honor of Haman (3:1–5)

¹After these events, King Xerxes honored Haman son of Hammedatha, the Agagite, elevating him and giving him a seat of honor higher than that of all the other nobles. ²All the royal officials at the king's gate knelt down and paid honor to Haman, for the king had commanded this concerning him. But Mordecai would not kneel down or pay him honor.

³Then the royal officials at the king's gate asked Mordecai, "Why do you disobey the king's command?" ⁴Day after day they spoke to him but he refused to comply. Therefore they told Haman about it to see whether Mordecai's behavior would be tolerated, for he had told them he was a Jew.

⁵When Haman saw that Mordecai would not kneel down or pay him honor, he was enraged.

COMMENTARY

1 The narrative is stunningly understated as this chapter commences. In fact, five years have elapsed between the foiled coup at the end of ch. 2 and Haman's rise to power (cf. 3:7), and there are hints at significant changes in the interval. The plethora of named advisers surrounding the king has disappeared and Haman is singularly empowered in their place, perhaps as the result of security measures imposed by the threatened king (Hazony, 44–51).

Haman's full identification occurs four times in the book of Esther (3:1, 10; 8:5; 9:24), two at the outset of his career as "enemy of the Jews," and two after his death. The king makes Haman great, lifts him up, and seats him *over* others, thus creating a hierarchy. The use of three verbs instead of the usual two indicates the significance of this elevation. In addition, it is Haman who is honored (*giddēl*, "to make great") instead of the expected promotion of Mordecai. No reason is given for his advancement, but it is conceivable that he schemed to make this happen. In the complex web of gate politics, he may have had connections with the two eunuchs whose plot Mordecai uncovered; the LXX suggests as much in the First Addition.

2 In contrast to Haman's singular elevation, this verse begins with the picture of all the royal officials (lit., "servants of the king") kneeling and paying homage to Haman. "Kneeling down and paying honor" is another in the pattern of doublets, and the interpretation is critical for the narrative. The terms specifically mean "to bend [the knee]" and "to fall on one's face." The participles may suggest a continual bowing and scraping, perhaps an intentionally ludicrous and humiliating posture. Because the king has commanded this exercise, it has his approval and does not mean something untoward from the political standpoint. The implication of v.4 is that Mordecai's refusal has to do with his being Jewish. Given the pervasive pattern of dyads, the two terms may simply be stylistic and lack any overtones of worship or idolatry. If so, the primary issue is simply the longstanding enmity between Israel and Amalek and the corporate honor of Mordecai's people.

Nevertheless, both actions show humility and recognition of a superior. While there are instances in the biblical text when Israelites bowed to kings (1Sa 24:8; 2Sa 14:4; 18:28; 1Ki 1:16) and to other superiors (Ge 23:7; 27:29; 33:3), the expressions are not the same. Here the terms are *kōr^eʿîm* *ûmištaḥ^awîm*. The same pair of words does not occur in any of the passages describing homage to another human. Instead, when these two verbs are used together, the individual is performing them in the presence of God (2Ch 7:3; 29:29; Pss 22:29; 95:6). This event takes place in the gate complex, which is sufficiently expansive as to prevent Haman's noticing the noncompliance of Mordecai until informed.

3 The "servants of the king" take upon themselves the role of gate "police," making certain that those who frequent the gate area meet all the demands of court protocol. There is clearly an enforced uniformity, and Mordecai's behavior is both civil disobedience of the king's law and a public affront to the honor of Haman. Their question is a challenge. Not only is Haman's honor at stake — theirs is, too, if one of their rank or lower is going to get by without submitting to what may have been an indignity.

4 In that spirit they keep after Mordecai day after day, but he (lit.) "did not listen to them," an expression that often denotes disobedience. Nevertheless, he does give the servants an explanation. His not bowing has everything to do with his Jewish identity. In reporting this information to Haman, the servants want to determine "if the *dibrê* [of] Mordecai will stand." *Dibrê* (GK 1821) is variously interpreted as "words," "attitude," or "actions." If it intimates "words," his claim of Jewishness might imply that he is depending on an ethnic and religious exemption. If the general idea is attitude and the accompanying action, the servants are keen to see whether perceived defiance will be tolerated.

Their decision to tell Haman represents malevolent intent. Up to this point, Haman has not noticed and may have gone on being oblivious, but once the servants know Mordecai is Jewish, they not only cease trying to persuade him to bow as they have been doing, but they also turn the matter over to Haman. Perhaps there are in the crowd some who retain resentment over Mordecai's having informed against Bigthana and Teresh — their tattling would be a means of avenging that perceived treachery. Perhaps something is afoot in the empire and being Jewish is problematic.

Mordecai has been hiding his identity for the same reasons that he told Esther to keep her Jewishness secret. Whenever it is that he divulges the information and why, the narrative links the divulgence directly with the report of the servants to Haman. They do not need any further explanation, but on the basis of his Judaism they understand the reason for his opposition to the king's decree, report it seemingly immediately, and do not hesitate to identify the issue as a "Jewish problem" (note v.6).

5 Haman's rage may stem from several points. For one thing, this public affront to his honor has been taking place for some time (lit., "was not kneeling or bowing down"), and he has failed to notice it—a true humiliation. If the ethnic feud contributes equally to his antipathy as well as Mordecai's, that feud may also explain why he is "enraged."

NOTES

1 That Haman came to be representative of Israel's archenemy no matter what the time period is indicated by the LXX's rendition of his name as "Haman, son of Hammedatha, a Bougean" (3:1) and "the Macedonian" (9:24). See Jobes, "How an Assassination Changed the Greek Text of Esther," *ZAW* 110 (1998): 75–78; and Michael Wechsler, "The Appellation BOUGAIOS and Ethnic Contextualization in the Greek Text of Esther," *VT* 51/1 (2001): 109–14.

2 See Paton, 196–97; Moore, *Esther*, 36; Fox, 42–45; and Laniak, 70, n. 7, 75–78, for reviews of the proposed reasons why Mordecai refuses to bow. Persians regularly bowed to high-ranking officials (Herodotus 1.134). Herodotus reports, however, an incident in which Spartans who, when they came into the presence of the king and were commanded to "fall down and do obeisance" to the king, refused because it was not their custom to do obeisance to humans (7.135–36). Jewish sages and medieval scholars almost uniformly claim that some form of idolatry was involved in the act (Walfish, 178–79).

4 עָמַד דָּבָר (ʿmd dābār) is a late biblical Hebrew idiom referring to the validity of the word (Bush, 379). It is on the basis of the officials' treachery that Joseph Fleishman ("Why Was Haman Successful at Winning King Ahasuerus' Approval to Exterminate the Jews in the Persian Empire?" *HUCA* 68 [1997]: 35–49 [Hebrew]) and others maintain that already there were strong currents of anti-Judaism spread throughout the empire.

B. Haman Threatens the Existence of Mordecai and His People (3:6–4:3)

1. Haman's Plan for Vengeance (3:6–9)

> [6]Yet having learned who Mordecai's people were, he scorned the idea of killing only Mordecai. Instead Haman looked for a way to destroy all Mordecai's people, the Jews, throughout the whole kingdom of Xerxes.
>
> [7]In the twelfth year of King Xerxes, in the first month, the month of Nisan, they cast the *pur* (that is, the lot) in the presence of Haman to select a day and month. And the lot fell on the twelfth month, the month of Adar.

> [8]Then Haman said to King Xerxes, "There is a certain people dispersed and scattered among the peoples in all the provinces of your kingdom whose customs are different from those of all other people and who do not obey the king's laws; it is not in the king's best interest to tolerate them. [9]If it pleases the king, let a decree be issued to destroy them, and I will put ten thousand talents of silver into the royal treasury for the men who carry out this business."

COMMENTARY

6 Having been humiliated, Haman formulates a massive retaliation by which he intends the ultimate dishonoring of Mordecai and his people's utter annihilation. "People of Mordecai" is repeated twice. First, Haman is informed of their relationship to Mordecai; then they become the object of his vicious intent. Something—perhaps the long-standing ethnic enmity between the descendants of Saul and those of Agag, or more widely brewing anti-Semitism—so inflames Haman that he hatches a plan for ethnic cleansing. His plan for comprehensive destruction is the lashing out of injured pride.

7 The Hebrew text begins, "in the first month, the month of Nisan," a pointed reminder of Passover and that great deliverance. It is in the twelfth year of the king's reign, five years since the events of ch. 2—both the accession of Esther to the throne and Mordecai's unacknowledged exposure of the assassination attempt. On the significance of *pûr* (GK 7052) and the wider cultural practices of consulting the gods regarding the fate of humans, see the Introduction: Purposes of the Text. That *pûr*, noticeably without the definite article, is identified as "the lot" (*haggôrāl*; GK 1598) indicates that initial audiences would have been unfamiliar with *pûr* but knew well the practice of casting lots.

In fact, the biblical text attests to the use of lots in regard to a wide range of activities (Lev 16:8;

Jos 15:1, 17:1; Jdg 20:9; Ne 11:1; Jnh 1:7). It was a mechanism for determining the Lord's direction (Pr 16:33). Casting lots was a common practice in the ancient Near East at large. "Cast" in this context has an indefinite subject, which could be read as equivalent to the passive, "the lot was cast" (Bush, 377), or as referring to a nameless "professional" called in for the occasion (Fox, 47).

The verse as it stands in the MT does not indicate the full determination produced by the lot. Literally it reads, "from day to day and from month to month, twelfth." The LXX added an indication of which day of the month, in other words, the thirteenth. A line may have fallen out by *homoioteleuton*, resulting from the eye of the scribe moving from one *ḥōdeš* to a second one (Torrey, 19–20 n. 9; Bush, 381). It may be, however, that the text tersely identified the month of the proposed slaughter but the narrator chose to sustain the suspense through Haman's audience with the king before indicating that it will indeed be the thirteenth day, as written in the edict. In any case, Haman is methodical in arranging his murderous plan.

8 Haman has unrestricted access to the king, a privilege not extended to the rest of the people, including the queen. Haman's keeping his charge vague is indispensable to gaining the permission he is seeking. His description is insidious, and the opening line carries a double edge. "A certain people" (ʿam-ʾeḥād) makes the Jews sound sinister, in that they are unnamed, and yet they are only "one" people and therefore insignificant and dispensable. Repressing the name of the people precludes identifying *individuals*, such as Mordecai, who is known as "the Jew."

Haman's presentation starts with the truth; they are indeed a "dispersed" (mᵉpuzzār) people and, in some ways, separated. The Pual participle (mᵉpōrād) is used only here and may be intended to stress that they are intentionally unassimilated (Bush, 381). The accusation then moves to a half-truth — that they have different customs — and finally to an outright lie — that they do not keep the laws of the king. Haman carefully does not tell the king which laws are not kept. If pressed, the only one he may have cited would be the command to bow to him!

Haman's final ploy is to put the matter in pragmatic terms; "it is not in the king's best interest to tolerate them" (lit., "it is not worthwhile for the king to let them rest"). The final word of the verse is an adumbration of the "rest" the Jews do indeed finally experience, but at this point it is a long way off. Haman's tantalizing carrot of "worthwhile" will be followed up with concrete means for addressing the problem that will, at the same time, enrich the king (v.9).

9 Prefaced by the obligatory "if it pleases the king," Haman proposes a decree as the solution. The passive "let it be written for their destruction" removes responsibility from any one person (the king or Haman) and places it with the unnamed bureaucracy (Fox, 51). Haman's offer of 10,000 talents is estimated to have been approximately 60 percent of the annual revenue of the Persian Empire. Its total revenue under Darius had been 14,560 talents (Herodotus 3.95; Olmstead, 297–98). Clearly Haman, as the second person in a kingdom where despots likely amassed huge amounts of wealth, has

considerable resources. The stated sum, however, seems to be even beyond those bounds.

One possible explanation is that he intends at least part of this payoff to come from looting the property of the Jews, even though he makes it sound as though the money will come from his own coffers. The literal rendition of the Hebrew is, "I will weigh to the hands of those who do the work, to bring to the royal treasuries." Haman thus expects to be able to pay further reward; the loot will pour in, and he can use it to pay those who bring additional plunder — a scam from antiquity with lethal consequences. This is a clear appeal to the greed of the king and, if Xerxes' resources had been seriously depleted by the war effort, it would be quite tempting (Paton, 206). It is also an indication of the ferocity of Haman's hatred of the Jews.

There is a further possible devilish facet to Haman's presentation to the king, and here we must presume that the narrator of the Hebrew text is careful to preserve in translation a significant wordplay in the original dialogue. Haman may have intentionally played on the similar sounds of lᵉʾabᵉdām ("to annihilate them") and laᶜăbādîm ("for slaves"). If that intent was indeed purposeful, it would explain Haman's appeal in the preceding verse to the value of not allowing this unnamed people to "rest." It may also provide an interpretive framework for understanding Esther's later reference to the effect that if they had only been sold into slavery, she would have kept silent (7:4). Finally, this wordplay may also explain why the king seems so obtuse in ch. 7 about the decree to which Esther refers. He was led to believe Haman's intent was enslavement when it really was wholesale murder.

It is significant that in speaking to the king, this term is the only one Haman uses; when the decree is written with its triple terminology, there is no mistake as to what he means. (See Berg, 101–2; Bechtel, 42–43; and Walfish, 185–89, who notes that the alternative connotations of this word were the focus of at least one medieval exegete.)

NOTES

7 On the use of lots in the ancient Near East, see Herodotus 3.128; Xenophon *Cyropaedia* 1.6.46; Hallo, "The First Purim," *BA* 46/1 (1983): 19–26. Paton, 201–2, suggests that Haman's reason for casting the lot was not initially to determine the day for the slaughter but to find a propitious day for approaching the king with his scheme.

8 The paradox of diaspora identity is reflected in the accusation, to be *dispersed and one* at the same time (Beal, 58–59). "One" implies a "threatening solidarity" that was peculiar and exclusivist on top of being scattered and rebellious. This position was obviously a severe threat to the empire and to the king (Laniak, 85–86). The Second Targum puts into the mouth of Haman a litany of venomous and inflammatory accusations that reflect anti-Semitic rhetoric from that period and ever since. Likewise, the accusation in the Greek *A*-Text calls them warlike, disobedient, and wicked (Clines, 223).

9 "The men who carry out this business" refers to officials in the king's administration (cf. 9:3) responsible for handling the monetary aspects of this exchange. Such wholesale massacres, particularly of groups perceived to be different and threatening, have been endemic throughout human history. Contemporaries of Xerxes would have known of the slaughter of the Magi after the discovery of Smerdis the Magus's usurpation of the throne (Herodotus 3.64–80).

2. The Royal Machinery Operates (3:10–15)

[10]So the king took his signet ring from his finger and gave it to Haman son of Hammedatha, the Agagite, the enemy of the Jews. [11]"Keep the money," the king said to Haman, "and do with the people as you please."

[12]Then on the thirteenth day of the first month the royal secretaries were summoned. They wrote out in the script of each province and in the language of each people all Haman's orders to the king's satraps, the governors of the various provinces and the nobles of the various peoples. These were written in the name of King Xerxes himself and sealed with his own ring. [13]Dispatches were sent by couriers to all the king's provinces with the order to destroy, kill and annihilate all the Jews — young and old, women and little children — on a single day, the thirteenth day of the twelfth month, the month of Adar, and to plunder their goods. [14]A copy of the text of the edict was to be issued as law in every province and made known to the people of every nationality so they would be ready for that day.

[15]Spurred on by the king's command, the couriers went out, and the edict was issued in the citadel of Susa. The king and Haman sat down to drink, but the city of Susa was bewildered.

COMMENTARY

10-11 The cavalier manner in which the king accepts Haman's request to destroy an entire people accompanied by a monumental bribe is shocking. If he is under the illusion that this is a sale for enslavement and that it is for the good of his realm because this people pose some sort of threat (see comments on v.9), his response may be somewhat more understandable. Nevertheless, he does dismiss them with a wave of the signet ring, while addressing first the money and then the people! At the point that Xerxes hands over his signet ring, in which was vested the royal authority, Haman's full name reappears, followed by the epithet, "adversary of the Jews." The term is stronger than "enemy" (*sōnēh*, "one who hates"); it is *ṣōrēr*, "one who causes distress."

The king's response regarding the financial arrangements may reflect a delicate and perhaps protracted bargaining process in which a polite refusal ("the money is given to you") is simply the first stage (Gordis, *Megillat Esther*, 36). In the final round, it seems that the king does accept Haman's offer in some form as Mordecai will report a financial transaction (4:7) and Esther declares that her people have been "sold" (7:4). While there may have been some purposeful ambiguity regarding the money and the meaning of *ʾbd*, once the king tells Haman to keep the money and deal with the people as he wishes, Haman's decree adds the chilling and unmistakable "kill" and "destroy." The king never asks for clarification but gives Haman free reign to do as he wishes; he consigns an entire people to slaughter or slavery and promptly forgets about it—as indicated in ch. 7.

12 The previous mention of Nisan (v.7) was a veiled allusion to Passover. Now the implications are brought full force; the decree is written on the thirteenth of Nisan, the day before Passover. At the time when the children of Israel traditionally recited the narrative of deliverance from the bondage of Egypt, they will instead face the horrifying prospect of annihilation under another foreign oppressor.

The bureaucratic machinery moves back into action. The scribes are summoned, and everything that *Haman* demands is written in the name of the king and sealed with his signet ring; the text uses a passive verb to indicate each action. The all-inclusive list of recipients starts at the top with the satraps, followed by governors of provinces, and finally the nobles or princes of each ethnic entity. The process for dealing with linguistic differences is standardized (cf. 1:22); each province again receives a dispatch in its script and each people group according to its spoken language. Nevertheless, there is more emphasis this time on assuring comprehensive distribution.

13 *Nišlôaḥ* ("sent") is another of the pattern of infinitive absolutes that continues the movement of the narrative. Although *rāṣîm* originally meant "runners," here in keeping with the efficiency of the Persian postal system (Herodotus 5.52–53; 8.98), they are mounted (cf. 8:10). In contrast to the sense of distance and noninvolvement created by the repeated use of the passive voice, the decree enjoins action. They are to destroy, to kill, and to annihilate all Jews, young and old, women and children, in one day—and to take spoil. With so much of the text in doublets, the force of *three* verbs in quick succession followed by the comprehensive list of victims is unmistakable. The closure granted free-for-all looting after all the rightful owners and potential heirs are disposed of in one day.

It has been objected that the issuance of the decree eleven months ahead of time is nonsense because it would allow the Jews time to escape, but this decree is comprehensive of the empire; defining and traveling to a safe haven would not be that easy. In addition, if some decide to leave, they forfeit all their property and Haman accomplishes his goal of ridding the empire of Jews and confiscating their goods. The situation has had its counterparts throughout subsequent history.

14 This verse serves to instruct the designated political leaders at each level who receive the dispatches (cf. v.12). The contents are to be made public so that everyone will be prepared for this day. Haman's vicious scheme depends on the suspicions and hatred between those who differ from Jews and the Jews themselves, fueled by the promise of plunder (Bush, 387). The waiting period of eleven months will serve to inflame passions more and create added fear among the Jews because there is no place to which to escape.

15 The verse structure in Hebrew is unusual in that all four clauses begin with nouns instead of the standard verb, and each of these nouns is positioned to highlight the complexity of responses. The couriers are pressed to the far reaches of the empire where, as we learn from ch. 9, huge numbers of people rally to the cause, even after the counter-decree. At the same time the edict is issued in the citadel. The king and Haman have a private celebration, notable for its callous tone after the immensity of their crime.

The population of Susa, significantly last in the list, is genuinely agitated (*nābôkâ*) about the decree, although we are not told why or what form this takes. In fact, a significant part of the confusion may be due to a vast and tangled complex of varying responses, from horror to unrestrained glee. They are distinguished from the elite of the citadel—a minority that has mandated the bloodshed from where the edict was initially promulgated.

NOTES

11 That נתן (*ntn*) may have multiple and ambiguous implications in a bargaining process is evident from Abraham's negotiating with the sons of Heth and Ephron for the cave of Machpelah. The word is used with both the connotation of "sell" (Ge 23:9, 13) and the supposed-but-not-real intent to give (Ge 23:11).

13 At this juncture, the LXX includes a significant addition purporting to be the text of the king's letter. In the LXX, the king is Artaxerxes. It is self-congratulatory regarding peace and quiet in the empire; it heaps praise on Haman for his wisdom, goodwill, and fidelity; it presents the threat to the aforementioned stability that is posed by the "certain malignant people"; and it confirms the destruction decreed by Haman for the *fourteenth* day of the month of Adar. Levenson, 75, notes that it is like a first-century text in 3 Maccabees 3:12–29, a letter of Ptolemy Philopater slandering the Alexandrian Jews and decreeing their annihilation. (On the use of the infinitive absolute, see GKC 113z; Joüon 123x,y.)

14 פַּתְשֶׁגֶן (*patšegen*) is only used in Esther and is a Persian loanword meaning "copy." A variant of it, *paršegen* appears four times in Ezra, both in the Aramaic and the Hebrew sections.

15 Even this chapter contains the structurally important banquet theme as the king and Haman sit down to "drink." נְבוֹכָה (*nābôkâ*) implies an agitated and tumultuous state (cf. Ex 14:3; Joel 1:18).

3. The Jews in Mourning (4:1–3)

> [1]When Mordecai learned of all that had been done, he tore his clothes, put on sackcloth and ashes, and went out into the city, wailing loudly and bitterly. [2]But he went only as far as the king's gate, because no one clothed in sackcloth was allowed to enter it. [3]In every province to which the edict and order of the king came, there was great mourning among the Jews, with fasting, weeping and wailing. Many lay in sackcloth and ashes.

COMMENTARY

1–2 As in 3:15, the normal Hebrew syntax of verb first, followed by subject, is reversed; Mordecai's name is first. The intelligence network in the gate area is thorough; he knows more than the general contents of the decree. "All that had been done," a continuation of the passive, indicates his sources have provided him with the details, even to the payment for the extermination (4:7).

Mordecai's response is visibly and audibly evident. Torn garments and sackcloth made of coarse goat- or camelhair were the clothing of exposure and self-humiliation. Dust and ashes were reminders of death's destruction of the flesh. These practices symbolized ritual impurity and separation from God (Laniak, 92–94). Because of the inherent shame signified by sackcloth, it was not allowed to sully the arena of power in the king's gate. The extreme bitterness of Mordecai's outcry (lit., "he cried a great cry") is due not only to the threat posed to his people, but also to the weight of his own responsibility in the circumstances that led to this point. His refusal to bow to Haman has been escalated to a crisis for the entirety of his people. His choice of location, however, is also indicative of a further motive in his public outcry. It is the best way to get Esther's attention and move her into action. In the seclusion of the palace, she is not even aware that anything has happened.

3 Mordecai's grieving on the individual level is mirrored and amplified as entire Jewish populations lament openly. Fasting was a prominent feature of their mourning and is a counterpoint to the feasting that is prevalent throughout the text. The fast is particularly striking in light of the proximity of Passover, which commences the following day. While the events in Susa unfold immediately, it is left to the imagination to contemplate the effect of the edict's arriving on or shortly after Passover. The final clause of the verse is literally "sackcloth and ashes spread out by many," again employing the passive mode and suggesting that the sackcloth is spread out as the Jews prostrate themselves in mourning (Baldwin, 77). There is nothing subdued about their response to this horrifying news.

NOTES

1 Because sackcloth was characteristically made of goats' hair, it would have been black (*HALOT*), thus adding to the symbolism. It was either bound about the person or covered him. Rending garments as an expression of deep anguish appears repeatedly throughout Israelite history, from Reuben's dismay at the absence of Joseph from the pit (Ge 37:29) to the siege of Jerusalem in Hezekiah's time (2Ki 18:37) and Ezra's grief at his people's sin (Ezr 9:3). The prophetic testimony incorporated dramatic actions in calls for repentance, particularly echoed in Joel 2:12−14. The torn garments were not only part of Israelite culture but also more widely indicative of mourning (Herodotus 8.99; M. E. Vogelzang and W. J. van Bekkum, "Meaning and Symbolism of Clothing in Ancient Near Eastern Texts," in *Scripta Signa Vocis* [ed. H. L. J. Vanstiphout et al.; Gröningen: Egbert Forsten, 1986], 269−71).

3 The passive יֻצַּע (*yuṣṣaʿ* [Hophal]) is followed by the *lamed* of agency, meaning "by many" (Torrey, 37). The verb occurs twice in Isaiah: in 14:11, where the bed of the nefarious ruler of Babylon will be spread out in Sheol, and 58:5, in conjunction with people lying in sackcloth and ashes as part of a fast.

C. Mordecai and Esther Face Off (4:4−17)

1. Esther Challenges Mordecai (4:4−5)

⁴When Esther's maids and eunuchs came and told her about Mordecai, she was in great distress. She sent clothes for him to put on instead of his sackcloth, but he would not accept them. ⁵Then Esther summoned Hathach, one of the king's eunuchs assigned to attend her, and ordered him to find out what was troubling Mordecai and why.

COMMENTARY

4 The communication network that has allowed Mordecai to keep watch on Esther and maintain some kind of contact with her through the years since her accession to the throne has been low profile. At this point, however, Mordecai's actions are dangerously unsuitable given her position. The Hebrew uses the title "the queen" as the subject of "was in great distress" (*tithalḥal*, a *hapax legomenon*), and her reaction hints of embarrassment.

By dispatching clothing to Mordecai Esther attempts to quell his outburst as effectively and quickly as possible, lest it have bad ramifications for her. His traditional reaction appears extreme, and the ritual sackcloth appears acutely distasteful and unseemly. Esther has spent five years functioning according to court protocol and is undoubtedly concerned for what the *king* will think and how he will respond (cf. 4:11). At this point, the dis-

tance between Mordecai the Jew and Esther the Persian queen is significant. That Mordecai refuses to remove his sackcloth is indicative of his complete identity with the national crisis.

5 Cutting through what is probably a flurry of attendants, Esther summons Hathach, appointed to serve her, and sends him to Mordecai. She must have a high degree of trust in Hathach and will have even more cause to do so as the sensitivity of this situation unfolds. *Ṣawwēh ʿal* (cf. the preposition here) has the sense of "to enjoin upon" (Haupt, 134). The same expression recurs in v.17 as Mordecai sets out to do as Esther commands.

In *mah-zeh wᵉʿal-mah-zeh*, *zeh* strengthens the interrogative "what?" That strengthening plus the repetition of the phrase constitutes the equivalent of, "What on earth are you doing?"

NOTE

4 The Qal stem of the verb translated "in distress" (חוּל, *ḥûl*; GK 2655) means "to writhe"; there is also a Hitpolel form meaning "writhing" or "whirling." It indicates a physical reaction from deep shock with a derivative meaning "to be deeply disturbed" (Bush, 390).

2. Mordecai Challenges Esther (4:6–9)

OVERVIEW

Here begins an extraordinary exchange mediated by Hathach. His continued presence slows the pace of the narrative and thus heightens the tension. In his first venture, the discourse is indirect as the circumstances of the edict are repeated for Esther's benefit.

> ⁶So Hathach went out to Mordecai in the open square of the city in front of the king's gate. ⁷Mordecai told him everything that had happened to him, including the exact amount of money Haman had promised to pay into the royal treasury for the destruction of the Jews. ⁸He also gave him a copy of the text of the edict for their annihilation, which had been published in Susa, to show to Esther and explain it to her, and he told him to urge her to go into the king's presence to beg for mercy and plead with him for her people.
> ⁹Hathach went back and reported to Esther what Mordecai had said.

COMMENTARY

6 The location may indicate that Mordecai has removed himself slightly from the gate of the king once he knows he has Esther's attention. He is in the city square—*rᵉḥôb hāᶜîr*, the same expression that appears in 6:9, 11 when Haman first describes and then carries out the ceremony to honor Mordecai.

7 Mordecai first explains what has happened to *him*, no doubt including the edict to bow before Haman, his refusal to do so, and the harsh consequences that have resulted in his mourning on behalf of the Jewish people. Then he presents the substantiating details that his sources have provided, even to the amount of money Haman has offered for their extermination. *Pārāšâ* is only found in Hebrew in this verse and 10:2 and has to do with defining or specifying, in this case the amount of money. Mordecai demonstrates that his concern is not based on vague information but on precise knowledge.

8–9 To confirm further the gravity of the situation, Mordecai produces for Hathach a copy of the written edict. That this object comes first in the Hebrew indicates its significance; it is followed by another passive verb repeating that the text has been published in Susa. In contrast, the following six

Hebrew infinitives, starting with "to show," "to tell," "to command [tell]," are succinct and emphatic. The first three are directed to Hathach in his position as intermediary. The second set addresses Esther. Mordecai expects her to absorb the report and act accordingly—to plead for mercy and beseech the king on behalf of *her people*. At this point, Mordecai is calling on Esther to reveal the identity he has commanded her to hide until now. This is the last time Mordecai issues a command to Esther.

3. Esther Responds to Mordecai (4:10–11)

> [10]Then she instructed him to say to Mordecai, [11]"All the king's officials and the people of the royal provinces know that for any man or woman who approaches the king in the inner court without being summoned the king has but one law: that he be put to death. The only exception to this is for the king to extend the gold scepter to him and spare his life. But thirty days have passed since I was called to go to the king."

COMMENTARY

10 From here on Hathach mediates, but the words of Esther and Mordecai are presented as direct dialogue. Literally, "Esther *commanded* him [Hathach]" as he returns to Mordecai. Esther's role as authoritative queen begins to emerge at this point and will be fully operative in short order.

11 Esther's first articulated words constitute a valid apologetic for inaction in the face of almost certain death. She expresses reluctance on the basis of what is common knowledge about a comprehensive restriction; the text specifies "any man or woman." Furthermore, *everyone knows*. The implication is that Mordecai should know this too, especially since he seems to have known everything else! Esther's concern for her own well-being is founded on her not having been called to the king for thirty days—a fact that Mordecai would not have known. Esther is likely aware of other ruthless acts on the king's part, and the added provocation of admitting she is *Jewish* will, in her estimation, make the case hopeless.

There is evidence in Herodotus of a "no approach" policy in the Persian palace—a policy designed to enhance the king's honor and also to protect him from assassination attempts (Herodotus 1.99; 3.77–84). There were exceptions (3.118), however, and one could make an appeal for an audience (3.140). Nevertheless, it is likely that, while messengers would be sent by men in regard to affairs of state, a woman would not have recourse to a messenger.

NOTE

11 There is a parallel mention of thirty days in Daniel 6:8, 13 [Aram.] as a significant interval. Xenophon recorded the presence of a golden scepter as part of the royal trappings of Cambyses (*Cyropaedia* 8.7.13).

4. Mordecai Responds to Esther (4:12–14)

> [12]When Esther's words were reported to Mordecai, [13]he sent back this answer: "Do not think that because you are in the king's house you alone of all the Jews will escape. [14]For if you remain silent at this time, relief and deliverance for the Jews will arise from another place, but you and your father's family will perish. And who knows but that you have come to royal position for such a time as this?"

12 Literally, "*They* told to Mordecai the words of Esther." Again, the use of the plural is the equivalent of the passive voice and may prepare for the subtle change in narrative style in the next verse. As the crux of the exchange approaches, the narrator dispenses with the mediating role of Hathach and the rest unfolds as direct discourse.

13 Mordecai's response is searing, pitting the privilege of her royal position against her Jewish identity and intimating the danger is so great that even being the favored queen will not save her. Once Haman discovers she is both Jewish and related to Mordecai, her fate will be a terrible one. Mordecai does *not* say how he anticipates Haman might discover that detail, or precisely from what "quarter" this treachery might come.

There may be a double meaning intended in (lit.) "escape … from all the Jews." Either Esther will not escape because her identity will become known along with those of the other Jews, *or* she will not escape retribution at the hand of the Jews themselves who *will* be delivered from another quarter and then perhaps attack those who were turncoats (Beal, 72). Esther may have been tempted to think that having concealed her identity for six years, she can continue. Mordecai shatters that illusion. Esther's dilemma is one repeated throughout history; she is hemmed in by circumstances and forced to take courageous action and exercise faith (see Baldwin, 79; Berman, 653).

14 An initial reading of this verse seems to indicate Mordecai's unwavering hope in the providence of God. Even if Esther keeps silent, deliverance will arise from another place, but Esther herself has the opportunity to be a significant player in the deliverance of her people. Nevertheless, it is not at all clear how to read the statement about deliverance by itself and then how to read it in the context of the rest of the verse and the potential threat at the end of v.13. For whatever reason, Mordecai has just warned Esther that she is not immune in the king's household, and he repeats the warning here: "you and your father's house will perish." The latter warning includes him, as he is her only "family." That would be particularly poignant for her as she has been nurtured by him in the absence of her "father's house."

Furthermore, his challenge to consider the reason she has been brought to the royal position has its force only if there were no other alternative! Otherwise, she could easily be tempted to do nothing but simply rest in the hope that relief will indeed come from somewhere else. One way of addressing the issue is to posit that help might arise ($ya^{ca}m\hat{o}d$), but elsewhere, and the proximity of the royal palace to Haman and the center of the maelstrom would mean that Esther and Mordecai will get swept away.

John M. Wiebe ("Esther 4:14: 'Will Relief and Deliverance Arise for the Jews from Another Place?'" *CBQ* 53/3 (1991): 409–15) interprets the second clause of this verse as a rhetorical question that assumes a negative response. The relevant portion would read, "if you keep silent at this time, will help and deliverance come for the Jews from another place? [Answer: 'No, it won't …;] and you and your father's house will perish ['as well']." This rendition addresses the problems that are incumbent in the traditional reading of the text, namely, that if help does arise from (whatever is meant by) "another place," why would not Esther's family, and especially Mordecai, also be delivered by this agent? As a result of the truly dire nature of Mordecai's challenge, Esther's mood changes dramatically, and the narrative takes a decisive turn.

The use of "who knows" in this context is not an ambivalent expression of doubt but rather a strong statement that Esther is indeed the Jews' only hope and that she has been brought to this point for this time. On the confidence of the expression, see Joel 2:14 and Jonah 3:9. Mordecai's closing statement may be an oblique acknowledgment that Esther's experience in getting to that point has been a horrifying one for her and for him as her guardian.

NOTES

13 The Hebrew rendered "do not think" captures the mental anguish Mordecai perceives within her. אַל־תְּדַמִּי בְנַפְשֵׁךְ (*ʾal-tᵉdammî bᵉnapšēk*) suggests that she will be ruminating silently as internally she processes all the options. This internal struggle may underlie the developing plan that will "buy her time" to expose her identity.

One would expect the preposition "in" (בְּ־, *bᵉ*) prior to "palace" in the Hebrew. מכל (*mkl*) in this case means "alone, singled out" (Haupt, 136).

14 Although rabbinic texts characteristically employed *HaMaqom* ("the Place") as a substitute for God, it is not the meaning here, although Laniak ("Esther's *Volkcentrism* and the Reframing of Post-Exilic Judaism," in *The Book of Esther in Modern Research* [ed. Sidnie White Crawford and Leonard J. Greenspoon; London: T&T Clark, 2003], 82) suggests the veiled allusion may be intended.

5. Esther Takes Charge (4:15–17)

> ¹⁵Then Esther sent this reply to Mordecai: ¹⁶"Go, gather together all the Jews who are in Susa, and fast for me. Do not eat or drink for three days, night or day. I and my maids will fast as you do. When this is done, I will go to the king, even though it is against the law. And if I perish, I perish."
> ¹⁷So Mordecai went away and carried out all of Esther's instructions.

COMMENTARY

15–16 At this critical moment, Esther chooses publicly to identify with her people even at the probable cost of her life. She has been adept at managing the delicate balance of obedience to her guardian and responsiveness to the demands of the pagan court. At this point, however, her strength of character is manifested in her resolve to defy the king's law, reveal her Jewish identity, and confront the second most powerful person in the empire.

With the knowledge that fasting was an ancient and venerable part of her tradition, she calls for a corporate and comprehensive fast, thus continuing the communal participation in this crisis that began as a response to the edict. A radical appeal for God's intervention, this call exceeds all mandated fasts for severity; there is to be *neither eating nor drinking* for three days and nights! So even though prayer is not mentioned, it is likely part of the enterprise.

At the outset of her public identity with Judaism, Esther subjects herself to one of its most rigorous disciplines. She further determines that her young women (who may not have been Jewish) will fast in the same manner along with her. Afterward, she will enter into the king's presence. Because 5:1 indicates that Esther crosses the threshold into the king's presence in royal attire "on the third day," her call for the three-day fast presumably means parts of the three distinct days. If the narrative reflects events in rapid succession, it is implied that this fast will

have begun on the eve of Passover. Instead of feasting and rejoicing over the dramatic deliverance that was paradigmatic for all Israelite history, the Jews will be renewing the appeal for God's intervention "in their day."

Esther's closing words to Mordecai are telling; in spite of this astonishing corporate appeal for divine mercy, she expects the enterprise to fail because it is contrary to Persian law. Her statement might be translated, "When I perish, I perish," indicating her recognition that death is the likely outcome of either choice. The irony is that her decision moves her from passive recipient to actor and initiator in the rest of the drama.

17 Because the verse literally says that Mordecai "crossed over," early rabbinic interpreters suggested that he transgresses the commandment of God by ordering a fast on the thirteenth and fourteenth of Nisan (*b. Meg.* 15a; both Targums). However, he may simply have left the citadel for the city of Susa to assemble the Jews and start the fast. In fact, both implications may be knit into the choice of the word. Mordecai's response is to do all that *Esther has commanded*; the tables are turned so that he now obeys her.

NOTE

16 The Torah is reticent in regard to fasting; the command in conjunction with the Day of Atonement (Lev 16:29–31) to "afflict oneself" (עָנָה, ʿānâ) was the only mandate. Nevertheless, throughout Israel's history there were significant occasions on which both individuals and the nation engaged in fasting (צוֹם, ṣôm) to demonstrate repentance and to beseech God to avert some impending disaster (2Sa 12:16–22; 1Ki 21:27; Joel 2:15). After the exile, it seems that the practice was institutionalized, perhaps because there was a communal dread that disobedience would bring a repeat of that disaster (Zec 7:2–3; see also Ne 9:1). Daniel fasted on behalf of his sinful people (Da 9). According to the book of Jonah, fasting was a recognized practice in the ancient Near East (Jnh 3:5), as the king of Nineveh called for a society-wide fast.

Just as the Jews' fast of mourning is a counterpoint to the casual drinking feast of the king and Haman, so also the discipline of this three-day fast contrasts with the theme of Persian revelry. Fasting will continue to hold an important place, as is evident in the commemorative activities (Est 9:31). For an explanation of calendrical differences that allow for three full days of fasting as well as Esther's entrance into the king's presence "on the third day," see N. L. Collins, "Did Esther Fast on the 15th Nisan?" *RB* 100 (1993): 533–61. Gordis (*Megillat Esther*, 40) suggests that this is not a seventy-two-hour fast but three periods of twelve-hour fasts.

At this critical juncture the LXX includes long and impassioned prayers of Mordecai and Esther. Mordecai reminds God that his motives for refusing to bow to Haman are not pride but concern for the glory of God. Esther sets aside her royal apparel, dons garments of humiliation along with ashes and dung, and cries out to God to accept her confession of the people's sins, intervene against their enemies, and grant her the necessary boldness and eloquence in order to effect deliverance. Part of this prayer is her declaration that everything associated with her position has been repulsive to her. In the LXX, these additions are followed by an expanded description of Esther's approach to the king.

III. REQUESTS, REVELATIONS, AND REVERSALS (5:1–7:8)

A. The First Banquet of Esther (5:1–8)

1. Esther's Grand Entrance (5:1–2)

¹On the third day Esther put on her royal robes and stood in the inner court of the palace, in front of the king's hall. The king was sitting on his royal throne in the hall, facing the entrance. ²When he saw Queen Esther standing in the court, he was pleased with her and held out to her the gold scepter that was in his hand. So Esther approached and touched the tip of the scepter.

COMMENTARY

1 After the critical exchanges between Esther and Mordecai, the narrative resumes with *wayᵉhî*, the same construction with which the book started (1:1). To prepare for her encounter with the king, Esther clothes herself in royal attire (*malkût*) and takes her position. In clothing herself, she goes beyond simply dressing up—she presents herself on the king's footing (Fox, 68).

Esther stands; the king sits. The structure of the sentence focuses on the palace in such a way as to build the suspense with the repetition of *bêt-hammelek* ("palace" and "king's hall"), followed by *bêt hammalkût*

("hall") and *petaḥ habbāyit* (lit., "the entrance of the house"). The two actors are positioned opposite the critical point of the doorway; the king is ensconced *in* the palace; she is approaching it. The word *nōkaḥ* ("in front of/facing") is used in regard to the position of each of them. The Persian court under Darius had created the separation of the king in order to enhance his majesty and dignity (Herodotus 1.99). For Esther to cross the threshold of the entrance is a recognized invasion of an almost sacred space.

2 The king sees Esther the queen. Her regal demeanor again wins "his favor" (see comments on

2:9, 15, 17), and he demonstrates the evidence of that favor by extending the scepter. That there is a precise and unchangeable protocol is suggested by the measured and careful language; the king "held out to [Esther] the gold scepter that was in his hand. So Esther approached and touched the tip of the scepter."

NOTES

1 As an indication of the importance of this deliverance for the sages and rabbinic audiences, a stock rabbinic piece on biblical events that occurred on the third day appears in *Midrash Esther Rabbah*. The LXX has Esther delicately leaning on her maids as she approaches, her heart filled with fear in the presence of the fierce anger of the king.

2 Perhaps thinking that the MT lacks sufficient spice, the translations/interpretations continue the melodramatic additions. Esther falls down, turns pale, and faints, and three angels come to her rescue. One lifts up her head, the second grants her grace, and the third lengthens the king's scepter. Although the king is incensed, God changes his heart and instead he leaps from the throne to her assistance and comforts her in his arms while she heaps on him appropriate acknowledgments of his royal majesty and glory (see the LXX, both Targums, and *b. Meg.* 15b). With regard to extending the scepter, archaeologists have uncovered a relief from Persepolis of Darius I holding a scepter in his right hand (Baldwin, 86).

2. Invitations and Promises (5:3–8)

[3]Then the king asked, "What is it, Queen Esther? What is your request? Even up to half the kingdom, it will be given you."

[4]"If it pleases the king," replied Esther, "let the king, together with Haman, come today to a banquet I have prepared for him."

[5]"Bring Haman at once," the king said, "so that we may do what Esther asks." So the king and Haman went to the banquet Esther had prepared. [6]As they were drinking wine, the king again asked Esther, "Now what is your petition? It will be given to you. And what is your request? Even up to half the kingdom, it will be granted."

[7]Esther replied, "My petition and my request is this: [8]If the king regards me with favor and if it pleases the king to grant my petition and fulfill my request, let the king and Haman come tomorrow to the banquet I will prepare for them. Then I will answer the king's question."

COMMENTARY

3 The king is obviously aware that something critical has made Esther risk her life and transgress court protocol. His question commences with *mah-lāk* (lit., "What is to/with you?"). This idiom is used elsewhere (Jos 15:18; Jdg 1:14; 18:3, 23–24; Eze 18:2; Jnh 1:6) and may mean simply "What do you want?" or "What are you doing?" It is not, however, the patterned rhetoric that the king uses on subsequent days. Perhaps he is moved by her appearance and part of the question inquires into her own distress. While it sounds brusque, he follows with the further standard question, "What is your request?" The promise of "up to half the kingdom" seems to have been a convention (cf. Mk 6:23), but an interesting one nevertheless. Even though he holds the power of life and death in the form of his own scepter, he is ready to be dominated by her request and, in fact, promises to grant it before she even speaks.

4 Esther's request that the king and Haman attend a private banquet she has already prepared indicates that she has carefully devised her strategy. Given her venture into the king's presence, for her merely to invite him to a banquet signals to him that the real issue is yet to be divulged. Undoubtedly, this maneuver piques his curiosity.

The feast, in addition to fitting both court "culture" and textual themes, will provide a less rigid and public place for addressing the difficult and delicate nature of her request. The occasion will also provide an appropriate venue to which to invite Haman, as second to the king, without "tipping him off" that something is amiss. The Hebrew form of Esther's invitation is in keeping with the stature of the two intended guests: "Let the king come [singular] and Haman...." The same formula appears in v.8.

5 The king complies with Esther's request. Haman is brought hastily, and the king enters (again the singular verb, perhaps setting him apart) along with Haman. At this point, the three ostensibly most powerful people in the Persian Empire are together in one room.

6 There apparently is a separate course for the consumption of wine (*mištēh hayyayin*) toward the

end of the banquet. Perhaps it served as the occasion for addressing issues that were deemed inappropriate during the main dinner. The king's first abbreviated query (v.3) comes partly in response to Esther's uninvited entry and her evident distress. In this context, his manner is more measured, perhaps in keeping with protocol. If indeed the doublet ("petition" and "request") is standard court rhetoric, Esther would know the pattern and may have prepared her critical request (7:3) ahead of time to fit perfectly.

7 This doublet rhetoric shapes both the narrative framework and Esther's first patterned response. A literal rendition is, "She answered and said, 'My petition and my request....'" This verse is an incomplete sentence, which may be intentional, though most modern translations read v.8 as the continuation of *this* request. Clearly, however, her request is not simply that they come to the next banquet. A sensitive audience can imagine her pause, perhaps to steady herself if she is faltering under the pressure. On the one hand, it may be that she spontaneously puts off the moment when she has to expose the treachery of the king's favorite adviser and declare her own identity. On the other hand, the pause may represent the next step in her calculated scheme to undo Haman systematically.

8 Here Esther is in full command of the rhetoric, the consummate diplomat using the full extent of the double forms as the king himself has articulated them. She phrases the matter exquisitely, thus obligating the king to grant the request when it will finally come—(lit.) "if it *seems good to grant my request* ... then let him come...." Furthermore, she prefaces it with her own flourish: "If I have found favor ... and if it seems good...." The first expression ("to find favor," as opposed to her "winning favor") is the more common idiom (see comment on 2:9) and indicates a certain deference on her part. The invitation to a second banquet, if planned from the outset, will further lull Haman into a mindset that will make him stunned when the announcement is made and perhaps prevent a clever political evasion on his part.

Esther's promise is (lit.) "to do according to the word of the king," an interesting declaration in the light of his having said he will do anything for her up to giving her half the kingdom! In contrast to her first invitation, here Esther says she will prepare the banquet "for them"—an unexplained inclusion that may have piqued twinges of jealousy on the king's part and kept him awake the following night. At this point, the narrator masterfully leaves the audience in suspense as the relationship between Haman and Mordecai is resumed.

NOTES

3 Even though בַּקָּשָׁה (baqqāšâ; NIV "request") is feminine, the promise ("it will be given …") is third masculine singular. Note a parallel promise of Xerxes to grant a request that had a gruesome outcome (Herodotus 9.110–11).

4 The rabbis extensively explored the question of why Esther invites Haman (b. Meg. 15b). Paton, 234, discounts all the possible reasons for Esther's delaying tactics in inviting Haman and claims that the invitation is simply literary artifice; a day is needed for Haman's humiliation.

7 "Answered and said" (lit.) is typical of Semitic expression but also serves here to contribute to the doublets in the text.

B. Haman's Mood Reversals (5:9–14)

⁹Haman went out that day happy and in high spirits. But when he saw Mordecai at the king's gate and observed that he neither rose nor showed fear in his presence, he was filled with rage against Mordecai. ¹⁰Nevertheless, Haman restrained himself and went home.

Calling together his friends and Zeresh, his wife, ¹¹Haman boasted to them about his vast wealth, his many sons, and all the ways the king had honored him and how he had elevated him above the other nobles and officials. ¹²"And that's not all," Haman added. "I'm the only person Queen Esther invited to accompany the king to the banquet she gave. And she has invited me along with the king tomorrow. ¹³But all this gives me no satisfaction as long as I see that Jew Mordecai sitting at the king's gate."

¹⁴His wife Zeresh and all his friends said to him, "Have a gallows built, seventy-five feet high, and ask the king in the morning to have Mordecai hanged on it. Then go with the king to the dinner and be happy." This suggestion delighted Haman, and he had the gallows built.

COMMENTARY

9 This verse is also built on dyads, with joy and high spirits (*ṭôb lēb*) characterizing Haman in contrast to Mordecai's refusal to rise or tremble. Previously, the command that Mordecai defied was to bow and prostrate himself before Haman. Now, having completed the three days of fasting and likely aware that Esther has successfully entered the throne room, he is back to sitting in the gate, possibly intent on gathering every shred of information he can discover. Seeing Haman coming, he refuses to stand up as the first step in the mandated procedure. The additional verb is telling. Haman has intended by his decree to arouse terror, but Mordecai doesn't flinch. As a result, Haman's state of mind changes to fury.

10–11 Haman pretends to be indifferent, but his emotion pours out in his overwrought boasting to his friends and the final eruption of his injured pride. Craving an audience, he summons his friends and Zeresh, his wife, who have to listen to a recital of information they already know—and perhaps have heard numerous times before. The order in the verse may hint at what is most important to Haman; he speaks first of his great wealth and then of his many sons. After that, he waxes eloquent about his own exalted status, especially above everyone else of any comparable stature. His friends serve as advisers (cf. 5:14; 6:13); it seems that neither the king nor Haman can function without them. The text names his wife, who, summoned along with his friends, also serves ably as an adviser.

12 If the friends have heard all his boasts before, this one *is* new. He alone has been privileged to dine privately with Queen Esther and the king. Literally, he was "brought" to the banquet, just as he will be to the second one (6:14). And if that were not enough, the same will happen the next day!

13 Haman here reveals the great flaw of his self-centered pride. Even though he is second to the king, he craves the obeisance of one person who withholds it and whose very people he despises—Mordecai *the Jew*. By this time Haman is so overwrought that Mordecai's very existence makes him lose control. *Šwh* can mean "to be equal/similar/in accordance with," or "to be appropriate/satisfactory." In this case it is best to read, "None of this is satisfactory for me as long as...."

14 It seems that Zeresh takes the lead in advising Haman how to proceed. The verb is singular (as in vv.4, 8) even though the friends are also part of the consultation. As with the other women in the narrative, Zeresh acts and speaks in ways that elicit responses, all quite amusing in the light of the decree that men are to master their own houses. Her counsel is designed to shame Mordecai and the people he represents and, in so doing, address the humiliation and wounded pride that nags at Haman every time he sees Mordecai.

The request to have Mordecai impaled on a ludicrously high pole (*ʿēṣ*) indicates Haman's frenzy to debase him completely. The pole will be seen all over Susa. The height may also reflect the fact that everything "official" in this setting is done on a grand scale. For a parallel "grand scale," see Daniel 3:1 (the ninety-foot statue). On the matter of hanging, see comments on Esther 2:23. The word "tree" (*ʿēṣ*) repeatedly surfaces in the book (2:23; 6:4; 7:9–10; 8:7; 9:13, 25).

Haman's advisers may have congratulated themselves on the irony they have created. In ch. 3 Mordecai would not bow; now he will not rise, so Haman will elevate him seventy-five feet high! That being done, they know Haman will be able to wine and dine joyfully with the king and queen. The suggestion is (lit.) "good in his eyes."

NOTE

12 The use of יָכּ ...ףַא (ʾap ... kî) is emphatic, not interrogative. It is a "done deal." The *lamed* after the passive אֵרְקִ (qārîʾ) denotes the agent, "summoned by her" (Torrey, 37).

C. "What Should Be Done for the Man the King Delights to Honor?" (6:1–13)

1. Revelation of a Minor Catastrophe: Mordecai's Honor Neglected (6:1–3)

OVERVIEW

The pervasive coincidences in this section are clear indications that something more is afoot. The king just happens to have insomnia; the chronicles just happen to be open to the point of Mordecai's good deed; Mordecai just happens to have waited for five years without saying a thing; Haman just happens to be outside at the propitious moment when the king determines that this matter needs to be set right; and the king just happens *not* to name the person whom he desires to honor, so that Haman presumes it can be none other than he. The reversals are the hand of divine providence; insomnia turns the story on its head—if it hadn't set in, Mordecai would have been dead before Esther's second banquet.

¹That night the king could not sleep; so he ordered the book of the chronicles, the record of his reign, to be brought in and read to him. ²It was found recorded there that Mordecai had exposed Bigthana and Teresh, two of the king's officers who guarded the doorway, who had conspired to assassinate King Xerxes.

³"What honor and recognition has Mordecai received for this?" the king asked. "Nothing has been done for him," his attendants answered.

COMMENTARY

1 That very night the sleep of the king "fled," a remarkably apt picture of the frustration of sleeplessness. The verb *nādad* means "flee, wander," or "be disturbed or shaken" (*HALOT*, BDB). Commentators, both ancient and modern, have speculated on why the king is afflicted in this manner. Caught in the tangled web of his thoughts might be apprehension that he has promised Esther up to half the kingdom, suspicion of Esther's motives for inviting Haman to both private banquets, her intimation that she is equally solicitous of Haman and the king (5:8), and the memory of an assassination attempt that brewed just outside of his door some years earlier (*b. Meg.* 15b; Walfish, 165).

The reading material is (lit.) "the book of the remembrances, the matters of the days." This descriptor is an expansion of *sēper dibrê hayyāmîm* (see 2:23), the expression commonly used for "chronicles," and is another example of the excesses of language when the action returns to the sphere of the Persian court. The same may be said of the following passive verbal form, "they were read." The periphrastic form (*wayyihᵉyû* plus the passive participle) suggests a process of some duration. The court reader(s) may have been droning on for a good part of the night. That the Persian court maintained such records is attested also in Ezra 6:1–5.

2 The record of the assassination attempt, with names and titles, is "found written"—two passive verbs reflecting the impersonal court and serving as a subtle indicator of the providential unveiling of these matters at just the right time.

3 The passive voice continues: [lit.] "what ... was done [*naᶜᵃśâ*]? ... nothing was done [*naᶜᵃśâ*]." The

young attendants provide the answer, as they did in ch. 2.

The specific reference to "honor" (*yᵉqār*) and "greatness" (*gᵉdûllâ*) in this context is an echo of Haman's promotion in 3:1; the misdirected honor there was an injustice that needed to be addressed. As a general rule, special services to the king were immediately honored (Herodotus 3.138–41; 5.11; 8.85; 9.107). Five years is a long time, and the king may be more concerned here with his own shame in neglecting to reward Mordecai than for Mordecai's well-being (Laniak, 105–6). If the king has been nurturing any suspicions of Haman, honoring Mordecai will create a counterweight to Haman's power (Hazony, 161–62). Mordecai will be honored in this chapter but not specifically promoted until 8:2.

NOTES

2 "Bigthana" is a variation of "Bigthan" in 2:21. The comment of Paton, 245, on this verse ("This is the way things happen in storybooks, but not in real life") seems to indicate little acquaintance with the oddities of real life!

3 On "benefactors" of the king, see comment on 2:23.

2. "Who Is There That the King Would Rather Honor Than Me?" (6:4–9)

⁴The king said, "Who is in the court?" Now Haman had just entered the outer court of the palace to speak to the king about hanging Mordecai on the gallows he had erected for him.

⁵His attendants answered, "Haman is standing in the court."

"Bring him in," the king ordered.

⁶When Haman entered, the king asked him, "What should be done for the man the king delights to honor?"

Now Haman thought to himself, "Who is there that the king would rather honor than me?"

⁷So he answered the king, "For the man the king delights to honor, ⁸have them bring a royal

robe the king has worn and a horse the king has ridden, one with a royal crest placed on its head. ⁹Then let the robe and the horse be entrusted to one of the king's most noble princes. Let him robe the man the king delights to honor, and lead him on the horse through the city streets, proclaiming before him, 'This is what is done for the man the king delights to honor!'"

COMMENTARY

4 Neither the king nor Haman has slept that night, and both have Mordecai on their minds—but with entirely different objectives! One wonders why the king is going to address his question to whatever unknown person is in the court, unless that location is restricted solely to trusted advisers. If so, by this time such a person can only mean Haman, who continues to be confident of his access to the king. As he enters the outer court, Haman is also *very* early, indicative of the unseemly haste with which he is intent on doing away with Mordecai. He also comes to *tell* (*lēʾmōr*) the king, not to ask—truly a brash attitude (Gordis, *Megillat Esther*, 45).

5 Haman has stationed himself in the courtyard to be ready for the earliest moment of access. That his entrance into the king's presence comes on the heels of the all-night soporific reading suggests Haman is ushered into the king's bedroom.

6 Regal prerogative means that the king's concern comes first. That he does not reveal the identity of Mordecai here is providential. Had the king done so, it would have gone ill with Mordecai, given Haman's influential position! The expression "the king delights to honor" lodges firmly in Haman's mind. He first savors it *bᵉlibbô* ("in his heart") and then returns to it repeatedly to define precisely what should be done for, as he assumes, *himself*. The character of Haman is the most transparent one through the entire narrative; here the audience has a window into his innermost thoughts and one sees overweening pride.

7 Although the NIV translation smoothes out this verse by attaching it to the following one, it should be read independently. Haman, relishing the phrase, repeats it and then begins describing the honors he so ardently desires, while continuing to interweave "the man whom the king delights to honor." Little does Haman realize he is practicing the announcement for repeated and public acclamation of Mordecai!

8–9 There are three critical aspects to Haman's response, and he repeats each element with increasing detail, thus making it clear that he intends the king to understand the full import of his advice. There is to be a public declaration that symbols of royal power and position are shared by someone of great importance to the king. Both the royal horse and the regal garment are to be ones the king himself has used, thus investing them with a significant degree of sovereign power. If Xerxes were to think that Haman is speaking with reference to himself, Haman's comments could be construed as the first step in a plan to usurp the throne (Abraham D. Cohen, "'*Hu Ha-goral*': The Religious Significance of Esther," *Judaism* 23 [1974]: 93; Levenson, 97; Baldwin, 90).

Perhaps as a result of his nighttime ruminations, the king is suspicious of Haman. If so, in addition to proposing the necessary ceremony for Mordecai, the king takes advantage of the timely appearance of Haman to test him and see what designs he has in mind. Haman, for his part, may have counted on the king's trust that his proposal is simply a maneuver to elevate the king further and to solidify his position in a context that is always potentially uncertain.

Some scholars have suggested that the proposed event is not a parade through the streets but rather a stationary demonstration in the city square (*birḥôb hāʿîr*). The verbs that are translated "has ridden" and "lead … through" (*rākab* and *hirkîb*) are better understood as "mount," implying the symbolic position to which Haman will be required to raise Mordecai as a public act of honor. Because the mount will be a horse ridden by the *king*, the honoree will share the king's own glory and honor (W. Boyd Barrick, "The Meaning and Usage of *RKB* in Biblical Hebrew," *JBL* 101 [1982]: 488–90).

A crest (lit., "crown") on the horse's head was not an unusual ornamentation in ancient Near Eastern art; such equine headpieces appear regularly in royal Assyrian reliefs from Nineveh on display in the British Museum in London. The pattern continued into the Persian period, as demonstrated in reliefs from Persepolis (Briant, 223). Nevertheless, the syntax of the final clause of v.8 is ambiguous because, unlike the preceding two *ʾašer* clauses, this one does not have an immediate antecedent; therefore, it might be read as "the king who wears the royal crown while riding the royal horse" (see Oswald T. Allis, "The Reward of the King's Favorite [Esther vi.8]," *PTR* 21 [1923]: 621–32; Berg, 62).

NOTES

6 יוֹתֵר מִן (*yôtēr min*) is late biblical Hebrew (see also Ecc 12:12) and should be understood as "apart from," indicating that Haman cannot imagine anyone else's being even remotely qualified. "More than" in biblical Hebrew is generally simply מִן (*min*). See Haupt, 143.

9 Wearing the king's robe and riding his horse were demonstrations of honor (Laniak, 106–7; cf. Herodotus 3.138–41). There is evidence that Xerxes himself asked one of his advisers to wear his royal robe, even though in that circumstance the intent was to "trick" whatever force was causing dreams that were troubling Xerxes (Herodotus 7.15–18).

רְחוֹב (*rᵉḥôb*) is used forty-two times in the MT, has the basic meaning of "open place," and is best translated "city square" (*TWOT*).

The third masculine plural verbal forms and the accompanying infinitive absolute keep the focus on the object of the honor, not on who will carry it out, even though that person will be a member of the nobility (Bush, 415–16). For further evidence that Persian monarchs allowed mere mortals to sample their royal means, see Xenophon's account regarding things personally sampled by Cyrus the Younger (ca. 400 BC) that were sent to friends as personal favors (*Anabasis* 1.9.20–26), and Plutarch's lighthearted rendition of a transgression of such royal boundaries (*Artaxerxes* 5).

3. Mordecai Honored; Haman Humiliated (6:10–13)

¹⁰"Go at once," the king commanded Haman. "Get the robe and the horse and do just as you have suggested for Mordecai the Jew, who sits at the king's gate. Do not neglect

anything you have recommended." [11]So Haman got the robe and the horse. He robed Mordecai, and led him on horseback through the city streets, proclaiming before him, "This is what is done for the man the king delights to honor!"

[12]Afterward Mordecai returned to the king's gate. But Haman rushed home, with his head covered in grief, [13]and told Zeresh his wife and all his friends everything that had happened to him.

His advisers and his wife Zeresh said to him, "Since Mordecai, before whom your downfall has started, is of Jewish origin, you cannot stand against him — you will surely come to ruin!"

COMMENTARY

10 Hearing "Mordecai the Jew" must have frozen every fiber of Haman's being. He despises that name above all others, and Mordecai is the person whose end has been, in his mind, tantalizingly close. In the public sphere, the plot turns at this point. There is a great deal that this verse does *not* say; thus it leaves much to the imagination of the audience.

How does the king know Mordecai is Jewish, and how can he have forgotten that the Jews have been doomed to destruction? Mordecai's identity may be written into the chronicles, but more likely the attendants who clearly know the circumstances (v.3) fill the king in on this detail as well. Haman has carefully avoided naming the objects of his decree, and the king has turned the whole sordid business over to Haman. Thus, even though the decree names the Jews, Xerxes may never have bothered to read it.

The events to this point forcefully demonstrate Xerxes' ability to miss just about everything of significance. Equally puzzling is the question of why the king is eager to honor "Mordecai the Jew" if anti-Semitism is lurking in the empire. Perhaps he is also oblivious to that sentiment. The king's parting shot not to "neglect anything" says literally, "Do not let anything fall"—a prescient directive in the light of what is forthcoming for Haman.

11 After Haman's extended description of the recommended ceremony, the actual event is reported with great economy, as though to suggest that Haman does it as quickly and perfunctorily as possible. The narrator leaves to the audience's imagination what the display in the city square is like both for Haman and for Mordecai. While the king may have been unaware of the antipathy between Haman and Mordecai, everyone in the public sphere who watches the spectacle knows the preceding incidents. Their knowledge is Haman's crowning humiliation as the proclamation is repeated with reference to Mordecai, that this is "the man the king delights to honor." At the same time, it must have felt like a cruel irony to Mordecai, for the seemingly inevitable and deadly decree is still in effect. Perhaps he, not knowing any of the precipitating events, construes the scene as a mockery in which he is forced to be the passive recipient.

12 While nothing is noted about Mordecai's response, Haman flees home in mourning with a covered head—an adumbration of the final covering of his face in 7:8. This indication of mourning contrasts entirely with what he has anticipated. The symbolism of the covered head appears in 2 Samuel 15:30 to describe David's mourning and shame as he exited Jerusalem at the time of Absalom's rebellion, and in Jeremiah 14:3−4 to indicate the mourning of Jerusalem.

13 Haman's description of his humiliation uses the same language that appears with regard to Mordecai's lowest moment (4:7). After hearing his narrative, Zeresh and the advisers ("the wise ones"), whose distance from him is indicated by their no longer being called "friends," recognize that his fate is sealed. He has begun to fall, and there is no stopping it; the verbal root of *nāpal* occurs three times,

the last being the emphatic infinitive absolute with the finite form. Because Mordecai is Jewish, Haman will not be able to prevail. The *ʾim* clause is not conditional ("if" he is Jewish—they know that he is) but causal.

The next verse (v.14) skillfully gets the reading audience back to the banquet after this most important tangent. The declaration of Zeresh and the advisers fits the pattern of non-Israelites aware of God's support for Israel (see Nu 22−24; Jos 2:8−11; 1Sa 4:8).

NOTE

10−12 In the rabbinic expansion of this section, Haman's daughter sees the procession and, thinking that Mordecai is Haman and vice versa, she empties a chamber pot onto Haman's head. When she realizes it is her father, she throws herself down to the ground and kills herself. Thus Scripture says, "and Haman hastened … mourning," which indicates that he hastens home in mourning for his daughter (*b. Meg.* 16a).

D. The Second Banquet of Esther (6:14−7:8)

1. Arrival of the Guests (6:14−7:1)

¹⁴While they were still talking with him, the king's eunuchs arrived and hurried Haman away to the banquet Esther had prepared. ⁷:¹So the king and Haman went to dine with Queen Esther.

COMMENTARY

14 One can just imagine the previous scene with Haman's tormented recital of events, perhaps prolonged as each is revisited, and the sobering responses of all his "comforters." Any hope that he might have sought from them is dashed, so it would be understandable if he had not prepared himself in a timely manner for the next banquet. The escort of eunuchs may have been court protocol for someone of Haman's stature, but when

they arrive, they find him still in the midst of the agonizing conversation and are compelled to hurry him to the queen.

7:1 The lower status of Haman vis-à-vis the king is again indicated by the singular verb, as it refers to the king's entrance. Literally, they come "to drink" (*lištôt*), but no doubt it is an entire sumptuous banquet. From this point on, Esther is repeatedly called *Queen* Esther.

2. The Royal Requests and Questions (7:2−5)

²...and as they were drinking wine on that second day, the king again asked, "Queen Esther, what is your petition? It will be given you. What is your request? Even up to half the kingdom, it will be granted."

³Then Queen Esther answered, "If I have found favor with you, O king, and if it pleases your majesty, grant me my life — this is my petition. And spare my people — this is my request. ⁴For I and my people have been sold for destruction and slaughter and annihilation. If we had merely been sold as male and female slaves, I would have kept quiet, because no such distress would justify disturbing the king."

⁵King Xerxes asked Queen Esther, "Who is he? Where is the man who has dared to do such a thing?"

COMMENTARY

2 On *mištēh hayyayin*, see comment on 5:6. If indeed this conversation occurs during a course toward the end of the meal, there has been a significant amount of time for tension to build. For the third time, the king asks to know Esther's request, and though the rhetoric determines the form of the question, it changes slightly again. He addresses her directly as "Queen Esther" and uses the expected feminine form of the verb (*tinnātēn*, "it will be given," to correspond to the feminine subject, *šᵉᵒēlâ*) instead of the masculine (see 5:3, 6), which may have been less personal. For the second time, Xerxes promises to grant her petition entirely.

3 Following the lead of the king and perhaps in keeping with court etiquette, Esther shapes her entire response, which is narrated as a doublet ("Esther the queen answered and said") in pairs. The first set includes the two conditionals, "if I have found favor with you, O king" and "if it pleases your majesty." Even these remarks are exquisite preparations for what follows. Esther uses the more deferential "find favor" as opposed to "won favor" and appeals directly to the king's relationship with her — a factor to which she returns in the next phase.

Knowing that her own life is more significant than her people's as far as the king is concerned, Esther first petitions that her life be spared and then requests the sparing of her people's lives. His honor will, after all, be profoundly damaged if the queen were killed in conjunction with Haman's edict against the Jews.

4 The next part of her plea is a masterpiece in diplomacy. She has to set the stage for the accusation of Haman without implicating the king, who is, to be sure, equally culpable in the matter. Haman is the king's choice as second in the realm, and the king has granted him free reign to unleash his fury against the Jews. In declaring (lit.) "we have been sold, I and my people," Esther identifies herself with the Jews, even though she does not yet name them. Her direct quotation of the language of the decree does away with any ambiguity; at this point Haman must realize with mounting horror what Esther's ethnic identity means for him.

In light of the possibility that Haman had exploited the convenient similarity between verbs meaning "to annihilate" and "to enslave" (see Notes on ch. 3), Esther's use of the term "sold" has multiple layers of meaning. They have been "sold" for destruction, a term used repeatedly of God's response to Israel's disobedience (cf. Jdg 2:14; 3:8; 4:2); they have literally been sold, as Haman has offered the king money for their annihilation and Xerxes appears to have accepted (Est 3:9; 4:7); and the king may have been "sold a bill of goods" by Haman's deceitful pun, which has lulled the king into thinking this matter has to do with slave trade.

Even sale into slavery, Esther goes on to maintain, would have been sufficiently tolerable to have prevented her bringing the matter to the king's attention. This maneuver is also clever because, while it is quickly becoming manifestly clear that she *could* keep quiet, her being sold into slavery by an edict the king himself has sanctioned would have been unthinkably shameful—for him! He has to respond.

The final clause is difficult because the three key words have multiple and ambiguous meanings—perhaps the very reason Esther chooses to use them at this necessary apex of her diplomatic endeavor. *Ṣār* ("distress" or "calamity") can also mean "adversary," an interpretation that would personalize the problem and connect with v.6, in which Esther identifies Haman with that very word.

Šōweh ("would justify," NIV) means "to be like/equal" and could imply both monetary value and the value of an action, particularly appropriate for the messy situation here (Laniak 113, n. 30). The word occurred previously at the end of Haman's

accusation of "a certain people": it wasn't worthwhile to the king to let them rest (3:8). In both cases, Haman and Esther express their concern to maintain some sort of equilibrium for the king, who was known to be a bit volatile.

Nēzeq ("disturbing"), only used here in biblical Hebrew, is generally a strong term, meaning "damage," in rabbinic texts. It could also have financial overtones, referring to the "loss" to the king of a sizable bit of income. A literal rendition of this clause would be, "there is no calamity [or 'adversary'] that is equivalent to damage to the king." If *ṣār* refers to a person, it would be a disdainful comment on Haman: he is so worthless that disrupting the royal equilibrium in order to accomplish his punishment would be too high a price to pay, thus implying utmost respect for the king and utmost contempt for Haman.

5 The Hebrew literally reads, "Then said King Ahasuerus, and he said to Queen Esther, 'Who is he? And where is he who has filled his heart to do such a thing?'" The awkward repetition of "said" is not a textual error. Instead, it works very well to indicate the "sputtering" of the king. He is so shocked that he has to catch his breath and start all over again. Both the description of his talking and his direct question indicate his dismay. Notably, the king does not recognize the language of the decree or make the connection between Esther's reference and Haman. Because he has been negligent in knowing about Haman's real activities and the Jewish identity of his queen, he asks the question that allows Esther to point at Haman.

NOTES

4 "Sold" also implies a change in "ownership," which would trouble the king, whose property Esther is, because that change in ownership would affect his honor as well (see Laniak, 112, n. 28). אִלּוּ (ʾillû) is an Aramaic particle used only here and in Ecclesiastes 6:6. For a comprehensive summary of the possible ways to translate the final clause, see Paton, 261−62. The medieval rabbis were also stymied by the clause; the number of interpretations proposed is just about equal to the number of interpreters (Walfish, 20−22).

5 אֵי־זֶה (ʾê-zeh) is only used with a person in the book of Esther. Generally the word means "where," but it can also mean "which" (BDB). "Who has filled his heart" (NIV, "who has dared") implies great audacity (Haupt, 149).

3. Haman's Perfidy Revealed and His Fate Sealed (7:6−8)

> ⁶Esther said, "The adversary and enemy is this vile Haman."
> Then Haman was terrified before the king and queen. ⁷The king got up in a rage, left his wine and went out into the palace garden. But Haman, realizing that the king had already decided his fate, stayed behind to beg Queen Esther for his life. ⁸Just as the king returned from the palace garden to the banquet hall, Haman was falling on the couch where Esther was reclining.
> The king exclaimed, "Will he even molest the queen while she is with me in the house?"
> As soon as the order left the king's mouth, they covered Haman's face.

COMMENTARY

6 Esther starts with general terms (lit.), "a man, an adversary and enemy," and proceeds to *"this* evil Haman." It is a terse indictment. She calls him an "enemy," not "the enemy of the Jews," thus intimating it is a much bigger problem. In effect, Haman is a traitor to the king as well as an enemy of the Jews (Baldwin, 93). It is horrifying news to Haman that the *queen* is Jewish and therefore condemned by his edict to die. Face to face with the king and queen, who are noted together at this point, he is gripped with sudden terror (*nibʿat*). The next events are compressed; Haman's fate is quickly sealed.

7 This revelation infuriates the king. He has been duped by Haman in more ways than one, and Esther's own subterfuge may have irritated him to a degree. How humiliating that his own queen identifies herself with a people officially consigned to destruction! His enraged exit matches his character.

The Hebrew is a "dramatic ellipsis"—"he got up in his rage from the wine course ... to the palace garden"—suggesting both haste and confusion. Haman turns to Esther to plead for his life. The king's mind is made up, but perhaps Haman hopes that the king again will not act on his own. If so, Esther is his only, very slim hope.

8 In the final irony of Haman's life, he falls onto the couch where Esther, the Jewish queen, is reclining, and he is in that posture of entreaty when the king returns and finds him there. Paton, 264, castigates Esther for not showing mercy, but that judgment betrays an astonishingly poor memory regarding Haman's intended genocide. To spare Haman's life would have been an act of folly (Gordis, *Megillat Esther*, 50).

Whether the king deliberately misinterprets Haman's action or actually thinks Haman is assaulting Esther is unclear. To violate the queen would be tantamount to tyranny, a practice that is evident at other points in Israel's history when potential usurpers slept with royal concubines (cf. 2Sa 16:21–22; 1Ki 2:13–22). What the king sees allows him to make a charge that will resolve his dilemma about the dishonorable implications for him of the edict. Everything can be blamed on Haman (Fox, 87; Bush, 433). In a tidy demonstration of measure-for-measure justice, Haman will die because of a false accusation just as he has falsely accused the Jews (Laniak, 115, n. 33). The exclamation ("word") from the mouth of the king may refer to the statement about assault and not his judicial condemnation of Haman. If so, covering Haman's face would be the mark of shame, not the immediate prelude to death (Baldwin, 93; Bush, 430).

The extreme brevity of the narrative suggests the blur of activity and haste with which these traumatic last moments of Haman's life pass. As in numerous earlier instances, the indefinite plural subject indicates passivity; Haman's face is covered.

NOTES

7 Haman (lit.) "stood" (עָמַד, *ʿāmad*), meaning that he remains or stays behind, in contrast to קוּם (*qûm*), which indicates that the king gets up and exits. On Haman's perception of *his* status at that point, the Hebrew literally reads, "harm was intended for him from the king."

8 לִכְבּוֹשׁ (*likbôš*), translated "molest," generally means in biblical Hebrew "to subdue [with force]" (see *HALOT*, BDB). Daniel F. Polish ("Aspects of Esther: A Phenomenological Exploration of the Megillah of Esther and Origins of Purim," *JSOT* 85 [1999]: 88) notes that a sensitive reading of this verse raises the question as to Esther's complicity in Haman's precarious position. Perhaps in the king's absence, she duplicitously invites Haman to her in order to seal his fate.

Numerous references in the biblical text demonstrate that covering has to do with shame (e.g., Ge 3:7, 21; Jer 51:51; Ps 35:26; see Laniak, 117, 120). Clines (195, n. 2) concludes that references to the Greco-Roman custom of covering the head of a person condemned to death (Livy 1.26.6, 11; Quintus Curtius, *History of Alexander* 6.8.22; Cicero, *Pro Rabirio* 4:13) are misleading. They speak of covering the head, while the reference in Esther is to Haman's face; a death sentence has not passed yet at this point.

IV. EFFECTING JUSTICE (7:9–9:17)

A. Measure for Measure (7:9–8:2)

⁹Then Harbona, one of the eunuchs attending the king, said, "A gallows seventy-five feet high stands by Haman's house. He had it made for Mordecai, who spoke up to help the king." The king said, "Hang him on it!" ¹⁰So they hanged Haman on the gallows he had prepared for Mordecai. Then the king's fury subsided.

8:1 That same day, King Xerxes gave Queen Esther the estate of Haman, the enemy of the Jews. And Mordecai came into the presence of the king, for Esther had told how he was related to her. 2 The king took off his signet ring, which he had reclaimed from Haman, and presented it to Mordecai. And Esther appointed him over Haman's estate.

COMMENTARY

9 Given its excessive size, the hastily erected pole (ʿēṣ) could not be missed. Undoubtedly, curious inquiries prompted Haman to disclose his intent of getting rid of Mordecai. Harbona is shrewd and, having heard what has happened in the interval to both Haman and Mordecai, he weighs in against the man whose star is falling. His words resolve a ticklish situation for the king by supplying a second reason for imposing the death penalty on Haman (see Herodotus 1.137 for possible context) while reminding the cluster of eunuchs and other court functionaries that Mordecai has just been celebrated as a benefactor of the king. Attacking someone of that stature is deadly business (Fox, 88; Laniak, 110, n. 23). Xerxes commands that Haman be hung.

10 Haman's "fall," noted with foreboding by Zeresh and the advisers, is completed when his body is hoisted on the pole for the final humiliation. The measure-for-measure justice is also noted; he is hung on the pole he had prepared for Mordecai. Notably, even though this king is superficially concerned to operate according to law, one of the charges against Haman is, contrary to appearances, not true.

The significance of the king's anger subsiding must not be overlooked. It means that his attention is focused solely on the events and persons as they affect *him*. The fate of Haman, whose plot has threatened the king's own honor, is sealed. The fate of Esther's people, still unresolved, does not concern him.

8:1–2 Esther's identities as ruling queen, the recipient of what was Haman's estate, and the cousin of the honored benefactor of the king all converge at this point. In effect, she receives more than "half the kingdom" previously offered to her (Wyler, "Esther: The Incomplete Emancipation," in Brenner, 129)!

Mordecai's advance is parallel. Whereas the king's previous recognition of Mordecai was a temporary display, at this point he comes into the presence of the king, a place reserved for very few. He is given both Haman's political power, indicated by the signet ring (retrieved by the king in a moment of lucidity before the death of Haman), and his economic resources as newly appointed custodian of Haman's estate.

Even though he is dead, Haman is still identified as "the enemy of the Jews," perhaps as a sobering reminder that the forces continuing to plan for their destruction have not been defanged. Given the nature of virulent hatred of any stripe, Haman's death may have made his "disciples" more bloodthirsty. The task of Esther and Mordecai will be to change that situation, and the measures necessary to deal with evil are themselves destructive.

NOTES

9 Harbona had served the king a long time—he was one of eunuchs sent to fetch Vashti (1:10).

8:1 בַּיִת (*bayit*; lit., "house") refers to Haman's "estate" (see Ge 39:4; 44:1). Even though Esther earlier reported Mordecai's loyal deed, only at this point does she note his kindred relationship to her. It is appropriate that Haman's property goes to Esther as queen; under Darius, the Persian state confiscated a criminal's property (Herodotus 3:128–29).

B. Esther's Appeal for Justice for the Jews (8:3–6)

³Esther again pleaded with the king, falling at his feet and weeping. She begged him to put an end to the evil plan of Haman the Agagite, which he had devised against the Jews. ⁴Then the king extended the gold scepter to Esther and she arose and stood before him.

⁵"If it pleases the king," she said, "and if he regards me with favor and thinks it the right thing to do, and if he is pleased with me, let an order be written overruling the dispatches that Haman son of Hammedatha, the Agagite, devised and wrote to destroy the Jews in all the king's provinces. ⁶For how can I bear to see disaster fall on my people? How can I bear to see the destruction of my family?"

COMMENTARY

3 It is possible that this scene is a continuation of the same day's events (cf. Moore, *Esther*, 82; Bush, 439–40, 444; Clines, 98). In that case, the Hebrew idiom "she added and spoke" suggests a continuation of the high-level political exchanges that have already taken place. It seems more likely, however, that some time has elapsed. The quick succession of events necessary for that reconstruction does not seem likely in a Middle Eastern context and particularly in this court governed by excessive protocol. Mordecai's appointments alone may have taken considerable time.

The reference in v.9 to writing the counterdecree in the third month also suggests significant delay, during which time Esther and Mordecai grow increasingly anxious as they see nothing transpiring in regard to the fate of the Jewish people. Thus Esther again faces the prospect of entering into king's presence unannounced and uncertain as to whether he will extend to her the golden scepter. Her impassioned appeal is marked by falling at his feet, weeping, and imploring him for mercy, particularly with regard to the diabolical scheme of Haman, of whose lineage the audience is reminded.

While the narrator does not use the term *dāt* ("law"), this summary of her plea refers to its irrevocability with the causative form of the same word employed in 1:19. It is notable that Mordecai, even though he wears the king's ring, has not taken it upon himself to approach the king. Perhaps they conclude that only Esther, because of her relationship to the king, can possibly succeed in the endeavor. Nevertheless, Esther does venture into the king's presence fully aware that Mordecai wields significant power as second to the king. As a result, Xerxes gives the matter over to both of them (v.8).

4 Esther's posture in this appeal is noticeably different from her first entreaty. In that case, she stood at a distance, and only when the king extended the scepter did she approach and touch it. Here Esther, perhaps already ensconced in the king's presence, falls in supplication at his feet; after being assured of a hearing, she rises and stands before him.

5 Esther's artful plea, initiated with not a two-part but a four-part formula, appeals both to what is recognizably good (*tôb*) and right (*kāšēr*), and to the king's regard for her. Each of these aspects appears twice, and her appeal to goodness takes priority in each set. Her reference to what is right implies that the previous decree decidedly is not. In requesting that the evil decree of Haman be revoked, she follows good court form: (lit.) "let it be written to cause to return [*lᵉhāšîb*] the dispatches," followed by a further full naming of Haman. These carefully chosen words get the king off the hook, even

though the dispatches have been issued in his name, and put the blame for the edict squarely on Haman, now deceased. It is important to note that Esther's primary request is the revocation of the decree. When that request is refused, other means must be adopted.

6 Again there are two parallel expressions in this continuation of Esther's plea. The first has to do with her "people" in general, and the second addresses "my kindred" (a better translation of *môladtî* than "my family")—reversals of Mordecai's command to Esther not to reveal either (2:20). Because the king has evidenced little concern for her people, she grounds her appeal for them also in how it will affect *her* since her personal welfare seems to be what has moved the king. Her anguish was apparent in "How can I bear...?"

NOTES

5 The expression כָּשֵׁר ... לִפְנֵי (*kāšēr ... lipnê*) was used primarily in later Hebrew. The idiom occurs only here in biblical Hebrew.

6 The syntax of Esther's appeal is rugged—literally, "how would I be able ... when I have seen...?" She intentionally breaks off regarding her own fate, as she observes the destruction of her people and her kindred. רָעָה (*rāʿâ*) is a feminine noun, but the verbal form is masculine singular. אֵיכָכָה (*ʾêkākâ*) is used only here and in Song of Songs 5:3.

C. Over-writing the First Edict (8:7–14)

⁷King Xerxes replied to Queen Esther and to Mordecai the Jew, "Because Haman attacked the Jews, I have given his estate to Esther, and they have hanged him on the gallows. ⁸Now write another decree in the king's name in behalf of the Jews as seems best to you, and seal it with the king's signet ring—for no document written in the king's name and sealed with his ring can be revoked."

⁹At once the royal secretaries were summoned—on the twenty-third day of the third month, the month of Sivan. They wrote out all Mordecai's orders to the Jews, and to the satraps, governors and nobles of the 127 provinces stretching from India to Cush. These

orders were written in the script of each province and the language of each people and also to the Jews in their own script and language. [10]Mordecai wrote in the name of King Xerxes, sealed the dispatches with the king's signet ring, and sent them by mounted couriers, who rode fast horses especially bred for the king.

[11]The king's edict granted the Jews in every city the right to assemble and protect themselves; to destroy, kill and annihilate any armed force of any nationality or province that might attack them and their women and children; and to plunder the property of their enemies. [12]The day appointed for the Jews to do this in all the provinces of King Xerxes was the thirteenth day of the twelfth month, the month of Adar. [13]A copy of the text of the edict was to be issued as law in every province and made known to the people of every nationality so that the Jews would be ready on that day to avenge themselves on their enemies.

[14]The couriers, riding the royal horses, raced out, spurred on by the king's command. And the edict was also issued in the citadel of Susa.

COMMENTARY

7 Titles are prominent at this point: Esther *the Queen* and Mordecai *the Jew*. The word order of the king's response in Hebrew may hint at a slight degree of exasperation with this further request. Xerxes frontloads his own actions of justice by saying, "Look, I gave Haman's estate to Esther and he has been hung...." Implicit in that statement might have been, "What more do you want?" Another interpretation might be, "Haman is completely off the scene; you are free to do as you wish."

8 This verse begins with "*you* [pl.] write concerning the Jews whatever seems good to you," which suggests that Xerxes wants nothing more to do with the affair. That reading would fit his comprehensive indifference to anything that did not impinge directly on his own personal world. It may also imply that he knows he is trapped and again hands the responsibility over to someone else (Clines, 18–19).

Theoretically, his reference to the irrevocability of an edict officially written in the name of the king and sealed with his ring refers to both

Haman's decree and whatever is forthcoming. With this maneuver, Xerxes allows the precedent established by Haman to stand but also makes a way, tortuous though it is, to address the problem. In this exchange, there may also be simply a bit of realistic assessment. Runners have gone out to the entire kingdom giving permission to act on well-entrenched prejudices. How can the effects of such a decree ever be prevented? The only recourse is presumably the one he indicates here.

9 The narrative regarding the issuance of the decree (vv.9–14) bears distinct verbal parallels to 3:12–15; this decree is an explicit countermeasure. The changes, however, are noteworthy. This edict is written on the twenty-third day of the third month—seventy days after the first one, so perhaps a subtle reminder from the narrator that just as the return from exile had occurred as promised, so the Jews can be certain of this deliverance (Bush, 442). This decree is in accordance with everything that Mordecai, now in Haman's position, commands, and the first recipients on the list are the Jews, absent from the preceding roll of addressees.

Even though the Jewish population quickly became aware of the first decree, it was the intent of its malevolent framer that they be excluded and therefore caught unprepared. In this decree, the rest of the address list is compressed and the presumptuous titles removed, as though the satraps, governors, and nobles are all of a kind. The extent of the kingdom as articulated in the first chapter is here repeated, likely to indicate that this decree has the widest coverage governmentally possible, and its delineation is followed by a repetition that this edict is directed to the Jews in their writing and their language.

10 An additional subtle change from the preceding edict is that the verbal forms are active. Mordecai takes responsibility; he writes the edict in the name of the king, he seals it with the ring, and he sends it by means of the governmental couriers ("runners"). In contrast to the couriers delivering the previous decree, however, these couriers have excellent "horsepower" at their disposal. While it is clear that they ride the best horses the government can provide, even the ancient commentators were perplexed by the description (cf. *b. Meg.* 18a). Two of the words, *rammākîm* and *ʾaḥašterānîm*, are *hapax legomena*. The first part of the latter term, *ʾaḥaš*, appears in both the king's name and the title of the satraps. It is clear that these horses are animals reserved for imperial use.

11 Mordecai's edict says that the king permits the Jews in every city to organize themselves in order to take action and literally to "stand for their lives." The rest of the verse has prompted extensive commentary, particularly the reference to "little children and women" (lit. trans. of *ṭap weⁿāšîm*), which syntactically can be read as either the potential objects of Jewish action of slaughter or as Jewish women and children attacked by enemy forces.

To determine which interpretation is better, it is important to note the critical contrasts with the preceding decree as well as the terms that have been carried over precisely. In the prior decree the objects of "to destroy, kill, and annihilate" were "all the Jews — young and old, women and little children" (3:13). The present decree uses the same three verbs as Haman did in his decree; here these verbs have as their immediate objects "any armed force [*ḥêl*] [GK 2657] of any nationality or province that might attack them," which is then followed by (lit.) "little children and women."

In each case, "little children and women" is not connected by a conjunction to what has preceded. In the first decree, they clearly represent the most vulnerable objects of enemy attack. Here, these words immediately follow "those attacking [*haṣṣārîm*] them" and thus suggest the Jews are given permission to kill those in every location still intent on carrying out the original decree by "attacking them, little children and their women." Because the direct focus of the Jewish self-defense is armed adversaries, it is illogical to think that the governmental mandate is being issued against those least likely to be in that category.

A further direct quote of the previous edict comes at the very end with the permission to take plunder (8:13c). Given the fact that the following narrative emphasizes that the Jews do not take plunder even though they are permitted to do so, it seems that if there had been a legal allowance to slaughter women and children, some comment would have been made in that regard as well. But there is no such summary. Instead, it says how many "men" were killed in Susa — 800 in two days (9:12, 15) — and many "enemies" throughout the empire — 75,000 (9:16). In sum, Mordecai cites specific phrases from the previous decree to emphasize that this edict is specifically a countermeasure. Because of the irrevocability of these laws, the terms of the second edict must reflect those of the first as protection for the Jews. Both the description of the circumstances and the text itself substantiate the claim that the Jews are not given wholesale permission to slaughter. Instead, they are allowed to respond to the provocations that that will come as a result of those acting on the first decree.

12 Reiterating that the defensive measures are to occur in all the royal provinces, the edict closes with the already-established date, the thirteenth day of Adar.

At this point the LXX includes a full text of the edict, most likely encouraged by the first word of v. 13, "a copy." The A-Text inserts it after 8:7. It is ostensibly from the king (Artaxerxes in the LXX), describes the danger of people like Haman, and warns the recipients not to participate in the actions enjoined in the first decree because its author is dead. In the letter, the Jews are exhorted to live under their own laws, the populace is encouraged not to follow the previous decree while provision is still made for Jewish self-defense, and Haman is represented as a Macedonian, likely a product of reading into the text the high-profile contemporary enemy. It then institutes the holiday of Purim.

13 The text of 3:14 is reproduced here with two additions. First, "the Jews" are to be ready for this day. Second, they are to be ready in order "to avenge themselves on their enemies." Whereas the interpretive problems with v. 11 stem from syntactical ambiguity, this one is blatantly troubling. There is nothing that seems more foreign to a Christian

worldview than vengeance. Nevertheless, several important observations are in order.

The Hebrew root *nqm* (GK 5933) and its related verbal and nominal forms refer not only to personal revenge that is reprehensible (cf. Lev 19:18; Jdg 16:28) but also to God's vengeance, which is necessary in an evil world (Dt 32:41). It is an action that first presupposes a wrong and then sets it right. It is distinctly and appropriately punitive and is therefore a source of encouragement for those who suffer unjustly (cf. 1Sa 24:12). While God himself most frequently executes vengeance (Na 1:2; Lev 26:25; Isa 1:24; 34:8), there are occasions on which he uses agents to do so (Ex 21:20; Nu 31:2). Haman's crime against the Jews was heinous, all the more so because its effects have not ceased with his death. That edict was designed to unleash pogroms across the empire. On the level of state, national, and international relations, provision for self-defense is a necessary prerogative of governments to protect their people. To be avenged means for the Jews to be vindicated and, in this case, to live instead of die (see Baldwin, 100–102).

14 The extra urgency behind this decree is evident in the repeated fact that the "runners" are actually riders of the government-issued horses. They go out both hastened and pressed (passives), an expanded statement from that of 3:15. Finally, the law is also given in Susa, which experiences its own reversal. This law produces no consternation. Instead, the city goes wild with joy (v. 16).

NOTES

9 Perhaps to compress the events, the LXX has this action on the twenty-third day of the first month. The A-Text gives no indication of the date.

10 רֶכֶשׁ (*rekeš*) is a synonym for סוּסִים (*sûsîm*; 1Ki 5:8 [Heb.]), and from its use in Micah 1:13 it seems that these are chariot horses and likely powerful. See Gerald Klingbeil ("רכשׁ and Esther 8,10.14: A Semantic Note," *ZAW* 107 [1995]: 301–3) on the use of the term in an administrative context.

11 לְהִקָּהֵל (*lᵉhiqqāhēl*), a derivative from "to assemble," is best interpreted as organizing for the purpose of action (Haupt, 158).

For varying treatments and summaries of potential ethical problems with this text, see Gordis ("Studies in the Esther Narrative," 50–52), Moore (*Esther*, 81–83), and Bush, 447. See particularly Fox, 284–85, who attempts to show that the Hebrew simply does not allow the reading proposed above. The predominant view of the "little children and women" clause is that this edict *does* allow for the "slaughter of the innocents." From that perspective, the discussion then ranges to the ancient Near Eastern context in which women, children, livestock, and property all suffered the ravages of war, and to some parallels with the concept of holy war, in which all associated with certain enemies were given over for destruction.

D. "It's Good to Be Jewish!" (8:15–17)

> ¹⁵Mordecai left the king's presence wearing royal garments of blue and white, a large crown of gold and a purple robe of fine linen. And the city of Susa held a joyous celebration. ¹⁶For the Jews it was a time of happiness and joy, gladness and honor. ¹⁷In every province and in every city, wherever the edict of the king went, there was joy and gladness among the Jews, with feasting and celebrating. And many people of other nationalities became Jews because fear of the Jews had seized them.

COMMENTARY

15 Mordecai's sackcloth and ashes of ch. 4 and the temporary robe from ch. 6 are replaced with permanent accoutrements of royalty. What Haman craved, Mordecai is given and, in fact, is given in abundance. One robe becomes an entire ensemble, and instead of a paltry crown on a horse's head, Mordecai wears his own large, golden crown. Even so, a distinction is maintained between this diadem of gold (*ᶜᵃṭeret zāhāb*) and the crown (*keter malkût*) worn by the Persian royalty (1:11; 2:17; see also 6:8). In fact, the narrator may have subtly emphasized Mordecai's Jewishness at this point since *ᶜᵃṭārâ* is the word most frequently used in the Hebrew Bible for "royal diadem." The colors blue, white, gold, and purple are indicative of royalty. Whereas earlier he had been given the position of first minister, now he receives official investiture. Susa is exultant and rejoices (the reversal from 3:15), expressed with another set of dyads.

16 In contrast to mourning, fasting, weeping, and wailing (4:3), the Jews now have (lit.) "light, gladness, rejoicing, and honor"—obvious reactions to reprieve from genocide. The description starts with light, symbolic of goodness as opposed to evil, and moves through the emotional responses to the restoration of honor.

17 The spontaneous joy turns into an outright holiday with its own accompanying *mišteh* ("feast") for the Jewish communities everywhere.

The phrase *ᶜam hāʾāreṣ* (lit., "people of the land") is used frequently throughout the biblical text with reference to both Israelite inhabitants of Judah (cf. 2Ki 11:14, 18, 20; 24:14; Jer 1:18; Eze 45:22; Hag 2:4; Zec 7:5) and non-Israelites with whom they have contact (Ge 23:7, 12–13; Nu 14:9). The plural (ʿammê hāʾāreṣ) refers to non-Jews (1Ch 5:25; Ezr 3:3; 9:1, 2, 11), and here it indicates those people who choose to identify themselves with the Jews.

Just what such an identification means, however, is a question. The word mityaḥᵃdîm (from yāhad, GK 3366, "become a Jew") only occurs in Esther, and it was a direct response to "fear of the Jews" falling on them. The same fear is noted in 9:2 along with the "fear of Mordecai" in 9:3. Both the nominal and verbal forms of pḥd (GK 7064, "to fear") indicate intense and sudden fear to the point of trembling, and they appear predominantly, though not exclusively, in prophetic and poetic texts with reference to dread of the Lord or a nameless, numinous ter-

ror. This fact may, therefore, indicate that this identification is prompted by something more than a concern for political security, though that concern may play a part (cf. Clines, 40–41; Bush, 448–49).

It is uncertain, however, that true conversion is implied here. The best interpretation seems to be that they profess to be Jews for a wide variety of motives, one of which may have been fear of the God of the Jews. Given the intertextual connections with the Passover and the exodus that surface repeatedly through the text, it is of interest that numerous non-Israelites also joined the people leaving Egypt (Ex 12:38) and that one of the poetic renditions of those formative events notes that "dread of Israel had fallen on [the Egyptians]" (Ps 105:38).

NOTES

15 עֲטֶרֶת (ʿᵃṭeret) comes from a word meaning to encircle and may be rendered "wreath" or "diadem." תַּכְרִיךְ (takrîk), which described the second item of the royal garments, is used only here in biblical Hebrew. In Aramaic, the root כרך (krk) also means "to encircle" or "to twine around." Here the word could refer to some sort of cloak, or it might be a second term referring to a diadem that is wrapped around a tiara. This possibility is suggested by the LXX, which has two terms, both "crown" and "diadem" (De Troyer, "On Crowns and Diadems from Kings, Queens, Horses, and Men," in *IX Congress of the Internatioanl Organization for Septuagint and Cognate Studies, Cambridge 1995* [ed. B. Taylor; Atlanta: Scholars Press, 1997], 360–61).

On the explosion of joy in Susa, note that צָהֲלָה (ṣāhᵃlâ) means "she roared" or "shouted" (Haupt, 161).

17 The LXX interpreted מִתְיַהֲדִים (mityaḥᵃdîm) as conversion and states that the peoples "circumcised themselves and became Jews." Also of interest is the possible implication in the *A*-Text that some Jews had avoided circumcision, perhaps as a result of assimilationist tendencies; it reads, "many of the *Jews* circumcised themselves" (8:41, Addition E).

E. Self-Defense and Relief from Enemies (9:1–17)

1. Events of Day One (9:1–10)

¹On the thirteenth day of the twelfth month, the month of Adar, the edict commanded by the king was to be carried out. On this day the enemies of the Jews had hoped to overpower them, but now the tables were turned and the Jews got the upper hand

over those who hated them. ²The Jews assembled in their cities in all the provinces of King Xerxes to attack those seeking their destruction. No one could stand against them, because the people of all the other nationalities were afraid of them. ³And all the nobles of the provinces, the satraps, the governors and the king's administrators helped the Jews, because fear of Mordecai had seized them. ⁴Mordecai was prominent in the palace; his reputation spread throughout the provinces, and he became more and more powerful.

⁵The Jews struck down all their enemies with the sword, killing and destroying them, and they did what they pleased to those who hated them. ⁶In the citadel of Susa, the Jews killed and destroyed five hundred men. ⁷They also killed Parshandatha, Dalphon, Aspatha, ⁸Poratha, Adalia, Aridatha, ⁹Parmashta, Arisai, Aridai, and Vaizatha, ¹⁰the ten sons of Haman the son of Hammedatha, the enemy of the Jews. But they did not lay hands on the plunder.

COMMENTARY

1 The Hebrew text highlights the date and the developing tension with one complex sentence. Because the two conflicting decrees had established this day, the resulting bloodshed is inevitable, and there are key stylistic indicators in the Hebrew text of the impending crisis. Even though there were two edicts issued in the name of the king, the expression is singular here. Each side could appeal to "the word of the king." The hope of the enemies of the Jews to dominate (*lišlôṭ*) is matched as the Jews dominate (*yišlᵉṭû*, from the same verb) those who hate them.

The centerpiece between these two statements is *nahᵃpôk hûᵓ*, "it was overturned" (NIV "tables were turned"), emphasizing the complete reversal and summarizing the victory to be described. At the same time, the bitter truth is that the deadly edict issued by Haman is not overturned in the same way that the gallows intended for Mordecai was revisited or the honor that Haman planned for himself was given to Mordecai. God did not intervene directly by eradicating the existing decree. Instead, it had to be overturned with armed battles, which were costly. It is telling that there were significant numbers of those who "hoped to overpower" the Jews.

2 The Jews were given the right to organize ("be assembled together") in order to "stand for their lives" (8:11). As the events unfold on the thirteenth of Adar, they attack those seeking their harm. The expression for "attack" (lit., "to send the hand") is the same one used to describe the assassination attempt against Xerxes. In fact, that no one can stand before them suggests the possibility of offensive action on the part of the Jews (cf. Jdg 2:14 for the same use of the idiom). The language accurately portrays the complexity and "messiness" of situations such as this one. A somewhat undefined horror had fallen on the non-Jewish inhabitants in anticipation of the day when Jews could defend themselves, and now there is a real dread as the result of seeing their power and the effective measures of self-defense.

3–4 Just as common folk dreaded the Jews, leadership at every rank had come to dread Mordecai. As a result of his decree, attacking the Jews was no longer officially sponsored (cf. 3:12). In fact, Mordecai's decree commanded these authorities to permit Jews to defend themselves and to kill those who would attack them (8:11). The rulers throughout the realm, being politically astute, chose to go with the second decree because in the intervening months Mordecai had become increasingly powerful (*hôlēk weˡgādôl*).

The order of the titles of Persian government officials is varied from 3:12 and 8:9. The earlier lists were in order of descending rank, while this one lists first the nobles, who may have been actively assisting local Jewish populations. In addition, those functionaries who did the work of the king also aided the Jews. These were the same workers whom Haman had expected to participate in effecting the financial arrangements of his decree (3:9).

5 This verse is central in the ethical discussion that rages over the events at the end of Esther. Simply put, is this a massacre of Gentiles that is no different from any other ethnically based offensive? There are those who claim that it was indeed a harsh preemptive strike; after the second decree, no one would have been intent on attacking the Jews. Instead, the Jews strike all their enemies, there is wholesale killing and destruction of life, and they do "what they please" to their foes.

This last comment has an undefined but repugnant sound to it. Nevertheless, this attack, for such it was, is a response to those attacking them, who were intent on harming them (9:2) and who viewed this occasion as an opportunity to destroy them completely. The Jews' offensive action is necessary in the light of the irrevocable decree that officially sanctioned their demise. The unfolding of these events intimates that there was a strong anti-Semitic sentiment that had been brewing all along.

The victims of the Jews were enemies, people who hated them (Levenson, 121; Baldwin, 104; Bush, 463–64). The verbal pair *hrg* and *ˀbd* recurs throughout this description of the Jewish attack on their attackers (vv.5–6, 12) and represents the measured response put precisely in the terms of the decrees. Once the bloodshed subsides, the narrative repeatedly emphasizes that the Jews got *rest* from their enemies (9:16–18); the relief was palpable.

6 If the five hundred men (*ˀîš*) killed in Susa represent those who attacked Jews, there was great hostility to Jews right in the capital. Some interpreters view this number and the figures that follow as further indications of exaggeration in the text (Fox, 110; Bruce Jones, "Two Misconceptions about the Book of Esther," *CBQ* 39/2 [1977]: 180). It is likely, however, that long-festering hatred, having been nurtured by the leadership, had a life of its own apart from rationality and blazed in the Persian "street" after Haman's death. The order of words in the Hebrew text "forefronts" Susa to prepare the reader for the distinction between it and other locations and the subsequent institution of two days' worth of festival observance (Bush, 472, 474).

7–10 In the MT (Hebrew text), the names of Haman's ten sons are placed in two columns—possibly an allusion by the ancient copyists to the sons' ultimate suspension on poles (9:14). The sons may have attacked Jews to avenge their father's death and as a result lost their own lives. They may also have been leaders in an anti-Jewish and anti-Mordecai insurgence. The name and honor of Haman would have been carried on by his descendants; thus this action cuts off his posterity, and the point is driven home by reiterating the title that had defined his presence in the book: "Haman, son of Hammedatha, the enemy of the Jews." Publicly hanging their bodies was a form of humiliating the name of Haman (cf. the Philistines' exposing the bodies of Saul and his sons [1Sa 31:10, 12]).

Finally, three separate statements stress that the Jews do not lay their hands on the enemy's plunder (vv.10, 15–16), thus demonstrating extraordinary restraint. Mordecai's generation succeeds where Saul himself failed. In his encounter with the Amalekites and King Agag, Saul had kept the best of the animals instead of giving them over to the Lord for destruction (*ḥērem*) and then piously but shamelessly tried to rationalize that maneuver when Samuel challenged him (1Sa 15:2–23).

NOTES

1 After the extensive temporal description comes נַהֲפוֹךְ (*nahápôk*), an infinitive absolute, followed by the pronoun—likely not sequential with the preceding clauses but standing independently as the main point of the verse.

"Those who hated [the Jews]" is repeatedly used synonymously with "enemies of the Jews." Hatred in the biblical world was not solely an emotional response; bound up with it was rejection and, in the case of persons, active intent to harm (see Laniak, 140, n. 38).

2 The fear of God's people by nations who have observed the mighty acts of God in his people's behalf is a familiar motif (Ex 15; Jos 2:8–11). What is different here is the absence of any direct attribution of these developments to the power of God.

5 מַכַּת־חֶרֶב (*makkat-ḥereb*; NIV "struck down … with the sword") is not used anywhere else in Scripture in contexts of self-defense.

6 The expression "killed and destroyed" again has the finite verb followed by an infinitive absolute (cf. 2:3) that carries on the sense of the first verb.

7–9 The names of the sons may suggest some relationship to Daiva, an eastern term that came to be associated with demonic powers (see Moore, *Studies in the Book of Esther*, xxxix; Jobes, 198). Why certain of the Hebrew letters in the names are smaller is unknown.

2. Conference between the King and Esther (9:11–14)

¹¹The number of those slain in the citadel of Susa was reported to the king that same day.

¹²The king said to Queen Esther, "The Jews have killed and destroyed five hundred men and the ten sons of Haman in the citadel of Susa. What have they done in the rest of the king's provinces? Now what is your petition? It will be given you. What is your request? It will also be granted."

¹³"If it pleases the king," Esther answered, "give the Jews in Susa permission to carry out this day's edict tomorrow also, and let Haman's ten sons be hanged on gallows."

¹⁴So the king commanded that this be done. An edict was issued in Susa, and they hanged the ten sons of Haman.

COMMENTARY

11 "That same day" stands first in the verse in Hebrew, emphasizing again the time factor that is so important for eventually establishing the festival.

12 In reporting to Queen Esther, the king repeats Susa's casualty list in the same words as it was originally narrated (9:6), followed by the specific reference to the sons of Haman. The next clause about the rest of the provinces, rather than being a direct question, might rather be, "I wonder what they have done in the rest of the provinces." "They" is ambiguous here; it could refer to either the adversarial forces or the Jews, or both. The uncertainty embedded in the "question," along with the unexpectedly large numbers in Susa, may have contributed to the king's reiteration of his promise to grant Esther further action.

Perhaps it has begun to dawn on the king that this unrest is an exceedingly serious problem *for him* as well as for the Jews. Forces that attacked Jews are attacking two people who are now closest to him, one of whom he has publicly honored as "Mordecai the Jew." In court contexts that seem always to be brimming with intrigue, the consequences of the turmoil set in motion by Haman's decree are alarming. In his response to Esther he slightly alters the formal question, no longer promising half the kingdom but asking, "What more...?" and allowing her to define the necessary measures.

13–14 A hint of Esther's boldness may lie in the fact that she no longer prefaces her request with the twofold condition including an appeal to the king's attachment to her. This time she simply places it in the context of "if it pleases the king."

From this point on, two issues intertwine in the narrative developments. First, it is evident that the threat of hostilities lingers; a deterrent action is advisable. Second, from the standpoint of legislation, the two-day festival has to have a firm foundation. The latter has its beginnings here and is expanded considerably in the rest of the chapter. Regarding the former, both the initial decree of Haman and Mordecai's counterdecree limited the fighting to one day. The day has come and gone with the Jews victorious, *as far as they know*, only in the citadel of Susa, with fighting sufficiently fierce that five hundred men have been killed. Esther's request may have been formulated within the framework of the continuing uncertainty.

Just as the report dealt with the citadel of Susa and Haman's ten sons, so also does her request, although the first one expands to the entirety of Susa. Both parts of the plan are designed to forestall further attack. In Susa, the Jews can act the following day "according to the *dāt* of today," which meant self-defense when attacked, and the bodies of Haman's sons will be hoisted high on the poles. What the king and Esther do not know at this point is the extent of the Jewish resistance throughout the empire. Those figures no doubt come in slowly. At this point, the king's response comes in the context of the known events in Susa.

3. Relief from Those Who Hated Them (9:15–17)

¹⁵The Jews in Susa came together on the fourteenth day of the month of Adar, and they put to death in Susa three hundred men, but they did not lay their hands on the plunder.

> ¹⁶Meanwhile, the remainder of the Jews who were in the king's provinces also assembled to protect themselves and get relief from their enemies. They killed seventy-five thousand of them but did not lay their hands on the plunder. ¹⁷This happened on the thirteenth day of the month of Adar, and on the fourteenth they rested and made it a day of feasting and joy.

COMMENTARY

15 The expansion to the entire city of Susa is initially puzzling. The confusion in the city at Haman's edict (3:15) and its rejoicing when it was overturned (8:15) may indicate that Susa was sympathetic to the Jews. Even so, it appears there was a minority that harbored malevolent intentions. Since the mandate (9:13) was that they act according to the law, the three hundred people killed by the Jews the fourteenth of Adar in Susa are those who initiated the attack—a sobering commentary on the tenacity of hatred. As before, the narrative emphasizes the point of honor that the Jews refrain from taking plunder.

16–17 If Esther is to be read within any kind of historical framework, then to be just to its characters it is necessary to assess these developments in the context of their access to information. As events unfold in Susa into the fourteenth day, the narrative resumes its summary of the empire-wide confrontations that occurred the previous day, even though those results may not have been known for some time in the power center of Susa. The rest of the Jews organized and "*stood* for their lives" (as in 8:11).

The theme of "the rest/remainder" resounds in the next three verses. That the text is so emphatic in this regard is a commentary on the fierceness of the anti-Jewish sentiment that has compelled 75,000 persons in the empire to act with sufficient aggression toward the Jews that they get themselves killed. Although this number is widely dismissed as an exaggeration, along with other aspects of the

narrative, Perisa was a vast empire and there were extensive Jewish populations in major cities both in the eastern and western parts of the realm; once the statistics filtered back, the large number does not strain credulity. That no Jewish casualties are mentioned does not mean there were none. The point to be taken from this figure is the depth and breadth of anti-Jewish hatred.

Four centuries later, the Persian ruler Mithridates VI ordered satraps and overseers of cities in western Asia Minor to kill all Italian residents, including women and children, with the royal treasury sharing the plunder of the victims. Depending on the source, the latter massacre claimed between 80,000 and 150,000 persons (John G. F. Hind, "Mithridates," in *Cambridge Ancient History* [2nd ed.; ed. J. A. Crook, Andrew Lintott, and Elizabeth Rawson; Cambridge: Cambridge Univ. Press, 1994], 9:148; Appian [*Roman History, Mithridatic Wars,* Book 12.4.22–23] narrates the details; Plutarch [*Life of Sulla* 24] gives a figure of 150,000 thousand; Valerius Maximus [9.2.4] gives the number 80,000).

Just as the relief is emphasized, so also is the fact that the Jews do not take any plunder from their enemies, even though they have been permitted to do so by the measure-for-measure form of the decree. This last detail is stated three times following the number of persons slain (vv.10, 15–16). The time factor is the focus of v.17; it is important to underscore that the conflict in the provinces is limited to the thirteenth day and that it is followed by cessation on the fourteenth day. In spontaneous response to the great relief, the day is marked with feasting and joy.

These two features characterize the subsequent, formally established institution of the festival. Already after Mordecai's elevation and the issu-

ance of the decree, rejoicing occurs and honor is restored for the Jews (8:16). There continues to be, however, a cloud of uncertainty with the edicts still impending. The thirteenth and fourteenth of Adar are necessary to accomplish the "rest."

NOTE

16–17 The structure of these verses is unusual. That the subject ("the remainder of the Jews") of the first clause appears first suggests a deliberate turn of attention outside Susa. The perfect verb ("they had organized") is followed by three infinitive absolutes, to "protect themselves," "get relief," and "kill." The relief comes as a result of the killing in self-defense. Perhaps the infinitive absolutes, in addition to sustaining a pattern familiar in Esther, are a way of indicating the chronological complexity of these events in the manifold locations throughout the empire. There is no intention of indicating that these are successive events.

S. R. Driver's suggestion that וְנוֹחַ (wᵉnôaḥ) should be emended to וְנִחֹם (wᵉniḥōm, "and avenged themselves") because the former contradicts what follows is unnecessary ("Problems and Solutions," *VT* 4 [1954]: 237; see also Paton, 291). This verbal pattern continues in v.17, which is mirrored in v.18 as it begins to articulate the basis for the Susan distinction in celebrating the festival. In each case, the verbs follow temporal clauses. The main point of this structure and its repetition (more doublets) is to give credence to the two days of festival celebration.

V. ESTABLISHING THE FESTIVAL (9:18–9:32)

A. The Distinctives in Days (9:18–19)

> **18**The Jews in Susa, however, had assembled on the thirteenth and fourteenth, and then on the fifteenth they rested and made it a day of feasting and joy.
> **19**That is why rural Jews — those living in villages — observe the fourteenth of the month of Adar as a day of joy and feasting, a day for giving presents to each other.

COMMENTARY

18 At this point, because "legislation" is forthcoming regarding the days of celebration, the distinctions between Susa and the vast empire are reiterated. The actions in Susa echo those from the provinces; they *assembled* for two days, *rested* on the

fifteenth, and *observed* that day with feasting and joy. The time indicators are important, as they are woven into the verbal pattern of finite verb followed by two infinitive absolutes.

19 "That is why" (*ʿal-kēn*; "therefore") indicates a forthcoming summary statement of practice based on the preceding recital of events. This summary reappears in v.26 with the naming and final authorizing of the festival. In contrast to the urban Jews of Susa, those living in outlying villages celebrate their festival on the fourteenth day. These rural contexts are defined in terms of the Jews who are *peruzîm* (the written form in the MT)/*perāzîm* (the form that was read; NIV "rural") living in towns that are *perāzôt*.

The meaning of *prz* is not easily determined, as it is not frequently used. The halakic expansions in the Mishnah (*m. Meg.* 1:1–3) and the Talmud (*b. Meg.* 19a) later interpreted this word as "unwalled town" or "village." Because the distinction here has to do with Susa as opposed to points outside, the most logical explanation is that Jews who were *peruzîm* were in jurisdictions outside the capital, as were towns that were *perāzôt* (Bush, 477; see also Gordis, "Studies in the Esther Narrative," 57.

In addition to the immediate feasting and joy of the holiday, the tradition begins to solidify with the sending of "presents" to each other. The Hebrew word is *mānôt* (pl.; GK 4950), the same term used to indicate the "portions" that Hegai arranged for Esther to have (2:9). This care to make verbal connections is another indication that the book has been authored as a unit (Baldwin, 112–14).

The wider biblical usage of this term indicates the special nature of these portions. The *mānâ* was the part of the offering waved before the Lord (Ex 29:26; Lev 7:33; 8:29). Elkanah gave *mānôt* to both of his wives (1Sa 1:4–5); Samuel reserved a *mānâ* in anticipation of Saul's coming (1Sa 9:23); and priests and Levites received *mānôt* from the contributions brought to the temple (2Ch 31:19). When Ezra read the Torah, the people were told to rejoice, eat and drink, and send *mānôt* on this day set apart for the Lord (Ne 8:10–12). Psalm 16:5 links together "portion" and "lot" (*gôrāl*), and the following verse, "lines have fallen in pleasant places," attests to God's providence in the life of the psalmist—a point of connection with the Esther narrative (see Berg, 45–46; Baldwin, 112–13).

Starting the verse with "therefore" and noting the traditions that developed serves as a transition from the events of the original Purim to the narrator's temporal context (Bush, 477–78).

B. Writing to Confirm (9:20–32)

OVERVIEW

The focus of the text moves from the narrative of deliverance to rejoicing and rest and, finally, to the means for perpetuating the memory of that tremendous occasion. It appears that the Jews had immediately set aside particular days and began "doing" the observances associated with the festival. It is, however, with the intent to preserve the memory that Mordecai now writes (vv.20, 23)

"these events" of Purim, and they are established, confirmed, or imposed (*leqayyēm*).

There are seven uses of *leqayyēm*. It occurs three times without the following *ʿal* ("upon") and in these cases means "confirm" or "validate." When used with *ʿal* it means "to make binding/impose on someone." These occurrences uniformly appear after some indication of writing (vv.21, 27, 29, 31

[3x], 32). The repetitious element in these verses and the general tangle of language to "establish" this new tradition come together in a remarkably apt form to convey the monumental effort to confirm the observance of Purim. In the commentary that follows, the intent is to explain how these sections make a statement as a unit rather than betray disparate and irreconcilable sources. On the relationship of this section to what precedes and the possible sources that Mordecai and the author use, see Clines, 39–63, and the evaluation of Clines' position by Levenson, 125–32.

1. The Impetus to Write (9:20–23)

> [20]Mordecai recorded these events, and he sent letters to all the Jews throughout the provinces of King Xerxes, near and far, [21]to have them celebrate annually the fourteenth and fifteenth days of the month of Adar [22]as the time when the Jews got relief from their enemies, and as the month when their sorrow was turned into joy and their mourning into a day of celebration. He wrote them to observe the days as days of feasting and joy and giving presents of food to one another and gifts to the poor.
> [23]So the Jews agreed to continue the celebration they had begun, doing what Mordecai had written to them.

COMMENTARY

20 While there is some question as to what exactly Mordecai writes and what he sends out, the repetition of "he wrote" in v.23 followed by the summary of events from Haman's evil scheme to his demise (vv.24–25) suggests that the intervening material (vv.21–23) serves as another recapitulation that stresses the need for commemoration.

Undoubtedly the essence of it is in Mordecai's summary. Verse 24 begins with *kî* ("that"), indicating that what follows forms the contents of Mordecai's dispatch to the Jews near and far summarizing the events leading up to the fateful decree. Those Jews in more distant locales may not have clear knowledge of how all the tumultuous events have occurred. If this particular document includes only that material, that factor might explain the necessity of subsequent memoranda to clarify all the details

about observance. Mordecai's writing of the end of Haman the Agagite is an echo of Moses' record that the memory of Amalek would be erased (Ex 17:14). There is a subtle contrast between Mordecai, who himself writes (thus suggesting that he is literate), and the king and Haman, who had scribes write for them (Klein, 173–74). Esther also writes for herself (v.29).

21 The Hebrew ("to impose upon them to be observing ... ") suggests that what follows is the intended *result* of Mordecai's sending out his dispatch, not necessarily what is in that communication. The communication from Mordecai enjoins on them the continued annual observance of both days. Presumably the recipients know which of the two to celebrate, depending on where they live and what they have experienced.

22 This two-part statement engages Jewish memory of the roots of the festival. Echoing key words, it harks back to the days when they got rest from their enemies (9:16–18) and to the month of the great turnabout (9:1). Subsequent generations are to celebrate these days with the same vitality and in the same manner as those original communities who experienced deliverance. The fourteenth and fifteenth days and the month of Adar will be freighted with meaning because anguish turned to joy and mourning to a festival.

It was all too extraordinary; the narrator does not want to lose that sense of wonder, and the activities that were spontaneous are now to serve as equally vibrant reminders. They are to have days of feasting, rejoicing, exchanging *mānôt*, and, in an addition that makes certain no one is excluded, sending them to the poor. The last instruction may have been a reminder of Esther's originally marginalized status.

23 In developing the tradition, the Jews receive (*qibbēl*) information from two sources that are equally authoritative in defining what will become a new festival. First, allowing popular practice to define future observance, they accept what they have already begun to do. The activities that are immediately part of the celebrations are summarized in vv.19, 21–22. Second, the Jews receive what Mordecai has written regarding the events that led up to the crisis, the historical précis in vv.24–25.

NOTES

20 Early commentators, among them Rashi, determined on the basis of this verse that Mordecai was the author of the entire text. Paton, 293, concludes that the letter consisted of vv.21–22, urging the Jews to observe both days and to celebrate as indicated.

21 See *HALOT* on קִיֵּם (*qiyyēm*) and its implications when used with varying prepositions.

23 The singular verb along with "the Jews" suggests a corporate unity about this enterprise of receiving tradition; the same form recurs in the *Kethiv* of v.27. In later Hebrew, קִבֵּל (*qibbēl*) developed the connotation of receiving authoritative tradition (see *m. ʾAbot* 1).

2. Linking the Narrative and the Celebration (9:24–28)

24For Haman the son of Hammedatha, the Agagite, the enemy of all the Jews, had plotted against the Jews to destroy them and had cast the *pur* (that is, the lot) for their ruin and destruction. 25But when the plot came to the king's attention, he issued written orders that the evil scheme Haman had devised against the Jews should come back onto his own head, and that he and his sons should be hanged on the gallows. 26(Therefore, these days were called Purim, from the word *pur*.) Because of everything written in this letter and because of what they had seen and what had happened to them, 27the Jews took it upon themselves to establish the custom that they and their descendants and all who join them should without fail observe these two days every year in the way prescribed and at the time appointed. [28]These days should be remembered and observed in every generation by every family, and in every province and in every city. And these days of Purim should never cease to be celebrated by the Jews, nor should the memory of them die out among their descendants.

COMMENTARY

24–25 Verse 24 begins with *kî* ("that"), suggesting that the next two verses are intended as the summary of Mordecai's communication. In this public document, Mordecai demonstrates that he is an exceedingly skillful diplomat by fully implicating Haman while carefully reshaping the king's part in the events to present him as the hero of the narrative. In the process Mordecai avoids any reference to the parts that he and Esther played. This tactic is a delicately executed maneuver to restore the significantly tarnished honor of the king.

Mordecai's letter also compresses the details considerably. As the events originally unfolded, Haman cast *pûr*, the lot, in order to determine the *day* for the annihilation of the Jews. In this abbreviated summary, the lot was cast to crush and destroy them. Likewise, the succinct statement here makes it sound as though Haman and his sons were hung on the poles at the same time. Mordecai states outright Haman's full lineage and the designation, "the enemy of all the Jews," followed by a terse description of his intent and methodology. The description serves notice that the festival is designed to celebrate deliverance from the terrible evil of Haman and not the paramilitary victory.

As Mordecai turns to the king's part (v.25), his choice of words obfuscates the issue considerably and likely intentionally. The first Hebrew word of v.25 is *ûb^ebōʾāh*, translated, "and when she/it [feminine suffix] came." This word might refer to Esther's initial venture into the king's presence (5:1) or to

the news of Haman's plot (*maḥ^ašabtô*, a feminine noun) coming before the king, *or*, ambiguously, to both as Esther made her second impassioned plea to the king—a context that refers to "the evil plan of Haman the Agagite, which he had devised against the Jews" (8:3). In the last case, with some small degree of compression, Mordecai can successfully make it appear as though the moment the king discovered Haman's plot, he ordered that this evil be addressed.

Thus Mordecai avoids any mention of that embarrassing first decree that had to be overturned. Further, by using the expression (lit.) "he [the king] said with the edict [*sēper*] let his [Haman's] evil plan return," Mordecai subtly puts together his own written decree, issued in the name of the king, to counter Haman's edict and the king's command to display the bodies of Haman and his ten sons. In this presentation, the end of Haman comes to represent the end of the crisis initiated by his criminal decree. As an intriguing parallel, Haman had modified the truth about the Jews when he brought the matter to the king in ch. 3; here Mordecai reshapes the truth about the king as he presents it to the Jews.

26–27 At this point there is another summary statement, ostensibly to bring further focus to the flurry of details that lies behind the legislation for a new festival. "Therefore" in v.19 had to do with the important distinction of two days. "Therefore" at the beginning of v.26 addresses the official name of the festival. A culminating "therefore" precedes the statement in v.27 (untrans. in NIV) that the Jews do actually take on themselves and their posterity the obligation to observe the two days of Purim without fail every year.

There are several possible reasons for substituting the plural "Purim" even though *pûr* is singular. First, the original casting of *pûr* determined one day for the slaughter of Jews. As the events unfolded, there were ultimately two days occupied with the events. For that reason, the name recognizes the multiple days. No doubt these elements are an intentional part of the doubling pattern throughout the book. Second, the plural name is a way of recognizing the reversals themselves. In effect, there were two lots; one was cast by Haman to determine a day of disaster, and the second came from God in behalf of the Jews (see Introduction: Purposes of the Text).

The third "therefore" in this lengthy and convoluted legislative piece draws together a final statement that the Jews both obligate themselves and accept (*qiyyᵉmû wᵉqibbᵉlû*, v.27) the obligation. There is nothing new here; it reiterates the prior material but in yet another formal statement presented with the proper rhetorical dyad. Their resolve to establish the festival is based on all the words of "this letter" (just quoted), what they have seen in this regard, and what has happened to them.

Again, the written testimony is augmented by the experience of the people as already noted

(v.23). The force of this commitment extends to their descendants and to those who join them. From the exodus onward, there was a consistent pattern of non-Israelites' being welcomed and likewise accepting the attendant religious obligations (Ex 12:48-49). The term used here (*nilwîm*; NIV "[all] who join them") appears in Isaiah 14:1 and 56:3-6. In a clear parallel to the irrevocability of the laws of the Persians and the Medes (Est 1:19), this obligation will not pass away (*lōʾ yaᶜᵃbôr*). The permanent establishment of this two-day festival on the basis of written word and developing ritual is assured.

28 This finale emphasizes the boundless nature of the celebration in terms of time, social structures, and geographical locations. There is a return to the passive form here, hinting that what has been active legislative process has now moved into the category of accepted law. The components of the verse emphasize the "two-ness" with the repetition of generation, family, province, and city. The days themselves are mentioned twice, and they are to be both remembered and observed. Memory is also invoked two times. There is a second reference to these days not passing away, and the mention of Jews in that context is matched with "their descendants" in the clause that follows. In sum, these factors comprise forceful testimony to the power of memory within community to sustain that community.

NOTES

24 There is a difference of opinion on how to interpret לְהֻמָּם (*lᵉhummām*). *HALOT* suggests that the root המם (*hmm*; GK 2169) is best understood as "confuse" or "disturb." The parallelism with לְעַבְּדָם (*lᵉʾabbᵉdām*) as well as the connotations of Jeremiah 51:34 suggest, however, that it should be "rout," "defeat," or "crush." Further, the verb is used in contexts of war, and particularly holy war (Ex 14:24; 23:27; Dt 2:15; Jos 10:10; Jdg 4:15; see O'Connell, *NIDOTTE*, 1:1046-48). The word's similarity of sound to Haman's name may have been intentional.

26 It has been suggested that the plural name for the festival is the result of assimilation to the pattern of Jewish festivals, most of which are plural (Clines, 201, n. 43). Of particular interest in this regard are Passover, called Pesaḥim in rabbinic literature but *pesaḥ* and *ḥag hammaṣṣôt* (Lev 23:5–6) in the biblical text, and *yôm hakkippurîm*. The latter, designated day of "atonements" (Lev 23:27–28; Nu 29:11), has several intriguing connections with Purim. The high priest cast lots over the two goats — one for the Lord and one for Azazel, a clear dichotomy between good and evil. There is further a phonological similarity between the two festival names. See Gershom Scholem, *The Messianic Idea in Judaism* (New York, Schocken, 1971), 54–55.

3. Esther and Mordecai Authorize the Festival (9:29–32)

²⁹So Queen Esther, daughter of Abihail, along with Mordecai the Jew, wrote with full authority to confirm this second letter concerning Purim. ³⁰And Mordecai sent letters to all the Jews in the 127 provinces of the kingdom of Xerxes — words of goodwill and assurance — ³¹to establish these days of Purim at their designated times, as Mordecai the Jew and Queen Esther had decreed for them, and as they had established for themselves and their descendants in regard to their times of fasting and lamentation. ³²Esther's decree confirmed these regulations about Purim, and it was written down in the records.

COMMENTARY

29 With all the emphatic and repeated language of confirmation and obligation that accompany the writing and distribution of Mordecai's first letter (9:20, 23, 26), Queen Esther's composition of a second letter, to which Mordecai also contributes, is puzzling, especially since it initially sounds as though she (they) write(s) a second letter to confirm (*leqayyēm*) the second letter!

Several observations may help sort this out. First, there is a louder ring of authority with this letter. Esther adds the weight of her Persian royal position and her Jewish patrimony to the standing of "Mordecai the Jew," and together they write as forcefully as possible (*'et-kol-tōqep*). This is an admittedly awkward grammatical construction, but the main point is that they recognize the challenges of establishing a new festival amidst the venerable collection of already existing ones, and they do not hesitate to bring their authority as two members of

the Jewish community to establish, institute, affirm, confirm, and make obligatory this newly minted festival! Thus the text includes extensive repetitions of imposing and accepting the obligation to observe these days. The significance of this process of institution cannot be overstated. That Esther writes authoritatively is repeated in v.32. Mordecai's presence here is to prepare for the specific reference to his sending these documents.

Second, just as the narrative refers to Mordecai's writing and sending his letter (v.20) significantly before addressing the details of that letter (vv.24–25), so also the contents of this second letter, which constitute the material that Esther affirms, may yet be forthcoming. These matters include Mordecai's "words of goodwill and assurance" (v.30), the repeated confirmation and exhortation to accept the obligation, and the added details about fasting and lamentation (v.31). These last two items are new and may give a further indication of the need for another authoritative letter. Given the potential for confusion regarding days, locations, and appropriate practices, certain aspects are articulated more thoroughly, while the overall shape of the festival is reiterated.

30 Mordecai oversees the distribution of this official document as he did the preceding one (v.20). Noting the 127 provinces at the end of the book balances their mention in ch. 1. Both *šālôm* ("peace"; NIV "goodwill") and *ʾemet* ("truth"; NIV "assurance") are fundamentally significant concepts in the biblical worldview. It may be that part of the forceful and authoritative tone of these texts for the Jewish communities also is the result of their being laced with already existing and recognized biblical language. In deliberately using scriptural "words of goodwill and assurance," Mordecai sets the widely flung Jewish community at ease.

There are echoes of Zechariah 8:19, which indicates that institutionalized fasts would become festivals of joy and urges the people of God to love truth and peace. The people have been through disruptions and trauma caused by insidious lying. By contrast, *šālôm*, related to the verbal root *šālēm*, implies setting matters right by means of recompense. Thus the victory of the Jews has contributed in some small way to the righting of the social order (Laniak, 161–63).

31 Most of this verse restates the sense of obligation to keep the festival of Purim. It is both imposed by Esther and Mordecai and acknowledged as self-imposed as well. In both cases the expression is *leqayyēm ʿal*. Esther's letter, however, adds the matter of fasting and lamenting, perhaps giving credence to a practice that developed to mark the danger they experienced. This memorializes the great three-day fast (*haṣṣōmôt*, an intensive plural) as well as the outcry as they mark the Jewish response to the initial crisis (see Haupt, 77–78; Samuel E. Loewenstamm, "Esther 9:29–32: The Genesis of a Late Addition," *HUCA* 42 [1971]: 123). Because anguish and mourning were noted in 9:22 as elements of the great reversal, Esther and Mordecai may have thought it appropriate that the ritual serve to remind participants of both the weeping and the joy.

32 The power of Esther's word (*maʾamar*), the first word in the Hebrew of this verse, is evident in that it establishes these commemorative aspects (*dibrê*) of Purim and is written, made permanent, and therefore accessible (Fox, 127). *Maʾamar*, used only in Esther, indicates the authoritative word of the king (1:15), Mordecai (2:20), and now Esther. In effect, her words are on a par with those of Xerxes and Mordecai. Here we have another example of the inclusios that signify the unity of the text (cf. B.W. Jones, "The So-Called Appendix to the Book of Esther," *Semitics* 6 [1978]: 36–43, esp. 41).

NOTES

29 It is possible to read אֶת־כָּל־תֹּקֶף (*ʾet-kol-tōqep*) as a direct object that is not an abstraction, such as power, might, or authority, but something that is written, has legal strength, and is a valid document. If this reading is correct, Esther authors a legally binding text (see Loewenstamm, "Esther 9:29–32," 119–20). While that possibility is interesting, it still does not fully address the problem of the "second" letter. For a summary of views in that regard, see Bush, 469–70, who suggests deleting it along with "Mordecai the Jew."

30 Gordis ("Studies in the Esther Narrative," 57–58) suggests that "words of peace and truth" may have been the standard formula for the beginning of a letter. In that case, the rest of the letter is summarized in v.31.

VI. HONOR IN THE REALM OF AHASUERUS (10:1–3)

> [1]King Xerxes imposed tribute throughout the empire, to its distant shores. [2]And all his acts of power and might, together with a full account of the greatness of Mordecai to which the king had raised him, are they not written in the book of the annals of the kings of Media and Persia? [3]Mordecai the Jew was second in rank to King Xerxes, preeminent among the Jews, and held in high esteem by his many fellow Jews, because he worked for the good of his people and spoke up for the welfare of all the Jews.

COMMENTARY

1 Although these final verses are not in the *A*-Text and have been designated another of the additions (Clines, 57), they bring appropriate closure to the text. Xerxes, the magnitude of his realm, and *his* power are key themes in ch. 1. Here they are restored after having experienced some shock waves. To close the text with accolades to Esther and Mordecai but no acknowledgment of the king would be a serious lapse.

At the same time, however, the point must not be missed that Mordecai shares significantly in that honor. Xerxes imposes "tribute" or "forced labor" (*mas*), indicating his control to the farthest reaches. This imposition affects (lit.) "the land and the islands of the sea," a possible inference that the western "border" stopped at that point instead of reaching to Athens. David Daube proposes that the *mas* is designed to address the potential loss of revenue from Haman's failed scheme and is a more stable economic measure than a round of pillaging ("The Last Chapter of Esther," *JQR* 37 [1946/47]: 139–47). The idea is discounted by Fox, 129; Clines, 57–58; and Bush, 494, but that rejection may be due to their preconceived notion that these chapters are additions to the original text. In any case, it indicates that the kingdom is back to stability (Levenson, 132; Laniak, 164, n. 91).

2 The reference to the authority and power of Xerxes serves as a backdrop for the real focus on Mordecai. In closing, this encomium awards him a place in the annals of the kings of Media and Persia and draws explicitly on the stock phrase describing the deeds of the kings of Israel and Judah (1Ki 11:41; 14:19, 29; 2Ch 32:32; 35:26–27; etc.). It also echoes the record established in Esther 2:23 and revisited in 6:1, although that chronicle seems to have been something less official. Up to this point, even though Mordecai had been a leader in the Jewish community with his position in the gate and his public mourning, Esther had arranged for each of his political advances. Here the record indicates that he is an excellent grand vizier of his own accord.

3 The introductory "that" (*kî*) at the beginning of the verse indicates the basic contents of the record about Mordecai. He is second to the king—a fact clearly echoing Joseph's role—and he is a benefactor to the Jews. This notation may be linked to the indication in v.1 about the tax/tribute. By urging Xerxes to reestablish regular taxation, Mordecai assists the king in creating a system for economic stability and providing a context for his own people to contribute to their government in a systematic way rather than as the target of plundering assaults (Daube, "The Last Chapter of Esther," 145).

Mordecai's prominent position sets the stage for the historical roles of Ezra and Nehemiah, who will follow him as leaders both in the Persian court and in the struggling Jewish community in Judah. He continues as an advocate and spokesperson in the government for the Jewish community.

The text closes with (lit.) "speaking peace [šālôm; NIV "welfare"] for all his descendants"—a poignant reminder of the necessity for Jews through-out the succeeding centuries to have someone able to intercede for their well-being. While Mordecai had expressed the confidence that help would arise from "another place," the grim reality is that persecution also continues to arise from "other places" (Beal, 106). That great need for shalom for Mordecai's descendants ("his seed") lies in the shadow of the greater One of those descendants who both spoke and made shalom. The events of Esther mean that God's people, through whom blessing will come to all nations (Ge 12:3), are preserved for the coming Intercessor.

NOTES

1 In biblical Hebrew, מַס (mas) implies "forced labor" (Ge 49:15; Dt 20:11; Jdg 1:30–35; 1Ki 5:14). Nevertheless, by the Assyrian period tribute paid to the ruling empire was monetary (cf. 2Ki 18:14). While the term *mas* does not appear in that context, Hezekiah was obligated and, in fact, promised to "lift up" whatever the king of Assyria demanded. In this regard, note the option of translating מַשְׂאֵת (maśʾēt) as relief from taxation or tribute (Est 2:18).

2 Arguing for the unity of the text, Daube ("The Last Chapter of Esther," 139) noted that פָּרָשַׁת גְּדֻלַּת (pārāšat gᵉdullat; NIV "account of the greatness"), not used elsewhere in biblical Hebrew, occurs in 4:7 (pārāšat hakkesep; NIV "amount of money") and in this contested section.

There is a subtle touch of historical authenticity in the reference to the chronicles (NIV "annals"). Whereas the phrase "laws of Persia and Media" (1:19) places the dominant force of that era (Persia) first, it seems that their chronicles may have spanned possibly even centuries. Thus Media, as the initially prominent power, is given priority here.

3 The LXX has its own sense of closure. The dream of Mordecai about the warring dragons, reported in the first chapter of the Greek text, is interpreted at the end. Haman is one of the dragons; Mordecai is the other. The Lord is responsible for the salvation of Mordecai's people.

JOB

ELMER B. SMICK

REVISED BY TREMPER LONGMAN III

Introduction

1. BACKGROUND

The uniqueness of the book of Job derives from its depth and thoroughness in dealing with the relationship of human suffering to divine justice, commonly called theodicy (from Gk. *theos* ["god"] and *dikē* ["justice"]). Numerous documents, especially from ancient Mesopotamia and Egypt, demonstrate that this genre of wisdom writing was well established in the OT world;[1] but none touch on these matters so eloquently and fully as this OT book. In a Sumerian document he calls "Man and His God," Jacob Klein relates the tale of a man who in his affliction complained to his "personal" god while wailing for mercy:[2]

> My companion says not a true word to me,
> My friend renders my words,
> truthfully spoken, a lie.
> The man of deceit speaks
> insulting words to me;
> (But) you, my god,
> do not thwart them!

Like the biblical Job, this "Job" was restored; "his god harkened to his bitter tears and weeping," which "soothed the heart of his god."

---

1. For a general survey of the issue, see R. G. Albertson, "Job and Ancient Near Eastern Wisdom Literature," in *Scripture in Context II* (ed. W. W. Hallo; Winona Lake, Ind.: Eisenbrauns, 1983), 214–30.
2. See *COS*, 1:573–74; see also S. N. Kramer, " 'Man and His God': A Sumerian Variation on the 'Job' Motif," in *Wisdom in Israel and in the Ancient Near East* (ed. M. Noth and D. W. Thomas; Leiden: Brill, 1955), 170–82.

Another poetic monologue also written in the second millennium BC is commonly called "I Will Praise the Lord of Wisdom" (*Ludlul Bel Nemeqi*; *ANET*, 434–37; *COS*, 1:486–92). This Babylonian "Job" is like the Sumerian one. As a righteous sufferer he also reckoned with the thought that Marduk, the cosmic god, allowed him to suffer. Yet he hoped that by means of ritual piety he would obtain mercy; but he had his doubts: "Oh that I only knew that these things are well pleasing to a god!" (2.33). He too was restored and ended with a thanksgiving hymn and offerings that "made happy their [i.e., the gods'] mood" and "gladdened their heart" (4.40).

These documents share literary structures and lament language in common with the biblical book of Job but deal with the meaning of suffering in a way that expresses their own social, ethical, and cultic standards—all polytheistic. Job is emphatically monotheistic, but the sufferer's predicament is the same, so similar issues and solutions are discussed. For example, in "A Dispute over Suicide" (*ANET*, 405–7), a man of Egypt debates with his BA ("soul" may be the closest English equivalent) over suicide because times (between the Old and Middle Kingdoms) are so bad that there is no more justice or love.[3] He finally decides death is better because men then become like gods in the netherworld. As Job longed for an advocate (Job 9:33; 16:19, 21; 19:25–27), so this man pleads for the advocacy of the gods and feels that he is presenting his case before a divine tribunal (*ANET*, 405, n. 2).

As for literary structure, this document bears a striking likeness to the book of Job in its A–B–A pattern, which begins, as does Job, with a short prose prologue, followed by a long poetic section, and ending with an epilogue in prose. This pattern finds expression in other ancient Near Eastern documents.

Still another document, from as early as 1000 BC, is called "A Dialogue about Human Misery" (*ANET*, 438; also known as The Babylonian Theodicy [see *COS*, 1:492–95]). This is even more like Job. It is a dialogue involving a friend who accuses the sufferer of imbecility and evil thoughts and suggests that he put aside such thoughts and seek the gracious favor of a god. The sufferer complains that animals do not have to make offerings, and that even people who get rich quickly do so without paying attention to the gods, while he who has done all the right things from his youth suffers. The friend warns him in these words:

> The mind of the god,
> like the center of the heavens,
> is remote;
> His knowledge is difficult,
> men cannot understand it. (lines 256–57)

The friend's view seems to be that the gods have made people perverse, and there is nothing that can be done about it. "Falsehood and untruth they [the gods] conferred upon them [men] forever" (line 280). The sufferer finally appeals to the gods for mercy, and the dialogue ends there on a fatalistic note.

So while the literary genre and overall format of the book of Job came from the world of which it was a part, there is really nothing extant that compares with the biblical book in its philosophical and theological

---

3. See H. Goedicke, *The Report about the Dispute of a Man with His BA* (Baltimore/London: Johns Hopkins Univ. Press, 1970).

profundity. Moreover, the book of Job cannot be forced into any single literary classification. It is generally called Wisdom literature, but that describes more the subject matter than the form. John Milton classified the book of Job as a subspecies of epic. C. S. Lewis, for one, considered this reasonable.[4] Although the book is not an epic, the Prologue has the stereotyped forms and expressions of an old epic tradition. The book also displays a dramatic intention that says something about its authorship and unity (see below). Job's antiwisdom in contrast to the wisdom of the counselors intensifies the dramatic aspect.

The book of Job is largely poetry of various genres (lament, wisdom, proverbs, hymns, etc.), and in places it is more difficult to understand than any other part of the OT. This appears to be due more to the language than to textual corruption, though critics still claim the text has suffered greatly in transmission. Pope considers chapters 24–27 thoroughly scrambled.[5] Job abounds in *hapax legomena* (words occurring only once in the Hebrew Bible). The grammar, syntax, and orthography (spelling) often stand outside the regular forms of classical Hebrew.

The more extensive literature of the cognate languages helps us interpret the difficult parts of the language of Job. Scholars have long used Arabic and Aramaic for help in vocabulary and elements of grammar. The Elihu speeches have an Aramaic flavor. Aramaic elements scattered throughout the book have led some to view it as originally written in Aramaic and later translated into Hebrew.[6] On the other hand, Dahood views the book as strongly influenced by earlier Canaanite patterns detectable through Ugaritic.[7]

Though his method and application have been seriously questioned, Dahood and his students attempted to use the poetic texts from Ugarit (Ras Shamra) to shed light on the language of Job.[8] The book has often been looked on as some form of Edomite work since Job is called a "man … of the East" (1:3). Edom was a reputed center of wisdom (cf. 1Ki 4:30), but we have no Edomite literary documents to test this view. Arabic, Aramaic, Hebrew, Ugaritic, and Phoenician are all northwest Semitic; and all may be included in what Isaiah calls "the language of Canaan" (Isa 19:18). We have no written Arabic from OT times, nor any appreciable amount of Edomite or Ammonite documents; but one of the oldest and longest documents from preexilic Transjordan is the Moabite Stone (Mesha Inscription). Being prose, it throws little light on Job. It does, however, show how this nearby language could have been understood easily by any Hebrew. So the unique Hebrew of Job and his counselors may fall into a similar category as another dialect perhaps of Edomite origin.

Since Ugaritic has a sizeable extant corpus of West Semitic poetic literature, it lends itself to comparative usage. Arabic grammar is instructive since it has preserved archaic forms (case endings, etc.), though

4. C. S. Lewis, *A Preface to Paradise Lost* (New York/London: Oxford Univ. Press, 1961), 4.
5. M. H. Pope, *Job* (AB 15; 3rd ed.; New York: Doubleday, 1973), xl.
6. N. H. Tur-Sinai, *The Book of Job: A New Commentary* (Jerusalem: Kiryath Sepher, 1957); cf. also Guillaume, "The Arabic Background of the Book of Job," in *Promise and Fulfillment* (ed. F. F. Bruce; Edinburgh: T&T Clark, 1963), 106–27.
7. M. Dahood, *Ugaritic-Hebrew Philology* (Rome: Pontifical Biblical Institute, 1965).
8. Cf. A. C. M. Blommerde, *Northwest Semitic Grammar and Job* (BibOr 22 ; Rome: Pontifical Biblical Institute, 1969); A. R. Ceresko, *Job 29–31 in the Light of Northwest Semitic* (BibOr 36 ; Rome: Pontifical Biblical Institute, 1980); and a variety of articles by M. Dahood in *Biblica* from 1957–1982 (for a listing, see E. Smick, "Job," *EBC¹* [Grand Rapids: Zondervan, 1988], 873).

its late date and large lexicon weaken its comparative value. Aramaic and Phoenician have little poetic material, though there are many documents from the OT period. Babylonian-Assyrian provides poetry for comparison, but it must be used cautiously since its morphology and syntax are East Semitic.

In this commentary I will use comparative linguistics to deal with difficult passages involving *hapax legomena*, rare meanings of homonyms, and rare syntax. Revocalizing will be resorted to only where a problem appears—that is, where the Hebrew as it stands is obviously strange or yields little sense.

2. AUTHORSHIP AND UNITY

Is Job of single or composite authorship? One critical approach makes it a gradual aggregation of materials on an original base.[9] The wisdom poem of chapter 28, the Elihu speeches in chapters 32–37, and the Yahweh discourses in chapters 38–41 are said to be additions. Much has been made of the supposed incongruities between the Prologue-Epilogue sections and the Dialogue. In the former Job is presented as a saint of God who will not curse God and die; in the latter his complaints are bitter to the point of being shocking, while his friends seem to be saying all the right things. Then come the unexpected rebuke of the friends and the commendation of Job in the Epilogue (42:7–8). Some scholars think this destroys the unity of the book. When considering these things along with the different literary form (prose vs. poetry) and Job's ritual piety in the Prologue-Epilogue (features missing in the Dialogue), they have concluded that the Prologue-Epilogue has come from a different source.

The Prologue-Epilogue, it is said, represents an old epic-tale used as a framework by the author of the Dialogue. This tale about a legendary figure named Job (Eze 14:14, 20) was used to give more advanced concepts about theodicy an impressive hoary antiquity. But Ewald says that it is not fully legitimate to ask "whether the work of the poet as we possess it contains history or fiction, as if a third thing were not possible."[10] His idea is that the book is an artistic masterpiece skillfully put together by a great poet who used materials available to him, and it is true that the book makes no claim of having been written by Job.

To return to the problem of the apparent incongruities mentioned above, the Israeli scholar Y. Kaufmann explains the problem of God's rebuking the friends and not Job himself by suggesting that the friends are guilty of clichés and empty phrases, while Job's challenge to God reflects a moral duty to speak only the truth before him.[11] This is more satisfactory than assuming, as some do, that the book has lost a large portion in which the friends, like his wife, tell Job to curse God and die. Job himself accuses his friends of currying favor with God by saying things they do not believe (13:7–8).

One cannot, of course, assume that there are no deletions or interpolations at all in Job. Yet a fair mind must recognize the singular organic unity of this extensive piece of OT literature. The brevity of Bildad's speech and the omission of Zophar in chapters 24–27, combined with Job's use of the argument of his detractors (27:13–23), may indicate such a deletion and/or interpolation. It is possible but by no means certain. Commentators cannot agree on how to handle the problem in chapters 24–27. Most shift

---

9. For different views of this, see P. P. Zerafa, *The Wisdom of God in the Book of Job* (Rome: Herder, 1978).

10. G. H. A. Ewald, *Commentary on the Book of Job* (trans. J. F. Smith; Edinburgh: Williams & Norgate, 1882), 20.

11. Y. Kaufmann, *History of the Religion of Israel from the Babylonian Captivity to the End of Prophecy* (trans. C. E. Froymsen; New York: Ktav, 1976), 335.

sections around to suit themselves. Pope claims the material was deliberately scrambled by someone who tried to refute Job's arguments by confusing the picture. This is only a guess, so it is just as satisfactory to work with the text as it is, assuming a breakdown in the debate and a final attempt by Job to be as eloquent as they are on the fate of the wicked. See the comments on chapter 27.[12]

Much is made of the fact that Elihu is ignored in the Epilogue as though this were proof that he was put in by an interpolater. But Satan is also ignored in the Epilogue; and even Pope, who takes a dim view of the authenticity of the Elihu speeches, admits they have been blended in with the rest of the book with great skill. Much depends on how one views the speeches themselves. On the role of Elihu, see the Overview to that section. The complaint against the first divine speech (ch. 38) on the basis that God is indifferent to the human predicament is a misunderstanding of the purpose of the divine speeches. (See Purpose; see also the Overviews to the divine speeches.)

Some critics accept as even more spurious the second divine speech, on Behemoth and Leviathan. But others regard it as the climax of the book and even more original than the first. Some writers have satirized the divine speeches, making God appear cruel and indifferent to human suffering.[13] Such abysmal lack of sensitivity to what many see as a literary and theological triumph is all too typical.

The overall A−B−A literary structure this book shares with other ancient compositions (see comments on "A Dispute over Suicide" above and also "The Code of Hammurabi," *ANET*, 164−80) is only the most obvious structural accomplishment of the author. There are other artful and balanced structures throughout the book, witnessing to a creative composition, not merely an arbitrary compilation. Job opens the Dialogues with a lengthy lamentation of his condition. This expected genre is used throughout by Job, but not in the specialized form of individual lament found in the Psalms.[14] The one exception is Psalm 88, which sounds much like Job (cf. Ps 88:8 and Job 19:13−19); but in keeping with the spirit of the Psalms, even Psalm 88 begins with a strain of hope (v.1). Job's laments, like Psalm 88, tend to be mostly negative (something like the grumbling tradition of Numbers); but the attempt to make them totally negative is an unfortunate scholarly quibble. The lengthy lament of chapter 19 clearly ends in hope.

Much of the book takes the form of legal disputation. Although Job's friends come to console him, they soon fall into a bitter dispute over the reason for his suffering. The argument breaks down in the third cycle, and Job is left to deliver a peroration on a theme he has repeatedly brought up: his own vindication (chs. 29−31). The wisdom poem in chapter 28 is the work of the unknown author who views the failure of the dispute as evidence of a lack of wisdom. In praise of true wisdom, he centers this structural apex between the three cycles of dialogue-dispute and the three monologues: Job's (chs. 29−31), Elihu's (chs. 32−37), and God's (chs. 38−41). In chapters 29−31 Job turns directly to God for a legal decision—that he is innocent of the charges the counselors have leveled against him. Elihu's monologue is another human perspective on why Job has suffered. More needed to be said on the value of divine chastisement and the redemptive purpose of suffering.

---

12. See also Zerafa, *The Wisdom of God in the Book of Job*, 1−28.
13. Cf. A. MacLeish, *Job, A Play in Verse* (Boston: Houghton Mifflin, 1957).
14. Cf. C. Westermann, *The Psalms: Structure, Content, and Message* (Minneapolis: Augsburg, 1980).

Architectonics of the
Book of Job[15]

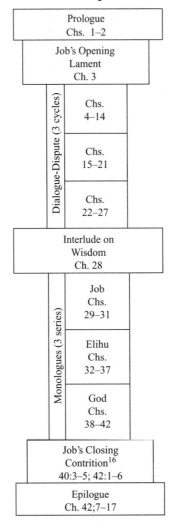

God's monologue presents the divine perspective. Job is not condemned as one who is being punished for sin, but neither is he given a logical or legal reason for his suffering. It remains a mystery to Job, though the reader is ready for Job's restoration in the Epilogue, because he has had the heavenly vantage point of the Prologue. So the architectonic and the theological significance of the book are beautifully tied together. (See the diagram above.)

15. Cf. J. F. A. Sawyer, "The Authorship and Structure of the Book of Job," in *Studia Biblica* 1978/1 (ed. E. A. Livingstone; JSOTSup 11; Sheffield: JSOT, 1979), 253–57; also C. Westermann, *The Structure of the Book of Job: A Form-Critical Analysis* (Philadelphia: Fortress, 1981), 6.

16. Job's words of contrition are divided to provide a response to each divine speech. The first is preparatory to the second.

It is neither prudent nor necessary to assume a view of the composition of the book that rules out the possibility of the use of source materials and some kind of literary development involved in the composition of the book of Job. But the fact is, any attempt to know exactly what that was is sheer guesswork. There is as much reason to believe that the book, substantially as we have it, was the work of a single literary and theological genius as to assume it is the product of numerous hands often with contrary purposes. We do not know who the writer was, but his work has witnessed to the spirits of the faithful through the ages that he was divinely inspired.

It is likely that the poet based the material on wisdom poetry passed down through the generations. The wisdom poetry of the speeches in Job includes poetic genres such as laments, hymns, proverbs, and oracles. Also, as in all Semitic poetry, parallelism is foremost. This comes from an artistic urge toward symmetry through balanced lines and other units of composition. The double line, or bicolon, tends to prefer a balance in form, that is, an equal weight of syllables (or accents) on either side of the line, except where unbalanced lines are used for other reasons. We call these unbalanced bicola "the lament form" (*qinah*), but it is not limited to lamentations. The balance of thoughts (meaning) on both sides operates similarly. The latter may be partially synonymous (the same) or antithetical (opposite) or may be entirely absent.

The poet, however, was a free spirit; so he created unique and intricate patterns of relationship between thought and form parallelism. Although the bicolon is usual, a rare monocolon and the more frequent tricolon are also employed, as is the double bicolon (quatrain). The patterns the poet creates with these principles are limitless, and they have given rise to many terms to describe the parallelism, such as introverted, stairstep, climactic, complete, incomplete, and void. The symmetrical urge also applies to strophes, stanzas, and whole poems where the climax is as likely to be in the middle as at the end. Structure on a wide scale that includes whole speeches and books has only recently begun to be appreciated. The strophic patterns play a role in literary and textual criticism and consequently in interpretation. See the commentary for various structures and patterns that often illuminate meaning. Line parallelism can only be fully appreciated on the basis of the Hebrew word order; so translations can only approximate what is there. The few samples below are an attempt (somewhat in vain) to overcome that problem.

Job 13:12 illustrates complete synonymous parallelism in a balanced bicolon with chiasm (crossing of elements):

> Your-maxims (are) • proverbs-of-ashes;
> defenses-of-clay (are) • your-defenses.

Hebrew syllables (form) 8 / / 8
Pattern (thought) a • b / / b' • a' (chiasm).

Job 5:9 illustrates incomplete synonymous parallelism in a balanced bicolon:

> He-performs • wonders • that-cannot-be-fathomed,
> miracles • that-cannot-be-counted.

Hebrew syllables (form) 7 / / 7
Pattern (thought) a • b • c / / b' • c'.

Job 8:20 illustrates incomplete antithetical parallelism in a balanced bicolon:

> Surely-God • does-not-reject • a-blameless-man
> or-strengthen the-hand-of-evildoers.

Hebrew syllables (form) 6 (8) / / 8
Pattern (thought) a • b • c / / B' • C'.[17]

Job 38:2 illustrates synthetic parallelism (no parallel thoughts) in a balanced bicolon:

> Who-is-this • that-darkens • my-counsel
> with-words • without-knowledge?

Hebrew syllables (form) 6 / / 6
Pattern (thought) a • b • c / / d • e.

Job 20:23 illustrates the balanced tricolon with synthetic and synonymous elements. Tricola are often formed by combining an opening line with a bicolon that completes the sense:

> When-he • has-filled • his-belly,
> (God)-will-vent • against-him • his-burning-anger
> and-rain-down • upon-him • his-blows.

Hebrew syllables (form) 8 / / 8 / / 8
Pattern (thought) a • b • c / / d • e • f / / d' • e' • f'.

Job 19:27 illustrates the tricolon with two synonymous lines completed with a synthetic line:

> Whom-I • will-see • for-myself
> my-eyes • will-see • and-not-another
> (How)-yearns • my-heart • within-me.

Hebrew syllables (form) 8 / / 8 / / 8
Pattern (thought) a • b • c / / a' • b' • c'/ / d • e • f.

---

17. The capital letters B and C indicate heavier elements originally used to balance the weight in syllables, but here the first line lost some final original vowels that contributed a number of additional syllables. This whole matter becomes somewhat theoretical; therefore, one should avoid dogmatism about the balance of lines and certainly should not emend the text on that basis.

Job 15:2 [1] illustrates a quatrain made of two synonymously parallel bicola that are tied together in thought and form:

<blockquote>

Would-a-wise-man • answer • with-empty-notions
or-fill • with-(hot)-east-wind • his-belly?
Would-he-argue • with-words • that-are-useless,
with-speeches • that-have-no-value?

</blockquote>

Hebrew syllables (form) 8 / / 7 / 8 / / 7
Pattern (thought) a • b • c / / b' • c' • a'; a • b • c / / b' • C'.

3. DATE AND SOURCE

As is true with much Wisdom literature, the actual composition of the book of Job as we have it is hard to date with precision. Suggestions range from the Mosaic era with Moses as author,[18] to the Solomonic era,[19] on into the seventh century BC and the unsettled and unfortunate times of Judah's king Manasseh after Sennacherib had besieged Jerusalem.[20] A. B. Davidson argues for a seventh-century date by observing that the questions of providence entered a new phase when God's laws were no longer calmly expounded but subjected to doubt, and a condition of great disorder and misery forms the background of the book of Job.[21]

Buttenweiser asserts that Job was written by "at least 400 BC"; and at the same time he insists that arguments purporting to show that the existence of a folk tale of Job was current in the sixth century BC,[22] during the time of Ezekiel's ministry,[23] are ultimately mistaken.

Doctrinal clues are mentioned by some authors as considerations one must take into account in trying to establish a probable date for the book of Job. Delitzsch, in support of his view of a Solomonic date,

---

18. Gleason Archer (*A Survey of Old Testament Introduction* [Moody, 1964], 464) approvingly cites the early Jewish tradition that the book was either authored or rewritten by Moses; so also the Talmud (*y. Soṭah* 5.8; *b. B. Bat.* 15a), Origen, Jerome, and other church fathers.

19. F. Delitzsch, *Job: Biblical Commentary on the Old Testament* (K&D; repr. Grand Rapids: Eerdmans, 1971), 1:21.

20. Ewald, *Job*, 76.

21. Davidson (*The Book of Job* [CBC; Cambridge: Cambridge Univ. Press, 1918], lx) argues that the "new phase" is seen in that one scarcely finds trace of the problems and questions that fill the book of Job in Proverbs, even though the same general subjects are treated in both books. An interesting and rather extended contrast with Delitzsch's view is found in Davidson (ibid., lx–lxx). The reader of these two views is left with the impression that either era is still open as a possibility, rather than that one sufficiently negates the other to the point of becoming a preferable view.

22. "All that follows from this bare reference is that alongside Noah and Daniel, Job had enjoyed the renown of exemplar piety ... the likelihood must be granted that the Job of the story current at the time of Ezekiel had little, if anything, in common with the suffering hero of the Book of Job. Ezekiel, who most consistently developed the view that there can be no punishment without sin and who made this the basis of his preaching, could not but have viewed Job's calamity in exactly the same light as the friends did" (M. Buttenweiser, *The Book of Job* [London: Hodder and Stoughton, 1922], 8–9).

23. Argued by K. Budde (*Das Buch Hiob* [Nowack Handkommentar; 2nd ed.; Göttingen: Vandenhoeck and Ruprecht, 1913], xii–xiii) on the evidence of Ezekiel 14:14–20.

claims that in 19:29 Job reflects only a personal belief regarding future judgment of humanity, whereas later Wisdom writings (e.g., Ecc 12:14) expressed it as a "settled element of general religious consciousness."[24] Nor is Job 19:25–27 "an echo of an already existing revelation of the resurrection of the dead," but it is an "acknowledgment of revelation which we see breaking forth and expanding throughout Isa. xxvi.19, comp. xxv. 8, and Ezek. xxxvii. comp. Hos. vi. 2, until Dan. xii.2."[25] The representations of the future in the book of Job are the same as those in Psalms, which come from the time of David and Solomon, and in the Proverbs of Solomon.[26]

Jastrow hypothesizes a religious evolution from an early conception of the gods as arbitrary figures to be appeased on a changeable, sometimes whimsical basis to a later conception of rule by God according to his self-imposed laws of righteousness and justice; through this he argues for a postexilic date of approximately 400 BC. He feels that Job contrasts what is with what ought to be. The problem of Job is thus "one which directly arises out of the basic doctrine of post-exilic Judaism ... and it was inevitable that the question would sometime be raised, whether what the prophets taught of the nature of God which the people accepted as guidance in their lives was compatible with the facts of experience."[27]

Davidson contrasts Wisdom as perceived in Job and Proverbs 1–9.[28] In Proverbs 1–9 Wisdom earnestly presses herself on human beings: she loves them that love her. Even when she rises to the highest conception of herself as architect of the world, she still offers herself to us and may be embraced by us (Pr 8:32). But the speaker in Job 28 despairs of wisdom: it can nowhere be found, neither in the land of the living nor in the place of the dead, neither by humanity nor by any creature.

Jastrow agrees and feels that Job and Proverbs 1–9, "being two such opposing representations, can hardly be contemporaneous."[29] But in stating this view, Jastrow perhaps unwittingly lends additional support to Delitzsch's position. It does indeed seem improbable that two such opposing views would be contemporaneous, but Delitzsch maintains that there are three Wisdom periods: (1) Proverbs and Song of Solomon (Solomonic era); (2) Proverbs 1–9 (Jehoshaphat's time); and (3) Ecclesiastes (postexilic).[30]

---

24. Delitzsch, *Job*, 1:22.

25. Ibid. A case may be made that the resurrection in Isaiah, Ezekiel, and Hosea is not personal but national. But compare M. J. Dahood (*Psalms 1* [AB 16; New York: Doubleday, 1965], xxxvi) on the concept of resurrection and immortality in preexilic times.

26. Delitzsch (ibid., 1:23) lays stress on Heman's being the author of Psalm 88:

> Besides, the greatest conceivable fullness of allusion to the book of Job ... is found in Ps. lxxxviii, and lxxxix, whose authors, Heman and Ethan ... [were] the contemporaries of Solomon mentioned in 1 Kings v. 11 [4:31 EV]." The agreement in either thought or expression of these Psalms and Job has "no such similarity as suggests a borrowing, but an agreement which, since it cannot possibly be accidental, may be most easily explained by supposing that the book of Job proceeds from much the same Chokma-fellowship to which, according to 1 Kings v. 11, the two Ezrathites ... belong.
>
> "One may go further, and conjecture that the same Heman who composed Ps. lxxxviii, the gloomiest of all the Psalms, and written under circumstances of suffering similar to Job's may be the author of the book of Job."

27. M. Jastrow Jr., *The Book of Job* (Philadelphia: J. B. Lippencott, 1920), 36.

28. Davidson, *Job*, lxi.

29. Jastrow, *Job*, 36.

30. Delitzsch, *Job*, 1:21.

A postexilic date for Job is rejected by Pope on the grounds that Job's suffering would have been seen as a parable of the nation's fate, and there is no hint of this or of any nationalistic concerns in the book. Moreover, the choice of an Edomite hero would be extremely unlikely because of the strong feeling against Edom by the prophets as a result of their aiding and abetting the enemy at the fall of Jerusalem (cf. the book of Obadiah).

Modern views have been many and varied, but the most recent tendency supports an early date. Urbrock points out that

> evidence is mounting for the antiquity of both the poetic and prose portions of Job. Robertson has shown that "verbal patterns of early poetry occur extensively in …Job" and that a clustering in Job of other linguistic forms characteristic of archaic Hebrew verse points similarly to an early date … he suggests as a working hypothesis the dating of Job to the "eleventh-tenth centuries." Again, Dahood and Pinar, Pope's commentary, Blommerde's grammatical analysis, and Michel's studies of mythological expressions in Job … have all demonstrated the usefulness of interpreting Job in the light of linguistic principles and thematic motifs exhibited in the Ugaritic texts from the fourteenth century BC. On the other hand, the prose prologue and epilogue have been shown to be "saturated with poeticisms in vocabulary and style" and to employ "some unique forms explicable by reference to Ugaritic," so that "the considerable amount of epic substratum indicates that our present narrative framework is directly derived from an ancient Epic of Job (Sarna, *JBL* 76:25)."[31]

In his dissertation Urbrock suggests that the formulaic nature of the poetry, when considered along with the thematic structure of the dialogue, indicates that a traditional oral song-cycle of Job lies behind the book of Job now preserved in the OT. This is quite convincing in itself as an argument for the possible antiquity of Job. Such a traditional oral song-cycle may indeed have very early roots, perhaps even preceding the eleventh-tenth century BC date mentioned by Urbrock.[32]

It is possible, then, that the book of Job, or perhaps parts of the book, existed outside Israel for a long time as oral tradition or even in written form until an unknown Israelite author under divine inspiration gave it its present literary form. This would account for the non-Israelite flavor of the book as well as for its unquestioned place in the Hebrew canon. It seems likely that Job himself lived in the second millennium BC (between 2000 and 1000 BC) and shared a tradition not far removed from that of the Hebrew patriarchs. Job's longevity of 140 years, his position as a man whose wealth was measured in cattle and who acted as priest for his family, and the picture of roving Sabean and Chaldean tribesmen fit the second millennium better than the first. The book, however, may not have reached its final form until the first millennium. Anywhere in the OT biblical period is a possible date, but attempts to place the authorship of Job as late as the second or first century BC have been dealt a decisive blow by the discovery of parts of a Targum of Job in the Qumran caves.[33]

---

31. W. J. Urbrock, "Oral Antecedents to Job: A Survey of Formulas and Formulaic Systems" (*Semeia* 5 [1976]: 132 *passim*). See also his "Evidences of Oral-Formulaic Composition in the Poetry of Job" (Ph.D. diss., Harvard University, 1975).

32. Urbrock, "Oral Antecedents," 132.

33. See comments in the section on Text.

In conclusion to the study of the possible date of Job, our sentiments lie in the direction of an early date for the book. But when all is said and done, the book is anonymous, and there are no definitive indicators of a specific date. Fortunately, the exact date of the book does not affect its interpretation in the least.

The exact place of origin is as difficult to determine as the exact date and is equally irrelevant to its message. As mentioned already, the book shows a considerable Aramaic flavor, which may mean Job and his friends lived near centers of Aramaic influence. Aram-Naharaim was such a center in northern Mesopotamia. At the end of the millennium, some Aramean tribes moved south and settled on the borders of Babylonia and Palestine, but Arameans continued to control the caravan route through the Khabur River area. This was the time when Aleppo and Damascus became Aramean centers and when the Chaldean tribes invaded Babylonia (*CAH*, 3:4). If Job 1:17 means that Chaldean tribes were still roving, the event could reflect a time before they settled at about 1000 BC.

Job himself lived in the land of Uz (1:1). Genesis 10:23 ties Uz with the Arameans, as does Genesis 22:20–22. The latter passage (v.22) also ties in Kesed (the Chaldeans) with the Arameans and the Uzites but does not make them identical. These passages refer to nations or tribes that were related sometimes mainly by their proximity. The land of Uz lay east of Palestine, but its precise location cannot be determined. Job had great influence in an unnamed town (29:7–11). According to Lamentations 4:21, Edom was in the land of Uz. It seems, then, that Uz might have been the name of a region east of Palestine and including the Edomites and adjacent tribes.

4. CANONICITY

Presently the book of Job is found in printed Hebrew Bibles in the second place among the eleven books of the third division of the Hebrew Scriptures, the Writings, following Psalms (cf. *b. B. Bat.* 14b), but it has not always been so. In some Hebrew Bibles it is placed after Psalms and Proverbs, and Jerome's list places Job before Psalms and Proverbs; but generally in Jewish lists it is grouped with the Psalms and Proverbs after the Prophets at the head of the Writings.

The Targum, however, and certain Greek and Latin texts (having abandoned the tripartite Hebrew division of Scriptures) have given Job many assignments, sometimes with the poetical books, sometimes with the historical, and sometimes after the Prophets. Since the thirteenth century, Job has come after the historical books, before Psalms, as in the Greek Vaticanus codex. Sinaiticus, however, bowing to the theories that connect Job with Moses, places the book between Deuteronomy and Joshua.

Childs in his "canonical" approach looks at Job as Israel and the church have traditionally done,[34] from the perspective of a community whose religious and theological confessions are being addressed by a divine word. The implication of this is to allow the book to perform a variety of different roles within the one community whose unity is not threatened by the presence of tension.

The tension in Job, resulting from the reader's awareness of the scene in heaven and Job's ignorance of it, serves to address the continuing community with basic issues of faith. The book poses two sets of questions, one for the reader who views the Dialogue from the framework of the Prologue, the other for the reader

---

34. Brevard S. Childs, *Introduction to the Old Testament as Scripture* (Philadelphia: Fortress, 1979), 533.

who chooses to share Job's stance of ignorance of the divine will in order to pursue his probing questions. One can agree with Childs's consideration that

> it is a serious misunderstanding of the diversity of the book's canonical role when someone, such as Rowley (*New Century Bible Commentary*, 13) sets these two perspectives in irreconcilable conflict and eliminates one. Because the reader is told in the prologue why Job is suffering, the truth of another solution is not ruled out which arises from the perspective of an ignorance of God's purpose in which the Job of the dialogue has been placed.[35]

Childs still agrees, however, with those who question the book's literary unity but maintains that that has nothing to do with its canonical integrity. This leads him to the pertinent statement, "the issue at stake is whether or not the reader who stands within the community of faith is given sufficient guidelines from the book to obtain a clear witness for a variety of different issues of faith."[36]

It is amazing that a book about a man who is outside the sphere of Israel's covenantal bond and whose experience illustrates both the highest and the lowest levels of faith became part of the Hebrew canon and was never seriously challenged. This proves that the Hebrews recognized the superior spiritual message of this book. The book did not become authoritative by an edict of an official body such as the rabbinical synod at Jamnia in AD 90. It was accepted as a divine word by the community of God's people at a time well before the Septuagint (LXX) was completed or else it would not have been included. Some books, such as Song of Songs and Ecclesiastes, were under discussion at Jamnia; but even the criticisms of Ecclesiastes were merely academic, and there were no such attacks on Job.

As Gordis notes, however, it would have been easy "to point to passages in Job's speeches that incline to skepticism and heresy."[37] Gordis's view is that Job was readily accepted because "only the Job of the prose tale impinged on the consciousness of ancient readers. ... The disturbing ideas were couched in difficult poetry."[38] This may be true for the later community, but it begs the question of why the earlier community accepted Job and for that matter the Song of Songs and Ecclesiastes as well. The theological tensions within Job were purposeful and were included to lift the teaching of the book to a new level of theological profundity.

The authority of the book of Job is tied to its place in the Hebrew canon: the Jewish community, in common with Jesus and the early church, held it as Scripture. Despite its difficulties theologically and linguistically, Job's place in the canon was never seriously challenged. The book itself, however, remains one of the greatest exegetical challenges facing the biblical scholar.

5. TEXT

The great Greek manuscripts of the OT (Vaticanus, Sinaiticus, and Alexandrinus) have approximately the same number of verses for Job as the MT, but both Origen and Jerome make it clear that the oldest Greek

---

35. Ibid., 534 (see pp. 534–43 for Childs' extended description of this diversity of canonical function).
36. Ibid., 543.
37. R. Gordis, *The Book of God and Man: A Study of Job* (Chicago: Univ. of Chicago Press, 1966), 221.
38. Ibid., 222.

text of the LXX of Job was shorter than the MT by about one-sixth.[39] Everyone agrees that the old Greek was free and interpretative, but some have held that the theologically offensive passages were toned down or omitted.[40] Others stress the ignorance of the translators;[41] for example, the Hellenistic Jews did not appreciate the earlier discursive Hebrew style, so they often chose to give a simplified summary. Orlinsky disagrees with both positions and maintains that in numerous passages the Hebrew pattern of the LXX differed from the preserved Hebrew text, and that in many places the divergences are simply stylistic Greek.[42]

Some believe there were two versions of Job and that the shorter version was the original. But this too is seriously disputed.[43] Origen, who expressly tells us about the omissions and additions, filled in the missing lines largely from Theodotion's minor Greek version, using diacritical marks to show the differences. But the manuscripts on which this knowledge is based yield conflicting evidence as to the exact extent of these additions.[44] The Coptic (Sahidic) version, based on the Greek, is thought to preserve the pre-Origen text. It was particularly in Job where Jerome felt the greatest need to make a translation directly from the Hebrew. Jerome was influenced by the rabbis who taught him Hebrew, but also by Origen's hexaplaric version of the LXX that he translated into Latin.

Jerome's attitude can be appreciated only when a comparison of the MT and the LXX is made. In the LXX Job 5:4–5, 14–16, Eliphaz tells what ought to happen (optative) to the wicked instead of asserting what does happen. This makes Job's irony lose its point in 6:8, 14. In general the LXX tends to make Job less defiant and more patient. In 32:1 the MT says that the friends ceased to answer Job "because he was righteous in his own eyes." The LXX presents a better view of Job by translating "because Job was righteous before them." The *Testament of Job*, a pseudepigraphal work based on the LXX, goes all the way in

39. On this matter cf. E. A. Dhorme (*Commentary on the Book of Job* [Paris, 1926; trans. H. Knight; London: Nelson and Sons, 1967], cxcix–cciii), S. R. Driver and G. B. Gray (*A Critical and Exegetical Commentary on the Book of Job* [ICC; 2nd ed.; Edinburgh: T&T Clark, 1950], lxxi–lxxvi).

40. See D. H. Gard, "The Exegetical Method of the Greek Translation of the Book of Job," JBL Monograph Series 8 (1952): 71–83. But Orlinsky ("Studies in the Septuagint of Job," *HUCA* 30 [1959]: 153–57; 32 [1961]: 268–93) corrects the notion that the Greek translation demonstrates a broad theological or philosophical bias.

41. See, e.g., G. Gerleman, *The Book of Job* (Studies in the Septuagint; Lund: Gleerup, 1946), 1:25–26.

42. See Orlinsky, "Studies in the Septuagint Book of Job," *HUCA* 35 (1964): 58. Orlinsky's "Studies in the Septuagint Book of Job" are the most definitive yet to appear. But in 1982 H. Heater Jr. (*A Septuagint Translation Technique in the Book of Job* [CBQMS 11; Washington, D.C.: Catholic Biblical Association of America, 1982], 41–42) made an important contribution toward a better understanding of the Greek text by demonstrating an anaphoric translation technique used in the LXX of Job. The technique was to adopt words or phrases from other passages of Scripture into the translation where the underlying idea was the same or similar. For example, the LXX of Job 3:16—"Or as a stillbirth coming from the mother's womb"—is not a paraphrase of the Hebrew (Dhorme) but an anaphoric translation coming verbatim from Numbers 12:12a. The much awaited Göttingen edition of the LXX of Job will be an important step forward for OT text critical studies.

43. The oral precedents that underlie the written composition of Job, according to Urbrock ("Oral Antecedents," 113), have had a role in producing the two versions of Job, the longer of the MT and the shorter of the Old Greek. But cf. Pope, *Job*, xliv.

44. F. Buhl (*Canon and Text of the Old Testament* [Edinburgh: T&T Clark, 1892], 129–30), citing Field's work on Origen's *Hexapla*, notes that Job had 1,600 lines (stichs), but 2,200 with the additions marked by asterisks. He maintains, however, that filling up the gaps from Theodotion began before Origen. See Driver and Gray, *Job*, lxxii.

simplifying the theology. The LXX translators were not above making additions. Many of these are exegetical comments. A rather lengthy one is attached to 2:9, involving Job's wife's complaint of her own sorrows.

In other places the translator adapts the text to his audience—the Alexandrian Jews of Hellenistic times. For example, in 42:11 the Hebrew says each of Job's friends brought him "a gold ring" (*nezem*, always translated *enōtion* ["ring"] elsewhere in the LXX). But here it is a *tetradrachma*, a coin common in Ptolemaic times; but to avoid any idolatrous overtones, the translator says it was "unstamped."

Despite the poor quality of the LXX as a translation, it still has value for textual criticism when used along with other ancient versions. On occasion the LXX translation is completely wrong and yet is still a good witness to the consonants of the Hebrew text (cf. Notes on 18:15). Sometimes the LXX handles difficult lines in Job by translating *ad sensum* (according to the general sense of the context). In such a case it is a paraphrase and has no divergent Hebrew text behind it, though the latter is always a possibility.

A good paraphrastic example is in 8:14a. The NIV has rendered the word *yāqôṭ* as "fragile" with some but little linguistic support (see NIV margin) and translates the line, "What he trusts in is fragile." The LXX has, "For his house shall be uninhabited." Did the LXX see the word "house" in the text in the first line? It is not likely. It is more likely that they did not know how to render this line and so made an *ad sensum* paraphrase, based on the second line, that speaks of "the spider's house" (web). The Syriac is much closer to the Hebrew: "Whose confidence [Heb., 'What he trusts in'] shall be cut off." Here the Syriac was based on the same Hebrew as our MT with a unique choice for the root of the dubious word. Gesenius-Buhl lists this as *qṭṭ* ("to cut off").[45] In this case the Syriac is a good witness to the original text and the LXX is unreliable.

A reversal of this situation appears in 15:23a. Here the RSV follows earlier versions, all of which were led astray by the MT vocalization (*ʾayyēh* ["where"] for *ʾ ayyâ* ["vulture"]). They therefore had to paraphrase: "He wanders abroad for bread, saying, 'Where is it?' " Even though the LXX paraphrases some of this context, it alone caught the correct idiom in the Hebrew text with the words "food for vultures." Partly following the LXX the NIV reads, "He wanders about—food for vultures." The Syriac uses an *ad sensum* meaning that fits the context but omits the difficulties by reading, "He flees because of the threat of judgment." See Note on 6:7 for another good example of the LXX's providing a superior reading.

No general rule can be formulated on how to use these ancient versions. Each line of each text must be independently evaluated, and even then room must be left for difference of opinion. The Syriac Peshitta version was translated directly from the Hebrew and, more than is generally realized, shows an understanding of numerous rare Hebrew forms or words. Like the LXX, even where it gives an erroneous translation, the Syriac may confirm the consonants of the MT. Such is the case in Job 35:11, where the Syriac reads *mn qdm* ("from before"), as though the Hebrew read *millipnê* ("from before"). This confirms the consonants of the MT, where we have a contracted form of the root *ʾlp* ("teach"; cf. Notes on 35:11).

The MT is still overwhelmingly the best source for the text of Job. This conclusion receives additional support from the several pieces of a lost Targum (Aramaic paraphrase) of Job found in Cave 11 at Qumran and published in 1971. The Aramaic of this Qumran Targum appears to be from some time in the second

---

45. F. Buhl, *Willhelm Gesenius' Hebraisches und Aramaisches Handwörterbuch über das Alte Testament* (Berlin/Göttingen: Springer-Verlag, 1949).

century BC, though the document may not have received its present form until the first century AD.[46] The MT order of chapters 24–27, which scholars have disputed (see comments below), is confirmed by this Targum; and the document ends the book at 42:11 in contrast to the LXX, which adds a lengthy and highly interpretative paragraph beyond v.17 of the MT. The document proves some Targumic material was already written down in pre-Christian times. Since the Targums were the Jewish community's attempt to put the Scriptures in a language the people could understand, it may be that the book of Job was chosen early on because of its great difficulty.

Studies in comparative Semitic linguistics have shed light on rarer meanings and unusual grammar and often support the MT. Evidence for this will be supplied in the Notes along with the commentary. An unknown nuance or little known homonym may be obscured by a common meaning of a word. An interesting example is in the last line of Job 30:13. Following many scholars, BHS suggests emending the word ʿōzēr ("one helping") to ʿōṣēr ("one hindering"). The RSV's "no one restrains them" did not need to follow this emendation, for G. R. Driver had already pointed out that in both Arabic and Akkadian ʿzr can mean "hinder."[47] So the presence of ʿzr as a homonym or as a verb with opposite meanings—"help" and "hinder"—is likely.[48] The Hebrew text needs no adjustment. The NIV rejected this option, but its footnote shows uneasiness about the choice.

In the Massora (notes of the Jewish scribes of the Middle Ages) we have information concerning several places in Job where the pre-Masoretic scribes emended the text for theological reasons. These *tiqqune sopherim* ("guides for the scribes") should be seriously considered for establishing the original text. One of these is in Job 7:20, where the simple omission of one Hebrew letter *kaph* (*k*) made Job say, "I have become a burden to myself" (cf. KJV), instead of "Have I become a burden to you" (cf. RSV, NIV, also LXX). The latter was felt by the scribes to verge on blasphemy; so the pronoun "you" was dropped, but a record was kept.

Another example in 32:3 is an even more substantive change. It lacks the support of the LXX; so the NIV has stayed with the MT, which says, "and yet had condemned Job." Again this was considered blasphemous (see Notes on 32:3); so "Job" was substituted for "God."[49] That there are only eighteen such emendations in the entire Hebrew Bible, and that a record was kept of them is a tribute to the Masoretic diligence in preserving the text they had inherited.

Frequently the Masoretes put in their marginal notes variants that came about when they observed a difference between texts coming from the two Masoretic schools (the Eastern and Western) or even within a school. These are usually minor vocalization or accent variants. Rarely a *Qere* (what is read) will substantively change the meaning of the *Kethiv* (what is written). An example of such a substantive change

46. J. P. van der Ploeg and A. S. van der Woude, *Le Targum de Job de la Grotte XI de Qumran* (Leiden: Brill, 1971). For a brief evaluation in English, see Pope (*Job*, xlv–xlvi); cf. also A. York, *A Philological and Textual Analysis (11QtgJob)* (Ann Arbor, Mich.: University Microfilms International, n.d.); M. Sokoloff, *The Targum to Job from Qumran Cave XI* (Ramot-Gan, Israel: Bar-Ilan Univ. Press, 1974).

47. G. R. Driver, "Problems in Job," *AJSL* 52 (1935–36): 163.

48. Pope, *Job*, 221.

49. For more information see C. D. Ginsburg, *Introduction to the Massoretico-Critical Edition of the Hebrew Bible* (repr. 1897; New York: Ktav, 1966), 347–67.

may be found in the last word of 19:29 (see Notes). On even rarer occasions our increased lexical knowledge (from extrabiblical sources) enables us to revocalize (make a different choice of vowels) the correctly preserved consonants and thus make good sense of the text. See, for example, 28:11, where *mibb^ekî* does not mean "from overflowing (weeping)," as in the KJV, but refers to the "sources" of the rivers (see Notes).

6. PURPOSE

The purpose of the book of Job cannot be reduced to a single, simple statement. The author appears to have had a multifaceted purpose under the general theme of wisdom teaching about God and human suffering. The various parts of the book speak with somewhat different purposes in mind. The Prologue teaches the wisdom of human beings' total submission to the will of the Creator. Readers view the drama from the divine perspective where they learn of God's secret purpose to expose the falsehood of the Accuser and prove Job's faith.

The Dialogue, by contrast, gives the human perspective. Job knows nothing of what has transpired in the heavenly council. The author's purpose there is to teach the believing community some profound lessons positively and negatively about honesty and reality in our relationship with God and about humanity's limited knowledge of the divine purposes. Here we see a deeper probing into the problem of evil than current views of theodicy have given.

The author of Job purposes to show how the theological position of Job's friends represents a shallow and only partial observation of life; that is, human suffering is always in proportion to one's sins. Overall there is no studied attempt to justify God with regard to the suffering of the innocent. But the author finally demonstrates that God does not abandon the sufferer but communicates with him at the proper time.

Another subsidiary purpose of the book is to show that though people are often sinful, weak, and ignorant, they can, like Job, be relatively pure and upright even when in the midst of physical distress, emotional turmoil, and spiritual testing. In the divine speeches the purpose is to prove to Job that God is Creator and Sustainer of all things and yet is willing to communicate with Job as his friend, not his enemy, as Job had imagined him to be. While this does not answer all Job's questions, it is all Job needs to know.

The Accuser is permitted to afflict Job and then test him through the instrumentality of would-be helpers, who use all the words of traditional piety. Job's major problem is this vexing question of theodicy. How can God be both good and sovereign in the light of the suffering of the innocent and the prospering of the wicked? The book pursues a middle course between the concepts of an evil deity on the one hand and a limited deity on the other.

But there is no attempt to give a rational or philosophical solution. The picture is the same as that given in Genesis, where the Serpent as a creature of God and subject to his will is also in rebellion. Here the Accuser bears the responsibility for Job's trouble, though he is permitted to do so by God. The problem of theodicy is left on the note that God in his omnipotence and omniscience can and does use secondary means to bring about his higher and perfect purposes. One such purpose in Job's suffering is to humiliate the Accuser, which thus proves Job's devotion to God is pure.

Initially Job stands the test even when his wife says, "Curse God and die!" (2:9). But as his troubles multiply, Job has second thoughts; he wrestles with God, challenges God, and sinks into depths of despair, with moments of trust and confidence, only to fall again into despair. Throughout, Job defends his own essential innocence (not sinlessness; see 9:2) against the view of his friends, who rarely move from the single theme that suffering is the immediate corollary of sin, and that because Job has grievously sinned God has become his enemy. But Job's own view of why he is suffering is in a state of flux. So he says many unfortunate things and yet in it all does not do what the Accuser said he would do; he does not curse God to his face (2:5).

While the counselors make no progress in their arguments, Job grows somewhat less belligerent. He appears to us to be self-righteous in his peroration (chs. 29–31), but this must be understood in its cultural context. He persistently calls for an audience with God to argue his case. He also calls for a friend in heaven to plead his cause at the divine tribunal. He is confident he will be vindicated (13:18; 19:26). The counselors consistently stand on God's side, sometimes uttering beautiful hymns; but they cannot seem to move from their fallacious notion that the righteous always prosper and sinners always suffer, and conversely that suffering proves sinfulness and prosperity proves righteousness.

Eliphaz is not quite so crass; but he still insists that though the righteous suffer a little and the unrighteous prosper a little, the righteous never come to an untimely end (4:7; 5:16–19), and the wicked, even when they prosper, are in dread of calamity (15:20–26). Bildad is convinced that Job's children died for their sins and warns Job that he will receive the same fate unless he gets right with God (8:4–6). Zophar is bent on denouncing Job as a mocker of God. Job's suffering is ample proof of his sinfulness, and repentance is his only hope (11:13–15).

Much of what Job's counselors say is theologically sound and true in the abstract, but it does not necessarily apply to Job. It is not so much what they say but what they leave out that makes their counsel so shallow. They all finally reach the conclusion that Job is obstinate and that his refusal to humble himself and repent proves he has committed sins of great enormity. The OT accounts of the innocent sufferers, such as Abel, Uriah, Naboth, and others, question this simplistic approach. Jesus, of course, taught his disciples that the innocent do suffer to accomplish God's higher purpose. "Neither this man nor his parents sinned," said Jesus of a man born blind (Jn 9:3), "but this happened so that the work of God might be displayed in his life."

Some have suggested that normative OT theology also teaches the counselors' erroneous view. For example, Psalm 1:3 says of the righteous, "Whatever he does prospers"; and Psalm 37:25 says, "I was young and now I am old, / yet I have never seen the righteous forsaken / or their children begging bread." The tension is real; but the discrepancy is superficial since the Psalms are not making specific applications, as were the counselors of Job, but are expressing general truth.

Job agonizes over how to integrate this general truth with his own experience. He has no answer, for he does not have the heavenly perspective given in the Prologue. Therefore, he blows hot and cold. Sometimes he blames the Lord for tormenting him (13:21, 25) and wishes God would leave him alone (7:17–21; 10:20; 19:22). At other times he yearns for God to communicate with him (14:15) that he might be vindicated (13:15). Job's emotional instability arises from his internal conflict over the fantasy that God is unjustly punishing him for sins he has not committed (9:21–24). So there are moments when he perceives God to be his enemy (7:20; 10:16–17; 16:9).

As noted, the book does not attempt to formulate a rational solution to the problem of evil, especially that aspect of the problem that tries to relate God's goodness and sovereignty to the suffering of the innocent. Although Job is exercised about God's justice, his ultimate concern is more practical than theoretical. His practical concern is not healing and restoration but his own vindication as an upright man. Job does not ask for rational answers; nor does God give such to him when he appears, though Job is finally vindicated (42:7–9). There were no heinous sins for which he was being punished. When God does rebuke Job, it is for his ignorance (38:2) and presumption while arguing his case (42:2), not for a profligate life. God is apparently telling Job in chapters 38–41 that human beings do not know enough about God's ways to make judgments concerning his justice.

In his appearance to Job, God ignores the problem of theodicy. He gives no rational explanation or excuse for Job's suffering, but Job is not crushed; he is only rebuked and then shown to be basically right, while the friends are condemned for their presumptive and arrogant claim to know God's ways (42:7). Job thus realizes that God does not need his creature's advice to control the world and that no extreme of suffering gives human beings the right to question God's wisdom or justice, and at this realization he repents (42:2–6).[50] On seeing the power and glory of God, Job's rebellious attitude dissolves and his resentment disappears. Job now gets what he sought for. His friends do not see him pronounced guilty, so their view of his suffering is refuted.

Job is not told why God has tested him. He comes to accept God on God's own terms; while we know the full story, Job has to walk by faith even after he is vindicated. That God never impugns Job's character proves that the Accuser has failed and that Job's testing has come to an end. Though he has not demanded restoration, God, having achieved his higher purpose through Job, now does restore him. Job in his suffering, despite moments of weakness, surpasses in righteousness his detractors, who have not suffered as he has. After all his doubts and bitterness, Job arrives at that point of spiritual maturity where he can pray for those who have abused him (42:10; cf. Lk 6:28).

The issues raised in the book are among the most profound and difficult of human existence. The answer was already on Job's lips in the Prologue when he said, "The LORD gave and the LORD has taken away; / may the name of the LORD be praised" (1:21b), and "Shall we accept good from God, and not trouble?" (2:10). The truth Job learns is that God must be God and that of all values and all existence, only God and his glory must ultimately prevail.

7. MAJOR CHARACTERS

Job

Apart from the Bible nothing is known of Job. He was not an Israelite (Uz is a location in Edom; La 4:21) and showed no knowledge of the covenant between Yahweh and his chosen people. Indeed there is not in the book the slightest hint of any acquaintance with the history of the Hebrew people.

The English name "Job" comes from the Greek *Iōb*, which derives from the Hebrew form *ʾîyôb*. Earlier attempts to determine an etymology of the name have given way to evidence from a well-attested West Semitic name in the second millennium found in the Amarna Letters, Egyptian execration texts, Mari, Alalakh, and Ugaritic documents. The original form of the name was *ʾAyyāb(um)*, which can mean

---

50. On Job's repentance see the discussion in the commentary on 42:2–6.

"Where is [my] father?" or possibly "no father." Either form might suggest an orphan or illegitimacy. The word ʾiy, from an original ʾay ("where" or "no"), was often connected with other substantives, such as "brother" (ʾāḥ) instead of "father" (ʾāb). Compare the name Ichabod (ʾî-kābôd), which might be translated "no-glory" (1Sa 4:21 margin). In the Hebrew ʾîyôb, a weak aleph (glottal stop) between vowels is dropped out.[51]

Job assumes two roles, but this does not imply there are two "Jobs," as critics have often maintained. The author of this masterly work is not that clumsy. He has purpose in the apparent discrepancy between Job's role as one who "did not sin in what he said" (2:10) and his role as the protester who shocks the somewhat discreet Eliphaz into saying, "Your own mouth condemns you … you vent your rage against God" (15:6, 13). Job in either of these roles alone would have produced just another statement on suffering, of which there were several in the ancient world. What lifts the book to literary and theological greatness is the author's deft presentation of a truly righteous man whose commitment to God is total, yet who can still struggle with God to the point of rage over the mystery of God's ways.

Job does not know what the reader knows—that God honors him by testing, thus expressing his total confidence in Job. But Job must remain ignorant of this for it to be genuine. For the intended message of the book, the raging Job is just as important as the patient Job, though it is true that in the history of interpretation one side of characterization has often been presented to the exclusion of the other, beginning with "Job's perseverance" in James 5:11.[52] In his suffering Job serves God supremely, not as a stoic, but as a man of feelings who has to come to terms with the mystery of the divine will.

The Three Counselors

These men play a unique role. They have the same underlying theory of suffering, but the speeches of each reflect a slightly different personality and approach.

Eliphaz. Based on a variety of passages, we have good reason to believe Eliphaz was an Edomite. According to Genesis 36:4, a man named Eliphaz was the firstborn of Esau, the progenitor of the Edomites, and Teman was his son (v.11). A number of prophets mention Teman as a place, an Edomite city or district (Jer 49:7, 20; Eze 25:13; Am 1:12; Ob 8–9). Jeremiah assumes Teman was known for its wisdom. The site may be the same as the Arabian town of Tema mentioned in Babylonian sources.[53]

Apparently Eliphaz is the senior member, since he speaks first. Throughout his speeches, at least until his final speech in chapter 22, he shows a broader spirit than the others by accepting Job as a pious man gone astray. Though failing in compassion, he alone of the three shows some consideration and respect.

Bildad. This non-Hebrew name is not mentioned in any other OT book. Bildad considers Job's struggle over the justice of God as blasphemy and uses his erudition, his knowledge of ancient wisdom tradition, to prove to Job that his family has gotten what they deserve and warns him of a similar doom.

---

51. For extrabiblical sources see Pope, *Job*, 5–6. For the negative meaning of ʾiy, cf. Notes on 22:30.
52. See Joel Allen, "Job: History of Interpretation," in *The Dictionary of the Old Testament: Psalms, Wisdom and Writings* (ed. T. Longman III and P. Enns; Downers Grove, Ill.: InterVarsity Press, 2008): 361–71.
53. Cf. W. F. Albright, "The Name of Bildad the Shuhite," *AJSL* 44 (1927–28): 36.

Genesis 25:2, 6 provides some helpful information about his tribe, the Shuites. They were descendants of Abraham through Keturah and inhabitants of "the land of the east." There is a land of Suhu on the Middle Euphrates mentioned in Assyrian records (*ANET, passim*); but apart from a possible phonetic problem, Genesis 25:3 suggests this tribe lived near Dedan, which Jeremiah locates near Tema and Buz (Jer 25:23), far from the Euphrates. Bildad's name is probably a combination of Bil (*baʿal*, "Lord"; cf. LXX's Baldad) and Adad (Hadad, Dadda), the well-known storm god. Compare Ben-Hadad, the Aramean royal name, and the Edomite kings Hadad the son of Bedad (Ge 36:35) and Baal-Hanan (v.38).

Zophar. Zophar is from Naamah, but not the little Israelite town in the western foothills (Jos 15:41). The LXX took the liberty to identify him with a known kingdom by calling him Zophar the king of the Minaeans (2:11; 11:1; 20:1; 42:9), which has led to the conjecture that there was a transposition of the consonants *n* and *m* in the MT. This is unlikely. The LXX also has "Zophar" for Zepho the son of Eliphaz ben Esau (Ge 36:11, 15). The fact is that scholars cannot agree either on the derivation of Zophar's name or on the location of the place. But it must have been somewhere in northern Arabia or Edom. Dhorme gives several possible locations based on data from Eusebius's *Onomasticon* and from topographical surveys.[54] Zophar is the most caustic of the counselors. His message to Job is to repent or die the horrible death the wicked deserve.

Elihu

This character appears only in chapters 32–37, where his speeches are recorded. Some critics have banished him as nongenuine, a late addition. He has the distinction of having his father's name recorded, which G. B. Gray takes as evidence of different authorship.[55] It is just as likely that the name "Barakel the Buzite" (32:2) is given to identify Elihu as one whose father was a leading figure in a clan more closely related to Job. Uz and Buz were brothers according to Genesis 22:21. Elihu's name means "He is my God" and is the only one of the five names (including Job) used by Israelites (cf. 1Sa 1:1; 1Ch 12:20; 26:7; 27:18).

The Aramaisms in Elihu's speeches fit the statement that Buz was the son of Abraham's brother Nahor, whose son Laban speaks Aramaic (Ge 31:47). Elihu gives his youth as the reason he dared not speak while the older men held forth. The character of his speeches and the author's intended use of them will be discussed later.

8. MYTHOPOEIC LANGUAGE

The book of Job, like a microcosm of the OT, bears witness to the will and purpose of the one God who created and rules over nature and all creatures, especially his crowning work of creation—human beings. In Genesis 3, as a result of the work of the Tempter, God put in effect the death penalty recorded in Genesis 2:17. Along with immediate punitive effects, the man and woman suffer alienation from God as a token of the death penalty.

---

54. Dhorme, *Job*, xxvii.
55. Driver and Gray, *Job*, 1:278.

The book of Job brings us a step closer to the mystery of godliness by adding a new dimension to the concept of punitive suffering. The ancient Near Eastern documents from Babylonia and Egypt agree with this punitive aspect of suffering but, as mentioned above, are shallow in the way they deal with the problem. In those documents people must humble themselves before the gods, who are often perverse or not interested, or they are incapacitated. Job's problem is the opposite. He thinks God is too interested and too powerful for him. Job is a strict monotheist (9:8; 23:13). He disavows any false worship (31:26–28) and yet is knowledgeable of many mythological concepts of the pagan religions current in the ancient Semitic world. H. W. Wolff says:

> The more distinctly the old Oriental religions are reconstructed before our eyes, the more clearly we see that the O.T. actively resists the attempt to understand it in analogy to the cults of its environment. This is all the more surprising since the connection of Israel with its environment in matters of a general world view, of profane and sacral usage, of Cultic institutions, yes even of prophetic phenomena, is constantly becoming clearer.[56]

To this may be added the observation that the mythological elements in Job conform remarkably well to the religious expressions from contemporary sources. But careful attention to certain features in context will show that any special problem these allusions may appear to pose for the monotheistic outlook of the author of this book is superficial.

My present purpose is to defend this last statement. Here I use the term "myth" in its traditional sense — not as another way of expressing the truth,[57] but as the way a polytheistic people understood deity. In this sense, to see wide mythological commitment, as some have been prone to do,[58] results in as much misinterpretation as does the attempt to ignore mythological expression to protect the Scriptures from such "contamination." Reading primitive meaning into a piece of monotheistic literature because the language is infused with the idiom of a primitive substratum is poor methodology. It is true that sometimes it is impossible to tell when the terms are mere figures and when they represent the view of the speaker.[59] We must be guided by the thrust of the context.

The language of mythology is inherent in every language from every age and is often used in religious contexts that are strongly monotheistic.[60] The Jews in Babylon borrowed pagan festival names for their religious calendar. Fanatically monotheistic Jews embellished their synagogues with zodiacal mosaics borrowed from Roman art and depicted the sun god riding his chariot.[61] Matthew 12:24 uses the pagan deity name Beelzebub (2Ki 1:3) for Satan simply as an idiom without a thought given to its origin. Isaiah and

---

56. H. W. Wolff, "The Hermeneutics of the Old Testament," in *Essays on Old Testament Hermeneutics* (ed. C. Westermann; trans. J. L. Mays; Atlanta: John Knox, 1963), 167.

57. John L. McKenzie ("Myth and the Old Testament," *CBQ* 21 [1959]: 265–82), following Cassirer, defines myth in this way, but the definition assumes a unique set of presuppositions.

58. Pope seems to hold this position. He objects to Gordis's statement that Job takes monotheism for granted (Pope, *Job*, xxxix).

59. See T. H. Gaster, *Myth, Legend, and Custom in the Old Testament* (New York: Harper & Row, 1969), xxxvi.

60. John Milton drew heavily on Greek mythology to enrich his poetic imagery even in his picture of creation.

61. Rachel Hachlili, "The Zodiac in Ancient Jewish Art: Representation and Significance," *BASOR* 228 (1977): 61–63.

Ezekiel, both monotheists, were prone to using mythological allusion as a vehicle through which they communicated their messages.[62]

Nature is a theme that frequently evoked mythological language: the storm, fire, the sea, the heavens and the earth, and creatures in both spheres. Job 3:8 begins with a reference to an occultic practice involving the celebrated Leviathan. Regarding the day of his birth, Job says, "May those who curse days curse that day, / those who are ready to arouse Leviathan."

Dhorme says that "those who curse days" may refer to other sufferers like Job who also cursed the day of their birth.[63] But in light of the parallelism, the expression more likely refers to professional cursers like Balaam. Job appears to be making a play on the similar sound of the words *yām* ("sea"; GK 3542) and *yôm* ("day"; GK 3427) and the parallel between Leviathan, the sea monster, and the Yam as a deity in Canaanite mythology.

Job, in a cursing mood, employs the most vivid and forceful proverbial language available to call for the obliteration of that day.[64] There is no way of knowing how valid Job considered the work of such cursers, but in his negative confession Job presents himself as a monotheist who rejects current mythological conceptions of the sun (31:26–28). Job's error, for which he can scarcely be excused, is in damning the day of his birth, questioning the sovereign purpose of God. But we must not be like his friends who fail to understand his frustration. He feels compelled to speak out what he truly feels and so comes perilously close to cursing God to his face, as Satan predicted.

Many of Job's words, then, are not normative; that is, they are not meant to teach a doctrine but are to show us the extent of Job's disturbance. Even where a passage may be considered normative, however, mythic language may be used.

These mythological expressions uniquely serve the purpose of the book. The way they are used sometimes reverses the effect of the polytheism and shows that Job's God is the Sovereign Lord over all creation. Notice what Job says in 9:13: "God does not restrain his anger; / even the cohorts of Rahab cowered at his feet." Who are these cohorts of Rahab? Are they literal sea monsters? Why then is God angry with them? It is more likely a metaphor describing those great cosmic powers that oppose God's will.

Sometimes these terms are simple metaphors, and at other times the biblical author is consciously antimythologizing. Psalm 121 appears to be, for example, a polemic against the hill shrines and the notion of many patron deities. Since the pagan deities are no-gods (Ps 4:2; 106:28), where can one turn for help? The psalmist says in 121:1:

> I lift up my eyes to the hills—
>   where does my help come from?
> My help comes from the LORD,
>   the Maker of heaven and earth.

---

62. See Isaiah 14 and 27; Ezekiel 28.
63. Dhorme, *Job*, 29.
64. Although the NEB renders 3:8b, "those whose magic binds even the monster," the same stem of the verb *ʿûr* means "to rouse" the dead in Sheol in Isaiah 14:9.

The psalmist goes on to reinforce this with his concept of the Lord as the only true patron deity:

> He will not let your foot slip—
> > he [Yahweh] who watches over you will not slumber ...
> The LORD will keep you from all harm. (Ps 121:3, 7)

We think immediately of Eliphaz's taunt of Job in 5:1:

> Call if you will, but who will answer you?
> > To which of the holy ones will you turn?

The "holy ones" are the *bᵉnê hāᵉlōhîm* ("the sons of God") of the Prologue.

The divine council concept may be considered in ideologic continuity with Canaanite religion,[65] but the author of Job and Psalms 82 and 89:5–8 have introduced a discontinuity in the way they handle the concept. The discontinuity can be appreciated in terms of the Hebrew hierarchy of *ᵉlōhîm* (godlike beings; GK 466). There is only one Creator; all the *qᵉhal qᵉdōšîm* ("council of holy ones") fear him, and none can be compared with him (89:7–8). Humans are *ᵉlōhîm* to the animals, and the heavenly beings are *ᵉlōhîm* to humans.

In the Canaanite mythology there were lesser divine beings created by the cosmic gods to serve them. They were sometimes available as patron deities or personal intercessors and were generally lackeys in the divine assembly. In Job 33:23 Elihu speaks of such an intercessor, calling him a *malᵖāk*[66] ("messenger"; NIV, "angel"; GK 4855) and a *mēlîṣ* ("interpreter"; NIV, "mediator"; GK 4885). Both Job and his friends believe that among such "holy ones" a man might find a defender. Three times Job mentions such a one: first as an arbiter (9:33), then as a witness to his integrity (16:19–21), and finally as his (redeemer) vindicator (19:25–27). This is certainly evocative and part of the ideological preparation for the mediatorial work of Christ, who could stand between God and man, sharing the nature of each, as Job says in 9:33: "to lay his hand upon us both."

The book of Job is replete with vivid imagery based on the colorful mythic literature deeply ingrained in the language and passed on through generations. There are many themes, but we will only sample a few.

A widely used theme is the quelling of Chaos, known in West Semitic literature as Yam ("Sea") and in Babylonia as Tiamat ("the Deep"). The sea monsters variously called Rahab ("the boisterous"), Tannin ("the dragon"), and Leviathan ("the serpent") also play a part.

In 7:12 Job speaks out in anguish over his imagined harassment by God and says, "Am I the sea [Yam] or the monster of the deep [Tannin], / that you put me under guard?" The tales of the conquest of Yam, Tannin, and Lotan (Leviathan) by Baal and Anat are well known (*ANET*, 137–38). The Babylonian Tiamat is killed by the hero god Marduk, who then proceeds to create the land and sea from the pieces. The West Semitic literature provides no creation account but stresses the control of the sea by the weather god,

---

65. See H. L. Ginsberg's translation of Ugaritic mythological texts in *ANET*, 130–55.

66. The same term is used in Ugaritic for the lackey gods; cf. A. Herdner, *Corpus des tablettes en cuneiforms alphabetiques découvertes à Ras Shamra-Ugarit de 1929 a 1939* (Paris: Imprimere Nationale, 1963), 1.2.17–21; 3.4.76–80; et al.; also C. H. Gordon, *Ugaritic Textbook* (AnOr 38; Rome: Pontifical Biblical Institute, 1965), 137:40–41; cf. *ANET*, 130.

Baal (*ANET*, 131). (Many scholars believe there was a creation account that followed the account of Baal's defeat of the Sea, though the text is broken.[67]) Job and his friends knew well the West Semitic myths. But they were not committed to them as part of their view of deity. This we know from the total thrust of their words.

A look at the Chaos terminology in the first part of chapter 9 will help us capture the thrust of Job's concept of deity. According to Job, El (one of Job's epithets for God) is indeed the God of profound wisdom and cosmic force and as such is too much for mere mortals. In vv.5–13 he moves mountains and shakes the earth off its foundations—the earthquake. He speaks and the sun does not rise—the eclipse. He seals up the stars from sight—movement of the stars and planets. He stretches out the heavens and tramples on the back of Yam (*bom°tê yām*; NIV, "the waves of the sea"; v.8)—creation and the overcoming of Chaos. He made the Bear, Orion, Pleiades, and the southern chambers; and when he is angry even the cohorts of Rahab (the boisterous sea monster) cower at his feet. Job here described his Deity as one who is unique and all-powerful when compared with the description of any single contemporary god.

The Ugaritic El (the head of the pantheon) is a character variously represented. Sometimes he is a forceful patriarch living in a tent, at other times a frightened deity who is forced to give up the young Baal to the messengers of Yam. Baal can take things in his own hands and destroy Yam with the weapons supplied by the craftsman god, Kothar wa-Hasis (*ANET*, 131). But then Baal is killed by Mot. The issue is always sovereignty. El and the divine assembly are faced with the question of ascribing kingship to Yam. Baal asserts kingship not only by eliminating Yam but also by demonstrating his power in the storm. This West Semitic story was imported to the East, where Marduk, chosen as king by the gods, asserts kingship by slaying Tiamat.[68]

The point is that Job's God assumes all the functions of the gods, whether Baal, El, or Yam. Job's El is never subordinated to any of the *b°nê hā°elōhîm* ("sons of God"). In 9:8 he exercises his creative power all by himself (*l°baddô*). The line in Hebrew is the same as a line in Isaiah 44:24. He is not only a deity who does not share his power and authority, but he performs his numberless wonders while being invisible (Job 9:11): "When he passes me, I cannot see him; / when he goes by, I cannot perceive him."

The psalmist expresses a similar discontinuity in Psalm 89:5–8:

The heavens praise your wonders, O LORD,
    your faithfulness too, in the assembly of the holy ones.
For who in the skies above can compare with the LORD?
    Who is like the LORD among the heavenly beings?
In the council of the holy ones God is greatly feared;
    he is more awesome than all who surround him.
O LORD God Almighty, who is like you?
    You are mighty, O LORD, and your faithfulness surrounds you.

---

67. See T. Jacobsen, "The Battle between Marduk and Tiamat," *JAOS* 88 (1968): 104–8.
68. Yahweh's lordship over Chaos is the theme of Psalm 29. There the *b°nê °ēlîm* (v.1) are called to honor the one who controls and sits enthroned over the flood (29:10).

As in Job and Isaiah, this theme is linked to God as Creator; for it is precisely at this point that the psalmist describes "the LORD" (Yahweh) as Creator of the heavens and earth and the one who rules over the surging sea, crushing Rahab and all his enemies. In his creating and saving power he is unique and incomparable.

The psalmist's God also had that mysterious quality of invisibility. Was it not this quality that disturbed his idolatrous contemporaries when they chided, "Where is your God?" (42:3, 10; 79:10). Psalm 115:2 reads:

> Why do the nations say
>> "Where is their God?"
> Our God is in heaven;
>> he does whatever pleases him.
> But their idols are silver and gold,
>> made by the hands of men.

Even though the Hebrew God is invisible, he exists in heaven and is supreme. Job likewise asserts that God is both invisible and all powerful.

Turning to another theme, in Job 5:7 most translations read, "Yet man is born to trouble / as surely as sparks fly upward." A more literal translation is, "Man is born to trouble / as sure as Resheph's sons soar aloft."

Who are "Resheph's sons"? Is this a metaphor for flames, sparks, or lightning? Resheph is equated with Nergal, the Mesopotamian god of pestilence and the netherworld. In Deuteronomy 32:24 the word is parallel with *qeṭeb* ("destruction") and in Habakkuk 3:5 with *deber* ("pestilence"), and the plural is used of lightning in Psalm 78:48. In Psalm 76:3 [4], however, "the reshephs" ("arrows"; GK 8404) of the bow are in apposition to the shield, the sword, and the battle. Resheph, like Baal, is a thunder god and a god of battle. In Ugaritic Resheph is called "lord of the arrow," either referring to his skillful use of lightning or his attendance on arrows in flight. Just as death's firstborn (Job 18:13) devours the bodies of wicked men, so here the sons of Resheph are active troublemakers. On Resheph, T. H. Gaster observes:

> When *Resheph* is said (Habakkuk 3:5) to attend upon Yahweh, or when the pangs of love are described as "fiery *reshephs*" (Song of Songs 8:6), do the writers really have in mind the figure of the Canaanite plague-god of that name, or is this simply a case of metonymy? This is a problem which I will not even attempt to resolve, but it must at least be mentioned.[69]

From my point of view, Gaster is asking the wrong question. It makes little difference whether the figure of the plague god is in mind or not. Habakkuk is using a highly anthropomorphic figure of Yahweh. The real questions are: Did Habakkuk believe Yahweh existed in the form of a warrior? Did Job and Habakkuk believe Resheph or Resheph's sons really existed as gods? These must be answered in the light of other things the writers say.

---

69. Gaster, *Myth, Legend and Custom*, xxxvi, as quoted in W. L. Michel, "The Ugaritic Texts and the Mythological Expressions in the Book of Job" (Ph.D. diss., University of Wisconsin, 1970), 8.

Job 26 is replete with mythological allusions—the denizens of Sheol, Zaphon the cosmic mountain, Yam, and Rahab—all in a cosmography with some rather sophisticated observations. Verses 5–14 may be translated:

> The spirits of the dead write,
>> the Waters below and their denizens.
> Sheol is naked in God's presence,
>> Abaddon is uncovered.
> He spreads out Zaphon over emptiness;
>> he hangs the earth on nothing.
> He wraps up the waters in his clouds;
>> yet the clouds do not burst under the weight.
> He covers the face of the full moon
>> spreading his clouds over it.
> He marks out the horizon on the face of the waters
>> for a boundary between light and darkness.
> The pillars of the heavens quake
>> stunned at his rebuke.
> By his power he churned up the sea,
>> by his skill he pierced Rahab.
> By his breath the skies become fair;
>> his hand pierced the gliding serpent.
> And these are only the outer fringes of is power;
>> how faint the whisper we hear of him!
>> Who then can understand the thunder of his might?

Buttenweiser, commenting on v.7, has written:

Our author, though naturally ignorant of the law of gravitation, had outgrown the naive view of his age about the universe, and conceived of the earth as a heavenly body floating in space, like the sun, moon, and stars. It is not surprising to meet with such a view in the book of Job when one considers the advanced astronomy in Babylonia, Egypt, and Greece. As early as 540–510 BC Pythagoras of Samos, in his travels in Egypt and the East, acquired the knowledge of the obliquity of the ecliptic and of the earth's being a sphere freely poised in space. ... Job 38:6 bears out rather than contradicts the conclusion that the writer of Job had attained a more advanced view of the universe, since the question, "Whereon were its foundations set?" shows that he no longer shared the primitive notion that the earth was resting on pillars erected in the sea.[70]

Both Buttenweiser and Dhorme contend "the north" (*sāpôn*, 26:7; GK 7600) is the celestial pole formed by the seven stars of Ursa Minor from which the movement of the universe was believed to proceed. Two observations are needed. First, the cosmography is not in itself the purpose of the passage. Again God's

---

70. M. Buttenweiser, *The Book of Job* (London: Hodder and Stoughton, 1922), comment on Job 26:7.

power is in focus. Second, we cannot ignore what Ugaritic literature tells about Mount Zaphon as the Canaanite Olympus.[71]

The cosmic-mountain concept is related to Sinai as the place God reveals himself from and Zion as God's dwelling place.[72] Psalm 48:1–2 says:

> Great is the Lord, and most worthy of praise,
>> in the city of our God, his holy mountain.
> It is beautiful in its loftiness,
>> the joy of the whole earth.
> Like the utmost heights of Zaphon is Mount Zion
>> the city of the Great King.

Eschatological Zion in Isaiah 2:2–4 is the place where the Lord's house is established at the head of the mountains with all the nations flowing to it, where the Lord is enthroned and rules over a world of universal peace (cf. Isa 24:23).

The passage that most closely approximates Job 26:7 is Isaiah 14:13–14. Here the king of Babylon desires to place himself where the Most High dwells. I translate it:

> You said in your heart,
> "I will ascend to heaven;
>> above the stars of God;
> I will set my throne on high;
>> I will sit on the mount of assembly.
> On the slopes of Zaphon,
>> I will ascend above the heights of the clouds
>> I will make myself like the Most High."

There is a difference in the way the two passages (Job 26:7; Isa 14:13–14) use Zaphon. In the mouth of the pagan king, it is used literally to mean the mount of assembly that indeed reaches into the heavens and is the divine abode. But in Job the choice of words points to metonymy. This is the conclusion Clifford makes in a similar observation:

> Zaphon's meaning seems to be practically "heavens." The verb *nōṭeh* elsewhere is used of "heavens" in the Old Testament (e.g. Ps 104:2), and it forms a reasonable merism with *ʾereṣ* in the passage from Job. It is easy to imagine the development of the meaning of Zaphon, under Israelite impulse, from "mountain (dwelling of God)" to "heavens (dwelling of God)."[73]

---

71. Now called *Mons Casius* due north of Israel. In Canaanite myth the god Baal-Hadad had his marvelous dwelling built there. This explains why the Hebrew word *ṣāpôn* means "north." Compare *negeb* ("dry") for south, *yām* ("sea") for west.

72. See Richard J. Clifford, *The Cosmic Mountain in Canaan and the Old Testament* (Cambridge, Mass.: Harvard Univ. Press, 1973).

73. Ibid., 162, n. 85.

So the mountain of all mountains is the mountain that God stretched out like a canopy, which is his dwelling place—the heavens.

Even though mythopoeic language is used, there is a hint that the author is demythologizing. In 26:12 he carefully placed the definite article on the word *yām* ("sea"; GK 3542), which shows that he did not consider it a proper name but "the sea."[74]

In this highly figurative language, "the pillars of the heavens" (26:11), like the pillars of the earth (9:6), are the mountains. In both cases God makes them quake. The writer does not have a rigid cosmography. His language is phenomenological, and his purpose is not to tell us how much he knows of the cosmos but how powerful God is. Job is saying El is the God of the heavens and the God of the earth—the God of all nature. Stretching out the heavens over emptiness and hanging up the earth on nothing are bold figures derived from actions common to humanity. The marvel is that he can do these things with nothing for support.

Other marvels of nature are also attributed to God's vast power and dominion. He fills the clouds with water, and they do not burst. He uses the clouds as a drape over the face of the full moon.[75] He marks out the circle of the horizon as with cosmic calipers. By a mere word he makes the mountains shake, and by his power he controls the raging sea and its monstrous creatures. All this is only a whisper of his power, only the fringe of his dominion.[76]

As noted above, understanding the mythological background sometimes accomplishes just the opposite of what some assume. Rather than showing ideological commitment to the pagan way of handling the mysteries of nature, it throws the discontinuity into relief and helps us appreciate how monotheistic the writer is. For example, Sheol is the realm of the god Mot (Death) in Ugaritic where Baal enters and is powerless. In 26:6 Sheol is open (NIV, "naked") before God so that its denizens tremble—a uniquely biblical concept that fits only monotheism.

Generally the mythology allots to the gods their separate domains. There are the gods of the heavens and the gods of the earth. With Baal dead, Ashtar, the rebel god, is permitted by El to attempt to sit on Baal's throne; but not having the stature, he does not succeed and must be content to reign on the earth.[77] Each god is powerful in his own domain. As personifications of nature, they are often in conflict with one another. The hero Baal faces a losing battle with Mot but has victory over Yam. Unlike the Ugaritic El, who sires deities but cannot control them, Job's "El" is the sovereign Lord over all natural forces—especially the domains of Mot, Yam, and Baal. This is what prompts Wolff to write:

> Following the signposts of the OT itself, we must seek to understand it on the basis of the peculiar nature of Yahweh, the God of Israel. In his essence, Yahweh is not a figure of mythology in the sense that one could speak

---

74. In contrast to 7:12, where *yām* is used without the definite article as a name: "Am I *Yam*?"

75. In 26:9 scholars differ over reading *kissēh* ("throne") or *kēseh* ("full moon"). The latter is on the basis of Psalm 81:3 4. and Proverbs 7:20. See R. Gordis, *The Book of Job: Commentary, New Translation and Special Studies* (New York: Ktav, 1978), comment on 26:9.

76. As early as 1957 Dahood suggested *derek* sometimes means "power" or "dominion" ("Some Northwest-Semitic Words in Job," *Bib* 38 [1957]: 306–20). In this he has since been generally supported (Pope, *Job*, 186).

77. Herdner, *Corpus des tablettes*, 6.1.39–65. Clifford (*Cosmic Mountain*, 168) mentions another place where Ashtar does exercise kingship from Zaphon.

of him in the manner of the myths of the neighboring lands, which chatter so much of the "private life" of their gods and of their life together in the pantheon. Yahweh is the one beside whom no other is god, and before whom all others are shown to be no gods.[78]

On this general subject W. F. Albright has made some cogent remarks, speaking of the OT as a "masterpiece of empirical logic not expressed in formal categories."[79] He claims the OT has demythologized the language on which some Hebrew literature is based. "Old words are kept but they have a new meaning, divested of all clear mythological connotations."[80]

There may be partial demythologizing in some cases. On 38:7 Andersen writes, "It is noteworthy that 11Qtg Job has completed the demythologizing making the stars shine instead of sing and calling the sons 'angels.' "[81] Is use of the plural in *ʾelōhîm* ("God") and *ʾadōnāy* ("Lord") demythologizing? In Hebrew this appears to mean the totality of all the manifestations and attributes of deity that polytheism broke down into single elements. In some Canaanite documents a single high god is referred to with the plural ending, the so-called plural of majesty (Amarna and Ugaritic). The Hebrews had no problem distinguishing between the plural of majesty for the true God and the same plural word for "the gods." Sometimes they are used in the same sentence (cf. Ps 82:1). The Chronicler in postexilic times heard no polytheism in Solomon's words to Hiram king of Tyre when he said, "Our God is greater than all other gods" (2Ch 2:5; cf. Pss 86:8; 95:3; 136:2). Despite this apparent attributing existence to the gods Psalm 96:5 says, "For all the gods of the nations are idols."

Albright observes that

much of the onslaught on early Israelite monotheism comes from scholars who represent certain theological points of view with reference to monotheism, i.e. who deny that orthodox trinitarian Christianity or orthodox Judaism or orthodox Islam are monotheistic. I do not need to stress the fact that neither of the last two religions can be called monotheistic by a theologian who insists that this term applies only to Unitarian Christianity or liberal Judaism. But no dictionary definition of monotheism was ever intended to exclude orthodox Christianity.[82]

9. BIBLIOGRAPHY

Books

Andersen, F. I. *Job, An Introduction and Commentary*. Downers Grove, Ill.: InterVarsity, 1976.
Blommerde, A. C. M. *Northwest Semitic Grammar and Job*. Biblica et orientalia 22. Rome: Pontifical Biblical Institute, 1969.
Burrell, D. B. *Deconstructing Theology: Why Job Has Nothing to Say to the Puzzle of Suffering*. Grand Rapids: Brazos, 2007.
Clines, D. J. A. *Job 1–20*. Word Biblical Commentary. Dallas: Word, 1989.

---

78. Wolff, "Hermeneutics of the Old Testament," 168.

79. W. F. Albright, *History, Archaeology, and Christian Humanism* (New York: McGraw-Hill, 1964), 94.

80. Ibid., 94.

81. F. I. Andersen, *Job: An Introduction and Commentary* (Downers Grove, Ill.: InterVarsity Press, 1976), 274.

82. Albright, *History, Archaeology, and Christian Humanism*, 155. For a more contemporary discussion of this issue from the perspective of Albright, see R. Hess, *Israelite Religions: An Archaeological and Biblical Survey* (Grand Rapids: Baker, 2007).

———. *Job 21–37*. Word Biblical Commentary. Nashville: Word, 2006.

Dahood, M. *Ugaritic-Hebrew Philology*. Rome: Pontifical Biblical Institute, 1965.

———. *Psalms*. Anchor Bible. Volumes 16, 17, 17A. Garden City, N.Y.: Doubleday, 1966–70.

Delitzsch, F. *Job: Biblical Commentary on the Old Testament*. K&D. Repr., Grand Rapids: Eerdmans, 1971.

Dhorme, E. A. *Commentary on the Book of Job*. Paris, 1926. Translated by H. Knight. London: Nelson and Sons, 1967.

Driver, S. R., and G. B. Gray. *A Critical and Exegetical Commentary on the Book of Job*. International Critical Commentary. 2nd ed. Edinburgh: T. & T. Clark, 1950.

Ewald, G. H. A. *Commentary on The Book of Job*. 1836. Translated by J. F. Smith. Repr., Edinburgh: Williams & Norgate, 1882.

Fohrer, G. *Das Buch Hiob*. Gütersloh: G. Mohn, 1963.

Gordis, R. *The Book of God and Man: A Study of Job*. Chicago: University of Chicago Press, 1966.

———. *The Book of Job: Commentary, New Translation and Special Studies*. New York: Ktav, 1978.

Guilleaume, A. *Studies in the Book of Job*. Annual of the Leeds University Oriental Society Supplement 2. Leiden: Brill, 1968.

Habel, N. C. *The Book of Job*. The Old Testament Library. Philadelphia: Westminster, 1985.

Hartley, J. E. *Job*. New International Commentary on the Old Testament. Grand Rapids: Eerdmans, 1988.

Jackson, D. R. *The Gospel According to Job: Crying Out for Vindication*. Phillipsburg, N.J.: Presbyterian and Reformed Publishing, 2007.

Kissane, E. J. *The Book of Job*. Dublin: Browne and Nolan, 1939.

Kline, M. "Job." Pages 459–90 in *Wycliffe Bible Commentary*. Edited by E. F. Harrison and C. F. Pfeiffer. Chicago: Moody Publishers, 1962.

Konkel, A. H. "Job." Pages 1–249 in *Job, Ecclesiastes, Song of Songs*. Edited by P. W. Comfort. Downers Grove, Ill.: Tyndale, 2006.

MacKenzie, R. A. F. "Job." In *Jerome Bible Commentary*. Edited by R. E. Brown et al. Englewood Cliffs, N.J.: Prentice-Hall, 1968.

Peake, A. S. *Job*. The Century Bible. Edinburgh: T. C. and E. C. Jack, 1905.

Pope, M. H. *Job*. Anchor Bible. Vol. 15. 3rd ed. New York: Doubleday, 1973.

Robertson, D. *The Old Testament and the Literary Critic*. Philadelphia: Fortress, 1977.

Rowley, H. H. *The Book of Job*. The New Century Bible Commentary. Grand Rapids: Eerdmans, 1980.

Tur-Sinai, N. H. *The Book of Job*: *A New Commentary*. Jerusalem: Kiryath Sepher, 1957.

Westermann, C. *The Structure of the Book of Job: A Form-Critical Analysis*. Philadelphia: Fortress, 1981.

Wilson, G. H. *Job*. New International Biblical Commentary on the Old Testament. Peabody, Mass.: Hendrickson, 2007.

Other Works

Clines, D. J. A. "The Arguments of Job's Three Friends." Pages 199–214 in *Art and Rhetoric in Biblical Literature*. Edited by J. G. Davies et al. Sheffield: JSOT, 1982.

Dahood, M. J. "Hebrew-Ugaritic Lexicography I–XII." *Biblica* 44 (1963) to 55 (1974).

Driver, G. R. "Two Astronomical Passages in the Old Testament." *Journal of Theological Studies* 4 (1953): 208–12; "Two Astronomical Passages in the Old Testament." *Journal of Theological Studies* 7 (1956): 1–11.

Fisher, L. R. *Ras Shamra Parallels*. 2 volumes. Rome: Pontifical Biblical Institute, 1972, 1975.

Fullerton, K. "Double Entendre in the First Speech of Eliphaz." *Journal of Biblical Literature* 49 (1930): 320–74.

Hummel, H. D. "Enclitic MEM in Early Northwest Semitic." *Journal of Biblical Literature* 76 (1957): 85–107.

Michel, W. L. "The Ugaritic Texts and the Mythological Expressions in the Book of Job." Ph.D. diss., University of Wisconsin, 1970.

Sarna, N. M. "Epic Substratum in the Prose of Job." *Journal of Biblical Literature* 76 (March 1957): 13–25.

Tsevat, M. "The Meaning of the Book of Job." *Hebrew Union College Annual* 37 (1966): 73–106.

10. OUTLINE

Text and Exposition

I. PROLOGUE (1:1–2:13)

OVERVIEW

The Prologue contains some epical features of a story passed on from generation to generation (cf. Sarna, 13–25). This does not necessarily remove it from the realm of history any more than the poetic features of historical psalms, such as Psalms 78 and 106, make them unhistorical. But it does help us appreciate the stylized and therefore identical phraseology of the two interviews with the Accuser (the Satan; 1:6–8, 12; 2:1–3, 6–7) and the consummate skill of the storyteller, who by repeating the simple phrase "while he was still speaking" (1:16, 17, 18), creates an effective tragic climax. Exegetical awareness of such features can be of value to the preacher and expositor.

The Prologue introduces us to Job as a man of faith and shows how his fortunes on earth are directed by heavenly forces beyond his control. But its full purpose lies even deeper. It is a deliberately planned foundation on which the spiritual message of the book is based. Without the Prologue, the Job of the Dialogues and Monologues might justly be considered a man of insufferable self-righteousness, and the reader would be left without a heavenly perspective much as in the other theodicies of the ancient Near East. With this Prologue the purpose of the book is clarified—to show that in a world where evil is a reality, good people may appear to suffer unjustly, but that such injustice is precipitated by the Accuser and, though permitted by God, it is an expression of God's total confidence that the faith of his servant will triumph.

Job, then, is like the guiltless sufferer in Psalm 22 and Isaiah 53. His attitude in the Prologue is an OT anticipation of the truth that God's servants are honored when they are "counted worthy of suffering disgrace for the Name" (Ac 5:41). Job starts with the triumphant spirit of the postresurrection disciples (1:20–21; 2:10); but like the prophet Jeremiah (20:7–9) and that greatest of prophets, John the Baptist (Lk 7:18–20), Job, as a man of like passions, is not above a struggle for faith. This is what creates the dramatic power of the book and provides courage for all faithful sufferers who also struggle to understand the mysteries of divine providence.

The Prologue consists of a series of vignettes. The opening scene introduces Job in his domestic felicity (1:1–5), and the closing scene introduces his three friends, who are moved to an extravagant display of mourning over the extent of Job's suffering (2:11–13). Between these two sections, the scenes shift back and forth from heaven to earth, unveiling the secret purpose for it all—a purpose unknown to Job.

A. Job's Felicity (1:1–5)

¹In the land of Uz there lived a man whose name was Job. This man was blameless and upright; he feared God and shunned evil. ²He had seven sons and three daughters,

³and he owned seven thousand sheep, three thousand camels, five hundred yoke of oxen and five hundred donkeys, and had a large number of servants. He was the greatest man among all the people of the East.

⁴His sons used to take turns holding feasts in their homes, and they would invite their three sisters to eat and drink with them. ⁵When a period of feasting had run its course, Job would send and have them purified. Early in the morning he would sacrifice a burnt offering for each of them, thinking, "Perhaps my children have sinned and cursed God in their hearts." This was Job's regular custom.

COMMENTARY

1–5 Job is presented as a blameless and upright man who worships (fears) God and shuns evil and whose life is crowned with prosperity. This way of describing Job uses vocabulary and phraseology that permeates the book of Proverbs. Fearing the Lord and shunning evil (v.1) are the controlling principles of wisdom (28:28). Although the author does not use the term wisdom (*ḥokmâ*) here, this repeated description of Job (1:1, 8; 2:3) labels him a truly wise man. The insertion of an excursus on wisdom in chapter 28 appears to be a deliberate structural feature of the book. Placed between the three cycles of dialogues and the three monologues, it tells the reader how a man so renowned for his wisdom cannot take it for granted. Wisdom is the essence of true religion in this OT literary genre.

That Job is "blameless" (*tām*) and "upright" (*yāšār*) should not be construed to imply he is sinless (cf. 13:26; 14:16–17). The former usually refers to a person's spiritual maturity and the integrity (purity) of his inner being. The latter, meaning "straight, right," is used in many contexts dealing with human behavior that is in line with God's ways. Together they provide an idiomatic way to describe Job's high moral character. As the book goes on to point out, Job is not completely and utterly devoid of fault, but his sin does not account for the incredible suffering he endures.

Job lives in Uz, a land somewhere east of Canaan on the edge of the desert (vv.1, 19). It is almost certainly to be identified with a city in Edom (La 4:21), which was renowned for its wisdom (see the mocking of the vaunted wisdom of Edom in Jer 49:7). He lives in an area where farming could be carried on (v.14) but is also near a town (29:7). In v.3 Job's wealth is described in terms similar to those used of the patriarchs, the stress being on animals and servants (Ge 12:16). Job is greater (richer) than any of "the people of the East," another indication that Uz is in Edom. This shows he was a well-known sage among the easterners. Such easterners may be contrasted with the Mediterranean people who came from the West, such as the Philistines.

Verse 5 reveals that Job, like the patriarchs, functions as a priest for his family. He takes his sacrificial obligation seriously, viewing it as expiation for sin. To Job this includes even sins of the heart, for he makes special offerings just in case his sons have secretly cursed God. The matter of cursing or not cursing God becomes a key theme in the development of this drama.

NOTES

1 The idiom אִישׁ הָיָה (ʾîš hāyâ, "there lived a man") indicates that the story has no connection with any earlier event. It is the Hebrew way to begin a totally independent narrative (Dhorme, 29). Clines (*Job 1–20*, 9–10) points out that the specific manner by which Job is introduced (lit., "there was a man … ") is only paralleled in parables (2Sa 12:1) and fables in the Bible. He also indicates that this does not decide the issue whether or not Job is a real person, but rather is a way of showing that he is not a part of the mainstream of Israel's redemptive-historical story.

Genesis 10:22–23; 22:21; and 1 Chronicles 1:17 tie עוּץ (ʿûṣ, "Uz") to the Arameans, but Genesis 36:28; Jeremiah 25:19–21; and Lamentations 4:21 tie it to Edom. The conflict may only be apparent since Genesis 10 (cf. 1Ch 1) is a table of nations, and Genesis 22:21 deals with Uz before the birth of Esau, the progenitor of the Edomites. Since, as Delitzsch notes, the Arabic name of Esau is ʿîṣ, Uz may be the place in what is now North Arabia where the two cultures (Aramean and Edomite) met or divided from a common origin. *Uṣṣa* in Shalmaneser III's annals is undoubtedly the same place.

5 וּבֵרֲכוּ (ûbērᵃkû, GK 1385; lit. "and blessed"; NIV, "and cursed") is a euphemism by the original writer, not a later scribe (so Pope, 8). For similar use of original euphemisms (cf. 2Sa 12:14) in Egyptian documents, see K. A. Kitchen, *Ancient Orient and Old Testament* (Downers Grove, Ill.: InterVarsity Press, 1966), 166 (cf. Job 1:11; 2:5, 9; 1Ki 21:10, 13; Ps 10:3).

B. Job Tested (1:6–2:13)

1. Satan's Accusations of Job (1:6–12)

⁶One day the angels came to present themselves before the LORD, and Satan also came with them. ⁷The LORD said to Satan, "Where have you come from?"

Satan answered the LORD, "From roaming through the earth and going back and forth in it."

⁸Then the LORD said to Satan, "Have you considered my servant Job? There is no one on earth like him; he is blameless and upright, a man who fears God and shuns evil."

⁹"Does Job fear God for nothing?" Satan replied. ¹⁰"Have you not put a hedge around him and his household and everything he has? You have blessed the work of his hands, so that his flocks and herds are spread throughout the land. ¹¹But stretch out your hand and strike everything he has, and he will surely curse you to your face."

¹²The LORD said to Satan, "Very well, then, everything he has is in your hands, but on the man himself do not lay a finger."

Then Satan went out from the presence of the LORD.

<h1 style="text-align:center">COMMENTARY</h1>

6–12 There are two scenes in heaven, each depicting the divine council (1:6–12 and 2:1–6). Each is followed by a series of events that result from the encounter between the Lord and Satan. The divine council (v.6) is made up of the *b^enê hā^{ʾe}lōhîm* ("the sons of God" [NIV, "angels"], which here refers to these supernatural beings who are above humans but created by God [Ps 8:5]). The heathen nations used the same terminology for their gods. The author of Job applies the term to the beings the Hebrews otherwise called the Lord's messengers (*maPākîm*, Ge 19:1; 24:7; 48:16; Ps 104:4; Mal 3:1; et al.). The Accuser (*haśśāṭān*, "the Satan") is such a being, but one whose business is to roam the earth (v.7) as the Accuser of those committed to serving God (1Pe 5:8; Rev 12:10).

Here we find the Accuser questioning Job's motive for religious devotion. "Does Job fear God for nothing?" (v.9). It is not the Accuser but the Lord who initiates the testing of Job, for the Lord says: "Have you considered my servant Job? There is no one on earth like him" (v.8). God's statement that Job is his servant implies more than mere servitude; it means God and Job are in a covenantal relationship based on solemn oaths.

As in Genesis 3, God sets the stage and allows Job to be put to the test. Here the Lord sees fit to use secondary means to accomplish his purpose. That purpose is not just to test Job as an end in itself but to give Job the opportunity to honor his Lord, to whom he has pledged his allegiance with a solemn oath. That allegiance becomes a significant part of the cosmic struggle between Job's adversary and the Lord. Will Job curse God or not?

Understanding this struggle is basic to understanding the book of Job as well as the whole historical-religious drama of the Bible (Ge 3:15; Ro 16:20). The Accuser insinuates that Job's allegiance is hypocritical (v.9). If only God would remove the protective hedge he has placed about Job (v.10), this "devout" servant would certainly curse God to his face. The attack is on God through Job, and the only way the Accuser can be proven false is through Job. So Satan is given limited but gradually increased access to Job—first to his possessions, then to his family, and finally to his physical well-being. But through it all, in the words of M. Kline, 461, "the primary purpose of Job's suffering, unknown to him, was that he should stand before men and angels as a trophy of the saving might of God, an exhibit of that divine wisdom which is the archetype, source, and foundation of true human wisdom."

<h1 style="text-align:center">NOTES</h1>

6 In וַיְהִי הַיּוֹם (*way^ehî hayyôm*, "One day … came … and"), stress is on the particularity of this day; the same is true in v.13.

The terminology לְהִתְיַצֵּב עַל־יְהוָה (*l^ehityaṣṣēb ʿal-yhwh*, "to present themselves before the LORD") is used of servants or courtiers who present themselves before their king. Sarna, 22–23, sees it as a Canaanite term used especially for the convocation of celestial beings.

In rendering הַשָּׂטָן (*haśśāṭān*, "the Satan"; GK 8477), the NIV has taken the liberty to leave out the definite article, which the Hebrew uses consistently here (1:6–12; 2:1–7). The article means the author wants the root meaning of this title to be emphasized. Whether this represents an earlier stage in the development of the doctrine of Satan is a debatable question. Both here and in Zechariah (3:1–2), a postexilic prophet, the definite article and the context emphasize the accusatory role of this superhuman adversary. The root is not used often in the OT and is usually of human adversaries (1Sa 29:4; 2Sa 19:22; 1Ki 5:4; 11:14, 23, 25; Ps 109:6). By the time of the Chronicler (cf. 1Ch 21:1, where no article is used), the LXX, and the NT, this term had become a proper name for the arch-adversary; but there is no data on when the concept originated. Here it should be rendered "the Adversary" or "the Accuser."

7 The Accuser is said to roam "the earth going back and forth." This may be part of a literary strategy to describe the heavenly court in analogy with royal courts on earth. Pope, 10, points to the connection with Persian spies, who were called "The King's Eye" and "The King's Ear."

2. Job's Integrity in Loss of Family and Property (1:13–22)

¹³One day when Job's sons and daughters were feasting and drinking wine at the oldest brother's house, ¹⁴a messenger came to Job and said, "The oxen were plowing and the donkeys were grazing nearby, ¹⁵and the Sabeans attacked and carried them off. They put the servants to the sword, and I am the only one who has escaped to tell you!"

¹⁶While he was still speaking, another messenger came and said, "The fire of God fell from the sky and burned up the sheep and the servants, and I am the only one who has escaped to tell you!"

¹⁷While he was still speaking, another messenger came and said, "The Chaldeans formed three raiding parties and swept down on your camels and carried them off. They put the servants to the sword, and I am the only one who has escaped to tell you!"

¹⁸While he was still speaking, yet another messenger came and said, "Your sons and daughters were feasting and drinking wine at the oldest brother's house, ¹⁹when suddenly a mighty wind swept in from the desert and struck the four corners of the house. It collapsed on them and they are dead, and I am the only one who has escaped to tell you!"

²⁰At this, Job got up and tore his robe and shaved his head. Then he fell to the ground in worship ²¹and said:

"Naked I came from my mother's womb,
    and naked I will depart.
The LORD gave and the LORD has taken away;
    may the name of the LORD be praised."

²²In all this, Job did not sin by charging God with wrongdoing.

COMMENTARY

13–19 Again the use of the article on the word "day" (v.13; cf. v.6) suggests the translation, "Now it was the day his sons and daughters were eating." According to v.5 Job's custom was to make offerings for them at that time. So the very day he makes these offerings, this devastation takes place. The meaning of the suffering then is even a deeper mystery for Job. As noted, the stylistic nature of the text indicates that the account is an old and frequently told story based on history. Indeed the coming of the messengers of misfortune each on the heels of the other (vv.14, 16, 17, 18), all on that one fateful day, has its dramatic effect heightened by the narrator's style.

We are informed, however, that it is really the work of the Accuser, this master of evil, who can and does use both the elements of nature and human beings to accomplish his purpose. Why does God allow such a devastating series of blows? Is it not a part of his higher purpose and design to humiliate the Adversary all the more?

As Delitzsch, 1:63, notes, Satan is a great juggler and has manifested himself as such in Paradise and in the temptation of Jesus Christ: "There is in nature as among men an entanglement of contrary forces which he knows how to unloosen because it is the sphere of his special dominion."

20–22 Tearing one's outer garment and cropping one's hair (v.20) were common gestures of violent grief in the biblical world (cf. Ge 37:34; Jos 7:6; Ezr 9:3, 5). Such response to grief, including weeping and wailing (Ps 42:3; Jn 11:33–35), is natural and beneficial to human needs.

The wisdom quatrain (v.21; cf. Ecc 5:15) introduces us to the poetic parallelism found in all the speeches, beginning in chapter 3. Here the attitude of Job, in contrast to that in the Dialogue section, is one of supreme faith and total resignation to God's sovereign will. Job does not understand why but he believes that his trouble come from God: "The LORD gave and the LORD has taken away" (v.21).

Job is ignorant of what has taken place in the divine council that God has allowed the Accuser to strike thus far. But Job is right—it is the Lord who has taken away. The use of secondary means does not solve the problem of evil, nor is it the purpose of the book of Job to solve this logical dilemma. In a real sense, Job's statement of trust in God goes as far as he or any human can go in solving this mystery.

When Job says, "May the name of the LORD be praised" (v.21), he is using, as noted, the same word that Satan used in v.11 as a euphemism with the opposite meaning. The play on the root *brk* ("bless") is forceful. It stresses how the Accuser is foiled at this point. Instead of cursing God to his face, Job praises him.

Here the author, being a Hebrew, uses that special covenantal name (*yhwh*) for God (see Notes). Job and his friends are not Hebrews; so they use other Hebrew epithets for God—most often the general epithet *ʾelôah*. Here in the Prologue the composer of the book carefully identifies the Job of faith and wisdom as the same Job with questions and defiance in the Dialogue and Monologue units. But more important is his identification of the God of the Dialogue with the true God, whom the Hebrews worshiped.

Up to this point (v.22), though deprived of family and possessions, Job does not sin with his lips (cf. 2:10) by accusing God of "wrongdoing" (*tiplâ*, see Notes).

NOTES

15 שְׁבָא (*šᵉbāʾ*, "the Sabeans"), nomads, are to be identified with the people of Sheba, who had a wealthy south Arabian kingdom and whose queen visited Solomon according to 1 Kings 10:1–13 (cf. Pope, 13).

16 אֵשׁ אֱלֹהִים (*ʾēš ʾᵉlōhîm*, "the fire of God") may be either lightning (Pope, 14) or brimstone (Delitzsch, 1:61). The terminology "of God" as part of a cliché does not mean God is considered the immediate source in this context. It is simply phenomenological language because it comes from heaven.

17 כַּשְׂדִּים (*kaśdîm*, "the Chaldeans") were roving marauders before they settled down in the south, west of the Tigris, in the ninth century BC.

שְׁלֹשָׁה רָאשִׁים (*šᵉlōšâ roʾšîm*, "three raiding parties") is an ancient military stratagem that is still used (Jdg 7:16, 20; 9:34, 43–45; 1Sa 11:11, 13:17).

לְפִי־חָרֶב (*lᵉpî-ḥāreb*, "to the sword"; lit., "to the mouth of the sword") reflects the custom of making swords with a hilt in the shape of a lion's head, with the blade coming from the mouth (see Pope, 13–14), just as Messiah is figured with the sword proceeding from his mouth (cf. Isa 11:4; Rev 1:16; 2:16; 19:15). To this may be added the reverse OT figure of words as sharp instruments of destruction (Ps 52:2–4; Hos 6:5), on which is based the NT figure of the Word of God as a sharp two-edged sword (Heb 4:12).

18 עַד (*ʿad*, "while") is an example of a defective spelling following plenary spellings. Compare Notes on 37:24.

21 The so-called Tetragrammaton יהוה (*yhwh*) is translated "the Lord" in the KJV, NASB, and NIV. Because it was considered too sacred to pronounce in post-OT Judaism, it was vocalized with the vowels of ʾᵃdōnāy ("Lord"; GK 151; cf. LXX *kyrios*). The original vowels were consequently lost, though scholars, on the basis of early transliterations (Epiphanius and Theodoret use the Gk. *Iabe*), pronounce it "Yahweh." The exact meaning is debated but always tied to some form of the Hebrew verb meaning "to be, become" (Ex 3:13–15). It was Israel's unique name for God and as such had special significance for their relationship to him in the covenant renewal at Sinai (Ex 6:2–5). The sage Job probably did not know God by this name, but the author of the book identifies Job's God as the very same God whom Israel worshiped.

אָשׁוּב שָׁמָה (*ʾāšûb šāmâ*, "will depart") is literally, "return there." In OT terminology the body is formed in mother earth; the womb is considered a place of darkness like Sheol (Ps 139:13, 15). So returning to it means going to the place where the departed go. It did not mean nonexistence as some have maintained. The ancient Semitic world viewed man as having an existence in Sheol, however drab it may have been. But Job here probably speaks merely of burial (Ge 3:19).

22 Much has been written about תִּפְלָה (*tiplâ*, "wrongdoing"). Dhorme's explanation (29) is the best. He links the word with the root *tpl* ("tasteless"; 6:6). As our words "insipid" and "insipient" are related, so the root *tpl* also means "worthless" in Lamentations 2:14. If Job does not charge God with doing anything worthless, he must believe God has a high purpose.

3. Satan's Further Accusations (2:1–6)

¹On another day the angels came to present themselves before the LORD, and Satan also came with them to present himself before him. ²And the LORD said to Satan, "Where have you come from?"

Satan answered the LORD, "From roaming through the earth and going back and forth in it."

³Then the LORD said to Satan, "Have you considered my servant Job? There is no one on earth like him; he is blameless and upright, a man who fears God and shuns evil. And he still maintains his integrity, though you incited me against him to ruin him without any reason."

⁴"Skin for skin!" Satan replied. "A man will give all he has for his own life. ⁵But stretch out your hand and strike his flesh and bones, and he will surely curse you to your face."

⁶The LORD said to Satan, "Very well, then, he is in your hands; but you must spare his life."

COMMENTARY

1–3 At a special time set aside, the Accuser again appears with "the sons of God" and as a subordinate presents himself before the Lord (v.1). The terminology is formulaic, using the same words as 1:6–9. The Accuser has continued to roam the earth (v.2), obviously looking for those whom he will take "captive to do his will" (2Ti 2:26). He has lost the first round of this contest. For the third time the Lord triumphantly describes Job as a unique servant ("no one on earth like him"), a pure and devout man who has become even stronger as a result of the testing. "He still maintains his integrity" (v.3). The stem (Hiphil) of the verb "maintains" indicates a strengthening of the grip he already has.

As though to add a bit of irony, the Lord says to the Accuser, "You incited me against him to ruin him without any reason" (v.3). The words are typical OT empirical logic. They should not be used to imply that God can somehow be stirred up to do things that are against his will. On the contrary, God suggested Job to the Accuser (1:8; 2:3) in the first

place. All Job's suffering is part of the divine purpose, as God says in 38:2: "Who is this that darkens my counsel with words without knowledge?" But when God uses a secondary cause to affect the life of a human, even Satan can be said to stir him up.

The word *ḥinnām*, sometimes translated "without cause" (KJV, RV, NEB; GK 2855), needs some clarification. Satan had a cause or reason—to discredit God—and certainly God was accomplishing his own cause or purpose. In 1:9 Satan used the same word to accuse Job of having an ulterior purpose for serving God. Now God taunts the Accuser with the counteraccusation that Satan himself is the one who wants to see injustice done. The translation of this key word (*ḥinnām*) as "without any reason" is good at this point. It means there was no immediate sinfulness in Job that called for punishment. Another possible translation for *ḥinnām* is "in vain" (cf. JB). This would suggest that Satan has wasted his energy on Job. But that meaning is rare in the OT (cf. Pr 1:17; Mal 1:10; NIV, "useless").

4–6 Satan does not consider his energy to have been wasted. His next move is to obtain permission to attack Job's body. With the adage, "Skin for skin! ... A man will give all he has for his own life" (v.4), Satan suggests that even Job's triumphant faith expressed in his doxology (1:21) is only a ploy by which he is purchasing his personal well-being. He is even willing to sacrifice the skin of his loved ones to save his own. If God would send his hand against Job's own body (i.e., permit Satan to do so), Job's verbal piety would prove to be a sham; and he will curse God to his face (v.5).

The contest is about to take on a new intensity. God places Job in the hands of their mutual adversary but limits his power—"you must spare his life" (v.6). The suffering of the innocent is a mystery that defies all human logic. The book of Job deals with this subject profoundly but does not attempt to give a neat logical solution.

NOTES

4 Scholars have pondered over the origin and precise meaning of the proverb עוֹר בְּעַד־עוֹר (ʿôr beʿad ʿôr, "skin for skin"). The sentence that follows it clearly explains its application. Satan is implying that Job is willing to give the life of another to save his own.

5 As a strong adversative אוּלָם (ʾûlām, "But"; GK 219) might be rendered "On the other hand." יְבָרֲכֶךָ (yebārakekkā, "He will ... curse you") is the same euphemism as in 1:11.

6 The verb שְׁמֹר (šemōr, "spare") means "to safeguard." Because of the choice of word, it would appear Satan is being made responsible for the life of Job.

4. Job's Integrity in Personal Suffering (2:7–10)

> [7]So Satan went out from the presence of the LORD and afflicted Job with painful sores from the soles of his feet to the top of his head. [8]Then Job took a piece of broken pottery and scraped himself with it as he sat among the ashes.
>
> [9]His wife said to him, "Are you still holding on to your integrity? Curse God and die!"
>
> [10]He replied, "You are talking like a foolish woman. Shall we accept good from God, and not trouble?"
>
> In all this, Job did not sin in what he said.

COMMENTARY

7–8 It is not important for us to know about Job's disease. The symptoms are many. The "painful sores" all over his body (v.7), from the soles of his feet to the tip of his head, are perhaps only the initial stage of the malady. Job speaks of other complications in 30:17, 27, 30. The Semitic root šḥn ("sores") denotes fever and inflammation, but in the OT it describes diseases that have symptoms appearing on the skin (Ex 9:9; Lev 13; Dt 28:27, 35). The scratching Job does with the potsherd (v.8) is because of the nature of his disease. He uses this only as a counterirritant and not for the ancient practice of laceration as a sign of mourning for the dead (Dt 14:1). If it were the latter, it would have been mentioned in conjunction with the loss of his family.

9–10 Not knowing the limitation God has put on the Accuser, Job's wife at this point diagnoses the disease as incurable and recommends that he curse God and die (v.9). Chrysostom's explanation of why Satan does not destroy Job's wife with the rest of the family is so that she can become his tool. Job's mental anguish is certainly intensified by his wife's advice. Had he followed it, the contest would have ended with the Accuser as the victor.

Job's reply is remarkable in the compassion he shows toward his wife and in his total accep-

tance of God's will for his life (v.10). He may have accused his wife of blasphemy but chose to accept it as a statement of desperation. Her "talking like a foolish woman" does not refer to intellectual foolishness but to religious apostasy as in Psalms 14:1 and 53:1, where "the fool [*nābāl*; GK 5572] says in his heart, 'There is no God.' " To curse God is essentially a way of denying he is God. Job is willing to believe that his wife is only talking like a blasphemer. Job's wisdom, however, is to receive with meekness whatever prosperity or disaster God might send. Such wisdom is not rooted in his intellectual capacity but in his fear (worship) of God.

Now the author repeats practically the same testimony of Job's verbal innocence given in 1:22. Despite all that has happened to him, up to this point Job does not err with his lips. This section of the Prologue provides the basis of the NT description of Job as a man of perseverance (Jas 5:11).

NOTES

8 Though somewhat messy, הָאֵפֶר (*hā'ēper*, "the ashes") was perhaps the most sterile place a man with sores could sit. That aspect may be only coincidental; but the ancients, by practice, may have found it physically advantageous.

9 בָּרֵךְ (*bārēk*, "curse") is the same as in 1:11 and 2:5.

10 The root of נְקַבֵּל (*neqabbēl*, "we accept") is not a late Aramaism (BDB), nor is it fully synonymous with *lqḥ* ("receive"; Dhorme). Canaanite evidence from the Amarna Letters shows it can mean "receive meekly/patiently" (Kline, 464).

5. The Coming of the Counselors (2:11–13)

11When Job's three friends, Eliphaz the Temanite, Bildad the Shuhite and Zophar the Naamathite, heard about all the troubles that had come upon him, they set out from their homes and met together by agreement to go and sympathize with him and comfort him. ¹²When they saw him from a distance, they could hardly recognize him; they began to weep aloud, and they tore their robes and sprinkled dust on their heads. ¹³Then they sat on the ground with him for seven days and seven nights. No one said a word to him, because they saw how great his suffering was.

COMMENTARY

11–13 It takes time, possibly months, for the news to pass by word of mouth and for the three sages, friends of Job, to come (cf. 7:3). Teman, an Edomite city, is the only place of the three that can be definitely located. The friends arrange a meeting (see Notes) so they can join together to console Job (v.11). Teman was a center of wisdom (Jer 49:7). Shuah was the name of an eastern tribe according to Genesis 25:2, 6. Pope, 24, puts Naaman at Rebel el Naʾameh in Arabia.

When the counselors join together near Job's home, they are stunned by what they see (v.12). Like the Suffering Servant of Isaiah 53, Job is disfigured beyond recognition, at least from a distance. The friends have come to show grief (*nûd*; GK 5653) and console (*nāḥam*) Job. The same words are used in 42:11, where other members of his house perform this eastern ritual after Job is restored. The verb *nûd* ("to show grief") means literally

"to shake the head." The three friends may have come largely to go through the proper motions. It does not appear that they are ready for what they encounter.

Instead of ritual-like acts that seem to take place in 42:11, the friends immediately go into a more drastic form of mourning usually reserved for death or total disaster. They tear their robes of nobility, wail, and throw dust into the air. Then they sit in silence before Job for seven days and nights (v.13; for mourning seven days over the dead, see Ge 50:10; 1Sa 31:13; Sir 22:12; cf. also Jos 7:6; 1Sa 4:12; 2Sa 13:19; La 2:10; Eze 27:30). Some consider the seven days of silence a display of grief in its most intense form (Dhorme, 23). Like the elders of fallen Jerusalem in Lamentations 2:10, Job's friends sit on the ground with dust on their heads and keep silent. For one of them to speak prior to the sufferer would have been in bad taste.

NOTE

11 אֱלִיפַז (*ʾĕlîpaz*, "Eliphaz") probably does not mean "God is fine gold" (Pope, 24) but possibly "God is the Victor," from the Arabic *paʾza* ("win, gain victory"). "Bildad" seems most likely to derive from *Bil-ʾada* ("Baal is lord"). See Pope, 24, for other suggestions on "Bildad." On "Zophar," Pope follows Dhorme, who sees a diminutive here meaning "little birds" (see the Introduction: Major Characters: The Three Counselors).

The verb וַיִּוָּעֲדוּ (*wayyiwwāʿᵃdû*, "by agreement") means more than simply "to agree" but rather "to have an appointment," including a time and place. Amos 3:3 proves the point (contrary to Dhorme), for two people cannot walk together unless they agree on a time and place.

II. THE DIALOGUE-DISPUTE (3:1–27:23)

OVERVIEW

The Dialogue is not strictly dialogue but alternating speeches given with an audience in mind. Sometimes they are directed toward what one or the other has previously said, but in Job's case they are also directed to God or given as soliloquy. Often there is highly emotional language with no closely reasoned argumentation. Each man gives a distinctive character to his utterances, and certain issues are taken up and often repeated. For example, Job repeatedly struggles over God's justice and his own vindication. And the friends often defend God and warn and condemn Job.

A significant difference between their speeches comes from a difference in relationship with God. Job is determined to be absolutely honest with God. Job tells God everything, every tear and every doubt. The three friends tell God nothing. They only talk about God, never to him. This should be kept in mind as we become impatient with Job, though it is true that it is Job who has the brief with God, not the three friends. We should also keep in mind that despite all the hair-raising things Job will say, he never asks for restoration. His main concern is about his relationship with God, and that is why he puts so much stress on vindication. Without vindication all that he is suffering is proof that God is his enemy.

The use of the poetic format beginning in 3:3 will help the reader remember that as Job breaks the silence, his words are highly figurative, poetic rhetoric. The reader has already seen this prosodic power and beauty in the doxology in 1:21. But now the genre is not blessing or praise but malediction replete with a full-bodied hyperbole and other poetic tropes.

The counselors will prove just as adept as Job in this media. Some of their poems are masterly,

and whole speeches show architectonic structure; each has a tone distinctively his own, and each has an overall coherence to his series of speeches. Discovering the tonality of a speech is aided by being sensitive to certain sentences that clearly express the speaker's mood. Clines ("Arguments," 199–214) calls these important features "nodal sentences" and lists some that he considers crucial for perceiving the real message (e.g., 4:6 and 5:8; for Eliphaz, 15:4–5; 22:21, 30; for Bildad, 8:4–6; 18:4; 25:4; and for Zophar, 11:4–5).

Clines also worries that failure to understand the practice of using stylized descriptions with certain rhetorical patterns as literary building blocks can lead the commentator astray. These rhetorical devices are subordinate and function in a way that is not always obvious. So the interpreter must not give a disproportionate emphasis to what is being used only as an aside, a rhetorical tool. For example, is Eliphaz insulting Job in 4:8–11, or is he merely giving an excursus on the fate of the wicked? At this point he really does not think Job is wicked and encourages him to be patient on that account (4:6; 5:19–26).

A further point made by Clines ("Verbal Modality and the Interpretation of Job 4:20–21," *VT* 30 [1980]: 354–57) is the importance of seeing the possible modal force of a verb in Hebrew (the language is not as precise as Greek in this respect), which may change one's understating of what the speaker is saying. For example, in 4:20–21 Eliphaz is talking about how fragile humans are, not about the brevity of life. He is saying that it is possible for people to die without even gaining wisdom.

As we get into the speeches, these rhetorical issues and a host of other linguistic challenges of this essentially atypical Hebrew will constitute an interpretative challenge. The so-called Dialogue itself has a structure. Job opens with a sizzling malediction (ch. 3), which brings on three cycles of emotive prosody that fades out with Bildad's brief poem in chapter 25. Job then closes the verbal duel with a final statement, employing both oath and imprecation (ch. 27) as big weapons to silence the arguments of his opponents.

A. Job's Opening Lamentation (3:1–26)

OVERVIEW

The spiritual tone of Job's life has changed dramatically here. The man of patience and faith sinks into a state of despondency and spiritual depression, so frequently a major problem to those who endure severe physical illness or impairment. (See my comments about the Job of the Prologue and the Dialogue in the Introduction: Major Characters.) In chapter 3 Job establishes an attitude that largely colors all he says in the succeeding chapters. In all his many words of despair, nowhere will he come closer to cursing God to his face (2:5) than here in chapter 3, where he sounds more like the grumblers in the wilderness described in the book of Numbers than the psalmists who approach God with their laments. By cursing the day of his birth, he is questioning the sovereign wisdom of his Creator. At this point the drama is intense, for the Accuser, whom we will never see again, seems to have triumphed. Whether he has or not will be determined by what follows.

D. N. Freedman ("The Structure of Job 3," *Bib* 49 [1968]: 503–8) and Habel, 102–3, have contributed enormously to the full appreciation of this chapter by analyzing its structure. Habel points to two poetic units: a curse (vv.3–10), followed by a complimentary lament (vv.11–26). Each unit has a framing device (inclusio). Each opens by announcing the subject and closes by giving the reason. So the following pattern emerges:

The Curses
    A: Subject: Day and Night (v.3)
      Curses on that day (vv.4–5)
      Curses on that night (vv.6–9)
    A':Reason for His Curse: His Misery (v.10)
The Lament
    A: Subject: Why Did He Not Die at Birth? (v.11)
      Laments on why God permits suffering (vv.12–24)
    A':Reason for His Lament (vv.25–26)

Worthy of note are the thematic similarities between Job 3 and Jeremiah 20:14–18 (see Habel, 103) and the cosmogonic connections suggested by M. Fishbane ("Jer. 4 and Job 3: A Recovered Use of the Creation Pattern," *VT* 21 [1971]: 151–67).

¹After this, Job opened his mouth and cursed the day of his birth. ²He said:

³"May the day of my birth perish,
   and the night it was said, 'A boy is born!'

⁴That day — may it turn to darkness;
    may God above not care about it;
    may no light shine upon it.
⁵May darkness and deep shadow claim it once more;
    may a cloud settle over it;
    may blackness overwhelm its light.
⁶That night — may thick darkness seize it;
    may it not be included among the days of the year
    nor be entered in any of the months.
⁷May that night be barren;
    may no shout of joy be heard in it.
⁸May those who curse days curse that day,
    those who are ready to rouse Leviathan.
⁹May its morning stars become dark;
    may it wait for daylight in vain
    and not see the first rays of dawn,
¹⁰for it did not shut the doors of the womb on me
    to hide trouble from my eyes.

¹¹"Why did I not perish at birth,
    and die as I came from the womb?
¹²Why were there knees to receive me
    and breasts that I might be nursed?
¹³For now I would be lying down in peace;
    I would be asleep and at rest
¹⁴with kings and counselors of the earth,
    who built for themselves places now lying in ruins,
¹⁵with rulers who had gold,
    who filled their houses with silver.
¹⁶Or why was I not hidden in the ground like a stillborn child,
    like an infant who never saw the light of day?
¹⁷There the wicked cease from turmoil,
    and there the weary are at rest.
¹⁸Captives also enjoy their ease;
    they no longer hear the slave driver's shout.
¹⁹The small and the great are there,
    and the slave is freed from his master.

²⁰"Why is light given to those in misery,
    and life to the bitter of soul,

²¹to those who long for death that does not come,
    who search for it more than for hidden treasure,
²²who are filled with gladness
    and rejoice when they reach the grave?
²³Why is life given to a man
    whose way is hidden,
    whom God has hedged in?
²⁴For sighing comes to me instead of food;
    my groans pour out like water.
²⁵What I feared has come upon me;
    what I dreaded has happened to me.
²⁶I have no peace, no quietness;
    I have no rest, but only turmoil."

COMMENTARY

1–2 The words "After this" (v.1), which typically mark a literary transition (Ge 15:14 [NIV, "afterward"]; 23:19; 25:26), introduce the Dialogue, a major division of the book. In fact, the entire third chapter, though a part of the Dialogue (in that it evokes a response from the three friends), is transitional.

3–10 The way Job curses the day of his birth has two interesting features here. First, he expressed a desire for the annihilation of that day, a would-be negation of God's creative act in bringing such a day into being (v.3). As God had said in Genesis 1:3, "Let there be light," so Job, using the same terminology in v.4, said, "As for that day, let there be darkness" (lit. trans.). All this is a logical absurdity; but it is poetry, and Job means to give full vent to his feelings. He wishes that day could be so annihilated that even God would forget it (v.4b). Job wants the day lost in total darkness, not even numbered any longer as a day in the calendar (vv.5–6).

The second feature is Job's use of personification. He personifies both the night of his conception and the day he was born. In Hebrew v.3b reads, "the night that said." That night speaks about what it has witnessed, the birth of a boy. It is more vivid to imagine the day perishing as a person (v.3a) than as a span of time. Jeremiah (Jer 20:14) also cursed the day of his birth but feeling the need for concreteness shifted the curse to the man who brought the news of his birth to his father. The first half of v.7 uses personification, but the second half does not. We must not press any figure too far. A barren night (figurative) unable to conceive results in a literal night in which no shout of joy will be heard.

Dhorme, 23, says that the phrase "those who curse days" in v.8 refers to other sufferers like Job who also cursed the day of their birth. But the expression more likely refers to professional cursers like Balaam (Nu 22–24). In v.8a Job appears to be making a play on the similar sound of the words *yām* ("sea") and *yôm* ("day") and the sound-alikes *ʾōrēr* ("curser") and *ʿōrēr* ("arouser"). Current mythology used the term Leviathan for a monster of chaos that lived in the sea, and the Sea itself was a boisterous deity who could be aroused professionally. But to Job, a strict monotheist (31:26–28), this was simply vivid imagery, the use of proverbial language tailored to his call for the obliteration of that day. The verb ʿûr means "to awaken" or "to arouse" the dead in Sheol in Isaiah 14:9. The figure, then, may be of an awakened monster of chaos that could perhaps swallow that day or even usher in the end of days.

11–26 Job continues his pitiable complaint with a series of rhetorical questions. There is a progression in his thought. Since the day of his birth did happen (v.10), the next possibility is a stillbirth (vv.11–12, 16). But since he is alive, he longs for a premature death (vv.20, 23). In vv.13–19 Job conceives of death as falling into restful sleep (v.13). It is clear that he does not consider it annihilation. The dead are in a place where there is no activity, where everyone finds rest; even the wicked stop making trouble there (v.17).

In addition to the progression of thought, there is also symmetry of ideas in these verses. Job wishes

he had been a stillborn child (vv.11–12) and then imagines himself joining the great (kings, counselors, rulers) who rest in Sheol (vv.13–15). Then in v.16 he repeats the issue and follows with a description of the small (the wicked, the weary, the captives) who also rest in Sheol. A concluding line wraps it up with the thought that the small and great are all alike (see Notes) in Sheol, where even the slave is freed from his master (v.19).

The last of Job's rhetorical questions comes in vv.20–23. To paraphrase: Why is light given to a person who is miserable (v.20a)? Why is life given to a person who has no future (v.23a)? His suffering is so intense both physically (v.24) and mentally (vv.20b, 23b) that death in comparison would be an exquisite pleasure, like finding hidden treasure (vv.21b–22). The very thing he dreads the most has happened. It thus appears to him that the very God who put a hedge of protection and blessing about him (1:10) has subsequently hemmed him in with trouble and distress (vv.23c, 26).

NOTES

3 The NIV takes אָמַר (ʾāmar) as a verb with an indefinite subject, namely, "it was [one] said."

4 The basic meaning of the root of יִדְרְשֵׁהוּ (yidreśēhû, "care about it") is "to seek, search for." The point is that the day might be lost in darkness.

The epithet אֱלוֹהַ (ʾelôah, "God"; GK 468) is used forty times exclusively by Job and the counselors. Except for one instance in 12:9 (and it is doubtful), the name yhwh ("Lord") is used only by the Hebrew author in the Prologue and Epilogue and in 38:1 and 40:1, 3, and 6.

5 Dhorme, following early Jewish interpretation, derives יִגְאָלֻהוּ (yigʾāluhû, "claim it once more") from a root that means "to pollute." "To claim" or "reclaim" is an extended meaning of gʾl I ("to redeem").

The vowels of צַלְמָוֶת (ṣalmāwet; GK 7516) make it read "shadow of death" (KJV); but these vowels, though ancient, probably do not reflect the original spelling. Other Semitic languages use the root ṣlm, meaning simply "darkness." The word is used ten times in Job; two of the contexts are about death (10:21–22; 38:17). We may conclude that from early on the word was used with "the shadow of death" etymology. Job 38:17 revolves around that meaning. That spelling in Psalm 23:4 may also have been deliberate by the original poet, but that does not seem likely in Job 3:5; 12:22; 16:16; 24:17; 28:3; and 34:22.

Most agree that the root of כִּמְרִירֵי (*kimrîrê*, "darkens"; NIV, "blackness") is *kmr* ("be dark, black"; cf. KJV). But the MT vowels read "like the bitternesses of," which some link to an eclipse. See Pope, 24, for data (cf. NEB).

6 For אַל־יִחַדְּ (*ʾal-yiḥadᵉ*, "may it not be included"), NIV reads *yēḥad* (*yḥd*), as in Genesis 49:6, literally, "be joined" (cf. KJV). BDB, 292, takes it from *ḥdh* ("rejoice"; cf. Driver and Gray, 278). KB and Holladay, 96, derive it from *ḥdh* II (cf. *ḥzh*), "be seen, appear," as does Blommerde, following Dahood.

The use of יְרָחִים (*yᵉrāḥîm*, "months") proves this is not standard OT Hebrew, which would use חֳדָשִׁים (*ḥᵒdāšîm*, "months" or "new moons").

10 If we understand בִטְנִי (*biṭnî*) in its usual genitive, "my womb" seems to mean the womb out of which he came, that is, his mother's. But Habel, 109, thinks it is deliberately ambiguous since Job's parents are left out of the earlier curse. The NIV avoids the issue by rendering the pronominal suffix in a rare dative relationship to the noun (cf. N. C. Habel, "The Dative Suffix in Job 33:13," *Bib* 63 [1982]: 258–59).

11 In this bicolon the principle of double duty usage of elements is applied on each side:

Why did I not [come out] from the womb and die;
[Why did I not] come out from the belly and expire?

14 The meaning of חֳרָבוֹת (*ḥᵒrābôt*) has been troublesome to some. Its ordinary meaning "ruins" is perfectly acceptable here, for it was considered a great achievement for kings to excavate, uncover, and rebuild the ruins of their ancestors. The verb בָּנָה (*bānâ*) can mean "rebuild" as well as "build." Nebuchadnezzar bragged in his building inscriptions: "Ebarra … abode of Samas which since distant days … was fallen to ruins. … Its ancient location I found and beheld … as of old I made and completed" (Stephen Langdon, *Building Inscriptions of the Neo-Babylonian Empire: Part I: Nabopolassar and Nebuchadnezzar* [Paris: Ernest Leroux, 1905], 443, 445).

19 It is now recognized that הוּא (*hûʾ*, "he"; GK 2085), like ὁ αὐτός (*ho autos*), can mean "the same." In Psalm 102:27 the heavens and earth change, but God is the same. Contrary to the NIV, the context would also favor the reading "There the small and great are alike [the same]."

B. The First Cycle of Speeches (4:1–14:22)

1. Eliphaz (4:1–5:27)

OVERVIEW

With artistic flare (see Notes), Eliphaz sounds the keynote for all else that he and his companions will say. Job in chapter 3 is so obviously wrong that it is not hard for Eliphaz to appear to be right. His words are so good that the apostle Paul quotes 5:13 in 1 Corinthians 3:19. But we must keep in mind that the overall purpose of the book includes the concept that the counselors are basically wrong even though their words are often right (42:7–8). Fullerton, 326–27, rightly warns that while on the surface the speech is orthodox and is given with "dignity and sobriety" in contrast to Job's "almost ungovern- able outbursts," yet there is "a subtle overtone" of flaws that can be easily missed by a casual reading.

¹Then Eliphaz the Temanite replied:

²"If someone ventures a word with you, will you be impatient?
　But who can keep from speaking?
³Think how you have instructed many,
　how you have strengthened feeble hands.
⁴Your words have supported those who stumbled;
　you have strengthened faltering knees.
⁵But now trouble comes to you, and you are discouraged;
　it strikes you, and you are dismayed.
⁶Should not your piety be your confidence
　and your blameless ways your hope?

⁷"Consider now: Who, being innocent, has ever perished?
　Where were the upright ever destroyed?
⁸As I have observed, those who plow evil
　and those who sow trouble reap it.
⁹At the breath of God they are destroyed;
　at the blast of his anger they perish.
¹⁰The lions may roar and growl,
　yet the teeth of the great lions are broken.
¹¹The lion perishes for lack of prey,
　and the cubs of the lioness are scattered.

¹²"A word was secretly brought to me,
　my ears caught a whisper of it.
¹³Amid disquieting dreams in the night,
　when deep sleep falls on men,
¹⁴fear and trembling seized me
　and made all my bones shake.
¹⁵A spirit glided past my face,
　and the hair on my body stood on end.
¹⁶It stopped,
　but I could not tell what it was.
A form stood before my eyes,
　and I heard a hushed voice:
¹⁷'Can a mortal be more righteous than God?
　Can a man be more pure than his Maker?

¹⁸If God places no trust in his servants,
if he charges his angels with error,
¹⁹how much more those who live in houses of clay,
whose foundations are in the dust,
who are crushed more readily than a moth!
²⁰Between dawn and dusk they are broken to pieces;
unnoticed, they perish forever.
²¹Are not the cords of their tent pulled up,
so that they die without wisdom?'

^{5:1}"Call if you will, but who will answer you?
To which of the holy ones will you turn?
²Resentment kills a fool,
and envy slays the simple.
³I myself have seen a fool taking root,
but suddenly his house was cursed.
⁴His children are far from safety,
crushed in court without a defender.
⁵The hungry consume his harvest,
taking it even from among thorns,
and the thirsty pant after his wealth.
⁶For hardship does not spring from the soil,
nor does trouble sprout from the ground.
⁷Yet man is born to trouble
as surely as sparks fly upward.

⁸"But if it were I, I would appeal to God;
I would lay my cause before him.
⁹He performs wonders that cannot be fathomed,
miracles that cannot be counted.
¹⁰He bestows rain on the earth;
he sends water upon the countryside.
¹¹The lowly he sets on high,
and those who mourn are lifted to safety.
¹²He thwarts the plans of the crafty,
so that their hands achieve no success.
¹³He catches the wise in their craftiness,
and the schemes of the wily are swept away.
¹⁴Darkness comes upon them in the daytime;
at noon they grope as in the night.

¹⁵He saves the needy from the sword in their mouth;
  he saves them from the clutches of the powerful.
¹⁶So the poor have hope,
  and injustice shuts its mouth.

¹⁷"Blessed is the man whom God corrects;
  so do not despise the discipline of the Almighty.
¹⁸For he wounds, but he also binds up;
  he injures, but his hands also heal.
¹⁹From six calamities he will rescue you;
  in seven no harm will befall you.
²⁰In famine he will ransom you from death,
  and in battle from the stroke of the sword.
²¹You will be protected from the lash of the tongue,
  and need not fear when destruction comes.
²²You will laugh at destruction and famine,
  and need not fear the beasts of the earth.
²³For you will have a covenant with the stones of the field,
  and the wild animals will be at peace with you.
²⁴You will know that your tent is secure;
  you will take stock of your property and find nothing missing.
²⁵You will know that your children will be many,
  and your descendants like the grass of the earth.
²⁶You will come to the grave in full vigor,
  like sheaves gathered in season.

²⁷"We have examined this, and it is true.
  So hear it and apply it to yourself."

COMMENTARY

1–11 Eliphaz, a man from Teman, an Edomite city noted as a center of wisdom (Jer 49:7), on the surface speaks as though he thinks Job is basically righteous and that his sufferings are temporary. But in reality Eliphaz is not so convinced of this. Later he openly agrees with a harder line against Job used by his other friends (22:1–11). His opening statement in 4:2 can be taken as a conditional sentence

(NIV) or as a question without the conditional sentence, namely, "Should one attempt to speak with you while you are (so) weary?" This opening line sounds like Eliphaz is truly concerned for Job's welfare but cannot resist the temptation to give Job some "proper" instruction—"But who can keep from speaking?" Some compliments are offered. Job is called a "wisdom teacher"—like himself (vv.3–4).

But the compliment is followed by a warning to Job (v.5), who instructed and strengthened those in trouble, that he must now be careful lest he fail to apply to himself the lessons he has taught others.

In v.6 Eliphaz was willing to affirm that Job is basically an upright man who only needs the wisdom to see that all deserve some punishment for sin, for no one is completely pure (4:17). Compare 22:4, where he speaks of Job's piety. Is it tongue-in-cheek?

According to Eliphaz, Job's faith in God and blameless conduct (1:8; 2:3) should have saved him; for "who, being innocent, has ever perished?" (v.7). Verses 8–11 may be an excursus about the fate of the wicked without reference to Job (cf. Clines, "Arguments," 201), or they may reveal that he really is not all that certain about Job. Moreover, Job's experience does not support the idea that the innocent never perish. With the perspective of the Prologue, the reader has insight that proves Eliphaz's statement in vv.7–8 is shallow. Although he is shallow especially with reference to Job, Eliphaz will also say things that are not so shallow. For example, he will admonish Job to be patient and see the disciplinary aspect of suffering (5:17–18).

12–21 At this point Eliphaz bolsters the authority of his words by an appeal to the supernatural—an eerie and hair-raising experience in which he received a divine oracle (vv.12–15). Uncertain about what it was he saw (v.16), he claims "a form" spoke in the silence of the night. The NIV runs the words of the oracle from v.17 through v.21. Others reduce the oracle to v.17 alone, with the balance of the verses being Eliphaz's comment on it. The NIV supports the traditional translation of v.17. But the thought that a man could be more righteous than God is hardly the issue. Many grammarians (e.g., Dhorme, Pope; cf. RSV) render it, "Can a mortal be found righteous in the presence of God?" (see Notes).

Eliphaz goes on to tell how far inferior the angels are to God (v.18). More so a human being, whose body is like a house of clay (v.19; cf. Ge 2:7), is as fragile as a moth. It is clear that Eliphaz sees humanity as almost zero in God's sight—hardly more than an insect that may perish unnoticed (v.20). Like collapsing tents people "die without wisdom" (v.21). This appears to be far more than a simple statement about the death of the ignorant. Eliphaz is saying, "They die and it is not by [of] wisdom." That is, there is no special purpose in it. To a God so transcendent that he does not even trust the angels, the death of a sinful man is of little consequence.

It would hardly seem possible to stress too much that God is transcendent. Eliphaz, however, succeeds in taking this important truth and misapplying it. In fairness to Eliphaz, the verbs in vv.19–21 may have an optative force. Hence they may only express possible consequences of man's sinfulness (see Notes), not what happens to every sinner. Eliphaz's point, then, is that since all deserve this, we should be patient when temporary suffering comes.

5:1–7 Eliphaz next directed his words more explicitly toward Job. There is no mediator among the "holy [servants]" of God (i.e., the angels) who would dare answer a plea from Job (v.1). Why? Because he is behaving like a fool (v.2). The fool in wisdom language is a man who pays no proper heed to God (Ps 14:1). What happens to such fools? Their houses are cursed, their children crushed, and their wealth depleted (vv.3–5; cf. 1:13–19). Eliphaz is not quite explicit, but Job no doubt gets the point; but see Cline's view ("Arguments") mentioned above. Similarly Habel, 121, makes a distinction between Eliphaz's role here as a friend and the poet's playing with his speeches. In vv.6–7 Eliphaz is establishing a connection between moral and physical evil. Trouble does not sprout up like weeds in the field. He is implying that one must sow and cultivate trouble.

Dhorme, 23, suggests v.7a should read "man engenders trouble" instead of "man is born to trouble." The suggestion is attractive and within grammatical bounds if one will allow a Hebrew vowel (pointing) change from passive to active (see Notes). Thus "man engenders trouble" emphasizes the point Eliphaz has already made: a person's active role as an evildoer rather than seeing him or her as a victim of circumstances.

The "sparks [that] fly upward" (v.7b) are literally "Resheph's sons" (see Introduction; also W. J. Fulco, *The Canaanite God Resep* [American Oriental Series 8; New Haven, Conn.: American Oriental Society, 1976]). The name is used seven times in the OT including this passage, mostly for flames or lightning (Dt 32:23–24; 1Ch 7:25 [proper name]; Pss 76:4; 78:48; SS 8:6; Hab 3:5). As I have noted above, this imagery from the current mythology is a literary trope and marks linguistic richness. Its use need not imply anything about the theology of the speaker or author. Eliphaz is probably saying that a human being, like the sons of this colorful and pestering figure, stirs up his or her own trouble or is the victim of uncontrollable natural forces such as disease, plague, and death.

8–16 Verses 9–16 are in the form a creedal hymn on the nature of God as the Lord of creation and salvation. So Job is admonished to appeal to God, who does only what is right. He punishes the unjust and delivers the lowly. This is, of course, exactly what Job believes, but such advice does not help him understand why his suffering is so intense. On the contrary, since it implies he is getting just what he deserves, it only adds to his confusion.

These lines are a fine example of hymn genre in OT poetry. A similar creedal hymn appears in Isaiah 44:24–28. That is why the apostle Paul could cite a line from 5:13 in 1 Corinthians 3:19: "He catches the wise in their craftiness." But in Eliphaz's case, what is absolutely true is misapplied—the sick room is not the place for theological strictures that may turn out to do more harm than good. Eliphaz as a counselor

is a supreme negative example. Great truths misapplied only hurt more those who are already hurting.

17–27 Eliphaz continues his lofty words with another unit of fine poetry. So the purpose of the creedal poem in 5:9–16 is to show a sinner (fool) how transcendent and holy God is. Sinners get what they deserve, and only the righteous have hope. It is a terrifying statement that God, because he is a holy God, hates sinners. But as a man dedicated to wisdom, Eliphaz balances this with another poem (vv.17–26) addressed to anyone who understands God's "discipline" (*mûsar*, v.17; cf. Pr 1:2, 7; 3:11; 23:12 [NIV, "instruction"], 23; et al.). The parallel expression in 5:17 and Proverbs 3:11 shows that in Wisdom genre such language is common. Typical gnomic truth (vv.19–26) maintains that the correcting wounds of God are temporary—the truly good man will always be rescued. The very God who injures him will heal him, and he will be blessed and again enjoy the good things of life.

In the light, however, of Job's experiences—the loss of his family, his economic ruin, his sickness—there is a thoughtless cruelty inherent in applying the words of vv.19–26 to him. For example, if Job benefits from God's discipline (v.17), then his "children will be many" (v.25); but Job's children are dead. Is it possible that the author of the book of Job includes this speech for a subtle reason? Perhaps it is meant to be a satire on all such mechanical use of theology with its heartless superiority. It is not what Eliphaz knows that is wrong; it is what he is ignorant of—God's hidden purpose—that makes all his beautiful poetry and grand truth only a snare to Job. Moreover, while things he says are good even for a sufferer to contemplate—such as the disciplining aspect of suffering—even these words, as we know from the Prologue, do not apply to the case in hand.

Eliphaz's patronizing attitude, revealed in his closing sentence (v.27), must have been galling to his peer Job.

NOTES

4:1 Andersen, 111, sees in Eliphaz's speech what he calls a symmetrical introverted (i.e., chiastic) structure. It is a keen observation and worth repeating:

    A. Opening Remark (4:2)
      B. Exhortation (4:3–6)
        C. God's Dealings with Human Beings (4:7–11)
          D. The Revelation of Truth (4:12–21)
        C'. God's Dealings Human Beings (5:1–16)
      B'. Exhortation (5:17–26)
    A'.Closing Remark (5:27)

For more on this subject, see E. B. Smick, "Architectonic Structured Poems, and Rhetorical Devices in the Book of Job," in *A Tribute to Gleason Archer: Essays on the Old Testament* (ed. W. C. Kaiser Jr. and R. F. Youngblood; Chicago: Moody Press, 1986), 87–104.

2 מִלִּין (*millîn*, "speaking") is a clear Aramaism used thirteen times. In the book of Job the Hebrew spelling *millîm* is used ten times. Compare v.10, where נָתַע (*nātaʿ*, "to be broken") would appear normally in Hebrew as נָתַץ (*nātaṣ*). Such Aramaic influence has little to do with dating the book. It simply reveals the dialect of the speaker. Dhorme, cv, has shown conclusively that Elihu's speech has an Aramaic color.

17 מִן (*min*), a preposition used commonly for comparison, here has the meaning "before" or "in the presence of." This meaning serves the context better and is attested in Numbers 32:22 (see Notes on 32:2).

20 Some render מִבְּלִי מֵשִׂים (*mibbʿlî mēśîm*, "unnoticed") as "nameless," reading שֵׁם (ם)מִבְּלִי (*mibbʿlî[m] šēm*) (Pope, 38). The NIV also considers the second *m* as enclitic but takes the word *śîm* ("put"; GK 8492) as it stands. The idiom שָׂם לֵב (*śîm lēb*, "put to mind, pay attention"; cf. 1:8; 2:3; 34:14) appears with ellipsis of *lēb* as in 23:6; 24:12; 34:23; and Isaiah 41:20; so here the NIV translates "without putting to mind," that is, "unnoticed." Compare Notes on 17:3 and 12.

21 יִתְרָם בָּם (*yitrām bām*, "the cords of their tent") is literally "their tent-cord(s) is pulled away from them" (a rare use of *b* meaning "from," as is common in Ugaritic). The KJV's rendering, which is scarcely intelligible—"Doth not their excellency *which is* in them go away?"—is based on some ancient versions (Targ., Vulg., Syr.).

5:4 For בַשַּׁעַר (*baššaʿar*, "in court, in the gate"), Andersen, 111, suggests reading *baśśaʿar* ("in the storm") as a cruel reference to the way Job's children were lost (1:19); this spelling of the Hebrew word meaning "storm" is attested in Isaiah 28:2.

5 The translation of וְאֶל־מִצִּנִּים (*wʿel-miṣṣinnîm*) as "even from among thorns" makes little sense and fails to do justice to all the Hebrew consonants. The line is difficult (Pope, 38, says "impossible"), but the Joseph story in Genesis may provide information to help us interpret the line. Genesis 37:7 uses the word אֲלֻמָּה (*ʾalummâ*, "sheaf") and Genesis 41:23 the word צְנֻמוֹת (*ṣʿnumôt*, "thin, emaciated"). The line would not require any change of consonants to read *wʿlm-ṣnym* with the meaning "the emaciated [cf. 'the hungry' in v.5a] take away ['consume' in v.5a] his [double duty pronoun from v.5a] sheaves ['harvest' in v.5a]." (For this I am partially indebted to Michel, 267–68.)

7 The Masoretes have vocalized יוֹלָד (*yûllād*, "is born") as a Pual perfect, but the presence of the *waw* creates a problem. The versions seem to read *yiwwālēd* (Niphal). Dhorme's suggestion (see comment) to read *yôlîd* accounts for the *waw* but then takes the preposition *l* on the preceding word as a sign of the accusative, a rarer Aramaism.

15 In addition to rendering מֵחֶרֶב (*mēhereb*) as "from the sword," the NIV has brought the word "needy" from v.15b to v.15a and inserted "them" in v.15b. It also renders *min* ("from") as "in" in the phrase, "in their mouth." The latter is perhaps possible; but neither expediency is necessary if we are willing to adopt Dhorme's pointing *mohᵉrāb* (Hophal participle from *ḥrb* III), which means "the desolate." The verse reads: "He saves the desolate from their mouth, the needy from the clutches of the powerful."

19, 21 The preposition ב (*b*), meaning "from"—בְּשֵׁשׁ (*bᵉšeš*, "from six"), בְּשׁוֹט (*bᵉšôṭ*, "from the lash")—is attested (4:21 [NIV, "without"]; Dt 1:44); but the reverse, that is, מִן, *min*, meaning "in" (as in NIV v.15a), is less likely. The Dead Sea Psalms scroll (11QPsᵃ) substituted *min* for *b* when they understood the meaning to be "from" (cf. Ps 119:87).

23 In the light of the parallelism with "wild animals," the א (ʾ, *aleph*) here could be understood as prothetic, rendering אַבְנֵי (ʾabnê, "the stones of") as "the sons [offspring] of the field." Pope, 38, carries the meaning a step too far with his "sprites of the field." For similar use of ʾabnê, see Isaiah 14:19; Ezekiel 28:14 (cf. Andersen, 122, n. 3). These are the same as v.23b—wild animals that kill domestic animals. The latter is the measure of one's wealth; so it is important to have a covenant with these beasts. It is important to take a count and find no sheep, goats, or cattle that have been killed.

2. Job's Reply (6:1–7:21)

OVERVIEW

Job attacks the counselors (ch. 6) and God (ch. 7), giving as his excuse for his rage the depth of his misery (6:2–3; 7:11). His words, disturbing as they are, arise from a limited knowledge (38:2) and his determination to speak only the truth as he sees it. "How painful are honest words!" (6:25). He views God as the author of his misery and opens (6:4) and closes (7:20) the speech with a figure of God shooting arrows in him. He finds life an unbearable arena of torment.

Once again Job's suffering is so intense that death will come as an exquisite release (6:8–10). Few have suffered as intensely as Job, so it is difficult for us to identify with his rage. But for those who have a similar experience, the words of Job can bring immense comfort for the simple reason

that many sufferers have felt rage but have been too ashamed to express it. That a man who had experienced such faith should speak from the depth of his being such words of anguish can only strengthen those in anguish. The psalms of lament (e.g., Pss 77; 88) also suggest that God allows for and even encourages honest expression of one's pain to him.

Job argues persuasively his case against the counselors. They have been no help. Their words are bad medicine or, as Job puts it, bad food (6:6–7). They are undependable (6:14–23) and cruel (6:27–30), and they view him as too great a risk to offer any help (6:21). Job challenges them to prove he is wrong (6:24) and pleads with them for the milk of human kindness (6:14, 28).

¹Then Job replied:

²"If only my anguish could be weighed
    and all my misery be placed on the scales!
³It would surely outweigh the sand of the seas —
    no wonder my words have been impetuous.
⁴The arrows of the Almighty are in me,
    my spirit drinks in their poison;
    God's terrors are marshaled against me.
⁵Does a wild donkey bray when it has grass,
    or an ox bellow when it has fodder?
⁶Is tasteless food eaten without salt,
    or is there flavor in the white of an egg ?
⁷I refuse to touch it;
    such food makes me ill.

⁸"Oh, that I might have my request,
    that God would grant what I hope for,
⁹that God would be willing to crush me,
    to let loose his hand and cut me off!
¹⁰Then I would still have this consolation —
    my joy in unrelenting pain —
    that I had not denied the words of the Holy One.

¹¹"What strength do I have, that I should still hope?
    What prospects, that I should be patient?
¹²Do I have the strength of stone?
    Is my flesh bronze?
¹³Do I have any power to help myself,
    now that success has been driven from me?

¹⁴"A despairing man should have the devotion of his friends,
    even though he forsakes the fear of the Almighty.
¹⁵But my brothers are as undependable as intermittent streams,
    as the streams that overflow
¹⁶when darkened by thawing ice
    and swollen with melting snow,
¹⁷but that cease to flow in the dry season,
    and in the heat vanish from their channels.

¹⁸Caravans turn aside from their routes;
  they go up into the wasteland and perish.
¹⁹The caravans of Tema look for water,
  the traveling merchants of Sheba look in hope.
²⁰They are distressed, because they had been confident;
  they arrive there, only to be disappointed.
²¹Now you too have proved to be of no help;
  you see something dreadful and are afraid.
²²Have I ever said, 'Give something on my behalf,
  pay a ransom for me from your wealth,
²³deliver me from the hand of the enemy,
  ransom me from the clutches of the ruthless'?

²⁴"Teach me, and I will be quiet;
  show me where I have been wrong.
²⁵How painful are honest words!
  But what do your arguments prove?
²⁶Do you mean to correct what I say,
  and treat the words of a despairing man as wind?
²⁷You would even cast lots for the fatherless
  and barter away your friend.

²⁸"But now be so kind as to look at me.
  Would I lie to your face?
²⁹Relent, do not be unjust;
  reconsider, for my integrity is at stake.
³⁰Is there any wickedness on my lips?
  Can my mouth not discern malice?

⁷:¹"Does not man have hard service on earth?
  Are not his days like those of a hired man?
²Like a slave longing for the evening shadows,
  or a hired man waiting eagerly for his wages,
³so I have been allotted months of futility,
  and nights of misery have been assigned to me.
⁴When I lie down I think, 'How long before I get up?'
  The night drags on, and I toss till dawn.
⁵My body is clothed with worms and scabs,
  my skin is broken and festering.

6"My days are swifter than a weaver's shuttle,
   and they come to an end without hope.
7Remember, O God, that my life is but a breath;
   my eyes will never see happiness again.
8The eye that now sees me will see me no longer;
   you will look for me, but I will be no more.
9As a cloud vanishes and is gone,
   so he who goes down to the grave does not return.
10He will never come to his house again;
   his place will know him no more.

11"Therefore I will not keep silent;
   I will speak out in the anguish of my spirit,
   I will complain in the bitterness of my soul.
12Am I the sea, or the monster of the deep,
   that you put me under guard?
13When I think my bed will comfort me
   and my couch will ease my complaint,
14even then you frighten me with dreams
   and terrify me with visions,
15so that I prefer strangling and death,
   rather than this body of mine.
16I despise my life; I would not live forever.
   Let me alone; my days have no meaning.

17"What is man that you make so much of him,
   that you give him so much attention,
18that you examine him every morning
   and test him every moment?
19Will you never look away from me,
   or let me alone even for an instant?
20If I have sinned, what have I done to you,
   O watcher of men?
Why have you made me your target?
   Have I become a burden to you?
21Why do you not pardon my offenses
   and forgive my sins?
For I will soon lie down in the dust;
   you will search for me, but I will be no more."

COMMENTARY

1–7 The two themes of Job's speech are introduced here. In vv.1–4 Job complains against God and in verses 5–7 against the counselors. First, he attempts to justify his own "impetuous" words (v.3) with an appeal to his overwhelming misery brought on by the arrows of God (v.4). Then he claims the right to bray like a donkey or bellow like an ox deprived of fodder and left to starve (v.5). Job starves for the right words that, like food (Am 8:11), can bring strength and nourishment. The food Eliphaz dishes out is absolutely tasteless; worse, it turns Job's stomach (vv.6–7). Despite his bodily misery Job's major concern is for the needs of his spirit. If only he could hear words that would nourish his soul rather than sicken him more!

8–10 Again (cf. 3:21) Job earnestly asks God to bring an end to his suffering by bringing an end to his life, a mercy killing! He would then have some joy even in pain. He would have one consolation left before he dies—that he has not denied the words of the Holy One, though he emphatically rejects the words of Eliphaz. Verses 1–10 form a unit based on a theme about the use of words: Job's words (v.3), Eliphaz's words (vv.6–7), and God's words (v.10).

11–13 Job complains that he has no reason to be patient, for he has nothing to look forward to (v.11). As a vulnerable creature made of flesh, he has no human resources left (v.12). Even his natural ability, the gifts that have contributed to his success, has been driven from him (v.13). This is a reply to Eliphaz's words in 4:2–6.

14–21 Turning, in despair, to his friends, Job pleads for kindness (ḥesed; NIV, "devotion"; GK 2876), even though they may think that he no longer fears God (v.14). Instead he finds them like wadis that run dry (vv.15–20). Verse 21 is the climax of Job's reaction to his friends' counsel. They

offer no help. The verse is like a sermon about the special strength needed to be willing to make oneself available when we see others in a truly dreadful condition. The risk involved makes us afraid.

22–23 Job never asked his friends for anything tangible (v.22). It is not as though they were being asked to pay a ransom to save him (v.23). The thought goes back to v.14, where he asked only for what would cost them nothing—their faithful love (ḥesed), despite what they thought he had done.

24–27 Job's words are a challenge and an indictment. His friends need to be specific about his sins and be sure they are right (v.24). He insists that they speak the truth just as he has affirmed a compelling desire to speak only the truth before God. His words may have been painful, but they were honest, even though his friends have treated them as wind (vv.25–26). In his mind it is their arguments that were specious (v.25b). He labels them as men of such severe cruelty that they could have cast lots for an orphan or bartered away a friend (v.27).

28–30 Here Job softens his tone and appeals to his friends as men of compassion (v.28). He pleads for justice, for a reconsideration of their indictment of him (v.29). His integrity is at stake, and that is more important to him than life itself. In v.30 Job again employs the figure of words as morsels of food. He reaffirms the honesty of his own words and claims for himself a discriminating taste for the truth.

7:1–2 These verses form a complaint to God. The life of human beings, so full of toil and suffering, is like hard military service, though the word may have a nonmilitary sense in this context similar to Job 14:14 and Isaiah 40:2—that is, like a toiling slave longing for the shade. He is a hireling laboring for his pittance. Certainly this negative view of life, this language of dejection, represents a feeling shared at times by almost every human being.

3–10 These are the words of a chronic sufferer. There have been months of futility and nights of tossing in misery, nights that seem to drag on endlessly (vv.3–4). Yet almost in the same breath Job describes his purposeless life as passing with incredible speed (v.6)—a complaint heard on the lips of the aging or any who feel their days are numbered (vv.7–10). In v.5 Job describes one of the symptoms of his disease—scabs that crack and fester. What kind of disease is this? We cannot be sure. But worse than the disease itself, Job has lost all hope of being healed. He believes his only release from pain is death.

Beginning in v.7 Job addresses God directly, and this continues throughout the chapter. His words are an empirical view of the human lot on this earth. Human life is only a breath (the same or a similar phrase occurs in a more hopeful context in Psalms 39; 89:45; and 144:4). He will go down to the grave and never return (v.9). Death is so final—a person disappears like a cloud, and his family sees him no more (v.10).

11–21 Again in v.11 Job asserts his determination to cry out in agony of spirit over the apparent injustice of God, who, it seems, will not leave him alone. Even when sleep does come, he blames God for his terrifying dreams (vv.13–14). This blaming of God brings up several theological issues.

First, does the book of Job teach a lesson about God's willingness to allow for Job's rage? Job's extreme language fits his cultural setting but was a source of great offense to postbiblical Jews who sometimes felt the need to theologically correct his words. That is exactly what was done in v.20 by scribes who preceded the Masoretes. Both an ancient scribal tradition and the LXX show the original reading of the final line to be "Have I become a burden to you?" (cf. NIV mg.). The present MT reads "I have become a burden to myself"—an early attempt to remove what was thought blasphemous. Fortunately a scribal note (*tiqqune sopherim*) was kept.

It is not only this verse but the whole passage that shares this raging attitude of Job. If reprehensible in the eyes of later readers, it is accepted by God (though not desired; cf. 38:2) as part of the struggle of a man who is determined to open himself wholly to God. In this way, Job is theologically in line with the lament psalms, which also honestly address God out of pain and suffering, even blaming God for the affliction (see Ps 77). However, in the lament tradition it was typical to express confidence at the end. Even in those psalms that do not move toward a positive conclusion, the fact that the psalmist is still speaking to God shows at least a flicker of hope (see Ps 88), which Job does not seem to share.

Second, is Job giving a parody of Psalm 8 (as Gordis [*God and Man*, 222] maintains)? Like the psalmist, Job asks, "What is man that you make so much of him?" (v.17). The biblical answer, of course, is that humans are the work of God's hands, created in his own image. God's purpose for the world centers on his human creatures, his crowning creation, to whom he has given the world. God makes much of humans, for they are meant to be God's surrogates on earth. But Job, in his current condition, believes God's interest in him is only negative—as though God's only interest were to torment him for his sin, not letting him alone long enough to swallow his spittle (v.19; see Note). God even uses him as a target for his arrows (v.20).

Contrary to all this, the reader knows from the Prologue that a loving God is waiting, with great concern, for that moment when Job's test will be over and the hand of the tormentor (the Accuser) will be removed. But at this moment it appears to Job that God is the tormentor. The reader knows God is using a secondary means and that Job's conception of God as tormentor is askew.

The reader also knows that because God is sovereign, the problem remains logically unresolved.

This age-old dilemma between divine sovereignty and divine goodness is a permanent backdrop throughout the book of Job. The dilemma is there, but it is not the purpose of the book of Job to attempt to resolve the problem. Job never receives logical answers to the questions he asks. Satan and humans may try to thwart the divine purpose. But that purpose can never be thwarted, for the one behind it is absolutely sovereign. It is precisely there that the book of Job and the entire Bible leave the question.

It is a mistake to think, however, that Job is wrestling with a purely intellectual problem. No, his concern is more experiential than cognitive, though he is also seeking a way to make his experience (suffering) agree with his theology (the justice of God). Hebrew sages in the OT were not trying to solve logical syllogisms. Job's pathetic words at the end of this chapter show that he still entertains doubts about his own blameworthiness, but they also suggest that he feels as if God is being unjust. These are words he will eventually regret (40:4).

NOTES

6:6 In rendering בְּרִיר חַלָּמוּת (bᵉrîr ḥallāmût) "in the white of an egg," the NIV follows the Targums, as does Dhorme. Pope, 38, says this means "slimy cream cheese." But A. R. Millard ("What Has No Taste? [Job 6:6]," *UF* 1 [1969]: 210) has pointed to the word *hilimitu* in the Alalakh Tablets, which means some kind of unknown vegetable, and this is close to the Syriac ("slime of purslane"). For *rîr* as "saliva" see 1 Samuel 21:13.

7 Various translations of נַפְשִׁי (napšî) are "my soul," "my throat," "my appetite." All are possible, but the NIV's "I" (lit. "myself") is a good choice.

The NIV's rendering הֵמָּה כְּדְוֵי לַחְמִי (hēmmâ kidwê laḥmî) as "such food makes me ill" may be excused for being a loose translation because the line as it stands in the MT is very difficult. But the witness of the LXX should be heeded, for it saw in the Hebrew text the letters *zhmh* (third feminine singular perfect) as the first word of v.7b. Two factors favor the LXX: (1) the usage in 33:20 of the verb *zhm* ("be loathsome") with *lḥm* ("food") and (2) that the paleo-Hebrew letters ' (y, yod) (preceding) and ז (z, zayin) were written almost identically in certain periods. The line can then be literally rendered: "It is loathsome like bad food." Pope, 38, suggests another attractive solution. Taking *lḥm* to mean "flesh" as in 20:23 (RSV mg.; NIV, "upon him") and Zephaniah 1:17 (RSV; NIV, "entrails"), he renders the line, "They [their words] are putrid as my flesh."

10 The NIV renders כִּי־לֹא כִחַדְתִּי (kî-lōʾ kiḥadtî) as "that I had not denied." The basic meaning of *khd* in Hebrew is "to hide" (15:18; 27:11); but in Ethiopic it means "to apostatize," which may be closer to its force in this context.

16 Since snow becomes dark as it melts, the NIV has captured the meaning of יִתְעַלֶּם־שָׁלֶג (yitʿallem-šāleg) as "with melting snow"; but the full force of ʿlm ("to be dark, conceal"; GK 6623) as parallel with *qdr* ("to become dark") in v.16a cannot be appreciated in English. Pope, 53, has shown that the Arabic cognate to ʿlm is used of overflowing wadis.

21 The Greek and Syriac paraphrase of v.21a to read "and you have been against me," understanding לֹא (lōʾ; NIV, "no help") as לִי (lî, "against me"). Another expedient in this difficult verse is to change כִּי (kî, "too") to כֵּן (kēn), reading "thus you have been to me." But there is no textual evidence for this. Others go with לֹו (*lô*), the *Qere* of a Western reading, and render, "For now you have become His" (JPS). The NIV has done well to stay with the MT, taking *lōʾ* to mean "nothing" (cf. KJV), that is, "no help."

7:6 Ibn Ezra noted long ago the play on the word תִּקְוָה (*tiqwâ*, "hope"), which can also mean "thread." Job's days move fast like a weaver's shuttle, and they come to an end through want of thread. Both meanings were equally intended. This is the kind of overtone in meaning that cannot be reflected in a translation without a footnote.

8 The precise meaning of this verse is problematic, not because the words are difficult, but because we are not sure who "the beholder" is in v.8a nor how v.8b relates to v.8a. There is an emphasis on both the finality of death and God's constant attention to humankind. Is Job repeating himself, saying in both lines that God will not be able to find him after he dies? Andersen (136, n. i; cf. also the note on 11:11) takes it this way, suggesting a rare assertive לֹא (*P*) in v.8a. But it is possible that the "beholder" is his fellow man, while v.8b gives the reason he will no longer be seen, for "God's eyes were against him and he will be gone."

12 This verse draws on mythological imagery. The Hebrew יָם (*yām*, "sea") is personalized and used like a proper name (Sea) without the article. It is also in apposition with תַּנִּין (*tannîn* "monster of the deep"), so it may be taken as a reference to the Canaanite god of the sea (*Yam* in Ugar.). The NIV by translating it "the sea" has rejected this meaning, probably because some felt it would imply Job believed in Yam (but see Introduction: Mythopoeic Language). According to the Canaanite myths, Yam was a boisterous opponent of Baal, who was taken captive by him. Job denies that he is like this. M. Dahood ("MIŠMR 'MUZZLE' in Job 7:12," *JBL* 80 [1961]: 270–71) has made a good case that מִשְׁמָר (*mišmār*) means "muzzle." In Ugaritic the goddess Anat boasts of muzzling the sea monster. But as Pope, 61, points out, the captive notion fits better with other OT texts (Ps 104:9; Jer 5:22) about the boisterous sea that is kept within bounds by God. Again we have overlapping semantic nuances that could be appreciated by those who felt the full range of meaning of a word like *mišmār* (GK 5464, 5465).

14 The parallel preposition בְּ (*b*) on בַּחֲלֹמוֹת (*baḥᵃlōmôt*, "with dreams") to the מ (*m*) in וּמֵחֶזְיֹנוֹת (*ûmēḥezyōnôt*, "with visions") suggests the overlapping meaning of these two prepositions. See DSS 11QPsᵃ on Psalm 119:87.

15 In rendering נַפְשִׁי (*napšî*) "I," the NIV takes *nepeš* to mean "I, myself." But in this context the more concrete meaning "throat" fits better with the idea of strangulation and the parallel word "bones." Sarna (cited in Andersen, 131; cf. also Hummel, 85–107) sees in the מ (*m*) prefixed to the word עַצְמוֹתָי (*ʿaṣmôtāy*, "bones") an enclitic *m* going with the preceding מָוֶת (*māwet*, "death"). He would read "so that my throat prefers strangling, my bones welcome death." Andersen, 137–38, follows this view but with mythological overtones. He sees Death (the god Mot) as the Strangler in Job's terrifying dream.

16 The NIV has added to מָאַסְתִּי (*māʾastî*, "I despise") the words "my life," but not without good reason. In 9:21 the same language is used including the object חַיָּי (*ḥayyāy*, "my life"), while in 42:6 the same word מָאַס (*māʾas*) in the imperfect tense is used as it is here, with the object suppressed.

19 Unfortunately the NIV in its attempt to give genteel English has paraphrased עַד־בִּלְעִי רֻקִּי (*ʿad-bilᵉʿî ruqqî*) as "even for an instant." This colorful figure is still used in Arabic, meaning a very brief moment, literally, "long enough to swallow my spit."

20 There is nothing in the Hebrew that demands the "if" in the verse, which suggests Job thinks God should be indifferent to sin, as in the NIV's rendering of חָטָאתִי (*ḥāṭāʾtî*, "If I have sinned"). No one in the

OT world would entertain such an idea. The key to the text is to understand that there are many kinds of sin. Job says, "I have missed the mark of perfection, but what have I done against you?" That is, have I committed the high-handed sin? His point is that the extent of his suffering goes beyond his sin.

For עָלַי (ʿālay; NIV, "to you") the MT reads "to myself." This is one of the *tiqqune sopherim* (see Introduction: Text) where the ancient Hebrew scribes recorded a change in the text. In this case it was made for theological reasons. Someone early in the transmission of the text felt it was sacrilegious for Job to say to God, "Have I become a burden to you?" (see also comments on 7:11–21). The BHS text critical note shows that the LXX also supports the second person singular.

3. Bildad (8:1–22)

OVERVIEW

Bildad's speech contains an important negative lesson about human nature in general and about the qualities of a good counselor. He has heard Job's words with his ears, but his heart hears nothing. This truth should be viewed in the light of Job's plea for compassion in chapter 6. All people under the most ordinary circumstances need compassion; how much more Job in his extremity!

Repeatedly in chapter 6 Job called himself a helpless (v.13) and despairing man (vv.14, 26) in need of the devotion of his friends. It seems almost incredible that Bildad replies so callously here. There is not only steely indifference to Job's plight but an arrogant certainty that Job's children have gotten just what they deserved and that Job is well on his way to the same fate. The lesson we must learn is that there are such people in the world and that they do their heartless disservice to humanity under the guise of being the special friend of God.

As he appears in the Dialogue, Job becomes a man whose frame of mind is not totally conducive to loving relationships with others. Anyone who curses the day of his birth and looks on death as preferable to life is in need of help. His three friends are there for that purpose, but Job comes to view them as part of his problem rather than as those who offer ther-

apy. Their view that people do suffer for their sins and need to be brought face to face with that reality is not wholly wrong. The assumption that Job is one of these is what leads them astray as counselors.

The lessons we learn from Job's friends about counseling are negative. None of them is able to accept Job unconditionally. It is true that Job is a stubborn patient, but they are unable or unwilling — or both — to become involved with him. Their advice is well-meant and often accurately and artistically stated, but it succeeds in making Job even more stubborn and resistive to them. No doubt a large part of the problem is their academic commitment to a viewpoint they refuse to alter, namely, that sin brings suffering and suffering is evidence of sin.

Job forces his counselors to accept or reject his contention that he is not suffering for his sins. In 6:24 he said, "Teach me, and I will be quiet; / show me where I have been wrong." That they do not accept Job's contention makes them unwilling to listen and hence miserable as counselors. Bildad can only reply, "God does not reject a blameless man" (v.20). However, had they accepted Job's contention, the book would have lost a major part of its message, a message that centers on the mystery of

God's purposes in dealing with his creatures. An important lesson to be learned from the book is that counselors must not be sacrosanct. They must be willing to listen, become involved, and have respect for the integrity of the human personality they are trying to help. And they must always bear in mind that they may not fully understand the nature of the case.

¹Then Bildad the Shuhite replied:

²"How long will you say such things?
    Your words are a blustering wind.
³Does God pervert justice?
    Does the Almighty pervert what is right?
⁴When your children sinned against him,
    he gave them over to the penalty of their sin.
⁵But if you will look to God
    and plead with the Almighty,
⁶if you are pure and upright,
    even now he will rouse himself on your behalf
    and restore you to your rightful place.
⁷Your beginnings will seem humble,
    so prosperous will your future be.

⁸"Ask the former generations
    and find out what their fathers learned,
⁹for we were born only yesterday and know nothing,
    and our days on earth are but a shadow.
¹⁰Will they not instruct you and tell you?
    Will they not bring forth words from their understanding?
¹¹Can papyrus grow tall where there is no marsh?
    Can reeds thrive without water?
¹²While still growing and uncut,
    they wither more quickly than grass.
¹³Such is the destiny of all who forget God;
    so perishes the hope of the godless.
¹⁴What he trusts in is fragile;
    what he relies on is a spider's web.
¹⁵He leans on his web, but it gives way;
    he clings to it, but it does not hold.
¹⁶He is like a well-watered plant in the sunshine,
    spreading its shoots over the garden;

> ^{17}it entwines its roots around a pile of rocks
>   and looks for a place among the stones.
> ^{18}But when it is torn from its spot,
>   that place disowns it and says, 'I never saw you.'
> ^{19}Surely its life withers away,
>   and from the soil other plants grow.
>
> ^{20}"Surely God does not reject a blameless man
>   or strengthen the hands of evildoers.
> ^{21}He will yet fill your mouth with laughter
>   and your lips with shouts of joy.
> ^{22}Your enemies will be clothed in shame,
>   and the tents of the wicked will be no more."

COMMENTARY

1–10 Bildad is blunt. Eliphaz might only "venture a word" (4:2), but Bildad opens with a blast. "Your words are a blustering wind" (v.2), he says as a preface to his one and only theological point: Job's suffering is the proof of his sinfulness. Since God cannot be unjust (v.3), there is only one conclusion—Job and his family (v.4) have received the punishment they deserve. Job should plead for mercy (v.5). Then, if he repents of his sin and lives a life that deserves it (v.6), God will restore him (v.7).

Eliphaz had appealed to revelation; Bildad appeals to tradition. To Bildad nothing less than the teachings of the ancients (vv.8–10) prove the orthodoxy of his viewpoint. If Job will only take the time to consider ancient tradition, he will find that God only does right. Sinners get just punishment, and good men are blessed with health and prosperity.

11–19 This poem on the destruction of the wicked has a literary quality similar to that demonstrated by Eliphaz in his masterly poem on the good man in 5:17–26. The person who ignores God, Bildad called a *ḥānēp* (NIV, "godless"; v.13; GK 2866). The word means something like our word "hypocrite." Such a person's hope is unreliable. Like a spider's web (v.14), it provides no support. The godless are like papyrus plants without water (vv.11–12) or a vine with shallow roots clinging to rocks, destined to be pulled up or left to wither and die (vv.16–19).

20–22 Bildad thinks he heard Job say that God perverts justice (v.3). Job has problems about divine justice; but he has not yet blatantly accused God of being unjust, though he has come close to it (6:20). Job finds it difficult if not impossible to understand God's justice. Although Job does not claim perfection (6:21), he considers himself a blameless man (*tām*, v.20). This is also God's view of him in the Prologue (1:8; 2:3), but Bildad is sure that God has rejected Job. Since God does not reject blameless men (8:20), Job cannot be one. So he must be a hypocrite (*ḥānēp*). The situation, however, can be remedied: if only he would turn to God, Job's lips might laugh again.

NOTES

6 The NIV renders נְוַת צִדְקֶךָ (nᵉwat ṣidqekā) as "your rightful place." "Estate" (or perhaps even "pasturage"; GK 5659) would be a better way to translate nāweh, which has pastoral overtones (also 5:3). The word ṣedeq has legal overtones yielding "your rightful (lawful) estate."

8 There is no need to emend כֹּנֵן (kônēn, "find out") to בֹּנֵן (bōnēn). Driver and Gray, and Dhorme understood it correctly. A colloquial ellipsis of לֵב (lēb, "mind") yields the meaning "fix (your mind) to," which fits with a similar colloquial use of the verb שִׂים (śîm, "to put"; 4:20; 23:6; 24:12; 34:23; GK 8492). The verb כּוּן (kûn, "fix"; GK 2922) appears with a similar meaning in Isaiah 51:13 (NIV, "bent") and probably in Job 28:27 (NIV, "confirmed") and Judges 12:6 (NIV, "pronounce"). The two verbs in this verse—שָׁאַל (šāʾal, "ask, inquire") and kûn—are used together with the same meanings in Ugaritic (Blommerde, 50).

11 The practical wisdom poem of vv.11–19 contains the words of instruction that come from the fathers. The rhetorical question is a common wisdom form Job has already used effectively in 6:5–6.

13 There is no need to amend אָרְחוֹת (ʾorḥôt, "paths"; GK 784) to אַחֲרִית (ʾaḥᵃrît) to get the meaning "destiny, fate." The Ugaritic evidence here is indirect (Blommerde, 52); but Dhorme has shown that ʾorḥôt in Proverbs 1:19 (NIV, "end") has the same meaning, and to that may be added Proverbs 24:14b (NIV, "future hope"; cf. Blommerde, 52).

14 The NIV margin says that the meaning of יָקוֹט (yāqôṭ, "fragile") is uncertain, but see our discussion of this in the Introduction. The various changes in the text suggested by commentaries accomplish nothing better than the *ad sensum* rendering of the NIV.

17 The NIV has added the words "a place" to יֶחֱזֶה (yeḥᵉzēh, "looks for") because the most common meaning of ḥāzâ is "to look." But nothing needs to be added if we understand the root to be אָחַז (ʾāḥaz, "to seize"), with a suppression of the א (ʾ, aleph) as in 2 Samuel 20:9 (tōḥez, NIV, "took"; cf. BDB, 28). The translation would read "It ['the plant' of v.16] takes hold among the stones." Pope, 61, makes the verb plural: "They [the roots] take hold." For the use of the word בֵּית (bêt, "among") as a preposition, see Holladay, 39.

19 The NIV renders הֶן־הוּא מְשׂוֹשׂ דַּרְכּוֹ (hen-hûʾ mᵉśôś darkô) as "Surely its life withers away." The MT is difficult because the two major words can be taken in more than one way. The NIV goes along with the NEB. The word mᵉśôś is identified with the same form in Isaiah 8:6 meaning "to wither (melt) away" instead of the other meaning, "joy" (so NIV, KJV, RSV, et al.), which does not fit the context at all. Dhorme (in loc.) may be right in giving derek a literal rather than a metaphorical meaning—"there by its path [derek] it rots."

4. Job's Reply (9:1–10:22)

OVERVIEW

In these chapters Job's words move from extolling God (9:1–13)—perhaps as a display of theological acumen to impress the counselors—to blaming God. Would God ever treat him justly? He doubts it (vv.14–31). Does God mock the innocent? Job thinks probably so (vv.21–24). "If it is not he, then who is it?" (v.24). These are hard words, but his question instead of a statement implies doubt. These words are followed in vv.32–35 with a yearning for someone strong enough to take up his cause with God. But in chapter 10 Job decides to plead his own cause and direct all his words to God. How can God, who has created him, want to destroy him—and that without any formal charges?

¹Then Job replied:

²"Indeed, I know that this is true.
    But how can a mortal be righteous before God?
³Though one wished to dispute with him,
    he could not answer him one time out of a thousand.
⁴His wisdom is profound, his power is vast.
    Who has resisted him and come out unscathed?
⁵He moves mountains without their knowing it
    and overturns them in his anger.
⁶He shakes the earth from its place
    and makes its pillars tremble.
⁷He speaks to the sun and it does not shine;
    he seals off the light of the stars.
⁸He alone stretches out the heavens
    and treads on the waves of the sea.
⁹He is the Maker of the Bear and Orion,
    the Pleiades and the constellations of the south.
¹⁰He performs wonders that cannot be fathomed,
    miracles that cannot be counted.
¹¹When he passes me, I cannot see him;
    when he goes by, I cannot perceive him.
¹²If he snatches away, who can stop him?
    Who can say to him, 'What are you doing?'
¹³God does not restrain his anger;
    even the cohorts of Rahab cowered at his feet.

¹⁴"How then can I dispute with him?
    How can I find words to argue with him?
¹⁵Though I were innocent, I could not answer him;
    I could only plead with my Judge for mercy.
¹⁶Even if I summoned him and he responded,
    I do not believe he would give me a hearing.
¹⁷He would crush me with a storm
    and multiply my wounds for no reason.

¹⁸He would not let me regain my breath
  but would overwhelm me with misery.
¹⁹If it is a matter of strength, he is mighty!
  And if it is a matter of justice, who will summon him?
²⁰Even if I were innocent, my mouth would condemn me;
  if I were blameless, it would pronounce me guilty.

²¹"Although I am blameless,
  I have no concern for myself;
  I despise my own life.
²²It is all the same; that is why I say,
  'He destroys both the blameless and the wicked.'
²³When a scourge brings sudden death,
  he mocks the despair of the innocent.
²⁴When a land falls into the hands of the wicked,
  he blindfolds its judges.
  If it is not he, then who is it?

²⁵"My days are swifter than a runner;
  they fly away without a glimpse of joy.
²⁶They skim past like boats of papyrus,
  like eagles swooping down on their prey.
²⁷If I say, 'I will forget my complaint,
  I will change my expression, and smile,'
²⁸I still dread all my sufferings,
  for I know you will not hold me innocent.
²⁹Since I am already found guilty,
  why should I struggle in vain?
³⁰Even if I washed myself with soap
  and my hands with washing soda,
³¹you would plunge me into a slime pit
  so that even my clothes would detest me.

³²"He is not a man like me that I might answer him,
  that we might confront each other in court.
³³If only there were someone to arbitrate between us,
  to lay his hand upon us both,
³⁴someone to remove God's rod from me,
  so that his terror would frighten me no more.
³⁵Then I would speak up without fear of him,
  but as it now stands with me, I cannot.

10:1"I loathe my very life;
　　therefore I will give free rein to my complaint
　　and speak out in the bitterness of my soul.
2I will say to God: Do not condemn me,
　　but tell me what charges you have against me.
3Does it please you to oppress me,
　　to spurn the work of your hands,
　　while you smile on the schemes of the wicked?
4Do you have eyes of flesh?
　　Do you see as a mortal sees?
5Are your days like those of a mortal
　　or your years like those of a man,
6that you must search out my faults
　　and probe after my sin—
7though you know that I am not guilty
　　and that no one can rescue me from your hand?

8"Your hands shaped me and made me.
　　Will you now turn and destroy me?
9Remember that you molded me like clay.
　　Will you now turn me to dust again?
10Did you not pour me out like milk
　　and curdle me like cheese,
11clothe me with skin and flesh
　　and knit me together with bones and sinews?
12You gave me life and showed me kindness,
　　and in your providence watched over my spirit.

13"But this is what you concealed in your heart,
　　and I know that this was in your mind:
14If I sinned, you would be watching me
　　and would not let my offense go unpunished.
15If I am guilty—woe to me!
　　Even if I am innocent, I cannot lift my head,
for I am full of shame
　　and drowned in my affliction.
16If I hold my head high, you stalk me like a lion
　　and again display your awesome power against me.

¹⁷You bring new witnesses against me
and increase your anger toward me;
your forces come against me wave upon wave.

¹⁸"Why then did you bring me out of the womb?
I wish I had died before any eye saw me.
¹⁹If only I had never come into being,
or had been carried straight from the womb to the grave!
²⁰Are not my few days almost over?
Turn away from me so I can have a moment's joy
²¹before I go to the place of no return,
to the land of gloom and deep shadow,
²²to the land of deepest night,
of deep shadow and disorder,
where even the light is like darkness."

COMMENTARY

9:1–24 In vv.1–13 Job intends to show that his problems are not due to gross ignorance of God's ways. Those ways are past finding out, but he knows as much about them as his friends do. His opening remark—"Indeed, I know that this is true" (v.1)—is a grudging admission that what Bildad has said contains the right theology. After all, Job does share the same basic idea as Bildad and the other three friends—that suffering is the result of sin—though he believes God is unjust to apply it in his case.

But Job had more than Bildad's words in mind. Job immediately calls to mind Eliphaz's rhetorical question in 4:17: "Can a mortal be more righteous than God?" Some think Eliphaz and Job are each using the root *ṣdq* ("righteous"; GK 7904–7907) in a slightly different sense. Eliphaz's righteousness is based on ontological superiority, while Job is thinking of juridical vindication, that is, innocence (see Robertson, 41). The word covers both meanings,

though it is likely that in these two instances in Job the root has the same juridical meaning.

Bildad's accusations in chapter 8 have turned Job's mind to the subject of legal vindication. In 8:20 Bildad said, "Surely God does not reject a blameless man." To Bildad God's justice requires punishing the guilty and blessing the innocent (see also 8:3–6). Job fervently believes that he is innocent of any sin that might warrant the kind of punishment he is enduring. But he is frustrated in his attempt to vindicate himself. God's wisdom is too profound and his power too great for Job to debate in court (9:3–4).

Verses 4–13 constitute a hymn in which Job describes God's awesome power. God shakes the earth from its place and makes its pillars tremble (v.6); he speaks to the sun, and it does not shine (v.7); he stretches out the heavens and treads on the waves of the sea—the creation and control of all natural forces (v.8). Job closes the hymn (v.10) with the words of Eliphaz used in 5:9: "He performs wonders that cannot be fathomed, miracles that cannot be counted." But Job is applying these words in a way opposite to how Eliphaz used them.

In chapter 5 Eliphaz was showing how God, by his power, does what is good and right. He lifts to safety those who mourn and delivers the poor from the clutches of the powerful. But Job sees God's power as though it were amoral, a sovereign freedom, an uncontrollable power that works mysteriously (v.11) to do whatever he wills so that no one can stop him and ask, "What are you doing" (v.12). Yes, God's anger makes even the armies of Rahab (the boisterous demonic power associated with the sea) cower at his feet (v.13). Job thinks such a God would overwhelm him in any attempt to show his innocence. He can only plead for mercy; even worse, Job doubts that God will give him even a hearing, but believes that for no reason at all God will crush him.

This awful indictment of God presents us with a contemporary theological issue. There are those within the bounds of the modern church who think that in the OT God is sometimes a bully and, therefore, this view of God must be written off as only a phase in human understanding. Because of Job's frustration and illness, these words (vv.14–31) must not be considered normative, but unfortunately even normative passages are sometimes written off as sub-Christian. All God's sovereign acts are rooted in his righteous character, even when they are outside the bounds of human ability to evaluate them. And that applies especially here as Job struggles to understand.

In verses 21–24 this God of Job's imagination is worse than morally indifferent (v.22), a God who even mocks the despair of the innocent (v.23) and blocks the administering of justice (v.24). Since everyone gets treated the same way—the blameless and the wicked—Job throws all caution to the wind: "I have no concern for myself; I despise my own life" (v.21). He adds, in effect, "If God is not responsible for this, then who is?" (cf. v.24).

These are the honest words of a sick and desperate man. They are a forceful reminder to anyone who has to counsel the sick, that people who face deep trials often say irresponsible things in their struggle to understand their suffering in the light of God's compassion. Not all Job's words are wrong, but it is a mistake to try to make them all represent valid theology rather than the half-truths of a person struggling to understand. They deal with the mystery at the heart of the book of Job: the problem of evil for which no human being has a logical explanation. So Job reasons, as many have, that if God is sovereign, truly sovereign, he is responsible for all evil.

Job does not mention the corollary: If there is evil beyond God's control, then he is not truly sovereign. Job stresses only God's irresistible might; and it appears to him that if God holds him to be guilty, there is nothing that he can do to establish his innocence. Yet he believes he is innocent and is concerned with disproving the contention of his friends that God only destroys the wicked and always cares for the righteous. Job's experience tells him that sometimes God crushes the innocent for no reason at all (v.17). Job believes that in so doing God is unjust; so he wants to meet with God and set him straight. We who are privileged to see the drama from the divine perspective know that Job is innocent and that God does have a cause, a cause beyond the purview of Job, a cause that cannot be revealed to Job at that moment.

25–35 Verses 25–31 combine as an expression of deep despair. Job is unable to suck sweetness from a single day; there is not a glimpse of joy, not a smile (v.27), only one unending blur of suffering (v.28). Since God has arbitrarily chosen to treat him as a criminal, what can he do to purge himself (v.29)? Even if he were able to purge himself (v.30), God would plunge him again into a slime pit so that even his clothes would detest him (v.31).

In vv.32–35 Job goes back to the theme of vv.14–20. He is so frustrated over the immenseness of God! No doubt Andersen, 151, is correct in saying that the real issue in the book of Job is not the problem of suffering but the obtaining of a right relationship between Job and God. What Job does not realize is that in wrestling with God, he is moving in the direction of a right relationship with his Maker. If he only understood what God is doing, that would have made his suffering bearable. But as it is, he bears a burden even greater than his suffering—his apparent inability to stand in God's presence as an upright and blameless man (v.32).

In v.33 Job touches on the mystery through which God willl eventually provide godliness for humanity. He yearns for a mediator between himself and God. A *môkîaḥ* ("someone to arbitrate") does not have to be one who stands over God and Job in order to judge between them (Pope, 61). As "one who argues a case," he is a mediator or negotiator who is able to bring parties together.

We should not infer from this that the book of Job here is directly predictive of the NT doctrine of Christ as mediator; W. C. Kaiser Jr. (*The Messiah in the Old Testament* [Grand Rapids: Zondervan, 1995], 61–64) is surely incorrect to argue that this passage, as well as 9:33 and 16:19–21, has an explicit connection with the messianic theme. For one thing, Job is not looking for a mediator to forgive him of his sins so that he might be received by God; Job is yearning for a mediator who can prove that he is innocent and can somehow be effective with God despite his infinite power and wisdom. But having said that, we have here a rudimentary idea that is certainly evocative of that NT concept. Even here in the book of Job the idea will move on to greater ramifications in 16:20–21 and 19:25–26.

10:1–22 In chapter 10 Job continues to bewail his sorrowful condition. Life has become an unbearable burden. In his bitter anguish he is determined to speak out (v.1), once again directing his words to God. He calls on God, not for healing and restoration (at least directly), which incidentally he nowhere ever asks for; but he wants to know again why he is suffering. "Tell me what charges you have against me" (v.2).

Job cannot understand how God, the Creator, who looked on his original creation and considered it good, can turn his back on the work of his hands (v.3). Has not Job dedicated his life to God, in contrast to the wicked who received God's smile? Job knows that God is not limited like human beings, who have mere eyes of flesh and a certain number of years (vv.4–5). Does God have to search out Job's faults when he knows that he is innocent (vv.6–7)? Job puts God on the witness stand and plies him with questions. Job cannot understand how the God who so marvelously made him in the womb, who gave him life and showed him such providential care, could be willing to destroy him (vv.8–12).

The NIV takes v.13 with what follows, but some do not agree (cf. Andersen, 153–54). If the NIV is correct (see Notes), then in v.13 Job is saying that God brought him into being so that he might hound him over his sin and let no offense go unpunished. It seems that Job is saying that it does not make any difference whether he is innocent or guilty because he is full of shame and drowned in affliction anyway (vv.14–15). No matter how much he tries to assert his integrity, it seems that God insists on stalking Job like a lion, showing his awesome power in wave after wave of oppression (vv.16–17).

Poor Job. The God who he imagines is so angry with him is not angry with him at all; but in his current state of mind, he reverts back to his original wish to have died at birth, to have been carried straight from the womb to the tomb (vv.18–19). In chapter 3 Job saw Sheol as a place where he might have found some rest from his troubles; here in chapter 10 he longs for a few days of release on earth before he has to go to that place of no return, which he envisions as a land of gloom and deepest night (vv.20–22).

Job has reached about as far as a human being can go into the depths of depression and despair, but it will do us well to be reminded that even the apostle of hope said in 2 Corinthians 1:8–9, "We were under great pressure, far beyond our ability to

endure, so that we despaired even of life. Indeed, in our hearts, we felt the sentence of death. But this happened that we might not rely on ourselves but on God, who raises the dead." In his despair Job still wrestles with God, but it is still to the living God that his cry is lifted up. An important question yet to be faced is: Does Job have any hope that transcends this life?

NOTES

9:2 Gordis (*Job*, 103) claims עִם־אֵל (ʿim-ʾēl, "before God") carries a double connotation: "in the estimation of God" and "in a contest with God." To passages using the latter meaning may be added Isaiah 7:14, where the rest of the chapter shows the prophet has a dual-cutting edge to that epithet Immanuel: God is with us—to bless—and God is in contest with us—to punish. Here in v.2 Job quotes Eliphaz in 4:17, but he substitutes ʿim for min. This lends weight to our contention that min means "before" spatially rather than expressing comparison in 4:17.

4 Is this verse a description of God or the man who would dare dispute with him? While the latter is possible (Pope, 61), it requires turning the line into a conditional sentence. Dhorme thinks the idea is too subtle. The same problem exists in v.3a, where Pope also goes against most by taking God as the subject "If he [God] deigned to litigate." The NIV considers the subject of v.3a to be indefinite, meaning "anyone." Verses 5–12 are clearly hymnic, extolling God's fearsome power. The NIV has chosen to include vv.4 and 13 in the hymn.

5 The NIV's rendering of וְלֹא יָדָעוּ (wᵉlōʾ yādāʿû, "without their knowing it") makes it sound as though the mountains do not know when they are moved. Again, an indefinite subject leads to the translation "and no one knows it"—that is, earthquakes in uninhabited places.

7 I have assumed the astronomical phenomena here are the eclipse of the sun and the periodic behavior of the planets and stars, but that may not be the primary reference. The Targum may have caught the intent of this context with its paraphrase, "The clouds seal up the stars" (Dhorme, 129). The NIV renders זָרַח (zārah) "shine," but its basic meaning is "rise." Is it a brief eclipse or sustained darkness? Verses 5–7 describe what God does in his anger—the quaking of the mountains often includes volcanic activity with clouds darkening the sky. In any case, the point is that God is sovereign even over the heavenly bodies, thought to be gods in pagan religion. How he seals up the stars is not really the issue.

8 The word לְבַדּוֹ (lᵉbaddô, "alone") stresses the monotheism of Job. Isaiah 44:24 uses identical language (see the Introduction). As many have noted, the rhetoric is mythopoeic (Pope, 70). The myth told of the defeat of the sea god; but since Job's God alone is God (v.8a), the meaning must be limited to his control over his creation. יָם (yām, "Yam"; NIV, "sea"; GK 3542) was a cosmic deity (a dragon). The back parts בָּמֳתֵי (bomᵒtê) of Yam is a metaphor for "the waves of the sea" (NIV).

9 Compare 38:31–33. The LXX shows the familiarity of the translator with Greek pagan literature. These heavenly phenomena are called "Pleiades, Hesperus, and Arcturus." For views on the identification of these constellations, see G. R. Driver ("Two Astronomical Passages," 5:208–12; 7:1–11); Pope (70–71, 301); Dhorme (131–32). Although their roots are obscure, Pleiades (כִּימָה, *kîmâ*) and Orion (כְּסִיל, *kesîl*) are generally accepted. But עָשׁ (ʿāš; cf. ʿayiš in 38:32) as "Bear" is uncertain. It may be "Leo" (cf. NIV mg. at 38:32). On "the constellations [chambers] of the south," G. Schiaparelli (*Astronomy in the Old Testament* [Oxford: Oxford Univ. Press, 1905], 63–67) notes that as a result of precession, many stars that were visible on the southern horizon in Palestine (the 32nd degree of north latitude) are no longer visible there. This heavenly display begins at the star Argus (Canopus) and ends with Centaurus and is the brightest part of the whole sky. In this area are five stars of the first magnitude (there are only twenty in the whole stellar sphere) and five more of the second magnitude. It actually produces a faint twilight illumination.

11 Job is frustrated—וְלֹא אֶרְאֶה (*welōʾ ʾerʾeh*, "I cannot see him")—because he wants to see God but cannot. What is this invisibility of God? Is Job's God by his very nature invisible compared with visible idols? In the Introduction I suggest this, but Job does finally "see" God in 42:5. It is my contention that even if the "seeing" is a literal viewing of something, it is only God's majesty and splendor (37:21–22), for the Lord speaks to Job out of the storm (38:1). Here and in 42:5 "seeing God" probably means a personal encounter that goes beyond head knowledge, which in 42:5 Job called "hearing with the ears."

13 Pope, 70–71, translates "a god could not turn back his anger." But the word אֱלֹוהַּ (*ʾelôah*, "God"; GK 468) is used forty-two times in Job of the true God; and 12:6 is the only additional passage where it could mean a god or an idol, but that, like this, is subject to the other interpretation (cf. NIV mg. at 12:6).

15–16 Andersen (147, n. 2) sees v.15 as pivotal for understanding the chapter. Job's claim to innocence makes it unlikely that he will appeal for mercy as admonished. He suggests לֹא (*lōʾ*) in v.15a does double duty and reads v.15b: "I do not need to plead with my judge for mercy." Andersen points out that Elihu later accuses Job of "justifying himself" and accuses the friends of failing to prove Job is willing. In v.16a Andersen finds difficulty in Job's accusation of God as cruel and unfair (also v.17). Not fairness but exposure to the divine presence (v.34) is Job's concern according to Andersen; so he turns the negative of v.16b into an assertive לֹא (*ʾl*). Of course, any negative can be made positive by turning it into a question. The text would read: "If I summoned him and he responded, would he not give me a hearing?" But this makes what follows seem unnatural.

19 On יֹועִדֵנִי (*yôʿîdēnî*, "summon him") with the third masculine singular suffix, see Note on v.35.

20 The NIV understands the subject of וַיַּעְקְשֵׁנִי (*wayyaʿqešēnî*, "it would pronounce me guilty") to refer back to "my mouth" rather than to "God." The Hebrew (masculine) will allow for either, but the NIV softens the overt injustice Job imputes to God, who would pronounce him guilty even if he were innocent.

27 Although against normal usage, *ʾim* with the infinitive and pronoun—אִם־אָמְרִי (*ʾim-ʾomrî*, "If I say")—is preferable to following the one MS that changes the verb to אָמַרְתִּי (*ʾāmartî*; cf. BHS mg.).

29 This verse is pure irony. Since the tone of irony cannot be conveyed in writing, the NIV has done next best—made it a hypothetical statement.

30 The Hithpael in אִם־הִתְרָחַצְתִּי בְמֵו־שָׁלֶג (*ʾim-hitrāḥaṣtî bemēw-šāleg*, "even if I washed myself with soap") may be iterative, not reflexive (cf. Andersen, 150, n. 1), meaning "Even if I repeatedly washed." The *Kethiv* and the LXX are right in reading *bemô*, the poetic preposition "with." Pope, 75, gives linguistic proof that *šeleg* here means "soap," not "snow"(GK 8920–8921).

33 The NIV goes with the LXX and other versions reading לוּ (*lû*), which expresses "desire," rather than the negative לֹא (*lōʾ*). The MT's pointing probably arose for theological reasons (cf. 16:4).

35 כִּי לֹא־כֵן אָנֹכִי עִמָּדִי (*kî lōʾ-kēn ʾānōkî ʿimmādî*, "but as it now stands with me, I cannot") is difficult. The NIV has rendered the line *ad sensum*. Blommerde, 8, suggests that *ʿimmādî* has the *yod* as a rare third person singular pronominal suffix on the basis of Phoenician and Ugaritic evidence. But Z. Zevit ("The Linquistic and Contextual Arguments in Support of a Hebrew 3 m.s. suffix -y," *UF* 9 [1977]: 315–28) argues against any such use in the OT. Zevit claims the Ugaritic evidence is questionable; and while the Phoenician evidence is well attested, the *yod* appears only with nouns or verbs ending in a long vowel and with singular nouns in the genitive case (cf. F. M. Cross and D. N. Freedman, "The Pronominal Suffixes of the Third Person Singular in Phoenician," *JNES* 10 [1951]: 228–30). Zevit claims all but five of Dahood's Psalms examples of third singular *yod* are either not necessary or impossible; so he falls back on the confusion between *waw* and *yod* during several periods when the two graphemes looked very much alike in the square script. If the third masculine singular *yod* were attested in Hebrew inscriptional material as it is in Phoenician, he would have to revise this opinion. Since this is not so, I accept only those passages in Job that are supported by the LXX as third singular or can be easily considered a graphic confusion of two similarly written letters.

The form *ʿimmādî* ("with me") here, however, creates a special problem since the form *ʿimmādô* ("with him") is not attested in the OT. This makes it difficult to see how the Greek arrived at the third singular. But Greek that reads "I do not think myself unjust with him" is too far from the MT. If *ʿimmādô* were possible, the line would render excellent sense: "but it is not so between us," reading the last two Hebrew words "I with him." Of the thirty-one examples of third singular *yod* in Job given by Blommerde, the following have a context clearly favoring the third person: 14:3; 19:28; 21:16; 22:18; 31:18.

10:2 The meaning of אַל־תַּרְשִׁיעֵנִי (*ʾal-taršîʿēnî*, "Do not condemn me") is literally, "treat a person as wicked." That is Job's problem with God. It appears to him that the Almighty is giving him what a wicked man deserves when he knows Job is not a wicked man ("guilty" in v.7 is the same verb).

3 הֲטוֹב (*hᵃṭôb*, "Does it please [you]") is literally "Is it good?" The idiom has overtones of Genesis 1, where God looked on all his creation and "it was good." How can he now despise the work of his hands?

8–12 Is this poem about the creation of a human being or on gestation? Verses 8–9 use the "potter" figure while vv.10–12 are figures of procreation and gestation—Job was poured out like milk (semen) and knit together in the womb.

15 Job claims it is his affliction that makes it appear he is guilty. This verse hardly means he is willing to concede that point. The two verbs at the end of this verse are imperative in form. The meaning then of v.15b is "be satisfied with my shame, be aware of my affliction" (see the NIV mg., which is closer to the MT). The NIV text has "drowned," from the root *nwh* ("be saturated"), instead of *rʾh* ("to see"). The difference in meaning is whether Job is calling on God for mercy or is stating his own sad condition.

16 The subject of the first verb is ambiguous. The Hebrew appears to be third masculine singular. The NIV goes with the Syriac (first person), but there are other ways to handle the problem. Beck's translation of the Bible takes *yigʾeh* as an adverb: "Bold like a lion you hunt me down." Pope, 75, does the same but reading *gēʾeh*.

20 יָשִׁית מִמֶּנִּי (*yᵉšît mimmennî*, "turn away from me") is literally "put from me," another example of ellipsis of either *lēb* (" heart") or *yād* ("hand"; cf. 38:11 for this verb and Note on 4:20 for ellipsis).

5. Zophar (11:1–20)

OVERVIEW

Zophar is a severe man. Like Bildad he lacks compassion and is ruthlessly judgmental. He thinks

Job, who is suffering to the point of despair, is getting much less than he deserves.

¹Then Zophar the Naamathite replied:

²"Are all these words to go unanswered?
  Is this talker to be vindicated?
³Will your idle talk reduce men to silence?
  Will no one rebuke you when you mock?
⁴You say to God, 'My beliefs are flawless
  and I am pure in your sight.'
⁵Oh, how I wish that God would speak,
  that he would open his lips against you
⁶and disclose to you the secrets of wisdom,
  for true wisdom has two sides.
  Know this: God has even forgotten some of your sin.

⁷"Can you fathom the mysteries of God?
  Can you probe the limits of the Almighty?
⁸They are higher than the heavens—what can you do?
  They are deeper than the depths of the grave—what can you know?
⁹Their measure is longer than the earth
  and wider than the sea.

¹⁰"If he comes along and confines you in prison
  and convenes a court, who can oppose him?
¹¹Surely he recognizes deceitful men;
  and when he sees evil, does he not take note?
¹²But a witless man can no more become wise
  than a wild donkey's colt can be born a man.

¹³"Yet if you devote your heart to him
  and stretch out your hands to him,
¹⁴if you put away the sin that is in your hand
  and allow no evil to dwell in your tent,
¹⁵then you will lift up your face without shame;
  you will stand firm and without fear.

> ^{16}You will surely forget your trouble,
>   recalling it only as waters gone by.
> ^{17}Life will be brighter than noonday,
>   and darkness will become like morning.
> ^{18}You will be secure, because there is hope;
>   you will look about you and take your rest in safety.
> ^{19}You will lie down, with no one to make you afraid,
>   and many will court your favor.
> ^{20}But the eyes of the wicked will fail,
>   and escape will elude them;
>   their hope will become a dying gasp."

COMMENTARY

1–12 Zophar considers Job's words pure mockery (vv.2–3), for he thinks Job is claiming flawless doctrine and sinless perfection (v.4). Job steadfastly maintains his innocence or blamelessness in contrast with wickedness (9:22), but he does not claim to be perfect (7:21). He does, however, feel that God has treated him much worse than he deserves. Though he complains bitterly of the treatment God appears to be giving him, to this point he has not been particularly sarcastic nor has he mocked God or even ridiculed his friends. He has accused them of being shallow in their arguments and callous in the way they have dealt with him (6:24–27).

Zophar speaks with eloquence about God's infinitude (vv.7–8), justice, and omniscience (vv.10–11). Job needs a stiff rebuke from the lips of God because God has favored him by forgetting some of his sin, or at least has allowed Job to forget some of his sin (see Note on v.6). Either way the words are designed to suggest the enormity of Job's sin. Zophar's only reason to believe Job has sinned to such an extent is derived from the extent of Job's suffering, which he takes to be God's way of exposing secret sin. That Job will not admit it is taken to be additional evidence of

his pride and hardness of heart. So Job needs to be humbled. The best way to humble him is to bring him face to face with God. In vv.7–9 he expounds on the immensity of God in spatial terms. If the limits of the created cosmos are beyond Job's understanding, how much more the mysteries of God!

In vv.10–11 Zophar touches on the omnipotence and omniscience of God, who sees through the deceit of people such as Job and keeps a permanent record of it. All this is designed to humble Job, but Zophar apparently doubts that it will. He then attempts heavy-handed shock treatment to get through to Job. The sharpness of his sarcasm is demonstrated in v.12. Zophar labels Job a witless, empty-headed man with as much chance to become wise as a wild donkey has to be born tame (see Notes).

13–20 Job's only hope is to stretch out his hands to God and repent (v.13). This is, of course, good advice for a person who has lived a life of sinful indulgence, but to Job's ears it is pious arrogance. And it is arrogant for Zophar to assume he knows why Job is suffering; he has reduced the solution of this complex human problem to a simplistic formula—every pain has a sin behind it. Zophar erroneously suggests that if one repents and gets right with God, this guarantees that the struggles and troubles of life will dissolve (vv.14–16).

This common error is made by many well-meaning Christians who fail to distinguish between forensic forgiveness that cancels the guilt of sin and the immediate consequences of a profligate life that often brings trouble and distress. But we know

from the Prologue that Job's troubles are not the result of a profligate life, so Zophar is wrong on both counts. Job's troubles do not come as a penalty from God; and even if they did, Job's repentance would not guarantee that life from then on would be "brighter than noonday" (v.17) and that people would stop molesting him and instead "court his favor" (vv.18–19).

NOTES

4 Used mainly in Proverbs, the word לִקְחִי (liqḥî, "my beliefs"; GK 4375) means "teaching." But in Deuteronomy 32:2, where it is parallel with אִמְרָתִי (ʾimrātî, "my speech"; NIV, "my words"), it may mean "my testimony" (cf. Habel, 207). But the subject here is Job's doctrine.

6 True, effective wisdom (תּוּשִׁיָּה, tûšîyâ) includes understanding the dialectical tension כִּפְלַיִם (kiplayim, "two sides") often involved in the balance of truth. But is this the meaning here? Zophar may mean the hidden (deeper) part of wisdom axioms. The precise meaning is not agreed on, but in Wisdom literature the מָשָׁל (māšāl, "proverb, riddle, parable"; GK 5442) had a hidden as well as an obvious meaning. Jesus frequently used this method of teaching. Zophar is chiding Job for being obvious and therefore shallow.

The NIV's translation of יַשֶּׁה לְךָ אֱלוֹהַ (yaššeh lekā ʾelôah)—"God has forgotten"—leaves out the force of the lekā. Literally it reads, "God has forgotten for you some of your sin." The verb našâ usually takes a direct object. If the lamed on lekā is a mark of the accusative (Aramaism), then we could read, "God has made (allowed) you to forget."

8 The NIV should not have used the word "grave" for שְׁאוֹל (šeʾôl) in this context. The stress is on a place that is opposite to heaven and very deep—the netherworld.

11 The NIV has chosen to make the readings positive with a question. This may be another case of the assertive or emphatic לֹא (lʾ; cf. BHS mg.; see also Note on 7:8).

12 The NIV's margin seems preferable. See Pope, 86, who claims עַיִר (ʿayir) means a male domesticated donkey, not a colt of a wild donkey. Dahood ("Zacharia 9:1, ʿên ʾādām," CBQ 25 [1963]: 123–24) claims פֶּרֶא אָדָם (pereʾ ʾādām) means "a wild ass of the steppe," reading ʾādām as ʾadāmâ; but see Speiser (Genesis [AB 1; New York: Doubleday, 1964], 118).

6. Job's Reply (12:1–14:22)

OVERVIEW

In the following speech, Job first answers his counselors (12:1–13:19), then he addresses God (13:20–14:22). With his patience running out, he

chooses to match Zophar's harshness with sarcasm— "Doubtless you are the people, / and wisdom will die with you!" (12:1). Job is sure he knows as much as they do and begs to differ with their view of suffering. Being comfortable themselves, they can afford to be contemptuous toward him. If only he were treated justly, Job would not be suffering the way he has been. He repeats the unanswerable question: Why does God treat him so badly? Why should a man who is righteous and blameless be made a laughingstock (v.4) when sinners and idolaters go undisturbed (v.6)? This is the kind of question that has made Job's friends brand him as a man whose feet are slipping (v.5).

¹Then Job replied:

²"Doubtless you are the people,
 and wisdom will die with you!
³But I have a mind as well as you;
 I am not inferior to you.
 Who does not know all these things?

⁴"I have become a laughingstock to my friends,
 though I called upon God and he answered—
 a mere laughingstock, though righteous and blameless!
⁵Men at ease have contempt for misfortune
 as the fate of those whose feet are slipping.
⁶The tents of marauders are undisturbed,
 and those who provoke God are secure—
 those who carry their god in their hands.

⁷"But ask the animals, and they will teach you,
 or the birds of the air, and they will tell you;
⁸or speak to the earth, and it will teach you,
 or let the fish of the sea inform you.
⁹Which of all these does not know
 that the hand of the Lord has done this?
¹⁰In his hand is the life of every creature
 and the breath of all mankind.
¹¹Does not the ear test words
 as the tongue tastes food?
¹²Is not wisdom found among the aged?
 Does not long life bring understanding?

¹³"To God belong wisdom and power;
 counsel and understanding are his.
¹⁴What he tears down cannot be rebuilt;
 the man he imprisons cannot be released.

¹⁵If he holds back the waters, there is drought;
   if he lets them loose, they devastate the land.
¹⁶To him belong strength and victory;
   both deceived and deceiver are his.
¹⁷He leads counselors away stripped
   and makes fools of judges.
¹⁸He takes off the shackles put on by kings
   and ties a loincloth around their waist.
¹⁹He leads priests away stripped
   and overthrows men long established.
²⁰He silences the lips of trusted advisers
   and takes away the discernment of elders.
²¹He pours contempt on nobles
   and disarms the mighty.
²²He reveals the deep things of darkness
   and brings deep shadows into the light.
²³He makes nations great, and destroys them;
   he enlarges nations, and disperses them.
²⁴He deprives the leaders of the earth of their reason;
   he sends them wandering through a trackless waste.
²⁵They grope in darkness with no light;
   he makes them stagger like drunkards.

^{13:1}"My eyes have seen all this,
   my ears have heard and understood it.
²What you know, I also know;
   I am not inferior to you.
³But I desire to speak to the Almighty
   and to argue my case with God.
⁴You, however, smear me with lies;
   you are worthless physicians, all of you!
⁵If only you would be altogether silent!
   For you, that would be wisdom.
⁶Hear now my argument;
   listen to the plea of my lips.
⁷Will you speak wickedly on God's behalf?
   Will you speak deceitfully for him?
⁸Will you show him partiality?
   Will you argue the case for God?

⁹Would it turn out well if he examined you?
　　Could you deceive him as you might deceive men?
¹⁰He would surely rebuke you
　　if you secretly showed partiality.
¹¹Would not his splendor terrify you?
　　Would not the dread of him fall on you?
¹²Your maxims are proverbs of ashes;
　　your defenses are defenses of clay.

¹³"Keep silent and let me speak;
　　then let come to me what may.
¹⁴Why do I put myself in jeopardy
　　and take my life in my hands?
¹⁵Though he slay me, yet will I hope in him;
　　I will surely defend my ways to his face.
¹⁶Indeed, this will turn out for my deliverance,
　　for no godless man would dare come before him!
¹⁷Listen carefully to my words;
　　let your ears take in what I say.
¹⁸Now that I have prepared my case,
　　I know I will be vindicated.
¹⁹Can anyone bring charges against me?
　　If so, I will be silent and die.

²⁰"Only grant me these two things, O God,
　　and then I will not hide from you:
²¹Withdraw your hand far from me,
　　and stop frightening me with your terrors.
²²Then summon me and I will answer,
　　or let me speak, and you reply.
²³How many wrongs and sins have I committed?
　　Show me my offense and my sin.
²⁴Why do you hide your face
　　and consider me your enemy?
²⁵Will you torment a windblown leaf?
　　Will you chase after dry chaff?
²⁶For you write down bitter things against me
　　and make me inherit the sins of my youth.

²⁷You fasten my feet in shackles;
    you keep close watch on all my paths
    by putting marks on the soles of my feet.

²⁸"So man wastes away like something rotten,
    like a garment eaten by moths.

^{14:1}"Man born of woman
    is of few days and full of trouble.
²He springs up like a flower and withers away;
    like a fleeting shadow, he does not endure.
³Do you fix your eye on such a one?
    Will you bring him before you for judgment?
⁴Who can bring what is pure from the impure?
    No one!
⁵Man's days are determined;
    you have decreed the number of his months
    and have set limits he cannot exceed.
⁶So look away from him and let him alone,
    till he has put in his time like a hired man.

⁷"At least there is hope for a tree:
    If it is cut down, it will sprout again,
    and its new shoots will not fail.
⁸Its roots may grow old in the ground
    and its stump die in the soil,
⁹yet at the scent of water it will bud
    and put forth shoots like a plant.
¹⁰But man dies and is laid low;
    he breathes his last and is no more.
¹¹As water disappears from the sea
    or a riverbed becomes parched and dry,
¹²so man lies down and does not rise;
    till the heavens are no more, men will not awake
    or be roused from their sleep.

¹³"If only you would hide me in the grave
    and conceal me till your anger has passed!
If only you would set me a time
    and then remember me!

¹⁴If a man dies, will he live again?
  All the days of my hard service
  I will wait for my renewal to come.
¹⁵You will call and I will answer you;
  you will long for the creature your hands have made.
¹⁶Surely then you will count my steps
  but not keep track of my sin.
¹⁷My offenses will be sealed up in a bag;
  you will cover over my sin.

¹⁸"But as a mountain erodes and crumbles
  and as a rock is moved from its place,
¹⁹as water wears away stones
  and torrents wash away the soil,
  so you destroy man's hope.
²⁰You overpower him once for all, and he is gone;
  you change his countenance and send him away.
²¹If his sons are honored, he does not know it;
  if they are brought low, he does not see it.
²²He feels but the pain of his own body
  and mourns only for himself."

COMMENTARY

12:1–25 After Job begins his speech with a self-defense of his wisdom and insults directed toward the friends (vv.1–3), this poem breaks neatly into three stanzas. The first (vv.4–6) states Job's problem: "Why me, God, and not those who really deserve misfortune?"

In the second (vv.7–12) Job complains that the whole world is afflicted with the same apparent injustice. Why should this be when all things, including the very breath of humanity, are in God's hands (v.10)? Bildad has already accused Job of attributing evildoing to God (8:3) and has appealed to the authority of past generations to prove Job is wrong. Now Job appeals to the experience of humanity and all creation to support his view that it makes no dif-

ference whether people are good or bad. God does not use morality as the basis for granting freedom from affliction. The issue over the problem of theodicy is joined, an issue every believer must eventually wrestle with. Job's counselors are so superficial that they have not yet struggled with this difficult problem. Their thoughts on the subject are simplistic. Job considers their words bland and superficial, certainly not a worthy part of the wisdom of elders (vv.11–12). He has already accused them of serving tasteless food (thoughts; 6:6–7).

In the third stanza (vv.13–25), Job expounds God's sovereign freedom—with his power and wisdom he does whatever he wishes (v.13). Job stresses the negative use God makes of his power.

God tears down what human beings build (v.14), sends drought and flood (v.15), makes fools out of judges (v.17), sends priests and nobles into captivity (vv.18–19), and deprives kings of their reason (v.24).

According to Robertson, 43, Job begins in v.13 to speak tongue-in-cheek. He is criticizing God for not being very wise. A wise man destroys in order to rebuild; but when God destroys, it is impossible to rebuild (v.14). A wise man may use the weather for good, but God "holds back the waters, there is drought; if he lets them loose, they devastate the land" (v.15). Robertson says Job is charging God with mismanaging the universe. Habel, 216, also labels this a satirical hymn that deliberately reverses the wisdom tradition of Proverbs 8:14–16.

The correct interpretation of this section probably lies in a more restrained view of what Job is saying. This may be a mockery of the lopsidedness of Eliphaz's creedal hymn in 5:18–26, where everything good happens to the righteous. It is hardly a parody on God's wisdom since in the introduction to the poem (v.13) Job ascribes wisdom to God in conjunction with his purpose and understanding. In this context Job's problem is with the counselor's wisdom, not God's. He is attempting to answer Zophar's question: "Can you fathom the mysteries of God? ... What can you know?" (11:7–8). He is saying that God's actions are indeed mysterious and strange. Job cannot figure them out, but he knows as much about them as the others.

In other words, Job believes the mystery is profound; and he is amazed that the "sages" would be so shallow (v.12). Job sees God so wise and powerful that he cannot be put in a box. He has sovereign freedom. Job illustrates this by drawing a word picture of the mystery of God's acts in the history of humanity. God humbles great men and nations, showing himself to be the only truly sovereign being (vv.16–25). However, it is also true, as mentioned above, that Job emphasizes the negative use

God makes of his wisdom and power. After all, he feels that God uses them against him with the same destructive consequences.

13:1–27 Job continues to show his irritation at Zophar's remark about his being an inane, witless person (11:12). His friends talk about God—Job maintains he can do that as skillfully as they (v.2). He is confident that given the opportunity, he can prove his case before God, for he knows their accusations are false (v.3). Despite the unfortunate things he has said about God in chapter 9—"He would not give me a hearing" (cf. v.16) but "would ... multiply my wounds for no reason" (v.17), and "he destroys both the blameless and the wicked" (v.22)—Job still hopes all this can be reconciled if only he can argue his case directly with God, though he also thinks he might die in the process (13:15). But his counselors smear him with lies. They are quacks and fake healers who will show their wisdom only if they keep quiet (vv.4–5; cf. Pr 17:28).

Job's argument in vv.6–12 has the following interesting twist. How dare his friends argue God's case deceitfully and use lies to flatter God? Job warns them about lying even while they utter beautiful words in defense of God. If they are going to plead God's case, they had better do it honestly. God will judge them for their deceit even if they use it in his behalf (vv.8–9). This proves what Job believes about God. We know from the Epilogue (42:7) that Job's assessment is right. Job's friends' words about God may be true, but they are worthless because they are empty maxims—mere clichés when applied to him (v.12). Their assessment of Job is wrong. If God would examine their lives, they would not be able to deceive him the way they deceive other humans. For their hypocritical partiality toward God and their dishonest charges against Job, God will surely punish them (vv.10–11).

By contrast, Job is so sure he will be vindicated that he repeats his desire for a hearing before God (vv.13–19). He views this boldness on his part as one of the evidences that what his counselors say about him is not true. If Job were a hypocrite, would he be willing to put his life in jeopardy in this way (v.16)? Such a person would not dare come before God. The much disputed v.15 (see Notes) expresses neither the trusting commitment of 1:21 nor the hopelessness of the NIV margin.

The negative should be maintained in v.15a, but Job is more positive than negative in this context. Even if slain he will not wait (*yāḥal*; NIV, "hope") but will defend his ways before God and is sure God will vindicate him. Although certain that his counselors' charges are false, Job does not claim sinless perfection. He admits the sins of his youth for which he hopes he has been forgiven (v.26). Why, then, does God keep frightening him with his terrors and treating him as an enemy, indeed, as an enslaved prisoner of war whose feet have been branded (v.27)? He sees himself as helpless, as swirling chaff or a wind-blown leaf. If God would only stop tormenting him and communicate, Job feels all will end well.

13:28–14:22 Job's mercurial mood changes again. At the end of chapter 13 he again loses grip on his confidence and regresses to a hopeless feeling. From 13:28 to 14:6 Job muses on human misery and humanity's pathetically brief life, uttering a brief but structured poem (see Notes), a literary device designed to introduce the theme of the plight of the human race. People are impure, so they are worthy of punishment. Job, however, utters a plea that the sovereign God, who gives to each a short span of numbered days, will let his poor creature alone until his hard labor on earth is over. Again we must be reminded that a key factor remains a mystery to Job — the presence and power, albeit limited, of the Accuser, who understandably is not mentioned at all in the Dialogue.

In 14:7–22 Job turns again to death as the only way out of his impasse. A tree may be cut down

and its stump appear to be dead (vv.7–8); yet at the scent of water, it springs to life and sends out new shoots (v.9). Such a phenomenological observation cannot be asserted for human beings. They are more like a lake run dry (vv.10–11). A human being's lifetime runs out and cannot be renewed (v.12). But Job suggests that God could provide a remedy by simply taking his life till his anger is over and then, by resurrection, call him back from Sheol.

Is Job being only hypothetical here while really rejecting all possibility of resurrection? Note his pessimistic assertions in vv.18–22. Critical scholars have held that a doctrine of bodily resurrection did not come into Hebrew theology until Hellenistic times, and even then it was resisted in the wisdom schools. It is sometimes noted that the LXX turns the question in v.14 into an assertion: "If a man dies, he will live again!" This was done despite the clear sign of the question in the Hebrew text.

While it may be true that a fully developed doctrine of resurrection and the afterlife came into Hebrew literature in Hellenistic times and later, Dahood (*Psalms*, 17A:xli–lii) has correctly shown that these concepts were not foreign to preexilic Israel. This chapter proves Job believes in the possibility of resurrection, though he sees humans differently from the tree that can be cut down and be immediately renewed. Humans lie down and will not rise till the heavens are no more (v.12). But the assumption is that humankind will be raised.

Job is not giving a general polemic against resurrection. On the contrary, he is saying that if God wanted to, he could hide Job in Sheol till his anger passes and then raise him (v.13). Job's pessimism arises, not from skepticism about resurrection, but from God's apparent unwillingness to do anything immediately for him. Therefore, his hopes are dashed and his life has become a nightmare of pain and mourning — with nothing to look for but death.

Job knows that eventually God will cover all his offenses and long for him as the beneficent Creator who delights in those he made. But despite his faith in God's power over death, Job is convinced that God will not even allow him the exquisite release of death (cf. Note on 14:14). The waters of suffering will continue to erode till his bright hope is a dim memory (v.19) and nothing matters anymore but the pain of his body and the continual mourning of his soul (v.22).

NOTES

12:2 Job starts out clearly speaking to his friends. אַתֶּם (ʾattem, "you") in the second person plural in vv.2–3, but the second singular appears in v.7. On this basis some have suggested that vv.7–12 are a redactor's insertion, pointing also to the use of יהוה (yhwh, "Yahweh") in v.9. This is the only place it is used in the entire Dialogue. Dhorme notes that some MSS have אֱלוֹהַ (ʾelôah), which he thinks is original, "Yahweh" having come in at an early time because the line is identical to Isaiah 41:20c.

But it is unlikely that vv.7–12 are an addition. Job's words at any point might be directed to what one of the counselors has said. In this case that one is Zophar, the last to speak who has just called Job an "evil" and "deceitful" man (11:11). Job wants Zophar to face the truth that instead of suffering, the wicked often prosper. Appalled at Zophar's lack of wisdom, he utters v.12, which might be translated, "The aged ought to have wisdom and the old understanding."

4 What can וַיַּעֲנֵהוּ (wayyaʿanēhû, "and he answered") mean when one of Job's major complaints has been that God will not even give him a hearing (9:16)? Although this is the Qal stem, hence meaning "answer," the solution may lie in understanding a double entendre. The homonym עָנָה (ʿānâ; GK 6699 and 6700) in the Piel stem means "to answer" or "to afflict." Job has become a laughingstock; the more he calls on God, the more God answers by afflicting him. Another possibility retains the understanding of the verb as coming from "to answer." He may be referring to the time before he was afflicted with suffering. In those days it would have been clear that he was someone who summoned or called on God and that God responded. He responded with a large family and wealth and health. But now such a characterization of Job is a matter of laughter among the friends. Indeed, Job now summons God, but God is silent (9:16, 19). Job is an object of dark humor.

5 For לַפִּיד בּוּז (lappîd bûz, "contempt for misfortune"), the MT reads literally "a contemptible torch belongs to the thought of one at ease." Though Rashi thought this torch (KJV, "lamp") was hellfire, the NIV correctly divides the first word into the preposition *l* ("for") and the word *pîd* ("misfortune"; GK 7085), which makes much better sense.

6 It is not the abrupt shift in number (common in Hebrew) but the use of the relative pronoun ʾašer that leads one to prefer the margin over the text in the NIV for לַאֲשֶׁר הֵבִיא אֱלוֹהַ בְּיָדוֹ (laʾašer hēbîʾ ʾelôah beyādô, "those who carry their god in their hands"). In the NIV text Job is saying that even idolaters who provoke God prosper. In the margin Job complains that God's hand provides security even for sinners who provoke him.

11–12 The NEB makes these two verses a parenthesis with some justification, but there is no justification in the dislocation of v.10. As noted above, Job is chiding his counselors for their lack of wisdom. He is talking about theodicy — a subject difficult only for those who have a sovereign God. Job has spoken honestly about the depths of his dilemma; he is amazed at the shallowness of their thinking and has uttered a hymn (not tongue-in-cheek; see above) in honor of God's sovereign control over all the affairs of human-kind and nations. It is much as though Job were saying, "I cannot understand God's apparent injustice, but I know he is wise and in control."

12 The root יָשֵׁשׁ (yšš, "aged, old") appears in the poetry of Job (15:10; 29:8; 32:6) and in 2 Chronicles 36:17. It does not prove that Job was necessarily written at the time of the Chronicles but is a good example of how a word spanning long centuries of usage may be attested only rarely in the extant literature. The date of Job has to be settled on other grounds. In this verse Job chides his counselors for being elders and yet so lacking in true wisdom. His tone must be caught.

18 The idea of וַיֶּאְסֹר אֵזוֹר (wayyeʾsōr ʾēzôr, "ties a loincloth") is that God frees those shackled by kings and sends kings into captivity.

21 וּמְזִיחַ אֲפִיקִים רִפָּה (ûmezîaḥ ʾapîqîm rippâ, "disarms the mighty") is literally "loosens the belt of." The word for belt (mezîaḥ) is a hapax legomenon as vocalized. Psalm 109:19 clearly limits it to something wrapped around a person. It may be an Egyptian loanword (cf. BDB, 561).

13:2 The second person pronouns in vv.1–12 are plural; e.g., כְּדַעְתְּכֶם (kedaʿtekem, "what you know"). Job is as theologically astute as his counselors are, but he is not satisfied with easy solutions.

11 Andersen, 165, cogently suggests that הֲלֹא (halōʾ, "would not") might be rendered "should not." If Job's counselors had true understanding of who God is, if they were truly wise men, their "fear of the Lord" would prevent them from indulging in such a perilous exercise as mouthing clichés in honor of the God they do not know. See Andersen's comments on Kierkegaard (165, n. 2).

14 Since the LXX does not have the expression עַל־מָה (ʿal-mâ, "why") and in the MT the same letters appear immediately before these (end of v.13), some consider this a scribal repetition or dittography and would translate the verse as a strong assertion: "I will!" But the question fits well with v.16: "Why? Because this could mean deliverance for me."

15 The interpretation of הֵן יִקְטְלֵנִי לֹא אֲיַחֵל (hēn yiqṭelēnî lōʾ ʾayaḥēl, "Though he slay me, yet will I hope in him") has produced considerable disagreement. Much depends on how one understands lōʾ. Most of the Hebrew MS tradition takes it as a negative, which would change the meaning from hope to despair: "Behold he will slay me; I have no hope" (RSV; a translation basically retained in the NRSV). Many other Hebrew MSS, some ancient versions, and the Hebrew oral tradition have לוֹ (lô, "in him"), which is the basis for the NIV (an approach continued by the TNIV). There are a number of ways, however, that one could translate the line positively. For example, Dhorme, Rowley, and Pope translate the verb "tremble, quaver": "I will not quaver." Andersen, 166–67, chooses to render the written tradition as לֻא (lāʾ), a rare assertive particle common in Arabic—"Certainly" (cf. M. Dahood, "Two Pauline Quotations from the Old Testament," CBQ 17 [1955]: 24, n. 23). Other positive renderings are Calvin's making the negative positive as a question: "Shall I not have hope?" The LXX probably read אֵל (ʾl) instead of לֹא (lʾ) and therefore translated it "the Mighty One" (ho dynastēs).

Dahood (Psalms, 16:144) understands the LXX to be the translation of a rare epithet of deity spelled לֵא (lēʾ; common as a description of Baal in Ugaritic), reading, "If the Victor should slay me, I will yet hope." This reading has been seriously questioned by, among others, Clines (Job 1–20, 282). Whatever the reading, the context appears to require a translation that expresses Job's faith, not his doubt. Though Job in other contexts (ch. 9) is troubled about it, here he expresses his conviction that God is just. Since Job is not a hypocrite ("godless man," v.16), if he can only argue his case in God's presence, he will be vindicated (v.18). We of course know from the Prologue that he is right.

17 אֲחַוֶּתִי (ʾaḥₐwātî, "what I say") is a noun with a "prothetic" *aleph* (cf. Note on 37:13).

20 The NIV renders אַךְ־שְׁתַּיִם אַל־תַּעַשׂ עִמָּדִי (ʾak-šᵉttayim ʾal-taʿáś ʿimmādî), "Only grant me these two things, O God." Since the MT is clearly negative ("Do not do to me"; cf. KJV), the NIV had to have a reason to repoint ʾal (negative; GK 440) to ʾēl ("O God"). There is no textual evidence, so the context is the compelling reason. It helps the reader to understand that God is now addressed. But more important, the things requested are positive acts, though the negative aspect of the first may have prompted the MT vocalization that produced the negative particle ʾal.

What are the two things? It is somewhat difficult to determine, but they seem to be, first, for God to withdraw his hand and stop terrifying Job (note the negative aspect). Job asks for deliverance from suffering but nowhere requests restoration to riches. Second, he is more interested in communication with God: "Then summon me and I will answer, or let me speak, and you reply" (v.22). Alternatively, it may be that the first is for God to withdraw his hand and the second to stop terrifying him. Then the result would be more open communication. There is little difference between these two options.

In אָז מִפָּנֶיךָ לֹא אֶסָּתֵר (ʾāz mippāneykā lōʾ ʾessātēr, "then I will not hide from you"), the Niphal ʾessātēr can be passive or reflexive. Andersen, 167, claims it is passive, an expression of Job's fear, and that it should be translated, "then I will not be hidden from your presence" (cf. Ge 4:14). In this context Job is not hiding from God but is seeking God's presence. However, it is more likely that Job is hiding from God until the two conditions he requests are granted. Compare v.24: "Why do you hide your face?"

25 תַּעֲרוֹץ (taʿₐrôṣ, "Will you torment") is open to two possibilities (1) "Do you wish to torment?" or (2) "Will you keep on tormenting?" In Job's mind the rhetorical questions require a negative answer. There is no list of sinful omissions or transgressions that can be brought against him. God should not consider himself Job's enemy, nor should he want to torment Job.

26 The Deity's record book—כִּי־תִכְתֹּב עָלַי מְרֹרוֹת (kî-tiktōb ʿālay mᵉrōrôt, "For you write down bitter things against me")—is an ancient concept well known in OT times (cf. Ex 32:32–33; Ps 69:28).

27 Job sees himself as a prisoner of war with his feet in stocks and branded as a slave, namely, עַל־שָׁרְשֵׁי רַגְלַי תִּתְחַקֶּה (ʿal-šorśê raglay tithₐqqeh, "putting marks on the soles of my feet"). For this practice see Hammurabi's Code (ANET, 176, n. 227), though here the brand is not said to be on the feet). Some (see Clines, *Job 1–20*, 322–23) seriously doubt that incisions on the soles of one's feet would function well as a slave brand. Hartley, 228–29, provides an interesting alternative when he suggests that incisions on the feet would lead to a more personalized footprint, allowing better tracking. The middle of this tricolon ("you keep close watch … ") applies equally to the colon that precedes and the one that follows. There is no dislocation (cf. Pope, 86).

28 It appears that the subject matter of chapter 14 begins here. The NIV assumes ʾādām ("man") in 14:1 is the referent of וְהוּא (wᵉhûʾ, "So he"; NIV, "So man"). Dhorme, Pope, et al. consider the verse misplaced and put it after 14:2.

14:3 The LXX, Vulgate, and Syriac all read וְאֹתִי תָבִיא (wᵉʾōtî tābîʾ, "Will you bring him?"), the antecedent being "such a one." The MT uses the first person. Contextually it makes little difference since in either case it is Job.

4 Gray, Pope, et al. think this verse is also out of place and unbalanced, but Andersen, 170–71, sees the verse as pivotal in this poem (vv.1–6) and therefore important. But I question Andersen's introverted structure (vv.3, 5 going together as do vv.2, 6). In subject matter I see v.2, 5 and v.3, 6 belonging together with v.4 as the apex. The introduction, which establishes the tone of the poem, is formed by 13:28 and 14:1. The poem would read as follows:

Man wastes away like something rotten, like a garment eaten by moths— man born of woman. (13:28–14:1a)	Introduction
Of few days and full of trouble he springs up like a flower and withers away; like a fleeting shadow he does not endure. (14:1b–2)	A
Do you fix your eye on such a one? Will you bring him before you for judgment? (14:3)	B
Who can bring what is pure from the impure? No one! (Or: "The Mighty One alone" [see Blommerde, 69]). (14:4)	Apex
Man's days are determined; you have decreed the number of his months and have set limits he cannot exceed. (14:5)	A'
So look away from him and let him alone, till he has put in his time like a hired hand. (14:6)	B'

6 Though one Hebrew MSS reads as a regular imperative—וַחֲדָל (waḥᵃdāl)—the consonants of 10:20 support the notion that וְיֶחְדָּל (wᵉyeḥdāl) may have an imperative force (so the NIV's "and let him alone").

10 The NIV has rejected the notion that וְאַיּוֹ (wᵉˀayyô) means "and where is he?" (KJV) and has gone with the LXX ("and is no more"). אַי (ˀî) is an old negative as in the name Ichabod ("No-glory," 1Sa 4:21; and Job 22:30, "one who is not innocent").

14 To capture the force of Job's meaning of חֲלִיפָתִי (ḥᵃlîpātî, "my renewal"), we must note that the same root is used in v.7 concerning the tree. There the NIV translated it "sprout." A basic meaning is "to have succession." In this verse Job is speaking of succession after death, not the healing of his body in this life.

It is important to see this verbal tie with v.7 because many commentators think Job has only relief in mind and any thought of life after death is considered impossible by Job. To make this idea clear, Pope, 86, uses the verbal auxiliary "would" instead of "will" in vv.14–17: "I would wait … you would call." The Hebrew text does not require such a rendering (though it is certainly possible), nor is it necessary to assume that Job gives a totally negative answer to his question, "If a man dies, will he live again?" Scholars have assumed this because of their preconceptions about OT theology, which rules out ideas of resurrection in preexilic and early postexilic Israel (cf. W. Kaiser Jr., *Toward an Old Testament Theology* [Grand Rapids: Zondervan, 1978], 99, 181, 249). It is, however, true that more and more evangelical scholars have argued that even if the Old Testament has the knowledge and occasionally the hope of resurrection, Job himself may not have believed it (see, e.g., Wilson, 155).

19 What is וְתִקְוַת אֱנוֹשׁ (*wᵉtiqwat ʾᵉnôš*, "man's hope")? It should be connected with the hope mentioned in v.7 and elaborated in vv.13–17. In vv.18–22 Job feels that the fulfillment of this resurrection hope is so far off ("till the heavens are no more," v.12) that for all practical purposes it offers no solution to his current dilemma. So he suggests that God hide him in the grave temporarily and then resurrect him when his anger subsides (v.13). But he does not believe this will happen; so he falls back to all the empirical evidence that contradicts his hope and thus ends his speech in the slough of despond.

C. The Second Cycle of Speeches (15:1–21:34)

1. Eliphaz (15:1–35)

OVERVIEW

In vv.1–13, Eliphaz plies Job with questions designed to shame him into silence. Most of the speeches start with some form of insult, but Eliphaz surpasses all others with his vitriol and theological flourishes. Verses 14–16 reveal again some interesting architectonics. These verses form an apex about which Eliphaz's words hinge. They derive from his vision in 4:17–19 and here state his thesis: God's holiness versus humanity's corruption. The remaining half of chapter 15 is a dramatic description of the dreadful fate of the wicked.

¹Then Eliphaz the Temanite replied:

²"Would a wise man answer with empty notions
  or fill his belly with the hot east wind?
³Would he argue with useless words,
  with speeches that have no value?
⁴But you even undermine piety
  and hinder devotion to God.
⁵Your sin prompts your mouth;
  you adopt the tongue of the crafty.
⁶Your own mouth condemns you, not mine;
  your own lips testify against you.

⁷"Are you the first man ever born?
  Were you brought forth before the hills?
⁸Do you listen in on God's council?
  Do you limit wisdom to yourself?
⁹What do you know that we do not know?
  What insights do you have that we do not have?

¹⁰The gray-haired and the aged are on our side,
    men even older than your father.
¹¹Are God's consolations not enough for you,
    words spoken gently to you?
¹²Why has your heart carried you away,
    and why do your eyes flash,
¹³so that you vent your rage against God
    and pour out such words from your mouth?

¹⁴"What is man, that he could be pure,
    or one born of woman, that he could be righteous?
¹⁵If God places no trust in his holy ones,
    if even the heavens are not pure in his eyes,
¹⁶how much less man, who is vile and corrupt,
    who drinks up evil like water!

¹⁷"Listen to me and I will explain to you;
    let me tell you what I have seen,
¹⁸what wise men have declared,
    hiding nothing received from their fathers
¹⁹(to whom alone the land was given
    when no alien passed among them):
²⁰All his days the wicked man suffers torment,
    the ruthless through all the years stored up for him.
²¹Terrifying sounds fill his ears;
    when all seems well, marauders attack him.
²²He despairs of escaping the darkness;
    he is marked for the sword.
²³He wanders about—food for vultures;
    he knows the day of darkness is at hand.
²⁴Distress and anguish fill him with terror;
    they overwhelm him, like a king poised to attack,
²⁵because he shakes his fist at God
    and vaunts himself against the Almighty,
²⁶defiantly charging against him
    with a thick, strong shield.

²⁷"Though his face is covered with fat
    and his waist bulges with flesh,

²⁸he will inhabit ruined towns
and houses where no one lives,
houses crumbling to rubble.
²⁹He will no longer be rich and his wealth will not endure,
nor will his possessions spread over the land.
³⁰He will not escape the darkness;
a flame will wither his shoots,
and the breath of God's mouth will carry him away.
³¹Let him not deceive himself by trusting what is worthless,
for he will get nothing in return.
³²Before his time he will be paid in full,
and his branches will not flourish.
³³He will be like a vine stripped of its unripe grapes,
like an olive tree shedding its blossoms.
³⁴For the company of the godless will be barren,
and fire will consume the tents of those who love bribes.
³⁵They conceive trouble and give birth to evil;
their womb fashions deceit."

COMMENTARY

1–6 Eliphaz is angry. He has run out of patience. The time to be polite (4:2) and indirect is over. He considers Job's words not only valueless but also deceitful and irreverent. In his opening lines Eliphaz accuses Job of belching out a hot wind of useless words (vv.2–3). Worse, his mouth spoke as it did because of the sin in his heart (v.5). Job has condemned himself by his ungodly talk. Such irreligion makes him a dangerous person able to lead others astray (v.4).

7–13 Here Eliphaz chides Job for arrogance. Note the questioning format, a motif used most effectively in the divine speeches in chapters 38–41. Is Job wise like the first person ever born (legendary Adam [Eze 28:12–13])? Was he, like Lady Wisdom (Pr 8:22–25), around before the hills? Was Job wise enough to sit in the council of God's angels (vv.7–8)? In reality he was not even wise enough to be in harmony with the elders and wise men on earth (v.10). "God's consolations" (v.11) are the gentle words Eliphaz tries to use with Job (see 4:1–6) only to receive a raging response (vv.12–13).

14–16 Eliphaz repeats the thought that came to him by "revelation" (4:17–19)—that a human being is too vile even to stand before God. That oracle has made a deep impression on the counselor.

17–20 Here Eliphaz bolsters this "revelation" with wisdom that comes from both observation and tradition—the wicked never escape the torment they deserve; and even if they do for a moment, trouble is just around the corner.

21–35 Eliphaz next presents a poetic discourse on the fate of the wicked. To the counselors Job's idea that the wicked prosper is a great heresy. The poem refutes this notion (compare his poem in 4:17–21, in which he describes the righteous man). He refuses to believe that any wicked person prospers, except perhaps for the briefest moment. Eliphaz believes that wicked people always suffer distress and anguish (vv.21–22). They know disaster is stored up for them (v.23). He pictures the wicked man as a quixotic figure who uselessly attacks God with full armor and thick shield (vv.25–26). No doubt it is all a caricature of Job, whose "eyes flash" as he "vents his rage against God" (vv.12–13).

In verses 27–35 the caricature continues with a variety of figures—the fat, rich, wicked man who finally gets what he deserves (vv.27–32). He is like a grapevine stripped before its fruit is ripe or an olive tree shedding its blossoms (v.33). As long as Eliphaz rejects the notion that the wicked prosper and its corollary that the innocent sometimes suffer, he will never have to wrestle over the disturbing mystery of how this fits with the justice of God. Eliphaz views humanity as either all good or all bad. He allows no room for a good man to have doubts and struggles, and those who are bad Eliphaz wants to reduce to zero.

In his query "What is man, that he could be pure?" (vv.14–16), Eliphaz's view of humanity comes through clearly. There is nothing in his words that leads one to the conclusion that God has any love for sinful human beings. Indeed, the deity Eliphaz worships is mechanical; he behaves like the laws of nature, so sinners can expect no mercy. The sinner always gets paid in full—trouble and darkness, terror and distress, the flame and the sword. God will see to it.

In describing such a fate, Eliphaz makes sure that all the things that have happened to Job are included—fire consumes (vv.30, 34; cf. 1:16), marauders attack (v.21; cf. 1:17), possessions are taken away (v.29; cf. 1:17), and houses crumble (v.28; cf. 1:19). Although the modern reader often misses the point that these barbs are all directed at Job, we can be sure that Job himself feels their sting.

NOTES

2 The Piel וִימַלֵּא (wîmalleʾ, "or fill") can also mean "to empty" or "to overflow" (cf. TEV).

4 יִרְאָה (yirʾâ, "piety"; lit., "fear" of God) is the OT term for true religion.

12 The root *rzm* is used only here in יִרְזְמוּן עֵינֶיךָ (yirzᵉmûn ʿêneykā, "your eyes flash"). Tur-Sinai cites an Arabic cognate "become weak, dim" with the meaning, "What has blurred your eyes?" The NIV has chosen to follow Dhorme, 131–32, who sees by metathesis the root *rmz* ("wink" or "flash the eyes"). More recently, Clines (*Job 1–20*, 342), citing L. Grabbe (*Comparative Philology and the Text of Job: A Study of Methodology* [SBLDS 134; Missoula, Mont.: Scholars, 1975], 66–67) agrees with Dhorme by citing via metathesis a postbiblical Hebrew *rmz* as well as the Arabic to gain a meaning of "flash" or "wink."

15 These created heavenly beings—i.e., בִּקְדֹשָׁו (biqdōšāw, "in his holy ones")—were referred to by Eliphaz in 5:1. If holy, why are they not trusted? The basic meaning of the root *qdš* is "to set apart" (the root is even used of temple prostitutes). Not all such beings are good (the Accuser; cf. 2Pe 2:4).

19 Andersen, 177, thinks וְלֹא־עָבַר זָר (wᵉlōʾ-ʿābar zār, "when no alien passed") may be "wisdom that is uncontaminated by foreign influence." That it refers to Israel's inheritance of the land is unlikely since it would be the only reference to Israelite history in Job.

21 קוֹל פְּחָדִים (qôl-pᵉḥādîm, "terrifying sounds") are reports of terrorism such as Job received in chapter 1.

23 The MT vocalization of לְלֶחֶם אַיֵּה (*lallehem ʾayyēh*) is followed in the RSV: "He wanders abroad for bread; saying, 'Where is it?'" The LXX failed to understand the first verb but correctly rendered this line: "He has been appointed food for vultures," seeing the object as ʾayyâ, "a vulture" (GK 370; cf. 28:7 and Introduction).

27–28 Being fat in that world was not objectionable; indeed, it was proof of a person's prosperity. Here Eliphaz is admitting that the wicked do prosper; but as he says in v.29, "His wealth will not endure." Sometimes being fat is an indication of God's blessing (Job 36:16; Pss 36:8; 63:5; 92:12–15), but here and elsewhere it is a sign of the arrogance of the wicked, insofar as their success and prosperity are the result of ill-gotten gain (1Sa 15:22; Pss 17:10; 73:7; Isa 1:11; Jer 5:28).

2. Job's Reply (16:1–17:16)

OVERVIEW

In these chapters we find a direct contradiction of what the counselors have said. Job's thoughts match, by means of contrast, those of Eliphaz in chapter 15; but his opening words are an answer to the opening words of all three (cf. 8:2; 11:2–3; 15:2–6). In 15:12–13, 25–26 Eliphaz accused Job of attacking God, but Job claims the reverse is true: God has assailed him (16:8–9, 12–14). Eliphaz saw all human beings as vile and corrupt in God's eyes (15:14–16); Job believes he has been upright and will be vindicated (16:15–21). Eliphaz thought the words of the wise supported him (15:17–18); Job is convinced that there is not a word of wisdom in what he had to say (17:10–12). Because God has closed their minds to understanding (17:4), they are incapable of doing anything but scold him (16:4–5; 17:2).

¹Then Job replied:

²"I have heard many things like these;
     miserable comforters are you all!
³Will your long-winded speeches never end?
     What ails you that you keep on arguing?
⁴I also could speak like you,
     if you were in my place;
I could make fine speeches against you
     and shake my head at you.
⁵But my mouth would encourage you;
     comfort from my lips would bring you relief.

⁶"Yet if I speak, my pain is not relieved;
     and if I refrain, it does not go away.
⁷Surely, O God, you have worn me out;
     you have devastated my entire household.

⁸You have bound me — and it has become a witness;
　　my gauntness rises up and testifies against me.
⁹God assails me and tears me in his anger
　　and gnashes his teeth at me;
　　my opponent fastens on me his piercing eyes.
¹⁰Men open their mouths to jeer at me;
　　they strike my cheek in scorn
　　and unite together against me.
¹¹God has turned me over to evil men
　　and thrown me into the clutches of the wicked.
¹²All was well with me, but he shattered me;
　　he seized me by the neck and crushed me.
He has made me his target;
　　¹³his archers surround me.
Without pity, he pierces my kidneys
　　and spills my gall on the ground.
¹⁴Again and again he bursts upon me;
　　he rushes at me like a warrior.

¹⁵"I have sewed sackcloth over my skin
　　and buried my brow in the dust.
¹⁶My face is red with weeping,
　　deep shadows ring my eyes;
¹⁷yet my hands have been free of violence
　　and my prayer is pure.

¹⁸"O earth, do not cover my blood;
　　may my cry never be laid to rest!
¹⁹Even now my witness is in heaven;
　　my advocate is on high.
²⁰My intercessor is my friend
　　as my eyes pour out tears to God;
²¹on behalf of a man he pleads with God
　　as a man pleads for his friend.

²²"Only a few years will pass
　　before I go on the journey of no return.
^{17:1}My spirit is broken,
　　my days are cut short,
　　the grave awaits me.

²Surely mockers surround me;
  my eyes must dwell on their hostility.

³"Give me, O God, the pledge you demand.
  Who else will put up security for me?
⁴You have closed their minds to understanding;
  therefore you will not let them triumph.
⁵If a man denounces his friends for reward,
  the eyes of his children will fail.

⁶"God has made me a byword to everyone,
  a man in whose face people spit.
⁷My eyes have grown dim with grief;
  my whole frame is but a shadow.
⁸Upright men are appalled at this;
  the innocent are aroused against the ungodly.
⁹Nevertheless, the righteous will hold to their ways,
  and those with clean hands will grow stronger.

¹⁰"But come on, all of you, try again!
  I will not find a wise man among you.
¹¹My days have passed, my plans are shattered,
  and so are the desires of my heart.
¹²These men turn night into day;
  in the face of darkness they say, 'Light is near.'
¹³If the only home I hope for is the grave,
  if I spread out my bed in darkness,
¹⁴if I say to corruption, 'You are my father,'
  and to the worm, 'My mother' or 'My sister,'
¹⁵where then is my hope?
  Who can see any hope for me?
¹⁶Will it go down to the gates of death ?
  Will we descend together into the dust?"

COMMENTARY

16:1–5 Job, with purpose, chooses a word (ʿāmāl) Eliphaz used to suggest Job had conceived his own misery ("trouble," 15:35); and he throws it back at him in the epithet "miserable [or 'trouble-some'] comforters" (v.2). He affirms how he would give real encouragement to them if the tables were turned, but all he has gotten are arguments and scoldings (vv.3–5).

The opening words of chapter 16 are full of meaning for all who aspire to counsel others. It is a powerful negative example. The counselors have become gadflies pestering Job, who is certain that they have no understanding of his real problem. Of course, it is easy to say what one would do if the situation were reversed. From what we know about Job, he may be deceiving himself since he does buy into their retribution theology.

6–14 In v.6 Job turns again to the enemy — the god his mind has created — the one who has worn him out and torn him in his anger. He views himself as one whom God has seized by the scruff of the neck and thrown into the clutches of the wicked (v.11). God has made Job his target, an object of attack; like a warrior he has pierced him without pity.

This figure has no doubt been suggested by Eliphaz's description of the wicked man (meaning Job) who shakes his fist at God, defiantly attacking the Almighty (15:25–26). Job sees it as just the reverse of that in vv.12–14. Job recognizes that God can do whatever he wishes. But Job is anguished by the thought that God acts like his enemy. So Job and Eliphaz are polarized in their respective views. Is God attacking Job, or is Job attacking God?

In v.7, because of a sudden shift in Hebrew to third person singular, the NIV has inserted the word "God" and changed the third person to the second person: "you have worn me out." It is possible, but less likely, that the Hebrew third singular refers back to the pain in v.6: "surely now it [my pain] has worn me out." In either case, there is no question in Job's mind that God has sent the pain — "you have devastated my entire household" (v.7).

A similar problem exists in v.8, where the antecedent in the clause "and it has become a witness" is Job's condition. So in vv.6–8 Job says it does not make any difference whether he speaks or does not speak — his pain is still there. It has worn him out

and has become the major witness against him, for on it his detractors have based their arguments. To them it is proof of his sinfulness. As though that were not bad enough, he thinks God has assailed him, crushed him, and turned him over to his detractors (vv.9–14).

15–17 Here we see a pathetic figure in sackcloth, sitting with brow in the dust, eyes sunken and face bloated with tears, avowing innocence. From this sad figure arises a baneful cry, but one that has not totally lost hope, as vv.18–21 show.

16:18–17:2 Job 16:18, 22, and 17:1 indicate that Job thinks he will die before he can be vindicated before his peers; so he is concerned that the injustice done to him should never be forgotten. That is what he means when he calls on the earth never to cover his blood or bury his cry (v.18). In Genesis 4:10–11 Abel's innocent blood was crying out to God as a witness against Cain. So Job is consoled to think his cry will continue after his death. And there is one in heaven who will listen to it (vv.19–21). He firmly believes that he has a friend, an advocate, an intercessor on high who will plead his cause. Those who say (e.g., Andersen, Dhorme) this is God himself must deal with v.21 — "he pleads with God."

There are indications, however, that Job considers this advocate to be greater than a human being. He is in heaven (v.19). In 9:33 the Arbitrator was a mere wish but was described as one who could put his hand on both God and Job. In 19:25 the Vindicator who lives must also be a heavenly figure since Job makes a special point of how he will eventually stand on the earth (dust). We must be careful how we apply all this as predictive. Certainly God has given Job this hope in the midst of his darkest hours to point to the one who will ultimately fulfill it. But Job probably understands only a limited part of its fullest meaning (contrary to Kaiser [*Messiah in the Old Testament*, 61–64; see comment on 9:25–35], who stretches the biblical material way too far).

Having a heavenly advocate is not a novel thought in that society, as may be inferred from 5:1 and 33:23, though it is clear that Job's hope for such a mediator is never realized in the book.

3–5 What pledge or guarantee is Job asking for? The translation of v.3 is difficult. The following paraphrase (cf. Notes) may help clarify the meaning: "Give attention (O God) to becoming my guarantor (that I am right) with you, / for who else will shake my hand to prove it?" If God puts up such a guarantee for Job, it will not only silence his mockers (the counselors, v.2) but will prove they are guilty of false accusation and deserve the sanctions and punishment they have implied Job deserves. Verse 5 is a proverb. Job is reminding his counselors of the dire consequences of slander.

6–9 Unfortunately such a guarantee from God is not evident. On the contrary, Job sees God as the one who has made him suffer humiliation (v.6). There are few who believe he is innocent. Most people think they are doing God a favor by spitting in Job's face. At least that is how Job feels.

But in vv.8–9 Job is saying that truly good men can pity him in his suffering without turning away from what is right. This is what his counselors cannot understand. To them every pain has a sin behind it, and God cannot be doing this to Job unless he deserves it. Another interpretation of vv.8–9 is that Job is being sarcastic, saying, as it were, "You upright men are appalled at this." He has already accused them of having contempt for sufferers like him (12:5).

10 Job is outraged at his friends' attitude, which he considers completely devoid of wisdom. He taunts them to come back and have another go at him. The verse lends added weight to the interpretation of vv.8–9 as sarcasm.

11–16 The counselors have said that night will be turned to day for Job if only he would get right with God (cf. 11:17). In vv.12–16 Job makes a parody of their advice. It is like going to the grave with the notion that all you have to do is treat it like home where warmth and loved ones are and it will become so. No, Job's fondest desires have been shattered (v.11); he has no hope but death. He closes this section as he opened it, with the despair of the grave (16:22–17:2). This despair is not quite as reprehensible as is their faulty advice.

NOTES

16:6 מַה (*mah*) may be negative as in the NIV ("not"; cf. Arabic and 1Ki 12:16), or it may mean "how much" (Isa 21:11).

7 הֶלְאָנִי (*helʾānî*; NIV, "you have worn me out") is third masculine singular perfect—"he (it) has made me weak." The reason the NIV has made it conform to the second half of the verse, which is clearly second person, is because such a shift in Hebrew is not unusual. But the subject could possibly, but not very likely, be his pain already mentioned in v.6.

כָּל־עֲדָתִי (*kol-ʿădātî*, "my entire household") means literally "all my company" or "all my assembly," and the concept is difficult to fit into this context.

9–11 These verses are impassioned Semitic hyperbole. Job views God as a beast of prey. He "assails" or possibly "sniffs out" (cf. שָׂטַם [*śāṭam*] in Ge 27:41; 49:23; 50:15; Job 30:21). It does not mean "hate" (KJV) or "hold a grudge" (BDB, s.v.; see T. L. Fenton, "Ugaritica-Biblica" [*UF* 1 [1969]: 65–66). And he "tears" (טָרַף, *ṭārap*) his victim. In 10:16 Job said, "You stalk me like a lion."

9 צָרִי (ṣārî, "my opponent"; GK 7640) is too mild for these blazing verses. Job looks on God as his enemy. In 13:24 and 19:11, Job thinks God considers him an enemy. In 13:24 the synonym אוֹיֵב (ʾôyēb, "enemy") is used, but in 19:11 the word is the same as here. Job never pictures himself as fighting God (v.17a), but as a pitiful victim (vv.12–14), even an innocent one (v.17b).

17 The preposition עַל (ʿal, "yet") is a shortened form of עַל אֲשֶׁר (ʿal-ʾašer, "although").

20 מְלִיצַי רֵעָי (mᵉlîṣay rēʿāy, "my intercessor is my friend"), as it is vocalized in the MT, may be read, "the ones deriding me [are] my friends." This would be based on a Hiphil participle of the root lîṣ ("to deride, scorn"). But in 33:23 and Isaiah 43:27 the word mēlîṣ (GK 4885)) means "an intermediary between God and man," a meaning that fits this context well. In several other passages it simply means "an interpreter or ambassador" (Ge 42:23; 2Ch 32:31). Other suggestions based on this meaning are "the interpreter of my thoughts" (cf. רֵעִי [rēʿî, "my thoughts"], Ps 139:2; BDB, 946) or "my cries [from רוּעַ (rûaʿ, 'cry out')] intercede for me." The latter carries on the thought of v.18, but v.21 goes on to describe a personal function of this one as an "intercessor" with God. So the NIV is justified in its choice of possible meanings.

In the light of v.21, one can hardly agree with Dhorme, 239, that the witness is God himself. The concept here should be tied to the גֹּאֵל (gōʾēl, "redeemer") of 19:25 and then probably to the מוֹכִיחַ (môkîaḥ, "advocate") of 9:33. Here is Job's answer to Eliphaz's taunt in 5:1: "To which of the holy ones will you turn?" Job believes there is a holy one he can turn to as his Intercessor.

22 The NIV has left a space to show that this verse goes better with chapter 17, leaving v.21 as a climax.

17:1 נִזְעָכוּ (nizʿākû, "are cut short") is used only here, but some MSS use the Aramaic spelling that comes from the root דָּעַךְ (dāʿak, "to extinguish"; see use of this verbal root in 18:5–6.).

The Hebrew reads "graves [קְבָרִים (qᵉbārîm)] (belong) to me." The grave is conceived as a dwelling place here (cf. Ps 49:11). The word is plural with singular meaning because of a peculiar grammatical feature that used this plural form for dwellings (cf. Pope, 384).

2 וּבְהַמְּרוֹתָם (ûbᵉhammᵉrôtām, "on their hostility") may not be about mockers and hostility but a continuation of Job's preoccupation with his impending death (see Clines, *Job 1–20*, 372–73). For slightly different approaches see Pope, 128, and Dahood (*Psalms*, 16:278–79).

3 The NIV's rendering of שִׂימָה־נָּא עָרְבֵנִי עִמָּךְ (śîmâ-nāʾ ʿārbēnî ʿimmāk, "Give me, O God, the pledge you demand") is somewhat paraphrastic and difficult to understand. Some vocalize ʿārbēnî as ʿērbōnî and read, "Put my pledge beside you" (Dhorme, 239), in which case Job is offering a pledge to God and in the next line is asking God for a mutual pledge (Pope, 128). But as the MT stands, it can be translated: "Consider [this, O God; see Note on this idiom on 4:20]; become my guarantee [go surely for me] with yourself. For who else is there that is prepared to strike [shake] my hand?" For handshaking as a way to ratify a pledge, see Proverbs 6:1; 17:18; 22:26.

4 Unless one changes the vowels or adds a מ (m), לֹא תְרֹמֵם (lōʾ tᵉrōmēm, "you will not let them triumph") does not include the pronoun "them." The text can be understood by seeing the prefix *t* as an indication of the third masculine plural as in Psalm 106:38 (wattehᵉnap) and Psalm 68:3 (tindōp). In Ugaritic the prefix *t* is so used (*UT*, 9.14). The JB has caught the sense by vocalizing it as passive: "and not a hand is lifted." Quite literally the text reads, "that is why they do not do anything [rise up to help]." For this use of רוּם (rûm), see Genesis 41:44.

5 יַגִּיד (*yaggîd*, "denounces"), a common word normally meaning "declare," clearly means "denounce" or "inform on" in Jeremiah 20:10.

12 יָשִׂימוּ (*yāśîmû*, "These men turn") could be the same idiom noticed above in v.3 (cf. Notes on 4:20). The verb *śîm* means "put (to heart)" or "consider" (suppressing the word *lēb*, "heart"). The idiom applies to both sides of the parallelism—"they think light is near"; so there is no need to supply the words "they say."

14 The NIV has followed the way the LXX translates לְשַׁחַת (*laššaḥat*, "to corruption") in Psalm 16:10. Here the LXX uses "death" but there "corruption." The NT interpretation of the psalm (cf. Ac 2:31–32) hangs on that meaning instead of the usual "pit." N. J. Tromp (*Primitive Conceptions of Death and the Netherworld in the Old Testament* [Rome: Pontifical Biblical Institute, 1969], 69ff.) has drawn on evidence from Ugarit and Qumran to support this meaning.

16 The NIV has seen fit to make the figure בַּדֵּי שְׁאֹל (*baddê šᵉʾōl*, "to the gates of death") more direct. The Hebrew has "the bars of Sheol." The figure (synecdoche) here uses the part (the bars) for the whole (the gates).

3. Bildad (18:1–21)

OVERVIEW

Following the pattern of Eliphaz and Zophar, only Bildad's opening lines are directly concerned with Job (cf. 15:2–3 and 20:2–5 with vv.2–4 here). In the rest of the speech, with typical redundant and discursive rhetoric, he launches into a poem on the fate of the wicked. In this chapter he makes no attempt to admonish Job as he did in 8:5–7, 20–22. The same is true of the words of Eliphaz and Zophar in chapters 15 and 20. The dispute intensifies (cf. 22:2–5), giving additional evidence of the planned structure of the Dialogue. For further observations on this compositional make-up and disputational form of the friends' speeches, see Westermann, 17–30.

¹Then Bildad the Shuhite replied:

²"When will you end these speeches?
    Be sensible, and then we can talk.
³Why are we regarded as cattle
    and considered stupid in your sight?
⁴You who tear yourself to pieces in your anger,
    is the earth to be abandoned for your sake?
    Or must the rocks be moved from their place?

⁵"The lamp of the wicked is snuffed out;
    the flame of his fire stops burning.
⁶The light in his tent becomes dark;
    the lamp beside him goes out.

⁷The vigor of his step is weakened;
    his own schemes throw him down.
⁸His feet thrust him into a net
    and he wanders into its mesh.
⁹A trap seizes him by the heel;
    a snare holds him fast.
¹⁰A noose is hidden for him on the ground;
    a trap lies in his path.
¹¹Terrors startle him on every side
    and dog his every step.
¹²Calamity is hungry for him;
    disaster is ready for him when he falls.
¹³It eats away parts of his skin;
    death's firstborn devours his limbs.
¹⁴He is torn from the security of his tent
    and marched off to the king of terrors.
¹⁵Fire resides in his tent;
    burning sulfur is scattered over his dwelling.
¹⁶His roots dry up below
    and his branches wither above.
¹⁷The memory of him perishes from the earth;
    he has no name in the land.
¹⁸He is driven from light into darkness
    and is banished from the world.
¹⁹He has no offspring or descendants among his people,
    no survivor where once he lived.
²⁰Men of the west are appalled at his fate;
    men of the east are seized with horror.
²¹Surely such is the dwelling of an evil man;
    such is the place of one who knows not God."

COMMENTARY

1–4 Bildad considers Job beside himself, a man no longer acting fully responsible (v.2; see Note for a slightly different interpretation). He resents Job's attitude toward them as belittling and accuses Job of being irrationally self-centered. The world is going to remain the same no matter how much Job rants against the order of things (v.4; for the second colon compare the image found at 14:18).

5–21 Bildad feels Job does not really understand the doctrine of retribution. He probably considers

Job weak on this subject because Job keeps harping on how the righteous suffer and the wicked prosper. In these speeches Job and his friends have nothing to say about future retribution at the day of final judgment or the balancing of the scales of justice after death. This is a truth that unveils gradually (progressive revelation) in the OT.

For example, in Psalm 73 the psalmist struggles like Job. He says, "For I envied the arrogant when I saw the prosperity of the wicked" (73:3). But through revelation the psalmist comes to understand their "final destiny" (73:16–17). Some dispute whether he means this life or the next, but the psalmist's triumph of faith in 73:23–28 sounds like a hope that transcends life itself.

Bildad's concern, however, is to establish in Job's mind the absolute certainty that every wicked person gets paid in full, in this life, for his or her wicked deeds. He says nothing of a final judgment but is sure the lamp of the wicked will be snuffed out (vv.5–6). As their step weakens (v.7), they are trapped and devoured (vv.8–10). "Terrors startle him on every side and dog his every step" (v.11). Death is part of the punishment, not a dividing line after which punishment comes. The only after-death retribution for Bildad is having one's memory (name) cut off, with no offspring or survivors. The only memory of the wicked, according to Bildad, will be the horrific fate that does them in (v.20).

Death is personified in vv.13–14. This king of terrors reminds us of the Canaanite deity Mot (Death), whose gullet reaches from earth to sky — the devouring deity (cf. *ANET*, 138). Isaiah reverses the figure and sees the Lord (Yahweh) swallowing up death forever (Isa 25:8; cf. 1Co 15:54). Bildad summarizes his speech with a confident affirmation that he has certainly described the fate of the wicked (v.21).

NOTES

2–3 The NIV (KJV) follows the LXX and 11QtgJob reading קֵץ (*qēṣ*, "end") as in 16:3 and 28:3. As spelled in the MT, קִנְצֵי (*qinṣê*, "end") is used only here. BDB, 890, suggests it means "a hunter's snare." So Gordis (*Job*, 190) translates: "How long will you go hunting for words?" W. Gesenius may have been right in viewing it as an Aramaic spelling of the word meaning "end" (BDB, 890). The next word, מִלִּין (*millîn*, "speeches"), is a clear Aramaism.

Notice the KJV's "ye (make an end)." Throughout vv.2–3 the Hebrew uses the second masculine plural. The text quickly shifts to the singular from v.4 on. Since the plural is repeated (both verb and pronoun), it is not a copyist's error. Dhorme, 239, thinks Bildad is addressing the audience that prevents him from speaking. But there is no evidence of this. Perhaps Bildad chooses to categorize Job as one of the problem people ("you people") who make life difficult by being unreasonable.

The NIV renders *tābînû* as "Be sensible," but it could be rendered "Reflect" (see NAB and NJB, "Think"). If so, then Bildad is accusing Job of speaking before he thinks — an error that Proverbs (15:28; 18:13; 29:20) warns against.

12 The jussive form of the verb (*yᵉhî*) in יְהִי־רָעֵב אֹנוֹ (*yᵉhî-rāʿēb ʾōnô*, "calamity is hungry for him") must be translated indicative. As *tertia*-weak, this verb would have originally ended in a diphthong (*yihyāy*). This vestige of the original dialect represents a contraction of the diphthong without the element *eh* common to the later spelling in Judah. The MT regularly treats a dangling consonantal *yod* by vocalizing it as í. Compare 20:23 and 24:14 for similar spelling. Although *ʾōnô* is open to several possibilities (Dhorme, "wealth"; Gordis, *Job*, 191–92, "child"), NIV takes it as parallel with אֵיד (*ʾēd*, "disaster"), though limited OT usage does not employ these words in parallel elsewhere. Dahood (*Psalms*, 16:237) sees here אָנָה (*ʾānâ*, "to meet"). This provides the meaning, "Famine has become (and continues to be) his partner." This provides a good parallel with the other half: "disaster is stationed at his side [lit., 'at his rib']." On the other hand, the MT takes it as the same word translated "vigor" in v.7, thus producing a translation like that found in the NRSV: "Their strength is consumed by hunger."

14 Justification for וְתַצְעָדֵהוּ (*wᵉtāṣʿidēhû*) to be translated "and marched off" depends on understanding the verb as a rare third person masculine plural imperfect with prefix *t* (cf. Blommerde, 15–16, 84–85). Other examples are found in 19:15 and Psalms 68:3; 106:38. The indefinite plural subject ("they march him off") is logically equivalent to a third masculine singular passive ("he is marched off").

15 The NIV has chosen to vocalize מִבְּלִי־לוֹ (*mibbᵉlî-lô*, "fire … ") as *mabbēl* + *l*, in which case the last letter introduces the second colon as emphatic *l* (*lamed*). The MT has preserved the consonants of a rare word meaning "fire." The root appears in both Akkadian and Ugaritic but nowhere else in the OT. This identification is now widely accepted (cf. BHS mg.) but was seen first by M. Dahood ("Some Northwest Semitic Words in Job," *Bib* 38 [1947]: 312–14). It has been accepted by Clines (*Job 1–20*, 407) and the REB. The parallelism with גָפְרִית (*goprît*, "burning sulfur") is compelling. The passage is also an example of how the LXX (and Theodotian) can completely misunderstand the Hebrew but still be a good witness to the original consonants (*en nukti autou* = *bᵉlîlô*, "in his night").

4. Job's Reply (19:1–29)

OVERVIEW

The chapter divides into four logical stanzas. In the first Job shows increasing irritation over his counselors' shameless attacks and his impatience with their superior claims (vv.2–5). Then follows Job's feeling of abandonment by God and perception that God's attack on him is wrong (vv.6–12). Then he blames God for alienating his kinsmen and household, even his wife (vv.13–20). In vv.21–27 he ends this lament, to our amazement, with a triumphant expression of faith in the one who will ultimately champion his cause and vindicate him (vv.23–27). This stanza is bracketed by words to his friends, who Job does not believe will ever have pity (v.21). So he warns them of the dire consequences of their false accusations (vv.28–29).

¹Then Job replied:

²"How long will you torment me
and crush me with words?

³Ten times now you have reproached me;
   shamelessly you attack me.
⁴If it is true that I have gone astray,
   my error remains my concern alone.
⁵If indeed you would exalt yourselves above me
   and use my humiliation against me,
⁶then know that God has wronged me
   and drawn his net around me.

⁷"Though I cry, 'I've been wronged!' I get no response;
   though I call for help, there is no justice.
⁸He has blocked my way so I cannot pass;
   he has shrouded my paths in darkness.
⁹He has stripped me of my honor
   and removed the crown from my head.
¹⁰He tears me down on every side till I am gone;
   he uproots my hope like a tree.
¹¹His anger burns against me;
   he counts me among his enemies.
¹²His troops advance in force;
   they build a siege ramp against me
   and encamp around my tent.

¹³"He has alienated my brothers from me;
   my acquaintances are completely estranged from me.
¹⁴My kinsmen have gone away;
   my friends have forgotten me.
¹⁵My guests and my maidservants count me a stranger;
   they look upon me as an alien.
¹⁶I summon my servant, but he does not answer,
   though I beg him with my own mouth.
¹⁷My breath is offensive to my wife;
   I am loathsome to my own brothers.
¹⁸Even the little boys scorn me;
   when I appear, they ridicule me.
¹⁹All my intimate friends detest me;
   those I love have turned against me.
²⁰I am nothing but skin and bones;
   I have escaped with only the skin of my teeth.

²¹"Have pity on me, my friends, have pity,
    for the hand of God has struck me.
²²Why do you pursue me as God does?
    Will you never get enough of my flesh?

²³"Oh, that my words were recorded,
    that they were written on a scroll,
²⁴that they were inscribed with an iron tool on lead,
    or engraved in rock forever!
²⁵I know that my Redeemer lives,
    and that in the end he will stand upon the earth.
²⁶And after my skin has been destroyed,
    yet in my flesh I will see God;
²⁷I myself will see him
    with my own eyes — I, and not another.
    How my heart yearns within me!

²⁸"If you say, 'How we will hound him,
    since the root of the trouble lies in him,'
²⁹you should fear the sword yourselves;
    for wrath will bring punishment by the sword,
    and then you will know that there is judgment.'"

COMMENTARY

1–5 Verse 4b literally reads "my error lives [remains] with me." Job implies his friends have no right to interfere, no right to behave as though they were God (cf. v.22).

By an unusual handling of v.6, Andersen, 191, claims Job is not accusing God of injustice but of no-justice (v.7b). This would be attractive if there were not so many other places where Job makes the same charge. Notice the following:

He mocks the despair of the innocent …
    if it is not he, then who is it? (9:23–24)
You must search out my faults …
    though you know that I am not guilty. (10:6–7)

God has turned me over to evil men
    … shattered me
    … crushed me….
Without pity, he pierces my kidneys. (16:11–13)

In the light of these lines, it is easy to render 19:6 "God has wronged me." These are the very thoughts that elicited Bildad's retort, "Does God pervert justice?" (8:3), and later Elihu's words, "It is unthinkable that God would do wrong, that the Almighty would pervert justice" (34:12). The only way to handle Job's words in 19:6 is along the lines already suggested, that it is Job's faulty perception or, better, his lack of full perception. The exasperated Job perceives things in this way. He does not know God's plan (42:2). But even without heavenly knowledge, Job's perception is better than Bildad's, who also lacks the heavenly knowledge that it is God who is permitting the Accuser to strike Job.

In a sense the Accuser is acting as the hand of God, for he said to God, "But stretch out your hand and strike his flesh" (2:5). And God replied, "Very well, then, he is in your hands" (2:6). So Job is not totally wrong when he says, "The hand of God has struck me" (19:21). Bildad with his truncated theological formula cannot begin to appreciate Job's predicament. And because he has reduced God and his actions to an impersonal formula, Bildad is incapable of showing any mercy toward Job.

6–12 In Job's mind God is at war with him. God's troops lay siege as though Job were a fortified city; but, alas, he is only a tent. In a series of largely military images the tension of Job's lament rises with each succeeding verse; but with poetic license the chronological sequence is in reverse of the way it really happened. In v.8 his paths (a metaphor for life's journey, well known from Proverbs) are blocked or walled up, that is, he is in captivity (cf. 3:23; 13:27). In v.9 he suffers royal dethronement — stripped of his honor and crown as a defeated king (see his words in 29:14, where Job claims righteousness and justice as his robe and turban). In v.10 he is torn down (like a wall) and uprooted (like a tree, more drastic than the figure in 14:7). Finally in vv.11–12 God's troops advance and build a siege ramp against him. Reverse this order and you have a step-by-step description of what happened in siege warfare. Job's perspective is not too far wrong. Perhaps it feels as if a whole army had been sent against him, but in reality God did send one of his soldiers against him (see the Accuser in chs. 1 and 2).

13–19 Leaving this compelling figure, Job speaks quite literally of how his family and friends have turned against him (vv.13–17). In any society

nothing hurts more than rejection by one's family and friends, but what could be worse in a patriarchal society than to have children ridicule the patriarch (v.18)? The point of this section is that Job has no one to support him. The only ones near him are his three "friends," who do not help but harrrass.

20 What does escaping with only the skin of one's teeth mean? The NIV takes this to mean that only Job's gums are left unaffected by his ailment. Since the word "only" must be inserted to get this meaning, many are not satisfied with it. The line is difficult. The KJV made a literal translation of it and thereby created an idiom in the English language for a narrow escape ("by the skin of my teeth"). But is Job talking about a narrow escape here?

Commentators list many attempts to find a suitable meaning for the line (see Rowley, 170). Rowley himself offers no solution but suggests Job is saying his disease has reduced him to a shadow of his former self and that he has barely survived at all. G. R. Driver ("Problems in the Hebrew Text of Job," in *Wisdom in Israel and the Ancient Near East* [eds. M. Noth and D. W. Thomas; Leiden: Brill, 1960], 80) offers some cogent lexical and grammatical reasons for rendering the line, "I gnaw myself on (the) skin (with) my teeth," like an unnerved person may gnaw at his lips.

Too often 19:21–29 has been isolated from what Job has said earlier. Job has stressed a number of themes that to a degree find their resolve here. Despite this resolve the dissonance of the dialogue continues after this; but Job's bitterness toward God, if not his puzzlement over what God is doing, is washed away as a result of the faith and hope expressed here.

Up to this point Job has come to the conclusion that he will soon die (10:20; 16:22–17:1). His experience has created in him a sense of amoral chaos in the world and in his life. His sense of being crushed causes him to look repeatedly toward death as a kind of hopeless release (14:18–22; 16:11–16).

He knows he is innocent and seeks above all else to be vindicated. His compassionless counselors have reiterated their impersonal theology that declares him guilty. He feels as if God is angry with him and has become the enemy who has attacked and crushed him. He perceives that he is alone in a cruel and amoral world. There is no one left who understands, no one to plead his cause or bear witness to his innocence. And this is what he wants most of all—not release, not retribution, but only justice, someone to vindicate him.

In two earlier chapters (chs. 9 and 16), where Job expressed deep bitterness toward God, he also touched on this same "Advocate" theme. In chapter 9 it was only a desire—"If only there were someone to arbitrate between us" (9:33). But in chapters 16 and 19 it becomes a firm conviction—"my witness is in heaven" (16:19) and "I know that my Redeemer lives" (19:25). As in 13:15, here in chapter 19 this hope extends to include Job himself as a participant in the process of vindication—"I myself will see him with my own eyes" (v.27; see Notes).

21 Deserted by loved ones Job needs radical friendship, not theological banter. This is not the first time Job has called for pity (cf. 6:14). It is necessary to feel with Job his sense of total desertion if we are to understand the passage. It is within this context that he turns to God in vv.25–26.

22 Job's appeal has failed. He thinks his counselors have joined forces with God as "the hound of heaven" to sniff him out and to be in on the kill (cf. 16:9). Although Job's perception of God may have been wrong (not understanding the role of the Accuser), his perception of them is correct. They have presumed to take on themselves the role of divine judicial authority, as is evident in Eliphaz's remark in 15:11a, where he assumed his words were God's words. As part of the "Chase" metaphor in v.22b, Job includes a typical Semitic idiom for slander—they devour his flesh.

23–24 These words arise from Job's desire to defend his integrity. Believing that he is at the point of death, Job feels he has nothing to lose by speaking out (7:7–11; 10:1; 13:3, 13–28; 16:18). But they are also a direct response to Bildad's taunt in 18:17 suggesting Job would be permanently forgotten. Both men were fully aware of Wisdom teachings such as Proverbs 10:7: "The memory of the righteous will be a blessing, but the name of the wicked will rot."

With no hope left of proving his righteousness, Job looks to the future, leaving his case with posterity (Ps 102:18). His wish to inscribe his words (v.24) is uttered with poetic expansiveness that contemplates several possible ways—in a scroll (copper? see Dhorme) or on a rock. Whether the lead is to be used on the rock or is another medium is not clear. Permanency is the issue—inscribed forever. These verses also underline just how important Job considers the following statement in vv.25–27.

25–27 Are these the only words Job wants inscribed, or does he mean all his words where he has over and over proclaimed his innocence? The conjunction that begins v.25 (not reflected in the NIV) may be the adversative "But." This would mean Job is leaving the thought of inscribing his words permanently to the even more favorable situation of having a living Redeemer (Vindicator) who will champion his cause even after he is gone (v.26). Job's hope in the midst of despair reaches a climax. Slandered by his friends and with death imminent, Job looks to the future where his Defender waits.

This time the Defender sounds like God himself, for there is no mention of his pleading with God (as in 16:21). But is it God? This is difficult to determine from the immediate context. The larger context (i.e., chs. 9 and 16), where the same third-party theme appears, lends weight to the notion that that theme finds its climax here. I have noted that the theme was already ancient in Job's day.

In pagan theology a personal patron deity acted as a champion for an individual human, pleading that person's cause in the council of the gods. In the book of Job the angels perform this role. In 33:23 Elihu clearly presents this theology of angels that takes the place of the pagan servant-deities. He employs the very root (*mlṣ*) used in 16:20 to describe Job's "Intercessor." In each of these Advocate passages, the third party is greater than a mortal; and in chapter 16 he lives in heaven. Yet he is fully capable of taking his stand to testify on earth (19:25). It is even possible, though not necessary, that Job uses the word "lives" (*ḥāy*) in its extended meaning "lives forever" (cf. Dahood, *Psalms*, 16:91; R. B. Y. Scott, *Proverbs and Ecclesiastes* [AB; vol. 18; Garden City, N.Y.: Doubleday, 1965], 91), just as he wishes his words will be inscribed forever (v.24).

The meaning of the word *gōʾēl* ("redeemer"; GK 1457) is fundamental to understanding this passage. The word is important in OT jurisprudence. It has both a criminal and a civil aspect. As "blood avenger," a *gōʾēl* had a responsibility to avenge the blood of a slain kinsman (Nu 35:12–28). He was not seeking revenge but justice. On the civil side he was a redeemer or vindicator. Here he had the responsibility to "buy back" and so redeem the lost inheritance of a deceased relative. This might come by purchasing from slavery or marrying the decedent's widow in order to provide an heir. As such he was the defender or champion of the oppressed (as in the book of Ruth). See Proverbs 23:10–11, where God is the Defender (*gōʾēl*) of oppressed individuals. In the exodus and the exile he is the *gōʾēl* of his oppressed nation (Ex 6:6; Isa 43:1). The Lord also as *gōʾēl* delivers individuals from death (Ps 103:4).

Here Job has something more in mind than one who will testify to his integrity. In 16:18 he cried, "O earth, do not cover my blood." Job saw himself a murder victim. He depends on his *gōʾēl* to testify for him but also to set the books straight. God who has become his enemy will become his friend, and those who have joined in the kill will be punished (vv.28–29).

In Hebrew the emphatic position of the pronoun "I" in v.25a shows Job has a settled conviction: "I, yes I know." The words "my Redeemer [Vindicator]" indicate a personal relationship, and the word "lives" must mean more than merely "alive" but implies he will continue his work of vindicating Job's integrity and avenging Job's death, as Job implied in vv.28–29.

In v.25b the Hebrew word *ʾaḥᵃrôn* ("in the end"; GK 340) does not have a preposition, though the NIV translation is permissible, being understood as an adverb meaning "afterward." Another possibility is to take it as a substantive referring to the Redeemer as "the Last." According to A. Schoors ("Literary Phrases," in Fisher, 1:12), the term is juridicial and refers to the one who has the last word at a trial. Dhorme, 239, recalls such passages as Isaiah 44:6 and 48:12, where God is called "the first and the last"; but the term never stands alone as an epithet of deity. It may be best to see it as an adjective "as the one coming after (me)." Job thinks his vindication will come after his death. The Hebrew alone in v.25b is not clear enough for us to determine whether Job is speaking of the end of his life or the end of the world. But since the latter concept is not mentioned elsewhere in the book of Job, the former is a safer interpretation.

Similarly, at the end of v.25, does "upon the dust" mean "upon the earth" (NIV) or does it refer to Job's grave (NIV mg.)? The term refers to the grave in 7:21; 17:16; 20:11; 21:26 and in Psalm 22:29 and Isaiah 26:19; but it can mean "the earth" as in Job 41:33. So Job could mean merely that the human arena here on earth is where his Vindicator will testify; but since the context is about Job's decaying body, it may be a specific reference to his grave.

Do the two succeeding verses, then, refer to Job's resurrection? In 14:10–14 Job says nothing about general eschatological resurrection; but there he believed in God's power to raise the dead and had a desire and hope that God will set a time and raise him. So here in chapter 19 we may see a similar resurrection in which Job will see God with his own eyes and as his friend. While he is anticipating the doctrine of resurrection, he is not spelling out the teaching of a final resurrection for all the righteous.

Verse 26a is a most difficult line. Literally it reads "after my skin they have struck off—this!" The general meaning alludes to the ravages of Job's disease, but the precise meaning is variously interpreted. Habel's understanding (216) of the line is appealing. He considers v.26a to be a continuation of the thought in v.25 and the word "after" (*ʾaḥar*) to be explanatory of the preceding "afterward" (*ʾaḥᵃrôn*; NIV, "in the end"), reading: "After, that is, my skin is peeled off!" This, then, emphasizes Job's confidence that even after he dies, his "redeemer" will arise to testify in his behalf. Dogmatism should be avoided and the precise meaning here perhaps held in abeyance (cf. Notes).

Verse 26b is clearer: Job expects to see God. Two verbs meaning "see" are used here and in v.27. The debate centers on whether it is "in the flesh" or

"apart from the flesh" that Job will have this experience. The Hebrew can go either way (cf. Notes); but since Job speaks of using his own eyes, and in the light of what has been said about Job's view of possible resurrection, the NIV's "in the flesh" is preferred. So Job is convinced that even if he dies, he will live again to witness his own vindication.

At the end of chapter 16 Job was obsessed with the notion that someone in heaven would stand up for him and plead his case. But here in chapter 19 he expects to witness his own vindication on earth. Indeed his own eyes will gaze on his Vindicator.

As it turns out, Job does not need the intermediary (*mēlîṣ*; GK 4885) mentioned in chapter 16 because his idea that God is against him proves to be without foundation. The lesson that suffering does not show that God is alienated is one of the most enduring themes in the book. Job's feelings of alienation and the condemnation by his friends produce in him a consequent feeling of need for a Redeemer (Vindicator), which is strongly evocative of sinful humanity's basic need before a holy God (cf. 1Ti 2:5–6). But in Job's case, as an innocent sufferer he finally realizes that God himself will appear to him and that he will see God with his own eyes (cf. 19:27 with 42:5); then Job will learn that his God is not alienated or unconcerned but is both his Vindicator (*gōʾēl*) and his friend.

NOTES

2 The alternation between the Hebrew plural with *mem* (ten times) and the Aramaic plural with *nun* (thirteen times) does not follow a particular speaker (in 26:4 Job used *n* [*nun*]).

מִלָּה (*millâ*, "word") is so common in Aramaic that its usage in Hebrew tends to be Aramaized.

11 For כְּצָרָיו (*kᵉṣārāyw*, "among his enemies") the RSV has "as his adversary," based on the Vulgate. The plural in the MT shows this to be dative rather than accusative, literally, "as (one) of his enemies."

15 In three places the second or third feminine plural with pronoun is vocalized as second masculine (Jer 2:19; SS 1:6; and here). The original vocalization of תַּחְשְׁבֻנִי (*taḥšᵉbunî*, "you count me") was probably *taḥšᵉbānnî* ("[my maidservants] count me"). Moreover, the poetic balance also favors taking "my guests" with the preceding line rather than following the Masoretic punctuation as does the NIV. The masculine plural pronoun at the end of the verse includes everyone from v.13 on.

17 לִבְנֵי בִטְנִי (libnê biṭnî, "to my own brothers") is literally "to the sons of my belly." What does it mean? The RSV and NIV take the belly to be his mother's. The fact that Job's sons were killed may simply mean these were the children of concubines, but not all agree. See Dhorme, 277–78, for a detailed discussion. He extends the meaning to include relatives.

18 The idiom וַיְדַבְּרוּ־בִי (wayᵉdabbᵉrû-bî, "they ridicule me") in Psalm 78:19 must mean "speak against." This weakens the case of those who see here an old meaning of a similar root evidenced in the Tell Amarna glosses. That meaning is "to flee" (G. R. Driver, "Hebrew Notes," *ZAW* 52 [1934]: 55–56). It was used widely in Old Babylonian and understood in the West. Since culturally it is more likely children would flee from rather than ridicule a sick patriarch, the case still has some merit.

22 In וּמִבְּשָׂרִי (ûmibbᵉśārî, "of my flesh"), the *min* clearly shows its overlapping quality with the preposition בְ (b, "with, in, from").

25 In Isaiah 44:6 the prophet speaks of God as the Redeemer or Vindicator (גֹּאֵל, gōʾēl), and in Isaiah 48:12 God calls himself "the first" (רִאשׁוֹן, riʾšôn) and "the last" (אַחֲרוֹן, ʾaḥᵃrôn; GK 340). Dhorme and Rowley see a similar meaning for (וְאַחֲרוֹן) (wᵉʾaḥᵃrôn) in v.25: "As the Last (One) upon the earth (dust) he shall stand (rise)." That the term does not stand alone as an epithet of deity should not rule against seeing God as the one who will have the last word in Job's trial. The NIV adds a preposition to capture an adverbial force since ʾaḥᵃrôn can mean "afterward," but the eschatological tone "in the end" is questionable.

As mentioned above, it is best to see ʾaḥᵃrôn as an adjective (BDB, 30, b), "as one coming after (me)." This fits the NIV margin where עַל־עָפָר (ʿal-ʿāpār) is rendered "upon my grave." The missing pronoun î ("my") may be due to haplography with the first letter י (y, yod) of the next word יָקוּם (yāqûm, "he will stand") or a case of single writing of a consonant where the morphology requires two (cf. Dahood, *Psalms*, 17A:371). Job has repeatedly lamented the fact that death is near (7:21b; 10:8–9; 14:10–12; 16:22–17:1).

26 וּמִבְּשָׂרִי (ûmibbᵉśārî, "yet in my flesh") is identical to the form in v.22, but here the meaning of the preposition is much more difficult. In its text and margin, the NIV has given the two major possibilities. They are opposite in meaning. The margin "apart from my flesh" (i.e., in the disembodied state) is at best a rare concept in the OT. In the next verse Job asserts he will see God with his own eyes (v.27). The preposition refers to the viewer's vantage point: "from (within) my flesh I shall see God."

27 In וְלֹא־זָר (wᵉlōʾ-zār, "and not another"), we may take zār ("stranger") as a genitive referring back to the "eyes," namely, "and not [the eyes] of a stranger." Equally defensible is the meaning "and not [as] a stranger." The latter expresses Job's desire for a friendly relationship with God.

28 The LXX, Theodotian, the Vulgate, and many Hebrew MSS take בִי (bî, "in me") as third masculine— בוֹ (bô, NIV, "in him"), which is another example of the confusion between the ו (w, waw) and י (y, yod) in the square script. In this case the context demands the third masculine meaning.

29 שַׁדִּין (šaddyyn, "judgment"), a *hapax legomenon* (note also it is a *Qere-Kethiv*) may be simply a variant of the divine epithet Shaddai. (For full treatment of this view, see L. R. Fisher, "sdyn in Job 19:29," *VT* 2 [1961]: 342–43). Most relate it to the noun דִּין (dîn, "judgment"), following the interpretation of Aquila, Symmachus, and Theodotian, and understand the שׁ (š) as the relative še (BDB, 979). But this use of še does not appear in Job. The LXX and the Hebrew oral tradition indicate ancient uncertainty, but Shaddai does appear in 29:5. The NIV margin is to be preferred.

5. Zophar (20:1–29)

OVERVIEW

This entire chapter is another poem on the ghastly fate of the wicked (see Bildad's words in 8:11–19 and in ch. 18, and Eliphaz's in 15:20–35). The poem must be read with full attention given to the use of figurative language, parallelism, and strophic structure, all basic elements of Hebrew poetry. Despite the error of Zophar's application, the poem itself ought to be appreciated as a masterly piece of literature.

We should also try to appreciate the elements of truth contained herein. As Gordis (*God and Man*, 90) notes, Zophar is "performing a vital task ... defending man's faith in a moral universe, a world governed by the principle of justice, which was not merely a deep desire of the human soul but an indispensable instrument of social control." It is unfortunate that one able to make such an eloquent statement of this truth should fail so miserably in properly applying it.

¹Then Zophar the Naamathite replied:

²"My troubled thoughts prompt me to answer
    because I am greatly disturbed.
³I hear a rebuke that dishonors me,
    and my understanding inspires me to reply.

⁴"Surely you know how it has been from of old,
    ever since man was placed on the earth,
⁵that the mirth of the wicked is brief,
    the joy of the godless lasts but a moment.
⁶Though his pride reaches to the heavens
    and his head touches the clouds,
⁷he will perish forever, like his own dung;
    those who have seen him will say, 'Where is he?'
⁸Like a dream he flies away, no more to be found,
    banished like a vision of the night.
⁹The eye that saw him will not see him again;
    his place will look on him no more.
¹⁰His children must make amends to the poor;
    his own hands must give back his wealth.
¹¹The youthful vigor that fills his bones
    will lie with him in the dust.

¹²"Though evil is sweet in his mouth
    and he hides it under his tongue,

¹³though he cannot bear to let it go
    and keeps it in his mouth,
¹⁴yet his food will turn sour in his stomach;
    it will become the venom of serpents within him.
¹⁵He will spit out the riches he swallowed;
    God will make his stomach vomit them up.
¹⁶He will suck the poison of serpents;
    the fangs of an adder will kill him.
¹⁷He will not enjoy the streams,
    the rivers flowing with honey and cream.
¹⁸What he toiled for he must give back uneaten;
    he will not enjoy the profit from his trading.
¹⁹For he has oppressed the poor and left them destitute;
    he has seized houses he did not build.

²⁰"Surely he will have no respite from his craving;
    he cannot save himself by his treasure.
²¹Nothing is left for him to devour;
    his prosperity will not endure.
²²In the midst of his plenty, distress will overtake him;
    the full force of misery will come upon him.
²³When he has filled his belly,
    God will vent his burning anger against him
    and rain down his blows upon him.
²⁴Though he flees from an iron weapon,
    a bronze-tipped arrow pierces him.
²⁵He pulls it out of his back,
    the gleaming point out of his liver.
Terrors will come over him;
    ²⁶total darkness lies in wait for his treasures.
A fire unfanned will consume him
    and devour what is left in his tent.
²⁷The heavens will expose his guilt;
    the earth will rise up against him.
²⁸A flood will carry off his house,
    rushing waters on the day of God's wrath.
²⁹Such is the fate God allots the wicked,
    the heritage appointed for them by God."

COMMENTARY

1–3 Zophar takes Job's words, especially his closing words in 19:28–29, as a personal affront. Job has dared to assert that on Zophar's theory of retribution, Zophar himself is due for punishment. To Zophar such can only happen to the wicked.

Zophar is the most emotional of the three friends; and he is not about to let Job's rebuke go unanswered, though in chapter 19 Job earnestly pleaded for a withdrawal of their charges. Here he has nothing new to say to Job but speaks with passion. The speech is full of terrifying imagery.

4–11 Zophar cannot abide the thought that the wicked prosper (cf. 9:22; 12:5–6). Beneath the words lies the comfortable fact that he is a healthy and prosperous man, which, in his view, is itself proof of his goodness and righteousness. To him the joy and vigor of the wicked will always be brief and like a fantasy (cf. Ps 73:19–20; Pr 11:4, 18; 21:6; 22:16).

Oppressing the poor is the mark of the truly wicked (vv.10, 19). On this subject Job has no quarrel with Zophar (see 31:16–23). But, of course, he denies being that kind of person.

12–19 The evil man's wicked deeds, especially robbing the poor, are tasty food that pleases his palate but turns sour in his stomach. God will force him to vomit up such ill-gained riches. Zophar's teaching conforms to Proverbs' point that the wealth of fools will not last, and even while they have wealth, it will not help, but even hurt them (Pr 11:4; 21:6). In v.19 Zophar claims that fools get rich off the backs of the poor, a practice condemned by Proverbs (Pr 28:27; 29:7). In his peroration (chs. 29–31) Job will stress his own social conscience and strongly deny Zophar's veiled accusation.

20–28 When a wicked man's belly is filled and there is nothing left for him to devour, God then vents his anger against him (vv.20–21). The man flees from an iron weapon only to be shot in the back by a glittering bronze arrow that must be pulled out of his liver (vv.24–25). Such attention to figurative detail is often overlooked as meaningless. On the contrary, the more eloquently it could be said, the more an ancient speaker was able to convey how deeply he felt and how sincerely he was trying to make his point.

But Zophar, despite his eloquence and sincerity, has no compassion. He leaves no room for repentance and puts all his stress on the importance of material possessions, while Job at this point is increasingly concerned over his relationship with God, no matter what happens to his body or possessions (19:23–27).

29 Like Bildad in 18:21, Zophar concludes his speech with a summary statement in which he claims all he has said is in accord with God's judicial order for the wicked.

NOTES

2 On חוּשִׁי (ḥûšî, "greatly disturbed"), see BDB (ḥûš II, 301–2).

3 The second colon may be translated "a spirit beyond my understanding gives me a reply." In other words, Zophar may not be appealing to his own understanding providing him inspiration, but something beyond him (presumably from the divine realm) is leading him to his conclusion (similar to Eliphaz's point in 4:12–17).

10 On יְרַצּוּ (yᵉraṣṣû, "must make amends"; GK 8355), compare 14:6. Contrary to its usual meaning, Dhorme, 277–78, has shown that the Piel form of this root means "to satisfy, pay off a debt," though in its usual meaning it could indicate that the wicked's children will "run after" the poor, either in the sense that they will run with them or will run after them to get something from them. In any case, the condition of their children will be unfortunate.

17 The deletion of נַהֲרֵי (nahᵃrê, "the rivers") or the addition of the word for "oil" is suggested by those who feel the first line in Hebrew is too short (cf. Pope). There is no textual evidence to help, so any corruption of the text was very early. Such unbalanced poetic lines do not always call for emendation. If one counts syllables, there are other unbalanced lines in the poem (vv.1, 16, 29). But the grammar is also difficult, if not impossible, which prompts BHS to call for the deletion of this word. A more satisfactory explanation comes from an understanding of paleography, that is, the early shape of the square letters נ (n, nun) and צ (ṣ, tsade). The error in our text could have come from the loss of a short diagonal stroke that changed the tsade to a nun (the additional vowel ending being secondary). For the basic root ṣhr meaning "fresh oil," see the denominative verb in 24:11. I render the text, "He will not enjoy the streams of oil, nor the rivers of honey and cream." This solves the problem of both balance and grammar.

19 There is a question whether בַּיִת (bayit, "houses") refers to "houses he did not build," or "houses he cannot rebuild," or "domains on which he cannot build a house." Andersen, 196, suggests the meaning is the last.

20 From לֹא יְמַלֵּט (lōʾ yᵉmalleṭ) the NIV gets "save himself" from comparing Amos 2:15. Here napšô ("himself") is suppressed.

23 On יְהִי (yᵉhî, "When he has"), compare the Notes on 18:12 and on 24:14. As in 18:12, here yᵉhî (jussive) really represents the indicative yihy(eh).

With some revocalizing and a different division of the letters, some scholars read בַּלְחוּמוֹ (bilḥûmô, "with his blows") either as mabbul ḥammô ("a flood of his wrath") or mabbēl ḥammô ("the fire of his wrath"; cf. BHS). The NIV derives this from the root lḥm, meaning "to fight" (cf. Pss 35:1; 56:2 [3], or as a noun in Jdg 5:8). It might also mean "with his flame" (Dt 32:24; NIV, "consuming") or even "into his intestines" (cf. the first line and Zep 1:17) or, with Arabic, "into his flesh" (see Dhorme); but KJV's "while he is eating" and RSV's "as his food" should be ruled out.

24 קֶשֶׁת נְחוּשָׁה (qešet nᵉḥûšâ, "a bronze-tipped arrow") literally reads "a bow of bronze." The NIV is not wrong, however, for no bows were made of bronze. It means either a bow that shoots arrows "tipped" with bronze or capable of piercing bronze targets (ANET, 244).

26 "A fire unfanned" does not sound very hot, but the point is a fire that needs no fanning by people to make it hot, which may be lightning.

6. Job's Reply (21:1–34)

OVERVIEW

In this closing speech of the second cycle, Job is determined to prove that he has listened to what his counselors have said. This he does by quoting or otherwise alluding to their words and then refuting them. Compare 20:11 with 21:7, 18:19 with 21:8, 18:5 with 21:17, 5:4 and 20:10 with 21:19.

¹Then Job replied:

²"Listen carefully to my words;
　　let this be the consolation you give me.
³Bear with me while I speak,
　　and after I have spoken, mock on.

⁴"Is my complaint directed to man?
　　Why should I not be impatient?
⁵Look at me and be astonished;
　　clap your hand over your mouth.
⁶When I think about this, I am terrified;
　　trembling seizes my body.
⁷Why do the wicked live on,
　　growing old and increasing in power?
⁸They see their children established around them,
　　their offspring before their eyes.
⁹Their homes are safe and free from fear;
　　the rod of God is not upon them.
¹⁰Their bulls never fail to breed;
　　their cows calve and do not miscarry.
¹¹They send forth their children as a flock;
　　their little ones dance about.
¹²They sing to the music of tambourine and harp;
　　they make merry to the sound of the flute.
¹³They spend their years in prosperity
　　and go down to the grave in peace.
¹⁴Yet they say to God, 'Leave us alone!
　　We have no desire to know your ways.
¹⁵Who is the Almighty, that we should serve him?
　　What would we gain by praying to him?'
¹⁶But their prosperity is not in their own hands,
　　so I stand aloof from the counsel of the wicked.

¹⁷"Yet how often is the lamp of the wicked snuffed out?
　　How often does calamity come upon them,
　　the fate God allots in his anger?
¹⁸How often are they like straw before the wind,
　　like chaff swept away by a gale?
¹⁹It is said, 'God stores up a man's punishment for his sons.'
　　Let him repay the man himself, so that he will know it!

²⁰Let his own eyes see his destruction;
  let him drink of the wrath of the Almighty.
²¹For what does he care about the family he leaves behind
  when his allotted months come to an end?

²²"Can anyone teach knowledge to God,
  since he judges even the highest?
²³One man dies in full vigor,
  completely secure and at ease,
²⁴his body well nourished,
  his bones rich with marrow.
²⁵Another man dies in bitterness of soul,
  never having enjoyed anything good.
²⁶Side by side they lie in the dust,
  and worms cover them both.

²⁷"I know full well what you are thinking,
  the schemes by which you would wrong me.
²⁸You say, 'Where now is the great man's house,
  the tents where wicked men lived?'
²⁹Have you never questioned those who travel?
  Have you paid no regard to their accounts—
³⁰that the evil man is spared from the day of calamity,
  that he is delivered from the day of wrath?
³¹Who denounces his conduct to his face?
  Who repays him for what he has done?
³²He is carried to the grave,
  and watch is kept over his tomb.
³³The soil in the valley is sweet to him;
  all men follow after him,
  and a countless throng goes before him.

³⁴"So how can you console me with your nonsense?
  Nothing is left of your answers but falsehood!"

COMMENTARY

1−3 If the counselors can give Job no other consolation, they should at least pay close attention to his words. They seem not to be listening to him since they keep repeating the same arguments in spite of his speeches. This is particularly the case with their statements about the fate of the wicked. Job will take on that subject again in this speech.

4-6 Job is appalled at the counselors' failure to have any compassion (v.5); but if his complaint were only against them (humans), his bitterness would not be justified. His rage is based on the idea that God may be responsible. Job is terrified either because he knows how awesome a task it is to complain against God or at the mere thought of the injustice implied by the prosperity of the wicked (v.6). Yet in all honesty, he can find no other way out of his predicament.

The scriptural lesson in these hard words can be understood only when we place them in their canonical context. God would rather have us complain than be indifferent toward him or handle his truths arrogantly and so reduce them to dead maxims. Job's anguish over not understanding what God has been doing is proof that Job is not indifferent or arrogant. It is the counselors who assume they know what is going on.

7-15 The counselors have elaborated the horrible fate of the wicked (15:20-35; 18:5-21) against Job's claim that the wicked often prosper. Those who wish to know nothing of God's ways, who even consider prayer a useless exercise (vv.14-15), flourish in all aspects of their lives. Far from dying prematurely, as Zophar said in 20:11, they live long and increase in strength (v.7). Job flatly denies (v.8) Bildad's claim that the wicked have no offspring or descendants to remember them (18:19-21). Job paints a word picture in vv.7-13 illustrating the domestic pleasantness and prosperity often enjoyed by godless people who dare to defy the Almighty (v.15). They even go peacefully to their grave (v.13), a fact that also irritated the Teacher (Ecc 8:10).

16 This verse as translated is difficult to understand. The NIV has not caught fully the correct interpretation. The way Eliphaz uses these words in 22:17-18 helps interpret Job's words (see Notes). Job knows God controls the prosperity of the wicked, and that is what makes it an enigma when the "counsel of the wicked" is so far from God (cf. Ps 1:1). "Why *do* the wicked live on ... and increase in power?" (v.7, emphasis mine).

17-21 Job alludes directly to Bildad's words in 18:5, with the retort "How often ... ?" (v.17). And if children have to pay for their father's sins, as Eliphaz (5:4) and Zophar (20:10) have said, then the wicked are encouraged to say, "What do we care?" (v.21). Job is disturbed at the apparent injustice of it all (cf. the Teacher in Ecc 8:11).

As noted earlier, the book of Job does not deal with the matter of final future judgment that will set right the tables of justice. Such revelation will come later. Job, therefore, feels that immediate punishment for the wicked would be the only just procedure; but he finds just the opposite in life. Again, failure to understand fully God's ways has led both Job and the counselors astray; but Job does not pretend to understand, and they do. Moreover, Job is suffering physically and emotionally, and they are not.

22-26 Job admits that his knowledge of God's ways is defective (v.22), but it is precisely his high view of God that has created a problem. Those who do not believe in an absolutely sovereign God cannot possibly appreciate the depth of the problem Job presents in vv.23-26. The answer still eludes us. Even with all our additional revelation (Ro 8:28), we often stand in anguish over the apparent injustice and seeming cruelty of God's providence.

27-33 Job realizes his counselors are going to repeat the same worn-out clichés that imply he is a wicked man. They have repeatedly suggested the destruction of his house as proof of it (cf. 8:15; 15:34; 18:15, 21). He calls these clichés schemes by which they wrong him (v.27). He challenges them to investigate the total experience of people throughout the world to determine whether he is right (v.29).

Job is saying that it is impossible to derive a just law of retribution from what we observe in this present world. His friends' simplistic view is wrong, claims Job, for all too often there is no one to denounce the wicked for what he has done, and there is no one to punish him (v.31, NEB; see Notes). Contrary to the description of the wicked in chapters 8 and 20, the ungodly man is often buried with the highest honors (vv.32–33). The Teacher in Ecclesiastes also questioned the justice in the honored burial of the wicked (8:10).

34 Job opened this discourse with a plea for a kind of consolation based on his counselors' quiet listening. He closes by returning to that thought with a blast at what they have offered as consolation, their answers riddled with falsehood and nonsense.

NOTES

3 תַּלְעִיג (talʿîg, "mock on") in the Hiphil probably has an elative meaning here, that is, not a little but increased mocking. The shift between singular and plural in Hebrew is merely a stylistic matter.

8 For לִפְנֵיהֶם (lipnêhem, "they see"), BHS wrongly suggests a deletion. It is tempting to repoint עִמָּם (ʿimmām, "around them") to ʿammān ("their kinsmen and their offspring"), but neither the Masoretes nor the LXX understood it this way. The NIV is on the right track even if a little loose. The Hebrew is asyndetic: "established before them, [even] around them."

13 יְבַלּוּ (yᵉballû, "they spend") is a good example of where the written (Qere) and oral (Kethiv) traditions diverge, each preserving a word with a different basic meaning: בָּלָה (bālâ, "wear out, use to full") versus כָּלָה (kālâ, "complete"). In this context the meanings converge, so either is possible.

The context witnesses against the common meaning for בְרֶגַע (bᵉregaʿ) as "in an instant" (NIV mg.). The NIV ("in peace") has followed the rarer meaning, usually in the Hiphil, "to be at rest." See Psalm 35:20 for the adjective with this meaning.

16 The words of this verse are easy to understand, and most translations have rendered them rather literally; but the problem lies with the strange result. Some attach it to what follows (RV). The latter inserts the words "ye say," as most translations do, for v.19 to solve the problem of Job's apparent agreement with the counselors in the middle of a speech in which he was so heartily in disagreement. Rashi took v.16a as a question, while Ibn Ezra felt the context was served better by a statement that implied God must be held responsible for allowing the wicked to prosper. There is no reason to question whether v.16b should be taken as Job's repudiation of all the words of the wicked recorded in vv.14–15.

It helps to compare 22:17–18 with 21:14–16. In chapter 22 Eliphaz uses Job's words to his own advantage. So Eliphaz's words are a commentary on these. Job is saying, "Look, the prosperity of the wicked is from God despite the fact that their counsel is far from him." While in 22:18a Eliphaz is using only the substage of Job's words, he clarifies the meaning of 21:16a. The words of 22:18b are identical with 21:16b. The relationship between the "a" and "b" clauses in both passages is concessive and refers to the distance between God and the wicked, not Job and the wicked. This implies reading מֶנִּי (mennî, "from me") as מֶנּוּ (mennû, "from him") or accepting a third singular pronominal suffix written with yod (9:19, 35 [note]; 14:3; 19:28; 21:16; 22:18). Compare Blommerde, 92–93, who interprets בְיָדָם (bᵉyādām) as "from his hand." This may be possible but is not necessary.

17 Whether כַּמָּה (*kammâ*, "yet how often") is an interrogative or exclamatory "how" cannot be determined from the Hebrew. See the NIV margin on vv.17–20. If it is exclamatory, we must assume Job is being ironic, as in 26:2–3, and has already begun to quote his friends (cf. the clarifying "it is said" in v.19). It is easier to take vv.17 and 18 as questions, if we realize that Job still has the words of Bildad in 18:5 in mind.

19 The corner brackets indicate that "⌞It is said⌟" is not in the Hebrew. But it clarifies the meaning. See Gordis on "The Use of Quotations in Job" (*God and Man*, 169–89). An alternative explanation is to understand the colon as a question: "Does God store up guilt for their children?" Job would then be responding to the view that even though the wicked don't suffer, their children will. He believes this would be quite unfair. The wicked should be punished and know they are being punished for their sin.

24 עֲטִינָיו (*ʿaṭînāyw*, "his body") is used only here. The NIV has loosely followed the ancient versions that rendered this word "thigh." The word חָלָב (*ḥālāb*, "milk") is taken as *ḥeleb* ("fat")—hence the RSV's "his body is full of fat." In Rabbinic Hebrew, *ʿaṭîn* probably means "a pail" or "bucket." But "his pails are full of milk" (BDB, 742) is contextually a problem.

25 Scholarly opinion (Driver and Gray, Dhorme) now sees the preposition בְּ (*b*) on בַּטּוֹבָה (*bāṭṭôbâ*, "anything good") as partitive, hence "anything." This fits the overlapping of the prepositions *b* and *min* as I have noted earlier (e.g., "from").

30 The problem with לְיוֹם אֵיד (*leyôm ʾêd*, "from the day of calamity") stems from the meaning given to the preposition לְ (*l*) and the verb יוּבָלוּ (*yûbālû*, "he is delivered") in v.30b. Because of the demands of the context, the NIV has chosen rare meanings for each. The margin—"man is reserved for the day of calamity, / that he is brought forth to"—is the more normal usage. Some feel the normal meaning fits Job's thesis in the sense that the wicked escape disaster during their lifetime even though they may have to face it after death. Gordis (*Job*, 234–35) solves the problem by considering the line a quotation of the friends' opinion. But if Pope, 128, and others are correct in giving the meaning "from" to the *l*, the problem dissolves.

34 The NIV translates מָעַל (*māʿal*) as "falsehood," a possible rendering; but the word more likely signifies "faithlessness" or "disloyalty." The three friends have shown themselves to be disloyal to Job by attacking him rather than consoling him.

D. The Third Cycle of Speeches (22:1–26:14)

1. Eliphaz (22:1–30)

OVERVIEW

Eliphaz, the least vindictive, is provoked to agree with his friends that Job has been a very wicked man (vv.4–5). He does not even attempt to answer Job's shocking statements in chapter 21 but moves on to accuse Job of various social sins (vv.6–11) and of failing to appreciate the wonderful attributes of God, especially God's omniscience (vv.13–14) and his justice, goodness, and mercy (vv.16–18). All Eliphaz feels he can do for Job is to make a final plea that he repent (vv.21–30).

¹Then Eliphaz the Temanite replied:

²"Can a man be of benefit to God?
　　Can even a wise man benefit him?
³What pleasure would it give the Almighty if you were righteous?
　　What would he gain if your ways were blameless?

⁴"Is it for your piety that he rebukes you
　　and brings charges against you?
⁵Is not your wickedness great?
　　Are not your sins endless?
⁶You demanded security from your brothers for no reason;
　　you stripped men of their clothing, leaving them naked.
⁷You gave no water to the weary
　　and you withheld food from the hungry,
⁸though you were a powerful man, owning land—
　　an honored man, living on it.
⁹And you sent widows away empty-handed
　　and broke the strength of the fatherless.
¹⁰That is why snares are all around you,
　　why sudden peril terrifies you,
¹¹why it is so dark you cannot see,
　　and why a flood of water covers you.

¹²"Is not God in the heights of heaven?
　　And see how lofty are the highest stars!
¹³Yet you say, 'What does God know?
　　Does he judge through such darkness?
¹⁴Thick clouds veil him, so he does not see us
　　as he goes about in the vaulted heavens.'
¹⁵Will you keep to the old path
　　that evil men have trod?
¹⁶They were carried off before their time,
　　their foundations washed away by a flood.
¹⁷They said to God, 'Leave us alone!
　　What can the Almighty do to us?'
¹⁸Yet it was he who filled their houses with good things,
　　so I stand aloof from the counsel of the wicked.

¹⁹"The righteous see their ruin and rejoice;
　　the innocent mock them, saying,

20'Surely our foes are destroyed,
    and fire devours their wealth.'

21"Submit to God and be at peace with him;
    in this way prosperity will come to you.
22Accept instruction from his mouth
    and lay up his words in your heart.
23If you return to the Almighty, you will be restored:
    If you remove wickedness far from your tent
24and assign your nuggets to the dust,
    your gold of Ophir to the rocks in the ravines,
25then the Almighty will be your gold,
    the choicest silver for you.
26Surely then you will find delight in the Almighty
    and will lift up your face to God.
27You will pray to him, and he will hear you,
    and you will fulfill your vows.
28What you decide on will be done,
    and light will shine on your ways.
29When men are brought low and you say, 'Lift them up!'
    then he will save the downcast.
30He will deliver even one who is not innocent,
    who will be delivered through the cleanness of your hands."

COMMENTARY

1–3 What is Eliphaz's argument here (cf. Elihu in 35:7)? Is it that God could have no ulterior motive in dealing with Job, since there is nothing Job could do to benefit God (Pope)? That may be part of it. But Eliphaz is here reacting to Job's notion that God allows human wickedness to go unpunished (ch. 21), and in his reactionary mood he goes to the opposite extreme by suggesting there is nothing human beings can do to benefit God. It is the now-familiar unbalanced stress on divine transcendence: the concept that people are nothing in God's eyes, that even their virtue is use-

less. God does not need people; it is people who need God. Since everything has its origin in God, mortals' giving it back — even in service — does not enhance God in any way.

Verse 3 carries the thought a step further. A translation that fits well into the context might be: "Would it please the Almighty if you were vindicated? / Would he gain anything if you did live a blameless life?" Two observations are in order. First, Eliphaz does not know of God's contest with the Accuser over Job's former, blameless life. The Almighty has especially chosen Job to be an instrument through whom he will gain glory and the Accuser be humiliated. Second, Eliphaz seems so convinced of Job's wickedness—even to the point of exaggeration (v.5)—that he does not believe Job can be vindicated. So in his mind Job's blamelessness is hypothetical nonsense. For Job to be vindicated would be a lie; so how could God take pleasure in that?

4–11 Verse 4 is pure irony. In 4:6 Eliphaz had been sincere about Job's piety, but here he speaks of it tongue-in-cheek. He no longer believes Job is basically a God-fearing man. Job's troubles are God's rebuke. That they are great testifies to the extent of his sin. So Eliphaz feels free, perhaps obligated, to expound the possible nature of those sins (vv.5–9).

Job's sins are described in terms of social oppression and neglect. In other words, Eliphaz feels that Job has deceived himself by trusting in his ritual piety (what he had done for God), while his real sin is what he has failed to do for his other people. For this God has sent snares and peril, darkness and floods (vv.10–11). These are not literal but commonly used figures of trouble and distress in the OT (cf. Pss 42:7; 91:3–6; Isa 8:7, 22; 43:2). That these charges are not true and that Job's suffering is not a result of such sins is clear. In chapter 31 Job himself recounts his past in such a way as to undermine Eliphaz's assertions (see esp. 31:16–23, 32–33).

12–20 As noted, Eliphaz's tone has been more positive and sympathetic than that of the others, but here he throws the weight of his argument with Bildad and Zophar, though not completely. He believes that though Job agrees with him that God is "in the heights of heaven" (v.12), he suspects Job thinks the distance means that God is not in touch with what is going on in human affairs, with the clouds blocking his view of heaven (vv.13–14). Eliphaz has become convinced that Job is a man who follows the path of the ungodly (v.15), so he uses Job's own words to refute him. Has not Job complained that the blessing of the wicked is God's

doing (21:13–16)? Eliphaz turns that around by saying that the wicked are destroyed before their time (v.16), that is, before they can fully enjoy the good things God has provided (vv.18–20).

21–30 Eliphaz is, no doubt, sincere in this his last attempt to reach Job through a call to repentance. Some feel the author of the book, through a subtle "double entendre," has used Eliphaz to show the incapacity of the standard wisdom ideas to handle the realities of human experience (Fullerton, 320–41, has developed this notion for Job 4 and 5). At any rate, this call for Job to submit; to be at peace with God (v.21); to hear God's Word and hide it in his heart (v.22); to return to the Almighty and forsake wickedness (v.23); to delight in God rather than in gold (vv.24–26); and to pray, obey (v.27), and become concerned about sinners (vv.29–30) cannot be improved upon by prophet or evangelist.

There are some problems, however, that beset these powerful words. They assume Job is an ungodly man and that above all he wants to return to health and prosperity (v.21). Most interesting is Eliphaz's insistence that Job turn from his love of wealth to a love of God, an implicit charge that is clearly not true (see Job's own words in ch. 28). The fact is that Job is not ungodly and that he has already made clear his desire to see God and be his friend (19:25–27).

But Job's words have not always sounded friendly toward God, and Eliphaz does not have the capacity to understand the nature of Job's wrestling with God where Job expresses to God his deepest feelings of fear and bafflement over what appears to be an unjust and cruel providence. To Eliphaz's black-and-white mentality, those words (backed by Job's troubles) are sad proof of Job's need to repent and "get right" with God. His assumption that Job does not know how to pray aright will be controverted by God himself, and Eliphaz will have to depend on Job's prayers (42:8).

NOTES

8 Again see Gordis's view on "The Use of Quotations in Job" (*God and Man*, 169–89). Some think this verse is out of place since Job is being addressed directly. Gordis adds the words, "For you believe." The Qumran Targum also felt this need and added "and you say." But Pope, 165, thinks it is "an oblique reference to Job as a land-grabber." This is essentially the way the NIV interprets it.

11 For אוֹר־חֹשֶׁךְ (ʾô-ḥōšek, "so dark"), the LXX reads "light" (ʾôr), which would make the Hebrew read "light becomes darkness so you cannot see." But also possible is the reading "the land becomes dark" (cf. Isa 24:15; 26:19; and possibly Job 33:30 for ʾûr meaning "land").

12 In גֹבַהּ שָׁמָיִם (gōbāh šāmāyim, "in the heights of heaven"), the Hebrew has no preposition "in" (cf. NEB, "at the zenith of the heavens"). Dahood (*Psalms*, 16:62) reads gāboah (adjective) instead of the MT noun and רֹאֵה (rōʾeh, "see") (participle) instead of the MT imperative rᵉʾēh (LXX has third singular indicative). The MT asks Job to see how high the stars are. Dahood (ibid.) reads, "Is not God the Lofty One of Heaven, and the One who sees the top of the stars though they are high?" Andersen's view (204) that v.12a is comparative—"Is not God higher than the heavens"—also seems to fit the context well. The point is that God is so lofty that he looks down on the top of the stars. Eliphaz uses this thought to accuse Job of believing God is so far away and so separated by thick clouds that he cannot see what evil people are doing. Job has complained that God seems indifferent to wickedness, but he has also complained of the opposite problem—God's overbearing surveillance.

15 As noted by Pope, 166, the meaning of הָאֹרַח עוֹלָם (haʾōraḥ ʿôlām, "the old path") may be "the dark path," based on a homonymous root common in Ugaritic (ġlm) but also attested in 42:3: מַעְלִים עֵצָה (maʿlîm ʿēṣâ, "makes dark [obscures] my counsel").

17 The LXX, Syriac, and Qumran Targum appear to go against the MT's לָמוֹ (lāmô, "to them"). These versions have "to us." Dahood claims lmw can mean "for (to) us" ("Hebrew-Ugaritic Lexicography III," 46:324; 47:409). The NIV follows the ancient versions without a footnote.

18 For רָחֲקָה מֶנִּי (rāḥᵃqâ mennî, "I stand aloof"), the LXX reads "the counsel of the wicked is far from him." The NEB and JB go in this direction. The NIV, Pope, Gordis, et al. do not and so make this line a parenthesis. Andersen, 204, thinks v.18 is a quote of Job's words (who claimed God blesses the wicked) in order to refute them (see above). That the MT uses the *yod* instead of the *waw* here and in 21:16 brings up again the question of a third singular pronominal suffix written with the *yod* (see Notes on 9:35; on 14:3; on 19:28; on 21:16; on 31:18).

20 Instead of קִימָנוּ (qîmānû, "our foes"), the ancient versions, following an otherwise unattested root (Arab. qiyām), render this "their substance" (cf. NEB, "riches"); but the root (qûm) often means "to rise up against," even without an accompanying preposition (cf. Ex 15:7: "those who opposed you").

23 Just how the LXX arrived at "and humble yourself" (perhaps from תֵּעָנֶה, tēʿāneh) instead of "you will be restored" (from תִּבָּנֶה, tibbāneh) is a mystery; but the NEB, JB, and RSV all adopt the LXX's reading. The Niphal of bnh means literally "be rebuilt," but that it can mean "be made prosperous" is clear from Jeremiah 12:16 and Malachi 3:15. Here it has the meaning to simply "be restored."

25 תּוֹעָפֹת (tôʿāpôt) is used four times in the OT, but its meaning is still dubious. For the NIV's "choicest," see KB, 1022. BDB, 419, gives "eminence" based on "the horns" in Numbers 23:22 and 24:8 and "the mountains" in Psalm 95:4 (opposite "the depths of the earth"). Pope guesses "piled up [silver]" is the meaning.

29 This verse is notoriously difficult, and there are many solutions; but it seems the simplest is to take the ו (*û*, sign of the plural) on הִשְׁפִּ֫ילוֹ (*hišpîlû*) as dittography (with the following word) and translate, "He [God] will bring [you] low if you speak in pride, but the humble he will save."

30 אִי־נָקִ֑י (*ʾî-nāqî*, "one who is not innocent") is an excellent example of how modern linguistic studies have clarified the meaning. The reader need only compare the KJV's "the island of the innocent." The use of *ʾî* as a negative in both Hebrew and Phoenician can no longer be doubted. Both Pope, 169, and Gordis ("Corporate Personality in Job: A Note on Job 22:29–30," *JNES* 4 [1945]: 54–55) stress the fact that v.30b requires a negative meaning since the innocent have no need of the clean hands of the righteous man. See, however, Clines (*Job 21–37*, 547) for alternative readings that allow for what he considers to be a better contextual reading that God saves the innocent.

2. Job's Reply (23:1–24:25)

OVERVIEW

While the meaning of chapter 23 is quite clear, scholars have seen serious problems in chapter 24. In addition to the difficulties in making sense of the text, there is the issue of determining whose words these are. There is no general agreement about what should be done. Some leave the verses as they are and consider the whole a disconnected series of short pieces that cannot be put together with any certainty. Others try to create a complete third cycle by rearrangement. For example, Pope puts vv.9, 21 between v.3 and v.4, and v.14c after v.15. He shifts vv.18–20 and vv.22–25 to follow 27:8–23 and labels them Zophar's words, since Zophar does not reply for a third time. The NAB suggests that vv.18–25 cannot be ascribed to Job with certainty, while Habel, 37–38, considers all of chapter 24 and 27:13–23 the words of Zophar.

All the above is done on the basis of what appear to be the thoughts of the counselors, not of Job. Some even claim that there is early scribal doctoring of the text to make Job sound more orthodox. One must not overlook the practice of unannounced quotations. The RSV added "You say" before 24:18 and looked on this as a quotation by Job of what the counselors have said (cf. Gordis, *God and Man*, 169–80). Such an ancient rhetorical device is disturbing to us because we are not used to it, but it may be the correct approach to these verses. Since there is no agreement about handling chapter 24, it seems wiser to let the text stand and above all refuse to force modern categories of logic and rhetoric on it (though see P. P. Zerafa, *The Wisdom of God in the Book of Job* [Rome: Herder, 1978], for the best arguments for attributing portions of the speech to the friends).

Job's statements about God in these chapters must be constantly evaluated in the light of the wider canonical context. Job has wrestled with the concept that God is free to do anything he pleases (23:13). For example, in 9:12 Job complained, "Who can say to him, 'What are you doing?'" What God does appeared unjust and led Job to fantasize about God as though God were his enemy (16:7–14). But such words are not normative, and a correct hermeneutic begins with the principle of the analogy of

Scripture (comparing Scripture with Scripture) and continues with the principle of contextualization. We must allow Job the right to use the language of feeling rejected (23:14−17) just as the psalmist freely does (e.g., Ps 88:3−18).

In the final verses of chapter 23, Job makes his apology for his emotional language, which has been so misunderstood by his friends. He has been terrified by what he has come to accept as God's plan for his life (vv.14−16). The mystery, however, is still there. Job does not understand what God is doing. So in all honesty he still needs to speak out and call for the thick darkness to be removed (v.17).

¹Then Job replied:

²"Even today my complaint is bitter;
    his hand is heavy in spite of my groaning.
³If only I knew where to find him;
    if only I could go to his dwelling!
⁴I would state my case before him
    and fill my mouth with arguments.
⁵I would find out what he would answer me,
    and consider what he would say.
⁶Would he oppose me with great power?
    No, he would not press charges against me.
⁷There an upright man could present his case before him,
    and I would be delivered forever from my judge.

⁸"But if I go to the east, he is not there;
    if I go to the west, I do not find him.
⁹When he is at work in the north, I do not see him;
    when he turns to the south, I catch no glimpse of him.
¹⁰But he knows the way that I take;
    when he has tested me, I will come forth as gold.
¹¹My feet have closely followed his steps;
    I have kept to his way without turning aside.
¹²I have not departed from the commands of his lips;
    I have treasured the words of his mouth more than my daily bread.

¹³"But he stands alone, and who can oppose him?
    He does whatever he pleases.
¹⁴He carries out his decree against me,
    and many such plans he still has in store.
¹⁵That is why I am terrified before him;
    when I think of all this, I fear him.

¹⁶God has made my heart faint;
   the Almighty has terrified me.
¹⁷Yet I am not silenced by the darkness,
   by the thick darkness that covers my face.

^{24:1}"Why does the Almighty not set times for judgment?
   Why must those who know him look in vain for such days?
²Men move boundary stones;
   they pasture flocks they have stolen.
³They drive away the orphan's donkey
   and take the widow's ox in pledge.
⁴They thrust the needy from the path
   and force all the poor of the land into hiding.
⁵Like wild donkeys in the desert,
   the poor go about their labor of foraging food;
   the wasteland provides food for their children.
⁶They gather fodder in the fields
   and glean in the vineyards of the wicked.
⁷Lacking clothes, they spend the night naked;
   they have nothing to cover themselves in the cold.
⁸They are drenched by mountain rains
   and hug the rocks for lack of shelter.
⁹The fatherless child is snatched from the breast;
   the infant of the poor is seized for a debt.
¹⁰Lacking clothes, they go about naked;
   they carry the sheaves, but still go hungry.
¹¹They crush olives among the terraces;
   they tread the winepresses, yet suffer thirst.
¹²The groans of the dying rise from the city,
   and the souls of the wounded cry out for help.
   But God charges no one with wrongdoing.

¹³"There are those who rebel against the light,
   who do not know its ways
   or stay in its paths.
¹⁴When daylight is gone, the murderer rises up
   and kills the poor and needy;
   in the night he steals forth like a thief.

¹⁵The eye of the adulterer watches for dusk;
    he thinks, 'No eye will see me,'
    and he keeps his face concealed.
¹⁶In the dark, men break into houses,
    but by day they shut themselves in;
    they want nothing to do with the light.
¹⁷For all of them, deep darkness is their morning;
    they make friends with the terrors of darkness.

¹⁸"Yet they are foam on the surface of the water;
    their portion of the land is cursed,
    so that no one goes to the vineyards.
¹⁹As heat and drought snatch away the melted snow,
    so the grave snatches away those who have sinned.
²⁰The womb forgets them,
    the worm feasts on them;
evil men are no longer remembered
    but are broken like a tree.
²¹They prey on the barren and childless woman,
    and to the widow show no kindness.
²²But God drags away the mighty by his power;
    though they become established, they have no assurance of life.
²³He may let them rest in a feeling of security,
    but his eyes are on their ways.
²⁴For a little while they are exalted, and then they are gone;
    they are brought low and gathered up like all others;
    they are cut off like heads of grain.

²⁵"If this is not so, who can prove me false
    and reduce my words to nothing?"

COMMENTARY

1–2 Job is becoming less fractious and insulting to his friends. Here he expresses his own sorry mental condition. His play on words in v.2 leaves somewhat open the question of whether he is still rebellious or just bitter (see Notes).

3–7 Job's spiritual movement during this dispute is evident again when we compare his attitude about a hearing with God in chapter 9 with his thoughts on the same subject here. Job still wants a fair trial, for he is certain he is blameless, that is, above the charges that have been made (23:3–4).

In 9:14–20 Job doubted that God would even give him a hearing and that even while pleading for mercy, he would be crushed. At that point he admitted he was not totally innocent (9:15–20), though he still considered himself blameless (*tām*; 9:21). After Zophar's abuse in chapter 11, where he was flatly labeled a wretched sinner (11:5, 14), Job reacted with a bolder assertion of his blamelessness (13:13–15). In chapter 22 we noticed how Eliphaz, the least accusatory of the three friends, had moved closer to the others with his quip, "Are not your sins endless?" (22:5). So here in chapter 23 Job reasserts his claim to be an upright man with renewed confidence that God agrees with him. This is why having an audience with God is important to Job (v.5). He continues to be positive (13:18) about the outcome of such an encounter (23:6–7).

Our knowledge of the doctrine of justification by faith with its premise of human depravity (Ro 1–3) makes it difficult for us to understand this part of the message of this book. It is helpful to look on Job as illustrative of Christ, who also suffered unjustly to fulfill the purpose of God (cf. Joseph, Ge 37–50). We have seen how Job's upright life was so rooted in the fear of God that even God himself used Job as an example of godliness (1:8; 2:3). So Job is not wrong in calling for his own vindication. The psalmist does the same (Pss 17:2–3; 26:1–3; 139; et al.).

8–12 Job is still frustrated, however, over the matter of finding God (cf. v.3). Job cannot find him, though he has searched for him in every direction (vv.8–9). God is absent. Later in 42:5 Job will say, "But now my eyes have seen you." But at this point, though he wrestles with God verbally (as he did in chs. 7; 10; 13–14; 17), he has no immediate sense of God's presence or of God's voice communicating with him. Yet in reply to Eliphaz (22:21) Job claims

to have heard God's words and treasured them in his heart (v.12), though this probably refers to God's law rather than to a personal dialogue. He rejects Eliphaz's call for him to return to God (22:23), for he feels he has never turned away from God.

Job does not think God is testing him (v.10b) as a means to purge away his sinful dross. It is rather to prove he is pure gold. Job's words in vv.11–12 have to be the words either of a terrible hypocrite or of a deeply committed believer. They remind us of Psalm 119:11, 101, 168.

The Hebrew of v.10 is difficult to interpret. Does "the way" mean the way Job has taken (NIV) or God's way with Job? If it means the latter, Job is being submissive to God's will—an answer to the stricture "Submit to God" in 22:21. Eliphaz had in mind Job's earlier demand to know why God was afflicting him (7:20–21; 10:2). With this interpretation Job is accepting his testing but with assurance that he will come forth as gold (a veiled rebuke of Eliphaz's accusation in 22:24). The NIV has taken the verse in the other sense, that God knows Job is following God's way. This he expresses more fully in vv.11–12. In either case Job answers Eliphaz's strictures.

13–17 Verse 13 is a monotheistic affirmation. Job says, "He [God] is the unique [one]," though as we will see in what follows the thought does not comfort him. The Hebrew expression is rare in the OT but idiomatic. A preposition is used between two words to express equivalence (see Notes). Job's God is the same as Israel's God—he is the only one; there is no other (Dt 6:4). As the all-powerful, sovereign Deity, God does what he pleases (v.13b). Job's fear (vv.15–16) is the necessary corollary to the truth that God is sovereign and therefore cannot be put in a box and be told what he can and cannot do by human beings.

What might this God who does what he pleases have had in mind for Job (v.14)? A real part of the living faith Job expresses in vv.8–12 is his determination not to be silenced despite the darkness he feels over the intention of God, who has no one to answer to for his behavior. This has led to M. Tsevat's observation (73–106) about God's being viewed as amoral. There is a sense in which God is above human conceptions of what is moral or right, but we must be careful in a formulation like Tsevat's lest we sound as though God is pictured as immoral, which Tsevat does not mean. See my comments below on this subject under the theophany.

24:1 Job begins by expressing in one bicolon (v.1) the mood that dominates here—a complaint on why God does not set straight the balance of justice. Why does not his promised retribution come at set times against all ruthless oppressors? The chapter alternates in a discursive way between a description of the criminals (vv.2–4, 9) and their victims (vv.5–8, 10–12).

This theme is an exceedingly important part of the major message of the book. Job feels God should demonstrate his justice by openly punishing the wicked. In the divine speeches God will teach him a tremendous lesson about this, which Job does not now understand. That lesson centers around the idea that the principle of retribution does not operate mechanically in this world but according to the divine will. Although God is free to do as he pleases, Job knows he does not deserve his suffering. But how then does the age-old principle of retribution fit in?

In this chapter Job presents a picture of a world that is still a deep enigma to him. His courageous honesty leads him to expound the mystery of how the wicked get by unpunished while they perform their evil deeds against the innocent. The touching pathos of these word pictures should be felt by the reader, for they give us some insight into Job's contempt for wickedness and his ability to empathize with those in distress (cf. 31:13–22).

2–12 The wicked are so brazen they pasture stolen flocks on stolen land, or possibly as the LXX has it, they dare to seize the shepherd along with his flock (v.2). Since the orphan (v.3) is without inheritance, his donkey represents everything he owns. Job appreciates those ancient civil laws that protected widows and the fatherless (cf. Ex 22:22). In contrast to this passage, the psalmist stresses how God himself is "a father to the fatherless" and the "defender of widows" (Ps 68:5) and the dispenser of justice to the wicked (Ps 68:1–2).

This section is a moving description of the ruthless exploitation of the poorest of the poor. Note the pitiful case of the destitute, who must carry food while they go hungry (v.10) and tread the winepress while they suffer thirst (v.11). The climax is v.12c, which returns to the theme of v.1. The great enigma is that all this is going on and God does nothing (cf. Ps 73:2–3; Hab 1:13; Mal 3:15). Also see the Notes on an alternative reading: "God does not pay attention."

13–17 The tone-setting bicolon (v.1) is followed by a stanza stressing the deeds of the wicked (vv.2–4). Then in vv.5–12 Job stresses the suffering and misery of the poor, and in vv.13–17 he returns to the deeds of the wicked. The murderer (v.14), the adulterer (v.15), and the thief (v.16) share a characteristic that is self-condemning: they all love darkness rather than the light (cf. 38:12–15; Ps 82:5; Jn 3:20; Eph 5:8; 1Th 5:5).

18–24 As stated in the Overview, many have insisted that these are not Job's words because they do not sound like his sentiments about the wicked. But there is nothing wrong with viewing them all as Job's words, since he never claims the wicked always prosper or never come to a bad end. His problem is that God treats the good and bad alike. But here again (cf. Gordis, *Job*, 253) this may be an unannounced quotation of the conventional view of the friends. Gordis supports this by showing how

Job cited their words in order to refute them in 21:19, where the quote is definitely unannounced, and in 21:28, where Job announced the quotation with the words "You say."

But the problem here in 24:18–24 is that the refutation is missing. Gordis thinks that is because this third cycle of speeches has become disarranged. I believe Job has a good reason for mouthing his friends' view here (see below). However, another possible way of understanding these as Job's words is to translate the verbs as jussives expressing his wishes rather than as indicatives expressing what he thinks is the state of affairs (Hartley, 350–54; Wilson, 272).

25 It is curious that in v.25 Job speaks as though he has just made an argument against the views of his friends rather than partially agreeing with them. The verse is a clue to the rhetoric of the chapter. It is not a disconnected assemblage of pieces put together by scribes who wanted to make Job sound more orthodox. An argument based on this verse can be made for literary unity in this chapter. We must go back to the nodal statement in v.1 and examine it carefully. The verb ṣāpan (GK 7621), there translated "set," means literally "store up." Job's query there is, "Why is there not a storing up of judgment by the Almighty so that his friends

can eventually see the day [v.2] of his wrath on the wicked?" Job is anticipating "the day of the LORD," a theme stressed by some of the prophets (cf. Joel).

The query of v.1 fits with Job's view that the wicked prosper. After developing a series of vignettes, with as much pathos as possible, about the deeds of the wicked and the sufferings of their victims (vv.1–17), Job finally mouths the view of his friends about God's judgment on the wicked. Job may either be quoting them with irony or complaining that this judgment comes piecemeal, a little here and a little there (see esp. vv.23–24).

Eventually the wicked die and are forgotten; they lack security and have their day only for a little while (22:16–18) — but where are the great days of stored-up judgment so the righteous can be sure that justice for such horrors is meted out? Job is not convinced that piecemeal judgment is truly just since the righteous often suffer the same. So v.25 is not a disconnected verse. Literally it forms an inclusio with the original query in v.1. Here the book of Job again anticipates a step forward in theological understanding (cf. 14:14–15; 19:25–27). There is no direct teaching of final judgment to set right the balance of justice, but there is a concept here that anticipates the teaching that God must have his day.

NOTES

23:2 In מָרִי שִׂחִי (merî śiḥî, "my complaint is bitter"), the consonants mry point not to mrr ("bitter") but to mrh ("to be contentious"); and the primary meaning of śiḥî is "to speak." So read "my speech is contentious (for) his hand, etc." But there may be a wordplay between Job's being defiant and resentful (cf. Andersen, 108).

On יָדִי כָּבְדָה עַל (yādî kābedâ ʿal, "his hand is heavy in spite of"), the NIV agrees with the LXX and Syriac. The MT reads "my hand" or possibly "the hand on me" (dative suffix, see NIV mg.). If we follow the LXX, either the likeness between the two letters yod ("my") and waw ("his") in late script or the rare third singular yod is a viable explanation (cf. Blommerde, 92–93, but see Notes on 9:35). For a similar use of ʿal meaning "notwithstanding, in spite of" in Job, see 10:7 and 24:9.

3 תְּכוּנָתוֹ (tekûnātô, "his dwelling") means a place prepared or arranged. A good translation would be "his tribunal, courtroom."

6 Commenting on הַבְּרָב כֹּחַ (*habbᵉrāb-kōaḥ*, "would he … with great power"), Tur-Sinai (*Job*) cogently shows that *rāb-kōaḥ* means "an attorney." The meaning is "Will he argue against me through an attorney?"

On יָשִׂם בִּי (*yāśim bî*, "press charges against me"), the NIV is paraphrastic because of failure to appreciate the Hebrew idiom *śîm lēb* ("put to mind, pay attention to"), with *lēb* suppressed as in 4:20; 24:12; 34:23; and Isaiah 41:20. Job answers his own question: God would not use an attorney but "surely he, himself [אַךְ־הוּא, *ʾak-hûʾ*] will give me full attention."

7 Instead of מִשְׁפָּטִי (*miššōpᵉṭî*, "from my judge"), some Hebrew MSS and the versions read *mišpāṭî* ("my case"). Combining this with the verb פָּלַט (*pālaṭ*, "to deliver"), Job is certain he will be vindicated. He says, "I will permanently bring my case to a successful conclusion" (delivery or birth; cf. *plṭ* in 21:10b).

9 The stress of בַּעֲשֹׂתוֹ (*baʿᵃśōtô*, "when he is at work") is not on God's working but on his being there, passing the time as in Ecclesiastes 6:12. Some say the root is *ʿšh*, which has a cognate that means "to turn" in Arabic and Ugaritic (cf. 1Sa 14:32, *Kethiv*).

13 On וְהוּא בְאֶחָד (*wᵉhûʾ bᵉʾeḥād*, "But he stands alone"), Budde's emendation (*Das Buch Hiob* [Nowack Handkommentar; 2nd ed.; Göttingen: Vandenhoeck and Ruprecht, 1913] from *bʾḥd* to *bḥr* (dropping *aleph* and changing *dalet* to *resh*) is thought justified by the fact that *bḥr* ("choose") and *ʾwh* ("desire"; v.13b) appear in Psalm 132:13 as parallel synonyms. Here the first line says, "When God chooses, who can oppose him?" I prefer to let the text stand and view the preposition as *beth essentiae* (GKC, par. 119 i; cf. Job 37:10; Ps 68:5), meaning "he is unique." Dahood (*Psalms*, 16:325) calls it *beth emphaticum*.

17 In כִּי־לֹא נִצְמַתִּי (*kî-lōʾ niṣmattî*, "Yet I am not silenced"), the verb in Hebrew consistently means "to be exterminated, put to an end" (cf. KJV). But in the Arabic and Syriac it means "becoming speechless"; and the NIV has followed the NEB in choosing this meaning. The verse is very difficult.

24:1 יָמָיו (*yāmāyw*, "such days") is literally "his days," that is, the Almighty's. This strengthens my view that Job anticipates the "day of the LORD" concept.

6 On בְּלִילוֹ (*bᵉlîlô*, "fodder"), the MT says, "his fodder they cut [harvest]." The words mean "mixed fodder," not as it grows in the field. The LXX has a doublet witnessing to a dual reading of the MT consonants. Dhorme, 277–78, and Fohrer chose the first half of the LXX "[they reap] at night" (בְּלֵילוֹ, *bᵉlêlô*), while the Vulgate, Syriac, and Targum chose the other half "[in a field] not his" (בְּלִי לוֹ, *bᵉlî lô*). Pope and others emend to בְּלִיַּעַל (*bᵉlîyaʿal*, "they reap in the field of the villain"), which fits the parallelism but may be too drastic.

9 Instead of MT's עַל (*ʿal*, lit., "upon"), the LXX provides a better reading—*ʿul* ("in front of"). But best of all is to emend to *ʿûl* ("infant"), as the NIV does.

11 שׁוּרֹתָם (*śûrōtām*) may mean "walls" or "terraces" (cf. Ge 49:22; 2Sa 22:30; Ps 18:29; Jer 5:10). It is probably a figure of speech (synecdoche) for "oil presses" (cf. NIV mg.).

12 וְנֶפֶשׁ (*wᵉnepeš*, "and the souls of") almost certainly means "and the throats of" (the wounded)—a generally accepted primitive meaning for *nepeš*. Alternatively, the expression *nepeš-ḥᵃlālîm* could possibly mean "the living dead."

For תִּפְלָה (*tiplâ*, "with wrongdoing"), the Syriac and two Hebrew MSS read *tᵉpillâ* ("the prayer"). This appears to be an attempt to make Job's theology more acceptable.

יָשִׂים (*yāśîm*, "charges") is another example of the ellipsis of *lēb* ("heart") in the idiom *śîm lēb* ("pay attention"; cf. 4:20; 23:6; 34:33): "God does not pay attention to wrongdoing."

14 The translation of לְאוֹר (lāʾôr) as "when daylight is gone" depends on the *l* being negative or separative ("from the light"), as in Ugaritic.

The NIV makes יְהִי (yᵉhî, "he steals forth") more colorful than it is. It literally says, "He becomes" (like a thief). But this jussive form of the verb "to be" appears several times in Job as an indicative (cf. Notes on 18:12 and on 20:23).

17 The words כִּי יַחְדָּו (kî yaḥdāw, "For all") seem strangely out of place. The Hebrew reads, "For together morning to them [is] deep darkness." Some (e.g., Rowley, NEB) suggest the first two words go with the preceding line. Pope omits them as a marginal comment. Following the plural in v.16, this may be a case where revocalization is in order. In 3:6 (see Notes) I saw the root חדד (ḥdh II) used and meaning "be seen, perceive, view" (cf. KB). It may be vocalized יֶחְדּוּ (yeḥᵉdû), meaning "the morning is seen by them as deep darkness" or "they view deep darkness as morning to them."

18 The third masculine singular pronoun is awkward here—הוּא (hûʾ, "they are"). In 37:6 the verb הֱוֵא (hᵉwēʾ) means "fall." We may vocalize this as a participle from the same root and render it, "Like scum falling on the surface of the water, may their portion ... be cursed."

24 Combining the force of the parallelism in the following line—"they are cut off like heads of grain"—with the witness of the ancient versions leads to the conclusion that the meaning of כַּכֹּל (kakkōl) is not "like all others." The LXX transliterates μολόχη (molochē), which in Hebrew is מַלּוּחַ (mallûaḥ, "saltwort" or "mallow"). Compare the NEB—"they wilt like a mallow flower." The Qumran Targum reads in Aramaic *kybl* ("like crabgrass").

3. Bildad (25:1–6)

OVERVIEW

This is the last we hear from Job's three counselors. Some think they have exhausted their arguments (e.g., Ewald, 246). Others (e.g., K. Fullerton, "The Original Conclusion of the Book of Job," *ZAW*, N.S., 1 [1924]: 121) consider this an unlikely solution. Most modern critical scholars lengthen this short speech by including 26:5–14, but there is no obvious reason why this should be done. The theme is similar but not the same. Indeed Job in 9:4–13 looked in awe at nature (cf. 26:5–14), while Bildad looks here at God's transcendence to show his purity and dominion over the moral order so that he (Bildad) can prove the impurity of humanity. R. A. F. MacKenzie ("The Purpose of the Yahweh Speeches in the Book of Job," *Bib* 40 [1959]: 435–45) notes that in celebrating God's power, Job stresses arbitrary power, the friends stress justice, and God in his speeches stresses mystery and love.

¹Then Bildad the Shuhite replied:

²"Dominion and awe belong to God;
  he establishes order in the heights of heaven.

> ³Can his forces be numbered?
>   Upon whom does his light not rise?
> ⁴How then can a man be righteous before God?
>   How can one born of woman be pure?
> ⁵If even the moon is not bright
>   and the stars are not pure in his eyes,
> ⁶how much less man, who is but a maggot—
>   a son of man, who is only a worm!"

COMMENTARY

1–3 Bildad in these few lines does not bother to answer Job's recent argument, nor does he present a new one. As Wilson, 280, points out, "Bildad makes but a weak and truncated response to Job's long, impassioned plea." He only repeats what has already been said by Eliphaz (4:17–21; 15:14–16). In 9:4–13 Job demonstrated his penchant for answering Bildad's moral argument with a lengthy description of God's arbitrary power in the universe. As noted above, each has his own reason for dwelling on the power of God. Here Bildad wants to show how God's power established order in the heavenly realm and that his dominion extends to all created beings.

4–6 God's majesty palls everything (moon and stars, v.5), and it reaches everywhere (v.3b). So how can any person be considered righteous or pure in God's eyes? We can recognize the truth here; but as we have seen earlier, it is the next statement that reveals what Bildad really has in mind. His point is that humans are maggots (v.6). Unlike the apostle Paul, who developed the doctrine of total depravity in Romans 1–3 to prepare the way for grace, we know from the rest of Bildad's remarks that he leaves no room for mercy or forgiveness.

Eliphaz was the first to question the possibility of anyone's purity before God (4:17). In chapter 8 his words left the door open only for those who were truly blameless (8:20). Job, repeating the issue in 9:2, wanted to know how he could prove his blamelessness since God was so inaccessible. In 15:14–16 Eliphaz came close to a nihilistic view of human beings—they are hopelessly "vile and corrupt, who drink up evil like water!" Yet in chapter 22 Eliphaz left the door open for Job to be restored, but not on the basis of mercy, for he must bear the penalty for whatever he has done. Then if there is repentance, Job could be restored (22:21–23). But Bildad here repeats the old question of 9:2 with an implied negative answer. If God is inaccessible, it is because he is too pure; and a human being is, like Job, a hopeless worm.

NOTES

3 Instead of אוֹרֵהוּ (ʾôrēhû, "his light"), the LXX reads as though it saw אוֹרְבוֹ (ʾôrēbô, "his ambush"). This parallels "his forces" and would read "against whom does not his ambush rise up?" NEB chose this reading, but most reject it.

5 It is unlikely that there is any such root as אהל (*ʾhl*) meaning "be bright." The MT's וְלֹא יַאֲהִיל (*wᵉlōʾ yaʾᵃhîl*, "is not bright") could be an example of *aleph* as an internal *mater lectionis*, reading יָהֵל (*yāhēl*) from the root הָלַל (*hālal*, "shine"; Job 31:26, cf. also 41:18 [10]; supported by Clines, *Job 21–37*, 621–22).

4. Job's Reply (26:1–14)

OVERVIEW

The chapter clearly breaks into two parts: Job's reaction to Bildad (vv.1–4) and a poem celebrating God's omnipotence (vv.5–14). The poem is frequently regarded as reflecting a line of argument inconsistent with Job's general position (but compare with 9:5–10 for many of the same arguments); and it is felt that, as such, it more properly should be assigned to one of the other speakers. Before giving the reason for leaving this poem where it is, a word might be said about the generally agreed-on disruption of the text in chapters 24–27.

Kissane, xli, who does not hesitate to move passages, complains that "the text has suffered much more at the hands of some modern critics than it had suffered throughout the ages of its history." One cannot help but wonder about such wholesale rearrangements as that of Tur-Sinai (*Job*) or M. P. Reddy's reconstruction ("Reconstruction," *ZAW* 90 [1978]: 49–94). Reasons put forth to "explain" such a corruption of the text are speculative and range from scribal errors, such as "accidental displacement" of lines or "straying" of a passage because it became attached to the wrong column of the text (Kissane, xlii–iii; and J. Strahan, *The Book of Job* [2nd ed.; Edinburgh: T&T Clark, 1914], 219), to the suggestion by N. H. Snaith (*The Book of Job: Its Origin and Purpose* [SBT, 2nd series; London: SCM, 1968], 61) that Job represents an unfinished work by an author who died before he proceeded very far. For

summaries of the host of scholastic opinions, see Rowley, 215–16, and Driver and Gray, xli. There is little to be gained by attempting to interact with such variety on an individual basis. I will simply note some arguments in support of accepting the text as it stands and call for the reader to draw his or her own conclusion.

Pope, xlvi, calls attention to the fact that the Qumran Targum (11QtgJob), dating to the first half of the second century BC, supports the Masoretic order of chapters 24–27.

Long ago Ewald, 249–50, saw chapter 26 as befitting Job's lips because it demonstrates his superiority over his "friends" and seems to show that he is in fact striving after higher knowledge with resignation and diffidence. Certainly Job assumed an attitude of "outdoing" his friends' knowledge in 12:1–4 and 13:1–2. But in 26:14 he gives a modest confession that he is able to do no more than describe the barest and most distant outlines of divine power. Here Job's contention is that in God there remains so much that is incomprehensible. Seen as such it would be strange indeed to hear such an admission coming from the lips of one such as Bildad, whose primary concern has been to keep God neatly packaged and demystified so that nothing remains "problematic." In earlier speeches it was Job who dwelt on God's mysterious ways (9:4–13; 12:13–25). Zophar mentioned the subject only as a way to rebuke Job (11:7–9).

¹Then Job replied:

²"How you have helped the powerless!
　　How you have saved the arm that is feeble!
³What advice you have offered to one without wisdom!
　　And what great insight you have displayed!
⁴Who has helped you utter these words?
　　And whose spirit spoke from your mouth?

⁵"The dead are in deep anguish,
　　those beneath the waters and all that live in them.
⁶Death is naked before God;
　　Destruction lies uncovered.
⁷He spreads out the northern skies over empty space;
　　he suspends the earth over nothing.
⁸He wraps up the waters in his clouds,
　　yet the clouds do not burst under their weight.
⁹He covers the face of the full moon,
　　spreading his clouds over it.
¹⁰He marks out the horizon on the face of the waters
　　for a boundary between light and darkness.
¹¹The pillars of the heavens quake,
　　aghast at his rebuke.
¹²By his power he churned up the sea;
　　by his wisdom he cut Rahab to pieces.
¹³By his breath the skies became fair;
　　his hand pierced the gliding serpent.
¹⁴And these are but the outer fringe of his works;
　　how faint the whisper we hear of him!
　　Who then can understand the thunder of his power?"

COMMENTARY

1–4 Bildad has struck a most sensitive nerve. In all Job's speeches nothing has been more important to him than his determination to be vindicated, to be shown blameless, in God's tribunal (10:1–7; 13:3, 13–19; 16:18–21; 19:23–27; 23:2–7). Bildad has just labeled that impossible. Job cannot restrain himself. He levels a sarcastic reply directly at the speaker (Hebrew second singular). He has nothing but contempt for Bildad's wisdom. In his colorful, ironic exclamations, Job considers himself powerless, feeble, and without wisdom, but not a maggot (vv.2–4). If Bildad would only impute to him the dignity every human being deserves, he could have some compassion. The RSV (continued in the NRSV) already caught this ironic tone departing from the question format in the KJV (LXX). Understanding vv.2–3 as sarcasm makes Job's question about the source of such wisdom equally tongue-in-cheek.

Job wants to know who "wrote" Bildad's material (v.4). He certainly knows Bildad was mouthing Eliphaz's words (4:17). Job considers inane Bildad's argument that the majesty and power of God are the reasons why humans cannot be righteous before him. It is proof of the poverty of his thought. It angers Job because he knows they all agree that he is a reprobate sinner and so has given up the idea that he is an upright person temporarily suffering for sins. No, he is a worm whose case is hopeless. So Job dares to remind them that they too are hopeless as counselors.

The sharp transition to a poem about God and the cosmos has led to the conclusion that these verses belong with Bildad's short speech. But there are two additional reasons this is not so. First, this lofty poem does not appear to have the kind of material we are used to hearing from Bildad. Second, sharp transitions are common in these discourses. All the speeches tend to be discursive. Some think this belongs to Bildad because its theme is like his, but that may be the very reason Job presents his view of the subject.

The controlling theme is indeed similar to Bildad's — God's vast power. Job takes up where Bildad left off. Bildad has used the theme to reduce sinful humans to the status of worms. Job wishes to correct what he sees as an unwarranted connection. He does not see God's power related to the possibility or impossibility of human reconciliation with God. Both men deal with the cosmos, but Job ends on a note that leaves humans standing before the mystery of God's power with unanswered questions (v.14), but not as a maggot (25:6).

5–6 The term $h\bar{a}r^e p\bar{a}^{\,}\hat{\imath}m$ ("the dead," v.5; GK 8327) in this and other OT passages means "shades or spirits of the dead" (see P. Johnston, *Shades of Sheol* (Downers Grove, Ill.: InterVarsity Press, 2002), 127–31, 134–41). Isaiah 14:9 pictures the Rephaim in Sheol rising from their thrones to greet the king of Babylon on his descent. Here they tremble as God casts his eye on them in Sheol (v.6).

But who are those that live "beneath the waters"? Some (e.g., Pope, 183) take it as the "watery abyss" that Sheol is thought to be. Rowley, 217, asserts that the mention of the waters is in reference to the netherworld, "entrance to which is often depicted in terms of being overwhelmed by waters." He cites 2 Samuel 22:5: "the waves of death ... torrents of destruction." Jonah was in Sheol in the belly of the great fish (Jnh 2:2). But this language is metaphorical for life-threatening situations (cf. 27:20). Job's earlier allusion to Sheol as "the land of gloom and deep shadow" (10:21) is more like this passage. It is possible that those "beneath the waters" (v.5) are those conceived of as buried in "the lowest pit, in the darkest depths" (Ps 88:6). Many commentators take those in the waters as the fishes, etc. Others feel this does not do justice to this context and believe it refers to the forces of creation (see below on the "Sea").

The thrust of these verses is that there is no place hidden from God. Job's remark is an emphatic rejoinder to Bildad's statement (25:3) that the light of God shines on everyone. Job heightens the observation dramatically by drawing attention to the searching eye of God from which even Sheol (Johnston, *Shades of Sheol*, 69–98) and Abaddon (from the Hebrew word "Destruction"; see Note) provide no hiding place. The proverbist, whose purpose is different from Job's, takes it a step further: "Death and Destruction lie open before the LORD; how much more the hearts of men!" (Pr 15:11).

7–8 The word "skies" (v.7) is a justifiable insertion. Although $\d{s}\bar{a}p\hat{o}n$ (GK 7600) means "north," the verb *nōṭeh* ("spreads out"; GK 5742) is never used of the earth and is often used in reference to the heavens. As in 9:8, where "[God] alone stretches out the heavens," *nōṭeh* carries the idea of "stretching out" as a tent (see Ps 104:2). This imagery is continued by the words "over empty space," or "over the void." It is difficult to postulate what "void" might be intended by Job if he is referring to a northern region of the earth where the majestic mountains rise.

In the Introduction I drew attention to two points worthy of consideration here again. First, cosmography is not in itself the purpose of the passage; God's power is in focus. Second, we cannot ignore what Ugaritic literature tells about Mount Zaphon as the Canaanite Olympus. The Canaanite "cosmic mountain" concept is paralleled in the OT by both Mount Sinai and Mount Zion as the dwelling place of God and the place from which he chooses to reveal himself. But here it is that holy place where God dwells, that greatest of tents that he spreads out and where he dwells, the heavens.

Is there any substance to the suggestion that "the north" is the celestial pole formed by the Ursa Minor constellation? Such a view would imply the text refers to spreading out the stars, for only at night is the "void" (absence of stars) noticeable. Other passages that describe the heavens stretched out like a tent do not limit it to the stars (cf. Jer 10:12, et al.). Job points to God's power as incomprehensible. The heavens are visible, yet they do not fall to earth; there is no visible means of support. Even the earth itself can be said to hang on nothing.

While it is doubtful whether we should ascribe with M. Buttenwieser (*The Book of Job* [London: Hodder and Stoughton, 1922]) much significance to Job's scientific insights, Fohrer's interpretation is also highly questionable. The earth, he thinks, was thought of like a plate over empty space supported with pillars at the edges. He uses 9:6 as evidence, but there earth's pillars are clearly the mountains.

Such an explanation destroys the mystery Job is seeking to present.

The fact that God can spread out the heavens over empty space, hang the earth on nothing, and fill the clouds with water without their bursting is intended to make us stand in awe (v.8). Job is boldly expressing in poetic terms the marvelous, majestic power of God. Those clouds, though they contain an impressive quantity of water, do not split and dump all the water at once. Even with today's scientific explanation of cloud formation in terms of temperature, pressure, condensation, etc., one is still moved to wonder at the extreme complexity and yet ingenious simplicity of such a phenomenon.

9 Does God cover the face of "his throne" or "the full moon" (see Notes)? If the text is speaking of God's throne, then this line can be tied to God's appearance in the storm (38:1). God uses the clouds to enshroud him in his lofty abode (Ps 104:3–13; Am 9:6). He appears in heaven in golden splendor and awesome majesty. But people can no more look at him directly than they can the sun (37:21–22). So the clouds must cover the face of his throne— an apt word picture of a theophany.

10 The NIV interprets the literal Hebrew "he draws a circle" as God's establishment of the horizon, which acts as the line of demarcation between light and darkness (day and night). Job is ascribing to God, and not to the incantations and rituals of the nature cults, the authority and dominion over night and day.

11 The Akkadian term for "the horizon" was *isid šamê* (lit., "the foundation of heaven"; cf. *The Assyrian Dictionary* [ed. E. Reiner; Chicago: The Oriental Institute, 1956–], 7:240). Here the mountains are called the "pillars of the heavens," while in 9:6 they are the "pillars" of the earth. They are pillars because their foundations go beneath the waters of the sea (Jnh 2:6) and reach to the clouds as though supporting the vault of the sky. The thought was common in the ancient world that the earth shook at its foundations when God expressed his anger (Ps 18:7, 15; Isa 2:19, 21; 13:13; Eze 38:19; et al.). Such phenomenological language was based on volcanoes and earthquakes. The force exerted by a thunderclap (Ps 77:18) is perceived as "the blast of the breath from your [God's] nostrils" (Ps 18:15).

12–13 Job continues his exaltation of God as Creator and Ruler of all nature. In the process he demythologizes the language of the popular myths that described creation as the overcoming of chaos (see J. N. Oswalt, "The Myth of the Dragon and Old Testament Faith," *EvQ* 49/3 [1977]: 163–72). The Akkadian creation epic (*ANET*, 66–69) tells of the defeat of the chaotic goddess Tiamat (the Deep) by the hero god Marduk (Bel). In west Semitic literature, Tiamat's counterpart was boisterous Yam (the Sea), who fought Marduk's counterpart Baal.

Job's intent to demythologize is quite evident. Here the sea that God subdues is not the deity Yam. Job depersonalizes Yam by using the definite article ("the" sea), thus expressing his innate monotheistic theology. Marduk employed seven winds (*ANET*, 66) to overthrow Tiamat; here God's own breath clears the heavens. All the power of the wind is his breath. Further, by his own wisdom, skill, and power he "cut Rahab to pieces" and "pierced the gliding serpent," unlike Marduk, who depended on the enablement of the father-gods.

A study of the OT names for the well-known Canaanite mythological sea monsters shows how purposefully the OT authors used the language to enrich their own poetic conceptions of the supremacy of the one and only true God. This is especially true of poetry that deals with cosmological, histori-cal, and eschatological themes. For example, Psalm 89:9–10 reads:

> You rule over the surging sea;
>> when its waves mount up, you still them.
> You crushed Rahab like one of the slain;
>> with your strong arm you scattered your enemies.

Compare also Psalm 74:13–14; Isaiah 27:1; 51:9–10.

Making the heavens beautifully bright by his breath could be a reference to the creation account of Genesis, when God separated the light from the darkness of the initial chaos (Ge 1:2–4), but it more likely refers to the clearing of the skies after a storm. Job, then, demonstrates God's authority over the domain of Mot (the god of death) in vv.5–6 and over the domain of Baal (the cosmic storm god) in vv.7–10. And in vv.12–13 Job draws attention to God's awe-inspiring power over the domain of Yam (the stormy sea-god). The same imagery is evoked and the same theology taught when Jesus stilled the waves (Mt 8:23–27), a powerful demonstration of the deity of the Son of Man.

14 For Job these manifestations and deeds are but mere shadows or whispers of the smallest part of God's might. We stand merely at the fringe of his majestic power. Who among us can even begin to comprehend this fully, let alone fully realize the thunderous might of which he is capable? How beautifully and humbly Job asserts the majestic omnipotence of God! But he ends the poem convinced of the mystery that surrounds that omnipotence.

NOTES

2 Andersen's translation, 217 ("How have you saved with your arm the strengthless?"), of זְרוֹעַ (zᵉrôaᶜ, NIV, "the arm") is good. In poetry prepositions are often not written. In OT literature "the arm" saves, it is not itself saved. So read "saved by [your] arm the feeble."

5 On the use of רְפָאִים ($r^e\bar{p}\bar{a}$'îm, "the dead"; GK 8327) in Ugaritic and the Bible, see J. C. de Moor ("Rapiuma-Rephaim," *ZAW* 88/3 [1976]: 323–45), C. L'Heureux ("The Ugaritic and Biblical Rephaim," *HTR* 67 [1974]: 265–74), and more recently H. Rouillard, "Rephaim," *DDD*, 1308–24, as well as *NIDOTTE*, 3:1173–80.

Both the Hebrew and resultant translations of מִתָּחַת (*mittaḥat*; NIV, "those beneath") are difficult to understand. Blommerde's solution should be given serious consideration. He takes the *mem* as enclitic with the preceding word and vocalizes *tḥt* as Hiphil of *ḥtt* ("be dismayed"; GK 3169). Thus *tēḥat* is third feminine singular followed by a subject considered collective (cf. BDB, 565, for "waters" with singular subject), giving the meaning "the waters and those living in them are dismayed" (cf. Pope, 182).

6 אֲבַדּוֹן ($^a\!baddôn$, "Destruction, Abaddon," from the root ʾābad, the "place of destruction"; GK 11) is the netherworld; and only rarely does this word mean general "destruction" (see Job 31:12 and perhaps also in 1QM fragment 9:3, *TDOT*, 23), though often so translated in modern versions. Gordis (*Job*, 279) suggests that the term Abaddon came into use later than Sheol and may carry the meaning "the land of destruction of evildoers," as against the older idea of Sheol as the undifferentiated domicile of the dead. Among the plethora of suggestions for the etymology of Sheol, Gordis thinks the proposal that it derives from the Hebrew שָׁאַל (*šʾl*, "ask, inquire"; GK 8626) has the most support. As "the place of inquiry," Sheol does not refer to necromancy but to "the place of God's inquiry" (M. Jastrow Jr., "The Babylonian Term šuʾalu," *AJSL* 14 [1897]: 170).

7 Concerning צָפוֹן עַל־תֹּהוּ (*ṣāpôn ʿal-tōhû*, "the northern [skies] over empty space"), in the Introduction and comments above, I have preferred to render צָפוֹן (*ṣāpôn*; GK 7600) "the heavens" (the celestial mountain) as God's abode. Though תֹּהוּ (*tōhû*) can mean "wasteland" (cf. 6:18 and 12:24 and possibly Ge 1:2), here and in Isaiah 40:17, 23 it means "the void, nothing," as proved by the parallelism.

9 Gordis (*Job*, 279) disagrees with many—including the NIV—who render כֶּסֶה (*kisseh*) "full moon," which he claims should be read as in the MT: "throne" (not *kēseh*, which he claims means "the day of the full moon" in Psalm 81:3 [4] and in Phoenician and Syriac). The NIV needs a marginal note (such as the NLT provides), for the KJV's "throne" is still a viable translation (cf. comments above; see also Konkel, 164, for this view). Habel, 372, points out that it is "his cloud" ($^c\!nānô$)—that is, "God's own cloud, not clouds in general"—that covers his throne.

The quadriliteral פַּרְשֵׁז (*paršēz*, "spreading") is unique. There is no consensus on its origin, but all agree it is a variant of the word *pāraś* ("spread"; GK 7298). It may be a combination of *pāraz* and *pāraś*, both of which mean "to spread" (so Clines, *Job 21–37*, 623).

12 The RV margin adopted by the RSV is based on a homonym of רָגַע (*rāgaʿ*, "churned up"), which has the opposite meaning "to still" (see BDB, 921). But the NIV has been guided by the similar texts of Isaiah 51:15 and Jeremiah 31:35.

13 In שָׁמַיִם שִׁפְרָה (*šāmayim šiprâ*, "the skies became fair"), the masculine plural noun going with the feminine singular verb raises a question about the translation of *šiprâ* ("brightness") as "became fair." Some see the preposition בּ (*b*) at the beginning of the line as dittography with the final consonant in v.12. Therefore "his breath [wind]" is the subject of a verb *šiprâ* (Piel), meaning (from Arabic) "sweeps clean" (Dhorme). Others feel the parallel line "pierced the gliding serpent" is mythopoeic language, so this line cannot be the clearing of the sky after a storm but something that goes with the parallel. Dhorme, Gordis, and Habel view the ב (*b*) before רוחו (*rûḥô*) as a dittograph; and Habel follows Gordis in reading: "his breath spread out [cf. *šaprîr* (Jer 43:10), BDB 1051] the heavens" (Gordis, *Job*, 279). Tur-Sinai (*Job*), followed by Pope, resorts to the Akkadian *sapāru* ("net" or "bag") and completely redivides and revocalizes *šāmayim* ("the skies") to read *śîm yām śiprâ* ("he put the sea in a bag").

14 דְּרָכָו (*dᵉrākāw*) is literally "his ways." Dahood et al. (cf. *Psalms*, 16:2, for bibliography) have extrapolated from the Ugaritic word *drkt* ("throne") the meaning "dominion, power," which they think is sometimes applicable to OT texts (cf. Pr 8:22). Here and in 40:19, the NIV has translated the word "work," since it frequently refers to actions (cf. BDB, 203).

E. Job's Closing Disclosure (27:1–23)

OVERVIEW

We are faced with the problem of how this speech fits in. Critics have given various reasons for the change from "Then Job replied" (6:1; 9:1; 12:1; 16:1; 19:1; 21:1; 23:1; 26:1) to "And Job continued his discourse" (27:1). Most feel the new formula was not original but was added because of a jumbled text. The same formula is used in 29:1 to mark off a clearly separate discourse. So here it also marks a separate discourse (ch. 27), probably as a concluding statement by Job to balance the introductory statement in chapter 3 (cf. Andersen, 219).

The poem is mainly about God's just punishment of the wicked. Job opens by denying he is such, though his counselors have so labeled him. The chapter divides into two major parts: vv.1–12, where Job speaks directly to his friends with words

a falsely accused victim would utter before an ancient Semitic tribunal—including oaths and an imprecation. Then in vv.13–23 he closes with a poem about the fate of the wicked, a favorite theme of the counselors.

Many take these latter verses to be a fragment of Zophar's final speech (cf. Gordis, *Job*, 291; Dhorme, 386; Clines, *Job 21–37*, 651–77). But as Andersen, 219–20, says (see also Konkel, 167–70; Wilson, 292–94), we do not need to take this as a sudden change in Job's point of view, nor as a later scribe's attempt to make him sound orthodox, nor as Zophar's words. Job has never categorically denied God's justice but simply differed with his counselors on how it is carried out in particular cases, especially his own.

¹And Job continued his discourse:

²"As surely as God lives, who has denied me justice,
　　the Almighty, who has made me taste bitterness of soul,
³as long as I have life within me,
　　the breath of God in my nostrils,
⁴my lips will not speak wickedness,
　　and my tongue will utter no deceit.

⁵I will never admit you are in the right;
    till I die, I will not deny my integrity.
⁶I will maintain my righteousness and never let go of it;
    my conscience will not reproach me as long as I live.

⁷"May my enemies be like the wicked,
    my adversaries like the unjust!
⁸For what hope has the godless when he is cut off,
    when God takes away his life?
⁹Does God listen to his cry
    when distress comes upon him?
¹⁰Will he find delight in the Almighty?
    Will he call upon God at all times?

¹¹"I will teach you about the power of God;
    the ways of the Almighty I will not conceal.
¹²You have all seen this yourselves.
    Why then this meaningless talk?

¹³"Here is the fate God allots to the wicked,
    the heritage a ruthless man receives from the Almighty:
¹⁴However many his children, their fate is the sword;
    his offspring will never have enough to eat.
¹⁵The plague will bury those who survive him,
    and their widows will not weep for them.
¹⁶Though he heaps up silver like dust
    and clothes like piles of clay,
¹⁷what he lays up the righteous will wear,
    and the innocent will divide his silver.
¹⁸The house he builds is like a moth's cocoon,
    like a hut made by a watchman.
¹⁹He lies down wealthy, but will do so no more;
    when he opens his eyes, all is gone.
²⁰Terrors overtake him like a flood;
    a tempest snatches him away in the night.
²¹The east wind carries him off, and he is gone;
    it sweeps him out of his place.
²²It hurls itself against him without mercy
    as he flees headlong from its power.
²³It claps its hands in derision
    and hisses him out of his place.

COMMENTARY

1–6 An oath based on the existence of God is the most extreme measure available (the last resort) in Job's society for a condemned person to plead innocent. Either he is innocent, or he will suffer the divine sanctions; for if Job is a liar, he has blasphemed God. He is saying that his integrity (blamelessness, not sinlessness) is more important to him than life itself (v.5).

But Job does not fear death, for he has spoken the truth. He knows he can swear before God without forfeiting his life. He feels God has denied him justice but inconsistently still knows that somehow God is just; so he can swear by his life. This same incongruity applies also to his earlier fantasies, when with highly emotional words he viewed God as his enemy (9:14–31; 16:7–14; 19:7–12). Refusal to accept the possibility of incongruous rhetoric baffles interpreters and makes them want to attribute Job's remarks to the counselors. It also baffles Elihu in 34:5–9.

We can all agree with Elihu that God never does wrong (34:10) — we can agree until tragedy comes into our lives. Then we may begin to ask ourselves what we have done wrong, or we may even question God's goodness. Deep down we know that neither question is right. So Job too emphatically denies either alternative. He is throwing the mystery into God's lap, as it were, and leaving it there. Andersen, 220, calls it Job's paradoxical appeal to God against God. Here at the very heart of the problem of evil, the book of Job lays the theological foundation for an answer that Job's faith anticipates but which Job does not fully know. God, the Sovereign and therefore responsible Creator, will himself in the person of his eternal Son solve this human dilemma by bearing the penalty of the sins of humankind, thus showing himself to be both just and the Justifier (Vindicator) of all who trust in him (Ro 3:26).

7–10 Job's oath is followed by this imprecation against his detractors (v.7). Imprecatory rhetoric is difficult for Westerners to understand. But in the Semitic world it is still an honorable rhetorical device. The imprecation has a juridical function and was frequently a hyperbolic means (cf. Pss 109:6–15; 139:19–22) of dealing with false accusation and oppression. Legally the false accusations and the very crimes committed are called down on the perpetrator's head.

Since the counselors have falsely accused Job of being wicked, they deserve to be punished like the wicked. They know nothing of mercy though Job pleaded for it (19:21). They spoke only of God's justice and power; yet they will become the objects of God's mercy despite Job's imprecation, which is later changed to prayer in their behalf (42:7–9). The imprecation, however, still serves a purpose. It is a dramatic means by which Job, as a blameless man, declares himself on God's side.

11–12 Here Job adds a warning and makes an application directly to his "friends." He reminds them of an issue on which they all agree — that the wicked deserve God's wrath. But they have put Job in that category falsely. He does not have to explain to them about God's ability to set things straight. Verse 11 can and should be understood as a question: "Must I teach you about God's power to punish? Indeed, I could never conceal from you a subject on which you have expounded at length."

13–23 Job expounds eloquently the subject the counselors know so much about. We might say he is giving this stanza on the fate of the wicked to dramatize in "living metaphor" the punishment they deserve for their false and arrogant accusation.

The stanza has an *inclusio* structure; that is, the opening and closing lines answer to each other. But this can only be seen when two items in v.23 are understood. First, the verbs and pronoun should be taken as third masculine singular. The reference is to God in v.13, not to the storm in the preceding verse. Second, "his place" at the end of v.23 means "heaven," God's place. Both prepositions in the Hebrew text, then, make sense. The verse reads: "He claps his hands against them and hisses at them from his dwelling [heaven]" (see Notes).

NOTES

1 מְשָׁלוֹ (meṡālô, "his discourse") means a poetic discourse, but no single English word can express fully its meaning (see *NIDOTTE*, 2:1134–35). The etymology is "a similitude or comparison" that many of the proverbs (māṡāl; GK 5442) in the book of Proverbs are. In usage the term includes parables, riddles, and other difficult sayings. Jesus frequently used māṡāl language (cf. Jn 4:13; 6:53–58; 10:6–10; 11:25). There were also the professional singers (mōṡelîm, Nu 21:27) and oracular poems of Balaam (Nu 23:7, 18; 24:3, 15, 21–23) where the same verb is employed (נָשָׂא, nāṡāʾ; GK 5951 as here in Job—"he took [lifted] up his māṡāl" (cf. Isa 14:4; Hab 2:6). The verb expresses the public aspect of this communication, and the auxiliary verb יָסַף (yāsap, "to add") shows this is a continuation of what Job has been doing.

6 There is a problem translating לֹא־יֶחֱרַף (lōʾ-yeḥerap) as "'will not reproach me" since there is no "me" in the text and the verb in this root would have to be Piel for this transitive meaning. This is the only place it appears in the Qal imperfect. Guilleaume, 109, relates it to the Arabic ḥarafa ("to change the mind"). This gives the reading "my mind will not change as long as I live." But using the Arabic dictionary in this way can be precarious (cf. Pope, Dhorme). Another alternative is that Job is asserting that he "will not reproach his days"; that is, he does not regret anything he has done, for he has led a blameless life (see NRSV).

7 The jussive establishes יְהִי כְרָשָׁע (yehî kerāṡāʿ, "may my enemies be like") as an imprecation. This terminology (hāyâ + k, "be like") here means "suffer the fate of."

11 Pope ignores אֶתְכֶם (ʾetkem, "you"), the second masculine plural pronoun, when putting these words into Zophar's mouth. At least Dhorme does not begin Zophar until v.13. But I have given reasons for leaving these as Job's words. Clines (*Job 21–37*, 651) says that vv.11–12 are part of Job's ninth speech and follow 27:6.

In בְּיַד־אֵל (beyad-ʾēl, "about the power of God"), the term yād ("hand"; GK 3338) should not be limited to "power." It could be rendered "his dealings, what he does" with his hand, which may be used for blessing or punishment. Job seems to be warning them.

15 Those who escape war and famine (v.14) will die בַּמָּוֶת (bammāwet, "the death"), which can be any tragic death, not just "the plague" (NIV and many other translations). Even worse than tragic death is the absence of mourning for the dead.

19 In rendering וְלֹא יֵאָסֵף (welōʾ yēʾāsēp) "but will do so no more," the NIV has followed the LXX (yôsîp) without a footnote. The MT says, "And he shall not be gathered." It is probably a rhetorical question and therefore refers to a person's dying with his eyes still open.

23 The grammatical difficulties with which Pope wrestles are solved if the verse is understood as an *inclusio* with v.13, as argued above. For מָקוֹם (māqôm) as God's "place, abode," see 1 Kings 8:30; 2 Chronicles 6:21; Isaiah 26:21; Hosea 5:15; Micah 1:3.

III. INTERLUDE ON WISDOM (28:1–28)

OVERVIEW

The purpose and function of this poem has brought about considerable debate (see A. Lo, *Job 28 as Rhetoric: An Analysis of Job 28 in the Context of Job 22–31* [VTSup 97; Leiden: Brill, 2003]). Many view it as extraneous and make no effort to integrate it with the rest of the book. Although it stresses a typical theme (the inaccessibility of wisdom except through piety), it appears to be more than that. There is a deeper reason it is in the book. Dhorme, 1, suggests that it is to express a judgment on the previous chapters. Since the dialogue has reached an impasse, the author now makes his own comment on the powerlessness of human efforts to penetrate secrets that belong only to God.

No speaker is identified at the beginning of the poem, though one might assume the author meant it to be Job. But the change goes beyond the usual discursiveness to a complete change in literary genre. The tone is so irenic that one need not assume Job is speaking. When we hear Job again in chapter 29, he is still in the midst of his struggle. As both Dhorme and Andersen, 222–24, observe, this is a calm meditation compared with Job's hot words.

The unknown author who composed the entire book in its present ABA (prose-poetry-prose) pattern now uses another trifold symmetrical pattern within the poetry. He inserts between the Dialogue in chapters 3–27 (three rounds corresponding to the three counselors) and the Monologue format in chapters 29–41 (three speeches based on three characters) his own wisdom poem as an apex. Chapter 28 is not the climax; that is reserved for the theophany at the end. The drive toward symmetry is an important aesthetic principle of OT poetry. Parallelism appears at every level. It is imbedded in lines, stanzas, poems, and books. The structure of this poem is as follows:

Introduction: The Source of All Treasure (vv. 1–2)
   I. First Stanza: The Discovery of Treasure (vv. 3–11)
      Refrain and Response: Wisdom Elusive (vv. 12–14)
  II. Second Stanza: Wisdom as Treasure (vv. 15–19)
      Refrain and Response: Wisdom Elusive (vv. 20–22)
 III. Third Stanza: God and Wisdom (vv. 23–27)
      Conclusion: The Source of Wisdom (v. 28)

The content of the chapter about the elusiveness of wisdom is climaxed with the admonition that wisdom may be attained only through submission to God. The theme is stated twice in the refrain, which appears in vv. 12, 20. Job was frustrated and unable to find a wisdom solution to the mystery behind his suffering. The counselors had been only a hindrance. So this theme—"Where can you find wisdom?"—is certainly not extraneous.

The poem develops the theme with skill by first concentrating on humans' inquisitive nature and technological ability, which enable them to find the riches of the earth no matter how difficult they are to obtain (vv. 1–11). The second stanza dwells on the value of wisdom and its scarcity compared with even the greatest treasure on earth (vv.15–19). The third stanza (vv.23–27) finally addresses the question asked in the refrain. Wisdom has a source, but it is so elusive that only God knows the way to it. That is because he is omniscient (v.24) and is wisdom's Master (v.27).

People find it only when they fear God and honor him as God (v.28).

The chapter as the literary apex of the book anticipates the theophany but does so without creating a climax. God alone has the answer—or better, is the answer to the mystery Job and his friends have sought to fathom.

> [1]"There is a mine for silver
>   and a place where gold is refined.
> [2]Iron is taken from the earth,
>   and copper is smelted from ore.
> [3]Man puts an end to the darkness;
>   he searches the farthest recesses
>   for ore in the blackest darkness.
> [4]Far from where people dwell he cuts a shaft,
>   in places forgotten by the foot of man;
>   far from men he dangles and sways.
> [5]The earth, from which food comes,
>   is transformed below as by fire;
> [6]sapphires come from its rocks,
>   and its dust contains nuggets of gold.
> [7]No bird of prey knows that hidden path,
>   no falcon's eye has seen it.
> [8]Proud beasts do not set foot on it,
>   and no lion prowls there.
> [9]Man's hand assaults the flinty rock
>   and lays bare the roots of the mountains.
> [10]He tunnels through the rock;
>   his eyes see all its treasures.
> [11]He searches the sources of the rivers
>   and brings hidden things to light.
>
> [12]"But where can wisdom be found?
>   Where does understanding dwell?
> [13]Man does not comprehend its worth;
>   it cannot be found in the land of the living.
> [14]The deep says, 'It is not in me';
>   the sea says, 'It is not with me.'

¹⁵It cannot be bought with the finest gold,
  nor can its price be weighed in silver.
¹⁶It cannot be bought with the gold of Ophir,
  with precious onyx or sapphires.
¹⁷Neither gold nor crystal can compare with it,
  nor can it be had for jewels of gold.
¹⁸Coral and jasper are not worthy of mention;
  the price of wisdom is beyond rubies.
¹⁹The topaz of Cush cannot compare with it;
  it cannot be bought with pure gold.

²⁰"Where then does wisdom come from?
  Where does understanding dwell?
²¹It is hidden from the eyes of every living thing,
  concealed even from the birds of the air.
²²Destruction and Death say,
  'Only a rumor of it has reached our ears.'
²³God understands the way to it
  and he alone knows where it dwells,
²⁴for he views the ends of the earth
  and sees everything under the heavens.
²⁵When he established the force of the wind
  and measured out the waters,
²⁶when he made a decree for the rain
  and a path for the thunderstorm,
²⁷then he looked at wisdom and appraised it;
  he confirmed it and tested it.
²⁸And he said to man,
  'The fear of the Lord—that is wisdom,
  and to shun evil is understanding.'"

COMMENTARY

1−2 Verses 1−2 state what appears to be a truism—earth's material riches have a source. But these two verses accomplish a rhetorical purpose by asserting that humans are able to plumb the depths of the earth to discover precious metals and ores. They set the tone without explicitly stating the theme. Dahood (*Ugaritic-Hebrew Philology*, 67) has missed the real parallelism by assuming *môṣā'* ("place of going forth") does not mean "mine" or "source" but "smelter," derived from an obscure root. The quatrain (vv.1–2) is clear. The first line of each bicolon refers to mining and the second to smelting.

3–11 These verses illustrate ancient people's technological ability in mining. Our scant knowledge of mining technique in the OT world has increased in recent years. B. Rothenberg's *Timna: Valley of the Biblical Copper Mines* (London: Thames & Hudson, 1972) presents the evidence for six thousand years of metallurgy in the Arabah. There smelting was done near the mines, but shaft mining is not evident till Roman times. A more sweeping summary of what we know about ancient mining and metal technology in the ancient Near Eastern world is provided by J. Muhley, "Mining and Metalwork in Ancient Western Asia" (in *Civilizations of the Ancient Near East* [ed. J. Sasson; Hendrickson, 1995]: 3:1501–21).

Searching in the blackest darkness requires light (v.3). This could be accomplished by cutting a shaft and letting in sunlight or by torches. We know mining lamps were used in Nubia in the first century BC (Gordis, *Job*, 304). The ability to cut shafts through rock is seen in the elaborate "waterworks" in cities such as Jerusalem and Megiddo. It began long before the tunnel of Hezekiah, whose Siloam Inscription tells of the rigors of boring through limestone. The mines at Serabitel Khadem demonstrate the same ability to cut through long distances of solid rock. Copper was mined in Edom and the Sinai Peninsula from Chalcolithic times on.

While there was no gold in Palestine, Egypt controlled rich mines in Nubia. Tushratta, king of Mitanni, wrote Amenhotep III that the gold in Egypt was like dust in the streets (*CAH*, 2.3, pt. 1, 486). As for iron, it was not used widely in Palestine till shortly before 1200 BC, but there is evidence of working terrestrial iron (as opposed to meteorite iron) back to about 6000 BC (see W. Kaiser Jr., "The Literary Form of Genesis 1–11," in *New Per-* *spectives on the Old Testament* [ed. B. J. Payne; Waco, Tex.: Word, 1970], 55). The OT reflects Israel's lack of technical knowledge in smelting and smithing iron before the time of David. The Philistine monopoly is mentioned in 1 Samuel 13:19–21. Iron mining was developed on the plateau east of the Jordan Valley, and clay in the floor of the valley was used in making large bronze castings for Solomon's temple (1Ki 7:46). He also imported (1Ki 10:11) large quantities of gold and precious stones from Ophir (Africa?; v.16).

Apart from the translation difficulties at the beginning of v.4 (see Notes), we now have knowledge of miners' being lowered down deep shafts in cages or baskets. Verse 5 could be a reference to volcanic action, but there is ancient evidence of shaft mining where fire was used to split rocks and to reach ore (see below).

Discoveries at Vinca, near Belgrade, and Rudna Glava, in Yugoslavia, reveal advanced knowledge of metallurgy dating back to 4500 BC (carbon–14 dating). Mining was a well-developed art in Europe long before the age of metals and on a small scale existed ten thousand years ago. This information fits the remembrance of early metallurgy reflected in Genesis 4:22. Shaft mining is evident, showing that the miners used ropes to haul out ore. Smelting was done with goatskin bellows. The often-vertical shafts varied in diameter up to five feet and followed the veins of ore (see B. Jovanovic and B. S. Ottaway, "Copper Mining and Metallurgy in the Vinca Group," *Antiquity* 50 [1976]: 104–13).

In the Late Bronze Age, an interesting form of shaft mining was carried on in the Austrian Alps at Mitterberg, where ore was separated by setting fire to the shafts and letting them burn for days and weeks. They also used small fires in the shafts to facilitate quarrying by alternating heating and cooling with water to crack the rock. In the Early Bronze Age in Iran (Veshonveh) and in Central

Turkey (Koslu), underground shafts over 150 feet long were worked. All these things happened in places far removed from the biblical scene, but their early date makes the knowledge in Job 28 far from surprising (see B. Jovanovic, "The Origins of Copper Mining in Europe," *Scientific American* 242/5 [1980]: 152−67).

Humans, the dauntless technologists, in their search for treasure reach paths that even a falcon's eye (one of the best eyes in nature) cannot see (v.7). Where beasts at the top of the food chain (v.8) cannot set foot, human hands touch as they "lay bare the roots of the mountains" (v.9).

12−14 The refrain states the theme and is followed by a response. (It is also possible that the refrain in v.12 concludes the section and vv.13−14 begin the next stanza, which concludes with a repeat of the refrain in v.20.) Compare the refrain followed by response in Psalm 107:8 and 9; 15 and 16; 21 and 22; 31 and 32.

In v.13 the response is clearer when the Hebrew translated "comprehend its worth" is rendered "know its abode" (see Notes). It is important to observe how as a refrain vv.12−14 are parallel in form and meaning with vv.20−22. In v.14 "the deep" and "the sea" give the same negative response as do "Destruction" and "Death" in v.22. The thrust is that even if one were able to probe these inaccessible places, wisdom cannot be found.

15−19 Unlike Proverbs 1, 8, and 9, wisdom here is not personified but is hypostatized—that is, given substance and objectivity so that the author can compare the search for it with the human search for treasures of gold and the like. The point is that human intelligence and determination enable people to accomplish amazing feats of technical ingenuity, but left to themselves they cannot find wisdom. Wisdom as a treasure is rarer than any other. Even with a wealth of technical knowledge, people cannot purchase wisdom.

The author piles up words for precious metals and stones to lay stress on how exceedingly rare and costly wisdom is. He uses four different terms for gold, of which the exact nuances elude us: the finest (red?) gold (*segôr*, v.15), gold of Ophir (*ketem ʾôpîr*, v.16), fine gold (*pāz*, v.17), and pure gold (*ketem tāhôr*, v.19). To emphasize his point he adds eight kinds of precious jewels in vv.16−19. Human beings may be clever, even ingenious and wealthy, but they are rarely wise.

20−22 Verses 12 and 20 are identical except for the verb. But there is no special significance to the change in verbs and no reason to change the text. They are clearly the same refrain. Verse 13 (see Notes) and 21 give the same answer to the questions, though in different terms. Verse 13 stresses human ignorance of wisdom and v.21 nature's blindness to wisdom. That Destruction (Abaddon, the place of the dead) and Death have a rumor about wisdom (v.22) probably means those who reach that place have a belated understanding they have missed in life (cf. the rich man in Lk 16:19−31).

23−27 The poem reaches its climax. God alone knows where the wisdom is (v.23), for he is omniscient. Humans must search for their treasure (vv.3−11), but God sees everything without searching (v.24). When he brought order out of the primeval chaos (vv.25−26), he used wisdom to do it. Wisdom is the summary of the genius God used to fashion the universe. In some sense it is objective to God (Pr 8:22), for he looked at it as though it were a blueprint of creation. He examined and approved it (v.27), and

> By wisdom the LORD laid the earth's foundations,
>> by understanding he set the heavens in place;
> by his knowledge the deeps were divided,
>> and the clouds let drop the dew. (Pr 3:19−20)

28 Having shown God as the Source of wisdom, the author now makes his application to humans.

They must look to God for wisdom. Humans may share in it only through knowledge of the revealed mind of God. To acknowledge him as God and live within the sphere of his life-giving precepts is wisdom for human beings (Dt 4:5–6; Ps 111:10; Pr 8:4–9; 9:10).

In the process of studying God's revelation, human beings learn that the price of wisdom—perfect obedience to God—is still beyond their reach.

In the spirit of Job 28, the apostle in Romans 11:33 speaks of "the depth of the riches of the wisdom and knowledge of God" and of "how unsearchable [are] his judgments." He assures us this mystery is hidden in Christ, through whom is revealed "the full riches of complete understanding" and "all the treasures of wisdom and knowledge" (Col 2:2–3). And in Ephesians 3:8–10 he calls the gospel "the unsearchable riches of Christ" and "the manifold wisdom of God."

NOTES

1 The initial particle כִּי (*kî*) is asseverative and does not need to be translated.

2 The passive participle יָצוּק (*yāṣûq*, "is smelted") has adjectival force. This is an example of a double-duty preposition. The מִן (*min*, "from") is carried over (cf. Blommerde, 92–93).

3 In this verse the third line lacks a verb and prepositions. As in v.2 the verb is implied from line 2 and prepositions are supplied as the context requires. Gordis (*Job*, 305) takes this third line with what follows. He sees "the rock of darkness and gloom" as lava.

4 מֵעִם־גָּר (*mē'im-gār*, "far from where people dwell") is difficult. Ancient and modern versions vary greatly. The KJV flooded the mines by taking *nahal* (NIV, "shaft") as a flowing wadi. Gordis (*Job*, 305) takes *gār* as a "crater" and reads, "the lava ... cleaves a channel from the crater." Dhorme (cf. NEB) vocalize *'im* as *'am* ("people") and use the initial *mem* to pluralize *nahal*, rendering "a foreign people has pierced shafts." Clines (*Job 21–37*, 896) provides a full discussion of all the many possibilities.

9 For הָפַךְ מִשֹּׁרֶשׁ (*hāpak miššōreš*), the NIV reads *hāpak-ma* (enclitic *mem*) followed by the direct object—"he lays bare the roots of" (Hummel, 103).

11 On מִבְּכִי נְהָרוֹת (*mibbᵉkî nᵉhārôt*, "the sources of the rivers"), compare the KJV's, "He bindeth the floods from overflowing." The Ugaritic *mbk nhrm* ("the source of the two rivers," that is, the place of the god El's abode; cf. H. L. Ginsburg, "The Ugaritic Texts and Textual Criticism," *JBL* 62 [1943]: 111; Pope, 203) has provided clarity for this passage, which the NIV has followed. But the NIV margin, following the RSV, is unnecessary; the Hebrew text does not have to be translated "dams up" (from *hbš*, "binds") for פ (*p*) and ב (*b*) can interchange. As Hebrew *npš* can be *nbš* in Phoenician, so *hpš* ("searches") might be written *hbš* in this dialect.

12 There is no discrepancy in meaning between תִּמָּצֵא (*timmāṣē'*, "be found") and תָבוֹא (*tābô'*, "come from") in v.20. Hosea 14:8 [9] shows *mṣ'* can be used with *min* (as here) with the meaning "comes from." The variation is most likely intentional in order to avoid the monotony of a strict repetition.

13 On עֶרְכָּה (*'erkāh*), in my comments above I have not gone along with the NIV's translation ("its worth"), for there no longer need be a choice between the LXX (presumably based on original Hebrew *darkāh*, "its way"; cf. RSV and BHS mg.) and the MT ("worth, price"). Dahood ("Hebrew-Ugaritic Lexicography VII," 355) has shown that the root *'rk* can mean "house, abode" (cf. Pope, 203, for additional information). This fits beautifully our idea that vv.12–14 and vv.20–22 are refrain units that parallel each other.

16 The exact identification of most of these precious stones — e.g., בְּשֹׁהַם (bešôham, "with … onyx") is guesswork.

17 On זְכוֹכִית (zekôkît, "crystal"), Pope's note is illuminating. This is glass (cf. Arab., Syr.), which at that time was considered precious enough to be considered jewels.

21 Concerning וְנֶעֶלְמָה (wenecelmâ, "it is hidden"), Blommerde, 92–93, notes the presence of the emphatic *waw* (cf. 31:30), which ties this verse nicely to v.20, answering, "It is hidden, indeed."

23 Instead of הֵבִין (hēbîn, "understands"), six MSS and the LXX would have us read הֵכִין (hēkîn, "establishes"); but the parallel with יָדַע (yādac, "knows") rules it out (cf. Fisher, 1:198).

26 חֹק (ḥōq) can mean "a decree" in Proverbs 8:29 and Jeremiah 5:22; however, NIV renders it "boundary" in reference to God's limitation of the sea. But here "rain" is in view, as in Job 38:25, where different words are used; but the idea is the same: "Who cuts a channel for the torrents of rain?" The force of the parallelism in v.26b and of the root חקק (ḥqq, "to engrave, cut") allows one to render ḥōq as "conduit, channel."

27 The existence of a few MSS and editions reading הֱבִינָה (hēbînâ, "he understood") instead of הֱכִינָהּ (hekînāh, "he confirmed it") has led Dhorme and Pope to accept the former. But the ellipsis use of kûn is similar to this in Judges 12:6. That also could be a mistake for bîn except that the Hiphil of kûn ("direct") + lēb ("the heart") means "give attention" (cf. Job 11:13; Ps 78:8 et al.). Just as śîm lēb ("pay attention") sometimes appears with ellipsis of lēb (see Notes on 4:20; 23:6; 24:12; and 34:23), the idiom here and in Judges 12:6 might better be translated, "he gave attention to it" (cf. BDB, 466).

28 Reasons presumed to be strong are listed for taking this verse as an editorial appendage, making the poem an agnostic statement about humans and wisdom (Fohrer). The arguments, however, are not as strong as they appear to be (see Habel, 400–401).

(1) The introductory formula "And he said to man" is said to be too short for a poetic line and hence was a splice (Pope). But Psalm 50:16 is the same kind of formula followed by a series of synonymous bicola. Including the formula in the balance of lines creates a tricolon (cf. vv.3–4) with an acceptable syllable count of 6/9/6 (cf. Pr 4:4).

(2) The form of the divine name as ʾadōnāy, used here only in Job, is supposed to prove this verse was added. It merely supports our contention that this entire chapter must be the words of the author who is using this term for God in contrast to those used by the non-Israelite characters. Many MSS have yhwh (cf. BHS mg.).

(3) It is also said that there is too sharp a cleavage between "metaphysical wisdom" and "practical wisdom." The latter (v.28) was supposedly added by the conservative school as an antidote to the agnostic tenor of the poem. But note how "wisdom" (ḥokmâ) is balanced by "understanding" (bînâ) in vv.12, 20, and 28. By asking about the source of wisdom, the refrains set the stage for the conclusion. Moreover, the poem opened with a statement about the source of human treasure and closes with a statement about the source of humans' greatest treasure.

Clines (*Job 21–37*, 925) adds that without v.28 the chapter simply says that wisdom is with God and unattainable to human beings. He rightly argues that such a message is not appropriate to this context of the book no matter who is thought to utter these words.

IV. THE MONOLOGUES (29:1–42:6)

A. Job's Peroration (29:1–31:40)

1. His Past Honor and Blessing (29:1–25)

OVERVIEW

Like a lawyer summing up his case, Job begins his monologue with an emotional recall of his former happiness, wealth, and honor (ch. 29) and proceeds to lament, not the loss of wealth, but the loss of his dignity and God's friendship (ch. 30). He completes this trilogy with a final protestation of innocence (ch. 31). This chapter is sometimes called a negative confession. It is really an oath of innocence that effectively concludes with Job's signature in 31:35. There is no more Job can say; his case rests in God's hands. Job has to be shown to be a liar and suffer the punishment he calls upon himself or be vindicated.

Chapter 29 is a classic example of Semitic rhetoric with one of the elements of good style being a symmetrical structure. Unfortunately, scholars have imposed their own notions of what the rhetoric should be and so have changed its order and obscured its beauty (cf. Dhorme, Pope, NEB; NJB). These authors all move vv.21–25 up to follow v.10. In this writer's opinion, the order of the verses in the Hebrew text presents the author's original symmetrical intention. The pattern is as follows:

Blessing (vv.2–6)
Honor (vv.7–10/11)
Job's benevolence (vv.11/12–17)
Blessing (vv.18–20)
Honor (vv.21–25)

Chapter 29 deals with both active and passive aspects of Job's former life. He was blessed by God and honored by people. But he was also socially active, a benefactor and leader. His benevolence was an important part of the high position he held in his society, where social righteousness was expected of every ruling elder. The Ugaritic literature and Hammurabi's Code both stress the responsibility of rulers to protect the poor and champion the cause of widows and orphans. So a description of Job's benevolence is in the climactic position in this oration, with the key line (v.14) in the exact middle of the poem. This verse sums up his benevolence in a striking metaphor about his being clothed with righteousness. Such benevolence establishes his right to the honor and blessing that the surrounding verses describe. This chapter, then, is setting the stage for chapter 30.

¹Job continued his discourse

²"How I long for the months gone by,
   for the days when God watched over me,
³when his lamp shone upon my head
   and by his light I walked through darkness!

⁴Oh, for the days when I was in my prime,
  when God's intimate friendship blessed my house,
⁵when the Almighty was still with me
  and my children were around me,
⁶when my path was drenched with cream
  and the rock poured out for me streams of olive oil.

⁷"When I went to the gate of the city
  and took my seat in the public square,
⁸the young men saw me and stepped aside
  and the old men rose to their feet;
⁹the chief men refrained from speaking
  and covered their mouths with their hands;
¹⁰the voices of the nobles were hushed,
  and their tongues stuck to the roof of their mouths.
¹¹Whoever heard me spoke well of me,
  and those who saw me commended me,
¹²because I rescued the poor who cried for help,
  and the fatherless who had none to assist him.
¹³The man who was dying blessed me;
  I made the widow's heart sing.
¹⁴I put on righteousness as my clothing;
  justice was my robe and my turban.
¹⁵I was eyes to the blind
  and feet to the lame.
¹⁶I was a father to the needy;
  I took up the case of the stranger.
¹⁷I broke the fangs of the wicked
  and snatched the victims from their teeth.

¹⁸"I thought, 'I will die in my own house,
  my days as numerous as the grains of sand.
¹⁹My roots will reach to the water,
  and the dew will lie all night on my branches.
²⁰My glory will remain fresh in me,
  the bow ever new in my hand.'

²¹"Men listened to me expectantly,
  waiting in silence for my counsel.
²²After I had spoken, they spoke no more;
  my words fell gently on their ears.

> ²³They waited for me as for showers
>   and drank in my words as the spring rain.
> ²⁴When I smiled at them, they scarcely believed it;
>   the light of my face was precious to them.
> ²⁵I chose the way for them and sat as their chief;
>   I dwelt as a king among his troops;
>   I was like one who comforts mourners.

COMMENTARY

1–6 These words are charged with emotion. Job longs for the precious days when he enjoyed God's watchful care (v.2) and guidance (v.3). God was his friend (vv.4–5a). Job enjoyed the blessings of family and wealth (vv.5b–6?). Like the key line (v.14), v.6 sums up the blessing in figurative language that reminds us of the words used to describe Israel's blessing in the land of promise—there it was "milk and honey," here "cream" (or "butter"; see *NIDOTTE*, 2:166–67] and "olive oil." In Deuteronomy 32:13, Israel was blessed with oil and honey from the rock; in Psalm 81:16 the figure is honey flowing from the rock. The point Job is making is not just that he had cream and olive oil but that he had it in such abundance that only hyperbole can describe it— "drenched with cream" and "streams of olive oil."

7–11 The "public square" (v.7) was the business center, town hall, and courthouse combined. We have no idea what city this is, but any city that had a gate and public square was a major urban center. Job is a city father who occupies a prominent seat (v.8). The reaction to Job in the square seems exaggerated to the western mind, but it is fully in keeping with his culture and times. This deference to Job from young and old, princes and nobles (vv.8–10), shows he is a ruler, or at least the most highly respected.

In the Prologue Job was described as "the greatest man among all the people of the East" (1:3).

Correct protocol demanded silence till the most honored person had spoken. The language excels in its descriptive power: Hushed, with their tongues sticking to the roofs of their mouths, all used to wait in silence for Job to speak (v.10). Verse 11 implies that he had spoken and registers the effect. Seeing v.11 as transitional is another good reason for not disrupting the pattern by jumping to v.21. While it is true that v.21 picks up again the story of Job's honor, so does v.18 continue the theme of v.6.

12–17 There may be good reason to make the stanza break after v.11 with the word "because" (*kî*) of v.12 toned down to "for." This is not certain, but it is clear that these verses are a unit (stanza) about Job's social benevolence. The stanza is both the apex (structurally) and the climax (conceptually) of this first unit of the trilogy. Verse 14 stands in the center of the stanza and the poem. It sums up in a metaphor what the surrounding verses present in action, thus describing his character as righteous. The entire stanza is the climax because it presents Job's major point in the trilogy as well as the reason he was so honored and blessed.

In these few verses Job covers a large area of the social responsibility of rulers who aspired to be godlike (Ps 68:5). The figure in v.14 is striking. Literally Job said, "I put on righteousness and it robed me," implying a veritable incarnation of righteousness. Other passages in both the Old Testament (Isa 52:1; 59:17) and the New Testament (Col 3:9–10) may be cited as using the metaphor of clothing to indicate one's spiritual condition (see *DBI*, 319).

This passage should be read as instruction, as a stimulus to our social conscience. Job responded to the poorest of the poor, gave comfort to the dying and joy to widows, assisted the blind and lame, and assumed the role of father and advocate for those who had no one else to look to. He was not just a protector but militantly opposed the wicked. It is important to see that Job did not concentrate on ritual righteousness (though see 1:5) nor other ethical or religious responsibilities but on that area where humans most often fail—in their response to the sufferings of others. Compassion that knew no bounds is what characterized the life of the one who was truly the righteousness of God incarnate, Jesus Christ, who "took up our infirmities and carried our diseases" (Mt 8:17).

There is not even a hint that Job had any power to perform miracles. The dying blessed him (v.13), not because he could keep them from dying, but perhaps because he provided a way for them to die with dignity. He even found ways to make a widow's heart sing.

This stanza is to be accepted, not as self-righteousness, as some insist, but as an eloquent testimony to the tenor of Job's life as "a blameless and upright" man who "feared God and shunned evil" (1:1, 8; 2:3).

18–20 The man who had provided for others now faces the prospect of a shortened life instead of the patriarchal ideal of 110 years with family gathered about (cf. Ge 50:22). He had hoped to flourish "like a tree planted by streams of water" (Ps 1:3) and to remain strong and virile. But is Job thinking of his family in v.18? Should the Hebrew word translated "nest" be taken figuratively (metonymy) and rendered "house" (NIV)? The problems in v.18

are formidable. The verse reads literally: "I thought, 'With(in) my nest I will expire (die).' " The LXX has "my age will grow old," which has led to surmising that the Hebrew text behind the LXX had *zqny* ("my old age") instead of *qny* ("my nest"). But the Greek translators had a habit of simplifying what they did not understand. The Targum saw the same letters as the MT, giving the Aramaic for "nest" (Pope, 214).

Some translators accept the old rabbinic opinion that the second half of the line speaks of the phoenix (cf. K&D, 2:127; cf. NAB, NEB mg., et al.). The question seems to hinge on whether the word *ḥôl* (usually "sand") can mean "phoenix" at all. Pope, 214–15, rejects Dahood's (originally Albright's) Ugaritic derivation. If this bird with legendary long life and power to renew itself is in view, then "nest" fits the figure: "I shall die in my nest and multiply my days as the phoenix." If not, then the NIV's *ad sensum* translation may be acceptable (but see Notes). In view of the figurative language already used in vv.14, 17, 19, and 20, rendering *qny* ("nest") as "house" certainly impairs the poetic effect.

In v.20 Job thinks of his former "glory" as a warrior and hunter. His "glory remaining fresh" means his continued prowess, vehemence, and splendor with weapons. The parallel "the bow ever new" proves the point (cf. Isa 21:15, *kōbed* ["vehemence"]; NIV, "heat"]; BDB, 458).

21–25 To bring to a balanced conclusion this first of the three connected poems, Job returns to the theme of vv.7–11. Again I emphasize the importance of seeing the stanza in its place, not only for the strophic parallelism mentioned above, but because it must stand immediately before the theme of chapter 30 to create the desired contrast between the high honor Job has enjoyed with the extreme dishonor he presently suffers.

The language on both subjects is choice. Job's effect on others was charismatic. Men waited expectantly to drink in his words (v.23). Even his smile carried a blessing. The terminology of v.24 is not unlike the priestly blessing of Numbers 6:24–25 and the words of Psalm 4:6: "Let the light of your face shine upon us, O LORD." So in this way Job again was godlike, so much so that his counsel was valued (vv.21–23), his approval sought (v.24), and his leadership accepted with gratitude (v.25).

NOTES

2 יַרְחֵי (*yārḥê*, "the months"; cf. 3:6; 7:3; 39:2) as used is typically archaic or Canaanite (Edomite?) since the Israelites regularly used חֹדֶשׁ (*ḥōdeš*, "new moon"), never used in Job. The chapter reveals such language in a number of places—for example, the archaic (full) form of the preposition עֲלֵי (*ʿᵃlê*, vv.3–4, 7; used ten times in Job) and the word קָרֶת (*qāret*) for "city" (v.7; cf. Pr 8:3; 9:3, 14; 11:11).

3 The NIV renders חֹשֶׁךְ (*ḥōšek*) "through darkness." An implied preposition is normal in poetry.

4 "Prime" (*ḥorpî*) is literally "my winter," but here it is used figuratively (see *NIDOTTE*, 2:279).

For בְּסוֹד (*bᵉsôd*, "when [God's] intimate friendship"), the ancient versions have a variety of *ad sensum* readings, but all based on the root *swk* (*skk*), from which some arrive at the meaning, "When God *protected* my tent." This was the verb used when the Accuser said to God, "Have you not put a hedge around him?" (1:10). Most recently Clines (*Job 21–37*, 934–35) has argued from this reading, citing the LXX specifically. But the NIV has stayed with the MT as an infinitive or noun form *swd*, meaning "to counsel or hold council." The problem has been the preposition עֲלֵי (*ʿᵃlê*, "upon" [Pope]; NIV, "blessed"), but compare Rowley's simple rendering: "When the friendship of God was upon my tent."

6 The MT has "anger" (*ḥēmâ*) where the NIV translates "cream," which rightly on the basis of context emends to *ḥemʾâ*.

7 If Gordis and Pope are correct in their claim that public squares were outside the gate as implied in 1 Samuel 31:12; 2 Samuel 21:12; Nehemiah 8:1, then *ʿᵃlê* may mean "from," as in Phoenician (cf. 30:2, 4, and, following Dahood). Another rendering, however, could be: "When I went out the gate [cf. 31:34, *lōʾ-ʾēṣēʾ pātaḥ*, 'I ... would not go outside'] to the city." קָרֶת (*qāret*, "city") may be used metaphorically to mean the people of the city as in Proverbs 11:10–11.

11 The particle כִּי (*kî*) is asseverative and thus not represented in the translation of the NIV.

12 Here the כִּי (*kî*) may or may not be asseverative, depending on whether the verse should be closely tied to v.11.

16 "Stranger" is a translation of the phrase *lōʾ-yādaʿtî* that could be understood as "something I did not understand," but is rightly taken by the NIV as "someone I did not understand" = a stranger.

18 In עִם-קִנִּי (*ʿim-qinnî*, "in my own house"), the preposition is thought to be a problem. Driver and Gray, 201–4, followed by Gordis, see no problem rendering *ʿim* as "within" (cf. Ex 22:24; Lev 25:35–36, 39, 47). There is no linguistic support for the translation "with my nestlings" (cf. Rowley, 238–39).

24 For לֹא יַפִּילוּן (*lōʾ yappîlûn*), the NIV has given a paraphrase: "was precious to them." The Hebrew words say, "They did not allow to fall." Dhorme's paraphrase is better: "Nor was my smile lost on them!" Both amount to the same idea, that Job's approval encouraged them. But others (e.g., Rowley) take it to mean that Job's cheerfulness was not clouded by their despondency. Indeed, Rowley sees both sides of the colon in this sense, reading: "I smiled on [laughed at] them when they had no confidence; / and the light of my countenance they did not cast down."

25 The last line of this verse is awkward as currently translated, but there is no need to drop the line as NEB does, nor to emend the text. Not a single consonant or word needs to be changed. Only a change in the vowels of the last two words creates the line *kaᵃšer ʾōbîlem yonḥu(ma)*, which reads: "as I conducted them they were led." This concludes with the use of enclitic *mem* (cf. Hummel, 85–107) and builds on the Hiphil of יָבַל (*yābal*, "to conduct") and the Hophal of נָחָה (*nāḥâ*, "to lead"; GK 5697; cf. Pope, 212). The verse, then, is a chiasm: a b // b' a'.

2. His Present Dishonor and Suffering (30:1–31)

OVERVIEW

The contrast between chapter 29 and chapter 30 is purposeful and forceful. The threefold use of "But/and now" in 30:1, 9, 16 ties the chapter together and reveals the author's contrastive intention. Moreover, the first verb seems to be used to heighten the contrastive effect. In 29:24 Job said (lit.), "I laughed [śḥq] at them" (at his people who were discouraged) and now (30:1) a brood of ruffians (lit.) "laugh [śḥq] at me." This is the second of the two possible interpretations of 29:24 mentioned above. Throughout 30:1–15 Job expands this theme: the loss of his dignity. If one feels he has exaggerated his honor in chapter 29, the hyperbole on his loss of honor in chapter 30 is even more extreme. Verses 3–8 are typical. Having your peers mock you is bad; but to prove how honorless he is, Job tells how boys, whose fathers

he could not trust to handle his sheepdogs, mock him.

This lengthy description of these good-for-nothing fathers is a special brand of rhetoric. The modern Western mind prefers understatement; so when Semitic literature indulges in overstatement, such hyperbole becomes a mystery to the average Western reader. To define every facet of their debauchery, to state it in six different ways, is not meant to glory in it but to heighten the pathetic nature of his dishonor.

To achieve a full measure of contrast, Job dwelt on the negative side of the three themes of chapter 29 in the following order: honor, blessing, and benevolence. The removal of God's blessing is far worse than affliction by people, so it is put in the climactic central position. The contrastive arrangement is as follows:

I. No Honor from Men (vv.1–15)
  A. Young mockers and their elders (vv.1–8; cf. 29:7–11)
  B. Job assaulted (vv.9–15; cf. 29:21–25)
II. No Blessing from God (vv.16–23; cf. 29:2–6, 18–20)
  A. Job suffers (vv.16–17)
  B. God afflicts (vv.18–19)
  C. Job pleads (v.20)
  D. God afflicts (vv.21–23)

III. No Benevolence for Job (vv.24–31; cf. 29:12–17)
    A. Plea for mercy and help (v.24)
    B. Reminder of his benevolence (v.25)
    C. No benevolence for Job (v.26)
    D. Result: his present condition (vv.27–31)

[1]"But now they mock me,
    men younger than I,
whose fathers I would have disdained
    to put with my sheep dogs.
[2]Of what use was the strength of their hands to me,
    since their vigor had gone from them?
[3]Haggard from want and hunger,
    they roamed the parched land
    in desolate wastelands at night.
[4]In the brush they gathered salt herbs,
    and their food was the root of the broom tree.
[5]They were banished from their fellow men,
    shouted at as if they were thieves.
[6]They were forced to live in the dry stream beds,
    among the rocks and in holes in the ground.
[7]They brayed among the bushes
    and huddled in the undergrowth.
[8]A base and nameless brood,
    they were driven out of the land.

[9]"And now their sons mock me in song;
    I have become a byword among them.
[10]They detest me and keep their distance;
    they do not hesitate to spit in my face.
[11]Now that God has unstrung my bow and afflicted me,
    they throw off restraint in my presence.
[12]On my right the tribe attacks;
    they lay snares for my feet,
    they build their siege ramps against me.
[13]They break up my road;
    they succeed in destroying me—
    without anyone's helping them.

¹⁴They advance as through a gaping breach;
  amid the ruins they come rolling in.
¹⁵Terrors overwhelm me;
  my dignity is driven away as by the wind,
  my safety vanishes like a cloud.

¹⁶"And now my life ebbs away;
  days of suffering grip me.
¹⁷Night pierces my bones;
  my gnawing pains never rest.
¹⁸In his great power ⌞God⌟ becomes like clothing to me;
  he binds me like the neck of my garment.
¹⁹He throws me into the mud,
  and I am reduced to dust and ashes.

²⁰"I cry out to you, O God, but you do not answer;
  I stand up, but you merely look at me.
²¹You turn on me ruthlessly;
  with the might of your hand you attack me.
²²You snatch me up and drive me before the wind;
  you toss me about in the storm.
²³I know you will bring me down to death,
  to the place appointed for all the living.

²⁴"Surely no one lays a hand on a broken man
  when he cries for help in his distress.
²⁵Have I not wept for those in trouble?
  Has not my soul grieved for the poor?
²⁶Yet when I hoped for good, evil came;
  when I looked for light, then came darkness.
²⁷The churning inside me never stops;
  days of suffering confront me.
²⁸I go about blackened, but not by the sun;
  I stand up in the assembly and cry for help.
²⁹I have become a brother of jackals,
  a companion of owls.
³⁰My skin grows black and peels;
  my body burns with fever.
³¹My harp is tuned to mourning,
  and my flute to the sound of wailing.

COMMENTARY

1–10 The conceptual correspondence with 29:7–11 is striking. Note the emphasis on the young and old (29:8) and on the chief men and nobles (29:9–10). The highest strata in society had stood hushed in respect (29:9–10) and then had spoken well (29:11) of Job. Here the lowest riffraff mock him.

Verses 2–8 develop a description of these despicable people who treat Job like a low-life. They are scavengers in the hinterlands, braying like donkeys and barely surviving, but still they feel superior to Job. Indeed they cannot be kept quiet, for he has become "a byword" among them (v.9). In 29:11 men had commended Job; here they detest him (v.10). There they had covered their mouths with their hands (29:9); here they spit in his face (v.10)

11–15 These verses begin with a line that takes us right back to 29:20, where Job mused on his former life as a hero with his bow ever new in his hand. But here God has unstrung his bow, resulting in the opposite situation as pictured in 29:21–25. Job's tribe had gathered about to hear every good word that fell from the lips of their benevolent leader. But here he is no longer leading the way like "a king among his troops" (29:25). Instead, he sees himself like a city under siege (civil war?).

Verses 12–14 use the terminology of siege warfare known from other biblical passages (Hab 1:10). Job has already used similar language of God's imagined attack on him (19:10–12). Here the language is even more precise. The "siege ramps" at the end of v.12 are called literally "roads of ruin." Verse 14 is vivid. Job thinks of himself as a city with a wide, gaping breach in its wall. The stones come crashing down, and amid the rubble the instruments of siege warfare roll through. The tranquility and dignity he had so enjoyed have vanished like a cloud.

16–23 Job shifts from this sorry relationship with people to an even sorrier subject, the removal of God's blessing from his life. He cries out to God but gets no answer. When God was his friend, it was like having a light over him in the midst of darkness (29:3). But at this time his days are full of suffering and his nights of misery (v.16). These verses are important in that they show us that Job's basic complaint still remains. It is not only God's silence (v.20) but especially his violent treatment of Job that has become the sufferer's greatest problem. It would be no problem at all if only Job's concept of God were limited. That not being the case, in Job's mind, it must be God who is responsible for all this.

The figure in v.18 is strange as it appears in the NIV. Most believe the agent in v.18 is God; but since the subject is hid in the verb, some take it as the pain of v.17 (cf. RSV, though see change in NRSV). Some commentators suspect that the difficult v.18 has been disturbed by a well-meaning, pious scribe who could not abide what appeared to him blasphemous (Pope, 223). The problem with this is that the succeeding lines are just as bad if not worse, and they are not disturbed. The Qumran Targum now supports the LXX in reading "seizes my garment" (see Notes). This greatly simplifies the text (RSV).

The NIV's translation of v.18 does not do justice to the key word (*ḥpś*; GK 2924), which it renders "becomes." The Hithpael of *ḥpś* can mean "to disguise oneself" ("let oneself be searched for"; cf. 1Sa 28:8; BDB, 344). The point may be that since God is all powerful, he can do anything. He can even disguise himself as Job's clothing and bind Job's neck at the collar (NIV). But this is unlikely. The use here is more like the Niphal of *ḥpś* as in Obadiah 6, where Esau "is ransacked" or "exposed." Here perhaps Job's clothing "is ripped off," and in the process he is choked by the collar of his tunic and hurled into the mud. Or perhaps we should emend *yithappēś* "to disguise oneself" (supported by LXX, see Clines [*Job 21–37*, 953–54] and NRSV).

Job sees his problem with God as twofold. First, God will not answer him; and, second, God actively afflicts him. This is exactly the bifold nature of his complaint in 13:20–27, even including the point of his being tossed about by the wind (13:25). As reflected in that speech (chs. 13–14), Job's only prospect for the future is death (v.23). What is so devastating to Job is not the fear of death, for he has already asked for it as a relief (6:8–10; 14:3), but that he should have to face it with God as his enemy (13:24). God's constant attack, his ruthless might (v.21), is so completely the opposite of Job's "intimate friendship" with God in those bygone days when he still perceived that God was on his side (29:4–5).

24–31 These verses complete the contrast with chapter 29. Here Job is in the position of those poor wretches to whom his heart and strength went out in 29:12–17. As a summation of his case, he packs his argument with emotion and righteous indignation. Justice is all on his side. The very benevolence he so freely had dispensed (v.25) he now looks for in vain (v.26). Verse 26 also reminds us of his expectations in 29:18–20. So here (vv.27–31) he presents himself to the court as he is, his body marred and burning with fever; he himself is exhibit A. As he often does, Job closes the stanza (v.31) with a strong figure of speech (cf. 29:6, 14, 17, 25; 30:15). His "path [had been] drenched with cream" (cf. 29:6), now his "harp is tuned to mourning and [his] flute to the sound of wailing" (30:31).

NOTES

2 That *kālaḥ* means "vigor" or "strength" in עָלֵימוֹ אָבַד כָּלַח (*ʿālêmô ʾābad kālaḥ*, "since their vigor had gone from them") seems clear from its only other use in 5:26. No doubt the KJV derived "old age" from the same connection, but "old age" makes no sense with the verb *ʾābad* ("perish"). There is a general consensus on the meaning but not on the derivation of *kālaḥ* (cf. Rowley, 191; Pope, 219; *NIDOTTE*, 2:652–54).

Even more vexing is how to fit these verses into Job's thought. Andersen, 235, does not think Job is still talking about the fathers of v.1, which would imply Job refuses to employ them simply because they are decrepit. Verses 2–8, then, are a commentary on these young scoundrels. The NIV rejects this line of reasoning by inserting the words "their sons" (not in the Hebrew) into v.9, though Andersen's views are quite reasonable.

3 Did the men "gnaw" or "roam" the parched land? The root word in הַעֹרְקִים (*haʿōreqîm*) in v.17 means "gnaw." Although the spelling is the same, we cannot be certain they are the same root; for the *ayin* in Hebrew can represent two different Semitic phonemes. On the basis of an Aramaic root, the verse is rendered "flee" in the KJV. This is also the origin of the Targum's "roaming," whence came the NIV's "they roamed." Verse 17, however, unquestionably means "gnaw."

The RSV attaches אֶמֶשׁ (*ʾemeš*; NIV "at night") to what precedes and omits the last two Hebrew words in the verse in an effort to create good poetry since the lines are said to be unbalanced (cf. RSV mg note). Pope, 219, observes that the alliteration here is too striking to be emended away (cf. 38:27). Moreover, the final idiom שׁוֹאָה וּמְשֹׁאָה (*šôʾâ ûmešōʾâ*, "desolate wastelands") also appears in 38:27 and Zephaniah 1:15 in contexts that demand a similar meaning.

But the tricolon is not unbalanced as supposed and therefore should not be changed. The Psalms present numerous lines like this where a short middle element of a tricolon applies equally to both the preceding and the following lines as here (cf. Pss 84:3; 98:2; 121:6).

4 Because לָחְמָם (laḥmām) is used in Isaiah 47:14 (as an infinitive of the root ḥmm, "to warm oneself"), and because it is claimed that "broom tree roots" are not edible and are used to make charcoal, Gesenius (BDB, 328) long ago rejected "their food" (NIV) as the meaning here (cf. RSV, NIV mg.). Andersen, 220, appeals to 11QtgJob, which supports the general idea of "eating." The Qumran Targum, then, is an excellent witness to the ancient Masoretic oral tradition. In light of the Isaiah passage (which has the same vowels), the interpretation here must be left open. In either case, the line describes the destitution of these individuals.

8 נִכְּאוּ (nikkᵉ'û, "they were driven") is thought to come from nkh ("to strike") and therefore to mean "to whip or scourge," but this is not certain. It may mean they were driven from the arable land to the steppe.

11 Because the context of כִּי־יִתְרוֹ פִּתַּח (kî-yitriw pittaḥ, "now that God has unstrung my bow") is about the deeds of these degenerate sons, and because the first two verbs in this verse are singular, Pope wants to emend them to plurals. Most translations assume God is the subject. What is not certain is what kind of "cord" (yeter) this is and whether it is God's or Job's. The oral tradition (Qere) says "my cord," the written (Kethiv) "his cord." But what does "God loosens his cord" mean? "My cord" could be Job's "tent cord" as in 4:21 (cf. K&D, 2:127, "the cord of life"). But since the word is clearly used for a "bowstring" in Psalm 11:2, the NIV has the most satisfactory interpretation, especially in the light of Job's statement in 29:20 and the relationship I have sought to establish between these two chapters.

12 The meaning of פִּרְחַח (pirḥaḥ, "the tribe") is conjectural. The KJV based its "youth" on a similar word in 39:30; Deuteronomy 22:6; and Psalm 84:3, which means "young birds." Gordis (Job, 333) suggests it is used contemptuously here as is our word "bird." Perhaps "brood" or "mob" would be better.

13 G. R. Driver ("Problems in Job," AJSL 52 [1935–36]: 163) pointed out long ago that עֹזֵר ('ōzēr, "helping") appears in Arabic as one of those verbs that carries opposite meanings. So the RSV's "no one restrains them" is better without any emendation to 'ṣr (see Introduction: Text). But the term could mean to help, and we could translate, "no one needs to help them," in the sense that they can handle dismantling Job on their own.

14 In תַּחַת שֹׁאָה הִתְגַּלְגָּלוּ (taḥat šō'â hitgalgālû, "amid the ruins they come rolling in"), šō'â connotes the noise as well as the devastation that may have a variety of causes. Here it is not the storm but the battle. The verb has nothing to do with "billows" (Andersen, Rowley) but is a verbalizing of the word גַּלְגַּל (galgal, "wheel"; cf. the war chariot in Isa 5:28; Jer 47:3).

18 Concerning יִתְחַפֵּשׂ לְבוּשִׁי (yitḥappēś lᵉbûšî, "becomes like clothing to me"), the Qumran Targum agrees with the LXX: "grasps my clothing." This does not mean the MT should be emended, for there may be a meaning of the root ḥpś that we do not know. The usual meaning is "to disguise oneself," but see the comment above on v.18, based on Obadiah 6, where it means "ransacked." A clue to the meaning may lie in a West Semitic gloss found in a letter to the king of Tyre among the El Amarna tablets, where the word ḥapśi means "arm, force" (J. A. Knudtzon, Die El-Amarna Tafeln [2nd ed.; Aalen: O. Zeller, 1964], 147:12; so W. F. Albright, "Canaanite hofsi, 'free,' in the Amarna Tablets," JPOS 4 [1924]: 169–70). The verb תָּפַשׂ (tāpáś, "to seize, grasp") seems to be behind the LXX and the Qumran Targum. If yittāpēś (Niphal, "is seized") was the original form, then an auditory corruption (addition of ה, h) took place after 11QtgJob was written (ca. 100 BC).

20 The problem with the NIV's translation of וַתִּתְבֹּנֶן בִּי (*wattitbōnen bî*) as "but you merely look at me" is that the verb in this stem is "to give diligent attention," which hardly fits the notion "merely look at." Andersen, 236–37, is on the right track. We have here a double-duty use of the negative: "but you do not give diligent attention."

24 This is a difficult verse. Indeed, Clines (*Job 21–37*, 957–58) calls this "one of the most unintelligible verses in the book." Many solutions have been suggested. (Clines has an extensive discussion.) The NIV is about as accurate as possible except that it seems to ignore לָהֶן (*lāhen*, "to them" [feminine]), which might mean "with regard to these things," that is, his affliction (cf. RV). The words "on a broken man" is a paraphrase of "on [against] a ruin." See Rowley, 197, for a summary of the many interpretations of this verse.

3. His Negative Confession and Final Oath (31:1–40)

OVERVIEW

We now arrive at the climax of the peroration. The material is similar in form, if not in content, to the negative confession given by the deceased who stands before Osiris in the Egyptian Book of the Dead (*ANET*, 34). Under oath the subject lists the evil things he has not done with the hope he will be vindicated and pass through the portals unscathed. Although the form is negative, Job's oration has a positive purpose as an attestation of loyalty to God as his sovereign Lord. To make this effective he calls down curses on his own head if his words are proved false. It is easy to interpret this passage as a prime example of self-righteousness, but to do so would fly in the face of Job's just call for vindication. Indeed, he has been doing this throughout the dialogue, and it reaches a climax in 27:5–6.

I will never admit you are in the right;
  till I die, I will not deny my integrity.
I will maintain my righteousness and never let
    go of it;
  my conscience will not reproach me as long
    as I live.

Job fleshes out that statement with a recital of the details of his virtuous life before God's hand strikes him. This is the "shun evil" aspect of the description of Job that God repeated to Satan in the Prologue (1:8; 2:3). As stated before, because such was God's view of Job, he must not be labeled as self-righteous when he speaks the truth, even though it is about himself.

This chapter, then, as to its literary format, is a negative testament, a protest of innocence, by which Job closes the matter of whether he is being punished for his sins. After such a statement, in the jurisprudence of the ancient Near East the burden of proof falls on the court. That is why v.40 says that "the words of Job are ended." Each disavowal must be accompanied by an oath that calls for the same punishment the offense deserves on the basis of the principle of *lex talionis*, that is, "an eye for an eye and a tooth for a tooth" (cf. vv.5–10). Since the charges against Job are wide and varied, he must give a similarly wide disavowal. He has already done this in a general way (cf. 23:10–12), but here he specifies and calls for condemnation and punishment from both God and humans (vv.8, 11–12, 14, 22–23) if he is guilty of any of those sins.

Even though this is a poetic statement and should not be interpreted as though it were a legal brief, Job adds his signature as a gesture to show his intentions to make it an official disclaimer of any indictment brought against him (v.35).

Some critical scholars have rearranged the contents of the chapter by putting together any verses that touch on the same subject. I agree with Andersen, 239, that by moving whatever annoys "their tidy minds," they do harm to the "living art of the whole poem." He points out, however, that this is poetry from a sufferer sitting on an ash heap. I have sympathy for such a sentiment, but we must keep in mind the goodly measure of orderly rhetoric we have seen even in Job's passionate and explosive utterances. Too much order should not be pressed; but even where the order is incomplete, it always seems to be present in these poems.

In this poem a structure of themes is built around the repeated-oath formula. The formula does not always have to have an apodosis to follow the "if" clause. It can be implied (vv.29–34). Also several totally different "if" clauses may be given before a single apodosis completes the formula (vv.16–22; vv.24–28). In vv.5–8 the formula is used with two "if" clauses on basically the same theme followed by one apodosis. Verses 9–12 have a complete formula with protasis and apodosis followed by moral observation tied to a divine sanction. In vv.13–15 the "if" clause has a moral observation also coupled to a word of divine sanction, which serves as an apodosis. The following is an attempt to show the thematic structure:

Job's Oaths of Allegiance to God

Introduction: No idolatry toward the fertility goddess—see below (vv.1–4)

Covenant ban
Divine sanction (vv.2–4)   Lust of the eye//God's eye

A. First list of sevenths oaths (vv.5–22)
Oath (v.5)
Self-imprecation (v.6)
Oath (v.7)
Self-imprecation (v.8)   Falsehood and deceit//God's scales

Oath (v.9)
Self-imprecation (v.10)
Divine sanction (vv.11–12)   Adultery//God's fire

Oath (v.13)
Self-imprecation (v.14)
Moral observation (v.15)   Mistreatment of slaves//God's court

Oath (vv.16–18)
Oath (vv.19–20)   Neglect of needy

Oath (v.21)
Self-imprecation (v.22)   Abuse of helpless//God's terror

B. Divine sanction v.23)   The fear of God

C. Second list of seven oaths (vv.24–34)
   Oath (v.24)
   Oath (v.25)
   Oath (vv.26–27)

   Divine sanction (v.28)

   Oath (v.29)
   Oath without ʾim (v.30)

   Oath (vv.31–32)

   Oath (vv.33–34)

> Idolatry (gold or gods)

Unfaithfulness to God

> Hatred of enemy

Selfishness

Hypocrisy

D. The climax: Job presents his signed defense
   and challenges God to indict him on specific charges (vv.35–37)

E. The anticlimax: literary device (vv.38–40)
   Oath (v.38)
   Oath (v.39)
   Self-imprecation (v.40)

> Avarice

¹"I made a covenant with my eyes
   not to look lustfully at a girl.
²For what is man's lot from God above,
   his heritage from the Almighty on high?
³Is it not ruin for the wicked,
   disaster for those who do wrong?
⁴Does he not see my ways
   and count my every step?

⁵"If I have walked in falsehood
   or my foot has hurried after deceit—
⁶let God weigh me in honest scales
   and he will know that I am blameless—
⁷if my steps have turned from the path,
   if my heart has been led by my eyes,
   or if my hands have been defiled,
⁸then may others eat what I have sown,
   and may my crops be uprooted.

⁹"If my heart has been enticed by a woman,
  or if I have lurked at my neighbor's door,
¹⁰then may my wife grind another man's grain,
  and may other men sleep with her.
¹¹For that would have been shameful,
  a sin to be judged.
¹²It is a fire that burns to Destruction;
  it would have uprooted my harvest.

¹³"If I have denied justice to my menservants and maidservants
  when they had a grievance against me,
¹⁴what will I do when God confronts me?
  What will I answer when called to account?
¹⁵Did not he who made me in the womb make them?
  Did not the same one form us both within our mothers?

¹⁶"If I have denied the desires of the poor
  or let the eyes of the widow grow weary,
¹⁷if I have kept my bread to myself,
  not sharing it with the fatherless —
¹⁸but from my youth I reared him as would a father,
  and from my birth I guided the widow —
¹⁹if I have seen anyone perishing for lack of clothing,
  or a needy man without a garment,
²⁰and his heart did not bless me
  for warming him with the fleece from my sheep,
²¹if I have raised my hand against the fatherless,
  knowing that I had influence in court,
²²then let my arm fall from the shoulder,
  let it be broken off at the joint.
²³For I dreaded destruction from God,
  and for fear of his splendor I could not do such things.

²⁴"If I have put my trust in gold
  or said to pure gold, 'You are my security,'
²⁵if I have rejoiced over my great wealth,
  the fortune my hands had gained,
²⁶if I have regarded the sun in its radiance
  or the moon moving in splendor,
²⁷so that my heart was secretly enticed
  and my hand offered them a kiss of homage,

²⁸then these also would be sins to be judged,
  for I would have been unfaithful to God on high.

²⁹"If I have rejoiced at my enemy's misfortune
  or gloated over the trouble that came to him —
³⁰I have not allowed my mouth to sin
  by invoking a curse against his life —
³¹if the men of my household have never said,
  'Who has not had his fill of Job's meat?'—
³²but no stranger had to spend the night in the street,
  for my door was always open to the traveler —
³³if I have concealed my sin as men do,
  by hiding my guilt in my heart
³⁴because I so feared the crowd
  and so dreaded the contempt of the clans
  that I kept silent and would not go outside

³⁵("Oh, that I had someone to hear me!
  I sign now my defense — let the Almighty answer me;
  let my accuser put his indictment in writing.
³⁶Surely I would wear it on my shoulder,
  I would put it on like a crown.
³⁷I would give him an account of my every step;
  like a prince I would approach him.) —

³⁸"if my land cries out against me
  and all its furrows are wet with tears,
³⁹if I have devoured its yield without payment
  or broken the spirit of its tenants,
⁴⁰then let briers come up instead of wheat
  and weeds instead of barley."

The words of Job are ended.

COMMENTARY

1–4 These verses need to be examined from the standpoint of subject and form. Why does the chapter begin like this? Why would a statement concerning sexual lust be at the head of the list, and why is not the oath formula used here? Some have emended the text; others have considered v.1 misplaced, belonging with vv.9–12 (NEB). Pope's observation (228) that this would leave vv.2–4 unconnected is worthy since these verses form a poetic unit. The covenantal ban on Job's eyes (v.1) parallels God's all-seeing eye (v.4), and these verses enclose vv. 2–3, which speak of God's judgment on the wicked, whose sins he sees.

The lines are, then, an introduction to Job's catalog of oaths protesting his loyalty to God. Job, by declaring a covenantal ban on his own eyes in conjunction with his Sovereign's ability to see all, appropriately brings to the fore the covenant theme that underlies and gives meaning to the oaths he is about to make.

There is, however, still more to it. Job's making a covenant with his eyes is not merely a promise not to lust after a girl. The sin he has in mind is more fundamental, or it would not command this position in the poem. Job is emphatically denying an especially insidious and widespread form of idolatry: devotion to the *bᵉtûlâ* ("the girl [maiden]"), the goddess of fertility. As the Venus of the Semitic world, she was variously known as the Maiden Anat in Ugaritic (*ANET*, 132–33), Ashtoreth in preexilic Israel (Jdg 2:13; 10:6; 1Sa 7:3–4; 1Ki 11:5, 33), and Ishtar in Babylonian sources, wherein she is described as "laden with vitality, charm, and voluptuousness" (*ANET*, 383). She is probably the Queen of Heaven mentioned in Jeremiah 7:18 and 44:16–19.

G. Jeshurun already suggested this interpretation in 1928 (cf. Pope, 228). Pope, 229, still chooses to emend 31:1, even though he admits that with this interpretation the difficulties that led to the emendation vanish (cf. D. N. Freedman, "Review of *Job 29–31 in the Light of Northwest Semitic*," by Anthony R. Ceresko, *JBL* 102 [1983]: 143). Even token worship of the sun and moon is disavowed in the middle of the poem (vv.24–34), so a disavowal of the temptation to even look at the sex goddess is rendered likely when we keep in mind that *btlt* ("the maiden") in Ugaritic is the very word used here. The Hebrews were constantly warned about this ubiquitous fertility cult (cf. Dt 16:21–22; Hos 4:14). Clay plaques and figurines of the virgin's nude form may be seen in museums of archaeology (cf. *ANEP*, 160–65; R. Hess, *Israelite Religions: An Archaeological and Biblical Survey* [Grand Rapids: Baker, 2007], 98–99 and footnoted bibliography).

See Hans Walther Wolff (*Hosea, A Commentary on the Book of the Prophet Hosea* [Hermenia; trans. G. Stansell; ed. P. D. Hanson [Philadelphia: Fortress, 1974], 14) for material on the sex cult. It would strengthen the case if a reference to the goddess using only *btlt* were available. However, in Proverbs 6:25 lusting (*ḥmd*) in the heart after a prostitute is not unlike Job's statement. Job used here the Hithpolel of *bîn* ("to give full attention to"). Earlier (9:11) he had used the Qal/Hiphil of *bîn* parallel with *rāʾâ* ("to see") to complain about his inability to see God. By contrast, the fertility goddess was everywhere to be seen.

The covenantal-ban language (v.1) is a forceful way for Job to stress his allegiance to God, and the divine sanction in vv.2–3 is equivalent to the self-imprecation in the oath format (vv.6, 8, 10, 14, 22). Indeed, that is the force of the imprecations, as may be seen by the references to God's judgment in almost every case.

Not all accept the text here as a reference to the goddess. Driver and Gray understand vv.1–4 as a general claim to a virtuous life, giving God's judgment on evil as the grounds that have led to a choice virtue. Such an understanding of v.1 is rather narrow to express such a general claim, but on this point Andersen, 240–41, agrees with Driver and Gray.

5–8 In Job's world there were no atheists or even secularists. Everyone believed in the validity of divine sanction. This made the oath the ultimate test of integrity (cf. Nu 5:20–22). Job opens the series of oaths by clearing himself of being false (Ps 26:4) and deceitful (Hos 12:8). In v.6, which may be either a parenthesis (NIV, RSV) or a "then" clause (Pope), Job mentions commercial dishonesty and moves on in v.7 to clear himself of avarice ("my heart has been led by my eyes"). Clearly v.7 is talking about any evil deed his hands may do. But the verb *dābaq*, translated "defiled," really means "cling to." If we follow the Oriental *Kethiv* (see Notes), then the text says, "if anything has stuck to my hands"—referring to thievery. With God's honest scales in mind, Job completes the oath with a self-imprecation that would balance the scales: May he not get any gain from what his hands have planted (v.8)!

9–12 From here to v.23 Job clears himself of social sins. The sin of adultery heads the list (v.9). In the biblical world adultery was heinous, because it struck at the roots of the family and clan. It meant, as is clear here, relations with another man's wife. In Hammurabi's Code it did not have to be a capital offense, but in the Mosaic Law it was (Lev 20:10). Here Job's hypothetical sin calls for "eye-for-eye" justice—the same would happen to his wife. In the versions and the Talmud, v.10a is also thought to have sexual connotations since the parallel in v.10b is explicit (Pope, 231; Gordis, *Job*, 346).

The moral observation that follows states that adultery is an offense punished both by human law (v.11) and the law of God (v.12). We are also reminded of the extensive teaching in Proverbs concerning adultery (and in particular allowing oneself to be enticed by a woman, v.9; see Pr 5–7). In v.12 Job uses a striking figure also found in Deuteronomy 32:22, in which fire kindled by God's wrath "burns [to Sheol]" and "devours the earth and its harvests." The figure is, no doubt, common poetic rhetoric. "It" refers to the sin but by metonymy means "God's wrath on the sinner." On the problem of the wife as victim when she is sinned against in v.10, see Gordis (*Job*, 346–47), who explains it on the basis of the ancient Semitic concept of corporate responsibility.

13–15 We may truly stand amazed at Job's egalitarian spirit, for he has taken seriously the rights of his servants (slaves?). He does not just admit their right to have grievances but to openly express them and expect justice (v.13). Even more amazing in terms of what we know about slavery in the OT world, Job bases this right on the principle that all human beings are equal in God's sight, because he who created them all is both their (his servants') Master and his, and that Master shows no favoritism (vv.14–15; cf. Pr 22:2; Eph 6:9). So Job considers any act of injustice to those under him as an affront to God (v.14).

16–23 Eliphaz already accused Job of gross sins against the poor in 22:6–9, and in 29:12–17 Job spoke positively about the depth of his social conscience. Here he closes the issue with a series of oaths of clearance enforced by a final fierce self-imprecation (v.22).

There are several interesting touches to his phraseology that should be noted. In v.16 "the desires of the poor" parallel "the eyes of the widow" and present a touching picture suggesting sensitivity to their wants beyond merely meeting basic needs for survival. The word *ḥēpeṣ* ("desires"; GK 2914) is never translated "needs" since the root means "take delight in." In v.20 "his heart" really means "his loins." The force of the parallelism is lost unless one can feel the pathos of a shivering body thankfully warmed by Job's fleece. In v.21 the verb "I have raised" comes from *nûp* ("to swing"). So it means literally "cuffing" the fatherless with impunity because of one's political power.

On the principle of *lex talionis*, the breaking off of the offending arm creates a dramatic imprecation (v.22). The hyperbolic language of Christ as he called for holiness (a God-fearing life) has its roots in this self-imprecatory rhetoric (Mt 5:29–30). Verse 23 is pivotal. It is meant as a statement that applies to all the oaths; for it contains a necessary ingredient for such clearance oaths to have meaning—the fear of God, that is, complete faith in his power to effect the curses. Thus his terror sets Job to trembling.

24–28 Job begins again with another firm denial of idolatry. But here the temptations are different. Instead of the appeal of the ever-popular sex goddess, it is the appeal of gold (vv.24–25) and the apparent luster of two of the most commonly worshiped astral deities, the sun and moon (v.26). Job denies even secret homage to them (v.27; see also 2Ki 23:5, 11 and Eze 8:16 for a criticism of solar and lunar worship).

29–34 Verses 31–32 as given in the NIV are somewhat difficult to understand because of the double negative. It can best be understood as Job's oath that his servants have never complained about his lack of generosity (cf. Notes on v.31). He has freely shared food and home with all who came his way. Despite the inconvenience, Job's servants are of one mind with him. Pope, following Tur-Sinai (*Job*), sees in v.31 a denial of homosexual intentions in Job's household like those against strangers in Genesis 19:1–10. The interpretation has some merit but is difficult to prove, since the Hebrew is so difficult.

Job denies hypocrisy in vv.33–34. Linguistically it is impossible to determine whether or not he is making a reference to Genesis 3 (cf. KJV, NIV mg.: "as Adam did") since the word *ʾādām* can be generic in meaning (NIV). Kline, 482, takes it as an allusion to the fall of Adam because then the imprecation in v.40 that "invokes the elementary primeval curse upon the ground" follows naturally. But Job is dealing with hypocrisy here—hiding one's sins. Adam hid himself in shame, but not his sins, as a hypocrite does. Also, Job does not typically refer to earlier biblical history. That Job admits to sin is important to see since one might easily assume he is claiming perfection in this chapter. Reading behind the

lines in v.34, one can appreciate how important an issue general knowledge of his sins might be and how great the temptation would be to maintain his public image (cf. v.21).

35–37 Job strategically brings his oration to its climax with a sudden change in tone. In 13:14–16 he was not so certain about his innocence and thought he might even put his life in jeopardy by calling for a hearing. But even then he affirmed that "no godless man would dare come before him [God]!" Now he is sure of his innocence, so confident of the truthfulness of these oaths that he affixes his signature and presents them as his defense with a challenge to God for a corresponding written indictment.

How does this brash attitude (vv.36–37) toward his "accuser" fit the statements accompanying the oaths about Job's fear of God's terror? This strange paradox in Job's mind that God, to whom he appeals for support, is also his adversary is the main point of the chapter. Fearing the terror of God (v.23) is meant for those who break covenant with him. Job knows he has not done this. But he cannot deny the existential reality that he stands outside the sphere of covenantal blessing. Something is wrong.

There is only one way Job knows to make this absurd situation intelligible. That is to appeal to his just and sovereign Lord as a vassal prince who has been falsely accused. Even though he has repeated it often, he obstinately refuses to accept as final that God is his enemy.

There is always a place in the lament rhetoric of the OT for the sufferer to remind God of his justice and covenantal love. But Job is not just reminding God. He wants God to reply to his defense with a list of the charges against him so whatever doubts are left might be publicly answered.

Verse 36 has been called a gesture of equality (S. Terrien, "The Book of Job: Introduction and Exegesis," *IB*, 3:11–24), where Job approaches God as a prince to force God to accept his unblemished record and prove the counselors are wrong about his being punished for his sins. Commentators have never been able to agree on whether Job is doing right or wrong. Some are satisfied to leave it as the poet's (the author's) responsibility. He has chosen to present "the problem of the relationship between God and man in the sharpest possible delineation" since "nowhere in the ancient Near East does man approach the deity as a prince" (Terrien, 3:11–24).

Others believe Job is putting himself in a false position. Neither his blamelessness nor his suffering gives him the right to tell God what he ought to do. Thus MacKenzie, 527, argues that "Job's precious integrity has become a barrier between him and God—a condition God must accept. Job overshot the mark."

The opening words of the theophany (God's answer to Job in chs. 38–41) throws some light on the posture of Job in these verses. God rebukes Job's brashness (38:2–3) as a darkening of his counsel. And as for the proud prince wearing the indictment like a badge of honor, God sets aside his majesty and assumes a human stance, calling on Job to brace himself and prepare to wrestle with the Almighty.

38–40 These verses are clearly anticlimactic, but that does not mean they belong in another place in this chapter (see the REB, NAB, and NJB, which relocate these verses earlier in ch. 31). In several places before, Job has shown his penchant for anticlimax (e.g., 3:23–26; 14:18–22).

Job denies avarice in these verses. He has not eaten of the produce of his land without paying for the labor or by cheating the tenant farmers (NIV). The second line of v.39 might mean "causing the death of the owners" (cf. RSV, Dhorme, Pope). In that case it is something similar to Jezebel's illegal seizure of Naboth's vineyard in 1 Kings 21 (see Notes). That the land personified as a witness cries out and weeps over the horrible deeds done there (v.38) lends support that murder as well as avarice is in mind. And that in turn is why the primeval curse on the land is invoked. This is like Genesis 4:8–12, where Abel's blood cried out to God, who then cursed the land so that it no longer yielded its crops to Cain.

NOTES

1 On מָה (*mâ*, "not"), compare the KJV, RSV, et al. The NIV has handled this in keeping with *mâ* in 16:6 (cf. Arab., rare in Heb.). However, it is more likely (contra the NIV) to take the *mâ* in its normal sense and translate, "How would I look lustfully on a girl?" See Clines (*Job 21–37*, 961).

7 מְאוּם (*mu'ûm*) as spelled means "spot, blemish." The Syriac, Targum, and Oriental *Kethiv* read *m°ûmâ* ("anything"). The MT would read, "A spot stuck to my hands." The NIV has combined the noun with the verb to produce the meaning "defile."

9 Note the secret enticement to idolatry in v.27.

11 "Shameful" is hardly strong enough for זִמָּה (*zimmâ*). The term is used with some of the worst sexual aberrations in Leviticus 18:17 and 20:14. The RSV's "heinous" is better. The second half of this verse is literally "a sin of the judges," stressing the human court, while v.12 is God's judgment.

18 גְּדֵלַנִי (*g°dēlanî*) is literally "he grew up with me," which means essentially what the NIV has: "I reared him."

23 This statement of the certainty of God's sanctions against all who violate his law need not be limited to the preceding verse. Like vv.2–3 (cf. אֵיד [ʾêd, "disaster, destruction"] in vv.3, 23), the concept is foundational to the validity of the oaths in this chapter.

27 On the kissing of idols, compare 1 Kings 19:18 and Hosea 13:2. The MT has "and my hand kissed my mouth." Since the heavenly bodies are remote, the kiss is not direct as with idols. So I read, "my hand passed a kiss from my mouth." This assumes the rare meaning "from" for the preposition לְ (*l*). See R. Hess (*Israelite Religions: An Archaeological and Biblical Survey* [Grand Rapids: Baker, 2007], 101) for more about solar and lunar religion in Israel.

31 This translation of אִם־לֹא (ʾim-lōʾ) as "if ... have never" obscures the meaning with the use of the word "never" to represent the *lōʾ* in the second colon. The *ʾim-lōʾ* of the first colon is an oath formula and as such is positive, not negative. So it would mean, "If the men of my house have ever said."

On מִי־יִתֵּן ... לֹא (*mî-yittēn ... lōʾ*, "who has not"), certainly the idiomatic meaning of *mî-yittēn* ("would that") should be preserved; and there is no problem if the *lōʾ* is vocalized *laʾ*, indicating a rare assertive (cf. Andersen, 136, n. 1): "Would that we might eat of his flesh until satisfied."

33 Concerning כְאָדָם (*kᵉʾādām*, "as men do"), as noted above, *ʾādām* can be "humankind" or "Adam." In this context Job denies hypocrisy—the hiding is not from God but from his fellow human beings.

בְחֻבִּי (*bᵉḥubbî*, "in my heart") is from *ḥbb*, is an Aramaism, and is also found in postbiblical Hebrew. Its Hebrew equivalent is *ḥeq* ("bosom").

35 תָּוִי (*tāwî*, "my signature") is literally "my mark"—that which authenticates a document. סֵפֶר (*sēper*, "indictment") simply means "a scroll." Some have suggested the translation "acquittal." "Let my prosecutor [ʾîš rîbî] write out an acquittal." But why would a prosecutor, opponent, or accuser do what is not his duty? It is better to leave the brash Job intact.

39 The NIV has rendered וְנֶפֶשׁ בְּעָלֶיהָ הִפָּחְתִּי (*wᵉnepeš bᵉ ʿāleyhā hippāḥtî*) "broken the spirit of its tenants." In 11:20 נָפַח (*nāpaḥ*) with *nepeš* was translated "dying gasp." It would be better to render it in a similar way here. The RSV has "caused the death of its owners." If *baʿal* means "owner," then it must mean the former owner, implying exploitation of the land (cf. 1Ki 21). Dahood ("Ugaritic Studies and the Bible," *Gregorianum* 43 [1962]: 75; "Book Review on *Le Livre de Job* by Jean Steinmann," *Bib* 41 [1960]: 303; and "Qoheleth and Northwest Semitic Philology," *Bib* 43 [1962]: 362) maintains "workers," not "owners," are in view. This is based on the shift between *b* and *p* as attested in Ugaritic and Phoenician—the usual Hebrew *pʿl* ("to work") being spelled *bʿl* here.

B. Elihu's Speeches (32:1–37:24)

OVERVIEW

Some critics tend to be fierce in their opposition to Elihu. Peake, 29, held the author of this section dissents with the Prologue and attacks the original poet for permitting God to participate in the debate. According to Peake, this author thinks he can solve the problem. To Rowley, 266, the original author made Elihu self-important and banal as a parody on such people. Pope, xxvii, considered the speeches diatribes that echo what has already been said but is offered by Elihu as novel and decisive; J. Barr agrees with Pope ("The Book of Job and Its Modern Interpreters," *BJRL* 54 [1971–72]: 28–46).

Generally the criticisms of those who find Elihu too long and drawn out are too severe. For example, Elihu's pride in his "superior knowledge" may not be a claim to superior knowledge but only to eloquence ("speech"; see comment on 36:4). Eloquence was highly regarded in the OT world; but like any aesthetic judgment, it is personal. What makes Elihu sound insufferably prolix to us might then have been considered the essence of good style. Scholars had to learn about the tautological style of the Ugaritic poems before they were willing to stop emending Hebrew poetry for this reason.

The list of those who see this section as a later addition is impressive and includes Delitzsch, 2:309. According to J. Strahan (*The Book of Job* [2nd ed.; Edinburgh: T&T Clark, 1914], 24–25), the speeches were the first commentary on the book of Job. As such they have high doctrinal value but are extraneous to the book. The view that the chapters were added by the author of the book has been stated in several ways. Gordis (*Job*, 548–49; *God and Man*, ch. 9) believes the author may have learned through his life the lessons of the disciplinary aspect of suffering and woven this into the already completed book with which he was occupied throughout his life. D. N. Freedman ("The Elihu Speeches in the Book of Job" *HTR* 61 [1968]: 51–59) thinks these speeches were written by the author but never fully integrated into the book, that being done by another hand.

Other critics go so far as to say Elihu's words represent the climax of the book, since only here do we find an answer given to the problem of suffering—that it is disciplinary and redemptive (see C. H. Cornill, *Introduction to the Canonical Books of the Old Testament* [trans. G. H. Box; London: Williams and Norgate, 1907], 426–27). Rowley finds

this a problem because the reader is told in the Prologue why Job is suffering, and it is not to discipline him but "to vindicate God's trust in him." So Rowley considers all that Elihu says irrelevant to the purpose of the book. The point is quite legitimate and deserves real consideration.

I have suggested in the Introduction (Purpose) the answer to Rowley. The canonical book of Job does not have a single purpose. It is true that Elihu is not mentioned elsewhere in the book, so his speeches could be left out. But at the beginning (ch. 32) and at the end (ch. 37), they are skillfully woven into the fabric of the book and made to play a legitimate role. Whether put in immediately or later by the same author or added at an even later time by another, the speeches are part of the canonical book and serve as a transition leading to the theophany. They give another human perspective in which we find a more balanced theology than that of Job's three counselors.

This differs from the view that Elihu is the divine forerunner whose role is to prepare Job for the theophany. How could that be, since Elihu sees no need for a confrontation between Job and God (34:23–24)? The idea should not be totally discarded but tempered with the thought that Elihu is merely human. So we need not assume everything he says is normative even though he claims a special inspiration (32:8, 18). Elihu's attack on Job is limited to his statements during the dialogue. He does not accuse Job of a wicked life for which he is being punished. So Elihu is not guilty of false accusation, and that may be the reason he is not rebuked by God (42:7).

Elihu tries to be sensitive to Job but deserves some criticism for a weakness common to people—his overconfidence in his ability to do what the others could not. This makes him sound sanctimonious; but once Elihu gets into his message, he seems to improve as he goes along. His poems in chapters 36–37, while at points difficult to understand, have a masterly quality similar to other great poems in the book.

Dhorme is correct in seeing a different mode of discussion here. The counselors and Job did not quote each other directly. Elihu has the debate before him and quotes Job, frequently using his name (cf. 32:12; 33:1, 31; 34:5–7, 35–36; 35:16; 37:14). The Yahweh speeches call into question Job's words in totality but not in particular as Elihu does. So here the author's purpose is to deal with Job's extreme language.

Job was extreme at times (cf. 9:14–24), but it was due to his determination to be honest. He was also inconsistent. He questioned God's justice on the basis of his experience but was deeply committed to it since he laid all his hope for vindication on it. Elihu senses this inconsistency and scores Job for wanting vindication while also accusing God of indifference to human behavior (35:2–3).

Elihu assures Job that God's wisdom coupled with his power to carry out his wise purposes guarantees his discipline will ultimately prove redemptive (36:11–16).

Despite his anger (32:2–3) and wordy lecturing style, Elihu never gets bitter as did Bildad and Zophar. Nor does he stoop to false accusation about Job's earlier life (cf. Eliphaz, 22:4–11). He presents God as a merciful teacher (33:23–28; 36:22–26). Suffering is disciplinary (33:19–22), not just judgmental. The counselors glorified God with their hymns but remained cold and detached. Elihu has a warmer personal response to the greatness of God (37:1–2). He includes himself as one who should be hushed in awe before God. Elihu says God reveals both his justice and his covenantal love in his sovereign control of the world (37:13, 23); this is the reason the wise of heart should worship him. That is a fitting note of introduction for Yahweh's appearance.

1. Introduction (32:1–5)

¹So these three men stopped answering Job, because he was righteous in his own eyes. ²But Elihu son of Barakel the Buzite, of the family of Ram, became very angry with Job for justifying himself rather than God. ³He was also angry with the three friends, because they had found no way to refute Job, and yet had condemned him. ⁴Now Elihu had waited before speaking to Job because they were older than he. ⁵But when he saw that the three men had nothing more to say, his anger was aroused.

COMMENTARY

1–5 Job closed his peroration with a final flourish of bravado. He was so certain of his blameless life that he would be willing to march like a prince into the presence of God and give an account of his every step. The attempts of his friends to convince him of his sinfulness have failed. Job could have no

more to say, having challenged God. The friends have no more to say because they consider him a hopeless hypocrite (v. 1; 22:4–5).

The book at this point introduces Elihu, a young man who in deference to age has waited with increasing impatience for the opportunity to speak (vv.2–4). Four times in the Hebrew text we are told he is angry. First at Job (v.2 [2x]) for justifying himself rather than God and then at the friends because of their inability to refute Job (v.3; cf. v.5).

We are not told explicitly why or under what circumstances he is there. The Prologue says nothing of bystanders, though it implies Job sat in an open public place where the friends could see him at a distance (2:12). These verses simply imply that Elihu is among bystanders who have been listening to Job and his counselors. One must assume a fictional quality to this narrative if the Elihu speeches are by a later author or even by the same author as an afterthought (see Overview). Authorship itself is not the crucial issue since we do not know who authored the book. What is important is that this is an authentic part of the canonical text and was accepted as such by successive communities of faith.

This introduction that stresses Elihu's anger has led to the conclusion that he is the original "angry young man" (MacKenzie). But his tone is not full of anger compared with some of the counselors' speeches. Andersen, 51, sees him as an adjudicator who gives the human estimate of what has been said in chapters 3–31. There is no reason to believe the speeches were intended as an alternative answer inserted much later because someone felt the divine reply was inadequate (see Pope, xxviii). However one may judge their quality, the speeches are only presented as a human reaction to Job's apparent "self-righteousness" and the counselors' ineptitude.

Elihu's concern is not that they have falsely condemned Job (v.3) but that in failing to disprove Job's claims about his blameless life, they have succeeded in condemning God. After all, they hold that God never afflicts the innocent and always punishes the wicked. This interpretation follows the ancient scribal tradition mentioned in the NIV margin (see Notes for other interpretations). Verses 4–5 reveal clearly that Elihu's major target is Job. He "waited before speaking to Job." Elihu's reply to the counselors is secondary, as is evident in his speeches.

NOTES

1 Instead of בְּעֵינָיו (beʿênâyw, "in his own eyes"), the LXX, Symmachus, and the Syriac have "in their eyes." Dhorme follows this, but nothing in the counselors' words even hints at such a change of mind to show that they are now convinced that Job is righteous. See also Clines (*Job 21–37*, 683).

2 Concerning מֵאֱלֹהִים (mēʾelōhîm, "rather than God"), on 4:17 I suggested that the preposition מִן (min) can also mean "in the presence of" (cf. Dhorme). Both the LXX and the Vulgate so translate it here. Rowley, 207, argues that Job was not only prepared to vindicate himself before God but also to bring an indictment against God, but he does not back that up with a specific reference. Job has certainly questioned God's justice but always relied on it for ultimate vindication.

3 Concerning וַיַּרְשִׁיעוּ אֶת־אִיּוֹב (wayyaršîʿû ʾet-ʾîyôb, "and yet had condemned him"), Jewish scribal tradition says that out of reverence the text was changed (cf. Introduction: Text). Originally it read, "and so had condemned God" (NIV mg.). That is, because the counselors failed to prove their case against Job, they made God responsible for being unjust to him. Most modern commentators accept this reading. However Tur-Sinai (*Job*) and Rowley accept the MT, but not as the NIV has it. They read, "They would not refute Job and so show him to be wrong" (a mere repetition). Andersen, 241, wants to apply the negative to both verbs: "They didn't find an answer and (didn't) prove Job wrong."

2. The First Speech: Part 1 (32:6–22)

OVERVIEW

Driver and Gray feel the major division here is not in 33:1 but in 33:8, where Elihu shifts from preliminary remarks to the substance of his speech. Up to 33:8 he tells why he has to speak and how he will go about it. His opening words (vv.6–14) are mainly an apology to the friends but also a rebuke for their failure with Job. Verses 15–22 take the form of a soliloquy about his urgency heard as part of his apology.

⁶So Elihu son of Barakel the Buzite said:

"I am young in years,
    and you are old;
that is why I was fearful,
    not daring to tell you what I know.
⁷I thought, 'Age should speak;
    advanced years should teach wisdom.'
⁸But it is the spirit in a man,
    the breath of the Almighty, that gives him understanding.
⁹It is not only the old who are wise,
    not only the aged who understand what is right.

¹⁰"Therefore I say: Listen to me;
    I too will tell you what I know.
¹¹I waited while you spoke,
    I listened to your reasoning;
while you were searching for words,
    ¹²I gave you my full attention.
But not one of you has proved Job wrong;
    none of you has answered his arguments.
¹³Do not say, 'We have found wisdom;
    let God refute him, not man.'
¹⁴But Job has not marshaled his words against me,
    and I will not answer him with your arguments.

¹⁵"They are dismayed and have no more to say;
    words have failed them.
¹⁶Must I wait, now that they are silent,
    now that they stand there with no reply?

¹⁷I too will have my say;
  I too will tell what I know.
¹⁸For I am full of words,
  and the spirit within me compels me;
¹⁹inside I am like bottled-up wine,
  like new wineskins ready to burst.
²⁰I must speak and find relief;
  I must open my lips and reply.
²¹I will show partiality to no one,
  nor will I flatter any man;
²²for if I were skilled in flattery,
  my Maker would soon take me away.

COMMENTARY

6–14 Elihu's reason for daring to intrude in an area usually reserved for sages is the fact that wisdom comes from God—the old may lack it, the young may have it—if the Spirit of God grants it (vv.6–9). Obviously Elihu believes he had been thus blessed. "Therefore," he says, "listen to me" (v.10).

The counselors' reasoning has not impressed him. He caricatures them as groping for words and unable to handle bombastic Job. In v.13 Elihu seems to be accusing them of using a falsely pious appeal to let God handle Job as a way out of their responsibility to refute him. But they have not made any such statement. Rowley, 209, following Peake, thinks the verse is a polemic against the author for including the divine speeches. But it is unlikely he would suggest there is no need for God because he (Elihu) can handle the situation. He has just said how dependent on the Spirit of God he is. The NEB goes the opposite direction, making v.13b Elihu's own claim that God, not people, will rebut Job.

In v.14 Elihu avows that he would have used a different set of arguments had he been in the dialogue with Job. Some critics have accused Elihu of

saying absolutely nothing new, of using the counselors' old traditional arguments all over again as though they were novel (cf. Pope, xxvii). Others see the Elihu speeches as authentic and meaningful (Gordis, *Job*, 358, 546–54). His speeches, though verbose and pompous from our standards, are not diatribes (Pope); and while they contain some of the thoughts already mentioned by the counselors, they are given in a different spirit (cf. 33:1–7).

This is why the NIVs "your arguments" for *ʾimrêkem* ("your words") may not be a wise translation. Elihu certainly does use some of their arguments as well as some of Job's, but one's words often convey more than an argument. In the light of the increasingly biting tone and mood in the dialogue, it seems unfair to accuse Elihu, however overconfident he may be, of continuing in the same vein as the counselors.

15–22 The shift to the third person in v.15 shows how Elihu uses the same discursive style as in the Dialogue. Here he launches a soliloquy all about words—his words. Words have failed Job's counselors, but here he is standing by with so many words inside him that he is fairly bursting at the seams (v.18). There is no way that he can hold them back (v.19). He promises himself (and anyone listening) that he will be absolutely impartial (v.21). As is usual in Semitic rhetoric, he carries the matter of impartiality to a hyperbolic extreme (v.22; cf. Job in 13:8−9). He will not even use honorific titles (see Notes on v.21), something he never learned to do skillfully for fear of God's punishment.

Almost all modern interpreters have found Elihu to be insufferably wordy. MacKenzie says it takes him twenty-four verses to say, "Look out, I'm going to speak." He even suggests the Elihu speeches may be a parody on "some particular 'younger school' of wisdom teachers." Whether successful or not from the modern viewpoint, Elihu means to be eloquent, and wordiness is the essence. This loquacious style to some degree makes all the speeches in chapters 3−41 difficult for the modern reader to appreciate. In Egypt even judges were impressed by the lengthy rhetoric of a defendant called The Eloquent Peasant (*ANET*, 407−10). The peasant was brought in before the magistrates nine times just to keep him talking; and when the Herakleopolitan king of Egypt (twenty-first century BC) heard of it, the peasant's speeches were put into writing for his majesty to enjoy. No doubt Aaron possessed some of this gift that Moses feared he himself lacked.

Elihu then appears on the scene to present eloquently a human viewpoint free of the acrimony that ultimately binds the thoughts of the three friends. Whether we see him as prolix or not, his intention is noble. See comments on 36:1−4, which suggest Elihu is referring to his "speech," not his "knowledge" here in 32:6 and 10.

NOTES

6 זָחַלְתִּי (*zāḥaltî*, "I was fearful") is another Aramaism found only here in the OT, attested as early as the ninth century Zakir inscription (see H. Donnerr and W. Rollig, *Kanaanäische und Aramäische Inschriften* [3 vols.; Wiesbaden: Otto Harrassowitz, 1968], 3:32, text 202). It also occurs in the Aramaic portion of Daniel (2:31; 4:5 [2]; 5:19; 6:26 [27]; 7:7, 19).

9 For רַבִּים (*rabbîm*, "the old"), the NIV margin reads, "Or *many*; or *great*." The versions (Greek, Syriac, Latin) understood the word to mean "older men." Genesis 25:23, where *rab* means "older," supports this, as does lQS, where *rabbîm* are the senior members (cf. v.7, where *rōb šānîm* ["great in years"] means "old"). The NIV's use of "only" avoids a categorical assertion that no old people are wise (cf. Andersen, 247).

10 Two Hebrew MSS and the Versions make שִׁמְעָה (*šimʿâ*, "Listen") plural and thus harmonize the grammar with the second plural pronouns in v.6. The MT is an emphatic imperative and should not be changed.

On דֵּעִי (*dēʿî*, "what I know"; lit., "my knowledge"), see Pope's comment (243) based on the Qumran Targum and H. L. Ginsberg's studies ("The Legend of King Keret, A Canaanite Epic of the Bronze Age," *BASORSup* 2−3 [1946]: 42−43), which point to the root *dw* (Arab.) meaning "speech" (also in vv.6, 17). In 36:3−4 this may also be the meaning (see below; cf. 37:16). Even if one insists this is from the familiar root *yd* ("to know"), it is still a mark of Elihu's distinctive style since in the Dialogue the infinitive is always *daʿat*.

11 הוֹחַלְתִּי (*hôḥaltî*, "I waited")—here and in v.16 Elihu again reveals a difference between his speech and that of Job and the friends. They consistently used the Piel and not the Hiphil of this root (cf. 6:11; 13:15; 14:14; 29:21, 23; 30:26). There is no difference in meaning, but the Piel is used widely in poetry of the Psalms and Isaiah. The Hiphil is another evidence of Elihu's style.

תְּבוּנֹתֵיכֶם (*t^ebûnōtêkem*, "your reasoning") is still preferred, despite the Syriac and the Qumran Targum translation "(until) you finish," based on the root *klh*.

13 Concerning אֵל יִדְּפֶנּוּ (*'ēl yidd^epennû*, "let God refute him"), the verb is stronger than mere refutation; it means "drive" or "beat" (as the wind does). This is the only place it is used of words. The Arabic "strike" (as with a mallet) fits this context.

14 The book of Job shifts back and forth with the plural spelling מִלִּין (*millîn*, "swords") and *millîm* (note *millîm* in v.15). Although the Hebrew reads smoothly in v.14a, Dhorme unnecessarily sees a difficulty in understanding why Elihu says Job did not marshal words against him when he was not even present. That is certainly no reason to see two haplographics in this verse. Elihu may have been pointing out the reactionary nature of their arguments of which he intends not to be guilty. Or, as Pope suggests, לֹא (*lō'*, "not") might be read לוּ (*lû'*, "would that").

17 The Hebrew of חֶלְקִי (*ḥelqî*, "my say") is literally "[speak] my piece."

18–19 In the second half of v.18, the Hebrew clearly reads "wind swells my belly," which should be kept as a figure in the light of v.19. This figure was used by Eliphaz in 15:2 as derogatory of Job's "hot wind." It is only from the parallelism that we know אֹבוֹת (*'ōbôt*) means "wineskins" (cf. Mt 9:17).

21–22 The use of אַל־נָא (*'al-nā'*) is hardly indicative mood. Elihu seems to have been saying, "Please do not expect me to show partiality." In the second half of this verse and in the first half of v.22, the verb כָּנָה (*kānâ*; GK 4033) means "to call someone by his honorific title," a practice Elihu feels God disapproves.

3. The First Speech: Part 2 (33:1–33)

OVERVIEW

Elihu speaks directly to Job, appealing to him by name (vv.1, 31). He ends the speech admonishing Job to reply (v.32). At the very end of his speeches (37:14, 19–20), Elihu makes another such appeal. And in 34:5, 7, 35–36, and 35:16 he refers again to Job by name. The three counselors studiously avoided even mentioning Job's name, which indicates how formal their relationship was. From chapter 12 on Job had lost all confidence in the sincerity of his friends (cf. 12:2; 13:4–5; 16:2–5; 19:2–6, 28–29; 21:3, 34; 26:1–4). Elihu is aware of this; so he opens his speech by stressing his own honest intent (cf. 1Ch 29:17; Ps 119:7). Of course, Job never responds to Elihu, which may indicate that though Elihu extends a more personal relationship,

Job does not find his comments worthy of reflection. Alternatively, we might understand Job's lack of reply a function of the fact that God intervenes and finally addresses Job directly.

The refutation of Job beginning in v.8 immediately reveals Elihu's style—direct quotation of Job's words. In the Dialogue Job and his friends replied in a more general way to one another's ideas. Elihu is not satisfied with this. Even though he says, "I heard the very words," some feel Elihu has the advantage of also seeing them. Whether that is so or not, he is concerned with the very words and quotes them fairly accurately three times (33:9–11; 34:5–6; 35:2–3) as the starting points for his rebuttal of Job's claim to innocence.

¹"But now, Job, listen to my words;
   pay attention to everything I say.
²I am about to open my mouth;
   my words are on the tip of my tongue.
³My words come from an upright heart;
   my lips sincerely speak what I know.
⁴The Spirit of God has made me;
   the breath of the Almighty gives me life.
⁵Answer me then, if you can;
   prepare yourself and confront me.
⁶I am just like you before God;
   I too have been taken from clay.
⁷No fear of me should alarm you,
   nor should my hand be heavy upon you.

⁸"But you have said in my hearing—
   I heard the very words—
⁹'I am pure and without sin;
   I am clean and free from guilt.
¹⁰Yet God has found fault with me;
   he considers me his enemy.
¹¹He fastens my feet in shackles;
   he keeps close watch on all my paths.'

¹²"But I tell you, in this you are not right,
   for God is greater than man.
¹³Why do you complain to him
   that he answers none of man's words ?
¹⁴For God does speak—now one way, now another—
   though man may not perceive it.
¹⁵In a dream, in a vision of the night,
   when deep sleep falls on men
   as they slumber in their beds,
¹⁶he may speak in their ears
   and terrify them with warnings,
¹⁷to turn man from wrongdoing
   and keep him from pride,

¹⁸to preserve his soul from the pit,
  his life from perishing by the sword.
¹⁹Or a man may be chastened on a bed of pain
  with constant distress in his bones,
²⁰so that his very being finds food repulsive
  and his soul loathes the choicest meal.
²¹His flesh wastes away to nothing,
  and his bones, once hidden, now stick out.
²²His soul draws near to the pit,
  and his life to the messengers of death.

²³"Yet if there is an angel on his side
  as a mediator, one out of a thousand,
  to tell a man what is right for him,
²⁴to be gracious to him and say,
  'Spare him from going down to the pit;
  I have found a ransom for him'—
²⁵then his flesh is renewed like a child's;
  it is restored as in the days of his youth.
²⁶He prays to God and finds favor with him,
  he sees God's face and shouts for joy;
  he is restored by God to his righteous state.
²⁷Then he comes to men and says,
  'I sinned, and perverted what was right,
  but I did not get what I deserved.
²⁸He redeemed my soul from going down to the pit,
  and I will live to enjoy the light.'

²⁹"God does all these things to a man—
  twice, even three times—
³⁰to turn back his soul from the pit,
  that the light of life may shine on him.

³¹"Pay attention, Job, and listen to me;
  be silent, and I will speak.
³²If you have anything to say, answer me;
  speak up, for I want you to be cleared.
³³But if not, then listen to me;
  be silent, and I will teach you wisdom."

COMMENTARY

1–7 As vv.1–3 form a unit of thought, so do vv.4–7. There is no need to shift v.4 (Dhorme) since the verses form an a • b/a' • b' pattern. Verse 4 goes with v.6 and v.5 with v.7. Having in mind Job's earlier words to God in 13:21—"Withdraw your hand far from me, and stop frightening me with your terrors"—Elihu says that he, like Job, is only a creature of God nipped from clay; so Job needs to have no fear in marshaling arguments against him. But the words "if you can" in v.5 belie an attitude of superiority despite his attempt to allay Job's fears (see Notes on v.7 on the linguistic play on words between 13:21 and 33:7).

8–22 Finally Elihu begins his argument. He has already shown an awareness of Job's precise wording. Now with some freedom he quotes the sufferer, picking out lines from various speeches. In 9:21 Job had claimed to be "blameless" (*tām*). In 10:6–7 he had complained, asking why God had to probe for sin in him when God knew he was not guilty. In 13:19 he had challenged anyone to bring charges against him and in 13:23 had requested God to show him his sin. We can be sure that chapter 13 is referred to because 33:10b–11 are virtually identical to 13:24b and 27a. However, quoting accurately does not necessarily mean verbatim. The NIV's "the very words" (v.8) unfortunately give that impression (see Notes on v.9).

Some of Job's words, especially out of context, sound like a claim to sinlessness. For example, in 23:10–12 Job said that he never had turned aside from God's steps or departed from his commands. Eliphaz certainly had that impression from Job's words (15:14–16). But the precise words of v.9 here were not uttered by Job, and on occasions Job admitted to being a sinner (7:21; 13:26). His words in chapters 9; 10; 13; 19; and 23:7, 10–12 have in mind sins for which he was being punished; and

he claimed nothing more for himself than what (unknown to him) God already had pronounced him to be (1:8; 2:3). Elihu, then, does not understand what is happening from the divine perspective, nor can we expect him to. His defense of God is like that of the counselors, especially in their earlier speeches, but without their rancor against Job.

In v.12 Elihu appeals to God's transcendence as the reason Job is wrong to dispute with him. His words sound banal, for hymns have already been uttered about God's greatness (4:8–16; 9:2–13; 11:7–9; 12:13–25; 25:2–6); but his purpose is commendable. God's thoughts and purposes are beyond human ability to comprehend, so how can anyone know what God is doing? But for the moment, beginning in v.13, Elihu sets aside the issue of Job's guilt or innocence and of God's transcendence (to both of which he will return) to answer Job's frequent complaint, that God will not give him a hearing (cf. 9:16, 35; 13:22; 19:7; 23:2–7).

God does communicate with people in various ways (v.14) and often (vv.29–30). Elihu expounds on two of these ways—through dreams (vv.15–18) and through illness (vv.19–22). The dream was considered an important channel for divine revelation in the ancient world. A repeated dream (vv.14–15) confirmed the revelation (Ge 41:32). Dreams and visions continued as legitimate means to determine God's will in Israel (1Sa 28:6) and in the early church (Ac 10:9–16).

Elihu tailors the possibility of this kind of revelation to Job's case. Job has already experienced dreams and visions from God, but they have only terrified him (7:14). This is, however, just the kind of revelation Elihu thinks Job needs, and Job should have interpreted this as God's instruction to keep him from ultimate destruction. Although v.16b is somewhat of a problem, it would be closer to the

MT to translate it "and he sets the seal on [confirms] their discipline" (cf. Notes). Unfortunately Elihu overlooks the real question about which Job wanted an audience with God, namely: What are the sins I am accused of?

The second, but nonverbal, way Elihu finds God revealing himself is even more tailored to Job's case: "Or a man may be chastened on a bed of pain" (v.19). As C. S. Lewis (*The Problem of Pain* [New York: Macmillan, 1943], 93) effectively observes, "God whispers to us in our pleasures, speaks in our conscience, but shouts in our pains: it is His megaphone to rouse a deaf world." God's purpose in suffering is to chasten us for our own good lest we find ourselves face to face with death (on v.22, "the messengers of death," see Notes). But Elihu does not make the crude claim so often on the lips of the counselors—that Job's sufferings are the proof of a wicked life.

Elihu's message is not exactly new, for Eliphaz had at least touched on the disciplinary aspect of suffering in 5:17-18. The subject, however, has not been broached again till now. Its emphasis by Elihu is commendable, but it is not exactly the kind of communication from God Job has had in mind.

In chapters 3; 6-7; 10; 14; 16-17; 29; and 30, Job spoke about death, either longing for it or complaining that it was his only hope. The emphasis is not lost on Elihu. After each of the two descriptions of how God communicates with humanity, Elihu ends on the theme that God does so to redeem people's life from the pit. In vv.18 and 22, after describing symptoms just like Job's (vv.19-21), Elihu pictures the sufferer at the edge of the pit—exactly where Job found himself—about to go on "the journey of no return" (16:18-22). There can be no question that Elihu has in mind chapter 16 as he picks up the subject of an interceding angel.

23-30 Eliphaz was convinced that there was no heavenly mediator who would listen to Job (5:1). In 16:18-21 Job dared to suggest that he had

such a witness, an advocate in heaven who would intercede for him, pleading as a person does for his friend. The word translated in 16:20 as "my intercessor" (but see Notes on the vocalization) is rendered here (v.23) as "mediator" (GK 4885). It also means "interpreter," as one who stands between two others to make communication possible.

The life of the "hypothetical" sufferer here hangs in the balance; no mere mortal can save him. Elihu considers such an event only a possibility, and even then this heavenly mediator would be "one out of a thousand"—a rare one indeed—who might do the job. His job is first "to tell a man what is right for him" (but see Notes). So in a sense this "angel" becomes a third means of revelation from God to humans. He also provides for mercy in behalf of the sufferer and even provides a ransom to save his life (v.24). All this will happen only if one listens to the revelation and turns to God for grace (v.26a). Such a redeemed person will openly admit his sin and praise God for his grace (v.27).

So Elihu has both agreed and disagreed with Job and with the counselors. He has added the element of God's mercy, a subject avoided by the counselors, who constantly appealed to God's justice. We must reap what we sow even when we repent and are healed. Elihu feels there is a place for grace. A ransom may have to be paid, but the man is restored and only then comes to make his public confession.

Verses 26-28 present a person who has truly had a conversion experience. He has joyous communion with God; he is thankful and contrite. In vv.29-30 Elihu makes a case for the patience of God, who will favor a man even when he falls away two or even three times. This should encourage Job, who has not yet even experienced it once.

31-33 Unfortunately like so many well-meaning messengers of grace, Elihu is so fully convinced of his good intentions toward Job that he becomes insufferably overbearing.

NOTES

5 עֶרְכָה (ʿerkâ, "prepare yourself"; GK 6885) means "set things in order," usually troops in battle array; here it is arguments. Elihu wants to do battle with Job, but only as his equal. Yahweh, in his later challenge to Job (38:3; 40:7), uses a significantly different figure and different word for "answer" (see Notes on those verses).

6 קֹרַצְתִּי (qōraṣtî) means "I ... have been taken from." In Assyrian the verb means "nipped off" (BDB, 902; GK 7975). It is what the potter does with clay. In Hebrew it can also have the basic meaning of "to pinch" (*NIDOTTE*, 3:994), and in Proverbs 6:3 and 10:10 it means to "pinch," that is, "to wink" the eye.

7 In rendering אַכְפִּי (ʾakpî) as "my hand," the NIV has followed the LXX (cf. KJV); but the verb of this rare root (ʾkp) is attested in Proverbs 16:26 and Sir 46:5, where it means "to press on." So the RSV's "my pressure" is better. The line is a play on 13:21, where Job called for God "to withdraw his hand" (kap). Elihu may have considered it elegant to substitute the rarer "like-sounding" word. See discussion in Clines (*Job 21–37*, 692).

9 Elihu announced in v.8 that he was quoting Job and yet he uses חַף (ḥap, "clean"), which is found nowhere else in the OT, though in Aramaic and late Hebrew the verb ḥāpap means "to wash." This suggests that the NIV of v.8—"the very words" for "the sound of the words"—may be overdone. It certainly reveals that modern verbatim quotation was not a feature of the ancient Semitic mentality. The NT quotations of the OT share that viewpoint.

13 דְּבָרָיו (dᵉbārāyw, "man's words") is literally "his words." The question here is what is the antecedent of the pronoun "his"? The NIV has made it refer to "man's words," but it may refer to human inability to answer God's words. That, however, contradicts the next verse.

The interpretation in the NIV margin, where it is God who does not answer for his actions, does not fit the context at all. Dahood ("The Dative Suffix in Job 33:13," *Bib* 63 [1982]: 258–59) sees here the participle with the dative suffix reading, "Why do you complain to him that he answers none who speak to him?" That fits both the wider and the immediate contexts well. The NRSV emends the pronominal suffix to first person singular and renders (as a quote from Job): "He will answer none of my words."

16 וּבְמֹסָרָם יַחְתֹּם (ûbᵉmōsārām yaḥtōm, "and terrify them with warnings") has been variously interpreted. As vocalized, the MT reads "and seals their fetters." With the vowel change to mûsār, we get "and seals [confirms] their discipline" (cf. KJV). Most modern English versions (NIV, RSV, et al.) follow the vocalization of the LXX in the second word (yᵉḥittēm), yielding "he terrifies them with mûsār [disciplinary warning]." The suffix ām is considered objective genitive (Gordis, *Job*, 375): "with warnings to them."

17 Understanding the use of מַעֲשֶׂה (maᶜᵃśeh, "from wrongdoing") as implicitly evil (cf. Ge 44:15) in this context is supported by the use of the synonym pōᶜal ("deed"), parallel with pešaᶜ ("transgression") in 36:9. We see here also the aforementioned tendency in this poetry to omit prepositions.

18 Both the parallelism and the root ᶜbr ("pass over, on, or by") support the identification here— מֵעֲבֹר בַּשֶּׁלַח (mēᵃbōr baššālaḥ, "from perishing by the sword")—of the Akkadian cognate šalḫu ("a water channel") used in Mesopotamian mythology with reference to the river of death (see Rowley, Pope, Tsevat, "The Canaanite God šalaḥ," *VT* 4 [1954]: 43). If we read "sword," "javelin," or "missile," we must justify the use of the verb ʿbr. It is used consistently in this idiom by Elihu (cf. 34:20; 36:12; cf. also Ps 37:36) and in Nahum 1:12, where it clearly means "to die."

21 יָכֵל (yikel, "wastes away") is again in Job clearly the apocopated form of the weak verb, not the jussive (see Notes on 18:12).

22 לַמְמֵתִים (lamᵉmitîm, "to the messengers of death") is a reference to the angels of death as in 2 Samuel 24:16; 2 Kings 19:35; 1 Chronicles 21:15; and Psalm 78:49, whose work can be accomplished by plague. Pope revocalizes, assuming the use of enclitic *mem*. But that involves questionable methodology. When a text is grammatically clear and fits culturally, one should not emend or revocalize to support a thesis over which there is some disagreement. The "waters of death" as the netherworld is not that well attested in the OT. The line only appears unbalanced until one counts the syllables.

24 Concerning פְּדָעֵהוּ (pᵉdāʿēhû, "spare him"), there is no known word pdʿ meaning "to spare." Gordis (*Job*, 377–78) follows the two MSS that read prʿ, but his attempt to show that the meaning in Proverbs 4:15 ("avoid") fits here is not convincing. Dhorme, also unconvincing, says the *ayin* stands for *heh* in pdh ("to ransom"). Guilleaume (see Pope) sees the conjunction p ("and"; Arab., Aram., Ugar., et al.) followed by the root wdʿ ("to release"), which, it is claimed, is used in 1 Samuel 21:3 (cf. J. Barr, *Comparative Philology and the Text of the Old Testament* [London: Oxford Univ. Press, 1968], 20–21).

25 Gordis gives four explanations of רֻטֲפַשׁ (ruṭᵃpaš, "is renewed"). Guilleaume, 119, relates it to the Hebrew rṭb ("be soft, tender"), with the final sibilant as used in Arabic. Others say it is from ṭpš ("grow fat") with prefixed *resh*. It may be a combination of the two verbs like paršēz ("spreading") in 26:9 (see Notes). All are guesses, but the context makes the general meaning of the word clear.

26 For וַיָּשֵׁב (wayyāšeb) the MT reads "And he restores man." The NIV assumes the subject is God: "he is restored by God." Because of the sudden shift in subject, some emend it to read yᵉbaššēr ("he [the man] announces [to men]"; cf. RSV). The NEB moves the line up to v.23. Gordis (*Job*, 379) attempts to show šwb ("return") can mean "proclaim." If this is so, the RSV is preferred.

27 Most revocalize יָשֹׁר (yāšōr, "then he comes") to yāšîr ("he sings," RSV), but the NIV takes it as is from šûr II (KB, 957).

30 בְּאוֹר הַחַיִּים (bᵉʾôr haḥayyîm, "that the light of life may shine on him") might possibly read, "that he may be given light in the land of the living" (see Notes on 22:11).

4. The Second Speech (34:1–37)

OVERVIEW

Elihu claims he wants Job to be cleared. It seems Elihu had repentance in mind when he called on Job "to speak up" (33:32) or else listen and learn wisdom. He sees himself as a teacher of wisdom (33:33). As he proceeds to do that in chapter 34, he believes even the wise can benefit from his chosen words (vv.2–4). Once again his method is to quote Job (vv.5–6), and his purpose is to show that Job's words are theologically unsound. He does not always claim to quote the very words of Job

(33:8–11). Sometimes he gives only a summary of what the sufferer has said (vv.5–6, 8).

As we examine this chapter, we should keep in mind that Elihu has picked out of Job's speeches those words and ideas that sound particularly damaging. Job has had questions about the justice of God, and he has emphatically asserted his innocence. But none of this should be viewed independently of Job's total statement. His claim to innocence is always given in the context of his reason for suffering. And while he has questioned the mystery of theodicy, he has also made clear he believes in God's justice so much that he is willing to rest his entire case, all his hope, on that one issue (13:13–19; 23:2–7). Like the counselors, Elihu picks out only those words of Job that he needs in order to prove his point.

Elihu, however, is not in all respects like the three counselors. For example, he does not express their view of suffering. As we have seen in chapter 33, he considered the disciplinary aspect of suffering to be one of the ways God communicates with humans. Unlike the counselors, Elihu does not totally condemn Job. He thinks Job, through association with the wicked, has picked up some of their views (vv.8–9). The counselors in defending God have stressed his transcendence almost to the point of denying his concern over humans. They viewed people in their sin as nothing. Elihu accuses Job of talking like a wicked person (v.36) and of being rebellious rather than submissive (v.37). But in 33:23–28 Elihu showed some understanding of God's free grace in dealing with human waywardness.

Like the counselors, Elihu has a compelling desire to uphold the truth that God always does what is right (vv.10–12). They saw this only in terms of black and white; God punishes and rewards. Elihu presents the sovereign Creator as one who intentionally and momentarily exercises benevolence toward all humankind (vv.13–15). Elihu is zealous to counter Job's complaint that God treats the wicked and the righteous alike (9:22; 10:3; 21:7–8; 24:1–12). This would mean God does evil (vv.10–30). Elihu is convinced Job needs to repent over such a rebellious notion (vv.33–37). He, like Job and the counselors, reveals no knowledge of the events in the divine council. So it appears Elihu is not an angelic messenger from God, for he has a limited perspective and presents, therefore, only a human estimate of Job's spiritual condition.

Apart from the introductory statement (vv.2–4), the chapter divides into three main themes. The quotation of Job and the condemnation of his views (vv.5–9) are followed by a long defense of God (vv.10–30) and then a return to his polemic against Job (vv.31–37).

---

¹Then Elihu said:

²"Hear my words, you wise men;
 listen to me, you men of learning.
³For the ear tests words
 as the tongue tastes food.
⁴Let us discern for ourselves what is right;
 let us learn together what is good.

⁵"Job says, 'I am innocent,
   but God denies me justice.
⁶Although I am right,
   I am considered a liar;
although I am guiltless,
   his arrow inflicts an incurable wound.'
⁷What man is like Job,
   who drinks scorn like water?
⁸He keeps company with evildoers;
   he associates with wicked men.
⁹For he says, 'It profits a man nothing
   when he tries to please God.'

¹⁰"So listen to me, you men of understanding.
   Far be it from God to do evil,
   from the Almighty to do wrong.
¹¹He repays a man for what he has done;
   he brings upon him what his conduct deserves.
¹²It is unthinkable that God would do wrong,
   that the Almighty would pervert justice.
¹³Who appointed him over the earth?
   Who put him in charge of the whole world?
¹⁴If it were his intention
   and he withdrew his spirit and breath,
¹⁵all mankind would perish together
   and man would return to the dust.

¹⁶"If you have understanding, hear this;
   listen to what I say.
¹⁷Can he who hates justice govern?
   Will you condemn the just and mighty One?
¹⁸Is he not the One who says to kings, 'You are worthless,'
   and to nobles, 'You are wicked,'
¹⁹who shows no partiality to princes
   and does not favor the rich over the poor,
   for they are all the work of his hands?
²⁰They die in an instant, in the middle of the night;
   the people are shaken and they pass away;
   the mighty are removed without human hand.

²¹"His eyes are on the ways of men;
    he sees their every step.
²²There is no dark place, no deep shadow,
    where evildoers can hide.
²³God has no need to examine men further,
    that they should come before him for judgment.
²⁴Without inquiry he shatters the mighty
    and sets up others in their place.
²⁵Because he takes note of their deeds,
    he overthrows them in the night and they are crushed.
²⁶He punishes them for their wickedness
    where everyone can see them,
²⁷because they turned from following him
    and had no regard for any of his ways.
²⁸They caused the cry of the poor to come before him,
    so that he heard the cry of the needy.
²⁹But if he remains silent, who can condemn him?
    If he hides his face, who can see him?
Yet he is over man and nation alike,
    ³⁰to keep a godless man from ruling,
    from laying snares for the people.

³¹"Suppose a man says to God,
    'I am guilty but will offend no more.
³²Teach me what I cannot see;
    if I have done wrong, I will not do so again.'
³³Should God then reward you on your terms,
    when you refuse to repent?
You must decide, not I;
    so tell me what you know.

³⁴"Men of understanding declare,
    wise men who hear me say to me,
³⁵'Job speaks without knowledge;
    his words lack insight.'
³⁶Oh, that Job might be tested to the utmost
    for answering like a wicked man!
³⁷To his sin he adds rebellion;
    scornfully he claps his hands among us
    and multiplies his words against God."

COMMENTARY

1–4 In 12:11–12 Job was sarcastic about the bad "food" the counselors had been dishing out to him under the guise of "the wisdom of the aged." Elihu here is determined to show where real wisdom lies, where food may be found that is really good. He calls for all who are wise to join him in his banquet of words to find out how good they are.

5–9 The quotation in v.5 is accurate. Job used the very words of himself. For v.5a compare 12:4; 13:18; 27:6; and for v.5b compare 27:2. Where Job has not used the very words, he did use the thoughts of v.5; but he never labeled himself as in v.6, a person "without transgression" (*bᵉlî-pāšaʿ*; NIV, "guiltless"). Despite Elihu's claim in 33:32 that it would please him if Job were shown to be in the right, we were told by the narrator that Elihu had already made up his mind; he was angry at Job for justifying himself rather than God (32:2). Now his anger surfaces.

The first half of v.6 presents a special problem. The NIV's "I am considered a liar" (cf. RSV) does not say who considered Job a liar. If it means Job accused God of calling him a liar, there is no evidence for that. If it means the counselors accused Job of this, there is some evidence. Eliphaz said Job had a "crafty tongue" (15:5). Certainly Job accused them of lying about him (13:4). Here in v.6 some modern translations follow the LXX, which reads "He [God] lies about my case" (Pope, NEB). Some scholars thus claim that a pious scribe changed the Hebrew text for theological reasons. But there is no scribal tradition to support this (as in 32:3). The LXX has its own propensity to change the text for theological reasons; it is interesting that it has a theologically more difficult reading here. What makes it unlikely is the absence of any such remark by Job.

The MT is clearly first person. The RV margin (cf. Rowley) is perhaps a better way to handle v.6a: "Should I lie against my right [i.e., when I am innocent]?" The latter is close to what Job said in 6:28–29 (cf. 6:14): "Would I lie to your face? ... my integrity is at stake." Their implication that Job was lying is what drew this comment, so Elihu may have both 6:28–29 and 15:5 in mind. God's "arrow [that] inflicts an incurable wound" (v.6) is surely based on 16:13 (see Notes on v.6).

In v.7 Elihu draws again from the words of Eliphaz. The latter said that Job "drinks up evil like water" (15:16), and he censured Job for venting his rage against God, for shaking his fist at the Almighty and defiantly attacking him (15:25–26). Elihu does not go as far as Eliphaz in accusing Job of this, but it is enough that Job has kept company with such people.

Verse 9 is not a direct quotation of Job. In 21:15 Job imagined wicked people saying this, and then Job complained that calamity did not come very often on them (21:17). So it is only by implication that Elihu can accuse Job. His accusation is based on Job's sentiment that the righteous get the same treatment as the wicked.

10–15 Intrinsic to v.9 is the accusation that God is not just. From this point on throughout the next twenty-one verses, Elihu expounds on the theme that "God only does right." Notice how he repeats himself to emphasize this theme in vv.10 and 12. Job had wailed "that those who provoke God are secure" (12:6) while one who is "righteous and blameless" is made "a laughingstock" (12:4; cf. 10:3; 21:7–8; 24:1–12). To Elihu this is nothing else than an accusation that God does wrong, and it is unthinkable that God would do wrong.

But that does not solve the mystery. Job was probing when he questioned, "Why do the innocent suffer?" Job saw that "the fatherless child is snatched from the breast; the infant of the poor is seized for a debt" (24:9), "the murderer ... kills the poor and needy" (24:14), "but God charges no one with wrongdoing" (24:12). "No!" said Elihu, "[God] repays a man for what he has done" (v.11). Whether Job has seen it or not, Elihu insists on that most basic truth: "For truly God cannot perpetrate evil" ('It is unthinkable that God would do wrong!' NIV, v.12).

Up to this point Elihu has not attempted to use logic but has countered Job's problem with a strong affirmation of God's righteousness. Without this affirmation all his words are meaningless. The righteousness of God is self-evident as truth because of the image of God in people. That is the reason people understand justice. Indeed, that Job has a problem on this issue is in itself a reflection of his Creator's justice, and God cannot be inferior to Job. Elihu's next words get us deeper into the mystery. They infer that God is the Creator and therefore not accountable to Job (v.13). Further, in vv.14–15 he asserts humanity's complete dependence on the continuing exercise of God's free grace to continue his existence.

16–20 From all this Elihu maintains that people are not in a position to stand as God's judge (v.17). Without God's impartial judgment, especially on those who hold power (vv.18–19), the world would dissolve into hopeless anarchy. Because of his omnipotence, no one can influence him as he actively governs.

21–30 Such impartial governance of the world is typified by God's punishment of the wicked rulers who disregard his ways. This justice lies behind all the order there is, and it is confirmed and guaranteed by God's omniscience as well as his omnipotence. Job had complained over the delay

of justice (21:19; 24:1). Elihu maintains that God does not have to set times for inquiry and judgment. His omniscience enables him to judge all the time. God hears the cry of the poor and needy and punishes the wicked openly, but it is his prerogative to remain silent if and when it pleases him (v.29). Even then he keeps his control over individuals and nations for the common good (vv.29c–30?). And even then he may use the wicked to punish the wicked and so keep the godless from ruling. But on vv.29–30, see Notes.

31–37 Having closed his defense of God, Elihu resumes admonishing Job. That much is clear, but vv.31–33 are among the most difficult to put together. The NIV has taken some small liberties with v.33 in order to make it a simple and direct call to repentance. The Hebrew of v.33 reads, "Should he pay back [reward] on your terms because you object?" It appears that Elihu is trying to show Job how untenable his position is by means of an illustration. If a person should repent after God has disciplined him, must God be subject to his or her wishes as he governs the world? The implied answer is "Of course not!" But this is what Job expects by making himself equal with God, by accusing God of injustice and demanding God present to him an indictment. Elihu is certain that any wise person he might consult would agree that Job's behavior is like the wicked's multiplying words against God. So Job deserves to be tested to the utmost.

Furthermore, the illustration in vv.31–32 is probably given to shame Job for lack of contriteness (see Notes for some variations in the way the verses should read). The question in v.33 could be meant to startle Job. Must God recompense (šlm) him for unfair treatments? Obviously not. Again, Job's sin is that he has arrogantly made himself equal with God and played the part of a rebel (v.37).

NOTES

6 For עַל־מִשְׁפָּטִי אֲכַזֵּב (ʿal-mišpāṭî ʾᵃkazzēb, "although I am right, I am considered a liar"), the LXX has "he [meaning God] lies." Some maintain the MT was changed to avoid the offensive theology (Dhorme, Pope, NEB, et al.). This fits nicely with ʿal-mišpāṭî ("concerning my case"). The NIV may be based on the intransitive Piel (cf. GKC, par. 52 k), but for this reading Gordis (*Job*, 386) has a better explanation: the indirect quotation, reading "In spite of my right, they say that I lie." Some want to change the vowels to Niphil (ʾekkāzēb, "I am proven a liar"), as in Proverbs 30:6 (Duhm); but Rowley's suggestion—following the RV margin—"should I lie" seems best. Clines (*Job 21–37*, 746–47) has a full discussion of all the options. See comments above.

חִצִּי (ḥiṣṣî, "his arrow") is literally "my arrow [is incurable]." Gordis (*Job*, 386) calls this a transferred epithet, meaning "the arrow that is in me" (cf. 6:4). For other options see Clines (*Job 21–37*, 747).

11 On יַמְצִאֶנּוּ (yamṣᵉPennû, "he brings upon him"), compare the use of *mṣ* in 31:25.

13 אָרְצָה (ʾārᵉṣâ, "the earth") is possibly an old accusative.

14 אִם־יָשִׂים אֵלָיו לִבּוֹ (ʾim-yāśîm ʾēlāyw libbô, "If it were his intention") is the idiom (lit., "if he set his heart to himself") used in 1:8 and 2:3. See also v.23 below. The RSV follows the LXX and the Oriental *Kethiv* in reading yāšîb ("take back") and dropping lēb ("heart, mind").

18 For הַאֲמֹר (haᵃmōr, "Is he not the One who says"), the MT has the interrogative *heh* with the infinitive construct, which means "Is it right to say" (Pope has "Does one say … "). The NIV seems to be a combination of the interrogative and the active participle ʾōmēr. The ancient versions (LXX et al.) have the participle with the article: "The One who says" (RSV, NEB, Dhorme). The participle with the article is preferred since v.19 continues the idea with the relative pronoun אֲשֶׁר (ᵃšer).

21 Compare 14:16; 24:23; 31:4.

23 It is usually assumed that יָשִׂים עוֹד (yāśîm ʿôd, "to examine men further") is a haplography and there were two *mem*'s, the second word being mōʿēd ("appointed time"; cf. BHS mg.). "For he has not appointed a time for anyone" (NRSV). Modern versions and commentaries (Dhorme, Pope, Hartley, Clines) have followed this since it was proposed by Reiske (*Conjecturae in Jobum et Proverbia*, 1779). Gordis (*Job*, 390) drops the *yod* and reads śîm (infinitive, "to set"): "It is not for man to set the time." The NIV keeps the MT with yāśîm as the idiom "pay attention" (cf. v.14) with the ellipsis of lēb, as in 4:20; 23:6; 24:12; and Isaiah 41:20 (cf. Driver and Gray, 299).

29–33 These verses are extremely difficult. Dozens of emendations are suggested, and some critics even leave blank spaces in their translations. The NIV attempts to stay reasonably close to the MT. Below I suggest some readings that will improve the NIV. The LXX omits these verses.

29 וְעַל גּוֹי וְעַל־אָדָם יָחַד (wᵉʿal-gôy wᵉʿal-ʾādām yāḥad, "Yet he is over man and nation alike") fits the context much better if we see in yāḥad ("alike") the third masculine singular of the root ḥdh II (KB; Holladay, 96), meaning "to see" (Aram.). We see this root in 3:6 (see Notes). Thus: "He watches over each nation and each man to keep a godless man from ruling, etc."

31 The NIV's rendering of כִּי־אֶל־אֵל הֶאָמַר (kî-ʾel-ʾēl heʾāmar) as "Suppose a man says to God" is based on reading kî-ʾel-ᵉlôah ʾāmar ("If [suppose] to God one says").

869

Concerning נָשָׂאתִי לֹא אֶחְבֹּל (nāśāʾtî lōʾ ʾeḥbōl, "I am guilty but will offend no more"), the idiom nśʾ ʿwn ("bear guilt") is what the NIV has in mind with ellipsis of ʿwn, because the idiom is common. Dhorme, Pope, et al. repoint the text, rendering niśśēʾtî ("I have been led astray"). The words "no more" could be based on the frequentative use of the imperfect; but considering the unbalanced line, Dhorme (525–26; cf. Pope) takes the first two letters (bl) of the next verse as dittography and ends this line with ʿadê ("still"). With the negative this yields the meaning "no more." He also sees haplography here and so begins the next line with ʿōd ("until"). See below. Alternatively, it could also be a shortened form of "I have endured punishment" (see NRSV).

32 Concerning בִּלְעֲדֵי אֶחֱזֶה (bilʿadê ʾeḥĕzeh, "what I cannot see"), Gordis (*Job*, 393) disagrees with Pope, who says bilʿadê is meaningless here. It is a preposition with a clause as *nomen regens* (Gordis), reading literally "apart from what I see." Dhorme reads: "Until I see, do thou instruct me."

33 In הַמֵעִמְּךָ יְשַׁלְמֶנָּה (hamēʿimmᵊkā yᵊšalmennâ, "reward you on your terms"), the use of ʿim ("with") in 10:13 and 27:11, where "with you" suggests what is in the mind of someone, what he thinks, permits the meaning "in your opinion" or "on your terms" (Dhorme). But "you" in "reward you" is not in the Hebrew. The person is hypothetical, "a man" (v.31; though Job may be in mind), and the feminine suffix may refer to God's punishment (v.26). Thus read: "Should God make amends for it [his punishment] because you [object]?" Furthermore, the end of the line does not have the word "repent." So if it is a call to repentance, it is being given in a very oblique way.

36 In עַל־תְּשֻׁבֹת בְּאַנְשֵׁי־אָוֶן (ʿal-tᵊšubōt bᵊʾanšê-ʾāwen, "for answering with a wicked man"), it is not necessary to change the preposition b to k with the LXX and a few MSS ("like," NIV). Job has been accused of keeping company with evil men (34:8) and so giving answers with their help.

5. The Third Speech (35:1–16)

OVERVIEW

Job had raised questions that really disturbed Elihu. In this speech he deals with several important issues that arose out of Job's problem about God's justice. Elihu begins (vv.1–3) by showing Job how inconsistent he has been to claim in one breath that God will vindicate him and then in another to complain he gets no profit out of not sinning (cf. 34:9). In other words, if God is so unjust, why does Job want to be vindicated by him? A colloquial way of phrasing the question would be: What is the use of being good if God does not care? Elihu has missed Job's point, namely, that he wants to be vindicated because he does believe God is just. Of course Job, in his struggle to understand what God is doing, has sent out two signals, one of which Elihu, like the others, has not been able to hear.

In answer to Job's inconsistency (vv.4–8), Elihu claims it is God who gets no benefit from Job whether or not he does right. God is far too transcendent for humans to affect him by their little deeds. Job's righteousness or lack of it affects only people like himself (v.8).

Another issue grows out of that last statement and centers around Job's concern over God's apparent indifference to the cries of the oppressed (cf. 24:1–12). Elihu maintains that God is not indifferent to people, but people are indifferent to God. People want God to save them; but they are not interested in honoring him as their Creator, Deliverer, and Source of wisdom (vv.9–11). Human arrogance keeps God from responding to the empty cry for help (vv.12–13). That is why God has not answered Job. The silence from God derives from Job's complaints, questions, and challenges that reveal the same kind of arrogance (vv.14–15). They are words without knowledge (v.16).

Modern interpreters tend to find Elihu's advice shallow. Andersen, 257–58, sees Elihu as a perfectionist with cruel advice. Should the oppressors in v.9 arouse the anger of God no matter what the spirituality of those who call for help? Andersen thinks that Elihu is as mechanical in his theology as were the counselors, with answers to prayer as well

as God's judgments being automatic, and that to Elihu God is manageable and predictable while to Job God has sovereign freedom (but see 36:22–23). All this is a matter of theological balance. Any stress on God's justice at the expense of his grace or on his transcendence at the expense of his immanence is wrong.

No doubt there is a lack of balance in Elihu's advice, but there are also some commendable aspects if we are willing to allow him a margin of error in his overly zealous comments, as we allowed Job in his fits of rage. Zealots tend to be heartless, so we should not be surprised at Elihu's cold analysis of Job's complaints. Job has certainly minimized human responsibility in some of his remarks (7:20) and sounded arrogant enough in 31:35–37 to arouse the ire of a moralist such as Elihu.

---

¹Then Elihu said:

²"Do you think this is just?
　　You say, 'I will be cleared by God.'
³Yet you ask him, 'What profit is it to me,
　　and what do I gain by not sinning?'

⁴"I would like to reply to you
　　and to your friends with you.
⁵Look up at the heavens and see;
　　gaze at the clouds so high above you.
⁶If you sin, how does that affect him?
　　If your sins are many, what does that do to him?
⁷If you are righteous, what do you give to him,
　　or what does he receive from your hand?
⁸Your wickedness affects only a man like yourself,
　　and your righteousness only the sons of men.

⁹"Men cry out under a load of oppression;
　　they plead for relief from the arm of the powerful.
¹⁰But no one says, 'Where is God my Maker,
　　who gives songs in the night,

> [11]who teaches more to us than to the beasts of the earth
> and makes us wiser than the birds of the air?'
> [12]He does not answer when men cry out
> because of the arrogance of the wicked.
> [13]Indeed, God does not listen to their empty plea;
> the Almighty pays no attention to it.
> [14]How much less, then, will he listen
> when you say that you do not see him,
> that your case is before him
> and you must wait for him,
> [15]and further, that his anger never punishes
> and he does not take the least notice of wickedness.
> [16]So Job opens his mouth with empty talk;
> without knowledge he multiplies words."

COMMENTARY

1–3 Job did not use these very words, but Elihu tries to reproduce two of Job's viewpoints. There is no doubting the first—Job is sure he will be vindicated (v.2; cf. 13:13–19). But where did Job ask, "What do I gain by not sinning" (v.3)? This is derived from his constant complaint that God treats the righteous and wicked alike, a major bone of contention with the three counselors. Job felt that according to the principle of retribution, his suffering is not just. He is found guilty (9:28–29) without charges (10:2). So to Job, a desire to be cleared made sense. But Elihu can only see in Job's words the accusation that God is unjust.

4–8 Many feel Elihu's answer is just a borrowing of material already said (but see Gordis, *Job*, 546–53). Verse 4 along with chapter 32 makes it clear that Elihu does not view this as a restatement. The relationship between divine transcendence and human behavior was often on Job's mind. Here also Job sounded inconsistent. He saw God as too attentive— the Watcher of humans (7:17–20)—and yet so tran-

scendent that he could say to God, "If I have sinned, what have I done to you?" (7:20). And Eliphaz had said, "Can a man be of benefit to God?" (22:2–3).

To Elihu God is too transcendent to be either helped by righteousness (v.7) or hurt by sin (v.6). And this is further refined by alluding to two kinds of sin, omission (*ḥṭ*) and commission (*pš'*), which can neither deprive God nor hurt him in any way.

There is no place in Elihu's theology for doing God's will out of love for him. Humans affect only their fellows by being good or bad (v.9). And though God may punish or reward people as Judge, there is no place for him in the role of a Father who can be hurt or pleased by humans.

9–16 Earlier Job devoted an entire speech to the subject of God's apparent indifference to his plight (ch. 23) and the plight of all who suffer and are oppressed (ch. 24). Elihu states the issue in v.9 and then sets out to give an answer. We must keep in mind what this young man has already said about God's purpose in human suffering. God uses it to teach (discipline) and warn (33:16–22). Or he may remain silent because he is using a tyrant as his instrument of punishment (34:29–30; cf. Isa 10:5–15). Or he may only be restraining his wrath in hope for repentance (33:29–30).

It seems as if Elihu is not totally rigid in his moralistic justice since he allows for the possibility of a mediating angel who could provide a ransom for the sinner and plead for grace (33:23–24). There is the possibility that those who cry for relief are also sinful and unwilling to bow before God as their Creator (v.10a) and Savior (v.10b). They cry only because of physical pain and not out of spiritual hunger (v.11; see Gordis, *Job*, 551).

The "songs in the night" of v.10 are most likely songs of praise as a result of deliverance (cf. "at night his song [*šîr*] is with me," Ps 42:8; but see Notes on *zᵉmirôt*). Verse 11 in the NIV (but see NIV mg. and Notes) refers to the capacity of the divine-image bearer (humanity) to hear the voice of God in contrast to brute beasts. As Elihu sees it, God does not listen to the cry of people when it comes to him as the empty sound of a brute beast (v.13).

Elihu feels that the failure of suffering people to see that their Maker is also the author of wisdom and joy is a sign of arrogance on their part. The interpretation of v.12 is crucial. Are people crying because of the arrogance of the wicked? Or is he saying that God does not answer because of the arrogance of the wicked? A comma after the first line of v.12 changes the meaning to the latter thought that continues in v.13.

Job might not be wicked, but he shares this arrogance and so gets no answer (v.14). Elihu seems offended by the idea that Job should consider himself a litigant at God's court. With his multiplicity of empty words, Job should not expect to be heard (vv.14–16). Even worse is Job's rebellious spirit chiding God for hiding his face (13:24; 23:3; cf. v.14) and seeking to march into his presence as an impatient litigant (13:15; 31:35–37). And now, with his case before God, Job dares to complain about waiting for an answer (30:20; cf. v.14c–d) and continues to accuse God of injustice (21:4; 24:1–12; cf. v.15, but see Notes).

NOTES

2 The NIV's marginal reading is unlikely as an option (though see Clines [*Job 21–37*, 788] for a recent defense of this view). Even though the preposition מִן (*min*) may express comparison, it is not used that way here in מֵאֵל (*mēʾēl*, "by God"). The MT says literally, "my vindication [will be] from [*min*] God."

3 The NIV has rendered לָךְ (*lāk*, "to you") as "to me" because it views this first line in Hebrew as indirect discourse and the second as direct (cf. 19:28). So to make the translation smooth, both are made direct. Some take it all direct and understand the "to you" as a reference to God, which, it is felt, fits Elihu's response in vv.6–7 better (cf. Driver and Gray, 304–5).

The preposition מִן (*min*) in מֵחַטָּאתִי (*mēḥaṭṭāʾtî*, "by not sinning") is partitive (separative), hence "by not."

6 The verbs תִּפְעַל־בּוֹ ... תַּעֲשֶׂה־לּוֹ (*tipʿāl-bô ... taʿăśeh-lô*, "that affect him ... that do to him") may be either second or third person (cf. RSV, "what do you do to him?").

10 Pope renders זְמִרוֹת (*zᵉmirôt*, "songs") "strength" based on the use of *dmr* ("mighty") in Arabic and in Ugaritic as an epithet of Baal as "the mighty one." The word also appears in OT proper names such as Zimri (Pope, 264). No doubt it fits as an epithet of Yahweh in Exodus 15:2; Psalm 118:14; and Isaiah 12:2;

but there is room for doubt here. Clines (*Job 21–37*, 790) and Hartley, 464, go with "songs," while the NRSV translates "strength." Both meanings fit the context.

11 In מַלְּפֵנוּ מִבַּהֲמוֹת (*mallĕpēnû mibbahămôt*, "[he] teaches more to us than to the beasts [of the earth]"), the verb as Piel participle of *ʾlp* is no problem, though the consonant *aleph* has contracted. Once again, the meaning of the preposition *min* is in question. The two NIV marginal notes on v.11 present a possible alternative. The meaning would be that God teaches human beings from (by) nature (cf. Pope). But keeping the comparative force of *min* does not necessarily yield the banal meaning suggested by Pope. That people are wiser than the beasts and birds could mean they alone can hear the voice of God.

12 For the usual local sense "there" for שָׁם (*šām*, untranslated in NIV), see the NRSV; but some see a temporal sense like the Arabic *tumma* ("then"; Driver and Gray, 268; Gordis, *Job*, 402). Dahood (*Psalms*, 16:81) suggests from an Amarna gloss *šumma*, "behold."

13 Since שָׁוְא (*šāwʾ*, "empty [plea]") is masculine, the feminine suffix on לֹא יְשׁוּרֶנָּה (*lōʾ yĕśûrennâ*, "pays no attention to it"), translated "it," refers to all the pleading in the preceding verse (cf. Dhorme, "a pure waste of words"). Gordis's translation (*Job*, 402), "But it is not true that God does not hear," seems unlikely.

15 For בַּפַּשׁ (*bappaš*), NIV's "of wickedness" follows the ancient versions (see margin), reading פֶּשַׁע (*pešaʿ*, "transgression"). Gordis (*Job*, 391, 403) has made a good case for occasional elision of *ayin* in biblical orthography. Two clear cases are in Amos 8:8, where *nišqĕhā* (*Kethiv*) stands for *nešqᵉʿāh* (*Qere*), and Hosea 7:6, where *yāšēn* stands for *yaᶜăšēn*.

6. The Fourth Speech (36:1–37:24)

OVERVIEW

Elihu needs a little more time to develop fully his defense of God's justice. His earlier apology was designed to disarm Job by a spirit of self-abnegation (32:1–33:7). Here, still full of words, he wants Job to become aware of his credentials as God's messenger (vv.1–4).

First Elihu presents his premise that God is mighty and firm of purpose (v.5). That purpose is stated: God will not grant life to the wicked but always grants the rights of those who are wronged (v.6). He then proceeds to tell how that purpose is carried out (vv.6–10). No matter what life may bring, whether chains or affliction, God never takes his eyes off the righteous but uses their troubles to give disciplinary instruction and to call them to repentance (vv.7–10). Responding to his call

determines the course of a person's life and his fate—obey and live under his blessing; disobey and die in bitter resentment (vv.11–14).

A new stanza begins in v.15 (or possibly v.16), in which Elihu applies his message to Job. Having forsaken his condemnatory spirit (35:14–16), Elihu seeks to comfort Job with the possibility of deliverance (v.15a). It is time for Job to see the hand of God in his suffering. God uses affliction to amplify his voice and thus obtain the attention of people (v.15). Job must understand that God is wooing him from the jaws of adversity, from slavery and oppression to freedom and comfort (vv.16–17).

Verses 18–21 are a further warning to Job probably about the dangers of prosperity and of turning to evil. But the translation of vv.18–20 is uncertain (see NIV mg. and Notes).

In v.22 Elihu completes his theme on God's purpose in human suffering by returning to his original premise: the greatness of God's power and the uniqueness of his ways (vv.22–23). Indeed, his power guarantees his purposes, for in his sovereign freedom he has no one to whom he must give an account (v.23). He is also the perfect teacher who makes no mistakes. Job would do well to sit at the Master's feet and learn that his hand never does wrong. Then Job will be prepared to extol God and his work (vv.24, 26).

Elihu, at this point, is so overwhelmed by the greatness of God that he bursts forth into a hymn of praise (36:27–37:13). Its theme is the mystery of God's ways in nature. But Elihu's real purpose is to impress Job with the mystery of God's ways in providence. The two sometimes coincide (37:13). The hymn extols the work of God in the autumnal rain. It is his hand that distills the drops, pours out the moisture on earth, and thus provides for the needs of humanity (vv.27–28). With flashing lightning and the crash of his thunder, God ushers in the winter season with its drenching rain and driving winds, its ice and snow, so that humans

and all God's creatures see his power on display (vv.29–30).

After this hymn Elihu asks Job a series of humbling questions about the mysteries of nature (37:14–18). If Job cannot understand how God performs these marvels, much less assist him, how then can he understand the far less obvious mysteries of God's providence (vv.19–20)?

A final lesson from nature captures Elihu's imagination. When the winter is past and the skies are swept of clouds, the sun reigns supreme, and so does God in his golden splendor (vv.21–22). With this suggestion of divine theophany, Elihu returns again to his original premise about God's power and good purpose for human beings (v.23) as the reason for us to worship him (v.24).

Elihu's fourth speech is clearly designed to prepare for the theophany that follows. Critics maintain it was written later and borrows from the divine speeches. Even if that were the case (cf. Gordis, who argues the same author wrote this later in life), the material is still an integral part of the book, consciously performing a literary purpose that appears to be twofold: to give another human perspective free from the heat of the debate and to prepare the reader (and Job) for the theophany.

¹Elihu continued:

²"Bear with me a little longer and I will show you
    that there is more to be said in God's behalf.
³I get my knowledge from afar;
    I will ascribe justice to my Maker.
⁴Be assured that my words are not false;
    one perfect in knowledge is with you.

⁵"God is mighty, but does not despise men;
    he is mighty, and firm in his purpose.
⁶He does not keep the wicked alive
    but gives the afflicted their rights.

7He does not take his eyes off the righteous;
    he enthrones them with kings
    and exalts them forever.
8But if men are bound in chains,
    held fast by cords of affliction,
9he tells them what they have done —
    that they have sinned arrogantly.
10He makes them listen to correction
    and commands them to repent of their evil.
11If they obey and serve him,
    they will spend the rest of their days in prosperity
    and their years in contentment.
12But if they do not listen,
    they will perish by the sword
    and die without knowledge.

13"The godless in heart harbor resentment;
    even when he fetters them, they do not cry for help.
14They die in their youth,
    among male prostitutes of the shrines.
15But those who suffer he delivers in their suffering;
    he speaks to them in their affliction.

16"He is wooing you from the jaws of distress
    to a spacious place free from restriction,
    to the comfort of your table laden with choice food.
17But now you are laden with the judgment due the wicked;
    judgment and justice have taken hold of you.
18Be careful that no one entices you by riches;
    do not let a large bribe turn you aside.
19Would your wealth
    or even all your mighty efforts
    sustain you so you would not be in distress?
20Do not long for the night,
    to drag people away from their homes.
21Beware of turning to evil,
    which you seem to prefer to affliction.

22"God is exalted in his power.
    Who is a teacher like him?

²³Who has prescribed his ways for him,
  or said to him, 'You have done wrong'?
²⁴Remember to extol his work,
  which men have praised in song.
²⁵All mankind has seen it;
  men gaze on it from afar.
²⁶How great is God — beyond our understanding!
  The number of his years is past finding out.

²⁷"He draws up the drops of water,
  which distill as rain to the streams;
²⁸the clouds pour down their moisture
  and abundant showers fall on mankind.
²⁹Who can understand how he spreads out the clouds,
  how he thunders from his pavilion?
³⁰See how he scatters his lightning about him,
  bathing the depths of the sea.
³¹This is the way he governs the nations
  and provides food in abundance.
³²He fills his hands with lightning
  and commands it to strike its mark.
³³His thunder announces the coming storm;
  even the cattle make known its approach.

^{37:1}"At this my heart pounds
  and leaps from its place.
²Listen! Listen to the roar of his voice,
  to the rumbling that comes from his mouth.
³He unleashes his lightning beneath the whole heaven
  and sends it to the ends of the earth.
⁴After that comes the sound of his roar;
  he thunders with his majestic voice.
When his voice resounds,
  he holds nothing back.
⁵God's voice thunders in marvelous ways;
  he does great things beyond our understanding.
⁶He says to the snow, 'Fall on the earth,'
  and to the rain shower, 'Be a mighty downpour.'
⁷So that all men he has made may know his work,
  he stops every man from his labor.

⁸The animals take cover;
    they remain in their dens.
⁹The tempest comes out from its chamber,
    the cold from the driving winds.
¹⁰The breath of God produces ice,
    and the broad waters become frozen.
¹¹He loads the clouds with moisture;
    he scatters his lightning through them.
¹²At his direction they swirl around
    over the face of the whole earth
    to do whatever he commands them.
¹³He brings the clouds to punish men,
    or to water his earth and show his love.

¹⁴"Listen to this, Job;
    stop and consider God's wonders.
¹⁵Do you know how God controls the clouds
    and makes his lightning flash?
¹⁶Do you know how the clouds hang poised,
    those wonders of him who is perfect in knowledge?
¹⁷You who swelter in your clothes
    when the land lies hushed under the south wind,
¹⁸can you join him in spreading out the skies,
    hard as a mirror of cast bronze?

¹⁹"Tell us what we should say to him;
    we cannot draw up our case because of our darkness.
²⁰Should he be told that I want to speak?
    Would any man ask to be swallowed up?
²¹Now no one can look at the sun,
    bright as it is in the skies
    after the wind has swept them clean.
²²Out of the north he comes in golden splendor;
    God comes in awesome majesty.
²³The Almighty is beyond our reach and exalted in power;
    in his justice and great righteousness, he does not oppress.
²⁴Therefore, men revere him,
    for does he not have regard for all the wise in heart?'"

COMMENTARY

1–4 Elihu is a little apologetic over the fact that he has even more to say in defense of God (v.2). Had he not claimed, however, to be bursting with words (32:15–20)? Interpreters have generally misunderstood the claim he is making for himself here (v.4). In 37:16 Elihu described God as "perfect in knowledge." That Elihu should so describe himself (v.4b) has elicited the remark from Rowley that "Elihu is a stranger to modesty."

Kline, 485, suggests the words "one perfect in knowledge" (v.4b) possibly refer to God, as similar terminology does in 37:16. It is certainly unlikely that Elihu would claim for himself the same perfection he attributes to God. Habel, 494, uses the word "reasoning" instead of "knowledge" here and uses "mind" in 32:6, 10, and 17. But H. L. Ginsburg long ago suggested that the word used here and in 32:6, 10 comes from a cognate root that limits Elihu's perfection to his speech (Arab. *ḏḵw*, "to call"; cf. Pope, 243, on H. L. Ginsberg and the Qumran Targum). That meaning is strengthened here by the feminine plural *millāy* ("my words") in v.4a, paralleling the feminine plural *dēʿôt* ("utterances") in v.4b. On this basis Elihu is claiming to be one "perfect of utterance" because his speech derives from God (see Notes on v.3), who is the source of perfect words.

It is interesting that in 37:16, where Elihu is speaking of God's perfect knowledge (words are not the subject), Elihu uses the masculine plural (cf. majesty) as a divine appellative. Here, however, he used the feminine plural in agreement with "my words" (*millāy*) in v.4a.

5–14 Everything Elihu says from here on rests on the affirmation in v.5. See the Notes below for the reasons for a slightly different translation that reads: "God is mighty, he does not despair [faint]; / he is mighty and firm in his purpose."

God's power assures the fulfillment of his purpose. In this purpose God will never grant life to the wicked but will always see that those who are afflicted receive justice. Verses 6–7 must be understood as God's ultimate purpose since vv.8–12 are conditional. Elihu is making room for Job's complaints about the suffering of the righteous and the prosperity of the wicked. He is also answering Job's frustration over God's surveillance (7:17–21). God never takes his eyes off the righteous. But in order to eventually enthrone them, he must discipline them for their own good.

The key word in this passage is *mûsār* ("correction") in v.10. As a wisdom word used often in Proverbs (1:2–3, 8; 3:11; 4:13; 5:12, 23; 6:23; 8:10, 33; et al.), it includes all that God does to teach human beings his wisdom by means of his commandments (v.10b) or by circumstances (v.8). God's unfainting purpose is to reach the hearts of people, if necessary by "cords of affliction" (v.8b). In v.10 he makes them "listen [Heb., 'uncovers their ears'] to correction," or perhaps "by the correction"; that is, he gets their attention and then calls for repentance.

Once attention is gained, obedience leads to life (v.11) and disobedience leads to death (v.12). These verses sound like a message of prosperity and doom not significantly different than that of Job's three counselors. But that might be an unfair judgment because Elihu is emphasizing the fact that the righteous are afflicted, a point mentioned by Eliphaz (5:17–18) but abandoned especially with reference to Job.

15–21 Elihu disapproves of Job's contention that the wicked prosper; and even though he agrees that the righteous suffer, it is only because of their waywardness, which needs correction. So there is hope for Job. Elihu does not really face the issue of the suffering of the innocent. He assumes in v.9 that the afflicted always have done something for which they are being punished. Job, however, can be rescued by (v.15a; the NIV has "in," but the preposition *b* could also mean "from") his suffering if he hears the voice of God wooing him away from the jaws of distress (v.16).

There are few verses in the entire OT that are more difficult to translate than vv.17–20 in this chapter. The difficulty does not arise from the meaning of individual words but from the fact that they are so difficult to put together. The text may be disturbed, but more likely it is the rare meaning of key words that escapes us (see Clines, *Job 21–37*, 817–23, for the most extensive study of the philology of this section). The translations vary greatly. Most make it a sharp rebuke of Job (Pope, JB, TEV) for being unjust and for misusing his power and wealth.

The following translation of vv.17–21 varies somewhat from the NIV by softening the tone without emending the Hebrew text. Explanations may be found in the Notes.

> Since you have had your fill of judgment due the wicked,
> > since judgment and justice have taken hold [of you],
> beware that no one entice you to want riches again.
> > Do not let the great price you are paying mislead you.
> Of what value was your wealth apart from affliction?
> > And of what value are all your mighty efforts?
> Do not long for the night,
> > when peoples will vanish from their place.
> Beware of turning to evil,
> > for that is why you are tested by affliction.

Elihu is admonishing Job to learn the lesson God is trying to teach him through his suffering. He warns Job not to allow his suffering to influence his judgment (v.17). Job will someday realize that his affliction is of more value to him than his wealth and all his efforts to justify himself (v.18). He should not long for the tribunal of the terrible Judge (the night) but learn the lesson of submission that God is teaching him through affliction (vv.20–21).

22–26 In a real sense these verses are both the climax of the preceding section and the first stanza of a hymn of praise. Elihu returns to the theme he began with—the power of God. The stanza has a chiastic pattern:

> A. God is great in power and a sovereign teacher (v.22).
> > B. Human beings cannot prescribe his ways or judge his purpose (v.23).
> > > C. Therefore praise him in song (v.24).
> > B'. Human beings see his power from afar (v.25).
> A'. God is great, beyond understanding (v.26).

Elihu considers God's power and wisdom as the themes Job should dwell on rather than God's justice. The wisdom of the great Teacher (cf. 34:32; 35:11) assures the justice of his actions, and his power makes certain his wise purposes will be fulfilled. God's ways derive from his sovereign freedom (v.23a), thus ruling out people's right to question God's moral conduct (v.23b). Because mortals see God's work at a great distance, they cannot understand it completely; so those who are wise will look on it with delight and praise (v.24). Elihu is here preparing the way for the theophany when Job will finally see his sovereign Lord and learn about his dominion. In v.26 Elihu is not saying that we cannot know God (NEB, RSV) but that we cannot fully understand his greatness.

From 36:27 to 37:13 the hymn continues by extolling God's power in the elements. Having admonished Job about praising God for his work (v.24), Elihu illustrates God's work in nature. The anthropomorphic terms are typical of this poetic genre (cf. Ps 18:7–15). Following the hymn Elihu closes his speech with admonitions to Job based on its contents (37:14–24).

27–33 God's active greatness in his creation is demonstrated by the rain cycle. Rain in the OT world was considered one of the most needed and obvious blessings of God. The phenomenon of condensation (v.27b) and precipitation (v.28), while not technically understood, was certainly observable. But evaporation (v.27) is not. Duhm therefore considers this proof that the Elihu speeches came a few centuries later than the divine speeches since such meteorological knowledge would have been obtained from the Greeks (cf. Driver and Gray, 315).

Pope sees in Genesis 2:6 and in the flood account a belief in cosmic reservoirs—above and below the earth—that rain comes from. But Pope's translation (267, 273) does not seem to fit completely with that notion: "He draws the waterdrops that distill from the flood." Elihu does not need a knowledge of physics, since God is the one who does this (an idea even we who know the physics can still affirm), but he may have known more about the phenomenon than Pope is willing to admit (see Notes).

The Hebrew word for "his pavilion" (v.29) is rendered "his canopy" in Psalm 18:11, which the parallel line in the psalm clearly defines as "the dark rain clouds of the sky." In v.30 "bathing the depths of the sea" might be rendered "lights up the depths of the sea" since "to cover [bathe]" with lightning is equivalent to lighting up (see Notes on v.30).

Verse 31 can be understood in the context if we allow the speaker the privilege of using a parenthesis; thus, there is no need to move the verse (NEB, Pope). Verses 29–30, as descriptive of the storm, form such a parenthesis; and v.31 refers back to the showers of v.28. The NIV margin (v.31) suggests the reading: "by them [the showers] he nourishes the nations," rather than "governs" them (see Notes). If

the latter meaning is chosen, it would be better rendered "to judge or punish," since the word rarely (if ever) means "govern." Judging or punishing by the storm is conceivable in terms of God's use of lightning. The parallelism in v.31 favors the rarer meaning of the margin, but v.32 would favor the text.

On v.32 Kline, 486, makes the anthropomorphism even more vivid. The Hebrew carefully uses the dual for "hands" (optional even for clapping, cf. 2Ki 11:12); this use of "both hands" produces the figure of "expertly hurled missiles of warriors in the elite ambidextrous corps (36:32; cf. *Iliad* 21:183; 1 Chr 12:2)." So when the lightning performs God's purpose in striking its mark, it is against those he chooses to punish (37:13).

Verse 33 is very difficult. Many interpretations are given. The NIV text has sought to follow the Masoretic vocalization but even so had to make an arbitrary choice for the precise meaning. "The coming storm" (lit., "concerning it [or] him") could mean God's approach (cf. NIV mg.). But the margin's rendering requires a different set of vowels for the second line (see Notes).

37:1–13 Andersen, 264–65, sees a unit in vv.1–5 formed by two bicola (vv.1, 5) and two tricola (vv.2, 4) centered about a single line about lightning (v.3b). But notice how the hymn moves from precipitation in 36:27–28 to lightning in 36:29–32 then to thunder in 36:33–37:5 and back to precipitation in 37:6. The stanza on thunder (36:33–37:5) has a chiastic pattern:

> A. God's voice thunders (36:33).
>> B. The terrifying sound of thunder (37:1–2).
>>> C. God unleashes lightning (37:3).
>> B'. The majestic sound of thunder (37:4).
> A'. God's voice thunders (37:5).

Elihu is impressed with God's voice as his word of dominion and power. By fiat he controls the snow and rain (v.6), and thunder is nothing less than the roar of his voice—a typical OT metaphor (cf. Ps 29). Elihu's heart pounds as God puts on an awesome display of his power. The passage continues to reveal a keen observation of atmospheric conditions and their effects. Possibly evaporation and clearly the distillation of rainwater are mentioned in 36:27. The clouds are reservoirs of moisture (37:11a) and arenas of lightning (v.11b). In their cyclonic movement (v.12) the clouds are subject to God's commands and perform his will.

Elihu sees a direct relationship between God's rule over nature and his dominion over the affairs of human beings (v.13). He has already begun to anticipate the reasoning in the divine speeches. Critics claim this is evidence of the plagiarism of a later author. Others find it in keeping with what is evident all through the dialogue (Andersen, 266, n. 2). Still others see Elihu's role as a divinely sent forerunner preparing the way for the theophany— a motif most notably expressed in Isaiah 40:3–5 and Malachi 4:5–6.

Verse 13 is a thematic climax that lists ways God may use the storm. Elihu wants to do more than impress Job with God's power in nature. Here he shows how the mystery of God's ways in nature coincides with the mystery of his ways in providence. When God's purpose is corrective, as punishment for the wicked (Ps 18:11–19), the storm is often connected with the deliverance of his people, thus demonstrating his covenantal love (ḥesed, v.13; cf. Jos 10:11; 1Sa 7:10–11; Ps 105:32–33). God may also, however, demonstrate his covenantal love by sending the rain in season (Dt 11:13–17).

The opposite (drought) is in view in vv.17–18, and that has prompted the NIV to insert the word "water" into the phrase "to his earth" (v.13). The addition is not needed, for there appear to be three

totally different purposes for the storm in v.13: to punish, to show his love, and for his own pleasure (lᵉʼarṣô; see Notes on v.13). The last anticipates a concept limited to the divine speeches (cf. 38:26)—one that could be missed without careful attention. Some things that God performs have no other explanation than that they please him. Having arrived at this amazing point, Elihu is prepared to apply this truth to Job's situation.

14–20 The questioning format anticipates the divine method in the upcoming speeches. Elihu wants Job to stop and think of how absurd his position is. Elihu asks him to supply knowledge he obviously does not have and is chided for his abysmal ignorance in the light of God's perfect knowledge (vv.15–16). Verses 17–18 go together. Sweltering in the heat of the dry season with the sky like a brazen mirror, Job sits helpless. He cannot do anything about the weather but endure it. How then can a mere creature, so lacking in knowledge and strength, expect to understand God's justice (vv.19–20)? Elihu's switch to the first person in vv.19–20 may be an attempt to soften the blow on Job's ego. Has Job not drawn up his case, affixed his signature, and called for an audience with God?

21–24 Elihu shifts his attention from his moral application back to a contemplation of the elements. But it is only to make an even more forceful moral application. After the storm, with the clearing skies (v.21), comes the sun in its brilliance; likewise in golden splendor and awesome majesty God comes from his heavenly abode (ṣāpôn, "the north," v.22; cf. 26:7 and Introduction). Elihu admonishes Job that he needs to see God as God, almighty and morally perfect (v.23), and prove he is wise in heart by worshiping (fearing) him (see Notes on v.24).

NOTES

36:3 Concerning אֶשָּׂא דֵעִי (ʾeśśāʾ dēʿî, "I get my knowledge"), it was noted above in the comments on vv.1–4 that in v.4 "speech" is preferred over "knowledge." But "knowledge" or "opinion" is more likely here.

5 Most emend וְלֹא יִמְאָס (wᵉlōʾ yimʾās, "but he does not despise"). Dhorme, Pope, Gordis, Driver and Gray, et al. complain of the lack of balance in the line and emend the second כַּבִּיר (kabbîr, "mighty") to בְּבַר (bᵉbār, "pure") and drop or transfer כֹּחַ (kōaḥ, "firm, strong"), reading: "He does not despise the pure in heart." A major reason given for the emendation is the lack of an object for yimʾās. The NIV's "men" is not in the text (cf. RSV's "any"). For a solution to this difficulty see 7:5, where the byform of mss ("melt") is spelled mʾs. Compare the same in Psalm 58:8: "the wicked melt like water." This word (root) "melt" is used figuratively meaning "faint" or "despair" in 6:14 and 9:23. That meaning fits this text beautifully: "God is mighty, he does not despair [faint]; / he is mighty and firm in his purpose."

6 It is better to render לֹא־יְחַיֶּה (lōʾ-yᵉḥayyeh, "he does not keep ... alive") as "he does [or 'will'] not grant life" with the parallel "he grants [or 'will grant'] justice." The tense is open. The same openness is true in v.7. The converted waws at the end of v.7 and in vv.9–10 have no tense significance.

12 For בְּשֶׁלַח (bᵉšelaḥ, "by the sword"), the NIV's margin—"will cross the River"—is preferred (cf. 33:18 Notes). See Hartley, 469.

14 בַּקְּדֵשִׁים (baqqᵉdēšîm, "among male prostitutes of the shrines") points to one of the horrors of the OT world, the temple prostitution tied to the fertility cult. No doubt children committed for ritual prostitution died young. In Deuteronomy 23:17–18 (cf. P. C. Craigie, *The Book of Deuteronomy* [Grand Rapids: Eerdmans, 1976], 301) the practice was forbidden in Israel (cf. 1Ki 14:24; 15:12; 22:46; 2Ki 23:7).

17 Concerning מָלֵאתָ (mālēʾtā, "But now you are laden"), Elihu's purpose is not to condemn Job but to try to get him to see the disciplinary value of God's use of judgment. I have therefore softened this verse by making it concessive and using the English perfect tense (see comments).

18 כִּי־חֵמָה (kî-ḥēmâ) literally reads "For anger." The NIV reads this as an imperative ḥᵃmēh ("see"), an Aramaism from the root ḥmy, hence "Be careful" (cf. Pope).

The NIV aligns בְּסָפֶק (bᵉsāpeq, "by riches") with śepeq ("riches, plenty") in 20:22 and not as rendered in 27:23, where the same three consonants mean "clap," whence the RSV gets "scoffing."

The NIV renders וְרָב־כֹּפֶר (wᵉrāb-kōper) as "a large bribe"; but the word kōper (GK 4111) is never used as "a bribe." It is usually "a ransom, a price," whether ritual or otherwise.

19 For הֲיַעֲרֹךְ שׁוּעֲךָ (hᵃyaʿᵃrōk šûʿᵃkā) the NIV arrives at "Would your wealth ... sustain you" by an inference from the common meaning "set in battle array" and therefore "protect." From this the translators arrived at "sustains." But this seems far-fetched and requires another "you" that is not in the text. The verb also means "to evaluate" (Hiphil), hence our "of what value was your wealth" (see comments).

For לֹא בְצָר (lōʾ bᵉṣār), the NIV has again inserted more into the translation ("so you would not be in distress") than the Hebrew warrants. For the meaning "apart from" (lōʾ + b), cf. 4:21; 34:20 (see our translation above).

20 Concerning לַעֲלוֹת עַמִּים (laʿălôt ʿammîm, "to drag people away"), in Psalm 102:24 (NIV) the same verb used clearly means in the Hiphil "to take away one's life." But since the noun ʿammîm ("peoples") usually refers to nations, Job is here being warned about a great catastrophe such as war or a plague.

21 בָּחַרְתָּ (bāḥartā, "you seem to prefer") includes the idea of making a choice by testing (cf. 34:4; Pr 10:20; Isa 48:10).

27 גָּרַע (gāraʿ) in the Qal means "to hinder" (15:4), "to limit" (15:8), and "to take away" (36:7). Here the Piel—יְגָרַע (yᵉgāraʿ, "he draws up"; GK 1757 and 1758)—seems to mean "withdraw" as in v.7. Andersen, 262–63 (cf. also Driver and Gray, 282), suggests the possibility that נִטְפֵי־מָיִם (niṭpê-māyim, "drops of water") be read נִטְפִים יָם (niptîm yām, ("drops [from] the Sea")), which is even more descriptive of evaporation.

The NIV's translation of לְאֵדוֹ (lᵉʾēdô, "to the streams") is in part based on the same interpretation of this rare word in Genesis 2:6. Pope, 273, ties the word to the subterranean flood of Akkadian mythology. He explains the suffix as a modification of the vocalic ending on the Akkadian (Sumerian) word ʾedû. The mythological imagery need not be carried as far as Pope carries it by positing two cosmic reservoirs, one above and one below the earth. Pope renders the line "that distill rain from the flood," with "from" being a rare possibility for the Hebrew ל (l) based on Ugaritic. The usual meaning for ʾēd ("mist"; KJV, RSV, NIV mg.), unfortunately, has no philological support according to E. A. Speiser (*Genesis* [AB 1; New York: Doubleday, 1964], 14, 16).

28 The NIV takes the antecedent of the relative pronoun אֲשֶׁר (ʾăšer) to be "the drops" in v.27a and for clarity supplies "their moisture." The verb is usually intransitive, so it may be better to read "which pour down from the clouds."

Concerning אָדָם רָב (ʾādām rāb, "abundant showers … on mankind"), the meaning "showers" for rāb (cf. rebîbîm, Dt 32:2) is proven by the parallel pair rb ("showers") and ar ("lightning") in Ugaritic (Fisher, 1:79). אוֹרוֹ (ʾôrô, "his lightning") in v.30 is an example of distant parallelism. Repointing ʾādam ("mankind") to ʾᵃdāmâ ("the ground"; Dahood, Pope) is possible but not necessary.

29 אַף אִם־יָבִין (ʾap ʾim-yābîn, "Who can understand") is more literally, "Indeed, can one understand?" But that means "Who can?" Emending to מִי (mî, "who") is unwarranted (cf. BHS).

30 Concerning וְשָׁרְשֵׁי הַיָּם (wᵉšoršê hayyām, "the depths of the sea"), many feel "he covers the roots of the sea" (with lightning) does not make sense. So many emendations are proposed, none of which are worth repeating. Pope's attempt to mythologize the verse by seeing the preposition עָלָיו (ʿālāyw, "about him") as *Aliy*, a Ugaritic epithet for the weather god, seems misguided from a book so dedicated to monotheism. Pope repoints כִּסָּה (kissâ, "he covers"; GK 4059) to כִּסְאוֹ (kissᵉʾô, "his throne") and reads "the roots of the sea are his throne." But the idea in this text is not farfetched. In Habakkuk 3:3 God's "majesty covers" (kissâ; NIV "glory covered") the heavens; so why should not his lightning flashes cover the roots (depths) of the sea?

31 The NIV renders בָּם יָדִין (bām yādîn) as "This is the way he governs." If, according to Pope, the roots of the sea are the throne of *Aliy*, why does he not govern the nations from them? Instead, Pope moves v.31 to follow v. 28 so that the nations can be "nourished" (yādîn is taken as a dialectical form of yāzîn, "nourish") from the drops of rain (v.27). I see no problem with the dialectical form's meaning "he nourishes" (cf. NIV mg.), with bām ("by them") referring to the clouds of rain.

32 For עַל־כַּפַּיִם כִּסָּה־אוֹר (ʿal-kappayim kissâ-ʾôr, "He fills his hands with lightning"), Gordis's resort (*Job*, 422) to Mishnaic Hebrew ("the double arch of heaven" for kappayim) to avoid the mythological imagery is just as misguided as Pope's attempt (276) to turn the text into mythic literature ("lightning … may seem … to prance in the palms of the storm-god"). For the imagery compare Psalm 18:14: "He shot his arrows ... great bolts of lightning." Again the verb *kissâ* ("he fills" ["covers"]) has caused some consternation. Dhorme emends to *níśśāᵓ* ("he lifts") and Pope to *naśśâ* ("it flickers, prances"). The "covering of both hands [dual] with lightning" is like the prophet's words—"rays flashed from his hand, where his power was hidden" (Hab 3:4)—but here the figure is probably drawn from the ambidextrous corps mentioned in 1 Chronicles 12:2, as noted above.

33 The NIV (text) understands עָלָיו (*ᶜālāyw*, "concerning it") to be "the storm"; but the margin, which reads "announces his coming— / the One zealous against evil," understands the antecedent as God. In this reading the second line requires *miqneh* ("cattle") be pointed *maqneh* (or *meqanneh*), "One zealous," and *ᶜôleh* ("[its] approach") becomes *awlâ* ("evil"). Gordis (*Job*, 424) makes a case on the basis of analogy, not direct usage, that *miqneh ᵓap* means "the wrath of indignation." He follows Perles in taking *ᶜal-ᶜôleh* ("concerning what rises") as the Aramaic *ᶜil ᶜolâ* ("whirlwind"), yielding: "His thunderclap proclaims his presence; his mighty wrath, the storm." This is an attractive possibility since it requires only slight vocalic change, but it is difficult to be dogmatic about a line with so many pitfalls.

37:2 The plural imperative with the infinitive שִׁמְעוּ שָׁמוֹעַ (*šimᶜû šāmôaᶜ*, "Listen! listen") may be a stylistic trait, since it occurred in 13:17 and 21:2. That it is plural rather than singular should not be stressed, for that is part of the idiom, with the implied subject being indefinite.

3 The verb יִשְׁרֵהוּ (*yišrēhû*, "he unleashes him") is usually taken as an Aramaic *šrh* ("to let loose"; cf. Da 5:16). The NIV substitutes "lightning" for the suffix "him." Gordis's *yôšer* ("strength"; *Job*, 425), while phonologically acceptable, must be rejected since it is not clearly attested; and Ugaritic uses this verb in the same way—*šrh larṣ brqm* ("he flashes lightning to the earth"; cf. Pope, 280; Hartley, 477). But whether it means "flashes" or "lets loose" is a moot question.

4 The problem with וְלֹא יְעַקְּבֵם (*welōᵓ yeᶜaqqebēm*, "he holds nothing back") is the suffix *ēm*. It is not the pronoun "them" ("the lightnings," cf. RSV), since in v.3 that is singular. The NIV agrees with Pope that it is an enclitic particle but disagrees with his changing the subject from God to men. Pope has "men stay not when his voice is heard."

6 Concerning הֱוֵא (*heᵂēᵓ*, "Fall"), BDB (217, *hwh*, and 224, *hyh*; GK 2092; 2218) notes the full meaning of the verb that includes "fall out," hence "to happen." But in Arabic the root simply means "to fall down, descend," which would be the meaning here (Clines, *Job 21–37*, 837–38). The observation of Rowley that it is found only here in the OT will need revision if I am correct in seeing it in 24:18 (see Notes).

11 The most popular modern emendation of בְּרִי (*berî*, "with moisture") to *bārāq* ("thunder bolt") or *bārād* ("hail"; Dhorme, Pope) is phonologically unnecessary. Driver and Gray, 291, note the regular contraction *rî* from *reŵî* ("saturation") from the root *nwh*, as *ᵓi, kî, ᶜi* are from *ᵓwh, kwh,* and *ᶜwh*. The emendation to *bārāq* is based on the parallelism, but not every parallel is synonymous, as is evident in the next verse. See Gordis (*Job*, 428) on the meaning of the verb *ṭrh* ("to load"; GK 3267).

13 In the NIV's rendering of אִם־לְאַרְצוֹ (*ᵓim-lᵉᵓarṣô*) as "or to water his earth," the words "to water" are supplied. The MT reads "whether for the rod, or for his earth [land] or for [his] love." Many have suggested the verb here is *rṣh* ("be pleased with"; GK 8354) with prefixed *aleph* as in *ᵓaḥᵃwātî* ("my declaration") in 13:17 (cf. Pope, 283) and Dahood ("Northwest Semitic Philology and Job," in *The Bible in Current Catholic Thought* [ed. J. L. McKenzie; New York: Herdner & Herdner, 1962], 72). The translation would be "he brings the clouds for correction, or for his own good pleasure, or to show his love." It seems reasonable here to assume Elihu anticipates an important idea found in the divine speeches—that some things God does simply because it pleases him, and no other explanation need be given (cf. Andersen, 266, esp. n. 2). The NIV margin assumes the same root but uses the nuance "to find favor" and makes the singular pronoun a collective for "men": "or to favor them and show his love."

15 For בָּשׂוֹם (bᵉśûm, "controls"), the idiom is (śûm + ʿal: "put [a command] upon" (cf. Ex 5:8). The object is understood. The idiom is not unlike the use of śîm with ellipsis of the object lēb ("mind"; cf. 4:20; 23:6; 24:12; 34:23).

16 On תְּמִים דֵּעִים (tᵉmîm dēʿîm, "who is perfect in knowledge"), compare the note on 36:4; but here the context is different. As an epithet of deity it is not so clear that dēʿîm means "speech" here. There is no parallel with "words" as in 36:4. The context is about "deeds," but compare Pope's references (285) to Akkadian divine epithets regarding the perfection of divine speech. God does his deeds by fiat (v.15a).

22 Concerning מִצָּפוֹן זָהָב (miṣṣāpôn zāhāb, "out of the north ... in golden splendor"), Dhorme defends the translation "golden splendor" or "rays" as the full meaning of zāhāb ("gold"). The supposed problem that the sun's rays do not come from the north neglects two matters. First, Elihu is here speaking of God, not the sun (cf. NIV); and, second, the word ṣāpôn is not here "the north" but God's heavenly abode (Isa 14:13–14), as I have observed in the Notes on 26:7 and in the Introduction. Pope gives the Ugaritic parallels to Baal's abode, but his literal interpretation of "gold" as the gold in Baal's palace on Mount Zaphon is hardly necessary. Gordis (*Job*, 433) follows the LXX, which has "the clouds shining like gold," but this leaves the other side of the line dangling.

In עַל־אֱלוֹהַּ (ʿal-ʾelôah, "God comes"), the ʿal is usually taken as the preposition "upon," thus "upon God is" becomes in the RSV's "God is clothed." Blommerde's treatment of ʿal as the divine epithet ʿēl ("The Most High") is likely. It is not clear whether the NIV is repeating "comes" from the first colon, or interprets ʿal as a verb, or takes it as a preposition without inserting the word "clothed."

24 Turning לֹא־יִרְאֶה (lōʾ-yirʾeh) into a question ("for does he not have regard for ... ?") is the NIV's way of handling a difficult problem. The NIV margin is hardly justifiable (cf. RSV). The idea that the truly wise of heart are beneath God's notice is contrary to all wisdom thinking. Andersen, 268, sees the line as an example of a repeated word where the second spelling was left defective (cf. his "Orthography in Repetitive Parallelism," *JBL* 89 [1970]: 343–44), making it look like the verb rʾh ("see") instead of yrʾ ("fear"). The full spelling would be yirʾuhû ("they [all the wise of heart] fear him"). The lōʾ may be either the assertive l ("surely"; Andersen) or a negative question, as in the NIV.

C. The Theophany (38:1–42:6)

OVERVIEW

Some modern interpreters of the book of Job see in the divine speeches a God parading his power and void of all moral responsibility. Indeed, some maintain the author of the book has created a brilliant caricature of the kind of god represented by those pedants, the counselors, who themselves are being caricatured by the author. The only hero is Job, who predicted in chapter 9 how God would act.

J. W. Whedbee ("Studies in the Book of Job," *Semeia* 7 [1977]: 23–24) takes issue with D. Robertson's contention that God acts in this way. Robertson maintains God's rhetoric in the theophany fulfills the prediction that he is the God of power and skill but one who cannot govern with justice. Even God's claim to put down wickedness in 40:9–14 is said to be only a parody of God's prerogatives, and Job's repentance is tongue-in-cheek. So the poet is like "a medicine man" who has developed a strategy for curing humanity's fear of the unknown by "ridiculing the object feared" (see D. Robertson and J. Curtis, "On Job's Response to God," *JBL* 98 [1979]: 497–511).

Others have held it is immoral by any human standards that there should be a game between the Almighty and Satan using as their pawn the soul of Job. Such a view overlooks the possibility I have already mentioned, that God does not meaninglessly allow Job to be tormented. On the contrary, he is honoring Job by putting his full confidence in the genuineness of Job's faith, which Satan has questioned. Tsevat, 73–106, suggests that in the divine speeches God is above human concepts of morality. As he says (105), "He who speaks to man in the book of Job is neither a just nor an unjust god but God." Rowley, 167–207, says God cannot be above morality. He maintains that the book of Job is concerned less with theology than with religion.

Many of the most recent interpreters (e.g., C. A. Newsome, *The Book of Job: A Contest of Moral Imaginations* [Oxford: Oxford Univ. Press, 2003]) do not hide their disappointment with the Yahweh speeches. Interestingly, they concentrate on the debate and find the resolution of the final chapters a problem. They believe that the single perspective offered in the Yahweh speeches brings a simplistic solution. There is no simple or dogmatic answer in a postmodern world, so they prefer to stay in the flux of the debate.

God offers to Job no theological explanation of the mystery of his suffering. The reader is told why Job was suffering in the Prologue, but that is to show that Job is innocent. Job is never told this; had he been told, the book would have immediately lost its message to all other sufferers. So the book is teaching us through the divine theophany that there is something more fundamental than an intellectual solution to the mystery of innocent suffering. Though the message reaches Job through his intellect, it is for his spirit.

Job's greatest anguish in the Dialogue Dispute was over the thought that he was separated from God. But why? Often sin was the reason, as the counselors perceived. But Job learns through the theophany that God has not abandoned him. And it gradually dawns on Job that without knowing why he is suffering, he can face it, so long as he is assured that God is his friend. Indeed, the reader comes to learn that it is not only Job who is to be vindicated, but God's trust in him is also vindicated. Job's past experience with God was nothing compared with the experience he finds through the theophany. It is like hearing about God compared with the joy of seeing him (42:5), by which he means something not literal but of the heart.

I differ with those who see in the divine theophany a God who is indifferent, cold, and aloof and almost making fun of Job. Irony is used, but the irony of God's questions is to instruct Job, not to humiliate him. Job has the high privilege here of sitting at the feet of the Lord. Had the Lord wanted to humiliate Job, he might have taken up his errors point for point as Elihu did. No, Job needs to learn something about the character of God by walking through all creation with him and contemplating his natural marvels. Far from being crushed, Job is being made wonderfully aware of who God is in a universe full of paradoxes for his human creatures and yet filled with joy and wonder. In this way Job learns to take God at his word without understanding hardly any of the mysteries of his universe, much less the reason why he is suffering. Andersen, 271, has a marvelous statement:

> Job is vindicated in a faith in God's goodness that has survived a terrible deprivation and, indeed, grown in scope, unsupported by Israel's historical creed of the mighty acts of God, unsupported by life in the covenant community, unsupported by cult institutions, unsupported by revealed knowledge from the prophets, unsupported by tradition and contradicted by experience. Next to Jesus, Job must surely be the greatest believer in the whole Bible.

Gray (Driver and Gray, 291), in speaking about the relationship of Yahweh speeches to the purpose of the book of Job, notes that what these speeches do not contain is almost as important as what they do contain. The speeches do not reverse the Lord's judgment in the Prologue about Job. Satan was wrong in impugning Job's inner reasons for being righteous, and the friends were wrong about Job's outward conduct as a reason for his suffering. God's rebuke of Job in 38:2 is for what he said during his intense suffering, not for earlier sins. The latter would have proved that the purely penal theory of suffering was correct. The friends by their theory implied they knew God's ways completely. One of the purposes of the Lord's speeches is to show that neither the counselors nor Job possesses such complete knowledge.

Indeed, the speeches show how limited human knowledge is. On the surface it would appear that the speeches concentrate only on the natural world, but careful reading reveals something else. In the first speech (chs. 38–39) God's works in the natural creation are in view. He introduces this with the words, "Who is this that darkens my counsel with words without knowledge?" (38:2). Then follow two chapters of proof that Job knows little of God's world—something modern people have learned

much more of only to discover how much more lies beyond. Job is humbled. He then agrees that his words have been based on ignorance: "I put my hand over my mouth. ... I will say no more" (40:4–5).

The second speech begins on an entirely different note. The introduction to the second speech in 40:8–14 tells about God's power and ability to crush the wicked, to look on all those who are proud and humble, and to bring them low. The purpose here goes beyond showing Job that God is Creator and Sustainer of the natural world. It is to convince Job that God is Lord also of the moral order, and appropriately Job's response this time is repentance (42:1–6).

G. K. Chesterton, in a chapter titled "Man Is Most Comforted by Paradoxes" (in N. N. Glatzer, *The Dimensions of Job* [New York: Schocken, 1969], 228–37), enlightens us considerably on why he believes God appears to Job with a battery of questions rather than answers. Chesterton was convinced that a trivial poet would have had God appear and give answers. By these questions God himself takes up the role of a skeptic and turns Job's rationalism (e.g., his doubts about God's justice) against itself. God ironically accepts a kind of equality with Job as he calls on Job to gird up his loins for a fair intellectual duel. Job had asked God to come into court with him and present a bill of indictment. God is willing but asks the right to cross-examine.

Both Socrates and Jesus used the methodology of asking questions of those who came to them with issues on their mind (e.g., Lk 14:1–5; 20:1–8, 27–44). The method is to ply the doubter with questions until he doubts his doubts. Job is simply overwhelmed with mysteries and paradoxes for which he has no answers; but in the midst of it all he comes to understand what is too good to be told, that God knows what he is doing in his universe.

Job has many questions to put to God, as do we all. Instead of God's trying to prove that it is an explainable world, however, he insists that it is stranger than Job has ever imagined. Yet in all the strangeness there is brightness and joy and opposition to evil and wrong; and the reader comes to understand that in a world of such paradoxes Job is suffering, not because he is the worst of men, but because he is one of the best. Indeed, he is a grand type. In all his wounds he prefigures the wounds of that One who is the only truly holy man ever to live, Christ the Lord!

1. God's First Discourse (38:1–40:2)

OVERVIEW

The broad structure of the divine speeches does not reveal the same drive toward symmetry found in some earlier speeches in Job. Although this first discourse opens and closes with a rebuke and challenge to Job, both really stand outside the discourse itself (38:2–3; 40:1–2). The following outline may help the reader navigate through the material.

Introductory Rebuke and Challenge (38:2–3)
      Subject: The Lord of Nature
  I. The Creator (38:4–15)
    A. Of the Earth (vv.4–7)
    B. Of the Sea (vv.8–11)
    C. Of Day and Night (vv.12–15)
  II. The Ruler of Inanimate Nature (38:16–38)
    A. The Depths and Expanses (vv.16–18)

    B. Light and Darkness (vv.19–21)
    C. Weather (vv.22–30)
    D. The Stars (vv.31–33)
    E. Floods (vv.34–38)
  III. The Ruler of Animate Nature
     (38:39–39:30)
    A. Nourishment (vv.39–41)
    B. Procreation (vv.39:1–4)
    C. Wild Freedom (vv.5–8)
    D. Intractible Strength (vv.9–12)
    E. Incongruous Speed (vv.13–18)
    F. Fearsome Strength (vv.19–25)
    G. Flight of the Predator (vv.26–30)
Closing Rebuke and Challenge (40:1–2)

¹Then the LORD answered Job out of the storm. He said:

²"Who is this that darkens my counsel
   with words without knowledge?
³Brace yourself like a man;
   I will question you,
   and you shall answer me.

⁴"Where were you when I laid the earth's foundation?
   Tell me, if you understand.
⁵Who marked off its dimensions? Surely you know!
   Who stretched a measuring line across it?

⁶On what were its footings set,
   or who laid its cornerstone —
⁷while the morning stars sang together
   and all the angels shouted for joy?

⁸"Who shut up the sea behind doors
   when it burst forth from the womb,
⁹when I made the clouds its garment
   and wrapped it in thick darkness,
¹⁰when I fixed limits for it
   and set its doors and bars in place,
¹¹when I said, 'This far you may come and no farther;
   here is where your proud waves halt'?

¹²"Have you ever given orders to the morning,
   or shown the dawn its place,
¹³that it might take the earth by the edges
   and shake the wicked out of it?
¹⁴The earth takes shape like clay under a seal;
   its features stand out like those of a garment.
¹⁵The wicked are denied their light,
   and their upraised arm is broken.

¹⁶"Have you journeyed to the springs of the sea
   or walked in the recesses of the deep?
¹⁷Have the gates of death been shown to you?
   Have you seen the gates of the shadow of death ?
¹⁸Have you comprehended the vast expanses of the earth?
   Tell me, if you know all this.

¹⁹"What is the way to the abode of light?
   And where does darkness reside?
²⁰Can you take them to their places?
   Do you know the paths to their dwellings?
²¹Surely you know, for you were already born!
   You have lived so many years!

²²"Have you entered the storehouses of the snow
   or seen the storehouses of the hail,
²³which I reserve for times of trouble,
   for days of war and battle?

²⁴What is the way to the place where the lightning is dispersed,
    or the place where the east winds are scattered over the earth?
²⁵Who cuts a channel for the torrents of rain,
    and a path for the thunderstorm,
²⁶to water a land where no man lives,
    a desert with no one in it,
²⁷to satisfy a desolate wasteland
    and make it sprout with grass?
²⁸Does the rain have a father?
    Who fathers the drops of dew?
²⁹From whose womb comes the ice?
    Who gives birth to the frost from the heavens
³⁰when the waters become hard as stone,
    when the surface of the deep is frozen?

³¹"Can you bind the beautiful Pleiades?
    Can you loose the cords of Orion?
³²Can you bring forth the constellations in their seasons
    or lead out the Bear with its cubs?
³³Do you know the laws of the heavens?
    Can you set up God's dominion over the earth?

³⁴"Can you raise your voice to the clouds
    and cover yourself with a flood of water?
³⁵Do you send the lightning bolts on their way?
    Do they report to you, 'Here we are'?
³⁶Who endowed the heart with wisdom
    or gave understanding to the mind ?
³⁷Who has the wisdom to count the clouds?
    Who can tip over the water jars of the heavens
³⁸when the dust becomes hard
    and the clods of earth stick together?

³⁹"Do you hunt the prey for the lioness
    and satisfy the hunger of the lions
⁴⁰when they crouch in their dens
    or lie in wait in a thicket?
⁴¹Who provides food for the raven
    when its young cry out to God
    and wander about for lack of food?

^{39:1}"Do you know when the mountain goats give birth?
  Do you watch when the doe bears her fawn?
²Do you count the months till they bear?
  Do you know the time they give birth?
³They crouch down and bring forth their young;
  their labor pains are ended.
⁴Their young thrive and grow strong in the wilds;
  they leave and do not return.

⁵"Who let the wild donkey go free?
  Who untied his ropes?
⁶I gave him the wasteland as his home,
  the salt flats as his habitat.
⁷He laughs at the commotion in the town;
  he does not hear a driver's shout.
⁸He ranges the hills for his pasture
  and searches for any green thing.

⁹"Will the wild ox consent to serve you?
  Will he stay by your manger at night?
¹⁰Can you hold him to the furrow with a harness?
  Will he till the valleys behind you?
¹¹Will you rely on him for his great strength?
  Will you leave your heavy work to him?
¹²Can you trust him to bring in your grain
  and gather it to your threshing floor?

¹³"The wings of the ostrich flap joyfully,
  but they cannot compare with the pinions and feathers of the stork.
¹⁴She lays her eggs on the ground
  and lets them warm in the sand,
¹⁵unmindful that a foot may crush them,
  that some wild animal may trample them.
¹⁶She treats her young harshly, as if they were not hers;
  she cares not that her labor was in vain,
¹⁷for God did not endow her with wisdom
  or give her a share of good sense.
¹⁸Yet when she spreads her feathers to run,
  she laughs at horse and rider.

¹⁹"Do you give the horse his strength
  or clothe his neck with a flowing mane?
²⁰Do you make him leap like a locust,
  striking terror with his proud snorting?
²¹He paws fiercely, rejoicing in his strength,
  and charges into the fray.
²²He laughs at fear, afraid of nothing;
  he does not shy away from the sword.
²³The quiver rattles against his side,
  along with the flashing spear and lance.
²⁴In frenzied excitement he eats up the ground;
  he cannot stand still when the trumpet sounds.
²⁵At the blast of the trumpet he snorts, 'Aha!'
  He catches the scent of battle from afar,
  the shout of commanders and the battle cry.

²⁶"Does the hawk take flight by your wisdom
  and spread his wings toward the south?
²⁷Does the eagle soar at your command
  and build his nest on high?
²⁸He dwells on a cliff and stays there at night;
  a rocky crag is his stronghold.
²⁹From there he seeks out his food;
  his eyes detect it from afar.
³⁰His young ones feast on blood,
  and where the slain are, there is he."

⁴⁰:¹The Lord said to Job:

²"Will the one who contends with the Almighty correct him?
  Let him who accuses God answer him!"

COMMENTARY

38:1 Job sees no "golden splendor" or even the "awesome majesty" imagined by Elihu (37:22). Indeed, it seems that he sees nothing but the storm from which he hears the voice of Yahweh. This Israelite covenantal name for God appears in the Prologue, in the divine speeches, and in the Epilogue; but "the men of the East" do not know God by this name. The only use of "Yahweh" in chapters

3–37 is in 12:9, where manuscript evidence may point to an original text with "Elohim" ("God"), not "Yahweh" ("Lord"). The reason, of course, is that the Israelite author was in those chapters preserving the authentic vocabulary of that earlier generation, or at least of a non-Israelite society.

Interestingly, Job 9:13–24 anticipates this scene where God appears in a whirlwind (9:17 uses a biform of $s^{e}\bar{a}r\hat{a}$). There Job said he wanted to question God, but that he would be crushed by God's whirlwind; and though he was innocent, God would prove him wrong. It turns out to be true that Job's optimism of coming before God like a prince (31:36–37) is not realized. But God does not condemn Job as much as simply puts him in his creaturely place.

2–3 How does Job "darken" (obscure) God's counsel (v.2)? There can be no doubt that this refers to the extreme language of Job during his moments of poetic rage, when he struggled with concepts of a deity who was his enemy—a phantom deity, one his own mind created. Here he needs to brace himself and wrestle with God as he really is (v.3).

The format God has chosen is to ply Job with questions (as a professor would do with a presumptuous student); but strangely he says nothing about Job's suffering, nor does he address the problem of theodicy. Job does not get the bill of indictment or verdict of innocence he has wanted. But neither is he humiliated with a list of the sins he has committed for which he is being punished. The latter would have been the case if the counselors had been correct. So by implication Job's innocence is established, and later it is directly affirmed (42:7–8).

It is important for Job to know that God is not his enemy as he has imagined. This encounter with the Lord to learn the lesson that God is God is Job's assurance that all is well. Job does not learn why he is suffering; but he does learn to accept God by faith as his Creator, Sustainer, and Friend. To learn this

lesson he must get rid of his ignorant fantasies—his "words without knowledge"—brace himself like a man, and learn who God really is. This he is about to do by walking with God through his created universe and being questioned about his limitations as a creature in comparison with God's power and wisdom in creating and sustaining the universe. The divine speeches, then, succeed in bringing Job to complete faith in God's goodness without receiving a direct answer to his questions concerning the justice of God.

4–7 The irony in the Lord's words "Surely you know" (v.5; cf. v.21) is sharp and purposeful. Job has dared to criticize God's management of the universe. Had he been present at the creation (an obvious absurdity), he might have known something about God's management of its vast expanses (vv.4–6). But even the angels who were there could only shout for joy over the Creator's deeds (v.7). And here Job, an earth-bound man, has lost sight of who this Creator is. As a man full of words often questioning what the Lord is doing, he is told of the celestial chorus that celebrated God's creative activity, which is beyond any mere creature's ability to improve on by comment. That Job is learning this lesson we may infer from his response in 40:4–5.

For personification of the stars (v.7) in parallel with "the sons of God," see Psalm 104:4, where the winds are God's messengers (angels) and the lightning bolts his servants (cf. Heb 1:7).

8–11 Those who literalize the "house-building" figure of vv.4–6 to fabricate an ancient cosmography must also literalize the figure of the sea's "coming forth from the womb" (v.8); but v.9 quickly moves from figurative to literal, making that impossible.

In the ancient Semitic world, control of the boisterous sea was a unique symbol of divine power and authority. The Lord controls the sea by his spoken word (v.11). In Luke 8:24–25 Jesus' ability to do the same identified him as God—as equal in power to Yahweh. That message is conveyed in vv. 10–11, where the "doors" are the bounds the Lord sets for the sea. But the "doors" of v.8 are not the same.

The meaning of the first verb in v.8 is seriously disputed (see Notes). Andersen, 274–75, presents an attractive approach to the verse, tying it with the use of the same verb in the same gestation figure in Psalm 139:13, translating, "Who constructed the sea within the doors? / Who delivered [it] when it burst from the womb?" The double doors here are the labia of the birth canal (cf. "the doors of the womb," 3:10), and God is the Creator of the sea as well as the midwife attending its birth. Although this calls for shifting the vowels in the verb translated "delivered" to make it causative (see Notes), the advantage to the context is enormous.

12–15 The morning and dawn (v.12) are personified. Surely Job did not give orders that caused these servants of the Lord to rise and seize "the earth by [its] edges and shake the wicked out of it" (v.13). The figure is based on the idea that daylight catches the wicked in the act and disperses them like one who shakes dirt from a blanket. The dawn flashes across the earth from east to west; and this, in the figure, is like seizing it by its edges and shaking it out.

Verse 14 pictures the long, deep shadows of early morning when the earth reminds us of clay taking the shape of the seal pressed into it or of the folds of a garment. Daylight deprives the wicked of the kind of "light" they need. Here we have a subtle figure (v.15), for "the light" the wicked are denied is certainly "the darkness" that is their element, indeed, "deep darkness is their morning" (24:17). The wicked "put darkness for light and light for darkness" (Isa 5:20). With the same powerful figure, Jesus warned, "See to it, then, that the light within you is not darkness" (Lk 11:35).

16–18 In vv.4–15 God questioned Job about his knowledge of the origin and function of the world. Here he turns to mysteries of created things

not visible to the human eye. Note the progression: journeying (v.16), then seeing (v.17), then understanding what you see (v.18). Each step in this progression is increasingly impossible for Job. Yahweh's control over this unseen netherworld is just as real as his control over the sea or the land of the living (cf. 26:5–6). If the names of various deities to whom the myths imputed control of these domains are here as an overtone (cf. Tsevat, n. 29), it is to suggest that neither they nor Job but only Yahweh really understands and controls "all this" (v.18). What does Job know about those realms where no living human being has ever been?

19–21 What does Job know about the mystery of light and darkness? Again personification creates a vivid figure of God's cosmic control. The irony of v.21 that focuses on Job's creaturely nature gives the clue to one of the purposes of the divine speeches — to show Job that God is God. To have been born before creation in order to know all this is a patent absurdity (v.21). But that is what makes the irony poignant. In 15:7 Eliphaz similarly chided Job for assuming he had knowledge older than the hills.

22–30 Again Yahweh questions Job about his ability to journey to those inaccessible places (cf. vv.16–17) where he can see the sources of nature's rich supply (v.22). The term "storehouses" (ʾôṣᵉrôt; GK 238) is used in Jeremiah 50:25 as a place for storing weapons (an armory). In this case the arsenal figure carries out the thought that snow and hail are often God's weapons (v.23; Pss 78:47–48; 148:8; Isa 30:30). Sometimes with them he controls the destiny of nations.

Ignorance of the mystery of God's control of nature was one of Elihu's themes (37:14–18). Here, however, the questions point to something more basic — it is the Lord's world, not Job's! The Lord is taking Job for an imaginary walk through the cosmic sphere (and later through the earth) to impress on him the grandeur and mystery, the order and complexity of his world. Some of the teachings are direct, others analogical, by way of similitude (*māšāl*; GK 5442). The lesson Job needs to learn is the most important one in the universe—God is God.

After querying Job about these cosmic mysteries, the Lord makes a statement in vv.25–26 that sounds trite on the surface but demands the attention of every human being. Elihu spoke of God's use of the elements to punish or bless (37:13), and there (assuming our interpretation is correct) he hinted at the point that the Lord makes here— that he has the right to display his power in nature for no other reason than his own good pleasure. When he "waters a land where no man lives," God demonstrates that people are not the measure of all things. He waters the desert only because it pleases him to do so.

Can Job give the Lord realistic answers to questions Job's contemporaries simplistically answered? Does the rain have a father or the ice a mother (vv.28–29)? The standard myths viewed the rain as the semen of the storm god. But the rhetorical question is there to impress on Job that these apparent male and female aspects of inanimate nature are God's doing and his alone.

In v.30 the freezing of the surface of the deep was a phenomenon unknown by common experience in and around the lands of the Bible. This is hardly a reason to reject the usual meaning for *tᵉhôm* ("the deep") as the ocean. Like other passages in Job (cf. 26:7–10), this text reveals an expanded knowledge of natural phenomena.

31–33 Job has moved with the Lord, in his mind's eye, from the "recesses of the deep" and "gates of death" (vv.16–17) to heavenly constellations. The terminology draws on the interpretation of those fanciful figures the ancients saw in the celestial constellations. Our language in this space age still uses the same terms. The antithesis of binding and loosening the imagined fetters that hold

together the cluster of stars called Pleiades or the belt of the hunter Orion rests on poetic license and literary convention. The message is about God's cosmic dominion over these stars as they seasonally move across the sky (see Notes on vv.31–32).

Verse 31 in the KJV reads, "the sweet influences of Pleiades." S. R. Driver (Driver and Gray, 307) doubted this was a reference to astrology. In v.33 the astrological approach, while accepted by a few interpreters (cf. Rowley, but see Notes), is not philologically or contextually necessary. There is a philological problem, however, with the NIV's "dominion" since this would be the only place *mištār* (GK 5428) has that meaning. As the Notes indicate, I prefer seeing here a pure antithesis. Job understands neither the laws of the heavenly bodies nor God's "inscription [signature]" (*mištār*) in the earth, and that is exactly what Yahweh is talking to Job about. In Psalm 19 the psalmist honors Yahweh as Lord of the heavens that "declare [his] glory"; and in Psalm 8 he sings, "O LORD, our Lord, how majestic is your name [*šēm*] in all the earth!"

34–38 These verses all refer to meteorological phenomena and related matters. The difference between them and vv.22–30 seems to be the time, place, and purpose of the weather. Verse 38 indicates that the seasonal rain is in view—after the long months of the dry season, Yahweh is the One who orders the clouds to release their moisture (v.34). Job and all humankind can only raise their voices in prayer to him who controls the former and the latter rain, that extension of the rainy season that provides a greater harvest.

The language used here has a playful humor. Imagine Job, if he were able, giving the clouds an order and suddenly being inundated with water (v.34b). Or Job might decide to dispatch the lightning bolts, if he could, and they would report like lackeys to him and say, "Here we are" (v.35). So even these seasonal rains result from the bidding of

Yahweh, who numbers every cloud and measures every jarful of rain (v.37).

In v.36 there are two words in Hebrew (one rendered "heart" in the NIV and the other "mind") whose meanings have been lost in antiquity. We can only guess at their meaning (see Notes). It is difficult to see how the words "heart" and "mind" have any relationship to this cosmic context. The NIV is based on ṭuḥôt as used in Psalm 51:6 [8], where the same spelling is rendered "inner parts" (see Notes). The word "mind" for śekwî is a pure guess since it is used only here. Of the many interpretations offered in the commentaries, all are tenuous. Some see here two birds reputed to have meteorological wisdom—the ibis (thought to be wise about the flooding of the Nile, the most important seasonal event in Egypt) and the cock (thought by the rabbis to forecast rain). See Dhorme for more details on this interpretation and the Notes for other opinions.

39–41 These verses really begin a new aspect of Yahweh's control over nature. From 38:39 to 39:30 the focus is on creatures of the animal world that are objects of curiosity and wonder to people. The choice is somewhat random, as though Yahweh is saying, "Here are only a few specimens of all my creatures, great and small, winged and earthbound, wild and tamed—but all are under my care and dominion." It has never crossed Job's mind to hunt prey for lions (v.39) or to stuff food into the outstretched gullets of the raven's nestlings (v.41). But are not their growls and squawks cries to God, on whom all these creatures ultimately depend?

39:1–4 Throughout the wild kingdom and its rich variety of creatures, God informs Job of his creative and sustaining activity. He provides for each species its own gestation period and ability to bear young in the field—without assistance and with a divinely ordered wisdom to provide for themselves and their young. The offspring of an ibex doe, unlike human infants who need years of care,

can stand within minutes of birth and soon gambol off to thrive in the wild.

5–8 The selection is only representative of familiar creatures; otherwise the words about them would have little significance. One of the most admired animals of the OT world was the wild donkey (or onager). It was a compliment and a promise of an enviable freedom when the angel declared that Ishmael (Ge 16:12) would become "a wild donkey of a man." The creature was admired for both its freedom and its ability to survive under the harshest conditions.

There is also a touch of humor in this passage. While its relative the domesticated donkey suffers the noise pollution of the crowded cities and the abuse of animal drivers (v.7), the wild donkey can laugh at that and somehow find green morsels in places humans cannot survive (v.8)—the salt flats and the barren leeward hills (v.6).

9–12 In vv.5–8 there was an implied contrast between the wild donkey and the tame donkey. Here there is an explicit contrast between the wild ox and the tame ox. This animal (Heb. rêm; "unicorn," KJV; "rhinoceros," Vul.; GK 8028) is believed to be the now-extinct aurochs (*Bos primigenius*). Next to the elephant and rhino, it was the largest and most powerful land animal of the biblical world. Most of the nine OT occurrences of the word make reference to it as a symbol of strength (cf. Nu 23:22; 24:8; Dt 33:17; Ps 29:6; et al.). It was already rare in Palestine in the time of Moses. Thutmose III tells of traveling far to hunt one, and the Assyrians often hunted them in the Lebanon mountains (see Assyrian relief in B. Mazar, *Views of the Biblical World* [Chicago: Jordan, 1959], 4:129).

Once again it is a bit of divine humor to even mention the possibility of this fearsome creature harnessed to Job's plow, working his fields, or tethered in his barn. For information on all the animals in this chapter, the reader can refer to G. S.

Cansdale's *Animals of Bible Lands* (Exeter: Paternoster, 1970).

13–18 The question format is now dropped, and the stanza speaks of God in the third person. Moreover, these verses are missing from the LXX. Some, therefore, see them as an interpolation. But considering the penchant of the LXX for omitting sections where the Hebrew is difficult, this omission should not be considered determinative (see Notes). The question format is used to impress on Job his impotence in performing deeds that take divine power and wisdom. But since the ostrich appears to be ridiculous in its behavior (v.17), it simply wasn't appropriate to ask Job whether he could match God's strength or wisdom, for neither is in view.

The ostrich has a tiny brain but is well programmed with instincts that assure its survival. It does not forsake its eggs (v.14; cf. KJV). The verb in this verse means "lay," though a homonym does mean "forsake" (cf. M. Dahood, "The Root עזב in Job," *JBL* 78 [1959]: 303–9). The seeming cruelty to her young (v.16; cf. La 4:3) derives from the practice of driving off the yearlings when mating season arrives. The ostrich has exceptional eyesight—the largest of any land animal, with 360 degree vision. But the text concentrates on the bird's most incongruous feature: tremendous legs. One kick can tear open a lion or a man.

The lesson is that God can and does make creatures that appear odd and crazy to us if doing so pleases him. Imagine a bird that can't fly. Though it has wings, it can run faster than a horse (v.18). Job cannot understand what God is doing in his life, and God is telling him the created world is just as difficult to rationalize.

19–25 The horse is the only animal in this poem that is domestic. This unexpected feature still serves the Lord's purpose, for only one kind of horse is viewed—the charger, the warhorse. The creatures of the wild in their proud freedom and curious behavior are obviously beyond Job's control, but even a creature that man has tamed can display fearsome behavior that excites our imagination. The lines burst with the literary energy needed to do justice to the performance of this amazing creature during the height of the frenzy of battle. Our increased lexical knowledge has enhanced the vividness of these lines. The reader need only compare the clarity of the NIV with the KJV to appreciate this. For example, in v.19 *ra'mâ* means "a flowing mane," not "thunder" (KJV) or "strength" (RSV). In v.20 the horse is not made "afraid" but made to "leap like a locust." And in v.21 he paws "fiercely," not "in the valley" (see Notes).

26–30 In v.26 the marvel for Job to contemplate is one we still view with amazement—the migratory instincts of birds. Our knowledge that some birds fly thousands of miles each year (cf. the arctic tern, which flies from the Arctic to the Antarctic) serves to validate this particular choice of God's faunal wonders. The two words used in vv.26–27 are the Hebrew generic names that include several species. The first (v.26) appears to be the sparrow hawk (*nēṣ*; GK 5891), a bird not resident to the Holy Land but known because it stops off there each year in its migration (Kline, 486). In v.27 the griffon vulture (*nešer*; GK 5979) is the largest bird of the area. The same word is used for the true "eagle" (NIV), but here a carrion eater is in mind. Several interesting characteristics of this bird are mentioned: its soaring ability, its aerie (nest) high on the crags, and its phenomenal eyesight.

40:1–2 These two verses conclude the first speech. Some omit v.1 (cf. LXX); others assume the Lord pauses to see whether Job has a reply, then hearing none goes on (Rowley, 235). Since Job has said nothing, a small problem arises because "the LORD answered Job and said" (v.1, lit. Heb.). This expression is formulaic throughout the Dialogue-Dispute, where we might expect it, but also in the monologue of Elihu, where no one was answering (cf. 34:1; 35:1). Here it announces a hortatory line (v.2). In 38:1 the same formula introduced this speech (though Job had not been speaking), and there also it was followed by words of exhortation; thus we find a kind of *inclusio* that ties together the entire first speech.

Understanding the formulaic nature of the expression weakens the contention of those who say 38:1 should follow immediately after 31:40 (cf. W. A. Irwin, "The Elihu Speeches in the Criticism of the Book of Job," *JR* 17 [1937]: 37–47). The beginning of each Yahweh speech is designated by adding to this formula the words "out of the storm" (cf. 38:1; 40:6).

Here, then, in 40:2 the Lord gets to the point. Job has set himself up arbitrarily as God's accuser. How can Job assume such a lofty position in the light of who God is? After this front-row seat surveying the marvels and mysteries of God's created universe, is Job still ready to make his proud insinuations and accusations about the nature of God's lordship over all things? It is Job's turn to speak again. But there will be no long speeches, no more rage, no more challenging his Creator.

NOTES

38:3 The figure in חֲלָצֶיךָ ... אֱזָר־נָא (ʾezār-nāʾ ... ḥᵃlāṣeykā, "Brace yourself") may be the ancient belt-wrestler. The hero girded his loins (that is, "tucked in the skirt of his robe," so Hartley, 492) with a warrior's belt that would be snatched from him as a trophy if vanquished (cf. Pritchard, *ANET*, fig. 219; C. H. Gordon, "Belt Wrestling in the Bible World," *HUCA* 23 [part 1; 1950–51]: 136). But it may be more general (1Ki 18:46; Isa 5:27).

8 The question וַיָּסֶךְ (wayyāsek, "Who shut up") is not explicit in Hebrew but must surely be carried over from what precedes. But there are two questions that precede "Where were you?" (v.4) and "Who?" (v.5). Driver and Gray prefer the former question, and Blommerde, following this, translates this verb "to pour out" (nsk). Thus "[Where were you] when the sea poured out of the two doors and went forth, erupting from the womb?" There is no problem in ascribing the meaning "from" for b (cf. Blommerde, 19). But Andersen's solution, 271, may be better: "Who constructed the sea within the doors?" This handles the verb as in Psalm 139:13 ("knit together in the womb"; cf. BDB, 651; GK 6114 and 6115). He also suggests we revocalize the verb יֵצֵא (yēṣēʾ, "burst forth") to Hiphil yōṣîʾ (written defectively) and read "Who delivered it?" This certainly strengthens the context by making God the Creator as in v.4, not just an observer of the sea's birth.

9 For חֲתֻלָּתוֹ (ḥᵃtullātô, "wrapped it"), the RSV has "its swaddling band." The word is used only here, but the verb is used in Ezekiel 30:21 of putting on a bandage.

10 It is obvious that the usual meaning "I broke" for וָאֶשְׁבֹּר (wāʾešbōr) does not fit the context. The NIV's "when I fixed" follows the RV, RSV, et al., which probably connected the root with the Arabic šbr ("prescribe boundaries"). Pope, 294, shows how the Qumran Targum also understood the verb as "set (bounds)." Gordis (*Job*, 428) uses semantic correspondence to show šbr can mean "decree, decide"; but there are no other OT examples for this meaning (see Hartley, 493).

11 Gordis (*Job*, 444–45) wisely notes וָאֹמַר (wāʾōmar, "when I said") as anacrusis—an introductory word outside the poetic balance.

Delitzsch (2:316) sees יָשִׁית (yāšît) as a logical passive with an indefinite subject and with a typical ellipsis of the direct object, probably חֹק (ḥōq, "limit"; cf. 10:20; 14:13 and Notes on 4:20 for ellipsis with śîm, "put"). The NIV's lucid word "halt" may be considered a way of handling the logical passive "[a limit] is set." BHS wants to borrow the preposition from the word גְּאוֹן (geʾôn, "proud") and metathesize it to get šbt ("to cease"), reading "here your proud waves cease."

13 The raised *ayin* in רְשָׁעִים (rešāʿîm, "the wicked") represents a proto-Masoretic correction that was faithfully preserved (cf. also v.15; Jdg 18:30; Ps 80:14). G. R. Driver's interpretation ("Two Astronomical Passages," 4:208–12; cf. NEB) that these are the "evil stars" (e.g., the Dog Star if one rearranges the letters) is not likely since they are shaken out of the earth, not the heavens. Furthermore, "wicked" works perfectly well in the context.

The verb נָעַר (nāʿar II; GK 5850) means "to shake, shake out/off." Its use in Psalm 109:23 is instructive for this passage: "I fade away like an evening shadow; / I am shaken off like a locust." Note how similar the figures of speech are to vv.13–14.

14 The NIV's rendering of וְיִתְיַצְּבוּ (weyityaṣṣebû) as "its features stand out" has "its features" inserted to account for the plural verb, which has only the "wicked" in v.13 as a reference. Scholars emend it to a feminine singular of ṣbʿ ("to tint or dye"). The RSV's "dyed like a garment" might refer to the color of the earth at dawn. As it stands, the text might mean "they stand forth [in the light] like [the folds of] a garment." If "they" are the wicked, that is the reason they can be shaken off (v.13). Such an idea leads into v.15, where the wicked are denied their kind of light (i.e., darkness; cf. 24:17) by the coming of the true light of day.

16 On נִבְכֵי־יָם (nibkê-yām, "the springs of the sea"), compare 28:11, where the MT's mibbekî reflects the Ugaritic nbk (npk) "(water) source" (UT, 441). S. R. Driver (Driver and Gray, 303) said the etymology was unknown, but see G. M. Landes ("The Fountain at Jazer," BASOR 144 [1956]: 31–32) and M. Mansoor ("The Thanksgiving Hymns and the Massoretic Text," RevQ 3 [1961–62]: 392–93).

17 צַלְמָוֶת (ṣalmāwet, "the shadow of death"; GK 7516) appears in some contexts meaning "darkness," as its use in extrabiblical documents proves. But even in biblical times its meaning as derived from the two words "shadow" and "death" was recognized and used, as this passage seems to confirm by using it in parallel with māwet ("death"). Of the ten times the word appears in Job, this is the only place the NIV renders it "shadow of death." It supports the same reading for Psalm 23:4.

18 In אֶרֶץ ... כֻּלָּהּ (ʾāreṣ ... kullāh, "the earth ... all this"), it may be better to take ʾāreṣ ("land"; GK 824) and kullāh ("all of it") both to refer to the land of the shadow of death. Even though Akkadian and Ugaritic use ʾāreṣ for the domain of the dead, it is at best rare in the OT. See Michel, 70–72, for passages in Job where he thinks ʾāreṣ might be translated "the underworld [netherworld]." Out of fourteen passages, including this one, only one is certain (10:21) and one other is possible but not probable (28:24).

24 Because of the parallel with קָדִים (qādîm, "[hot] east winds"), critics suggest various emendations for ʾôr ("lightning") in יֵחָלֶק אוֹר (yēḥāleq ʾôr, "lightning is dispersed"). The NEB's translation "the heat [is] spread abroad" (cf. Driver and Gray; see Rowley, 313) is possible. Some may feel "lightning" (NIV "light") is appropriate in 41:18 also. In Isaiah 44:16 and 47:14, ʾûr is fire that people kindle to warm themselves.

25 See 28:26.

27 The NIV took מֹצָא (mōṣāʾ [no equivalent in NIV]) to mean "the place or act of going forth" (BDB, 425; cf. 28:1). The meaning then is tautological: "to make sprout, the going forth of grass." The translation omits the repetition. Others see it as simple metathesis from *ṣāmēʾ*, reading "the thirsty (land)," yielding "to make the thirsty land sprout grass."

31–33 See Amos 5:8 and Notes on 9:9. The KJV's "sweet influences of Pleiades" for מַעֲדַנּוֹת כִּימָה (*maʿᵃdannôt kîmâ*, "the beautiful Pleiades") comes from the earlier English version that got it from Jewish sources in the Middle Ages (Nachmanides et al.). Driver (Driver and Gray, 306–7), after citing a note in the Geneva Bible, maintained no astrological meaning was intended (cf. Pope, 300), only that the heliacal rising of Pleiades coincides with the beginning of spring that is the time when flowers, etc. ("sweet delights") are stimulated. But all this is wide of the mark. Like the KJV, the NIV's "beautiful" is based on the root ʿ*dn* ("luxury, delight, dainty"; GK 6357–6361); but the root with this meaning is always used in the masculine, not the feminine.

The NIV margin suggests two out of a number of other possible alternatives: "the twinkling" that is based on מָעַד (*māʿad*, "to quiver, tremble"; GK 5048; at least Jerome, in the Vulgate, thought it meant "twinkle"); another is "the chains/bonds of," which requires a metathesis coming from ʿ*nd* ("to bind"; 31:36). The only other use of *māʿᵃdannôt*—in 1 Samuel 15:32—presents the same problem. According to some translations the resigned Agag comes to be slain "delicately" (KJV), "cheerfully" (RSV), or "confidently" (NIV). All these are based on a semantic stretch of the root עֶדֶן (ʿ*dn*). The NIV margin—"him trembling, yet"—is based on *mʿd* (cf. Beck). Pope, citing S. R. Driver's *Notes on the Hebrew Text and the Topography of the Books of Samuel* (2nd ed.; London: Oxford Univ. Press, 1966), accepts the metathesis in both passages; so Agag comes "in fetters." But G. R. Driver rejects "fetters" in 38:31, claiming support from Ugaritic and Arabic to show the word should be translated "company, group" (cf. NEB, "cluster"). The words "Can you bind the cluster ... and loose the cords" make excellent sense. Driver thinks the cords are Orion's belt ("Two Astronomical Passages," 7:1–11).

32 On מַזָּרוֹת (*mazzārôt*, "the constellations"), compare *mazzālôt* ("constellations," 2Ki 23:5). The two are usually identified on the basis of the interchange between *l* and *r* in Semitic dialects (Pope, 301). Both G. R. Driver ("Two Astronomical Passages," 7:6–8) and Dhorme, 589–90, question the identification. Driver sees the zodiacal constellations here in Job but the planets in 2 Kings 23:5. Dhorme, stressing etymology (*nēzer*, "crown"), finds this to be the Corona Borealis.

For עַל (ʿ*al*, "with") meaning "along with," cf. Genesis 32:11 [12]; 1 Samuel 14:32.

33 The root *šṭr* never appears as a verb and is found only here as מִשְׁטָרוֹ (*mišṭārô*, "God's dominion"; cf. *šōṭēr*, "official"). The root has to do with writing in Akkadian, Arabic, and Aramaic. On this nuance of the Hebrew root, see BDB, 1009.

Friedrich Delitzsch (cited in Dhorme, 591) was the first to point to the Assyrian *šiṭir šamāmi* ("the writing of the sky") meaning the stars (cf. also *mašṭāru*, "inscription"). Both the NIV and Pope think it means "God's dominion" here. But Gordis (*Job*, 451) finds a hidden plural (inscribed decrees = "order"), making the verse antithetic: "Do you know the laws of heaven; can you establish order on the earth?" N. H. Tur-Sinai ("*šiṭir šamê*: din Himmelsschrift," *Archiv Orientální* 17/2 [1949]: 419–33) ties the verse to Psalm 19 and sees the "language of heaven going out into all the earth." Rowley, 245, makes it purely astrological—the heavenly writing is the stars. Pope, 290, understands it as God's rule on earth.

The verb could be *śîm* with elliptical *lēb* (cf. 4:20; 23:6; 24:12; 34:23), giving the meaning "Have you considered his inscription in the earth?" i.e., God writes (reveals himself) not only in the heavens (Ps 19), but also "in all the earth" (Ps 8:1). The evidence of God's hand in the earth is precisely what he takes up throughout the rest of this speech.

36 בַּטֻּחוֹת (*baṭṭuḥôt*, "the heart") and לַשֶּׂכְוִי (*láśśekwî*, "the mind") have had a long history of attempts to interpret them, and there is still no consensus. Gordis (*Job*, 452–53) lists four major views and gives reasons for eliminating three, and a case could be made for eliminating the fourth. One of the three is the NIV's "heart" and "mind," which is essentially the same as the KJV and RV and has the distinction of being the first presented by Ibn Ezra. (The NIV margin needs correction since it implies only one word is under consideration.) That *ṭuḥôt* means "the heart" is based on one other passage where the word is used: Psalm 51:6 [8]; the parallel with *sātum* ("the inmost place") creates a reasonable assumption that, if this is from the same root, *ṭuḥôt* means something similar. But all attempts to arrive at a root in either case have been unsatisfactory. The same is true for *śekwî*, an OT *hapax legomenon*.

The second unsatisfactory explanation according to Gordis (*Job*, 453) is "clouds" and "mists" (cf. RSV, BDB). Here too the philological support is weak (cf. Pope, 302), and the context's reference to wisdom is left unexplained.

The third view is that of many modern scholars and is summarized and supported by Pope, 256. Its philological base is an attempt to show that the words *ṭuḥôt* and *śekwî* sound like the names of two Egyptian gods: Thoth, the scribe-god and founder of knowledge, and Souchi, the Coptic name for the god Hermes-Mercury. This fits the wisdom concept; and though the name Thoth was popular among the Phoenicians and Neo-Babylonians in OT times, there is no evidence that the same is true for Souchi. Gordis (*Job*, 453) is correct in questioning the notion that so uncompromising a monotheist as we have here would describe God giving wisdom to pagan deities. How can such be considered one of the wonders of God's creation (Gordis, 453)?

So the only interpretation that seems to have some philological support and that fits the immediate and overall context—though it too must be considered tentative—is the view reflected in TEV's paraphrase: "Who tells the ibis when the Nile will flood, or who tells the rooster that rain will fall?" Both Gordis and Dhorme, 591, support this view. The word *ṭuḥôt* then refers to the ibis bird, the symbol for Thoth, the Egyptian god of wisdom. Since the ibis was thought to foretell the rising of the Nile, by allusion we have a reference to one of nature's great wonders, though the text does not say that.

The philological support for *śekwî* as "the cock" that was believed to forecast rain is based on rabbinic references that are far from convincing, but Gordis (*Job*, 453) seems to accept it. This view fits the context if the allusion to a "wisdom" that these birds have but that humans lack is correct. But this interpretation ignores Psalm 51:6 [8], the only bit of OT philological evidence available. There is no satisfactory solution to the problem this text poses.

39:3 The literal meaning of חֶבְלֵיהֶם תְּשַׁלַּחְנָה (*heblêhem t°šallaḥnâ*, "their labor pains are ended") is "they cast off their pains." The "pains" need not be metonymy for what causes them (BDB, s.v.), since *ḥabal* means "fetus" in Arabic (Pope).

4 Seeing בַבָּר (*babbār*, "in the wilds") as an Aramaism corrects the KJV's "with corn," which is based on a common Hebrew homonym meaning "grain" (see Hartley, 506). Pope wishes to move the word up to v.3 on the basis of the Qumran Targum, which has no equivalent in either verse. The LXX has an equivalent; and though it misunderstood the word, it supports the MT.

12 The NIV's "to bring in your grain" follows כִּי־יָשׁוּב זַרְעֶךָ (kî-yāšiwb zarʿekā), the MT *Qere*: the Hiphil with the object "your grain." BHS margin, wanting a balanced bicolon, prefers the *Kethiv* (Qal): יָשׁוּב (yāšûb, "that he will come back"). But this leaves the second half difficult to translate; so BHS wants to emend it. To dispel the mystery one need only see anacrusis, namely, there are three parts to the line, with "Can you trust him" outside the balance and applying to both sides.

13 The obscurity of אִם־אֶבְרָה חֲסִידָה וְנֹצָה (ʾim-ʾebrâ hᵃsîdâ wᵉnōṣâ, "but they cannot compare with the pinions and feathers of the stork") disappears when ʾim is understood as a particle of wishing (BDB, 50). The bicolon has a twinkle of humor when translated literally: "When the wing of the ostrich flaps joyfully, would that it was a stork's pinion and feathers!" Another possible option for this difficult verse is to slightly emend to ʾim ʾebrâ hᵃsērâ nōṣâ and translate "though its pinions lack plumage" (see Hartley, 509).

13–18 On the omission of these lines in the LXX, Habel, 524, suggests, "It is much easier to see why the LXX would omit this awkward verse than to understand why someone would insert it later." He sees it as "a deliberate feature of the poet's plan."

19 On רַעְמָה (raʿmâ) as "flowing mane" (NIV), see KB, 901.

20 The NIV renders הְתַרְעִישֶׁנּוּ (hᵃtarʿîšennû) as "Do you make him leap … ?" The Qumran Targum translates rʿš as "leap," though it is not generally used this way. The common meaning "shake" or "quake" (cf. v.24; GK 8321) is used as in Isaiah 9:5 [4] and refers to the noise of an army ("battle," NIV; cf. KJV, "confused noise"). The warhorses' hoofs sound like the roar of locusts, but this is accomplished by running and jumping. The REB takes rʿš in its usual sense of "quiver" and likens the horses' quivering to that of locust wings.

21 The NIV's rendering of בָּעֵמֶק (bāʿēmeq) as "fiercely" is supported by both Ugaritic and Akkadian, which attest to ʿmq meaning "strength," used adverbially here (cf. *UT*, 457). However, it may also be understood as "valley," so that the horse is pawing the soil of the valley (see NJB; also NAB).

25 The MT vocalizes בְּדֵי (bᵉdê) as though this were the preposition *b* with the substantive *day* (construct *dê*; "sufficiency"), the combination meaning "as often as" ("when," RSV); but this combination appears only with the preposition *min* (BDB, 91). Here and in 11:3 the idiom is like the Ugaritic *bd* ("song") used adverbially, hence the NIV's "at the blast [song] of."

30 The verb יַעְלְעוּ (yᵉʿalʿû, "feast on") is treated as a Piel of ʿlʿ, an unknown root. BHS suggests a reduplicated form of lûaʿ ("swallow, lap"; cf. BDB, 534), but this entails adding another *lamed* after the *yod*. Others want to drop or explain away the first *ayin* (Dhorme). Pope, 314–15, claims he has an Arabic root meaning "to shake a thing [in order] to pull it out," which would be Aramaized in this way. But he gives no documentation. Hartley, 513, takes it as a Pilpel of lôaʿ in the sense of "extract."

40:2 The NIV understands יִסּוֹר (yissôr), a *hapax legomenon*, to be from ysr ("to correct"). This requires adding the pronominal object "him," which does not appear in Hebrew. Others make *yissôr* a rare noun: "Will the faultfinder [yissôr] contend with the Almighty?" (RSV). Most revocalize *rôb* to *rāb*, a participle ("the one who contends"), and make it the subject of the verb *sûr*, meaning "yield." So Dhorme has "Will he who argues with Shaddai yield?" (cf. Pope).

In rendering יַעֲנֶנָּה (yaʿᵃnennâ) as "answer him," the NIV has not followed the feminine form of the pronominal suffix, which has to be translated "it" or "this" (cf. RSV). No doubt the NIV has chosen to somewhat paraphrastic since "it" means Yahweh's argument.

2. Job's Humbling (40:3–5)

³Then Job answered the LORD:

⁴"I am unworthy—how can I reply to you?
  I put my hand over my mouth.
⁵I spoke once, but I have no answer—
  twice, but I will say no more."

COMMENTARY

3–5 Job, the challenger, in a hand-over-mouth posture that signifies his intention to remain silent (v.4), realizes how complex and mysterious God's ways are. In other words, the view of the things from God's perspective has chastened Job. His reply is based not so much on his unworthiness (NIV) as on his insignificance. God has not crushed Job. God has not done what the counselors wanted when they reduced Job to zero, but he has cured Job's presumption. The Hebrew verb translated "unworthy" means "to be light" or "lightly esteemed" (GK 7837) and in that sense "contemptible." Job sees how contemptible it must have appeared to God when he said "like a prince I would approach him" (31:37).

Job has been so moved by this experience, so taken out of himself by his vision of God, that he is released from his problem—his concern to be vindicated. And yet God has given him no explanation of his sufferings. Job will no longer alternate outbursts of rage and self-pity. But he is still on the rack; his suffering has not abated. Job has gone beyond it to see and trust God as his friend. As a friend God has brought Job out of his bitterness to a full realization that he must reckon with God as God. And yet Job still does not know how God put himself on trial when he allowed Job to be afflicted under Satan's instigation. So Job is humbled and thereby prepared for the Lord's second speech, which will pull together some important threads and bring the drama to a climax.

NOTES

4 In הֵן קַלֹּתִי (hēn qallōtî, "I am unworthy"), the particle hēn can mean "if" as well as "lo, behold." Dhorme takes the verb to mean "be light in speech or thought" rather than lightly esteemed (BDB, 886) and translates, "If I have been thoughtless." JB is similar: "My words have been frivolous." Pope stresses the Arabic meaning and is more literal: "Lo, I am small; how can I answer you?" But the idea of "being contemptible" fits the way this word is used as a Canaanite gloss in the Tell El Amarna tablets (cf. BDB, 886; Gesenius-Buhl, *Handwörterbuch*, 714) and in Genesis 16:4 and 1 Samuel 2:30.

יָדִי ... לְמוֹ־פִי (yādî ... lemô-pî, "my hand ... over my mouth") is a gesture of silence and submission that Job has used twice before (21:5; 29:9; cf. Jdg 18:19 [KJV]; Pr 30:32; Mic 7:16).

5 As a figure of speech the idiom אַחַת ... וּשְׁתָּיִם (ʾaḥat ... ûšetayim, "once ... twice"), so common in Semitic tongues (cf. Am 1:3, 6, 9, et al., a numerical parallelism; see J. M. LeMon and B. Strawn, "Parallelism," in

Dictionary of the Old Testament: Wisdom, Poetry and Writings [ed. T. Longman III and P. Enns; Downers Grove, Ill.: InterVarsity Press, 2008]: 502–15 [esp. 511]), should not be pressed unduly. Nor should the words "but I will say no more" be taken too literally (cf. 42:2–6). Job means he has no rebuttal.

3. God's Second Discourse (40:6–41:34 [41:26])

OVERVIEW

As with Yahweh's first speech, the following outline may help the reader navigate through the material of this second speech:

Introductory Challenge to Job (40:6–7)
Subject: The Lord of History
    I. Prologue: Lord over the Moral Order (40:8–14)
        A. Rebuke of Job (40:8)
        B. God's Majestic Wrath against All Wickedness (40:9–14)
    II. The First Monster (40:15–23)
        A. His Might—Four Bicola (40:15–18)
        B. A Primordial Creature under God's Control—Climax (40:19)
        C. His Security—Four Bicola (40:20–23)
    III. The Second Monster (40:24–41:34)
        A. Man (Job) and Leviathan (40:24–41:10)
        B. God and Leviathan (under God's Control)—Climax (41:11–12)
        C. Description of Leviathan (41:13–24)
        D. Other Mighty Beings and Leviathan (41:25–34)

The descriptions of Behemoth and Leviathan have been assailed by many who are doubtful of their authenticity. For example, Driver and Gray (351–52) see this section as out of balance with the animal descriptions of the first speech and present a list of reasons why this could not have been written by the author of the first speech: the beastly descriptions are longer; the question format is less frequent, which tends to lessen the vividness of this as God's words; the focus here is on the body parts of the beasts while there it was on their habits, activities, and tempers; Behemoth and Leviathan are said to be Egyptian (the hippopotamus and the crocodile) while the earlier animals were Palestinian, etc. But

Gordis (*Job*, 567) has shown how Driver and Gray's view is much too mechanical and does not allow for poetic creativity.

R. B. Y. Scott (*The Way of Wisdom* [New York: Macmillan, 1971], 159 n.) claims 40:15–41:34 is an anticlimax and adds nothing to the challenge of 40:6–14. Such a view overlooks a number of important matters. First, it is reasonable to assume the author intended a lengthy new speech to begin at 40:6 parallel to chapters 38–39. This is confirmed by the fact that the formula in 38:1 and 3 is repeated in 40:6–7 just as the new formula used in 27:1 is repeated in 29:1. The words "I will question you" (40:7) would be out of place only if there were no questions in the Behemoth and Leviathan sections (see Westermann's comment below). Second, 40:8–14 serves as a prologue to the rest of the speech. And the message of this prologue gives us the clue to the correct interpretation of the descriptions of Behemoth and Leviathan.

The Lord, acting as his own defense attorney, moves to the heart of his case: Job's misunderstanding of God's attitude toward wickedness. Verses 8–14 question the contention that the God of the book of Job is amoral and that one purpose of the book is to set aside the old biblical doctrine of justice and retribution (cf. Tsevat, 102–5). Here God addresses himself to the moral question and rebukes Job for daring to question his justice (v.8). Job has been discrediting (*pārar*, "to frustrate") God's justice by suggesting he is guilty of failing to run the world in the way Job imagines it should be run (e.g., 9:21–24; 24:1–12). Job's preoccupation with his own vindication has obscured the real issue—God alone has the power and majesty it takes to combat evil and turn it into good.

The imperatives in vv.10–11 that call on Job to display the attributes of deity are obviously intended to prove to him how helpless he is against the reality of the forces of evil in this world. Verse 14 places the emphasis on salvation from evil. The message is that Job's right hand cannot save, but God's can. Indeed, if Job could do what he claimed God failed to do, then he does not need God at all—a horrible implication since Job has never denied God is sovereign. Job's problems stem from that very belief.

Gordis's notion (*Job*, 475) that God is tacitly conceding he has not been able to achieve completely his goal of obliterating evil is just the opposite of what this speech is all about. God states the fact that wickedness exists and that he alone has the power to uphold his own honor by crushing it. Deliverance from all evil rests with God, not with humans (vv.9–14). Westermann, 105, has noted that

the imperatives in many of these verses really have questions behind them. The words "Then adorn yourself with glory and splendor" mean "Are you so adorned?" God has already pressed Job's own creatureliness on him in the first speech. Job thus needs to acknowledge God not only as Creator but also Savior (v.14b). It is precisely these two attributes of God that stand behind the Yahweh speeches.

This prologue in vv.8–14 shows how the lengthy descriptions of the two creatures, Behemoth and Leviathan, serve the purpose of the book in a subtle and yet forceful way. This time God will accomplish more than he had in the first speech, where he humbled Job by showing him how he is Creator and Sustainer of the natural world. Here God will convince Job that he is also Lord of the moral order—one whose justice Job cannot discredit. And appropriately Job's response this time is repentance (42:1–6).

The concentration on these two awesome creatures, placed as they are after the assertion of the Lord's justice and maintenance of moral order, lends weight to the contention that they are symbolic though their features are drawn from animals like the hippopotamus and crocodile (GK 990 and 4293). Both words are used often in the OT without symbolic significance (Pss 8:8; 50:10; 73:22; 104:26; Joel 1:20; 2:22; Hab 2:17; et al.). But Leviathan sometimes symbolizes evil political powers. In keeping with what I said above (Introduction: Mythopoeic Language), in Psalm 74:12–14 mythopoeic language about the many-headed Leviathan is historicized and used metaphorically to describe the Lord's great victory in history at the Red Sea. The monster here is Egypt.

> But you, O God, are my king from of old;
>> you bring salvation upon the earth.
> It was you who split open the sea by your power;
>> you broke the heads of the monster in the waters.

It was you who crushed the heads of Leviathan
   and gave him as food to the creatures of the
   desert.

The same is true of Isaiah 27:1, where again the mythic chaos-figure Leviathan is historicized to represent the final evil power in the end time. It is important to stress that this terminology in Mesopotamia and Canaanite myth is always tied to natural phenomena, never to historical events. Here in Job it is not a particular historical event; but as the poem's prologue in vv.8–14 suggests, the theme is God's actions against all creatures who dare assert themselves against him. Most important for this interpretation of Job 40–41 is Isaiah 26:21–27:1. Here the prophet says:

See, the LORD is coming out of his dwelling
   to punish the people of the earth for their
   sins.
The earth will disclose the blood shed upon her;
   she will conceal her slain no longer.
In that day,
the LORD will punish with his sword,
   his fierce, great and powerful sword,
Leviathan the gliding serpent,
   Leviathan the coiling serpent;
he will slay the monster of the sea.

Genesis 3:1 and Isaiah 27:1 present the OT view of the beginning and the end of the history of sin in the world. They mark a major ideological difference between the OT view of the origin and disposition of evil and that of Canaanite myth. Nevertheless, the serpent imagery shows a continuity between the

two that cannot be ignored (see *ANET*, 137–38). Imagery similar to Job is found in Revelation 12–13. There we see a beast (Behemoth) as well as a dragon (Leviathan), both of whom only God can subdue. Revelation 12:9 says: "The great dragon was hurled down—that ancient serpent called the devil or Satan, who leads the whole world astray. He was hurled to the earth, and his angels with him." There is no apocalyptic tone to this part of Job, merely a free use of the same Canaanite imagery that Isaiah and the psalmist knew so well.

Those who regard these creatures as literal animals must admit that the description given here in Job is an exaggeration of the appearance and power of hippopotamuses and crocodiles. A number of scholars (e.g., Gunkle, Cheyne, and Pope) understood them as mythological creatures. I claim only mythological terminology is used to present graphic descriptions of the powers of evil such as the Satan in the Prologue. But the Accuser cannot be openly mentioned here without revealing to Job information he must not know if he is to continue as a model to those who also must suffer in ignorance of God's explicit purpose for their suffering.

Both creatures share two qualities. First is the open (on the surface) quality of a beast with over-size bovine or crocodilian features. This meets the needs of the uninformed (as to events of the Prologue) Job, who is learning a lesson about the Lord's omnipotence. Second is the hidden quality of a cosmic creature (the Accuser of the Prologue), whose creation preceded (40:19) and whose power outranks (41:33) all other creatures.

⁶Then the LORD spoke to Job out of the storm:

⁷"Brace yourself like a man;
   I will question you,
   and you shall answer me.

8"Would you discredit my justice?
　　Would you condemn me to justify yourself?
9Do you have an arm like God's,
　　and can your voice thunder like his?
10Then adorn yourself with glory and splendor,
　　and clothe yourself in honor and majesty.
11Unleash the fury of your wrath,
　　look at every proud man and bring him low,
12look at every proud man and humble him,
　　crush the wicked where they stand.
13Bury them all in the dust together;
　　shroud their faces in the grave.
14Then I myself will admit to you
　　that your own right hand can save you.

15"Look at the behemoth,
　　which I made along with you
　　and which feeds on grass like an ox.
16What strength he has in his loins,
　　what power in the muscles of his belly!
17His tail sways like a cedar;
　　the sinews of his thighs are close-knit.
18His bones are tubes of bronze,
　　his limbs like rods of iron.
19He ranks first among the works of God,
　　yet his Maker can approach him with his sword.
20The hills bring him their produce,
　　and all the wild animals play nearby.
21Under the lotus plants he lies,
　　hidden among the reeds in the marsh.
22The lotuses conceal him in their shadow;
　　the poplars by the stream surround him.
23When the river rages, he is not alarmed;
　　he is secure, though the Jordan should surge against his mouth.
24Can anyone capture him by the eyes,
　　or trap him and pierce his nose?

41:1"Can you pull in the leviathan with a fishhook
　　or tie down his tongue with a rope?

²Can you put a cord through his nose
  or pierce his jaw with a hook?
³Will he keep begging you for mercy?
  Will he speak to you with gentle words?
⁴Will he make an agreement with you
  for you to take him as your slave for life?
⁵Can you make a pet of him like a bird
  or put him on a leash for your girls?
⁶Will traders barter for him?
  Will they divide him up among the merchants?
⁷Can you fill his hide with harpoons
  or his head with fishing spears?
⁸If you lay a hand on him,
  you will remember the struggle and never do it again!
⁹Any hope of subduing him is false;
  the mere sight of him is overpowering.
¹⁰No one is fierce enough to rouse him.
  Who then is able to stand against me?
¹¹Who has a claim against me that I must pay?
  Everything under heaven belongs to me.

¹²"I will not fail to speak of his limbs,
  his strength and his graceful form.
¹³Who can strip off his outer coat?
  Who would approach him with a bridle?
¹⁴Who dares open the doors of his mouth,
  ringed about with his fearsome teeth?
¹⁵His back has rows of shields
  tightly sealed together;
¹⁶each is so close to the next
  that no air can pass between.
¹⁷They are joined fast to one another;
  they cling together and cannot be parted.
¹⁸His snorting throws out flashes of light;
  his eyes are like the rays of dawn.
¹⁹Firebrands stream from his mouth;
  sparks of fire shoot out.
²⁰Smoke pours from his nostrils
  as from a boiling pot over a fire of reeds.

²¹His breath sets coals ablaze,
  and flames dart from his mouth.
²²Strength resides in his neck;
  dismay goes before him.
²³The folds of his flesh are tightly joined;
  they are firm and immovable.
²⁴His chest is hard as rock,
  hard as a lower millstone.
²⁵When he rises up, the mighty are terrified;
  they retreat before his thrashing.
²⁶The sword that reaches him has no effect,
  nor does the spear or the dart or the javelin.
²⁷Iron he treats like straw
  and bronze like rotten wood.
²⁸Arrows do not make him flee;
  slingstones are like chaff to him.
²⁹A club seems to him but a piece of straw;
  he laughs at the rattling of the lance.
³⁰His undersides are jagged potsherds,
  leaving a trail in the mud like a threshing sledge.
³¹He makes the depths churn like a boiling caldron
  and stirs up the sea like a pot of ointment.
³²Behind him he leaves a glistening wake;
  one would think the deep had white hair.
³³Nothing on earth is his equal—
  a creature without fear.
³⁴He looks down on all that are haughty;
  he is king over all that are proud."

COMMENTARY

6–14 Using the same formula of challenge (v.7) as in 38:3, God presents to Job another barrage of questions designed to bring him back to reality. After all, Job's subfinal words of his monologue were a challenge (31:35–37) that threw into question God's integrity by suggesting that any indictment God might bring against Job would prove to be false (40:8). But all such is hypothetical nonsense. It came straight from Job's imagination. God had no such indictment of Job in the first place; but Job's attitude has to be corrected, for he has wrongly assumed that he has to be vindicated by God.

To do this the Lord reminds Job of who he (God) is. Does Job have an arm like God's—is he almighty (v.9)? And where are Job's majesty and glory (v.10)? Job begins to realize why God has in his first discourse taken him through his garden of natural wonders. Could Job by his power and glory create and sustain all that? Obviously not! So Job needs also to leave to his Creator supremacy in the moral realm. Job has no power to crush wickedness finally; so obviously he needs to leave that ultimate exercise of justice to God. He needs to let God be God. He needs to cease his agitation over what God is doing and trust him to do right.

These verses are presented as an aggressive challenge to Job. "Unleash the fury of your wrath … crush the wicked. … Then I myself will admit that your own right hand can save you" (see vv.11–12, 14). But these words are lovingly designed to shake Job's spirit into realizing God is the only Creator and the only Savior there is. Job needs to and will learn to rest quietly and trustfully in that truth. To confirm this, the Lord proceeds to paint the word pictures of these awesome creatures that defy God and humankind. Indeed, the second is so awesome that nothing on earth equals it (41:33).

15–24 Only one other place in the OT uses the word *bᵉhēmôt* (GK 990), where it functions as a singular. The *-ôt* ending normally marks the feminine plural when the word simply means "beast." Here, however, the plural ending has an intensive force meaning the beast par excellence; that is, the beast becomes a monster. The other passage (Ps 73:22) is clearly metaphorical; the psalmist confesses to God: "I was a brute beast before you." But if Behemoth is a mere beast in Job 40, the language, apart from hyperbole, is difficult to understand.

What could possibly be the reason for such hyperbole? In v.19a Behemoth is labeled the "first among the works of God." Pope, 272, translates the line "a primordial production of God." This fits Pope's purely mythological interpretation, but I suggest it is mythopoeic language (cf. Ps 74:13–14), intended as another

way of referring to a unique cosmic creature such as the Accuser in the Prologue (see more recently R. S. Fyall, *Now My Eyes Have Seen You: Images of Creation and Evil in the Book of Job* [Downers Grove, Ill.: InterVarsity Press, 2002]: 117–38). He is beyond the pale of mere human strength, just as the Accuser is.

But, as noted above, this information cannot be revealed to Job, and that explains the extravagant language. The use of the two names Behemoth and Leviathan is a poetic repetition, just as Psalm 74 refers to the breaking of the heads of the monster (*tannînîm*) and the heads of Leviathan, both referring to the power of Egypt at the Red Sea. In Ugaritic the goddess Anat conquered the seven-headed Leviathan along with a bovine creature called "El's Bullock" (*ANET*, 137, l. 41). Since similar mythopoeic language is used for Leviathan (Ps 74:12–14), it is a small step to view the Behemoth figure in the same light.

41:1–34 [40:25–41:26] Verses 1–9 develop the thought that Leviathan is far too powerful for humans to handle. The first eight verses are addressed to Job, and they assert that any relationship Job may attempt to have with Leviathan will be doomed to failure — whether by treaty or by force. Linguistic problems in vv.10 and 12 make it necessary to be careful about their interpretation (see Notes), but most are agreed that at this point God states that he alone has the power to control Leviathan; therefore, he is the only Supreme Being. In these verses we reach the climax of the stanza. But this is not the original conclusion of the whole poem as Westermann, 119, claims. It is perfectly good Hebrew style to put such a climax in the middle of the poem.

Before this climax the stress was on human impotence before the Leviathan. After the climax (vv.12–34) the poem becomes a masterly description of this creature that goes beyond anything ascribable to a mere crocodile or whale. I translate beginning in 41:18:

His snorting flashes forth lightning;
    his eyes are like the glow of dawn.
Flames stream from his mouth;
    sparks of fire leap forth.
From his nostrils pours smoke,
    as from a pot heated by burning brushwood.
His breath sets coals ablaze;
    a flame pours from his mouth.

And I translate verse 25:

When he arises, the heavenly beings are afraid;
    they are beside themselves because of the
        crashing.

Swords, javelins, arrows, clubs, slingstones—all are ineffective against him according to vv.26–29. And in verse 33 we read:

On earth there is not his equal;
    he was made without fear.
He looks down on all that is lofty:
    he is king over all proud beings.

Is this merely a crocodile, or should it be understood in the light of Isaiah 27:1 and other such passages?

By telling of his dominion over Behemoth and Leviathan, the Lord is illustrating what he has said in 40:8–14. He is celebrating his moral triumph over the forces of evil. Satan, the Accuser, has been proved wrong though Job does not know it. The author and the reader see the entire picture that Job and his friends never know. No rational theory of suffering is substituted for the faulty one the friends have proffered. The only answer given is the same as in Genesis. God permits the Accuser to touch Job as part of his plan to humiliate Satan.

But now that the contest is over, God still does not reveal his reason to Job. Job does not find out what the readers know. That is why Job can be restored without destroying the integrity of the account. To understand this is to understand why the forces of moral disorder are veiled underneath mythopoeic language about ferocious, uncontrollable creatures. Once again I emphasize that if the specific and ultimate reason for his suffering had been revealed to Job even at this point, the value of the account as a comfort to others who must suffer in ignorance would have been diminished, if not cancelled.

In 41:9 the Hebrew Bible begins a new chapter. No doubt the scribes responsible for putting the break here noticed how the questions put to Job reached a climax in 41:8. I agree that a break exists here but I would put it after v.9 or possibly after v.10 (see Notes on v.10). After the lead-in (v.7; cf. 38:2–3), this speech has the following structure:

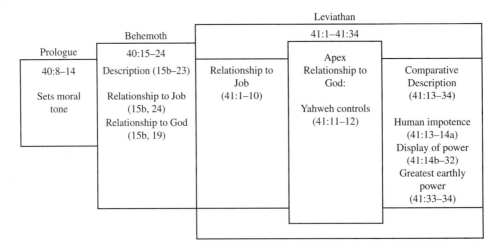

NOTES

40:11 The phrase כָל־גֵּאֶה (*kol-gēʾeh*, "every proud man") here and in v.12 need not be limited to human beings. "Proud one" is a tighter translation and allows for the interpretation that God alone can control the forces of evil, whether human or otherwise. Those forces include all the "proud" and "haughty" beings mentioned in 41:34. The same idea should be applied to the word "wicked" in v.12. Such an interpretation might include the Accuser of the Prologue, whom God, for good reason, does not see fit ever to mention to Job.

15 Although בְּהֵמוֹת (*bᵉhēmôt*, "the behemoth"; GK 990) looks like a plural, the singular verbs in this context prove it was understood as the plural of majesty or intensive plural, which, like אֱלֹהִים (*ʾᵉlōhîm*, "God"), is not plural at all. As Pope notes, it is the beast par excellence. In contrast to the OT use of Leviathan, the mythopoeic usage suggested above appears only here and not elsewhere in the OT when the plural form of *bᵉhēmâ* is used (cf. Pss 8:8; 50:10; 73:22; Joel 1:20; 2:22; Hab 2:17).

19 For רֵאשִׁית דַּרְכֵי־אֵל (*rēʾšît darkê-ʾēl*, "first among the works of God"), the KJV reads "chief of the ways of God." Dahood renders this line "the finest manifestation of God's power." He bases this on the possibility that the Ugaritic *drkt* can mean "dominion" or "power" (cf. Pr 31:3; Hos 10:13; GK 2006). See M. J. Dahood's "Ugaritic DRKT and Biblical DEREK," *JTS* 15 (1954): 627–31; idem, *Psalms*, 16:2. But see also Note on 26:14.

GKC (358, n. 1) calls הָעֹשׂוֹ (*hāʿōśô*, "his Maker") an anomaly "since a word determined by a genitive does not admit of being determined by the article." This problem dissolves if the pronominal suffix is logically conceived as the direct object of the verbal aspect of this participle, reading "the one making him."

20 Two interpretations of כִּי־בוּל הָרִים יִשְׂאוּ־לוֹ (*kî-bûl hārîm yiśʾû-lô*, "The hills bring him their produce") seem equally convincing. The NIV understands *bûl* as a short form of *yᵉbûl* ("produce"), in which case the stress is on the great amount of pasture this beast can devour. Pope calls attention to the bovine monsters of Ugaritic called "Eaters" and "Devourers" and the Gilgamesh Epic's Bull of Heaven, with its prodigious intake. A slightly different translation renders the verb as passive (by means of an indefinite subject): "The produce of the hills is brought to him."

The other interpretation follows Tur-Sinai (*Job*) in his comparison of the Akkadian *bûl ṣeri* ("beast[s] of the steppe") with *bûl hārîm* ("beast of the hills"). The strength of this lies in the parallelism with "the beast(s) of the field" in v.20b ("wild animals," NIV). But it is not necessary to follow Pope's insistence on emending the verb *yiśʾû* ("they lift up"), which may be understood as an elliptical expression meaning either "show respect" (with *pānîm*) or "rejoice" (with *qôl*) and thereby paralleling the verb *śḥq* ("play") in v.20b (cf. Gordis, *Job*, 478).

23 כִּי־יָגִיחַ יַרְדֵּן (*kî-yāgîaḥ yardēn*, "though the Jordan should surge") does not have the article, though the context uses the article (40:20: *haśśādeh*, "the wild"). So this involves something more than the poetic nature of this text. We would also expect an article with the word "river" in v.23a unless it is an epithet. In Ugaritic "River" was an epithet of Yam, the sea god (cf. *ANET*, 129); and the same may be true of Jordan if its basic meaning is "river" (cf. E. B. Smick, *Archaeology of the Jordan Valley* [Grand Rapids: Baker, 1973], 26–30; C. H. Gordon, *The World of the Old Testament*, [Garden City, N.Y.: Doubleday, 1958], 122, n. 19). So if "Jordan" and "River" are used as names in support of the mythopoeic overtone, this does not in the least deprive the text of the colorful literal figure of the surging Jordan. Rather, it suggests that underlying that figure and all this language based on a terrestrial mammoth is a cosmic creature that even cosmic beings cannot perturb; indeed, only his Maker can handle him (v.19).

24 Attempts to emend בְּעֵינָיו (bᵉʿênāyw, "by the eyes") to read "in his lair" (Kissane) or make it refer to "a water hole" (NIV mg.) are all misguided, since "eyes" and "nose," which open and close the couplet, are a parallel pair. Dhorme's citing of Herodotus on using plaster on a crocodile's eyes to control him has the merit of reasonably explaining the meaning, but it also means this line goes with what follows. Since 41:1 begins a whole series of questions about Leviathan and none have been asked regarding Behemoth, it seems appropriate to begin the questioning here. Another option is to take "eyes" as a reference to "hooks" (see NRSV). The NLT, by contrast, links "in his eyes" to the fact that since this animal only has its snout and eyes out of the water, it cannot be caught off guard and captured (see Konkel, 231).

41:9 [1] Instead of הֶן־תֹּחַלְתּוֹ (hēn-tōḥaltô, "any hope of subduing him"), one MS says "your hope"; but that merely shows how that editor struggled with the line. The NIV's paraphrase is based on understanding the third person pronoun as dative—"hope regarding him"—rather than as possessive—"his hope" (cf. KJV).

For הֲגַם (hᵃgam, untrans. in NIV), the NIV (cf. BHS mg.) considers h a dittograph and thinks the particle gam ("also") is not needed in English.

In rendering אֶל־מַרְאָיו יֻטָל (ʾel-marʾāyw yuṭāl) as "the mere sight of him is overpowering," the NIV treats the line as it appears in the MT, making the subject of the verb indefinite (cf. KJV, which inserts a negative: "Shall not one be cast down … ?"). Others (e.g., Pope; NRSV) have followed a lead suggested by the Syriac and Symmachus, which read ʾēl ("god") for the preposition ʾel. Pope likens it to the consternation of the gods over the monsters that Tiamat created (Babylonian Creation Epic [*ANET*, 64]) and following Cheyne emends to ʾēlîm ("gods"), which requires that the verb also be made plural. Pope, influenced by the KJV, also inserts a negative, reading: "Were not the gods cast down … ?" Since this use of the preposition ʾel with the verb ṭûl ("cast down") is unusual, ʾēl ("god" or "godlike being") may be correct as a reference, not to God or even El of the Ugaritic pantheon, but to a mighty being, angelic or human (cf. 41:25). The force of gam ("also, even") then may be significant—thus: "Even a mighty being [angel] is cast down at the sight of him" (cf. Kissane).

10 [2] Gray, Dhorme, and Pope all see לֹא־אַכְזָר (lōʾ-ʾakzār, "no one is fierce enough") as descriptive of Leviathan and make it a question: "Is he not fierce … ?" The KJV, RSV, NIV, et al. stress a slightly different point. The verse could be a contrast between the two powerful beings introducing the climax of the poem. I read: "Is he not fierce when one arouses him? / But who is it that can stand against me?"

Instead of לְפָנַי (lᵉpānay, "against me"), many Hebrew MSS and a LXX variant read "him" for "me." Blommerde, 8, appeals to the use of the third person suffix yod (see Notes on 9:35). Using the third person would keep the emphasis on Leviathan. This verse would go with v.9, and vv.11–12 would form the climax of the poem (see comments above).

11 [3] In מִי הִקְדִּימַנִי וַאֲשַׁלֵּם (mî hiqdîmanî waʾᵃšallēm, "Who has a claim against me that I must repay?"), the first verb (hiqdîmanî) means "to confront." The NIV uses šalēm ("to repay"; GK 8966), the second verb, to throw light on the first verb. Hence "confronting to claim a debt" or confronting to give a gift (cf. Dt 23:4) is the way it is construed. If Paul has this verse in mind in Romans 11:35, he is at best paraphrasing; for he follows neither the Hebrew nor the LXX fully. The LXX, which reads: "Who will resist me and remain

[safe]?" may have understood the second verb as an Aramaism. The so-called aphel stem (cf. Jer 25:3) would account for the *aleph* that normally would indicate the first person imperfect (NIV). But even in the Piel, the verb (*šlm*) can mean "remain" or "make safe" (cf. 8:6) as well as "repay." I agree, however, with Habel, 555, who wants to keep the first person and render the line, "Whoever confronts me I requite" (551).

The questions raised by Pope, Gordis, Dhorme, et al. against the way the KJV, RSV, and NIV translate לִי־הוּא (*lî-hûʾ*, "belongs to men") are legitimate. The Hebrew of this line does not say "under heaven all is mine" but "under all the heaven he [it] is mine," which is a problem as to both translation and context. Without emending the text the words can mean "he is against me," based on a similar syntax that appears in Genesis 13:13. The whole line would then read: "underneath all the heavens he [Leviathan] is against me." As the apex and climax of the poem, Yahweh is asserting his supremacy over this creature who uniquely opposes him because nothing on earth is his equal (v.33). Understanding vv.11–12 in this way ties the Leviathan picture to the important concept of Yahweh's supremacy in the speech's prologue (40:8–14). This climax is flanked first by questions about a human's (Job's) ability to overpower Leviathan (40:24–41:9) and then by a detailed description of the fearsome creature who terrifies even the mighty (angels?; 41:13–34).

12 [4] In the NIV the description of Leviathan begins here—בַּדָּיו וּדְבַר־גְּבוּרֹות וְחִין עֶרְכֹּו (*baddāyw ûdᵉbar-gᵉbûrôt wᵉḥîn ʿerkô*, "his limbs, his strength and his graceful form"). But is this verse about his strong and graceful body? Many feel it is about his boasting against Yahweh. Much depends on whether the word *baddāyw* ("his limbs") comes from a root meaning "a part, member, limb," as used in 18:13, or from a root that means "idle, vain talk," as used in 11:3 (cf. BDB, 94–95; GK 963 and 966). The last word in the line—*ʿerkô* ("his form")—can be used either way but is used often in Job for the arrangement (form) of words (13:18; 23:4; 32:14; 33:5; 37:19).

As for *ḥîn*, rather than making it a byform of *ḥēn* ("grace"), which is inappropriate for the context, I prefer to see here the root *ḥnn* II ("be loathsome, stale") as used by Job in 19:17, or from *hanaʾ* ("bend"), which appears in Arabic for anything "crooked" or "dubious" (cf. W. T. Wortabet, *Wortahet's Arabic-English Dictionary* [Beirut: Librairie du Liban, 1968], 121). Moreover, the objection that an animal (crocodile?) cannot speak is refuted by v.3, where it is attributed the ability to speak. Having established that Leviathan is too fierce for any human being, Yahweh now reaches his climax (apex) in vv.11–12. I translate:

Who can confront me and remain safe?
> When under all the heavens he dares oppose me,
will not I silence [cf. 11:3] his boastings,
> his powerful word and his dubious arguments?

22 [14] It is not really clear whether דְאָבָה (*dᵒābâ*) means "dismay" (NIV) or "faintness" from the Aramaic *dᵉb* ("to waste away"). The LXX confuses it with *ʾbd* ("destruction"), which fits the context better but not the root. The Qumran Targum renders it "vigor" (cf. Pope, 343), which tends to support F. M. Cross Jr. ("Ugaritic *dbʾat* and Hebrew Cognates," *VT* 2 [1952]: 163–64), who saw here a metathesis of the word *dbʾh* ("power" in Ugar.; cf. Dt 33:25, where it means "strength").

The NIV's "goes" is too weak for the Aramaism דּוּץ (*dûṣ*, "dance"). I read the line, "his power leaps before him."

24 [16] לִבּוֹ (*libbô*, "his chest") is literally "his heart." The NIV has unfortunately taken this as metonymy, thus losing the moral tone. If this creature can be "proud" (v.34), he certainly can be hard-hearted and so stubborn. See Ezekiel's contrast between the heart of stone and the heart of flesh (Eze 11:19; 36:26).

25 [17] The NIV, like the BHS conjecture, translates אֵלִים (*ʾēlîm*, "the mighty") as though spelled *ʾêlîm* from *ʾayil* ("ram, leader, chief"). The MT's *ʾēlîm* ("gods" or "heavenly beings") suggests again the cosmic (hidden) aspect of Leviathan.

D. Job's Closing Contrition (42:1–6)

> ¹Then Job replied to the LORD:
>
> ²"I know that you can do all things;
>   no plan of yours can be thwarted.
> ³⌞You asked,⌟ 'Who is this that obscures my counsel without knowledge?'
>   Surely I spoke of things I did not understand,
>   things too wonderful for me to know.
>
> ⁴"You said, ⌞'Listen now, and I will speak;
>   I will question you,
>   and you shall answer me.'
> ⁵My ears had heard of you
>   but now my eyes have seen you.
> ⁶Therefore I despise myself
>   and repent in dust and ashes."

COMMENTARY

1–2 Job's immediate response (v.1) shows that he understands clearly the thrust of the second divine speech. As I noted in the opening comments on that speech, the prologue (40:8–14) sets the tone — that God is all-powerful, especially as Lord over the moral sphere. He alone puts down evil and brings to pass his entire holy will. This, as I have tried to show, is the thought also of the climax (apex) of the Leviathan poem (cf. 41:11–12; see Notes).

Job now opens his mouth to tell God that he has gotten the message: God's purpose is all that counts, and since he is God, he is able to bring it to pass (v.2). There is nothing else Job needs to know except, perhaps, that this Sovereign of the universe is his friend (42:7–8).

3–4 There are two unannounced quotations, though not exact, in these verses (cf. the beginnings of v.3 and v.4 in the Hebrew). In v.3 Job appropriately agrees with the quotation from 38:2. He admits that he did, indeed, obscure God's counsel through ignorance. Chastened thus by the wonders of God (v.3c), he quotes in v.4 the line God himself saw fit to use twice on Job (38:3; 40:7, at the opening of each speech). The question is expressive of the nature of the divine discourses. God took the witness stand in his own behalf and cross-examined Job, who now records the final effect of this proceeding.

5–6 Job has heard about God (v.5). Finally his often-requested prayer to come into his presence has been answered, with the result that he withdraws his rash statements when he fantasized about God's failure to be just and loving. The verb translated "I despise myself" (v.6) can be rendered, "I reject what I said" (see Notes).

A major interpretative issue centers on the meaning of the second verb in v.6, translated "and repent." Andersen, 292, stresses the thought that Job "confesses no sins here," but that is true only in the sense that Job's integrity has been vindicated. Job does not need to repent over sins that brought on his suffering since his suffering is not the result of his sin.

One should not, however, assume that Job has nothing to be sorry for. His questioning of God's justice, for which God chided him in 38:2 (quoted in v.3), is enough to call forth a change of heart and mind. But the word *nāḥam* ("repent"; GK 5714) has a breadth of meaning that includes not only "to be sorry, repent" but also "to console oneself" or "be comforted." So it may be that Job is saying that because he has had this encounter with God (v.5b)—since he has really "seen" God—he has been delivered of his fantasy about God. Job thus rejects (despises) what he so recently said, for he now understands that God is his friend, not his enemy. So he is consoled and comforted though still suffering.

NOTES

3–4 The NIV's insertion of "You asked" and "You said" as indicators of unannounced quotations may be compared to the KJV, which leaves the text as is and thereby obscures the meaning, or to the NEB, which drops the first line of v.3 and suppresses v.4 to a footnote, suggesting the Hebrew has mistakenly added it.

6 Note the lack of an object on the verb עַל־כֵּן אֶמְאַס (*ʿal-kēn ʾemʾas*, "Therefore I despise myself"). We learn from its use in 7:16 and 36:5 that this verb leaves the object implied, to be supplied according to the needs of the context. "I despise myself" therefore is only one possible interpretation. Since the root often means "reject," the implied object in the light of v.3 is what he spoke in ignorance.

V. THE EPILOGUE (42:7–17)

OVERVIEW

Job has learned that humans by themselves cannot deduce the reason why anyone suffers. Still unknown to Job is the fact that his suffering has been used by God to vindicate God's trust in him over against the accusations of the Accuser. So without anger toward him, God has allowed Job to suffer in order to humiliate the Accuser and to provide support to countless sufferers who would follow in Job's footsteps. Once the purpose of the book has been fulfilled, Job's suffering cannot continue without God's being capricious. We see here the heart of the difference between the suffering of the wicked as punishment and of the righteous to accomplish God's higher purpose.

Job's lavish restoration (double all he had) is not based on Job's righteousness but on God's love for him as one who has suffered the loss of all things for God's sake and for no other reason. Here Job joins the Suffering Servant of Isaiah 53, who, "after the suffering of his soul," sees "the light of life" and is given "a portion among the great" and "will divide the spoils with the strong" (Isa 53:11–12).

A. The Verdict (42:7–9)

⁷After the LORD had said these things to Job, he said to Eliphaz the Temanite, "I am angry with you and your two friends, because you have not spoken of me what is right, as my servant Job has. ⁸So now take seven bulls and seven rams and go to my servant Job and sacrifice a burnt offering for yourselves. My servant Job will pray for you, and I will accept his prayer and not deal with you according to your folly. You have not spoken of me what is right, as my servant Job has." ⁹So Eliphaz the Temanite, Bildad the Shuhite and Zophar the Naamathite did what the LORD told them; and the LORD accepted Job's prayer.

COMMENTARY

7–9 Why does God commend Job for "speaking of him what is right" and condemn the counselors, who have always taken God's side, often with beautiful creedal hymns (v.7)? Some interpreters have taken this apparent incongruity as proof that the writer has in mind only the Job of the Prologue and that part of the story is lost where the counselors give advice similar to that of Job's wife. Such a view simplifies God's rebuke. Fortunately that approach to the book has been largely abandoned, but the question is still there. God has just rebuked Job for many wrong words during his dispute with the counselors; in what sense, then, is he here commended for saying what was right? Pope, 350, claims it will not do to take the word *nᵉkônâ* ("right") to mean "sincerity," since such a meaning cannot be sustained from usage.

Nᵉkônâ is based on the root *kûn* ("be established, made firm"; GK 3922), which has an adjectival derivative: *kēn*, meaning "upright" or "honest" (Ge 42:11, 19, et al.; GK 4026). That meaning fits Y. Kaufmann's claim (*History of the Religion of Israel from the Babylonian Captivity to the End of Prophecy* [trans. C. E. Froymsen; New York: Ktav, 1976], 335) that Job felt a moral duty to speak honestly before God (see Introduction: Authorship and Unity). But the derivative *kēn* is not used here. Of the wicked the psalmist says, "No truth [*nᵉkônâ*] is in their mouth" (Ps 5:9, lit. trans.). In 1 Samuel 23:23 the word means "definite information."

The counselors certainly lacked the right information about why Job was suffering. Job spoke without understanding (v.3) and was often fiery and emotional in his remarks (15:12–13; 18:4). His opinions and feelings were often wrong, but his facts were right. He was not being punished for sins he had committed. But the friends were claiming to know for certain things they did not know and so were falsely accusing Job while mouthing beautiful words about God. Job rightly accused them of lying about him and trying to flatter God (13:4, 7–11).

Pope, 350, mildly suggests that it may not be the words of the Dialogue that are in mind but that if they are, v.7 is "as magnificent a vindication as Job could have hoped for, proving that God values the integrity of the impatient protester and abhors pious hypocrites who would heap accusations on a tormented soul to uphold their theological position."

In v.8 the counselors, who are no longer with Job, are ordered by God to go back to Job with sacrificial animals sufficient to atone for their transgressions. The sacrifice, performed by Job, is an integral part of the worship in which Job prays for them. Praying for your enemy (Mt 5:43–44; Lk 6:27–28) is already taught and practiced in the OT (Ps 35:12–14; 109:4–5). And showing mercy to one's enemies is a faith principle clearly required

in Exodus 23:4–5. In the Wisdom literature such behavior is considered a mark of godliness (Pr 25:21–22). The psalmist believes that those who repay him "evil for good, and hatred for … friendship" (Ps 109:5) are opposing God, so he utters imprecations against them (Ps 109:6–20; cf. Job 27:7; Mt 23:13–36).

The two patterns of behavior are considered a problem only by those who do not think rebellion against God is serious. Since God had a high purpose for Job's suffering, the counselors made themselves enemies of God by accusing Job. The large sacrifice (v.8) shows how grave the Lord considered their sin. Grave as it was, he accepts Job's intercession (lit., "lifted up Job's face"). Job, who might have held a grudge, does not fail to love those who spitefully abused him when he was most helpless. This lofty and practical truth is a fitting theological finale to a book that calls forth a rigorous exercise of both soul and mind.

NOTES

8 The NIV has taken the liberty of adding to עֲשׂוֹת עִמָּכֶם נְבָלָה (‘*sôt ‘immākem nᵉbālâ*, "deal with you according to your folly") the extra pronoun "your," which avoids the anthropopathism that God should do folly. Pope, 350, wants to keep the striking figure, adding that *nᵉbālâ* ("wanton sin, folly"; GK 5576) is almost always sexual. Dhorme's position seems better. He renders the line "inflict on you something disgraceful" (Dhorme, 651–52). This is in keeping with the Prologue, where the Accuser is permitted by God to do just this to Job.

B. The Restoration (42:10–17)

¹⁰After Job had prayed for his friends, the Lᴏʀᴅ made him prosperous again and gave him twice as much as he had before. ¹¹All his brothers and sisters and everyone who had known him before came and ate with him in his house. They comforted and consoled him over all the trouble the Lᴏʀᴅ had brought upon him, and each one gave him a piece of silver and a gold ring.

> ¹²The Lord blessed the latter part of Job's life more than the first. He had fourteen thousand sheep, six thousand camels, a thousand yoke of oxen and a thousand donkeys. ¹³And he also had seven sons and three daughters. ¹⁴The first daughter he named Jemimah, the second Keziah and the third Keren-Happuch. ¹⁵Nowhere in all the land were there found women as beautiful as Job's daughters, and their father granted them an inheritance along with their brothers.
>
> ¹⁶After this, Job lived a hundred and forty years; he saw his children and their children to the fourth generation. ¹⁷And so he died, old and full of years.

COMMENTARY

10 The restoration, some claim, contradicts the purpose of the book, which is to present an alternative to the counselors' orthodox view of suffering held as normative in so much of the OT. When Job again receives his prosperity, righteousness is rewarded and his whole case is defeated. But I would remind the reader that the purpose of this book is not to contradict normative OT theology but to provide a balance of truth. All things being equal, sin brings suffering and righteousness blessing. Since Job has successfully endured the test and proved that his righteousness is not rooted in his own selfishness, there is no reason for Job to continue to be tested; his sufferings need to end.

God created humans so that he might bless them, not curse them. Job has been declared innocent of all those false accusations, so he cannot continue to suffer as punishment. And God's higher purpose has been fulfilled; thus, there is no reason why Job should not be restored.

11 Job's relatives, who kept their distance from the spectacle of suffering (19:13–15), here prove themselves to be fair-weather friends. Their comforting and consoling come a little late, but their presents are expensive (v.11): a "ring of gold" (for the nose [Ge 24:47; Isa 3:21] or the ears [Ge 35:4;

Ex 32:2]) and a "piece of silver" (*qᵉśîṭâ*). The latter is not money in the sense of coinage but an early designation of weight, like the shekel (see Notes).

12–15 Verses 12–13, as compared to the Prologue (1:3), highlight the twofold increase of Job's possessions. Everything is twofold except Job's sons and daughters. But Dhorme, 651–52, translates v.13 "fourteen sons," seeing an old Semitic dual form of the word for "seven" (but see Notes). This would leave only Job's daughters unmultiplied twofold. Pope, 352, claims that fits the general cultural pattern that frowned on a surplus of daughters. Whether or not that is the reason, it is curious that the author ignores the sons and concentrates on Job's daughters (vv.14–15). The Ugaritic literature proves this prominence of women is in keeping with the social milieu of the epic tradition (see Notes on v.13).

The daughters are named and granted an inheritance even when sons are available. Zelophehad's daughters in Numbers 36 were granted an inheritance only because he had no sons. The stress on the great beauty of Job's daughters is also characteristic of the epic tradition (Sarna, 24). Their names are indicative of their beauty: Jemimah means "turtledove"; Keziah is probably an aromatic plant as in the name cinnamon ("cassia" in Ps 45:8); and Keren-Happuch means "a jar [horn] of eye paint."

16–17 Job's longevity is in keeping with patriarchal tradition (possibly double the normal span of Ps 90:10). Certainly the wisdom ideal of seeing one's grandchildren is fulfilled twice over to the fourth generation (cf. Ge 50:23), and the patriarchal formula "old and full of years" expresses a completely fulfilled life (cf. Ge 25:8; 35:29).

NOTES

10 Gesenius (GKC, par. 91k) takes the singular noun רֵעֵהוּ (*rēʿēhû*, "his friends") to be collective. But it is also possible the author uses the singular to state a principle: "after Job prayed for his neighbor." This deed proves Job is spiritually ready for restoration.

11 קְשִׂיטָה (*qᵉśîṭâ*, "piece of silver") is used only here and in Genesis 33:19 and Joshua 24:32, which indicates it was an early (patriarchal?) unit of exchange. Its value is unknown, but the LXX (and other versions except Symm.) says each one gave him a lamb. Rabbis Akiba and Qimchi confirm its monetary meaning, and Dhorme notes that the lamb was used as a basis for uniformity in exchange so that a weight of gold or silver corresponding to the price of a lamb might have been called a *qᵉśîṭâ*. Compare the oldest Roman coins with a picture of an ox, sheep, or pig and the Latin *pecunia* from *pecus* ("cattle").

13 Concerning שִׁבְעָנָה בָנִים (*šibʿānâ bānîm*, "seven sons"), Dhorme defends the unique ending on *šibʿâ* as an old Semitic dual (*ān*), thus doubling the number of sons (see above). But Sarna, 18, sees only an archaism here related to the Ugaritic *šbʿny*, claiming the sociology of the story mirrors an epic background that tends to exalt the female, as in vv. 14–15. Even in the Prologue (1:4, 13) the daughters participated in the feasts. In Ugaritic, Baal has three daughters — *Pdry*, *Ṭly*, and *Arṣy* — and seven unnamed sons; and in the Epic of Kirtu the king's daughter shares her father's estate with her brothers (Sarna, 24).

Share Your Thoughts

With the Author: Your comments will be forwarded to the author when you send them to *zauthor@zondervan.com*.

With Zondervan: Submit your review of this book by writing to *zreview@zondervan.com*.

Free Online Resources at
www.zondervan.com

Zondervan AuthorTracker: Be notified whenever your favorite authors publish new books, go on tour, or post an update about what's happening in their lives at www.zondervan.com/authortracker.

Daily Bible Verses and Devotions: Enrich your life with daily Bible verses or devotions that help you start every morning focused on God. Visit www.zondervan.com/newsletters.

Free Email Publications: Sign up for newsletters on Christian living, academic resources, church ministry, fiction, children's resources, and more. Visit www.zondervan.com/newsletters.

Zondervan Bible Search: Find and compare Bible passages in a variety of translations at www.zondervanbiblesearch.com.

Other Benefits: Register yourself to receive online benefits like coupons and special offers, or to participate in research.

ZONDERVAN.com/
AUTHORTRACKER
follow your favorite authors